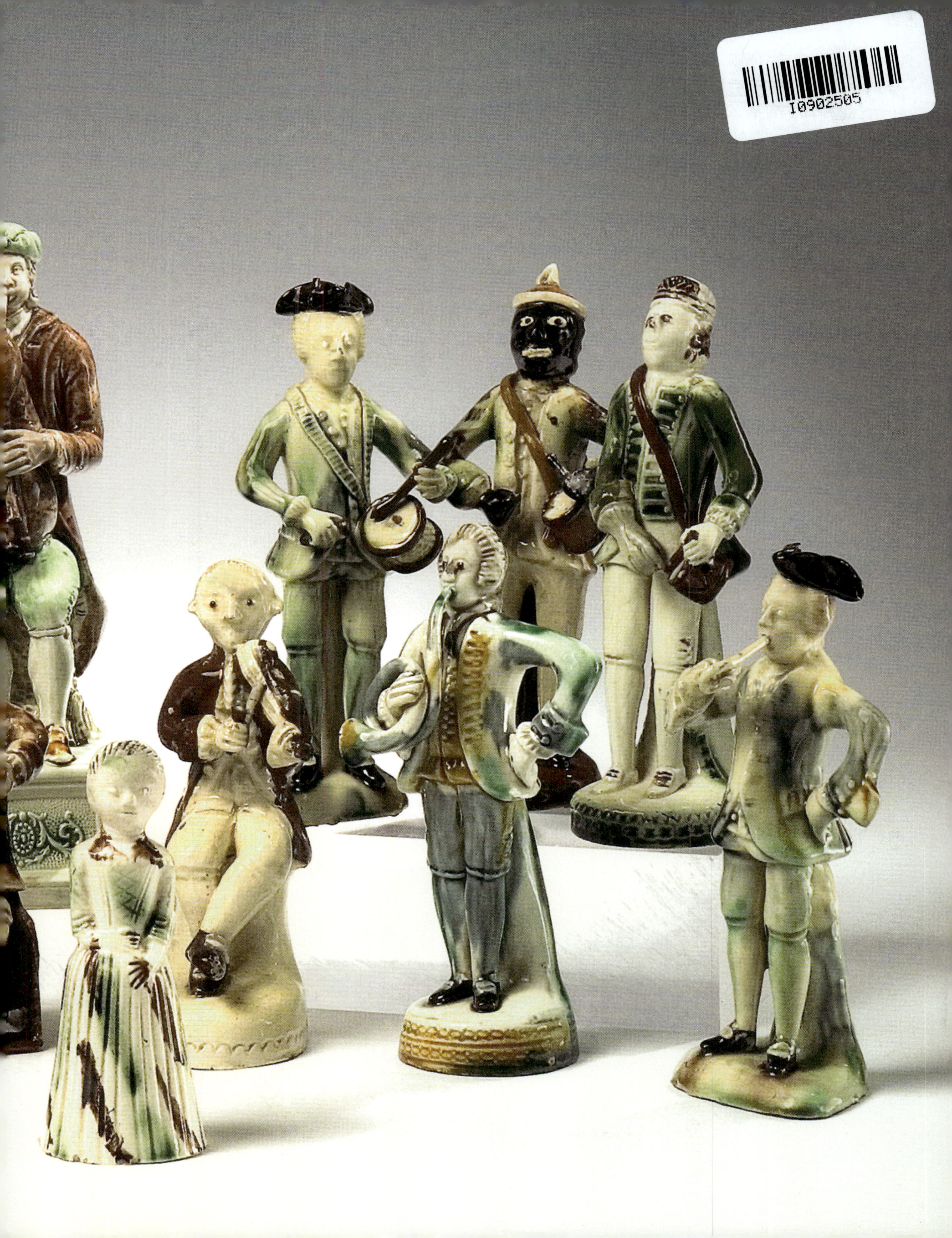

A Potted History

Henry Willett's Ceramic Chronicle of Britain

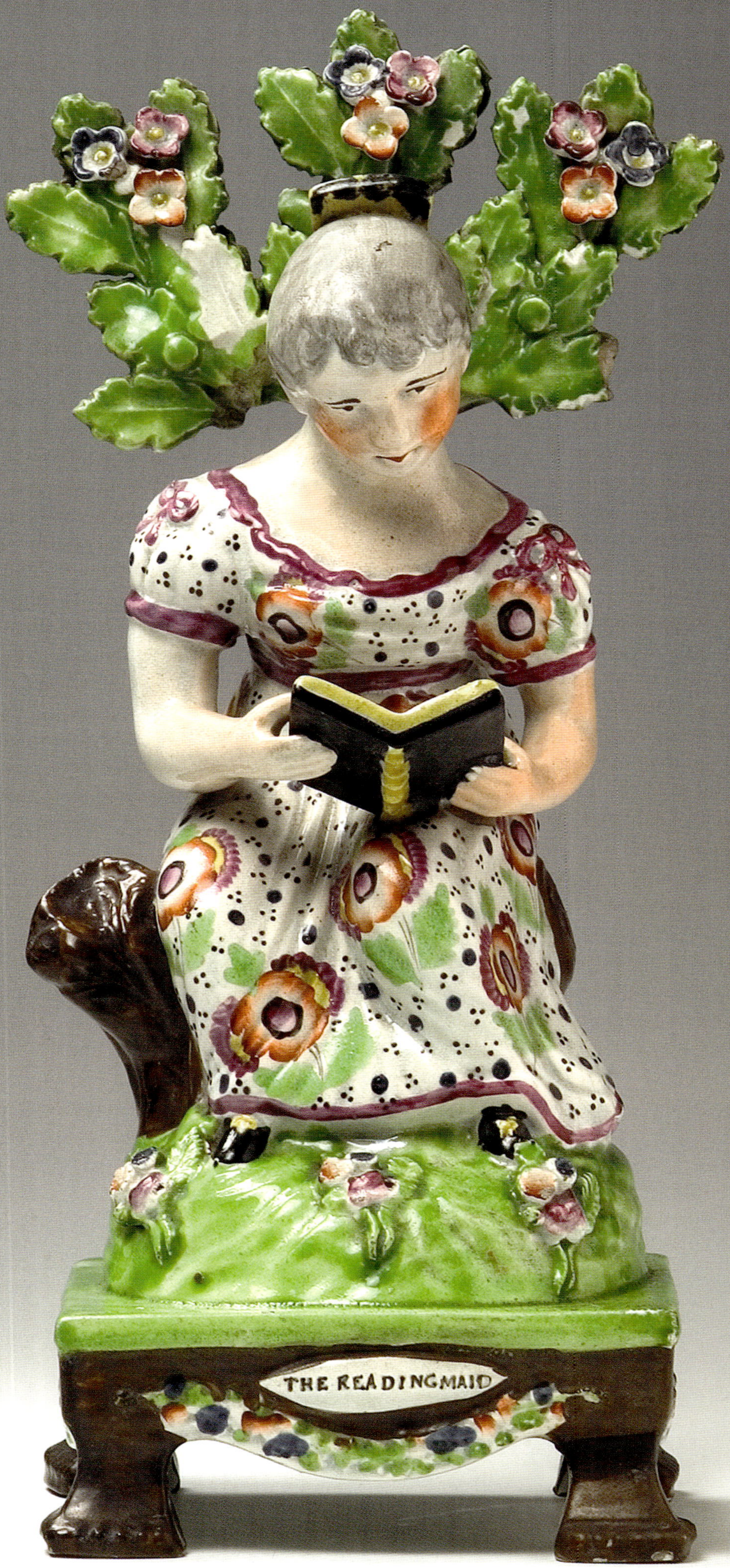
THE READINGMAID

A POTTED HISTORY

HENRY WILLETT'S CERAMIC CHRONICLE OF BRITAIN

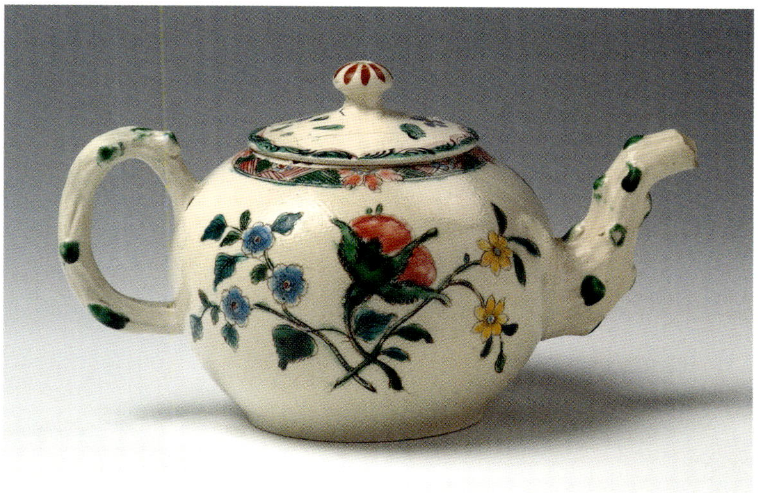

STELLA BEDDOE

ACC ART BOOKS

ISBN 978 1 85149 811 6

British Library Cataloguing-in-Publication Data

A catalogue record for this book is available from the British Library

MIX
Paper from responsible sources
FSC® C104723
FSC www.fsc.org

Photograph on Page 3: Teapot celebrating the lost cause of Charles Edward Stuart, salt-glazed stoneware, Staffordshire, c.1750 (see page 32).

Endpapers

Front: Figure group of fourteen musicians, earthenware, Staffordshire, c.1760 (see page 183).

Back: Twelve tiles (fire surround) depicting a global history of ceramic production, slip-decorated earthenware, Staffordshire, Stoke-on-Trent, Mintons, c.1878 (see page 137).

Illustrations to chapter headings taken from printed details on Willett's pots and from sheets of vignettes by Thomas Rowlandson, published by Fores, 1790. (Brighton & Hove Collections)

Printed in China for ACC Art Books Ltd, Woodbridge, Suffolk, England

CONTENTS

PREFACE

Henry Willett was one of the founding fathers of Brighton Museum & Art Gallery, which opened in rooms in the Royal Pavilion in 1861, moving to its current site in 1873. He was a prolific and innovative collector. It is thanks to collectors like Willett that, today, the city's museums have such a richness of collections; these are important in helping us to understand our past and to develop and inform our future. The author of this catalogue, Stella Beddoe, worked at Royal Pavilion & Museums in Exhibitions, and as Keeper of Decorative Art and later Senior Keeper, from 1978 to 2012. During this time, the Decorative Art collections, including the Willett Collection, were awarded Designated status by a government-backed scheme to identify and support collections of national and international importance. Stella, along with Jessica Rutherford, the then Director of Royal Pavilion & Museums, was instrumental in achieving this honour for the collections. Her early research on Willett informed a number of well-received lectures both at Brighton Museum and further afield, and we now hold an extensive bank of knowledge about the Willett Collection – a fitting legacy for Stella's years of dedicated work as Keeper. This knowledge and expertise have been captured in this wonderful book. The seeds of the project to develop this publication were planted by Jessica Rutherford and the Royal Pavilion & Museums Foundation (formerly the Friends of the Royal Pavilion, Art Gallery & Museums). I would like to thank Stella and our colleagues at ACC Art Books, with the support of Harold Blakey and the Paul Mellon Centre for Studies in British Art, for bringing this project to fruition.

Janita Bagshawe
Director, Royal Pavilion & Museums, Brighton & Hove

ACKNOWLEDGEMENTS

The publication of *A Potted History: Henry Willett's Ceramic Chronicle of Britain* would not have been possible without the late Harold Blakey. As my volunteer assistant, researcher and mentor he devoted time and enormous enthusiasm to the Willett Collection over several years. In addition, he donated a substantial sum towards the publication of this book. Generous funding was provided by the Royal Pavilion & Museums Foundation and the Paul Mellon Centre for Studies in British Art.

I have benefitted immensely, over more than thirty years, from the pioneering research of numerous other members of the English Ceramic Circle and the Northern Ceramic Society. In particular, I received invaluable advice and support from the following, who, sadly, did not live long enough to see the publication appear: David Drakard, Dr Minnie Holdaway, Jonathan Horne, Norman Stretton, Tom Walford and Bernard Watney.

At Royal Pavilion & Museums, Jessica Rutherford and Janita Bagshawe, successive Directors of the Royal Pavilion, and David Beevers, Sarah Posey, Gillian Smithson, Jonathan Whitson Cloud and Laura Williams gave their unstinting practical support. I must also acknowledge the long-term encouragement of late Councillor Andy Durr, Myrna Schkolne and Lars Tharp, and of David Bains and Louise Bains.

A number of colleagues from other museums have been extremely helpful, namely Aileen Dawson at the British Museum, Howard Coutts of the Bowes Museum, Nick Dolan, late of Tyne & Wear Museums, Ann Eatwell at the Victoria & Albert Museum, Robin Emmerson, late of the National Museums, Liverpool, Miranda Goodby at the Potteries Museum, Hanley, and Pat Halfpenny and Leslie B. Grigsby of Winterthur Museum, Delaware. Thanks also to Professor Julian Crampton.

Finally, I must thank Diana Steel, Sandra Pond and Andrew Whittaker at ACC Art Books for undertaking the project and Peter Greenhalf, for photographing a huge number of diverse ceramic objects with such sensitivity.

NOTE TO THE READER

Unless stated otherwise, objects are captioned from left to right.

Collection numbers are given for each item, distinguished as follows: **001–1715**: numbers given to entries in a catalogue of 1899, when the Willett Collection was lent to Bethnal Green Museum, referring to single pieces, pairs or larger groups (e.g. 888A–G); **R.603.1-13**: group donated some time after the main collection in 1903; **R2454…**: donated by Willett family members in 1923. **Six figure** numbers (e.g. 324613) were given to all items when the collections were computerised from 1970s onwards.

INTRODUCTION

Henry Willett, the Man and the Collector

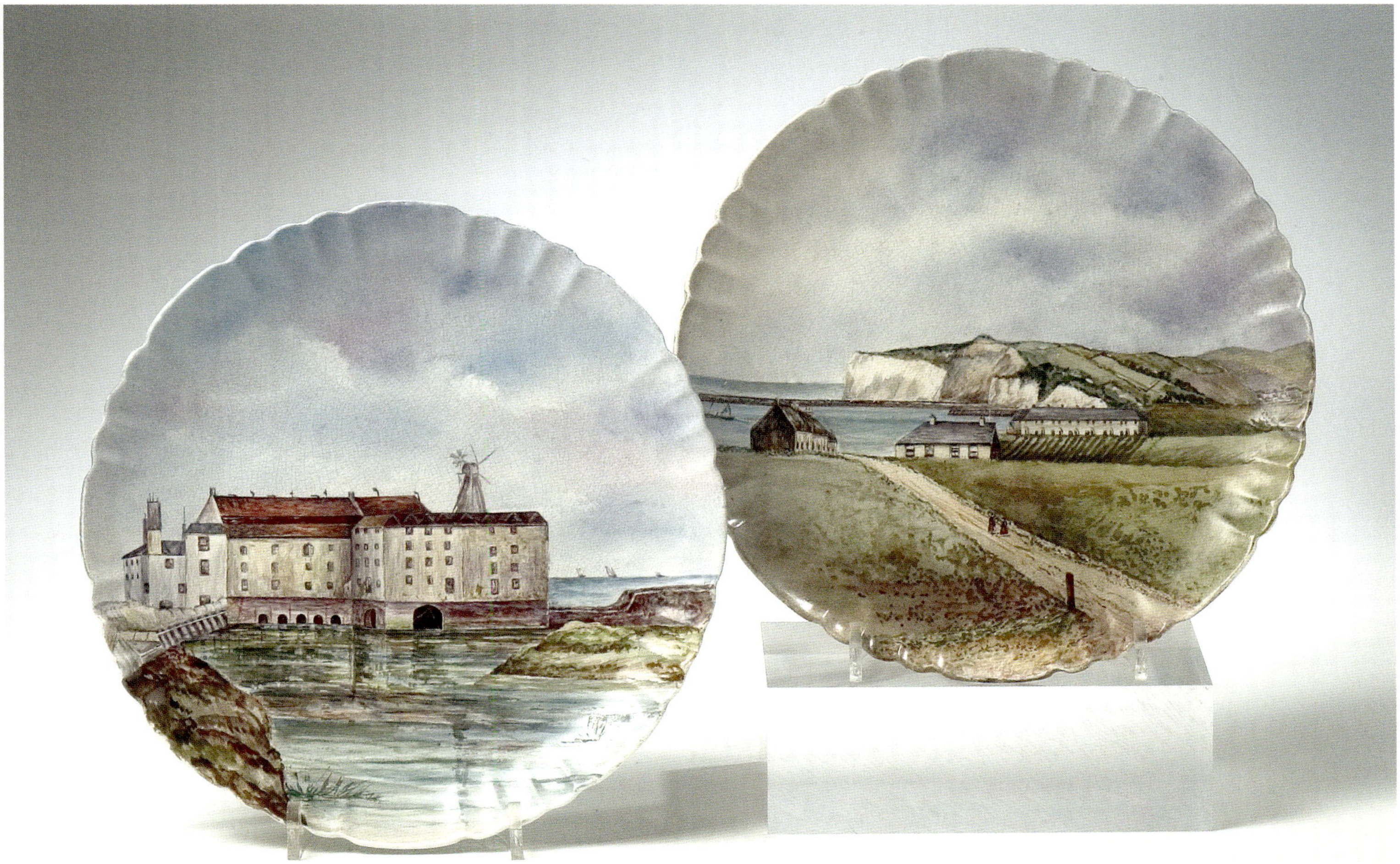

Pair of Dishes, (**666 & A**), c.1850, Stoke-on-Trent, Mintons, both diameter: 21.7cm, (8½in), enamelled bone china. Two blank dishes probably painted by a member of the Willett family. One shows Bishopstone Tide Mills, near Newhaven, Sussex, built by Henry Willett's father, William Catt, who was said to farm by day and mill by night, thus establishing the family fortune. The other shows the shore and cliffs at Newhaven, Sussex.

Henry Willett, 1823-1905

Henry Willett was born Henry Catt, the twelfth and last child of William Catt, a farmer and miller at Bishopstone, near Newhaven in Sussex, on 13 January 1823. His mother, the former Hannah Dawes, weakened by multiple pregnancies, died giving birth to him. His eldest sister Elizabeth, who was twenty-six when he was born, ran her father's household for the next forty years and was known at Miss Catt, even to her siblings. William, Henry's father, was the youngest of the four children of John Catt and Elizabeth Willett of Buxted in Sussex. Elizabeth was a woman of independent mind and means who believed she had married beneath her and the marriage appears to have been tense and unhappy. When she died in 1817 she left her considerable fortune to William's daughter, Elizabeth (her eldest grand-daughter), with the proviso that the name of Willett must continue. Four years later John hanged himself from a beam in the barn across the lane from their farmhouse in Robertsbridge.[1] William seems to have inherited his mother's dominant personality and drive. On his wedding day (26 January 1797) he is said to have risen at 5 a.m. to cut timber for hop poles and returned to work the next morning.[2] With £500 from his parents he purchased Stonehouse Farm and two years later bought a small mill at Lamberhurst.

Around 1803 William's family moved to Bishopstone where, on reclaimed land, he developed one of the first flour mills powered by the tides of the English Channel. The tide mill was the largest water mill ever constructed in Sussex. Henry and his siblings grew up here and swiftly learned to contribute to the family business. They farmed by day and milled at night, in rhythm with the ebb and flow of the tide and William Catt & Sons prospered. Described as a flour-mogul, William won contracts to victual the coastal barracks against Napoleon during the great invasion scare. He was even accused of profiteering during famine years, prompting the malediction scratched on the wall of a house in Southover, Lewes, 'Flour 2/11d. a gallon … God grant it may soon fall: and Cat may fall with it'.[3] With unstinting energy and acting as his own architect and engineer, William enlarged his existing mill and constructed new ones, together with additional workers' cottages, creating the village of Bishopstone Tidemills. His expertise was much in demand and in 1846 the French King Louis-Philippe invited him to the Chateau d'Eu, near Dieppe, to advise on milling in

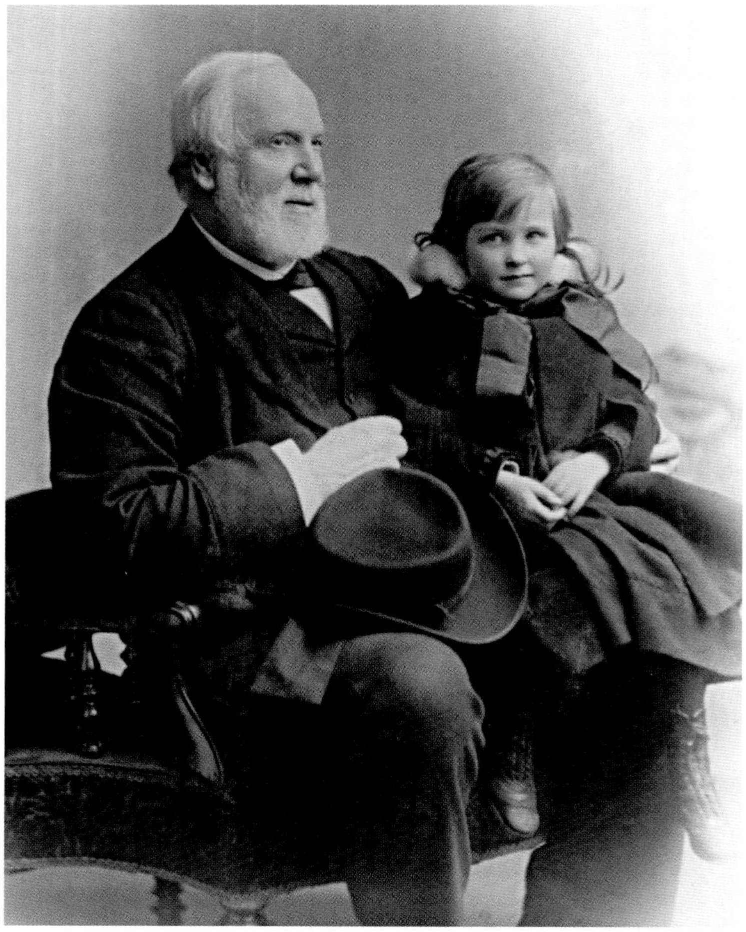

Henry Willett with his granddaughter, Joyce, c.1903.

France.[4] With canny foresight, he anticipated that coal-fired mills would supersede those powered by wind and water and diversified his interests, investing in the brewing industry. He bought maltings at Newhaven and Kingston Buci near Shoreham, together with the West Street, Ship Street and Kemp Town breweries in Brighton as well as a number of public houses. His only leisure interest appears to have been the cultivation of pears. Despite the bleak aspect of the tide mill he fanned pear trees against its east-facing wall and apparently succeeded in his aim to 'get a good pear all year round'.[5]

Henry's eldest sister Elizabeth Catt, died on a spring holiday in Rome in 1863 leaving £13,000 to her eight surviving siblings, on condition that they changed their surname to Willett, in accordance with her grandmother's wishes. George, Caroline and Charles challenged this in a high court case entitled 'Catt's Trusts'[6] and won the right to benefit from her will while retaining the name of Catt.[7] Henry, despite being an established businessman of forty, was the first to adopt the name of Willett, and was followed by Edmund, John and William. Their sister Hannah had long since married the Rev. James Smith.

Little is known of Henry's education except that he developed early passions for collecting and cricket. His very varied collections continued to grow throughout his life whilst he pursued a career as a successful businessman. He inherited money from his father as well as his sister and, by applying 'considerable commercial sagacity', was able to leave an estate worth around £250,000 when he died in 1905. As early as 1846, together with his brother Charles, he purchased a third share in a merchant brig, *Elizabeth,*[8] and in 1847 bought an eighth share in Vallance & Catt, West Street Brewery, which he helped save from destruction by fire in 1863. He acquired property in Brighton, Hove and West Sussex, the home area of his wife, Frances Coombe, whom he married in June 1851. He also had substantial holdings in the Blackpool Electric Tramway, the Midland Railway, electricity and water companies and utilities in Western Australia.

In 1858, Henry and Frances and their growing family established themselves at Arnold House on Upper North Street, Brighton. They had three sons and four daughters. He and his wife entertained regularly and were part of a large and influential social circle. His acquaintances included John Ruskin, who mentions him frequently in his writings. Willett had some of Ruskin's publications reissued at prices low enough to be affordable for the working classes.[9] He is also mentioned by the American writer, Oliver Wendell Holmes and was a close associate of Sir Augustus Franks, the influential collector and curator at the British Museum. Religiously he was very tolerant and it was said that; 'Catholic, Anglican, Jew and Greek could gather round his table, knowing that nothing harsher than trifling persiflage would arise to mar the pleasant exchange of ideas'.[10] In his leisure hours he played cricket and in 1856 was elected Brighton representative at the founding of the Sussex Cricket Club at the Egremont Hotel, kept by Tom Box, the legendary wicket-keeper. From 1859 he was also active in the Sussex Volunteer Artillery Corps, being swiftly promoted from Gunner Catt to Lieutenant Willett.

In 1865, he masterminded the difficult though ultimately successful election campaign for the Brighton constituency of the blind Liberal candidate, Professor Henry Fawcett.[11] He was mocked for his pains by the Tory press, punning on his still recent name-change: 'Mewsings on Cat-iline Willett's Cat-asstrophe' After his election, Fawcett joined a radical group in the House of Commons who campaigned, unsuccessfully, to win women the vote. He did, however, pioneer major reforms of the postal services. Willett was an active political supporter of the Liberal Party throughout his life, chairing the Brighton Liberal Association for many years. He championed several controversial left-wing causes, including the Land Tenure Reform Association, which opposed the enclosure of common land. In 1864 he supported the abolition of capital punishment. In 1873, in honour of his association with the Liberal politician Richard Cobden, Willett presented 500 of Cobden's papers to the newly opened Brighton Reference Library, which he had helped to found. Among his favourite charities were the YMCA, the Brighton Workhouse, which he helped to rebuild, the Brighton Grammar School and the Emigration Society, which encouraged young people, particularly women, to emigrate to Canada. He campaigned vigorously for the education of the poor. J.G. Bishop mentions a well-known churchman whom Willett spotted as a boy, washing pots in an inn, 'whiling away odd moments behind the bar by working conic sections on a slate'. Willett paid for his education. Sometimes Willett read aloud from morally uplifting books, such as Charles Kingsley's *Alton Locke.*[13] On more than one occasion he addressed an audience of working people in public places such as the Steine in Brighton, sheltered from the sun or rain by a large umbrella held by Sergeant Menzies, an artillery instructor. In 1861, Willett read from Charles Dickens's *A Christmas Carol* at Brighton's Town Hall in order to raise funds for the Brighton Mechanics' Institute.[14] In 1865 he was involved in the formation of the Brighton Working Men's Union.

Henry was a large man, standing well over six feet tall and weighing between eighteen and twenty stones in his later years. He had piercing grey eyes, a thick white beard and was fond of wearing a long, black, quasi-clerical coat and flat hat. With his boundless energy, dominant personality and sharp intellect some of his children found him rather intimidating. Henry Willett's burial at St Helen's, Hangleton, a fashionable church outside Brighton, was packed with mourners from all strata of Brighton society. 'The very poor were there … some of them had walked out all the way from Brighton to stand by the grave of their benefactor'.[15] He was also paid the singular honour of having a memorial plaque installed in the chancel of the church, decorated with a sculpted tondo of the pietà, perhaps a piece from his own collections.

Willett the Scientist and Collector

Willett's early academic interests were scientific. After moving to Brighton in 1841 he was bitterly disappointed to find that the famous fossil collections amassed by Gideon Mantell, had been sold to the British Museum in 1838. As a child Willett had met the great Brighton-based doctor and geologist and was inspired to begin digging for chalk fossils himself and paid others to do so. In 1846 he was a founder member of the Sussex Archaeological Society and later joined the Geological Society. He presented the chalk fossils to Brighton in 1861; they are now housed at the Booth Museum of Natural History. In the introduction to the *Catalogue of the Cretaceous Fossils* which he published privately in 1871, lies a key to his passion for collecting: 'The pleasure of a collector in meeting with a fossil fish in a chalk stone, is not surpassed by that of an angler who has hooked a living one'.[16]

In 1858 Willett became fascinated by the sinking of a well at Warren Farm on the summit of the downs just outside Brighton. Water was eventually located in 1862 at a depth of 1,285 feet, making it the deepest in the world at that time. Willett had medals struck for each of the workers and held a dinner for them at the Brighton Town Hall. On 31 August 1872, during the conference of the British Association held in Brighton, he took many of the delegates to view the quarry near Cuckfield, where Gideon Mantell was supposed to have found most of his geological specimens. Willett also drew attention to a major exploration of the sub-Wealden strata beneath South East England and appealed for financial support.[17] Willett even found dinosaur specimens himself, namely the bones of an iguanodon, excavated in the Cuckfield area. His many more recent natural history specimens, also deposited with the Booth Museum, range from pangolins from Africa and armadillos from South America, to rare birds and an incomplete skeleton and casts of the head and foot of one of the last dodos from Mauritius.

Amongst a small number of artefacts from cultures outside Europe is a very rare and important wooden memorial sculpture from Abeokuta in south-west Nigeria, presented in 1885. Made by the Yoruba people, it features a procession, which includes a Catholic missionary priest

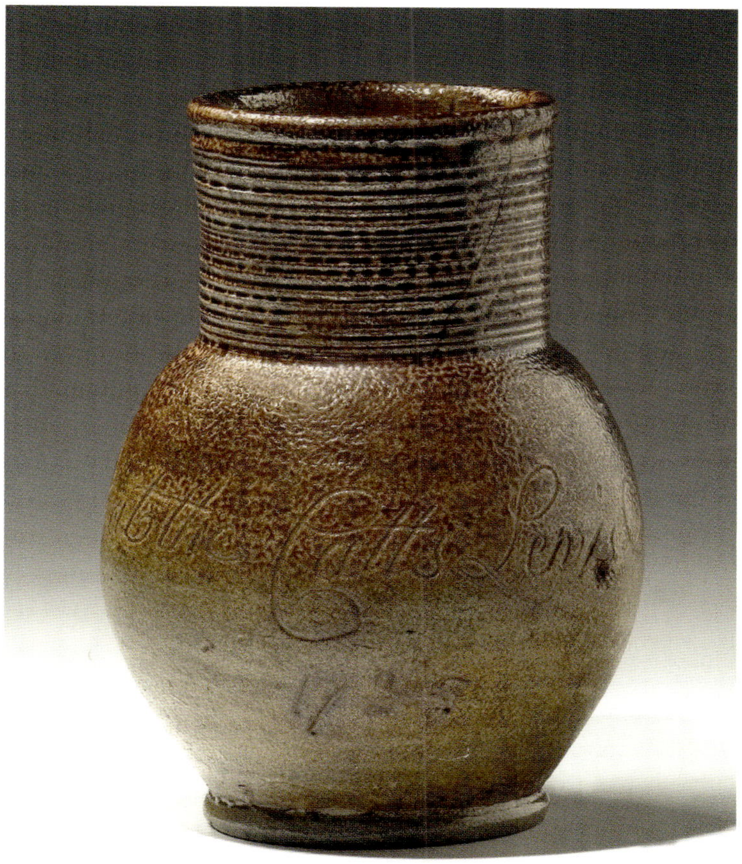

Jug, (1382), 1735, London, height: 19.1cm, (7½in), salt-glazed stoneware. Globular mug with cylindrical neck incised, 'Thos. Foord at the Catts Lewes Sussex/ 1735'. Apart from the link to Willett's original surname, 'The Catts' was an affectionate nickname for the Dorset Arms tavern in Cliffe High Street, Lewes, whose heraldic crest included two spotted leopard as supporters. The most likely landlord is Thomas Foorde [*sic*], who married one Mary Alchorn at Isfield, five miles from Lewes, on 12 August 1725.

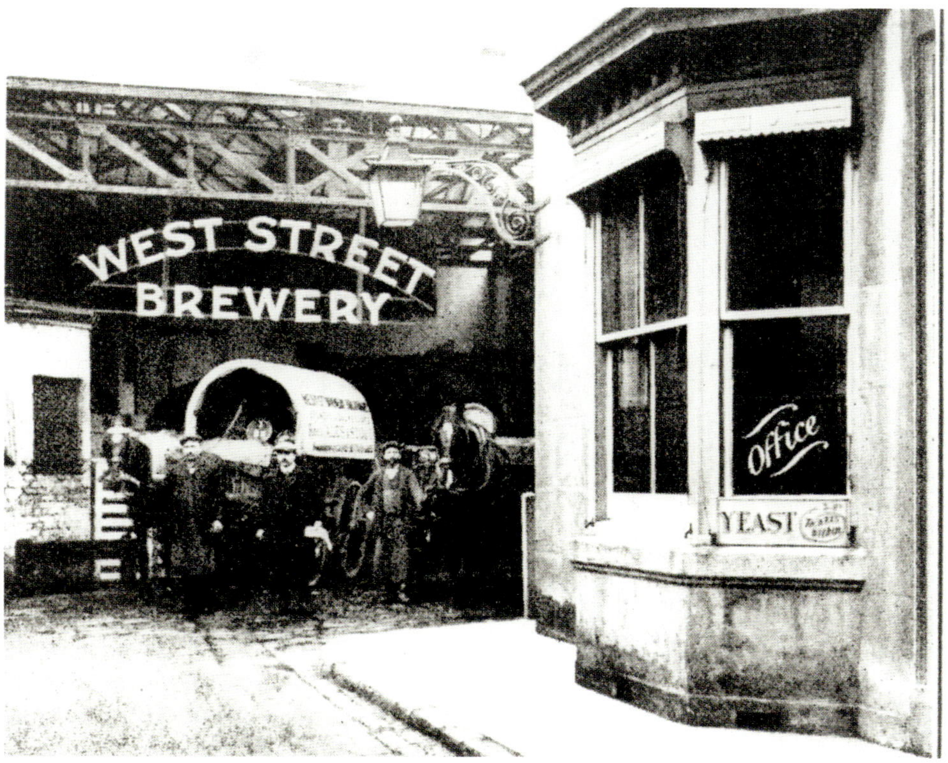

Premises of Vallance & Catt, West Street Brewery, Brighton.

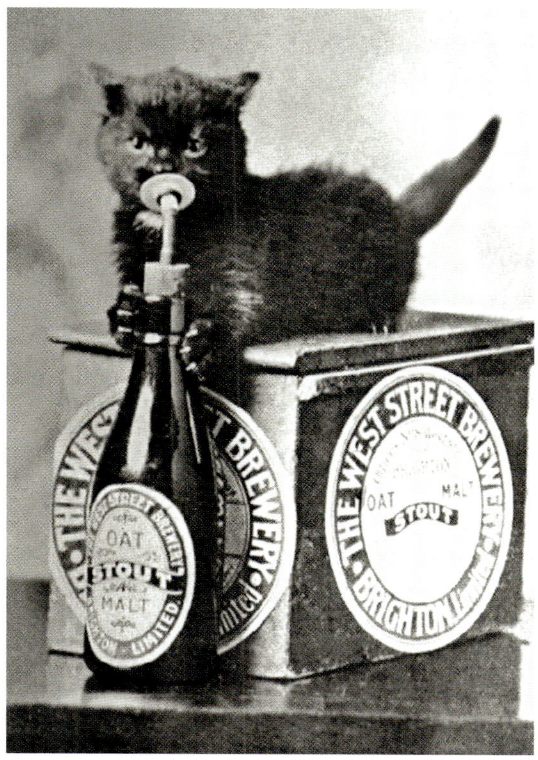

Postcard advertising the West Street Brewery. The unfortunate kitten is used as a pun on the name of Catt.

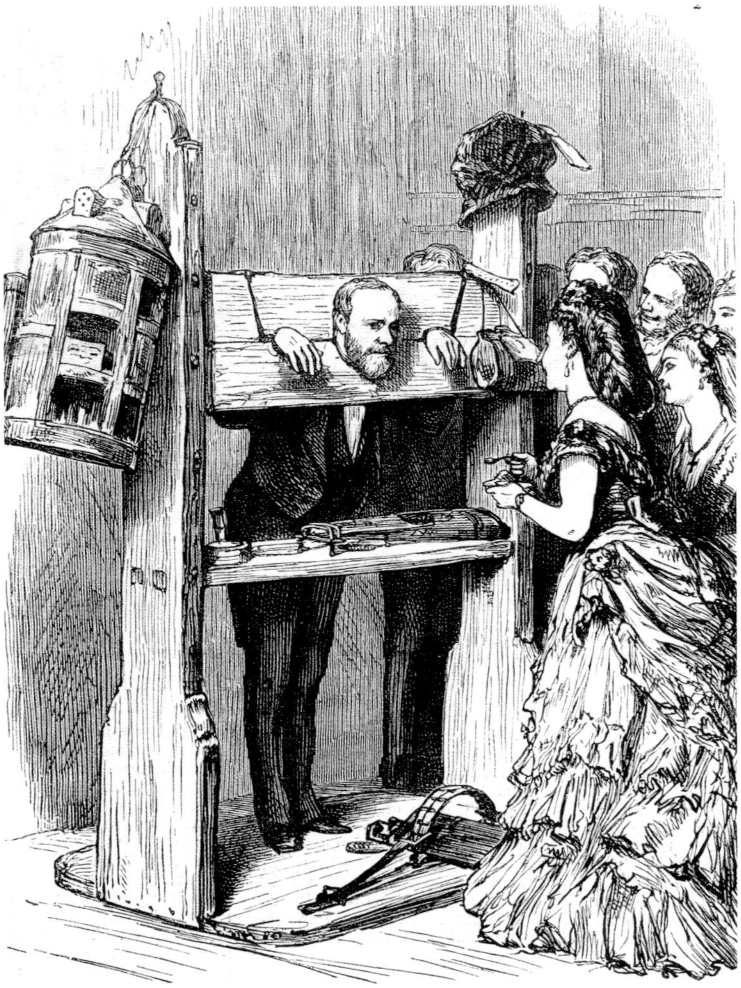

Willett poses in the stocks, wearing full evening dress, to promote Brighton's forthcoming museum and art gallery.

riding a mule.[18] Other pieces include iron tea kettles from Japan, a group of containers decorated in gold mosaic from Burma and a glass bowl and cover decorated in the Islamic style. This was, in fact, a piece of contemporary applied art, signed by the French glassmaker, P.J. Brocard, which Willett took for an antique.

Willett assembled an important collection of Old Master Paintings including major works from the Italian and Flemish Renaissance, which were sold in 1896 and are now in such national collections as the Metropolitan Museum in New York, the National Gallery in Washington, the Royal Museum, Brussels and the Thyssen Collection, Madrid. Some of these had to be sold to settle the costs of a court case in connection with his eldest son, Ernest. His remaining paintings were presented to the Brighton Museum after its refurbishment in 1903. The most important of these is Jan Lievens's *The Raising of Lazarus*.[19]

Willett and Brighton Museum

Willett had enthusiastically supported the proposal to found a dedicated museum in Brighton since displays were first mounted in the Royal Pavilion in 1861. He was instrumental in acquiring a marble statue of Captain Pechell, who died a hero at the Battle of Sebastopol in the Crimean and a bust of the Rev. F.W. Robertson, of Trinity Chapel, Brighton, whom he knew and admired, which were placed in the Pavilion's entrance hall. In 1874 he presented parian-ware busts of politicians Richard Cobden and John Bright and the writer Charles Dickens.[20]

In 1872, during the conference of the British Association, Willett promoted the idea of a custom-built museum, to be installed in buildings close to the Royal Pavilion. These, together with the Brighton Dome, constituted the Pavilion's former stables and riding school. A page from *The Graphic* shows visitors in the new reading room, at the aquarium and being treated to the sight of Henry Willett in virile middle age, wearing evening dress and posing in the stocks with some of his extensive collections of Sussex folk life and instruments of correction.[21] The free library, museum and picture gallery opened on 12 September 1873 and Willett hosted and probably underwrote a banquet in the Royal Pavilion to celebrate the occasion. Unusually, he failed to invite five of the seven local newspapers, which provoked a vitriolic outburst from those excluded.[22] He remained a member of the Museum Committee for much of his life.

In 1899 Willett read a paper at a meeting of the Museums Association held in Brighton. Entitled *Museums and their Uses*, in it he stated that regional museums should not attempt to compete with the 'National collections of the Metropolis' but should highlight local manufacture and, to this end, he assembled important collections of Sussex pottery and Sussex iron firebacks. That year Brighton Museum was emptied for refurbishment and the ceramics collection was lent to Bethnal Green Museum in east London, an institution Willett had earlier tried to persuade to acquire a collection of instruments of torture, allegedly used by the Spanish Inquisition! Willett's ceramics collection was at this time on loan to Brighton Museum. With its emphasis on peoples' history, it was also thought to be of particular interest to the inhabitants of the East End of London. It was here that the most comprehensive catalogue to date was compiled and published, listing nearly 2000 pieces under twenty-three subject headings.[23]

The collection returned in 1903 and was finally presented to Brighton Museum when it reopened. Willett stipulated that the collection must be kept together, 'distinct from all other ceramic productions' and be shown as originally intended, 'such as to represent the human and historical idea ... and it should be insured for £3000 with the proviso that if it be burned the proceeds should be used for local charities.' He died in 1905. Except for a short period in the 1950s when the collection was regrouped under identified factories and manufacturing techniques, Willett's conditions have been respected for over a century.

Willett the Ceramics Collector

Of his many varied collections, Henry Willett seems to have been particularly drawn to ceramics. His presentations to Brighton Museum included Islamic and Persian tiles, Chinese and Japanese vases and dishes as well as the famous collection of British pottery and porcelain. He was collecting ceramics and exchanging information and examples with the great collectors of his day. He is mentioned in the correspondence of Lady Charlotte Schreiber (whose collections form the basis of the holdings of the Victoria & Albert Museum). He dedicated his first catalogue of 1879 to Augustus Franks, of the British Museum, Robert Soden Smith, of the South Kensington Museum Library, Professor Arthur Church (who would write one of the first introductions to English ceramics)[24] and Dr Hugh Diamond, a fellow collector.[25]

Llewellynn Jewitt refers to several important pieces of early English delftware in Willett's collection (that are now lost) including a seventy-two tile panel representing Hogarth's *The March to Finchley*.[26] In 1874, Willett presented a Wrotham candlestick of 1651 to the British Museum. In 1878, examples of his white salt-glazed stoneware were published [27] and in 1887 Sir Augustus Franks recommended that the entire collection be bought for the British Museum. Willett compromised, selling Franks 176 pieces, including several fine slipware dishes.[28] Shortly before the opening of Brighton Museum, Henry Willett lent more than sixty pieces of Wedgwood creamware and Worcester and Derby porcelain to an exhibition at Alexandra Palace in London. This was a traditional connoisseurs' collection, featuring high quality

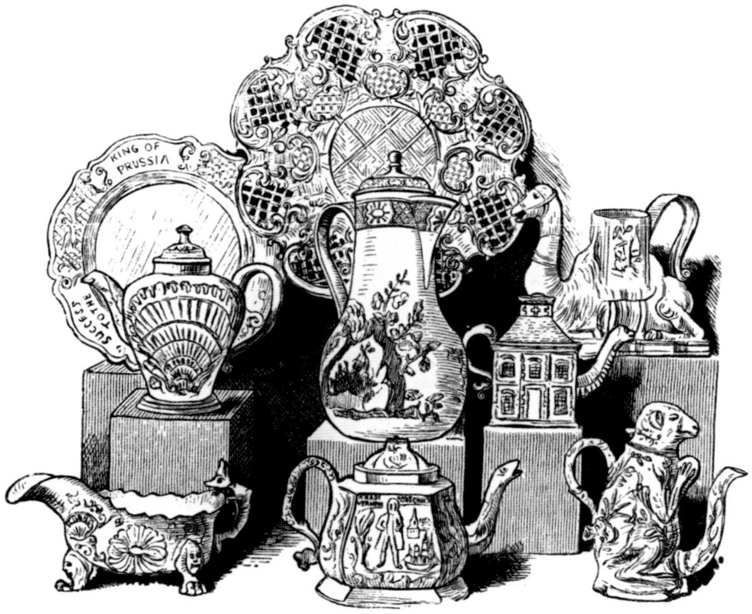

2.—SPECIMENS OF SALT-GLAZED WHITE WARE, EIGHTEENTH CENTURY.
(From the Collection of Henry Willett, Esq.)

White salt-glaze wares from Willett's collection, published 1878. Note the foreground teapot celebrating Admiral Vernon's victory at the battle of Porto Bello (see page 44 (HW165)).

products from renowned factories. On 9 June, 1873, within weeks of the opening of the reconstructed exhibition centre, they were all destroyed by fire together with several thousand other loans.[29]

Apparently unshaken, Willett lent an early version of his new ceramic collection to the new museum, which opened in September but he was unhappy with the displays. In May 1874 he wrote to the chairman of the Pavilion Committee, 'The temporary cases … are unsuitable both in shape and size so that the specimens cannot be properly classified or arranged and neither instruction nor interest can be derived … I have the opinion of Mr Frank [*sic*][30] of the British Museum … that no other Collection exists so extensive and complete (illustrative of bye gone habits and customs and of the popular impressions prevalent at the time when these specimens were manufactured)'.[31] He then offered to design and pay for alternative casing, to which the committee readily agreed. He also proposed to fund an illustrated catalogue of the collection, to be sold at less than 1/- in aid of the Museum Purchase Fund. The first (unillustrated) catalogue was duly published in 1879 and sold for 2d.[32] In these early days the collection was described as being 'totally unarranged, and … in an uncatalogued condition, the small and superficial catalogue … being quite inadequate to its purpose.'[33]

In 1899 an illustrated catalogue was published, which sold for 6d., produced when the collection was lent to the Bethnal Green Museum. The much enlarged, well-organised volume reflected Willett's refinement of the collection, after he had added and removed items for twenty years. After his death in 1905, there were sales of material from his varied personal collections including ceramics, which were either the victims of this process of refinement or the continued acquisitions of an addicted collector. The Struan Robertson Stoneware Collection, presented to Brighton Museum in 1927, included six or more pieces, mainly flasks moulded as politicians, bought from the Willett Collection in 1905. Free copies of the 1899 catalogue were presented to the delegates to the Congress of Curators, held in Brighton in 1899, in compensation for the collection's absence. In his paper, *Museums and their Uses*, Willett states how he intended to show,

> the minor features which were distinctive of the lives of our forefathers in the various aspects of their amusements, their religion, their political life, and their intense interest in the naval and military operations by which this nation has been permitted to keep its shores inviolate from the foot of the invader[34]

Willett's thesis was that 'the history of a country may be traced on its homely pottery' and he proceeded to assemble what could be found 'on the mantelpieces of English cottage homes, representations of what its inmates or their forefathers admired, reverenced, trusted in … a kind of unconscious survival of the Lares and Penates [household gods] of the ancients.'[35] The thematic assemblage could take the unwary visitor by surprise, 'Ancient pottery of artistic value, selected at the sale of some celebrated collection, stands side by side with vulgar crocks … the subjects represented upon them being the only cause of their present connection.'[36] Albert Lee, an American ceramic collector visiting in the 1920s, found it 'the most interesting ceramic collection in England'.[37] 'Aside from its wealth of portraiture, the Willett Collection is the most extensive and complete assemblage of English folk pottery'.[38] In 1902 a journalist mused on Willett's collecting methods,

> Mr Willett was a born collector and, with ample means and leisure, has prosecuted his curious hobby with incessant devotion. From many an old country village, secluded farm house, wayside hostelry and obscure auction room he has routed out his treasures, one by one, and the great collection he has accumulated, all stored and classified so perfectly.[39]

He contrived to tell the history of the British people, political, social and cultural, through their ceramic productions, with particular reference to their decorative subject matter. His achievement is one of the earliest and most eloquent and informative assemblies of English material culture.

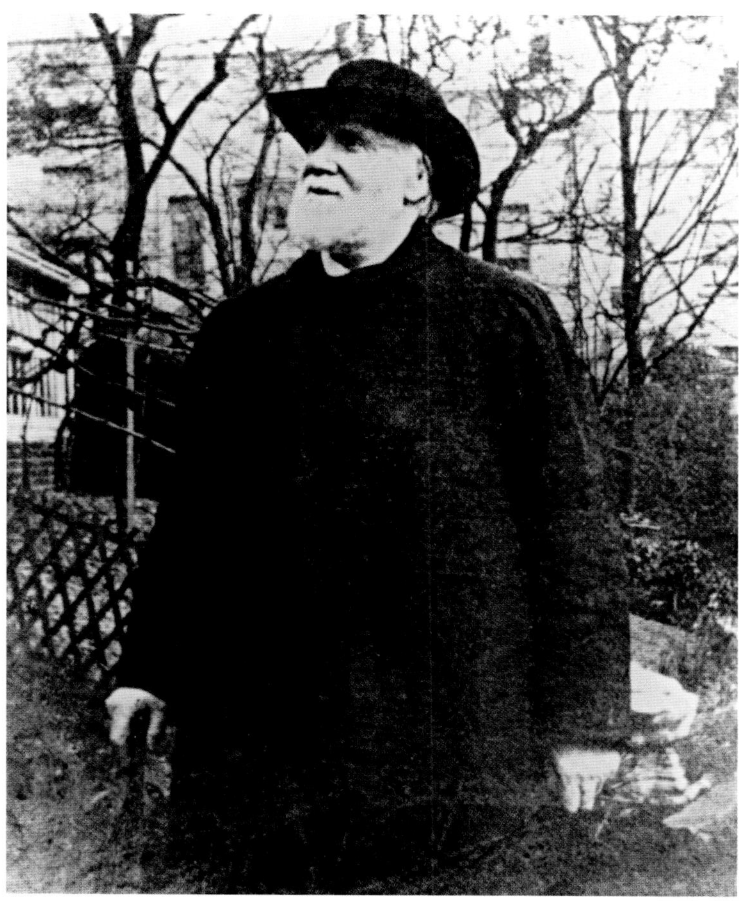

Willett in his characteristic black attire.

Chapter 1

ROYALTY & LOYALTY

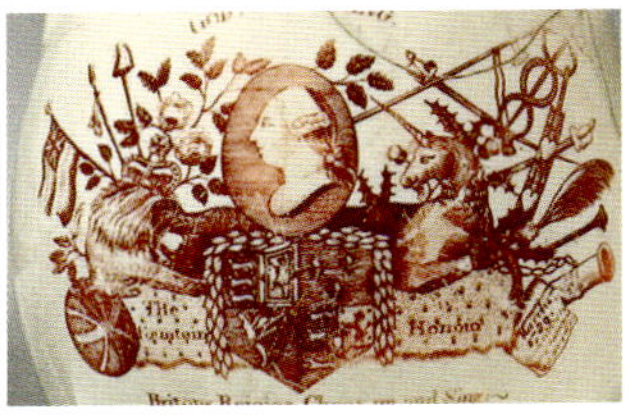

The Tudors

Henry Willett associated the first two items in his collection with Queen Elizabeth I. 'Good Queen Bess' enjoyed renewed popularity with the late-nineteenth-century revival of interest in the Tudors and the cult of 'Merrie England'. In fact neither item dates from her reign. Earthenware was the only ceramic body readily available in sixteenth-century England and it was used to construct simple vessels to hold liquids. Lead glaze was used to waterproof inner or outer surfaces and copper oxide could be added to tint the glaze green. Ceramics in a variety of bodies and with sophisticated decoration were imported from abroad before the English potters had acquired the technical skills to make them here.

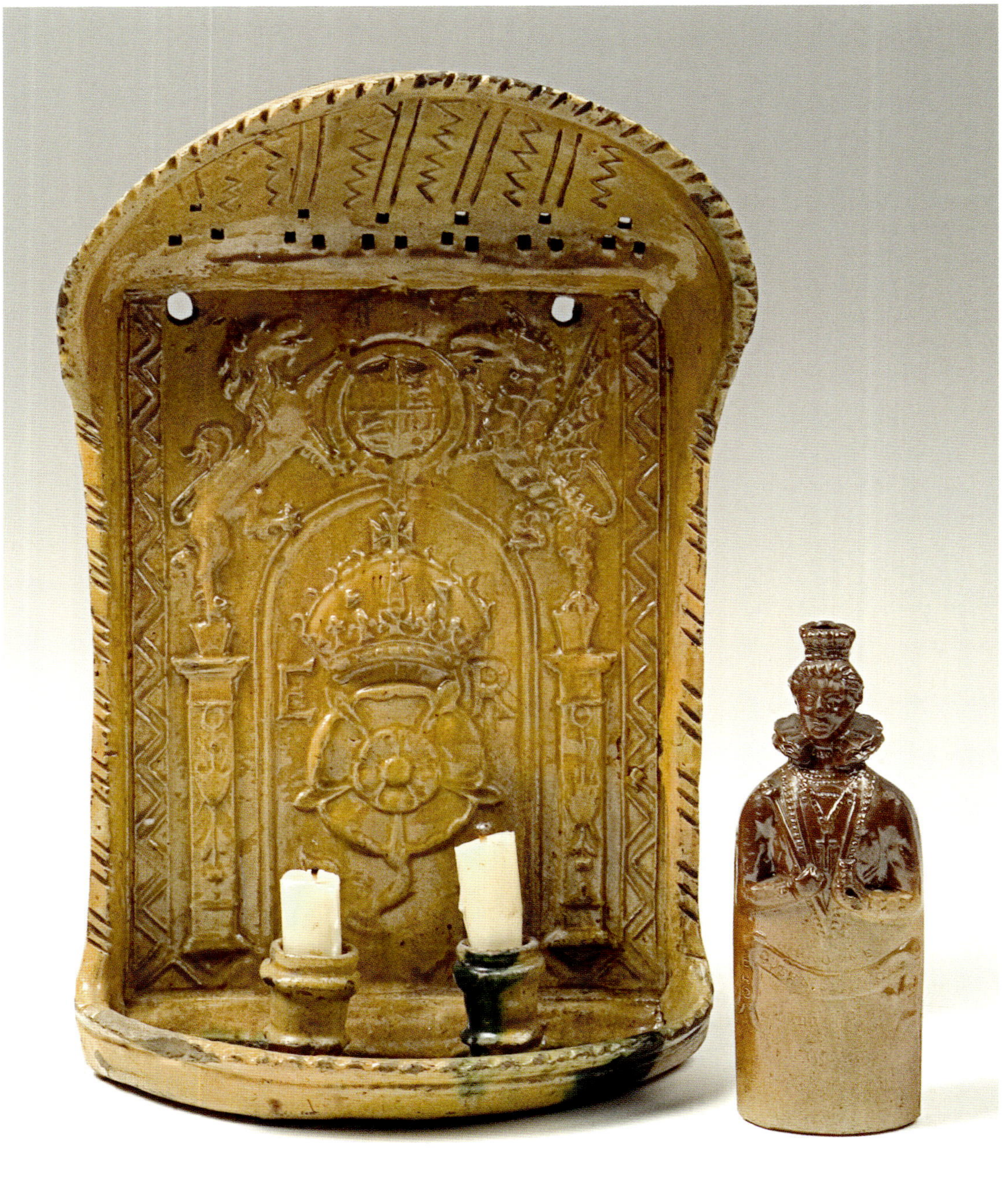

Candle Bracket, (001), mid-sixteenth century, possibly German, height: 45.7cm, (18in), yellow-glazed earthenware. Moulded with the Royal Arms and supporters and the Tudor rose flanked by initials 'ER' and 'AM', its integral canopy is pierced for hanging and its tray has two candle sockets.[1] Bernard Rackham suggests the few surviving examples may date from the reign of Edward VI and may be German, because of the high quality of the moulded decoration.[2]

Spirit Flask, (002), c.1830, London, height: 21cm, (8¼in), brown stoneware. Moulded as the figure of Elizabeth I. Inscribed, 'G. BROWNE / OLD QUEEN ELIZABETH HEAD/LOWER ROAD / ISLINGTON.' Other examples of this flask are inscribed, 'Pub by Wetherill July 27 1830 London'.[3]

Charles I (1625-1649) and Oliver Cromwell (1653-1658)

After nearly a decade of political conflict and the pitched battles of the English Civil War, the Parliamentarians defeated King Charles I's Royalist supporters and the king was executed in 1649. For eleven years Britain became first a Commonwealth then, in 1653, a Protectorate under the personal rule of Oliver Cromwell. The secret cult of the late king as 'Charles the Martyr' emerged among Royalists during the 1650s but commemorative objects became more common after the Restoration of Charles II. The only mementoes of Cromwell date from long after his time since his Puritan supporters destroyed religious art wherever they could and discouraged personality cults. Tin-glazed earthenware in the form of maiolica arrived in England from Italy in the early seventeenth century. It crossed the English Channel in 'Flanders galleys' and became known as 'galleyware' or delftware after the Dutch city that was a major producer.

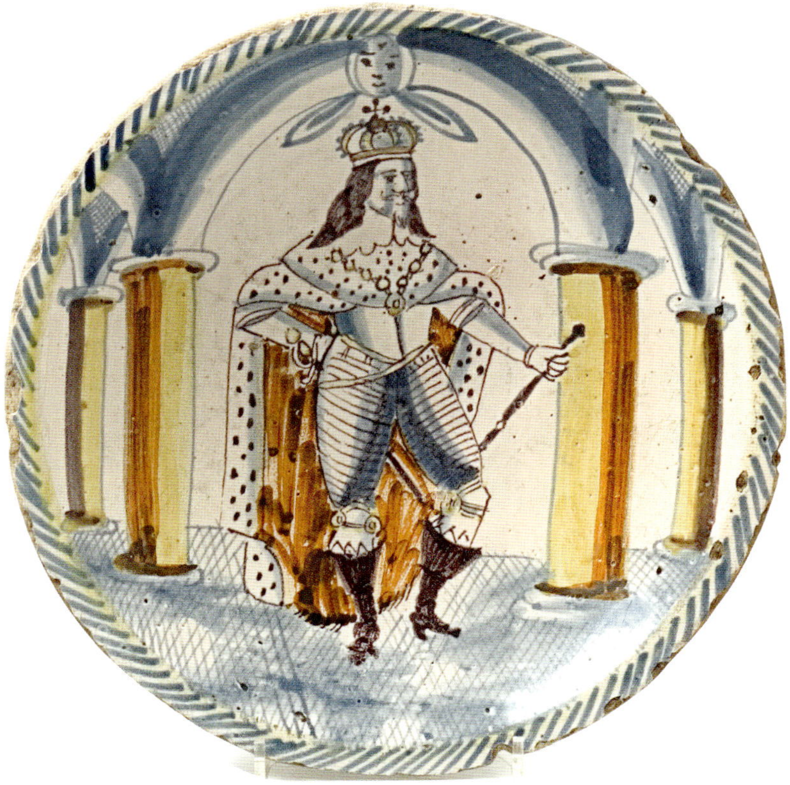

'Blue-dash' Charger, (003), c.1660, diameter: 30.5cm, (12in), tin-glazed earthenware. Charles I in a heroic pose, dressed in full armour stands in a cloister-like setting, a schematic face above represents God. The design reflects Charles's belief that kings were divinely appointed and answerable only to God. Such dishes were made from the 1650s, in support of the secret cult of 'Charles the Martyr'. It is safer to assume that this one was made after the monarchy was restored under his son, Charles II, in 1660.[4]

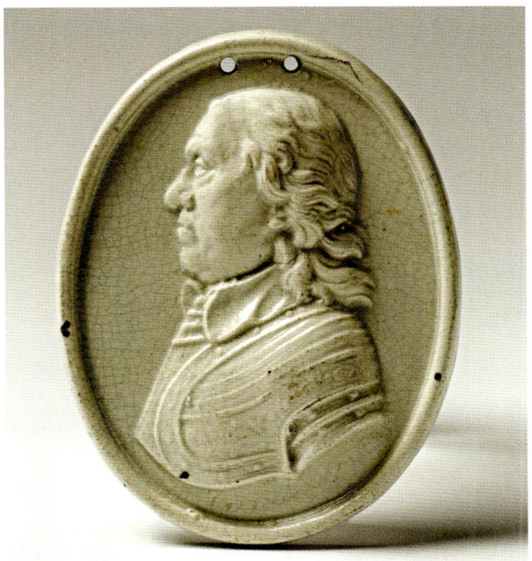

Plaque, (**005**), c.1810, possibly Swansea, height: 10.2cm, (4in), creamware. Relief-moulded with a profile portrait of Oliver Cromwell in armour. It may come from Swansea, since a similar piece was modelled for the proprietor, L.W. Dillwyn, from a bronze relief in his own collection.[5]

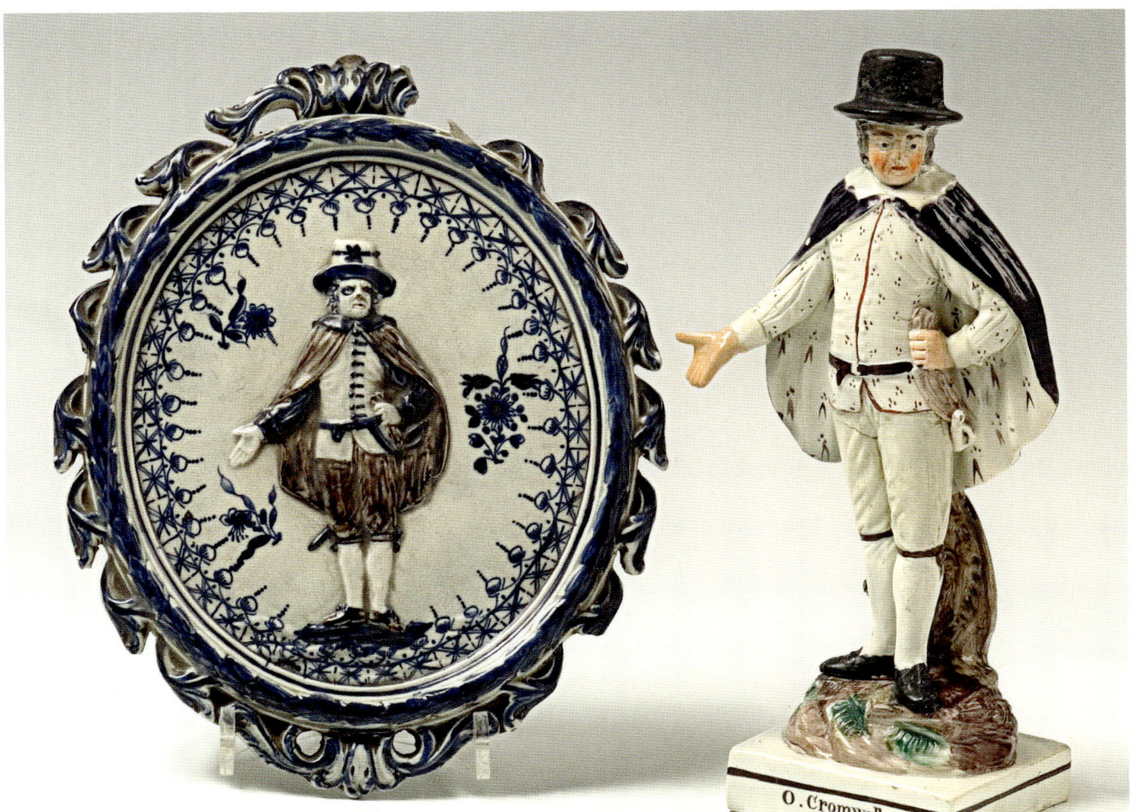

Figure, (004), c.1790, Staffordshire, height: 22.9cm, (9in), Enamelled pearlware.
Plaque, (0115), (c.1800, Staffordshire, height: 21.5cm, (8½in), Prattware. Two representations of Cromwell, the Lord Protector, are based on Charles Grignion's engraving (after Samuel Wale), used to illustrate G. F. Raymond's *A New Universal and Impartial History of England*, 1787. The inappropriate ermine lining of the cloak hints at Cromwell's late desire to establish a hereditary dynasty. The plaque is incorrectly incised on the reverse, 'Duke William'.

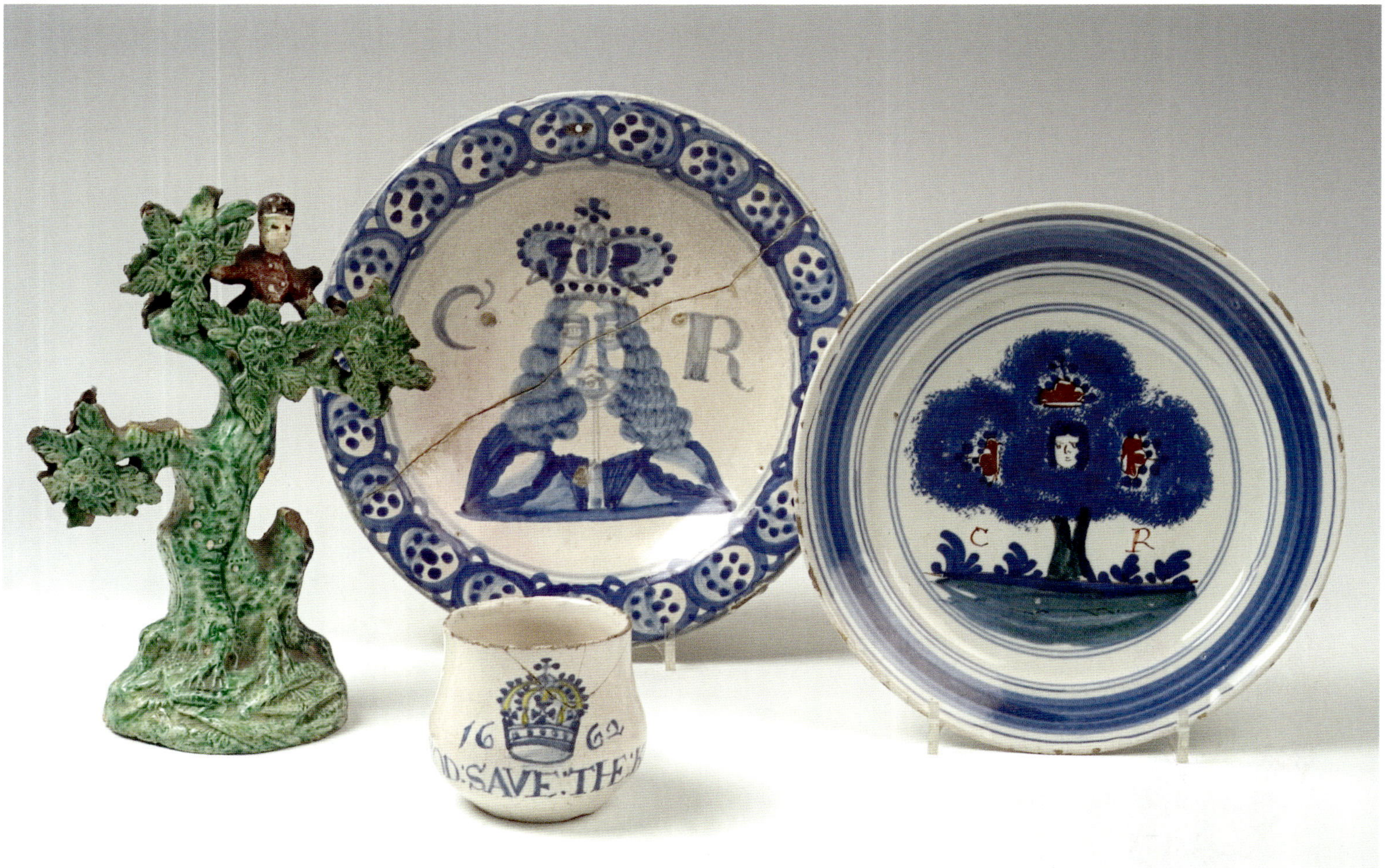

Figure Group, (007), c.1830, Staffordshire, height: 20.3cm, (8in), enamelled pearlware.
Plate, (008), c.1700, diameter: 21.6cm, (8½in), tin-glazed earthenware.
Plate, (006), c.1715, London or Bristol, diameter: 21.6cm, (8½in), tin-glazed earthenware. The crudely modelled group, thought to portray the prince hiding in the oak tree, more closely resembles popular bird's-nesting groups produced in the 1830s. The central plate is naively painted with a portrait of Charles II as king, inscribed 'CR'. The face of Charles, Prince of Wales, framed by three crowns (of England, Scotland and Ireland), inscribed 'CR' for Carolus Rex, peeps through the branches of the 'Boscobel Oak'. The technique of sponging oxide colour onto the plate's surface, to indicate the foliage, was not used until after 1700.
Cup, (009), dated 1662, London, height: 7.6cm, (3in), tin-glazed earthenware. Decorated with a crown and inscribed, 'GOD : SAVE : THE : KING', the cup celebrates the Restoration of Charles II. The interior inscription: 'Lambeth', is an early reference to this factory.

Charles II (1660-1685)

Following the execution of Charles I, his eldest son, Charles, continued to oppose the Parliamentarians until his defeat at the Battle of Worcester in 1651. According to tradition, after the battle, he hid in an oak tree on the estate of Boscobel House in South Staffordshire before fleeing to France. He embarked from what is now Hove Lagoon, an event commemorated annually in the Royal Escape yacht race from Brighton to Fécamp. The 'Boscobel oak', which gave its name to numerous 'Royal Oak' taverns, became popular with Stuart sympathisers after Queen Anne's death in 1714, when the German, George of Hanover, became King.

Charles II's Restoration to the English throne in 1660 was initially greeted with general rejoicing. It inspired production of the sort of commemorative objects and imagery previously suppressed by the Commonwealth. Slipware was perfected in Staffordshire and lively figurative scenes were applied in pale slip to the surfaces of impressively large dishes, in the manner of cake icing.

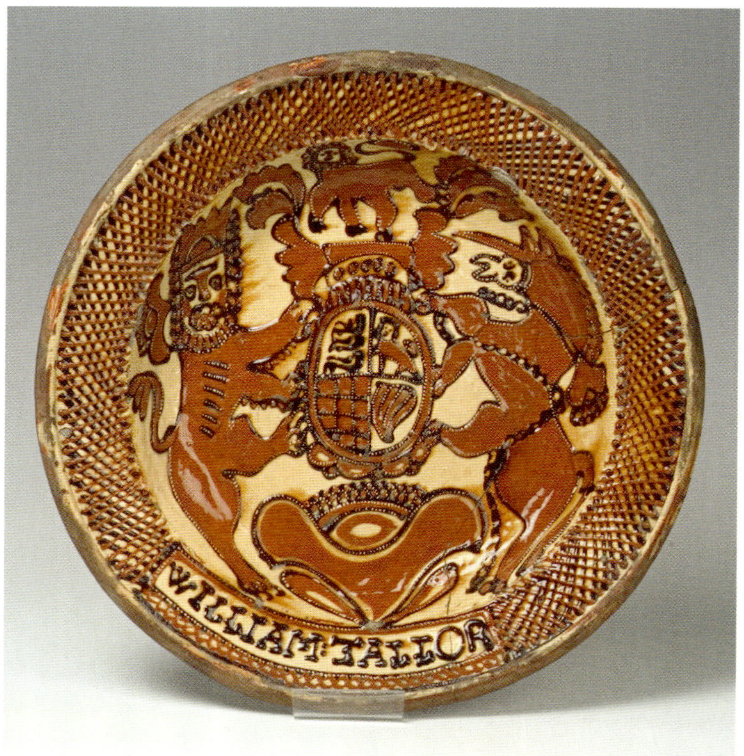

Dish, (010), c.1685, William Talor, Staffordshire, diameter: 43.2cm, (17in), slipware. An edict of 1660 decreed that the royal coat of arms, (depicted here), be displayed in every church. The dish is inscribed by its maker, 'WILLIAM : TALLOR'. Talor (the more usual spelling) was born in Burslem in 1624 or Wolstanton in 1632 and made dishes for the coronations of Charles II and later James II. He probably copied the design from dishes made by the better-known Thomas Toft but made mistakes in rendering the armorial bearings.

William III (1689-1702) and Mary II (1688-1694)

William of Orange was born in 1650 to Mary, Charles I's eldest daughter and the Protestant 'Stadtholder' prince of the Netherlands, who died eight days before he was born. His mother died when he was ten and although nominally a ward of Charles II, he was raised by his grandmother in Orange (one of the Netherlands states). In 1677 he married his first cousin Mary, elder daughter of Charles II's brother, James. Following the 'Glorious Revolution' of 1688, James II (who had converted to Catholicism) was deposed and William and Mary were invited to take the British throne. William reigned alone after Mary's death. Their marriage was childless.

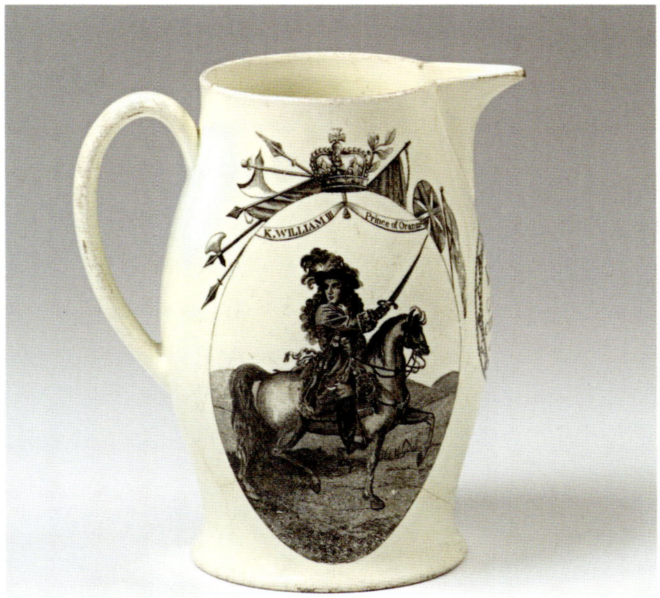

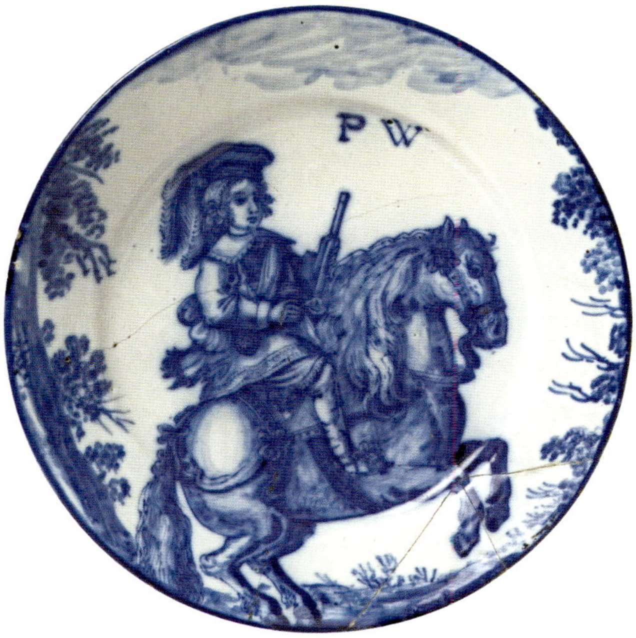

Jug, (016), c.1793, Wedgwood, printed in Liverpool, height: 17.8cm, (7in), creamware. Printed with William on horseback in full armour beneath the British crown and a festoon of weaponry. Image adapted from a print after Benjamin West, painted a century later, of the King victorious at the Battle of the Boyne in Ireland (1690).[6] He is depicted as a military hero and the saviour of Protestant Britain during the Glorious Revolution. The jug (which also features George III) was probably made to restate the legitimacy of the Protestant succession at a time of national emergency over war with France.

Dish, (011), c.1670, Netherlands, diameter: 38.1cm, (15in), delftware. Painted with a portrait of the young Prince William of Orange on a prancing horse and initials 'PW'. The image is reminiscent of Velasquez's equestrian portraits of Hapsburg monarchs, especially that of Infante Baltasar Carlos of Spain (1635, in the Prado, Madrid), which may have been known from engravings.

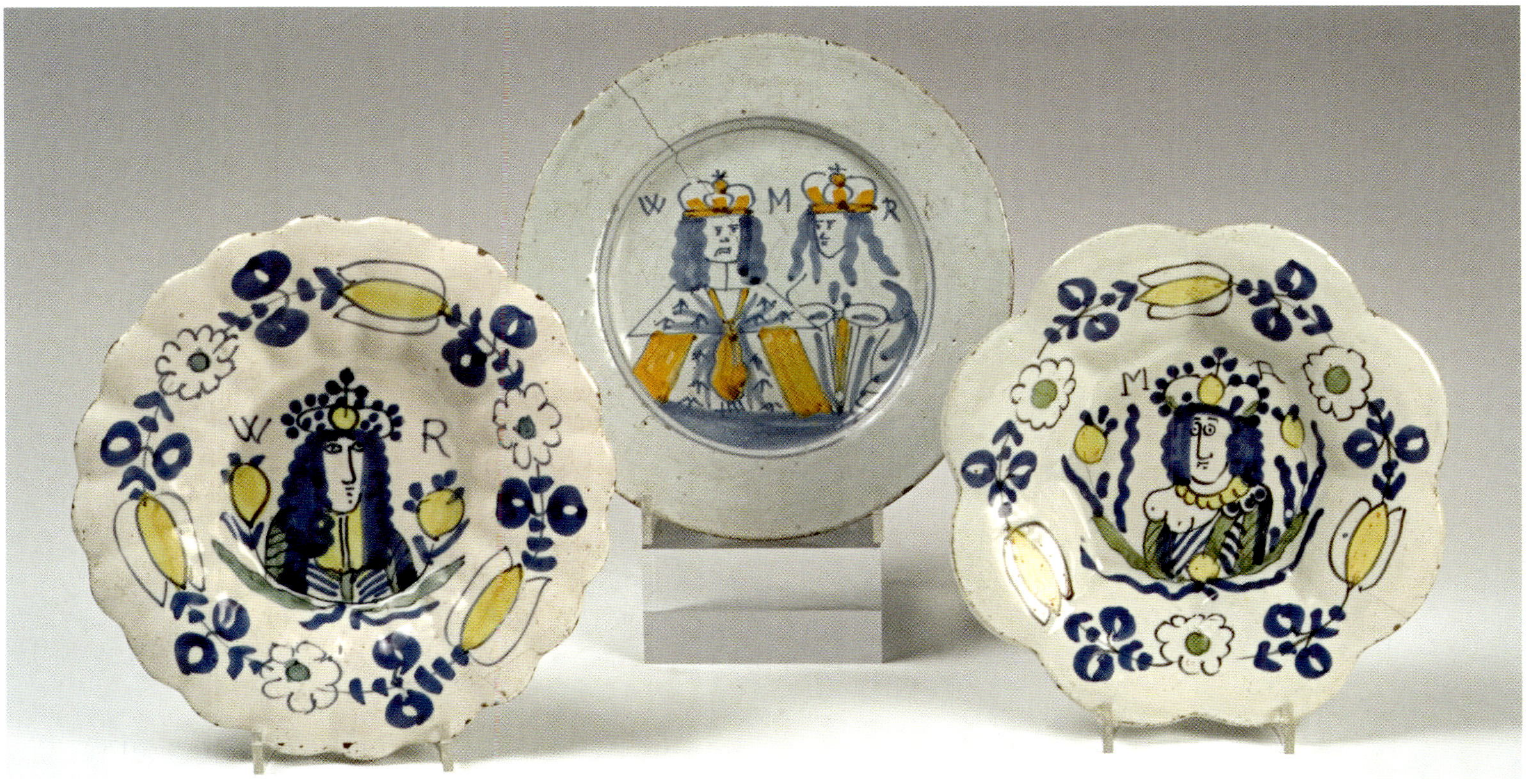

Pair of Dishes, (012 & A), c.1690-c.1700, Netherlands, each diameter: 20.3cm, (8in), delftware. The dishes are painted with caricatured portraits of the king and queen. The unusual lobed rims, decorated with tulips, suggest a Dutch origin.

Plate, (013), c.1690-c.1700, probably London, diameter: 21.6cm, (8½in), tin-glazed earthenware. Painted with portraits of William and Mary and the initials WMR. Other examples of this design are dated 1691, and are probably taken from a coronation portrait.

Queen Anne (1702-1714)

William III was succeeded by Mary's younger sister, Anne, who was married to Prince George of Denmark. Her reign was marked by the development of two political parties, the Whigs and the Tories. Although Anne and George had many children, none survived her.

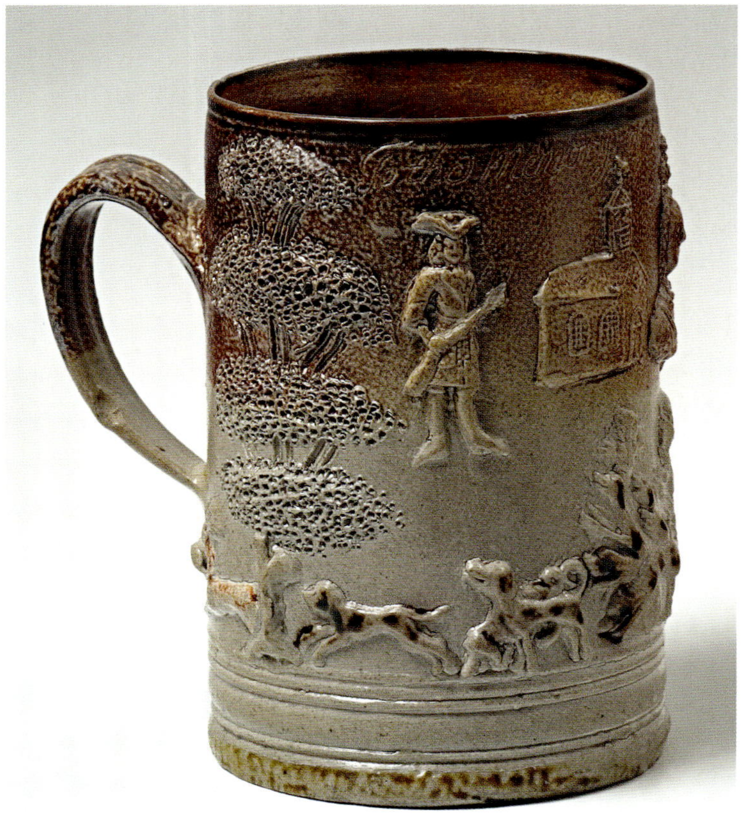

Giant Mug, (018), 1721, Vauxhall, London, height: 21.6cm, (8½in), salt-glazed stoneware.
Decorated with applied, relief sprigs including a portrait of the queen, a church, two soldiers with muskets, and a hunting scene where spotted hounds chase a stag amongst trees. Inscribed 'To the Memory of Queen Ann (*sic*) Made 1721'. Anne was a keen huntswoman and when too old to ride she would follow the hunt and her royal buckhounds through Windsor Forest in her carriage.[7]

George I (1714-1727)

After Anne's death, in the absence of any close Protestant heir, the throne passed to George of Hanover, Anne's distant cousin on his mother's side. Although he had the support of Parliament, George was never popular with the British people. He spent long periods in Hanover and never learned to speak English. His reign saw the emergence of Robert Walpole, Britain's first de facto Prime Minister.

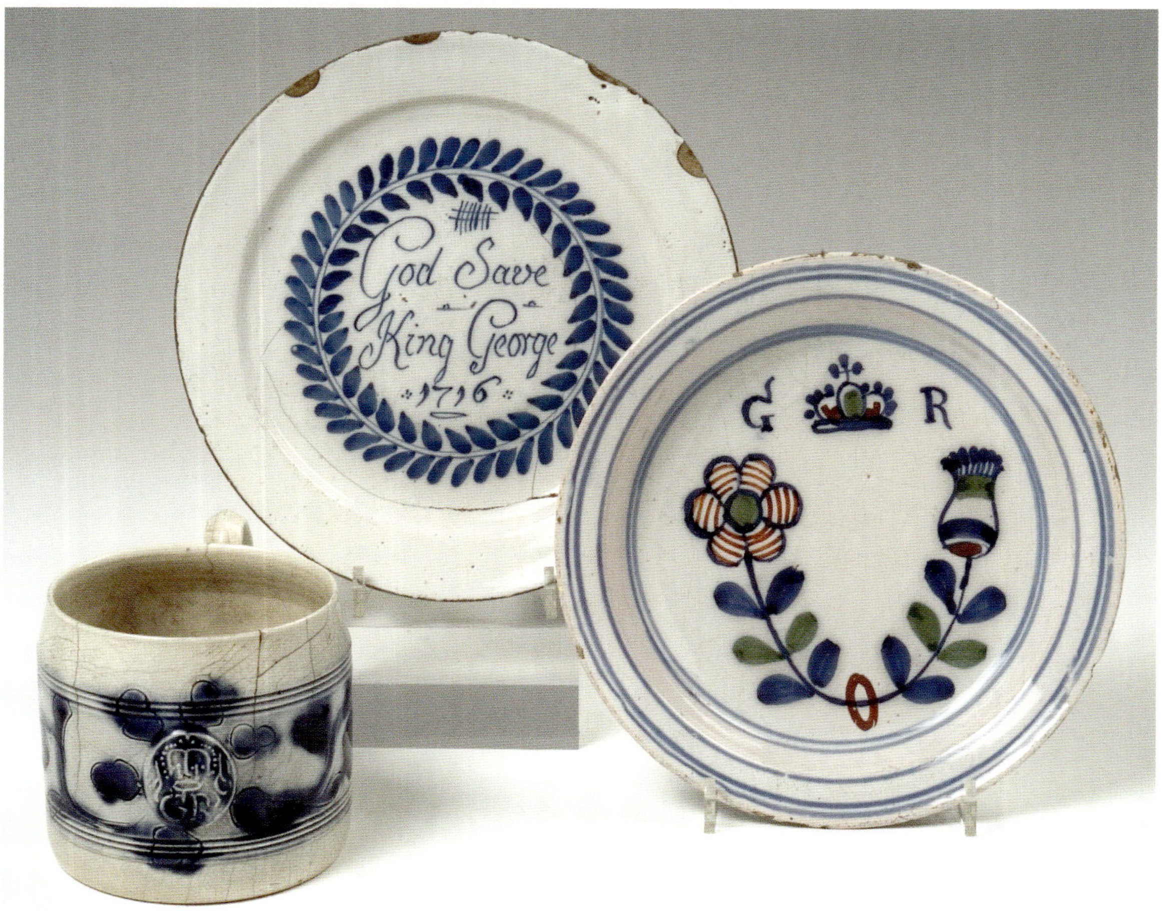

Mug, (023), c.1720, London, height: 10.2cm, (4in), stoneware. Moulded with medallion impressed with a crowned GR.
Plate, (021), 1716, Lambeth, London; diameter: 22.9cm, (9in), delftware. Painted inscription within a blue wreath, 'God Save / King George / 1716'.
Plate, (022), Lambeth, London; diameter: 21.6cm, (8½in), delftware. Painted initials GR and a crown are supported by the English rose and the Scottish thistle.

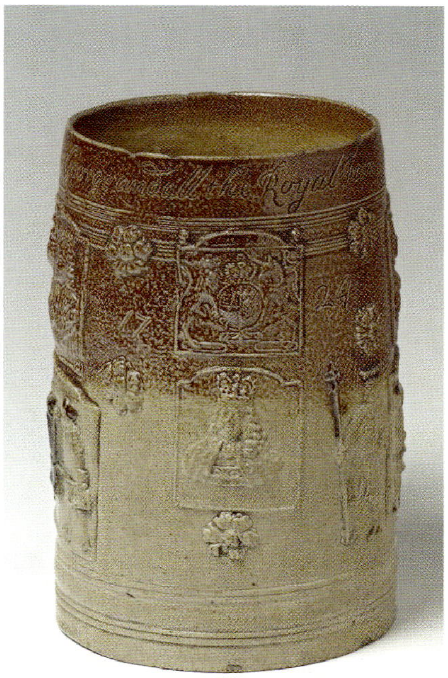

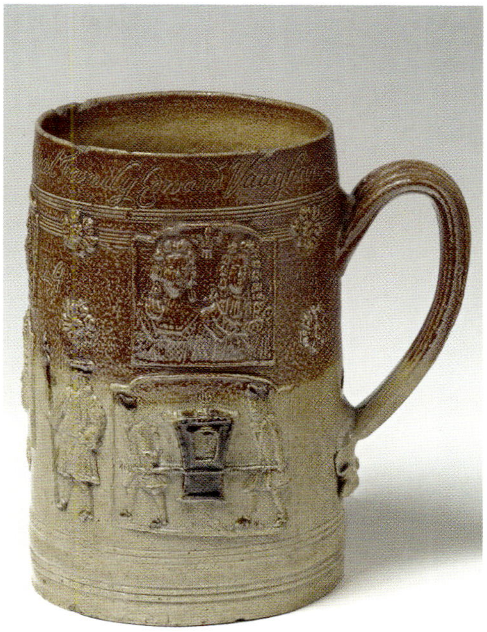

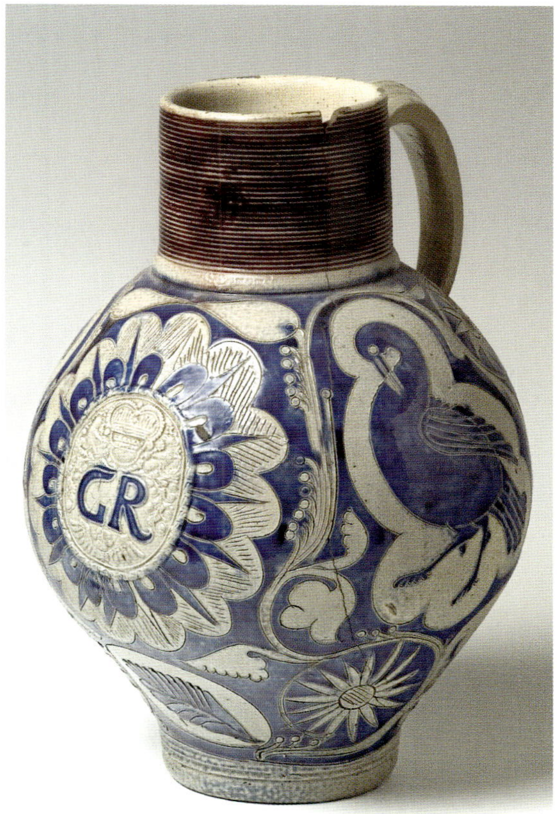

Giant Mug, (024), 1724, Vauxhall, London, height: 21.6cm, (8½in), salt-glazed stoneware
Front view; Relief decorations include applied inn signs moulded with the Royal Arms, flanked by incised date 1724 and a portrait of George I. Inscription 'God preserve King George and all the Royal Family Edward Vaughan / 1724' is incised around the rim.
Side view; Applied inn signs moulded with the Prince and Princess of Wales, sedan chairs with bearers, gentlemen yeomen and rosettes.
The mug may have been commissioned by or presented to one of two Vaughans who sat in Parliament as MPs for Welsh constituencies. Edward Vaughan was elected the member for Montgomeryshire in 1679 and served until his retirement in 1718, the year he became 'Father of the House'.[8] It was Richard Vaughan, however, member for Carmarthen and Merioneth from 1655 to 1734, who was declared Father of the House in 1724. Potters frequently made mistakes in their inscriptions.

Flagon, (020), c.1720, Germany, Westerwald, height: 31.8cm, (12½in), salt-glazed grey stoneware. Impressed with crown and GR monogram for George I, it is incised and decorated in cobalt blue with two large birds, possibly pelicans, symbolising self-sacrifice.[9]

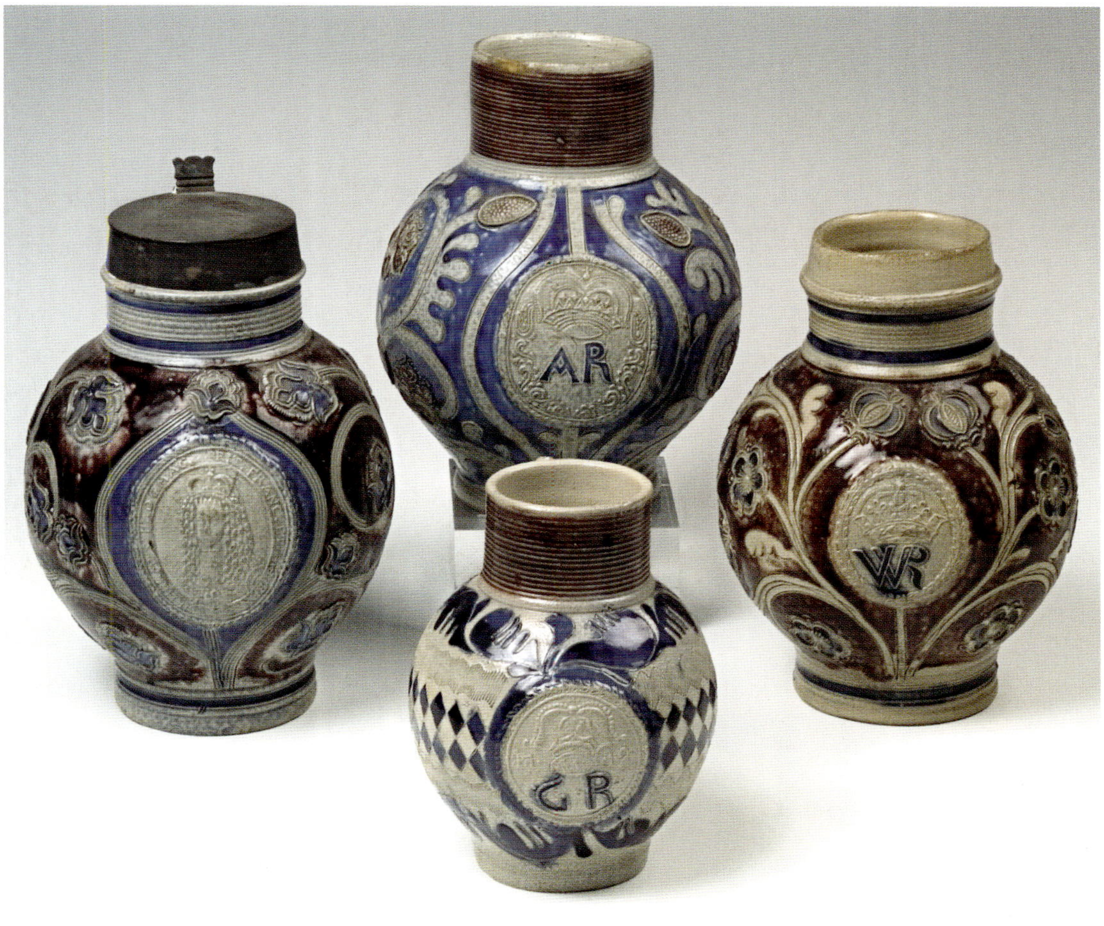

Four Flagons, Germany, Westerwald, salt-glazed grey stoneware, incised and decorated in cobalt blue and manganese purple. Clockwise: **(014)** with metal lid, height: 21.6cm, (8½in), impressed with portrait of William III; **(017)** height: 21.6cm, (8½in), impressed with crown and monogram AR for Anne; **(015)**; height: 21.6cm, (8½in), impressed with crown and monogram WR, dated 1719; **(019)** height: 15.3cm, (6in), impressed with crown and monogram GR for George I.

George II 1727-1760

George II was born and raised in Germany and married Caroline of Ansbach in 1705 with whom he had eight children. On his father's accession to the British throne in 1714 he accompanied him to London. Unlike his father, he was a fluent English speaker. He was also the last British monarch to lead his troops into battle, defeating the French at the Battle of Dettingen in 1743. In 1745 he had to face the Jacobite Rebellion, led by Charles Edward Stuart, the Catholic grandson of the deposed James II.

His reign saw important developments in British ceramic production. Soft-paste porcelain was pioneered at Chelsea and Bow in London in the 1740s and shortly after at Vauxhall, Derby and Worcester in the 1750s. In addition, the technique of transfer-printing engraved designs onto ceramics, enabling the mass reproduction of high-quality imagery, was patented by Sadler and Green of Liverpool.

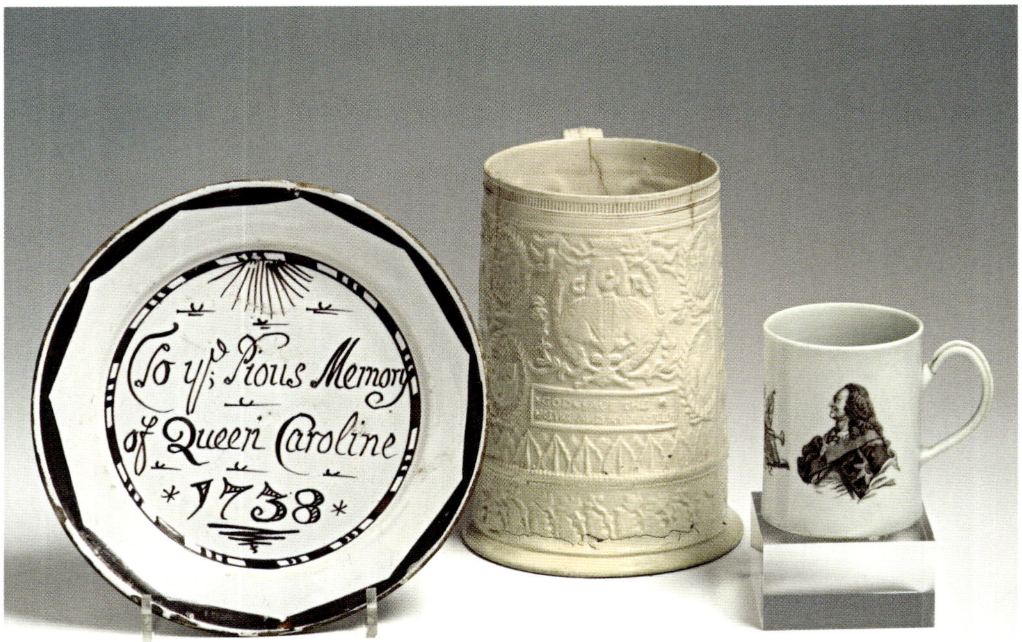

Plate, (031), 1738, probably London, diameter: 8.9cm, (3½in), tin-glazed earthenware. Inscribed in funereal manganese, 'To ye Pious Memory of Queen Caroline / *1738*', acknowledging the death of his wife, Caroline of Ansbach (1683-1737).[10]

Mug, (028), c. 1760, Worcester, height: 20.3cm, (8in), soft-paste porcelain.
Printed with a profile portrait of George II wearing the Star and Garter. The portrait was engraved by Robert Hancock after a 1753 painting by Thomas Worlidge.[11] On the reverse a boy sits amidst military trophies, holding a pole with the Phrygian Cap of Liberty and a banner inscribed 'Liberty'. This is marked with Hancock's monogram and the anchor symbol, a rebus for Richard Holdship, then manager of the Worcester factory and director of the print works.

Mug, (025), c.1756, Staffordshire, height: 17.8cm, (7in), white salt-glazed stoneware.
Moulded with a portrait of George II and the loyal declaration, 'GOD.SAVE.THE / KING AND MY MASTER' and the coats of arms of members of the George II's ministry of 1756. They include arms of the Leveson-Gower family, several of whom were prominent politicians and Lords Lieutenant of Staffordshire.[12]

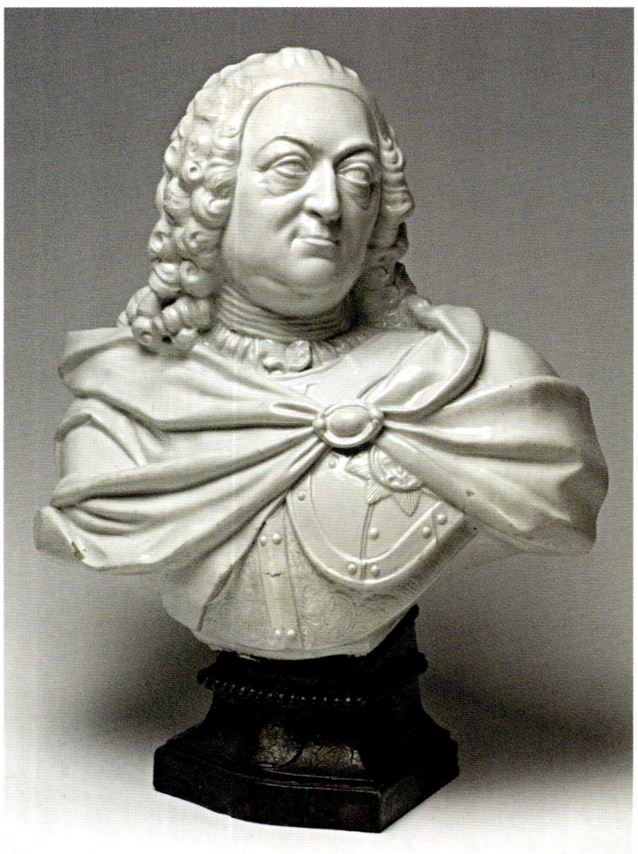

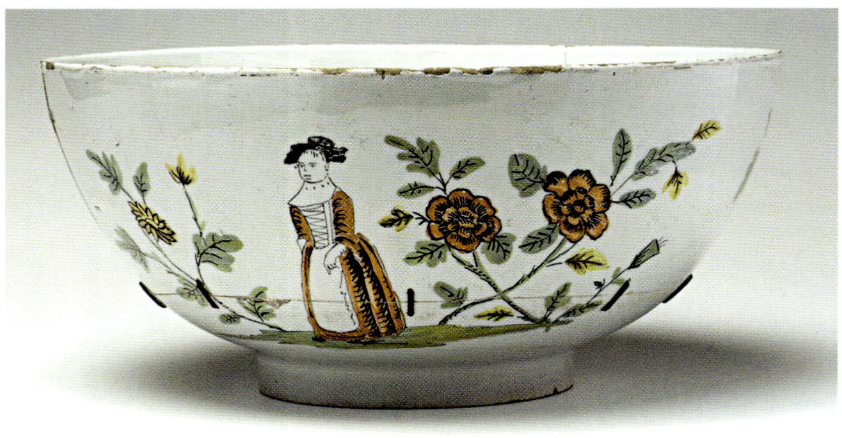

Punchbowl, (029), 1757, Liverpool, (base inscribed 'TB'), diameter: 26.7cm, (10½in), tin-glazed earthenware. Interior inscribed within a toast to the king; 'Now friends are Mett / Lets drink and Sing / A health to George / our Brittish [*sic*] King / Decb the 1-1757'. Exterior; floral decoration and a female figure painted in Fazackerly palette commonly found on Liverpool tin-glazed wares.

Portrait Bust, (030), c.1745-60, London, height: 39.4cm, (15½in), soft-paste porcelain, painted cast iron. This celebrated bust of George II, of which 19 variants survive, has been ascribed to most English porcelain factories. It is now thought most likely to have been made in London, possibly at Vauxhall but more likely at Bow.[13] The king, shown in vigorous late middle age, wears the Garter Star pinned to his cuirass, a light-weight breastplate, half hidden by his cloak. The original model may have been modelled by Roubiliac the style of whose posthumous portrait bust of the king it resembles.[14] This example has a waisted cast-iron socle painted matt black applied with a moulded medallion portrait, similar to that on a silver crown of 1745.

George III (1760-1820)

George III was the first Prince of Wales since Charles II to be born (in 1738) in England. George's father, the charismatic Frederick, Prince of Wales, died in 1751 when his son was only twelve. Frederick left his son a political testament, drafted in 1749, in which he advised separating Hanover from England, practising economy and reducing the national debt. It concluded by advising George to 'convince the nation that you are not only an Englishman born and bred, but that you are also this by inclination'.[15]

When George III succeeded his grandfather to the throne in 1760 he was initially seen to be weak and dominated by the unpopular Earl of Bute. Ceramic souvenirs were made to celebrate his marriage to Charlotte of Mecklenburg-Strelitz (1744–1818) and their joint coronation in 1761. It proved an enduring and affectionate marriage and they had fifteen children. George never took a mistress and the royal couple were models of decorum and frugality. Court life, however, was said to be tedious and fraught with protocol.

A range of ceramic commemoratives celebrated the King's recovery from his first bout of serious illness in 1788. A service to mark the royal recovery took place at St Paul's Cathedral on 15 March, and 23 April was declared a day of national thanksgiving. He was dogged by increasingly severe bouts of mental illness (long thought to be porphyria), for the rest of his life. He also survived several assassination attempts by deranged individuals. He was stabbed by Margaret Nicholson in 1786, stoned in the state coach on his way to Parliament in 1795 and shot at by James Hadfield in 1800.

George III was the first British king since Edward III to reign for more than fifty years. A Mrs Biggs wrote to Parliament to propose the novel idea of festivities to celebrate his Golden Jubilee. It was a measure of how popular the monarchy had become, despite the legacy of dislike for the Hanoverians and the loss of the American Colonies. Britons were recovering from the shock of the French Revolution and his Jubilee coincided with a period of economic prosperity. To support the military and naval reviews, royal pardons and local celebrations, a wide range of souvenir items was produced for the King's Golden Jubilee which was celebrated in 1809, in accordance with tradition, rather than 1810.[16]

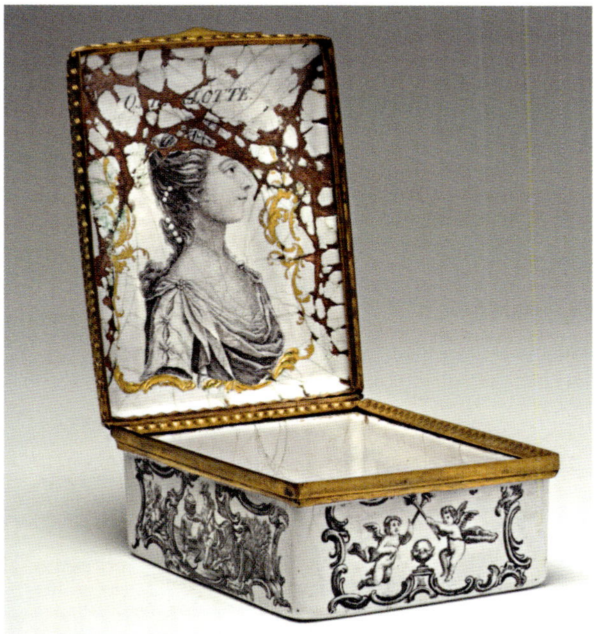

Snuff box, (033), c.1761, London or Birmingham, height: 3.5cm, (1⅜in), enamelled and printed copper. Such snuff boxes were produced as souvenirs of the royal wedding. It is printed with a profile portrait of George III on the outside of the lid and inside, a profile of Charlotte. The sides are printed with tiny vignettes of Britannia, Neptune and other figures and devices symbolising the arts and prosperity. The box is inscribed beneath, 'Let Him Love now / Who never Lov'd before, / Let Him who ever Lov'd / Now Love the more'. The portraits are by William Woollett (1735-1785) and the verse is a translation by Thomas Parnell from 'Pervigilium Veneris'.[17] There is a similar box in the Royal Collection.

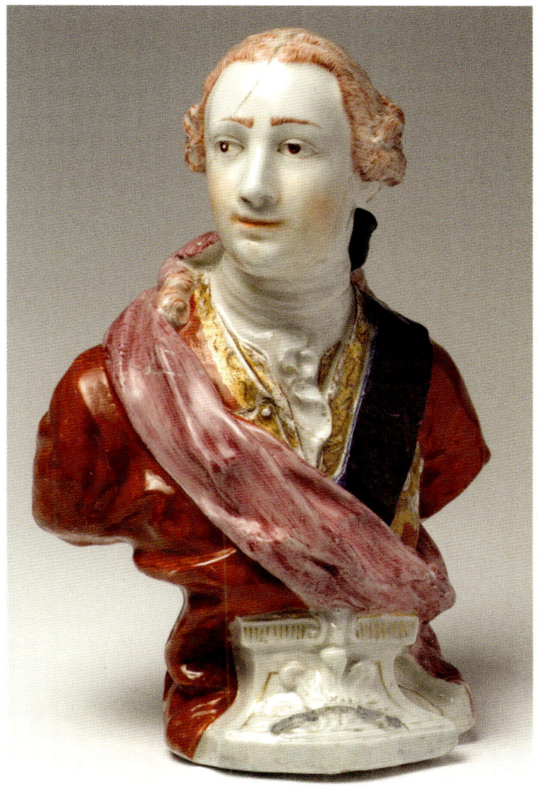

Portrait Bust, (032), c.1752, probably Longton Hall, Staffordshire, height: 27.9cm, (11in), enamelled, soft-paste porcelain.
The likeness of George, Prince of Wales, may be based on an engraving by James Macardell (pub.1751) after a portrait by David Luders. The bust, integral with its base, is moulded with the Prince of Wales's feathers. Previously ascribed to Chelsea, only two other (uncoloured) examples are known.[18] Extensive cracks beneath and on the reverse confirm the experimental nature of firing large pieces at this early date.

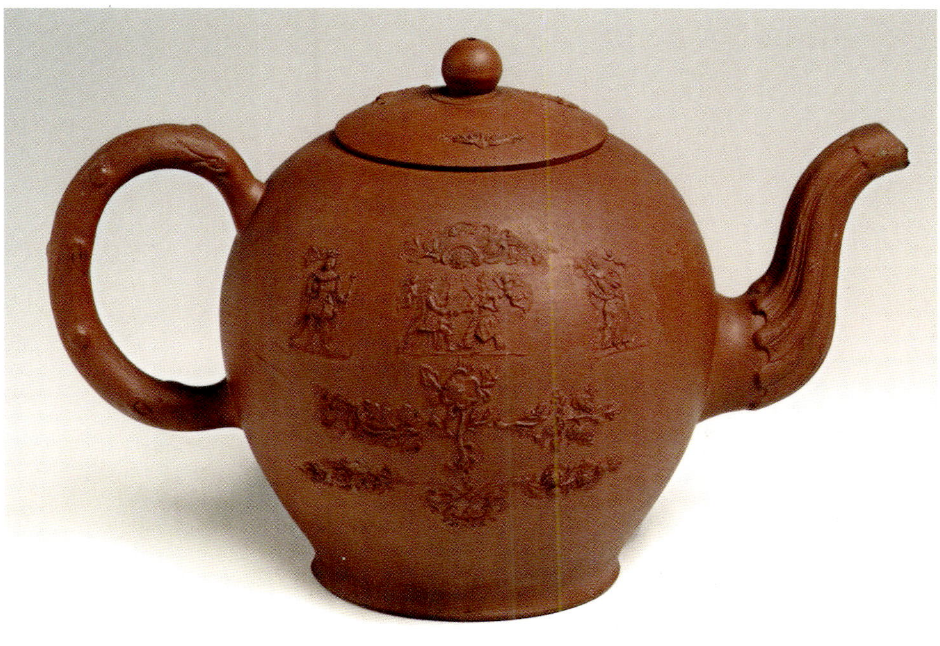

Punch Pot, (027), c.1761, Staffordshire, height: 16.5cm, (6½in), red stoneware.
Applied sprigs show the crowned king and queen sitting together between the initials 'GR', flanked by emblematic figures. The most likely event being commemorated is the marriage and (fifteen days later) the coronation of George III and Queen Charlotte in 1761.

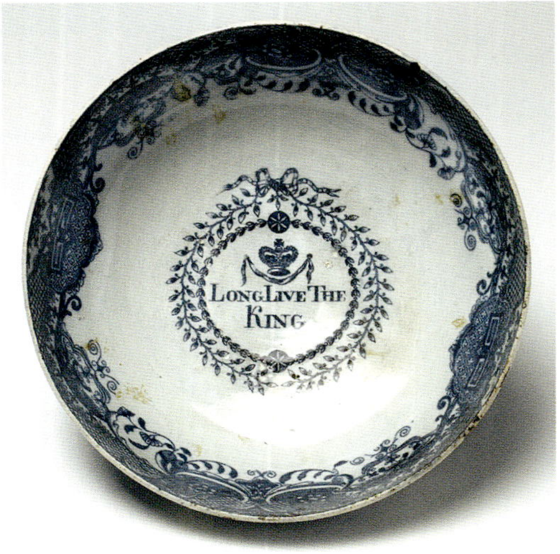

Punchbowl, (037), c.1790, Swansea, diameter: 25.4cm, (10in), printed pearlware. Exterior decorated with chinoiserie buildings and landscapes; interior with a broad band of foliage, latticework and scrollwork. At the centre a wreath encloses a crowned inscription 'LONG LIVE THE KING'.

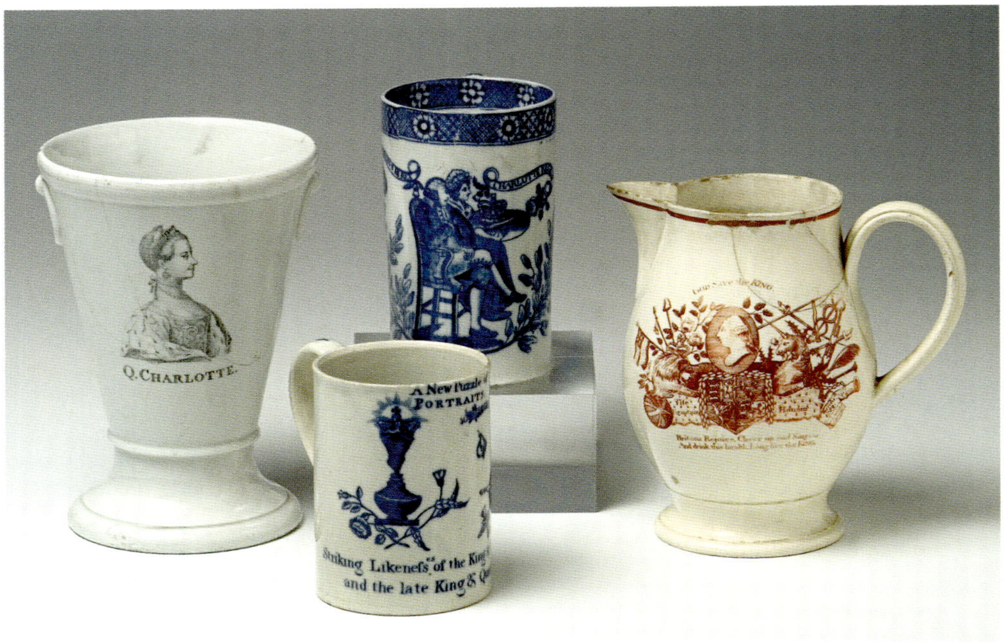

Clockwise: **Flowerpot, (034),** c.1761, Worcester, height: 16.6cm, (6½in), printed soft-paste porcelain. Printed with a profile portrait of Queen Charlotte in court dress (classical ruins on the reverse). The portrait, by Robert Hancock, is based on an engraving by James Macadell, (pub.1761), made at the time of her marriage and coronation. It was reused for the 1809 Jubilee.
Mug, (035), c.1790, Staffordshire or Swansea, height: 11.4cm, (4½in), printed pearlware. George III and Queen Charlotte sit side by side, flanked by laurel sprays. Two banners above are inscribed, 'GEORGIUS III REX / CHARLOTTE REGINA'.
Jug, (036), c.1789, probably Staffordshire, height: 14cm, (5½in), printed creamware. A medallion portrait of George III is supported by heraldic and other national symbols, beneath the motto, 'GOD save the KING'. Inscribed, 'The / Fountain/ Of / Honour/ March 17 1789' and 'Britons Rejoice, Cheer up and Sing / And drink this health. Long live the King'. It was produced to celebrate the King's recovery from his first bout of serious illness in 1788.
Mug, (038), Swansea, Cambrian Pottery, height: 8.9cm, (3½in), printed pearlware. Inscribed above, 'A New Puzzle of / PORTRAITS', and below, 'Striking Likenefses of the King & Queen of England / and the late King & Queen of France'. The design incorporates two hidden pairs of portraits and other symbols. The left side reveals *trompe l'oeil* silhouettes of George III and Queen Charlotte on the profiles of a vase.[19] Unlike the French monarchs (who had recently been executed), their crown is still intact and they are flanked by floral emblems of Great Britain. The design, taken from a print published by Orme on 18 January, 1794, highlights the vulnerability of the British monarchy, weakened by George III's illness and the unpopularity of George, Prince of Wales. Republican ideas and sympathies were spreading.

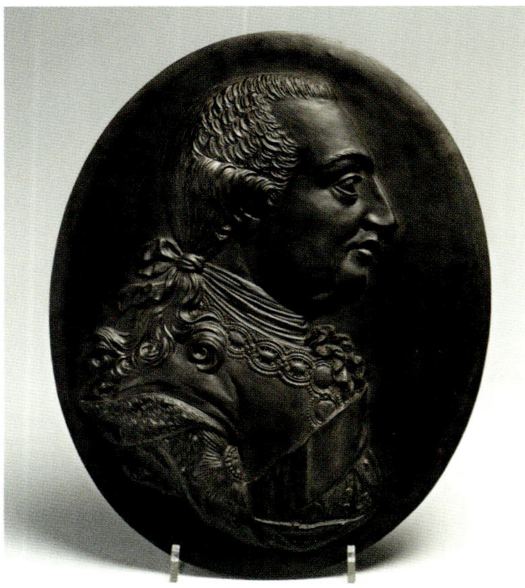

Plaque, (041), c.1780, marked Neale & Co. for James Neale, Hanley, Staffordshire, height: 30.5cm, (12in), black basalt. Moulded with a profile portrait of George III wearing a sash and the Garter Star embroidered on an ermine mantle. Based on a portrait medallion issued by Wedgwood, designed by William Hackwood after wax portraits by Isaac Gosset.[20]

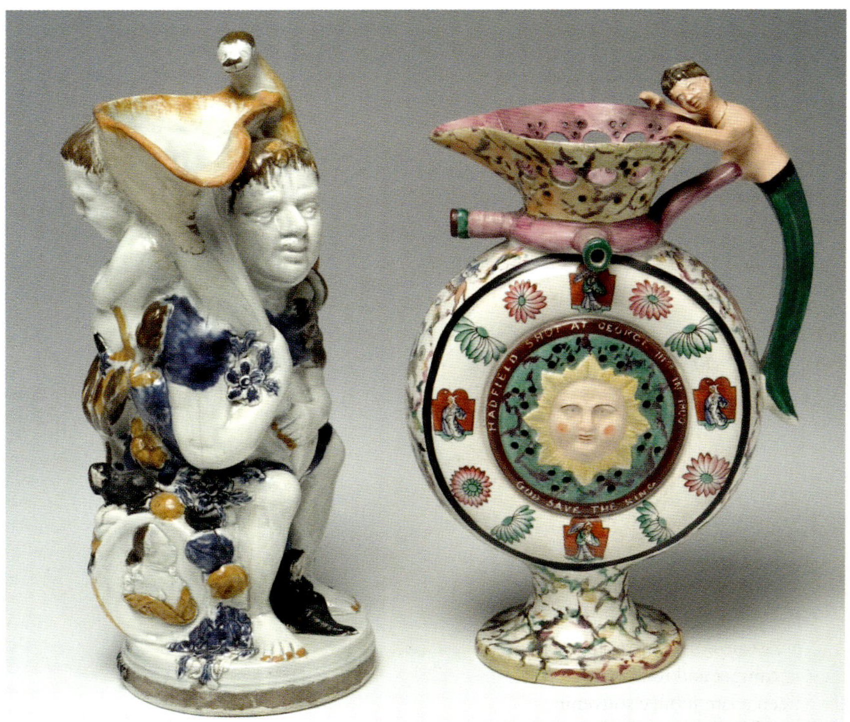

Novelty Jug, (040), 1800-20, probably Staffordshire, height: 30.5cm, (12in), Prattware. Modelled as Bacchus sitting on a barrel supporting a cornucopia (which forms the spout), the handle moulded as a chained weasel. On the reverse the figure of a satyr and on each end of the barrel are relief portraits of George III and Queen Charlotte.
Puzzle Jug, (042), c.1820, probably Staffordshire, height: 30.5cm, (12in), printed and painted pearlware. Jug has a wheel-shaped body applied with a central, moulded sun-face, a figurative handle and three spouts at the neck. Body printed with chinoiserie figures and enamelled. On one side only, a ring of dark red enamel is roughly incised: 'HADFIELD SHOT AT GEORGE III Rd IN 1800 / GOD SAVE THE KING'. This records the incident when, on 15 May 1800, the deranged James Hadfield shot at George III, as he entered his box at Drury Lane Theatre, London. Afterwards he slept, as usual, during the interval between the play and the afterpiece. The style of printing suggests that the jug long postdates the assassination attempt.

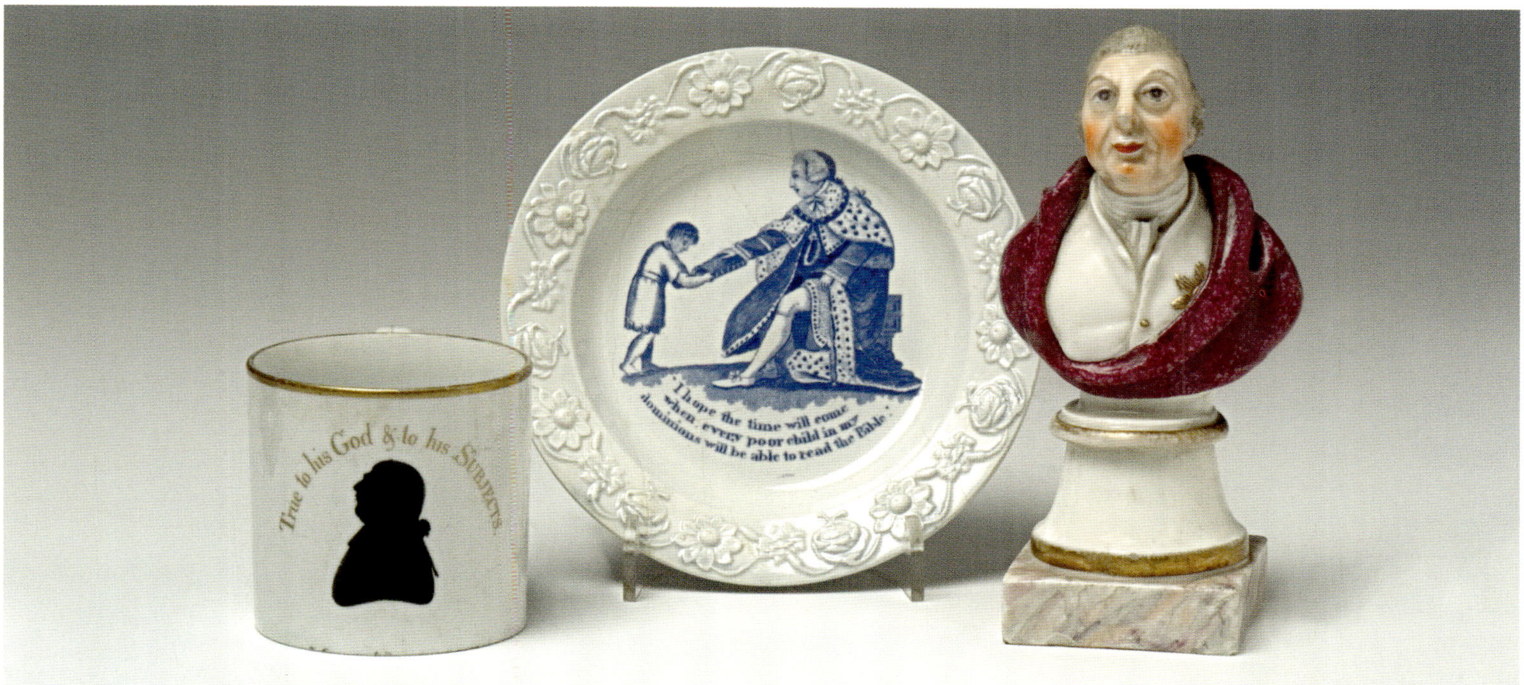

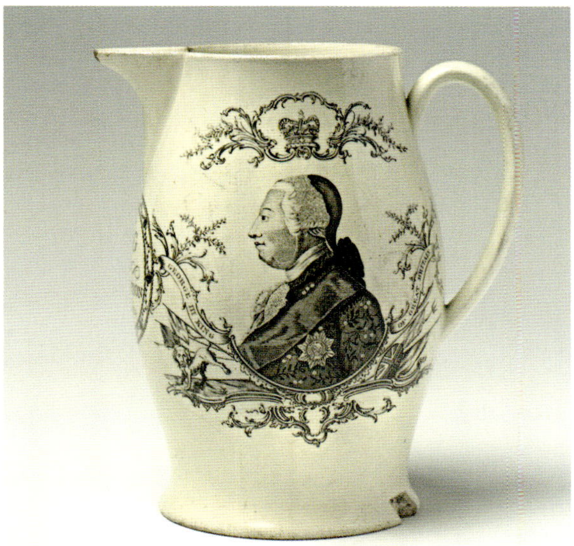

Coffee Can, (043), c.1809, probably Shropshire, Coalport, height: 6.2cm, (2½in), soft-paste porcelain, enamelled and gilt. Painted with silhouette portrait of George III, inscribed in gold, 'True to his God & to his Subjects.' Probably a souvenir item made to celebrate George III's Golden Jubilee.
Nursery Plate, (039), c.1805, probably Staffordshire, diameter: 13cm, (5¼in), printed pearlware. The king presents a Bible to a small child with inscription, 'I hope the time will come/ When every poor child in my/ Dominions will be able to read the Bible'.[21] The print is associated with the work of Joseph Lancaster, who pioneered a teaching method whereby monitors taught groups in classes of several hundred pupils, in schools for the poor. George III granted him an audience in 1805 and was sufficiently impressed to subscribe £100.
Portrait Bust, (044), c1809, probably Derby, height: 14cm, (5½in), soft-paste porcelain, enamelled and gilt. The bust, incised 'George III', is a good likeness of the elderly king. It may have been issued for the Golden Jubilee.

Jug, (016), c1793, Wedgwood, printed in Liverpool, height: 17.8cm, (7in), creamware. Printed with a profile portrait of George III, from an engraving after Jeremiah Meyer. Below the scroll inscribed 'GEORGE III KING' the small figure of the British lion urinates on the French fleur-de-lys.[22] Inscribed beneath the spout: 'King and Constitution', the motto of the Anti-Gallican Society (founded 1745), which campaigned against French influence in public life. The anti-French message suggests that the Anti-Gallicans, a Masonic lodge or other conservative interests may have commissioned such pieces at the outbreak of war with France in 1793.

Punchbowl, (046), c1809, Liverpool, diameter: 17.8cm, (7in), printed creamware. Interior printed with a view of Pembroke Place, Liverpool, where a crowd salutes a new equestrian statue of George III, whose plinth is embellished with Liverpool's Liver Bird. Emblematic figures, representing Britannia and the Spirit of History hover above them supporting a scroll inscribed: "Happy would England be/ could GEORGE/ But live to see another/ Jubilee." Beneath, interlaced with olive branches, denoting peace, is a long ribbon inscribed: "Debtors' Liberation/ Statue's Foundation,/ in celebration/ of the Jubilee, 25th Oct., 1809". The design, known as the 'Amnesty Print', marked the release of all prisoners of war (except the French), the issue of a general pardon for all offences, including desertion from the military, and the raising of a subscription to discharge all insolvent debtors. The exterior printed with rhymes and small figures of sailors.
Portrait Figure, (045), c1814, London, (impressed on back of base) reads, 'Pubd By A. Giacomelli / Oct 4th 1814 London'; height: 19.1cm, (7½in), painted and gilt plaster. George III, in old age, wears a frock coat applied with the Garter Star, holds an ear trumpet and rests on a metal cane. The original may have been a late Jubilee souvenir as Willett suggests in the 1899 catalogue.[23] The survival of a large number of these plaster figures, dated as late as 1818, indicates their popularity.

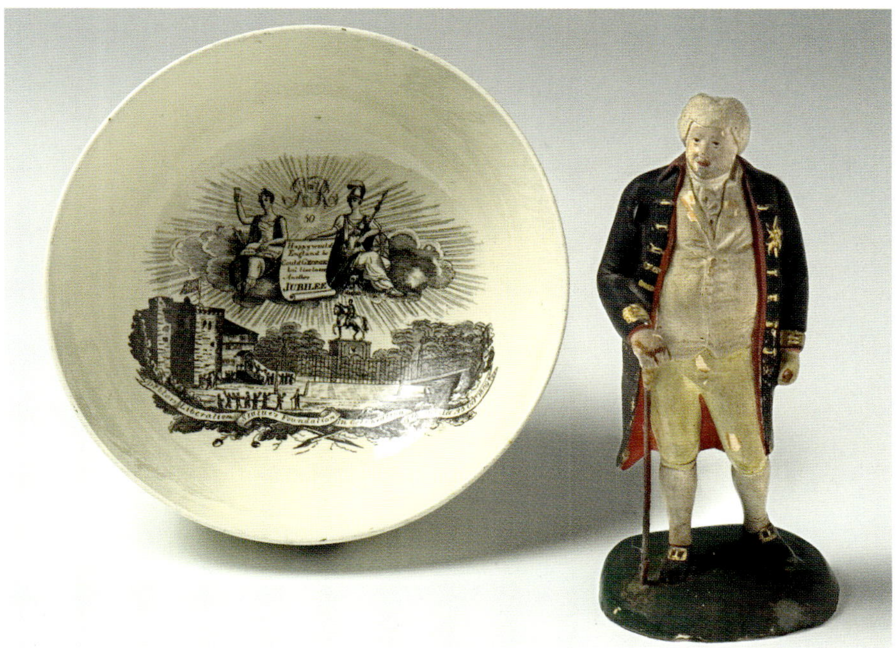

George IV (1820-1830)

George, Prince of Wales, reluctantly agreed to marry Princess Caroline of Brunswick (1768-1821) in April 1795, in exchange for clearing his enormous debts. Despite George III's efforts to mediate between the warring Prince and Princess of Wales, Caroline left Carlton House in 1797 and went to live in a rented house near Blackheath. Here she frequently entertained leading politicians from both parties, such as William Pitt, Lord Grey, Spencer Perceval and George Canning. From 1813 she travelled around the Mediterranean, exhibiting increasingly eccentric behaviour. Among her retinue of Italian companions was Bartolomeo Pergami, rumoured to be her lover.

George and Caroline's disastrous marriage produced one daughter, Princess Charlotte Augusta (1796-1817). To national rejoicing, Charlotte married Prince Leopold of Saxe-Coburg-Gotha (born 1790) on 2 May, 1816. Many ceramic souvenirs were produced to mark the occasion. When Princess Charlotte died giving birth to a stillborn son in 1818, the shock registered by the population was unprecedented. Henry Brougham, Charlotte's legal adviser, wrote: 'It really was as if every household throughout Great Britain had lost a favourite child.' Her death and the aftershock of the Napoleonic Wars provoked a wave of public grief and the production of a mass of souvenir ceramics, particularly tea services. The Romantic Movement in art and literature influenced the choice of imagery such as angels, willow trees and weeping figures.

George III was too ill to participate in government for the last ten years of his reign and a regency was declared in 1811, with his eldest son, George Prince of Wales, (born 1762) as Regent. As soon as George IV became king in 1820, he ordered the exclusion of his estranged wife from the prayers for the royal family in the Anglican liturgy. Incensed by this insult, Caroline returned to England to claim her position as queen. Henry Brougham (appointed her Attorney General), met her at St Omer to urge her to negotiate a financial settlement and to remain abroad but she refused. Under instructions from the king, the Cabinet unwillingly introduced, on 17 August, a 'Bill of Pains and Penalties' designed to strip Caroline of her title and to end her marriage by Act of Parliament. The queen's visits to Westminster to attend the so-called 'trial', were greeted by cheering crowds and Brougham and Thomas Denman discredited her accusers. The adoption of her cause by Whig politicians and radicals gave the private lives and morals of the royal family a public and political significance.

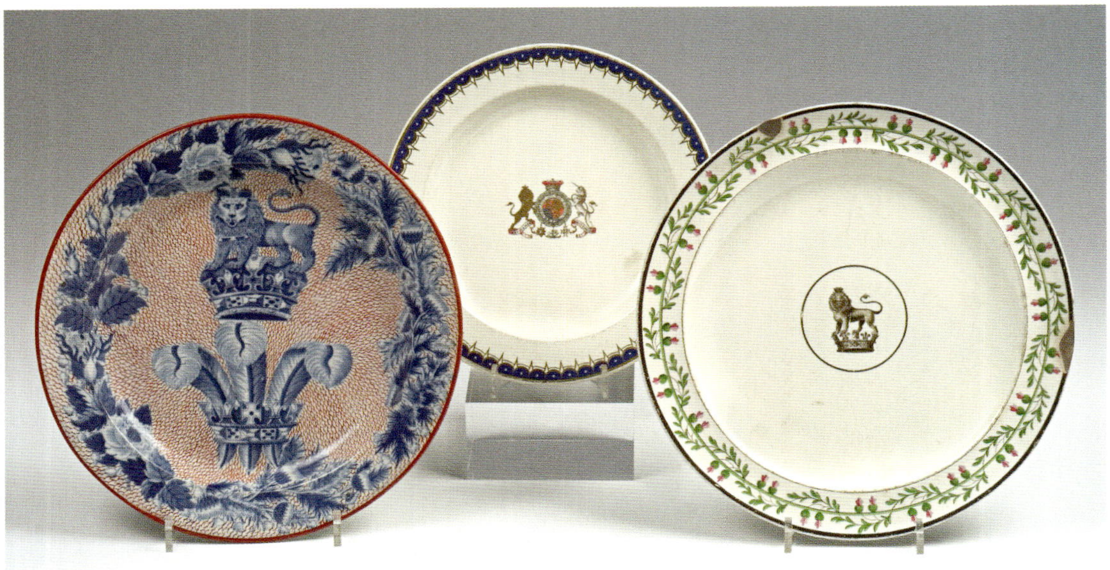

Plate, (052), c.1800, probably Thomas Lakin, Staffordshire, diameter: 25.4cm, (10in), printed, painted and gilt earthenware. A crowned lion crest surmounts the Prince of Wales's feathers, within a floral wreath. The ground is painted in red-brown with a herringbone network.
Plate, (048), c.1800, Wedgwood, Staffordshire, diameter: 20.3cm, (8in), enamelled creamware.
Egg-and-dart border (Wedgwood pattern 334) and in the centre, the Royal Arms within the Garter ribbon, hung with badges and mottoes.
Plate, (047), c.1800, Wedgwood, Staffordshire, diameter: 25.4cm, (10in), enamelled creamware.
Border of alternating pairs of thistles and a crowned lion crest in the centre.

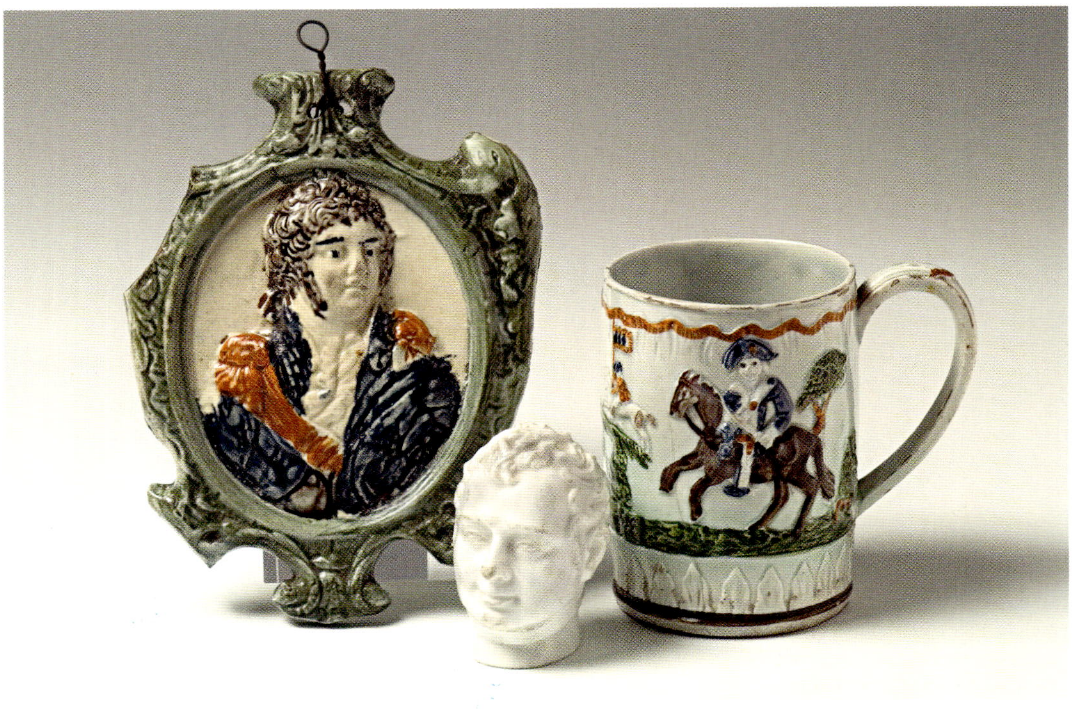

Plaque, (049), c.1800, Staffordshire, height: 16.5cm, (6½in), Prattware.
Moulded with a half-length portrait of the Prince of Wales within a (damaged) scrolling frame, pierced for hanging.
Head, (053), c.1820, Staffordshire, height: 7cm, (2¾in), soft-paste porcelain.
Slip-cast porcelain portrait of the Prince Regent in middle age.
Mug, (051), c.1820, Staffordshire, height: 11.4cm, (4½in), Prattware.
Appears to represent the Prince Regent on horseback.

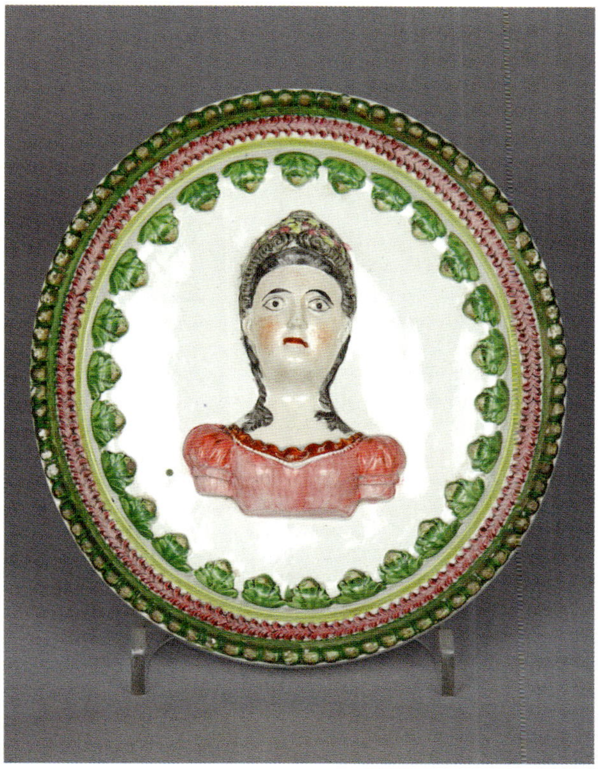

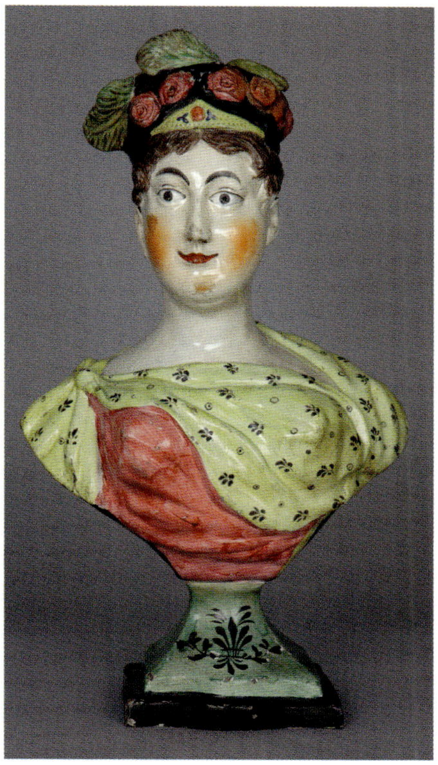

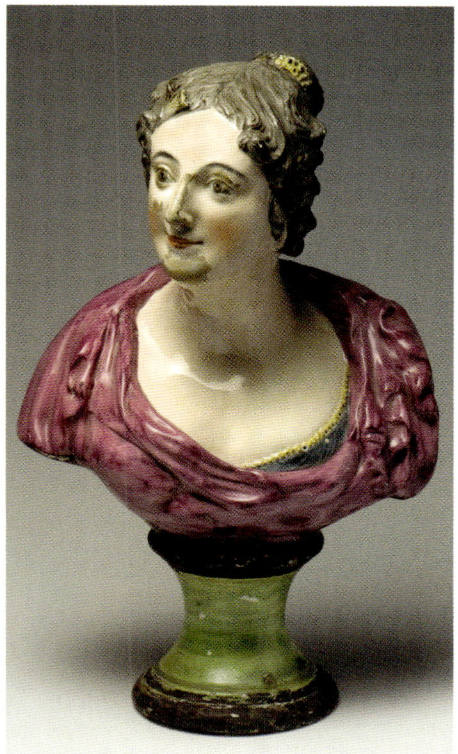

Plaque, (050), c.1817, height: 19.1cm, (7½in), enamelled earthenware. High relief portrait of Princess Charlotte within elaborately moulded oval frame.
Portrait Bust, (069), c.1817, Staffordshire, height: 48.5cm, (19in), enamelled pearlware. This portrait of Princess Charlotte on an integral waisted base, shows a young woman wearing a tiara and her hallmark wreath of roses and plumes in her hair The source is one of a number of prints after a portrait of the Princess (with Leopold) by George Dawe of 1817.
Portrait Bust, (070), c.1817, Staffordshire, height: 45.8cm, (18in), enamelled pearlware. Thought to represent Princess Charlotte, this bust lacks attributes to confirm her identity.

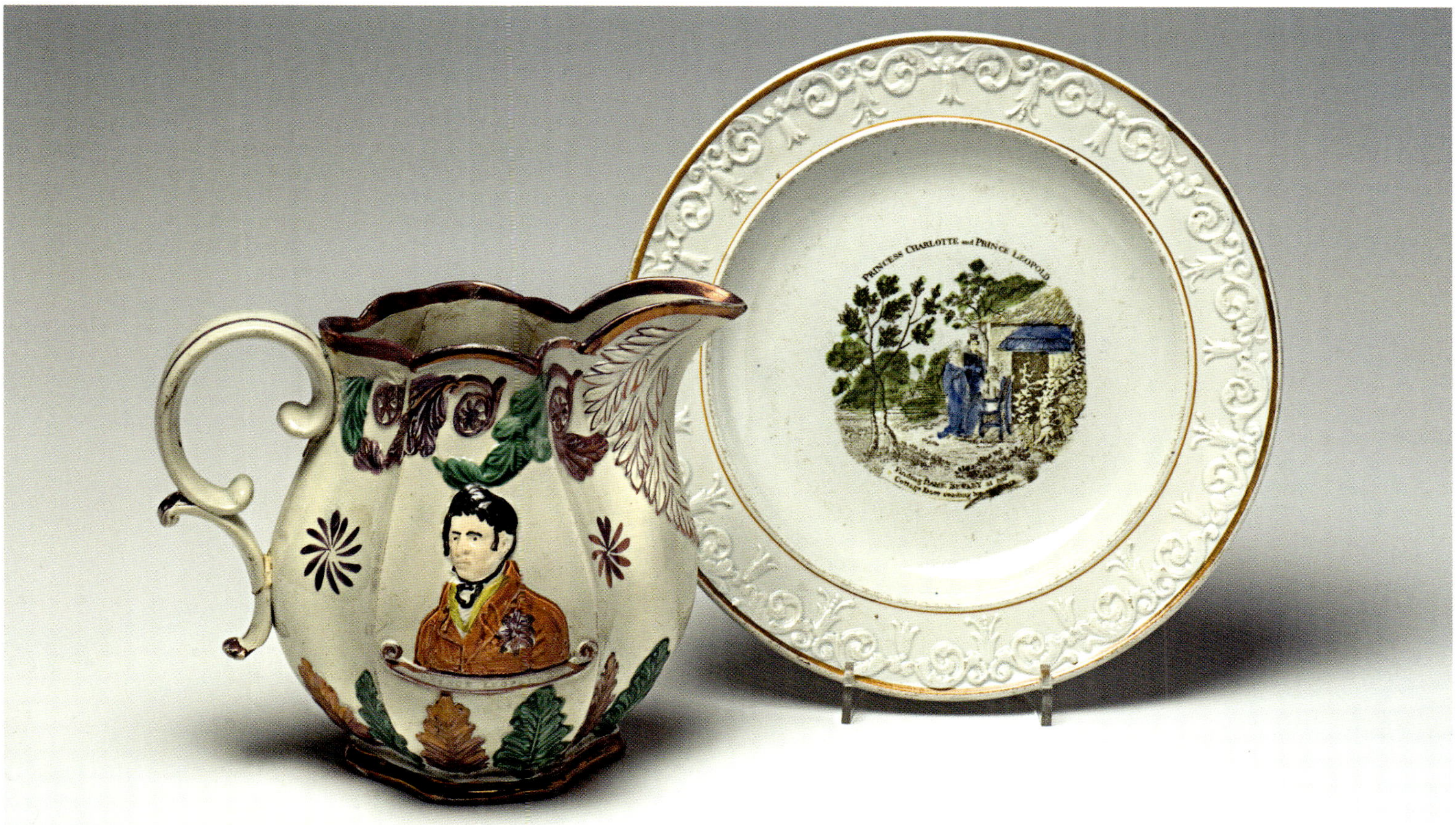

Jug, (054), c.1816, Staffordshire, height: 16.5cm, (6½in), pearlware, enamelled and lustred. Six-sided jug is relief-moulded with bust length portraits impressed, 'PRINCESS CHARLOTTE' and 'PRINCE LEOPOLD'. Such jugs seem to be the most common souvenirs of the royal wedding. Charlotte and Leopold were very popular and feature in many paintings and prints.

Plate, (055), c.1819, Staffordshire, imp: A. Stevenson of Cobridge, diameter: 22.2cm, (8¾in), pearlware, printed in brown and painted. A commemorative piece, printed, within a moulded scroll and bell flower border, with figures beside a cottage door, inscribed, 'PRINCESS CHARLOTTE and PRINCE LEOPOLD / , Finding DAME BEWLEY at her / Cottage Door reading her … BIBLE'.[24]

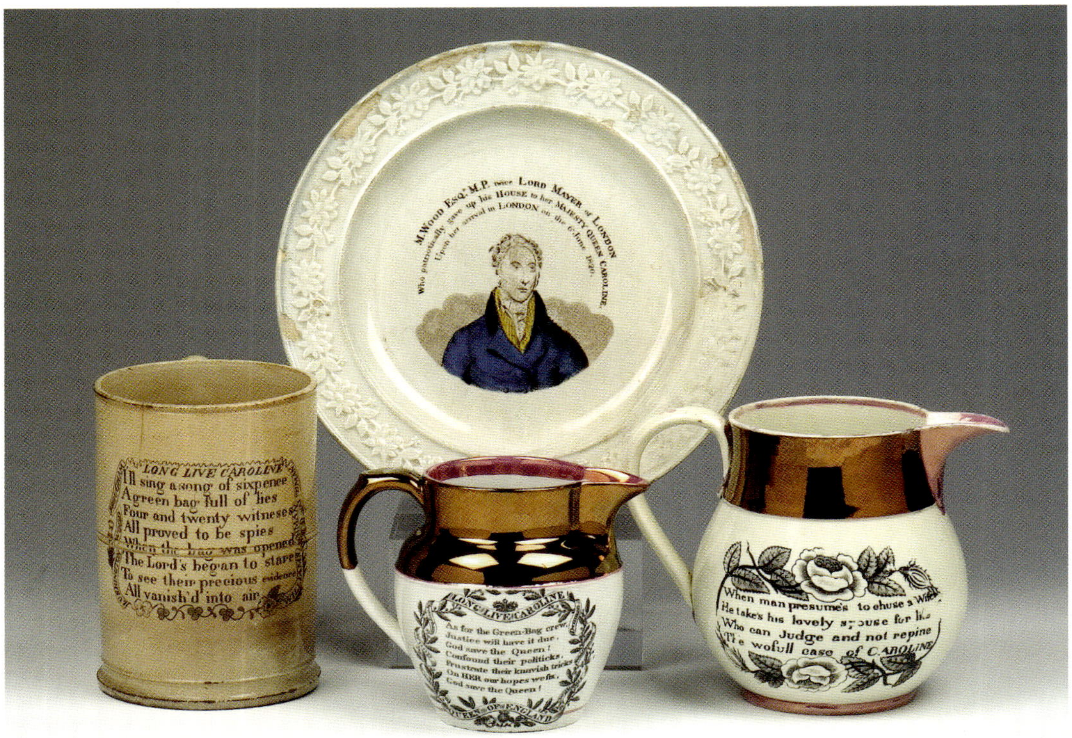

The evidence of the 'Milan commission' who had investigated Caroline's behaviour in Italy was presented to Parliament in sealed, green, legal-brief bags, which were exploited by the satirical press.

Clockwise:

Mug, (065), c.1820, Staffordshire or North East, height: 12.7cm, (5in), drab earthenware. Printed with a spiral ribbon listing her supporters: 'Brougham / WOOD / Lushington / Denman / Waithman [*sic* - for Whithman] / Williams' and a verse, intended to be sung to the tune of the nursery rhyme: 'LONG LIVE CAROLINE / I'll sing a song of sixpence / A Green bag full of lies / Four and twenty witnesses / All proved to be spies / When the bag was opened / The Lord's began to stare / To see their precious evidence / All vanish'd into air'.

Plate, (062), c.1820, imp: Staffordshire, Andrew Stevenson of Cobridge, diameter: 20.3cm, (8in), pearlware, brown-printed and enamelled. Within a relief-moulded floral border, a portrait inscribed, 'M.WOOD Esq. MP Twice LORD MAYOR of LONDON / Who patriotically gave up his HOUSE to her MAJESTY QUEEN CAROLINE / Upon her arrival in LONDON on the 6th June, 1820'. Alderman Matthew Wood was the former Lord Mayor of London.

Jug, (063), c.1820, Staffordshire, height: 11.4cm, (4½in), earthenware, printed and lustred. Printed between foliate borders, 'When man presumes to chuse a Wife / He takes his lovely Spouse for life / Who can Judge and not repine / The wofull [*sic*] case of CAROLINE', referring to Caroline's refusal to grant George a divorce.

Jug, (064), c.1820, Staffordshire, height: 10.2cm, (4in), earthenware, printed and lustred. Printed within a wreath, inscribed with the names of her supporters (as 065), 'LONG LIVE CAROLINE / QUEEN OF ENGLAND', and verse, 'As for the Green Bag crew / Justice will have its due / God Save the Queen! / Confound their politicks / Frustrate their Knavish tricks / On HER our hopes we fix / God Save the Queen!'

Pair of Plaques, (059 & A), c.1820, probably Coalport, Shrops., each height: 14.6cm, (5¾in), soft-paste porcelain, printed and enamelled and gilt. Within pink enamel frames, oval reserves printed with portraits inscribed, 'GEORGE IV / Born Aug 12 1762. Proclaimed King of Engld Jan 31. 1820' and Caroline, inscribed, 'HER MOST GRACIOUS MAJESTY / Queen Caroline'. The portrait of the king is taken from a print by R. Page, published by Kinnersley in 1818. That depicting Caroline is painted on the reverse in gold, with a florid monogram: ST.

Figure, (068), c.1825, Staffordshire, height: 16.5cm, (6½in), enamelled pearlware. George IV, wearing the Garter Star pinned to a long coat, carries a letter.

Figure, (058), c.1820, Staffordshire, height: 15.2cm, (6in), soft-paste porcelain, enamelled and gilt. Press-moulded in low relief and mounted on a two-tier base, an unusual figure of Queen Caroline, fashionably dressed, clutches her heart in distress. It is faintly inscribed beneath the base in brown, '42'.[25] It could be a chimney ornament intended for a narrow mantelpiece; early Minton catalogues list a dozen or so blocks for unidentified subjects.[26]

Jug, (067), c.1830, Staffordshire, printed:'G.B.H' for Goodwin, Bridgwood & Harris, Lane End, height: 17.8cm, (7in), printed earthenware. Printed in brown with sprigs of flowers inside and outside the neck and a portrait of George IV. Inscribed, 'TO THE MEMORY OF / HIS LATE MAJESTY / KING GEORGE IV / BORN. AUGT.12 1762 / ASCENDED TO THE THRONE. JANY 29. 1820 / PUBLICLY PROCLAIMED … / DEPARTED THIS LIFE. JUNE 26 1830 / AGED 68 YEARS'. Beneath the spout are the Royal Arms and supporters. It is printed in brown on the base.

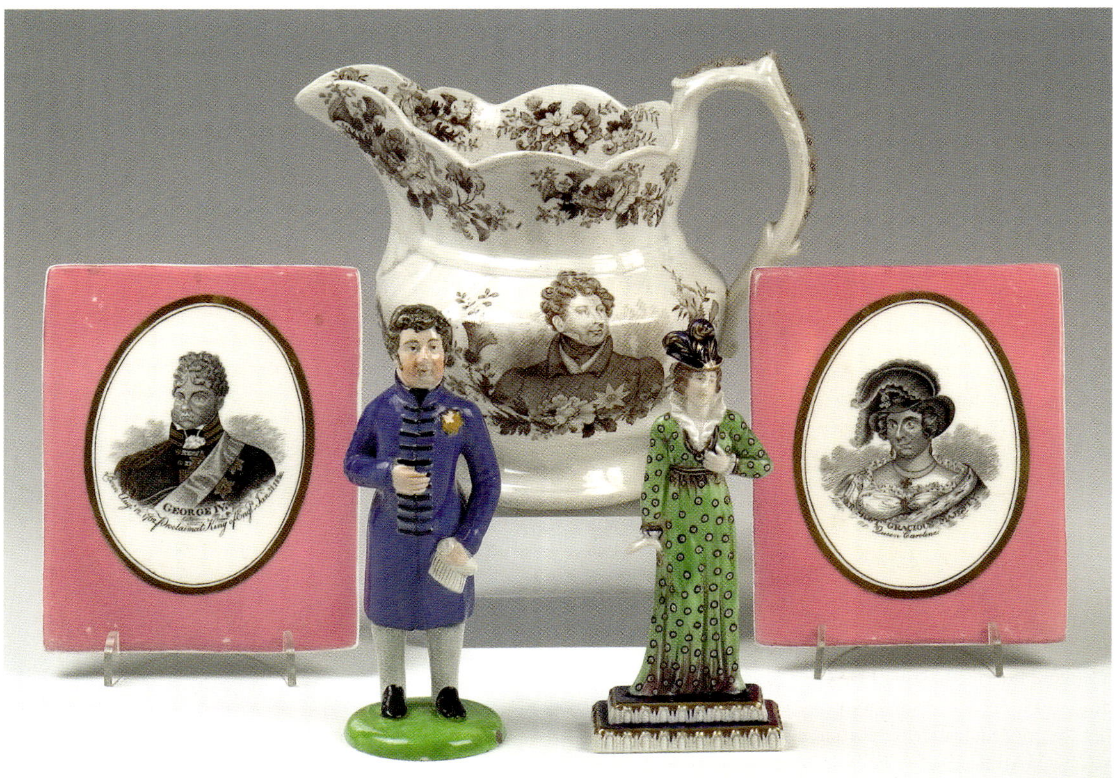

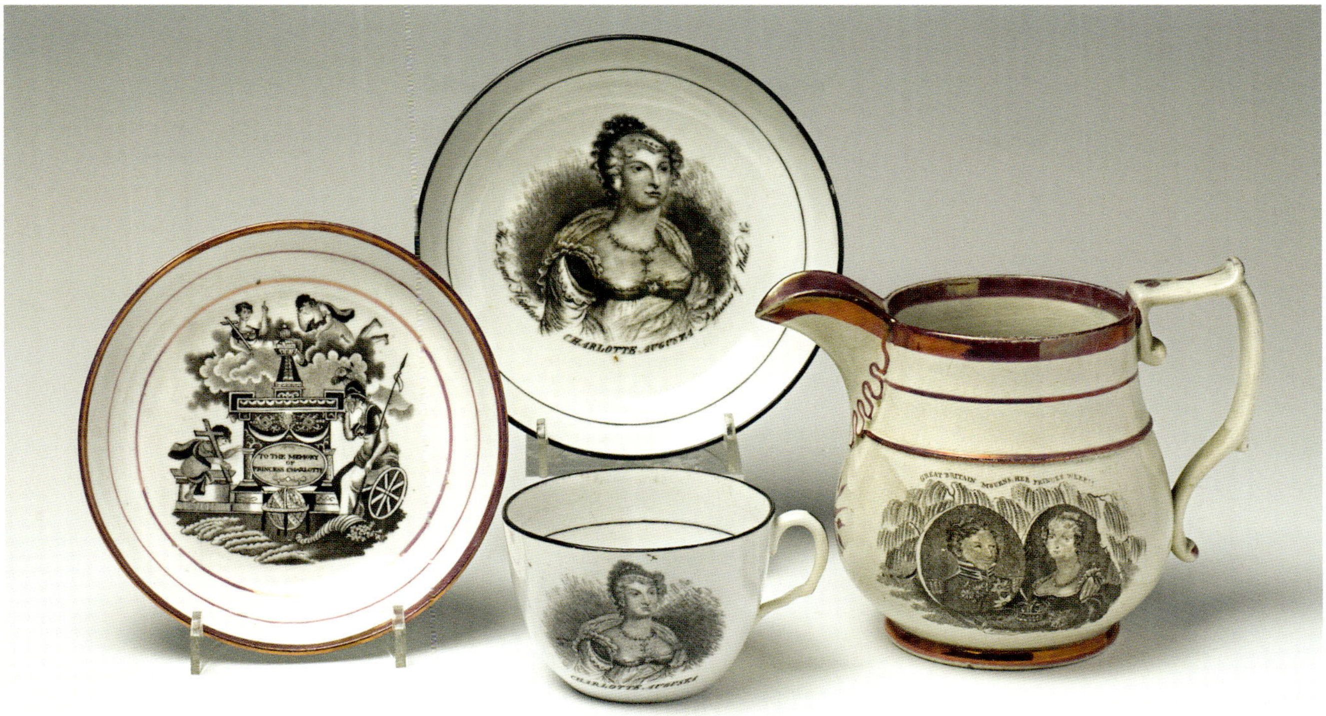

Saucer, (056), c.1818, Staffordshire, diameter: 14cm, (5½in), bone china, printed and lustred. Printed with Britannia and other figures mourning at the tomb of Princess Charlotte, inscribed, 'TO THE MEMORY / OF / PRINCESS / CHARLOTTE'. Mass-produced commemorative ceramics appeared after Princess Charlotte's untimely death.
Cup and Saucer, (R603.9), c.1818, Staffordshire, height: 8.5cm, (3⅜in), diameter: 14.7cm, (5¾in), printed bone china. Edged in black enamel, printed with half-length portrait.
Jug, (057), c.1818, Staffordshire, height: 12.7cm, (5in), earthenware, printed and lustred. Printed with portraits of Charlotte and Leopold framed by weeping willows, inscribed, 'GREAT BRITAIN MOURNS, HER PRINCES WEEP!!'. (On the other side is Charlotte's tomb attended by cherubs and Britannia, weeping.)

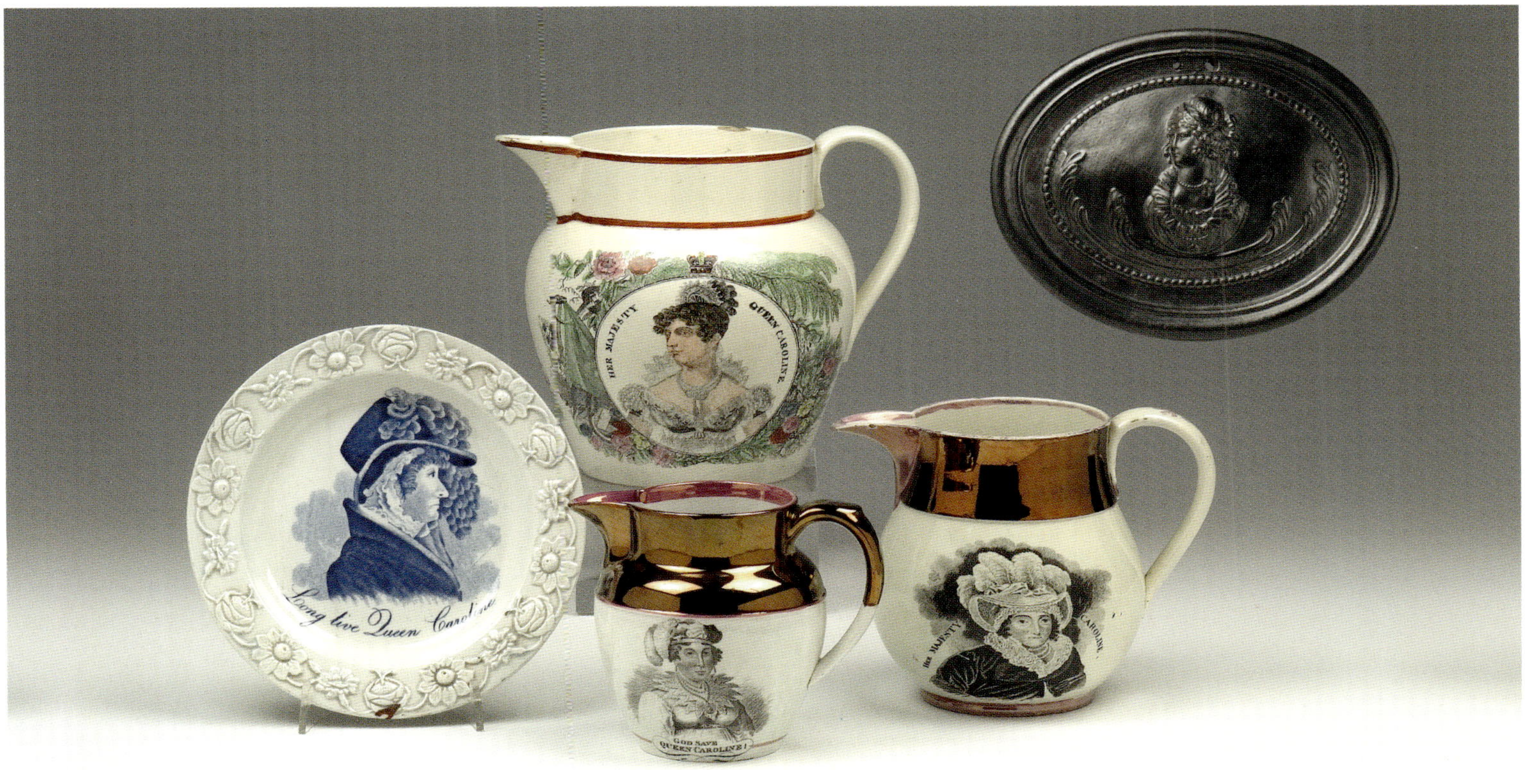

Clockwise:
Plate, (061), c.1820, Staffordshire, diameter: 15.3cm, (6in), enamelled pearlware. Relief-moulded border of roses and daisies, printed with profile portrait of Queen Caroline inscribed, 'Long Live Queen Caroline'.
Jug, (EH/A/10), c.1820, North East, height: 15cm, (5⅞in), creamware, printed and enamelled. Flattering portrait of youthful Caroline in circular frame, printed, 'HER MAJESTY / QUEEN CAROLINE'.
Plaque, (060), c.1820, Staffordshire, height: 11.4cm, (4½in), enamelled earthenware. Relief-moulded with bust portrait of Queen Caroline, impressed, 'SUCCESS.TO. QUEEN / CAROLINE'. Faintly incised on reverse, 'Miss Jane Barton'.
Jug, (063), c.1820, Staffordshire, height: 11.4cm, (4½in), earthenware, printed and lustred. Printed with a portrait bust of Caroline inscribed, 'Her MAJESTY / CAROLINE'.
Jug, (064), c.1820, Staffordshire, height: 10.2cm, (4in), earthenware, printed and lustred. Printed with a full-face portrait of Caroline inscribed, 'GOD SAVE / QUEEN CAROLINE'. The portrait is taken from Robert Cooper's engraving (pub. 1820) after Abraham Wivell.

William IV (1830-1837)

William, the third son of George III was born in 1765 and in 1789 he was created Duke of Clarence. He joined the navy in 1779, served in America and the West Indies but saw little military action although in 1811 he attained the rank of admiral. William lived for 20 years with the actress Dorothea Jordan, with whom he had ten illegitimate children. The death in 1817 of his niece, Princess Charlotte, and her stillborn son, obliged William to marry in the hope of producing a legitimate heir to the throne. Adelaide of Saxe-Meiningen (1792-1849) was half his age but the marriage, though happy, was childless. William IV's reign saw several important reforms; slavery was abolished throughout the British Empire and Parliament and the constitution were overhauled by the Great Reform Act of 1832. William's popularity among his subjects is reflected in his nicknames, Sailor Bill and Reform Bill!

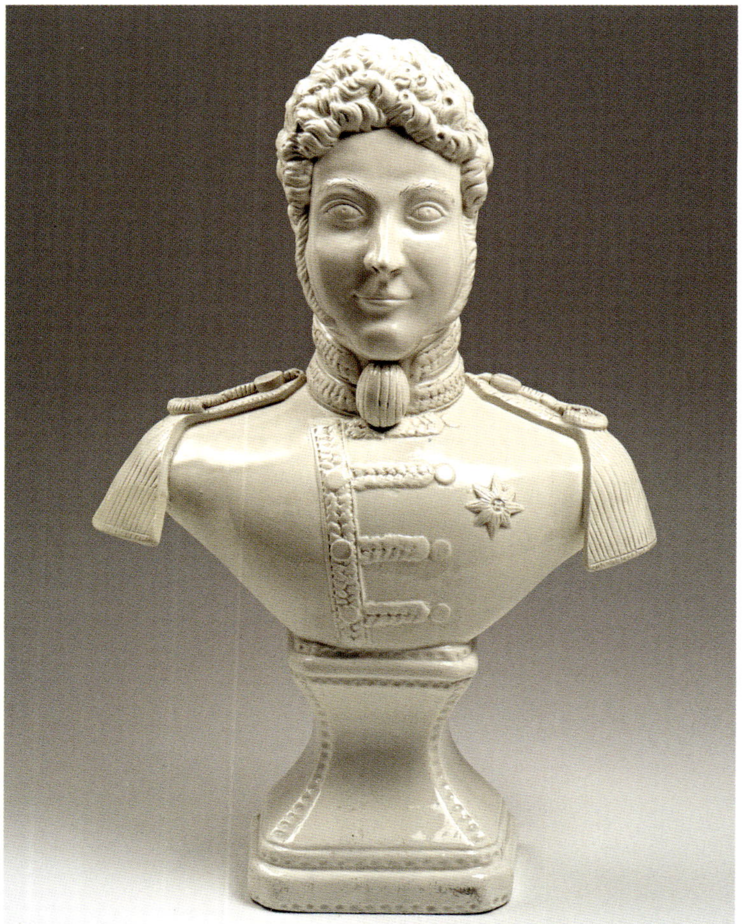

Portrait Bust, (072), incised on reverse: D. L. Sept 9th / 1832, Staffordshire, height: 49.5cm, (19½in), pearlware. This may represent a stylised portrait of William IV, wearing a naval jacket with braid and epaulettes and the Garter Star.

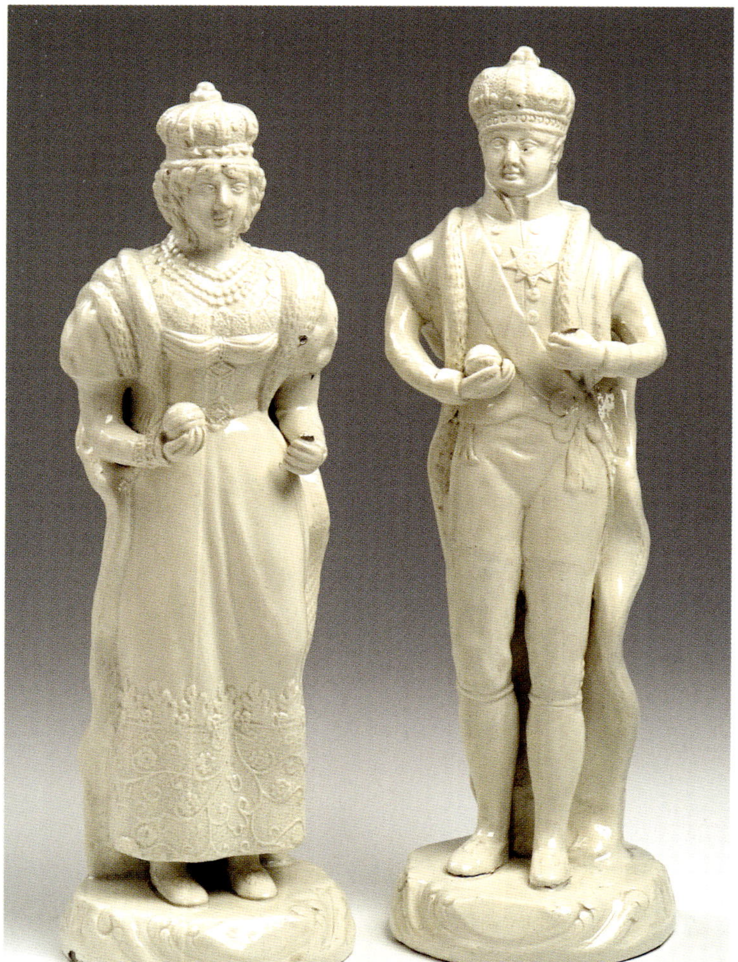

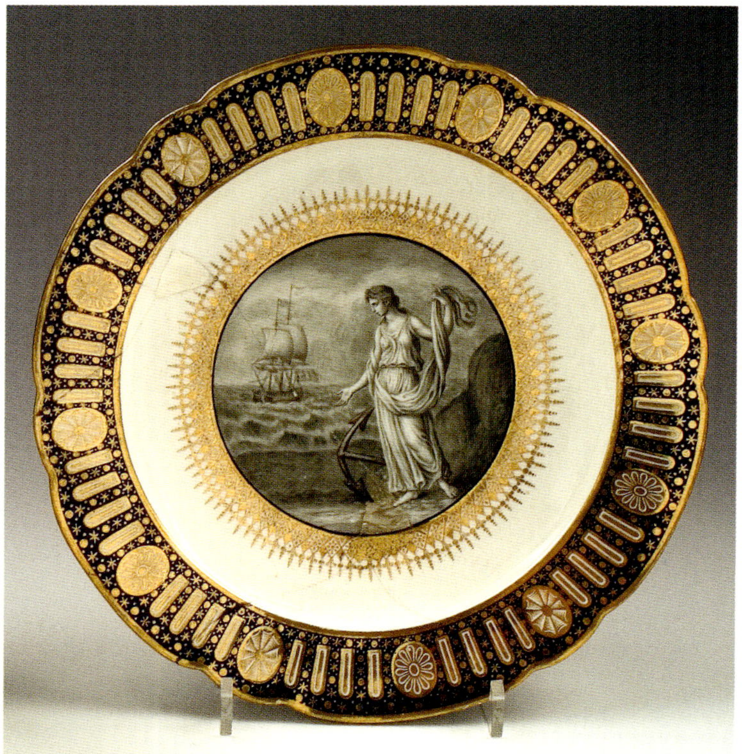

Plate, (073), c.1792, Worcester, painted: a crown / Flight / a crescent; diameter: 24.2cm, (9½in), soft-paste porcelain, enamelled and gilt. Densely patterned gilt borders frame central reserve, painted by John Pennington, in monochrome, with the figure of Hope with an anchor and a ship. The plate is part of an extensive service ordered from Worcester by William IV while Duke of Clarence. John Flight's diary for January 1790 notes that the Duke, then serving in the navy, had chosen Hope as the theme for a service to be completed within a year (it took three) that was to cost £700.[27] The *Reading Mercury* reported on 21 March, 1791, 'There are near 500 pieces and the price is to be 800 guineas. The ground is very antique and upon every piece there is painted a figure of Hope and in each drawing the attitude is varied'.

Pair of Figures, (071), c.1830, Staffordshire, each height: 33cm, (13in), earthenware. Slip-cast figures representing King William IV and Queen Adelaide crowned, clad in coronation robes and carrying orbs (and formerly sceptres).

Clockwise:
Portrait Bust, (075), c.1830, Mintons, Stoke-on-Trent, height: 12.7cm, (5in), biscuit porcelain. Geoffrey Godden identified this bust of Queen Adelaide as an early, unmarked, product of the Minton factory, recorded in the Minton pattern book as No.15.[28]
Plaque, (078), c.1817. Assumed to represent the Duke of Clarence, this is probably Prince Leopold, husband of the unfortunate Princess Charlotte (see (050) p. 23).
Portrait Bust, (074), c.1830, Mintons, Stoke-on-Trent, height: 19.1cm, (7½in), soft-paste porcelain, enamelled and gilt. Represents William IV in naval uniform wearing the Garter sash and Star.
Figure, (076), c.1835, Staffordshire or Derby, height: 12.7cm, (5in), biscuit porcelain. William sits crossed-legged on an upholstered sofa holding a book.

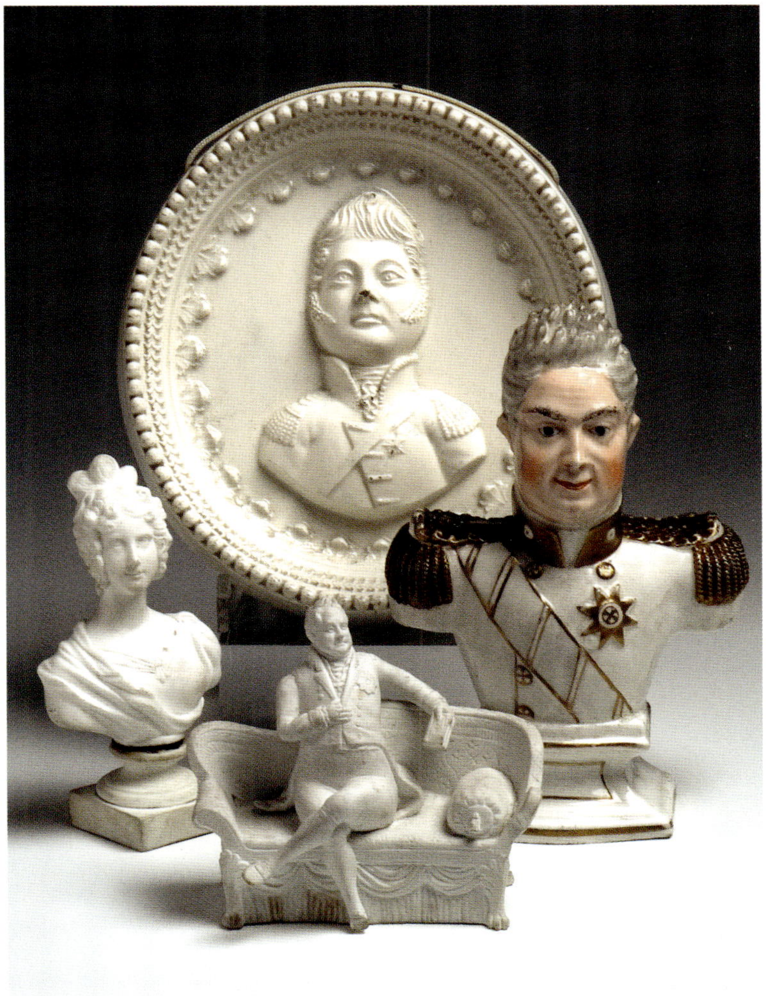

Queen Victoria (1837-1901)

Princess Alexandrina Victoria (born 1819) was the daughter of Prince Edward, Duke of Kent and Strathearn, (1767-1820) and Princess Victoria of Saxe-Coburg-Saalfeld (1786-1861). After her father's death in 1820 she was closely supervised by her mother until she succeeded her uncle, William IV in 1837. In 1840 she married her cousin Prince Albert of Saxe-Coburg-Gotha (1819-1861), who became Prince Consort. After the tragic death in childbirth of Princess Charlotte of Wales the happy and fruitful marriage of Victoria and Albert was a great relief to the British people. Their first two children were Victoria, the Princess Royal, (1840-1901) and Albert Edward, Prince of Wales, (1841-1910). Vicky would later marry Kaiser Wilhelm II of Prussia while the Prince of Wales eventually succeeded his mother as Edward VII. Arranging marriages for their nine children into the royal families of Europe led to Victoria being nicknamed 'the grandmother of Europe'. Following Albert's early death in 1861, she underwent prolonged mourning, shunning public life to the consternation of her government and the British people. Her popularity recovered in the latter part of her unprecedented 63-year reign. Her Golden and Diamond Jubilees were widely celebrated.

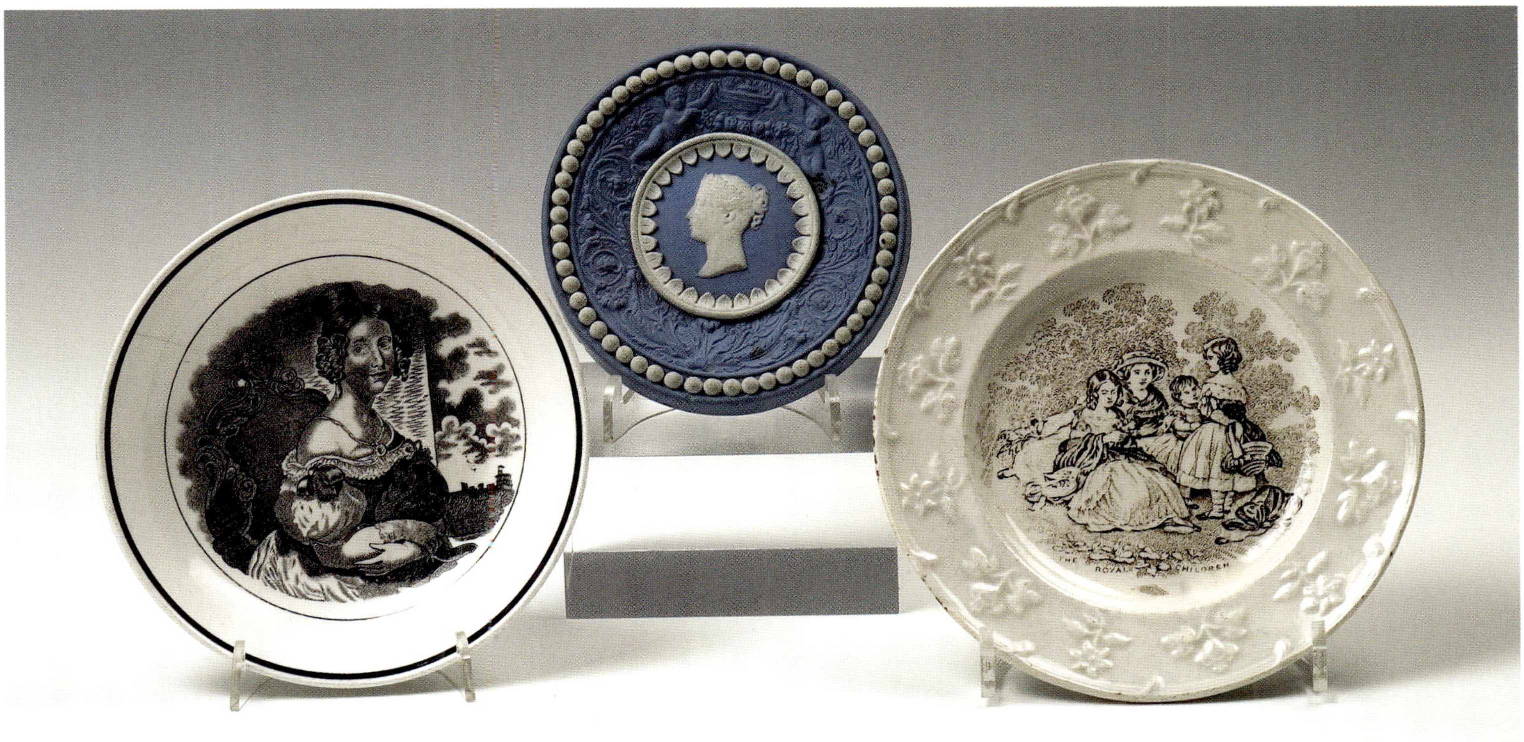

Saucer, (082), c.1838, Sunderland, imp: Dixon, Austin & Co., diameter: 15.3cm, (6in), printed earthenware. Enamelled rim, printed with image of the young Queen Victoria, loosely based on prints after the very popular portrait by Sir George Hayter (1833).[29]
Plaque, (087), c.1840, Staffordshire, diameter: 11.2cm, (4½in), blue jasperware. Relief-moulded with foliate decoration, a white pill border, and a central profile portrait in white of Queen Victoria, very similar to an anaglyptograph of 1839.[30]
Nursery plate, (098), c.1850, Staffordshire, diameter: 16.5cm, (6½in), printed earthenware. Relief-moulded floral border is printed in brown with design entitled, 'THE ROYAL CHILDREN'.

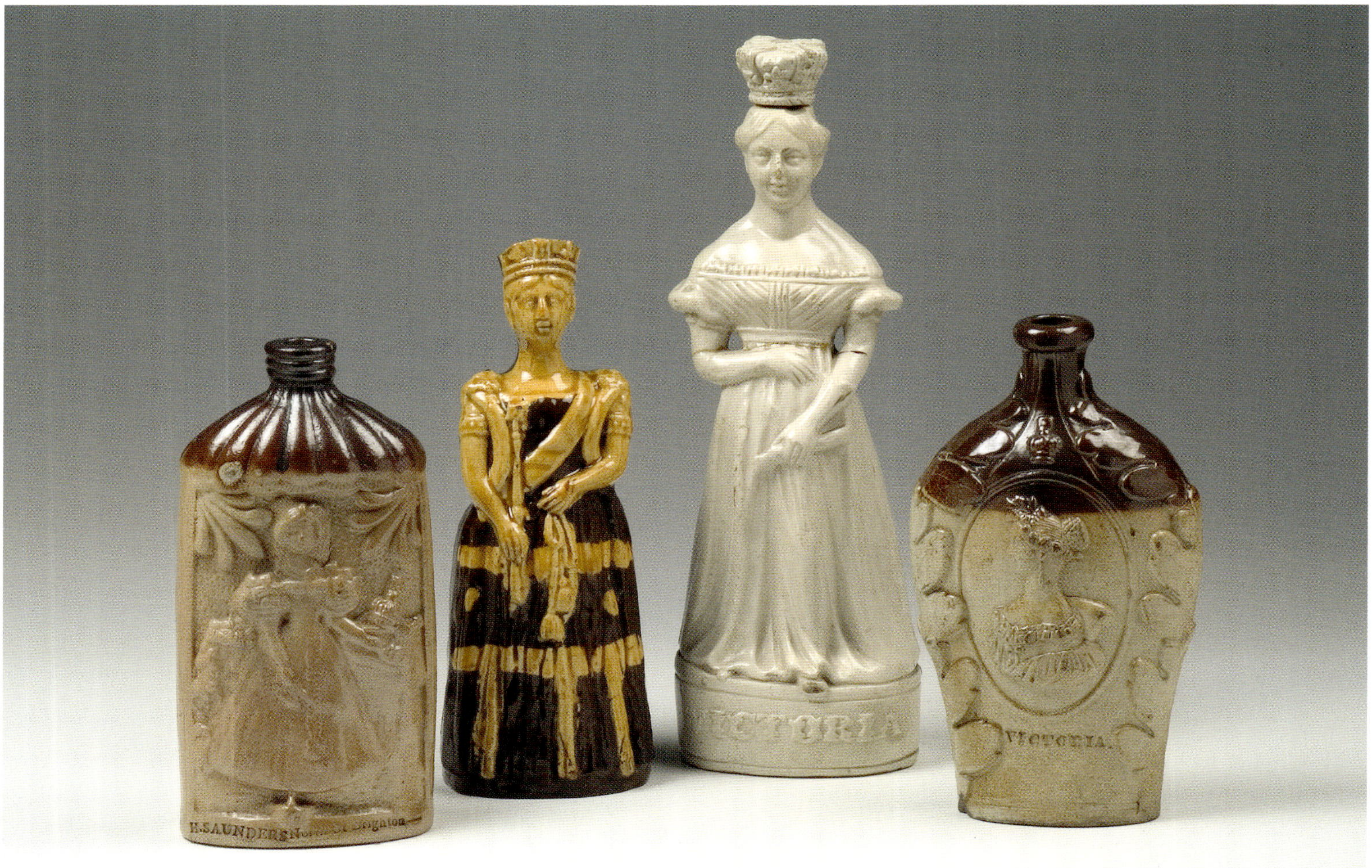

Flask, (085), c.1837, London, height: 21.6cm, (8½in), salt-glazed stoneware Moulded on both sides with a full-length image of Princess Victoria, based on a portrait of 1833 by Sir George Hayter.[31] Impressed on the base, 'H. SAUNDERS North St Brighton'. In Leppard & Co.'s *Brighton Directory,* (1845), Hugh Saunders is recorded as the landlord of the Blacksmith's Arms, 142 North Street, Brighton, from 1833 onwards.[32] Such pieces were ordered wholesale by wine and spirit merchants throughout the country.

Flask, (084), c.1840, probably Staffordshire, height: 25.4cm, (10in), red clay and cream slip. Crudely modelled as the young queen, a handle attached to her back.

Flask, (083), c.1837, London, imp.: Stephen Green, 'Lambeth, 20 July 1837', height: 33cm, (13in), cream stoneware. Modelled as a full-length figure, holding a letter; base relief-moulded, 'VICTORIA'; the stopper formed as a crown.

Flask, (R2454.4), c.1837, London, height: 21.6cm, (8½in), salt-glazed stoneware Moulded with a profile portrait bust, impressed, 'VICTORIA'. The Duchess of Kent, is shown on the reverse.

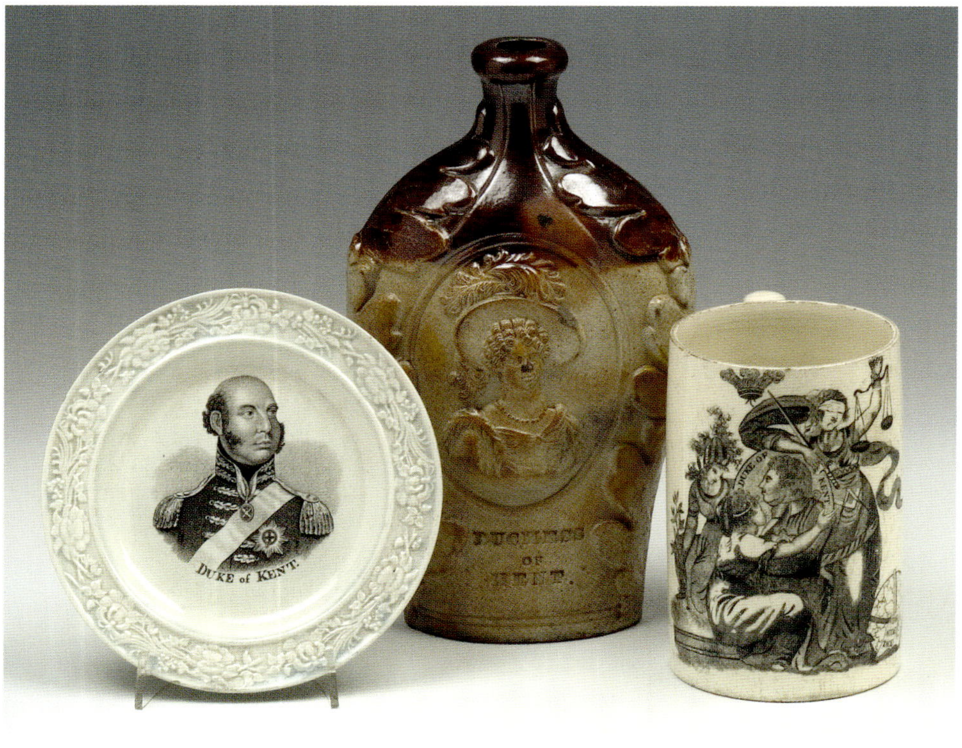

Nursery Plate, (080), Staffordshire, c.1820, diameter: 14.6cm, (5¾in), printed pearlware. Printed, within a moulded floral border, with a bust portrait of Victoria's father in military uniform, inscribed, 'DUKE of KENT'. The image is taken from a print of 1815 after a portrait by Sir William Beechey.[33]

Flask, (R2454.4), c.1837, London, height: 21.6cm, (8½in), salt-glazed stoneware. Moulded with a portrait of Queen Victoria's mother, impressed, 'DUCHESS OF KENT'.[34]

Mug, (079), c.1820, Staffordshire or the North East, height: 12.1cm, (4¾in), printed creamware. One of three allegorical female figures holds a sapling. Another kneels before an oval plaque with a profile portrait inscribed, 'DUKE OF / KENT'. The third represents blind Justice wearing a Masonic apron. (The Duke was elected Grand Master of the Atholl or Antients [*sic*] Grand Lodge in 1813). The Prince of Wales's feathers, a globe and an open book inscribed, 'VIDE / AUDE / TACE / G' also appear. The Duke died on 20 January, 1820, shortly after the birth of his only daughter and just six days before his father, George III.

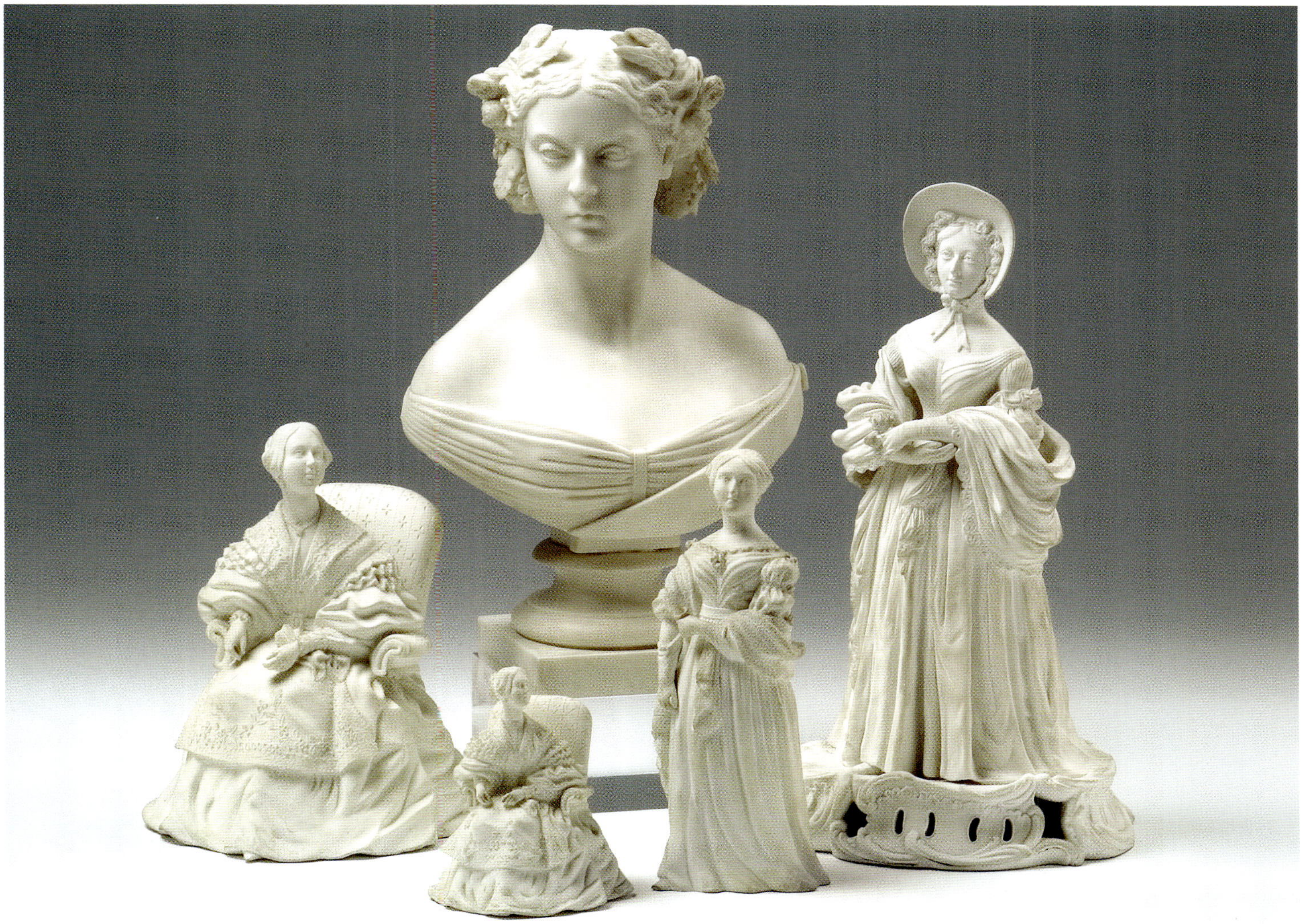

Clockwise:
Figure, (089), c.1840, Staffordshire, Mintons of Stoke-on-Trent, height: 14cm, (5½in), biscuit porcelain. The Queen sits in an armchair, its back applied with the Royal Arms, a crown, and a laurel and oak wreath in relief. The image is based on a print of 1838 by R.J. Lane after A.E. Chalon.[35]
Bust, (090), c.1855, Staffordshire, imp.: 'C. Marochetti' and, 'Victoria R. / Published by Minton & Co.'(symbols beneath), height: 29.2cm, (11½in). Parian-porcelain. The Queen wears a low-necked bodice, her hair decorated with laurel leaves, roses and sprigs of oak. The Italian sculptor, Baron Carlo Marochetti (1805-1867), showed work at the International Exhibitions from 1851 onwards. He was patronised by the Royal Family and Mintons adapted his royal portrait figures and busts for production in Parian ware.[36]
Figure, (081), c.1837, Staffordshire, Mintons (unmarked), height: 29.2cm, (11½in), biscuit porcelain. Queen Victoria, c.1840, is fashionably dressed with bonnet and shawl on a base embellished with rococo scrolls. The modeller based the image on a print by F.C. Lewis of 1838.[37] The model appears in the Minton design book as No.106, 'Queen with Veil'.
Figure, (091), c.1840, Staffordshire, probably Mintons, height: 17.8cm, (7in), biscuit porcelain. A similar but smaller version of (081) shows the Queen (without a bonnet) holding a rose. One of an unmatched pair with the Prince Consort.
Figure, (088), c.1840, Staffordshire, Mintons of Stoke-on-Trent, height: 10.2cm, (4in), biscuit porcelain. Smaller version of (089), the back of the chair applied with a crown in relief.

Flask, (086), c.1840, London, imp.: Stephen Green Imperial Potteries Lambeth', height: 27.9cm, (11in), stoneware. Moulded as a tipstaff, or constable's baton, mounted with an imperial crown moulded, 'V ⋆ R' and the Royal Arms.
Jug, (095), c.1860, probably Coalport, height: 15.2cm, (6in), bone china, enamelled and gilt. Simple scrolls surmount the Garter Star. Printed beneath, in puce pink: crown and a Garter band inscribed: 'WINDSOR CASTLE / MORTLOCK. 18.REGENT St.' John Mortlock (est. 1746 - ceased c.1930) was a leading London retailer during the nineteenth century, associated with several factories.

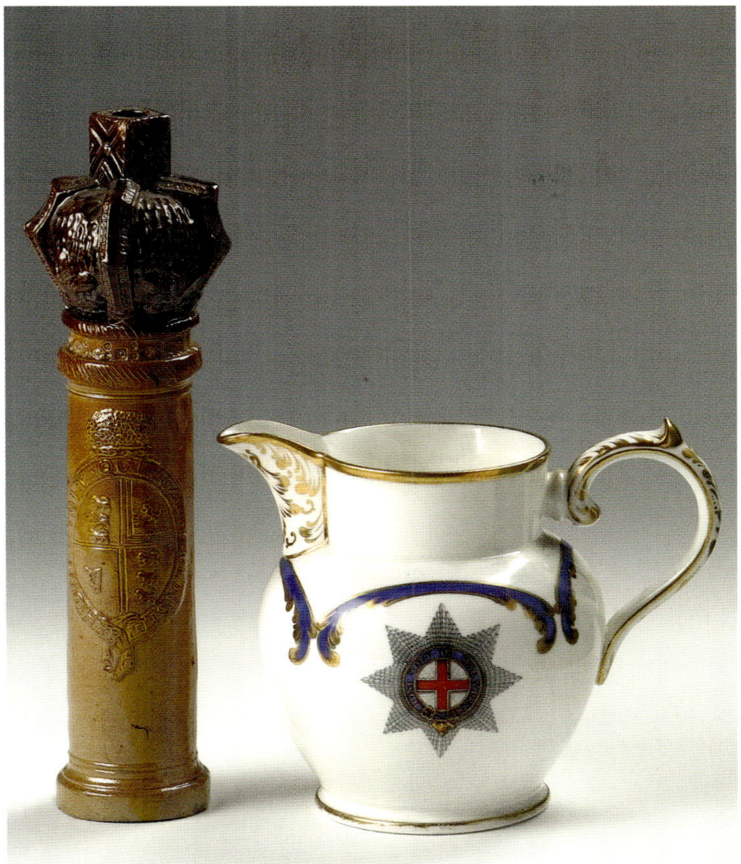

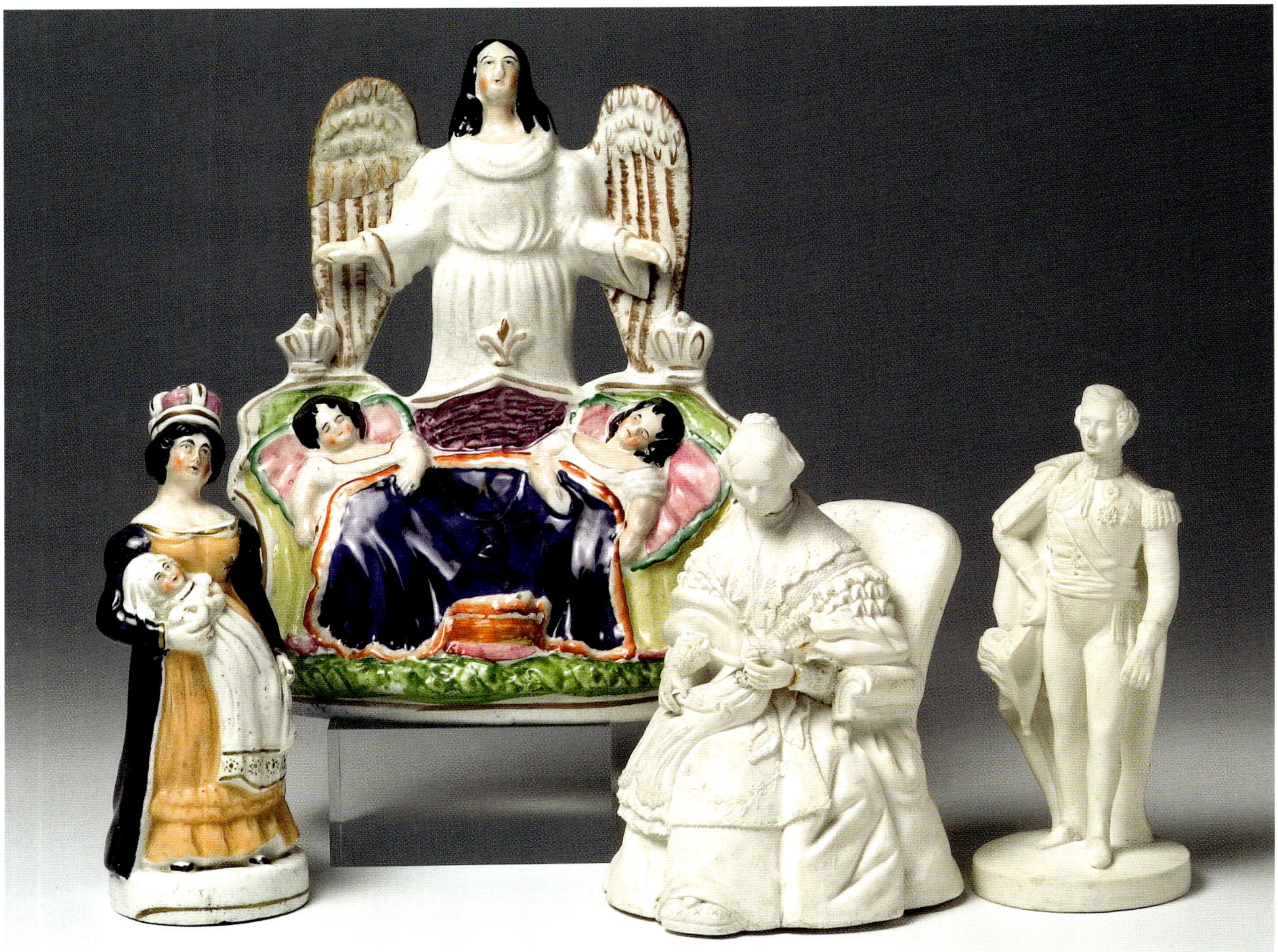

Figure Group, (097), c.1840, Staffordshire, height: 17.8cm, (7in), Earthenware, enamelled and gilt. Queen Victoria, wearing a crown, carries an infant, possibly the Princess Royal.

Figure Group, (096), c.1845, Staffordshire, height: 17.8cm, (7in), earthenware, slip-cast, enamelled and gilt. An angel watches over two of the royal children, sleeping on a double-ended couch marked with two crowns and a fleur-de-lys. The composition is based on George Dawe's popular print, *The Guardian Angel*. Two anonymous infants have been given crowns, to identify them as the eldest children of Queen Victoria.

Figure, (093), c.1844, London and Staffordshire, incised: 'Modelled by / D: Cocker / 8 Chenies St. / Bedford Sq.' Mintons of Stoke-on-Trent, height: 17.8cm, (7in), biscuit porcelain. The Queen sits in an armchair holding an infant. The back of the chair is applied with the Royal Arms, a crown and a laurel and oak wreath in relief. The reserve below the back seat rail is incised 'Douglas Potts Cocker' (c.1811-1846) lived at Chenies Street only in 1844, which dates this example. The image (like 089) is again based on a print of 1838 by R.J. Lane after A.E. Chalon.[38]

Figure, (091A), c.1840, Staffordshire, probably Mintons, height: 17.8cm, (7in), biscuit porcelain. Prince Albert, the Prince Consort, wears a general's uniform and carries a cocked hat.

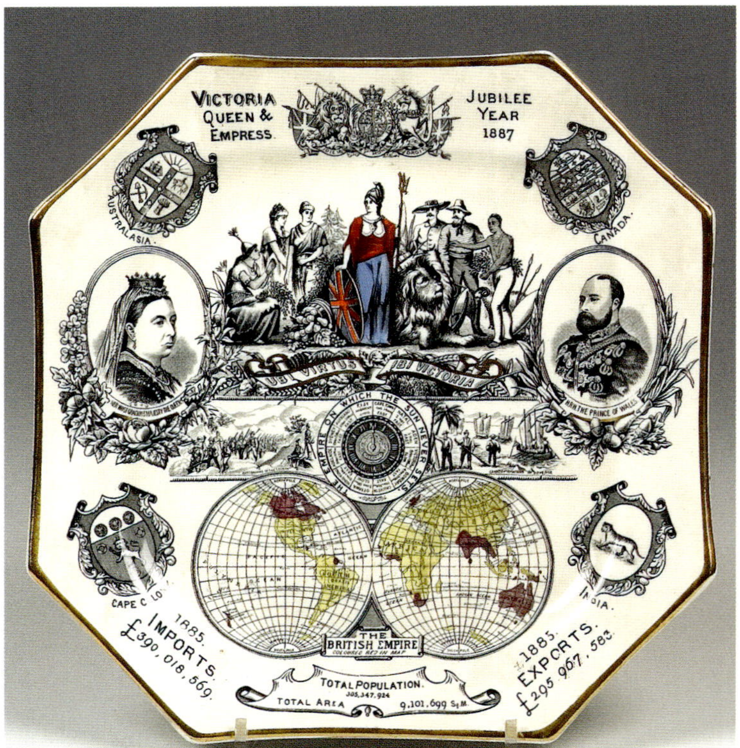

Octagonal Dish, (102), 1887, probably Staffordshire, height: 25.4cm, (10in), earthenware, printed and coloured.
Golden Jubilee souvenir, printed with designs including oval portraits of Queen Victoria and the Prince of Wales, scenes, symbols, statistics and maps representing the British Empire. Main inscription, 'VICTORIA QUEEN & EMPRESS / JUBILEE YEAR 1887'. Printed on reverse for maker or retailer, 'NESTLE & HUNTSMAN / rd. No.63164 / 5'.

Clockwise:
Mug, (R2454.9), 1897, Staffordshire, height: 8.6cm, (3⅜in), blue-printed earthenware.
Portrait Bust, (106), 1897, height: 16.5cm, (6½in), plaster. This is the only souvenir in Willett's collection for the Queen's Diamond Jubilee. It is impressed, 'VICTORIA / DIAMOND JUBILEE 1837 – 1897'.
Mug, (100), 1887, Staffordshire, height: 8.9cm, (3½in), earthenware, printed in red and gilt. Portrait of Queen Victoria framed by sprays of national flowers and foliage, inscribed, 'VR / THE QUEEN'S JUBILEE / BARCOMBE / JUBILEE FETE / 1887'. Such mugs were issued to school children to mark national celebrations.
Mug, (101), 1887, Staffordshire, printed: Edward Asbury & Co., Longton; height: 7.6cm, (3in), earthenware printed in brown and coloured. A wreath of national flowers frames the profile of the young Queen, inscribed, 'VICTORIA / JUBILEE 1887'.

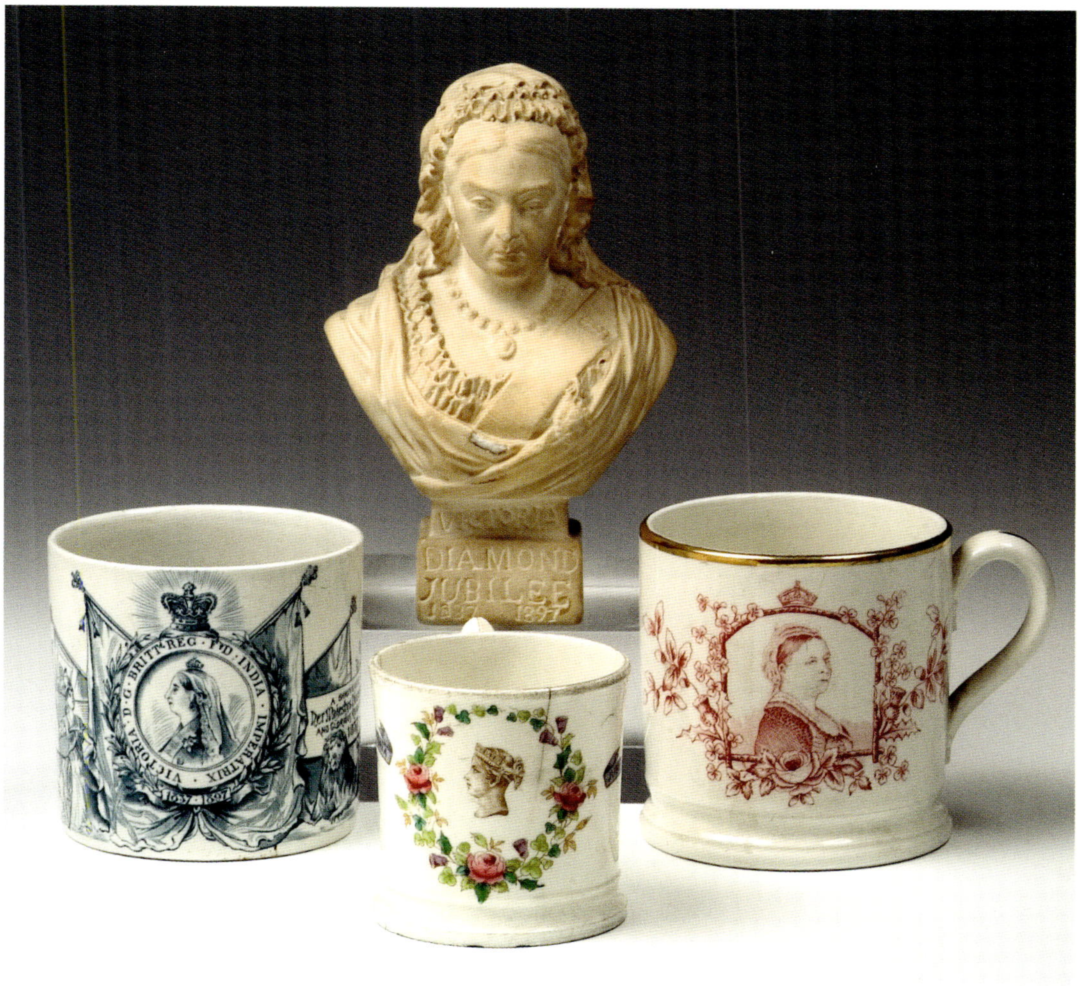

Jug, (099), c.1888, imp: 2/ painted in gilt: 71/ printed in red: Made in Germany, height: 14cm, (5½in), hard-paste porcelain, colour-printed and gilt. Printed on one side with oval portraits of Princess Alexandra and the Prince of Wales inscribed, 'IN COMMEMORATION OF / THE SILVER WEDDING / 1863-1888 / MARCH 10TH'. On the other: Prince of Wales's feathers and motto, 'ICH DIEN' within a shield.
Two-handled Mug, (104), 1894, imp: Made in Devon (probably Aller Vale), height: 20.3cm, (8in), slip-decorated earthenware. On one side incised design of a Tudor rose and inscription: 'Prince Edward of York / 1894 / Bryght be the stars on the eve of / St John / Luckie the babe that is born thereon'. On the other, incised design of floral grotesques. Edward was the first child born to the Duke and Duchess of York (Victoria's grandson)
Three Busts, (105), c.1887, Devon, probably Torquay Terracotta Company,[39] each height: 12.7cm, (5in), terracotta. Portraits of Queen Victoria and the Prince and Princess of Wales. Such busts were made as jubilee souvenirs.
Mug, (103), c.1893, Staffordshire, height: 7.6cm, (3in), earthenware, printed in brown with circular portraits of the Duke of York and Princess May of Teck (known as Mary) and the arms of Brighton, divided by Tudor roses and sprigs of may blossom. It is inscribed, 'IN COMMEMORATION OF THE WEDDING OF THE DUKE OF YORK & PRINCESS MAY JULY 6th 1893'. It is printed beneath for the retailer, 'COPELAND / CHEESEMAN.NORTH BRIGHTON / CHINA & GLASS WAREHOUSE'.

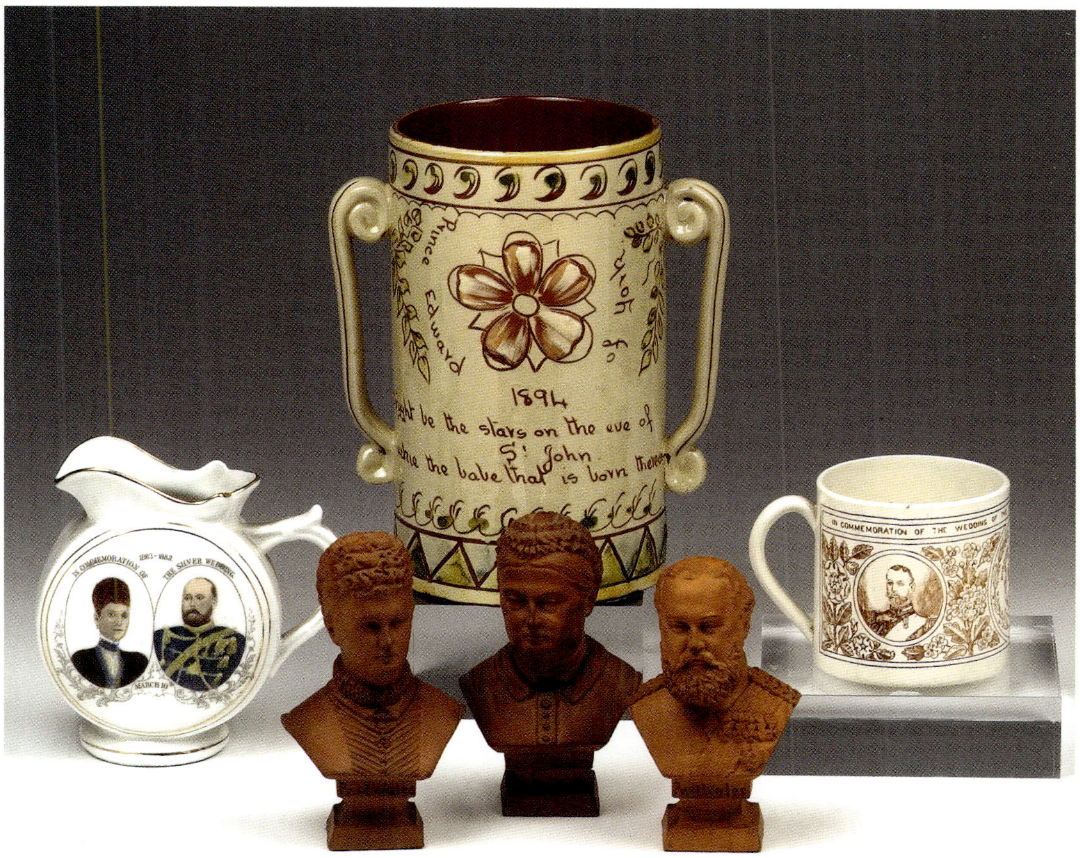

Chapter 2

MILITARY HEROES

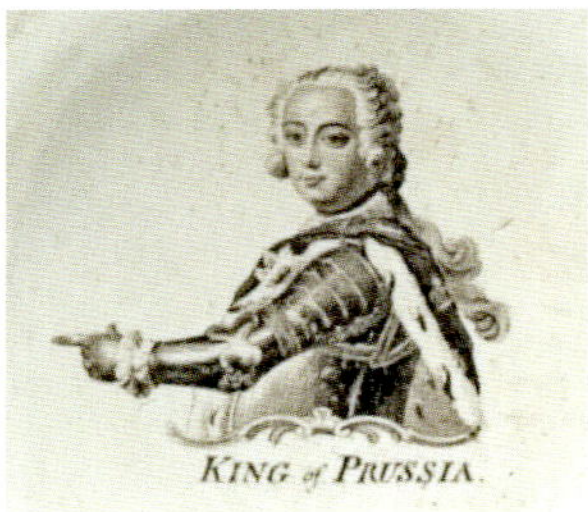

John Churchill, 1st Duke of Marlborough (1650-1722)

One of Britain's most successful commanders, Churchill is said to have taught himself military strategy from a book in St Paul's School library in London. After he deserted James II in 1688, William III made him an earl. Queen Anne appointed him Commander-in-Chief of the allied forces during the War of the Spanish Succession and made him a duke in 1703. He scored major victories over the French at Blenheim in 1704, and at Malplaquet in 1709. Queen Anne dismissed him in 1711 but George I reinstated him in 1714. The anonymous G.C. from Enfield wrote verses applauding,

> Marlborough's return unto the soldiers' sight,
> Welcome to all their eyes as wished for light,
> Renowned for council, and for courage great[1]

The Jacobite Rebellion

Charles Edward Stuart (1720-1788), better known as 'Bonnie Prince Charlie' or the 'Young Pretender', was the grandson of the exiled James II after whom his supporters were named. Jacobites considered him the rightful heir to the British throne. After he landed in the Hebrides with a handful of followers in 1745, Scottish clansmen flocked to him and he marched successfully on Edinburgh. Following defeat in 1746 at the battle of Culloden on Drumossie Moor near Inverness, Charles Edward fled and the Jacobite cause went underground. The battle ended his hopes of taking the British throne but for many years his supporters continued to observe secret rituals, toasting the King 'over the water,' from wine glasses engraved with the white rose or the oak tree. While most English people considered 'Bonnie Prince Charlie' a villain, for the Scots, some English border dwellers and for Catholics he remained a romantic folk hero.

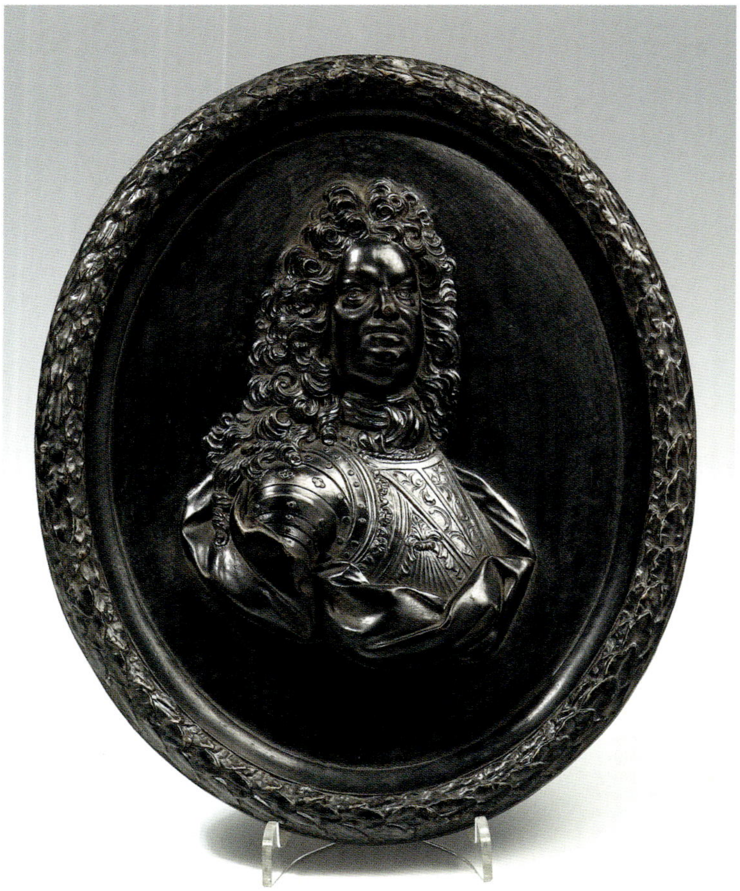

Plaque, (108), c.1800, probably Staffordshire, height: 26.7cm, (10½in), earthenware. Relief-moulded with a bust portrait in armour of the Duke of Marlborough. Painted black to imitate basalt or bronze. Superficially similar to prints after Sir Godfrey Kneller but closer to one engraved by Bartolozzi in 1794, after a portrait of 1703 by John Faber Snr.[2] The detailed body armour differs considerably from either of these.

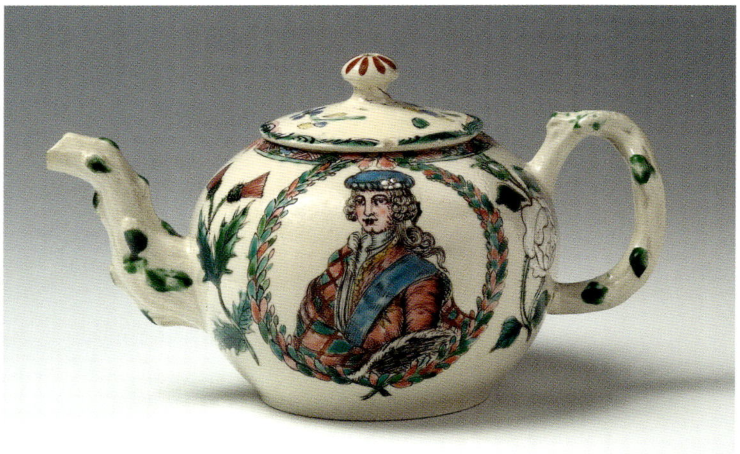

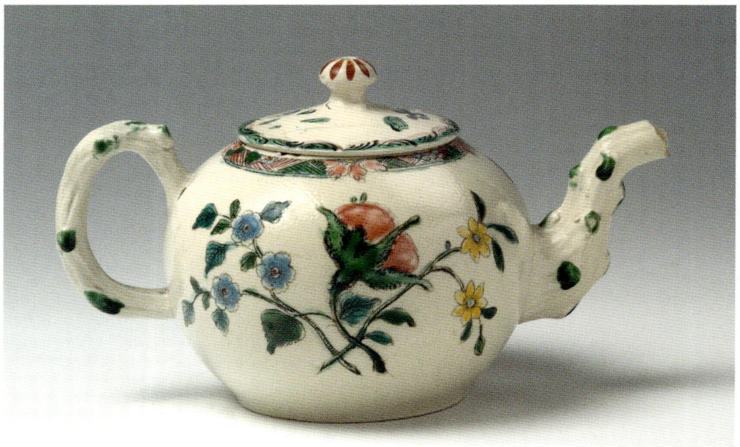

Teapot, (109), c.1750, Staffordshire, height: 11.5cm, (4½in), enamelled, white salt-glazed stoneware. This very rare teapot celebrates the lost cause of Charles Edward Stuart. The distinctive 'crabstock' (twig-like), spout and handle help to date it. The prince, framed by a thistle, (representing Scotland), and the white (Yorkist) rose, wears Highland plaid with a bonnet and a blue sash. Flower spray on the reverse.

William Augustus, Duke of Cumberland (1721-1765)

Cumberland, the second son of George II, commanded the British forces that vanquished Charles Edward Stuart at the battle of Culloden. He earned himself the nickname of 'Butcher' and the undying hatred of the Scots for his relentless pursuit of the Scottish rebels. The influence wielded by Scots Peers in Parliament, Scottish landowners and Scottish commanders in the armed forces reinforced this negative image. Cumberland was, in fact, a popular leader and a social reformer within the army. He founded the Chelsea Hospital near Buckingham House for invalid soldiers and enabled the passing of a Parliamentary bill protecting army pensions. He spent his later years cultivating an arboretum. At his death Horace Walpole considered, 'He would have made a great king, but probably too great a king for so corrupt a country.'[3]

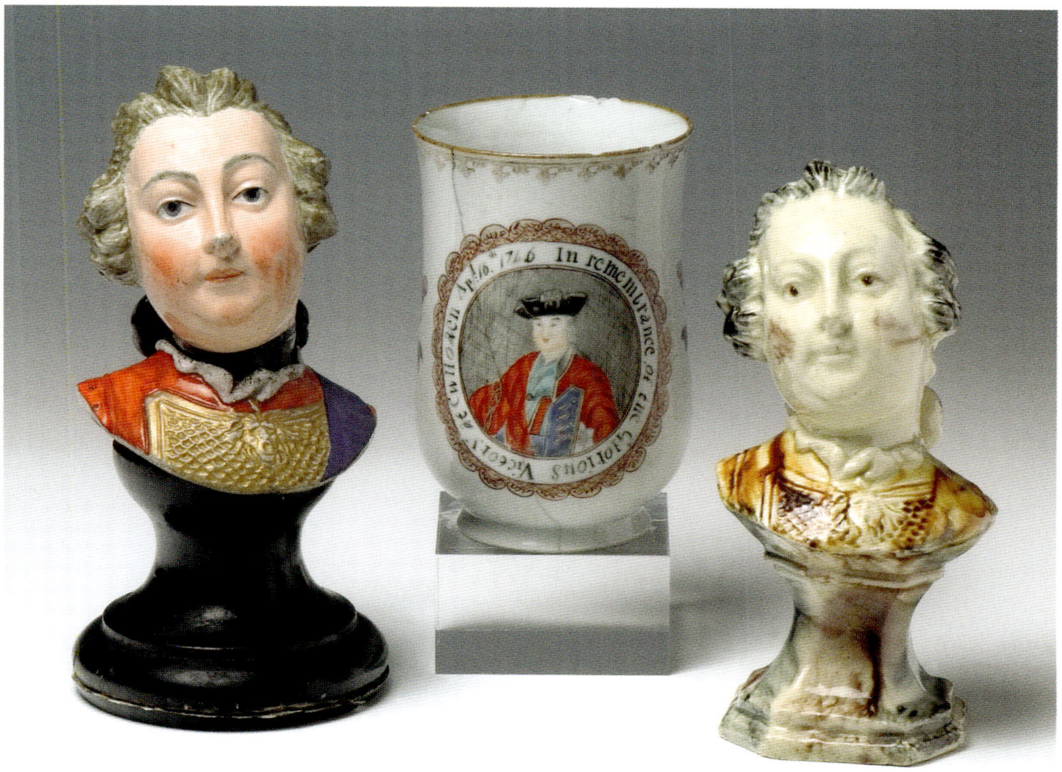

Bust, (112), c.1752, London, Chelsea, height: 17.8cm, (7in), soft-paste porcelain, enamelled and gilt.[4] Bust of Cumberland made to commemorate victory at Culloden and because Sir Everard Fawkener, the Duke's private secretary, was one of the directors of the Chelsea porcelain factory, in which the Duke also had a financial interest.[5] Perhaps based on a lead bust by John Cheere, or from a mass-produced cheap plaster cast.[6]
Mug, (110), c.1755, China, height: 13.3cm, (5¼in), hard-paste porcelain, enamelled and gilt with a portrait of the Duke, inscribed, 'In remembrance of the Glorious Victory at Culloaen [*sic*] Apl: 16th 1746'.[7] Image, probably taken from a famous equestrian portrait of 1744, by John Wootton.[8]
Bust, (111), c.1755, height: 17.8cm, (7in), Staffordshire, earthenware. Moulded with integral socle, lead glazed and lightly coloured with metal oxides. Examples of the Chelsea bust are also found in white salt-glazed stoneware.

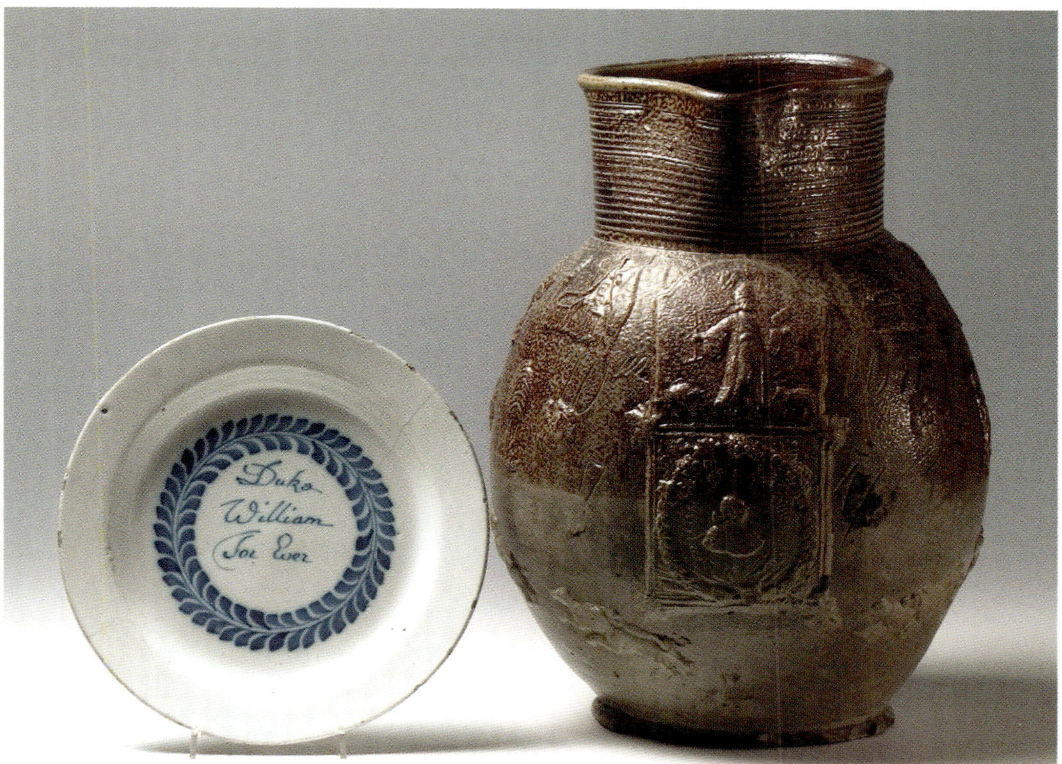

Plate, (114), c.1750, unknown, diameter: 20.3cm, (8in), tin-glazed earthenware Inscribed, within wreath, 'Duke William For Ever'.
Jug, (113), c.1747, height: 31.6cm, (12½in), Staffordshire, stoneware. Moulded images: (below spout) include inn sign with a bishop, flanked by sheep, profile portrait, entitled: 'WILLIAM DUKE OF CUMBERLAND'. Further sprigs of hunting scene, houses and trees. Inscribed: 'Wm Wright 1747'- a publican, perhaps?

Frederick the Great, King of Prussia (1712-1786)

Frederick II played a leading role in the break-up of the Holy Roman Empire and the rise of the small provincial kingdom that would eventually head a new, united Germany. In 1730, as an unhappy youth, he tried to flee to England. Later an esteemed British ally, he was regarded, not least by Willett, as an honorary Englishman. He succeeded to the Prussian throne in 1740 and indulged his passion for the arts, ruling as an enlightened, if absolute monarch. Surprisingly, he soon proved skilful in warfare, winning much of Silesia and taking Prague in the War of the Austrian Succession (1740-48) after which he was styled 'the Great'.

A secret pact between Austria and France led to an Anglo-Prussian alliance for the duration of the Seven Years War (1756-63). Despite fluctuating financial and military support from Britain, Hanover, Brunswick and Hesse-Kassel, Frederick won victories at Leuthen in 1757, Minden in 1759 and at Torgau in 1760. He gained an extraordinary following in Britain and was equally popular in the American Colonies.[9] Pastors in the Scottish kirk would pray for his soul (he was very relaxed about religion and tolerated Jesuits at court). William Ramsden, a Charterhouse schoolmaster, wrote in 1763 of his own happy home life, 'from the arm of my Wife's easy Chair, a Situation I wo'd not change [with] the King of Prussia',[10] while Horace Walpole marvelled at Frederick's popularity,

> All England kept his birthday: it has taken its place in our calendar next to Admiral Vernon's ... & the people, I believe, think that Prussia is part of *Old England'*, and again, as I was walking by the river the other night, a bargeman asked me for something to drink the King of Prussia's health.[11]

A large number of ceramic souvenirs survive.

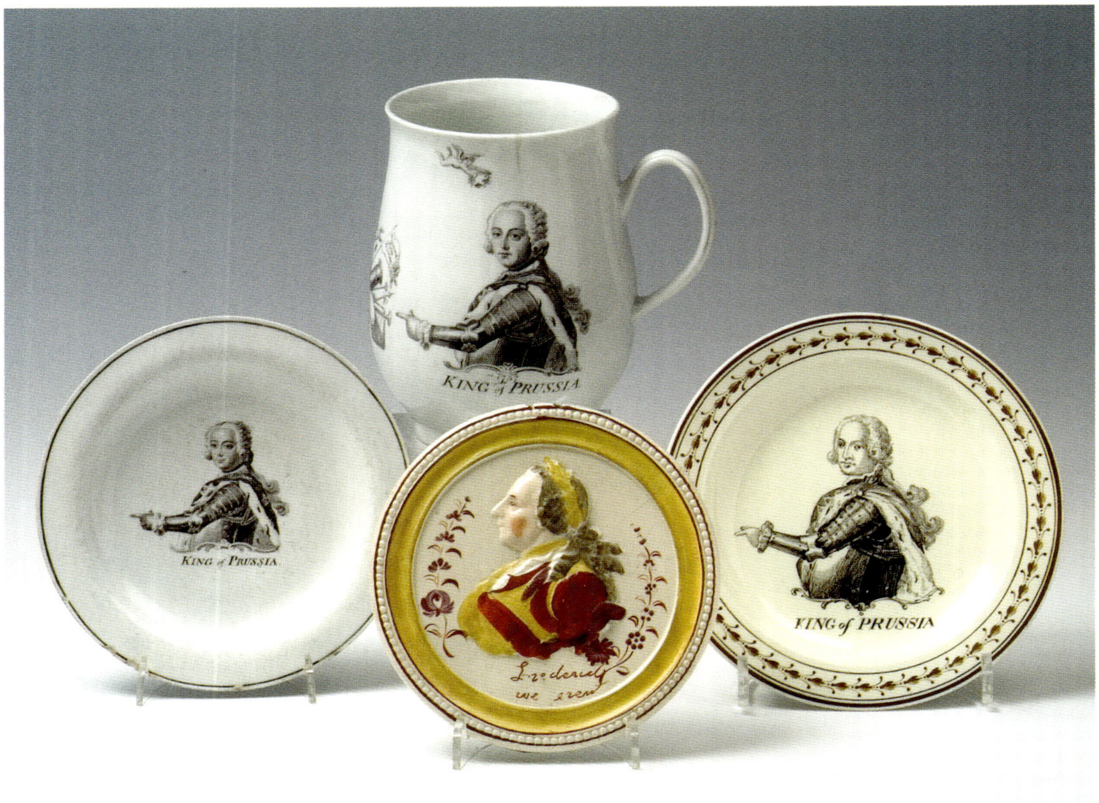

Clockwise:
Plate, (117), c.1760, Worcester, height: 15.3cm, (6in), soft-paste porcelain. Printed portrait of Frederick by Robert Hancock.
Mug, (116), dated 1757, Worcester, height: 15.3cm, (6in), soft-paste porcelain. Printed portrait by Hancock, (signed RH, + anchor rebus for Richard Holdship, director of the factory), adapted from one of Frederick as Crown Prince, painted in 1739, by Antoine Pesne.[12] Clad in armour, he points to a pile of battle trophies with flags inscribed, 'Reisberg, Prague, Collin [a defeat], Welbach, Rossbach, Breslaw'. A flying putto holds a crown of laurel and on the reverse Fame blows twin trumpets.
Plate, (118), c.1760, Staffordshire, diameter: 16.5cm, (6½in), creamware. Hand-painted with same portrait within a fine husk border (an arrow is painted on the reverse).
Plaque, (122), reverse incised: 'May 3 1827',[13] Staffordshire, diameter: 12.7cm, (5in), pearlware. Relief-moulded with profile portrait of King of Prussia and painted: 'Frederick for ever'. Likeness probably taken from a medal or coin (possibly the third 'taler' issued in 1774). Late date unexplained.

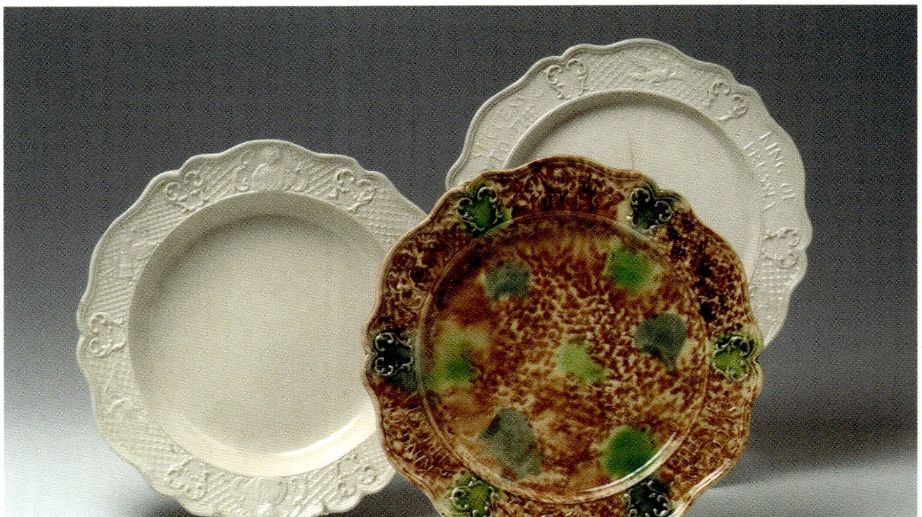

Clockwise:
Soup Plate, (120), c.1760, Staffordshire, diameter: 21cm, (8¼in), creamware.
Rim moulded with relief portrait of the king, an eagle and cannon.
Plate, (119), c.1760, Staffordshire, diameter: 22.9cm, (9in), salt-glazed stoneware.
Moulded in relief with inscription, 'SUCCESS TO THE / KING OF PRUSSIA / AND HIS FORCES'; and symbols (as 120 and 121).
Plate, (121), c.1760, Staffordshire, diameter: 21cm, (8¼in), creamware.
Moulded in relief (as 119 and 120), and sponged with metal oxide colours.

General James Wolfe (1727-1759)

Wolfe is one of those iconic military heroes about whom it is now difficult to separate fact from fiction. He died, like Nelson, at the climax of a momentous victory and at the age of only 32. He joined the Marines at fourteen, served in Flanders under his father, (General Edward Wolfe) in 1743 and fought at Culloden in 1746. Wolfe was tall, thin and had a long face and red hair. With his bulging eyes, a retroussé nose and a receding chin he was considered ugly; 'the singular form of his profile, ... might be nearly represented by two lines of an obtuse angle, meeting at the tip of the nose'.[14] He probably suffered from manic depression[15] but his mercurial personality made him attractive and endeared him to his troops. When the English Court branded the young brigadier general mad, King George II is said to have declared: 'Mad, is he? Then I hope he will bite some of my other generals!'[16]

After being credited with the victory at Louisbourg, Nova Scotia, in 1758 William Pitt sent him back to Canada in 1759, to capture Quebec. On 13 September, having scaled seemingly impregnable cliffs to the high Plains of Abraham, he surprised and routed the French in less than one hour. Though mortally wounded by a sniper's bullet, he lived long enough to learn of the victory. The French commander, the Marquis de Montcalm, survived him by only a few hours. The loss of Quebec led to the collapse of French power in the New World.

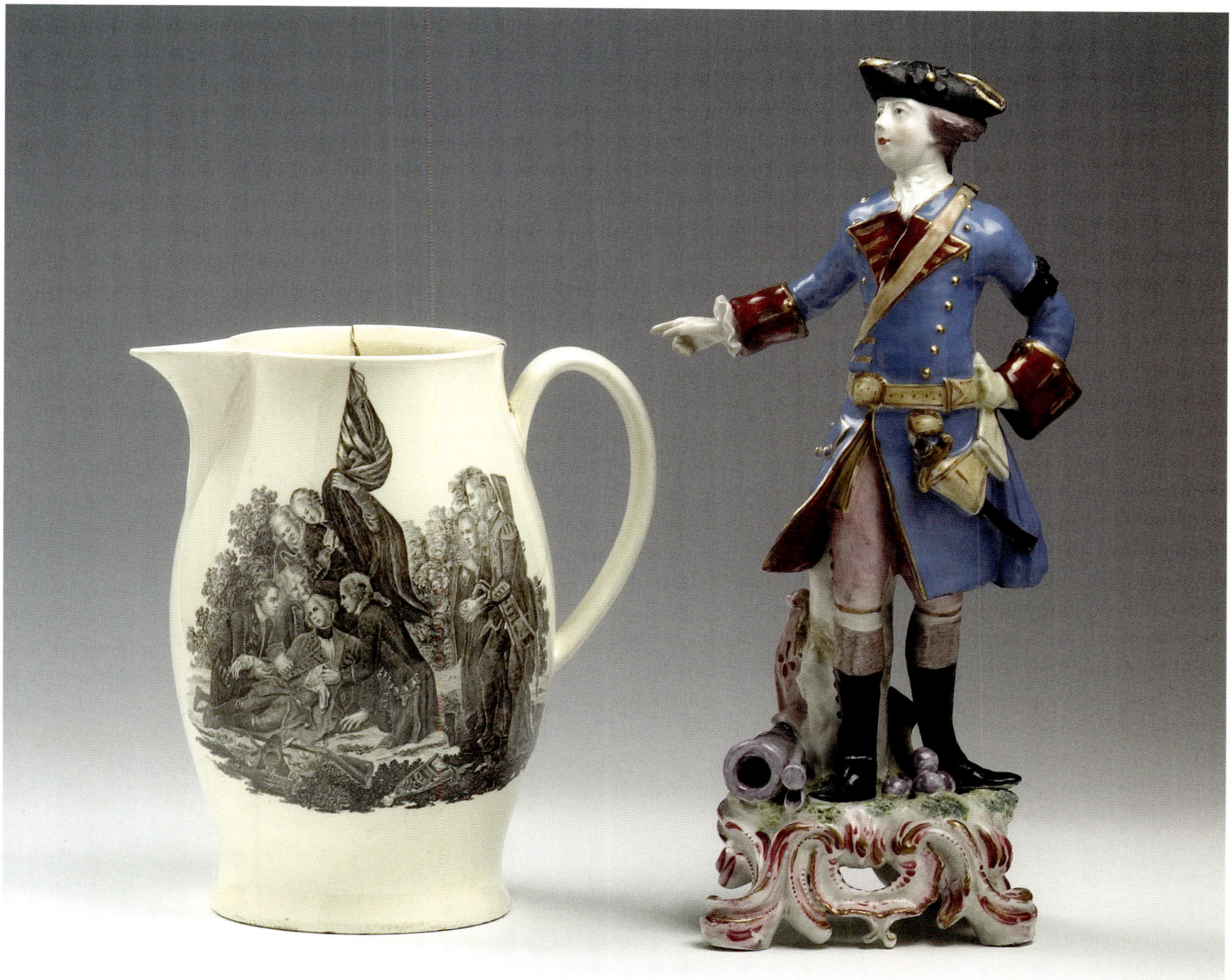

Jug, (125), c.1778, probably Liverpool, height: 24.2cm, (9½in), printed creamware. General Wolfe dying in the arms of his officers.[17] Taken from the right-hand side of Benjamin West's painting, *The Death of General Wolfe*, which was given a rapturous reception when it was shown at the Royal Academy in 1771. The Union flag is lowered in deference to the dying General, who slumps in the arms of his adjutants, Captain Hervey Smith and Colonel Barre. The doctor, Robert Adair (who was not present) holds a handkerchief to Wolfe's heart. Engraved by William Woollett in 1776, the image became the best-selling print of its era, earning the painter over £5,000 in foreign sales alone.[18]

Figure, (124), c.1770, London, Bow, height: 35.6cm, (14in), soft-paste porcelain, enamelled and gilt. A sword hangs from Wolfe's belt and a musket from his shoulder. A rolled map of Quebec, a cannon, cannon balls, a flag and a spontoon (an officer's signalling lance) lie at his feet. Black crepe armband probably indicates mourning for his father, who had died while Wolfe was at sea. In view of this detail, Wolfe is, surprisingly, incorrectly dressed. The most successful of the 'Redcoat' generals in North America is shown wearing a blue coat, matching that of his companion figure, the Marquis of Granby. Captain Hervey Smith is said to have sketched Wolfe from life and a full-length portrait was painted by J.S.C. Schaak,[19] engraved in mezzotint by Richard Houston, c.1770.[20]

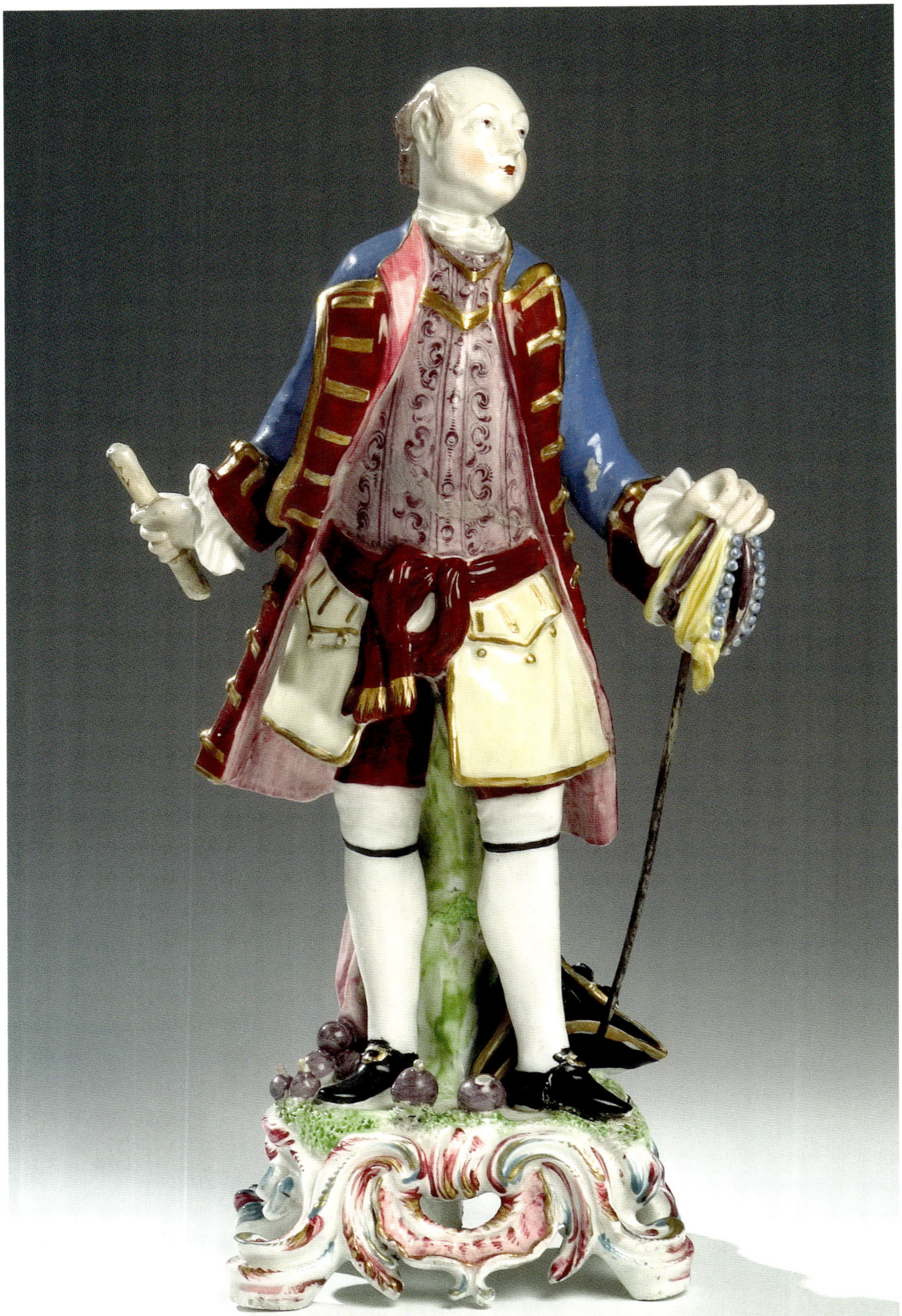

Figure, (124), c.1770, London, Bow, height: 35.6cm, (14in), soft-paste porcelain enamelled and gilt. Bow issued the figure of the Marquis of Granby as a pair to Wolfe. The most likely source is one of several copies of a 1758 portrait by Sir Joshua Reynolds. It was published in 1760 by three engravers, notably as a mezzotint by Richard Houston.[23] Probably painted after the capture of Warburg, (when his hat famously blew away), he is shown bare-headed and bald, leaning thoughtfully on a (metal) sword. The figure faithfully reproduces his regimental greatcoat but his waistcoat is oddly painted; the top is purple and the skirt and pockets lemon yellow.

John Manners, Marquis of Granby (1721-1770)

Manners, eldest son of the 3rd Duke of Rutland, attended Cambridge University before becoming an MP, first for Grantham in 1741, and later for Cambridge. He received his army commission in 1745 and, like Wolfe, saw action in the Highlands and in Flanders in 1747. He became a hero of the Seven Years War. He was despatched to Germany in 1758 as Colonel of the Royal Horse Guards (the Blues). As head of the British contingent of Prince Ferdinand of Brunswick's army he triumphed at the battle of Minden in 1759, stormed Warburg in 1760 and defended Vellinghausen in 1761, returning to Britain in 1763. A painting (and a best-selling print) of *The Marquis of Granby Relieving a Sick Soldier,*[21] 1764, by Edward Penny, emphasise his humanity and generosity to his troops.[22] The number of inns and public houses that took his name (some run by his demobilised soldiers), confirm his popularity.

Field Marshal Henry Seymour Conway (1721-1795)

Conway is better known as a key supporter of the controversial politician, John Wilkes, than as a military leader.[24] Handsome and charming, he was the nephew of Prime Minister Robert Walpole and a close friend of his cousin, Horace Walpole. Like Wolfe and Granby, he saw action in Scotland and Flanders, and was promoted to lieutenant general in 1759. He returned to England in 1763 and opposed the new King George III's action against Wilkes. The King dismissed him as 'Groom of the Bedchamber' and deprived him of his regiment, leaving him financially embarrassed. He later returned to the army, was made a full general in 1772 and Governor of Jersey.

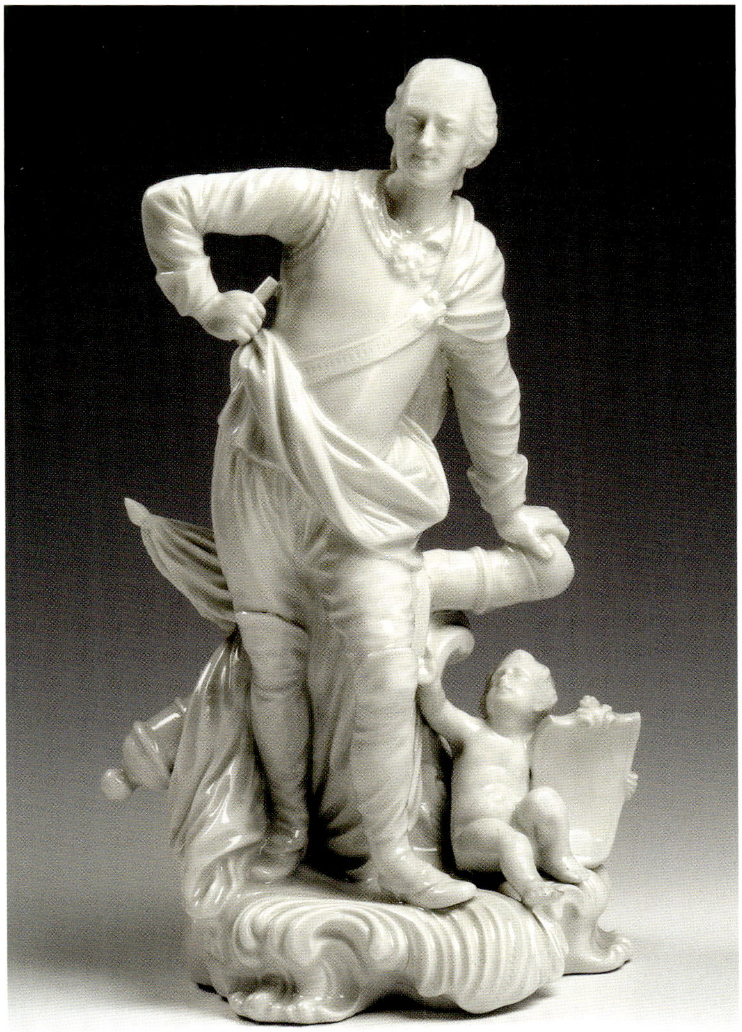

Figure, (123), c.1765, Derby, height: 29.8cm, (11¾in), soft-paste porcelain. Figure of Conway[25] made at Derby as a pair to one of John Wilkes. Conway, in armour, leans on a cannon while holding a baton in the other hand. At his feet a putto holds a shield.[26]

Frederick Augustus, Duke of York and Albany (1763-1827)

Frederick, second son of George III, was sent as a colonel to Hanover for military training in 1780. Following the outbreak of war with France in 1793, he commanded the British forces in Flanders and, with the assistance of experienced staff, drove the French from Belgium, capturing Valenciennes on 28 July 1794. The showman, Philip Astley, staged a re-enactment of the siege at Astley's Amphitheatre, firing a cannon captured there.[27] For this and other modest victories Frederick was nicknamed, 'the Grand old Duke of York', in the famous nursery rhyme. He was driven out of Belgium in 1794.

At home the Duke of York achieved real success in reforming abuses of the army. In 1809, however, he was forced to resign, following his involvement with the unscrupulous courtesan, Mary Anne Clarke (1776-1852), and her unproven allegations that he had sold commissions. The scandal broke when the embittered ex-Colonel Wardle, MP for Okehampton, (who had been refused a commission), challenged the Duke's ignorance of these transactions and presented evidence of Mrs Clarke's business dealings to Parliament. Charles Lamb wrote, 'The sensation in London about this nonsensical business is marvellous ... thousands of ballads, caricatures, lives, of Mrs Clarke, in every blind alley.'[30] In return for a generous annuity, Mrs Clarke destroyed the memoirs Col. Wardle had persuaded her to write. In 1811 the Duke was reinstated as Commander-in-Chief to popular acclaim and later founded a school in Chelsea for educating soldiers' sons. He died of dropsy in 1827.

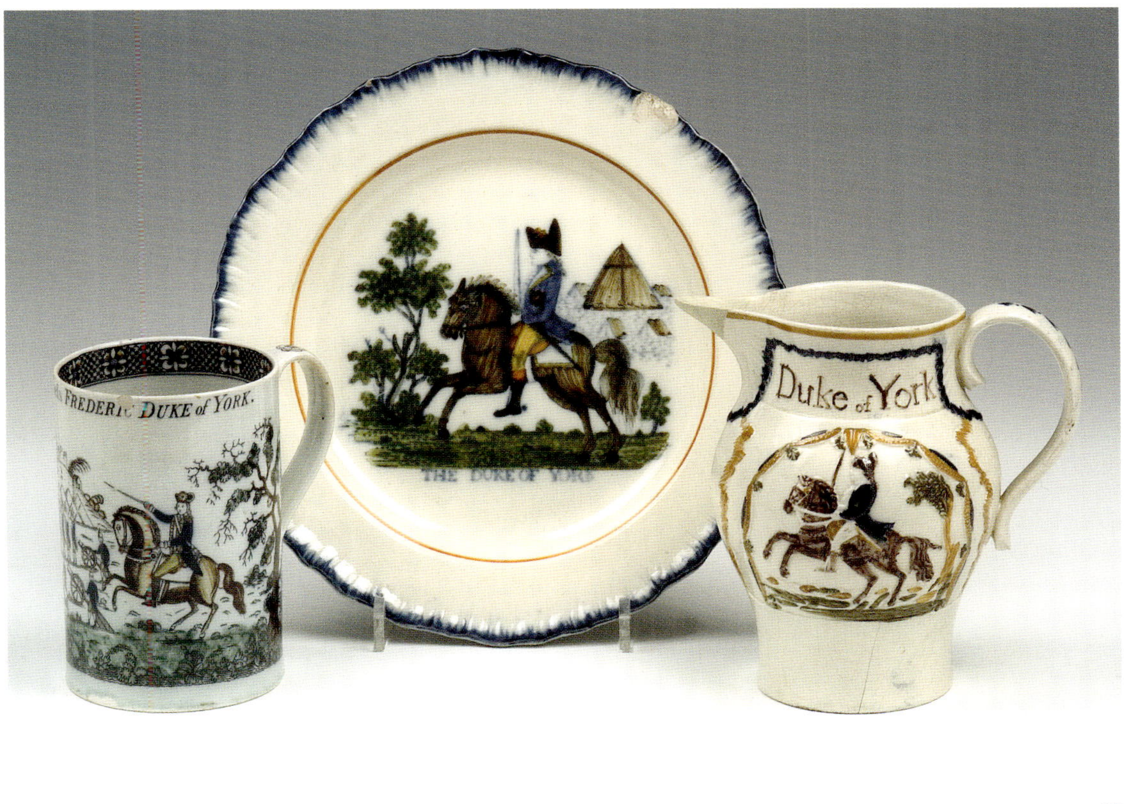

Mug, (129), c.1795, Staffordshire, height: 12.7cm, (5in), earthenware, printed and painted in high-temperature colours.
Wrap-around print, inscribed, 'His Royal Highness FREDERIC DUKE of YORK', shows him directing the assault on a French stronghold, probably Valenciennes. The image of the Duke on his rearing horse on all three pieces derives from a print of 1794 by John Fairburn.[28]
Plate, (127), c.1795, Staffordshire, height: 24.2cm, (9½in), earthenware, printed and painted in high-temperature colours.
Inscribed, 'THE DUKE OF YORK', shows an equestrian figure before a distant encampment.
Jug, (128), c.1795, Staffordshire, height: 15.3cm, (6in), earthenware, Prattware.
Relief-moulded with two equestrian portraits inscribed, 'Duke of York / Prince.Coburg' (an ally).

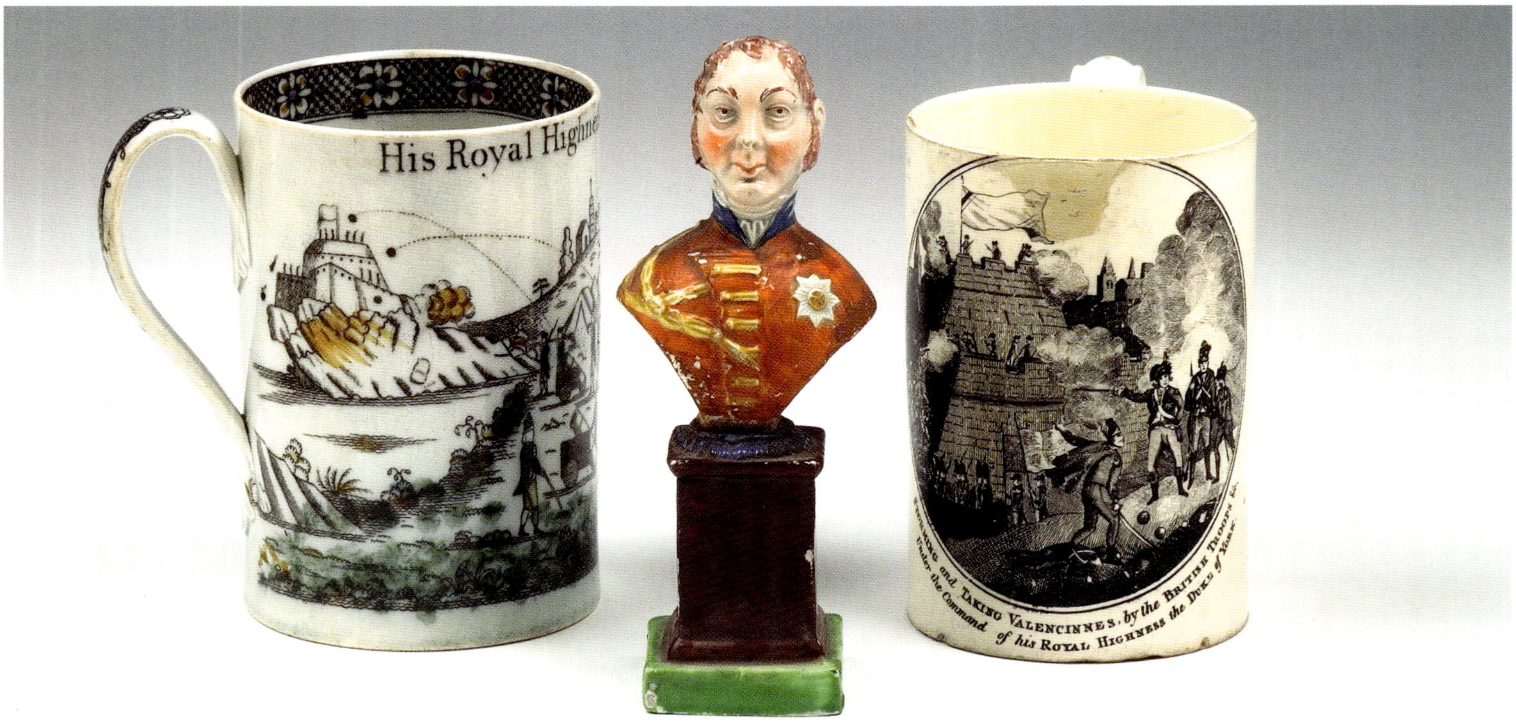

Mug, (129), c.1795, Staffordshire, height: 12.7cm, (5in), earthenware, printed and painted in high-temperature colours. Wrap-around print, inscribed, 'His Royal Highness FREDERIC DUKE of YORK'. Infantry with heavy field guns and cannon lay siege to a hilltop fort. The cartoon-style trajectories of the cannon balls are shown, flying towards their targets.
Bust, (131), c.1800, probably Staffordshire, height: 15.3cm, (6in), enamelled pearlware. The crop-haired Duke wears the uniform of the Coldstream Guards.
Mug, (130), c.1800, probably Staffordshire, height: 12.7cm, (5in), printed pearlware. Scene inscribed, 'STORMING and TAKING VALENCINNES [*sic*] by the BRITISH TROOPS … / Under the Command of His ROYAL HIGHNESS the DUKE of YORK'.[29]

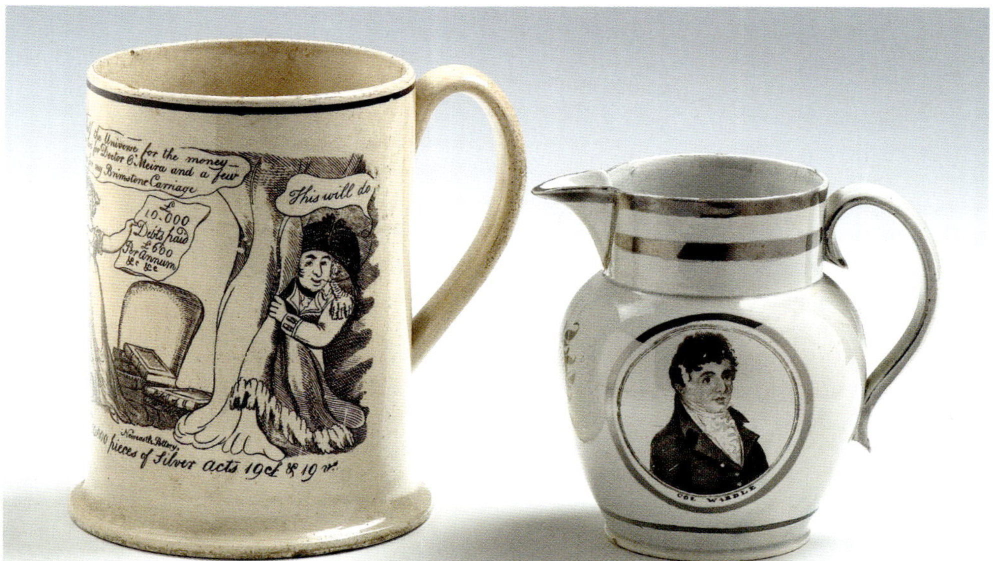

Mug, (133), c.1809, marked 'Newcastle Pottery', for Addison, Falconer & Co.,[31] height: 14.6cm, (5¾in), printed creamware. Satirical scene in a domestic interior. The Duke of York secretly watches Mrs Clarke who is, 'Burning the books of Curious Arts value 50,000 pieces of silver Acts 19ch and 19vs.' (the biblical reference is to the value of books of magic arts burned by magicians in Ephesus.) The print, after Rowlandson, appeared in 1809.[32]
Jug, (132), c.1809, probably Staffordshire, height: 11.5cm, (4½in), printed pearlware.
Portraits inscribed, 'COL. WARDLE' and 'MISS TAYLOR', in silver lustre frames.

General Lord Cornwallis (1738-1805)

Charles Cornwallis was a consummate career soldier and public servant who, in a long and distinguished career, saw active service on three continents. He served with distinction in Germany from 1759, notably at Minden and Vellinghausen. Posted to America as Major General in 1776, he won the battle of Brandywine and occupied Philadelphia in 1777 before conceding defeat at Yorktown in 1781. After returning to England in 1782, he reluctantly travelled to India as Governor General and Commander-in-Chief to reform the civil and military administrations. One of his most implacable enemies was Tipu Sultan (1750-99), the 'Tiger of Mysore', who precipitated the third Mysore War, culminating in the siege of Seringapatam. The defeated Tipu was forced to cede half his territories, a sum equivalent to £3,600,000 and, on 26 February 1792, two of his young sons as hostages, in order to ensure his compliance. In August Cornwallis was created Marquis in recognition of his services.

In 1798, at the age of 60, he agreed to accept the post of Viceroy and Commander-in-Chief in Ireland. There he suppressed a rebellion of Irish and French troops and oversaw the passing of the 1800 Act of Union by the Irish Parliament. Exasperation with the corruption and inefficiency of the Irish parliament, however, made him sympathise with the Catholics. Having resigned and retired in 1801 he was appointed British plenipotentiary to negotiate the Peace of Amiens with Napoleon in 1802. He was then persuaded to return to India in 1805 where he fell ill and died.

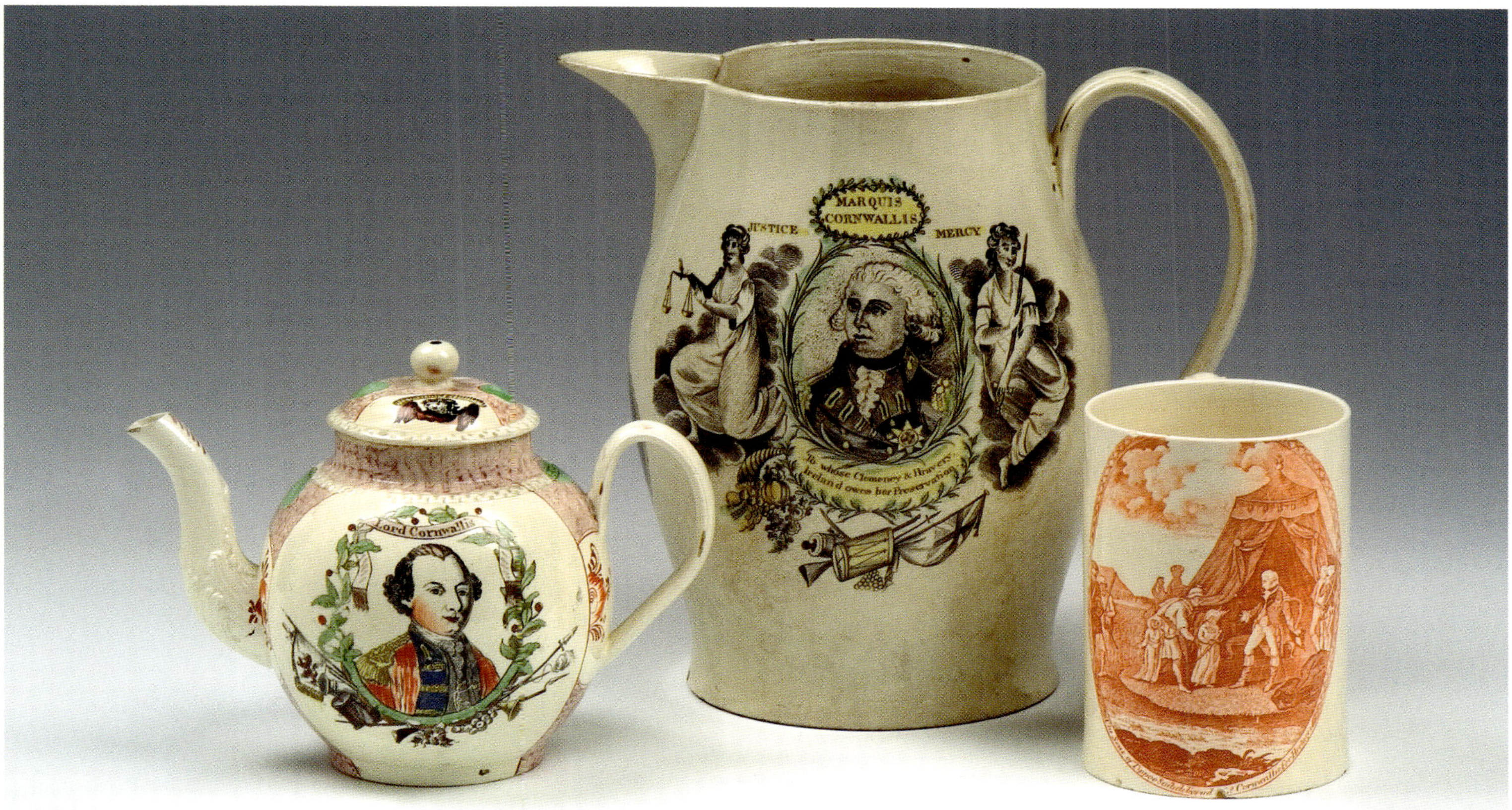

Teapot, (135A), c.1780, Staffordshire, William Greatbatch of Fenton, height: 11.5cm, (4½in), creamware, printed and enamelled. Wreathed portrait of 'LORD CORNWALLIS'.
Jug, (136), c.1800, Staffordshire, height: 21.6cm, (8½in), printed creamware, lightly coloured. Cornwallis's last posting to Ireland is commemorated on a large, jug, c.1800. Wreathed portrait, flanked by Justice and Mercy, entitled, 'MARQUIS CORNWALLIS / To whose Clemency & Bravery / Ireland owes her Preservation'. (Nelson, as hero of the Battle of the Nile (1798) is shown on the reverse).
Mug, (134), c.1800, Staffordshire, height: 12.1cm, (4¾in), creamware, printed in red.
The episode in India where Cornwallis took hostage Tipu's sons was painted by Robert Home (shown at the Royal Academy in 1797) and by Mather Brown.[33] The scene was freely adapted from several prints.

The Napoleonic Wars

Lieutenant-General, Sir John Moore (1761-1809).

The son of a Glasgow doctor, Moore served with distinction in America, in Ireland and in Egypt but was frequently wounded in action. At home he reformed army training and was made a Knight of the Bath in 1804. He led the British forces into Spain in 1808 but when Spanish reinforcements failed to materialise, he was forced to retreat to the coast at La Coruña, losing many men in the winter blizzards. They were attacked by the French but, against the odds, repulsed them. Moore, however, was fatally wounded, died, and was buried at La Coruña on 17 January 1809.

Arthur Wellesley, Duke of Wellington (1769-1852)

Wellesley was born in Dublin, the third son of the Earl of Mornington in the Irish peerage. After attending Eton and the French Académie d'Equitation at Angers, he and his brothers entered the British army and were posted to India in 1796, where Richard, the eldest, became Governor General. When Tipu, Sultan of Mysore allied with the French to escape the British stranglehold on his territories, the brothers led the attack on Tipu's capital, Seringapatam, in 1799.

Major General Arthur Wellesley returned to Britain in 1805 and

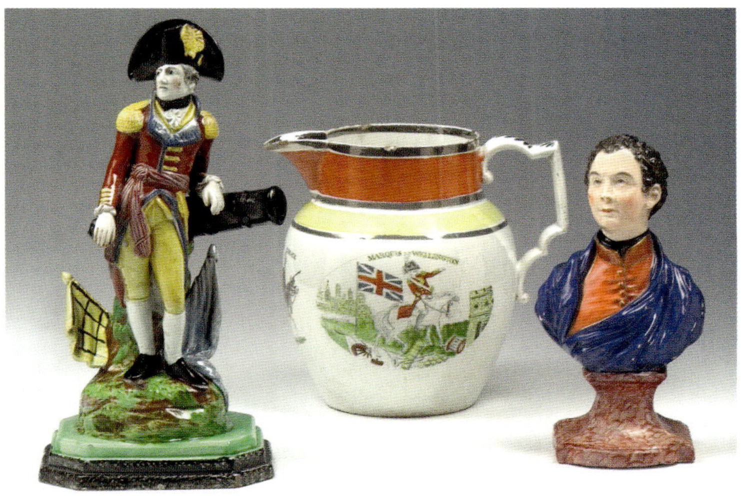

Figure, (139), c.1815, Staffordshire, height: 30.5cm, (12in), enamelled pearlware. Thought to represent Wellington, the figure rests on a cannon before crossed flags.[34] A similar figure in the V&A identified as modelled by Pierre Stephan.[35]
Jug, (406), 1812, Staffordshire, height: 20.3cm, (8in), pearlware, printed and enamelled. An officer on horseback, named 'MARQUIS WELLINGTON', stands with a large Union flag before the city of Salamanca.
Bust, (137), Staffordshire, height: 22.9cm, (9in), enamelled pearlware. Probably based on the portrait fragment of Moore painted in 1801 by James Northcote.[36] The bust was probably issued after the publication in 1815, of the Rev. Charles Wolfe's famous poem, 'The Burial of Sir John Moore at Corunna'.

entered politics as a military adviser and Chief Secretary for Ireland. He resumed his military career in the Iberian Peninsula, maintaining that Portugal could be defended with a British force of fewer than 30,000 men against Napoleon's 100,000, even if Spain were overrun. Following the death of Sir John Moore in 1809, he assumed command of the British army.

After Wellington's victory at Talavera on 28 July 1809, he was created Baron Douro, Viscount Wellington, and became an Earl on 18 February 1812. Having briefly liberated Madrid and trounced the French at Salamanca on 22 July he was made Marquess. A reserved and ruthless commander, he scored an even greater victory at Vittoria on 21 June 1813. The French were routed and driven from Spain.

Napoleon resigned in April 1814 and in June Wellington was awarded a dukedom and a grant of £400,000. In February 1815, Napoleon escaped from Elba and assembled a large veteran army on the Belgian border. He was finally defeated at Waterloo on 15 June by the combined British, Dutch and Hanoverian forces under Wellington, together with General Blücher's Prussian troops. After supporting the restored French monarchy in Paris from 1815-18, Wellington returned home and a grateful nation presented him with the estate of Stratfield Saye. He also leased Apsley House as his London base. After a stormy career in politics with three short spells as Prime Minister, he succeeded his old friend Lord Hill as Commander-in-Chief of the army, remaining in post until his death, aged 83.

General Rowland Hill (1772-1842)

The fourth of the sixteen children of John Hill, 3rd Baronet Hawkstone of Shropshire, Rowland Hill and four brothers joined the army and he served in Egypt before joining Wellington in Portugal in 1808. He proved an able commander and was made Lieutenant General in 1812, Baron Hill in 1814 and full General in 1825.

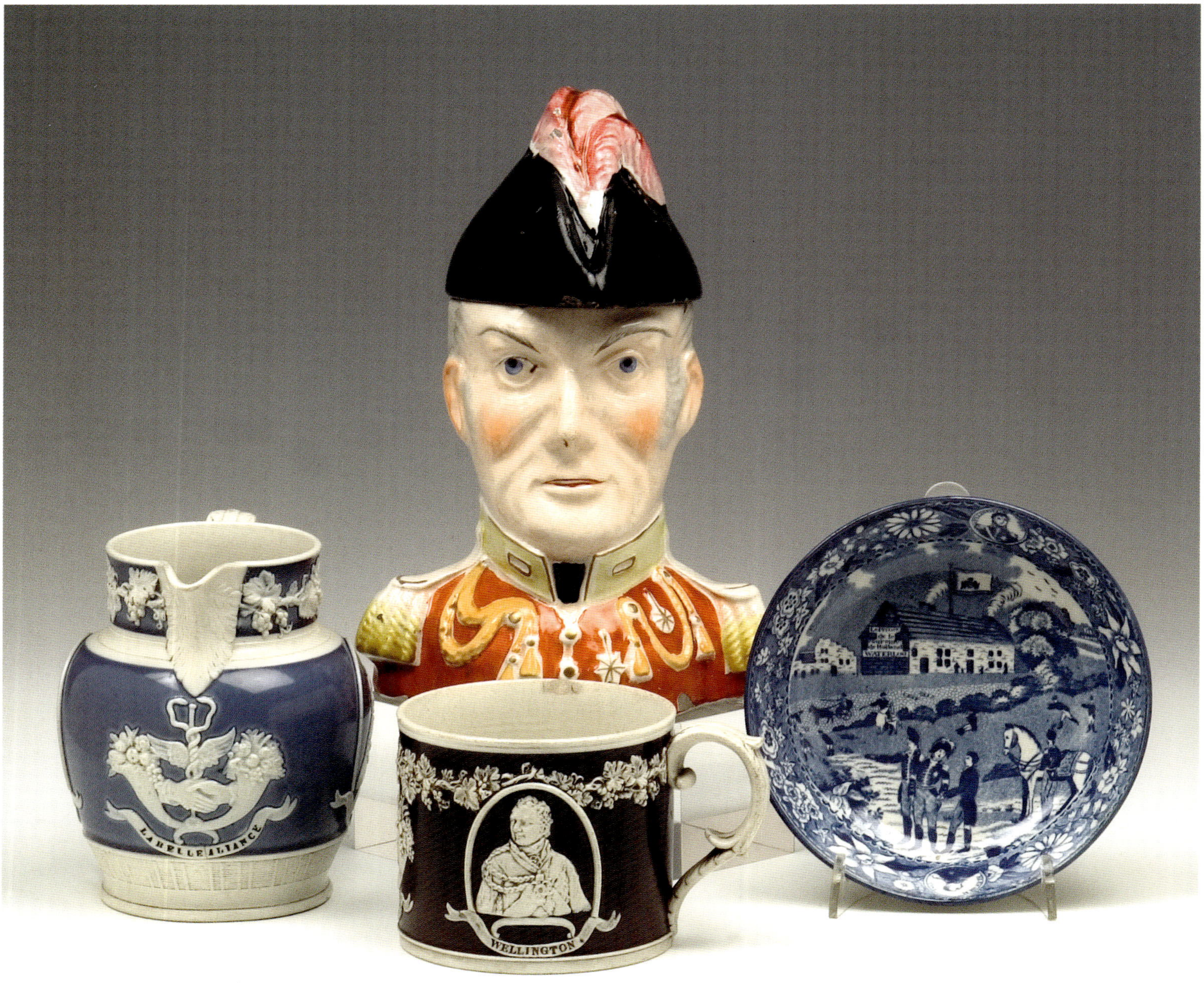

Jug, (140), c.1820, Staffordshire, height: 7.7cm, (3in), stoneware, slip-glazed in blue.
Mug, (141), c.1820, Staffordshire, height: 12.1cm, (4¾in), stoneware, slip-glazed in brown. Both decorated with white sprigs celebrating 'LA BELLE ALLIANCE' between vignettes of Wellington and General Blücher.
Tobacco Jar, (144), c.1840, Staffordshire, height: 12.7cm, (5in), enamelled pearlware. Moulded as a bust of the Duke of Wellington, his cocked hat forming the cover.
Saucer, (Hove 16.35), c.1820, Staffordshire, diameter: 7.7cm, (3in), blue-printed pearlware. Wellington before the Château d'Hougoumont farmhouse on the field of Waterloo.

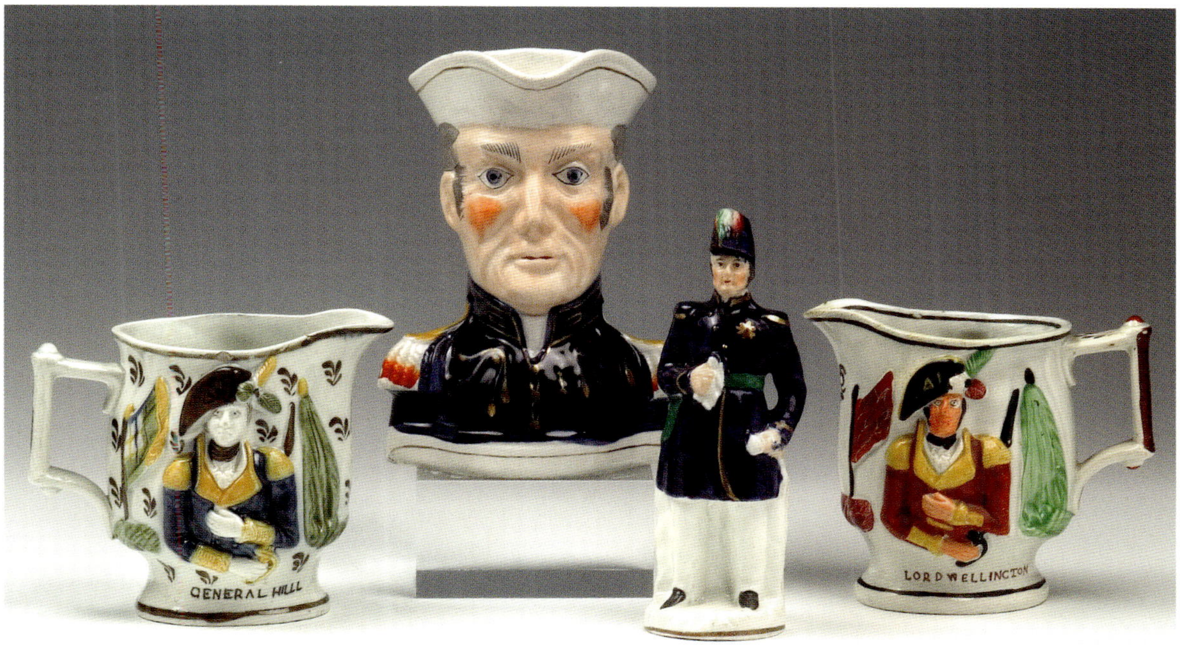

Two Jugs, (138 + 138A), Staffordshire, c.1830, each height: 12.7cm, (5in), Prattware. Relief-moulded with very similar half-length portraits, labelled 'LORD WELLINGTON' and 'GENERAL HILL'.
Bust Jug, (145), c.1850, Staffordshire, height: 18.4cm, (7¼in), earthenware, enamelled and gilt. Moulded as Wellington wearing a tricorne hat.
Figure, (142), c.1850, Staffordshire, height: 17.8cm, (7in), earthenware, enamelled and gilt. Moulded as Wellington wearing a cocked hat. Many of the Wellington commemoratives were made much later in his career, or possibly at his death.

The Crimea and After

A few items relate to the war of 1854-56 in the Crimean Peninsula. In 1853, after sending troops to defend Christians within the Ottoman Empire, Russian troops had occupied parts of Turkey and the Turks declared war. On 28 March 1854, looking to prevent Russian expansion, Britain and France (with Austrian support) also declared war on Russia. In September 1854, allied troops invaded Crimea and within a month were besieging Russian-held Sebastopol. British troops were poorly supplied and had little medical assistance (despite the publicity generated by the nurse, Florence Nightingale) and suffered heavy casualties. The French and British forced the fall of Sebastopol on 11 September 1855 and peace was ratified at Paris.

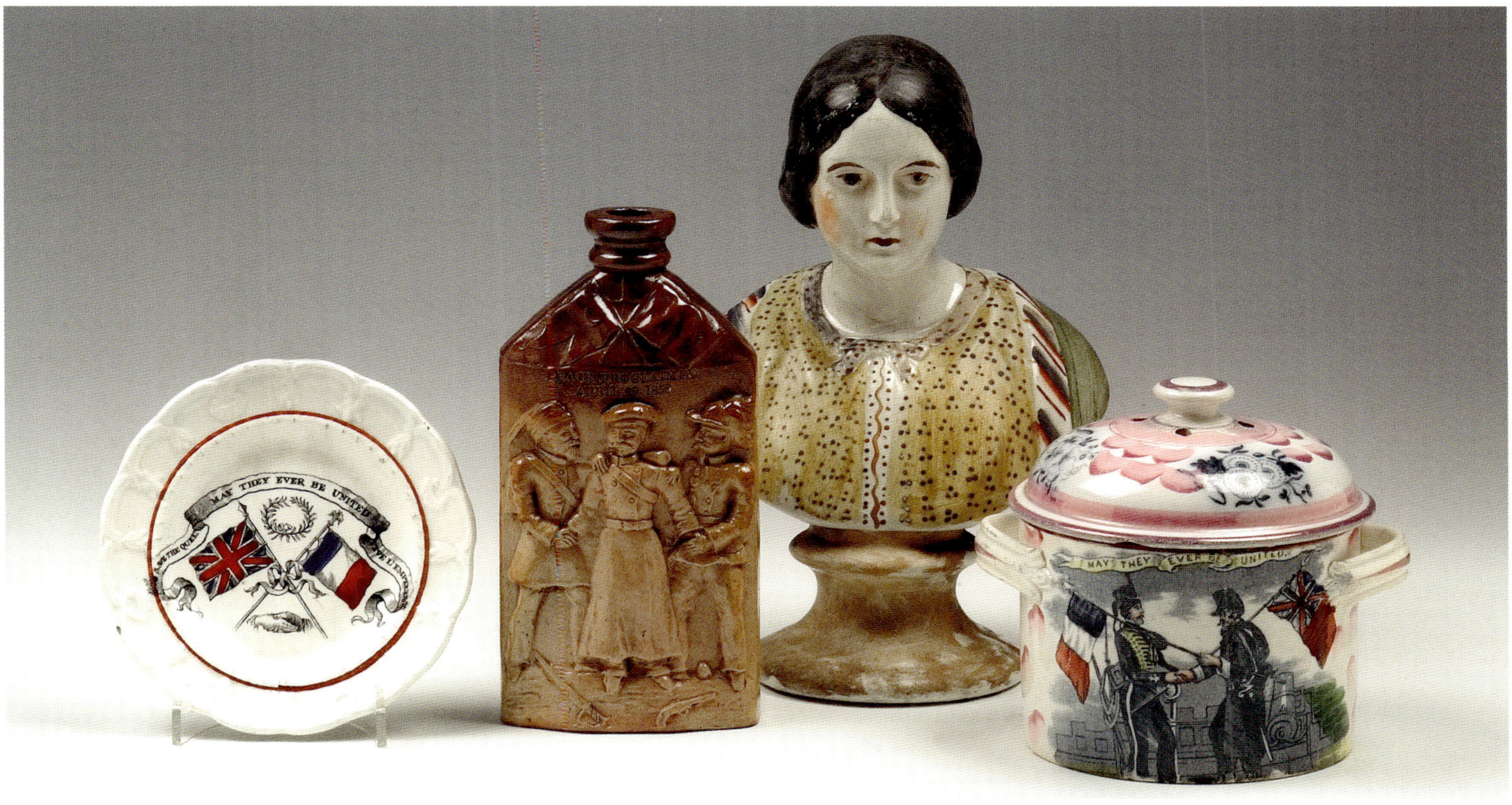

Saucer, (158), c.1855, Sunderland, Moore & Co., diameter: 12.7cm, (5in), earthenware, printed and enamelled. Inscribed, 'GOD SAVE THE QUEEN / MAY THEY EVER BE UNITED/ VIVE L'EMPEREUR' above the British and French flags.
Flask, (157), c.1856, London, height: 17.8cm, (7in), stoneware. Moulded in high relief (on both sides) with three soldiers shaking hands, having laid down their weapons. Impressed, 'WAR DECLARED / MARCH 28 1854' and 'PEACE PROCLAIMED / APRIL 29 1856'.
Bust, (160), c.1860, Staffordshire, height: 22.9cm, (9in), enamelled earthenware. Woman wearing a patterned, high-necked dress is said to portray Florence Nightingale.
Butter Dish and Cover, (159), c.1855, Sunderland, Moore & Co., diameter: 14cm, (5½in), earthenware, printed, enamelled and lustred. British and French soldiers shake hands, inscribed, 'MAY THEY EVER BE UNITED'.

Giuseppe Garibaldi (1807-1882)

Garibaldi, leader of the Italian Risorgimento, was first involved in revolutionary activities as an exile in South America. He returned to Italy in 1848 and again in 1854, in support of Victor Emmanuel, King of Sardinia. In 1860, inspired by uprisings in Messina and Palermo in Sicily he gathered a band of 1000 volunteers (*i Mille*), and landed at Marsala, conquering Sicily and driving out the Bourbon rulers. Unable to afford full uniforms, Garibaldi and his followers adopted red flannel shirts.[37] They marched through the mainland and declared Victor Emmanuel King of a united Italy. When he visited England in 1864, 500,000 Londoners turned out to cheer him and the radical *Reynolds's Newspaper* declared him 'the greatest man by whom England has ever been visited'. Fashionable ladies wore red blouses in his honour and babies were given his name. Large numbers of figures were made of Garibaldi, striking various poses.

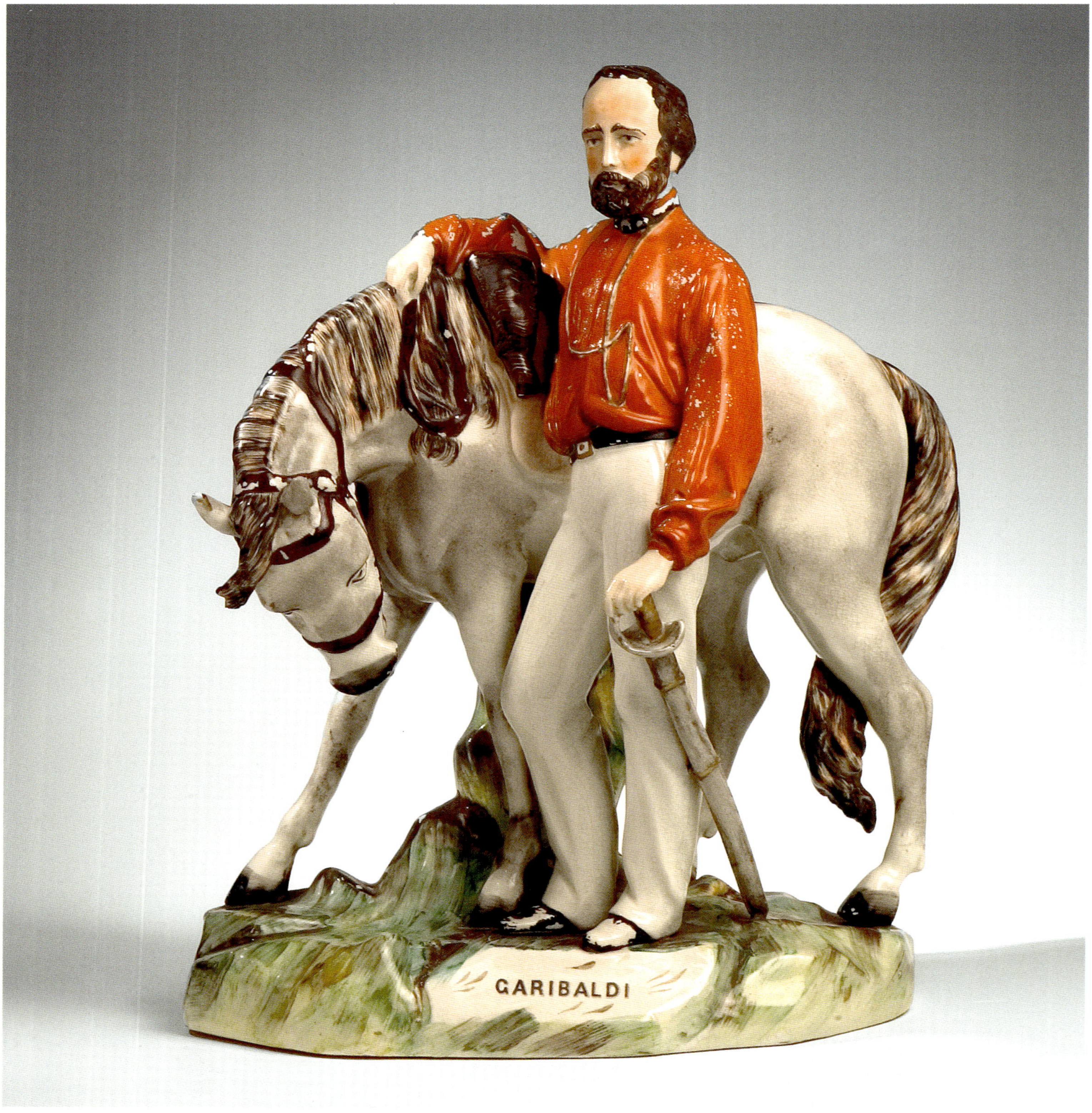

Figure Group, (161), c.1861, Staffordshire, height: 38.1cm, (15in), enamelled earthenware. Garibaldi, in a red shirt and white trousers, stands beside a grey horse. The likeness was based either on a portrait photograph by Gustave Le Gray of 1860 or a coloured engraving, published in a supplement to the *Illustrated London News*, 26 January 1861.

Major General Sir Henry Havelock (1795-1857)

Havelock was born in Sunderland, educated at Charterhouse and joined the army a month after Waterloo. He fought in Afghanistan in 1840 and in the Sikh wars of 1845-46. At the outbreak of the Indian Mutiny, he organised the relief of Cawnpore and Lucknow, witnessing the horror of the massacre there. He died of dysentery while besieged at Lucknow on 24 November 1857. A monument, sculpted by William Behnes in 1861, was erected to his memory in Trafalgar Square, London.

General Charles George Gordon (1833-1885)

A career soldier, Gordon served in Crimea before travelling to China in 1860. He helped to capture Peking and opposed the Taipings, earning the nickname 'Chinese Gordon'. From 1873 he served in Sudan, fought against the slave trade and was made Governor General. He returned to Sudan in February 1884 to evacuate Egyptian forces from Khartoum, where they were threatened by Sudanese rebels, under the brilliant military leadership of Muslim fundamentalist, Muhammad Ahmad al-Mahdi. On 26th January 1885, after a siege lasting 317 days, the rebels broke into Khartoum, beheading Gordon (against al-Mahdi's instructions) and the other defenders. The British relief force arrived two days later. The British public reacted to his death by acclaiming 'Gordon of Khartoum' a martyred warrior-saint and blamed the government for failing to relieve the siege. A statue of Gordon was placed in Trafalgar Square in 1888, but re-sited on the Victoria Embankment in 1953.

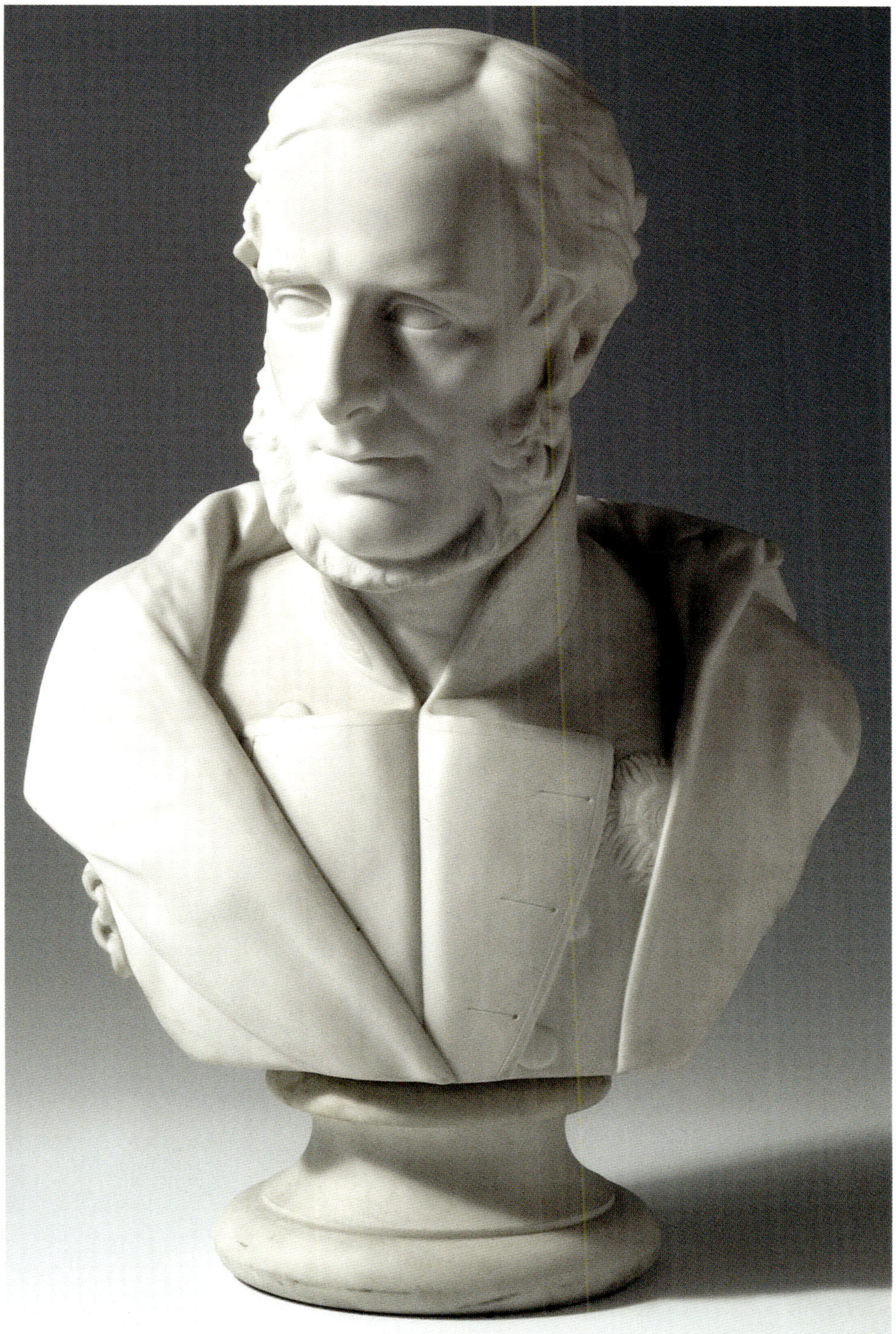

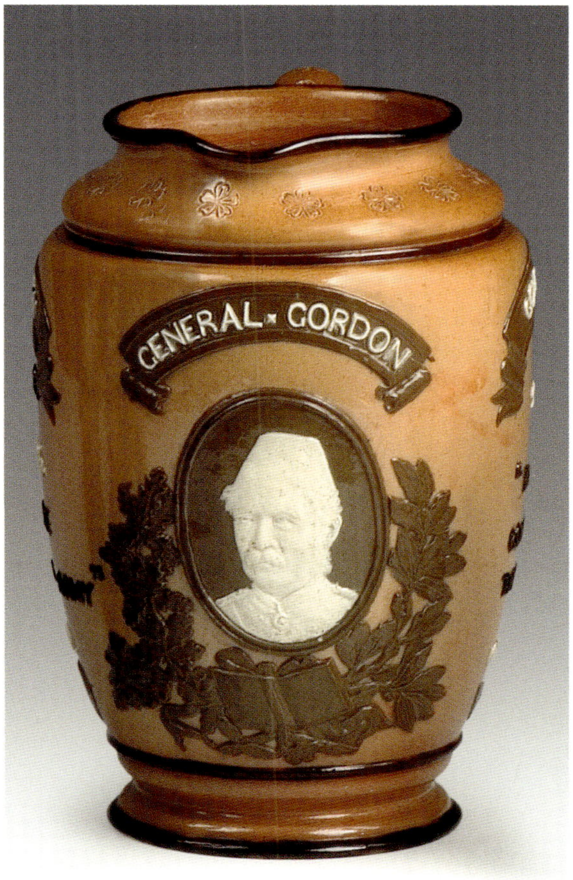

Jug, (164), 1884, London, Lambeth, Doulton & Co., height: 19.1cm, (7½in), stoneware. Sprigged portrait of Gordon, wearing the uniform of the Governor General of Sudan, including a fez. Taken from a celebrated photograph and inscribed: 'GENERAL GORDON ... 'CHINESE GORDON' BORN JAN.28. 1833 /', listing his achievements in Crimea, China, the Sudan and in Khartoum.

Portrait Bust, (162), c.1870, Staffordshire, height: 40.6cm, (16in), Parian porcelain.
Portrait of Havelock appears to be based on a drawing by Frederick Goodall of 1857, engraved c.1865.[38]

Chapter 3

NAVAL HEROES

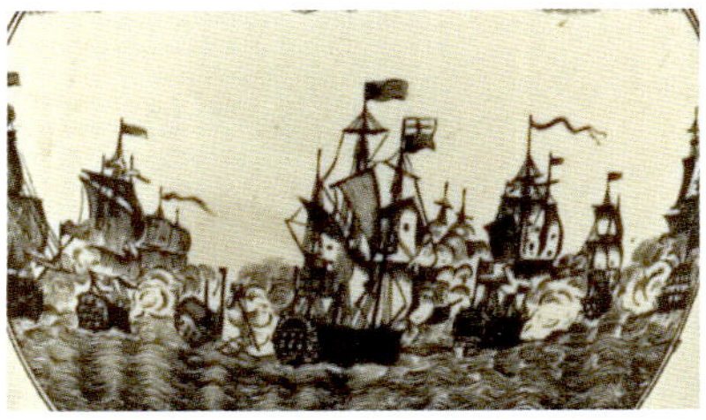

The later eighteenth century saw the expansion and modernisation of the British Navy resulting in increased success in sea battles and a rise in the social status of the sea service. During the American War of Independence the sons of dukes joined the Navy and in 1779 George III took the unprecedented step of sending his second son, Prince William Henry (later William IV) to sea.

Most of those commemorated on pots achieved notable maritime victories. Many of the most celebrated sea officers[1] joined up while they were still children. Duncan was fourteen, Jervis and Sidney Smith thirteen, Boscawen and Nelson twelve and Keppel was only ten years old. However well connected they were, they enjoyed no special privileges but gained the necessary experience, (including two years as a midshipman), to pass the lieutenant's examination by the age of 20. They were then in an ideal position to benefit from rapid promotion at the outbreak of major hostilities such as war with Spain during the 1740s, the Seven Years War with France (1756-63) the American War of Independence (1776-83) war with Revolutionary France (1793-1802) and with France under Napoleon (1803-15).

Admiral Edward Vernon (1684-1757)

Already an experienced naval commander, Vernon became MP for Penryn in 1722. Combative in parliamentary debates, he urged the renewal of war against Spain. Irritated by his criticisms and hoping to humiliate him, the government sent Vernon to the Caribbean in July 1739 with a tiny squadron of ships. He picked up five more ships in Jamaica and stormed the Spanish stronghold of Puerto Bello (on the

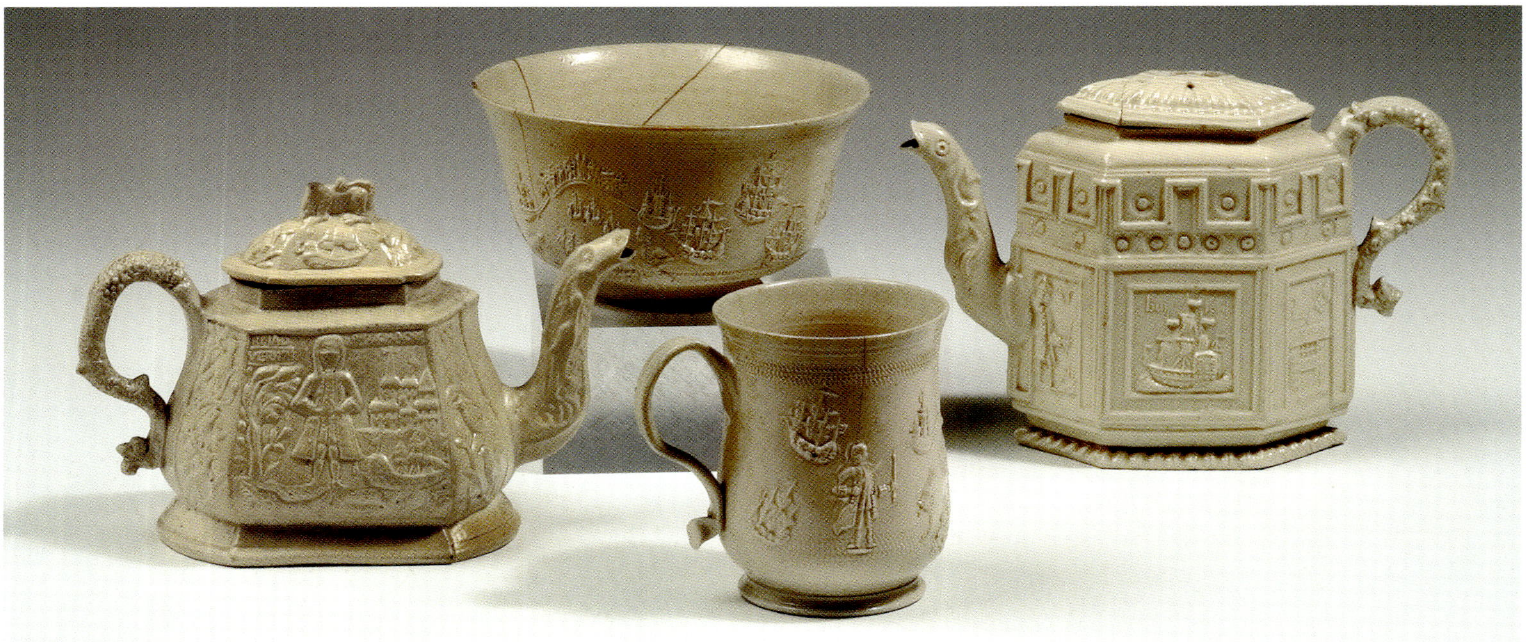

Teapot, (165), c.1740, Staffordshire, height: 12.7cm, (5in), white salt-glazed stoneware. Moulded with duck-bill spout and sea-snake handle and lid with a lion knop. Rounded body has low-relief panels showing a large figure standing before buildings entitled: 'BY/ AD/ VERNON / FORT / CHAGRE' and on the other side, a harbour and shipping, entitled: 'PORTO / BELLO / TAKEN'.

Mug and Slop bowl, (167 + 168), c.1740, Staffordshire, height: 9.6cm, (3¾in), height: 7.7cm, (3in), white salt-glazed stoneware. Both are relief-moulded with bird's-eye harbour views of Puerto Bello and Fort Chagre in Panama and feature a large figure of Vernon.[5] Moulded inscriptions read: 'THE BRITISH GLORY REVIV:D / BY ADMIRAL VERNON / HE TOOK PORTO-BELLO / WITH SIX SHIPS ONLY / NOV YE:22 1739'. The aerial view may derive from a print entitled *England's Glory*, published in 1739.[6] The figure of Vernon is taken from a commemorative bronze medal struck in 1739.[7]

Teapot, (166), c.1740, Staffordshire, height: 14cm, (5½in), white salt-glazed stoneware. Relief-moulded with duck-bill spout and sea-snake handle. The six flat sides are moulded with figures, a ship named *Burford* and a harbourscape, marked 'PB' (166).[8]

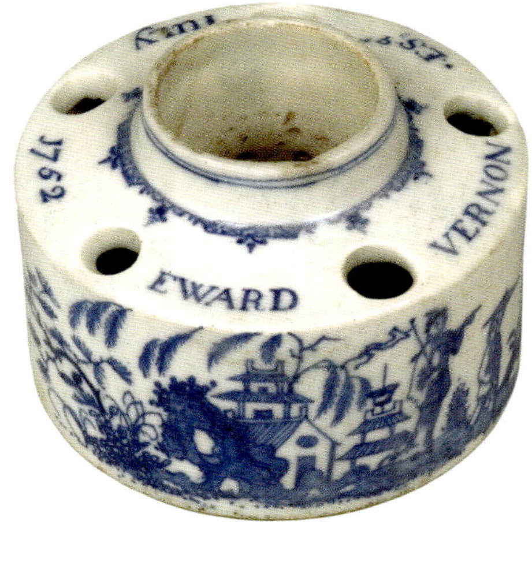

Inkpot, (169), 1752, London, Bow, height: 6.4cm, (2½in), soft-paste porcelain. Painted underglaze in blue with imaginary Chinese figures and buildings in landscapes. The Bow factory called itself 'New Canton', advertising its intention to replicate Chinese porcelain and reflecting the fashion for chinoiserie designs. Few inkpots survive; fewer are inscribed and dated as this one: 'Eward [*sic*] Vernon, Esqr., July, 1752'. This Edward Vernon was not the Admiral (as Willett believed) but a director of the Royal Exchange Insurance Company with whom Bow had a policy.[9] Vernon may have commissioned the inkpot, or it may have been presented to him.

north side of the Isthmus of Darien in Panama) He captured the Fort of San Lorenzo and the town of Chagre in 1740, with few losses.

In 1741 Vernon returned home a national hero, despite losing the battle for the Spanish port of Cartagena. He was made a Freeman of the City of London where taverns were renamed 'Vernon's Head' and more than 100 medals were struck in his honour. London stage productions of 1739-40 included songs such as, 'Singing by Beard in the Character of an English Man of War Upon the taking of Portobello' and 'A New Song by Parry in Praise of Admiral Vernon'.[2] Towns in Scotland and England and a farm in west London (it later gave its name to Portobello Road) were named after the victory. As a measure of the provincial response to his triumph, a Mr Ward of Squerries, in Kent, was said to have entertained 7,000 of his neighbours with strong beer to celebrate Vernon's (premature) claims of success at Cartagena in 1741.[3] Ceramic commemoratives of the early 1740s used a new clay body; white, salt-glazed stoneware.

Vernon was made full Admiral in 1745 but failed to become Commander-in-Chief. He was demoted in 1746 after publishing correspondence criticising the Admiralty. Despite noting that victory 'made him so popular that, … he was chosen into parliament for several places, had his head painted on every sign, and his birthday kept twice in one year', Horace Walpole dismissed him as 'a silly, noisy admiral'.[4] But Vernon also pioneered strategies for naval defence and marine economy, including diluting sailors' rum rations having noticed the pernicious effect of strong liquor on their behaviour in the tropics.

THE SEVEN YEARS WAR (1756-1763)

Admiral Edward Boscawen (1711-61)

The third son of the 1st Duke of Falmouth, Boscawen joined the navy at twelve. He shone at the battle of Porto Bello and was commended for bravery at the siege of Cartagena in 1741. As Rear Admiral, in India he helped take Madras from the French in 1748. In 1758 he captured the port of Cape Breton in Nova Scotia also from the French. Horace Walpole wrote of the event, 'Admiral Boscawen and General Amherst with a fleet of 150 sail and 14,000 men … by the end of July made themselves masters of [Louisbourg], after destroying or taking five men of war that lay to cover it'.[10] In 1759 Boscawen fought an action off Lagos in Portugal, which prevented the French squadron in Toulon from joining the Brest fleet. He was nicknamed 'Old Dreadnought' by his sailors whose conditions of service he did much to improve.

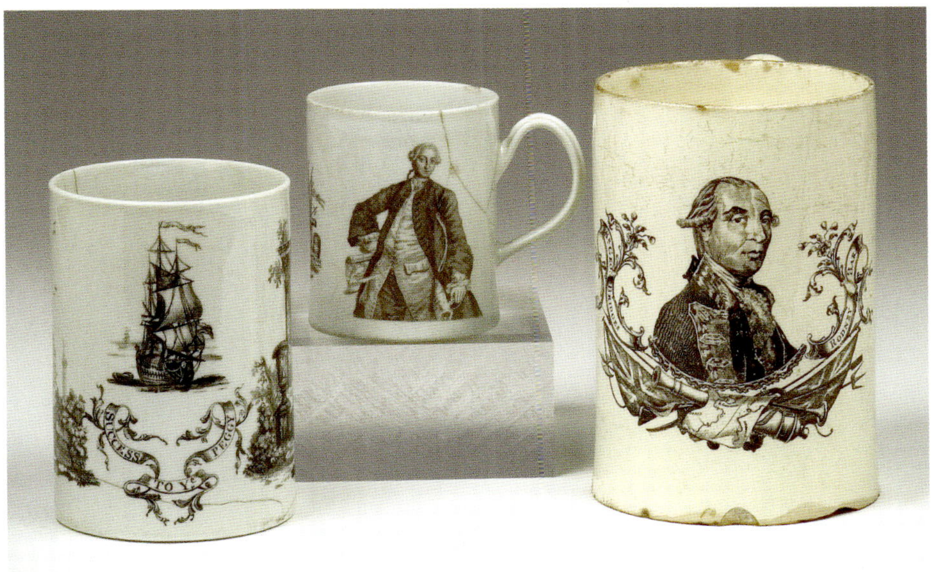

Mug, (325), c.1759, Worcester, height: 12.7cm, (5in), printed, soft-paste porcelain. Printed with a ship, inscribed on scrolls, 'SUCCESS / TO Ye / PEGGY', classical ruins and statues on the reverse. Probably designed by Robert Hancock. Unfortunately nothing is known of the *Peggy*.
Mug, (170), c.1759, Worcester, height: 8.9cm, (3½in), printed, soft-paste porcelain. Printed with a rare image of Boscawen with his coat of arms (Boscawen impaling Glanville) in the midst of trophies and two men of war. Although Boscawen's face resembles the portrait engraved by James Macadell in 1757, after Reynolds,[11] the pose is adapted from a mezzotint by John Faber the younger (published 1751),[12] after Allan Ramsay. The Admiral holds a partly rolled map, inscribed, 'LOUISBOURG'. On the reverse is a similar ship to that on (325).
Mug, (178), c.1781, Liverpool, height: 15.3cm, (6in), printed creamware. Printed by Guy Green with a portrait of Admiral Rodney, inscribed, 'Sr GEO BRIDGES [*sic*]/ RODNEY BART', commemorates the victory at Cape St Vincent in 1780. Union flags, swords and cannon are draped with a map of southern Spain, (referring to the relief of Gibraltar). The likeness is based on a popular engraving of 1778 by James Watson after Reynolds. A version was published by Fielding & Walker in the *Westminster Magazine* on 1 April 1780.

Admiral Augustus Keppel (1725-86)

Keppel, the second son of the Earl of Albemarle, went to sea aged ten and in 1740 sailed with Admiral Anson on his voyage around the world. He sat as MP for Windsor from 1761 to 1780. During the Seven Years War he served in France and in America, where he helped capture Havana in 1762. His 'share of the spoils' exceeded £25,000. He refused to serve against America during the War of Independence but was made Commander-in-Chief of the Channel Fleet.

Following a naval engagement off Ushant in July 1778, fellow Admiral Sir Hugh Palliser accused him of misconduct, leading to the court martial of both men which attracted national interest. News of Keppel's acquittal reached Newcastle upon Tyne on 15 February 1779, prompting 'a grand illumination in that town and Gateshead, which was kept up until two or three o'clock the next morning, during which time the bells were kept ringing, accompanied with frequent firing of guns.'[13] Keppel went on to serve as First Lord of the Admiralty from 1782 to 1783.

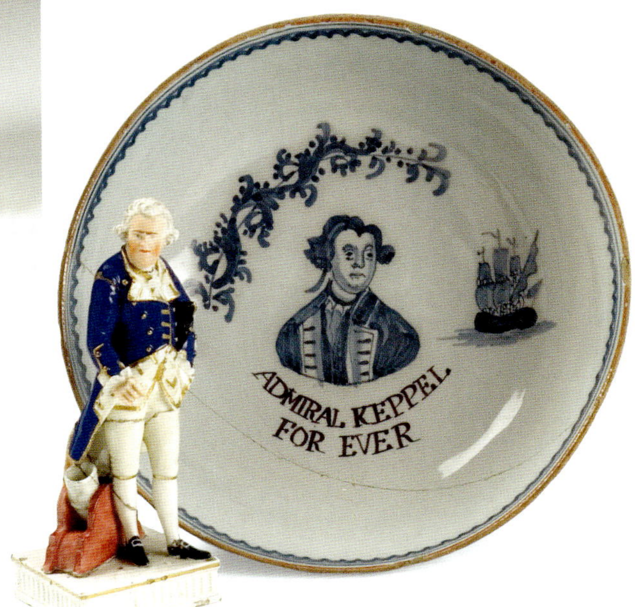

Figure, (171), c.1780, Derby, height: 21.6cm, (8½in), soft-paste porcelain, enamelled and gilt. Admiral Keppel stands with a cannon and shield at his feet. It is based on prints after Joshua Reynolds, who was a close friend.
Punchbowl, (172), c.1780, probably Bristol, diameter: 30.5cm, (12in), tin-glazed earthenware. Painted underglaze with a sketchy portrait inscribed, 'ADMIRAL KEPPEL / FOR EVER'. This is also from a print after Reynolds, probably by Cook, published 1 February 1779.[14]

Admiral George Brydges Rodney (1718-1792)

Rodney attended Harrow School before joining the Navy in 1732. During the Seven Years War he served with Boscawen at the taking of Louisburg in 1758 and was made Rear Admiral after blockading Le Havre the following year. In 1761 he was in Jamaica, as governor of the Leeward Islands, and in 1762 took the sugar islands of St Lucia, Grenada, Martinique and St Vincent from the French. Created Baron Rodney in 1764, he served at home from 1765 to 1770 as governor of Greenwich Hospital. In 1775 ruinous election expenses caused him to flee to Paris to escape his creditors.

On being recalled he returned to the Caribbean via the besieged British garrison of Gibraltar. In January 1780, having captured a Spanish convoy off Cape Finisterre he defeated Admiral de Langara off Cape St Vincent, allowing supplies to reach General Eliott, besieged in Gibraltar. Rodney's greatest triumph was the Battle of the Saintes off Dominica on 12 April 1782 when, together with Admiral Hood, he defeated the Comte de Grasse. Rodney boasted, 'Within two little years I have taken two Spanish, one French and one Dutch admiral'. He returned home in glory, was created Baron Rodney of Rodney Stoke (the family home) and retired with a pension of £2000 a year. Though a very able officer, Rodney was vain, cold and unscrupulous and was feared by his men.

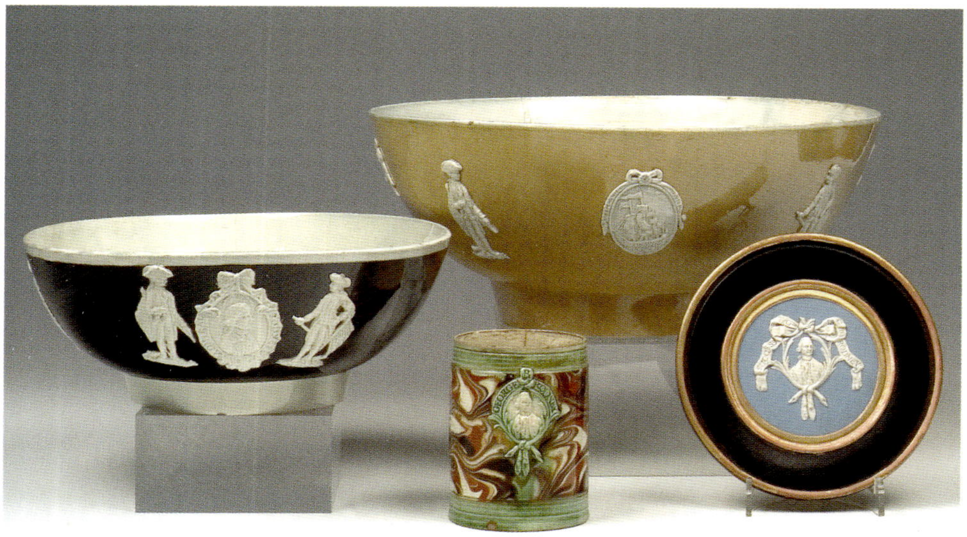

Clockwise:
Punchbowl, (180), c.1780, Staffordshire, diameter: 22.2cm, (8¾in), pearlware, slip-decorated in black. Applied with moulded white sprigs: medallion portrait inscribed, 'ADMIRAL RODNEY', flanked by sailors with flags, one of them impressed, 'LORD HOOD'.
Punchbowl, (181), c.1780, Staffordshire, diameter: 29.2cm, (11½in), pearlware, slip-decorated in buff. Applied with moulded white sprigs: medallion portrait, inscribed, 'SUCCESS TO GEL. ELLIOTT [*sic*]', and a ship inscribed, 'VILLA [*sic*] DE PARIS', flanked by soldiers with flags impressed, 'LORD HOOD' and 'LORD RODNEY'. This recalls when British ships broke through French lines to capture the Ville de Paris which surrendered to Admiral Hood on the Barfleur.
Plaque, (173), c.1780, Staffordshire, Enoch Wood, diameter: 10.2cm, (4in), blue jasperware. Moulded with white sprigged portrait of Rodney, framed with palm leaves and a ribbon and inscribed, 'SUCCESS / TO / G.B / RODNEY'
Mug, (174), c.1780, Staffordshire, height: 8.9cm, (3½in), slip-decorated creamware. Moulded sprigged portrait titled similarly to (173), set into a broad band of agate slip.

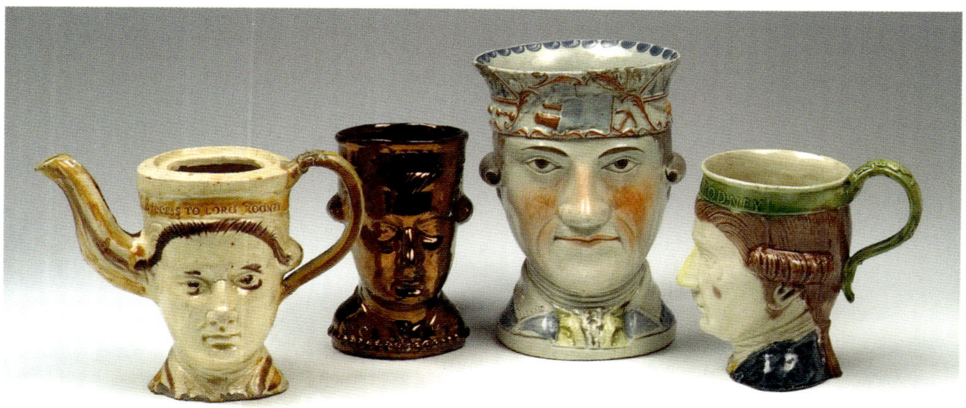

Curiously for such a severe man, mugs and teapots were comically modelled as Rodney's bewigged head.
Teapot, (176), c.1780, Staffordshire, height: 11.4cm, (4½in), Pratt-coloured creamware. Rodney's head, bizarrely applied with a spout and handle in place of ears. Impressed around the rim, 'SUCCESS TO LORD RODNEY'.
Mug, (177), c.1780, Staffordshire, height: 11.4cm, (4½in), earthenware, copper-lustred. Rodney's head, faintly moulded, 'LD RODNEY'.
Mug, (179), c.1780, Staffordshire, height: 15.3cm, (6in), enamelled pearlware. Rodney's head, its broad rim moulded with naval emblems. It deploys his plaited pigtail as a handle.
Cup, (175), c.1780, Staffordshire, height: 10.8cm, (4¼in), pearlware, oxide-coloured. Rodney's head, inscribed around the rim, 'SUCCESS TO LORD RODNEY'.

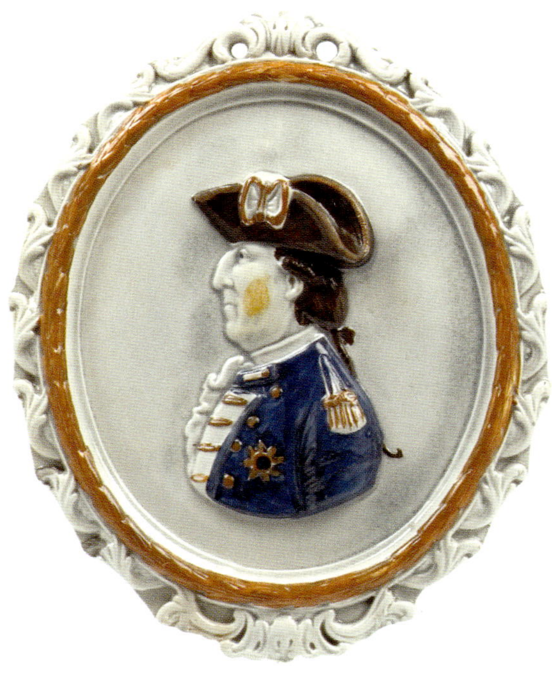

Plaque, (185), c.1786, possibly Scotland, height: 22.2cm, (8¾in), Prattware. Not Admiral Lord Howe as Willett believed, it is relief-moulded with Eliott's distinctive profile. Incised on reverse: 'John Monford'. The image is taken from a drawing of Eliott by Lieut. G.F. Koehler, issued as an engraving by Fores in 1786 (also used for a Wedgwood medallion).[16]

General George Augustus Eliott (1717-1790)

Eliott was born near Stobs Castle, in Roxburghshire on the Scottish Borders. A distinguished career soldier, he is best known for his defence of Gibraltar, besieged by the Spanish from 1779 to 1783, for which he was dubbed the 'Cock of the Rock'. 'The siege of Gibraltar' was a popular song performed on the London stage from 1789 to 1790.[15] He was made Knight of the Bath and in 1787, was created General Eliott of Stobs, 1st Baron Heathfield of Gibraltar.

Jug, (182A), c.1795, probably Staffordshire, height: 18.4cm, (7¼in), printed creamware Beneath a portrait medallion, inscription, 'LONG LIVE EARL HOWE / Commander in Chief of / THE VICTORIOUS BRITISH FLEET /... the glorious first of June / 1794.
Jug, (183a), c.1795, probably Staffordshire, height: 17.8cm, (7in), printed creamware. Half-length figure inscribed, 'EARL HOWE / Commander in chief of His Majesty's fleet in the Channel'. Howe gestures towards his flagship, the *Royal Charlotte*. Taken from a print by Charles Corbutt, first published in 1777 and reissued in 1794.[17]

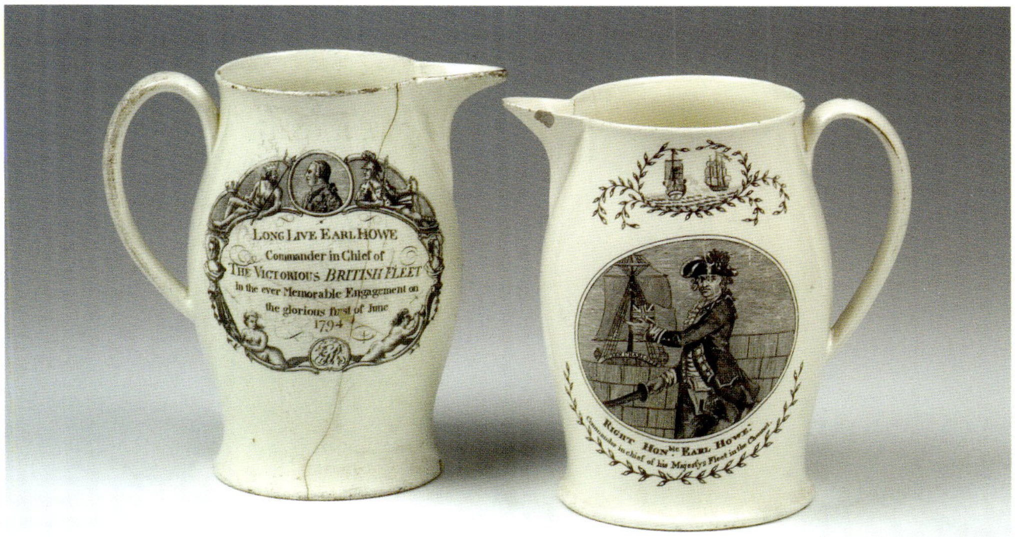

Jug, (182b), c.1795, probably Staffordshire, height: 18.4cm, (7¼in), printed creamware. The Admiral, looking old and careworn, (source unidentified), stands on deck holding a telescope.
Jug, (183b), c.1795, probably Staffordshire, height: 17.8cm, (7in), printed creamware. A naval battle inscribed, 'a Representation of the Glorious Defeat of the French Fleet / of Brest by EARL HOWE June 1st 1794'.

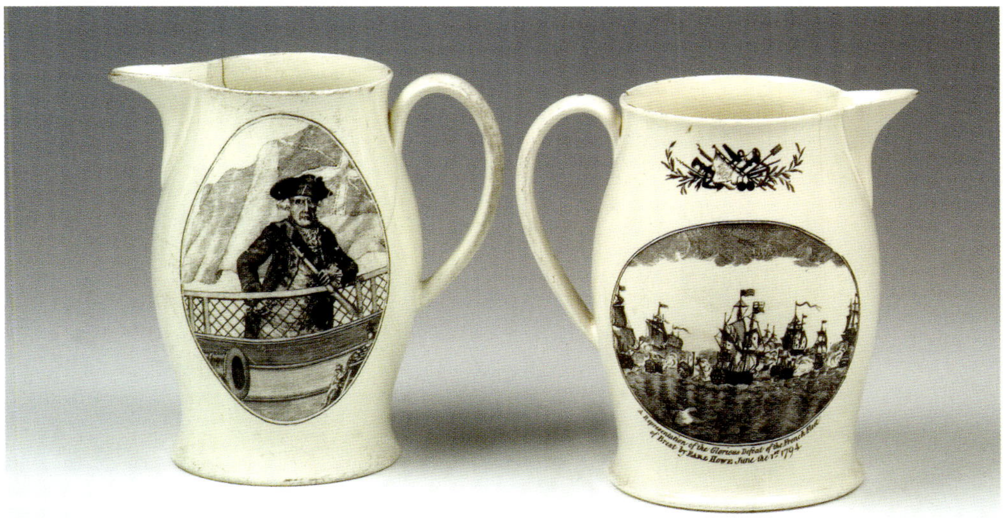

Figure, (184), c.1785, probably Staffordshire, height: 28.6cm, (11¼in), soft-paste porcelain. Painted matt black and gilt, Howe stands on a rock with a flag; incised beneath the base, 'Howe'. Its source is unidentified although it has a passing resemblance to an undated mezzotint portrait by Benjamin Killingbeck.[18] It may celebrate Howe's achievement at Gibraltar.

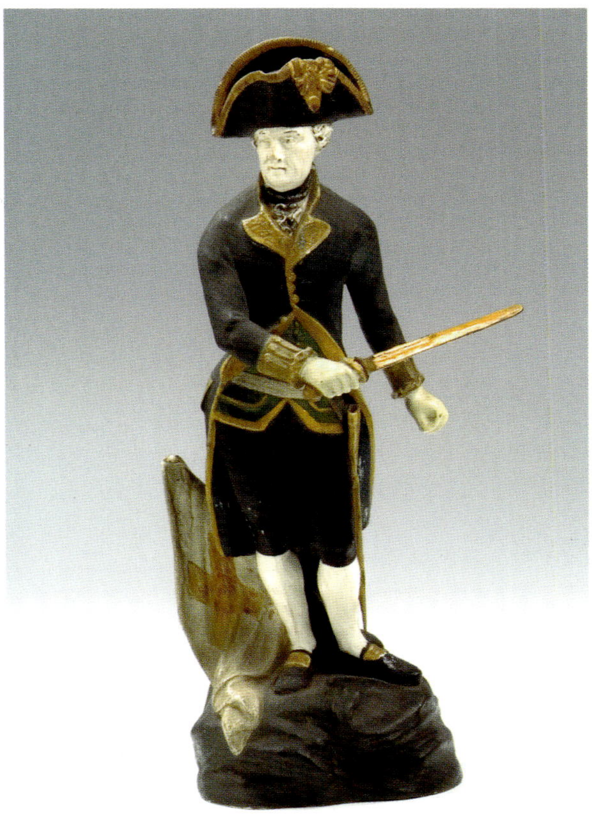

Admiral Richard Howe, 1st Earl Howe (1726-1799)

Howe was the second son of the 2nd Viscount Howe in the Irish peerage. Richard became 3rd Viscount after the death, in America, of his elder brother George. Both his brothers became generals and Richard's long naval career began in the West Indies in the 1740s. He was MP for Dartmouth from 1762, a member of the Admiralty Board from 1765 and Treasurer of the Navy from 1770. As Vice Admiral, he commanded the North American station in 1776, despite sympathising with the colonists. With his brother, General William Howe, he captured the city of Philadelphia. Both brothers are shown slumped at a table in Philadelphia in the background of a satirical print on a small creamware jug (436).[19]

In 1782 Admiral Howe assumed command of the Channel Fleet and effected the relief of Gibraltar, which had been blockaded for several years. He served as First Lord of the Admiralty from 1783 to 1788 but his finest hour came in 1794 when he was nearly 70. On 'the Glorious First of June', in charge of the Channel Fleet, he vanquished the French off Brest, in the Third Battle of Ushant. There was national rejoicing. In London, Richard Sheridan turned the stage of Drury Lane Theatre into a sea to re-enact the events of *The Glorious First of June*, while in Bury St Edmunds merchant James Oakes noted on 18 June, 'This evening very unexpectedly, the town was illuminated on acct of the Victory gaind over the French fleet on 1st June ... Ringing of Bells – firing of Guns &ca.'.[20] Nicknamed 'Black Dick', on account of his swarthy complexion, Howe was very popular with his men. In 1797 he was brought out of retirement to resolve the naval mutiny at Spithead.

Admiral Adam Duncan (1731-1804)

Duncan, born in Dundee, joined the navy as captain's servant to his kinsman Robert Haldane of Gleneagles. Having served with Keppel at Belle Isle and Havana during the Seven Years War, he reluctantly attended Keppel's court martial in 1779. He was with Rodney and later with Howe at the relief of Gibraltar in 1782. As Vice Admiral in 1795, he was given command of the British forces in the North Sea and instructed to contain the Dutch fleet (then allied to France) in the River Texel.

In 1797, following naval mutinies at Spithead, Duncan managed to quell the rebellion that had broken out on his flagship, *Venerable*. He led the fleet to the Texel and maintained an effective blockade until forced to resupply at Yarmouth. His fellow officer Captain Henry Trollope (1756-1839) sighted the Dutch fleet at sea and Duncan sped to accost them at Camperdown, off the Dutch coast. On 11 October he won a 'Glorious Victory', securing the surrender of three admirals, nine ships of the line and two frigates.[21] In December 1797 the government organised a solemn thanksgiving service at St Paul's Cathedral, attended by George III, to celebrate the combined naval victories at Camperdown, Cape St Vincent and the 'Glorious First of June'. Duncan, feted as a national hero in London, Edinburgh and Dundee, became the focus of a thriving souvenir industry.

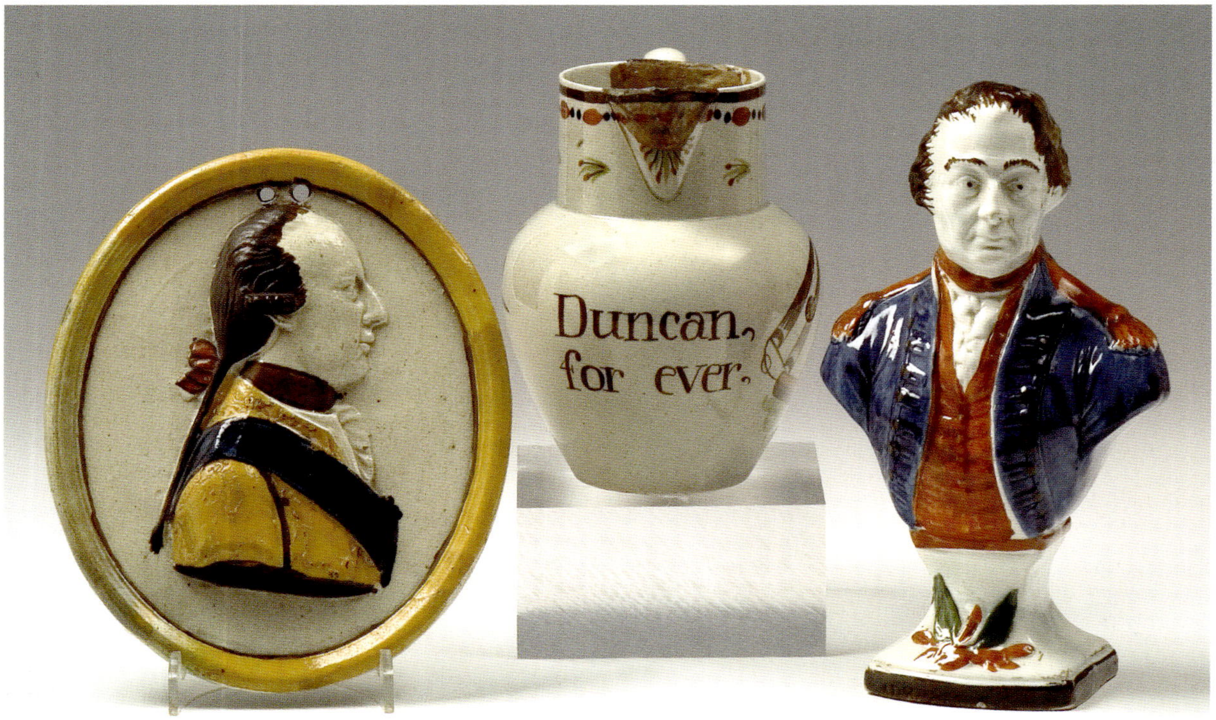

Plaque, (186), c.1798, Staffordshire or Scotland, height: 17.8cm, (7in), Prattware. Relief-moulded profile portrait, thought by Willett to be Duncan, actually represents Emperor Joseph II.
Jug, (191), c.1798, Staffordshire or Scotland, height: 13.3cm, (5¼in), pearlware. Painted in Pratt colours with a ship and anchor, and inscribed in brown, 'Duncan, for ever'.
Bust, (188), c.1798, Staffordshire or Scotland, height: 19.7cm, (7¾in), pearlware, painted in Pratt colours. Moulded on base, 'ADMIRAL DUNCAN', it was cast from one by Worthington, Humble & Holland at the Herculaneum Pottery, Liverpool.[22]

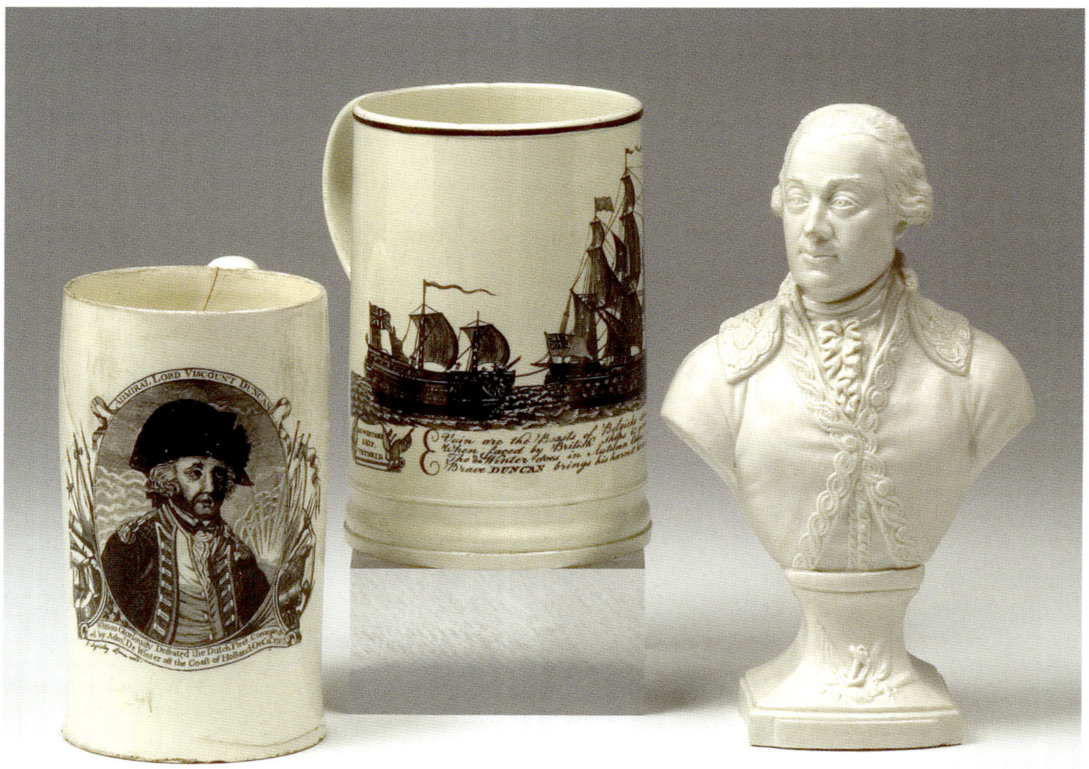

Mug, (192), c.1798, Staffordshire Lane End, height: 15.3cm, (6in), printed creamware. Portrait, signed by John Aynsley, of 'ADMIRAL LORD VISCOUNT DUNCAN', inscribed 'who so Gloriously Defeated the Dutch Fleet' .[23] The image and inscription are taken from print issued by Laurie & Whittle in November 1797.[24]
Mug, (187), c.1798, Sunderland, made by Dawson's Pottery at Low Ford, height: 15.3cm, (6in), printed creamware. Sea battle inscribed, 'Tho' de Winter does in Autumn come / Brave DUNCAN brings his harvest home' and two ships, 'DUNCAN'S SHIP VENERABLE' towing 'DE WINTER'S SHIP VRYHEID'.
Bust, (190), c.1798, Liverpool, Herculaneum, height: 21.6cm, (8½in), semi-porcelain. Represents Duncan's adversary, Admiral De Winter (1761-1812), whose name is incised inside the base. Duncan captured the Dutch commander at Camperdown.

Admiral Sir John Jervis, Earl St Vincent (1735-1823)

The son of a solicitor from Meaford, Staffordshire, Jervis assisted at the conquest of Quebec in 1759, served during the American War of Independence and fought in the Battle of Ushant in 1778. In 1782 he was made a Knight of the Bath after capturing a French ship and entered Parliament as a Whig. From 1796, one of his main duties as British Commander-in-chief in the Mediterranean was to monitor the Spanish fleet. In January 1797 the Spaniards set out to join the French fleet off Brest to invade Britain but were blown out into the Atlantic. They were returning to Cadiz when Jervis intercepted them off Cape St Vincent on the southern coast of Portugal. With a far smaller squadron of fifteen ships he split them into two groups and defeated them, ably assisted by Commodore Nelson. Jervis was created Baron Jervis, Earl St Vincent.

Jug, (193), c.1798, Staffordshire or Scotland, height: 19.7cm, (7¾in), Prattware. Relief-moulded with profile portrait impressed, 'Captain Trollope' on sash (Admiral Duncan on reverse).
Jug, (195), c.1798, Staffordshire or Scotland, height: 12.7cm, (5in), Prattware. Relief-moulded on both sides with figure holding a banner impressed, 'LORD JARVIS [*sic*]', flanked by ships.
Jug, (194), c.1798, Staffordshire or Scotland, height: 13.3cm, (5¼in), Prattware. Relief-moulded with profile portrait impressed, 'Admiral Duncan' on sash (two classical female figures on the reverse).

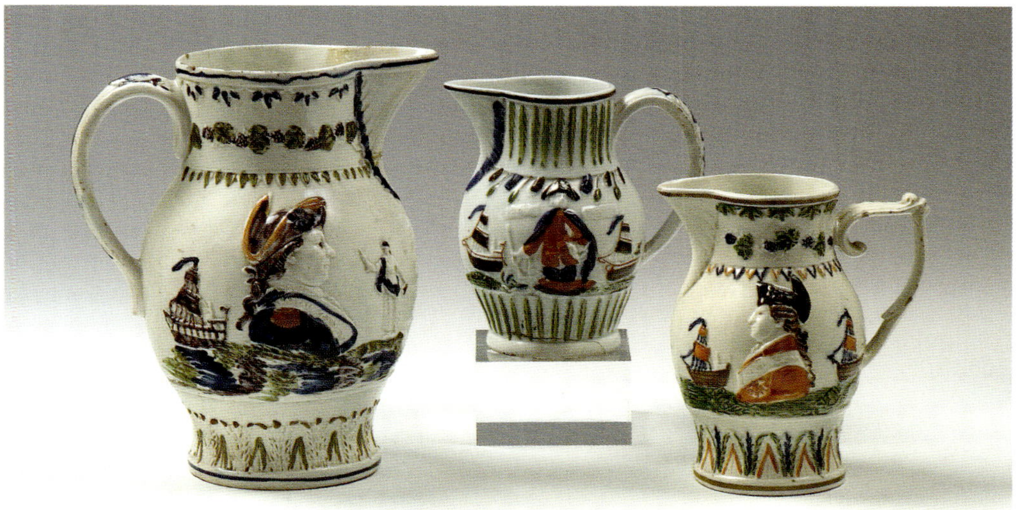

Admiral Sir William Sidney Smith (1764-1840)

Smith was born in Westminster into a military family. He served with distinction under Rodney at Cape St Vincent and at the battle of the Saintes. He later became involved in intelligence and travelled throughout Europe. In 1793 he attempted to set fire to the French fleet at Toulon. The French eventually captured him in 1796 and held him for two years at the Temple Prison in Paris. Royalist agents helped him to escape to England.

In 1799 Smith embarked on the captured French ship, *Tigre*, for Istanbul, where his brother was a minister pleni potentiary. Thence he sailed to Palestine to assist the Turkish commander, Jezzar Pasha, to reinforce the defences of Acre before Napoleon arrived from Egypt. Smith managed to capture the French seaborne siege artillery, and by bombarding French troops from the sea, prevented them from using the coastal road from Jaffa. Thanks to Smith, Acre managed to repel French assaults for two months and Napoleon withdrew to Egypt. On his return to England Smith received a pension of £1,000. Following the Congress of Vienna in 1815 he embraced the cause of anti-slavery but amassed considerable debts and emigrated to France where he died in 1840. He is buried in Père Lachaise cemetery in Paris.

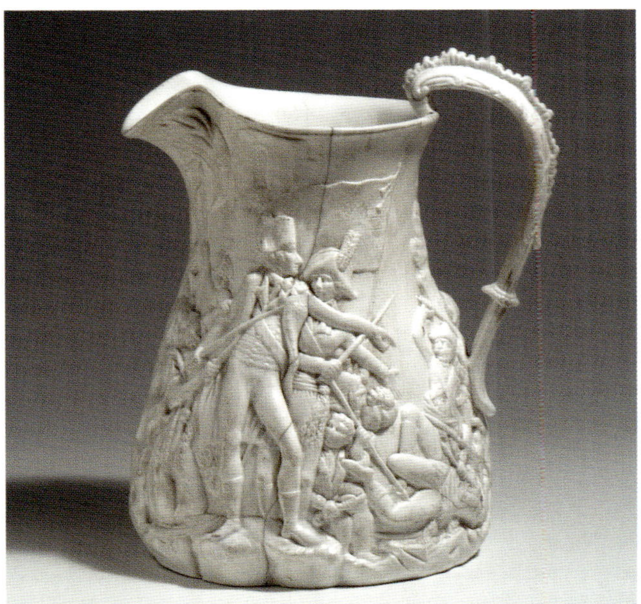

Jug, (196), c.1820, Staffordshire, height: 25.4cm, (10in), drab stoneware. Relief-moulded with Jezzar Pasha and Sir Sidney Smith defending the fortress of 'St. Jean D'Acre'. The image was adapted from a print by A. Smith, published by Evans, 12 March 1815, after a drawing by Laffert or from later copies.[25]

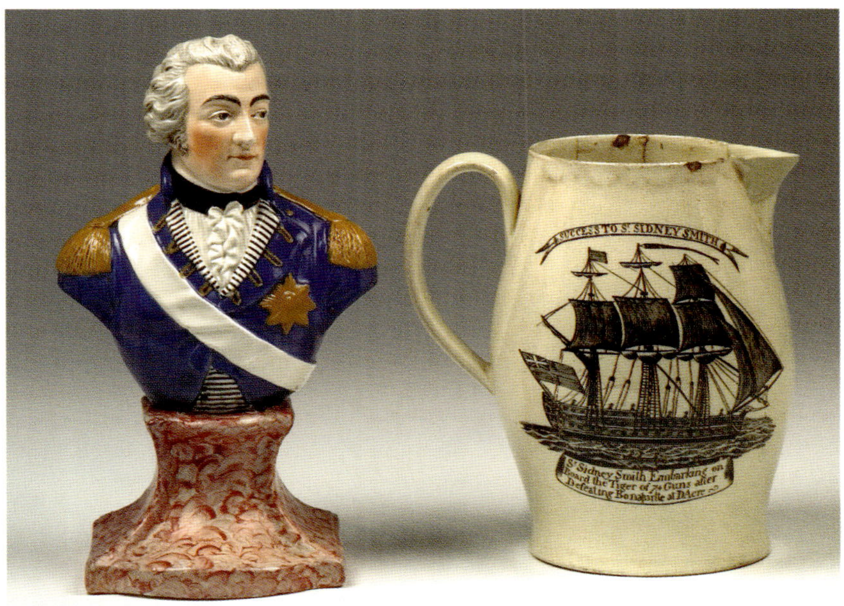

Bust, (198), c.1800, Staffordshire, height: 24.1cm, (9½in), enamelled pearlware. Portrait of Sir Sidney Smith.
Jug, (197), c.1798, Staffordshire, height: 17.8cm, (7in), printed creamware. Printed with a ship inscribed above, 'SUCCESS TO Sr. SIDNEY SMITH' and below, 'Embarking on / Board the Tiger [*sic*] of 74 Guns after / Defeating Bonaparte at DAcre'.

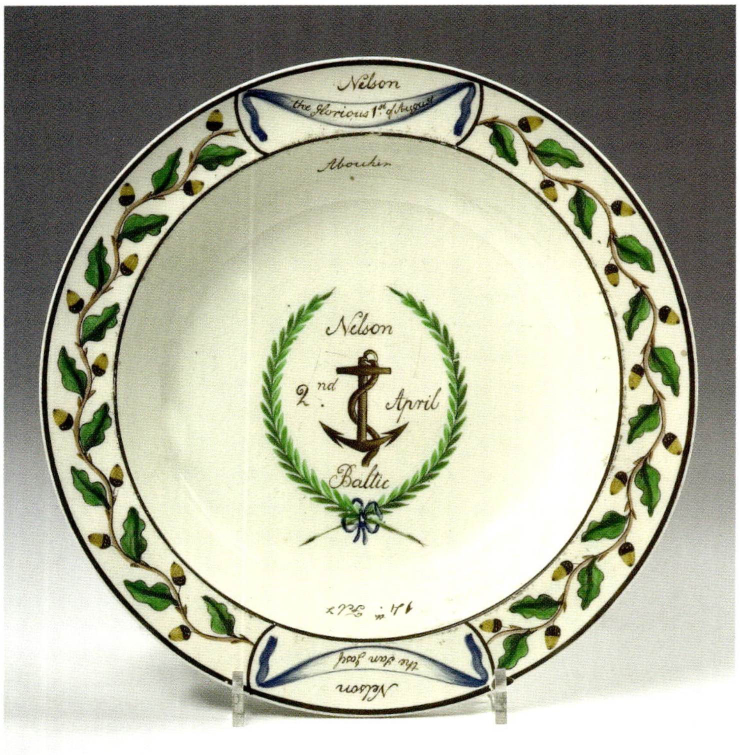

Soup plate, (201), c.1802, Staffordshire, David Wilson, diameter: 24.1cm, (9½in), enamelled creamware. Painted with Nelson's successes up to 1801.[26] In the centre, a wreath enclosing an anchor is inscribed, 'Nelson / 2nd April / Baltic'. In reserves within an oak leaf and acorn border, inscribed, 'Nelson / the Glorious 1st August / Aboukir / and Nelson / the San Josef / 14 Feby' (at Cape St Vincent).

Admiral Horatio Nelson (1758-1805)

Nelson was the sixth of the eleven children born to the rector of Burnham Thorpe in Norfolk. He joined HMS *Raisonnable* under his uncle, Captain Maurice Suckling, served on an Arctic expedition, in the East Indies, then in Jamaica during the American War of Independence. On Nevis in the West Indies he married the young widow, Frances Nisbet and returned to Norfolk to live on half pay for five years. At the outbreak of war with France in 1793, Nelson commanded the *Agamemnon* under Lord Hood and helped seize Corsica from the French, losing an eye during the siege of Calvi. He never wore an eye patch. As Commodore he captured two Spanish ships at the Battle of Cape St Vincent, was made Rear Admiral of the Blue and awarded the Order of the Bath. During an abortive raid on Tenerife his right arm was so badly damaged that it had to be amputated and he was invalided home.

He rejoined Admiral Jervis in April 1798, narrowly missing Napoleon's fleet as it left Toulon for Egypt. He caught up with the French after they had already taken Alexandria. On 1 August he confronted Admiral Brueys at anchor in Aboukir Bay, off the Rosetta mouth of the Nile and annihilated all but two ships. Admiral Brueys was killed at Aboukir and Nelson suffered a head wound. He recuperated in Naples as the guest of the British envoy, Sir William Hamilton and his wife Emma. He was showered with honours, made Baron of the Nile and Burnham Thorpe and ordered home. Instead, encouraged by Emma Hamilton, he stayed to meddle, unsuccessfully, in Neapolitan politics but was created Duke of Bronte by the King and Queen of Naples. Having accompanied the royal family as they fled to Vienna, he and the Hamiltons embarked on a triumphal return to England via Prague, Dresden and Hamburg. He arrived home as one of the most popular national heroes of all time but was coolly received at court for dallying on the journey.

On 17 January 1801, he was made Vice Admiral of the Blue and accompanied Admiral Sir Hyde Parker to the Baltic to suppress a hostile coalition of northern powers under Tsar Paul of Russia. Despite Parker's signal to desist, Nelson attacked and defeated the Danish navy at Copenhagen on 2 April. He was made Commander and created Viscount. In May 1803, with *Victory* as his flagship, he was given command of the Mediterranean fleet in order to monitor the French fleet at Toulon. The French proved elusive until Nelson managed to confine them together with the Spanish squadron at Cadiz. The blockade was enforced by his close colleague, Admiral Cuthbert Collingwood (1748-1810). Their careers had been linked from the West Indies in 1777 to the 'Glorious First of June', 1794, and Cape St Vincent.

In September 1805, Nelson joined Collingwood to set up a relay system of signals to ensure a close watch on movements in Cadiz

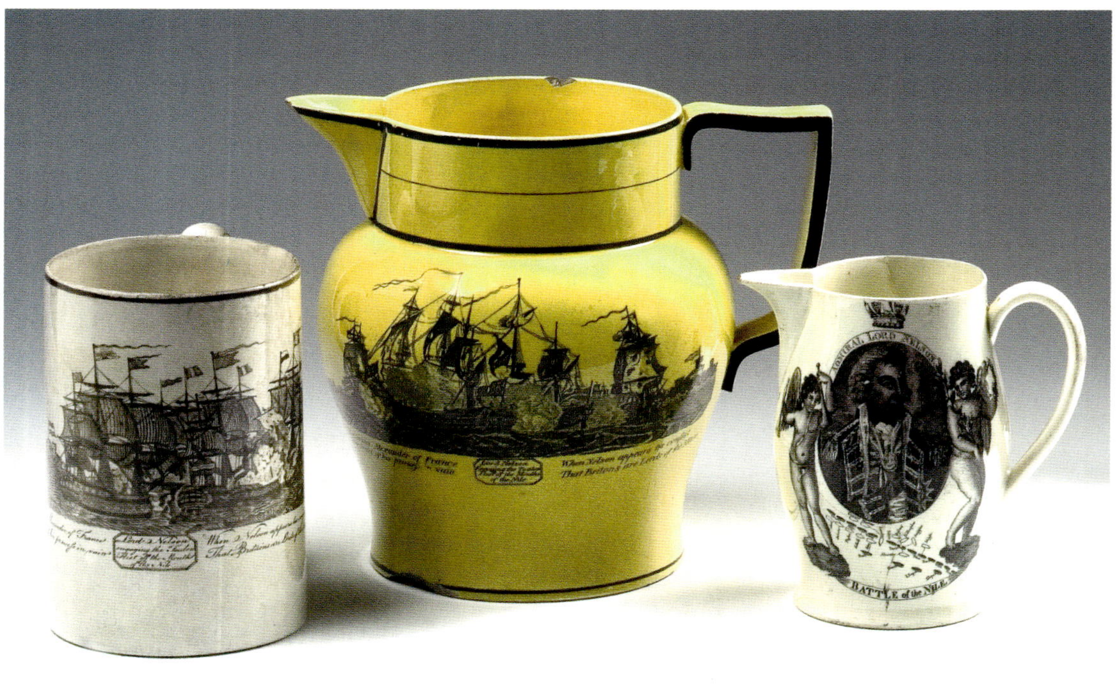

Mug, (202), c.1800, Sunderland, Dawson & Co., Low Ford, height: 15.3cm, (6in), printed creamware. Shipping, inscribed, 'Lord Nelson/ Engaging the Toulon / Fleet off the Mouth / of the Nile', and a verse, 'The Young Alexander of France / May boast of his prowefs in vain / When Nelson appears tis confest / That Britons are Lords of the Main'.
Jug, (204), c.1800, probably Dawson & Co., Low Ford, Sunderland, height: 20.3cm, (8in), printed, yellow-glazed earthenware. Sea battle inscribed, 'Lord Nelson / Engaging the Toulon fleet' and verse, 'The young Alexander of France / and 'A South East / VIEW / of the stupendous iron Bridge / over the Wear'.[27]
Jug (205), c.1800, Staffordshire, height: 14cm, (5½in), printed creamware. Portrait of Nelson flanked by two angels, above a battle plan inscribed, 'BATTLE of the NILE', with Nelson's Arms, supporters and motto, 'PALMAM / QUI MERUIT / FERAT', on the reverse.

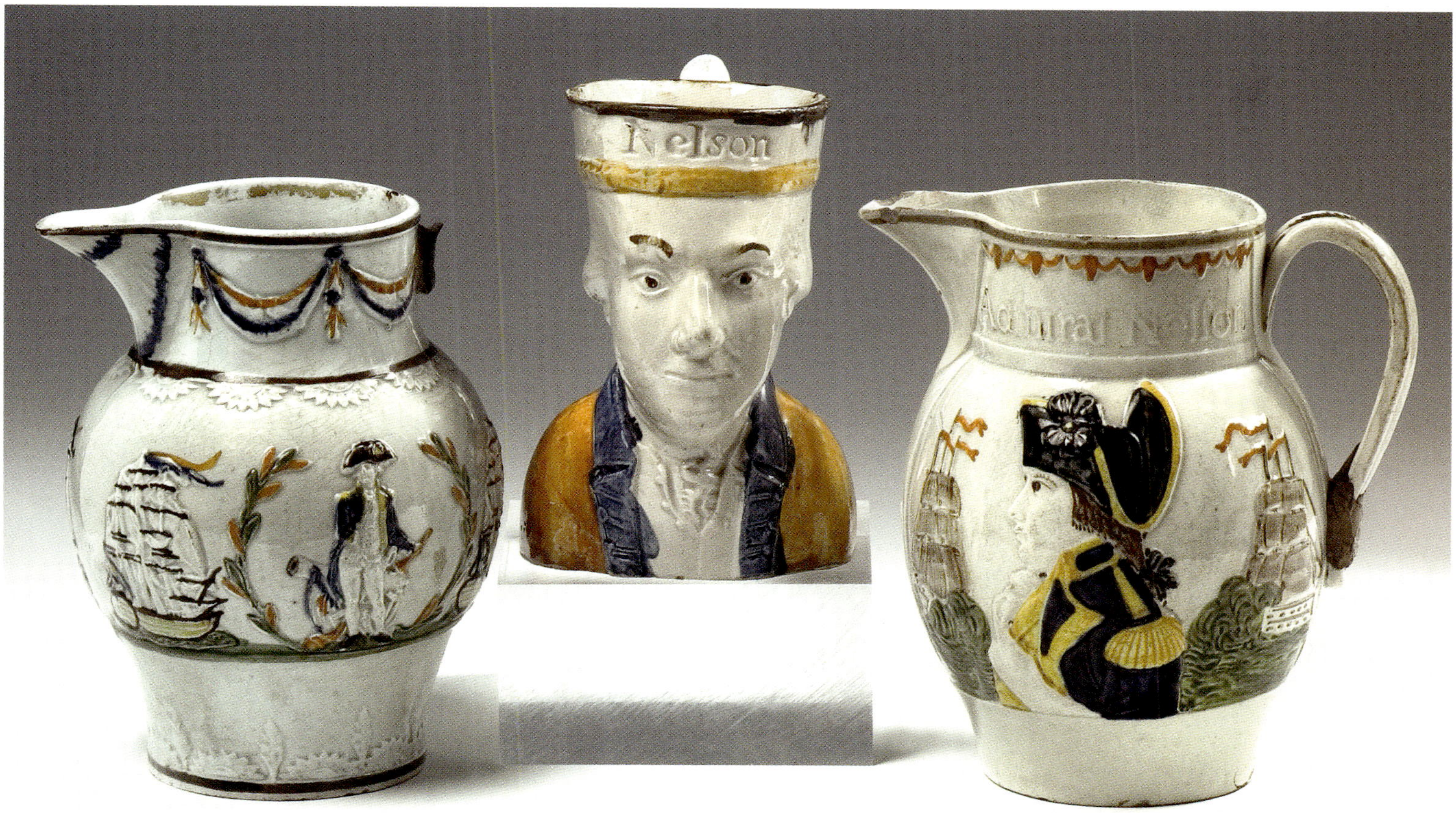

Jug, (203), c.1800, Staffordshire, height: 15.3cm (6in), Prattware. Jug (missing handle) moulded in relief with figures of Nelson (lacking a right arm) and ships.
Mug, (208), c.1800, Staffordshire, height: 12.7cm (5in), Prattware. Cast as a head and shoulders, impressed around the rim, 'Nelson'.
Jug, (207), c.1800, Staffordshire, height: 15.3cm (6in), Prattware. Relief-moulded with profile portraits of Nelson (Captain Berry on reverse).

harbour, so that Nelson was prepared and waiting when Admiral de Villeneuve set out. At 11.45 a.m. on 21 October, the most famous signal in British naval history, 'England expects that every man will do his duty', was hoisted up *Victory*'s mast. Nelson's pre-battle briefings were so thorough that Collingwood's first reaction on seeing the flags was to remark crossly that he wished Nelson would stop signalling since they all knew what they had to do.[28] Nelson directed 27 British ships in a two-columned attack on the line of enemy ships off Cape Trafalgar and defeated or captured 33 French and Spanish vessels. Nelson, like General Wolfe, fell at the moment of triumph, to a sniper's bullet fired from the French ship, *Redoubtable*. After Captain Thomas Masterman Hardy (1769-1839) managed to signal to Collingwood that Nelson was dying. Collingwood assumed command.

Trafalgar was the decisive naval engagement of the Napoleonic Wars, giving Britain control of the seas and removing all possibility of a French invasion and conquest. Under a lesser commander the risks taken could have proved disastrous. Nelson was a brilliant tactician and an enlightened leader who could delegate to gifted subordinates. He inspired the devotion of his men and the adulation of the public. A vain man who craved attention, he sat frequently for portraits. The ubiquity of his image and his four great victories ensured his immortality and account for the great number and variety of surviving souvenir items. His body (preserved in a cask of brandy) was brought home and lay in state at Greenwich. It was paraded through grieving crowds to St Paul's Cathedral (his own choice) where he was interred beneath the cupola on 8 January 1806. His tomb and his flagship *Victory*, installed in Portsmouth Harbour, continue to attract pilgrims.

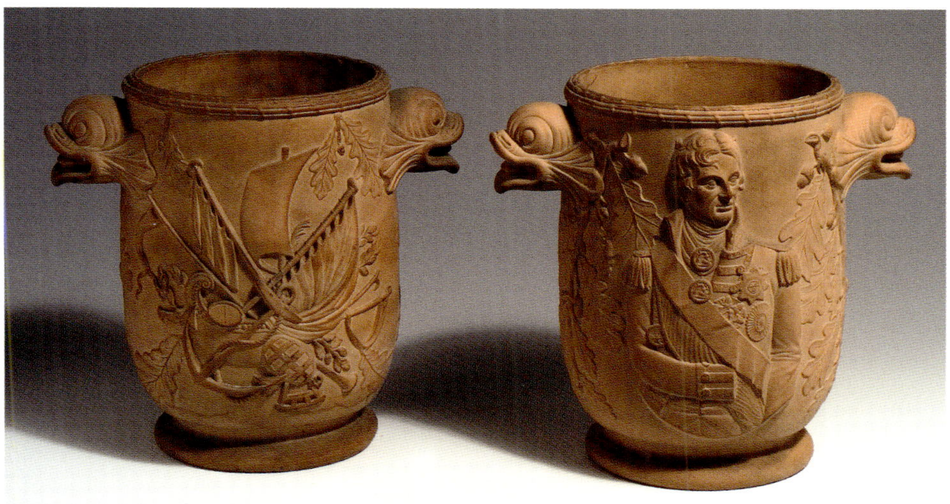

Pair of Wine Coolers, (209), c.1812, Staffordshire, Davenport of Longport, each height: 25.4cm, (10in), terracotta. Cast with dolphin-mask handles and each relief-moulded with a half-length figure of Nelson, (an arm missing) naval trophies, oak leaves and acorns. The motifs are inspired by the Egyptian campaign of 1798-9 but are difficult to date. Perhaps the Royal Order in the Davenport archive, dated 1807, for '24 Egyptian porouse Wine Coolers, Emboss'd. &c. 10/6 £12.12.0', refers to these items.[29] The portrait of Nelson, however, is said to be taken from the statue by John Flaxman in St Paul's Cathedral, not completed until 1812.

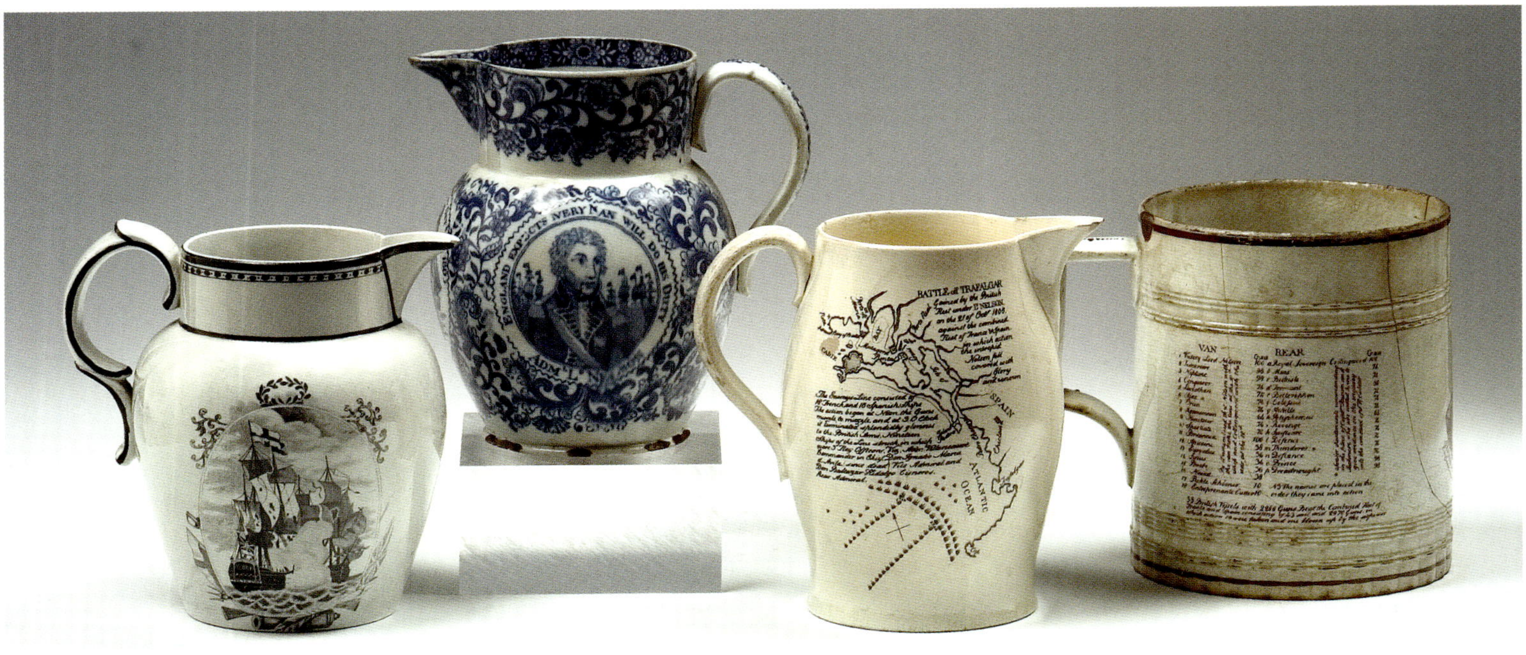

Jug, (213), c.1805, Staffordshire, height: 14cm, (5½in), pearlware, printed and enamelled. Two battleships, one marked 'VICTORY'.
Jug, (223), c.1805, Staffordshire, height: 15.3cm, (6in), blue-printed pearlware. Portrait of Nelson within dense foliage.
Jug, (210), c.1805, Staffordshire, height: 14cm, (5½in), printed creamware. Map of Southern Spain and explanation of the 'BATTLE off TRAFALGAR'.

Jug, (225), c.1805, Staffordshire, height: 14cm, (5½in), sepia-printed pearlware.
List of British vessels involved at Trafalgar and their tally of guns. Also a portrait of Nelson and a British ship with trophies and a medallion portrait of George III with a banner inscribed, 'LONG / LIVE / THE / KING' and 'SUCCESS TO COMMERCE'.

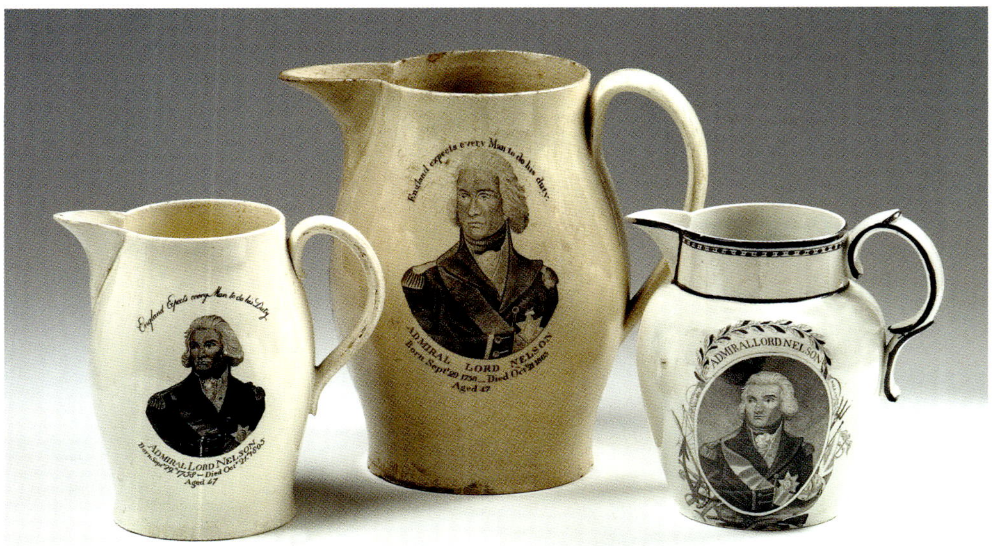

Jug, (210), c.1805, Staffordshire, height: 14cm, (5½in), printed creamware. Inscribed, 'England Expects every Man to do his Duty', above portrait and Nelson's birth and death dates.
Jug, (224), c.1805, Staffordshire, height: 20.3cm, (8in), printed creamware. Inscribed, 'England Expects every Man to do his Duty', above portrait and Nelson's birth and death dates. Reverse printed with a diagram and explanation of the 'BATTLE off TRAFALGAR'.
Jug, (213), c.1805, Staffordshire, height: 14cm, (5½in), printed pearlware. Sea trophies frame portrait inscribed, 'Trafalgar 1805 / Nile 1798'. The source of the image of Nelson on all three jugs is one of many prints after the 1797 portrait by Lemuel Francis Abbott, probably that engraved by J. Chapman and published 1 December 1798, after the Battle of the Nile.[30]

Jug, (207), c.1805, Staffordshire, height: 15.3cm, (6in), Prattware. Captain Edward Berry (1768–1831).[31] Berry was flag captain of Nelson's ship *Vanguard* at the Battle of the Nile, prior to his knighthood in 1798. He also commanded the *Agamemnon* at the Battle of Trafalgar.
Mug, (222), c.1805, possibly North East., height: 11.5cm, (4½in), pearlware printed and enamelled. Portrait of Nelson and ships and 'ENGLAND EXPECTS'.
Jug, (223), c.1805, Staffordshire, height: 15.3cm, (6in), blue-printed pearlware. Portrait of Admiral Collingwood, within dense foliage and an image of *Victory* inscribed, 'Off Trafalgar Oct 21 1805'.

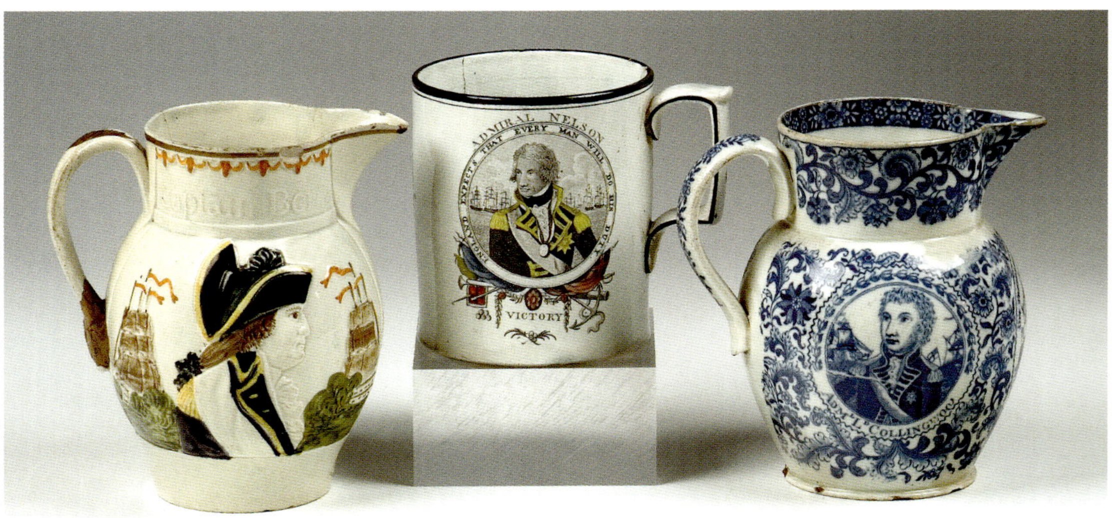

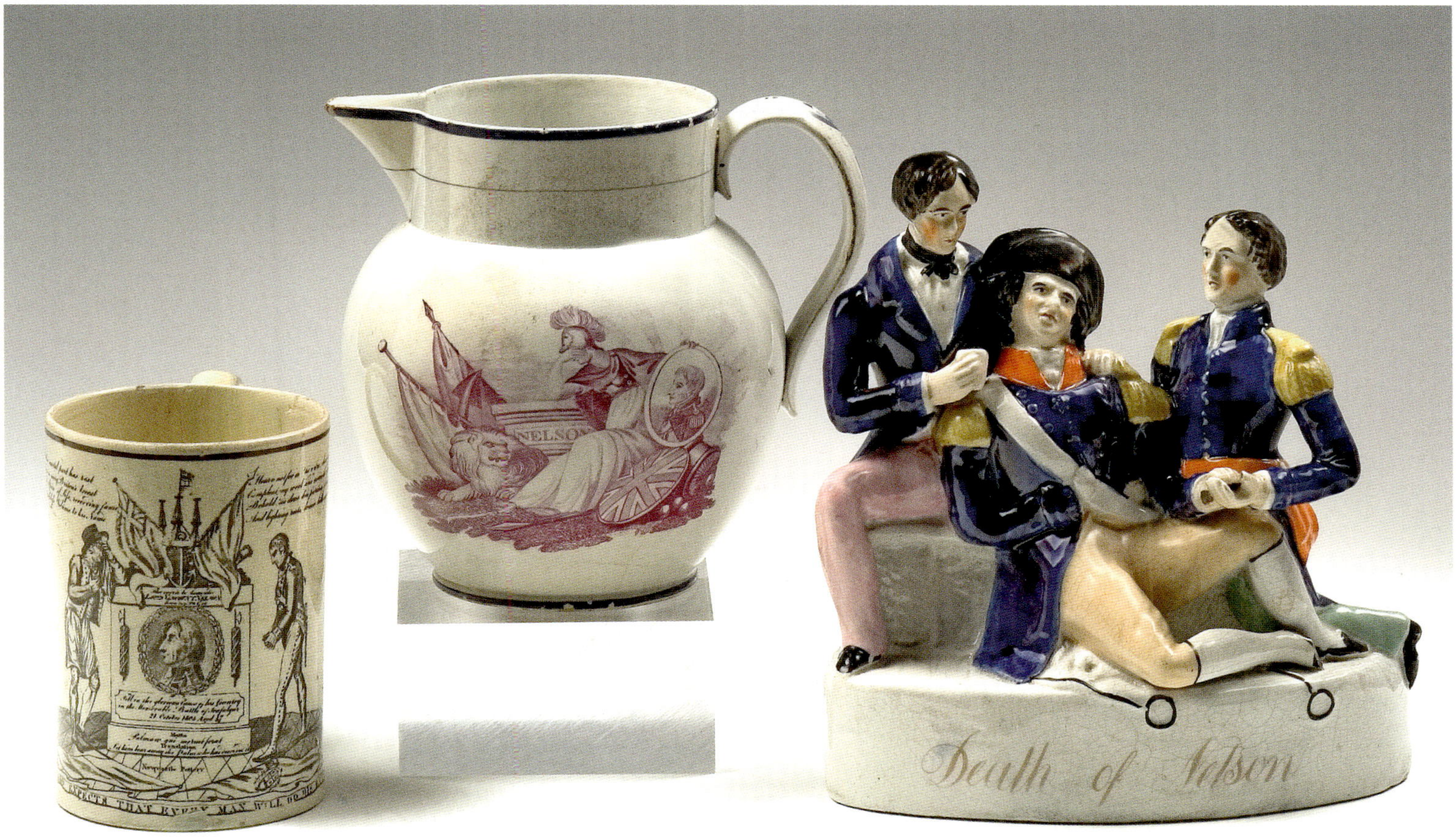

Mug, (214), c.1805, Newcastle Pottery, Addison, Falconer & Co., height: 12.7cm, (5in), printed creamware. Two sailors mourn at Nelson's tomb, inscribed, 'The ever to be lamented / LORD VISCOUNT NELSON,' Nelson's motto and verses, 'Remember whilst his mortal part has rest / Th'immortal lives in every Briton's breast'.[32]
Jug, (216), c.1805, Staffordshire, height: 15.3cm, (6in), purple-printed pearlware. Britannia weeps at Nelson's tomb, a figure of Fame and on reverse, Britannia's address on the death of Lord Nelson, beginning, 'Behold the PORTRAIT of my darling Son'.
Figure group, (212), c.1850, Staffordshire, height: 19.7cm, (7¾in), earthenware, enamelled and gilt. 'The Death of Nelson', based on prints after the celebrated painting of 1806 by Benjamin West.[33]

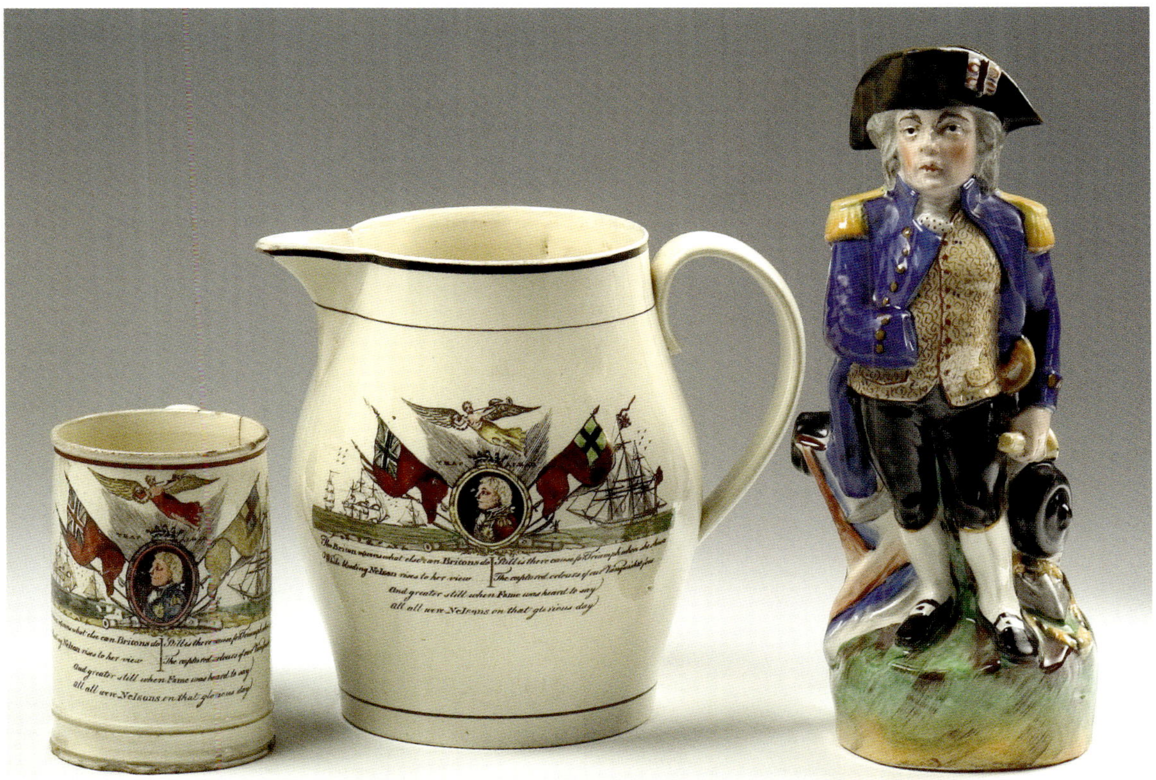

Mug, (215), c.1805, Sunderland, Phillips & Co., Garrison Pottery, height: 12.7cm, (5in), creamware.
Jug, (221), c.1805, Sunderland, Phillips & Co., Garrison Pottery, height: 19.1cm, (7½in), creamware. Both printed and enamelled with a winged Victory hovering over a medallion portrait of Nelson, (taken from a print by Edward Orme) flanked by flags and ships at Trafalgar. Verses read, 'The Briton mourns; what else can Britons do / While bleeding NELSON rises to her view'.
Figure, (R2454/6), c.1840, Staffordshire, height: 24.2cm, (9½in), enamelled earthenware. Nelson with an empty sleeve, stands before cannon.

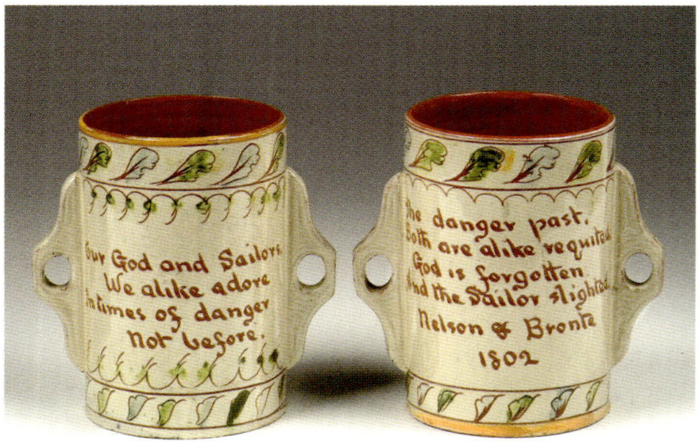

Pair of Mugs, (220), c.1890, Devon, Aller Vale, each height: 15.3cm, (6in), slip-decorated earthenware. Two-handled mugs, enamelled and incised, 'Our god and sailors we alike adore / In times of danger not before / ...Nelson & Bronte. 1802'.

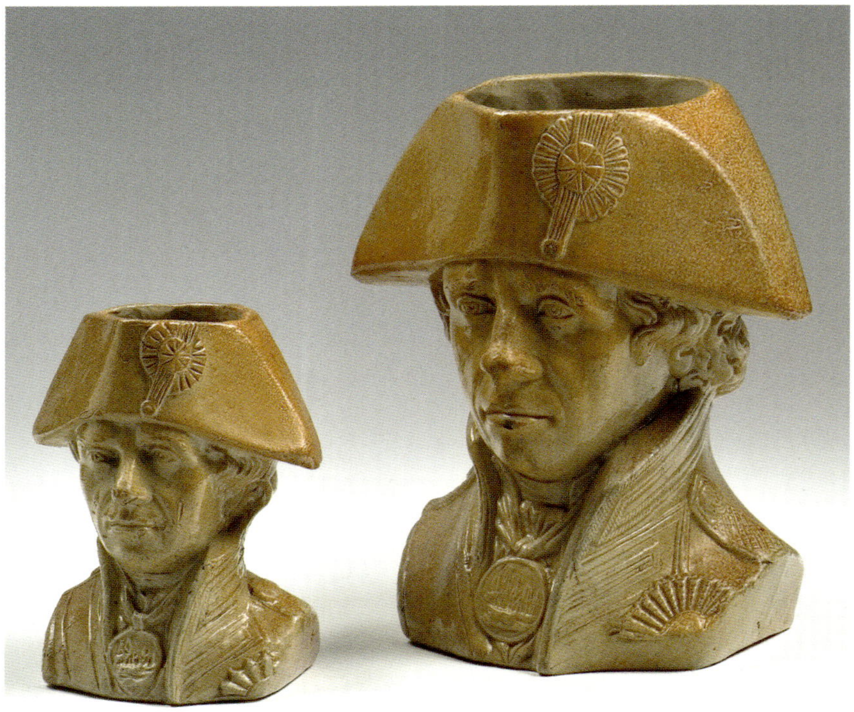

Jug, (217 & 218), c.1845, London, Doulton & Watts, height: 12.7cm, (5in) and 19.1cm, (7½in), salt-glazed stoneware.
Two similar jugs with twisted rope handles, moulded as busts of Nelson.
Jug, (219), c.1845, London, Doulton & Watts, height: 31.7cm, (12½in), salt-glazed stoneware. Moulded as half-length figure of Nelson. Moulded inscriptions, 'NILE 1798 / TRAFALGAR 1805 / England expects…'.
The marble bust by Franz Thaller and Matthias Ranson, for whom Nelson sat in Vienna in 1800, was shipped to London in 1801. It served as the model for many later sculpted portraits, including E.H. Bailey's full-length statue, placed on top of the column erected in Trafalgar Square in 1843.[34] It was also the source for these stoneware jugs.

Personifications of the Sea

Just as the Roman goddess Minerva evolved into Britannia, an embodiment of Britain as an emerging nation, so Neptune and Venus came to symbolise the growing might of British sea power. These deities appear frequently as printed decoration on Liverpool creamware around 1790, on items such as a bowl depicting Benjamin Franklin (453), and they also appear as ornamental figures.

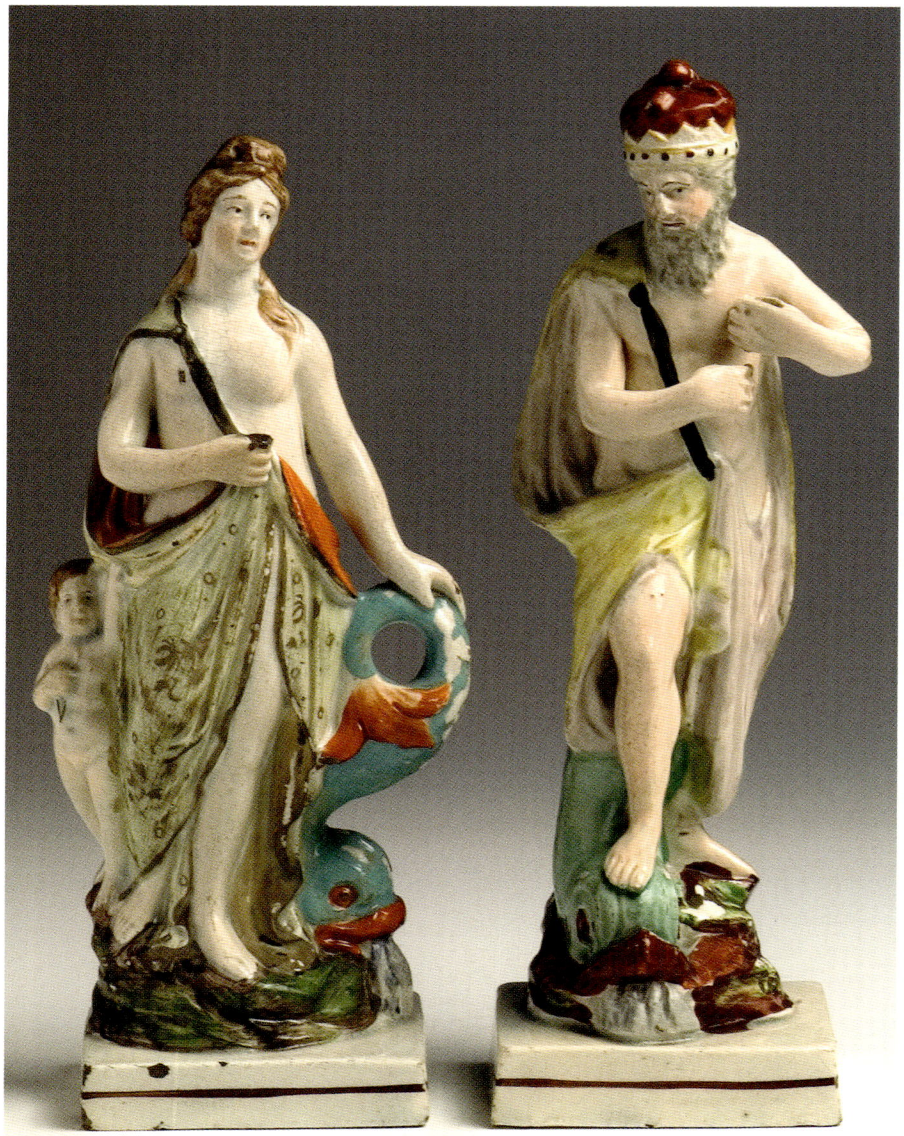

Pair of figures, (226 & A), c.1800, Burslem, Enoch Wood, each height: 24.1cm, (9½in), enamelled pearlware. Neptune wears a large crown and Venus is attended by Cupid. Both have dolphin supporters and stand on square bases.

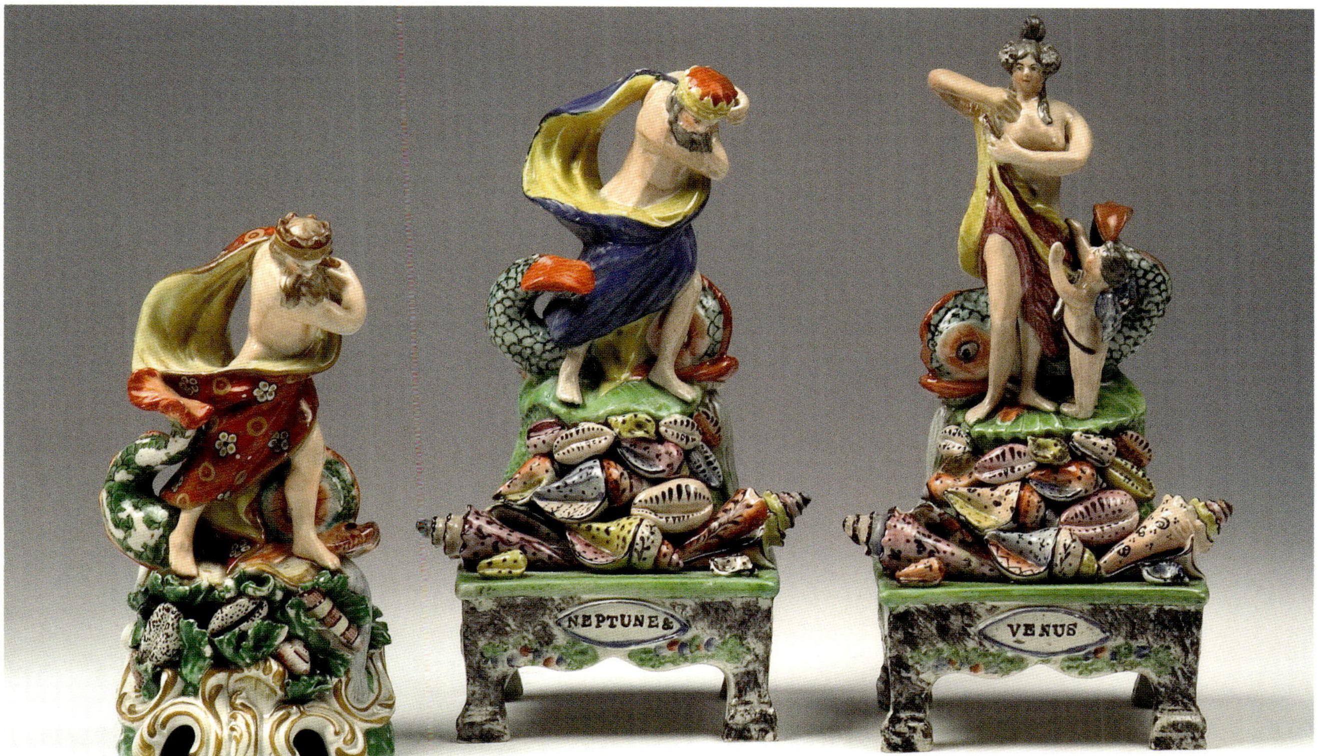

Figure, (227), c.1830, Staffordshire, height: 19.7cm, (7¾in), pearlware, enamelled and gilt. Stands on a scrolled base with seaweed and shells. Cast from a Derby porcelain figure, itself copied from a bronze figure by Michel Anguier.
Pair of figures, (229 & A), c.1830, Burslem, Enoch Wood, height: 24.8cm, (9¾in) and 22.9cm, (9in), enamelled pearlware. Neptune is based on the same source as (227) while Venus, more crudely modelled, has a fashionable coiffure from c.1830. Both have dolphin supporters. They perch on a mound of huge seashells mounted on table bases, inscribed, respectively, 'NEPTUNE &' 'VENUS'.

LATER NAVAL COMMANDERS

Rear Admiral Sir John Franklin (1786-1847)

Franklin served at Copenhagen in 1801 and at Trafalgar in 1804, before becoming an explorer. On his first, ill-fated trek into North West Canada in 1818 he lost eleven of twenty men and the survivors attempted to eat their own boots. His expedition of 1825 was better organized; he surveyed thousands of miles along the Mackenzie River and the Beaufort Sea. In 1825 he was elected a Fellow of the Royal Society and was knighted in 1829. In May 1845, after serving from 1834 to 1843 as governor of Tasmania, he embarked with two ships for the Arctic, to search for the North West Passage from the Atlantic to the Pacific. He was never seen again but his widow Jane (an intrepid solo traveller in her own right), was indefatigable in trying to discover his fate and personally financed several expeditions. Emotive articles were published, reporting on the search missions.[35] Between 1854 and 1859 evidence was finally discovered to account for his death and the fate of the expedition: a combination of poor planning, bad weather, poisoned food and illness.

Admiral Sir Charles Napier (1786-1860)

Napier served in the Mediterranean and in America during the War of 1812. He later settled in Paris whence he hectored the British Admiralty, who regarded him as an eccentric pest, urging naval reform. After serving in the Syrian campaign of 1840 he exhibited increasingly erratic behaviour, becoming known as 'Mad Charlie'. However he was made Commander of the Channel Fleet in 1847 and Vice Admiral of the Blue in 1853. At the outbreak of the Crimean War he was appointed Commander of the Baltic Fleet but was, by then, out of touch with modern marine warfare. Relieved of his command, he spent his later years quarrelling with the Admiralty.

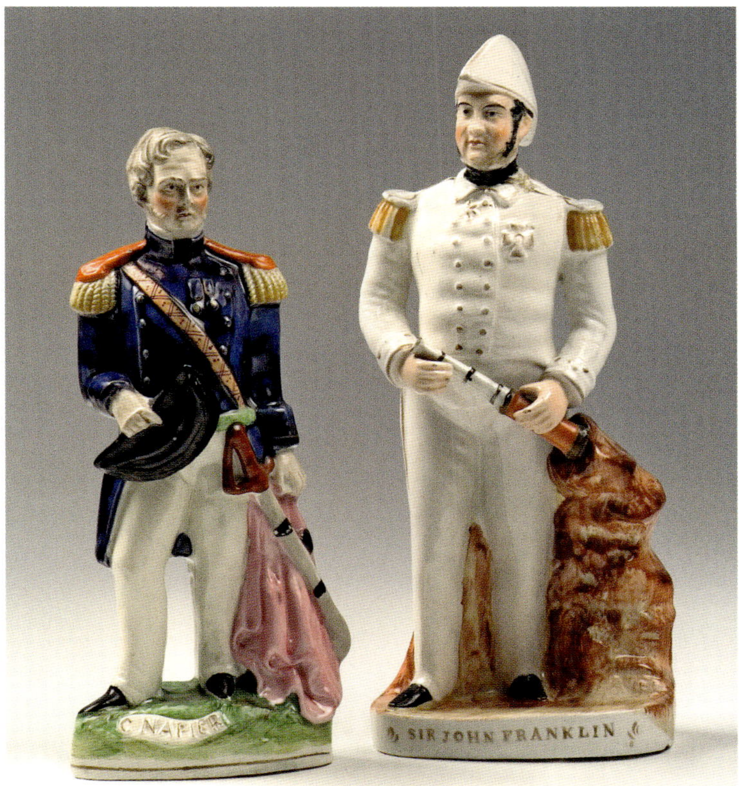

Figure, (199), c.1850, Staffordshire, height: 24.8cm, (9¾in), earthenware, enamelled and gilt. Represents Sir Charles Napier.
Figure, (200), c.1850, Staffordshire, height: 28 cm, (11in), earthenware, enamelled and gilt. A pair of figures of Sir John and Lady Franklin[36] was produced, possibly as part of the campaign to keep his memory alive. It appears to be a good likeness of Sir John, similar to an engraved portrait.[37]

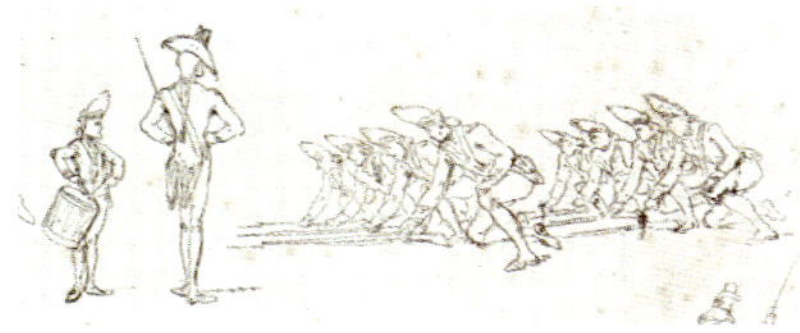

Chapter 4

SOLDIERS & SAILORS

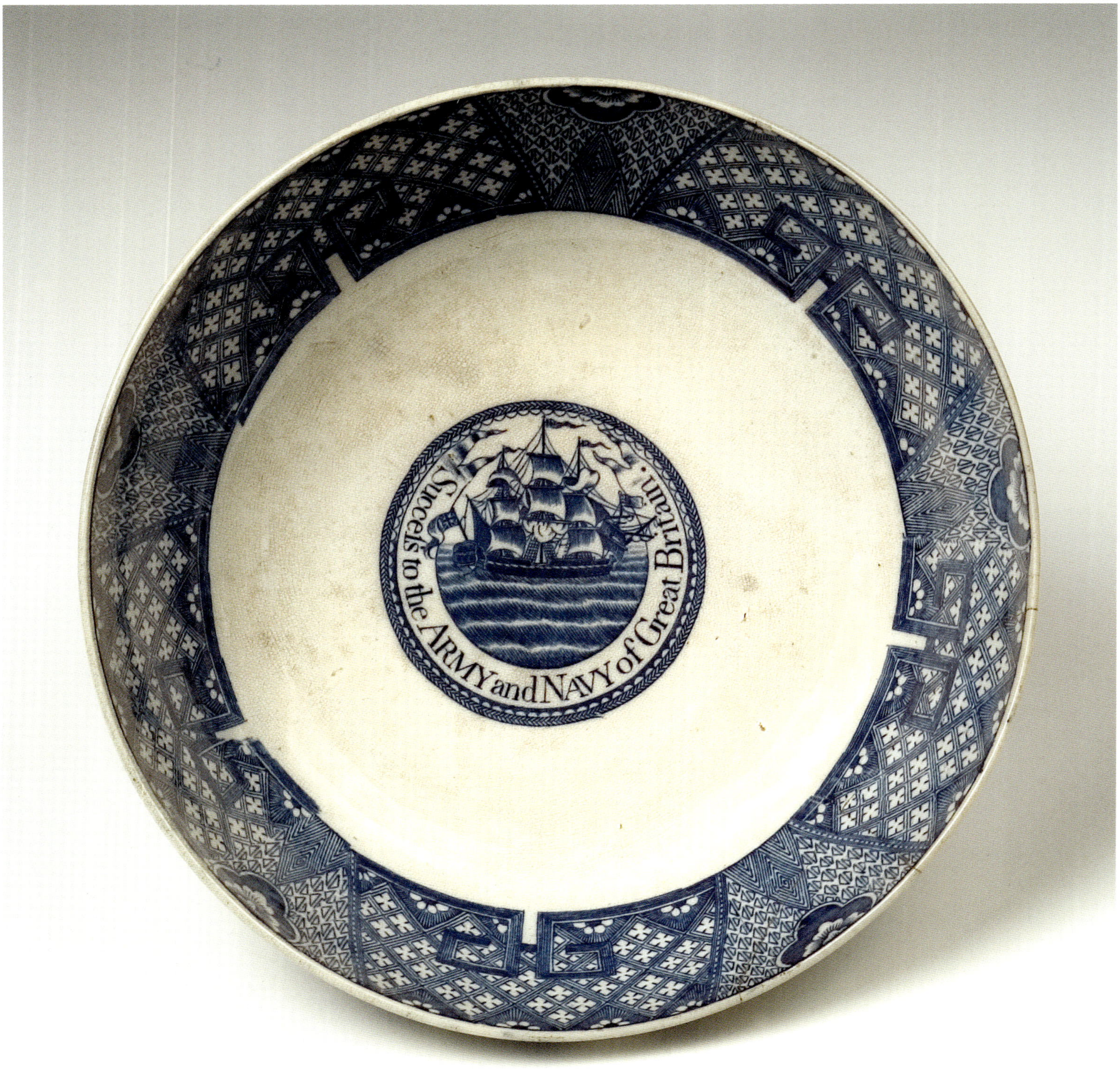

Punchbowl, (254), c.1810, probably Staffordshire, diameter: 22.9cm, (9in), blue-printed pearlware. Birds and flower sprays on the outside, ship motif in centre inscribed, 'Success to the ARMY and NAVY of Great Britain'.

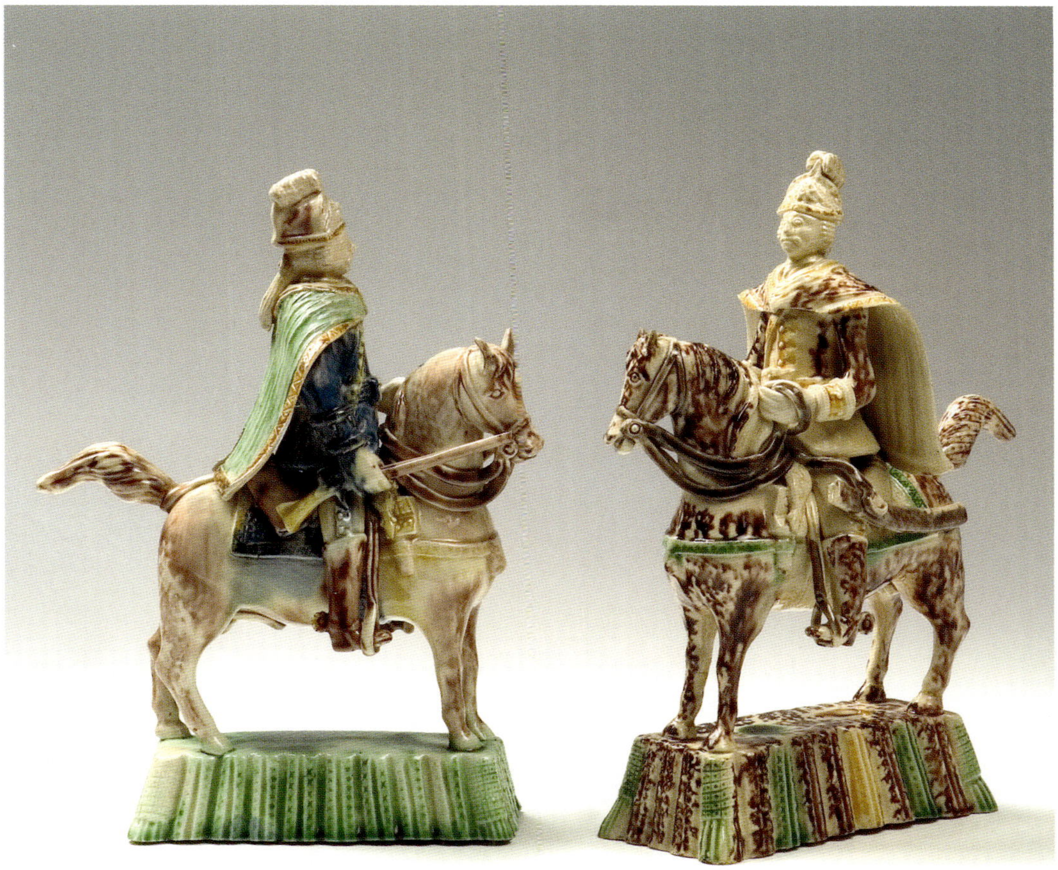

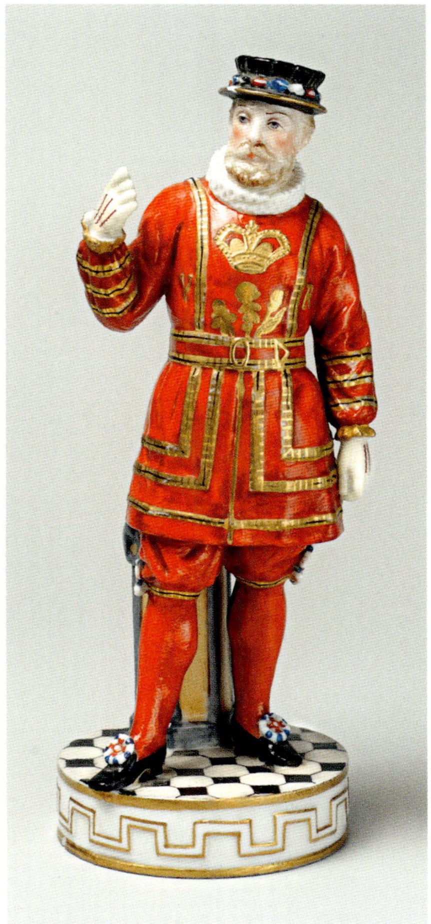

Figure Group, (237), c.1750-60, Staffordshire, height: 24.1cm, (9½in), earthenware.
Figure Group, (240), c.1750-60, Staffordshire, height: 26cm, (10¼in), earthenware. Two rare groups, lead-glazed and decorated with metal oxide colours. (The figure in 237 wears blue uniform and a green cloak). Modelled as cavalry officers on horseback, apparently from the same mould. Hand-modelled additions, e.g. muskets. Saddle pommels impressed with the royal cipher 'GR'. Uniform probably based on that of Light Dragoons.[1] These early horse and rider groups would have been difficult to mould and fire successfully, yet none has a supporting stump beneath the horse's belly.

Figure, (248), c.1870, probably Derby, height: 20.2cm, (8in), soft-paste porcelain, enamelled and gilt. A Gentleman Yeoman of the Guard from the Tower of London, holding a large lantern. Retailed by W. Toogood, of London, whose printed mark appears beneath.

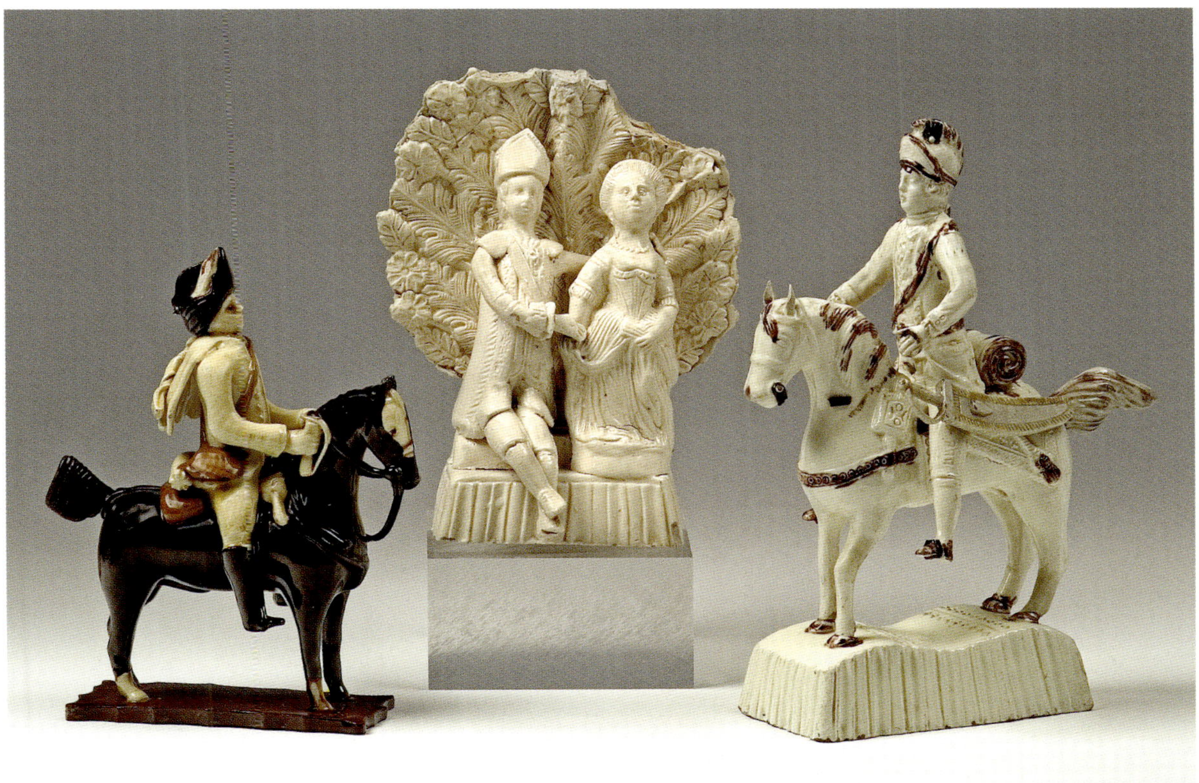

Figure Group, (238), c.1750-60, Staffordshire, height: 17.8cm, (7in), earthenware. Naively modelled hussar and rider group, on flat base, glazed dark brown.
Figure Group, (241), c.1750-60, Leeds or Staffordshire, height: 15.3cm, (6in), white salt-glazed stoneware. A soldier (wearing a grenadier's conical hat) sits with his sweetheart beneath a tree that radiates huge feathery branches.[2]
Figure Group, (239), c.1750-60, Staffordshire, height: 22.9cm, (9in), earthenware. Mounted hussar decorated with only sparse dabs of manganese colouring.

The Volunteer Movement

Militias were first raised under an Act of 1757 and strengthened by the Defence of the Realm Act in 1798. Their purpose was to provide some 60,000 extra troops to counter threats of invasion from France and Spain.[3] At the Peace of Amiens of 1802 the 340,000 serving Volunteers were disbanded but were soon recalled when a renewal of hostilities seemed likely. The Military Service Bill of 1803 that enabled a compulsory call-up of anyone fit to bear arms, proved unnecessary because half a million men volunteered. Local gentry usually took the lead and made themselves the officers. The government remained uneasy about having an armed citizenry especially of the 'lower orders' but the self-funding nature of the corps limited membership to those who could afford it.[4]

In 1801, when William Pitt was briefly out of office, he withdrew to Walmer Castle, his base as Lord Warden of the Cinque Ports and became Colonel of the Cinque Port Volunteers. He took his duties very seriously, raising three battalions when war resumed.[5] The illustrator George Cruikshank, a regular visitor to Brighton, was an officer in a volunteer regiment and took part in 'one of those good old sham fights on the Race Hill' in Brighton in the 1820s.[6] Some years later Henry Willett was equally committed, being promoted from Gunner Catt to Lieutenant Willett in 1864 (after his name change of 1863). Those who lived in the Staffordshire Potteries were as enthusiastic as any. Enoch Wood was involved with the formation of the Burslem Volunteers in 1798 and after 1803 there were Volunteer brigades in Lane End, Longport, Tunstall, Hanley and Shelton, Stoke and Fenton.[7] Commemorative ceramics reflect public enthusiasm for the Volunteer movement.

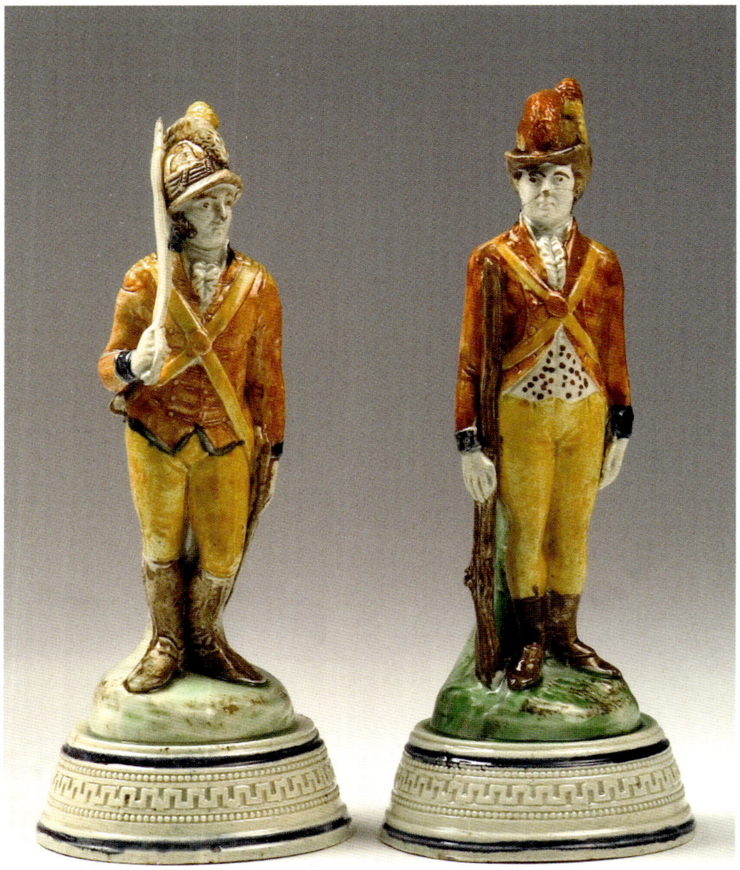

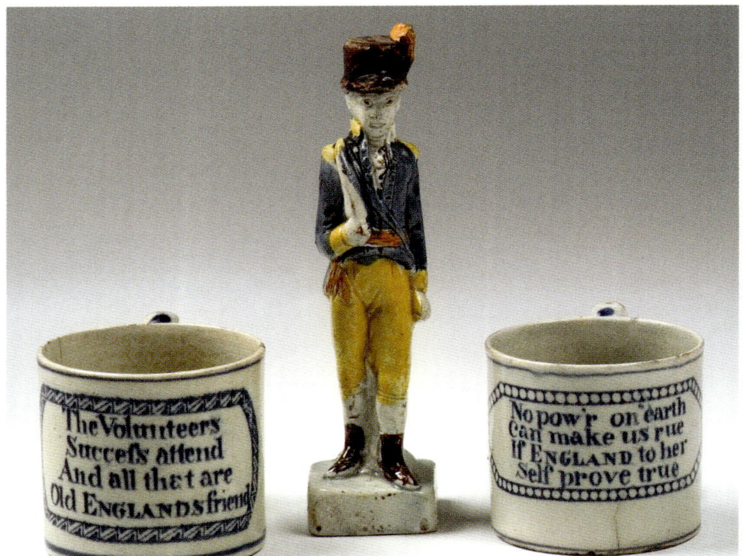

Pair of mugs, (230 + 231), c.1810, probably Staffordshire, height: 6.4cm, (2½in), height: 5.7cm, (2¼in), underglaze blue-printed pearlware. Patriotic mottoes relating to the Volunteer movement, 'The Volunteers / Success attend / And all that are / Old ENGLAND'S friend', and, 'No pow'r on earth / Can make us rue/ If ENGLAND to her / Self prove true.'
Figure, (233), c.1810, probably Staffordshire, height: 15.3cm, (6in), Prattware. Represents a volunteer soldier.

Pair of figures, (232 & A), 1800. Scotland, probably Prestonpans,[9] each height 22.9cm, (9in), Prattware. They stand on domed bases impressed with bands of roulette and Greek key mouldings, and appear to wear the uniform of the Grenadier Company of the Royal Edinburgh Volunteers.[10]

Jug, (234), c.1796, Staffordshire, impressed 'WEDGWOOD/6', height: 19.1cm, (7½in), enamelled creamware. Painted with a cavalry officer on a prancing horse, likely to be a portrait of Colonel Thomas Legh of Lyme Park.[8] Medallion with initials: W.C. (unidentified) beneath the spout. An assemblage of farm implements on the reverse.
Jug, (236), c.1790, impressed Wedgwood, printed in Liverpool, height: 22.2cm, (8¾in), creamware, printed by Guy Green. Finely printed cartouche surmounted by Hibernia (symbolising Ireland) with a harp, supported by two Irish soldiers (also used on jug (235) inscribed, 'Succefs to the / INDEPEN-DENT VOLUNTEER / SOCIETIES / of the Kingdom of / IRELAND' and 'FOR MY COUNTRY'. The 'Death of Wolfe' on the reverse.
Jug, (235), c.1790, Wedgwood, Liverpool, height: 21cm, (8¼in), creamware, printed and enamelled. Applied foot ring (and restored spout and handle). Three infantry soldiers in the uniform of the Irish Volunteers, who were recruited in 1779 after English troops were withdrawn from Ireland to serve in America. Inscribed beneath the spout, 'Succef to Colon. Conyngham AND THE Springhill UNION'. Henry, third Lord Conyngham in the Irish peerage (1766-1832), in 1794 married Elizabeth Denison, who became the last mistress of George IV. The 'Death of Wolfe' on the reverse.

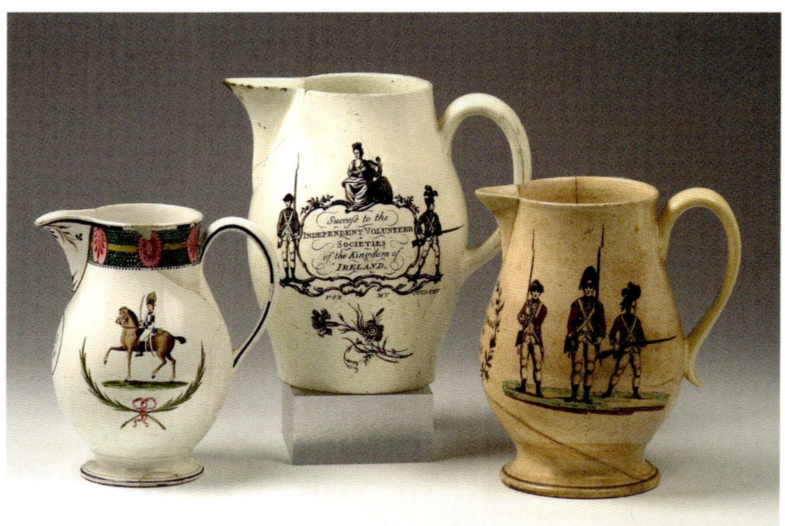

Scottish Soldiers

Scottish soldiers were and still are famously courageous and determined fighters. After the upheavals of the Jacobite rebellion, the Scots became a major force in British military life. Today, despite numbering 9 per cent of the population they constitute 12% of the British army. Many Scottish regiments fought at Waterloo, including the Gordon Highlanders and the cavalry of the Royal Scots Greys, of whom Napoleon is said to have commented, 'Ah! Ces terribles chevaux gris' ('Oh! those awful grey horses').

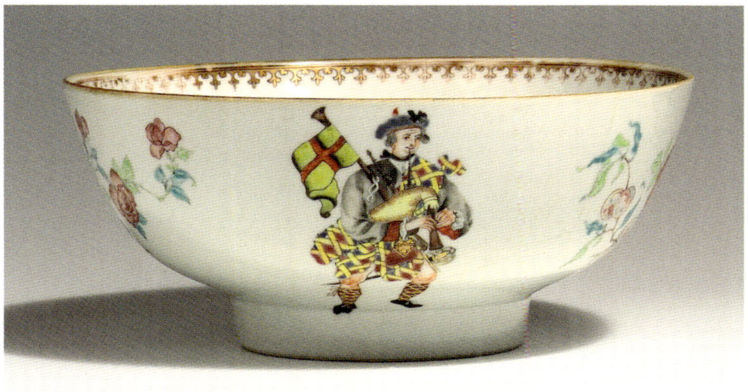

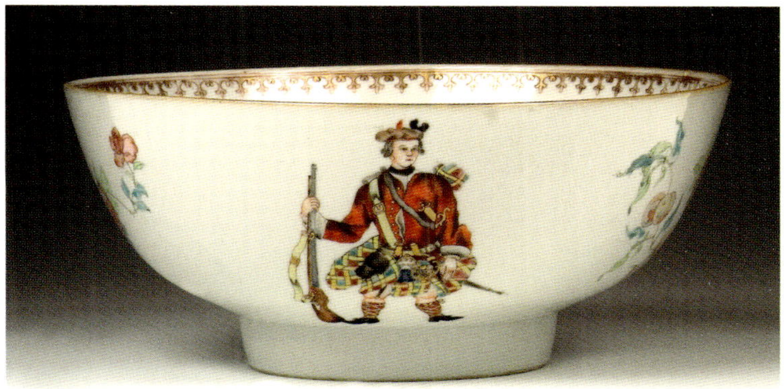

Punchbowl, (243), c.1745, China, diameter: 26cm, (10¼in), hard-paste porcelain. Enamelled with the figures of two Scottish soldiers, a musketeer (possibly Rifleman Shawe) and Piper Macdonnel. Copied from illustrations in George Bickham's *A Short History of the Highland Regiment*, (pub. 1743). Four riflemen of the Highland Regiment had mutinied and were executed at the Tower of London on 18 July 1743, becoming early martyrs to the Jacobite cause. These popular commemorative prints inspired a number of similar pieces, ordered from China by supporters of Charles Edward Stuart. By the time the consignments arrived, however, the rebellion had been crushed and the cause was lost. The wearing of Highland dress was banned in 1747, to help break the power of the clans and to secure peace. This proscription was not lifted until 1782.

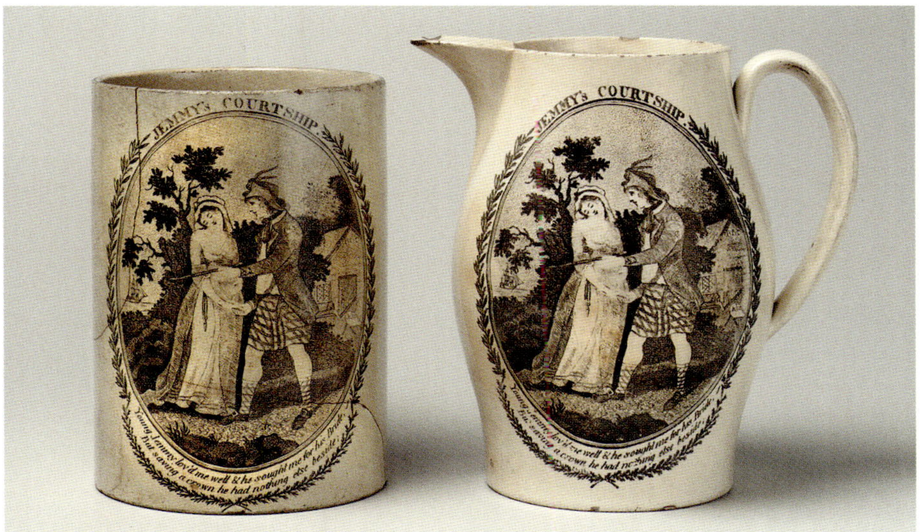

Mug, (301), c.1790, Staffordshire, height: 17.2cm, (6¾in), printed creamware.
Jug, (1666), c.1790, Staffordshire, height: 15.3cm, (6in), printed creamware. Both printed with scene entitled, 'Jemmy's Courtship'. An impoverished Scottish soldier, wearing a kilt, woos a young woman, accompanied by verse, 'Young Jemmy lov'd me well and sort [*sic*] me for his bride / But saving a crown he had nothing else beside'. The lines are taken from a long ballad, written by Lady Anne Ballard, published anonymously in 1771 under the title of the 'Song of Auld Robin Gray'.[11] The original Scottish hero was named Jamie though this was anglicised to Jemmy. The reverse of the jug printed with a British ship on starboard tack.

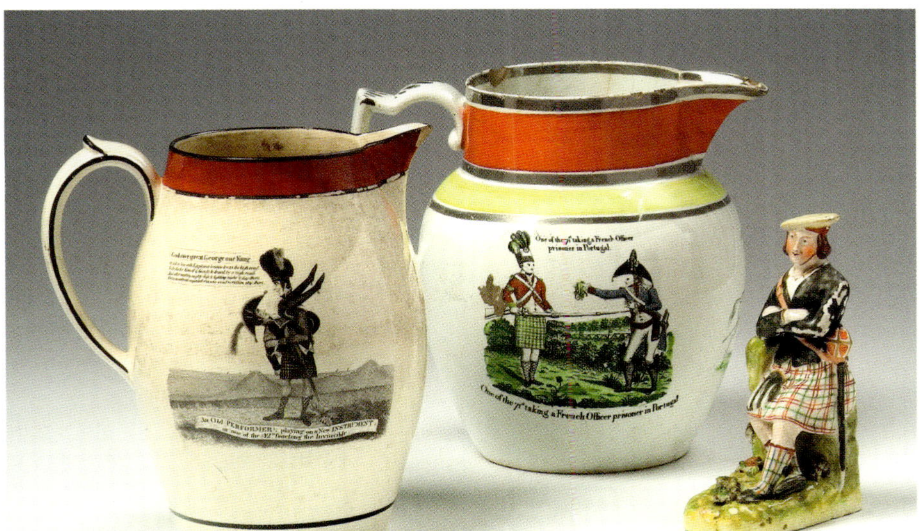

Jug, (399), c.1805, probably Staffordshire, height: 20.3cm, (8in), earthenware, printed and enamelled. Inscribed beneath spout, 'I. Topham 1804'. A Scottish soldier from the 42nd Highland Regiment (later the Black Watch), attempts to play Napoleon as a bagpipe. Inscribed, 'An Old PERFORMER playing on a New INSTRUMENT or one of the 42nd Touching the Invincible'.[12] This refers to Sir Ralph Abercrombie's victory over the French at Alexandria on 21 March 1801, where the regiment played a crucial role, including the capture of the eagle standard of Napoleon's 'Invincibles'.
Jug, (406), c.1810, probably Staffordshire, height: 20.3cm, (8in), pearlware, printed, enamelled and lustred. Printed with 'One of the 71st taking a French Officer prisoner in Portugal'. A French soldier hands over booty to a kilted Scottish soldier. It probably dates from 1808 to 1811 when the French were driven from Portugal.
Figure, (244), c.1840, probably Staffordshire, height: 15.3cm, (6in), enamelled pearlware. A kilted Highlander, of c.1840 leans against a grassy bank. It may be one of a pair of bookends.

Sauceboat and Stand, (242), c.1780, Staffordshire, Wedgwood, (impressed: WEDGWOOD and gothic 'a' height: 15.3cm, (6in), enamelled creamware. Finely painted for the Scottish Cameronian Regiment.[13] The vessel has side handles and an integral foot, a domed cover with loop handle and a larger oval stand. Decorated with bands of thistles and individual motifs; a sword, a pistol and a regimental forage cap.

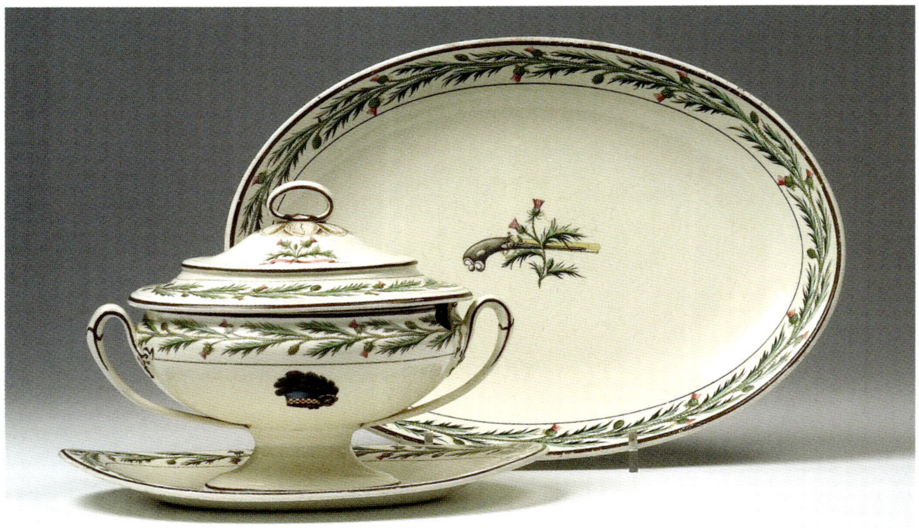

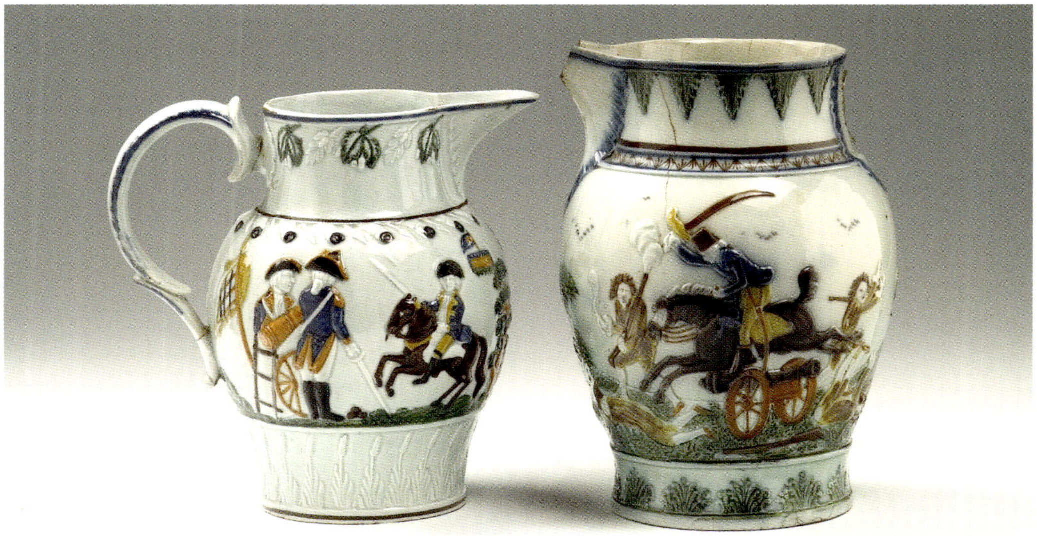

Jug, (245), c.1810, probably Staffordshire, height: 17.8cm, (7in), Prattware. Moulded with a military review between moulded friezes of oak leaves and bulrushes.
Jug, (246), c.1820, probably Staffordshire, height: 19.7cm, (7¾in), Prattware. Jug (missing handle) moulded with a scene from the Battle of Waterloo between friezes of foliate chevrons and palmettes.

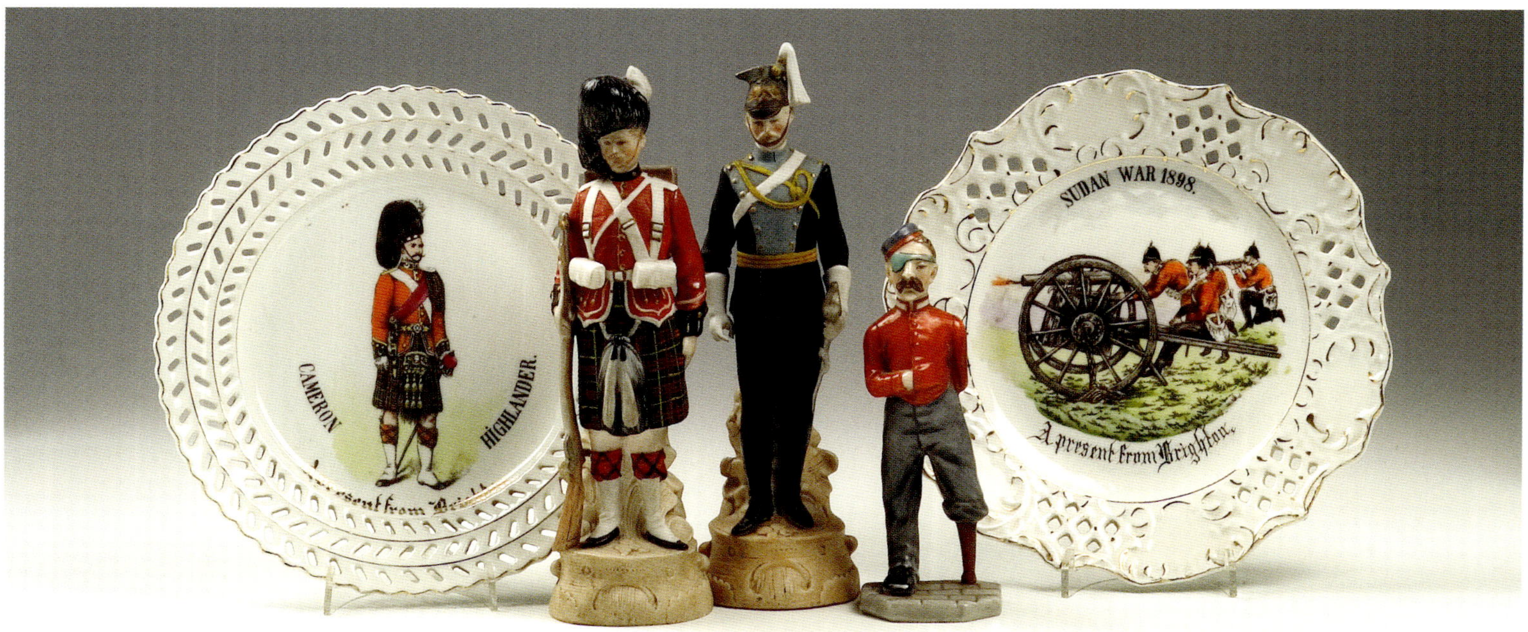

Plate, (250), c.1898, probably Germany, diameter: 21.6cm, (8½in), hard-paste porcelain. Printed with coloured image of a Cameron Highlander and inscribed, 'A Present from Brighton'.
Plate, (249), c.1898, probably Germany, diameter: 21.6cm, (8½in), hard-paste porcelain. Printed and painted with soldiers operating a field gun and inscribed, 'SUDAN WAR 1898'.

Two Figures, (R2454.23 + 24), c.1898, probably Germany, each height: 22.9cm, (9in), hard-paste porcelain. Modelled as a Scottish Highlander and a British Fusilier.
Figure, (247), c.1875, Royal Worcester (registration mark), height: 15.9cm, (6¼in), soft-paste porcelain. Enamelled figure of a wounded war veteran. One of a series (shape 440), incongruously modelled as 'Men Menu Holders' designed to wear menus as sandwich boards suspended front and back.[14]

Recruitment and Impressment

In the eighteenth and nineteenth centuries recruitment to the army and navy fluctuated according to need. Sometimes patriotic slogans and toasts were sufficient declarations of support for the armed forces. At other times fortunate events, such as the capture of enemy ships and the division of the spoils among the crew, were used as positive propaganda for the navy and incentives for joining up. Occasionally potters deployed satirical prints that portrayed the brutality and malpractice sometimes involved in drafting new recruits into the army and navy. There were few full-time military professionals at this time, so when war broke out or a new military campaign was planned, the armed services needed reinforcements.

Impressment into the navy was equally controversial, especially in ports where the press gang had not reached an accommodation with the local magistrates and was effectively operating outside local byelaws.[15] When hostilities ceased, the forces were disbanded and volunteers were laid off, usually without a retainer or pension. Both services used bribes and threats, often making men drunk before taking them away from their homes and families to fight abroad. Such scandalous ploys were eventually outlawed by Parliament.

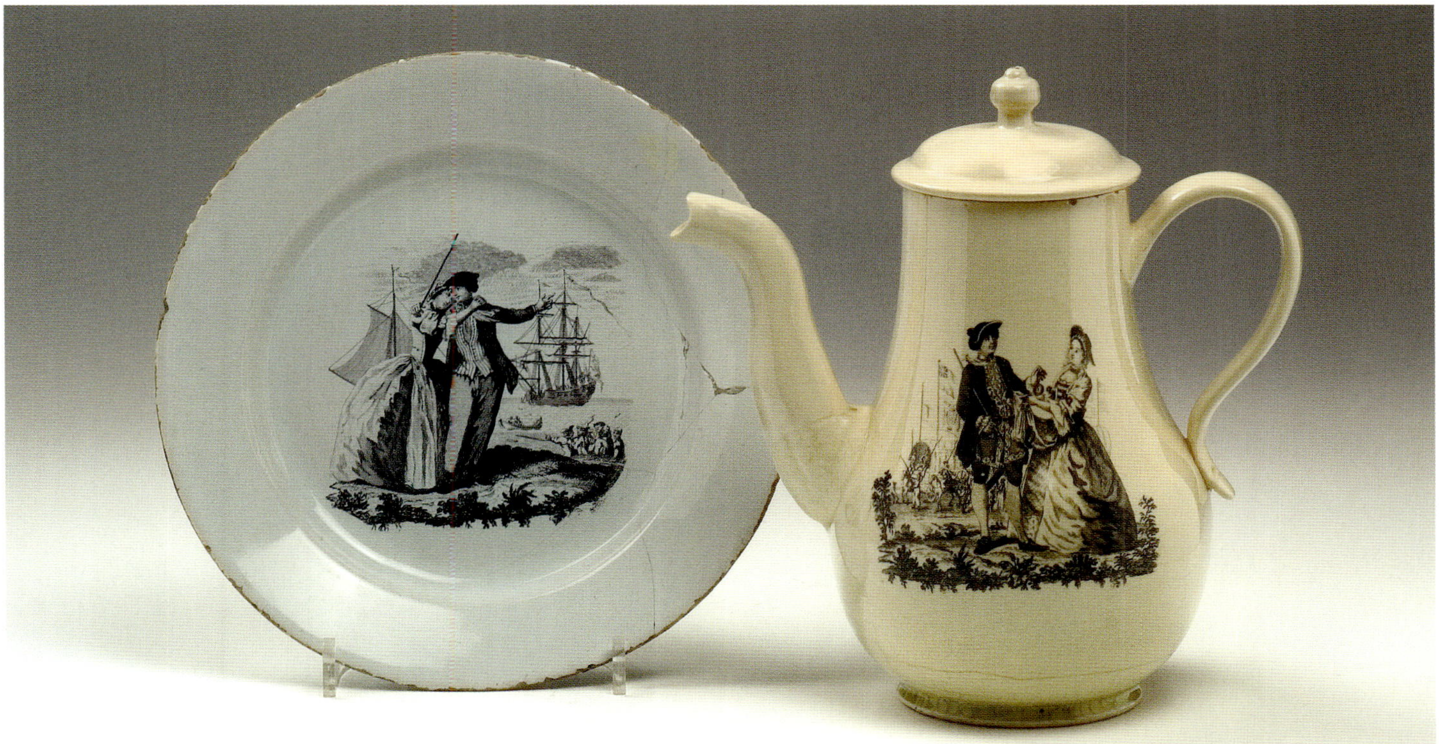

Plate, (286), c.1770, Liverpool, printed by John Sadler, diameter: 21.6cm, (8½in), printed tin-glazed earthenware. A sailor bids his sweetheart farewell, indicating the rowing boat, taking his shipmates to join their ship.
Coffee Pot, (287), c.1780, Liverpool or Staffordshire, height: 22.9cm, (9in), printed creamware. Coffee pot applied with companion print. The same sailor returns finely dressed, and presents his sweetheart with a watch and money while carts, bearing treasure, pass behind them. This pair of 'Sailor's Farewell' and 'Sailor's Return' prints, originally published in 1744,[16] celebrate Admiral Anson's eventful circumnavigation in the *Centurion*. Of the crew of 961 who set out, 743 were lost. The few who returned to Spithead in 1744 had encircled the globe and had fought major sea battles with the Spanish, successfully capturing the treasure ship the *Nuestra Senora de Cavadonga*. They came back with £500,000 in booty, and 32 wagons bearing the treasure were escorted in triumph from Portsmouth to London. The survivors were now so wealthy that they would never have to work again.

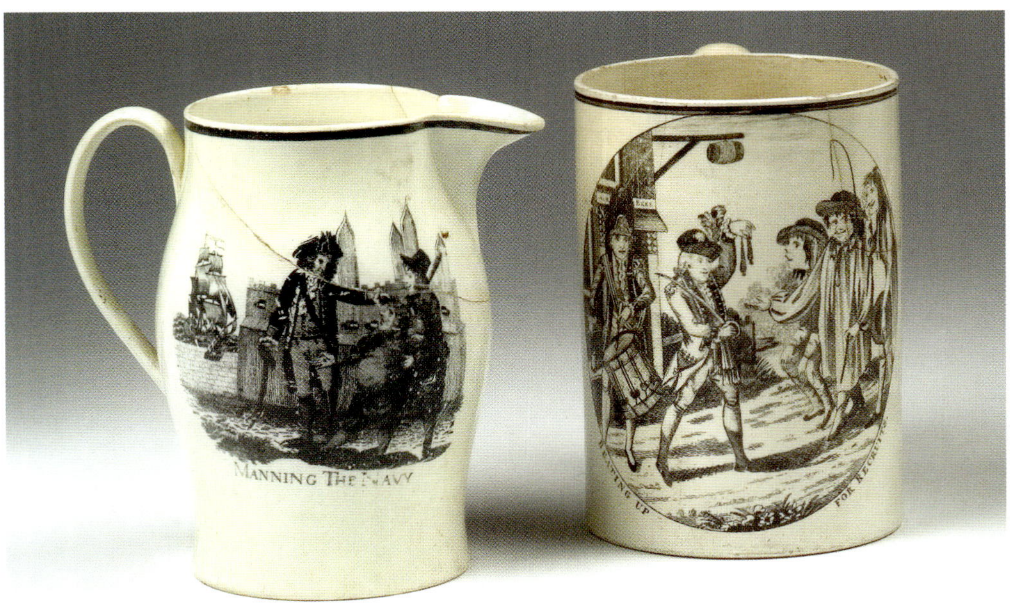

Jug, (256), c.1795, probably Staffordshire, height: 14.6cm, (5¾in), printed creamware. Jug has caricature entitled, 'MANNING THE NAVY', where an officer greets two unlikely recruits at the quayside. Design taken from part of print with same title, published 1 June 1790.[17] The original print shows the violence practised by the press gang. (On the other side, an officer gesticulates from the shore at two incoming vessels.)
Mug, (255), c.1795, probably Staffordshire, height: 14.6cm, (5¾in), printed creamware. The mug printed with a scene inscribed, 'BEATING UP FOR RECRUITS'; a soldier beats a drum while a scout with a sword over his shoulder dangles a purse full of money in front of a group of farm yokels, who wear smocks and rustic straw hats and carry switches over their shoulders, in imitation of weapons. The print was drawn by Robert Dighton and published by Robert Sayer, c.1790.[18]

Life on the Ocean Wave

'The great lesson of the eighteenth century was that the key to commerce was shipping and the ability to protect that shipping'.[19] There are myriad images of ships on all types of ceramics. Some are portraits of identified vessels, made to celebrate a launch or a maiden voyage, heroic deeds at sea or a change of command. At this time Britain and the Netherlands far outstripped France in developing their navies. In wartime Britain could muster more than twice as many skilled seamen as France; the census of 1801 recorded 135,000 sailors in the Royal Navy and 144,000 in the merchant navy. This was as crucial for Britain's success as a trading nation as for the great naval victories of the 1790s and 1800s. Consequently there are far more representations of sailors than of soldiers in the Willett Collection.

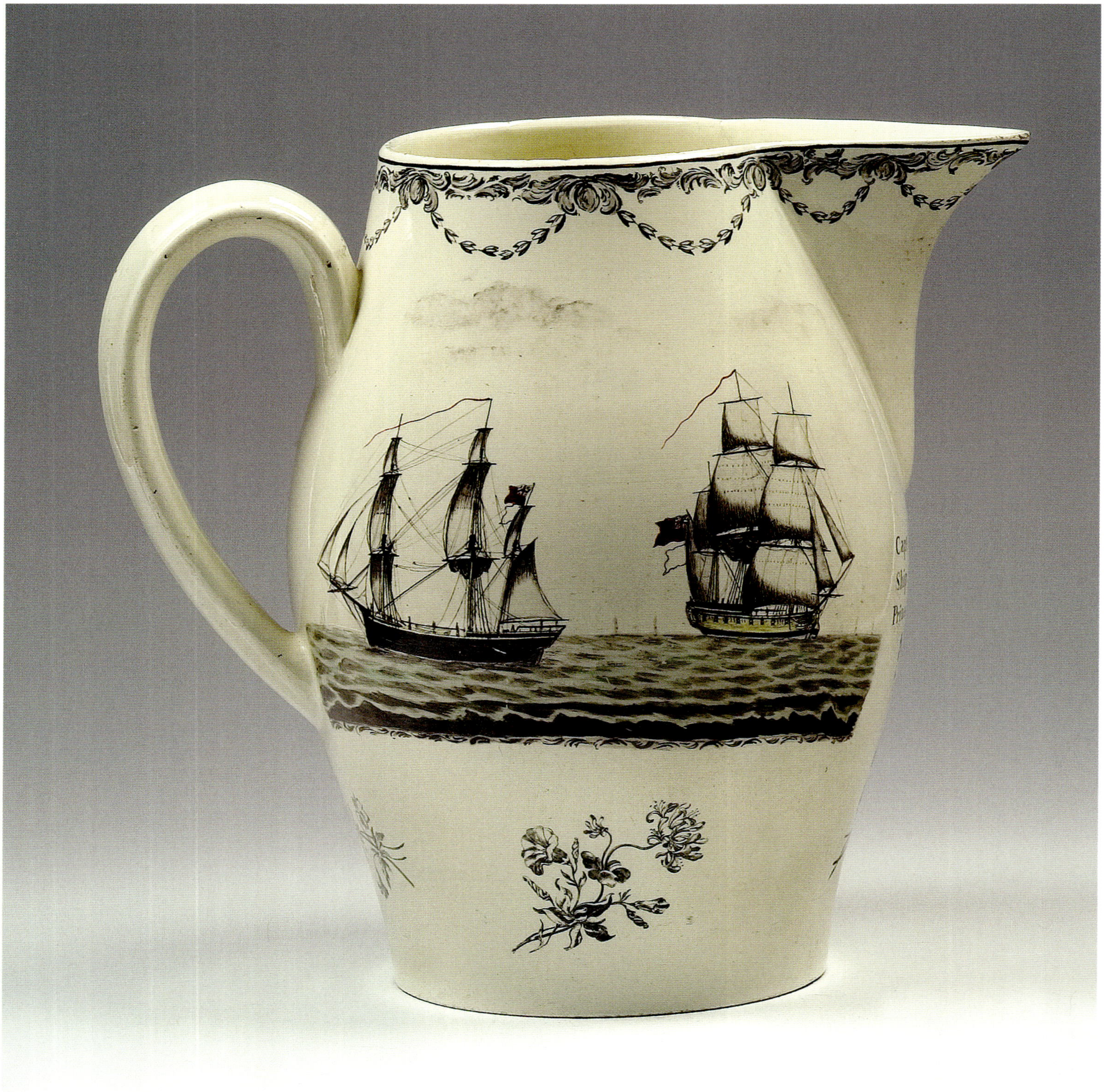

Large Jug, (339), c.1785, Liverpool, probably Guy Green, height: 29.2cm, (11½in), enamelled creamware. Scene of a British naval action; a single ship on one side and a pair on the other. Inscribed beneath the spout, 'Capt Joseph Anthony / Ship St Ann with her two / Prizes Le Pelerin & Consalateur [*sic*]'. The *St Ann* (built 1779), had been taken from the French in 1781. Its purchaser, Sir William James, hired it to His Majesty's Board of Ordnance as an armed store-ship trading out of the port of London. Returning alone from Gibraltar in September 1782, she encountered 70 French merchant ships returning from Saint Domingue (Haiti), without naval escort. The *St Ann* captured two vessels, laden with sugar, coffee etc. and took them to Plymouth. In June 1784 the Admiralty relinquished its claim to the proceeds and Captain Joseph Anthony received £3,185 from the total value of £22,445.[20] A companion punchbowl, similarly decorated, also survives.[21]

Large Mug, (327), c.1790, Liverpool Herculaneum, height: 11.4cm, (4½in), pearlware. Printed in puce; on one side a scene of warships in a panoramic seascape inscribed, 'Succefs to the British Fleet' (an image used on Wedgwood creamware). On the reverse, three children dressed as soldiers practise army drill.[22]

Jug, (334), 1788, probably Liverpool, height: 18.4cm, (7¼in), pearlware. Covered with blue slip but for narrow diaper bands around the neck and base. It is black enamelled and gilt with a ship with furled sails, the date 1788 and the monogram 'TMR'.

Plaque, (343), c.1810, probably Staffordshire, height: 15.3cm, (6in), Prattware, pierced for hanging, relief-moulded with portrait of a hussar, inscribed, 'Daniel Goostry'. A man of this name was christened on 15 Oct 1721 in Cheddleton, Staffordshire. Several men of this name were listed in the Stoke-on-Trent Parish registers around 1800.

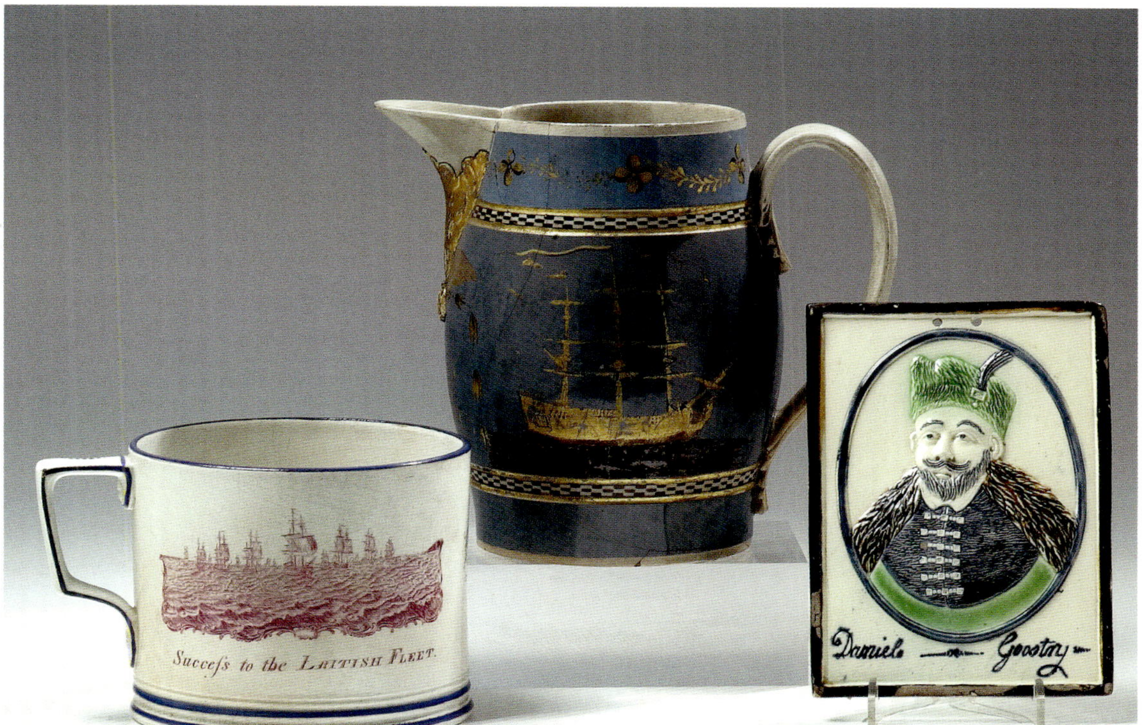

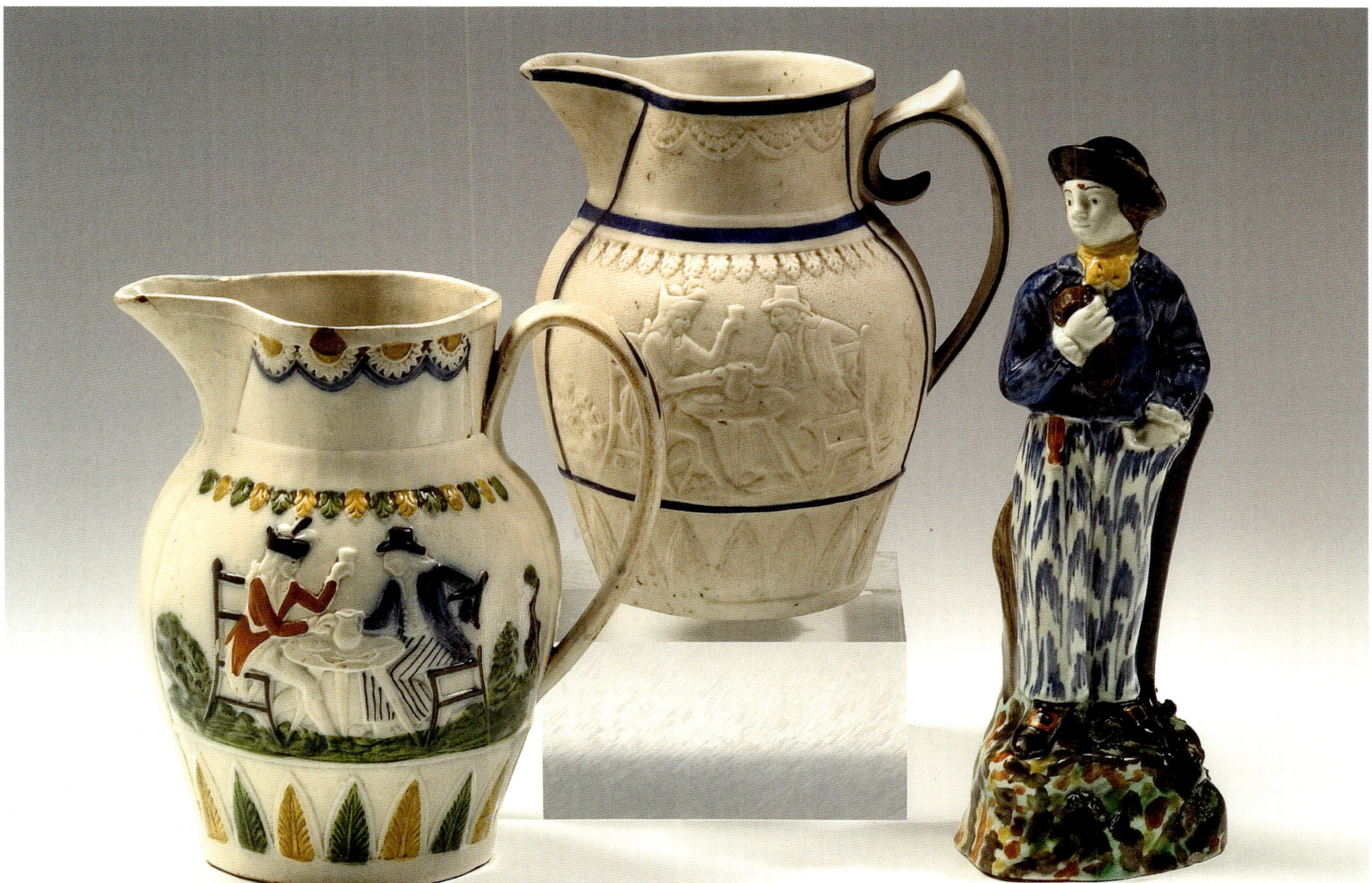

Jug, (252), c.1810, probably Yorkshire, height: 15.3cm, (6in), Prattware.
Jug, (253), c.1810, probably Yorkshire, height: 15.3cm, (6in), smear-glazed stoneware. Two relief-moulded jugs show similar scenes of a soldier and sailor carousing.

Figure, (289), c.1800, probably Staffordshire, height: 19.7cm, (7¾in), Prattware. Sailor leans on an anchor, holding a bag of money, probably his discharge wages.

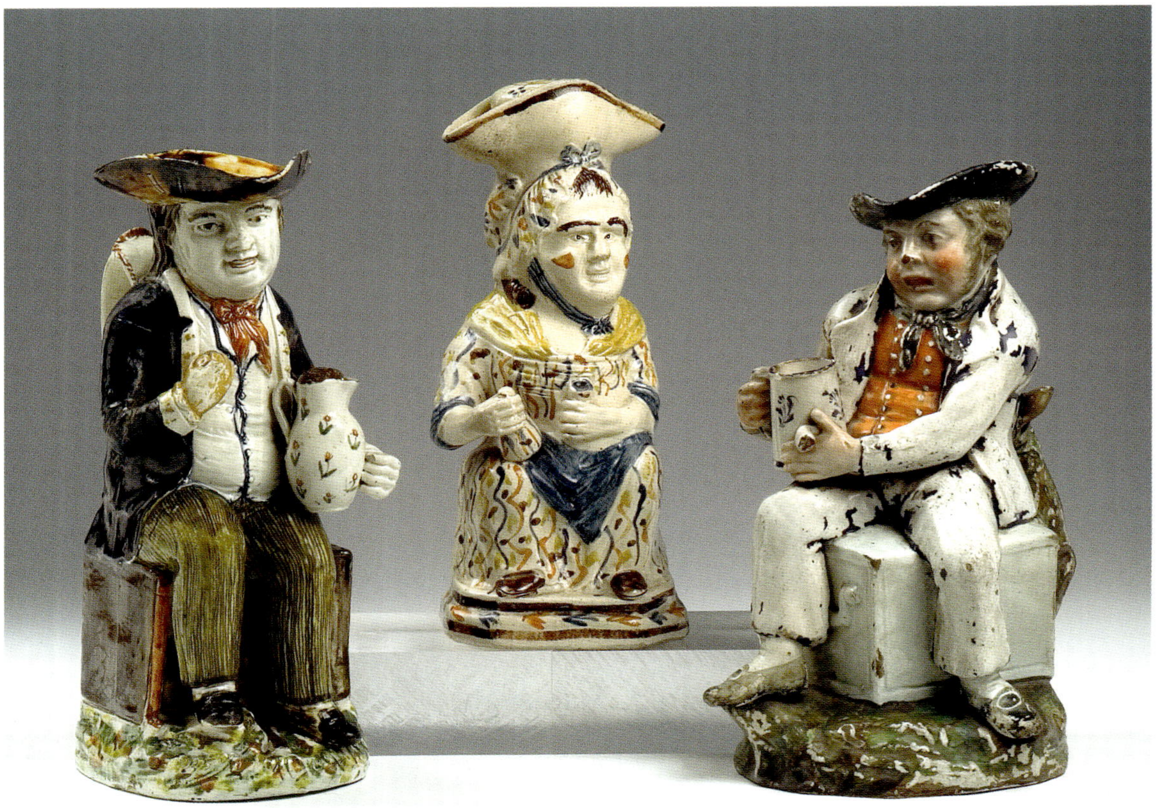

Toby jug, (297), c.1800, probably Staffordshire, height: 30.5cm, (12in), Pratt-coloured pearlware. Verse impressed on reverse, around the handle: 'Hollo Brother Briton / Whoever Thou be / Sit down on / That chest of/ Hand Dollors by me / And drink a health / To all sealors Bold [*sic*]'.
Female Toby, (1456), c.1800, probably Staffordshire, height: 26.7cm, (10½in), pearlware. Decorated in high-temperature colours; traditionally known as 'Martha Gunn', after the Brighton bathing woman.
Toby Jug, (278), c.1800, probably Staffordshire, height: 29.2cm, (11½in), pearlware. Badly fired so that enamel has peeled badly, sits on a chest moulded with a ship motif.

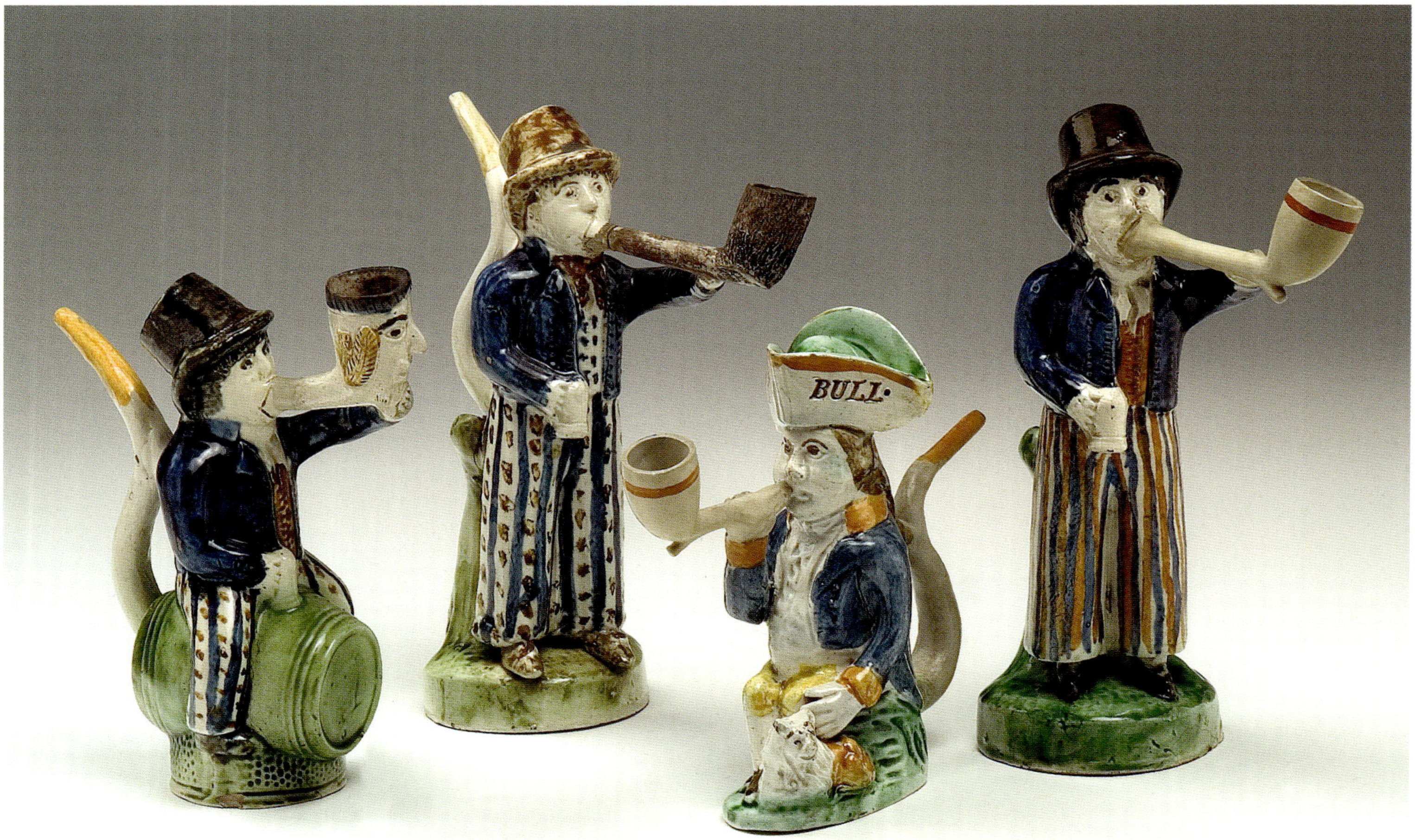

Clockwise:
Pipe, (274), c.1800, Staffordshire or Scotland, height: 15.3cm, (6½in), pearlware. Modelled as sailor sitting on a barrel. Pipe bowl specially modelled, with a face and thistle sprigs.
Two Pipes, (294 & 294A), c.1800, probably Staffordshire, each height: 17.8cm, (7in), pearlware. Two standing sailors fitted with real churchwarden clay pipes.
Pipe, (273), c.1800, probably Staffordshire, height: 14cm, (5½in), pearlware. Decorated in high temperature colours. Wears a tricorne hat impressed, 'JOHN BULL' and fitted with real churchwarden clay pipe.

Figure, (338), c.1800, probably Staffordshire, height: 14cm, (5½in), enamelled pearlware. Sailor leans on an anchor holding a bag of money.
Figure, (293), c.1850, London, height: 22.9cm, (9in), stoneware. Sailor leans on a coil of rope beside an anchor, holding a pipe; impressed, 'L. Dyer / Wine & Spirit Merchant / Kings Arms / Commercial Road East'.
Pepper or Pounce Pot, (259), c.1830, London, height: 14cm, (5½in), drab earthenware. Sailor, described by Willett as a boatswain, lightly enamelled and gilt.
Toby Jug, (258), c.1800, Staffordshire, height: 26.7cm, (10½in), enamelled pearlware. Sailor clutches a foaming mug of beer inscribed, 'SUCCESS TO OUR WOODEN WALLS' sits on a chest marked, 'DOLLARS'.
Figure, (279A), c.1854, Staffordshire, height: 19.7cm, (7¾in), enamelled earthenware. Sailor stands with arms akimbo.[23]

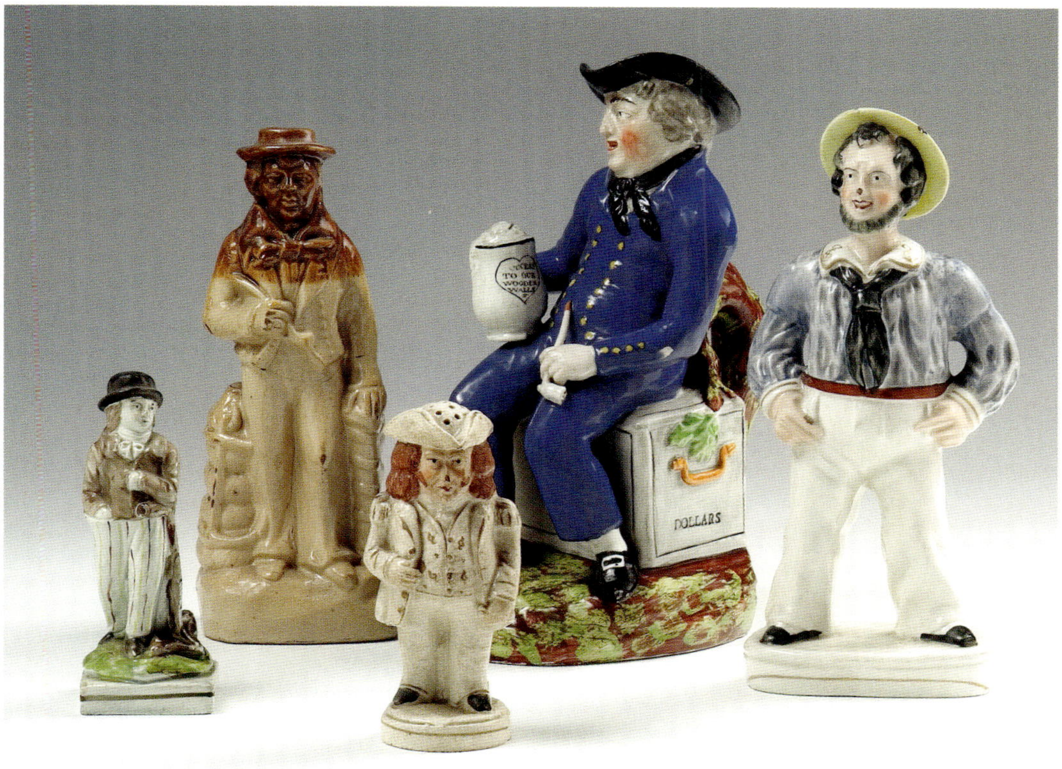

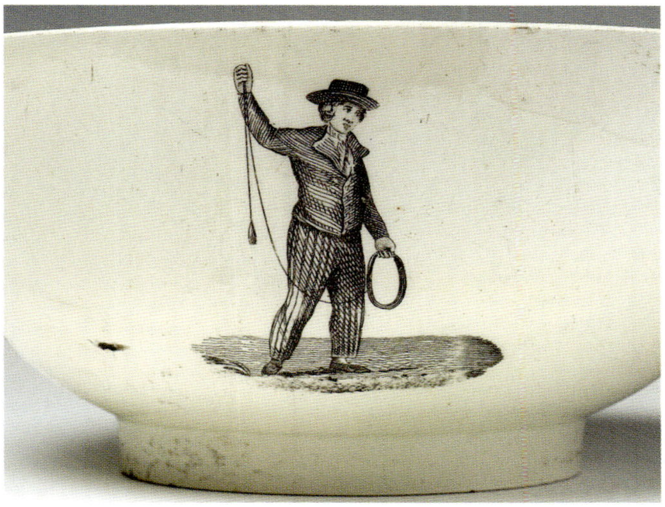

Punchbowl (detail), (046), c.1809, Liverpool, diameter: 17.8cm, (7in), printed creamware. Small vignettes of sailors at work; one reads a sextant (invented 1757), a refinement on the quadrant for calculating angles at sea, the sextant cost four times as much. The other figure 'heaves the lead'; the method for calculating water depth near coasts, to facilitate navigation or safe anchoring. A five-kilo lead weight, secured to a hemp rope of about twenty-five fathoms (up to fifty metres), marked at fathom intervals with leather strips, was tossed ahead of the ship and measured when vertical.

Jug, (340), c.1795, probably Staffordshire, height: 16.5cm, (6½in), printed creamware.
Jug, (335), c.1795, probably Staffordshire, height: 17.8cm, (7in), creamware, printed and coloured. Similar designs show sailors 'swinging the lead' beside prints of the mariners' compass.[24] Beneath title, 'COME BOX THE COMPASS' (to recite the compass points and quarter points), a potted history; 'Invented by Murphy a Dutchman / AD 1229 first exhibeted [*sic*] at Venice / 1260, improved by Giore of Naples / 1302 its declination discover'd by Hartman 1538'.
Jug, (318), c.1795, probably Liverpool, height: 21.6cm, (8½in), printed creamware. Signed in the compass centre by Joseph Johnson of Liverpool.
Jug, (333), c.1820, probably North East, height: 14.6cm, (5¾in), pearlware, printed and lustred. 'THE MARINER'S COMPASS' flanked by British ships, and patriotic verses.

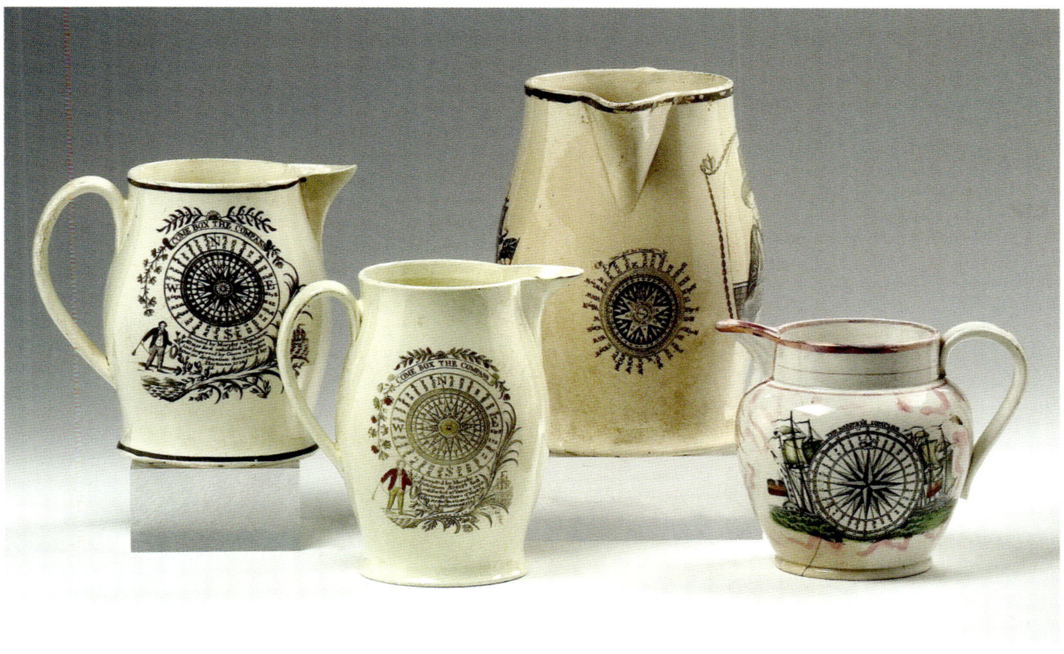

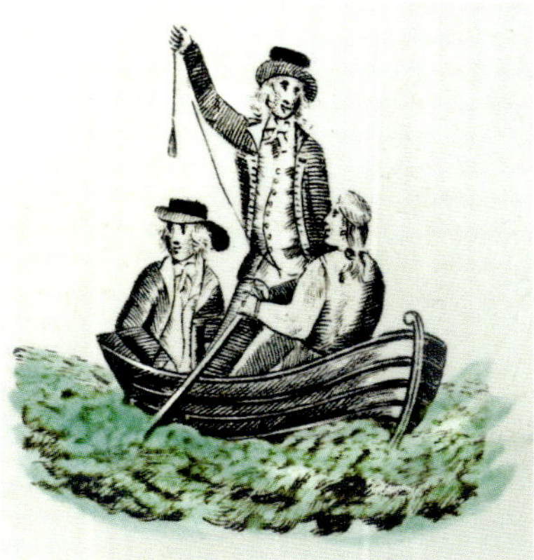

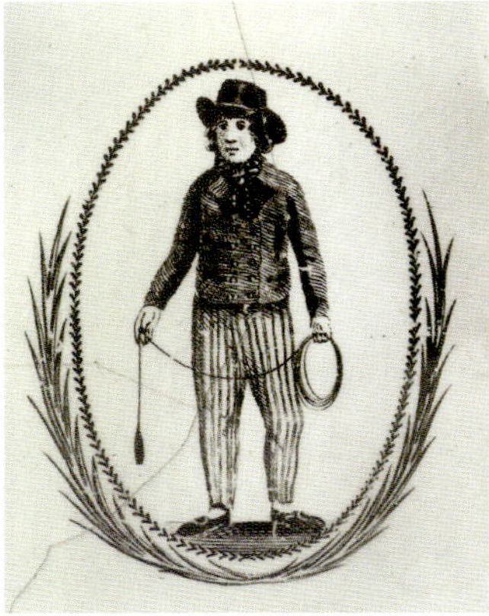

Vignettes of sailors at work with plumb lines appear quite often; three sailors in a rowing boat beneath the spout of one jug (302, see below), a singleton in an oval frame beneath the spout of another (285, see page 73).

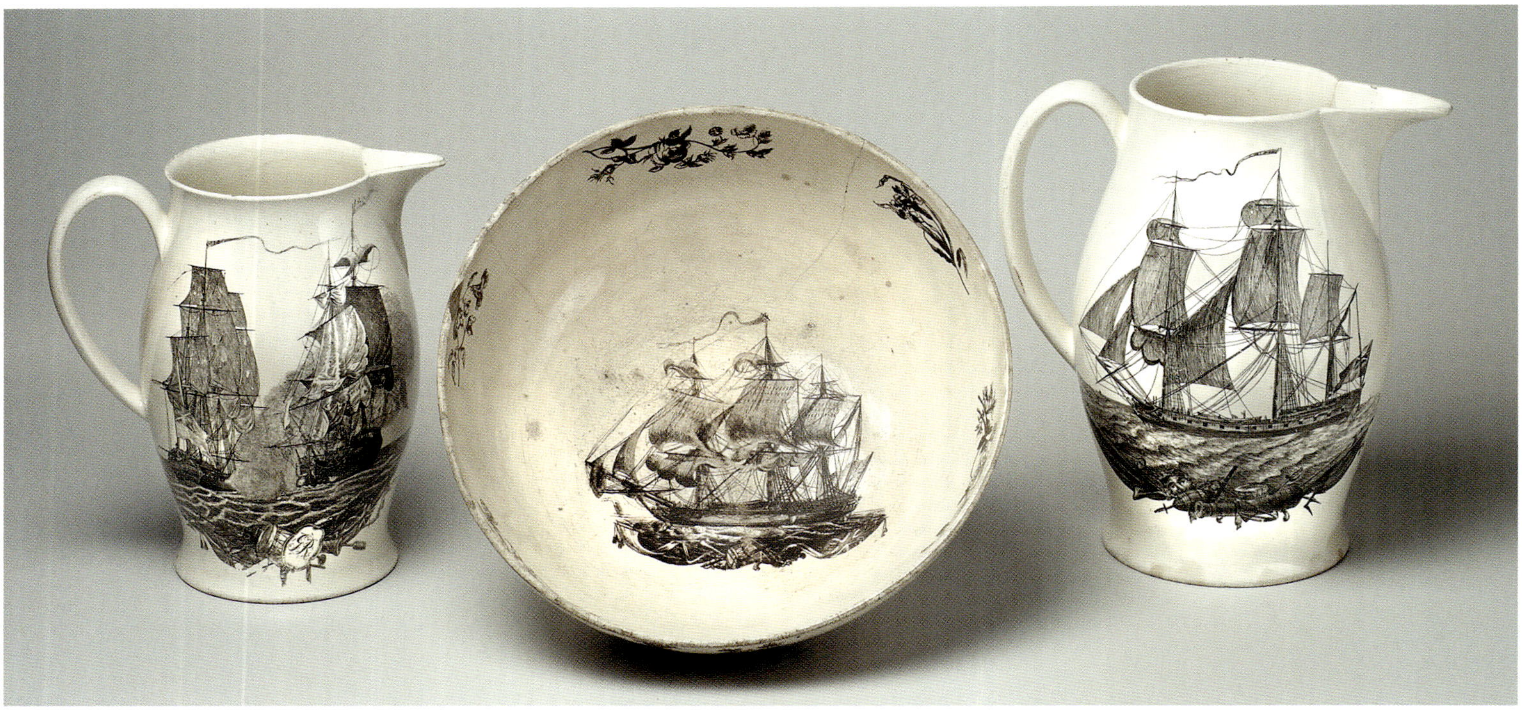

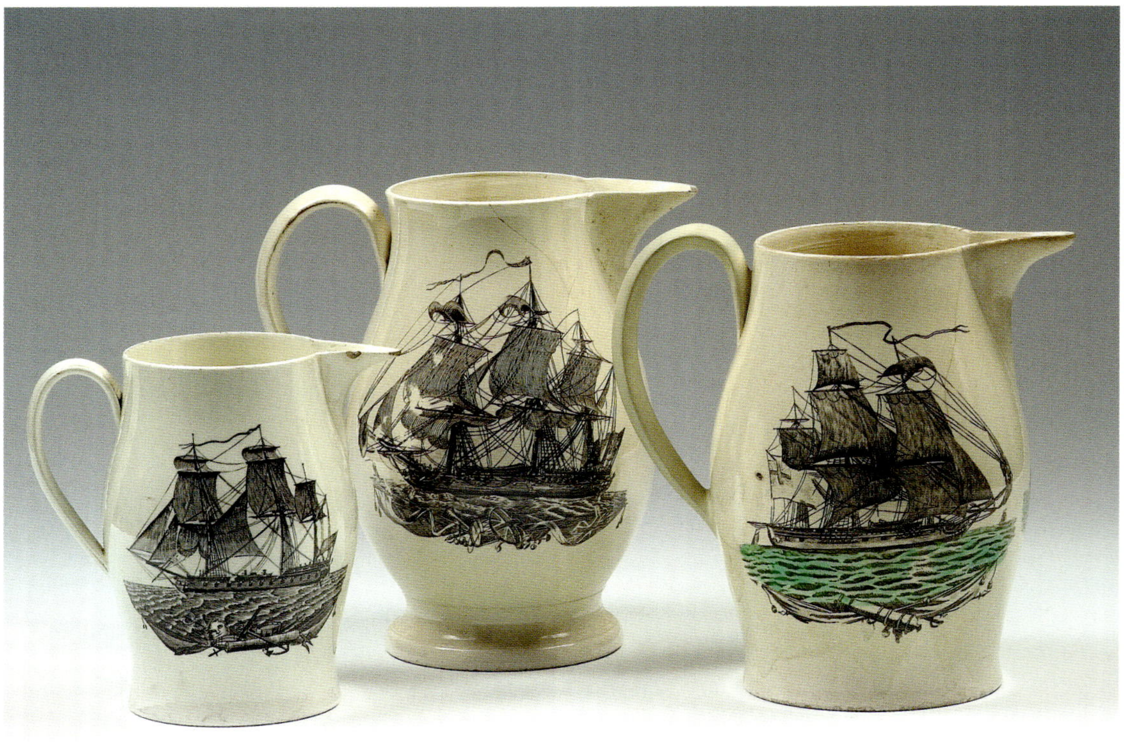

Two Jugs, (125 + 268), c.1778, Wedgwood probably printed in Liverpool, each height: 24.2cm, (9½in), printed creamware. Finely engraved scene of two ships engaged in battle on the reverse of a jug printed with the *Death of General Wolfe* and another large ship.
Punchbowl, (261), c.1790, Liverpool, printed by Sadler and Green, diameter: 27.3cm, (10¾in), printed creamware. A ship in full sail appears in the centre of bowl. Exterior with three river landscapes and scene with a nobleman flirting with a young woman.

Jug, (269), c.1795, Liverpool or Staffordshire, height: 15.3cm, (6in), printed creamware. A ship on port tack.
Jug, (337), c.1795, Liverpool or Staffordshire, height: 21cm, (8¼in), printed creamware. A ship on starboard tack.
Jug, (302), c.1795, Liverpool or Staffordshire, height: 19.1cm, (7½in), printed creamware. Printed and lightly enamelled with a British ship on port tack.

Jug, (337), c.1790, Liverpool or Staffordshire, height: 21cm, (8¼in), printed creamware. Entitled, 'The East View of Liverpool Light House' showing 53 signal flags. On the reverse, lists the 'BIDSTON / LIGHT HOUSE SIGNALS', surmounted by the Liver bird.
Jug, (319), c.1790, Liverpool or Staffordshire, height: 21.6cm, (8½in), printed creamware. Printed and enamelled with 'The East View of Liverpool Light House' showing 58 signal flags.
Mug, (320), c.1795, Liverpool, Joseph Johnson, height: 10.2cm, (4in), printed creamware. Entitled, 'The East View of Liverpool Light House & Signals on Bidston Hill 1789', shows the octagonal, stone lighthouse and 51 signals. In 1771 the Liverpool Corporation built the first lighthouse on Bidston Hill on the north side of the Wirral Peninsula, the highest point in the area, overlooking the main approach to the River Mersey. A navigational aid for shipping in the Rock Channel and a lookout and signal point, using ship-owners' flags, it heralded the return of vessels from America.[25]

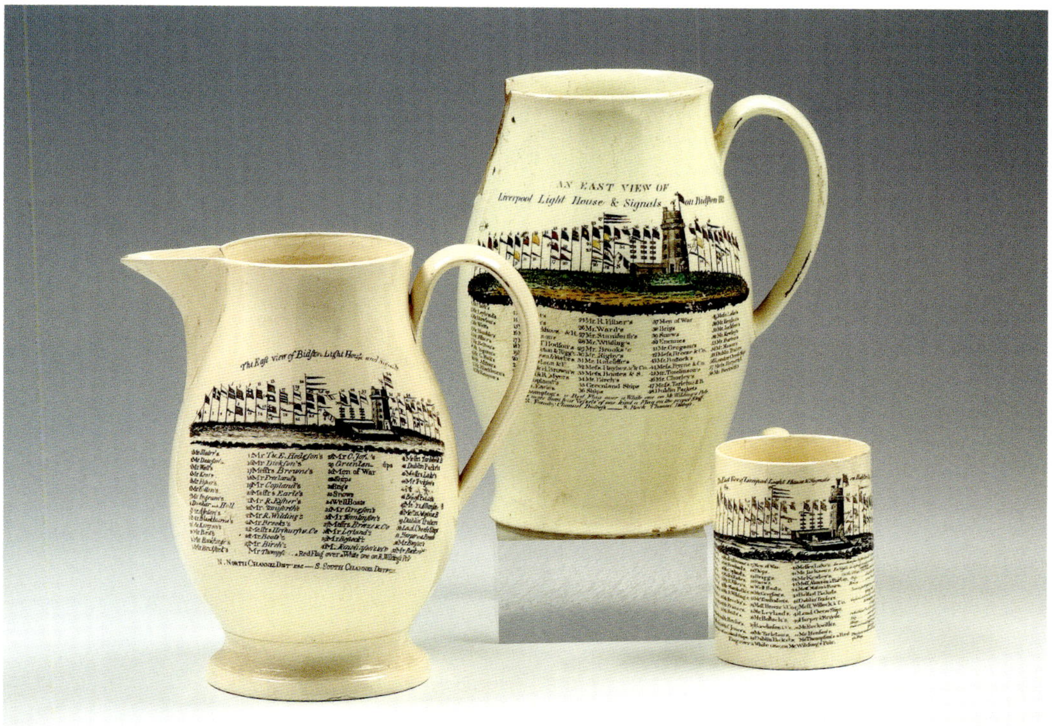

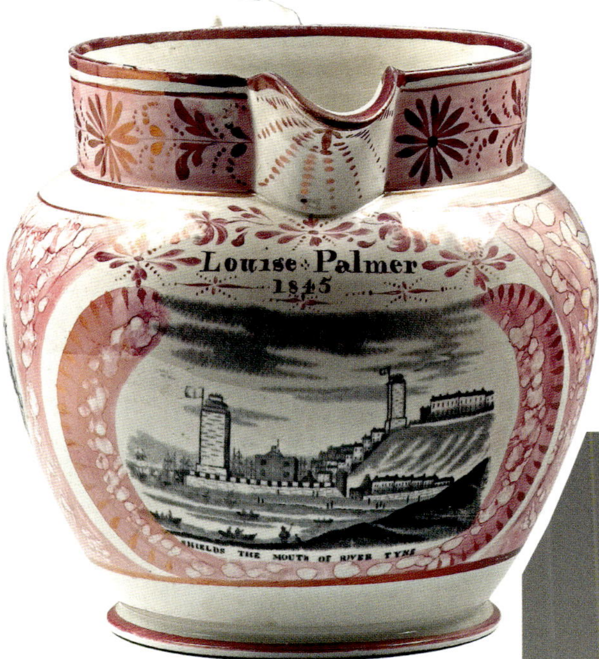

Jug, (308), c.1845, probably Newcastle upon Tyne, height: 22.9cm, (9in), earthenware, printed and lustred. Inscribed, 'Louise Palmer 1845' (to whom it was probably given), and printed with a city riverscape, entitled, 'SHIELDS THE MOUTH OF RIVER TYNE'. Small ships and lengthy verses on each side: 'The walls of old England are oak and they're strong / And our tars have the heart of the oak they belong / Oh! who is so brave so kind and so free / As he who defendeth the Queen of the Sea' and, 'How dear to the heart of the long absent tar / Is the home of his childhood to gaze on from far / When the cliffs of old Tynemouth appear to his view'.

Jug, (271), c.1800, probably Staffordshire, height: 17.8cm, (7in), Prattware. Relief-moulded with 'Sailor's Farewell' and on reverse, Britannia placing a wreath on the mast of a departing ship.
Jug, (291), c.1800, probably Staffordshire, height: 16.5cm, (6½in), Prattware. Sailor waves from the shore to a departing ship.
Jug, (292), c.1800, probably Staffordshire, height: 12.7cm, (5in), Prattware. Relief-moulded with sailor's sweetheart waving to him on his return.

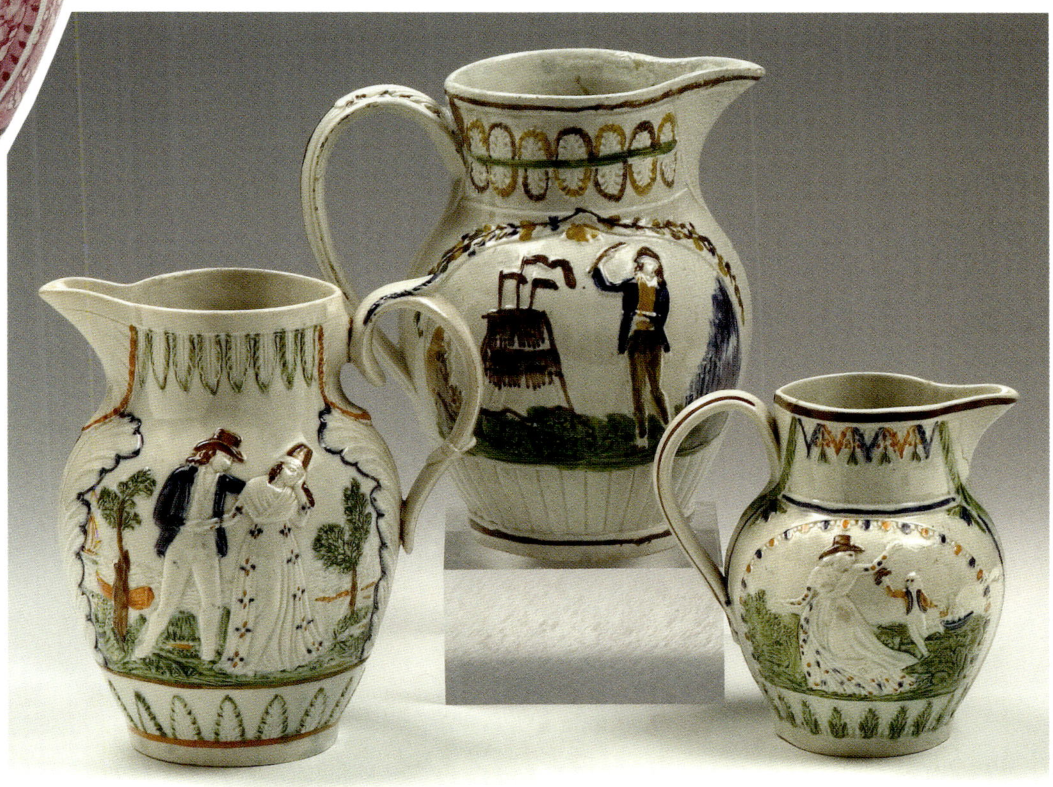

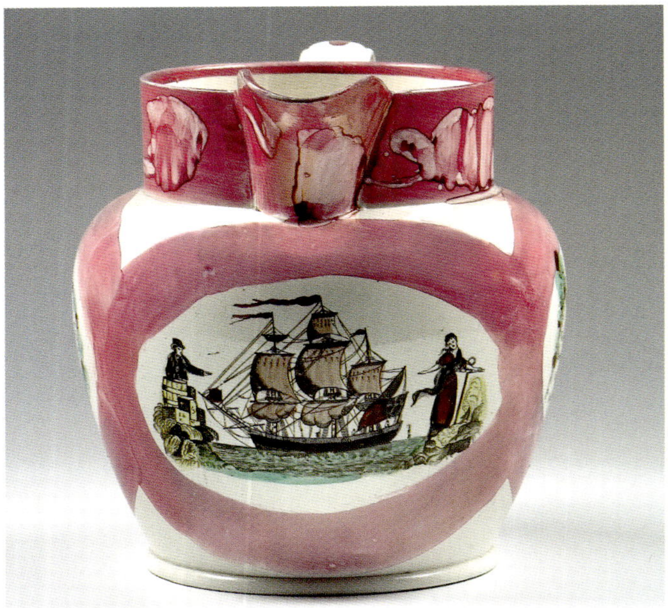

Jug, (309), c.1830, Newcastle upon Tyne, Collingwood & Beall, N Shields, height: 22.9cm, (9in), earthenware. Within broad bands of pink lustre, printed and enamelled with a British ship on starboard tack, flanked by a sailor sitting on crates and Hope with an anchor. Verses on each side, 'We sailors are born for all weathers / Great Guns let them blow high blow low / Our duty keeps us to our tethers / And where the gale drives we must go'.

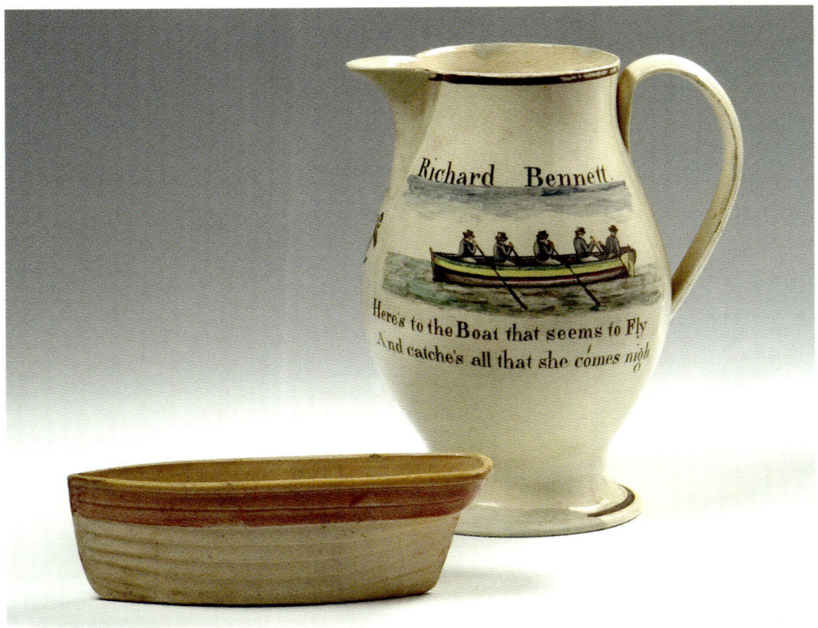

Boat Model, (321), c.1800, Staffordshire or Yorkshire, length: 21cm, (8¼in), drab earthenware. Rowing boat resembling models of cobles (fishing boats used mainly in the North East) attributed to the Stockton potteries, although this has a deeper keel.[26]
Jug, (296), c.1790, Staffordshire, height: 24.1cm, (9½in), enamelled creamware. Five men in a rowing boat inscribed above, 'Richard Bennett' and beneath, 'Here's to the Boat that seems to fly / And catches all that she comes nigh'. Printed with a ship on reverse and enamelled with an anchor beneath the spout.

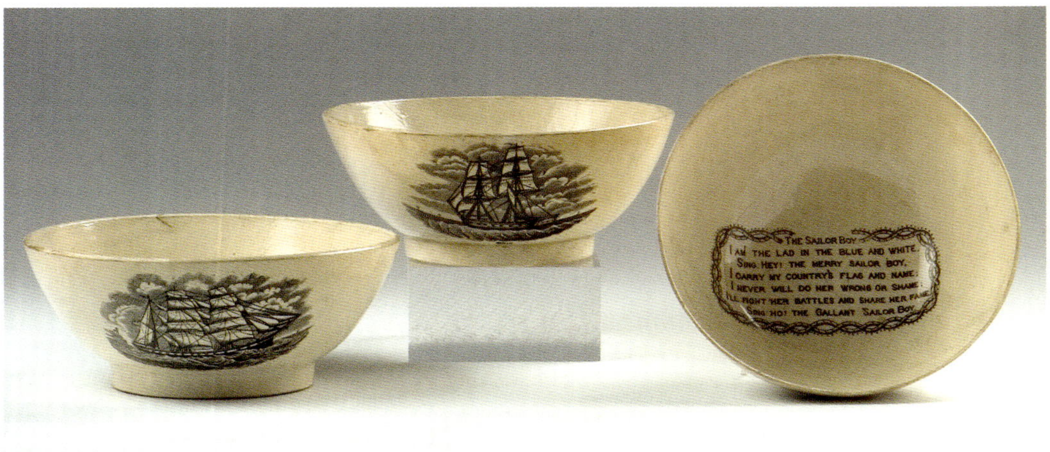

Three Bowls, (312, A & B), c.1830, Staffordshire, each diameter: 19.1cm, (7½in), printed creamware. Each printed with a different type of ship (one is identified as a 'BRIG') and shanties. These include 'The Sailor Boy', 'Look Aloft', (very popular with the American market), / 'In the tempest of life / when the wave and the gale / Are around and above / if thy footing should fail' and a patriotic British verse, 'There's one whose fearless courage / Yet has never failed in fight. / Who guards with zeal out country's weal / Our freedom and our right. / He's Britain's bost [*sic*], and claims a tost [*sic*]./ In peace my boys or war
Here's to the brave upon the wave / The gallant English tar.'

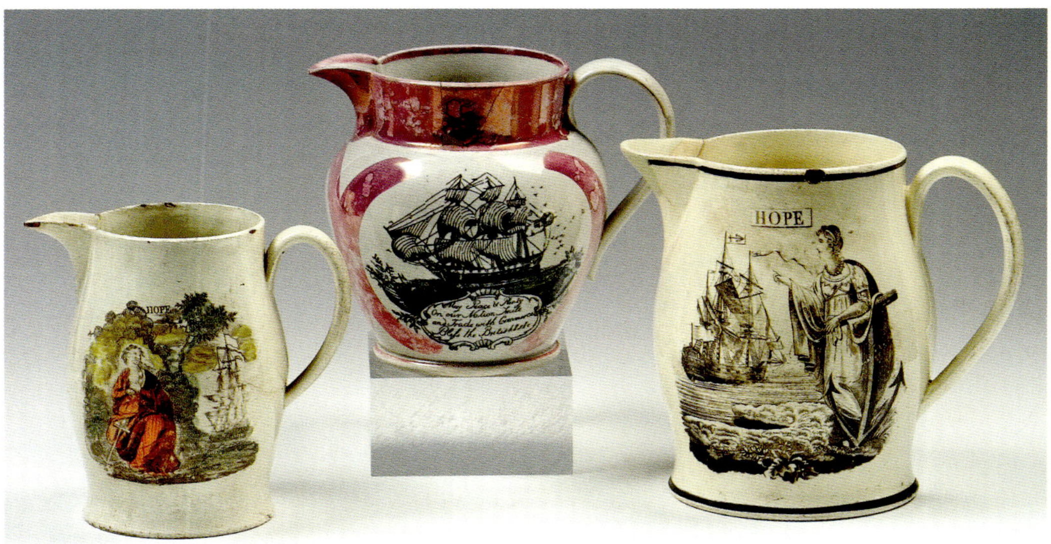

Jug, (476), c.1790, Staffordshire, height: 14.6cm, (5¾in), creamware, printed and enamelled. Hope kneels on seashore as a ship leaves harbour.
Jug, (315), c.1830, North East, height: 14.6cm, (5¾in), earthenware, printed and lustred. Within pink lustre bands, a ship on starboard tack and verses, 'May Peace with Plenty/On our Nation smile/ & Trade with Commerce / blefs the British Isle'... / 'The man doom'd to sail / With the blast of the gale/Through billows Atlantic to steer / As he bends o'er the wave / Which may soon be his grave/ Remembers his home with a tear'.
Jug, (340), c.1790, Staffordshire, height: 16.5cm, (6½in), printed creamware. Large figure of Hope points to a topmast pennant bearing a tiny anchor.

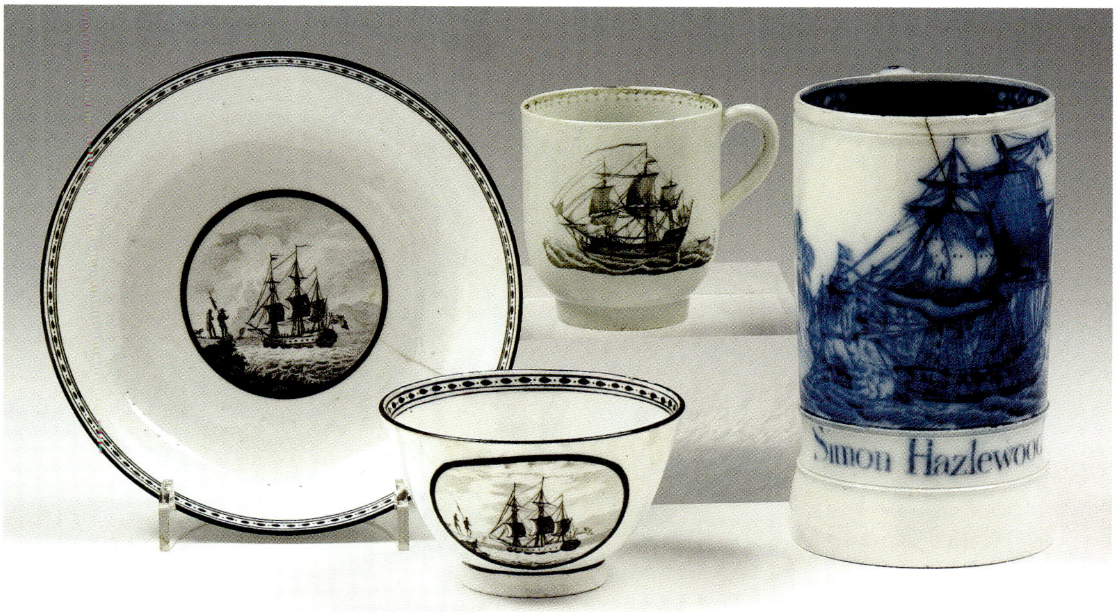

Tea Bowl and Saucer, (341 & A), c.1810, Staffordshire, Possibly Factory Z, height: 8.5cm, (3⅜in), diameter: 14cm, (5½in), soft-paste porcelain, printed and enamelled. Two figures and a dog watching a British ship.
Coffee Cup, (342), c.1775, possibly Liverpool,[27] height: 6.4cm, (2½in), soft-paste porcelain. Enamelled with views of ships, possibly made in Liverpool.
Mug, (317), c.1800, possibly made in Wales, height: 13.3cm, (5¼in), blue-printed pearlware. Printed with a warship in action and inscribed, 'Simon Hazlewood'. It is unknown whether the name refers to the ship, the owner or a member of the crew but it does not appear in Lloyds Register.[28]

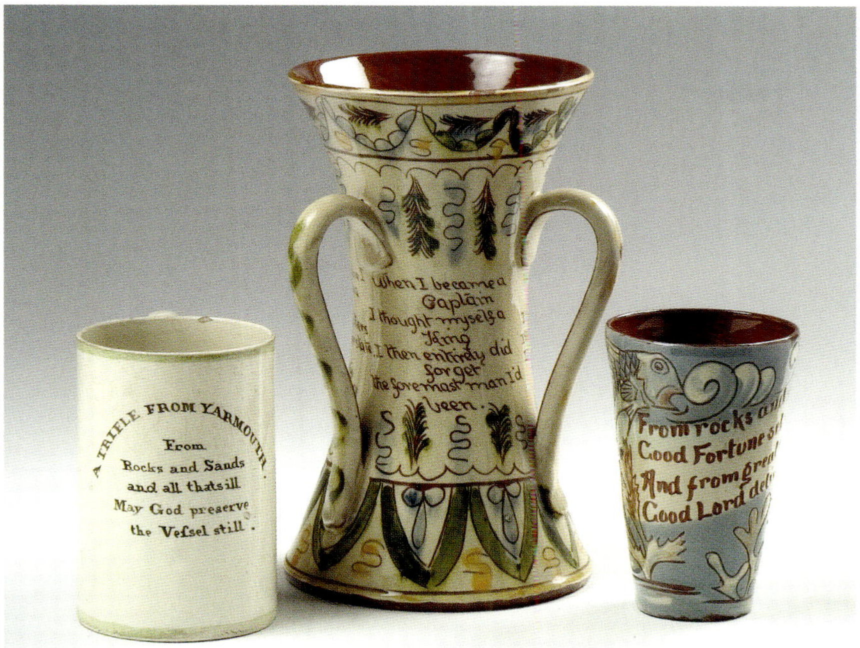

Mug, (326), c.1790, Staffordshire, height: 12.1cm, (4¾in), enamelled creamware. Inscribed (probably by Absolon of Yarmouth), 'A TRIFLE FROM YARMOUTH / From Rocks and Sands and all that's ill May God preserve the Vefsel still'.
Three-handled Cup, (329), c.1890, Devon, height: 22.2cm, (8¾in), coloured slipware. Based on the medieval tyg, sgraffito-incised, 'When first I was a foremast man / I often did pretend / If e'er I got promotion / I'd be a seaman's friend. / But in a little time / was promoted to be a mate / I then like many others / forgot my former state / When I became a captain / I thought myself a King / I then entirely did forget / the foremast man I'd been'.
Beaker, (324), c.1890, C.H. Brannam, North Devon, Barnstaple, height: 12.7cm, (5in), coloured slipware. Sgraffito-incised with design of a fish and seaweed and a verse, 'From rocks and sand and barren land / Good Fortune set me free / And from great Guns and Women's tongues / Good Lord deliver me'.[29]

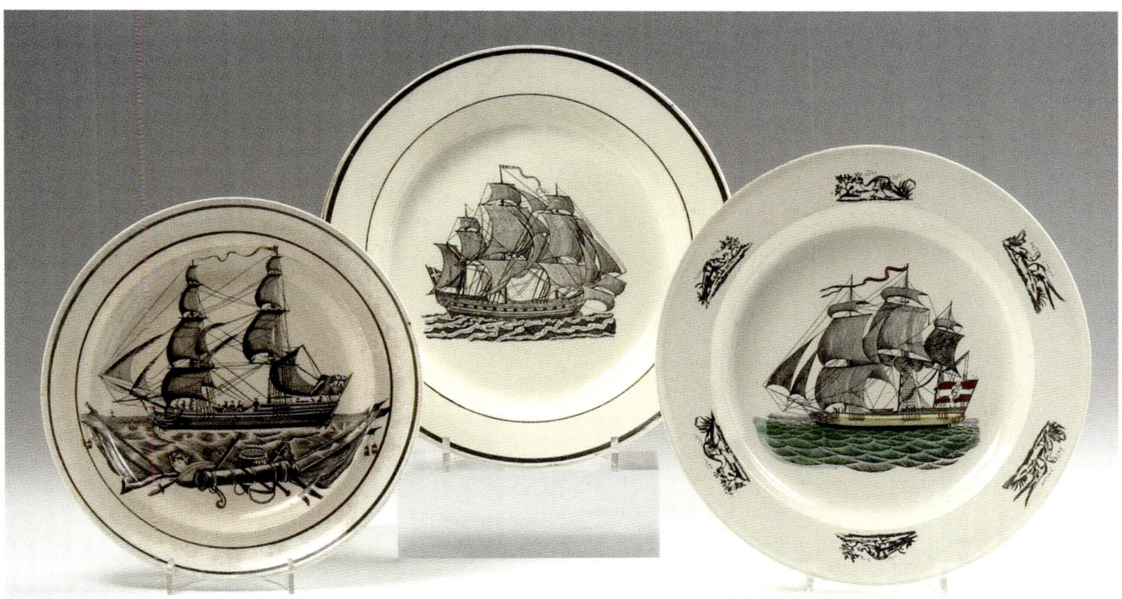

Plate, (R.603/7), c.1800, Swansea, Dillwyn's Cambrian Pottery, diameter: 21.6cm, (8½in), printed creamware. Printed with a ship on port tack and enamel bands.
Plate, (313), c.1800, Liverpool, diameter: 24.8cm, (9¾in), creamware. Printed with unnamed ship on starboard tack.
Plate, (328), c.1800, Liverpool, diameter: 24.8cm, (9¾in), creamware. Printed vignettes of birds around rim and unnamed ship on port tack flying what may be the Danish flag marked 'C7' (for Christian VII of Denmark; 1766–1808).

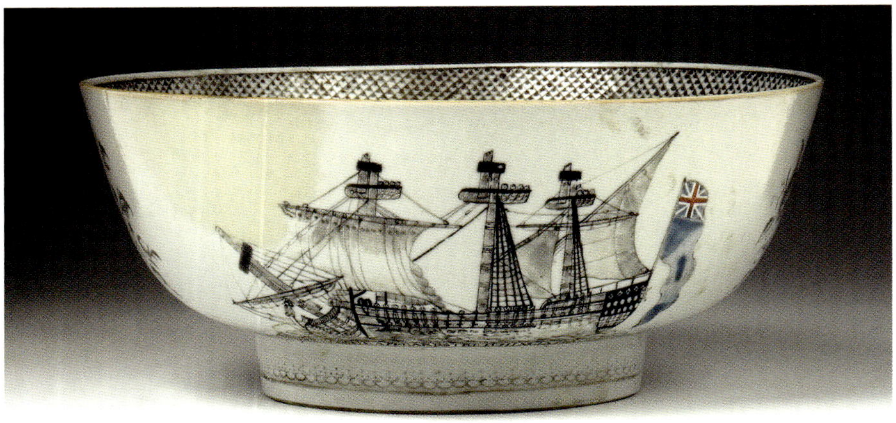

Punchbowl, (311), c.1776, China, diameter: 28cm, (11in), enamelled, hard-paste porcelain. Painted with two views of the same ship. Inscribed around the foot-ring junction, 'A SECOND VIEW OF THE EARL OF SANDWICH IN THE SAME GALE / A 3RD VIEW OF THE EARL OF SANDWICH AS SHE APPEARD STRETCHING IN FOR THE LAND NOV. 12TH, 1776. LATT21D.X12'. The *Earl of Sandwich* was probably named after the fourth Earl, three times First Lord of the Admiralty, lastly from 1771to 1782. The East India Company ship made four voyages and is listed in Lloyds Register of Shipping for 1776 as embarking for China on its second voyage under Captain Charles Dean, when it weighed 804 tons fully laden (she must have been unusually large).[30] The inscriptions suggest that the ship has been drawn directly from an engraved record of the voyage.

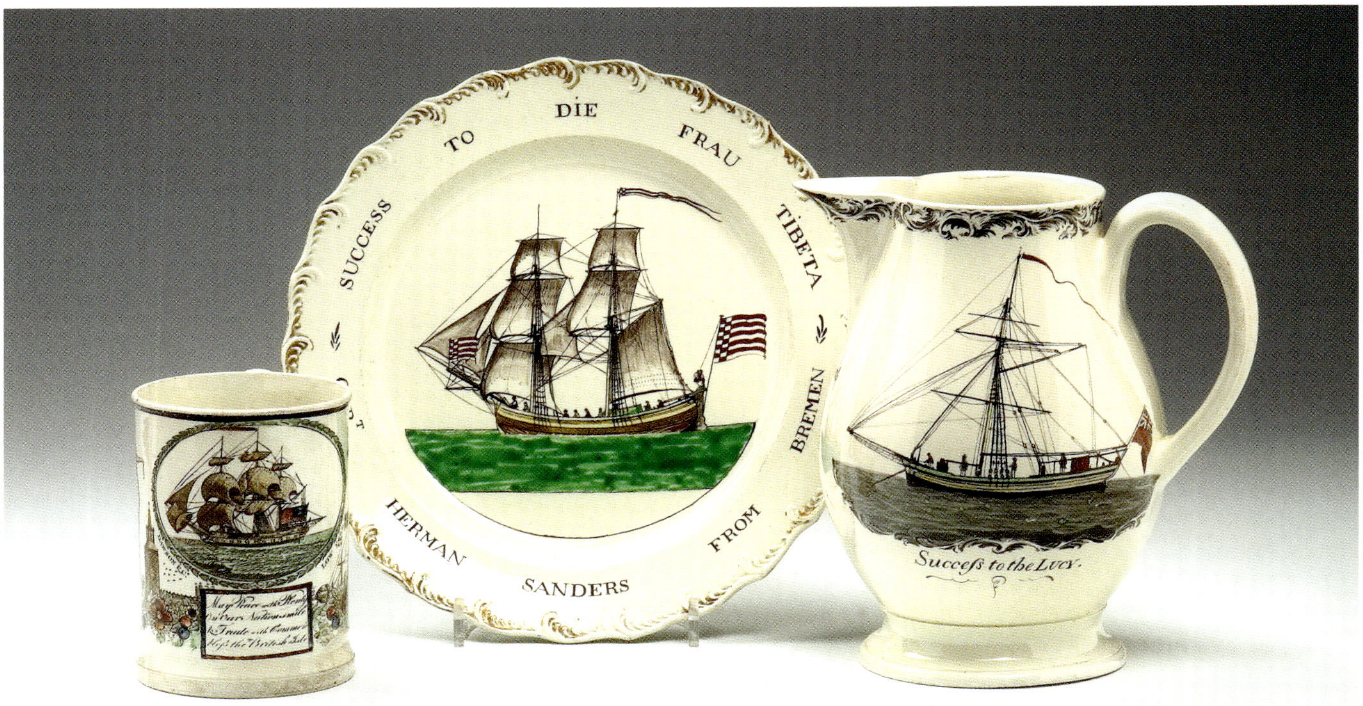

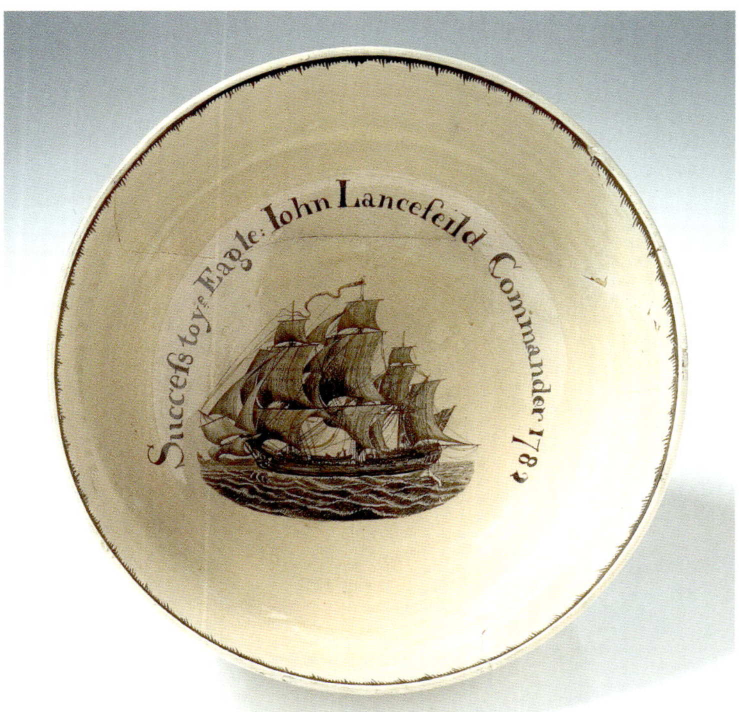

Mug, (322), c.1805, Sunderland, Dawson's, Low Ford, height: 11.5cm, (4½in), printed creamware. Ship and verse, 'May Peace and Plenty / On our Nation smile / & Trade and Commerce / Bless the British Isle'. Initials W.C. for Walter Cockburn, a silversmith and engraver of Bishopwearmouth, Sunderland, who worked for John Dawson & Co.[31]

Plate, (316), c.1780, Staffordshire, diameter: 24.2cm, (9½in), creamware, enamelled and gilt. Portrait of a German ship on port tack. Inscribed, 'SUCCESS TO DiE FRAU TIBETA / CAPT HERMAN SANDERS FROM BREMEN'. Probably commissioned as part of a service by or for the German captain while in a British port.[32]

Jug, (336), 1788, Staffordshire, Wedgwood, height: 19.7cm, (7¾in), enamelled creamware. Ship, inscribed, 'Succefs to the LUCY' and beneath spout, 'Mrs Elizabeth / Lear, / Portsmouth / Hants / 1788'.[33] The *Lucy*, described as a Revenue Cutter, is rigged but not yet fitted with sails. She flies the seagoing version of the Union Flag and is secured with anchors on both sides. *The Lucy* has not yet been identified. The date 1788 could be relevant to the unknown Mrs Lear or to the launch of The *Lucy* itself.

Punchbowl, (330), c,1782, Liverpool, diameter: 27.9cm, (11in), printed creamware. Exterior vignettes of figures in landscapes, in the centre a ship on starboard tack, inscribed in black enamel, 'Success to ye Eagle: John Lancefeild [*sic*] Commander 1782'. The *Eagle* (250 tons, of French origin) is recorded in Lloyds Register as being under the command of John Lancefield in 1782-3 when it went from London to Antigua. By 1783-4 it was commanded by J. Dearon and went from London to Greenland. One of the exterior vignettes, known as 'The Three Fishers' or 'The Bird Catchers', probably derives from a French or Dutch original, which was used on Worcester porcelain around 1760.[34]

Jug, (336), 1788, Staffordshire, Wedgwood, height: 19.7cm, (7¾in), creamware. Printed with figure of Hope leaning on an anchor.
Plate, (073), 1790-91, Worcester, diameter: 24.2cm, (9½in), soft-paste porcelain. Richly bordered in dark blue enamel and gilt, centre painted in grisaille with figure of Hope and a departing ship. Part of an extensive service made for William, (later William IV) Duke of Clarence and used by him at his home, Bushey Park. For 800 guineas, Flight and Barr's Worcester factory supplied over 260 pieces, each one painted by John Pennington with Hope in a variety of poses.

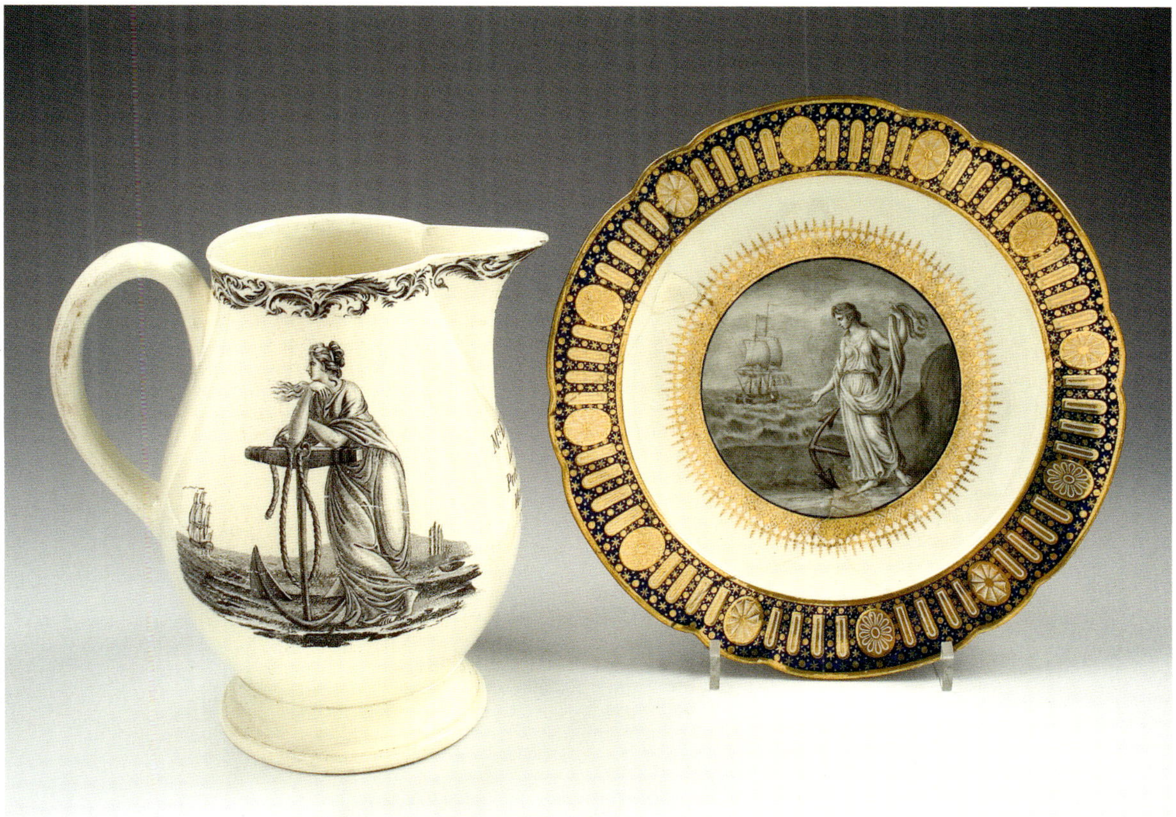

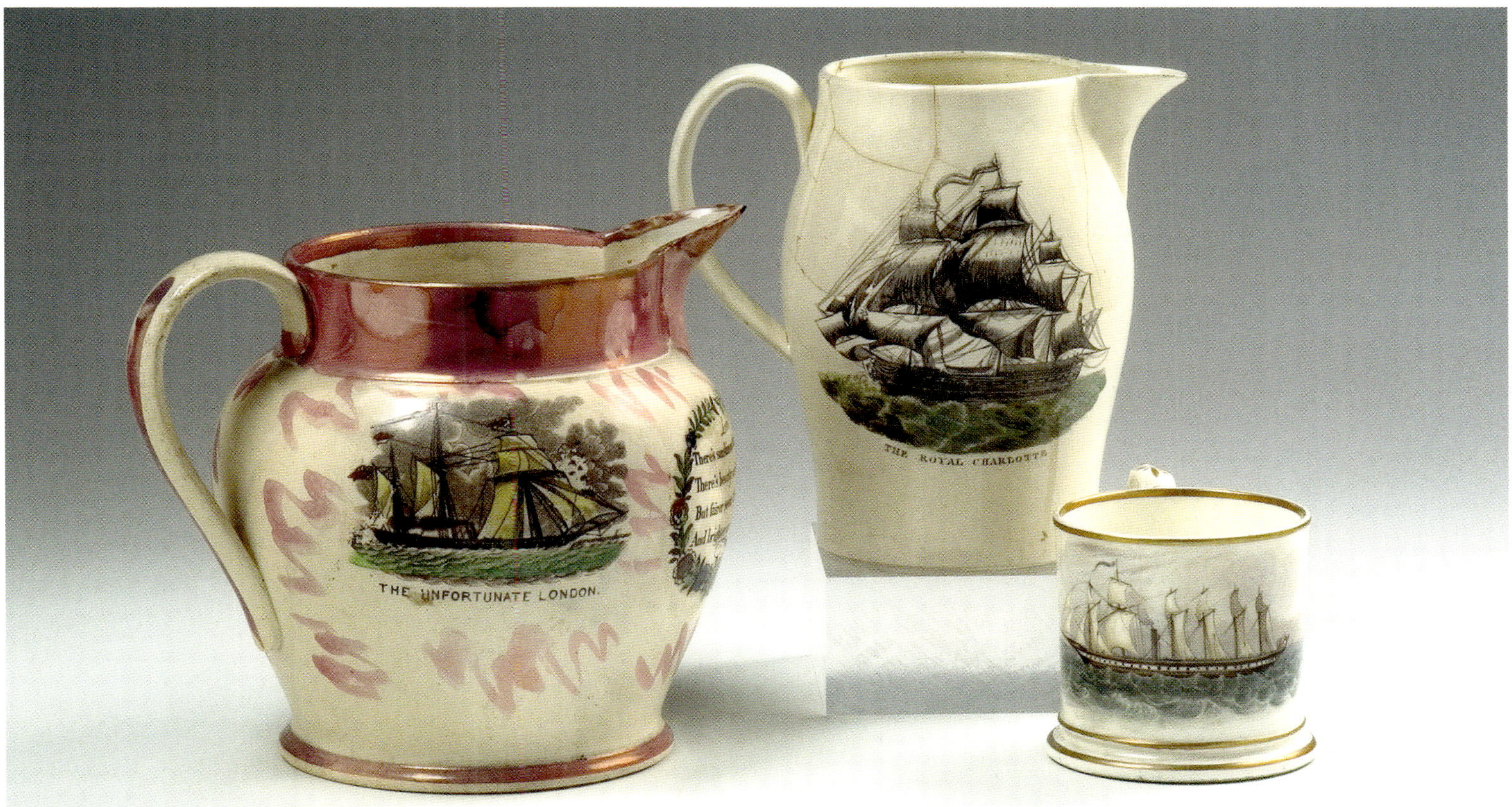

Jug, (332), c.1870, Sunderland, height: 19.1cm, (7½in), earthenware, printed and lustred. On one side, 'THE UNFORTUNATE LONDON', on starboard tack, and on the other 'THE GREAT AUSTRALIA CLIPPER SHIP', on port tack.[35] A short, sentimental verse beneath the spout. The *London* was indeed unfortunate. Lloyds Register notes that the huge iron, screw steamer (267 feet long, weighing 1752 tons), launched in 1864, sank in 1866, on a voyage from London to Australia. The *Australia* was one of the fast trading ships that transported tea or grain around the world.
Jug, (303), c.1785, Liverpool, height: 17.8cm, (7in), creamware. Printed with 'THE ROYAL CHARLOTTE', one of George III's ships. Launched in 1740 as the *Royal Caroline* (for his grandmother), it was a rigged vessel of 232 tons, armed with ten guns. Renamed in 1761, it led the fleet that brought Princess Charlotte of Mecklenburg-Strelitz to England to become the new Queen Consort.
Mug, (R2454.16), c.1843, possibly Staffordshire, height: 8.5cm, (3⅜in), bone china. Finely painted with the steamship *Great Britain* (inscribed beneath). A revolutionary, propeller-driven design by Isambard Kingdom Brunel, she was launched in 1843 and reached New York in 14 days. Unfortunately she ran aground in Ireland in 1846.

Wine, Women and Song

Sailors traditionally celebrated shore leave with gusto. Armed with pay or prize money they could dance hornpipes on terra firma, drink to excess and attract temporary female companions. They also danced at sea; 'Every moonlight night the sailors dance' wrote Admiral Collingwood.[36] Private Wheeler of the *Revenge* recalled, 'Two evenings a week is devoted to amusement… some [dance] to a fiddle, others to a fife … a select party immortalize the heroes of by days by singing songs to the memory of Duncan, Howe, Vincent and the immortal Nelson'.[37]

A number of ceramic subjects allude to sailors' weakness for prostitutes. Some episodes are archly described in euphemistic naval language while the scenes they depict are more direct.

Scenes of sailors making merry proliferated with the success of the maritime ballads written by Charles Dibdin (1745-1814).[38] The stage productions of this prolific composer and impresario were said to have brought more men into the Navy than the entire efforts of the press gang. Dibdin showed precocious musical talent and after an erratic early career, which included volatile partnerships with Isaac Bickerstaffe and David Garrick, he earned fame and fortune in the 1790s through successful stage shows and a profitable London shop. This enabled him to retain copyright of his most popular songs, of which he claimed to have written 900.

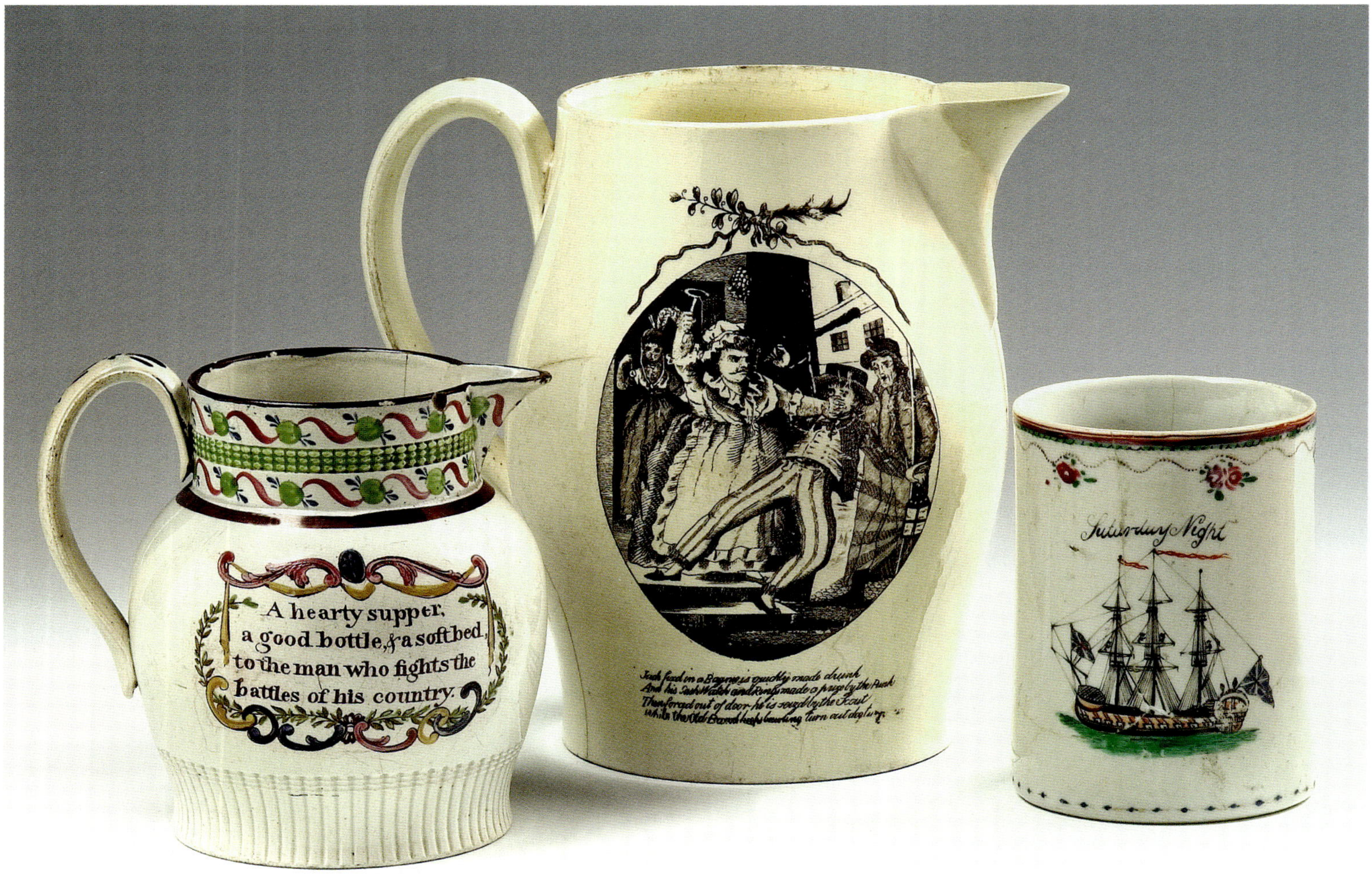

Jug, (284), c.1810, Staffordshire, height: 14cm, (5½in), pearlware. printed and enamelled with a spray of flowers and inscription, 'A hearty supper / a good bottle, & a soft bed, / to the man who fights the / battles of his country'.
Jug, (304), c.1780, Liverpool, height: 20.3cm, (8in), creamware.
A sailor is thrown out of a brothel by a stout madam, while a nightwatchman looks on. Verses explain, 'Jack fix'd in a Bagno[39] is quickly made drunk'.
And his Sash, Watch and Rings made a prize by the punk
Then forc'd out of door he is seiz'd by the Scout
While the Old Bawd keeps bawling, turn out dog, turn out.
Mug, (283), China, height: 11.4cm, (4½in), enamelled, hard-paste porcelain. A British ship at anchor entitled, 'Suturday [*sic*] Night' the preferred night for merry making. Handle missing but mug retains four elaborate (Leeds-style) floral terminals.

Opposite:
Tile, (299), c.1760, Liverpool, printed by John Sadler, height: 12.1cm, (4¾in), printed, tin-glazed earthenware. Happy sailors on shore leave drink with girlfriends at 'The King of Prussia' tavern, (from the inn sign that hangs above their heads). The image is a well-known version of the 'Sailor's Return', pendant to the 'Sailor's Farewell'.[40] Frederick 'the Great', King of Prussia, a British ally during the Seven Years War, enjoyed immense popularity in Britain, especially from 1757 to 1760.[41]
Jug, (305), c.1800, Liverpool , height: 22.9cm, (9in), printed creamware. Sailors carouse at a table, beneath a banner inscribed, 'WE ANCHOR ON OUR NATIVE SHORE'. This drinking scene shows a variant on the subject of Charles Dibdin's song, 'Sweetheart and Wives / Twas Saturday night'.
Mug, (281), c.1800, Staffordshire, height: 9.2cm, (3⅝in), printed creamware Entitled, 'THE WAND'RING SAILOR', sailors carouse at a waterfront inn with a verse, 'When round the bowl the jovial crew / The early scenes of youth renew May we, when toil and danger's o'er, / Cast anchor on our native shore!'

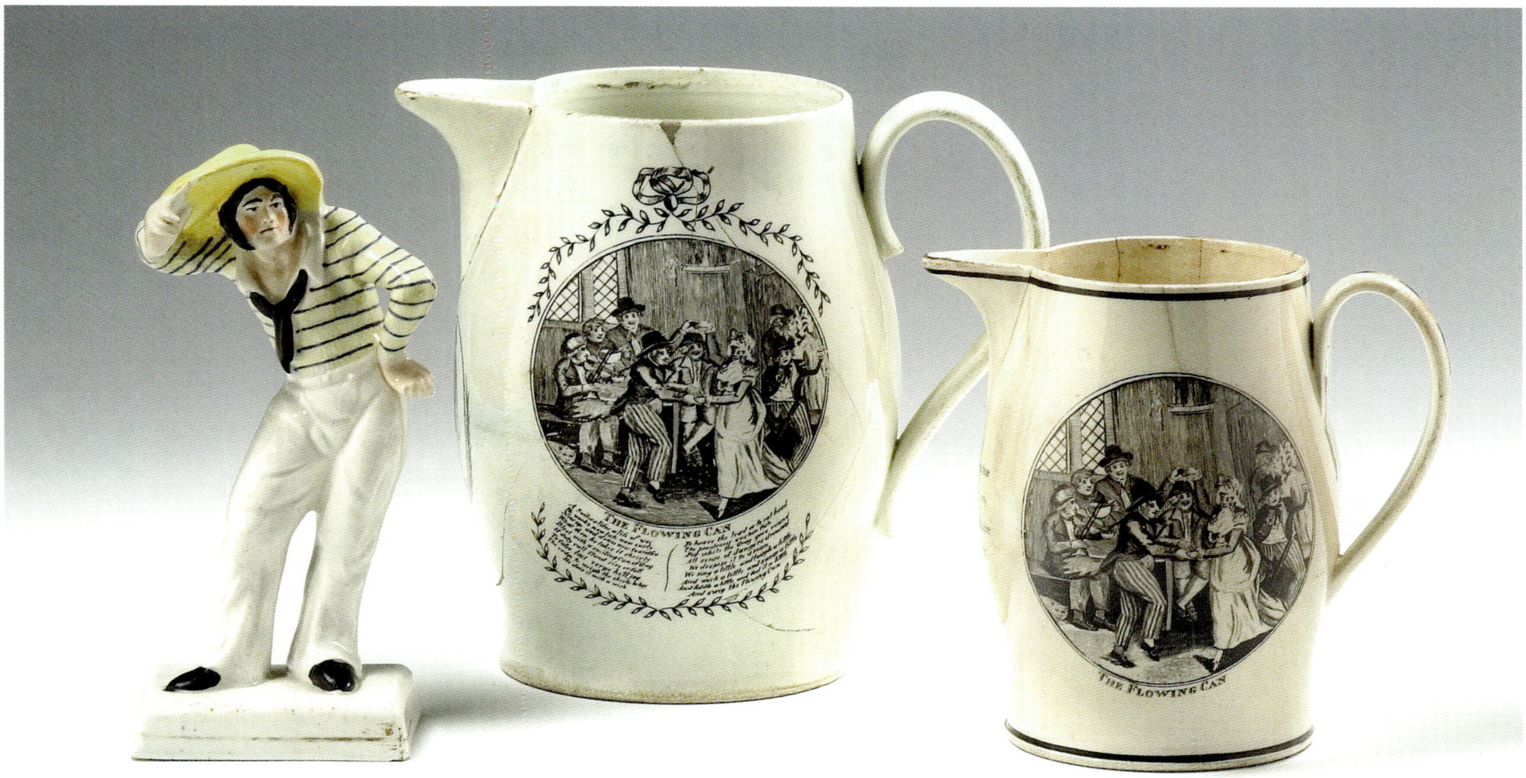

Figure, (279), c.1870, Staffordshire, height: 19.8cm, (7¾in), enamelled earthenware. A sailor in striped shirt, white trousers and a large straw hat, dances a hornpipe.
Jug, (285), c.1795, Liverpool, height: 21.6cm, (8½in), printed creamware. 'THE FLOWING CAN', an animated tavern dance scene, taken from a print published 1791, here accompanied by Dibdin's verses for his *Oddities* programme of 1789.[42] (There are ships printed on the reverse of both jugs here.)
'A sailor's life's a life of woe / He works now late now early
Now up and down, now to and fro, / What then he takes it cheerly
Blest with a smiling can of grog …
For while the grog goes round / All sense of danger's drown'd
We despise it to a man.
We sing a little, we laugh a little / And work a little and foot it a little
And swig the flowing can'.
Jug, (290), c.1795, Staffordshire, height: 16.5cm, (6½in), printed creamware. 'The Flowing Can', and inscribed beneath the spout,
'May Winsford continue / To flourish in Trade
Till the Globe shall dissolve, / Not leaving a shade.'
Winsford in Cheshire was important for salt production.

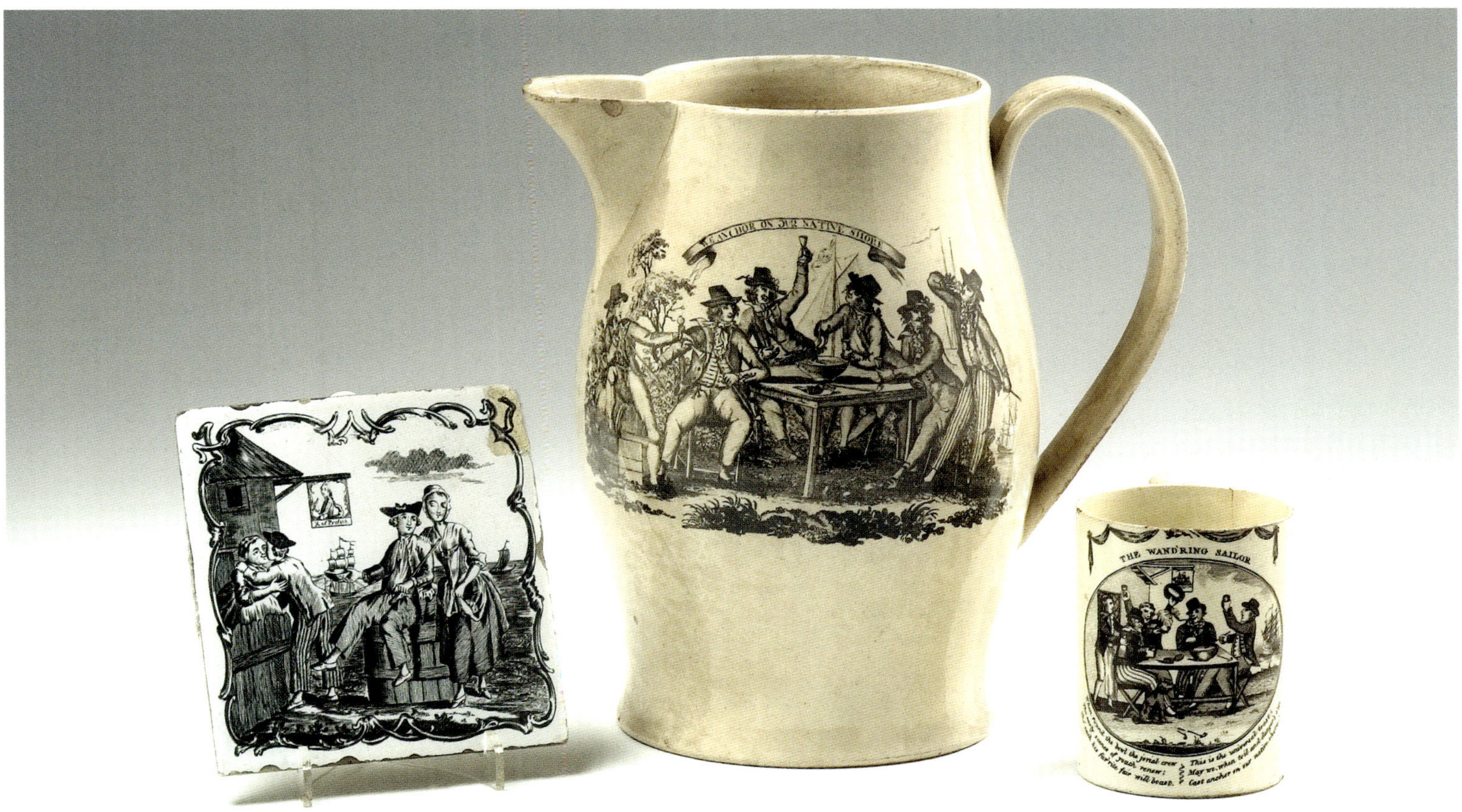

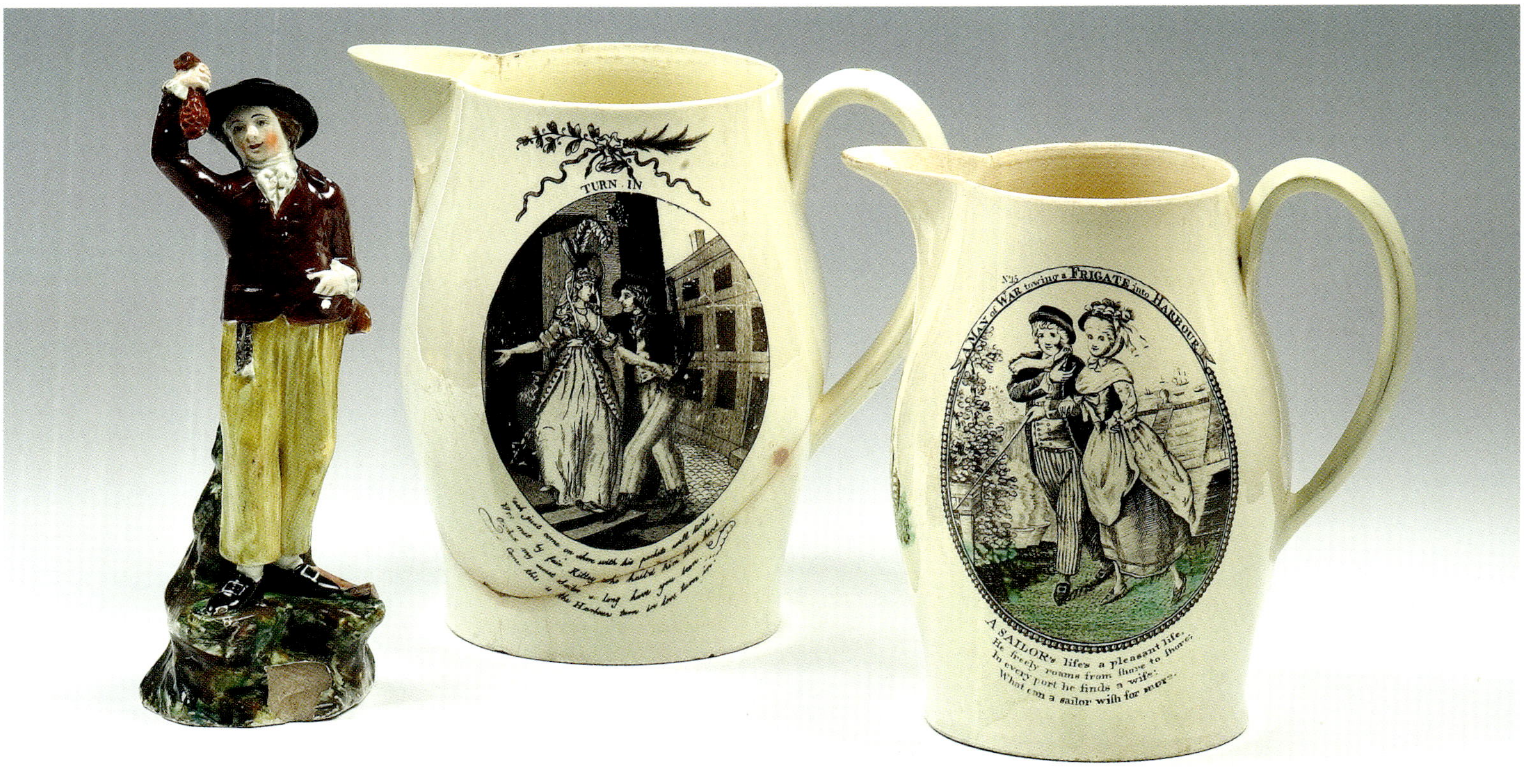

Figure, (288), c.1800 Staffordshire, height: 22.9cm, (9in), enamelled pearlware. A sailor leans on an anchor on a grassy mound, holding a bag of money. He could use this to pay for drink and a woman while on shore leave.

Jug, (304), c.1790, Liverpool, height: 20.3cm, (8in), printed creamware. A sailor is led into a house by an exotically-dressed prostitute, inscribed 'TURN IN', with verse, 'Jack just come on shore with his pockets well lin'd, / Was met by fair Kittey who hail'd him thus kind / Oh where my sweet sailor so long have you been / Come this is the harbour, turn in love, turn in'.

Jug, (302), c.1790, Liverpool, height: 19.1cm, (7½in), creamware, printed and enamelled. 'No 15. A MAN of WAR towing a FRIGATE into HARBOUR', shows a sailor and a young woman promenading, with a verse,
'A sailor's life's a pleasant life / He freely roams from shore to shore;
In every port he finds a wife; / What can a sailor wish for more'.
The print was one of a series published by Carrington Bowles around 1781 after designs by Robert Dighton.[43]

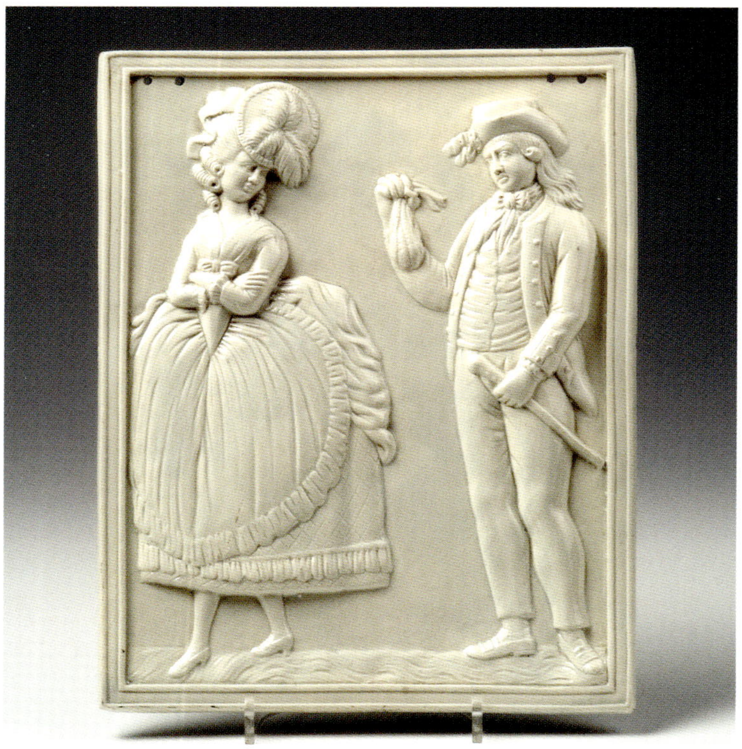

Plaque, (298), c.1785, Staffordshire, height: 28.6cm, (11¼in), pearlware. Relief-moulded with figures of a well-dressed young woman looking backwards at a sailor with a swagger stick (provocatively placed) and a bag of money. This popular subject is known as 'Jack on a Cruise', after a print by Sayer and Bennett that is probably the source for several scenes of the sailor ashore, seeking a prostitute.[44]

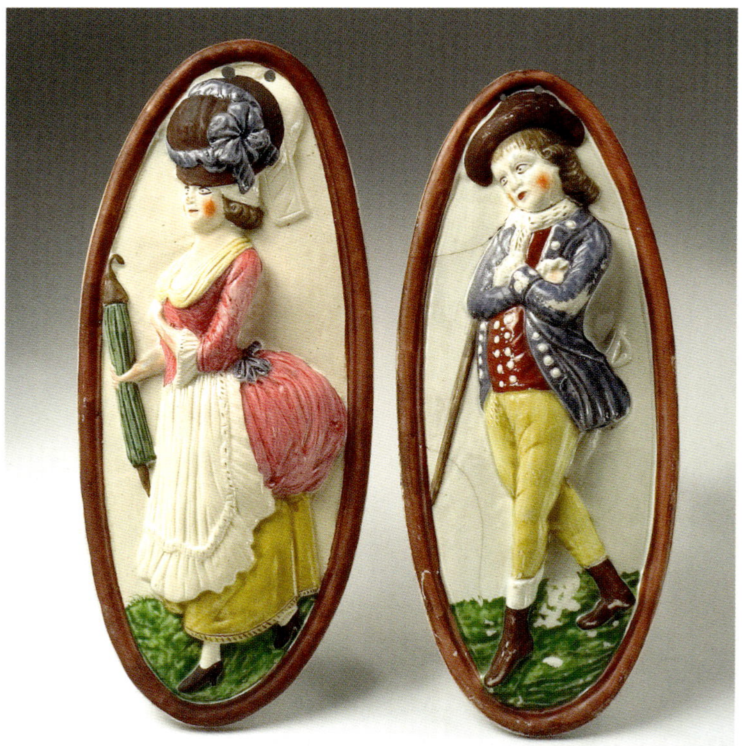

Pair of Plaques, (1665 & A), c.1790, Staffordshire, Burslem?, each height: 25.4cm, (10in), enamelled pearlware. Relief-moulded plaques, possibly by Wood family, of a sailor on shore leave and a fashionable young woman. Nicknamed, 'Patricia and her Lover', it is taken from a print entitled, 'Jack on a Cruise' published by Robert Sayers, c.1785.[45]

Sweethearts and Wives

Late eighteenth and early-nineteenth century literature is full of the excitement of the arrival of the regiment in a country town and the poignancy of its departure. As Mrs Bennet recalls, 'I remember the time when I liked a red coat myself very well – and indeed so I do still at my heart'.[46] Young women were very susceptible to young men in uniform. Such romantic encounters were frequently presented on the stage and are depicted on ceramics.

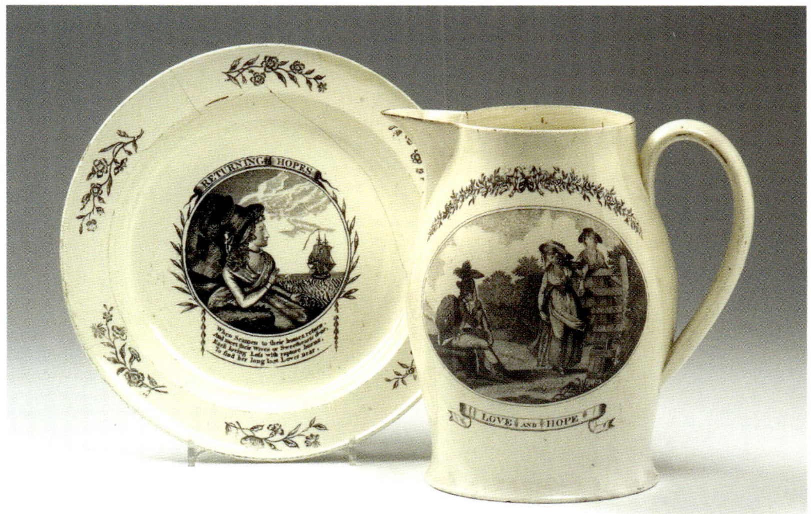

Plate, (295), c.1790, Liverpool Herculaneum, diameter: 25.4cm, (10in), printed creamware. A woman looks towards a ship on the horizon, entitled, 'RETURNING HOPES' and inscribed, 'When seamen to their homes return / And meet their wives or sweethearts dear, / Each loving Lass with rapture burns, / To find her long lost Lover near' The source (identified by Joyce Cockerill) is the second of a pair of prints (the pendant to 'Parting Wishes'), published by C. Taylor of Holborn, London, 1 April 1791.
Jug, (251), c.1790, probably Liverpool, height: 21.6cm, (8½in), printed creamware. 'LOVE AND HOPE' shows two young women climbing a stile beside a seated soldier. The print source is a stipple engraving by Knight after Bunbury, published by Dickinson on 1 December 1786.[47]

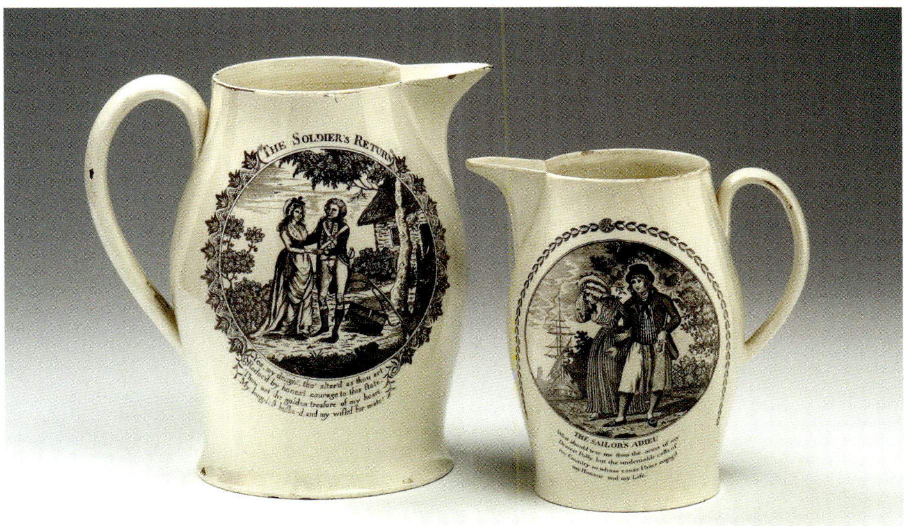

Jug, (251), c.1790, probably Liverpool, height: 21.6cm, (8½in), printed creamware. 'THE SOLDIER'S RETURN' shows a soldier clasping hands with a young woman, and verse,
'Yes my delight, tho' alter'd as thou art, / Reduc'd by honest courage to this state,
Thou art the golden treasure of my heart, / My long-lost husband, and my wished for mate!'.
Jug, (260), c.1790, probably Liverpool, height: 17.8cm, (7in), printed creamware. 'THE SAILOR'S ADIEU' shows a sailor leaving his weeping sweetheart. Inscribed,
'What should tear me from the arms of my / Dearest Polly but the undeniable calls of / my Country in whose cause I have engag'd / my Honour and my Life'.[48]

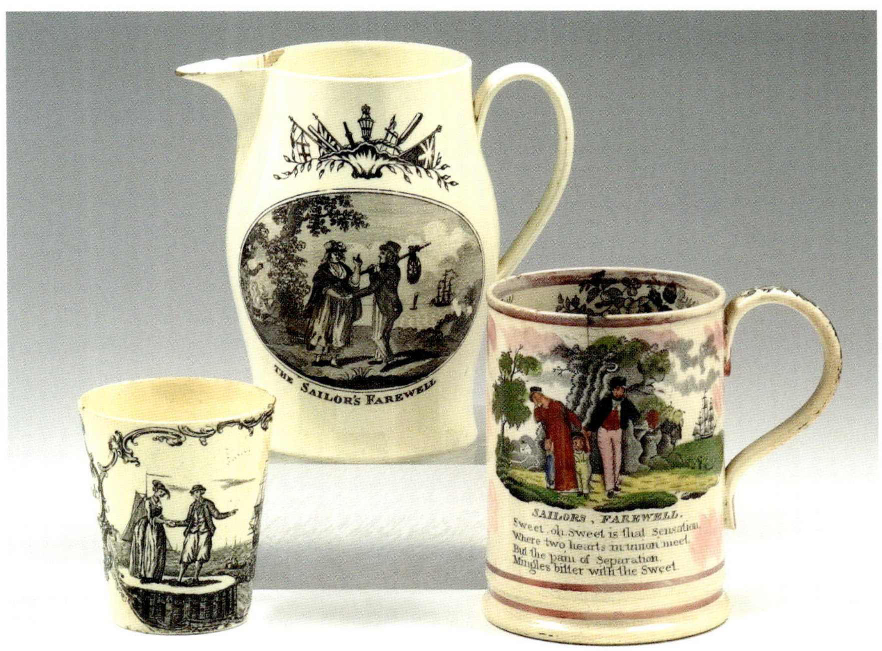

Beaker, (267), c.1790, possibly Ralph Wedgwood,[49] printed in Liverpool, height: 8.9cm, (3½in), printed creamware.
A sailor takes leave of his sweetheart at the quayside, boats in the distance, and a verse,
'When this you see remember me / And bear me in your mind,/ Let all the World say what they will, / Speak of me as you find'
Jug, (269), c.1795, Staffordshire, height: 15.3cm, (6in), printed creamware.
'THE SAILOR'S FAREWELL' shows a sailor carrying a bundle on the end of a stick, taking leave of an admonishing girlfriend.
Frog Mug, (266), c.1840, Sunderland, Southwick, Scott & Son, height: 12.7cm, (5in), earthenware, printed, coloured and lustred. 'SAILOR'S FAREWELL' shows a sailor parting from his family and verse,
'Sweet, oh sweet is that sensation / Where two hearts in union meet; / But the pain of Separation / Mingles bitter with the Sweet'. Enamelled frog inside.

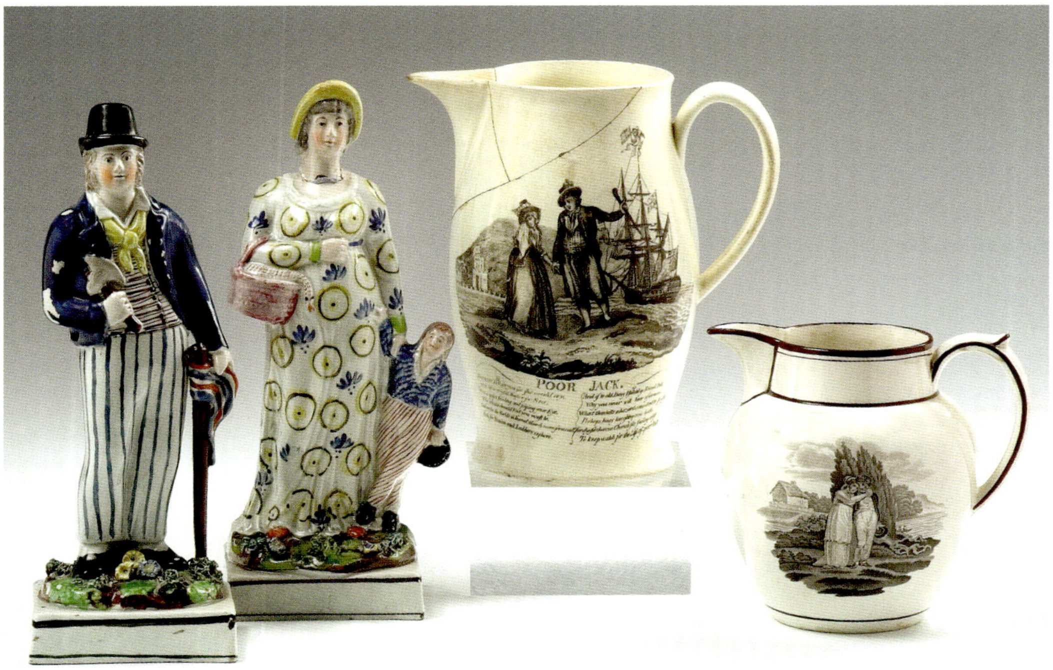

Pair of Figures, (272 & A), c.1810, Staffordshire, each height: 24.2cm, (9½in), pearlware. Decorated in high-temperature colours, a sailor holds an axe and a flag, while his wife has a small boy in tow.
Jug, (R.2454/13), c.1790, Liverpool, height: 18cm, (7⅛in), printed creamware.
'POOR JACK', shows a sailor indicating a ship flying Union flags, as he takes leave of his sweetheart, with verses,
'I said to our Poll, for you see she would cry, / When last we weighed anchor for sea
What argufies snivling and piping your eye / Why what a damn'd fool you must be …
What then, all's a hazard, come don't be so soft, / Perhaps I may laughing come back
For, d'ye see theres a cherub sits smiling aloft / To keep watch for the life of Poor Jack'
These are the last two verses of 'Poor Jack', probably Charles Dibdin's most famous song, from *Whim of the Moment*, performed at the Lyceum in 1788 and published in 1789.[52]
Jug, (270), c.1815, Staffordshire, Stoke-on-Trent, Spode, height: 13.3cm, (5¼in), printed bone china. A girl embraces her departing sailor.

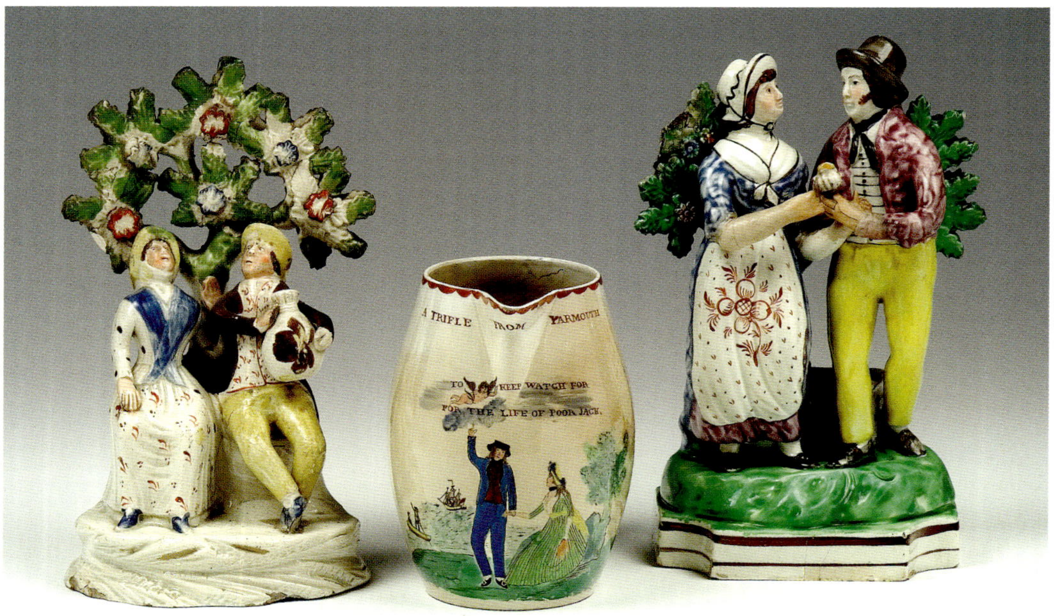

Figure Group, (344), c.1820, Staffordshire, height: 22.3cm, (8¾in), enamelled pearlware.
Jug, (323), c.1800, Staffordshire, height: 14cm, (5½in), enamelled creamware. Painted with a sailor taking leave of his sweetheart, inscribed, 'A TRIFLE / FROM / YARMOUTH' and, 'TO KEEP WATCH FOR / THE LIFE OF POOR JACK'. Decorated by William Absolon of Great Yarmouth.
Figure Group, (306), c.1820, Staffordshire, height: 24.1cm, (9½in), enamelled pearlware.
Sailors present bags of money to their wives as they sit beneath a tree or stroll.

Jug, (305), c.1800, Liverpool, height: 22.9cm, (9in), creamware, printed and enamelled. A British ship on starboard tack.
Jug, (277), c.1800, Liverpool or Staffordshire, height: 21.6cm, (8½in), printed creamware. A sailor parts from his sweetheart, who weeps into a handkerchief.[50] Entitled (in a ribbon scroll), 'POOR JACK', (see jug (R.2454/13). This illustration of Dibdin's most famous song was probably made for the United States market, since the ship flies the American flag and cherub holds an American pennant rather than the Union flag.
Jug, (318), c.1800, Probably Staffordshire, height: 21.6cm, (8½in), printed creamware. A grinning sailor clutches bags of money, inscribed, 'Tis Comical I know / To have all this Rhino' (slang term for cash).[51]

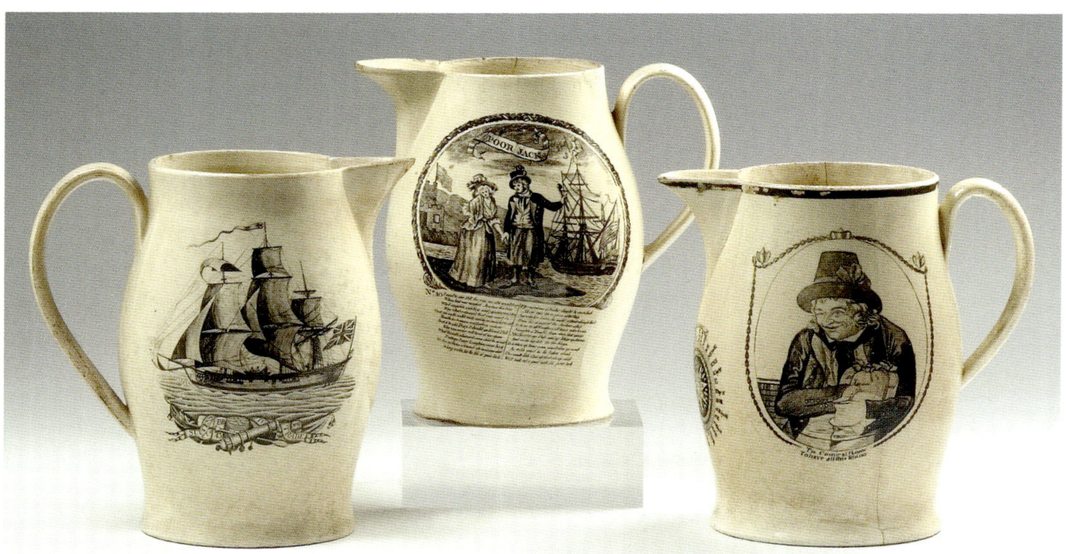

Pair of Figure Groups, (264 & A), c.1820, each height: 22.9cm, (9in), enamelled pearlware.
A sailor bids farewell to his seated sweetheart; his pack and a stick lie on the ground. Sailor returns with a chest inscribed, 'DOLLARS' and a purse bulging with gold, in consolation for his absence.

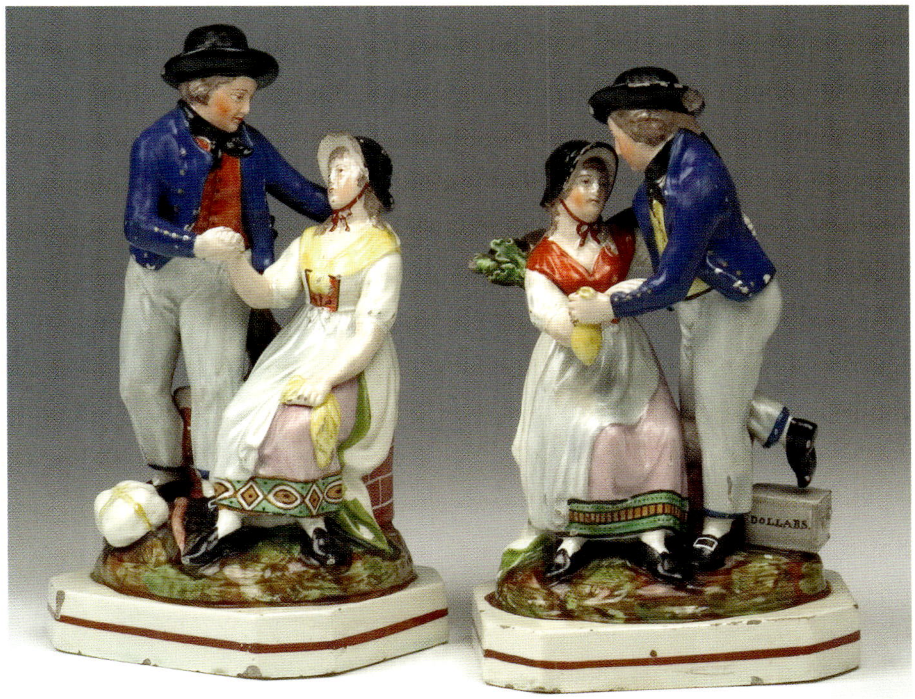

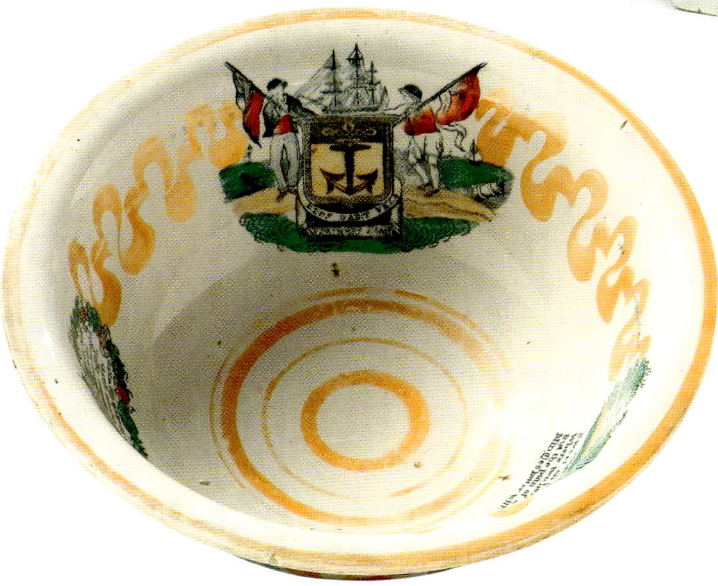

Punchbowl, (331), c.1880, North Shields, John Carr, diameter: 28.6cm, (11¼in), earthenware, printed, enamelled and lustred. Exterior printed with 'SAILOR'S FAREWELL', and interior with the Mariners' arms with motto, DEUS DABIT VELA (God will give a sail) and several verses, including, 'Glide on my bark the summer's tide / Is gently flowing by thy side; / Around they prow the waters bright, / Incircling [sic] rounds of broken light, / Are glittring as if ocean gave, / Her countless gems to deck the wave'. This evocative sea song is quoted (with many others) in Frederick Marryat's *Jacob Faithful* (1834) and seems to have been particularly popular in the North East.

Plaque, (265), c.1810, possibly Derby height: 11.4cm, (4½in), enamelled soft-paste porcelain. A distraught young woman waves a handkerchief as her lover's ship departs. Another woman restrains her as they stand on a rocky promontory at the harbour entrance.
Jug, (268), c.1800, Liverpool, height: 23.5cm, (9¼in), printed creamware. A large figure of a windswept woman waves a handkerchief to the departing fleet, entitled, 'SUSAN'S FAREWELL / Adieu she cry'd, and wav'd her Lily Hand'.[53] The inscription derives from John Gay's poem *Black Eyed Susan* of 1720, popularised as a song set to music by Charles Dibdin.
Jug, (300), c.1785, Liverpool, height: 18.3cm, (7¼in), printed creamware. 'SWEET POLL OF PLYMOUTH', a woman stands in a rowing boat, waving a large handkerchief at a departing ship while a man sits at the oars. Image taken from a print of 1786 after George Morland, illustrating (confusingly), 'Susan's Farewell'![54] The verses include, 'Our anchor weighed, for sea we stood / The land we left behind: / Her tears then swelled the briny flood / Her sighs increased the wind./And have they torn my love away? / And is he gone? she cry'd; / My Polly, sweetest flower of May / She languish'd droop'd and died'. / 'Sweet Poll of Plymouth' was another of Charles Dibdin's popular sailor songs that later became associated with the press gang.[55]

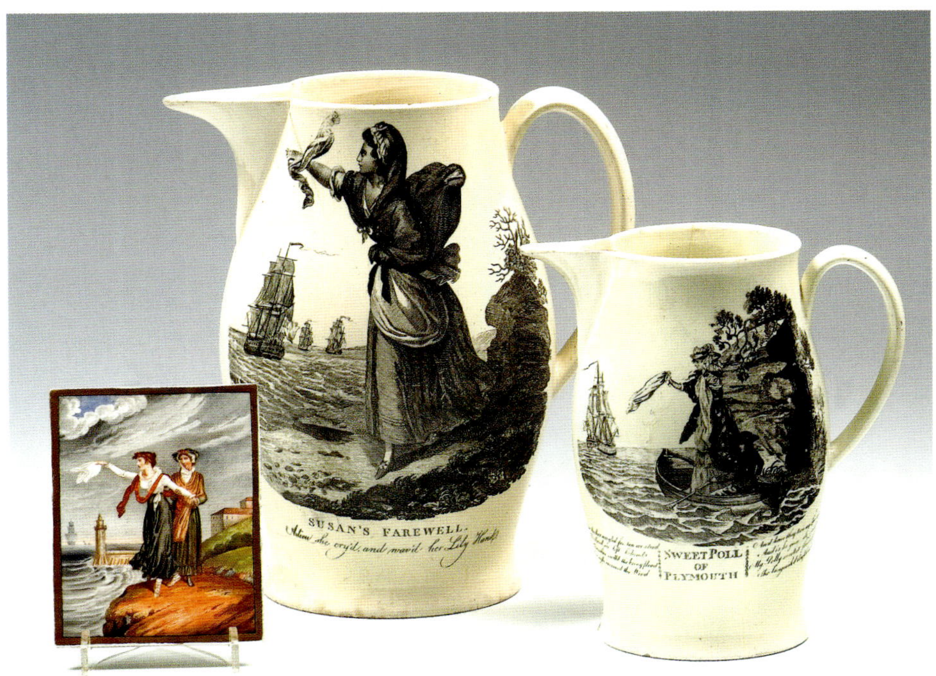

Disasters at sea

Life at sea in the eighteenth-century navy was insanitary, claustrophobic and fraught with danger from disease, enemy ships, unknown coastlines and inclement weather. At times even the sailor's homecoming was inauspicious and had tragic consequences.

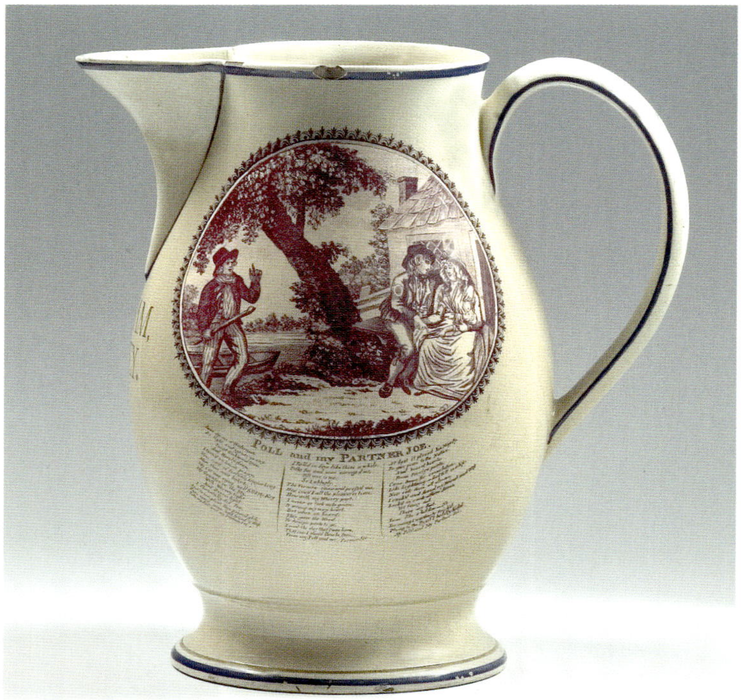

Jug, (310), 1797, Staffordshire, signed by Thomas Fletcher, Shelton, height: 33cm, (13in), purple-printed creamware. Large jug with waisted foot ring, painted beneath the spout, 'WILLIAM DAVEY 1797'. A returning sailor surprises a man and woman embracing. 'POLL and my PARTNER JOE', was another composition by Charles Dibdin, first performed in *Whim of the Moment* at the Lyceum Theatre, London, in 1788 and published in 1789. Verses describe the sailor's happy life with his wife Poll and his friend Joe, before he was seized by the press gang,
'I did my duty manfully while on the billows rolling;
And, night or day, could find my way blindfold to the main-top bowling.
Thus all the dangers of the main, quicksands and gales of wind
I braked in hopes to taste again the joys I left behind …
At last it pleased his Majesty to give peace to the nation,
And honest hearts from foreign parts came home for consolation.
Like lightening (for I felt new life now safe from all alarms)
I rush'd and found my friend and wife lock'd in each others arms!
Yet fancy not I bore my lot tame, like a lubber - no;
For, seeing I was fairly trick'd plump to the devil I finely kick'd
My Poll and my partner Joe.'

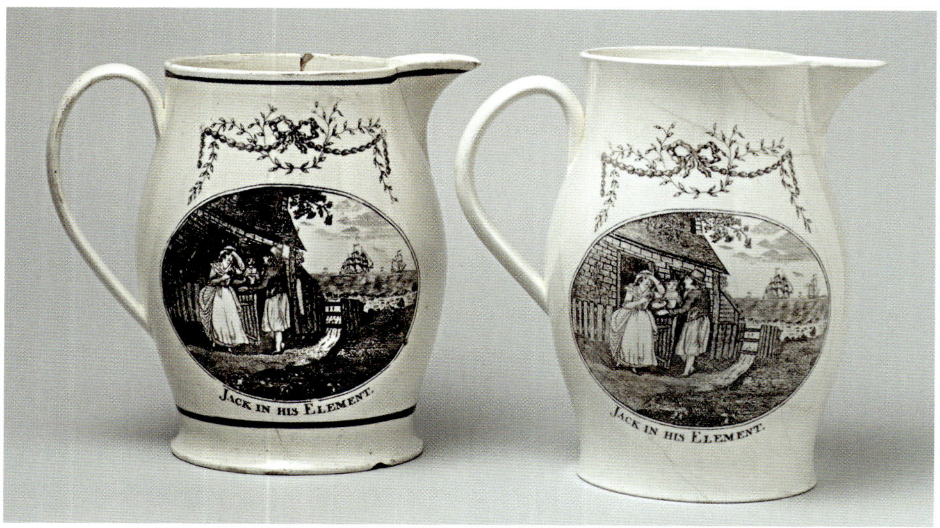

Jug, (276), c.1795, Staffordshire, signed by Thomas Fletcher, Shelton, height: 21.6cm, (8½in), printed creamware.
Jug, (442), c.1800, possibly Liverpool, height: 19.7cm, (7¾in), printed creamware. 'JACK IN HIS ELEMENT', is taken from a song by Charles Dibdin, from *The Camp of Pleasure,* performed at the Lyceum Theatre in 1790. Jack, the bringer of bad news (in this case, the death of fellow-sailor, Will Gast) offers more than sympathy to the stricken Poll, who puts her hand to her brow in horror, 'Will Gast by Death was ta'en aback, / I came to bring the news, / Poll whimper'd sore, but what did Jack, / Why stood in William's shoes'.[56]

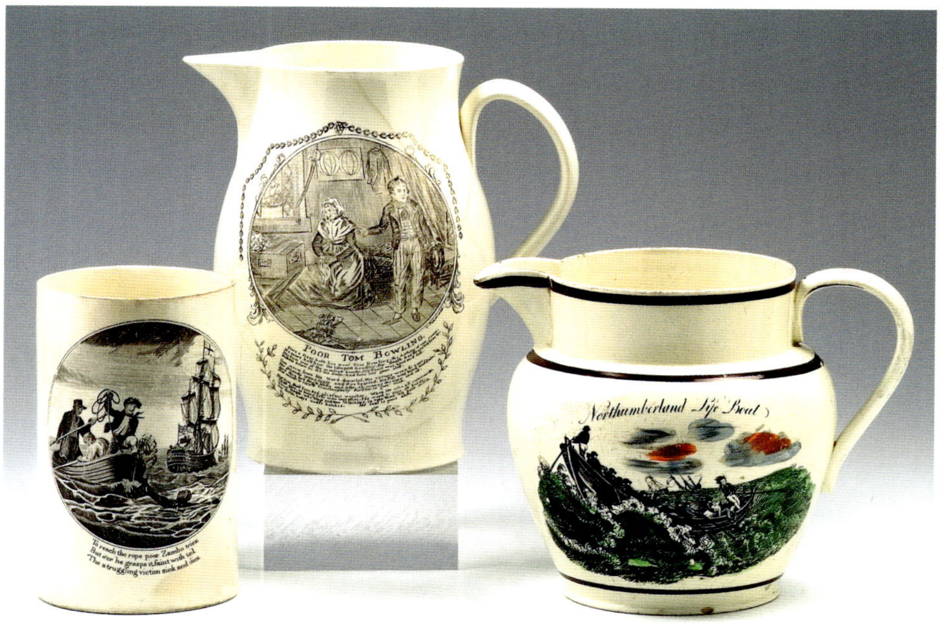

Mug, (262), c.1805, Liverpool, height: 15.9cm, (6¼in), printed creamware. Printed with sailors attempting to rescue a drowning black man (slave or sailor). Verse reads, 'To reach the rope poor Zambo tries / But e'er he grasps it, faint with toil / The struggling victim sink and dies'.[57]
Jug, (276), c.1795, Staffordshire, signed by Thomas Fletcher, Shelton, height: 21.6cm, (8½in), printed creamware. A widow views a coffin as a sailor tells her of the death of her husband, the saintly, 'POOR TOM BOWLING'.[58]
'Here, a sheer hulk, lies poor Tom Bowling / The darling of our crew, / No more he'll hear the tempest howling[58] / For death has brought him to/His form was of the manliest beauty / His heart was kind and soft/Faithful below he did his duty / And now he's gone aloft…'
The image is based on a print published in 1794 by Laurie and Whittle. Although the name, 'Tom Bowling', was taken from Smollett's *Roderick Random*, the song was written by Charles Dibdin as a tribute to his own brother, Captain Thomas Dibdin, who had been struck by lightning and died at sea. It was first performed among Dibdin's *Oddities* at the Lyceum theatre, London, in 1789-90.
Jug, (314), c.1825, possibly Newcastle upon Tyne, height: 16.5cm, (6½in), creamware, printed and enamelled. The 'Northumberland Life Boat' crests a steep wave. This image appeared on a public notice of 12 March 1823, threatening action if the vandalism and misuse of the North Shields lifeboat continued and ship owners failed to pay their dues.[59] The design is taken from Thomas Bewick's engraving which heads the notice.[60]

Veterans and Pensioners

If he were fortunate, an old or disabled soldier or sailor might become an in-pensioner at either of the two retirement hospitals founded by Charles II and William III, both designed by Sir Christopher Wren. By the end of March 1692, the full capacity of 476 former soldiers was in residence at the new Royal Hospital, Chelsea. Greenwich Hospital was designed in 1694 and began admitting sailor pensioners in 1705.

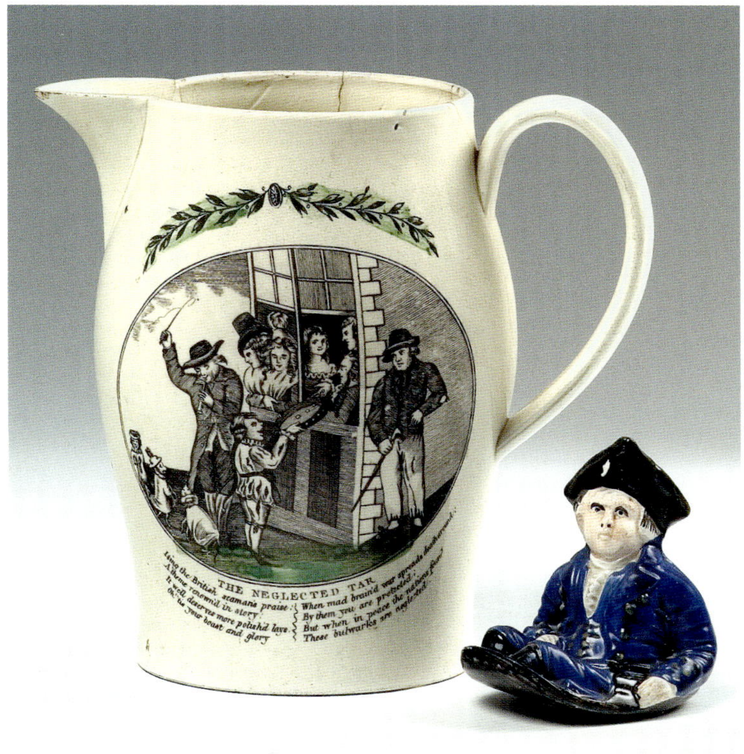

Jug, (303), c.1795, Liverpool or Staffordshire, height: 17.8cm, (7in), printed creamware. Well-dressed women lean from a town-house window to watch a group of street performers. A flautist directs a small group of dancing dogs in fancy dress while his companion takes round a collecting box.[61] Unnoticed, a destitute sailor leans against a wall nearby. Inscribed beneath the scene is 'The Neglected Tar':

> 'I sing the British seaman's praise / A theme renown'd in story … / … When mad brain'd war spreads death around,/ By them you are protected; / But when in peace the nation's found/ These bulwarks are neglected."

Taken from a song, written and performed in London in the 1790s by Charles Dignum.[62] It describes the plight of ex-servicemen, who were routinely discharged between campaigns or wars without an income or the skills to earn one. This was a particular problem between the end of the American War of Independence in 1783 and the outbreak of war with France in 1793.

Figure, (282), c.1800, probably Staffordshire, height: 7.7cm, (3in), enamelled pearlware. A veteran sailor, with both legs amputated at the knee, sits on a curved, coracle-shaped board, on which he probably wheeled himself around.

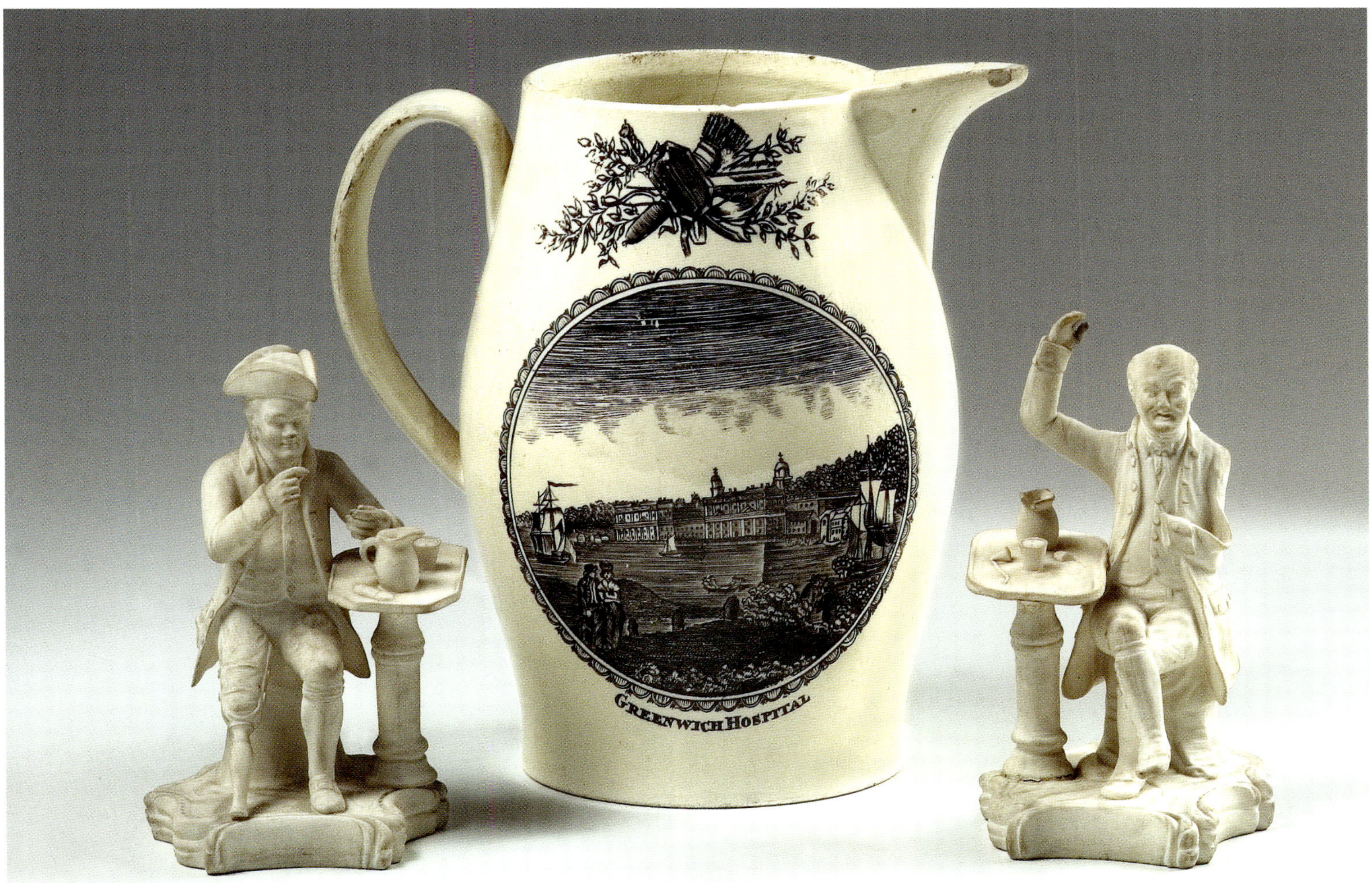

Pair of Figures, (257 & A), c.1835, Staffordshire, Stoke-on-Trent, Mintons, each height: 14cm, (5½in), biscuit porcelain. A pair of war veterans, described as a Chelsea pensioner and a Greenwich pensioner. The Greenwich pensioner wears a tricorne hat and has a leg amputated below the knee, the other has an arm missing.[63] A variant of the Chelsea pensioner (with both arms intact) has since been identified as Oliver Goldsmith's 'Old Soldier'.[64]

Jug, (260), c.1800, Liverpool, height: 17.8cm, (7in), printed creamware. A view of the Greenwich Hosptial. Charles Dibdin wrote the popular comic opera, *The Chelsea Pensioner* (1779) while the gifted baritone Charles Bannister was to move the audience at *A Divertissement* (1790) with his rendition of 'The Greenwich Pensioner'.[65]

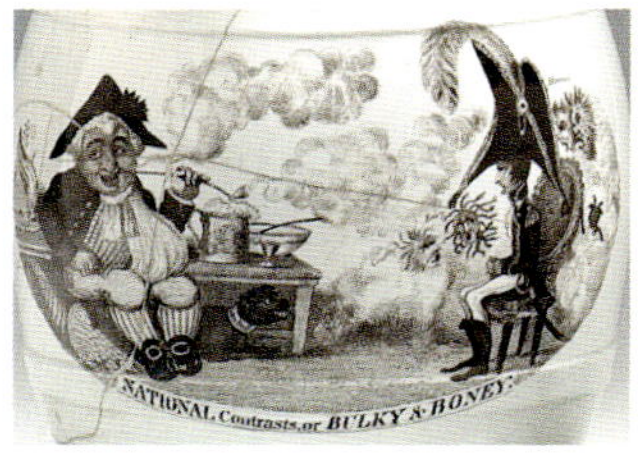

Chapter 5

ENGLAND & FRANCE

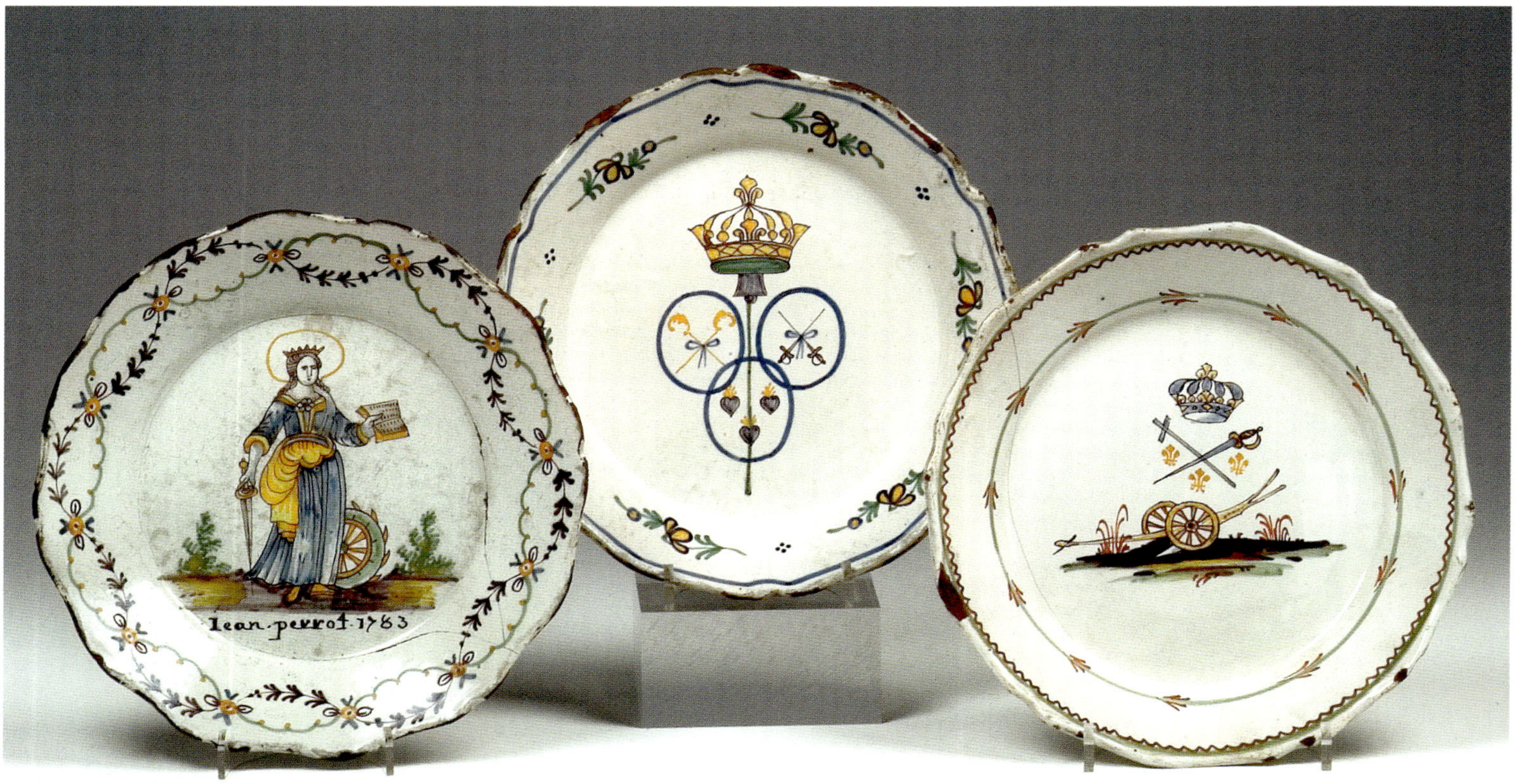

Plate, (345), 1783, France, Nevers, diameter: 20.3cm, (8in), faience. Inscribed for 'Jean Perrot', Saint Catherine shown with the wheel, the symbol of her martyrdom.
Plate, (347), c.1789, France, Nevers, diameter: 20.3cm, (8in), faience. Interlocking circles containing emblems of the church, the army and the unity of the nation (symbolised by flaming hearts) are shown here subject to the crown.
Plate, (346), c.1789, France, Nevers, diameter: 20.3cm, (8in), faience. The ploughshare here resembles a weapon of war.[4] It is shown beneath symbols of the monarchy, the church and the army.

Revolution

The unique power and impact of the French Revolution was precipitated by the coincidence of political and social crises in the late 1780s. On 20 August 1786 Calonne, the French finance minister, reported to Louis XVI that France was effectively bankrupt. Eventually the reluctant king called the Estates-General (the French parliament), to meet at Versailles in May 1789. Meanwhile a period of terrible weather culminated in the failure of the 1788 harvest in large areas of France. This caused the price of bread to soar and the demand for manufactured goods to collapse, so that the labouring poor were denied employment when they most needed it. An underlying suspicion that a conspiracy between government ministers and grain racketeers to starve the French people into submission led to the eruption of violence all over France.[1]

The town of Nevers in central France had been a major producer of tin-glazed earthenware since the late seventeenth century. From the late eighteenth century, the ornamental motifs used to decorate their popular line of faïences patriotiques changed. In place of the family coats of arms, figures of saints and royal fleurs-de-lys, the crown of the Bourbon monarchy began to share the central space on plates and salad bowls with a cross, a sword and a ploughshare. The cross of the Catholic Church, (occasionally shown as the regional Cross of Lorraine) was sometimes replaced by one or a pair of bishops' croziers. The swords of the French nobility recall the outdated weapons of medieval chivalry and indicate how out of touch with reality were the military elite. Together with the ploughshare of agriculture, these were the emblems of the Three Estates, the main sectors of society in the Estates-General.

There are no specific references to the Revolution on any of the French dishes in Willett's collection. Although contemporary souvenirs survive, including plates showing the storming of the infamous Bastille prison fortress in Paris, on 14 July 1789, the Revolutionaries were far too occupied to design and produce commemoratives.[2] The progress of the Revolution, however, was marked by other symbols, slogans and dates. Most important was the *bonnet rouge*, the red cap of Liberty. Derived from images on Roman coins, where former slaves were shown awarded a Phrygian Cap, together with their freedom, the bonnet had been widely used symbolically, for 200 years.[3] The difference was that a real cap now became obligatory headgear for the sans-culottes.

From 1790, however, the seething ferment of revolutionary France deployed increasingly unusual imagery. The heaps of weapons, drums and regimental standards previously used to depict military victories, were hijacked and subverted by the sans-culottes. Flags were replaced by the Revolutionary tricolour, whose invention, ironically, is credited to the king himself. When he rode to the Hotel de Ville to petition the National Assembly to restore order on 17 July 1789, he added the red and blue of Paris to the white of the Bourbon dynasty. Later, after the execution of the king had unlocked the floodgates of the Terror (1793-95), waves of prominent revolutionaries were executed without comment or commemoration.

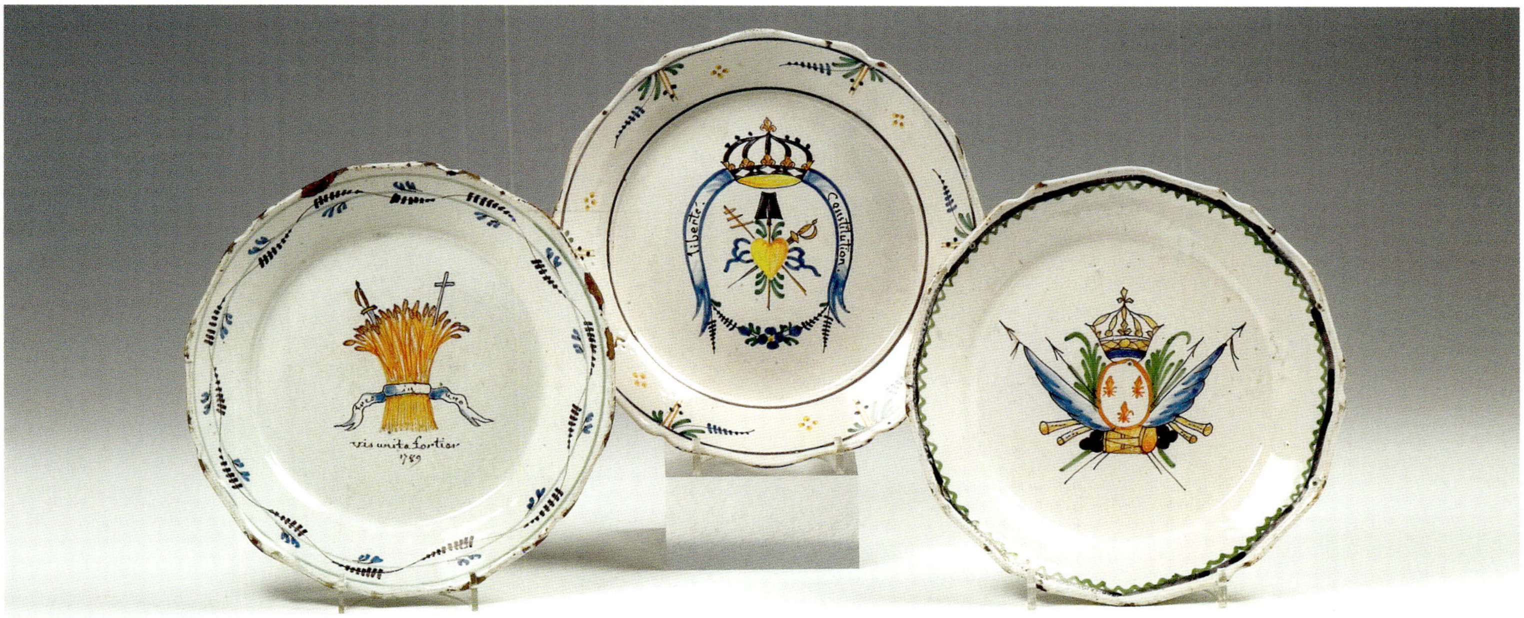

Plate, (350), 1789, France, Nevers, diameter: 20.3cm, (8in), faience. The church and the army are embedded in the wheatsheaf of agriculture. Ribbon inscribed, 'Tres in Uno' (three in one) and below, 'vis unita fortior' (stronger together).
Plate, (349), c.1789, France, Nevers, diameter: 20.3cm, (8in), faience.

The church (the Cross of Lorraine) and the army are united, under the crown, by Liberty and the French constitution.
Plate, (348), c.1789, France, Nevers, diameter: 20.3cm, (8in), faience. Traditional military trophies are shown beneath the crown and fleurs-de-lys.

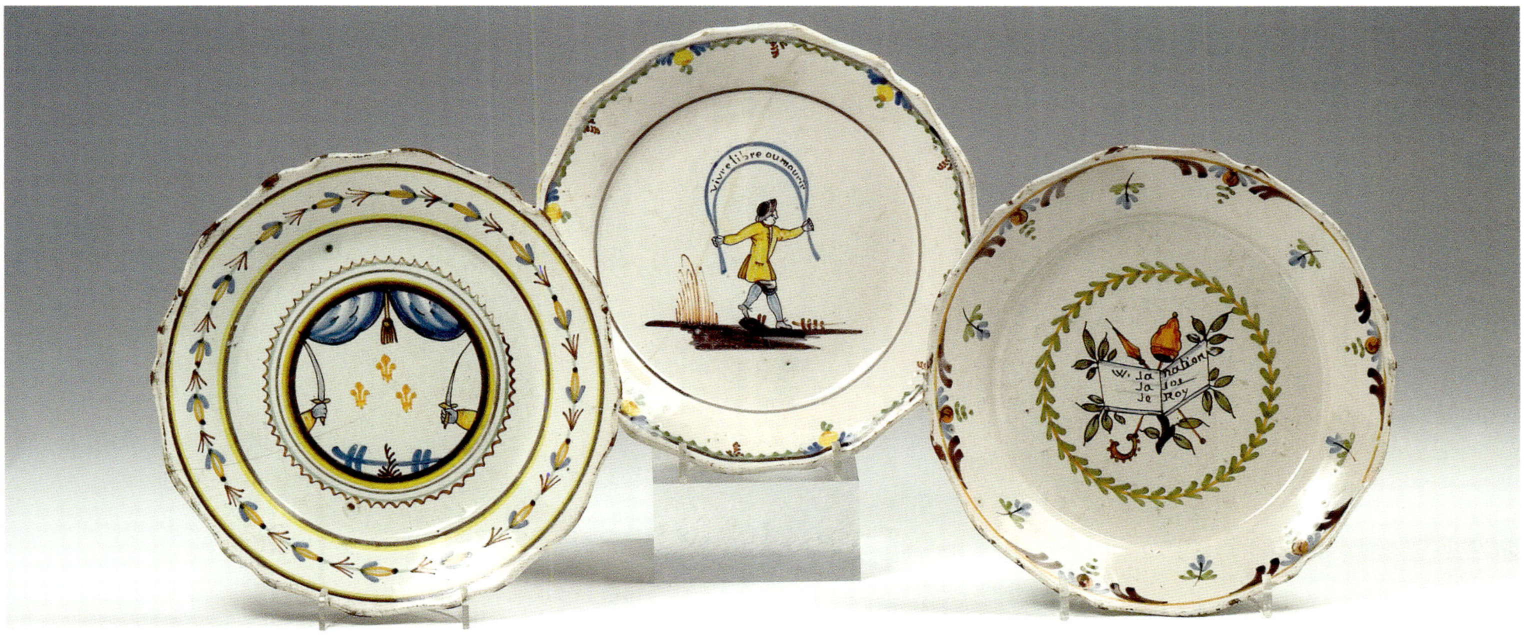

Plate, (351), c.1789, France, Nevers, diameter: 20.3cm, (8in), faience. The plate to the left shows military sabres saluting the fleurs-de-lys.
Plate, (352), c.1790, France, Nevers, diameter: 20.3cm, (8in), faience. A skipping peasant waves a banner proclaiming 'Liberty or Death'.
Plate, (353), c.1790, France, Nevers, diameter: 20.3cm, (8in), faience.

Although the Crown of monarchy was gradually replaced by the Liberty Cap, there was an uneasy truce between king and revolutionaries until after the Royal Family's disastrous attempt to flee the country in June 1791. This led to slogans such as, 'W[vive] le nation / la loi / le roy'[*sic*]; 'Long live the nation, the law, the king'.

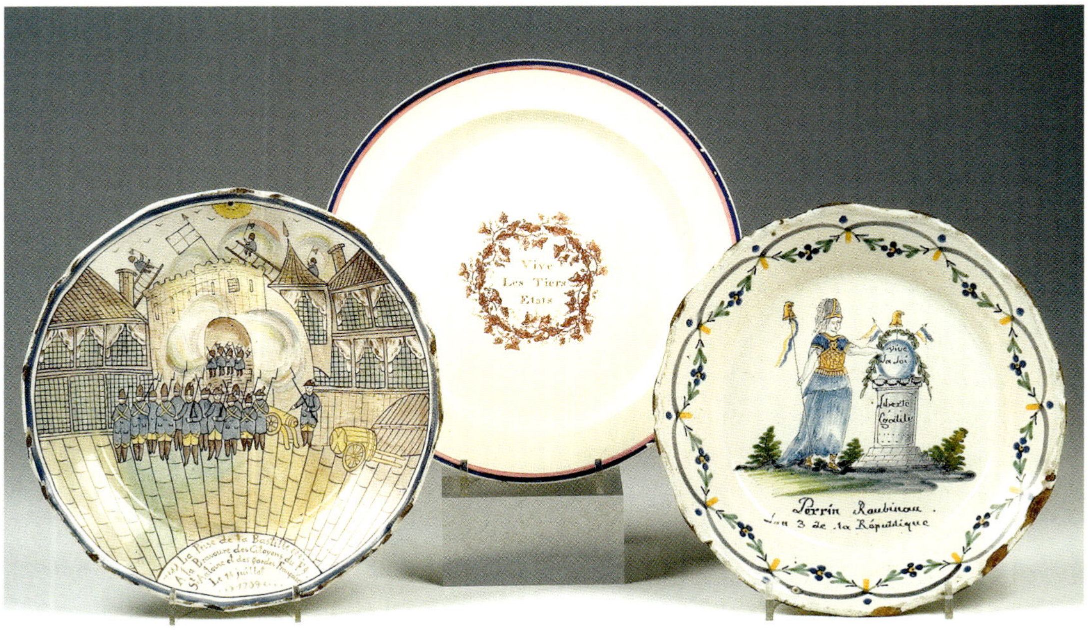

Plate, (355), 1889, France, diameter: 20.3cm, (8in), faience. A centenary souvenir plate; few contemporary ceramic souvenirs were made of the storming of the infamous Bastille prison fortress in Paris, on 14 July 1789.
Plate, (366), 1789, Staffordshire, T. & J. Hollins of Shelton, Hanley, diameter: 23.5cm, (9¼in), red-printed creamware. Printed within vine wreath with incorrect inscription, 'Vive les Tiers Etat', (instead of 'le Tiers Etat'). Made for the French market, probably between 5 May and 17 June 1789.[5] The Third Estate, comprising the vast majority of the French people, first declared itself in the French National Assembly (parliament) on 5 May 1789.
Plate, (354), c.1791, France, Nevers, diameter: 20.3cm, (8in), faience. Plate inscribed for 'Perrin Raubinau', in the third year of the Revolution. Minerva, Roman goddess of war, brandishes a Liberty Cap and tricolour mounted on a pole before a shrine to 'Law, Liberty, Equality'.

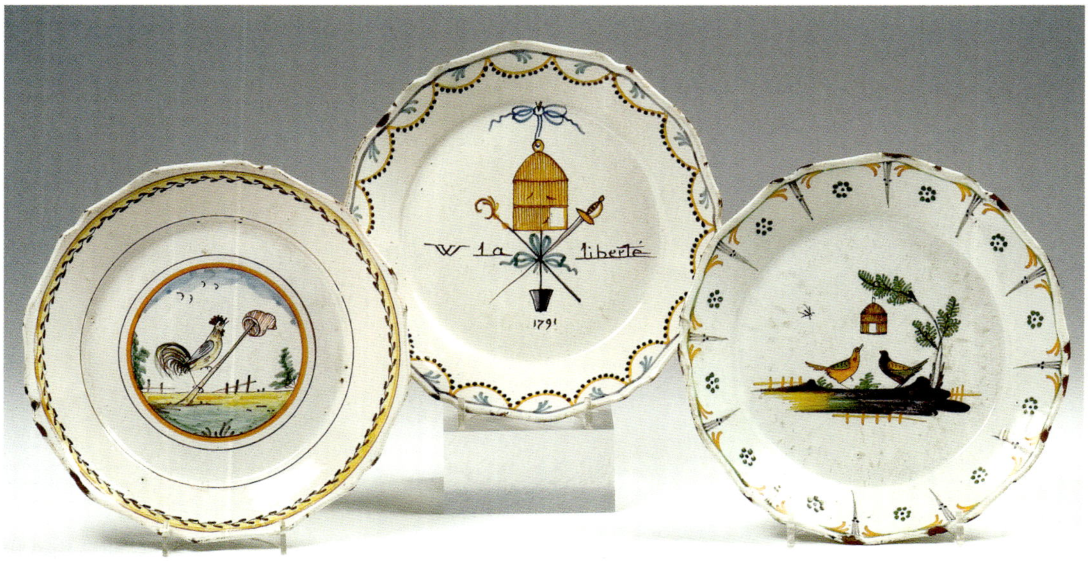

Plate, (358), c.1791, France, Nevers, diameter: 20.3cm, (8in), faience. The French Revolutionary cockerel stands on a pole bearing a Liberty Cap, crowing to 'wake the nation'.
Plate, (359), 1791, France, Nevers, diameter: 20.3cm, (8in), faience. Inscribed, 'W la liberté' (long live Liberty), birds are released from a cage.
Plate, (360), c.1791, France, Nevers, diameter: 20.3cm, (8in), faience. Birds, symbolising the French people, sing as they gaze at their empty cage.

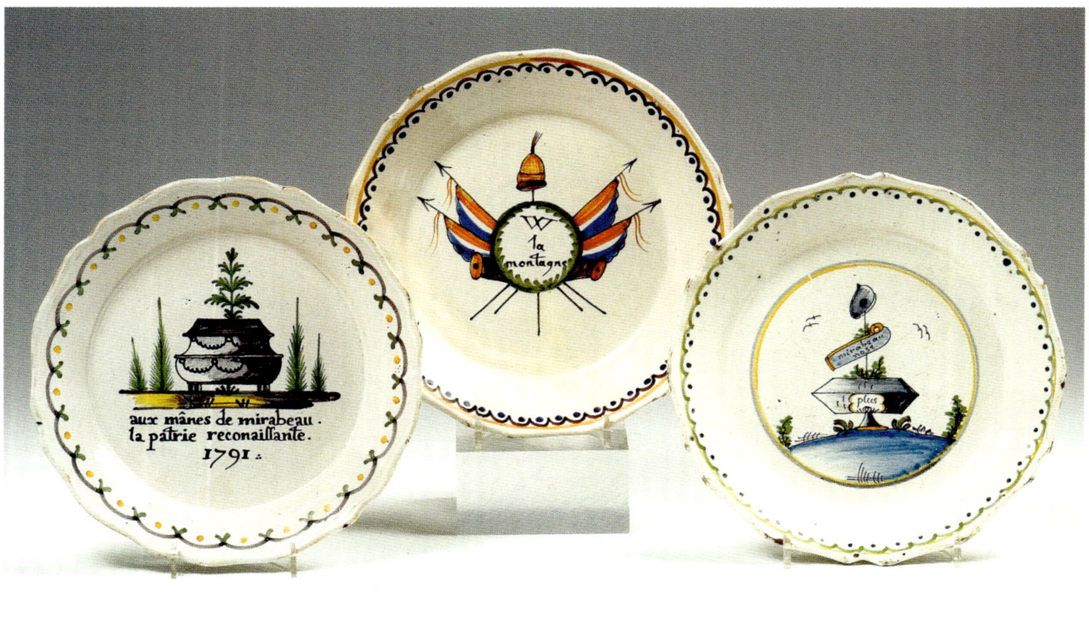

Plate, (363), 1791, France, Nevers, diameter: 20.3cm, (8in), faience. Painted with sarcophagus and inscribed 'the grateful homeland honours the spirit of Mirabeau,' plate marks the death of Honoré Gabriel de Riqueti, Comte de Mirabeau, (1749-1791), author of *Essai sur le despotisme*. An early revolutionary aristocrat who represented Provence, he collapsed and died on 2 April 1791, shortly after addressing the Revolutionary Assembly. Given an elaborate funeral, he was the only revolutionary to become a national hero.
Plate, (361), c.1791, France, Nevers, diameter: 20.3cm, (8in), faience. Plate salutes 'La Montagne' or the Mountain, the extreme radical Jacobin faction, who occupied the highest benches on the Revolutionary Convention and was led by Robespierre.
Plate, (364), c.1791, France, Nevers, diameter: 20.3cm, (8in), faience. Painted with sarcophagus, Liberty cap and banner, this plate commemorates the Comte de Mirabeau.

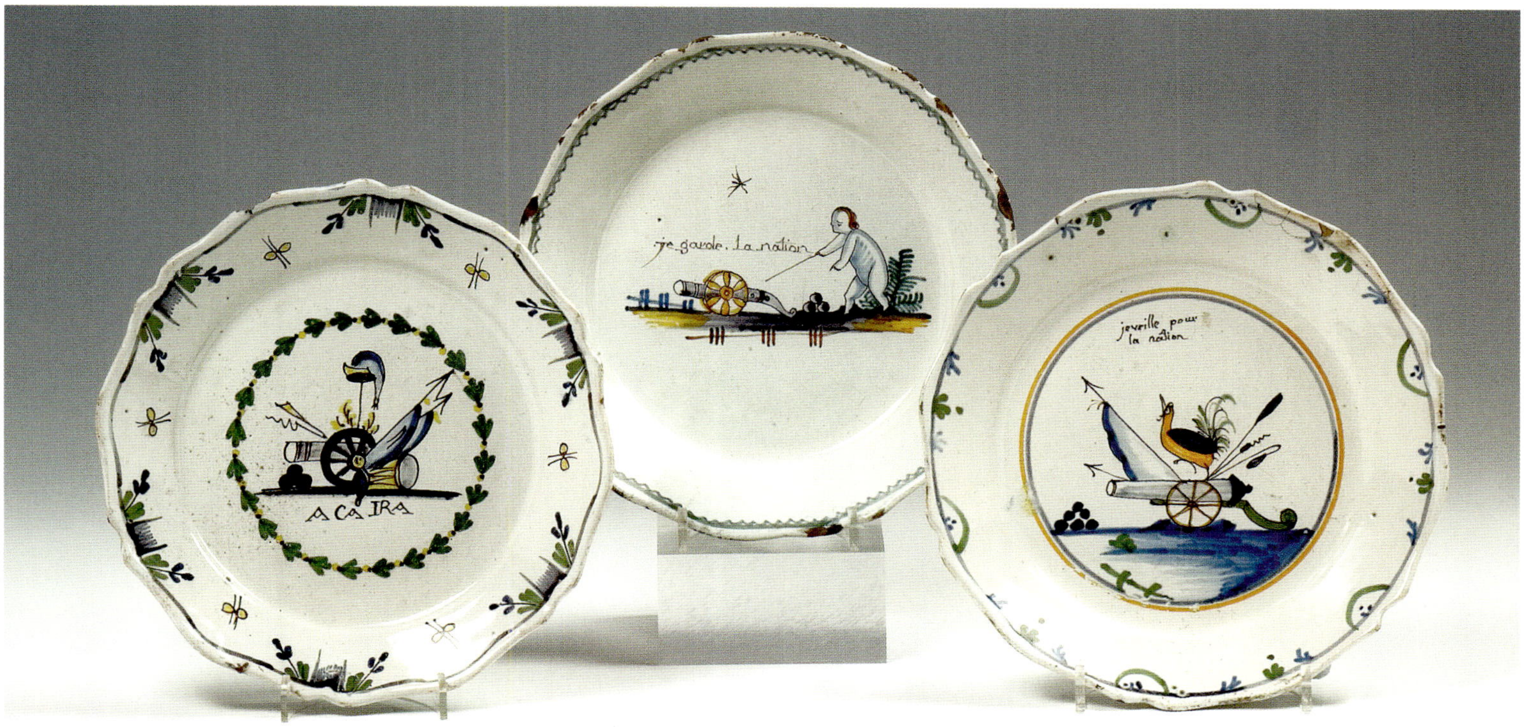

Plate, (362), c.1792, France, Nevers, diameter: 20.3cm, (8in), faience. Quoted beneath a trophy pile of cannon and Liberty cap, *A Ça Ira* the most blood-thirsty song of the Revolution, was composed in 1790 and remained popular throughout the Terror.
Plate, (356), c.1792, France, Nevers, diameter: 20.3cm, (8in), faience. A naked child ignites a canon inscribed, 'I look after the nation'.
Plate, (357), c.1792, France, Nevers, diameter: 20.3cm, (8in), faience. The Revolutionary cockerel uses his morning call to 'wake the nation'.

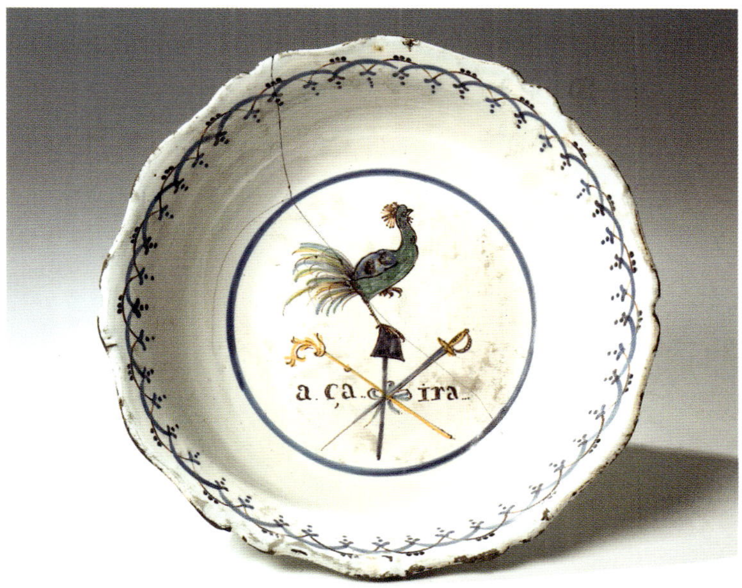

Bowl, (365), c.1791, France, Nevers, diameter: 30.5cm, (12in), faience. The Revolutionary cockerel perches on the Cap of Liberty between crossed sword and crozier. The blood-thirsty anthem, *A Ça Ira*, composed in 1790, boasted such lines as 'Tous les aristocrats on les pendra' (we'll hang all the aristocrats).

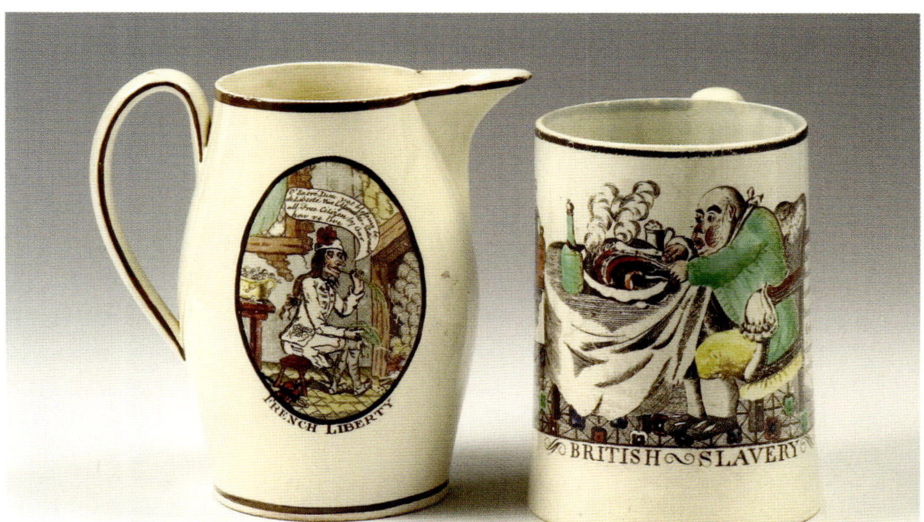

Jug, (375), c.1793, Staffordshire, height: 16.5cm, (6½in), printed creamware. Printed with a satirical scene entitled, 'FRENCH LIBERTY', showing a destitute Frenchman with a chamber pot full of snails, nibbling limp leeks and shivering before an empty hearth, but giving thanks that he is a Free Citizen. On the reverse is 'BRITISH SLAVERY'.
Mug, (R2454.49), c.1805, North East, height: 14.7cm, (5¾in), printed pearlware. In the pendant scene, 'BRITISH SLAVERY', a well-fed John Bull tucks into a large joint of roast beef while complaining bitterly of the present 'cursed Ministry' that has made him a slave to taxation. Designs taken from a contrasting pair of prints by James Gillray, published by Hannah Humphrey on 21 December 1792.[6]

The Execution of the French King and its Aftermath

At the centre of the national disaster in France were Louis XVI (1754-1793), last of the absolute monarchs and his extravagant wife, Marie-Antoinette (1755-1793). The Queen was the daughter of Francis, Duke of Lorraine (1708-1765) who was elected Holy Roman Emperor in 1745 and the Empress Maria Theresa of Austria (1717-1780).

On 3 February 1793, shortly after executing Louis XVI, the French Convention declared war on England, Holland and Spain. They had already been at war with Austria and Marie Antoinette's relations since 1792. William Pitt's government reluctantly prepared Britain for war, less in protest at the Revolution than to safeguard British interests in a Europe now dangerously unbalanced by French actions.[7] British poets' and radical politicians' admiration for the revolutionaries rapidly evaporated as publishers and print-sellers were prosecuted and imprisoned for selling seditious prints and tracts by radical republican sympathisers such as Thomas Paine.[8]

The 28-year-old Duke of York and Albany, second son of George III, was appointed commander of the British troops. He led the Hanoverians and reinforcements from Austria and Prussia, driving the French from Belgium, before capturing the northern French town of Valenciennes on 26 July 1793. These early victories were greeted enthusiastically and the potters produced a large number of commemorative souvenirs to satisfy demand.

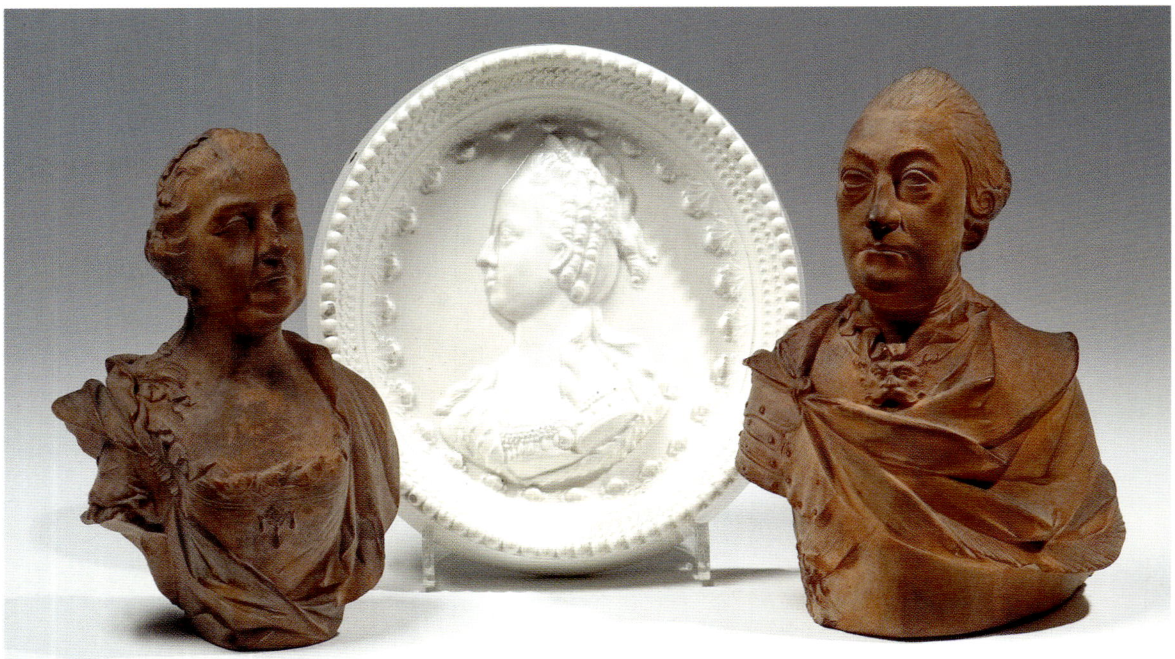

Pair of Portrait Busts, (369 & A), c.1780, France or Germany, each height: 19.1cm, (7½in), terracotta. Finely modelled likenesses of Francis of Lorraine (wearing armour) and Maria Theresa of Austria, the parents of Queen Marie Antoinette of France.
Portrait Plaque, (370), c.1800, Staffordshire, height: 19.1cm, (7½in), creamware. Relief-moulded profile of a plump-faced woman with an elaborate coiffure, is said to be Marie Antoinette, although it more closely resembles portraits of her mother, Maria Theresa, on thalers minted in the 1750s.

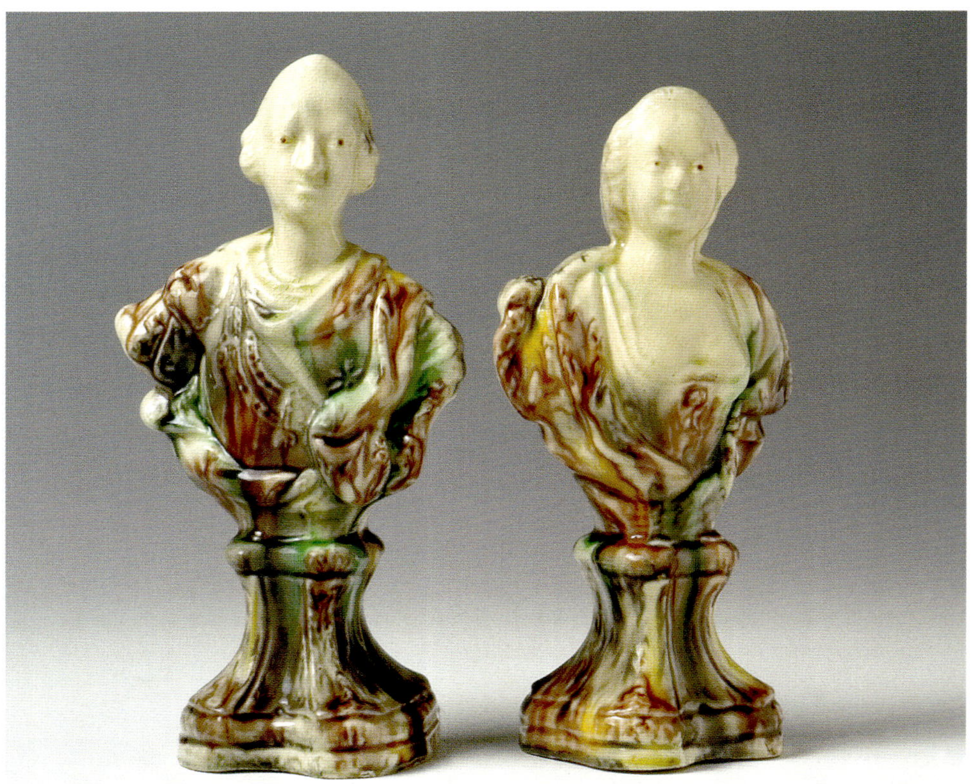

Pair of Portrait Busts, (367 & A), c.1760, Staffordshire, each height: 21.6cm, (8½in), creamware, lead-glazed and oxide-coloured. Likenesses of Francis of Lorraine and Empress Maria Theresa of Austria, the parents of Queen Marie Antoinette of France.[9] The production of such English souvenirs reflects their high profiles especially that of Maria Theresa who, after her husband's death, brought the Austrian Hapsburg Empire to international prominence.

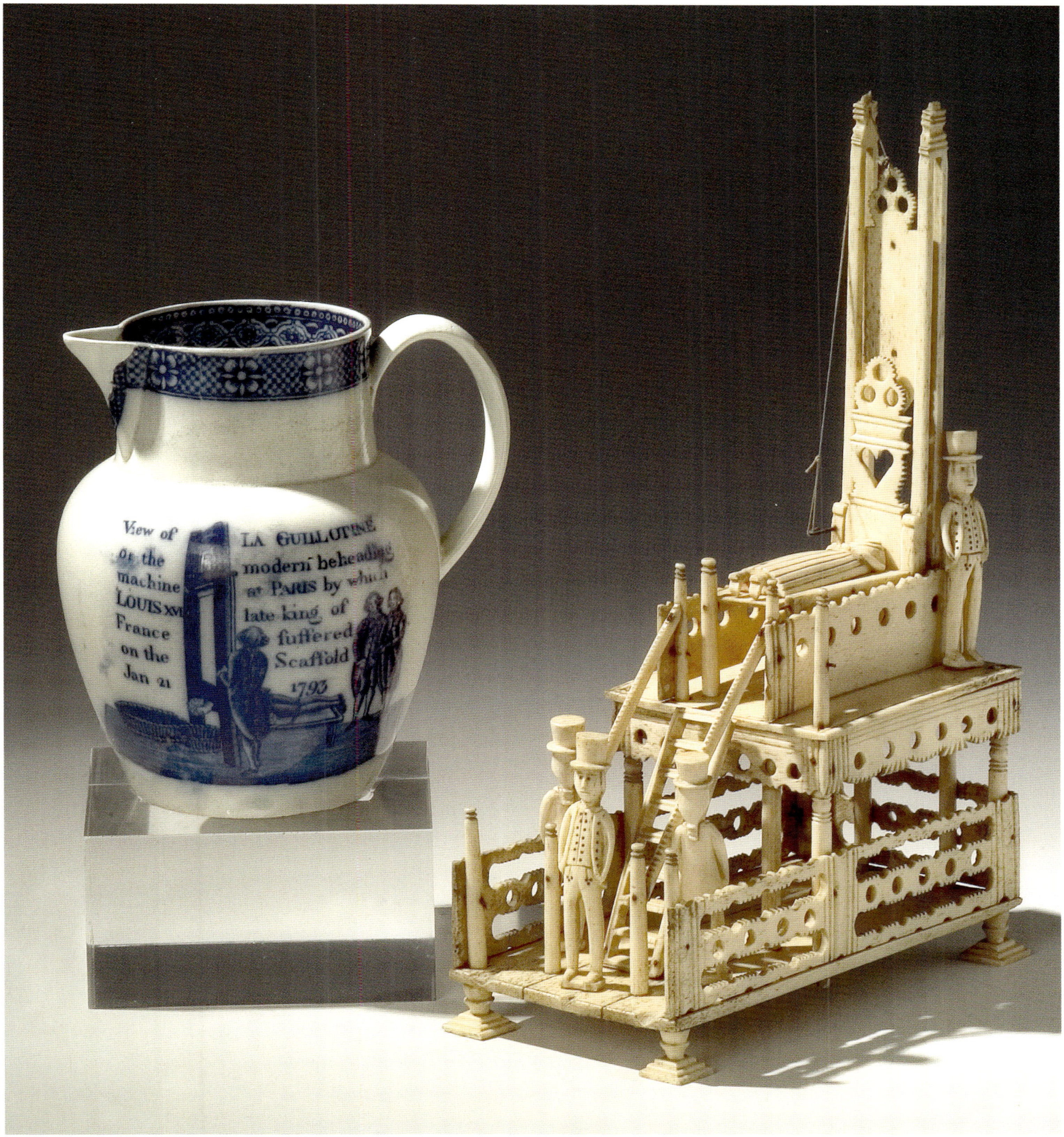

Jug, (372), c.1793, Staffordshire, height: 14 cm, (5½in), blue-printed pearlware. Louis XVI appears at his execution, which took place on 21 January 1793. The king's body is attended by two witnesses as one man operates the guillotine. Scene inscribed: 'View of LA GUILLOTINE / or the modern beheading / machine at Paris' taken from a woodcut design that headed a broadsheet printed by William Lane early in 1793. Lane had merely adapted an existing woodcut print illustrating Dr Guillotin's invention for humane (and efficient) execution.[10] Lane announced this shocking event under the title, 'Massacre of the French King!'.[11] On the reverse, a rare view of the heckling crowd that witnessed the event, assembled before a walled garden. **Model, (0374),** c.1810, England, made by French prisoners, height: 17.2cm, (6¾in), animal bone. Three-dimensional model of a guillotine, delicately carved and pierced similar to love spoons or busks. It was designed to work by means of pulley threads on thin chains. The prone figure of a woman, already beheaded, is attended by five soldiers. A number of such models survive, made by French prisoners of war, from beef or mutton bones between 1800 and 1815, the period of the Napoleonic wars. Napoleon refused either to exchange or to pay for the upkeep of French prisoners of war who represented a major responsibility. By 1814 there were over 80,000 French prisoners in Britain.[12] Betsey Fremantle, visiting Porchester Castle in 1797, noted in her diary that the French prisoners were 'very industrious and make all kinds of little works. We bought a Guillotine neatly done in bone'.[13] Porchester Castle, outside Portsmouth, was one of the nearest centres to Brighton to house such prisoners.

Mug, (038), c.1794, Swansea, Cambrian Pottery, height: 8.9cm, (3½in), blue-printed pearlware. The design entitled, 'A New Puzzle of Portraits … Striking Likenesses of the King & Queen of England and the late King & Queen of France' demonstrates British alarm at recent events in France.[14] Based on an engraving published by Edward Orme on 18 January, 1794, it derives from puzzle pictures such as *L'Urne Mysterieuse*, a *trompe l'oeil* of 1793 print by F.-J. Crussaire, popular at the French court. The contours of the urn and surrounding vegetation hide silhouettes of Louis XVI and Marie Antoinette outlined by the twisting bodies of two snakes.[15] The snakes have already split the royal crown and broken the sword of the nobility and the mace of state, as they tear leaves from the fleur-de-lys.

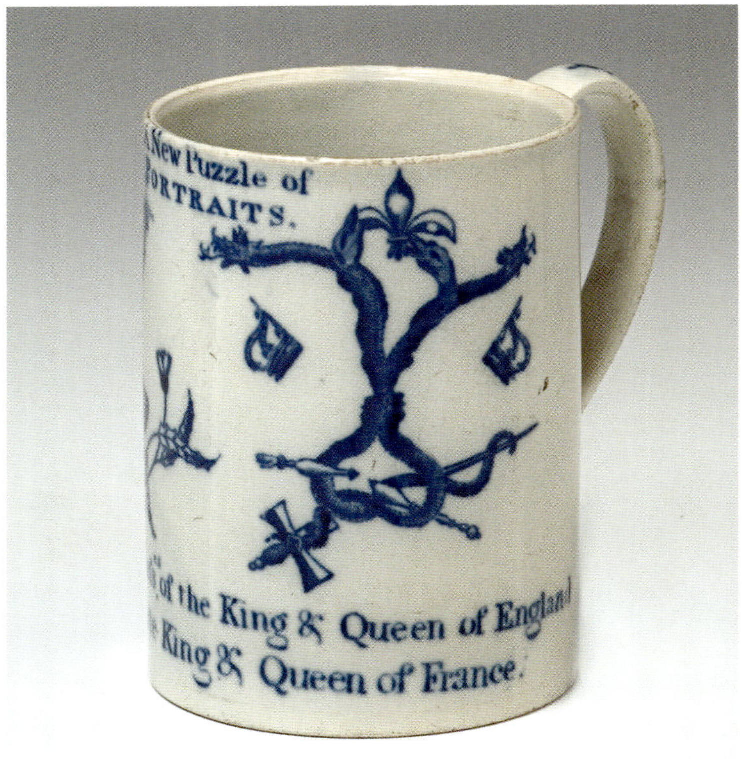

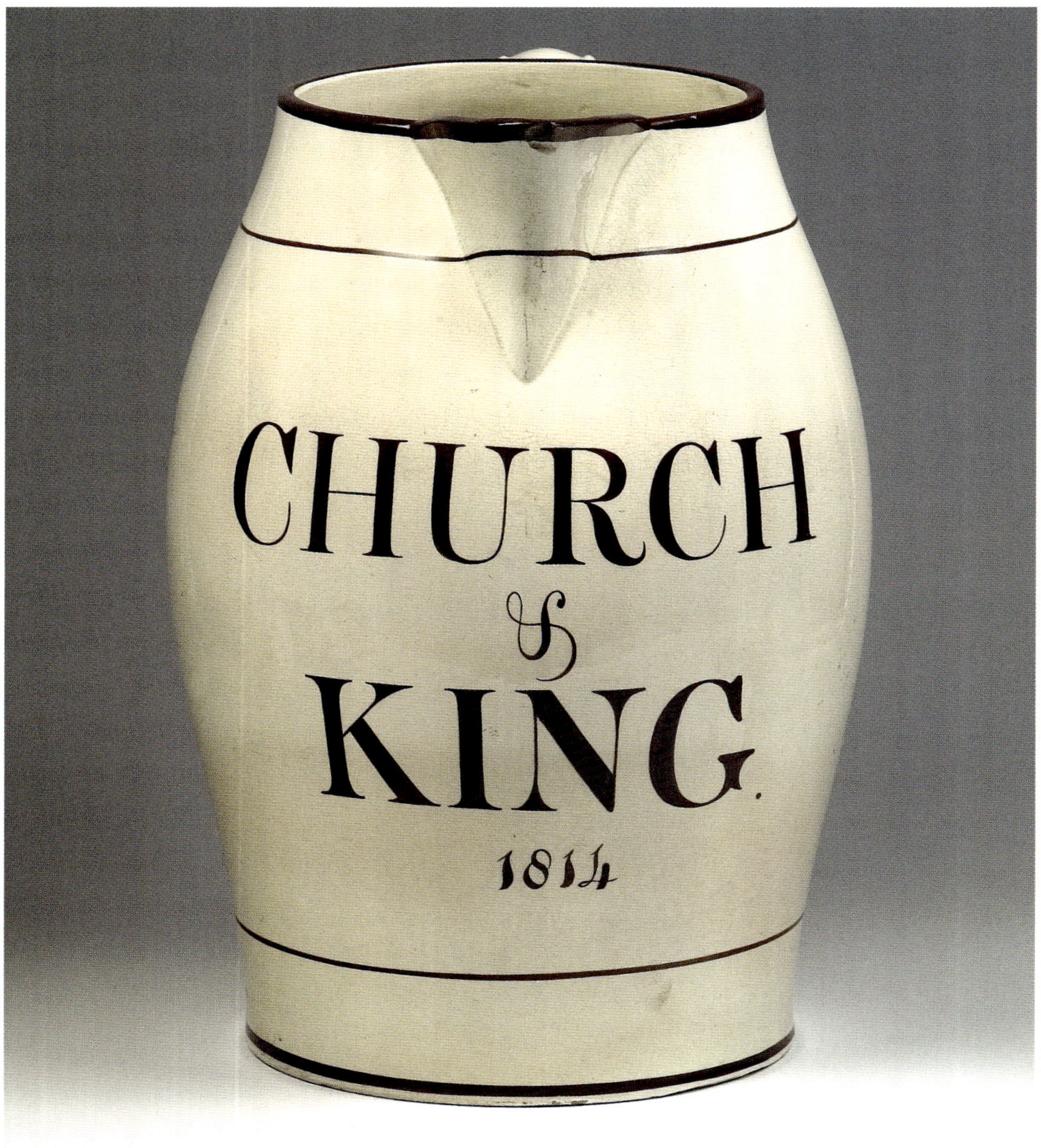

Large Jug, (864), 1814, Bristol Pottery, height: 36.8cm, (14½in), enamelled creamware. The red-painted inscription, 'CHURCH & KING 1814', is connected with the virulent anti-French sentiments that spread through Britain during the Terror. In May 1792 George III had approved a proclamation against sedition and by November, James Reeves had founded the Crown and Anchor Society to promote anti-radical (i.e. anti-French) propaganda, with the tacit encouragement of the government.

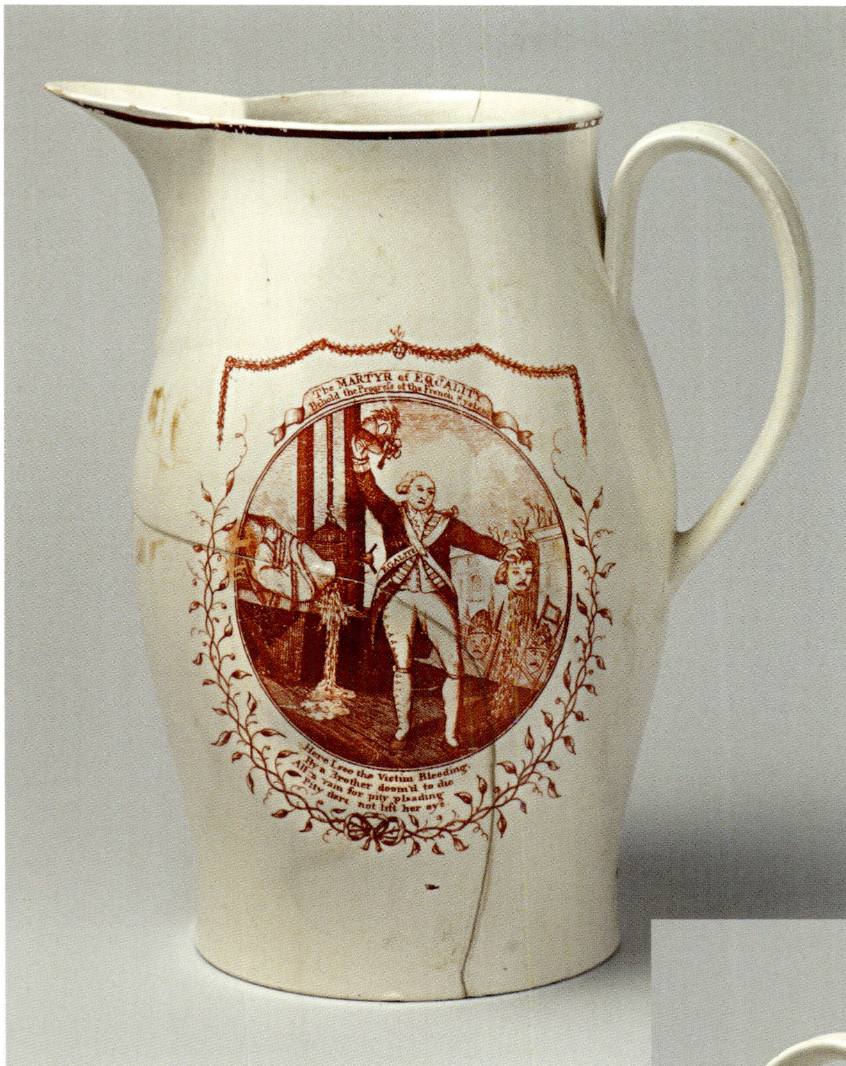

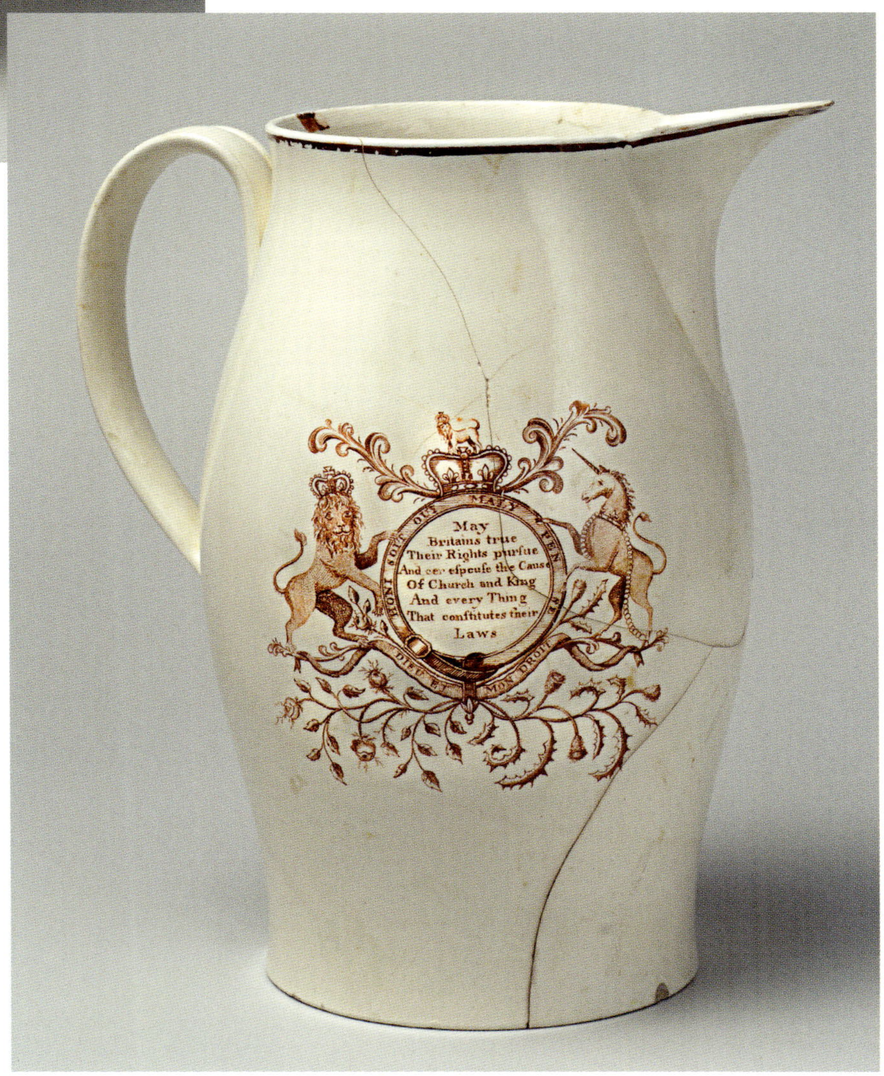

Jug, (373), c.1794, Liverpool or Wales, height: 24.8cm, (9¾in), red-printed creamware. The Revolutionary aristocrat, Louis-Philippe-Joseph, Duke of Orleans, (known as Philippe Egalité), holds up the severed head of his cousin, King Louis XVI. An emotional verse exhorts pity for the hapless victim, 'By a Brother doom'd to die'. The design is based on Isaac Cruikshank's etching, *The Martyr of Equality.*[16] Philippe Egalité, the man permitted by court protocol to hand the king his undershirt at his daily dressing ceremony, had visited Brighton in 1784 and 1790, taking Marlborough House for the social season.[17] He himself mounted the scaffold on 7 November 1793. On the reverse a quasi-heraldic assemblage; a crowned lion and unicorn supporting the Garter, inscribed with a verse: 'May / Britains true / their Rights pursue / And e'er espouse the Cause / of Church and King / And every Thing that constitutes their / Laws.' These rousing patriotic sentiments reflect the shocked response to events in France and their possible effect on a Britain where the king had only recently recovered from a debilitating bout of mental illness.[18]

Napoleon

The Corsican-born Napoleon Bonaparte (1769-1821) won a commission from the Paris Ecole Militaire into the French Royal Artillery in 1785. He was appointed Général de Brigade after the recapture of the port of Toulon in 1793, commanded the artillery in Italy in 1794 and by 1796 was in charge of the entire Italian army. Despite an unsuccessful foray into the Middle East, he was elected First Consul of France in December 1799 but it was not until the Peace of Amiens, signed in March 1802, that he first appeared on British ceramics.

Admiration for Napoleon as a commander was widespread in Britain at this time, particularly among those who leaned towards Republicanism. The celebrations that preceded the signing of the peace treaty included the projecting of 'transparencies' or large painted caricatures, onto the sides of London buildings. According to the Radical William Cobbett, many of these transparencies 'were expressive of attachment to Buonaparte's person, or to the cause of France'. One hailed Napoleon as the 'Saviour of the Universe'.[19]

The writer, Fanny Burney, was very impressed by Napoleon's appearance during a close encounter with 'Le Premier Consul' at a troop review in Paris in 1802,

> '[his face] is of a deeply impressive cast, pale even to sallowness, while not only in the Eye, but in every feature, Care, Thought, Melancholy & Meditation are strongly marked, with so much of character, nay Genius, & so penetrating a seriousness – or rather sadness, as powerfully to sink into an observer's mind'.[20]

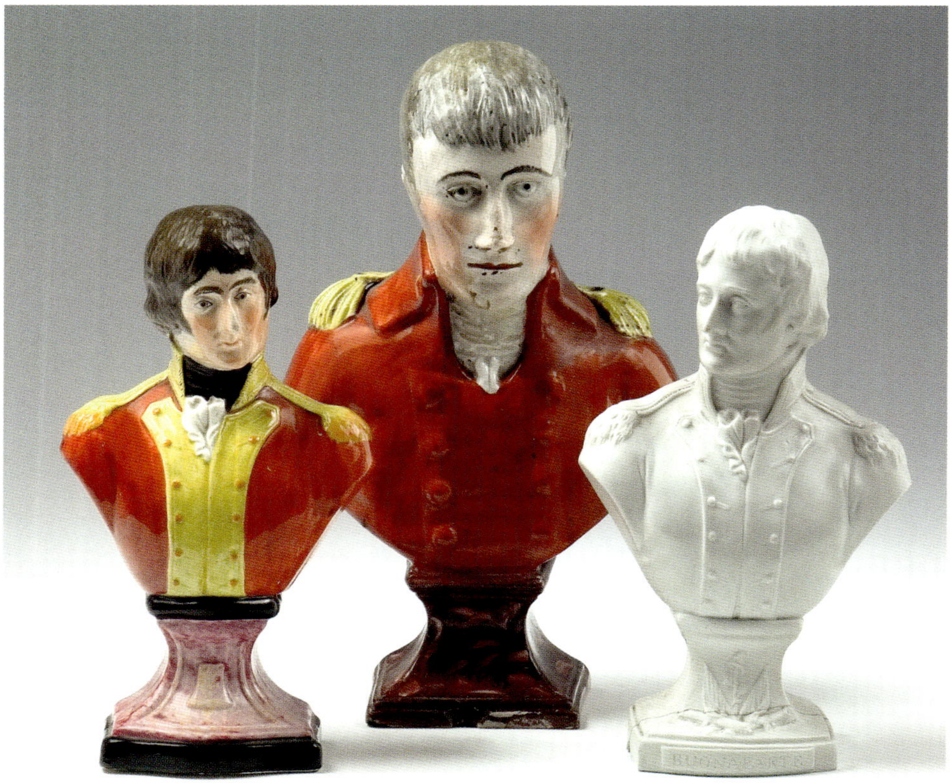

Portrait Bust, (400), c.1805, Staffordshire, perhaps Burslem, height: 21.6cm, (8½in), enamelled pearlware. Portrait of Napoleon as First Consul, perhaps by Enoch Wood.
Portrait Bust, (395), c.1805, Staffordshire, height: 26.7cm, (10½in), enamelled pearlware. Portrait of Napoleon as First Consul.
Portrait Bust, (403), c.1805, Liverpool, Herculaneum, height: 21.6cm, (8½in), porcellanous stoneware. One of a series featuring renowned military leaders, it retains traces of gilding. Mounted on a waisted rectangular socle, impressed 'Bonaparte' and moulded with military symbols including the Phrygian Cap.

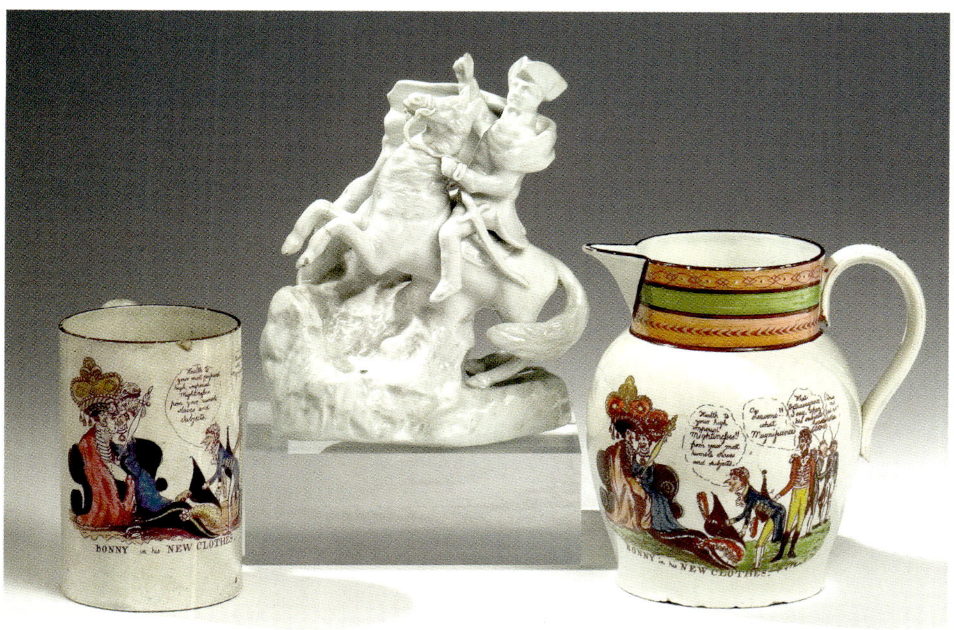

Mug, (377), c.1805, Staffordshire, height: 16.5cm, (6½in), pearlware, printed and enamelled.
Figure Group, (378), c.1805, France, height: 17.8cm, (7in), hard-paste porcelain. Equestrian portrait of Napoleon taken from Jacques-Louis David's dramatic painting of 1801, showing Napoleon crossing the St Bernard Pass, now at Versailles.[21]
Jug, (376), c.1805, Staffordshire, height: 12.1cm, (4¾in), pearlware, printed and enamelled. The comic satire, 'BONNY in his NEW CLOTHES', shows Napoleon in his new role as Emperor, following his proclamation of 18 May 1804. He wears an oversized crown and beams from ear to ear as he and Josephine receive their grovelling subjects. Both pieces made by Thomas Harley, and signed by John Henry Clive.[22]

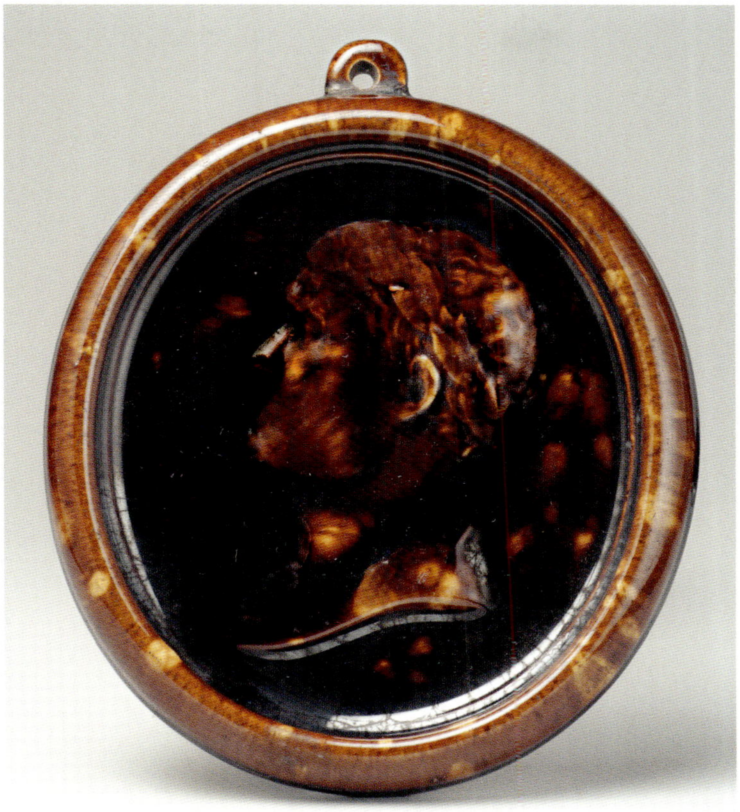

Plaque, (411), c.1805, Staffordshire, height: 16.5cm, (6½in), brown-glazed earthenware. Circular plaque, relief-moulded with Napoleon in profile wearing a laurel wreath, resembling an antique coin or medal. It dates from the time of his coronation.

Jug, (418), c.1845, London, Lambeth, height: 19.1cm, (7½in), stoneware. Moulded as the head of Napoleon; a fold in the rim of his cocked hat acts as a pouring lip. Stephen Green of Lambeth made these jugs in large numbers and different sizes during the 1840s, when the building of Trafalgar Square stirred memories of the Napoleonic Wars.

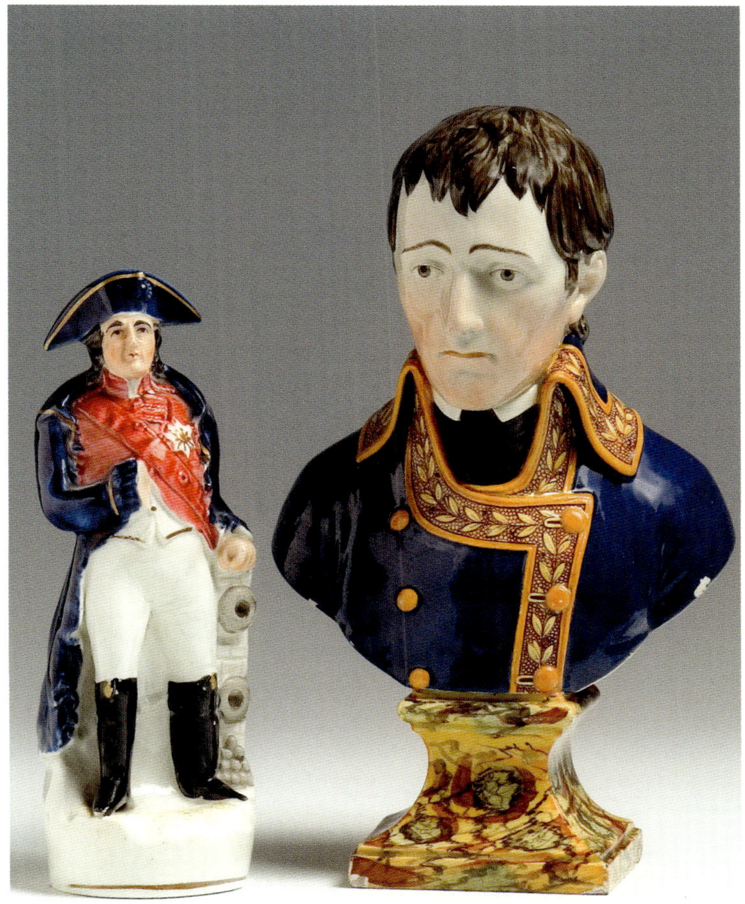

Figure, (402), c.1850, Staffordshire, height: 20.3cm, (8in), earthenware, enamelled and gilt the Emperor standing in characteristic pose, his right hand thrust into his left jacket opening, while his left rests on a gun emplacement.

Bust, (405), c.1802, Staffordshire, Burslem, height: 25.4cm, (10in), enamelled pearlware. The most accomplished portrait bust of Napoleon shows him as First Consul, wearing a richly enamelled military jacket.

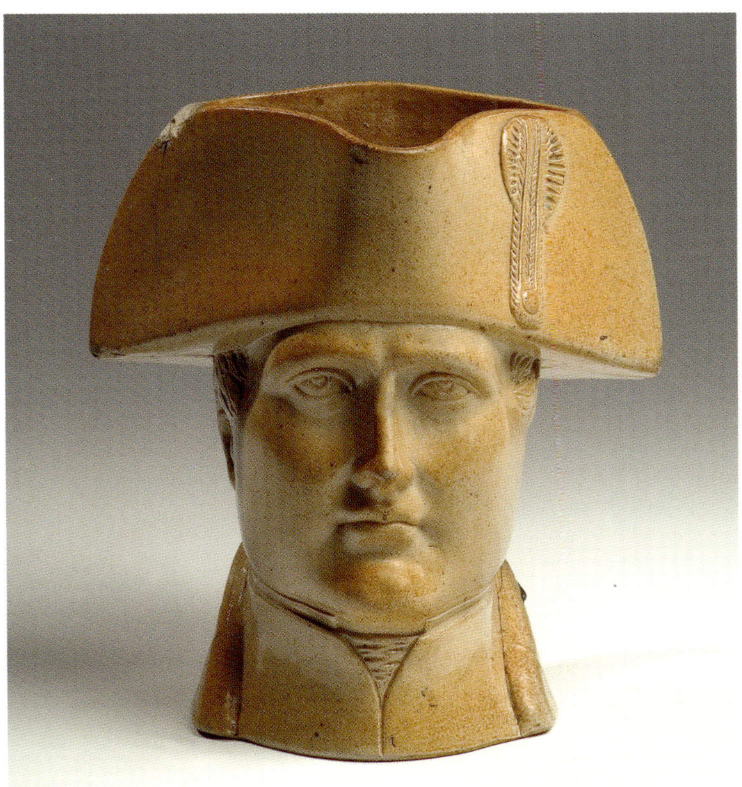

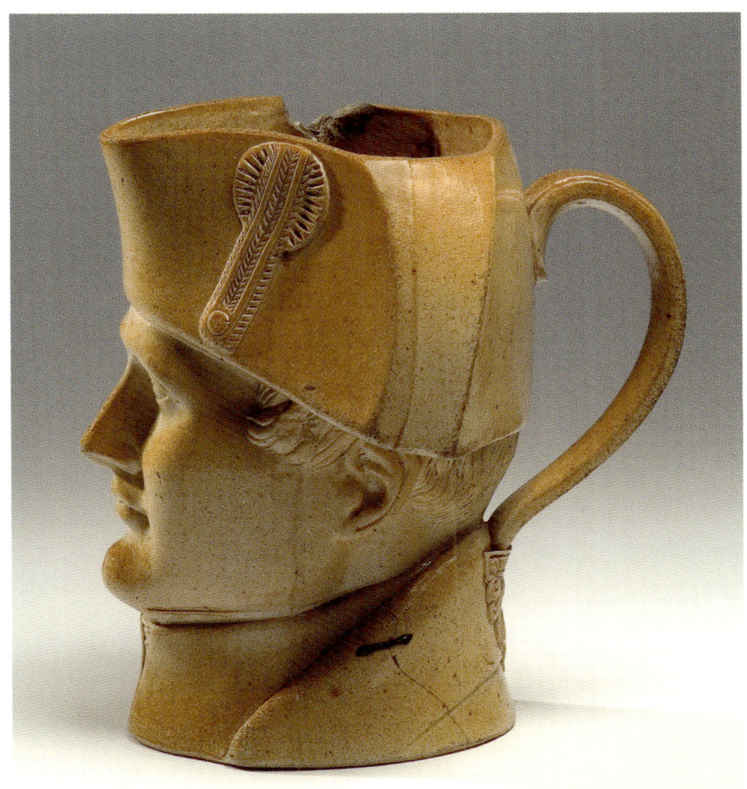

The Great Invasion Scare

Following the resumption of hostilities in 1803, hundreds of anti-Napoleonic caricatures were produced, whose subtext was to boost public morale during this uncertain period. A number of these caricatures, which portrayed Bonaparte in turn as ridiculous, arrogant, pusillanimous or the Devil incarnate, were used to decorate ceramic jugs and mugs.[23] The knockabout humour of these images and the easy slang of the captions were intended to play down very real anxiety and fear, as Britain faced the first prospect of invasion from France since the Norman Conquest. Huge contingents of troops were stationed along the South coast of England while a vast network of underground bunkers and defensive forts, (the Martello Towers) was built.

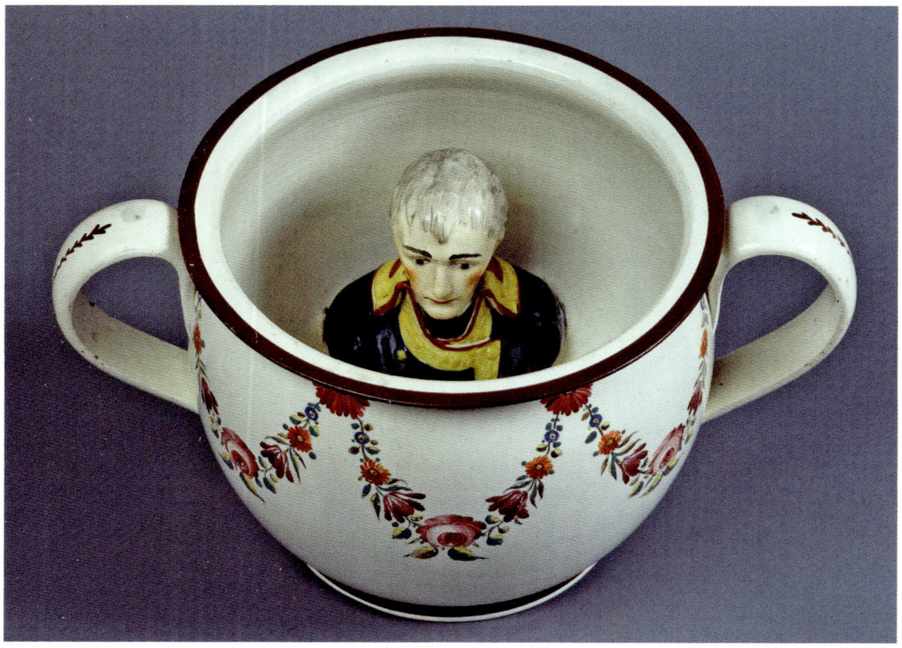

Chamber Pot, (R4554/7), c.1805, Liverpool or Staffordshire, height: 28.5cm, (11¼in), enamelled creamware with pearlware bust. Portrait bust of Napoleon cemented to base of chamber pot made in Staffordshire or Liverpool, 1810-15.[24] Exterior finely painted with swags of flowers while the word 'PEREAT' (Let him Perish!) is painted in front of the bust within. During the Napoleonic Wars a Briton could perform his patriotic duty every night, humiliating Public Enemy Number One by urinating on his head.[25]

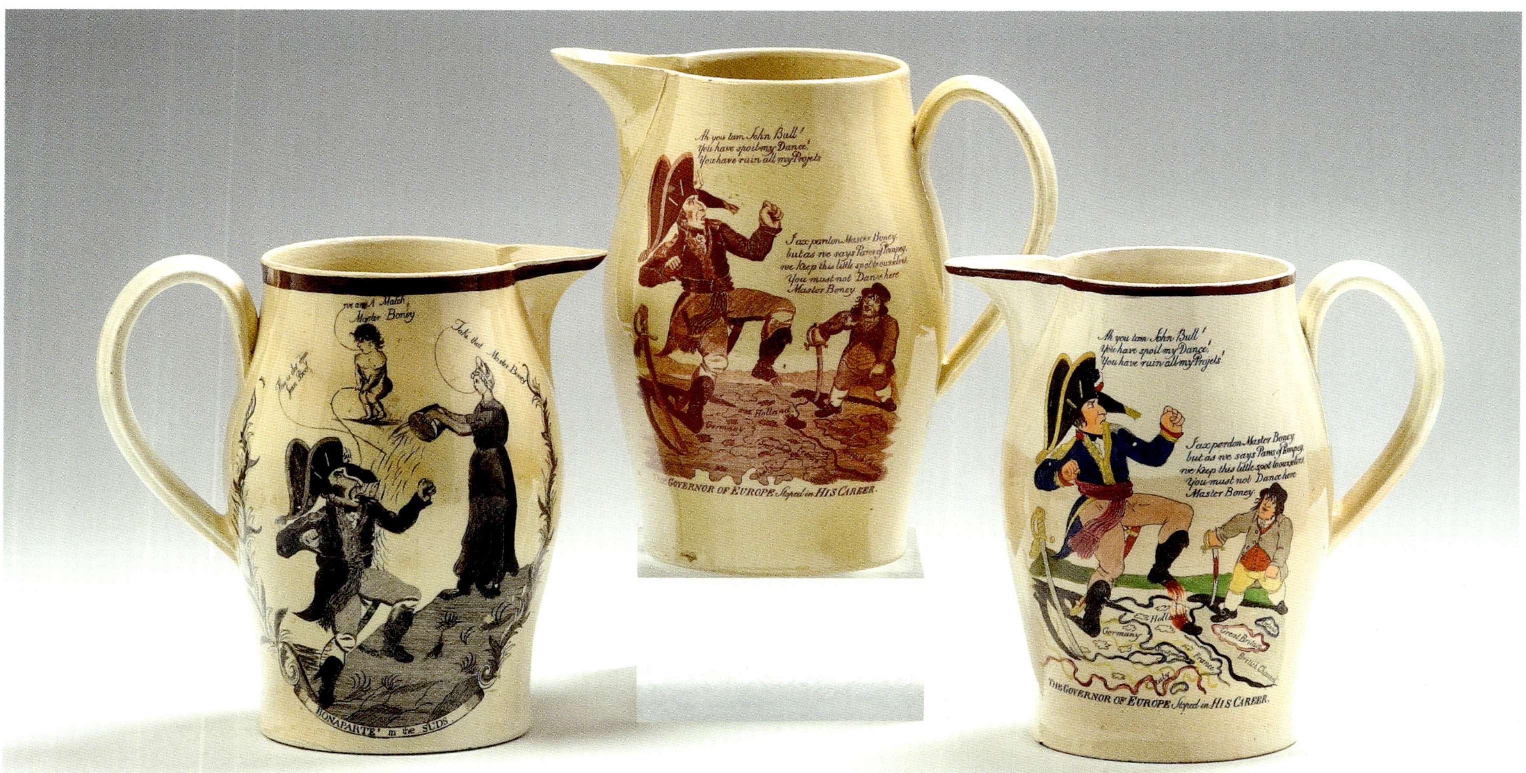

Jug, (410), c.1805, Staffordshire or Liverpool, height: 17.1cm, (6¾in), printed and painted creamware. 'THE GOVERNOR OF EUROPE Stoped [*sic*] in HIS CAREER', (see below). A crude but unusual altered version painted on the reverse, entitled 'BONAPARTES in the SUDS'. A woman empties slops onto Bonaparte and a child urinates on him.[26]
Jug, (404), c.1805, Staffordshire or Liverpool, height: 16.5cm, (6½in), red-printed creamware. 'THE GOVERNOR OF EUROPE Stoped [*sic*] in HIS CAREER', shows the small but plucky John Bull amputating Napoleon's toes as he dances across the Channel. The print was published a month before war was declared and proved enduringly popular.[27] The map of Europe on which the adversaries stand may be inaccurate but the message is clear. John Bull apologises politely but warns, 'Paws off Pompey / We keep this little spot to ourselves'.[28]
Jug, (422), c.1805, Staffordshire or Liverpool, height: 17.8cm, (7in), creamware, printed and enamelled. 'THE GOVERNOR OF EUROPE Stoped [*sic*] in HIS CAREER', (as above).

Clockwise:
Mug, (419), c.1805, Staffordshire, height: 9.6cm, (3¾in), red-printed creamware. Over-large version of 'JOHN BULL peppering BONAPARTE in the FRONT and REAR'.[29] John Bull, dressed as a Volunteer, quickly gains the upper hand as the Frenchman pleads for mercy.
Mug, (416), c.1805, Staffordshire, height: 8.9cm, (3½in), red-printed creamware. 'JOHN BULL peppering BONAPARTE' (as above) but reversed, entitled, 'John Bull Drubbing Bonaparte'.
Mug, (397), c.1805, Staffordshire, height: 12.7cm, (5in), red-printed creamware. 'JOHN BULL out of all PATIENCE!!', shows John Bull in full regimental uniform as a light-horse volunteer, crossing the Channel on the back of the British Lion, while a tiny Bonaparte flees.[30]
Mug, (396), c.1805, Staffordshire, Stoke-on-Trent, height: 9.6cm, (3¾in), printed creamware. A print entitled 'A COCK & BULL STORY' decorates a small mug from the Spode factory.[31] A Napoleon-headed cockerel turns to face an ox with the features of George III, comfortably positioned on the opposing cliffs.

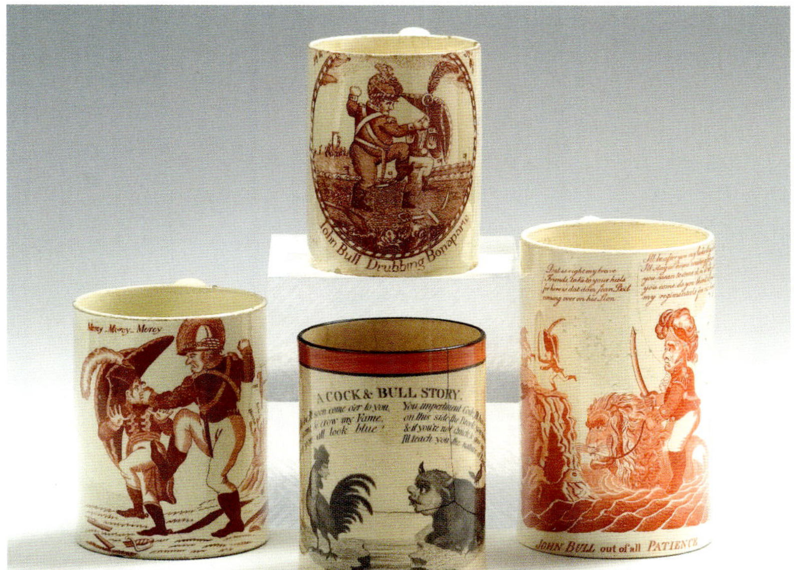

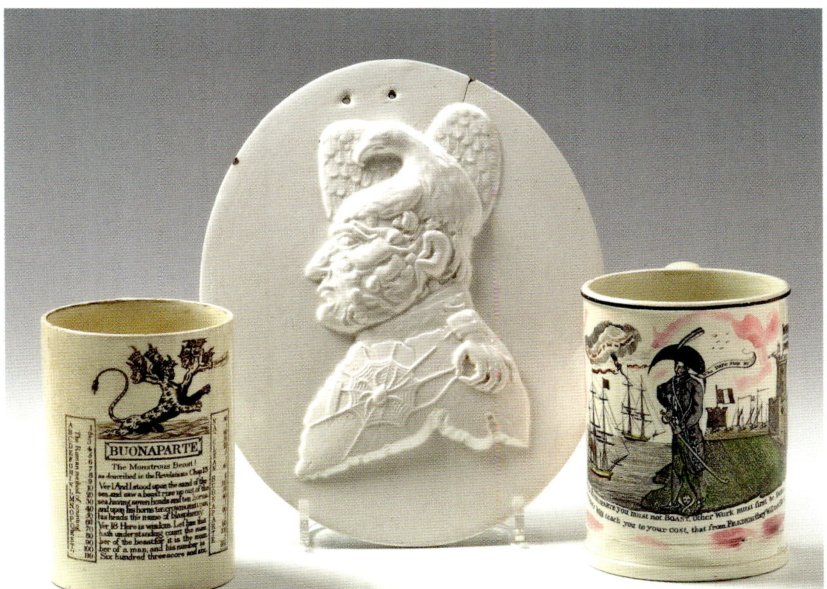

Mug, (417), c.1810, possibly Swansea, height: 12.1cm, (4¾in), printed creamware. 'BONAPARTE The Monstrous Beast!' (attributed to Baker, Bevans and Irwin) attempts to identify Napoleon with the Antichrist, as described in Revelation chapter 13.[32] A many-headed monster is flanked by tables allotting numerical values to letters of the alphabet. The total 666, (the 'Number of the Beast' in Revelation), is only achieved when his name is misspelled as 'Napolean'. The politician John Cam Hobhouse declared in 1816, 'preachers and politicians of the present age; who by helping out the Apocalypse with an anagram, behold in this warrior sometimes the Horned Beast,..'.[33]
Plaque, (420), c.1815, possibly Staffordshire, height: 23.5cm, (9¼in), bone china. Relief-moulded with a mysterious profile bust of Napoleon as a *trompe l'oeil* composition. Writhing human bodies compose his face, an imperial eagle his cocked hat, a hand serves for an epaulette and a spider for a military decoration. An explanatory print identifies the collar and shoulder of his coat as a map of the English Channel and North Germany.[34]
Mug, (394), c.1805, Newcastle upon Tyne, height: 12.7cm, (5in), pearlware, printed, coloured and lustred. 'STOP BUONAPARTE you must not BOAST' (signed: W.C. for Walter Cockburn) shows Napoleon standing on cliffs before a fortress flying a flag with the word 'LIBERTY' inverted, a skull and crossbones at his feet. He unsheathes his sword and defies the assembled British fleet, yelling 'Who Dare Stop Me'. The castle is that of Fort Qait Bey, outside Alexandria in Egypt, referring to Nelson's victory over the French at the Battle of the Nile in 1798.[35]

Jug, (414), c.1805, Staffordshire, Lane End, height: 15.3cm, (6in), pearlware, printed and enamelled. 'BONAPARTE and the QUAKER' has the Quaker reply to Bonaparte's accusations of cowardice (a reference to Quaker pacifism) that if the French come to Britain they will all be made 'Quakers' – from fear.[36] (All three engravings signed by Thomas Harley of Lane End. All three jugs printed with flower sprays on the reverse).
Jug, (409), c.1805, Staffordshire, Lane End, height: 15.9cm, (6¼in), pearlware, printed and enamelled. 'FACING the ENEMY', shows John Bull as a London Volunteer with a growling mastiff, glowering at a skinny Frenchman.[37]
Jug, (424), c.1805, Staffordshire, Lane End, height: 14cm, (5½in), pearlware, printed and enamelled. 'JOHNY BULL giving BONEY A PULL', mocks the helpless Frenchman's plea for mercy ('Misericordi'); his captor refuses to 'measure the cord' as he prepares to hang him.[38]

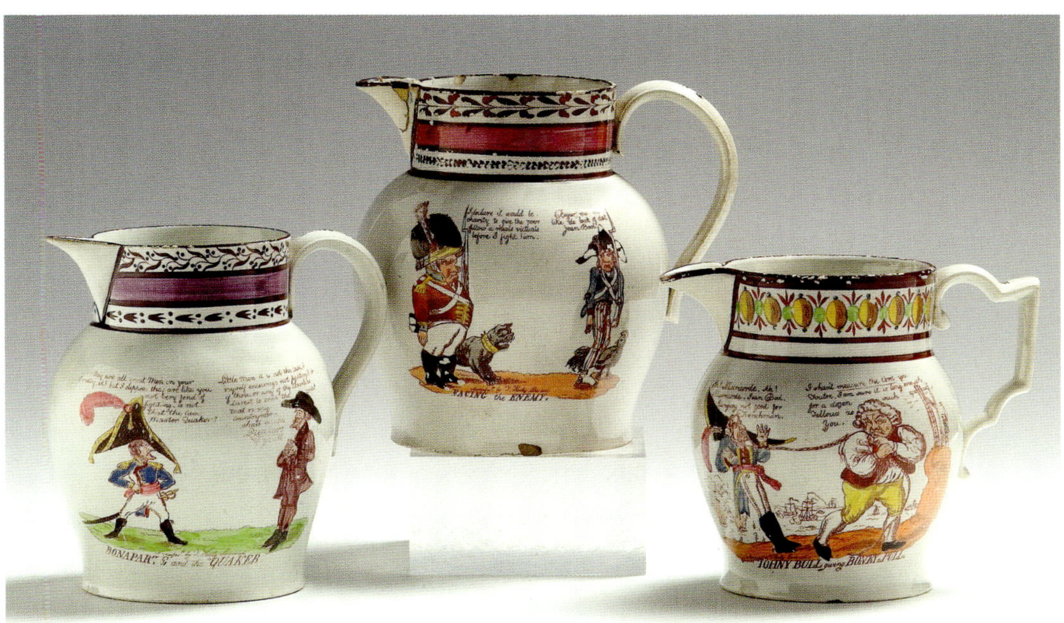

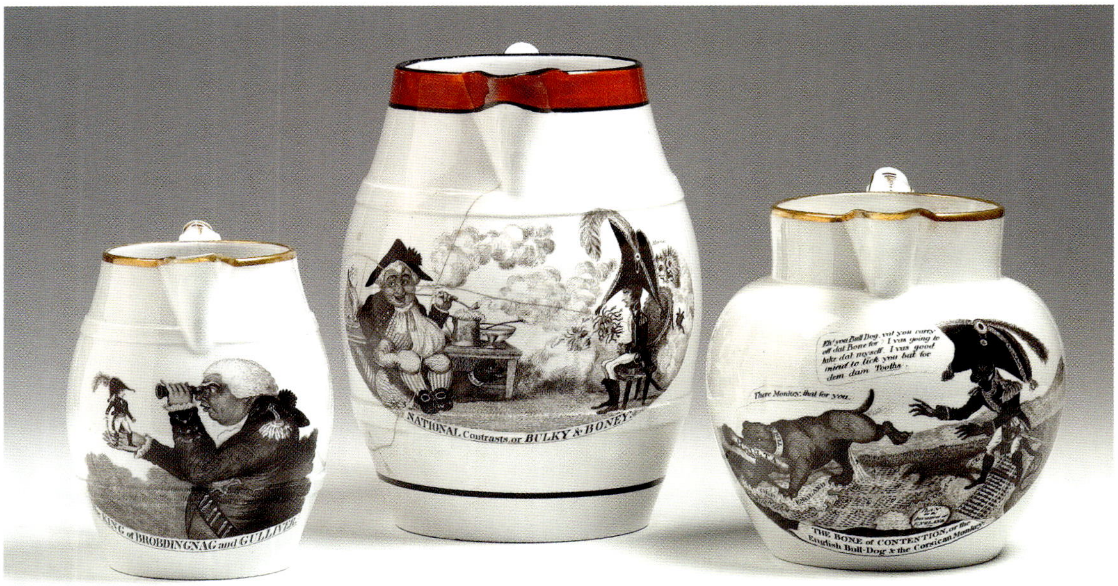

Jug, (399), c.1802, Staffordshire, height: 20.3cm, (8in), pearlware, printed and enamelled. 'The Centinel at his Post or BONEY'S peep into Walmer Castle!!'[43] shows William Pitt, dressed as Colonel of the Cinque Port Volunteers. While briefly out of office in 1801, Pitt withdrew to Walmer Castle, his base as Lord Warden of the Cinque Ports. When war resumed he raised three battalions, fully intending to lead them against the French who were expected imminently.

Jug, (393), c.1805, Staffordshire, Stoke-on-Trent, Spode, height: 12.7cm, (5in), printed bone china. 'The KING of BROBDINGNAG and GULLIVER'; the gentle, giant king/George III observes tiny, pugnacious Gulliver/Napoleon, standing on his hand. James Gillray's etching was published by Hannah Humphrey on 26 June 1803.[39] The satire was inspired by a voyage in *Gulliver's Travels* by Jonathan Swift (published 1726), one of the most popular novels of the eighteenth century. Alexander Pope declared, 'it is universally read, from the cabinet council to the nursery'. When George III saw the print, he is said to have muttered, (referring to the bag-wig) 'Quite wrong, quite wrong, no bag in uniform.'[40]

Jug, (401), c.1805, Staffordshire, Stoke-on-Trent, Spode, height: 19.7cm, (7¾in), printed bone china with enamel. 'NATIONAL Contrasts, or BULKY & BONEY', contrasts the Englishman's good nature and opulent physique with Bonaparte, shown with Cruelty, Envy and Horrors.[41]

Jug, (398), c.1805, Staffordshire, Stoke-on-Trent, Spode, height: 14.6cm, (5¾in), printed bone china with gilding. 'THE BONE OF CONTENTION' John Bull-dog, with a large bone (labelled Malta) in its jaws, urinates on Napoleon's invasion fleet assembled in the Channel, while the 'Corsican Monkey' screeches ineffectually from France.[42] This refers to the contest for control of Valletta's strategically important Grand Harbour in Malta.

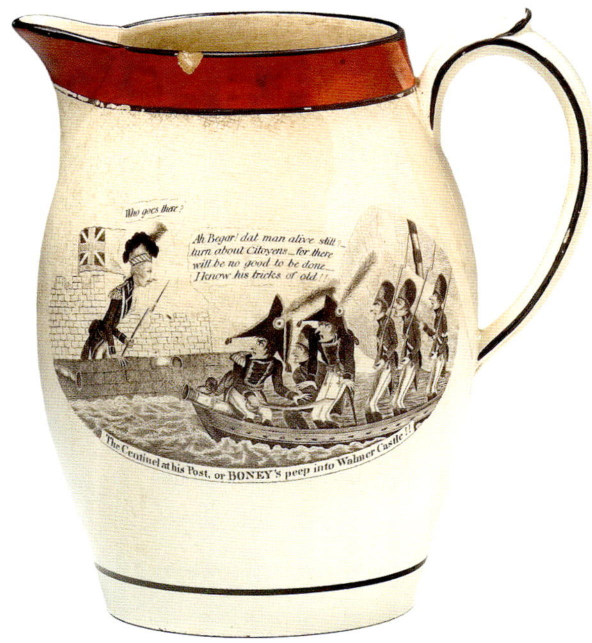

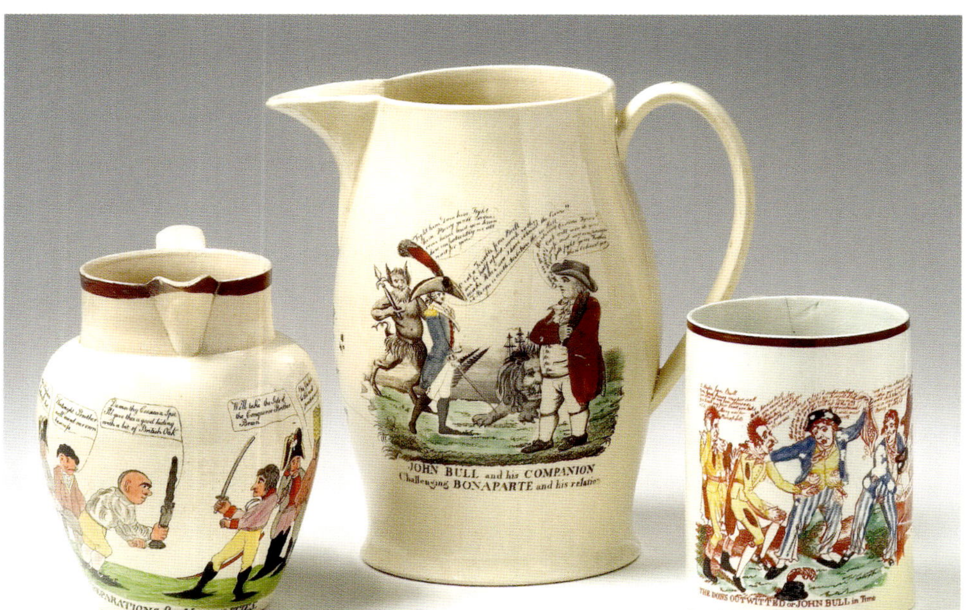

Jug, (413), c.1805, Staffordshire, height: 14cm, (5½in), pearlware, printed and enamelled. In 'PREPARATIONS for HOSTILITIES', a wigless John Bull brandishes a cudgel at a dapper Bonaparte with a sabre, while a Prussian, a Dutchman, an Austrian and a Russian watch from the sidelines.[44]

Jug, (415), c.1805, Staffordshire, height: 19.7cm, (7¾in), creamware, printed and enamelled. In 'JOHN BULL and his COMPANION / Challenging BONAPARTE and his relation', Napoleon is allied with the Devil, while John Bull stands beside the British Lion.[45] Napoleon's speech bubble refers to his recent coronation, so it must date between May 1804 when Napoleon was declared Emperor and September 1805, when the last of his troop units left their invasion camp at Boulogne.

Mug, (408), c.1805, Staffordshire, height: 11.8cm, (4⅝in), pearlware, printed and enamelled. 'THE DONS OUT-WITTED or John Bull in Time [for Once],' indirectly salutes the brother of the British hero, Sir John Moore. Captain Graham Moore commanded a group of British frigates that captured a Spanish treasure convoy from the New World on 3 October 1804.[46] It reflects the enthusiastic response to a questionable enterprise, since Britain was not at war with Spain, as one of the Dons points out.

The Invasion of Russia

Napoleon made slow progress into Russia during the summer of 1812 until, after the indecisive Battle of Borodino, the French took and occupied Moscow on 14 September. After the fire of Moscow, Napoleon decided to over winter in Smolensk. Pursued by the Russian army and totally unprepared for the severity of a Russian winter, the French army retreated in disarray, losing 500,000 men. Britain was incredulous and jubilant at Bonaparte's first major setback. Bonaparte abandoned his army in Russia on 5 December, to make a swift return to the French capital.

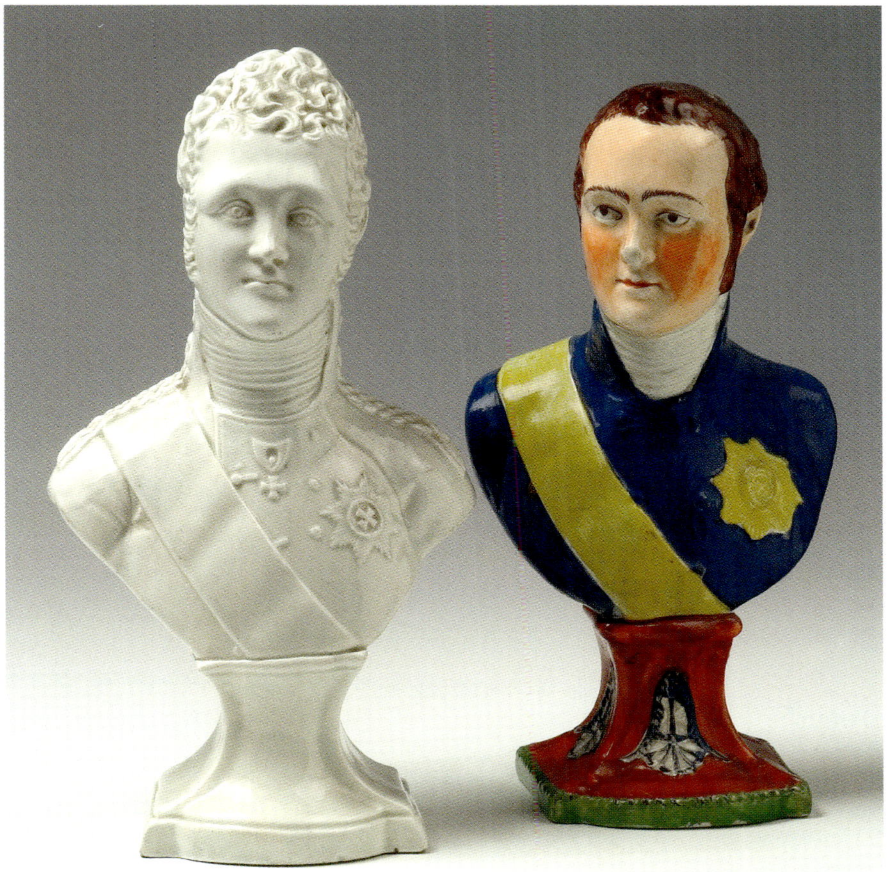

Bust, (385), c.1812, Staffordshire, height: 25.4cm, (10in), pearlware. Busts of Czar Alexander I of Russia were available before the disastrous Russian campaign of 1812 but when news of Napoleon's shambolic retreat from Moscow reached Britain he became a national hero.[47] This portrait, shown wearing the Garter Star, may represent the young Czar.
Bust, (380), c.1812, Staffordshire, height: 25.4cm, (10in), enamelled pearlware. In this portrait of Czar Alexander I, his hair is caught in a pigtail at the back. He also wears the Garter Star.

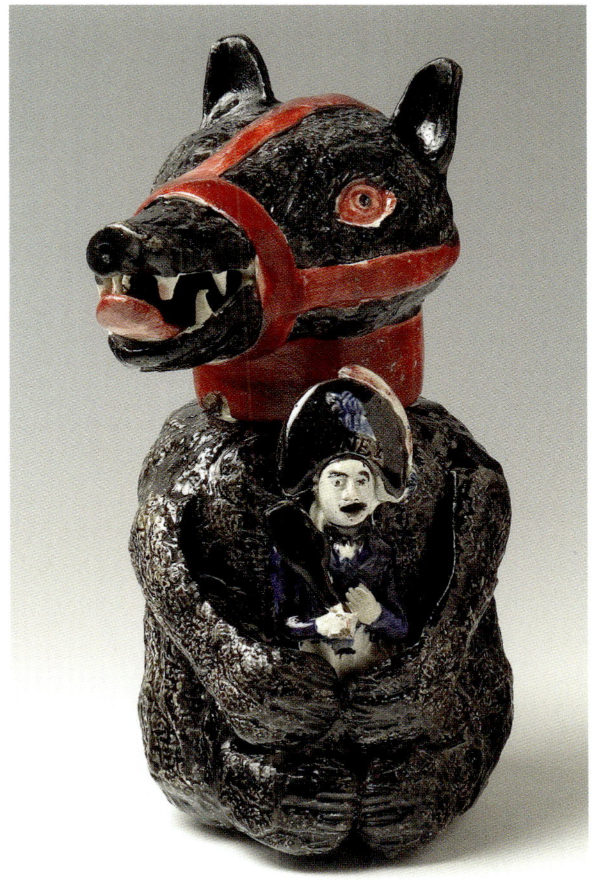

Jug, (383), c.1813, Staffordshire, height: 19.7cm, (7¾in), enamelled pearlware. This large bear jug subverts a traditional form, recalling bears kept for baiting and dancing. The bear now represents Russia and in place of an aggressive bull terrier, the bear grips and overpowers the tiny figure of Napoleon, his cocked hat clearly impressed: 'BONEY'.[48]

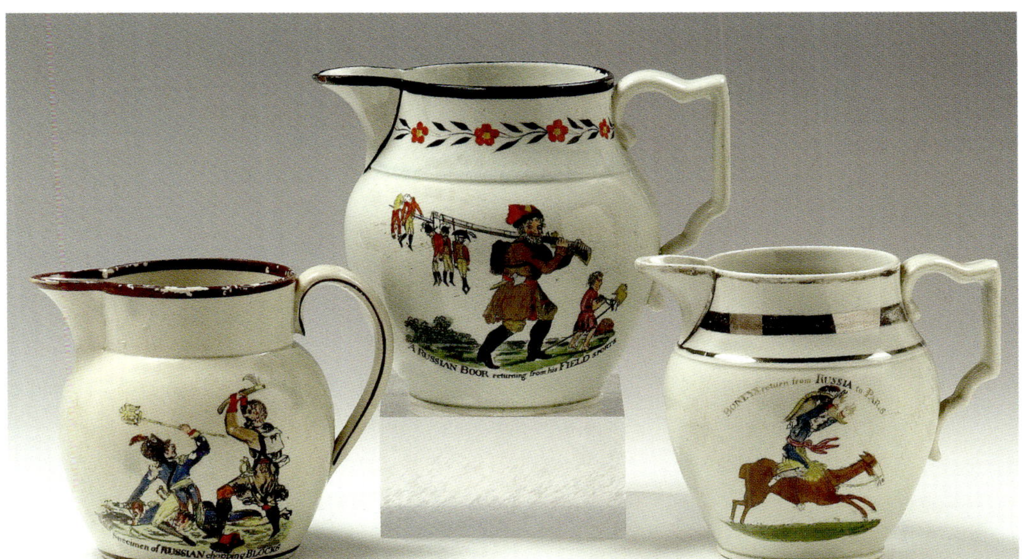

Jug, (381), c.1813, Staffordshire, height: 11.5cm, (4½in), pearlware, printed and enamelled. 'Specimen of RUSSIAN chopping BLOCKS' shows a Russian soldier disposing of the remains of the French army. On 13 January 1813, Hannah Humphrey published two adaptations by George Cruikshank (son of Isaac), of cartoons by the Russian artist, Ivan Terebenev, (first published in Russia the previous November).[49]
Jug, (391), c.1813, Staffordshire, height: 14cm, (5½in), pearlware, printed and enamelled. 'A RUSSIAN BOOR returning from his FIELD sports' carries a line of diminutive dead Frenchmen, suspended like rats from his bayonet. This was based on Cruikshank's adaptation of Terebenev's second print.
Jug, (388), c.1813, Staffordshire, height: 12.1cm, (4¾in), pearlware, printed, enamelled and lustred. 'BONEY sneaking into PARIS at MIDNIGHT' celebrates Bonaparte's shameful return from Russia. 'A RUSSIAN BOOR' appears on the reverse.[50]

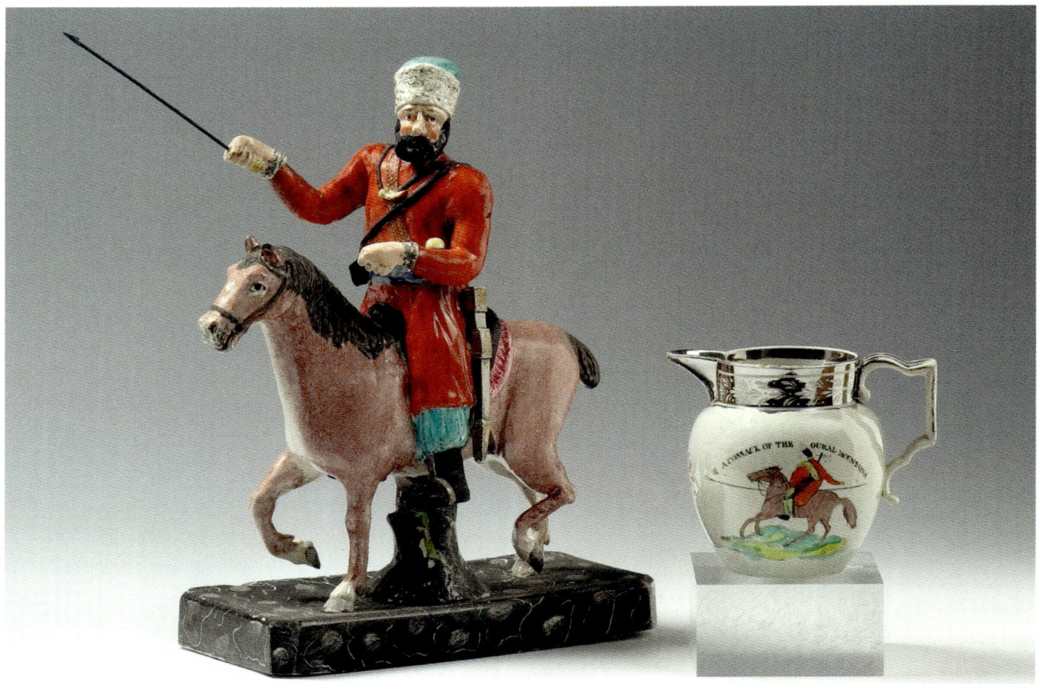

Figure Group, (392), c.1813, Staffordshire, height: 33cm, (13in), enamelled pearlware. A Russian Cossack is shown mounted on a stocky little pony, brandishing his pike.
Jug, (386), c.1813, Staffordshire, height: 12.1cm, (4¾in), enamelled pearlware. 'A COSSACK OF THE OURAL MOUNTAINS' is based on drawings by A. Orlovski, published 1813.

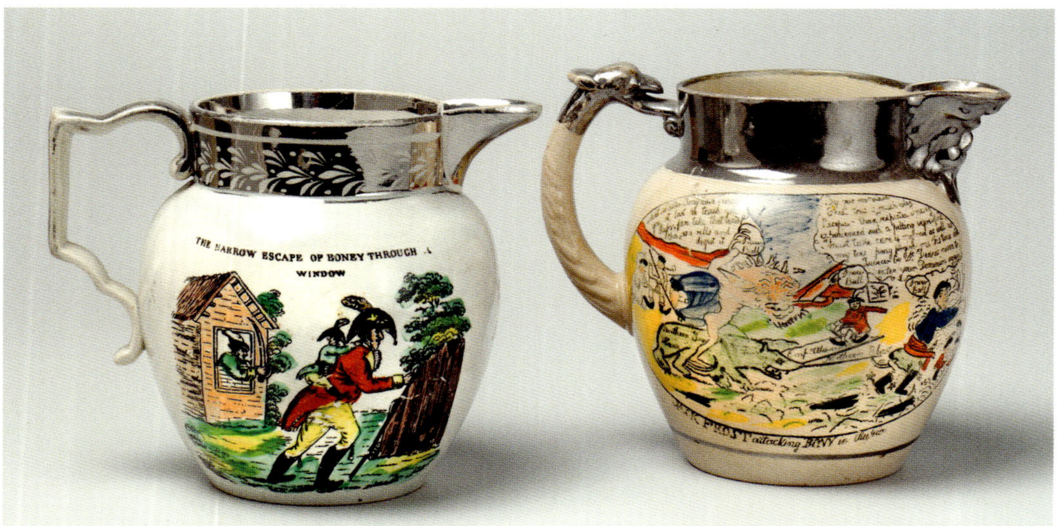

Jug, (386), c.1813, Staffordshire, height: 12.1cm, (4¾in), enamelled pearlware. 'THE NARROW ESCAPE OF BONEY THROUGH A WINDOW' is a totally fictitious incident.[51]
Jug, (390), c.1813, Staffordshire, height: 12.7cm, (5in), pearlware, printed, enamelled and lustred. 'JACK FROST attacking BONY in RUSSIA', shows the spiky, menacing figure of Frost, (evoking the Russian winter), mounted on a bear, blasting Boney's nose and toes.[52]

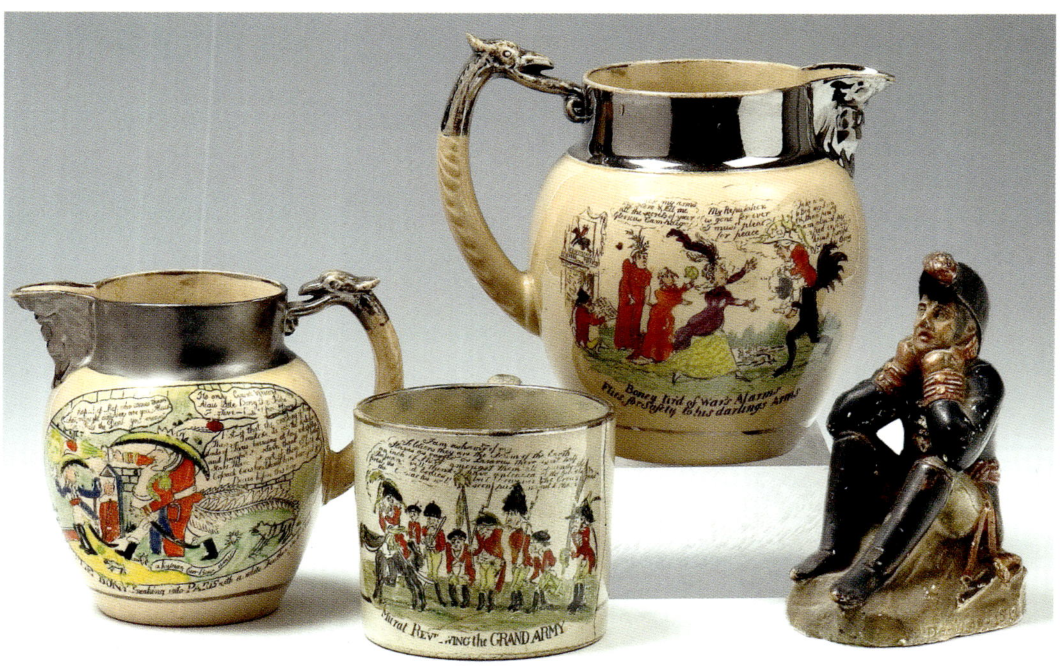

Jug, (390), c.1813, Staffordshire, height: 12.7cm, (5in), pearlware, printed, enamelled and lustred. A complex but crudely executed version of Napoleon's retreat to Paris appears on another Staffordshire jug, under a slightly different title, 'LITTLE BONY sneaking into PARIS – with a white feather in his tail'. It was drawn by Elmes, published by Thomas Tegg in January 1813.[53]
Mug, (379), c.1813, Staffordshire, height: 8.9cm, (3½in), pearlware, printed, enamelled and lustred. 'Murat, REVIEWING the GRAND ARMY' shows General Murat, Napoleon's brother-in-law, inspecting the pathetic remains of the French army entrusted to his charge when Napoleon left Russia.[54]
Jug, (388), c.1813, Staffordshire, height: 12.1cm, (4¾in), pearlware, printed, enamelled and lustred. 'Boney tir'd of War's Alarms / Flies for Safety to his darlings Arms' shows Napoleon being carried by the Devil to his wife, Marie Louise.[55]
Figure, (389), c.1813, London, height: 14cm, (5½in), pearlware, enamelled and lustred. A pensive French soldier sits on a mound with his chin in his hands, impressed, 'Decebr. 1 1812. Pub. As the Act directs.'

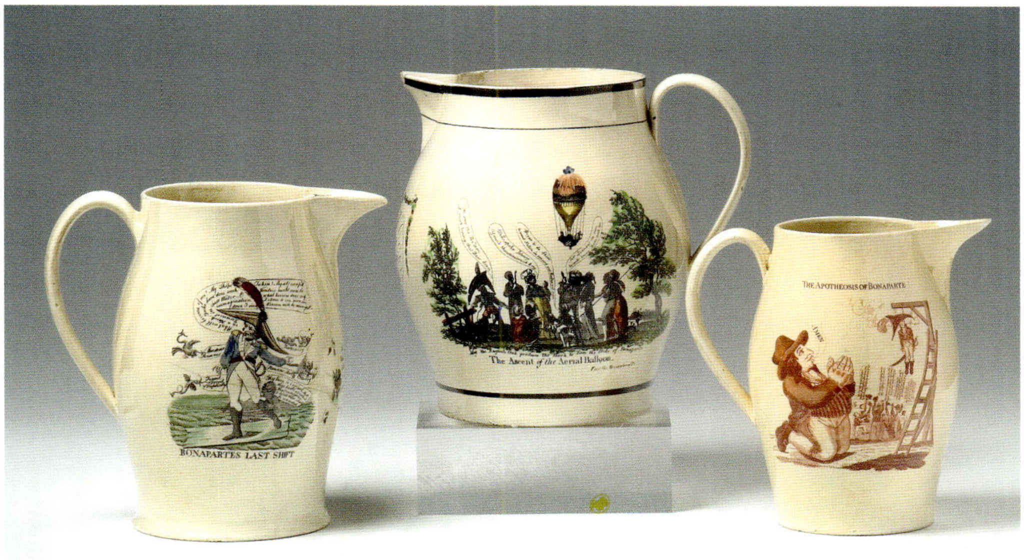

Jug, (415), c.1813, Staffordshire, height: 19.7cm, (7¾in), creamware, printed and enamelled.
'BONAPARTE'S LAST SHIFT' shows Napoleon escaping defeat on a raft, surrounded by little winged devils.
Jug, (412), 1813, Sunderland, Phillips & Co.'s Garrison Pottery, height: 20.3cm, (8in), pearl-ware, printed, enamelled and lustred.
One of the onlookers to 'The Ascent of the Aerial Balloon', (otherwise unrelated to European events[56]) exclaims, 'May the English oak produce the bark to tan the hide of Bonaparte.'
Jug, (422), c.1813, Staffordshire, height: 17.8cm, (7in), red-printed creamware. 'THE APOTHEOSIS OF BONAPARTE' (drawn by Woodthorpe, published by John Badcock's on 10 August 1803) shows John Bull, on his knees, giving thanks as Bonaparte hangs from the gallows.[57]

Flower Pot, (425), c.1815, Bristol Pottery, height: 14.6cm, (5¾in), printed pearlware. The design, celebrating the 'PEACE of EUROPE Signed at PARIS May 30, 1814' shows Peace and Plenty and national flags, including the fleurs-de-lys of the French monarchy, which replaced the tricolour. It also includes a tiny vignette of the pottery itself in the lower right corner.
Mug, (426), c.1815, Bristol Pottery, height: 11.5cm, (4½in), creamware, printed and enamelled. Similar design to (425). The Peace of Paris inspired only a limited range of ceramic souvenirs. The Bristol Pottery reused the print produced for the 1802 Peace of Amiens, on mugs, jugs and flowerpots.
Jar Lid, (424), c.1815, Staffordshire, height: 17.8cm, (7in), puce-printed pearlware. 'PEACE! May its duration equal the Years of the WAR', printed within a wreath of flowers, seems a little cautious!

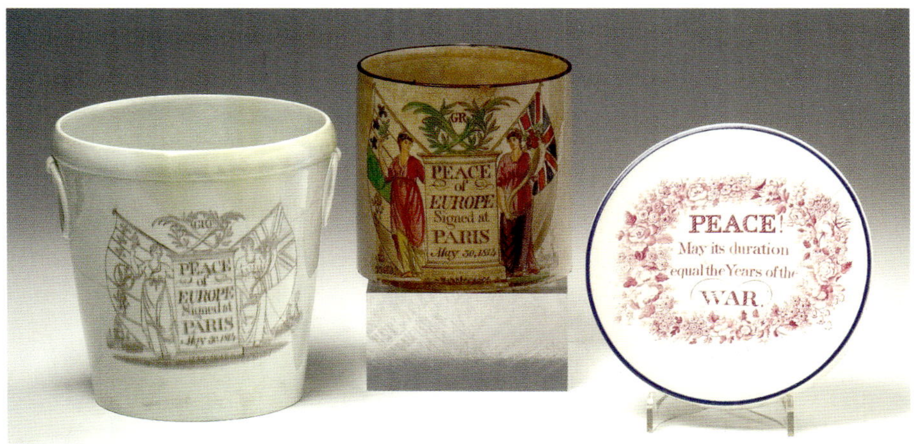

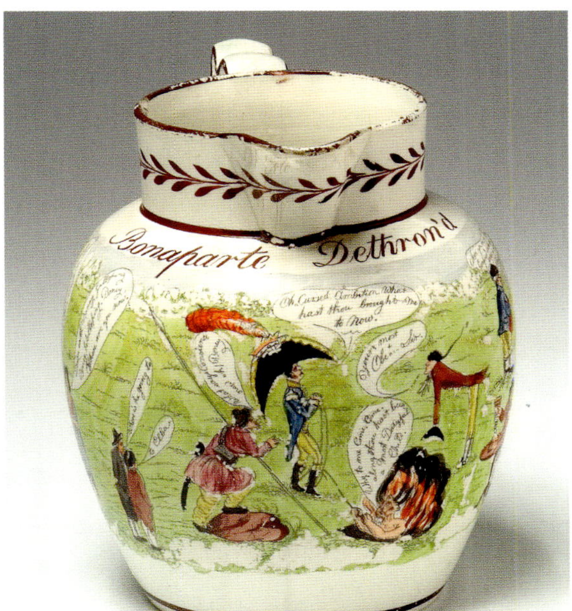

Jug, (423), c.1815, Swansea, height: 16cm, (6½in), pearlware, printed and enamelled. 'Bonaparte Dethron'd' shows Napoleon in chains, lamenting, 'Oh Cursed Ambition what hast thou brought me to Now', amid scenes of rejoicing.[58] Speech bubbles from two participants confirm that he is to be sent to Elba. The signature of James Brindley, an independent engraver who supplied prints to L.W. Dillwyn's Cambrian Pottery can just be seen.

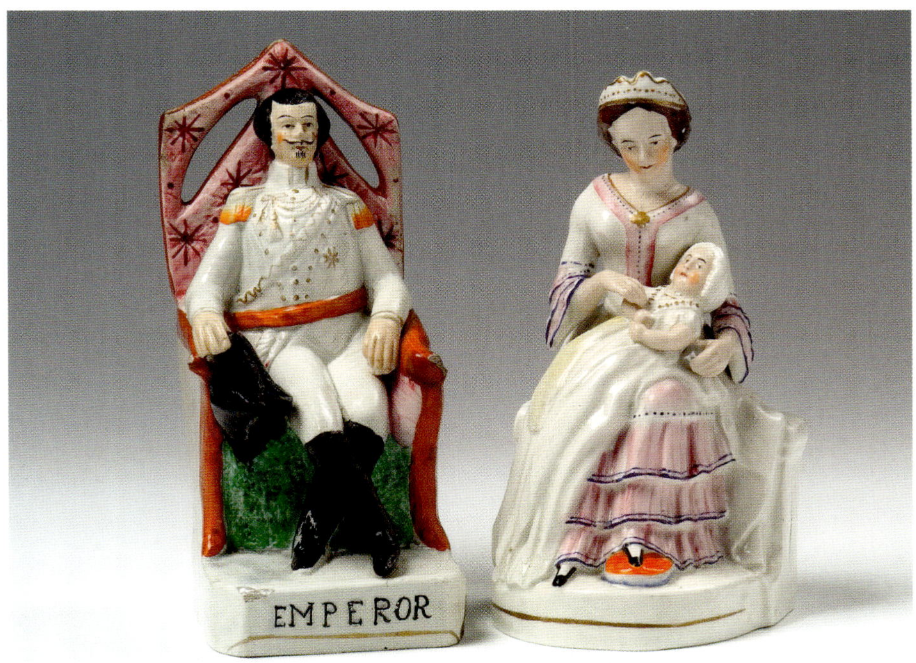

Figure, (382), c.1870, Staffordshire, height: 20.3cm, (8in), enamelled earthenware. Portrait figure of Napoleon III (1808-1873), entitled, 'EMPEROR', sitting in full dress uniform. Napoleon III was deposed after the Battle of Sedan in 1870; he and his family fled into exile in Britain.[59]
Figure, (094), c.1870, Staffordshire, height: 19.7cm, (7¾in), enamelled earthenware. Figure of Empress Eugénie (1826-1920), whom Willett mistook for Queen Victoria, cradles the Prince Imperial.[60] After their flight from France, the couple stayed for a time at the Grand Hotel in Brighton.[61]

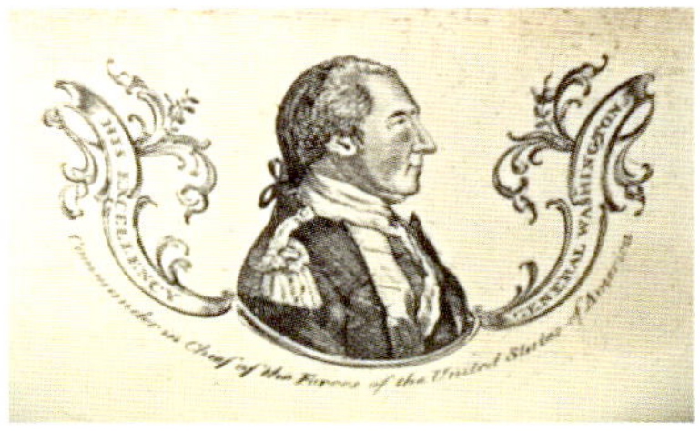

Chapter 6

ENGLAND & AMERICA

Early Colonists

The Pilgrim Fathers were far from the first people to leave Europe for America, nor indeed the first Englishmen[1]. Armed with a Patent to live in territory already settled by the Virginia Company, a disparate gathering of 102 Protestant dissenters (the core group from Scrooby in Nottinghamshire), set out aboard the *Mayflower* from Plymouth, Devon, on 6 September 1620. Having landed in Massachusetts on 22 December only half the Pilgrims lived through the first winter. However, in the autumn of 1621, the survivors assembled for a special meal, a gathering that would be repeated each year.

In 1635 Roger Williams, a church minister, was expelled from Salem, Massachusetts for challenging Puritan rules that interfered in religious matters and allowed the seizure of land without payment to indigenous people. In 1636 he and his followers founded Providence, Rhode Island, which, in 1644, was granted a charter from the English parliament as a new colony.

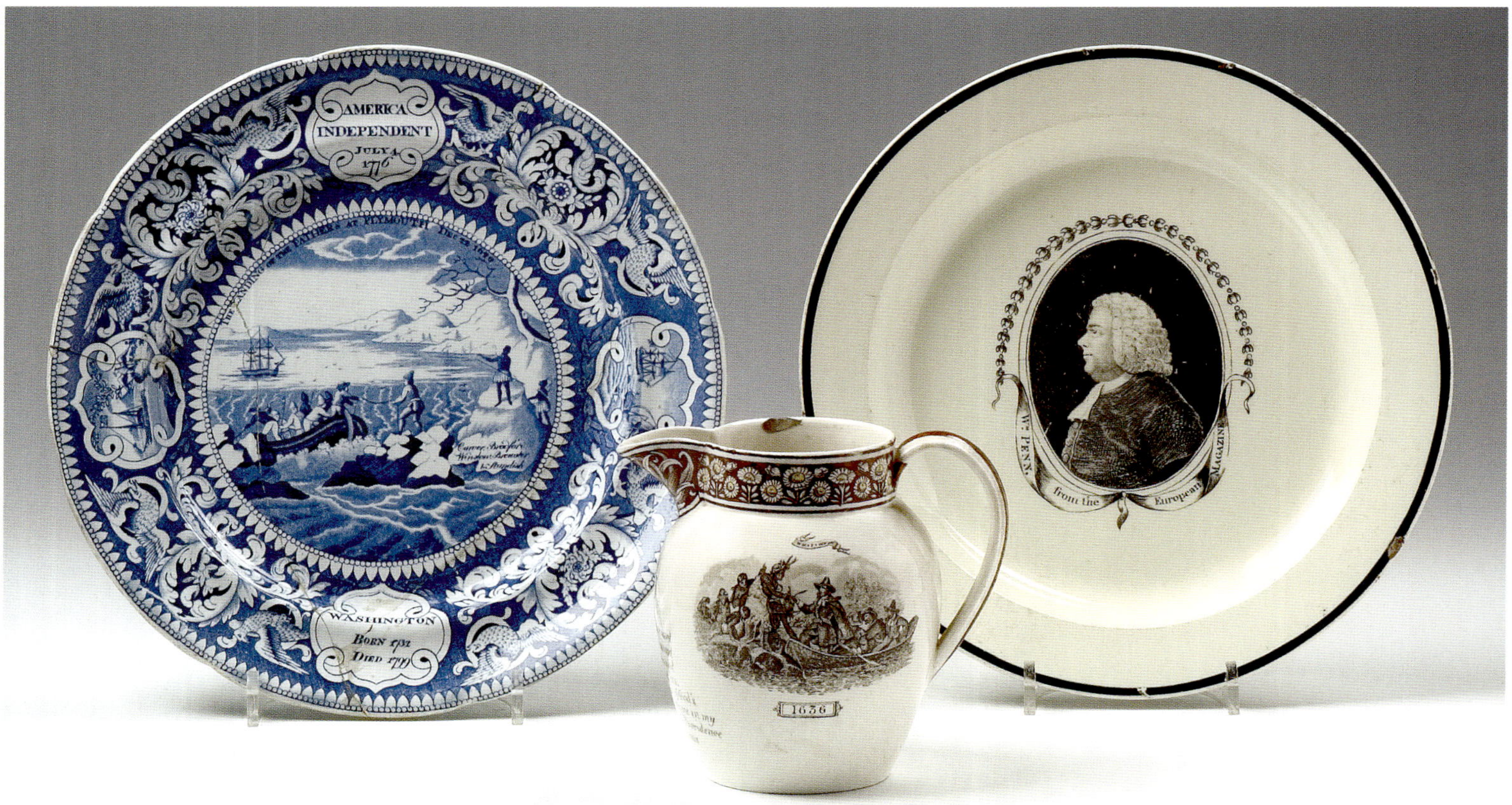

Plate, (428), c.1820, Staffordshire, Burslem, Enoch Wood, diameter: 25.4cm, (10in), blue-printed earthenware. 'THE LANDING OF THE FATHERS AT PLYMOUTH a DEC 22 1620 / Carver, Bradford, Winston, Brewster & Standish', shows the Pilgrim Fathers arriving in the New World. Image, taken from print by Samuel Hill, (a Boston engraver), decorated the invitation for the first annual Thanksgiving Dinner for the Sons of the Pilgrims, held on 2 December 1800.[2] It is probably a bicentenary commemorative.
Jug, (429), c.1886, Staffordshire, Wedgwood, height: 12.1cm, (4¾in), brown-printed earthenware. Roger Williams (1603-1683) shown landing among welcoming Native Americans, inscribed, 'WHAT CHEER … 1636'. Another portrait of Williams flanked by maize plants inscribed, 'I having made covenant /of peaceable neighborhood [*sic*] / with all the Sachems and / natives round about us; … called the place Providence. ROGER WILLIAMS'. Celebrates 250th anniversary of the settlment of Rhode Island.
Plate, (430), c.1791, Staffordshire, diameter: 24.1cm, (9½in), printed creamware. Profile portrait of William Penn (1644-1718), founder of Pennsylvania, for which he received the charter in 1681 in return for money owed him by Charles II. Founded as a haven for Quakers (the Society of Friends), it became a model of religious toleration whose capital, planned by Penn, was named Philadelphia, 'city of brotherly love'. The creamware plate, probably a centennial production, inscribed on a banner, 'Wm PENN / from the / European MAGAZINE'.[3]

The War of Independence

In 1773 Americans threw crates of imported tea (on which Britain levied tax) into Boston Harbour, challenging Britain's right to tax Colonists and precipitating the War of Independence. By 1778, when it became clear that Britain and the Colonists would not be reconciled, France, eager to avenge their defeat in the Seven Years War, made a treaty with the rebels. They were soon joined by Spain and Britain declared war on both nations. The war was finally concluded in 1783 with the Treaty of Versailles in which Britain formally acknowledged the independence of the United States of America.

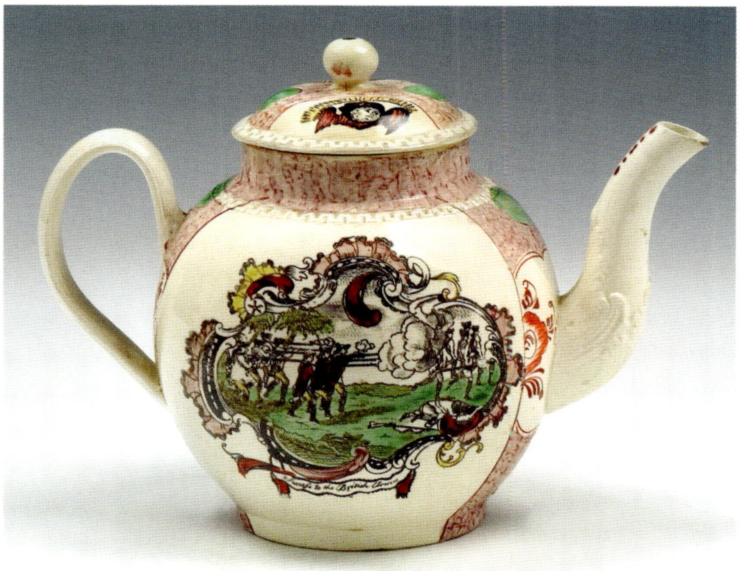

Teapot, (135), c.1781, Staffordshire, William Greatbatch of Fenton, height: 11.5cm, (4½in), creamware, printed and enamelled. View of troops firing muskets at a retreating enemy, inscribed, 'Success to the British Arms'. Portrait of General Cornwallis on reverse.

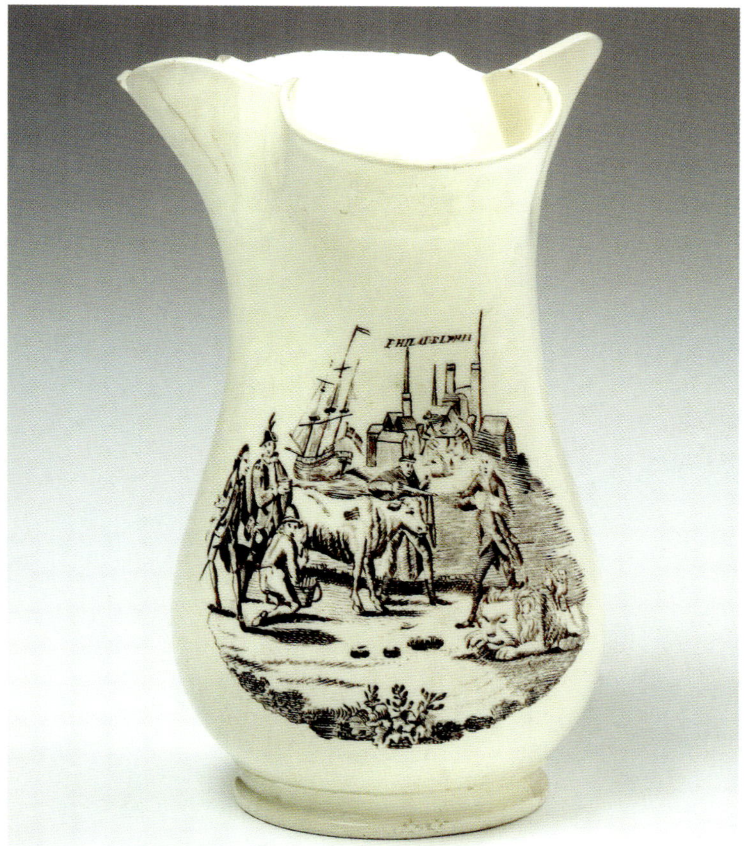

Jug, (436), c.1780, Leeds, height: 12.7cm, (5in), printed creamware. Jug with a three-lobed rim and ornate, double-twist handle, shows a satirical take on recent events against the backdrop of Philadelphia. 'A Picturesque View of the State of the Nation for February 1778', published in the *Westminster Magazine*, vol.VI, p. 66, refers to the ongoing war.[4] An Englishman wrings his hands helplessly while a Native American saws off the horns of the British cash cow and the Dutch, French and Spanish steal her milk. The British lion sleeps while the French pug urinates on the lion's back. Meanwhile, in the background, officer brothers General and Admiral Howe drink themselves to sleep in Philadelphia.

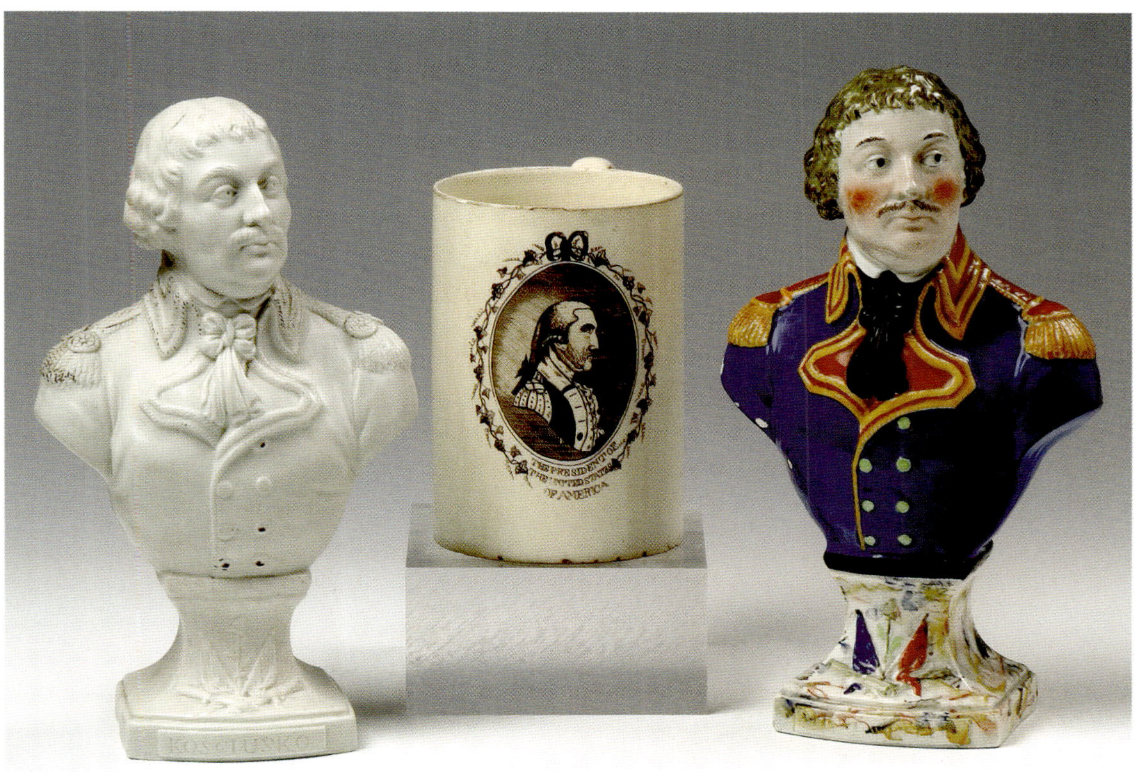

Bust, (439), c.1790, Liverpool, Herculaneum, height: 21.6cm, (8½in), porcellanous stoneware, traces of gilding. Polish patriot, Tadeusz Kościuszko (1744-1817), a brigadier General in the American Revolutionary Army, surrendered to Cornwallis at Guildford Courthouse but defeated him at Yorktown. One of a Herculaneum series of portrait busts of military leaders.[5] Willett has carefully annotated the back of the bust with biographical notes on Kościuszko.
Mug, (441), c.1800, Staffordshire, height: 12.1cm, (4¾in), printed creamware. Profile portrait of Washington as, 'THE PRESIDENT OF / THE UNITED STATES / OF AMERICA'. It is based on copies after a dry point by Joseph Wright, published 1790.
Bust, (189), c.1781, Staffordshire, height: 21.6cm, (8½in), pearlware, printed and enamelled. Cast from a Herculaneum mould of Kosciuszko and mounted on a base impressed for Admiral de Winter, the adversary of Admiral Duncan. The name has been deliberately obscured with enamelled marbling.

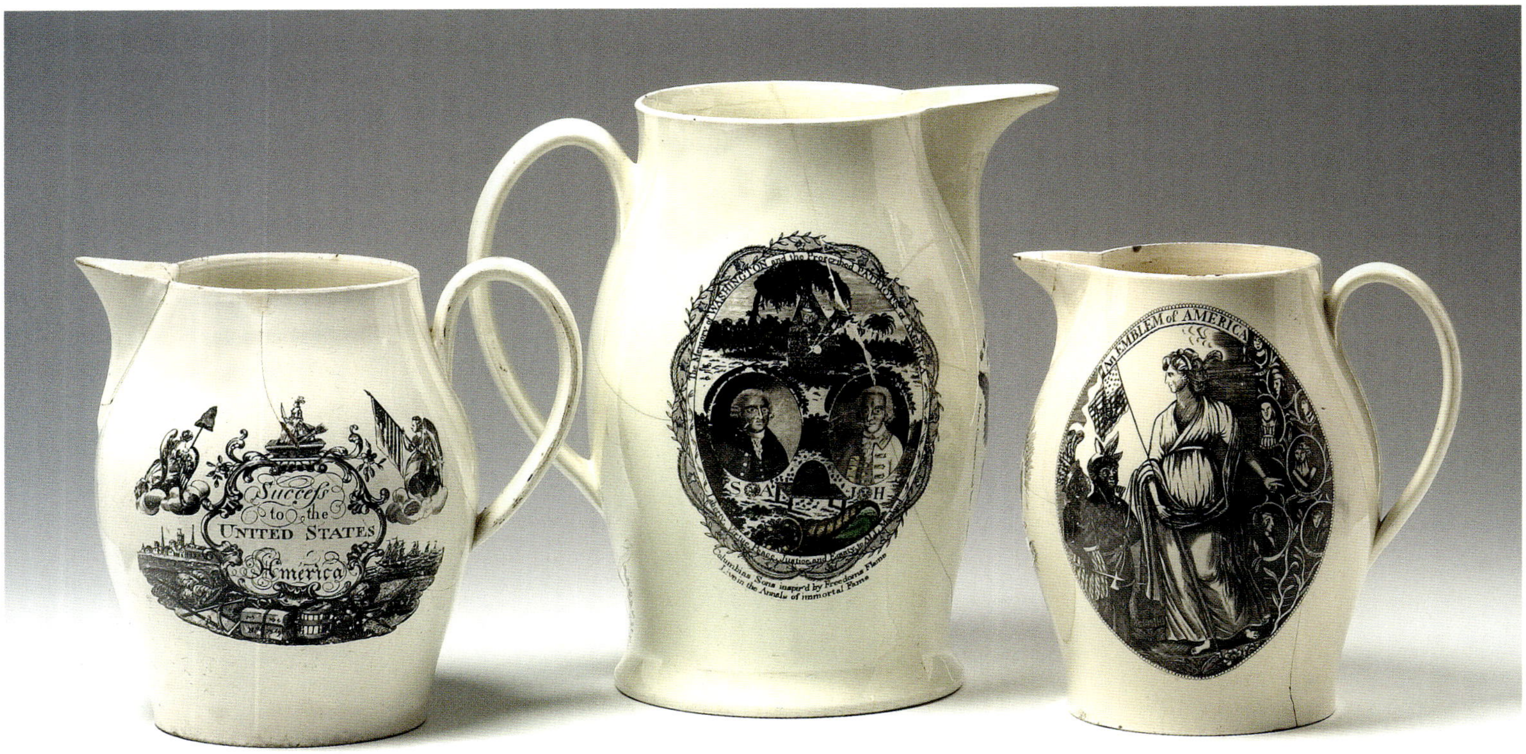

Jug, (431), c.1785, Staffordshire, height: 20.3cm, (8in), printed creamware. 'Success / to the / UNITED STATES / America', is flanked by winged figures with the Liberty Cap, the Stars and Stripes and other symbols. Probably made soon after US independence was ratified in 1783.
Jug, (461), c.1800, Staffordshire, height: 26.7cm, (10½in), printed creamware. 'In Memory of WASHINGTON and the Proscribed PATRIOTS OF AMERICA / Liberty, virtue, Peace, Justice and Equity to ALL mankind', inscribed around Washington's tomb and two oval portraits of Samuel Adams and John Hancock.
Jug, (444), c.1800, Staffordshire, height: 20.3cm, (8in), printed creamware. 'An EMBLEM of AMERICA' shows the symbolic figure of Columbia, carrying the Stars and Stripes, indicating portraits of the nation's founders to two small Native Americans.[6]

George Washington (1732-1799)

Washington was the best known and most iconic of all the Americans associated with the War of Independence. Born in Virginia, as commander of all Virginian forces from 1755 he defended the American Colonists' interests against French incursions. Having joined the rebels in 1775, he led the American army into New York as the British evacuated it. From 19 April 1783, he retired to his Virginia estate, Mount Vernon, until 1786. On 30 April 1789, a new Constitution was adopted and he was elected President of Congress.

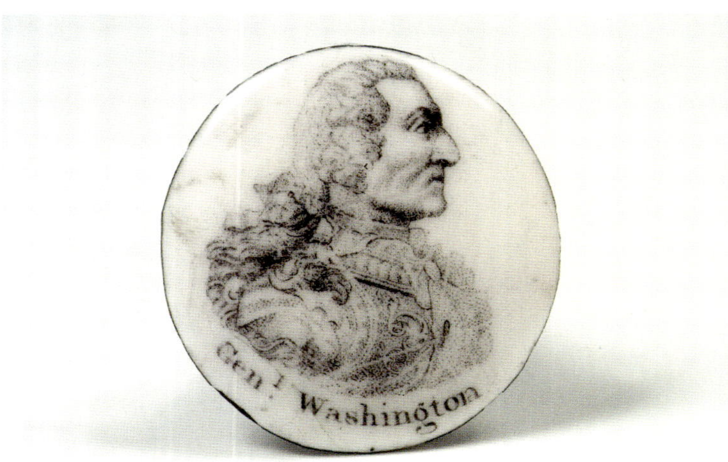

Watch-back, (447), c.1783, London or Birmingham, diameter: 3.8cm, (1½in), copper, enamelled and printed. Finely engraved profile portrait in armour, entitled 'Genl. Washington' may date from as early as 1783.

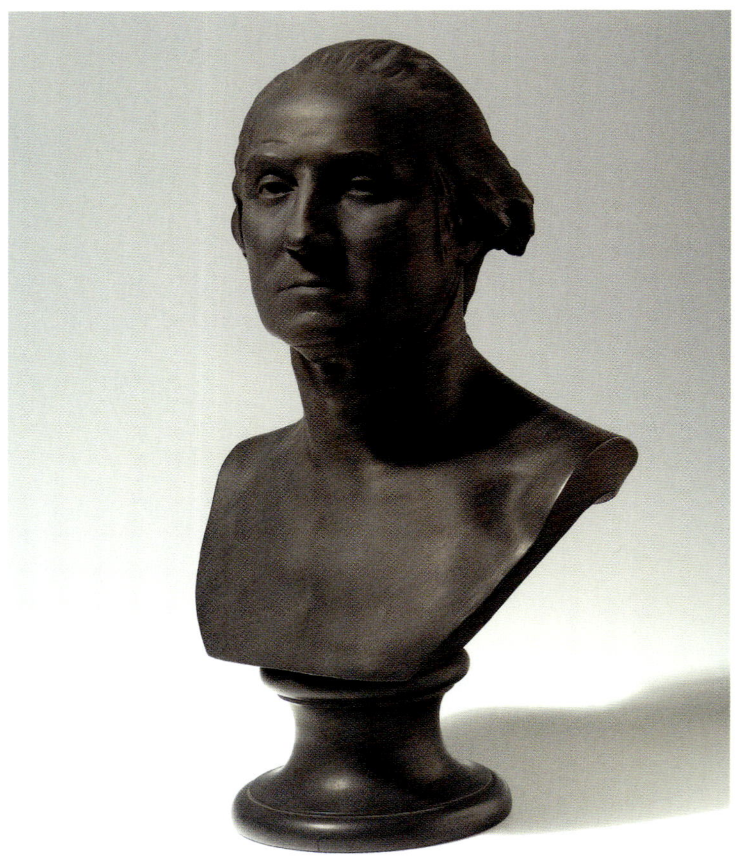

Portrait Bust, (434), Staffordshire, Wedgwood, height: 44.5 cm, (17½in), black basalt. Sculptural portrait bust of Washington on waisted circular plinth, impressed 'JBW / D', probably modelled posthumously.

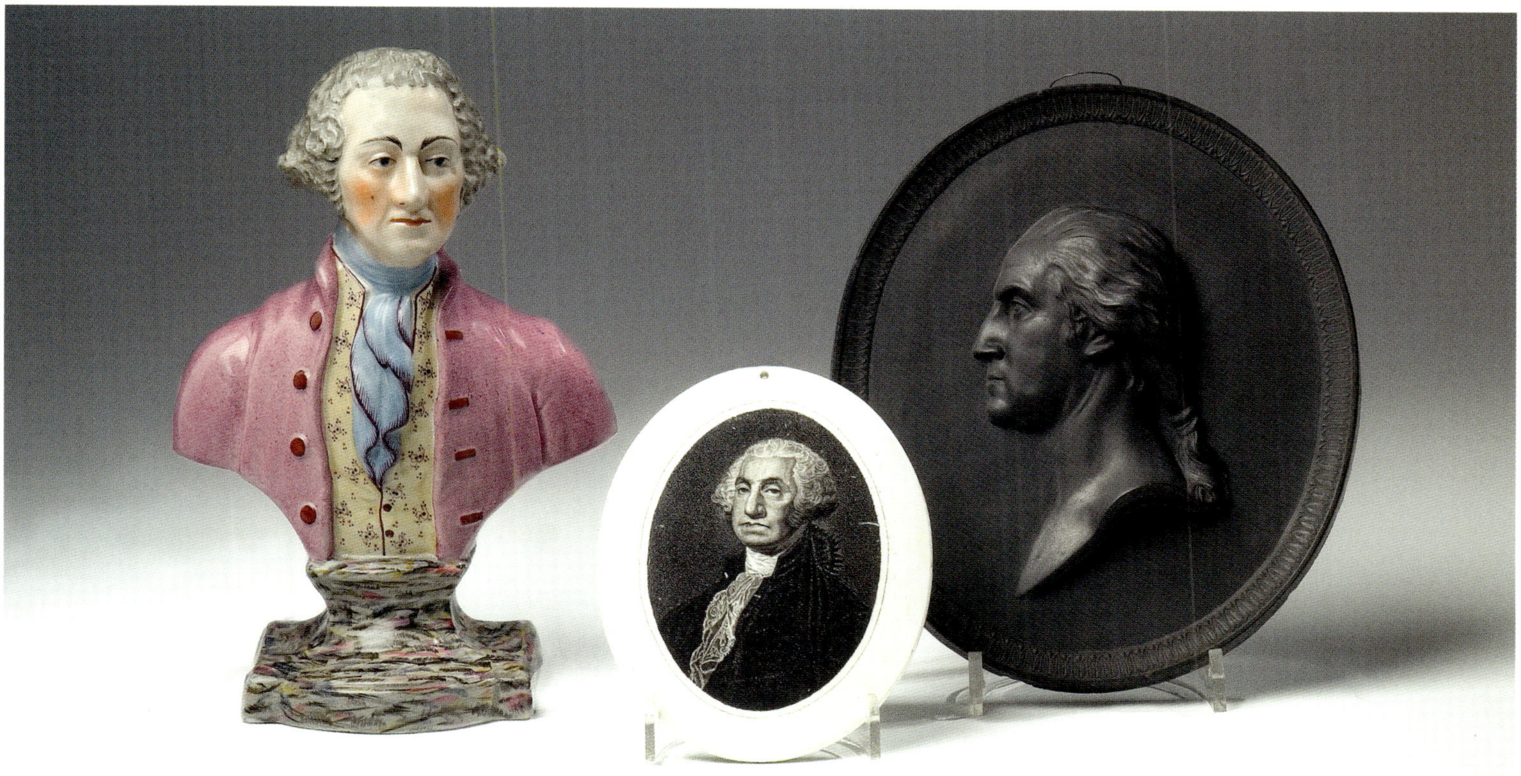

Bust, (432), c.1820, Staffordshire, height: 20.3cm, (8in), enamelled pearlware. A small black basalt portrait bust in Hanley Museum, marked and dated by Enoch Wood in 1818, is the model for the numerous pearlware busts exported to America in the 1820s.
Plaque, (438), c.1805, Liverpool, Herculaneum, height: 12.7cm, (5in), printed creamware. Finely engraved image of Washington after Gilbert Stuart's celebrated 'Athenaeum' portrait of 1796.[7] The plaque was probably produced as a commemorative souvenir after Washington's death in 1799.
Plaque, (433), c.1800, Staffordshire, Wedgwood, height: 19.4cm, (7⅝in), black basalt. Relief-moulded profile portrait of Washington, with moulded leaf border, probably based on the celebrated sculpture by Jean-Antoine Houdon.[8]

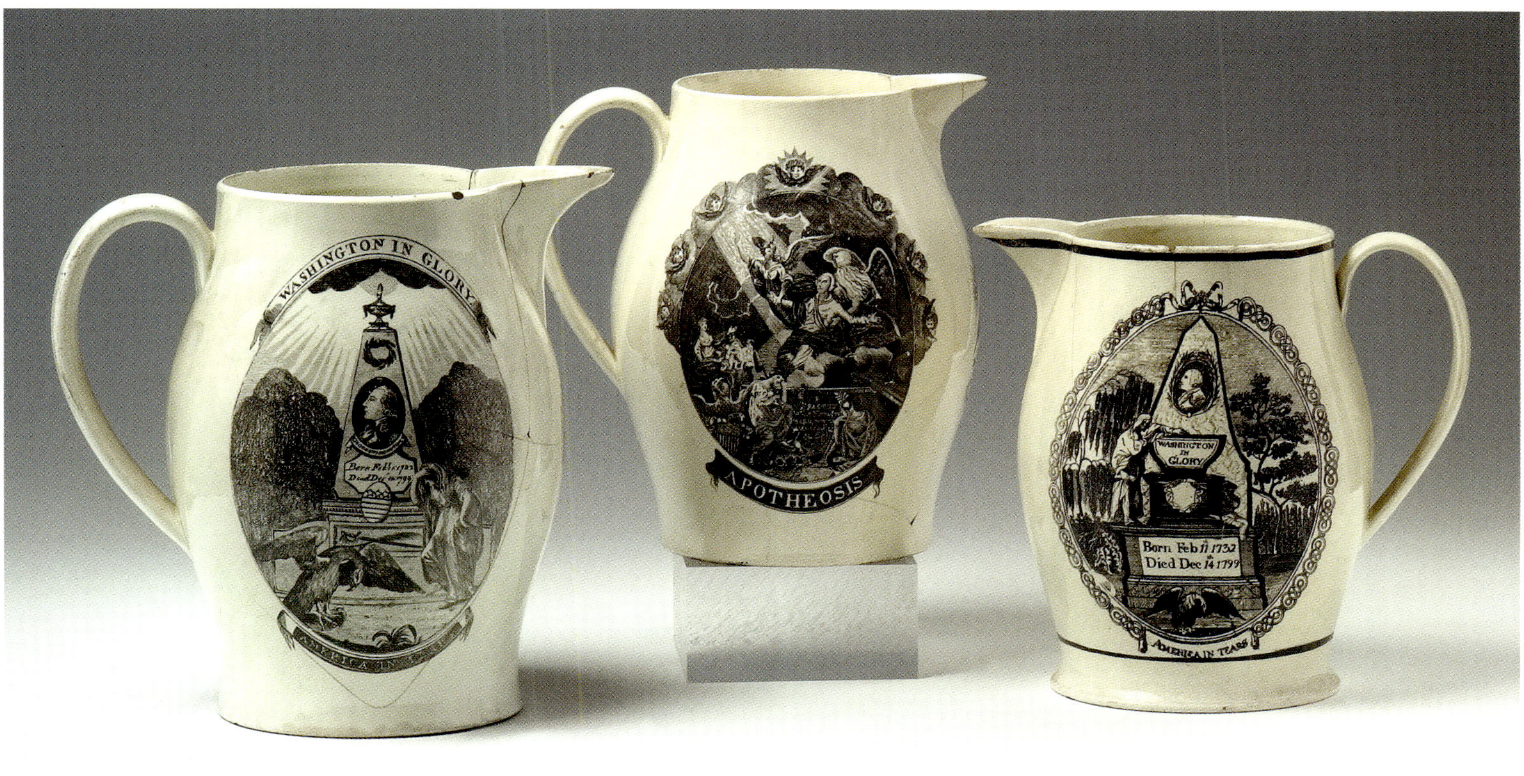

Jug, (442), c.1800, possibly Liverpool, height: 19.7cm, (7¾in), printed creamware. 'WASHINGTON IN GLORY … AMERICA IN TEARS' shows a shrouded female mourner and the American bald eagle at the base of Washington's tomb.
Jug, (444), c.1802, Staffordshire, height: 20.3cm, (8in), printed creamware. 'APOTHEOSIS', Washington carried aloft by angels in a shaft of heavenly light. It is based on a print drawn by J.J. Barralet in 1800 and published by Simon Chaudron in Philadelphia in 1802. Such imagery confirmed Washington's place in the new pantheon of American history.
Jug, (443), c.1800, Staffordshire, height: 22.9cm, (9in), printed creamware. 'WASHINGTON IN GLORY … AMERICA IN TEARS', a similar composition to (442) with willow and cypress trees (also symbols of mourning).

Benjamin Franklin (1706-1790)

Perhaps the greatest and best-loved of early Americans, on both sides of the Atlantic, was the energetic polymath, Benjamin Franklin. Having learned the printing trade in his home town of Boston, at twenty-four he owned the Philadelphia-based *Pennsylvania Gazette*. His business skills made him sufficiently wealthy to pursue his passion for scientific experiment. He improved designs for urinary catheters and storage batteries, invented bi focal lenses, the glass harmonica, watertight bulkheads for ships and the lightning conductor. He was the first person living outside Britain to be awarded (in 1753) the Royal Society's Copley Medal for his publication, *Experiments and Observations on Electricity*.

As a member of the Pennsylvania Assembly and Deputy Postmaster General for the Colonies he practised diplomacy in London in the 1750s and 60s, petitioning for a better financial and governmental deal for America and warning of growing disaffection. While in England he was very taken with English ceramics. He wrote to his wife in 1755 that he had bought 'a large fine Jugg for Beer' and urged her to, 'Look at the Figures on the [Bow] China Bowl and Coffee Cups, with your spectacles on … they will bear Examining'.[9] In 1775 he worked on the Declaration of Independence. He was sent to France as Commissioner for the new United States from December 1776 to 1785, negotiating both the Treaty of Paris and the Anglo-American peace treaty in 1783. In 1787 he helped write the American Constitution.

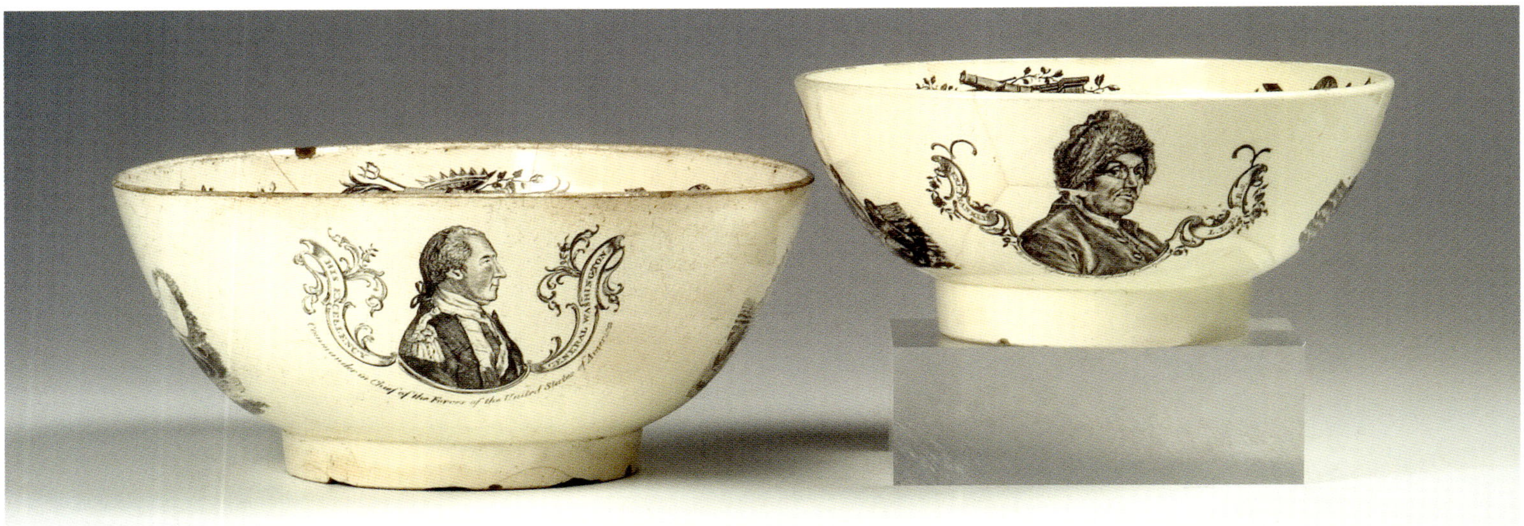

Punchbowl, (449), c.1790, Liverpool, diameter: 26cm, (10¼in), printed creamware. 'HIS EXCELLENCY / GENERAL WASHINGTON / Commander in Chief of the Forces of the United States of America' was probably engraved at Thomas Billinge's workshop and printed by Guy Green.[10] The portrait may be based on an engraving by Ellis.[11] There is also a portrait of Franklin, similar to that on (453).

Punchbowl, (453), c.1790, Liverpool, diameter: 22.9cm, (9in), printed creamware. Portrait of 'BENJ. FRANKLIN / L.L.D. F.R.S.', with his date of birth, (presumably produced before his death in 1790), based on a painting of c.1780 by Charles-Nicholas Cochin.[12]

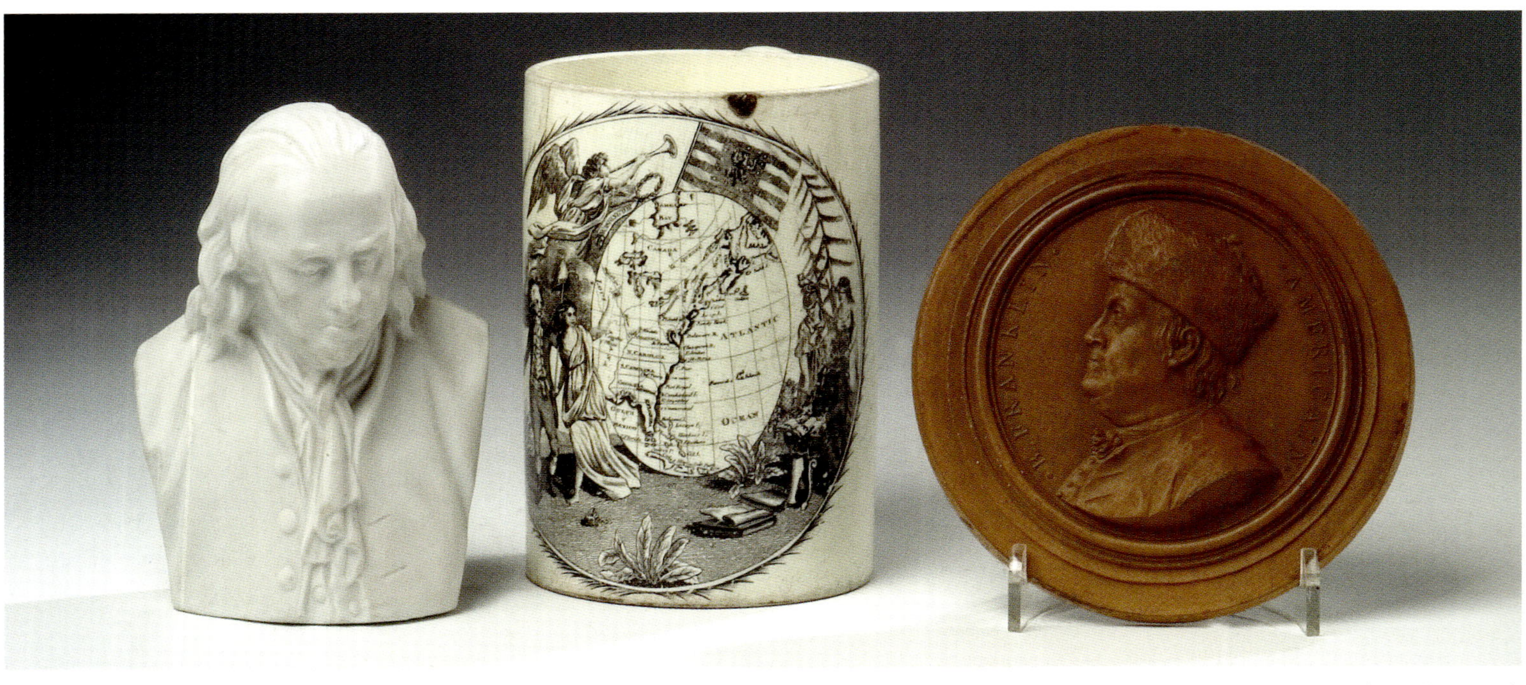

Bust, (454), c.1830, possibly Derby, height: 12.7cm, (5in), biscuit porcelain. Portrait of Franklin, bareheaded.

Mug, (448), c.1785, Staffordshire, height: 12.1cm, (4¾in), printed creamware. The so-called 'Washington Map', features the new United States; Washington walks with Liberty while Benjamin Franklin sits, flanked by Wisdom and Justice. Print based on an embellished title to a map published in London by John Wallis, 3 April 1783.[13]

Plaque, (450), 1777, France, Jean-Baptiste Nini, diameter: 11.5cm, (4½in), terra-cotta. Relief-moulded profile portrait of Franklin wearing a fur hat. Nini's plaque was issued in France in 1777, the year he negotiated a Franco-American Alliance.[14]

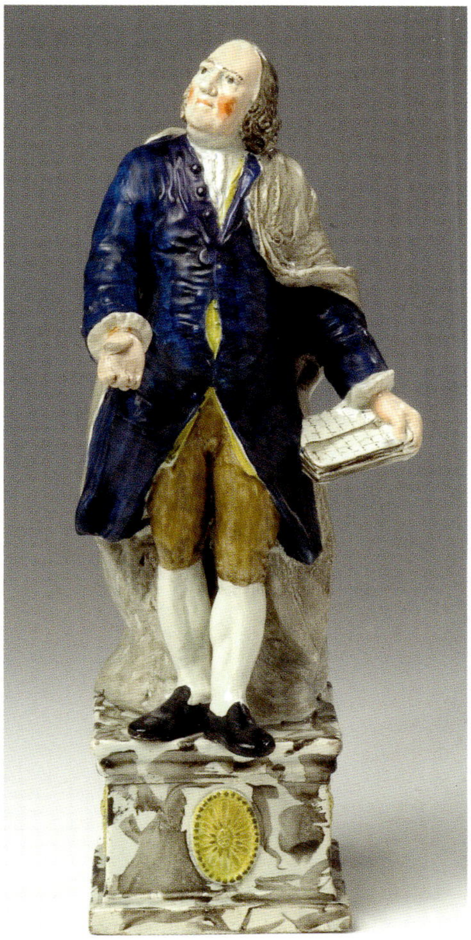

Figure, (451), c.1800, Staffordshire, possibly Enoch Wood, height: 33cm, (13in), enamelled pearlware. Franklin stands on a marbled plinth declaiming from a book.[15]

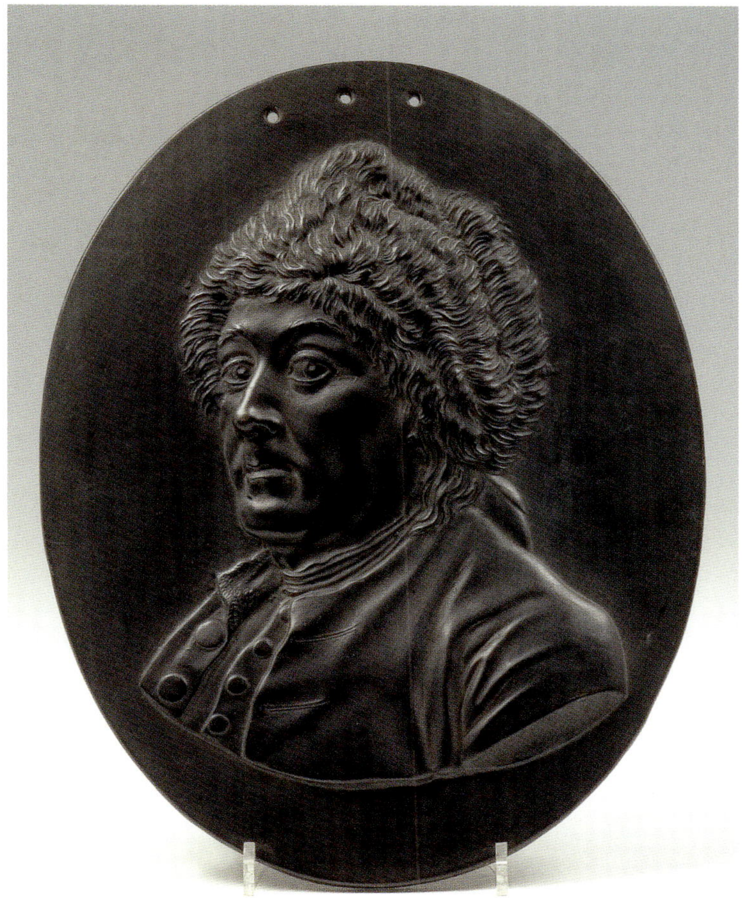

Plaque, (474), c.1790, Staffordshire, height: 33cm, (13in), black basalt. Relief-moulded portrait of Franklin, wearing his familiar fur hat, probably dating from the time of his death in 1790.

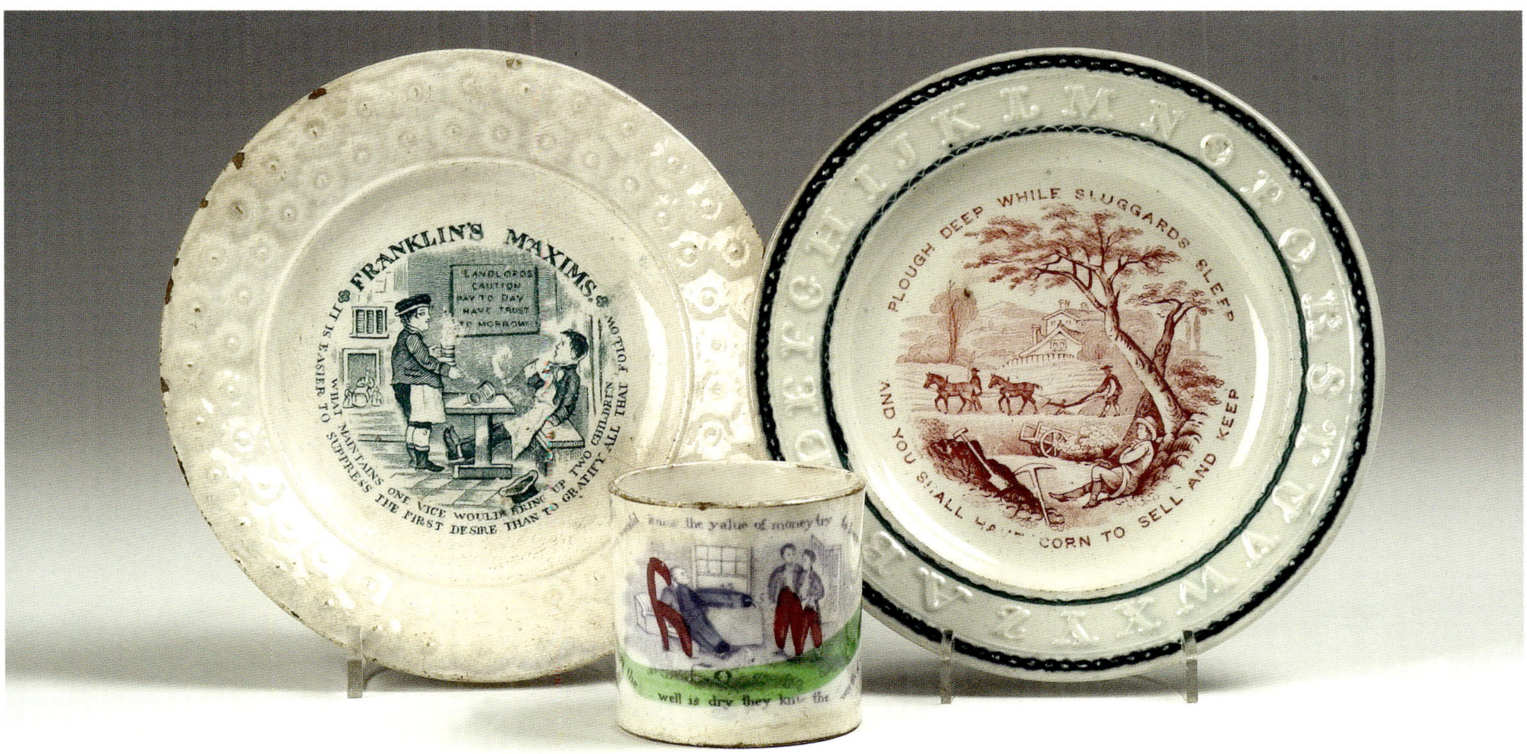

Plate, (456), c.1830-50, Staffordshire, diameter: 17.8cm, (7in), green-printed earthenware and a plate entitled 'FRANKLIN'S MAXIMS / WHAT MAINTAINS ONE VICE WOULD BRING UP TWO CHILDREN'.[16] 'Poor Richard's Sayings', (otherwise known as Dr Franklin's Maxims), were published for over 25 years in the *Pennsylvania Gazette*. Cheap nursery mugs and plates continued to be reproduce them long after Franklin's death. They had particular appeal for Victorian parents and educators.

Mug, (455), c. 1850, Staffordshire, height: 6.7cm, (2⅝in), blue-printed earthenware. 'THE WAY TO WEALTH / OR DR. FRANKLIN'S Poor Richard / ILLUSTRATED' is a poor quality print, crudely enamelled.
Plate, (1262), c.1830-50, Staffordshire, diameter: 17.8cm, (7in), red-printed earthenware. 'PLOUGH DEEP WHILE SLUGGARDS SLEEP AND YOU SHALL HAVE CORN TO SELL AND KEEP'.[17] (Willett included this alphabet plate with Agriculture).

Emblems of the United States

From the 1780s demand grew rapidly for ceramics to celebrate and document the new nation, as well as for use. A specifically American iconography was already established by 1800. In addition to adopting the Liberty Cap of the French Revolution, (which soon disappeared), the American bald eagle,[18] the stars and stripes of the American flag and rings representing the individual States of the Union made regular appearances.

Jug, (R2454.8), c.1800, Staffordshire, height: 17.4cm, (6⅝in), printed creamware. The bald eagle with wings and legs outspread, encircled by 15 rings printed with the names of 16 States[19] and 16 stars around its head.
Mug, (440), c.1790, Staffordshire, height: 15.3cm, (6in), printed creamware. 'UNION to the PEOPLE of AMERICA' and beneath 'CIVIL and RELIGIOUS LIBERTY TO ALL MANKIND' represents an emblematic scene where Washington, Jefferson and Adams (the first three presidents), join hands to support the Cap of Liberty on a pole.
Jug, (460), c.1805, Staffordshire, height: 17.8cm, (7in), printed creamware. 'THOMAS JEFFERSON PRESIDENT OF THE UNITED STATES OF AMERICA', shows Jefferson (1743-1826), the third president, framed with intertwining wreaths inscribed with the names of 15 States.[20]

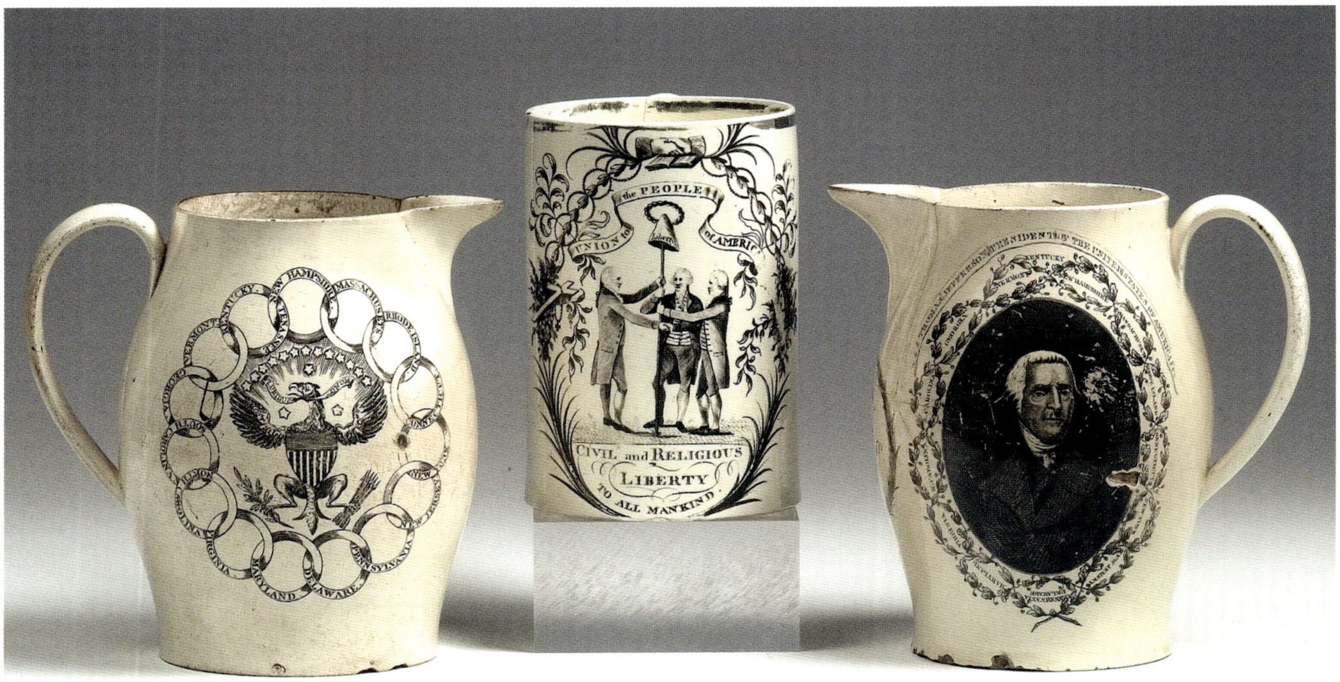

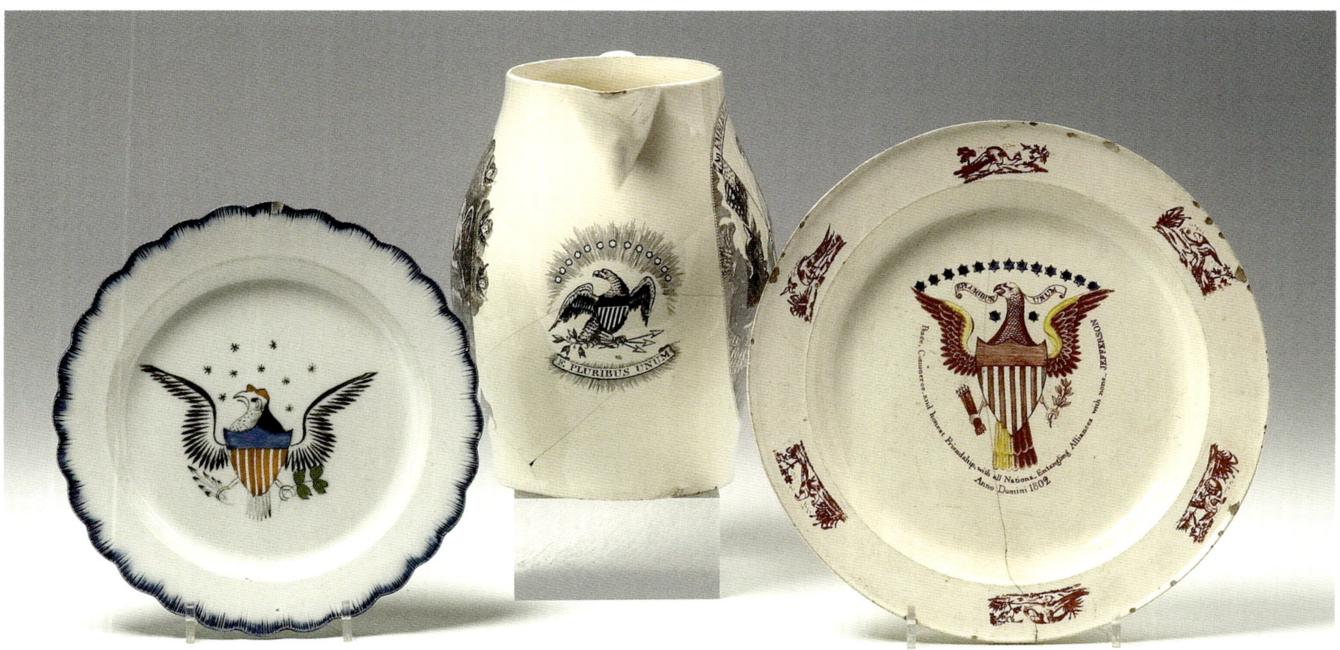

Plate, (435), c.1790, Staffordshire, diameter: 21cm, (8¼in), pearlware, painted underglaze. Naively painted eagle with a striped shield and nine stars.
Jug, (444), c.1790, Staffordshire, height: 20.3cm, (8in), printed creamware. Eagle grips three arrows and an olive branch, beneath arc of 13 stars. Banner reads 'E PLURIBUS UNUM'.

Plate, (459), c.1802, Liverpool., diameter: 25.4cm, (10in), brown-printed creamware underglaze. Spread eagle with ribbon inscribed 'E PLURIBUS UNUM' and an arc of 13 stars. Inscribed with a quotation from Jefferson, 'Race, commerce, and honest Friendship, with all Nations. Entangling alliances with none – JEFFERSON / Anno Domini 1802'.

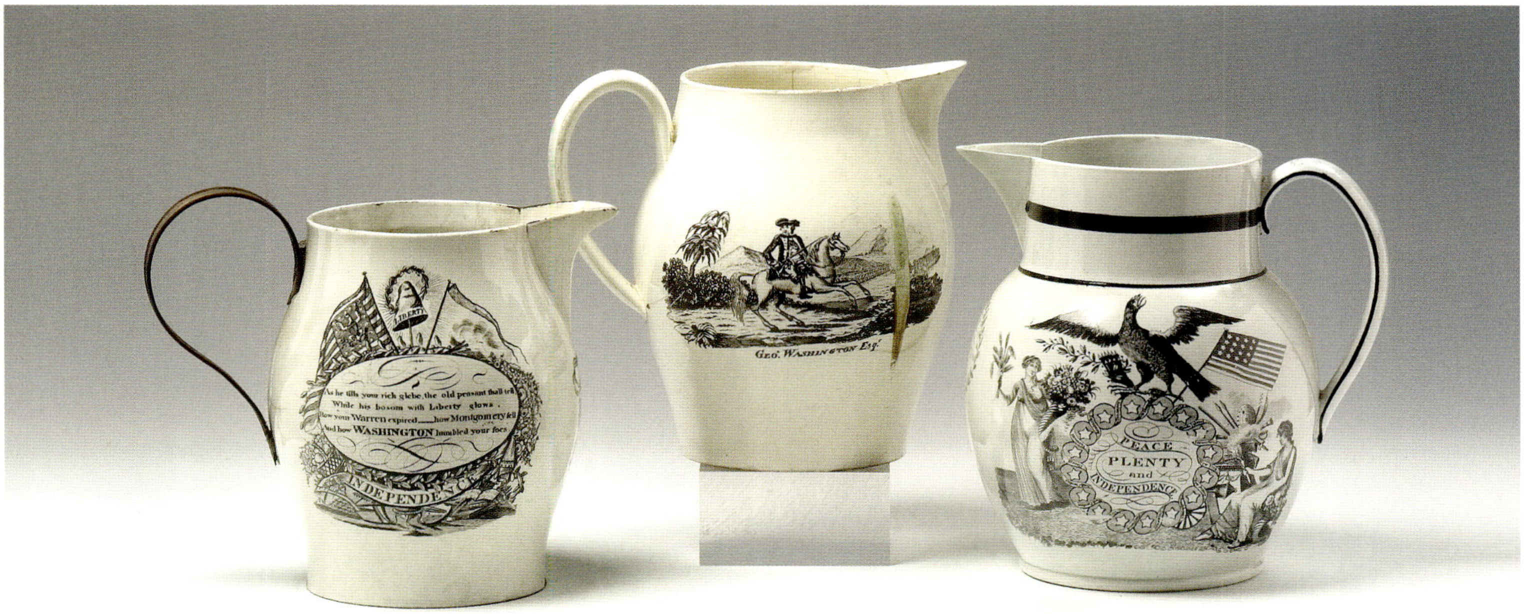

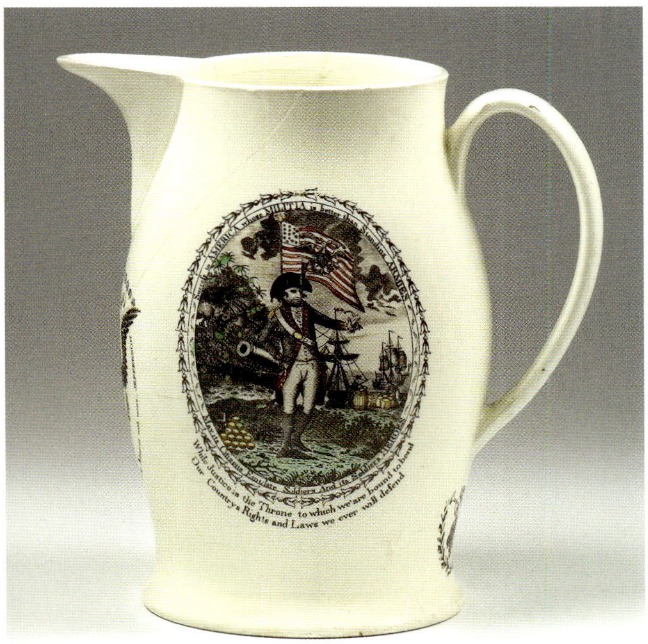

Jug, (457), c.1790, Staffordshire, height: 22.2cm, (8¾in), printed creamware. Entitled, 'INDEPENDENCE' with flags, Liberty Cap, agricultural tools and verse, 'as he tills your rich glebe, the old peasant shall tell, / While his bosom with Liberty glows / How your WARREN expired__how MONGOMERY fell / And how WASHINGTON humbled your foes.' Extract from *Ode on the Fourth of July*, (pub. 1806). Joseph Warren died while commanding forces at the Battle of Bunker Hill, 17 June 1775 and the Irishman Richard Montgomery died fighting the British in Canada.[21]

Jug, (431), c.1783-6, Staffordshire, height: 20.3cm, (8in), printed creamware. The equestrian portrait of Washington is based on a popular engraving, c.1775, by the fictitious 'Alexander Campbell'. The caption, 'GEOr WASHINGTON Esq', fits with the period when he briefly returned to civilian life.[22]

Jug, (458), c.1790, Staffordshire, height: 19.1cm, (7½in), printed creamware. Within a wreath of 16 stars, 'PEACE PLENTY and INDEPENDENCE', surmounted by the American eagle and flag and flanked by the symbolic figures of Prosperity (with cornucopia) and Peace, destroying the weapons of war.

Jug, (461), c.1790, Staffordshire, height: 26.7cm, (10½in), creamware, printed and coloured. 'Success to AMERICA / Whose MILITIA is better than Standing ARMIES / May its citizens emulate soldiers and its soldiers HEROES' with a military commander standing before the American flag, supervising the unloading of ships.[23] Eagle printed beneath the spout.

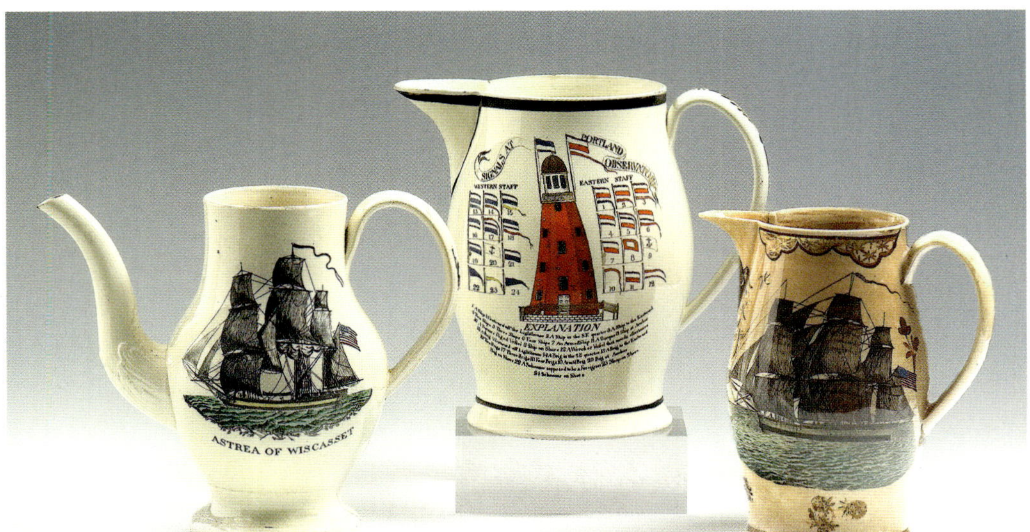

Coffee Pot, (452), c.1797-1803, Staffordshire, height: 21.6cm, (8½in), creamware, printed and enamelled. A ship on port tack, flying the American flag, is inscribed, 'ASTREA OF WISCASSET'. A ship of this name (weighing 458 tons), appears in Lloyds Register in 1792, sailing from Wiscasset, Maine, to Liverpool. It was owned or chartered by Wood & Co. and commanded by Tinkham and D. Kenny.

Jug, (475), c.1810, Liverpool, height: 22.2cm, (8¾in), creamware, printed and enamelled. 'SIGNALS AT PORTLAND OBSERVATORY', shows a boldly painted lighthouse and 24 different flag signals. The observatory was built on the highest hill in Portland, Maine, in 1807 to warn the town of approaching shipping.

Jug, (462), c.1790, Staffordshire, height: 20.3cm, (8in), creamware, printed, coloured and gilt. A ship on port tack flies the American flag.

The War of 1812 and After

On his re-election in 1812, James Madison, fourth president of the United States (1809-17), announced that the United States and Britain were at war. After years of trade restrictions, clashes over searching ships during the Napoleonic Wars, the desire to free Canada from British rule and to annex Florida from Spain, 'War Hawks', led by John Calhoun of South Carolina and Henry Clay of Kentucky, called for action. American attempts to conquer Canada were unsuccessful but so were British counter measures to invade the United States from Canada.

British naval squadrons were defeated by Captain Oliver Perry on Lake Erie and Commodore Thomas Macdonough on Lake Champlain. American warships claimed early victories, notably the *Constitution* under Captain Hull, but after defeating Napoleon British superior sea power proved decisive. Having stormed Chesapeake Bay the British captured Washington DC, burning government buildings. Fort McHenry at Baltimore, however, withstood British bombardment, inspiring Francis Scott Key to write *The Star-Spangled Banner*. The British attempt to invade the American south-west was thwarted by defeat at New Orleans. Hostilities were resolved at the Treaty of Ghent in 1814.

Years of trade embargo followed by wartime blockades had drastically reduced the import of British goods making Americans more self-reliant. As ship building and foreign commerce became unprofitable, businessmen invested capital in home industries, notably New England textile mills, where they could process the abundant cotton from the Southern States. But they still relied on English ceramics. Not a single piece is known recording a British success in this war but as soon as the trade ban was lifted, the Staffordshire and Liverpool potters were swift to meet demand for pieces immortalising American heroes.[24] Much of the English ware was decorated with prints supplied by American printers. Thirty years earlier, during the War of Independence, Josiah Wedgwood had overcome his scruples concerning the morality of trading with the enemy and they certainly did not worry the nineteenth-century potters; business was business.

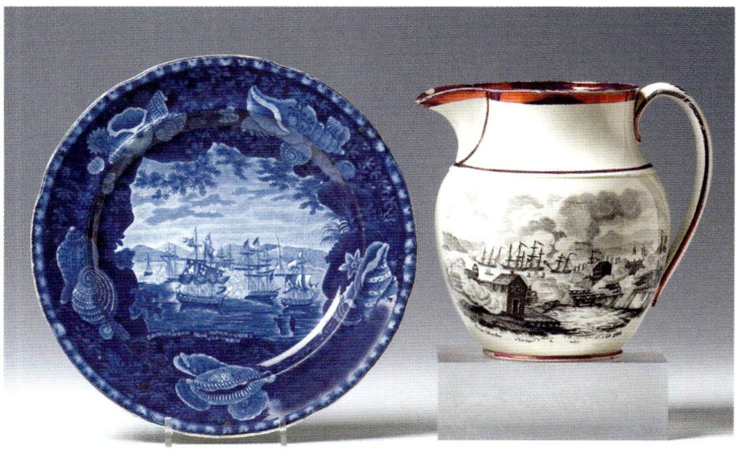

Plate, (465), c.1835, Staffordshire, Burslem, Enoch Wood, height: 26cm, (10¼in), blue-printed earthenware (marked, 'semi-china') 'COMMODORE MACDONOUGH'S VICTORY'; the sea battle at Lake Champlain is illustrated within a frame of exotic plants and tropical shells. It is based on an engraving of 1816 by Tanner after Reinagle.[25]
Jug, (466), c.1790, Staffordshire, Shelton, Bentley, Wear & Bourne, height: 17.8cm, (7in), creamware, printed and lustred. Naval battle scene, carefully copied from a print of 1815.[26] Caption only partly legible, 'Com. Macdon[ough]'s Victory [Lak]e [Champlain] S[eptembe]r11th 1814'. MacDonough's victory earned him a Congressional Gold Medal; it was the last engagement of the war to be celebrated.[27]

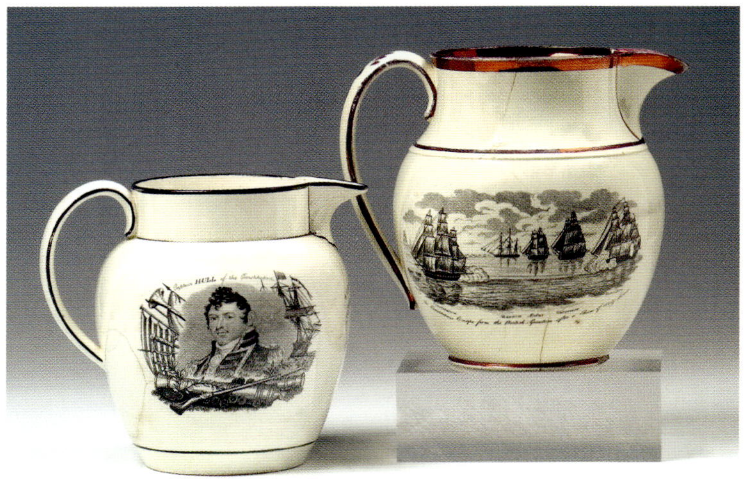

Jug, (463), c.1817, Staffordshire, height: 4½cm, (6½in), printed pearlware. A printed portrait of 'Captain HULL of the Constitution' appears amid battle trophies.[28] On 19 August, 1812, the 44-gun frigate, *Constitution*, commanded by Captain Isaac Hull, overcame the British ship *Guerrière* in one of America's greatest maritime victories.
Jug, (466), c.1790, Staffordshire, Shelton, Bentley, Wear & Bourne, height: 17.8cm, (7in), creamware, printed and lustred. Sea battle with ships firing, entitled, 'The Constitutions Escape from the British Squadron after a Chase of sixty hours' with named ships including *Constitution, Shannon, Aeolus* and *Guerriere*.[29]

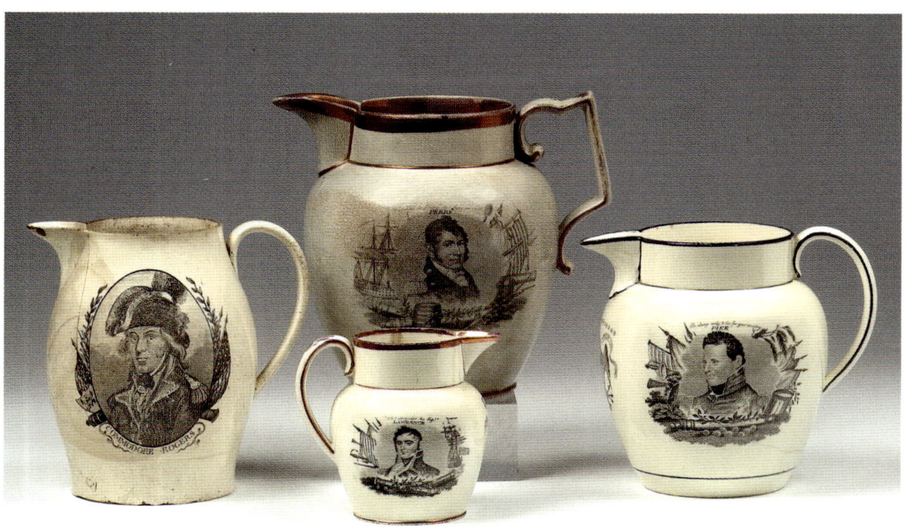

Clockwise: **Jug, (R2454.8),** c.1790, Staffordshire, height: 17.4cm, (6⅝in), printed creamware. A creamware jug commemorates Commodore John Rodgers who served in the US Navy from 1798 to 1837. Rodgers fired the first shot of the War of 1812 from his flagship, the USS *President*, and helped recapture Washington after the capital was burned by the British.
Jug, (467), c.1815, Staffordshire, height: 19.1cm, (7½in), creamware, printed and lustred. 'We have met the Enemy and they are ours / PERRY'.[30] Captain Oliver Perry devastated the British fleet on Lake Erie on 10 September 1813, even after he was forced to abandon his flagship. (Captain Hull features on the reverse).
Jug, (463), c.1815, Staffordshire, height: 16.5cm, (6½in), printed creamware. 'Be always ready to die for your Country / PIKE', portrait among battle trophies; heraldic spread eagle beneath the spout. Brigadier General Zebulon Montgomery Pike was killed leading his troops in a successful assault on Fort York (now Toronto) in Canada in April 1813.[31] (Captain Hull features on the reverse).
Jug, (464), c.1815, Staffordshire, height: 11.5cm, (4½in), creamware, printed and lustred. 'Don't Surrender the Ship / LAWRENCE'.[32] Captain James Lawrence's moment of glory came when the British brig *Peacock* surrendered to his ship *Hornet* on 24 February 1813. (Captain Stephen Decatur on the reverse).

Marquis de Lafayette (1757-1834)

Marie-Joseph Paul Yves Roch Gilbert du Motier de Lafayette was a close ally of General Washington during the War of Independence. Returning to France he commanded the National Guard during the Revolution (1789-91) but fell foul of the Jacobins. While serving in Austria he was captured (ensuring he escaped execution) and finally released in 1797. Following a Congressional Resolution of 1824, President James Monroe invited him to visit the United States, where he was given a hero's welcome. He arrived on 15 August 1824, remained until September 1825 and during his stay visited all twenty-four States of the Union. Congress voted him a grant of $200,000 and 24,000 acres of land, in recognition of his services during the Revolutionary War and he celebrated his 68th birthday at the White House.

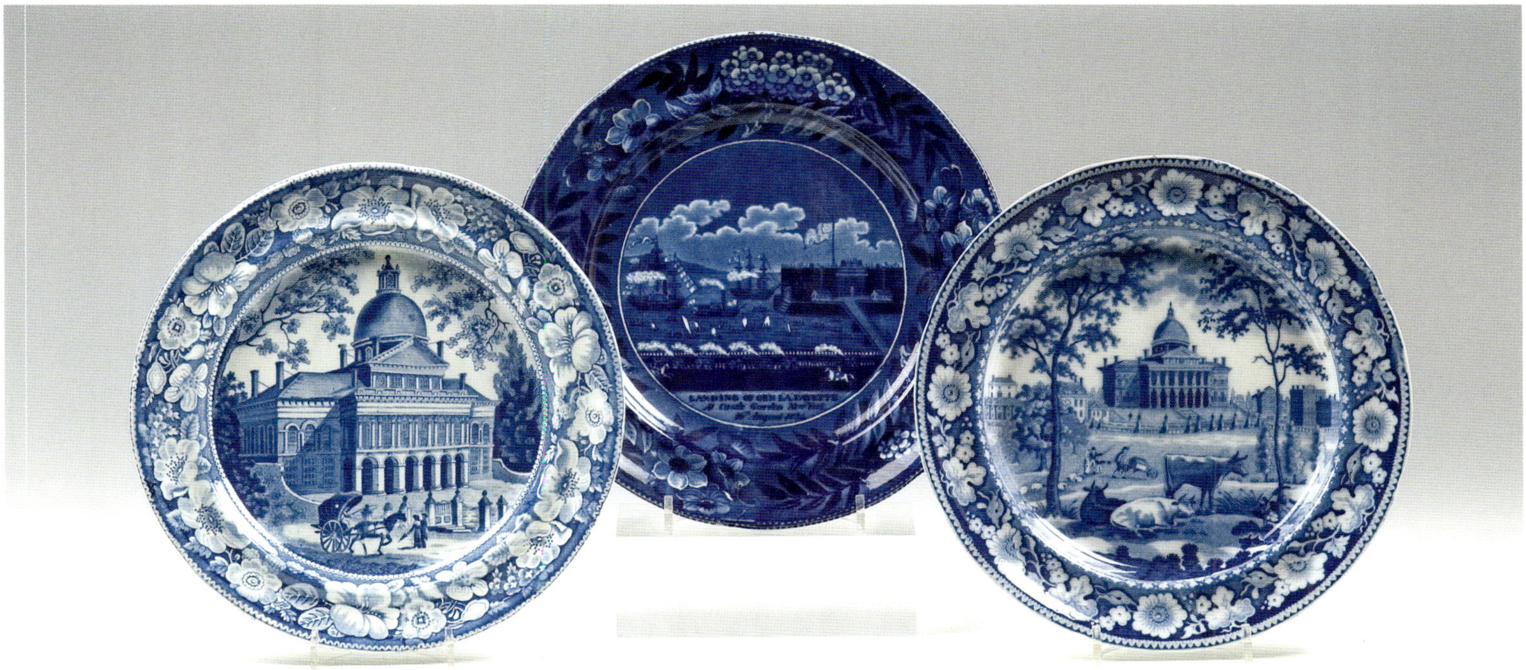

Plate, (470), c.1810, Staffordshire, Burslem, Enoch Wood, height: 24.8cm, (9¾in), blue-printed earthenware. The Massachusetts State House, Boston was designed by Charles Bulfinch, the first American-born professional architect, and built 1795-98. This view, c.1804 shows a gig in the foreground.
Plate, (468), c.1835, Staffordshire, Cobridge, Clews, height: 26cm, (10¼in), blue-printed earthenware. 'LANDING OF GENERAL LAFAYETTE At Castle Garden New York 16th August 1824'.[33] Central scene of a naval gun-salute in a harbour within a deep floral border.
Plate, (469), c.1835, Staffordshire, John Rogers & Son, height: 25.4cm, (10in), blue-printed earthenware. View of the Massachusetts State House with sheep and cattle in foreground.[34] Bulfinch based his designs on Somerset House (1776-86) in London.[35] It is fronted by an elevated portico with a series of Corinthian columns, facing out onto Boston Common. Governor Samuel Adams laid the cornerstone and in 1802 patriot and silversmith, Paul Revere rolled the copper sheathing for the central dome. Painted white in 1825, the red brick facade was revealed once again in 1928. For many years it was the grandest public building in the United States and served as a model for other state houses nationwide.

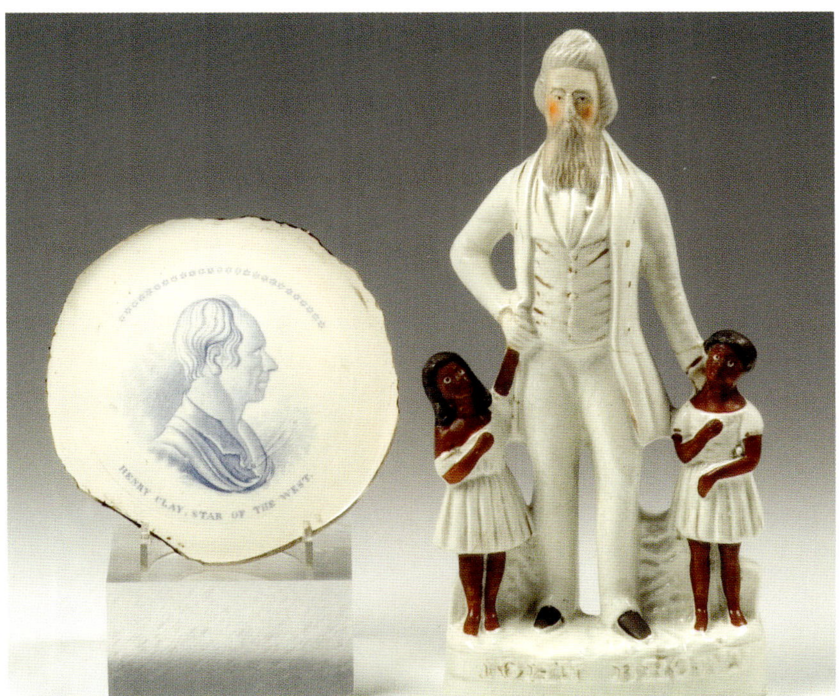

Plate, (471), c.1852, Staffordshire, height: 13.3cm, (5¼in), blue-printed earthenware. Profile portrait of 'HENRY CLAY, STAR OF THE WEST', beneath an arc of twenty six stars.[36] Printed on the reverse, 'James Tams & Co.' importers of Philadelphia. Clay, (1777-1852) the 'War Hawk' congressman of 1812, became Senator and Secretary of State from 1825 to 1829, leading the National Republicans. He made unsuccessful bids for the presidency in 1828, 1832 and 1844.
Figure Group, (472), c.1865, Staffordshire, height: 27.3cm, (10¾in), earthenware. John Brown (1800-1859), one of American history's most controversial figures, holds the hands of two black children. On Sunday 16 October, 1859, he led 16 white and five black men across the Potomac River from Maryland to Virginia. He intended to capture weapons stored at the US Arsenal at Harpers Ferry in order to attack slaveholders and liberate slaves. After seizing the arms, Brown's gang took hostage 60 townspeople. Federal troops, led by Robert E. Lee successfully stormed Brown's hiding place and he was seriously wounded. He was tried, convicted of treason and hanged on 2 December 1859, but 'his soul goes marching on'. John Brown's raid and subsequent trial inflamed the dispute between abolitionist and pro-slavery factions, hardening the lines between the Northern and the Southern United States.

Chapter 7

POLITICS: REVOLT & REFORM

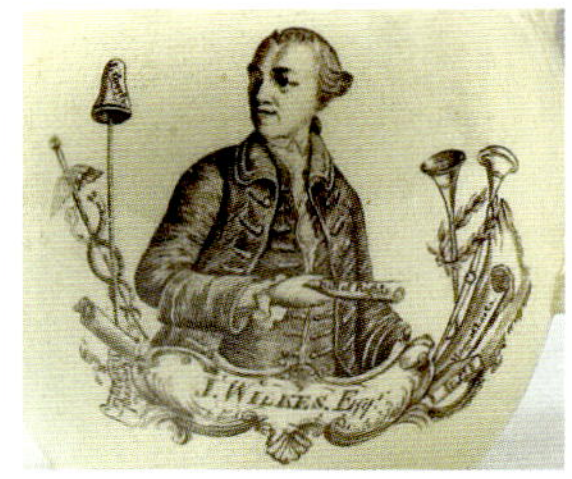

Henry Willett was a lifelong Liberal supporter and chaired the Brighton Liberal Association for many years. He was a shrewd and influential operator behind the scenes of Brighton political life but always resisted standing for office himself. His endorsement of Professor Henry Fawcett as Liberal MP for Brighton made him a target for spiteful Tory propaganda, but Fawcett was duly elected in 1864 and proved an active reformer in the House of Commons. Willett championed a number of radical causes, and in 1864 backed an unsuccessful attempt to abolish capital punishment.

In 1873, in honour of his friendship with the Liberal MP Richard Cobden, Willett presented five hundred of Cobden's papers to the newly opened Brighton Reference Library. The selection of pieces for the 'Statesmen' ceramic group may reflect his personal interests. They range from tributes to individual political grandees to propaganda items made to promote candidates in the infrequently contested elections of the eighteenth century. They also include mass-produced items for national political and social campaigns such as the abolition of slavery in the years around 1800, the Reform Bill of 1832 and the campaign for Irish independence.

William Pitt the Elder, (1708-78)

The William Pitts, father and his eponymous second son, dominated British politics during the second half of the eighteenth century. Pitt the Elder, a complex, mercurial character, was regarded as an incorruptible patriot when he took the post of Paymaster General to the army but refused its lucrative perks. As plain Pitt, from 1755 he dominated a largely titled cabinet and was a brilliant but malicious orator in Parliament where,

> the benches full of overgrown schoolboys watched gleefully as Pitt, tall and statuesque … pointed his beaky nose at some unfortunate timeserver, trapped him in the net of his irony and then jabbed away with Britannia's trident[1]

He pursued an expansionist foreign policy and was regarded as the architect and victor of the Seven Years War in which Britain triumphed over its European enemies (especially the French), and helped to bring Canada and India under British dominion. His fame peaked in 1759 when Horace Walpole wrote, 'our bells are worn threadbare with ringing at victories'.[2]

After the death of George II in 1760, Pitt fell out with his former friend, the Earl of Bute, mentor to the young King George III, and his patrons disappeared. In 1766 he ceased to be 'The Great Commoner' when he returned to head the government as the Earl of Chatham, accepting a title he had so long refused. He later earned the king's bitter enmity by actively supporting the rebellious American colonists in their fight against taxation. He ensured his immortality by collapsing in the House of Lords in May 1778 and dying shortly afterwards. An estimated 100,000 people filed past his coffin in the Painted Chamber of the Palace of Westminster on 8 June and even more lined the streets in pouring rain the following day, to witness the funeral procession.

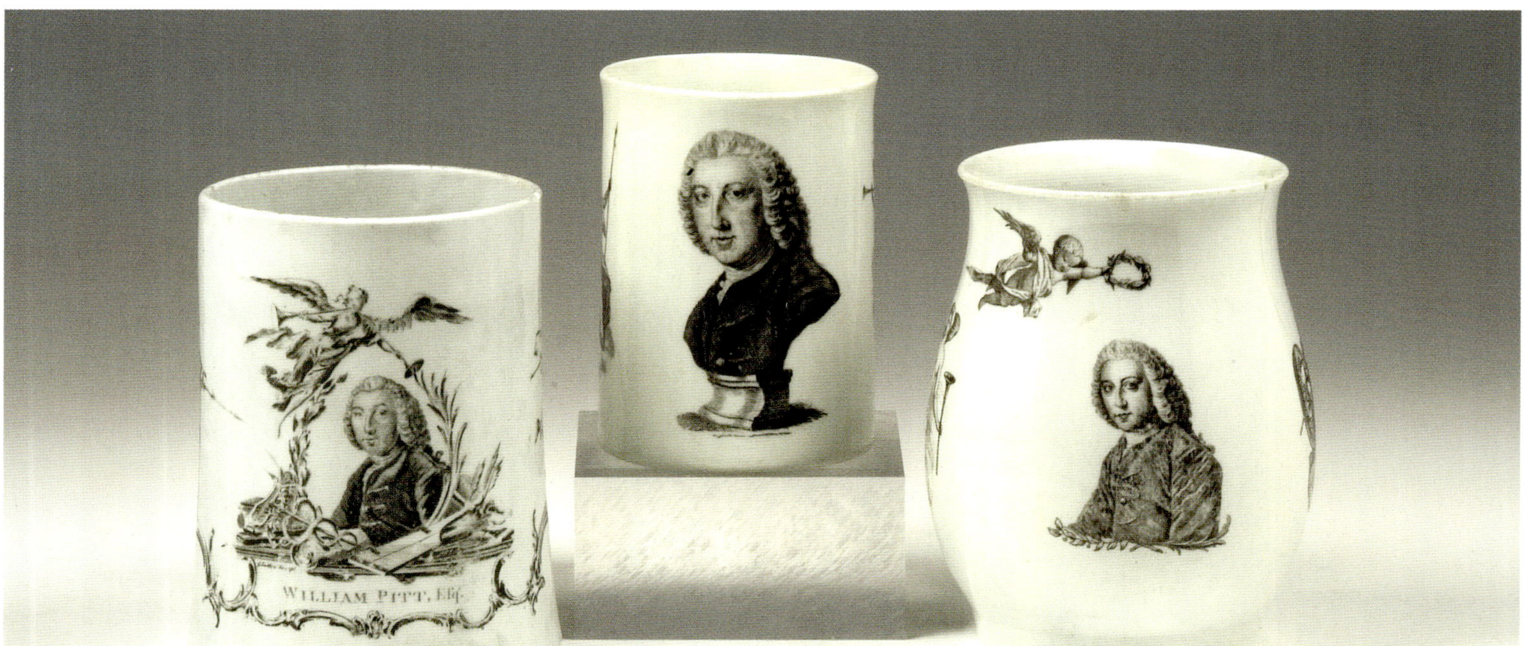

Mug, (481), c.1760, Liverpool, height: 14cm, (5½in), printed, steatitic porcelain. Pitt's portrait framed in laurel wreath, surrounded by attributes of learning and culture, while Fame blows twin trumpets above his head. Most souvenirs of William Pitt (while still 'The Great Commoner'), are based on a 1754 portrait by William Hoare.[3] The image on this tankard from Richard Chaffers's factory is signed by John Sadler, the pioneer of transfer printing.

Mug, (480), c.1760, Worcester, height: 14.6cm, (5¾in), printed, soft-paste porcelain. Printed with bust of Pitt, by Robert Hancock, perched on a short pedestal.[4] He is accompanied by Minerva and an androgynous figure of Fame.[5]
Mug, (477), c.1760, Worcester, height: 11.5cm, (4½in), printed, soft-paste porcelain. Print shows Pitt being crowned with a laurel wreath by a flying putto, also flanked by armed Minerva and Fame blowing trumpets.

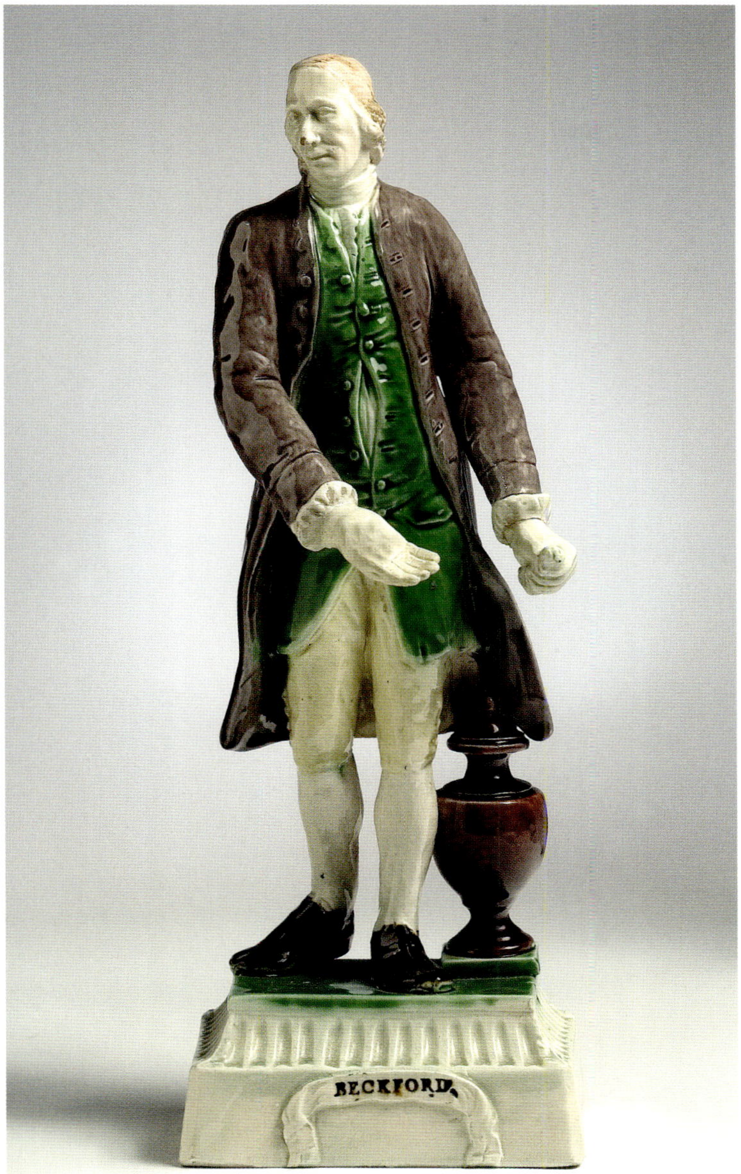

Figure, (**488**), c.1780, Staffordshire, Wood factory, height: 29.2cm, (11½in), lead-glazed earthenware, oxide-coloured. Beckford is shown embarking on his celebrated riposte to George III, a rolled scroll in his left hand. Figure loosely based on the Guildhall sculpture but with an urn at his feet rather than a plinth. His waistcoat is unbuttoned over his stomach (as in Moore's drawing) but he does not wear his Lord Mayor's chain of office.[6]

William Beckford (1709-1770)

Chatham's only political contemporary in Willett's collection is William Beckford, the immensely wealthy scion of a Jamaican sugar-planting dynasty, who returned from Jamaica in 1744. He was a London MP from 1754 until his death in 1770 and served twice as Lord Mayor of London, in 1763 and 1770. A lifelong friend of William Murray, later Lord Mansfield, the Lord Chief Justice, he also became an ally of the Earl of Chatham and an agitator for reform. On a famous occasion in 1770, only three weeks before his death, he embarrassed George III with the second of two loyal but reproachful addresses criticising royal interference in the recent Middlesex election.

John Francis Moore designed a monument dedicated to his memory, first shown in 1767,[7] engraved and published in May 1771 and installed in London's Guildhall in 1772. The statue shows Beckford in mid-speech flanked by grief-stricken figures representing the City of London and Trade and Commerce.

William Pitt the Younger (1759-1806) and Charles James Fox (1749-1806)

Chatham's son William was born in 1759, into a family steeped in politics for generations on his mother's as well as his father's side and he never contemplated any other career. He was Chancellor of the Exchequer before becoming, in 1784, First Lord of the Treasury (in effect Prime Minister), at twenty-four, the youngest ever. A popular rhyme commented that it was 'a sight to make all nations stand and stare: a kingdom trusted to a schoolboy's care'. With a short hiatus between 1801 and 1804, he continued to head the government in his twin offices until his death, at forty-six, in January 1806.

He was a brilliant orator and a supreme parliamentarian. 'He enjoyed redesigning the structures of government but would on no account risk their collapse. This is what would define him as a Tory in the eyes of future generations.'[8] He faced some of foreign policy's greatest challenges with a cool head, though in his later years he was worn down by operating with such a small majority and the ever-present threat of war with France.

Charles James Fox, the son of another famous political father, Henry Fox, was also precocious, becoming MP at nineteen and Lord of the Admiralty at twenty-four. He served briefly as Foreign Secretary in 1782 and in 1806 after Pitt's death, but otherwise spent his parliamentary career in opposition. Another great orator, Fox was larger than life, corpulent, charismatic, gregarious and a gambler. A passionate libertarian, he was life long opponent of slavery, an early supporter of the French Revolution, (for which he was much ridiculed), and a staunch opponent of George III.

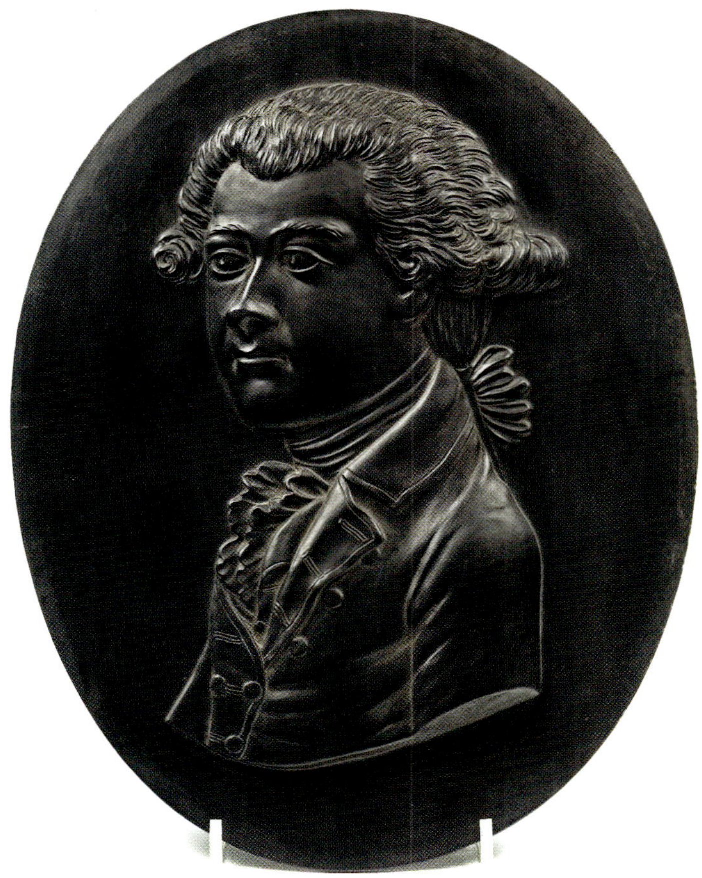

Plaque, (**489**), c.1785, Staffordshire, Neale & Co.; diameter: 31.8cm, (12½in), black basalt. A large plaque relief-moulded with a portrait of the young Pitt wearing a bob wig. It is a pendant to a portrait plaque of George III (041). Few ceramic images of Pitt were produced during his lifetime. Perhaps his austerity and lack of personal charisma made him an unmarketable subject whose achievements were recognised only after his death.

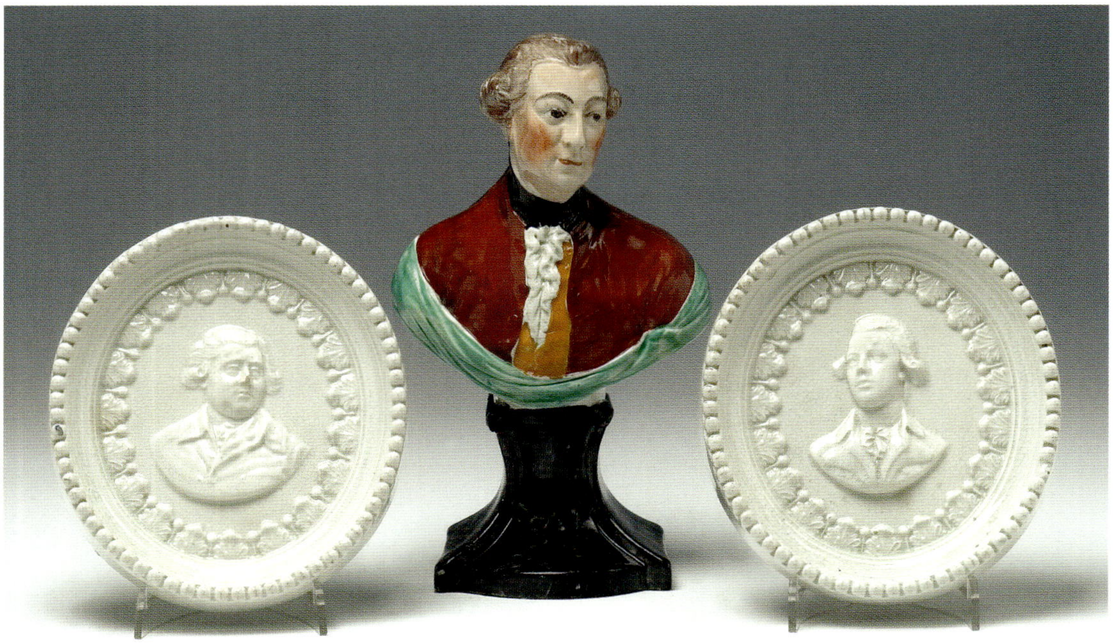

Pair of Plaques, (486 & A), c.1820, Staffordshire, each height: 15.3cm, (6in), creamware. Pair of portraits of Pitt (r) and his parliamentary adversary, Charles James Fox (l). Similar plaques with distinctive, deeply-moulded frames commemorate Princess Charlotte and Prince Leopold (050, 078).
Bust, (487), c.1800, Staffordshire, possibly Wood factory, height: 21.6cm, (8½in), enamelled pearlware. Portrait bust of Pitt produced in large numbers.

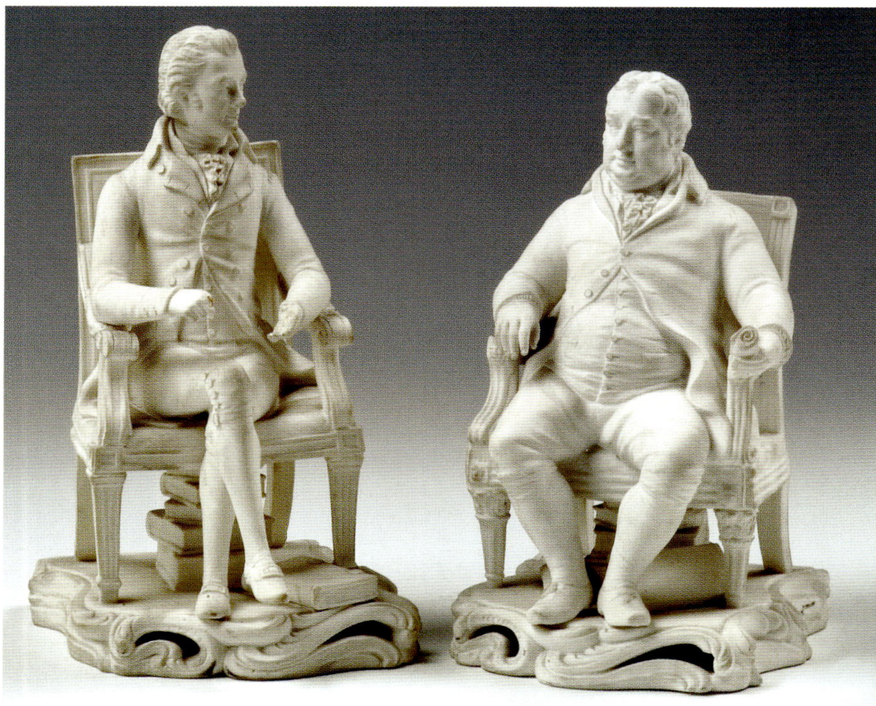

Pair of Figures, (482 + 483), c.1830, Staffordshire, Stoke-on-Trent, Mintons, height: 20.3cm, (8in), height: 21.6cm, (8½in), biscuit porcelain. Probably modelled by George Cocker, who had previously worked at Derby (incised 71 for Pitt and 72 for Fox), they sit in armchairs supported by piles of books. Pitt's slim angularity and his distinctive, retroussé nose are probably based on an engraving after a portrait painted on copper, c.1800, by Henry Edridge.[9] Fox's corpulent appearance derives from a pastel portrait of 1802 by John Raphael Smith.[10]

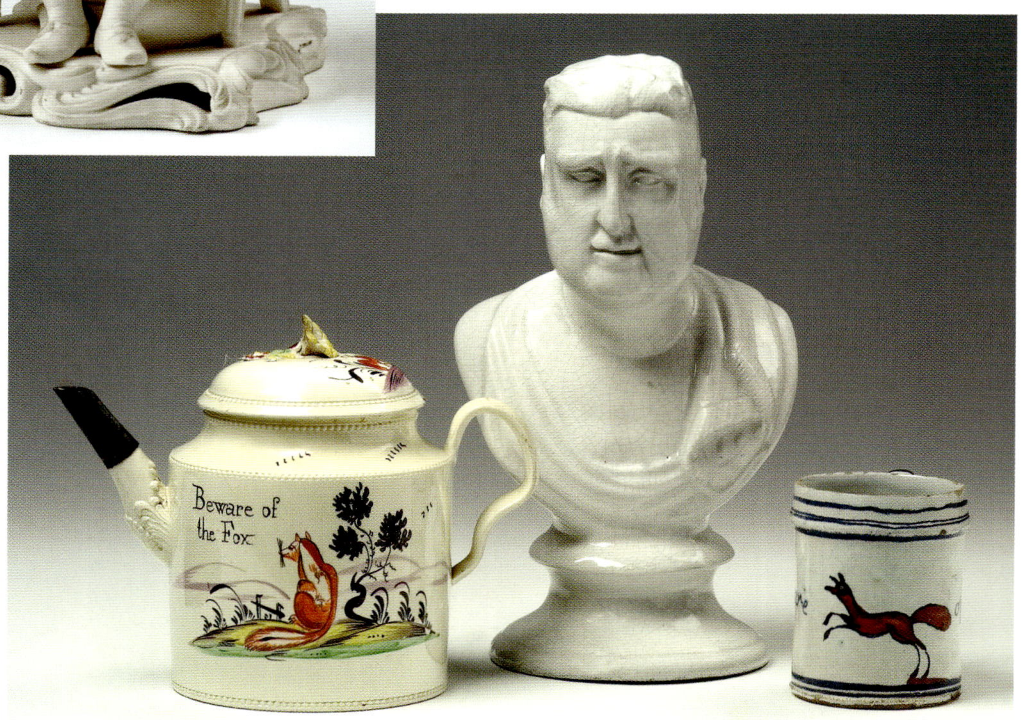

Teapot, (485), c.1770, Staffs, Greatbatch of Fenton, height: 15.3cm, (6in), creamware. See Mug (479).
Bust, (484), c.1805, London, height: 26.8cm, (10½in), pearlware. Bust shows Fox as 'a crop', with his hair cut short and a quasi-Roman toga draped about his shoulders in keeping with his republican credentials. Probably loosely based on one of a group of portrait busts by Joseph Nollekens, made for the fifth Duke of Bedford's famous 'Temple of Liberty' at Woburn Abbey[11].
Mug, (479), c.1740, London, height: 8.9cm, (3½in), tin-glazed earthenware. Both teapot and mug painted with charming images of foxes and inscribed, 'Beware of the Fox'. Willett assumed the phrase referred to the wily politician, who was occasionally caricatured as the animal but the term is now regarded as an idiomatic warning against intoxication. Delftware mugs of c.1730, similarly inscribed, confirm this interpretation.[12]

John Wilkes (1725-1797)

John Wilkes, the most controversial MP of the eighteenth century, played a critical role in the development of radical politics. The son of a wealthy London malt distiller, he was elected Member for Aylesbury in 1757. Within a decade he had set three significant precedents. He asserted the right of ordinary citizens to protection from arrest; he championed the freedom of electors to send their chosen candidate to Westminster and promoted the campaign for accurate reporting of Parliamentary proceedings.

In 1762 he launched his satirical weekly, the *North Briton*, targeting George III's mentor, the influential Scottish Earl of Bute, particularly for his handling of the Peace of Paris of 1763 that ended the Seven Years War. On 15 November 1763, Wilkes enraged both Houses of Parliament. In the Commons, he was accused of seditious libel for mocking the King's speech in issue no. 45 of the *North Briton,* at the opening of Parliament in April 1763. In the Lords he was newly accused of blasphemy over his *Essay on Woman*, an obscene travesty of the refined verses of Alexander Pope. He fled abroad to escape arrest, returning in 1768, partly to escape his French creditors and partly because he knew a general election was to be held. He was duly tried and convicted.

While serving twenty-two months in prison, he was elected and, despite efforts to have the result quashed, triumphantly re-elected three times as MP for Middlesex. He triumphed when the Duke of Grafton's government foolishly seated his defeated opponent in his place.[13] He gathered something of a following among Americans who were, in the 1770s, preparing for independence from Britain. Wilkes became a City of London magistrate, championing the cause of uncensored parliamentary reporting and was elected Lord Mayor of London in 1774. By the time he retired from public life in 1790 he was a staunch supporter of George III and his rehabilitation was complete.

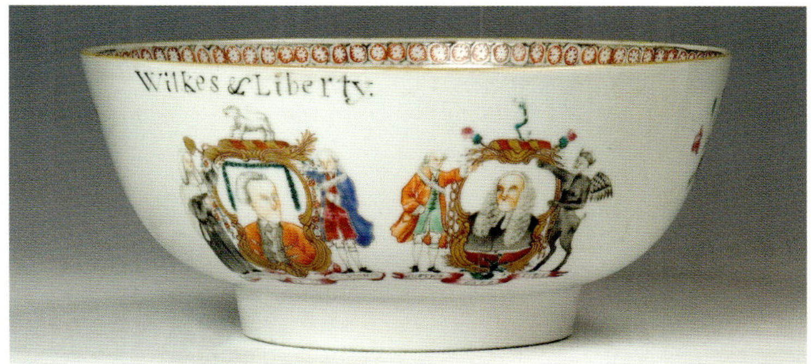

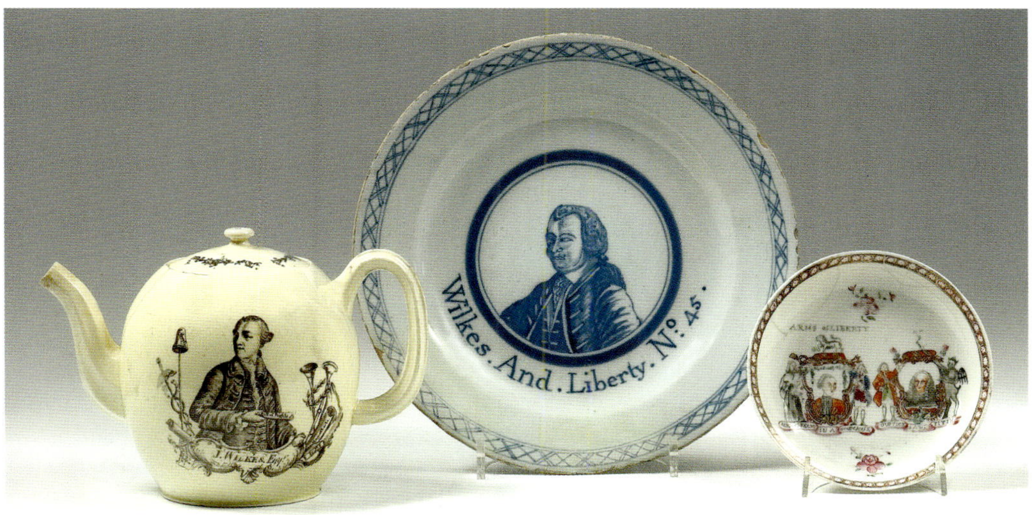

Punchbowl, (**491**), c.1765, China, diameter: 26cm, (10¼in), enamelled, hard-paste porcelain. Embellished beneath the famous slogan, 'Wilkes & Liberty', with framed portraits of Wilkes, with Sergeant Glynn, (who appeared for the defence at his trial) and Earl Temple, his political patron. Ribbon beneath inscribed 'ALWAYS READY IN A GOOD CAUSE'. The Judge, Lord Mansfield, is shown with the Devil and Lord Bute (who had now left office); the ribbon beneath reads 'JUSTICE SANS PITIE' (Justice without Mercy). The long-running interest in the Wilkes court case made it economically viable to have engraved satires copied onto porcelain in China. Large Chinese punchbowls, teapots and tea services survive commemorating Wilkes and his struggle against the Establishment. Image of Wilkes based on an engraving by J.S. Miller of 1763 that emphasised his famous squint.[14]

Teapot, (**496**), c.1770, Derbyshire, Cockpit Hill, height: 12.7cm, (5in), printed creamware. Wilkes holds a rolled 'Bill of Rights' in a print signed by Thomas Radford, who worked freelance at Cockpit Hill before moving to Staffordshire in 1778.[15] The image of Wilkes is very close to one published in a pamphlet of 1768, entitled 'English Liberty…'.[16] He is framed by the Liberty Cap on a pole, entwined serpents, a scroll of 'Magna Charta [*sic*]', twin bugles (of Fame) and the laurel wreath (of Victory).[17]
Plate, (**495**), c.1765, London or Bristol, diameter: 22.9cm, (9in), tin-glazed earthenware. Half-length portrait inscribed 'Wilkes.And.Liberty. No. 45'.
Saucer, (**492**), c.1765, China, height: 12.7cm, (5in), enamelled, hard-paste porcelain. Painted, like the punchbowl (491), with twin portraits of Wilkes and Lord Mansfield, under the banner proclaiming 'Wilkes & Liberty'.

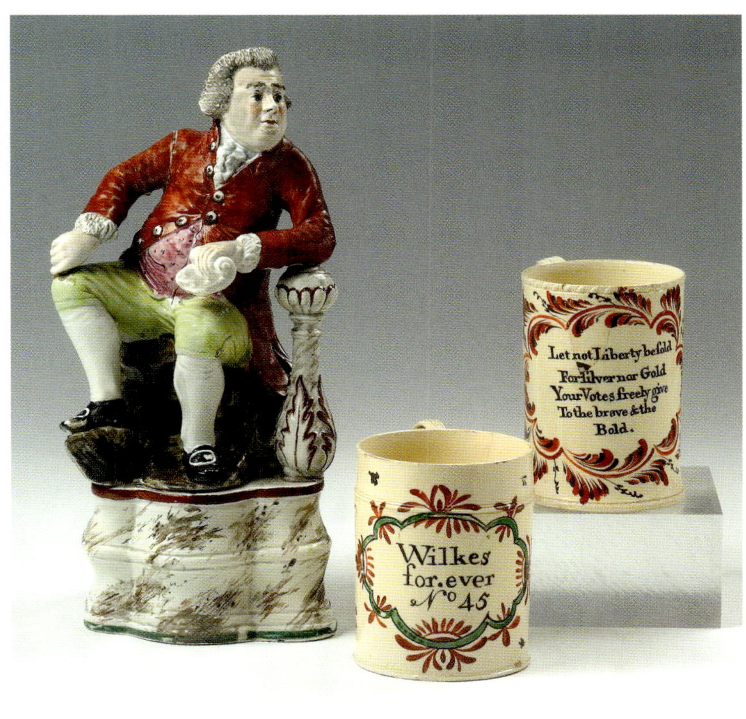

Figure, (**497**), c.1797, Staffordshire, height: 24.8cm, (9¾in), biscuit porcelain. From Staffordshire comes an enamelled, pearlware figure of Wilkes, seated on a rock. He is modelled as unusually stout but squints and holds a scroll marked 'The Rights of the People'. The piece may have been made at the time of his death in 1797.
Mug, (**493**), c.1770, Yorkshire, Leeds, height: 9.3cm, (3⅝in), enamelled creamware. Enamelled with floral sprigs and inscribed, 'Wilkes for ever No 45'. Mug has interlaced handle with flower terminals.
Mug, (**494**), c.1769, Yorkshire, Leeds, height: 10.2cm, (4in), enamelled creamware. Enamelled with floral sprigs and inscribed, 'Let not Liberty be sold / for silver nor Gold / Your Votes freely give/ To the brave & the / Bold'. Thought to be linked to Wilkes's electoral campaign of 1769.

George Canning (1770-1827)

Canning was William Pitt's political protégé and loyal supporter. Canning lived for some time on Marine Parade in Brighton, where he built a soundproofed tunnel from the house to the seafront. Here he held secret meetings with George IV and practised oratory 'to the music of the waves'.[18] Canning became Prime Minister but died after only four months in office. He was described by George Croly as 'the first debater, the most dextrous politician and the happiest wit in the house; but the most perplexed, unhappy and disappointed of ministers.'[19]

George Kinloch (1775-1833)

In November 1819 Kinloch gave an impassioned speech in Dundee in response to events at Peterloo in Manchester and two weeks later was charged with sedition. Fearful of deportation to Australia, he fled to France, returning secretly to Kinloch via London in 1823. In May of that year a pardon arrived and in 1832 he became MP for the new constituency of Dundee, created by the Parliamentary Reform Bill of 1832. He died a few months later.

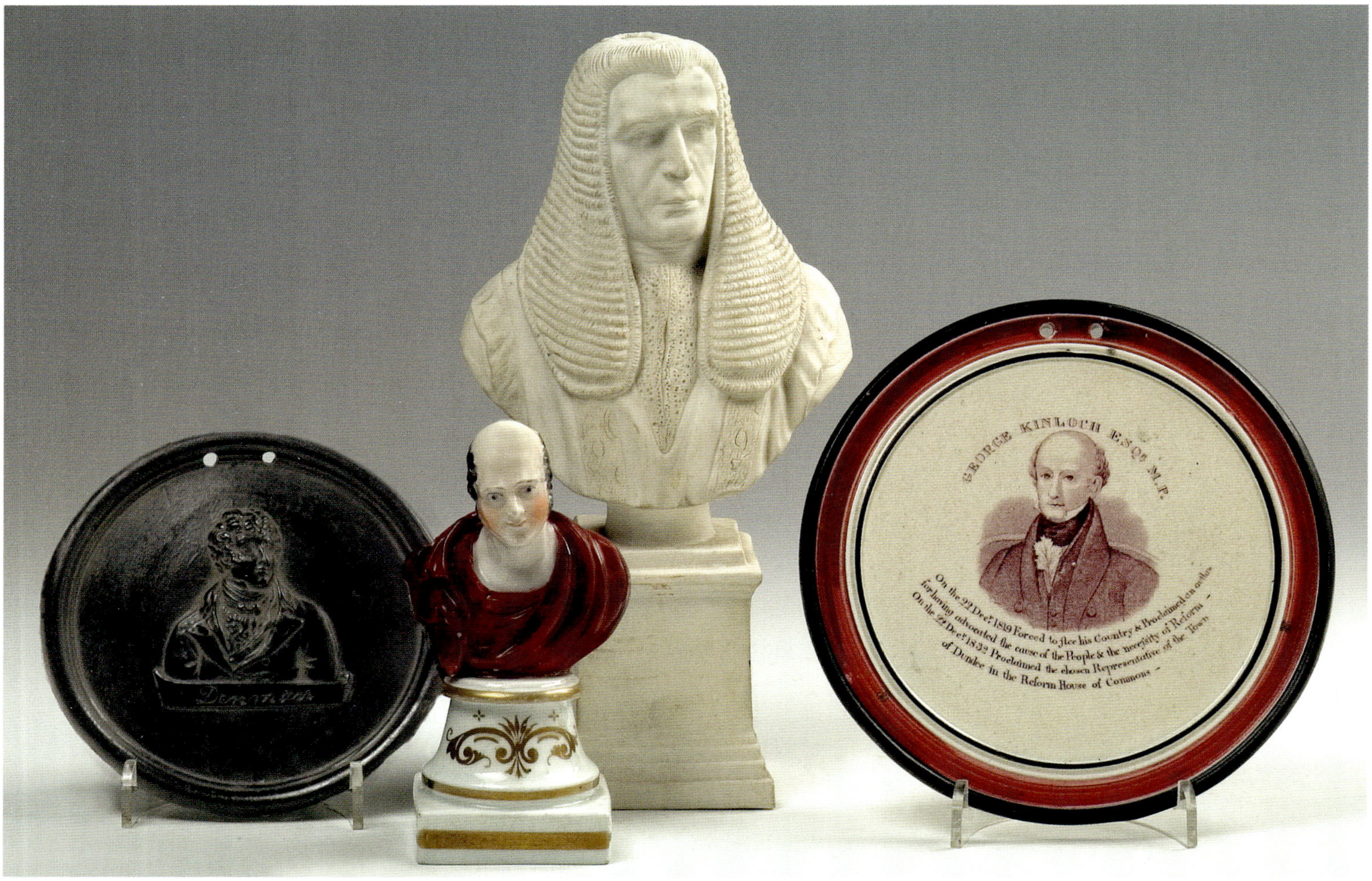

Plaque, (**524**), c.1820, Staffordshire, diameter: 12.7cm, (5in), painted earthenware. Relief-moulded with a half-length portrait of Thomas, 1st Baron Denman (1779-1854). Denman earned the enmity of George IV with his spirited defence of Queen Caroline in 1820 although he went on to serve as Lord Chancellor of England 1832-1850.

Bust, (**525**), c.1830, possibly Derby, height: 13.3cm, (5¼in), soft-paste porcelain, enamelled and gilt. Small bust, possibly made at the time of his death, commemorates Canning's brief tenure as Prime Minister.

Bust, (**526**), 1826, possibly Derby, height: 22.9cm, (9in), biscuit porcelain. Portrait of John Copley, 1st Baron Lyndhurst (1772-1863). Born in Massachusetts, the son of the painter, John Singleton Copley, he was called to the Bar in 1824, made Attorney General in 1824 and Master of the Rolls in 1826. He served as Lord Chancellor on three occasions.

Plaque, (**508**), c.1835, diameter: 15.9cm, (6¼in), pearlware, two-colour printed and enamelled. Portrait of Scottish MP, George Kinloch, known as the 'Radical Laird'.[20] Beneath his portrait is inscribed, 'On the 22Decr.1819 Forced to flee his Country & Proclaimed an Outlaw / for having advocated the cause of the People & the necessity of Reform'.

Election Ceramics

Corrupt political practice was endemic in mid-eighteenth century England. The interests of a small minority of landed gentry and aristocrats (usually Whigs) and their sparsely populated estates were represented in Parliament at the expense of the increasingly populous cities of the Midlands and the North. Leeds, Manchester and Birmingham remained unrepresented until the passing of the Reform Act in 1832. Although the term Tory was first used to describe any opposition to the Whigs, the Tory party tended to emerge from the growing urban middle classes.

Contested elections were avoided wherever possible since it was far more profitable for country magnates to divide the spoils between them without recourse to the voters. In the general election of 1761 only three counties went to the polls while Northamptonshire held only three elections during the entire eighteenth century! A number of pots refer directly to some of the more contentious elections of the period. It is not known whether such plates, jugs and mugs inscribed for Parliamentary hopefuls were commissioned by the candidates themselves, their supporters or were made speculatively by the potters.[21]

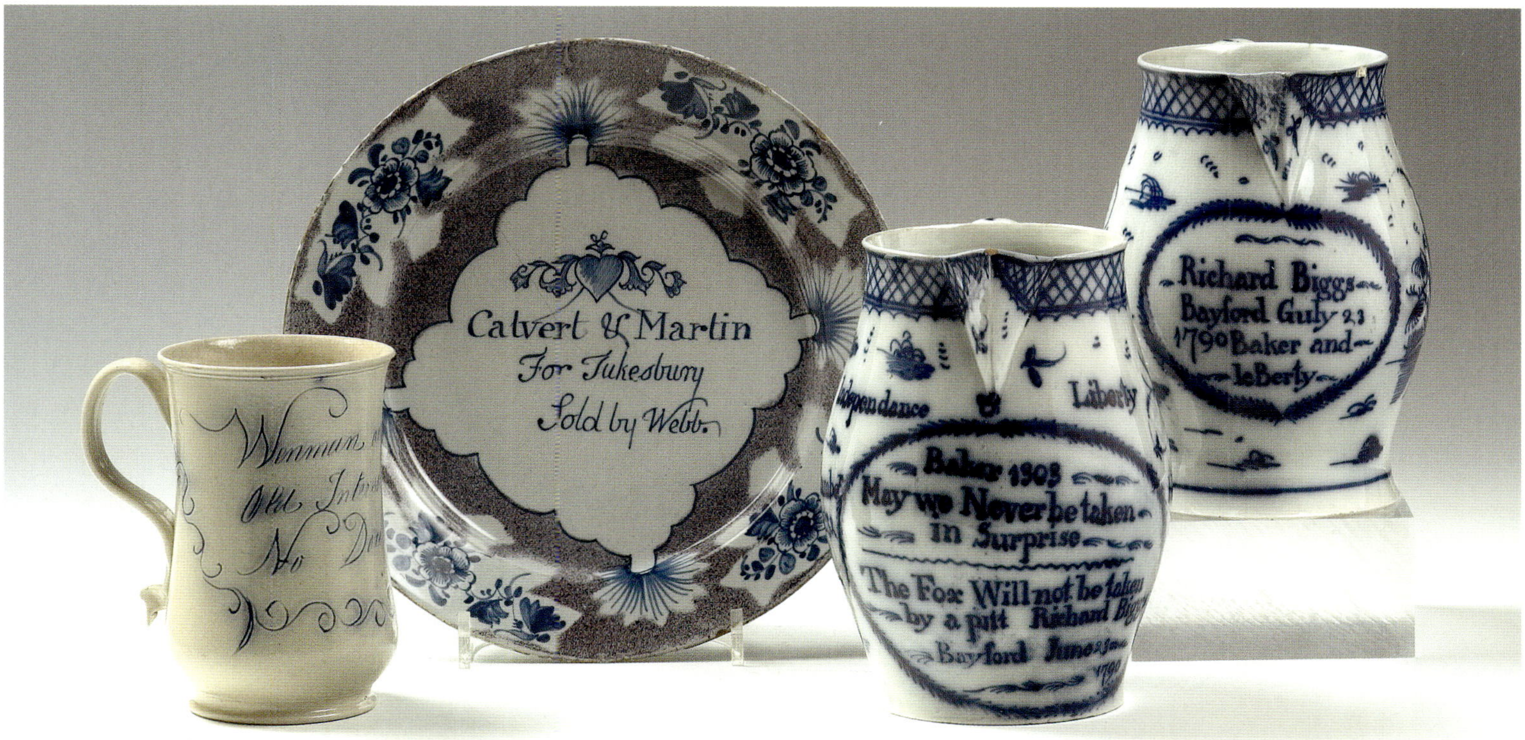

Mug, (**490**), 1754, Staffordshire, height: 9.3cm, (3⅝in), salt-glazed stoneware. Inscribed in 'scratch blue', 'Wenman and Dashwood / Old Interest for Ever', (Tory incumbents) and 'No Double Returns', intended to discourage the return of all four candidates to Parliament. The mug must have been made after the votes were counted.[22]

Plate, (**478**), 1754, Bristol, diameter: 22.9cm, (9in), tin-glazed earthenware. Inscribed 'Calvert & Martin / for Tukesbury / Sold by Webb', one of several plates, made by Richard Frank of Bristol, for the Tewkesbury election of 1754.[23] The last phrase suggests that the retailer Webb was selling such pieces.

Jug, (**499**), c.1790, Staffordshire, height: 15.9cm, (6¼in), pearlware, painted underglaze.

Jug, (**500**), c.1790, Staffordshire, height: 15.9cm, (6¼in), pearlware, painted underglaze. Jugs made for Richard Biggs, supporter of the Whig candidate William Baker, in the Hertfordshire election of 1790, one dated 23 June, the other 23 Guly [*sic*]. The Whigs duly won with 1,303 votes. The inscription, 'The Fox Will not be taken / by a pitt' makes this the first piece to invoke national political leaders.

From about 1724 to 1770 most pieces were made in delftware. The year of 1754 was particularly contentious. At the Bristol election, 'a novel mode of canvassing was adopted. Delft dinner plates, bearing the inscription, 'NUGENT ONLY 1754' were made and distributed, probably made by Richard Frank, 'gallypot-maker' of Redcliffe.[24] Delftware ceramics were also made for elections in Taunton and Barnstable the same year and punch bowls, jugs, plates and mugs were made in tin glaze and stoneware for the notorious Oxfordshire election.

The Tory seat of Oxford, held by Philip, Viscount Wenman and Sir James Dashwood, was contested for the first time by Thomas, Viscount Parker and Sir Edward Turner, Whig candidates supported by the Duke of Marlborough, the most powerful landowner in the area. Four paintings by William Hogarth, now in Sir John Soane's Museum, London, brilliantly satirised the proceedings. The week-long election in May 1754 was marred by such scandalous voting irregularities that another had to be held the following year. The Tories are thought to have spent £40,000 during the nine-month propaganda war to combat the Whig challenge but their majority was eventually overturned. They distributed leaflets and objects (probably given away rather than sold) in support of the two sitting MPs.

Jug, (**527**), c.1790, Shropshire, Coalport, height: 19.1cm, (7½in), soft-paste porcelain, enamelled and gilt. Inscribed in gilt, '1835 in Commemoration of the Twelve Conservatives of Shropshire' including the names of Lord Hill and the Earl of Powys and followed by the names of those elected, leading to the nickname of the 'Twelve Apostles' jug.[25]

Jug, (**498**), c.1796, Shropshire, Coalport, height: 22.2cm, (8¾in), soft-paste porcelain, printed underglaze. Inscribed, 'HONOUR and HONESTY / IOHN HILL for EVER / PROSPERITY to THE HOUSE OF HAWKSTONE' and 'MAJORITY of 44 / IN THE YEAR / 1796'. One of three survivors, thought to be the earliest dated pieces of Coalport porcelain.[26] The sitting Tory member John Hill of Hawkstone, was opposed by his cousin William Hill of Attingham. Their rivalry led to a contest, 'the bitterness of which can never be exceeded. Both parties … incurred a lavish expenditure in bringing voters to the poll'.[27] A jug at Attingham Park, Shropshire, is inscribed for the victorious William Hill. This seems to be the first election where ceramics were produced in support of rival candidates.

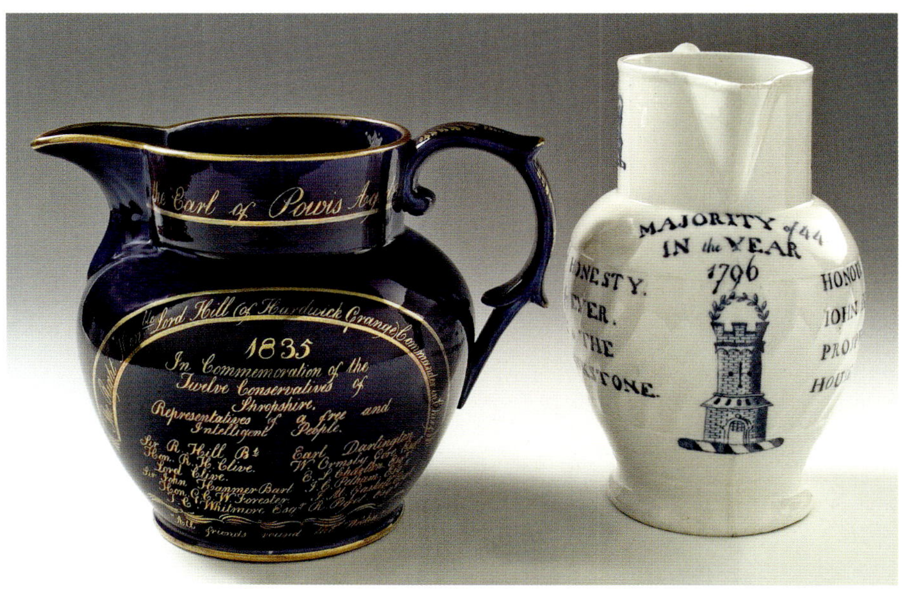

Thomas Paine (1737-1809)

Paine was born into a Quaker family in Thetford and trained as a staymaker before settling in London, working for the Excise Service and immersing himself in politics. His detractors referred throughout his life to his humble origins in corsetry. In 1774 he embarked for the American Colonies, where he edited the *Pennsylvania Magazine* and wrote the pamphlet, *Common Sense* (1774). This defined the character of the coming revolution and helped shape the Declaration of Independence. Following the Revolutionary War, he became Secretary for Foreign Affairs to the Congressional Committee.

On his return to England he became best known for *The Rights of Man,* (1791), a radical treatise supporting the principle of equality for all, written in response to Burke's *Reflections on the Revolution in France*. Fearing arrest, Paine fled to France where he was elected to the Revolutionary Convention although he spoke no French. He fled France when his criticism of the execution of Louis XVI and the publication of *The Age of Reason* earned him the enmity of Robespierre's regime and a spell in the Luxembourg prison. He returned to the United States but died in poverty in New York in 1809. In 1819 William Cobbett, a fellow radical, went to New York to bring home his bones.

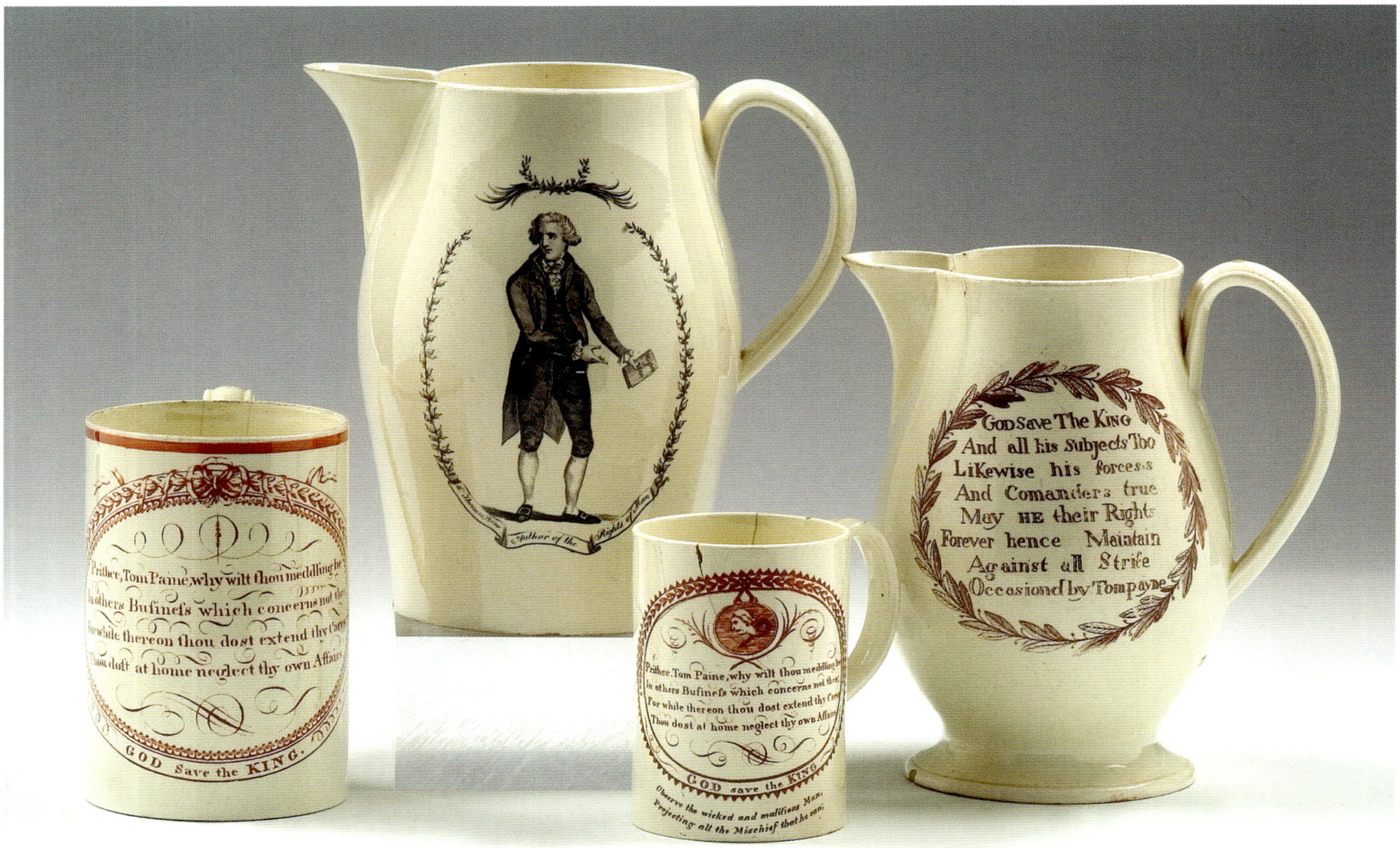

Mug, (**520**), c.1795, Staffordshire, height: 12.1cm, (4¾in), red-printed creamware. Inscribed, 'Prithee Tom Paine, why wilt thou meddling be/ In others Business which concerns not thee'. Thomas Paine was seen to be such a threat to national security and stability that pottery was produced denouncing him.

Jug, (**518**), c.1795, Liverpool, height: 17.8cm, (7in), printed creamware. Entitled, 'Thomas Paine / Author of the / Rights of Man', the jug is printed with an unusually sympathetic portrait of Tom Paine as hero.[29]

Mug, (**521**), c.1795, Staffordshire, height: 9.6cm, (3¾in), red-printed creamware. Inscribed, 'Observe the wicked and malitious [*sic*] Man / Projecting all the Mischief that he can,' there is a tiny portrait of Paine with a forked tail.

Jug, (**519**), c.1795, Staffordshire, height: 17.1cm, (6¾in), brown-printed creamware. Inscribed, 'God Save the KING / and all his Subjects Too Against all Strife / Occasion'd by Tom Payne'. Horace Walpole jokes that Paine could easily raise an army from 'the hosts of banditti' (murderous footpads) threatening the population.[30] Following the execution of the French king Louis XVI effigies of Tom Paine 'were shot through and through and then burnt'.[31] In the 1800s the musician Dr Burney, blamed his son James's inability to gain promotion in the navy on his subversive views, 'Painism & politics'.[32]

Edmund Burke (1729-1797)

Born into a middle-class Dublin family in 1744 Burke attended Trinity College where he set up a debating society and wrote a philosophical treatise on aesthetics which attracted attention among Enlightenment Europeans. He left Ireland in 1750 to study law in London but abandoned it for writing and politics, becoming an MP in 1765. He sided with the colonists in the American War of Independence and supported other democratic issues such as Catholic emancipation despite being a member of the Anglican Church of Ireland. He is best remembered for his pamphlet, *Reflections on the Revolution in France*, published 1790, in which he expressed serious misgivings about the aims of the revolutionaries and ideas of universal equality. Predicting that the revolution would lead to anarchy, bloodshed and the destruction of society, the publication was described as the 'manifesto of a Counter Revolution'.[28]

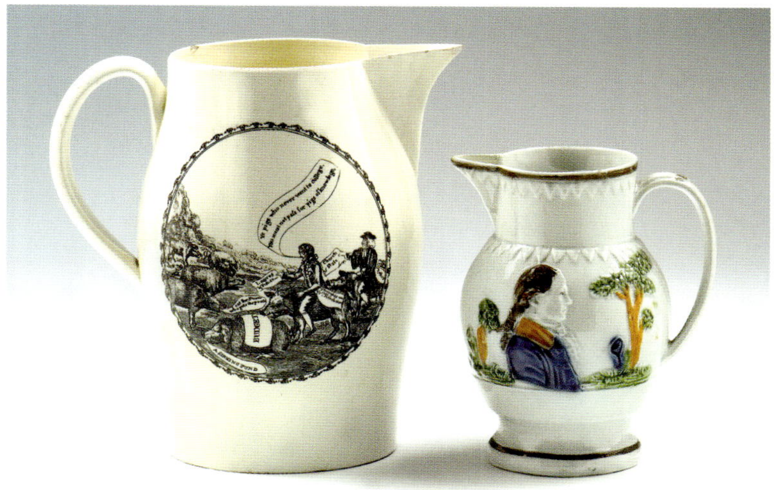

Jug, (518), c.1795, Liverpool, height: 17.8cm, (7in), printed creamware. A political caricature, inscribed, 'Ye pigs that never went to college / you must not pass as pigs of knowledge'. Paine's adversary Edmund Burke, is shown condemning 'the swinish multitude' to ignorance, in reference to remarks made in his treatise, *Reflections on the Revolution in France*, 1790; the cartoon's source has not been traced. This rare piece, supporting Paine and critical of Burke, (the first pair to symbolise the polarised politics of Left and Right) may have been produced for the American market.
Jug, (437), c.1800, Staffordshire, height: 14cm, (5½in), Prattware. Willett assumed the relief-moulded profile portrait on a pearlware jug, decorated in high-temperature colours, was that of the Marquis de Lafayette. Griselda Lewis identified it as Edmund Burke, taken from a very similar Wedgwood jasperware cameo portrait.[33]

Radical Politics and Public Unrest

The political and social upheavals of the American and French Revolutions and the dissemination of the ideas of visionaries and radicals such as William Blake, Tom Paine and William Cobbett, inspired a widespread demand for social change. A working-class movement developed, demanding the reform of Parliament and improvements to the living and working conditions of the urban and rural poor. It also led to protest and confrontation.

Sir Francis Burdett, Bart (1770-1844)

Cast in the mould of a hero of the Romantic Movement, Burdett was an early champion of political reform. He was handsome, theatrical and, as well as being independently wealthy, had married the daughter of Thomas Coutts the banker, reputed to be the richest man in England. An MP since 1796, having spoken out against political corruption, flogging and press censorship, in 1807 he fought a duel with John Paull, parliamentary candidate for Westminster. Both were hurt but Burdett, wounded in the thigh, was elected MP in place of Paull and processed in celebration into London as soon as he could walk on crutches. Mrs Mary Anne Clarke explained why she was late for dinner with her lover, the Duke of York, 'the occasion that had detained me was to see the procession of Sir Francis Burdett's electors arrive in town from Brentford.'

In 1810 Burdett published a letter in defence of a radical orator imprisoned in Newgate gaol, was considered to have breached parliamentary privilege and was himself committed to the Tower of London. By this time he had a huge popular following and his imprisonment provoked widespread rioting in London's West End.

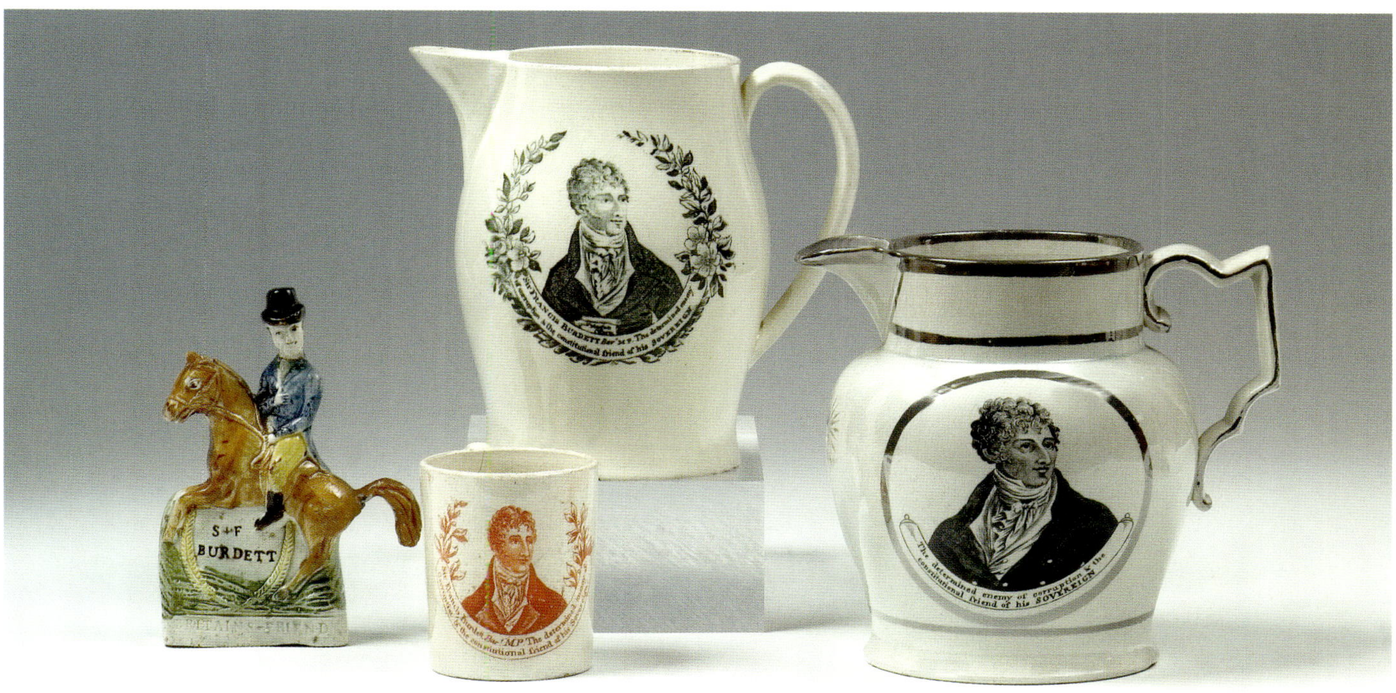

Figure, (502), c.1810, Staffordshire, height: 11.5cm, (4½in), Prattware. Staffordshire pots were produced in support of Sir Francis Burdett, together with a tiny figure of the baronet on horseback, impressed: 'S + F BURDETT' and 'BRITAINS + FRIEND'.[34]
Mug, (503), c.1812, Staffordshire, height: 6.6cm, (2⅝in), red-printed creamware. Printed, within a wreath, with portrait of Burdett.
Jug, (501), c.1812, Staffordshire, height: 14cm, (5½in), printed creamware. Printed, within a wreath, with portrait of Burdett.
Jug, (504), c.1812-30, Staffordshire, height: 14cm, (5½in), pearlware, printed and lustred. Printed, within a wreath, with portrait of Burdett, probably based on prints after a portrait by James Northcote.[35] All state that Burdett was imprisoned '...for firmly / and disinterestedly asserting / the legal rights of / the British / people' but remained, 'The determined enemy of corruption & the / constitutional friend of his SOVEREIGN'. Such pieces may have been reissued around 1830 in support of the Reform Bill. After it was passed in 1832 Burdett became Tory MP for North Wiltshire, disappointing his more radical followers by revealing that his real mission was parliamentary reform, not revolution.

The Peterloo Massacre

In 1817 Joseph Nadin, the Deputy Constable of Manchester wrote; 'The lower orders are everywhere meeting in large bodies and are very clamorous ... they talk of a general union of the lower orders throughout the kingdom.' In 1816, 12,940 men, women and children were employed in the Manchester textile factories. For a working day of up to 16 hours, spinners earned 30 shillings and weavers 12 shillings a week. In the economic depression that followed the Napoleonic Wars wages fell by half. Living conditions were squalid and life expectancy short. In the face of growing unrest, the government became obsessed with maintaining public order.

Against this volatile background, on 16 August 1819, around 60,000 people gathered at St Peter's Field on the outskirts of Manchester to hear the weaver, Samuel Bamford, and the charismatic Henry 'Orator' Hunt (1773-1835). Hunt was a Wiltshire farmer who moved, after eloping with a friend's wife, to farm near East Grinstead in 1811. Here he met William Cobbett and turned radical agitator. The Manchester Patriotic Union Society took pains to ensure that the gathering was orderly and peaceful and, under banners proclaiming 'Universal Suffrage', some sang Methodist anthems. Local magistrates, however, were determined to break up the gathering and the Manchester and Cheshire Yeoman Cavalry, their sabres unsheathed, together with the local constabulary stormed the meeting on horseback, dispersing the crowd by force.

Around a dozen people were killed including a little girl, trampled under the horses' hooves and 500 were injured, at least 100 of them women and children. The incident became known as the 'Peterloo Massacre', a satirical reference to the recent victory at Waterloo. The event was widely publicised in popular prints. A peep-show man was arrested in Chudleigh, near Exeter for showing such an image and describing it to the public using seditious expressions.[36] By late 1820 Hunt and Burdett were once again in prison.[37]

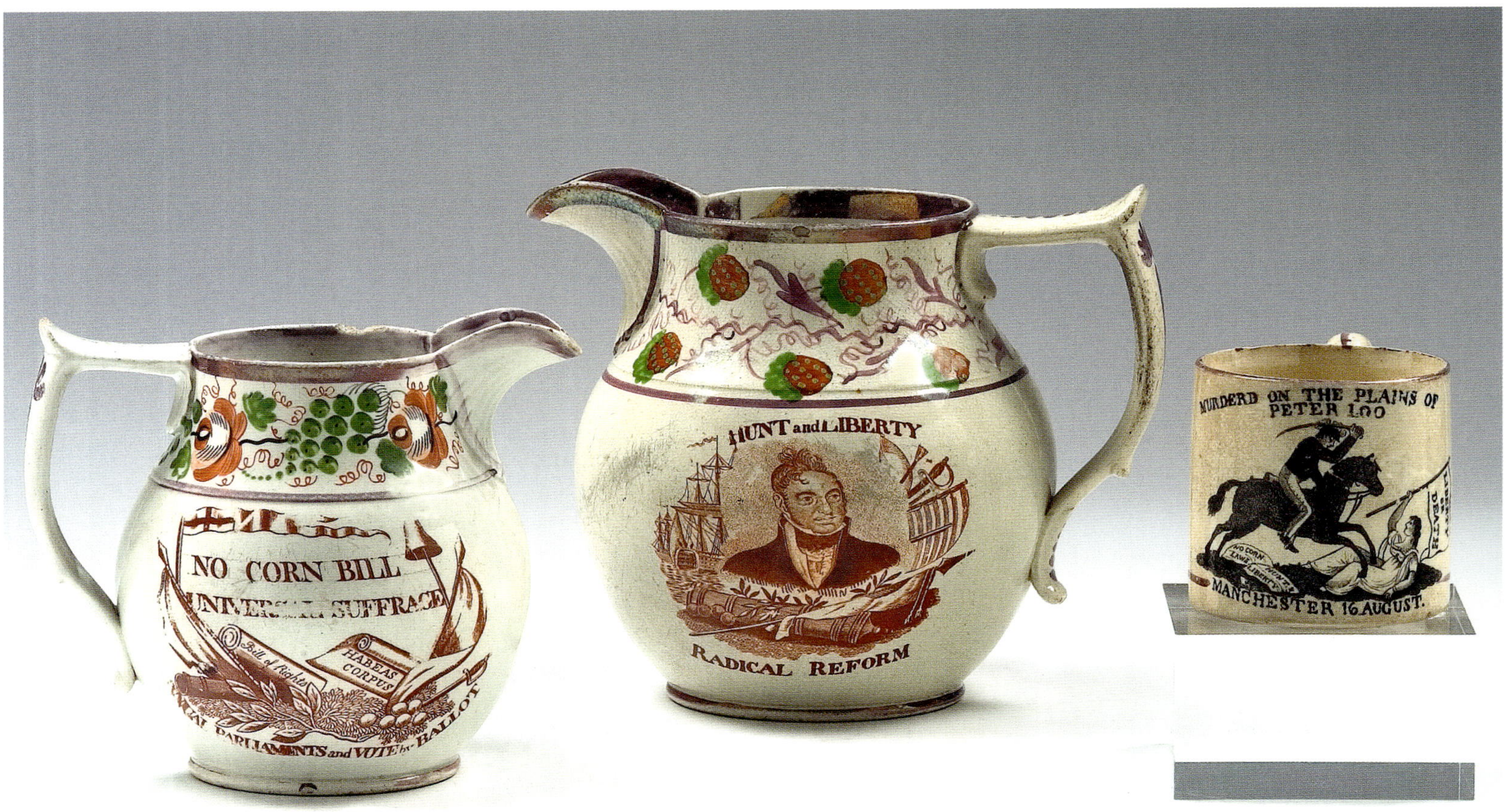

Jug, (**505**), c.1820, Staffordshire, height: 13.3cm, (5¼in), pearlware, printed and painted.
Jug, (**506**), c.1820, Staffordshire, height: 11.5cm, (4½in), pearlware, printed and painted. Both have portrait, labelled, 'HUNT and LIBERTY / RADICAL REFORM' and inscribed on reverse, 'Universal Suffrage / Magna Charta [*sic*] / No Corn Bill / Annual Parliaments and Vote by Ballot'. Portrait not an authentic likeness of Hunt. Surrounded by battleships and cannon, the print was left over from the War of 1812 and depicts the American, Commodore Bainbridge[38] – it was assumed that English customers were unlikely to know the difference.
Mug, (**507**), c.1822, Staffordshire, height: 6.4cm, (2½in), printed drabware. Entitled; 'MURDERD ON THE PLAINS OF PETERLOO / MANCHESTER 16 AUGUST', a mounted cavalryman tramples the symbolic figure of Liberty, who holds a banner proclaiming 'Liberty or Death'. The image may be taken from one of several prints by George Cruikshank. The design is closest to the woodcut header for the broadsheet *A Slap at Slop*, which the potters may have seen.[39]

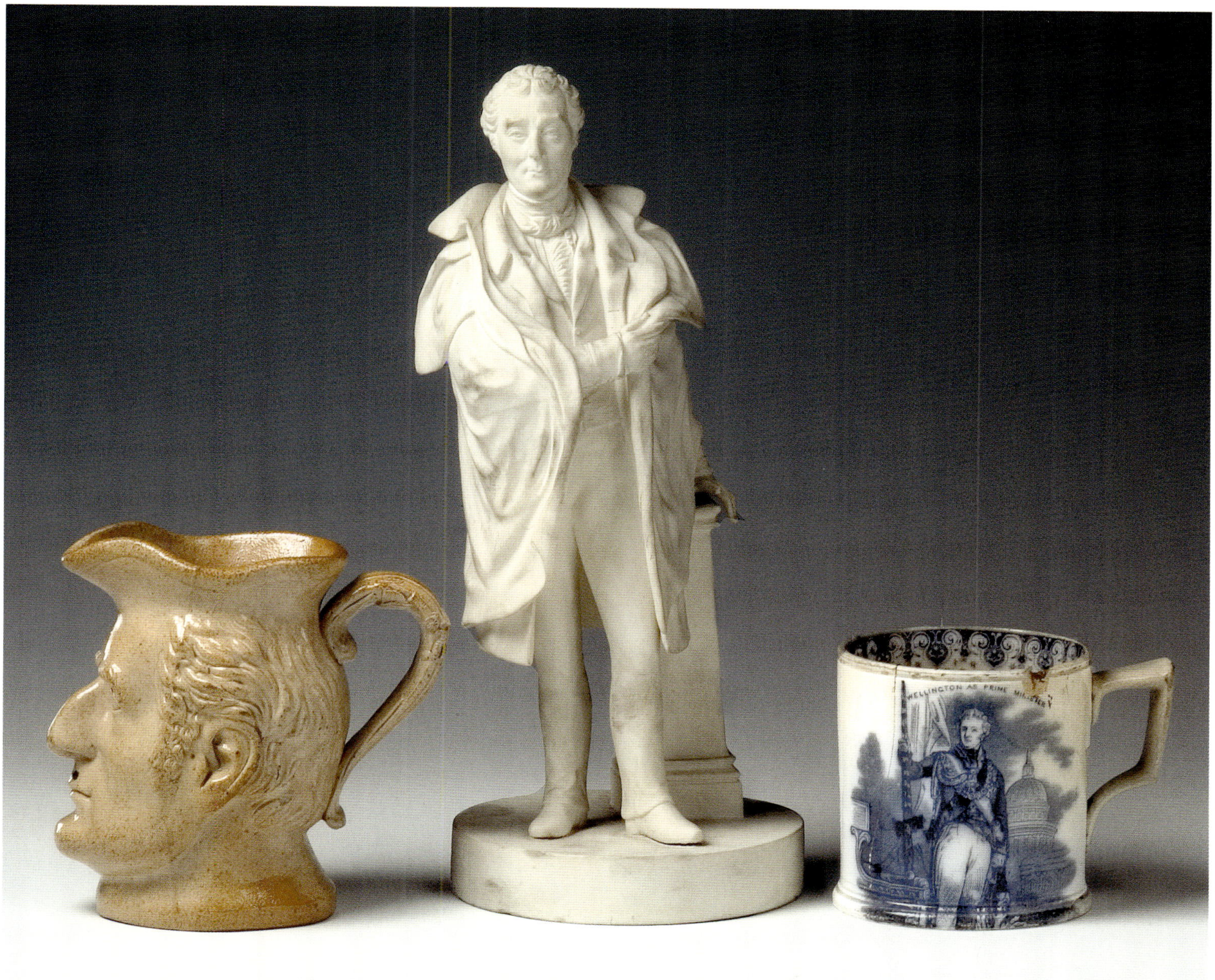

Jug, (143), c.1840, London, Stephen Green, height: 12.7cm, (5in), salt-glazed stoneware.Moulded as a fine portrait of 'Old Hooky'; Wellington's nickname on account of his aquiline nose.
Figure, (146), c.1830, Staffordshire, Stoke-on-Trent, Mintons, height: 27.5cm, (10⅞in), biscuit porcelain. One of few ceramic souvenirs of Wellington as Prime Minister, wearing civilian dress and a cape.

Mug, (147), c.1840, possibly North East England, height: 8.9cm, (3½in), blue-printed earthenware. 'WELLINGTON AS PRIME MINISTER' and 'WALMER CASTLE KENT' shows Wellington standing before St Paul's Cathedral and his residence as Lord Warden of the Cinque Ports.

Reform

After the sudden death of George Canning, the Duke of Wellington (1769-1852) became Prime Minister in 1828. In addition to other rewards for his military service he leased Apsley House in London and was made Lord Warden of the Cinque Ports, based at Walmer Castle in Kent. Despite his outstanding achievements on the battlefield, he was an inept politician. Although he grudgingly accepted the case for Catholic emancipation he was vehemently opposed to parliamentary reform. This made him very unpopular, led to public riots, an attack on Apsley House and the fall of his government in 1830. Parliamentary reform had been hotly debated under the Commonwealth during the 1650s. Eventually Cromwell, the Lord Protector, rejected radical ideas such as universal suffrage and sided with conservatives who held that an individual must own land worth at least £200 in order to qualify for the vote. His limited reforms, granting representation to Manchester and Leeds for instance, and increasing the number of members for some of the more populous counties, were reversed at the restoration of the monarchy in 1660.

The issue then lay dormant until the 1760s, when it was revived by the Earl of Chatham, who held that the borough system was 'the rottenest part of our constitution'.[40] His son, Pitt the Younger, later balked at the wholesale abolition of rotten boroughs and proposed more MPs for the counties. The electorate needed to expand to reflect the growing influence of the middle classes as well as the shift in population from the countryside to the cities, in line with the change from an agricultural to an industrial economy. Pitt's reform bill of 1786 was rejected, as were further bills, such as that proposed by Charles Grey in 1797.

In 1830, after the fall of the Tory Duke of Wellington, Earl Grey (a Whig) became Prime Minister and backed Lord John Russell's Reform Bill of 1831. This proposed disenfranchising 60 of the smallest boroughs, reducing representation for 47 others and redistributing the seats among the London suburbs, large cities, the counties, Scotland and Ireland. Championed by Russell, Earl Grey, Lord Brougham, the Lord Chancellor Lord Althorp, and Lord Lansdowne it received overwhelming support in the Commons but was rejected by the House of Lords. This prompted Grey's resignation followed by his reinstatement, the opposition of King William IV and later his covert support. The bill finally received royal assent on 7 June 1832.

By enfranchising householders and leaseholders with property over a certain value, the vote was increased by nearly 80 per cent. Many 'rotten boroughs' in rural areas lost their MPs while the big commercial and industrial centres of the North of England gained representation. The Reform Act prompted a sequence of social and economic reforms that unfolded throughout the nineteenth century. New municipal councils were created, an organised police force was inaugurated and religious toleration was extended.

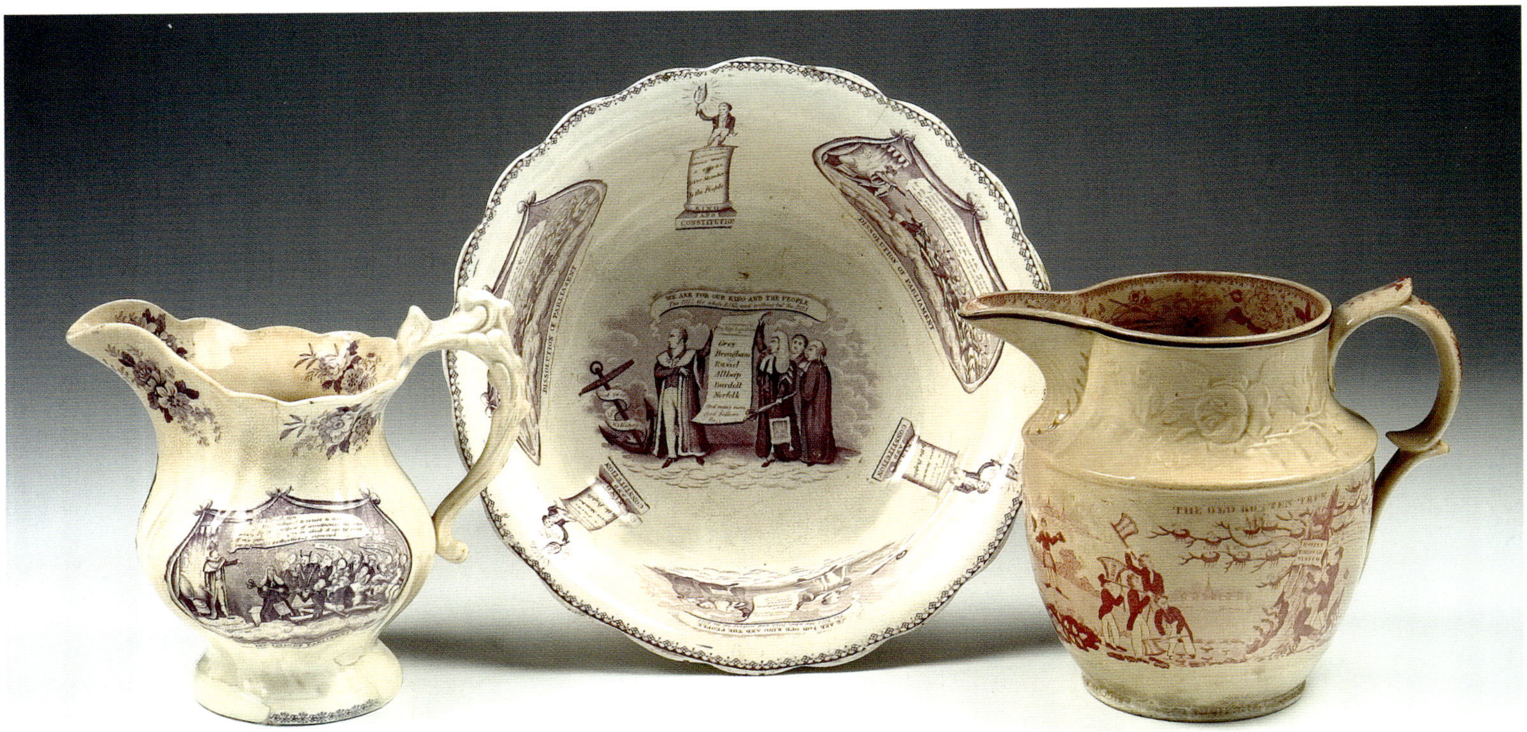

Jug and Punchbowl, (509 & A), c.1832, Staffordshire, height: 17.8cm, (7in), diameter: 28cm, (11in), purple-printed earthenware. Both pieces decorated with vignettes, including, 'DISSOLUTION OF PARLIAMENT';[41] a banner entitled, 'WE ARE FOR OUR KING AND THE PEOPLE' with the Whig Lords holding a scroll listing leading champions of the Bill;[42] and a figure on a column holding the torch of Truth, entitled, 'KING AND CONSTITUTION'.
Jug, (R2454.10), c.1832, Staffordshire, height: 17.8cm, (7in), red-printed drabware. Scene of the felling of 'THE OLD ROTTEN TREE' on Constitution Hill. Adapted from a caricature by Cruikshank, celebrates reform.[43]

Clockwise:
Beaker, (510), c.1832, Staffordshire, height: 10.2cm, (4in), blue-printed earthenware. Inscribed, 'Littledale and the Independence of Whitehaven', promotes the candidate, Littledale, in the 1832 election and celebrates the passing of the great Reform Bill.[44]
Flask, (077), c.1832, Derbyshire, Denby, height: 19.1cm, (7½in), salt-glazed stoneware Moulded as figure of William IV, impressed: 'WILLIAM IVTH'S REFORM CORDIAL' flask toasts 'Reform Bill' (nickname).
Jug, (511), c.1832, Wales, Glamorgan Pottery, height: 15.3cm, (6in), printed earthenware. Portraits of Reform champions, entitled, 'THE ZEALOUS & SUCCESSFUL PROMOTERS OF REFORM'.[45] They had ensured that 'THE PURITY OF THE CONSTITUTION RESTORED' with majorities of 84 in the Lords and 116 in the Commons.
Mug, (512), c.1832, Staffordshire, height: 10.2cm, (4in), red-printed earthenware. Portraits of Reform champions, Earl Grey and Lord Brougham & Vaux and national floral emblems.

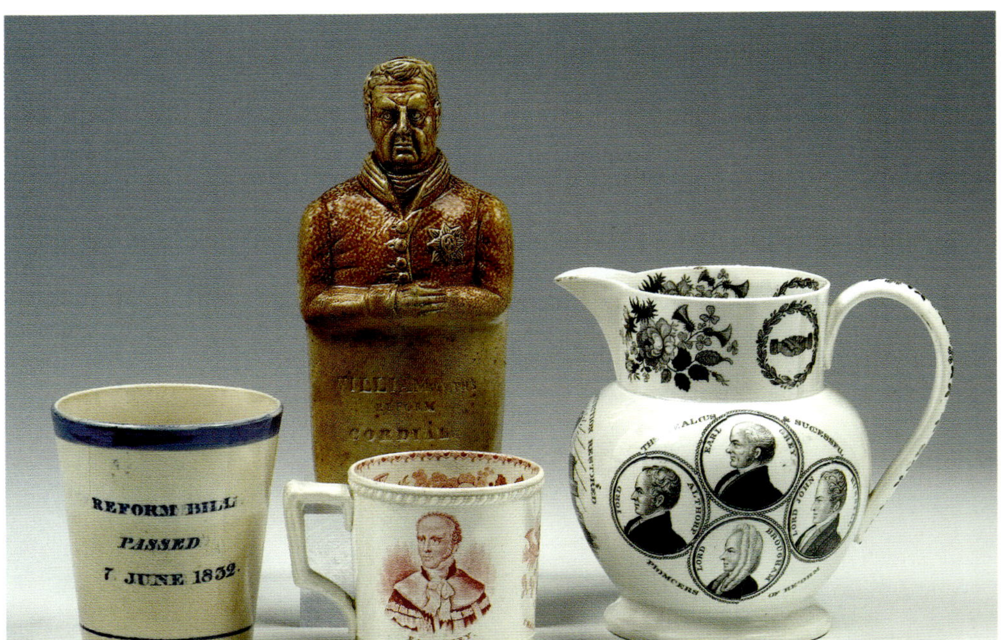

Lord John Russell (1792-1878)

Russell, third son of the sixth Duke of Bedford attended Westminster School and the University of Edinburgh, and entered Parliament in 1813. Sydney Smith said in the 1830s of the diminutive Russell (only 5' 4"), 'Before this Reform agitation commenced Lord John was over six feet high. But, engaged in looking after your interests ... he has been so constantly kept in hot water that he is boiled down to the proportions in which you now behold him.'

Henry Brougham, 1st Baron Brougham and Vaux (1778-1868)

Brougham studied natural science and mathematics at Edinburgh University, before qualifying as a lawyer. In 1802 he helped to found the *Edinburgh Review* before moving to London. Called to the English Bar in 1808, he became MP in 1810, devoted himself to libertarian causes and acted as the popular champion for Queen Caroline at her trial in 1820. As Lord Chancellor from 1830 to 1834, he assisted Earl Grey to draft the Reform Bill. Later he helped to establish the London Mechanics' Institute, the Society for the Diffusion of Useful Knowledge, and the non-denominational University College, London. He also gave his name to the one-horse enclosed carriage, which he designed in 1839.

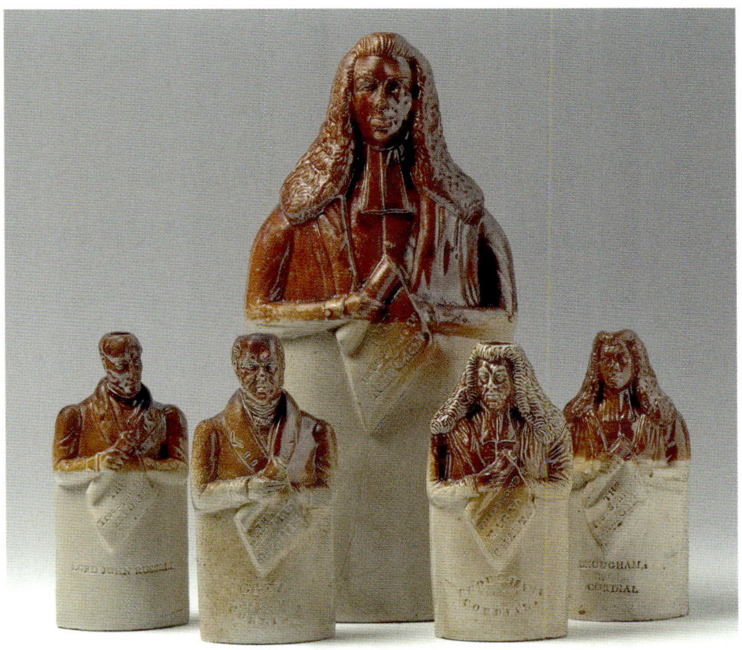

Ireland

Following the events of the French Revolution, Ireland was seen as a weak link in the chain of Britain's defences against a possible French invasion. After 1794 the Catholic 'Defenders' who were nationalist and 'Gaelic' merged with the secular, republican, United Irishmen.[46] The Westminster and Dublin Parliaments disagreed profoundly on policy and loose affiliations formed between Francophiles, excited by the Revolution, Catholics, eager for emancipation, Irish nationalists and Radical republican followers of Tom Paine, who was in the United States but was expected to return to Ireland. The Westminster government grew nervous and Pitt determined to suppress Radicalism at all costs. Volunteer regiments were drafted to strengthen Irish garrisons, dissident printers and journalists were arrested and imprisoned and networks of spies and informers were set up.

Matters came to a head in 1798 when United Irish revolutionaries openly rebelled and reactionary Protestants formed Orange Lodges (named after William of Orange), some siding with Westminster, others with Dublin Castle. British troops suppressed the uprisings with brutality, culminating in the deaths of over 30,000 Irishmen. After the decisive and bloody Battle of Vinegar Hill on 21 June, Lord Cornwallis, aged veteran of the American War of Independence and India campaigns, was appointed Viceroy. This was his last posting 'in a career devoted to cleaning up the messes of the British Empire'.[47]

In 1800 the Act of Union was passed, abolishing the Dublin Parliament since Irish members would now sit at Westminster. This was apparently achieved by bribing the Protestant Loyalists and giving unspoken hope of enfranchisement to Catholics.

Flask, (517), c.1832, London, Lambeth, height: 18.4cm, (7¼in), salt-glazed stoneware. Moulded as 'LORD JOHN RUSSELL', his scroll impressed, 'THE True Spirit of REFORM'.
Flask, (514), c.1832, Derbyshire, height: 18.4cm, (7¼in), salt-glazed stoneware. Impressed, 'GREY REFORM CORDIAL', his scroll impressed, 'THE PEOPLES RIGHTS'. Earl Grey served as Prime Minister from 1846 to 1852 and as Foreign Secretary from 1859 to 1865.
Flask, (513), c.1832, London, Lambeth, height: 36.8cm, (14½in), stoneware. Moulded as Lord Brougham and Vaux, his scroll impressed, 'THE TRUE SPIRIT OF REFORM'.
Flask, (516), c.1832, Derbyshire., height: 17.8cm, (7in), stoneware. Moulded as Lord Brougham and Vaux. Impressed, 'BROUGHAM'S REFORM CORDIAL', his scroll impressed, 'THE SECOND MAGNA CHARTER'.
Flask, (515), c.1832, London, Lambeth, height: 17.2cm, (6¾in), stoneware. Moulded as Lord Brougham and Vaux, impressed, 'BROUGHAM'S Reform CORDIAL', his scroll impressed, 'THE True Spirit of REFORM'.

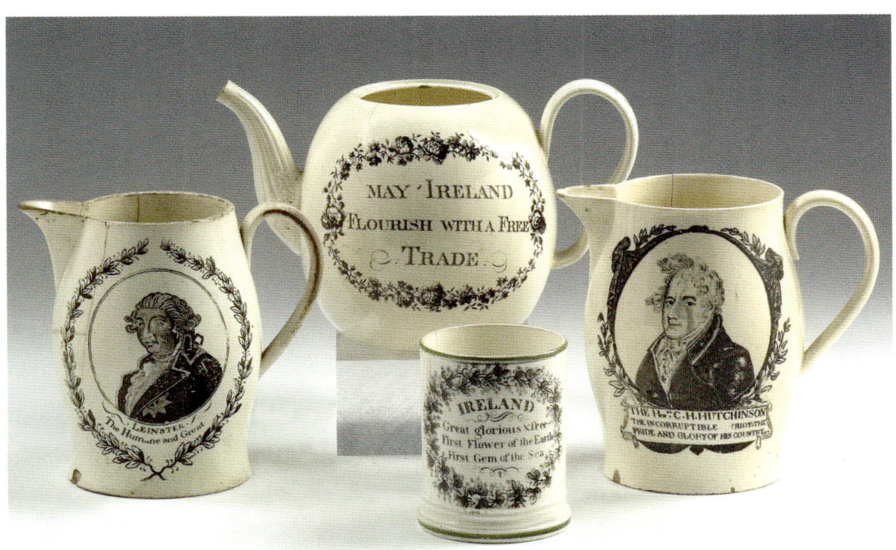

Clockwise: **Jug, (528)**, c.1810, Staffordshire, height: 14cm, (5½in), printed creamware. Portrait of the Duke of Leinster, the premier peer of Ireland, inscribed, 'The Humane and Great'. It is unclear whether this is the second Duke, who died in 1804, or his father the first Duke, a more influential figure.
Teapot, (535), c.1800, Staffordshire, probably Wedgwood, height: 12.7cm, (5in), printed creamware. Inscribed within a wreath, 'MAY IRELAND / FLOURISH WITH A FREE / TRADE'. (On the reverse, 'the lovers disturbed'.)
Jug, (529), c.1815, Staffordshire, height: 14.6cm, (5¾in), printed creamware. Portrait of Christopher Hely-Hutchinson (1767-1826), inscribed, 'THE INCORRUPTIBLE PATRIOT THE / PRIDE AND GLORY OF HIS COUNTRY'. He was MP for Taghmon, in County Wexford, and an Irish patriot. During the Irish Rebellion of 1798, he enlisted as a volunteer under his brother John.[48] At the Battle of Ballinamuck he helped capture the French generals Lafontaine and Sarrazin, and was commended for his bravery by Lord Cornwallis.
Mug, (536), c.1810, possibly Cumbria, Whitehaven Pottery, height: 9.6cm, (3¾in), printed creamware. Inscribed, within a wreath of shamrocks, 'IRELAND / Great glorious & free / First Flower of the Earth / First Gem of the Sea'.

Daniel O'Connell (1775-1847)

Six items in the Willett Collection celebrate Daniel O'Connell, regarded as the 'Liberator' of Catholic Ireland and perhaps the first person in Anglo-Irish history to use the political system, rather than violence, to achieve change.

O'Connell was the son of minor Catholic gentry in County Kerry, an area remote from English influence. A charismatic figure and a shrewd political player, he is saluted as 'the inventor of mass agitation' by reviving the old Catholic Association, and making it a popular movement for change.

George III had famously refused to compromise his coronation oath by 'putting Papists and Presbyterians in a state of equality with the Church of England'. This meant that members of the minority faiths were unable to vote or to stand for election to Parliament.

Despite the suppression of the Catholic Association, which was seen as a threat by Parliament, O'Connell himself was elected in 1829 for County Clare, with a large majority. Alarmed at the threat of public disorder, the hitherto anti-Catholic government of the Duke of Wellington and his Home Secretary, Sir Robert Peel, passed the Roman Catholic Relief Act, enabling O'Connell to take his seat. In becoming the first Irish Catholic to sit as an MP in Westminster and the champion of the rights of Catholics to vote, O'Connell proved himself a political leader of genius. Once in Parliament, he used his influence to lobby for similar emancipation for the Jews.

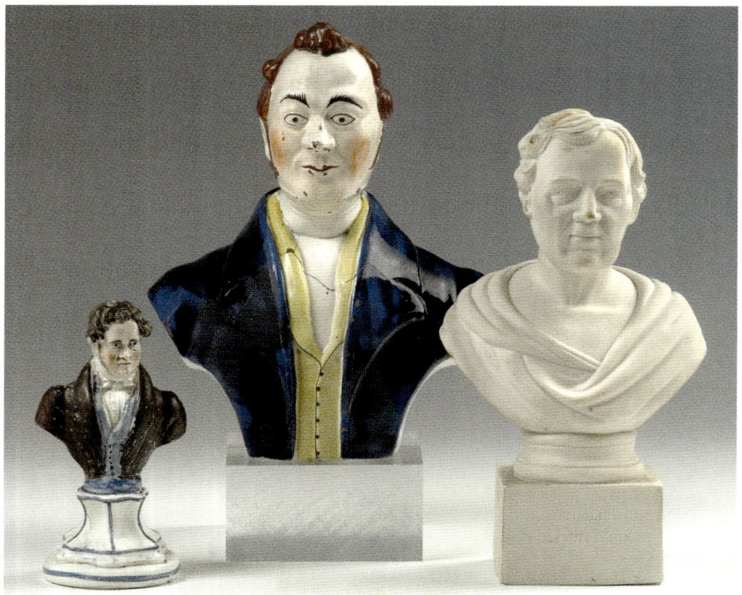

Bust, (533), c.1820, height: 14.6cm, (5¾in), pearlware, coloured under and overglaze. Portrait of Daniel O'Connell on waisted, faceted plinth
Bust, (534), c.1830, height: 22.3cm, (8¾in), enamelled earthenware. Lightly caricatured portrait of Daniel O'Connell.
Bust, (530), c.1830, height: 24.1cm, (9½in), biscuit porcelain. Inscribed, 'CATHOLIC EMANCIPATION', showing O'Connell robed as a Roman senator.

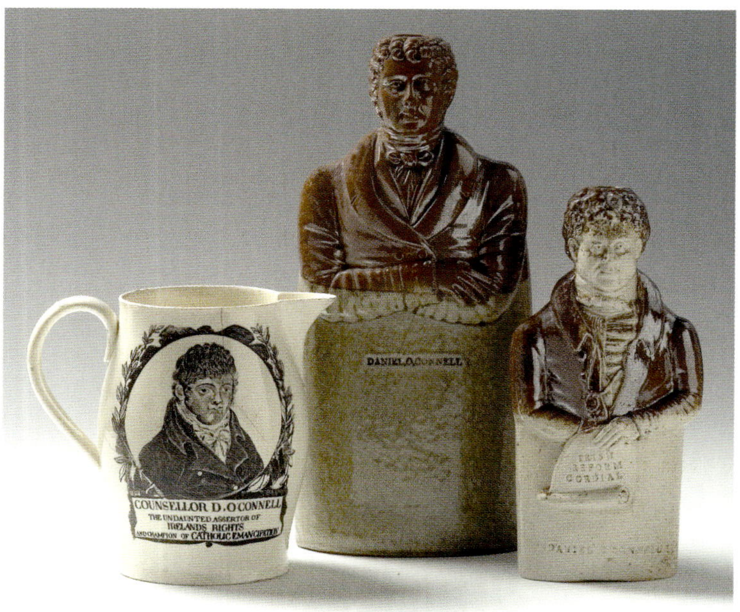

Jug, (529), c.1815, Staffordshire, height: 14.6cm, (5¾in), printed creamware. Portrait of Daniel O'Connell inscribed, 'COUNSELLOR D. O'CONNELL / THE UNDAUNTED ASSERTOR OF / IRELANDS RIGHTS...' It is probably based on one from the *Dublin Magazine* in 1813.
Flask, (531), c.1830, Derbyshire, Denby & Codnor Park, height: 27.9cm, (11in), stoneware. Moulded and impressed, 'DANIEL,O,CONNELL' [*sic*].
Flask, (532), c.1830, Derbyshire, Brampton, Oldfield & Co., height: 20.3cm, (8in), stoneware. Portrait of 'DANIEL O'CONNELL', with scroll impressed 'IRISH REFORM CORDIAL'.

Later Politicians

George Granville Leveson-Gower (1758-1833)

Willett considered a seated porcelain figure to be a likeness of Charles Lamb (1775-1834), the writer of such well-loved books as *Tales from Shakespeare* (1807), and the *Essays of Elia* (1823). The figure, with its distinctive aquiline nose, represents not Lamb but Leveson-Gower, first Duke of Sutherland, who was a millionaire landowner, politician and art patron.[49] He owned the Bridgewater Canal, constructed a vast network of roads and bridges and was infamous for clearing peasant farmers from the Scottish Highlands. He was also an early benefactor of the National Gallery and President of the British Institution.

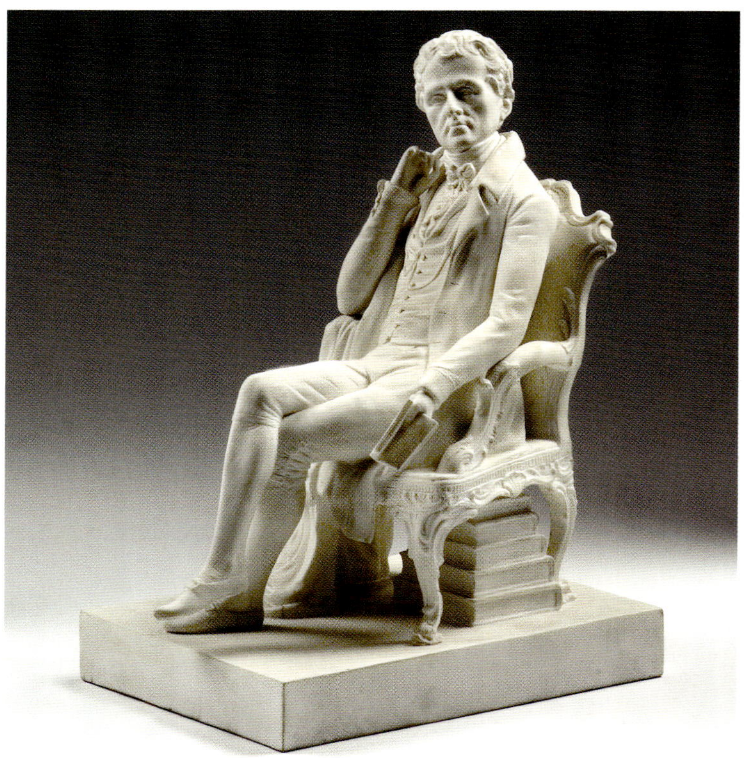

Figure, (978), c.1830, Derby, height: 25.4cm, (10in), biscuit porcelain. Portrait figure of Leveson-Gower, sitting reading, his chair supported by a pile of books.

Robert Peel (1788-1850)

As a reward for a double first (in Classics and Mathematics) at Oxford University, Peel's father, a wealthy cotton manufacturer bought the 21-year-old Peel the seat of Cashel in Tipperary in 1809. He later represented Tamworth, his father's old constituency. He made an immediate impact in the House of Commons; the Speaker described his maiden speech as the best since William Pitt's. In 1829, while serving as Tory Home Secretary under the Duke of Wellington he decided to reorganize law and order in London, setting up a new metropolitan police force, members of which became known as 'Bobbies' or 'Peelers'. Appointed Prime Minister in 1834 he was regularly outvoted and resigned in 1835. Having come to accept the policies of parliamentary reform and Catholic emancipation he marked the shift to a more enlightened Conservatism when he became Prime Minister again in 1841. When Ireland's population faced starvation in 1845, after the potato crop failed, he attempted to remedy the situation by removing the duty paid on cheap imported corn. The issue split the Conservative party and he resigned.

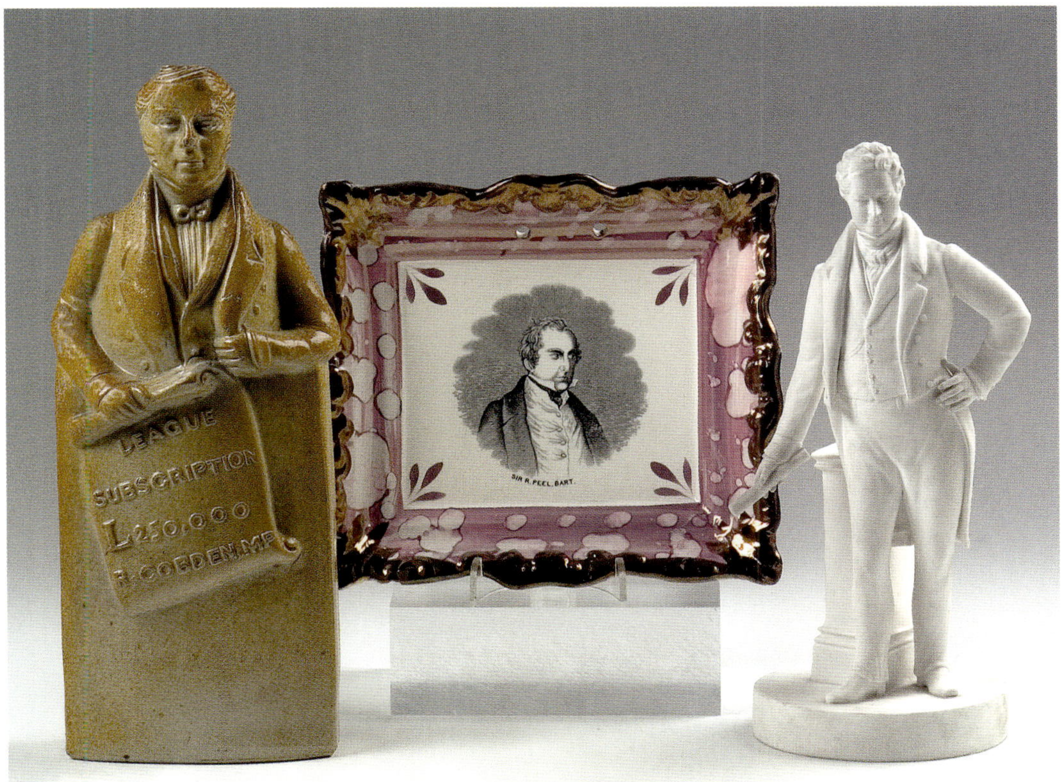

Flask, (537), c.1830, London, height: 30.5cm, (12in), salt-glazed stoneware. Portrait of Richard Cobden, his scroll moulded, 'LEAGUE SUBSCRIPTION £250,000 R.COBDEN MP'. Produced to promote the cause of the Anti-Corn Laws League. The Irish potato famine of 1845 allied him with Sir Robert Peel and led to the repeal of the Corn Laws.
Card Tray, (540), c.1830, Sunderland, height: 19.1cm, (7½in), earthenware, printed and lustred. Portrait of 'SIR R. PEEL BART.' printed on plaque or card tray, pierced for hanging.
Figure, (542), c.1835, Staffordshire, Stoke-on-Trent, Mintons, height: 27.9cm, (11in), biscuit porcelain. Portrait of Peel proffering a rolled scroll, (No. 77 in the Minton pattern book).

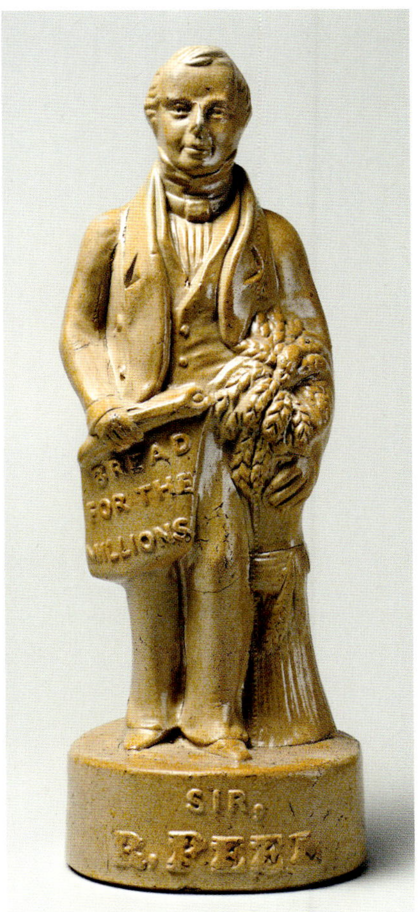

Flask, (R2878.41), c.1845 Staffordshire, height: 30.5cm, (12in), salt-glazed stoneware. Modelled as Peel clutching a large sheaf of corn and a scroll, moulded, 'BREAD FOR THE MILLIONS', in reference to the Corn Laws.

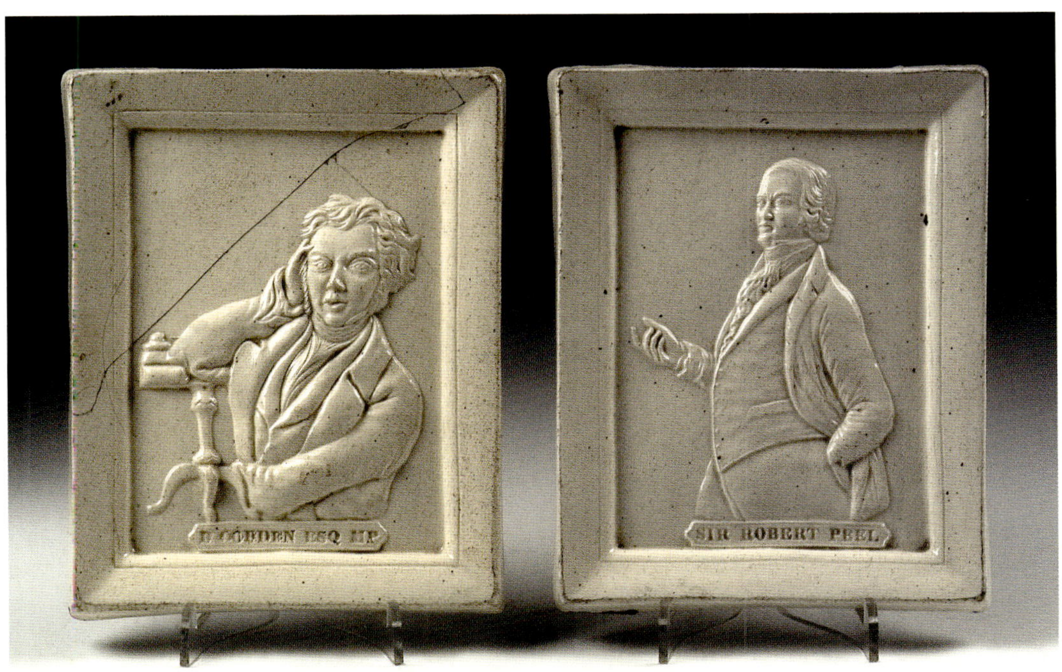

Pair of Plaques, (541 & A), c.1845 Staffordshire, each height: 17.1cm, (6¾in), earthenware. Relief-moulded portraits of Liberal Richard 'R.COBDEN ESQ.' and 'SIR ROBERT PEEL'. For a while Peel and Cobden formed an unlikely alliance to combat the Corn Laws.

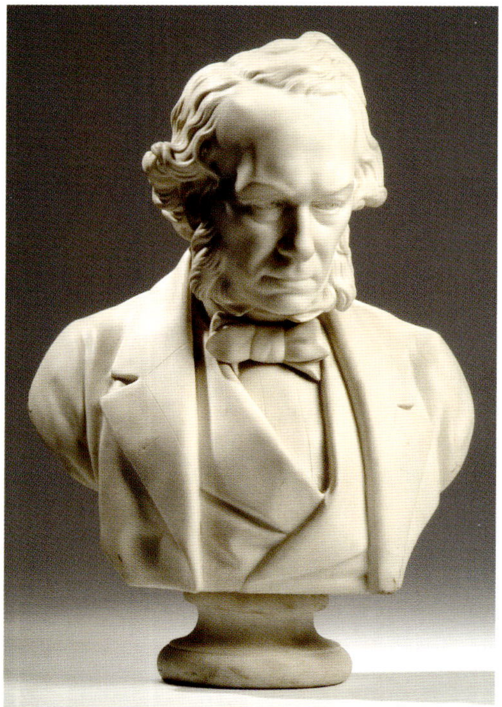

Bust, (**539**), 1865, Staffordshire, Hanley, Adams & Co. height: 35.5cm, (14in), Parian ware. Portrait of Richard Cobden, sculpted by E. Wyon. The crystalline Parian ware body used for these busts was an inexpensive substitute for marble of which the egalitarian Cobden would have approved.

Richard Cobden (1804-1865)

Cobden was born into extreme poverty and at fourteen was apprenticed as a clerk in the Yorkshire textile industry. In 1828, with his knowledge of the cotton trade, he set up a highly successful business selling calico prints in London. The profits enabled him to travel, between 1833 and 1837, throughout Europe and to America and Russia.

In 1835 he published *England, Ireland and America*, warning that Britain would struggle to compete with the emerging economic power of the United States. He also advocated free trade, low taxation and major reforms to the education system.[50] He became involved in Manchester politics and was elected MP for Stockport in 1841. In 1839 he set up the centralized Anti-Corn Law League and campaigned up and down the country against restrictive tariffs, together with the brilliant orator, John Bright.

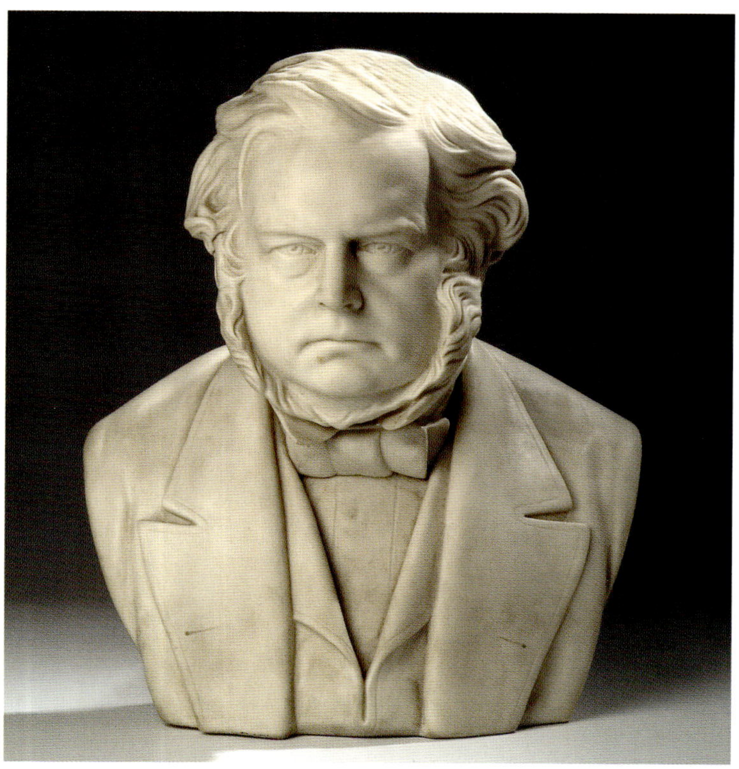

Henry John Temple, 3rd Viscount Palmerston (1794-1865)

Palmerston first entered Parliament as MP for the 'pocket' borough of Newtown on the Isle of Wight[51] and served as Secretary of State for War under five prime ministers. In 1830 he joined Earl Grey's Whig administration, served as Foreign Secretary until 1850 and was finally appointed Prime Minister in 1855 at the age of 70. He was 81 by the end of his second term of office, which lasted from 1859 to 1865. He refused to retire but died later that year. Queen Victoria recorded her difficulties with him in her journal,

'We had, God knows! terrible trouble with him about Foreign Affairs. Still as Prime Minister he managed affairs at home well and behaved to me well. But I never liked him.'

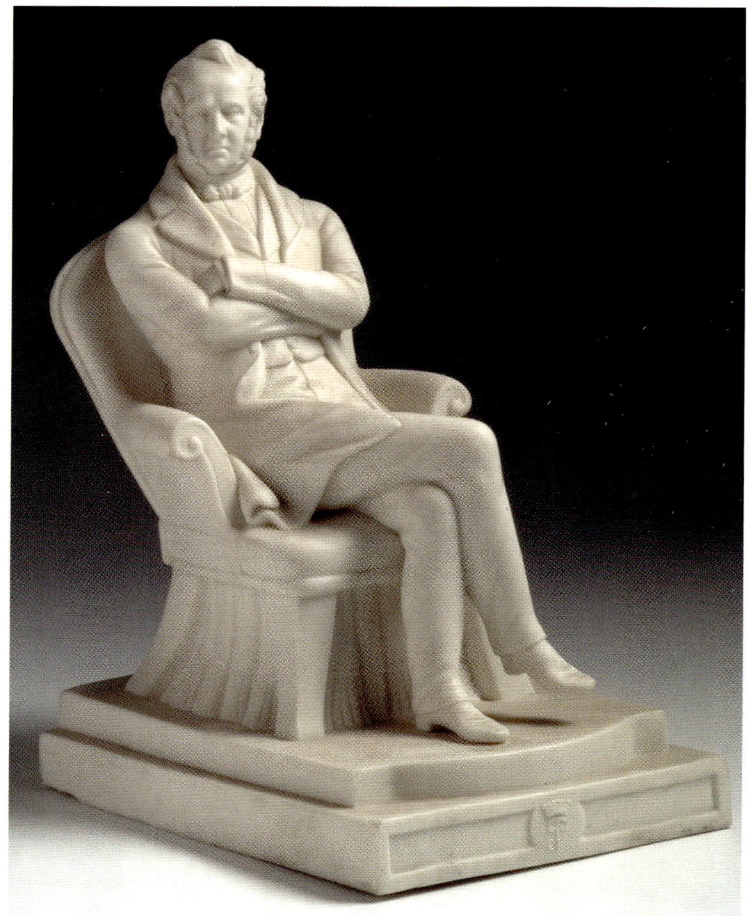

Figure, (**543**), c.1862, Staffordshire, Stoke-on-Trent, Mintons, height: 25.4cm, (10in), Parian ware. Portrait of Lord Palmerston, modelled by George Abbott. The source image is unknown but Palmerston's appearance, with his abundant hair and side whiskers would have been well known from early photographs and engravings after portraits such as that of 1855 to 1859 by Francis Cruikshank.[52]

John Bright (1811-1889)

Bright was the son of a prosperous cotton manufacturer in Rochdale. As a Quaker he was passionately committed to political and religious equality. As MP for Durham from 1843 he campaigned for universal suffrage and the secret ballot. In 1880, late in his career, he became Chancellor of the Duchy of Lancaster under Gladstone.

Bust, (**538**), 1867, Staffordshire, Hanley, Adams & Co. height: 39.3cm, (15½in), Parian ware. Portrait bust of John Bright sculpted by E. Wyon. There is an early photographic portrait taken by Maujean of Cobden and Bright (c.1860) in the collection of the National Portrait Gallery.[53]

Benjamin Disraeli (1804-1881)

One of the most charismatic and mercurial of Victorian politicians, Disraeli was, like his father Isaac, a prolific novelist. Despite remaining proud of his Jewish ancestry throughout his life, he was baptised into the Christian faith and was eventually elected Whig MP for Maidstone in 1837. He had little political success until, as a Tory, he was made Chancellor of the Exchequer under Lord Derby in 1852. Meanwhile he founded the Young England group to develop his ideas on social reform. In 1867, supported by Gladstone, he pioneered the new Reform Act, which gave the vote to every adult male in a borough constituency, extending the franchise by 1,500,000. He led the Tory party to a clear victory in 1874 and remained Prime Minister until 1880. His reformist legislation included the 1874 Factory Act, The Public Health Act (1875), the Climbing Boys Act (1875) and the Education Act (1876). As Lord Beaconsfield, Disraeli won great acclaim at the Congress of Vienna in 1878, for limiting Russian power in the Balkans.

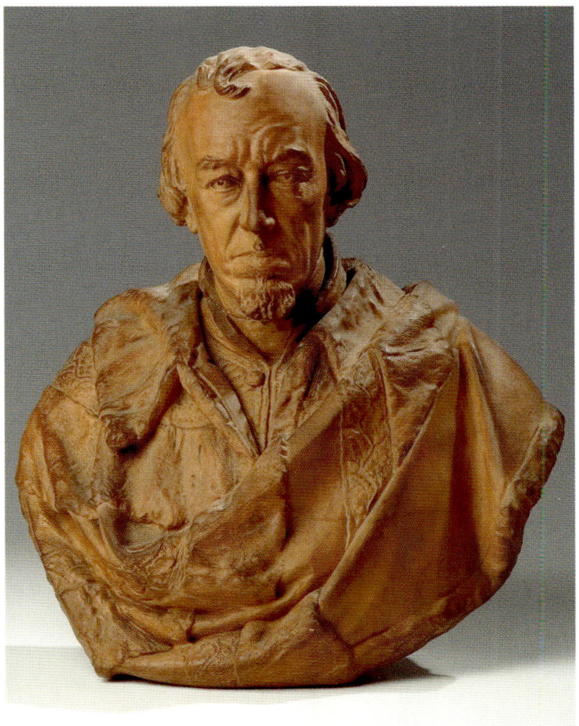

Bust, (R2454.33), 1883, Devon, Watcombe Pottery, height: 28cm, (11in), terracotta. Portrait bust of Disraeli modelled by the Italian sculptor Mario Raggi (1821-1907) who settled in England in 1880. Raggi's major commissions included a memorial for Disraeli in Parliament Square and another for Gladstone in Albert Square, Manchester.

Figure, (R2454.35), c.1885, Staffordshire, height: 34.2cm, (13½in), earthenware. Portrait of Gladstone wearing a waistcoat decorated with shamrocks, (demonstrating support for Irish Home Rule), shown with an axe since he liked to chop wood for relaxation.
Figure, (R2454.34), c.1885, Staffordshire, height: 35cm, (13¾in), earthenware. Portrait of Irish Nationalist, Charles Stuart Parnell (1846-1891), represented as a Celtic chieftain in tunic and cloak, brandishing a green flag defaced with an Irish harp and holding a stout shillelagh or cudgel.

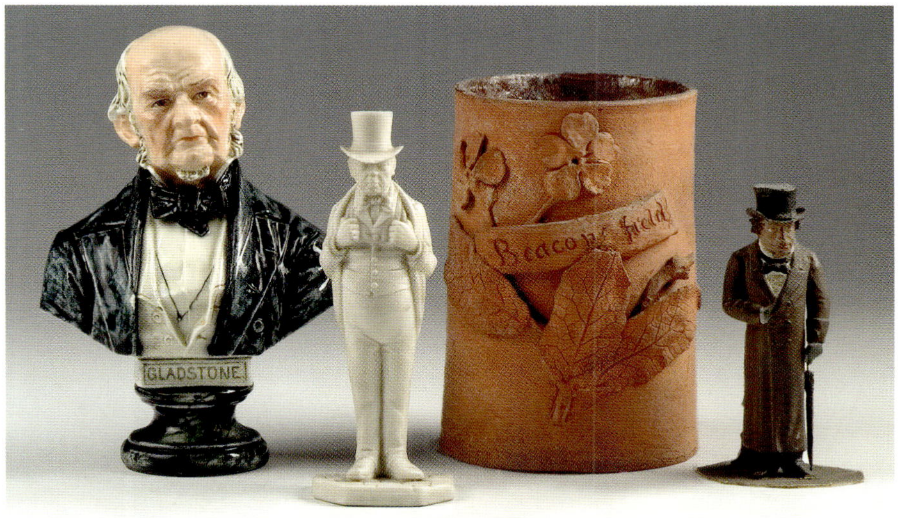

Bust, (545), c.1880, Austria, height: 17.8cm, (7in), enamelled earthenware. Portrait bust of Gladstone.
Figure, (544), c.1875, Worcester, height: 15.6cm, (6⅛in), biscuit porcelain. Portrait figure of Gladstone modelled by James Hadley, as a menu holder.
Beaker, (R603.12), c.1885, Sussex, Chailey, height: 15.2cm, (6in), terracotta. Incised 'Beaconsfield', and applied with moulded primrose sprig. After his death, in 1883, his Conservative followers founded the Primrose League (Disraeli's favourite flower) to develop Conservative thinking.[55]
Figure, (546), c.1880, height: 12.1cm, (4¾in), plaster. A tiny, cheap plaster figure was the only item related to Disraeli in Willett's early collection.

William Ewart Gladstone (1809-1898)

Gladstone, who attended Eton and Oxford University, was the son of a successful Glaswegian businessman.[54] He entered Parliament as a Tory but gradually aligned himself with the Liberals. He served as Chancellor of the Exchequer in the1850s and 1860s under three Whig prime ministers, including Lord John Russell, whom he succeeded as leader of the Liberal Party. He was four times prime minister (1868-74, 1880-85, 1886 and 1892-94, by then in his eighties and known as the 'Grand Old Man').

Gladstone was a renowned orator and campaigner for agricultural and land reform and most famously, for Irish Home Rule, an issue which split the Liberal Party. Intriguingly Gladstone was himself a passionate collector of china and was heartbroken when, in 1875, while short of funds, he had to sell his house at 11, Carlton House Terrace, together with his collections.

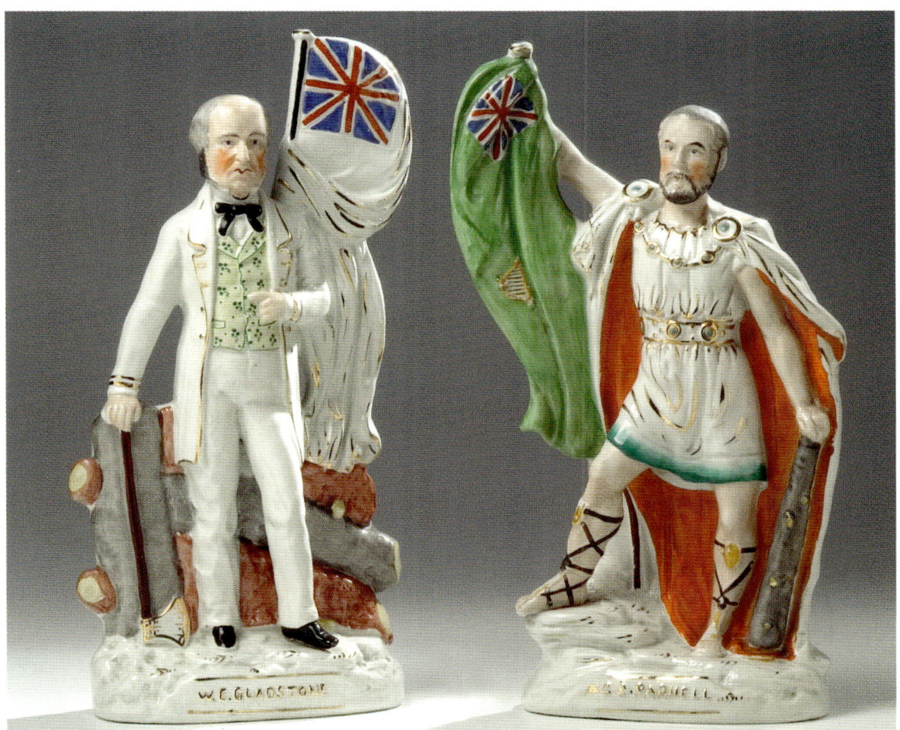

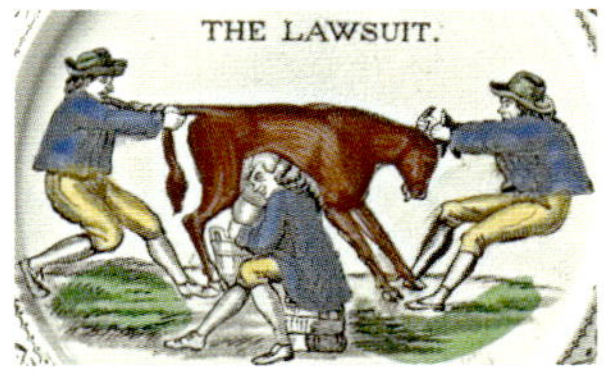

Chapter 8

PROFESSIONS & TRADES, CLUBS & SOCIETIES

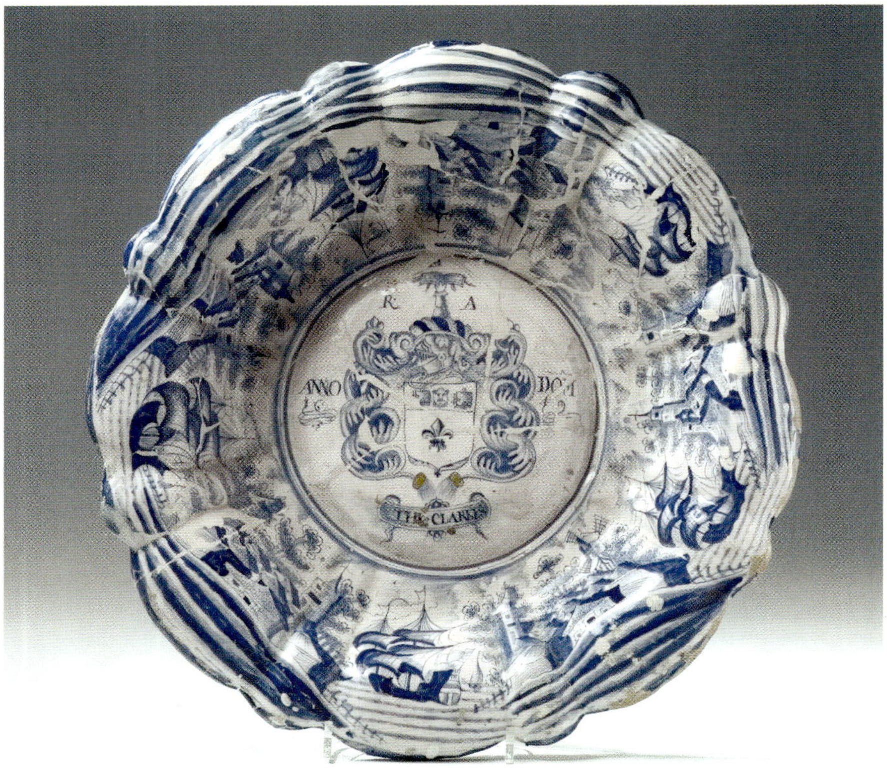

Dish, (**557**), 1649, London, Pickleherring factory, diameter: 38.7cm, (15¼in), tin-glazed earthenware.
Large dish, dated 1649, inscribed 'The Clarks' with initials, 'RMA' and the Arms of the Worshipful Company of Parish Clerks (a leopard's face between two songbooks over a single fleur-de-lys). Deep lobed rim decorated with buildings bordered by ploughed fields, alternating with Dutch 'Fluits' (long-distance cargo ships) at sea. Such vessels were often used as symbols of commercial success and affluence.[4] Although the form and decorative style of the dish owe much to Holland, this example was made in London.

Craft Associations

The medieval guilds were formed to maintain standards of conduct and quality control in skilled crafts and trades and to provide financial and social support for individual members. A charter document c.1200 states that, 'To become a gildsman … it was necessary to pay certain initiation fees … [and to take] an oath of fealty to the fraternity, swearing to observe its laws, to uphold its privileges, not to divulge its counsels, to obey its officers and not to aid any non-gildsman'.[1]

Over the centuries some of the wealthiest craft guilds in the City of London became established as City Livery Companies. Others evolved into more modest but practical 'benefit societies', formed for the mutual aid and insurance of their members. These voluntary associations included Friendly Societies, fraternal organisations such as the Freemasons and Oddfellows, and were the origins of the trade unions. The formation of such groups gained momentum during the onset of the Industrial Revolution. At this time a large proportion of the working population moved from the fields into factories in the fast-growing cities, where working conditions could be appalling, wages low and labourers were at the mercy of unscrupulous employers. Organisations strong enough to campaign for improved working conditions, that could provide a support network for their members, became essential.

British Trade

Holland had dominated northern European trade in the seventeenth century but the accession of a Dutch king of Britain in 1688 created the concept of 'the Maritime Powers', a natural alliance to defend Protestantism and commerce against the Catholic absolutism of Louis XIV in France. Gradually Britain overtook Holland in importance so that Daniel Defoe could proclaim in *The Complete English Tradesman*, that, 'We are not only a trading country, but the greatest trading country in the world'.

If that statement were not strictly true in 1726 it certainly was by 1800.[2] Over the century exports had grown steadily at 1.5 per cent per annum then rapidly accelerated to 5 per cent per annum from 1780. By 1818, when London boasted four miles of dockyards and thousands of ships, barges, dockers and navigators, England was not only the workshop but 'unquestionably the warehouse of the world'.[3]

Dish, (**555**), 1663, London, diameter: 40.6cm, (16in), tin-glazed earthenware. Large dish or blue-dash charger (for the striped decoration around the rim), initialled 'ICM' and dated 1663. It has a broad border of oranges and florid foliage in Italianate style surrounding the Blacksmiths' Arms (a chevron separating three hammers with ducal crowns).

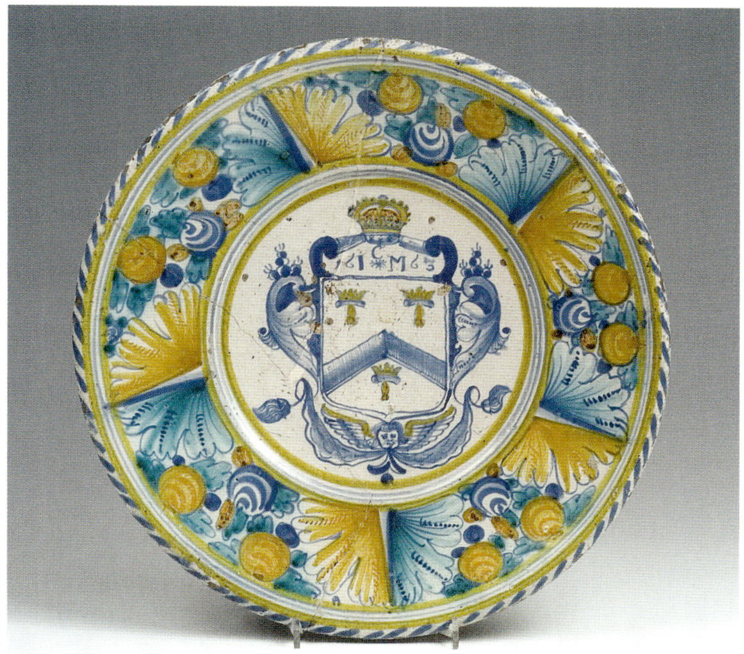

Mug, (**553**), 1682, London, height: 12.1cm, (4¾in), tin-glazed earthenware. Painted with the richly mantled coat of arms of the London Watermen's Company.[5] Ribbons inscribed 'IWS' and the date 1682. The shield, supported by dolphins, illustrates two cushions (for the comfort of passengers!) either side of crossed oars over a manned rowing boat.
Plate, (**554**), 1700, London, diameter: 21.6cm, (8½in), tin-glazed earthenware. Decorated with London Watermen's Company, initials, 'EBS' and dated 1700. The Company of Watermen was formed in 1566 to put an end to 'divers and many misfortunes and mischances [caused by] evil and ignorant persons who robbed and spoiled of their [passengers'] goods ... and also drowned them'.
Mug, (**571**), c.1790, North-east, height: 12.1cm, (4¾in), creamware, printed and enamelled. Printed with the Shipwrights' Arms.[6] Their shield, supported by a sailor and a ship-builder with measuring tools, shows a man-of-war, lacking masts, balanced on logs, beneath the cross of St George. The crest is Noah's Ark and the motto, 'WITHIN THE ARK SAFE FOR EVER'.
Jug, (**567**), c.1830, North-east, height: 12.1cm, (4¾in), earthenware, printed and lustred. Printed with the Mariners' Arms whose shield, flanked by sailors carrying red ensigns, shows an anchor and their crest is a frigate.

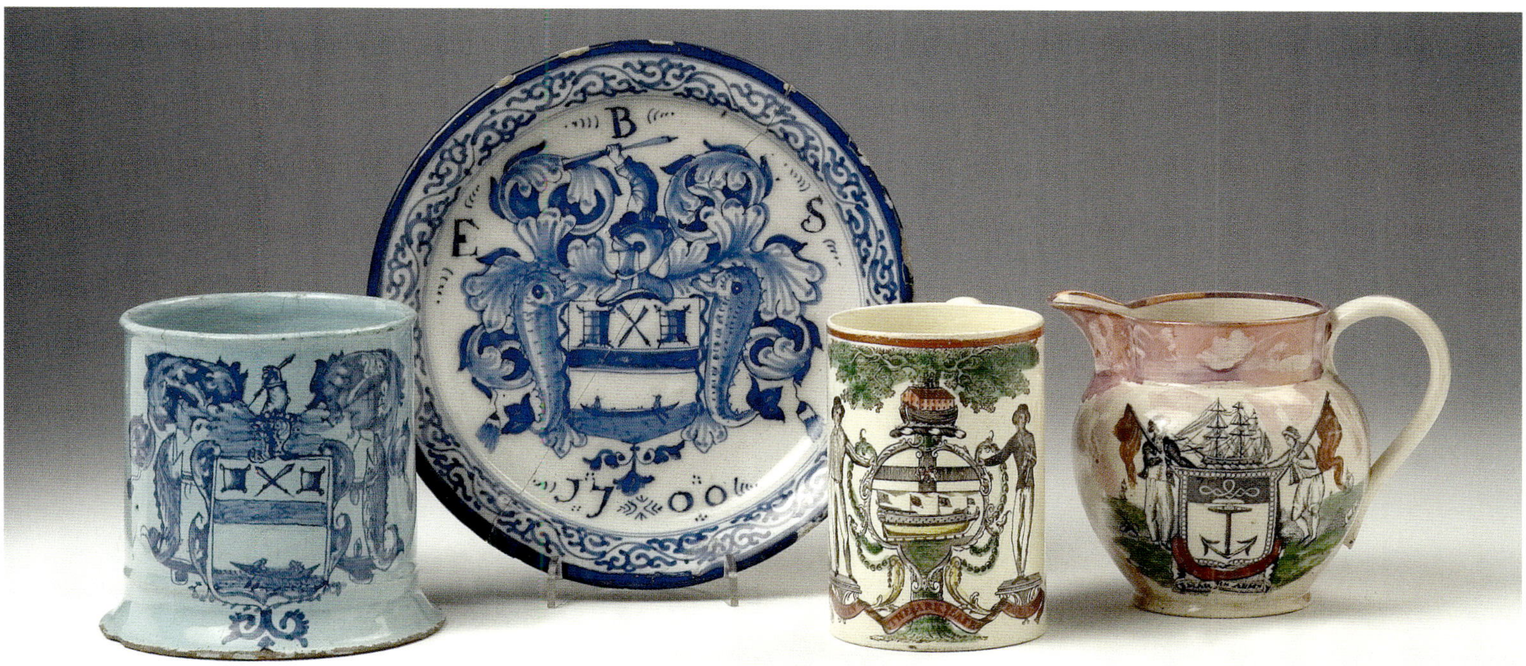

Plate, (**566**), c.1800, Swansea, Cambrian Pottery, diameter: 16.5cm, (6½in), blue-printed pearlware. Printed with St Michael's Mount in Cornwall, one of the county's best-known landmarks, together with a shield and mottoes.
Jug, (**565**), c.1815, Swansea, probably Dillwyn & Co.,[7] height: 16.5cm, (6½in), printed drab earthenware. Printed with the fifteen bezants (gold coins) from the Cornish Arms, a banner proclaiming 'ONE & ALL' and a shield inscribed 'FISH TIN & COPPER', together with mining structures and the famous Newquay pilchard.
Frog Mug, (**548**), c.1800, Sunderland, Low Ford, Dawson & Co., height: 12.7cm, (5in), creamware, printed and enamelled. Printed with an armorial shield supported by the naked figures of Adam and Eve, the first gardeners; beneath them the motto; 'From the Sweat of thy Face Shalt thou eat Bread'. The shield illustrates agricultural and garden tools and the figures stand in a landscape surrounded by animals and fruit.

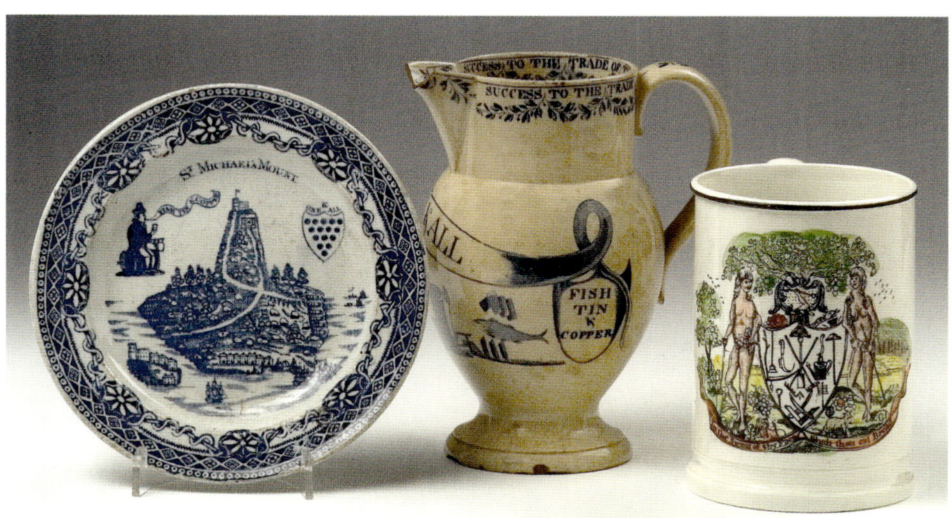

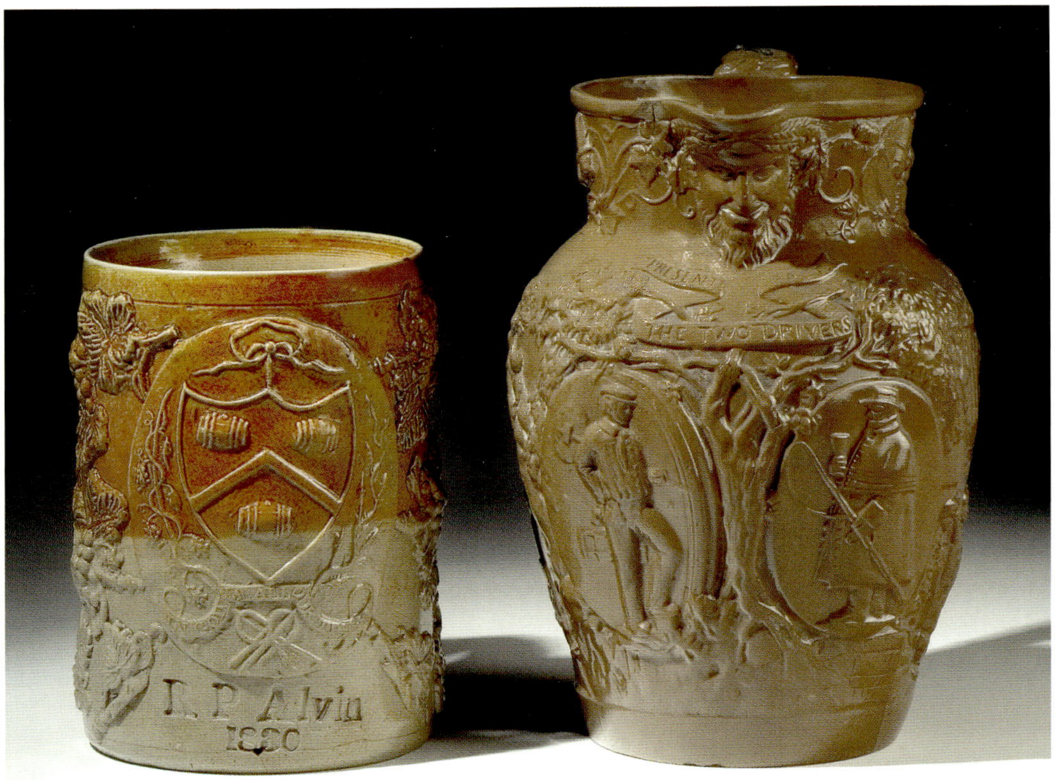

Mug, (**547**), c.1830, London, Mortlake, Kishere Pottery, height: 15.8cm, (6¼in), stoneware. Moulded in deep relief with heraldic shield, showing three wine casks or tuns and a chevron, adapted from the arms of the Vintners' Company, surrounded by hop flowers and foliage. The shield probably represents the Country Brewers Association, rather than the Worshipful Company of Brewers, whose motto appears below, 'In god is all our Trust'.[8] The mug is impressed for R.P. Alvin, 1830, a resident of Mortlake (who died in 1832) and: 'Kishere, Moatlake [*sic*]', for Joseph Kishere (1768-1834), founder of the Mortlake.
Jug, (**646**), c.1848, Staffordshire, Stoke-on-Trent, Mintons, height: 21.7cm, (8½in), stoneware. Jug relief-moulded with an engine-driver and coachman, inscribed 'THE TWO DRIVERS'. Designed by Henry James Townsend for Summerley's Art Manufactures to contrast modes of transport past and present. To one side a group of people cower on a bank as a train thunders out of a tunnel.

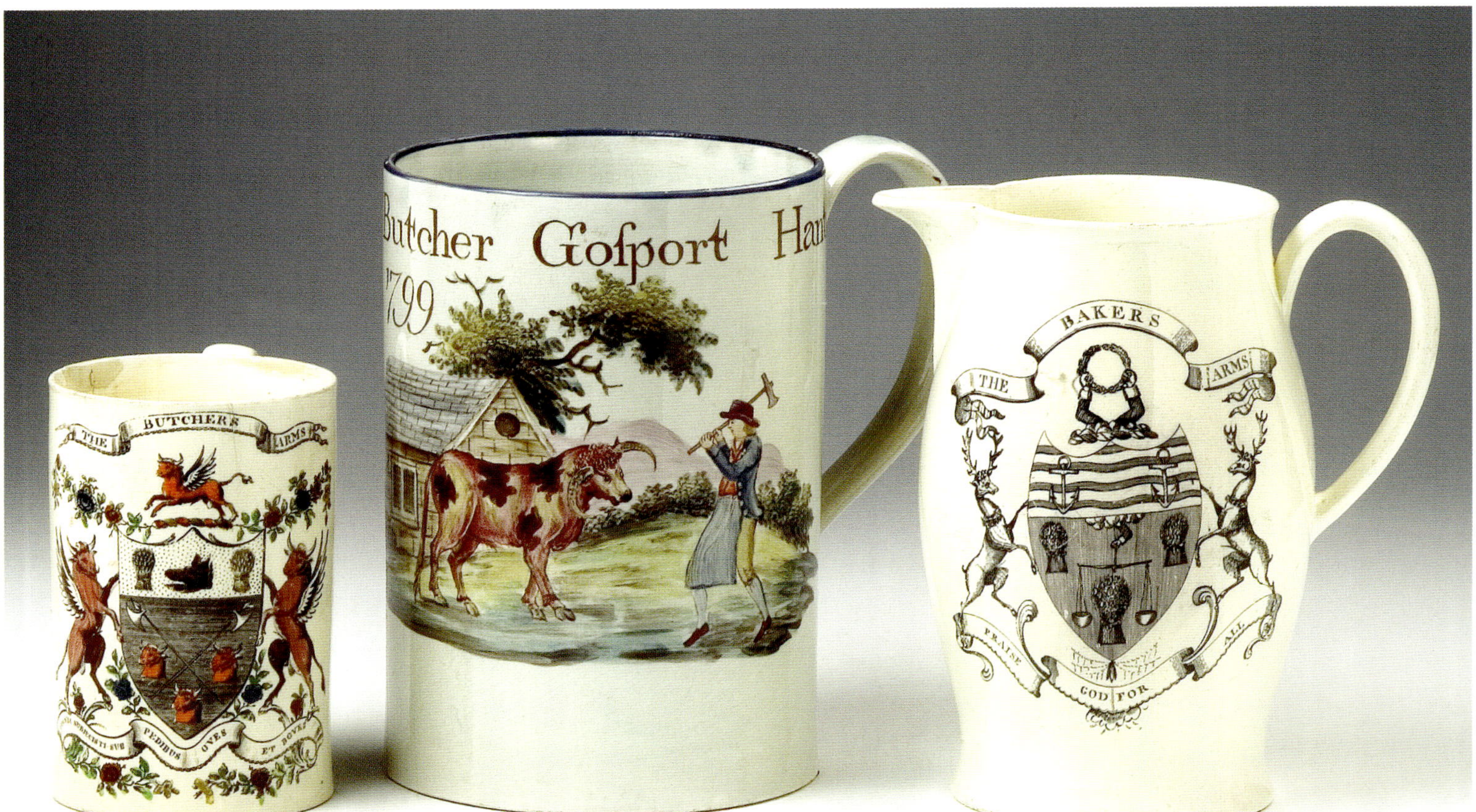

Mug, (**549**), c.1790, Staffordshire, height: 12.7cm, (5in), creamware, printed and enamelled. Printed with the Butchers' Arms supported by winged oxen. The shield has a boar's head between wheat sheaves over three ox heads, separated by crossed axes. Beneath is the Latin tag, '*Omnia Subjectisti sub Pedibus oves et boves*'. (You have put all things beneath the feet of sheep and oxen).[9]
Mug, (**673**), 1799, Staffordshire, height: 19.1cm, (7½in), enamelled pearlware. Inscribed, 'William Wavell Butcher Gosport Hants' and dated 1799, enamelled with a dramatic scene showing Mr Wavell about to slaughter an ox.
Jug, (**561**), c.1790, Staffordshire, height: 17.7cm, (7in), printed creamware. Jug printed with the arms of the Bakers' Company. Shield, supported by stags, has two anchors over sheaves of wheat and a pair of weighing scales. The motto is, 'PRAISE GOD FOR ALL', a popular form of grace before 'breaking bread'. The Bakers' Guild, one of the earliest, is first mentioned in the great 'Pipe Rolls' of Henry II.

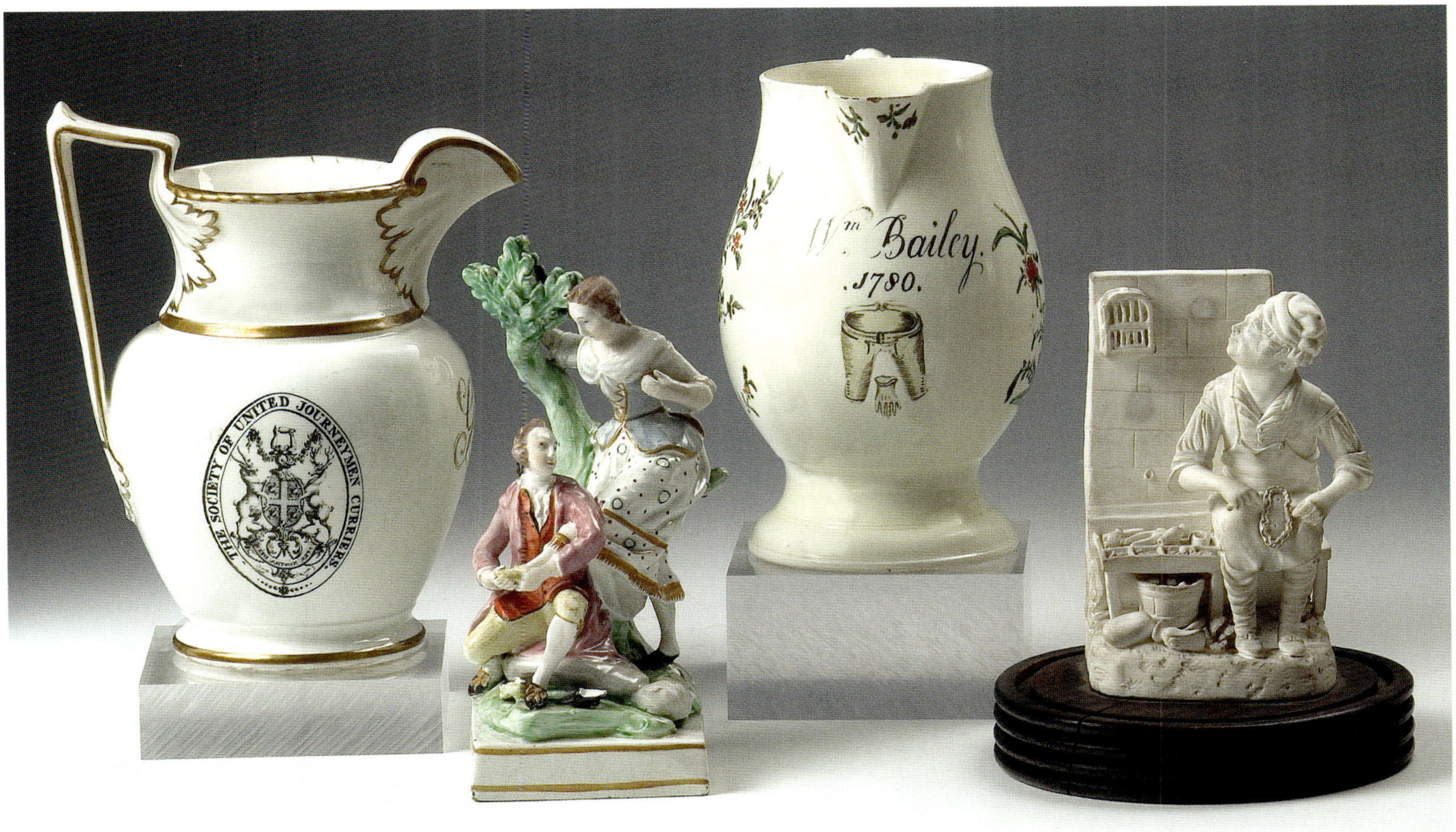

Jug, (**568**), 1831, Staffordshire, perhaps Daniel, height: 19.1cm, (7½in), soft-paste porcelain, printed and gilt. Gilt monogram 'GR' and printed with arms whose frame is inscribed, 'THE SOCIETY OF THE UNITED JOURNEYMEN CURRIERS' supported by a goat and a stag. The arms (signed by I. Howes of Birmingham) printed in reverse, including the motto, *'Spes Nostra Deus'* (God is our hope). Curriers were concerned with the curing of leather. They now share a London Livery Hall with the Cordwainers, representing cobblers and shoemakers.
Figure Group, (**665**), c.1800, Staffordshire, height: 17.1cm, (6¾in), enamelled pearlware. The group of a shoemaker fitting his client is based on Derby porcelain prototypes of the 1770s.
Jug, (**669**), 1780, Staffordshire, height: 16.5cm, (6½in), enamelled creamware. Sides painted with an elegant oriental-style woman in a garden, inscribed beneath the spout, 'Wm. Bailey, 1780' with vignettes of a pair of breeches and a glove. Mr Bailey was probably a leather worker.
Figure Group, (**663**), c.1830, Derby, height: 13.3cm, (5¼in), biscuit porcelain. A cobbler, distracted from his work by a bird in a cage, probably modelled by George Cocker. Closely based on an eighteenth-century faience group by Paul Louis Cyfflé of Lunéville for the Niderviller factory in Eastern France.

Jug, (**550**), 1780, Staffordshire, height: 15.3cm, (6in), printed creamware. Printed shield (containing three goat heads) entitled, 'THE CORDWAINERS ARMS' and motto, 'NULLA INVERTITUR ORDO' (nothing will topple our order). The supporters hold a riding boot and a lady's shoe.
Mug, (**551**), 1780, Worcester, height: 7.6cm, (3in), puce-printed porcelain. Similar composition (to 550) appears in reverse on a mug, substituting the arms of the City of Worcester for those of the Cordwainers. Further inscriptions include, 'We unite to maintain our Rights Inviolate / Prosperity attend ye Justness of our Cause', 'King and Constitution' and 'The Friendly Society of Cordwainers of England … Instituted the 22nd of June 1807'.
Mug, (**552**), 1780, Staffordshire, height: 15.2cm, (6in), printed creamware. Very similar shield and inscriptions (to 551) although here a lady holds a shoe. The Cordwainer derives from the Spanish leather-producing centre of Cordoba in Andalucia, where an alum dressing process was applied to goatskin to produce a fine white leather. The care and repair of footwear is a subject for several figure pieces.

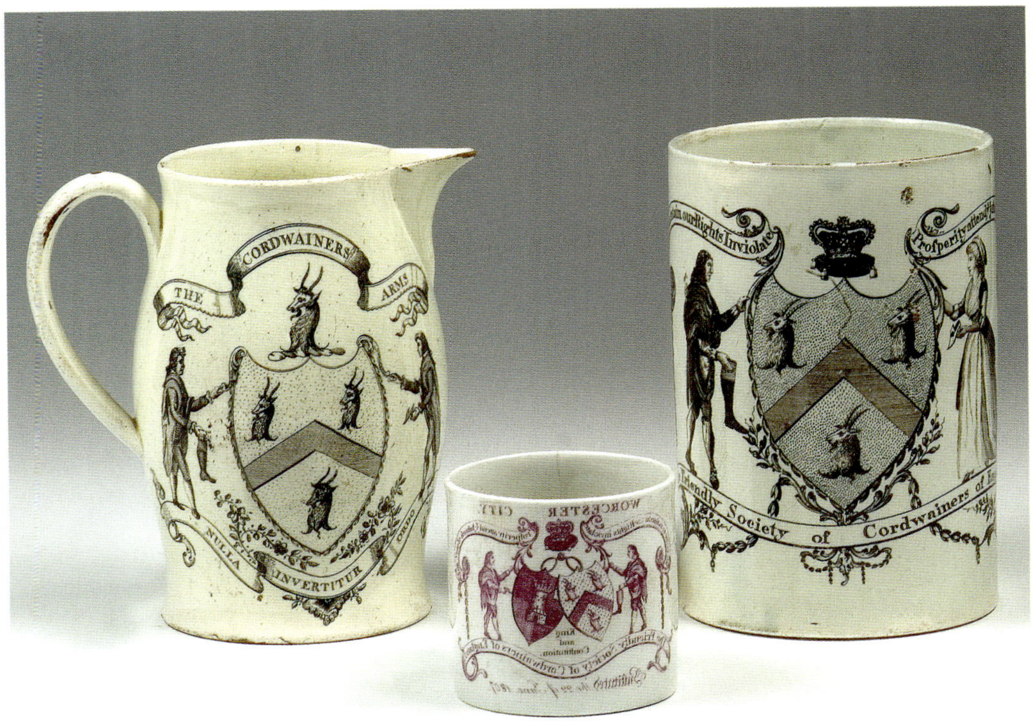

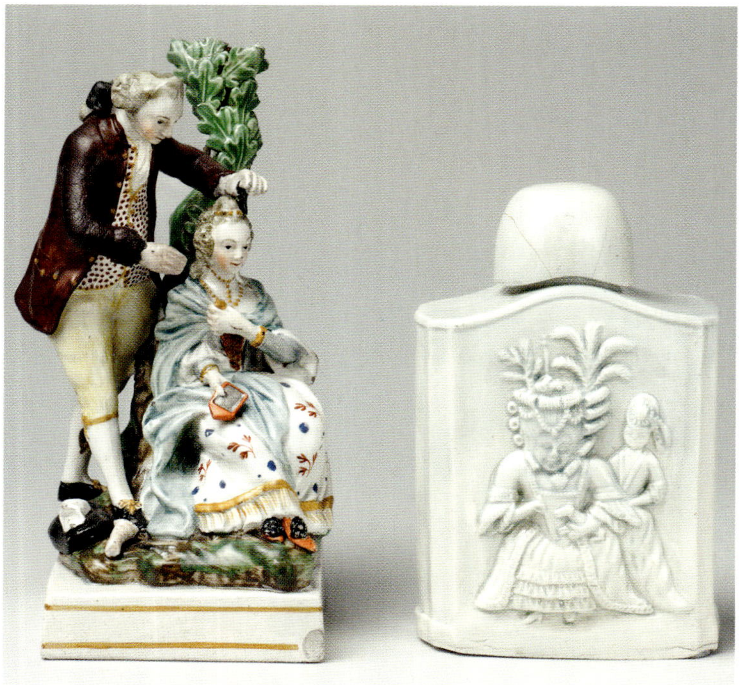

Figure Group, (**661**), 1780, Staffordshire, height: 17.1cm, (6¾in), printed creamware. A hairdresser and his client (pair to the shoemaker and his customer (665). They are based on Derby porcelain prototypes of the 1770s.
Tea Canister, (**633**), 1775, Staffordshire, height: 14cm, (5½in), pearlware. Relief-moulded canister shows a fashionable woman on one side, on the other a 'macaroni' dandy, both staggering under ludicrously large wigs, satirised by contemporary caricatures.[10]

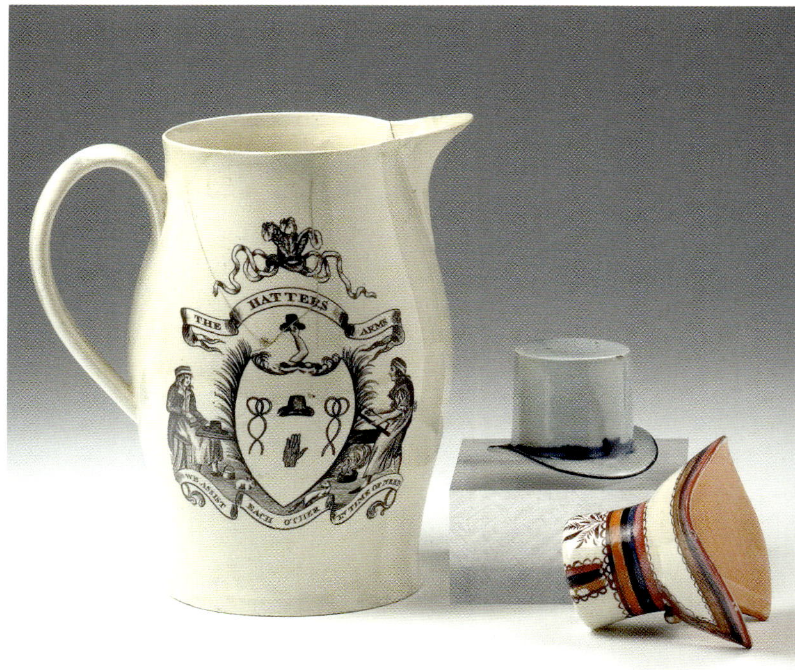

Jug, (**559**), 1810, Staffordshire, height: 21.6cm, (8½in), printed creamware. A rare print of the Hatters' Arms; the Prince of Wales's feathers float above the shield, decorated with ribbons, a glove and a hat. Figures at each side make millinery and motto below reads, 'WE ASSIST EACH OTHER IN TIMES OF NEED'.
Model, (**629**) c.1815, Staffordshire, height: 7.6cm, (3in), enamelled pearlware.
Model, (**630**) c.1815, Staffordshire, height: 5.1cm, (2in), enamelled pearlware. Miniatures of a large lady's straw bonnet and a little top hat, modelled in styles fashionable around 1810 to 1820. Perhaps samples or marketing accessories.

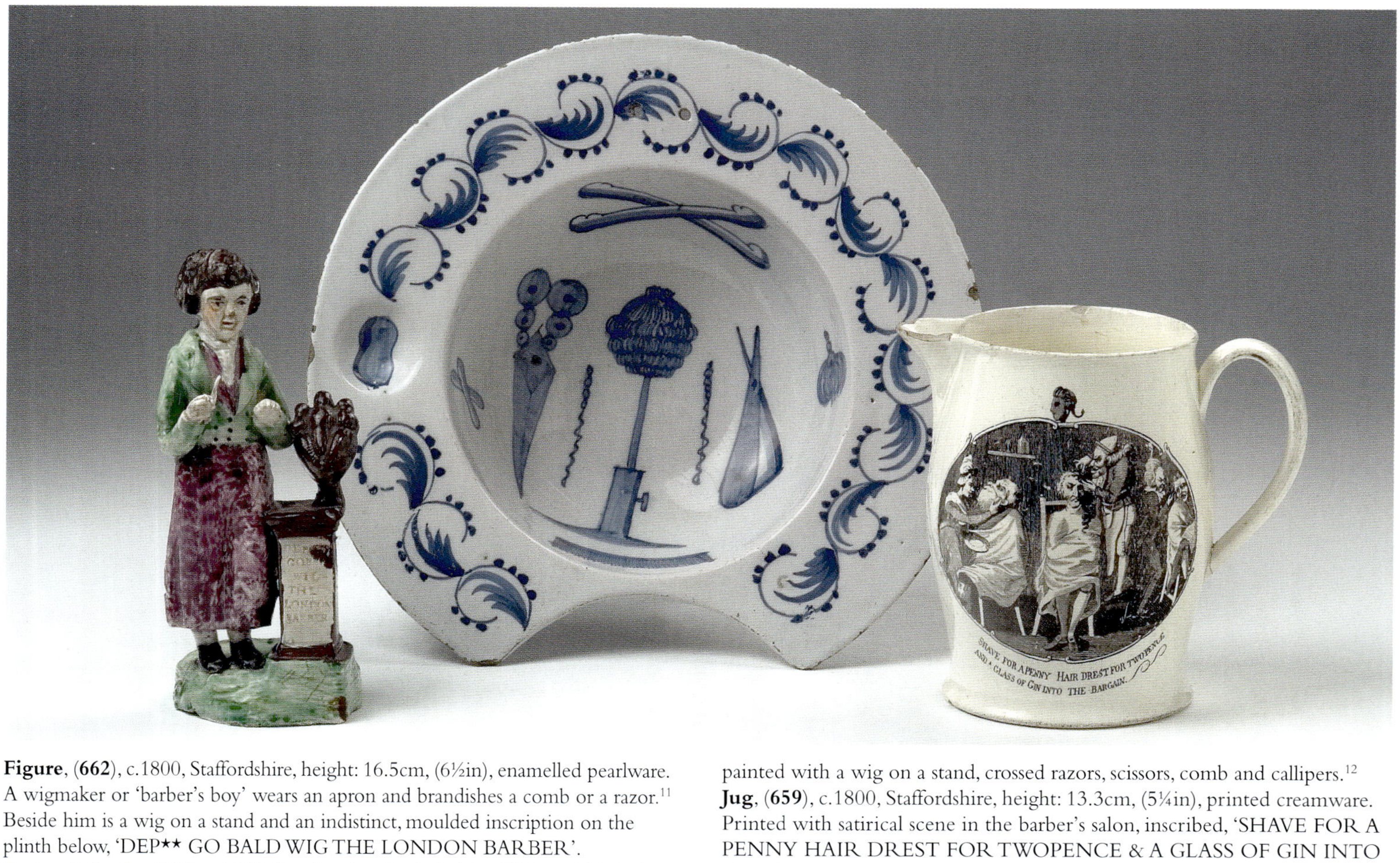

Figure, (**662**), c.1800, Staffordshire, height: 16.5cm, (6½in), enamelled pearlware. A wigmaker or 'barber's boy' wears an apron and brandishes a comb or a razor.[11] Beside him is a wig on a stand and an indistinct, moulded inscription on the plinth below, 'DEP** GO BALD WIG THE LONDON BARBER'.
Barber's Basin, (**660**), c.1700, London, Lambeth, height: 25.4cm, (10in), tin-glazed earthenware. Bowl has customary lunette removed to accommodate the customer's neck and a small depression in the rim to hold soap. Interior painted with a wig on a stand, crossed razors, scissors, comb and callipers.[12]
Jug, (**659**), c.1800, Staffordshire, height: 13.3cm, (5¼in), printed creamware. Printed with satirical scene in the barber's salon, inscribed, 'SHAVE FOR A PENNY HAIR DREST FOR TWOPENCE & A GLASS OF GIN INTO THE BARGAIN'. A woman shaves one man while a very short barber stands on a box to fit part of a wig on another client. The source print was published by Thomas Prattent in 1793.[13]

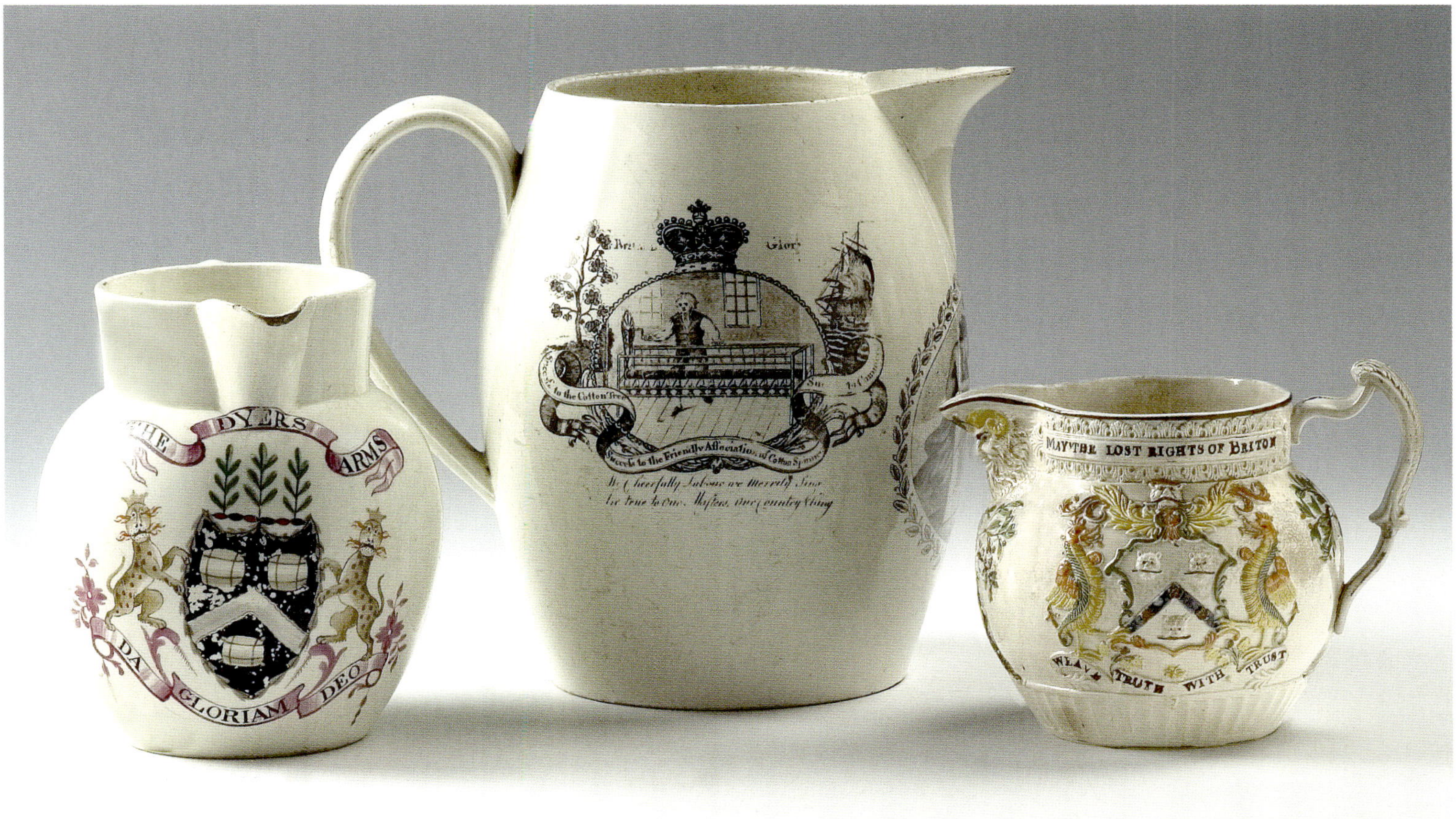

Jug, (**562**), c.1780, Staffordshire, height: 16.5cm, (6½in), enamelled creamware. The Dyers' Arms, comprising three bound bales of cloth, surmounted by plants, are supported by spotted leopards.
Jug, (**564**), c.1800, Staffordshire, height: 22cm, (8⅝in), printed creamware. Printed with a man operating a large spinning machine in a textile factory. The inscription wishes, 'Succefs to the Cotton Tree / Succefs to the Friendly Association of Cotton Spinners / Succefs to Commerce', with 'Britain's Glory' above and a loyal rhyme beneath. By 1800 there were over thirty cotton towns in Cheshire, Lancashire and Derbyshire and branches of the Cotton Spinners' Association were set up in Stockport (1785) Manchester and Preston (1795) and Oldham (1797). The protestations of loyalty may have been intended to allay any suspicions that these organisations may have raised.
Jug, (**563**), 1800, Staffordshire, height: 13.3cm, (5¼in), painted pearlware. Relief-moulded jug with satyr mask beneath the spout and the Weavers' Arms, decorated in high-temperature colours. The shield, supported by griffins, has three leopard heads, each with a weaver's shuttle in its mouth. Motto reads, 'WEAVE TRUTH WITH TRUST' and around the neck, 'MAY THE LOST RIGHTS OF BRITON [*sic*] SOON BE RESTORED'.

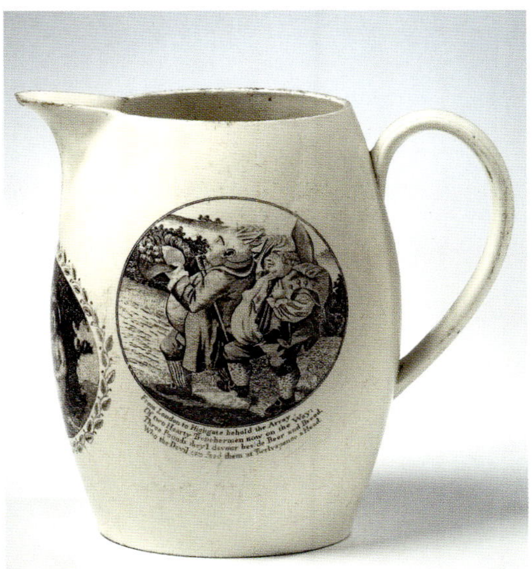

Jug, (**564**), 1800, Staffordshire, height: 21.7cm, (8½in), printed creamware. Two stout men mop their brows as they climb a hill. The source print, (published c.1795), is entitled, 'Two 3 Pounders in full speed to a Shilling Ordinary on Sunday', and refers to the Shilling Ordinary meals sold to visitors at the Gate House Tavern in Highgate in the late eighteenth century.[14]

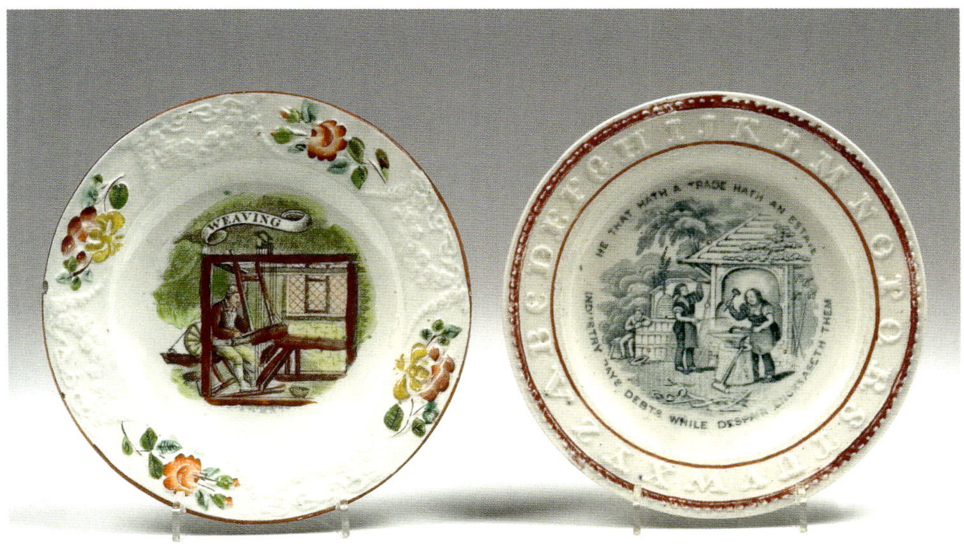

Plate, (**656**), c.1820, Swansea, Glamorgan Pottery, height: 17.8cm, (7in), pearlware, printed and enamelled. A weaver working at his loom. Image taken from a popular *Book of Trades or Library of the Useful Arts*, intended as an introduction to possible careers.[15]
Plate, (**658**), c.1830, Swansea, Glamorgan Pottery, height: 17.8cm, (7in), pearlware, printed and enamelled. Moulded alphabet plate printed with scene at a forge where the smiths wear protective leather aprons. Inscribed with two of 'Poor Richard's Rhymes', popular moralising ditties, one of which reads, 'HE THAT HATH A TRADE HATH AN ESTATE'.[16]

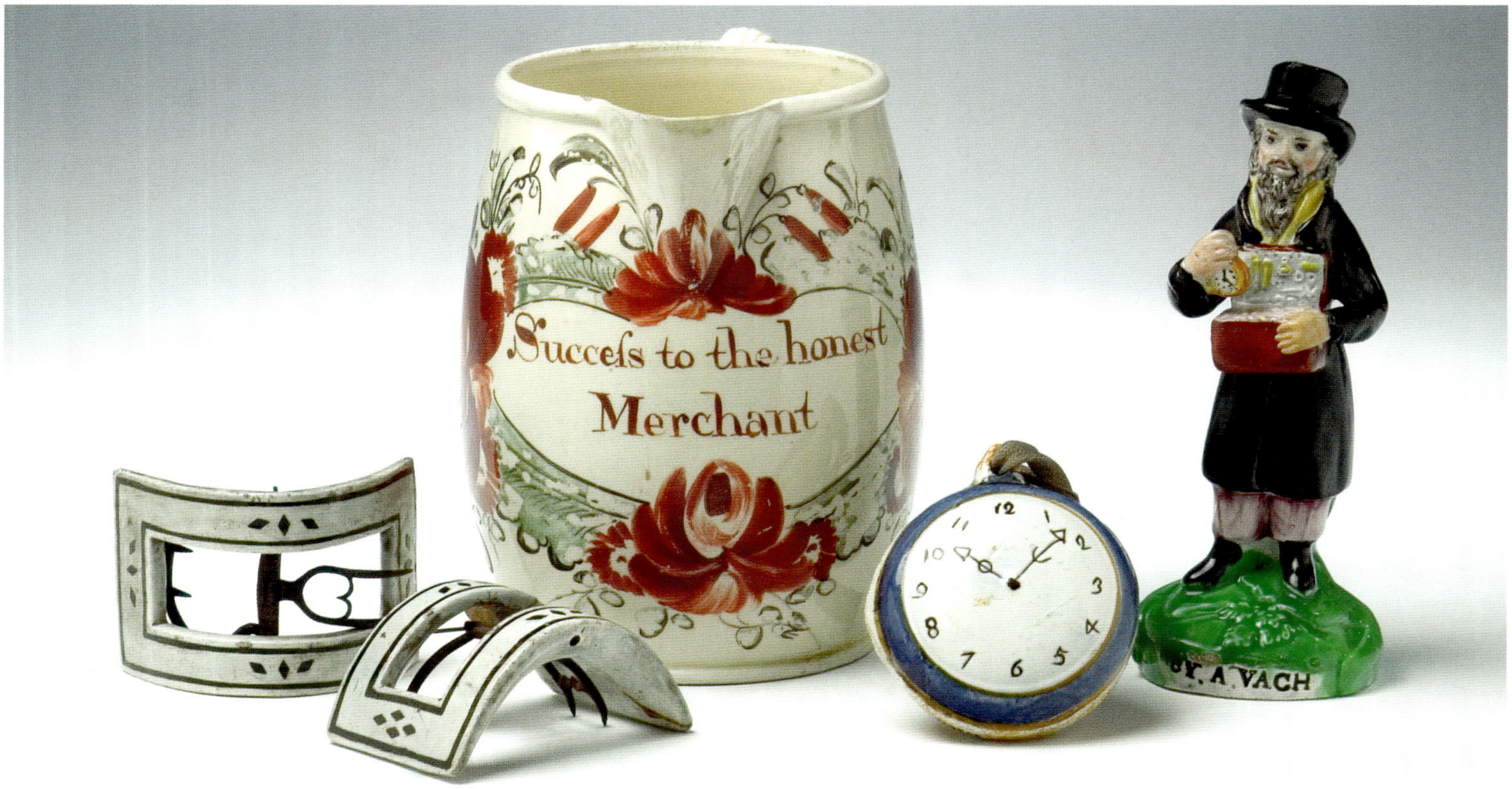

Pair of Buckles, (**632 & A**), c.1780, each height: 7.6cm, (3in), enamelled pearlware and metal. Pair of bowed, rectangular shoe buckles in pearlware, with metal fittings; novelty accessories but intended to be worn.
Jug, (**671**), 1790, Yorkshire, height: 15.3cm, (6in), enamelled creamware. Inscribed, 'Succefs to the honest Merchant', the jug, decorated with roses and peapods and its entwined handle with flower terminals, salutes salesmen of integrity.

Model Watch, (**631**), c.1800, Staffordshire, diameter: 7cm, (2¾in), pearlware, decorated in high-temperature colours.
Figure, (**678**), c.1825, Staffordshire, height: 15.3cm, (6in), enamelled pearlware. Figure represents an itinerant Jewish salesman, showing a pocket watch from his portable trinket stall.[17] Inscribed, 'BY A VACH', transcribing the salesman's central European accent.

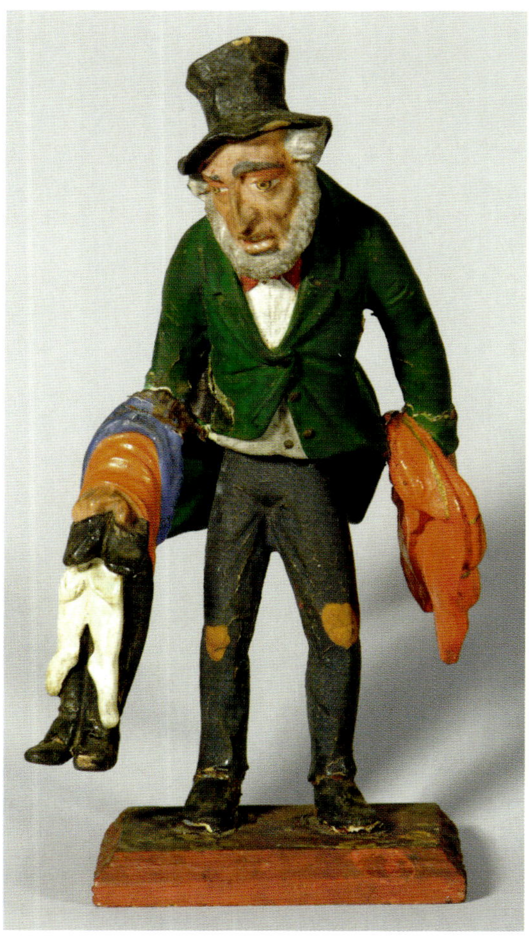

Figure, (**677**), c.1860, height: 17.8cm, (7in), painted wood. Wooden figure with hinged arms, representing a caricature of an itinerant, Jewish street vendor selling second-hand clothes.

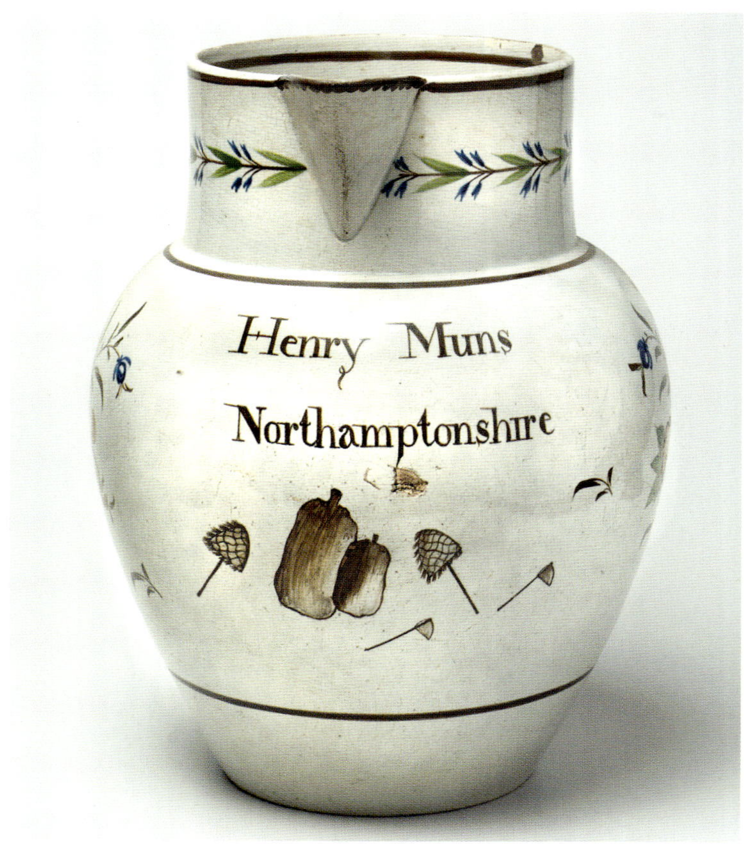

Jug, (**674**), c.1800, Yorkshire, height: 26.1cm, (10¼in), enamelled pearlware. Inscribed for 'Henry Muns' of Northamptonshire and decorated with soot sacks, nets and brushes, essential equipment for chimney sweeps.

Figure, (**676**), c.1850, Germany?, height: 12.7cm, (5in), enamelled porcelain. Figure of chimney sweep, wrapped in a black cloak. Climbing boys or 'chummies' were apprenticed from the workhouse and endured a miserable, dangerous and unhealthy life cleaning flues. Ironically they had very good teeth, kept clean by soot.[18]
Figure Group, (**664**), c.1825, Staffordshire, height: 23.5cm, (9½in), enamelled pearlware. A shoemaker and his customer; the crude modelling suggests the young woman has a badly dislocated knee!
Figure, (**675**), c.1825, Staffordshire, probably Wood, height: 17.8cm, (7in), enamelled pearlware. Figure of boy sweep, with a blackened face, based on a figure of Winter by P.L. Cyfflé.

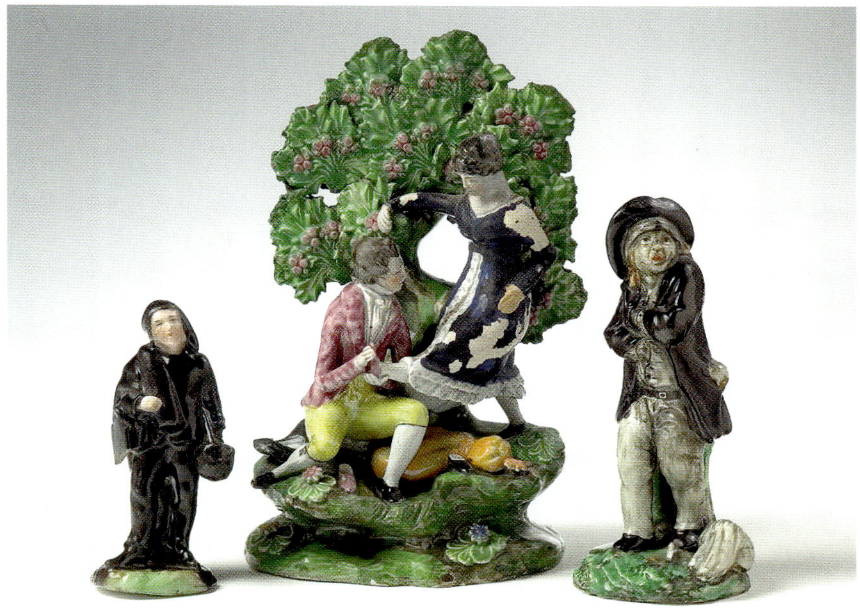

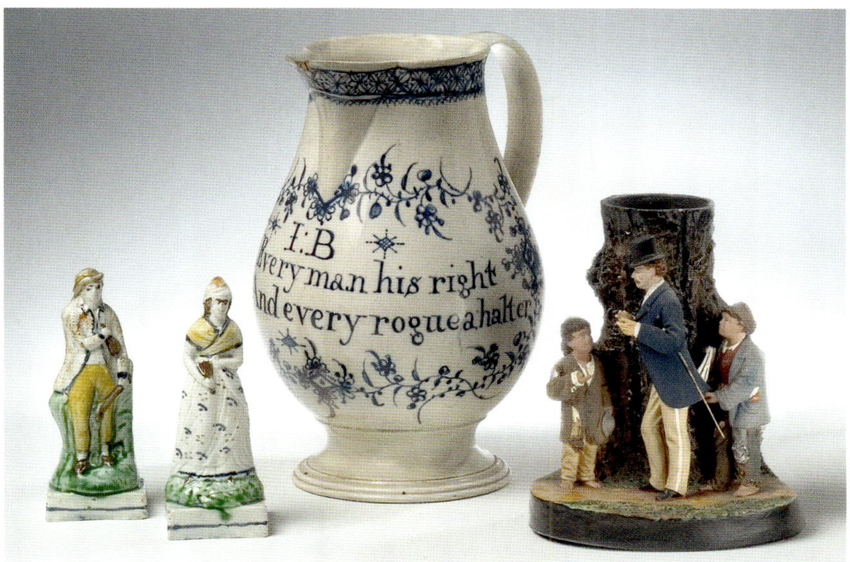

Pair of Figures, (**615 & A**), c.1800, Staffordshire, each height: 12.7cm, (5in), Prattware. They may represent a footpad, carrying a bag of money and his female victim or a sailor and his wife.
Jug, (**617**), c.1800, Staffordshire, height: 16.5cm, (6½in), pearlware, blue-printed underglaze. Inscribed, 'Every man his right And every rogue a halter' with initials, 'IB', it may be taking a swipe at dishonesty.
Matchholder, (**672**), c.1890, France, height: 22.9cm, (9in), hard-paste porcelain. Modelled as a tree stump before which a fashionably dressed man has his pockets picked by ragged boys.

Pair of Figures, (**639 & A**), c.1800, Germany?, each height: 17.1cm, (6¾in), enamelled hard-paste porcelain. Two caricatured figures of beggars, a regular feature of town life, relaxing.
Figure, (**638**), c.1830, Staffordshire, height: 15.3cm, (6in), enamelled pearlware. Man with a wooden leg holds out his hat for gifts.
Tobacco Jar, (**634**), c.1830, Germany?, height: 24.8cm, (9¾in), enamelled pearlware. Jar or biscuit barrel (impressed 'FCW' on the base), modelled as a beadle (a forerunner of the policeman) who monitored public behaviour.
Figure, (**635**), c.1760, Staffordshire, Longton Hall, height: 12.1cm, (4¾in), enamelled soft-paste porcelain. Intended to represent Winter, figure, lacking brazier or basket of embers and given a lantern, is assumed to be a night-watchman.
Figure, (**621**), c.1820, Staffordshire, height: 19.1cm, (7½in), enamelled pearlware. Events and local news were relayed by the town crier, who is shown with his bell.

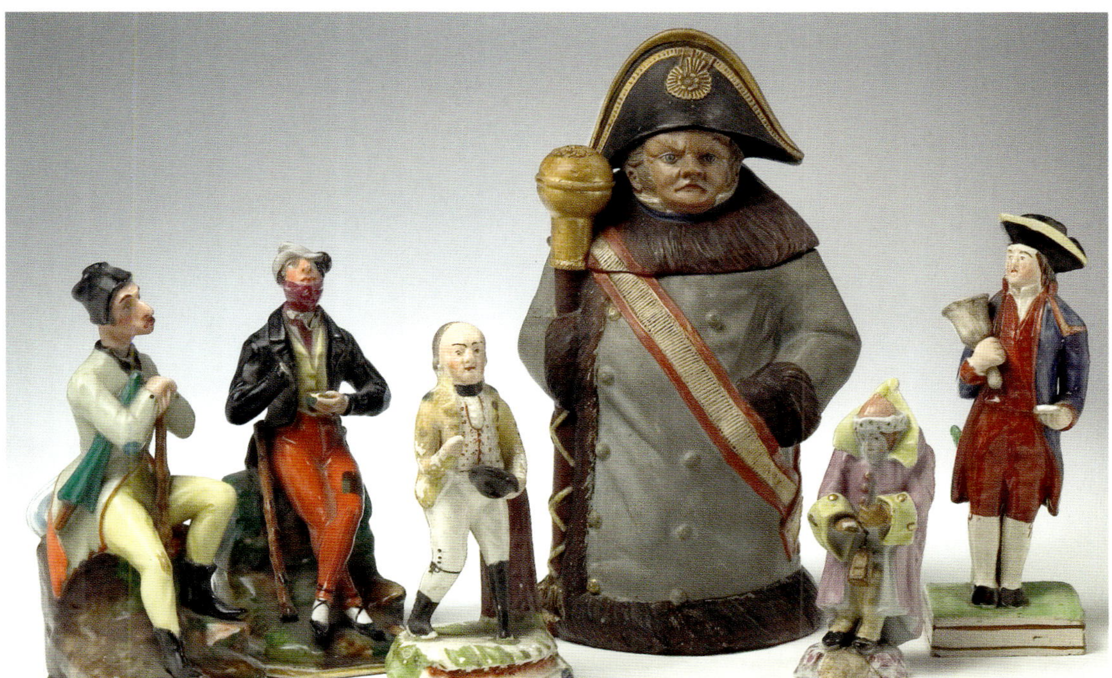

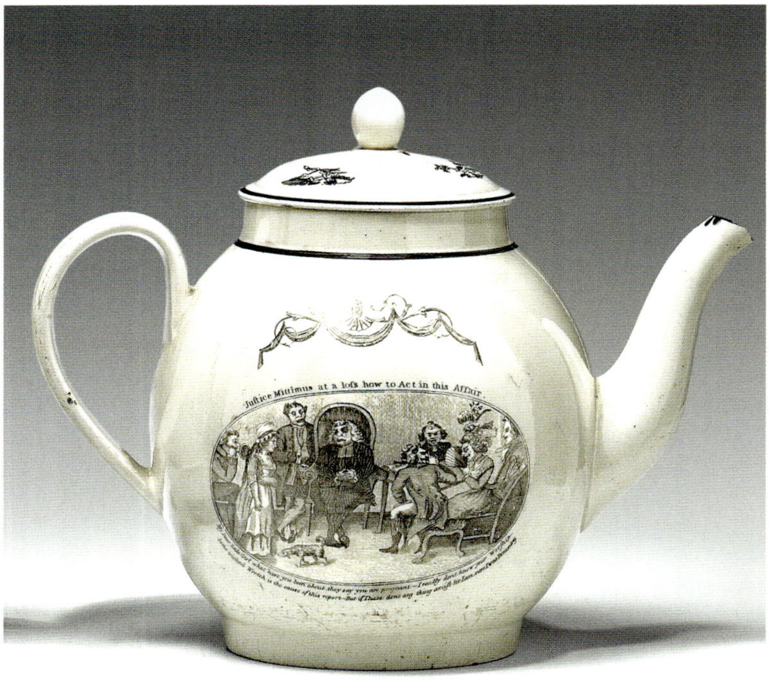

The Professions

Patchbox, (**622**), c.1795, London?, height: 5.1cm, (2in), enamelled copper. Inscribed, 'A Lawyer and his Agent', a dubious character holds papers as the Devil looks over his shoulder. This is probably based on a satire published 1793 by Carington Bowles after Robert Dighton.[19] The original is concerned with a case in Middlesex.

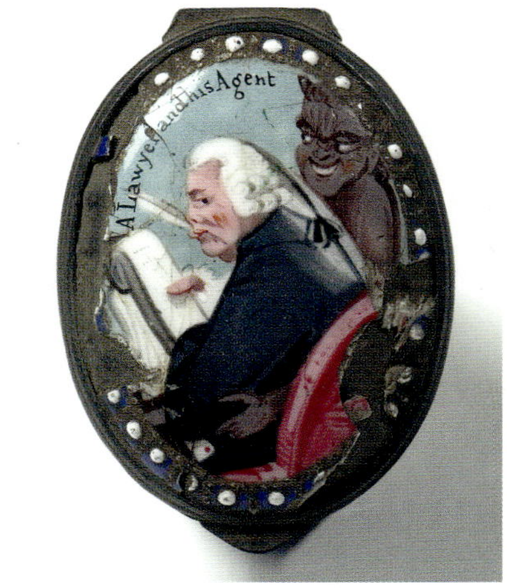

Teapot, (**1680**), c.1795, Staffordshire, height: 21.6cm, (8½in), printed creamware. Satirical scene, based on print by Isaac Cruikshank, shows 'Justice Mittimus at a loss how to Act in this Affair'.[20] A serving girl stands before a magistrate, who addresses her, 'My Dear little girl what have you been about, they say you are pregnant'. She replies, 'I really don't know your Worship, some wicked wretch is the cause of this report – but if I have done anything amiss, Sir, I am sure I was dreaming.'

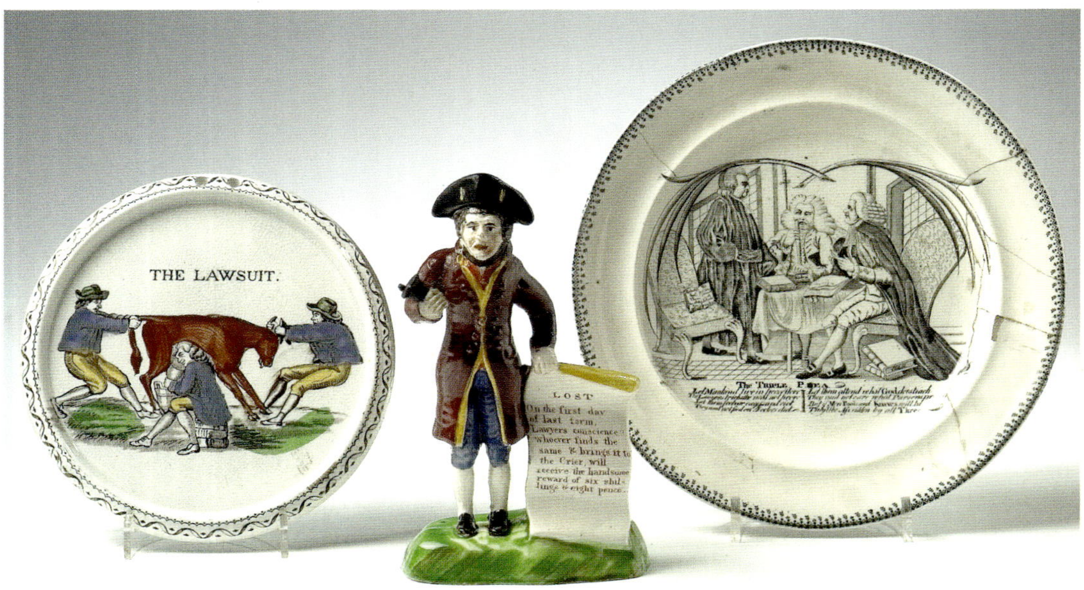

Plaque, (**624**), c.1820, Staffordshire, diameter: 16.5cm, (6½in), pearlware, printed and enamelled. Inscribed, 'THE LAWSUIT', two quarrelsome neighbours playing tug of war with a cow while the lawyer smugly milks her.
Figure, (**636**), c.1820, Staffordshire, height: 17.8cm, (7in), enamelled pearlware Figure of a town crier draws particular attention to the shortcomings of lawyers.[21] His scroll reads, 'LOST / on the first day of last term/ Lawyers Conscience!!'.
Plate, (**625**), c.1785, Staffordshire, diameter: 21.9cm, (8⅝in), printed creamware. Entitled 'The Triple Plea', the image is closely based on a print published by Bowles & Carver, 1780, after a painting by John Collet.[22] The characters represent the professions, 'Law, Physick and Divinity'; (from left) a priest a doctor and a lawyer who all fleece unsuspecting clients.

Tile, (**620**), c.1770, Liverpool, Sadler & Green, height: 12.7cm, (5in), printed tin-glazed earthenware. Scene of impromptu dental extraction taken from engraving after Andries and Jan Both, illustrating 'Feeling'.[23]
Plate, (**619**), c.1780, Staffordshire, diameter: 25.4cm, (10in), printed creamware. A helpless patient, wracked with pain, anticipates the extraction of a molar. The surgeon, relishing his work, waves tongs holding a red-hot coal in the patient's face. With his other hand he grips a taut thread, wrapped around the patient's tooth. The design is taken from No. 8 of *Human Passions Delineated*, (published 1773) by Tim Bobbin, contrasting Mirth with Anguish. John Collier of Urmiston, otherwise known as Tim Bobbin, the 'Lancashire Hogarth'.[24]

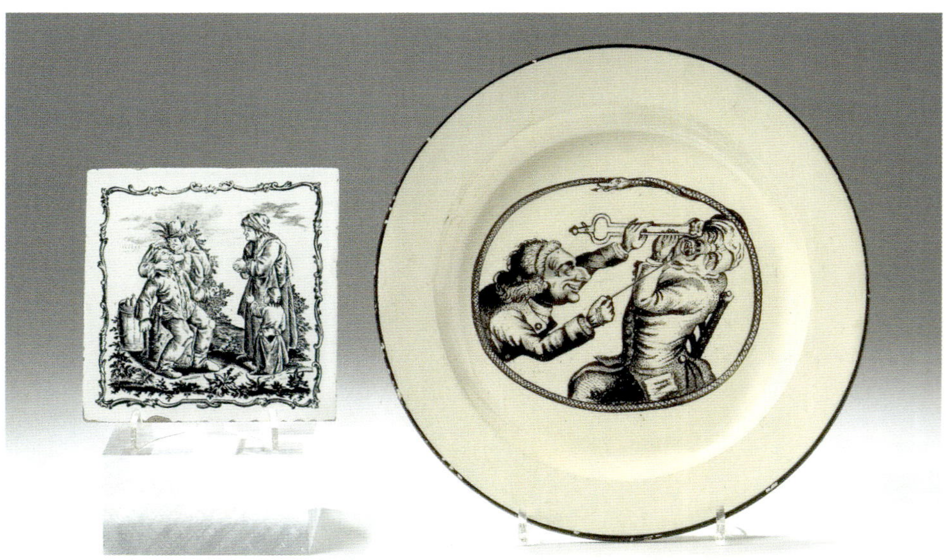

Construction and Industry

Jug, (**556**), c.1790, Staffordshire, height: 14.8cm, (5¾in), printed creamware. Printed with a version of the Blacksmiths' Arms; a chevron separating three hammers with ducal crowns, a phoenix crest and suits of armour as supporters. The Company's motto beneath; 'BY HAMMER AND HAND ALL ARTS DO STAND'.
Plaque, (**657**), 1814, North East?, height: 18.4cm, (7¼in), Prattware. Relief-moulded with image of blacksmith, naked but for a loin cloth and sandals, hammers a horseshoe. It could be intended as a portrait of the god, Vulcan. Incised behind, J. Phillips, 1814.
Jug, (**550**), c.1800, Liverpool?, height: 15.3cm, (6in), printed creamware. The ancient craft of coopering is celebrated on a rather battered creamware jug of around 1800. Printed with image of the cooper 'trussing a cask' of separate wooden staves with heated iron hoops. On reverse, the Coopers' Arms, the shield bearing three iron rings or annulets, supported by camels spotted with annulets. The motto reads, 'MAY PROSPERITY ATTEND THE INTEGRITY OF OUR CAUSE'.

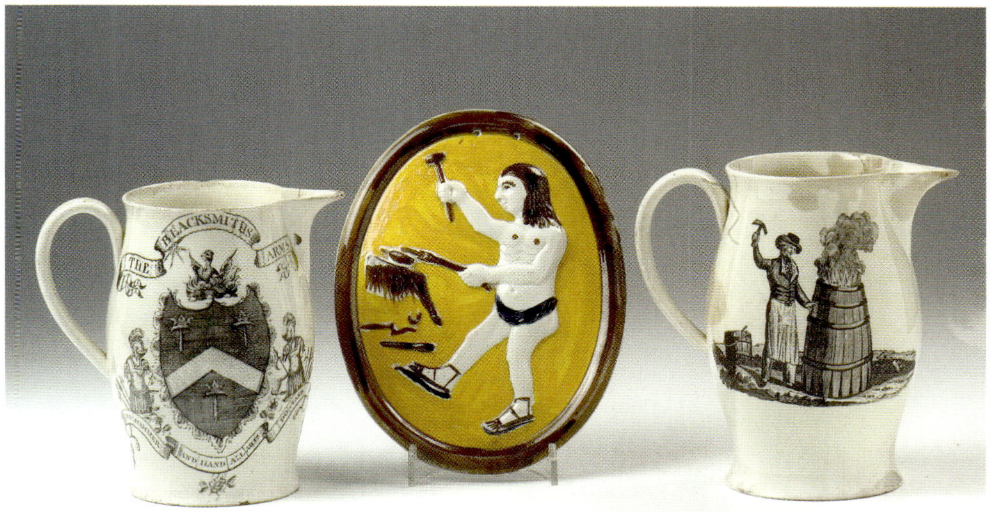

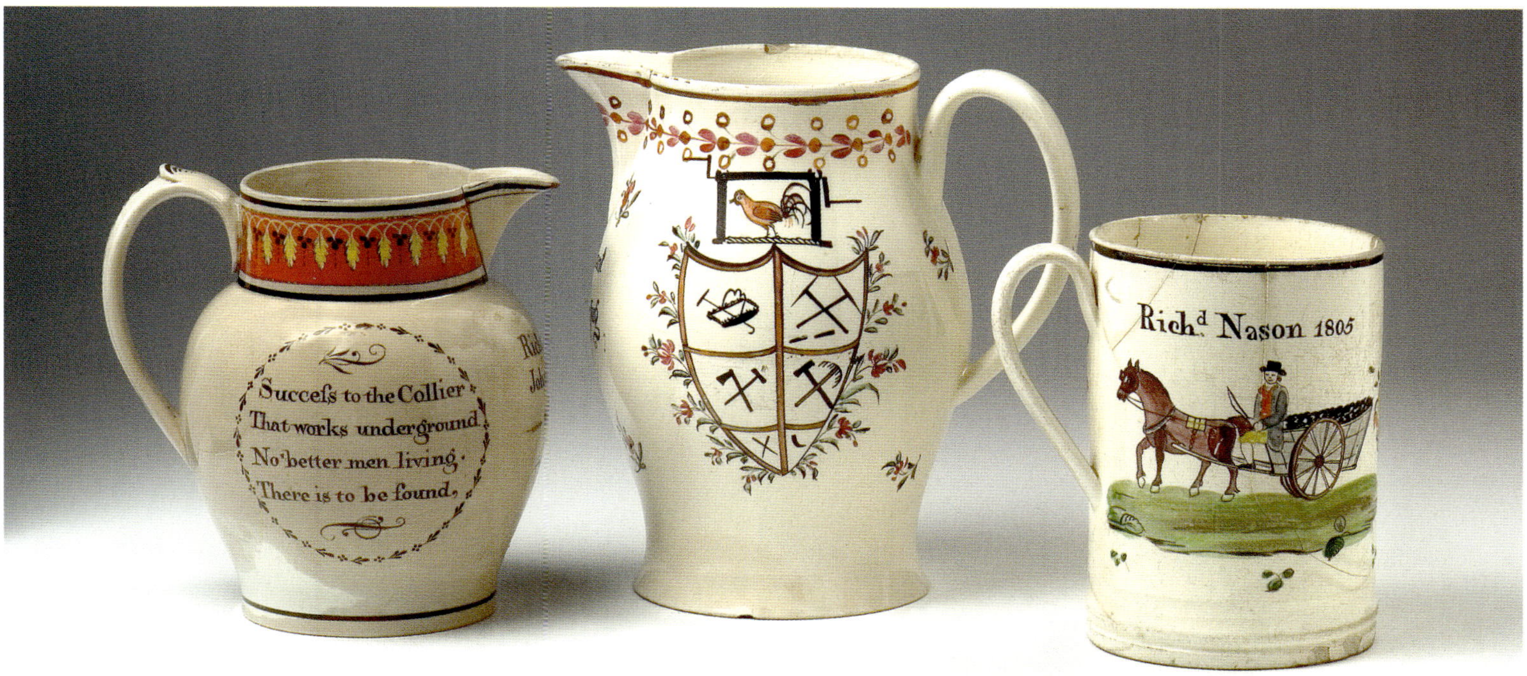

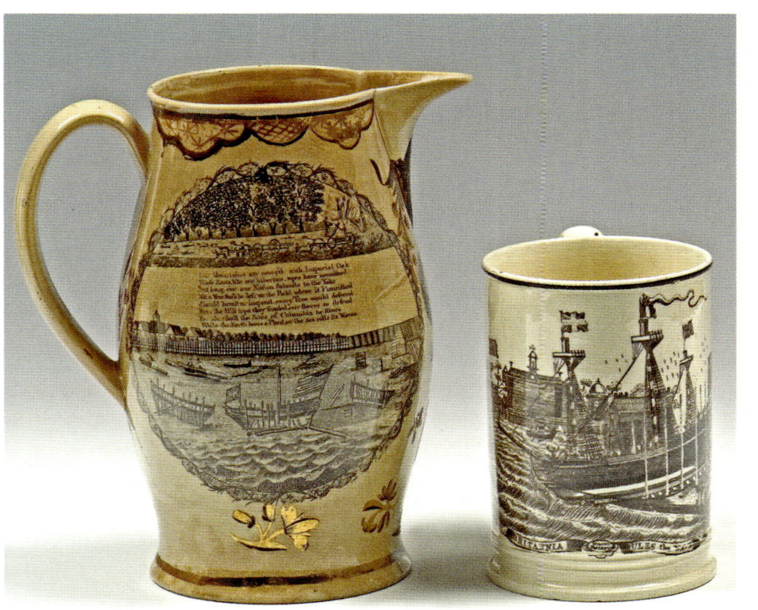

Jug, (**570**), 1808, Staffordshire, height: 16.5cm, (6½in), enamelled drabware Inscribed for 'Richard Johnson, 1808', with doggerel verse, 'Succefs to the Collier That works underground, No better men living There is to be found'. On the reverse the Colliers' shield, decorated with tools.
Jug, (**569**), 1796, Staffordshire, height: 20.3cm, (8in), enamelled creamware. Inscribed for 'Thomas Plant, 1796'. Painted with the Colliers' shield, decorated with pickaxes, rakes and mallets and a cockerel as a crest – possibly a forerunner of the canary used in the mine to detect toxic gases.
Mug, (**670**), 1805, North East?, height: 15.3cm, (6in), enamelled creamware Inscribed, 'Richd. Nason 1805', presumably a coal merchant painted with his horse and cart. On reverse a doggerel verse, 'Coals by the Bushel, Coals by the Peck, If you have not a Horse and Cart, You may carry them on Your Neck'.

Jug, (**462**), c.1800, Liverpool, height: 20.3cm, (8in), drabware, printed and gilt. Within a circular frame, felled trees being transported to a shipyard with several vessels under construction and verses, 'Our mountains are cover'd with Imperial Oak / Whose Roots like our Liberties, ages have nourished'.[25]
Mug, (**280**), c.1800, Sunderland, Southwick, Union Pottery, height: 14cm, (5½in), enamelled creamware. Wrap-around print shows the launch of a new ship, being rolled down a log ramp, before embarking on its maiden voyage. Below, a ribbon is inscribed; 'BRITANNIA / RULES [*sic*] the WAVES', misquoted from Thomas Arne's poem for the masque *Alfred*, (1740). It is a rare piece marked for the Union Pottery, Sunderland, which was only in production from 1789 to 1805.[26]

Transport: Coaching

Although Willett included 'coaching' as a Sport it seems more appropriate to consider here those pieces concerned with commercial transport for people, goods and mail. Before the 1780s the 'post boy', a mounted messenger, carried letters along the main postal routes. Having noted the unreliability of this service but the general improvement in road quality, in 1784 the Bath impresario John Palmer was authorized by his friend William Pitt, the new Prime Minister, to run a scheduled mail-coach service, carrying letters and passengers from Bristol to London. It was so successful that services were extended to other cities and by 1786 the travelling time from Edinburgh to London was shortened from 3½ days to 60 hours.[27]

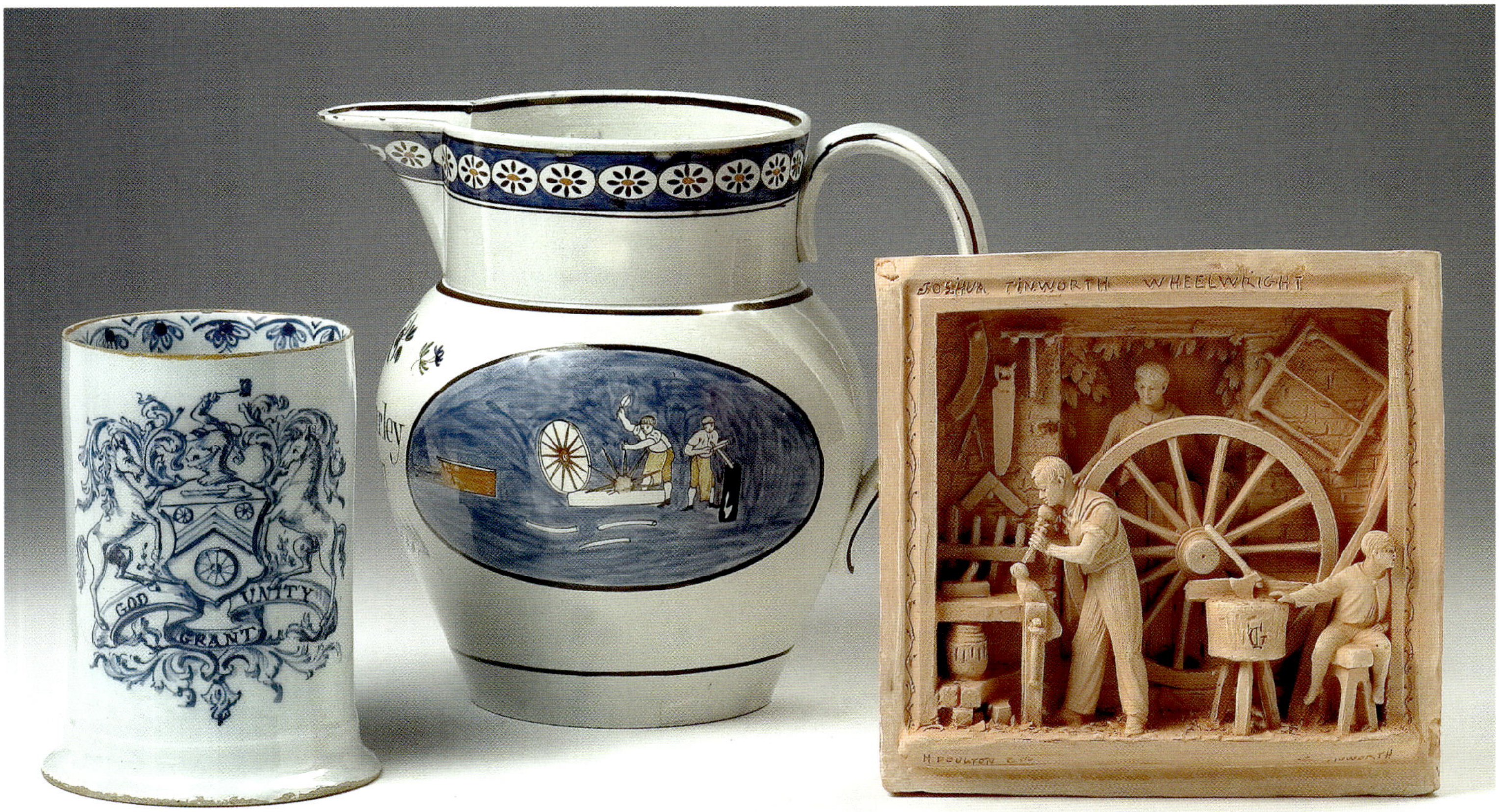

Mug, (**558**), 1763, London?, height: 15.9cm, (6¼in), tin-glazed earthenware. Arms of the Worshipful Company of Wheelwrights where carriage horses support a shield applied with an axe and three cartwheels. Motto, 'God Grant Unity'. Underside inscribed, 'IBM 1763'. Two different bands of floral decoration either side of the handle.
Jug, (**668**), 1807, Yorkshire, height: 22.3cm, (8¾in), pearlware, painted underglaze. Inscribed for 'W. Moayarley 1807'. Wheelwrights contruct a wheel. The jug may mark the setting up of a new workshop.
Sculpture, (**655**), 1880, Staffordshire, height: 19.1cm, (7½in), terracotta Animated scene created in terracotta by George Tinworth (1843-1913), Doulton's great modeller. George's father 'Joshua Tinworth, Wheelwright' shown at his workbench, surrounded by tools and a huge wheel. His wife enters through a central doorway while the young George sits on the right, looking out of the frame.

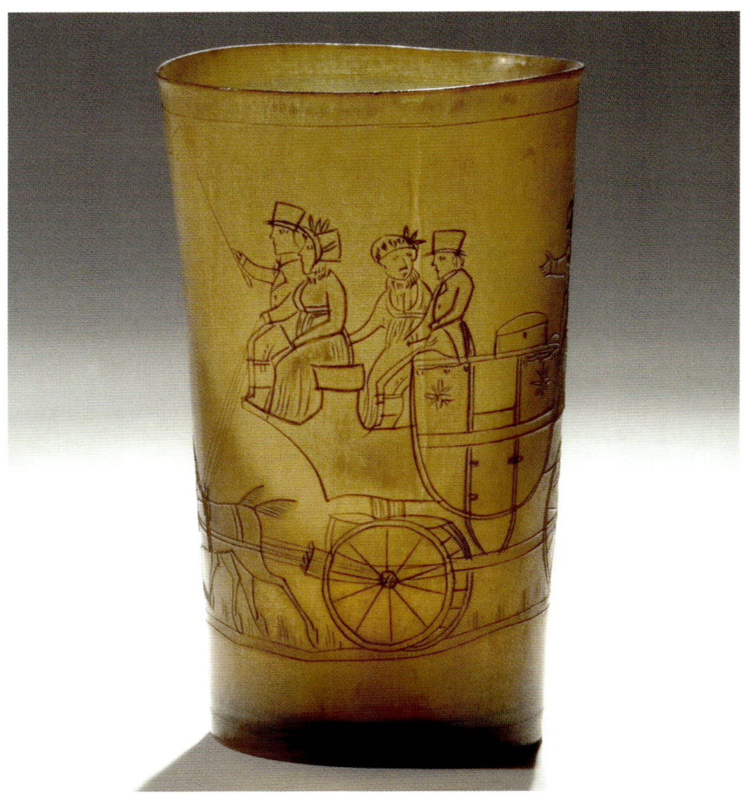

Beaker, (**1069**), 1810, height: 9.6cm, (3¾in), animal horn.
Engraved and stained with a scene of a four-horse coach passing a house.

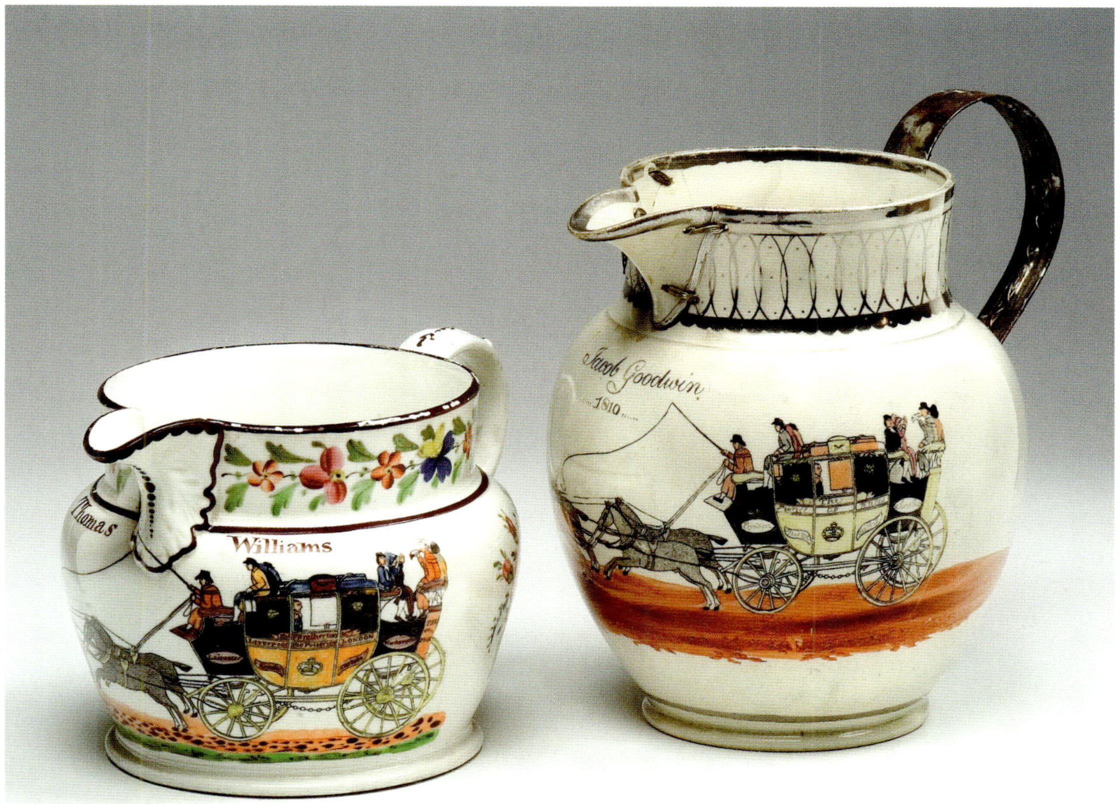

Jug, (**1066**), c.1820, probably Liverpool, height: 11.5cm, (4½in), bone china, printed and enamelled. Inscribed, 'Thomas Williams' and printed with a four-horse coach inscribed, 'the Royal Pilot/ by F. Bretherton & Co. / Liverpool / the Potteries / Leicester / Kendal / Carlisle / Northampton / London'.[28] The Brethertons were a celebrated family of Liverpool coach builders. F. Bretherton probably stood for Francis (1770-1833).[29]

Jug, (**1068**), 1810, probably Swansea, Cambrian Pottery,[30] height: 16.5cm, (6½in), pearlware, printed, enamelled and lustred. Inscribed, 'Jacob Goodwin 1810', and decorated with a four-horse coach, labelled, 'The Prince of Wales / Bristol / Cardiff / London / Swansea'. Handle replaced with a riveted metal strap.

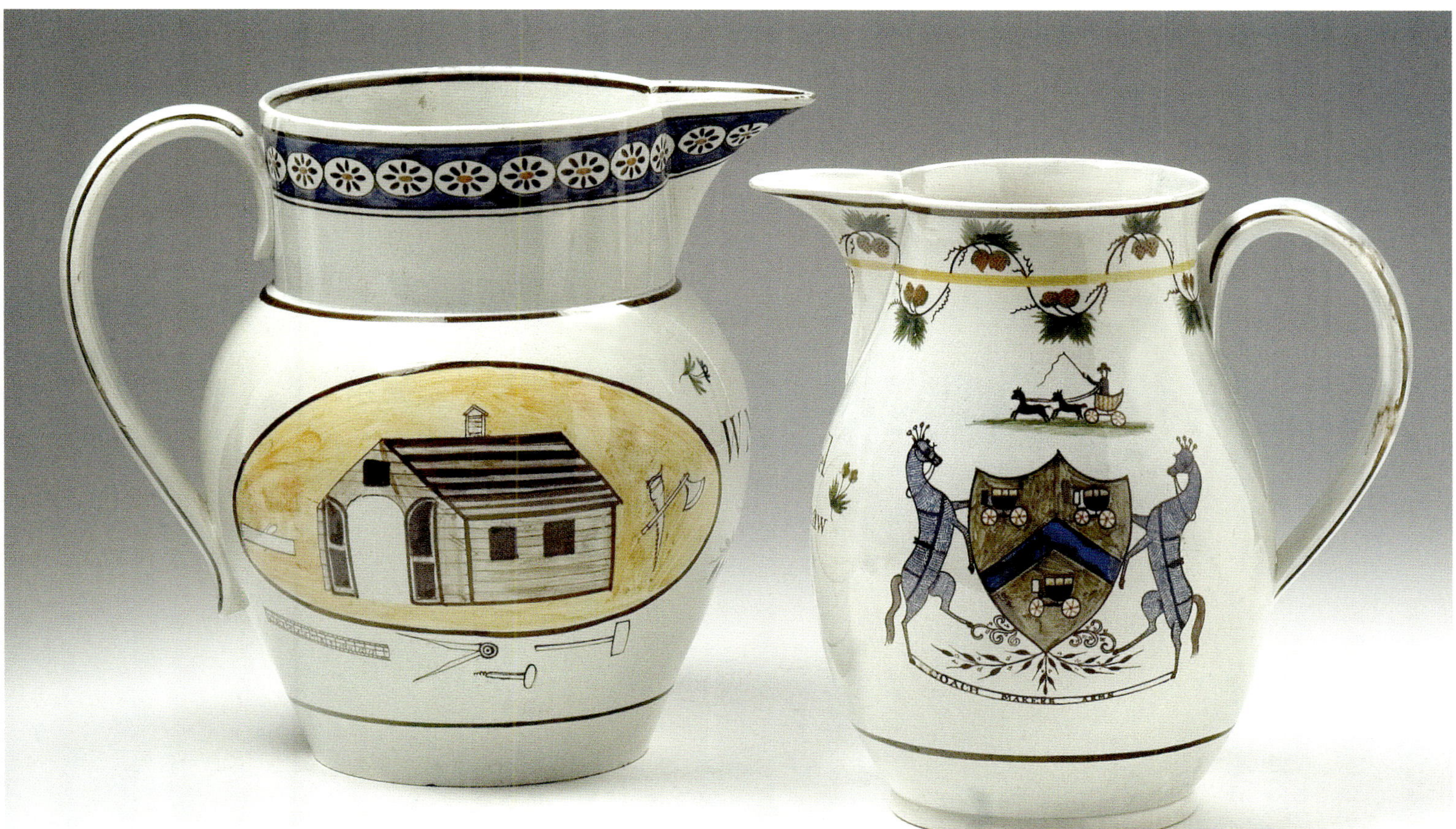

Jug, (**668**), 1807, Yorkshire, height: 22.3cm, (8¾in), pearlware, painted underglaze. On the other side of the jug inscribed for 'W. Moayarley 1807' a new barn or workshop is under construction, surrounded by builders' tools and a measuring rule. The jug may mark the setting up of a new workshop. Many trades depended on the wheelwrights, including the coachmakers.

Jug, (**572**), 1807, Yorkshire, height: 20.3cm, (8in), pearlware, painted underglaze. A pearlware jug, decorated in Pratt colours is inscribed for 'Samuel Wilshaw' and shows the Coachmakers' Arms. The shield, supported by two rearing carriage horses in harness shows three carriages separated by a chevron.

Marc Brunel (1769-1849) and Isambard Kingdom Brunel (1806-1859)

In 1825 the French engineer Marc Isambard Brunel began work on a tunnel that would enable horse-drawn carriages to travel under the River Thames from Rotherhithe to Wapping. He invented an iron 'tunnelling shield' to facilitate burrowing into the soft wet soil and to provide some protection for the diggers. He and his son Isambard completed the Thames Tunnel despite numerous setbacks, including floods, collapsing walls and explosions caused by pockets of methane gas. Isambard later pioneered the Great Western Railway, which ran from London to Bristol, designed innovative bridges, such as the suspension bridge over the River Severn at Clifton, near Bristol and great steamships such as the *Great Britain*, launched in 1843. He suffered a stroke just before the *Great Eastern* made its maiden voyage to New York in 1859.

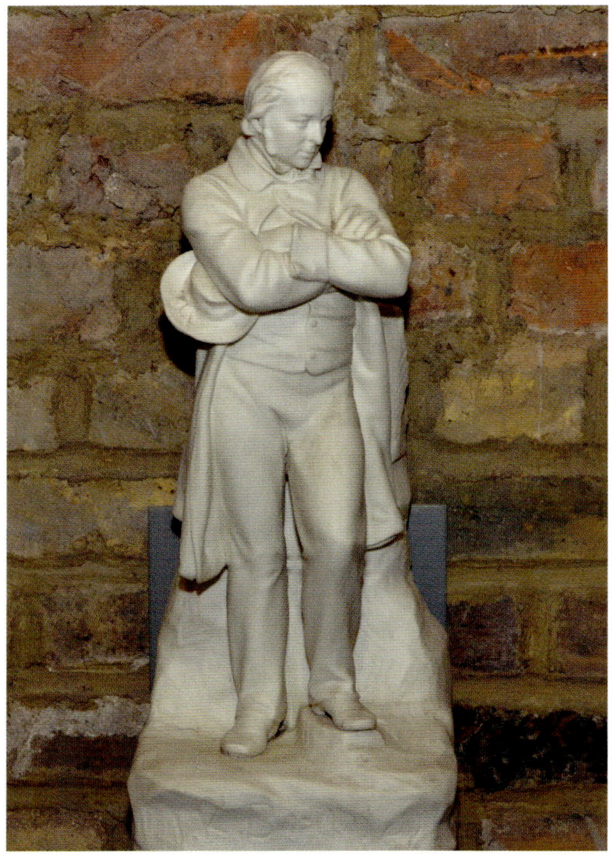

Figure, (**641**), 1860, Worcester, height: 51cm, (20in), Parian porcelain figure of I.K. Brunel, 50cm high, was modelled by the sculptor, J. Durham in 1860 for the Worcester factory. *Photo courtesy of The Brunel Museum, London.*

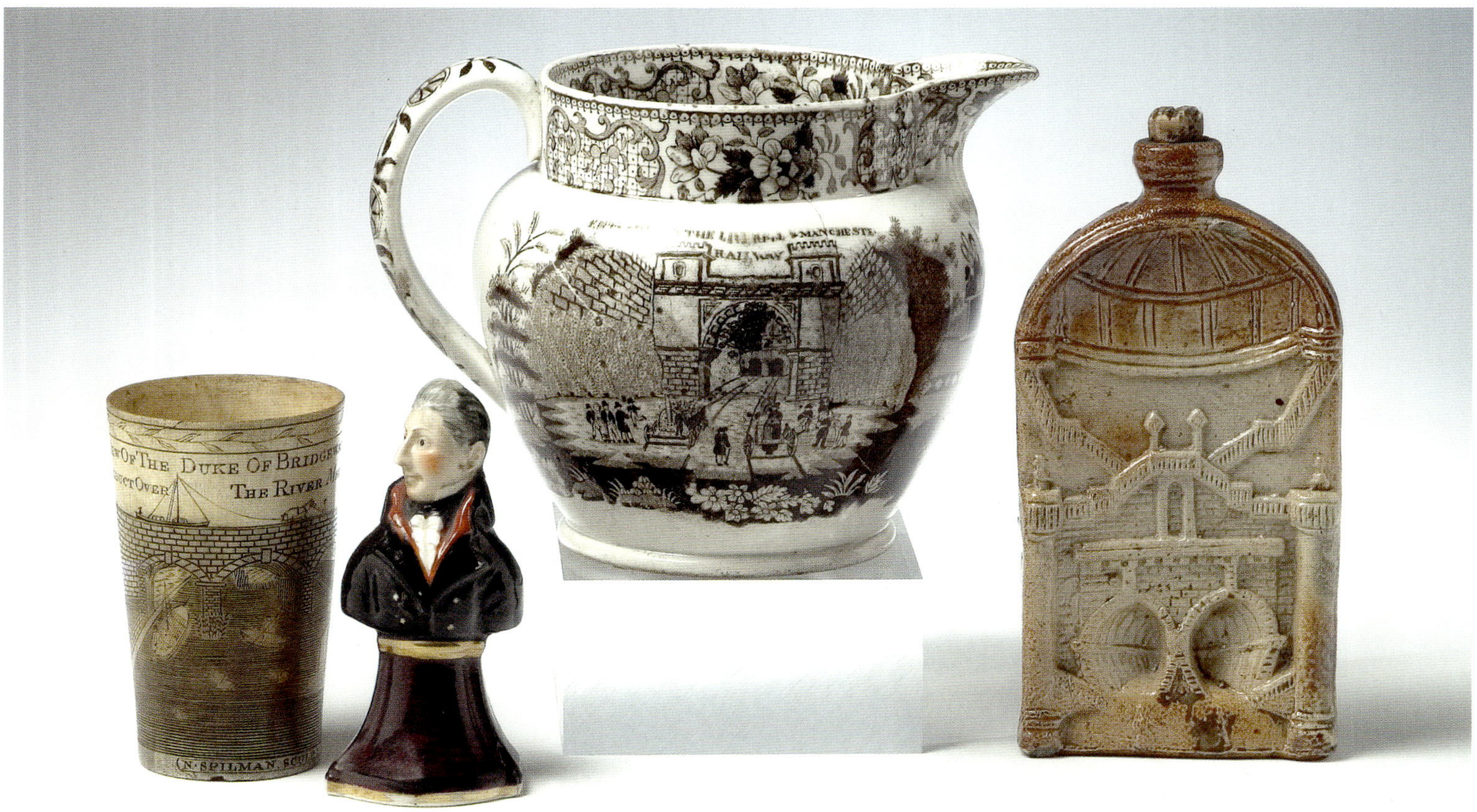

Beaker, (**648**), c.1810, signed, N. Spilman, height: 10.2cm, (4in), animal horn. Incised and stained with two scenes; a couple travel along the seaside in a one-horse carriage, or gig, inscribed 'A TRIP TO THE FORT',[31] and 'A VIEW OF THE DUKE OF BRIDGEWATER'S AQUEDUCT ACROSS THE RIVER MERSEY'.[32]
Bust, (**647**), c.1800, possibly Derby, height: 11.5cm, (4½in), enamelled soft-paste porcelain. Bust is said to be a portrait of the 3rd Duke of Bridgewater (see p.135)

Jug, (**643**), c.1830, Staffordshire, height: 14cm, (5½in), brown-printed earthenware. Print celebrates the opening of the Liverpool & Manchester Railway on 15 September 1830, with a view of its distinctive entrance .
Flask, (**640**), c.1845, London, height: 17.8cm, (7in), salt-glazed stoneware. Modelled in relief with the twin entrances to the Thames Tunnel, flanked by flights of steps. Celebrates the opening of the first river tunnel, designed and completed by I.K. Brunel, in 1843.[33]

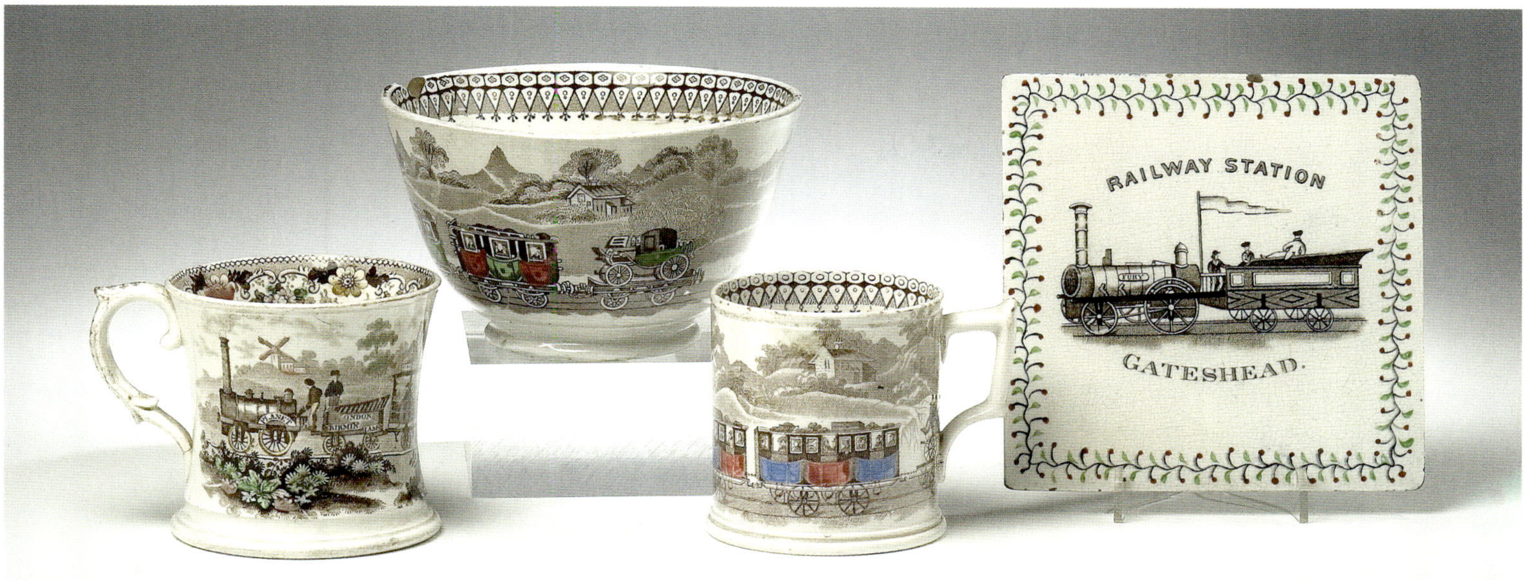

Mug, (**644**), c.1850, Staffordshire, height: 9.3cm, (3⅝in), earthenware, brown-printed and painted. Printed with steam locomotive *Planet*, shown pulling a London & Birmingham train. The original steam locomotive *Planet* was built in 1830 by Robert Stephenson for the Liverpool & Manchester Railway.
Bowl, (**R.603.8**), c.1880, Staffordshire, Burslem, height: 9.3cm, (3⅝in), earthenware, brown-printed and painted. Printed with passenger compartments and carriage. Marked 'Railway' B & T' for Blackhurst & Tunnicliffe.
Mug, (**645**), c.1845, Staffordshire, Cobridge, John & Robert Godwin, height: 8.9cm, (3½in), earthenware, brown-printed and painted. Train with locomotive *Fury,* a popular name embodying its observable behaviour.
Tile, (**642**), c.1845, North East?, height: 15.3cm, (6in), earthenware, printed and painted. Printed 'RAILWAY STATION' and 'GATESHEAD' with a locomotive named *Fury*.

Mechanisation and Engines

The eighteenth-century steam pumps and engines pioneered by Thomas Newcomen and James Watt brought about a revolution in engineering and transport. The steam locomotive was the great transport innovation of the nineteenth century. Using technology pioneered by Richard Trevithick for the Cornish mines, George Stevenson (1791-1848) built his first locomotive for the Stockton & Darlington Railway Line in 1814. In 1825, Stephenson was appointed chief engineer of the Liverpool & Manchester Railway, which opened, in the presence of the Prime Minister, the Duke of Wellington, on 15th September 1830. The day was marred when a government minister was knocked down and killed by one of the locomotives. Stephenson and his son Robert built the *Rocket* (1826-29), which later managed a top speed of 29 mph and he went on to work on the Manchester & Leeds, Birmingham & Derby, Normanton & York and Sheffield & Rotherham railways.

Francis Egerton, third Duke of Bridgewater (1736-1803) commissioned the engineer, James Brindley, to construct a canal that ran from Bridgewater's coal mines at Worsley to Castlefield in Manchester. This massive undertaking involved building an aqueduct over the River Irwell at Barton. By linking the Mersey to the Trent at Wilden Ferry, the 'Grand Trunk' canal joined the west and east coasts of Britain and inaugurated the 'canal age'. After the canal opened in 1761, Egerton was nearly bankrupted extending it towards Liverpool.[34] The Manchester-Liverpool Ship Canal took ten years to build, from 1762 to 1772. The economies of both Liverpool and Manchester greatly benefitted from the increase in trade brought by Bridgewater's canal.

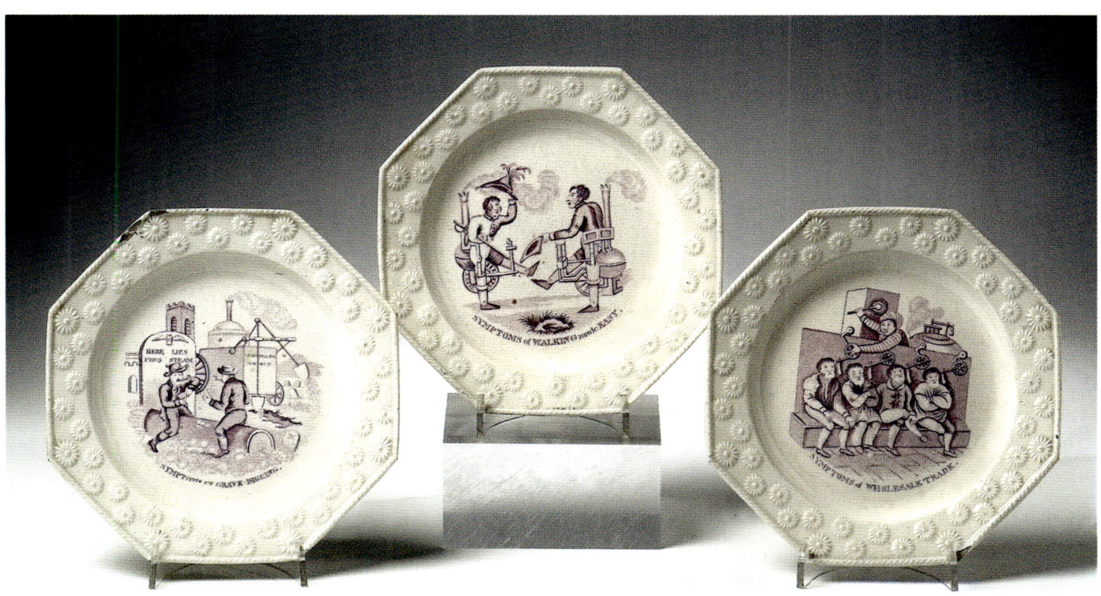

Three Plates, (**680, 681, 682**), c.1830, Staffordshire, each diameter: 15.3cm, (6in), puce-printed earthenware. Octagonal nursery plates, each printed with a parody of new technology, particularly the use of steam power.[35] 'SYMPTOMS of WALKING made EASY' shows men harnessed to steam engines and 'SYMPTOMS of GRAVE-DIGGING', shows men made redundant by a mechanical digger. 'SYMPTOMS of WHOLESALE TRADE' shows a row of clients being shaved simultaneously, taken from 'Shaving by Steam' by Richard Seymour (published by E. King, 1828).

Ceramic Manufacture

George Tinworth (1843-1913)

An ardent but eccentric Christian, from a non-conformist background, Tinworth studied alongside Robert Wallace Martin (Martin Brothers) under John Sparkes at the Lambeth School of Art. Sparkes persuaded Henry Doulton to employ Tinworth as a modeller at 30/- per week.

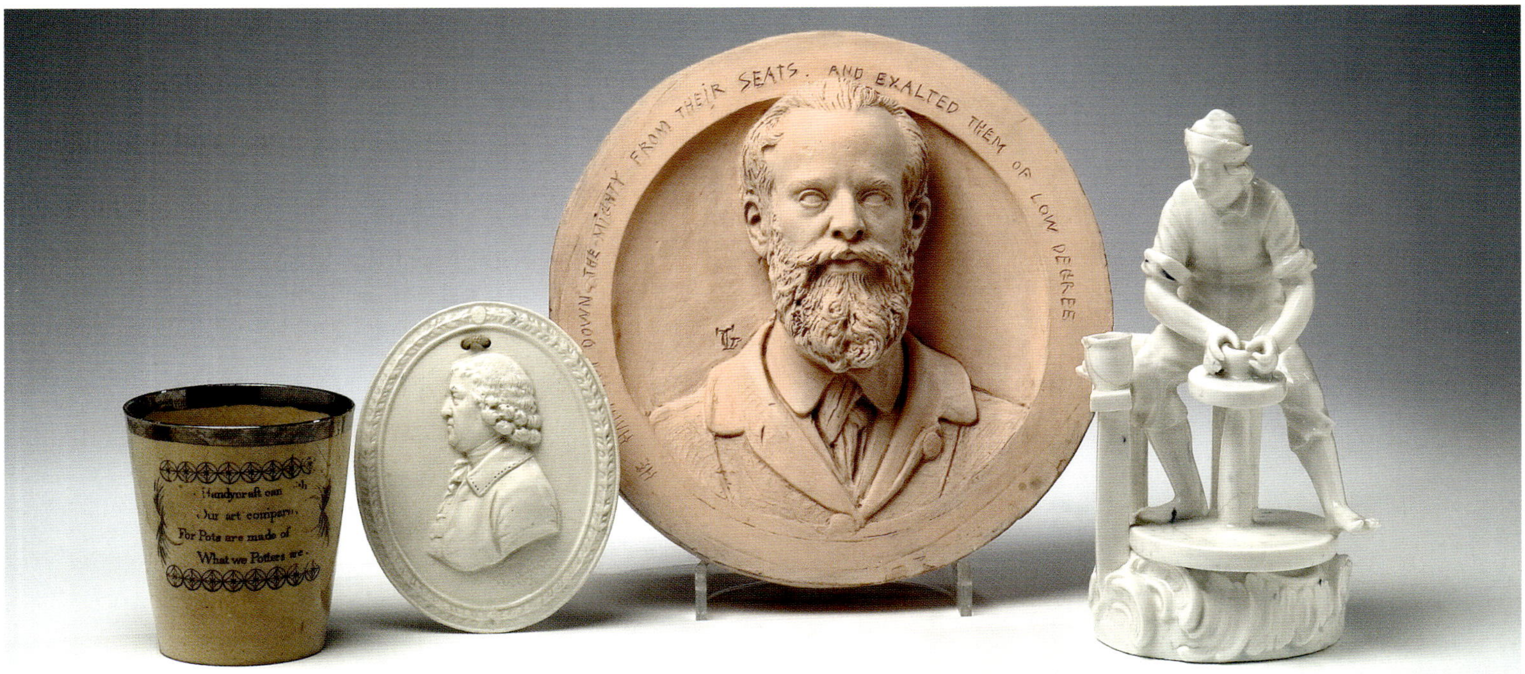

Beaker, (**651**), Staffordshire, height: 8.9cm, (3½in), drabware, printed and lustred. Printed with verses, 'No Handycraft can with Our art compare For pots are made of What we Potters are', alluding to human origins in primaeval clay.
Medallion, (**650**), Staffordshire, height: 12.1cm, (4¾in), creamware. Profile portrait of Josiah Wedgwood based on one modelled by John Hackwood for the Wedgwood factory.
Plaque, (**654**), London, Doulton, diameter: 21.6cm, (8½in), terracotta. Self-portrait of George Tinworth, modelled in high relief. Incised around the rim, 'HE HATH PUT DOWN THE MIGHTY FROM THEIR SEATS. AND EXALTED THEM OF LOW DEGREE'. (Luke 1:52). The self-portrait must have been inspired by John Flaxman's famous terracotta self-portrait of 1778, similarly annotated, which Tinworth probably encountered as a student.[36]
Figure, (**652**), c.1870, Derby, Stevenson & Hancock, height: 20.3cm, (8in), soft-paste porcelain. Figure of a potter kicking his wheel as he throws his pot.

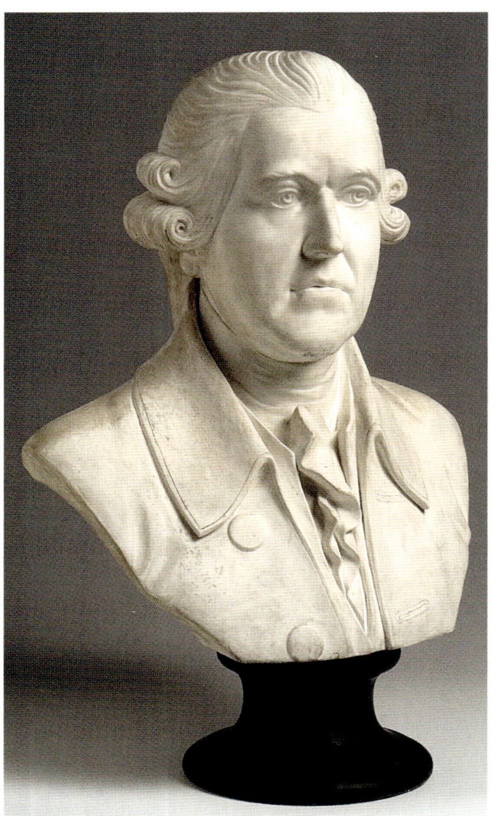

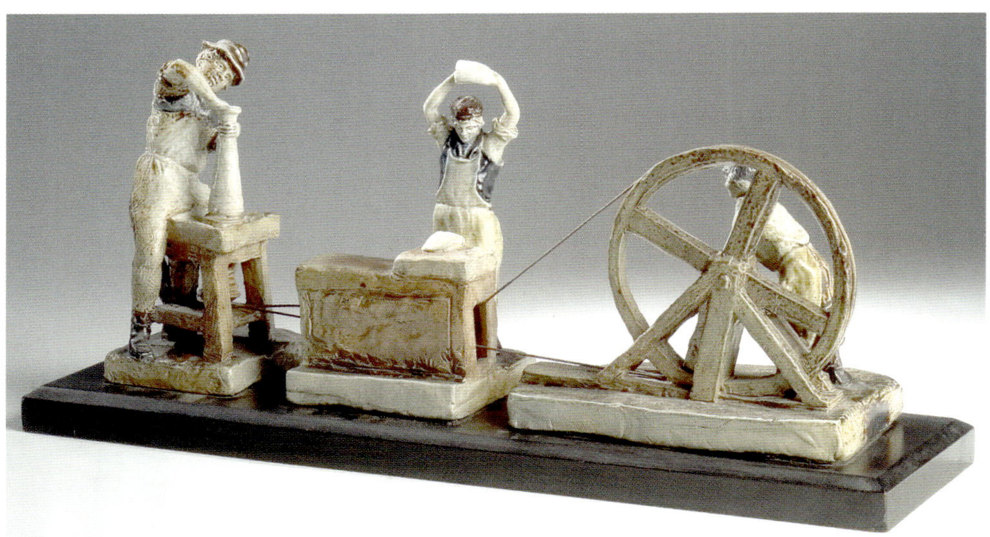

Figure Groups, (**653**), c.1880, Southall, Martin Brothers, height: 17.8cm, (7in), height: 17.8cm, (7in), height: 14cm, (5½in), coloured, salt-glazed stoneware. A three-part sculpture, (each piece signed by Robert Wallace Martin) makes up a complete demonstration of 'throwing' clay. The scene probably taken from an illustration, called 'The Thrower', published in 1877,[39] and from photographs taken of the Martin Brothers' own workshop. A relief plaque, illustrating the same subjects also identifies the wheelboy, who turns the potter's wheel and the benchboy at the centre, wedging the clay.

Bust, (**649**), c.1873, Mintons?, Toft, height: 53.4cm, (21in), soft-paste porcelain. Portrait bust of Josiah Wedgwood, based on the medallion in Stoke church by the sculptor, Charles Toft, (1839-1902). Incised beneath, 'C Toft'.

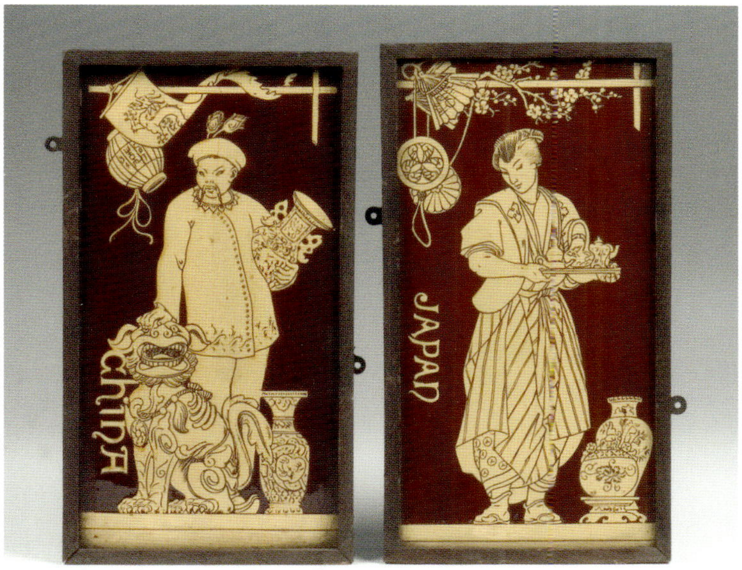

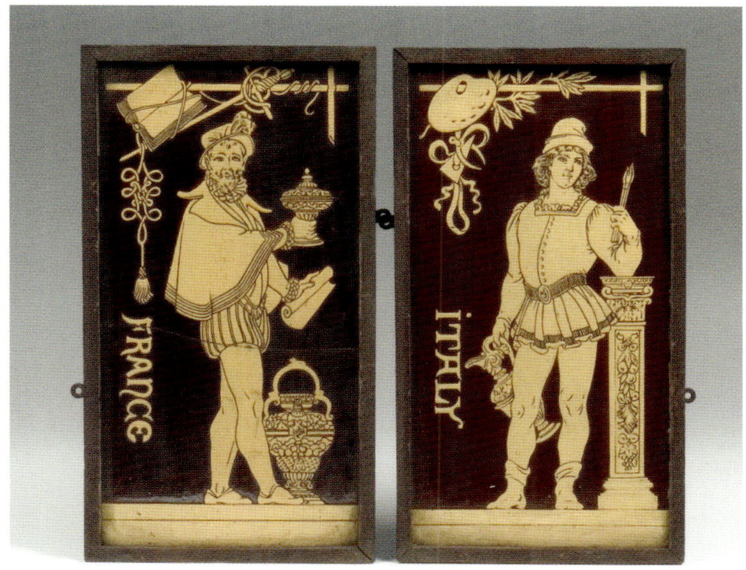

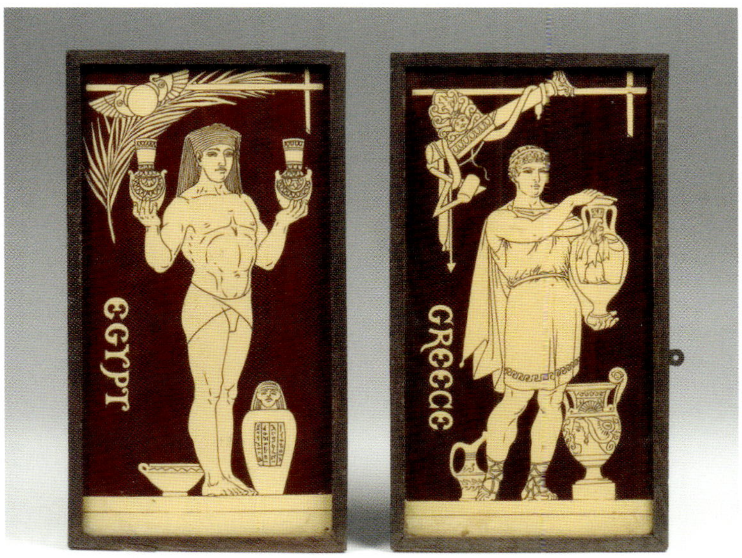

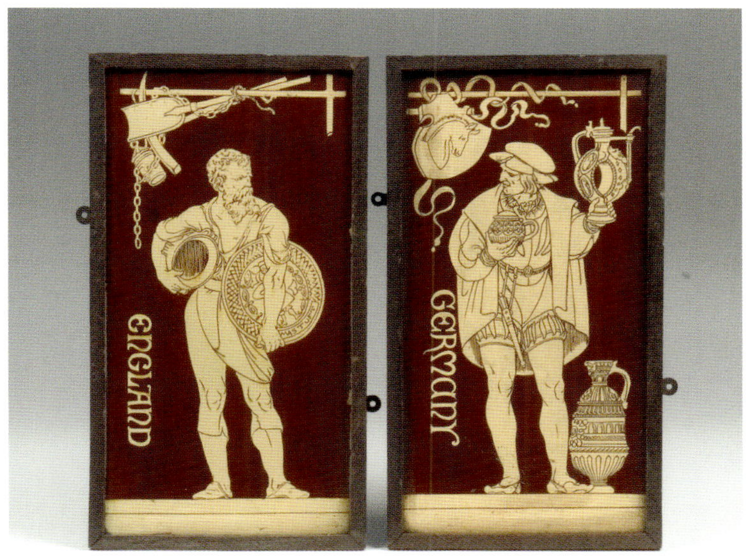

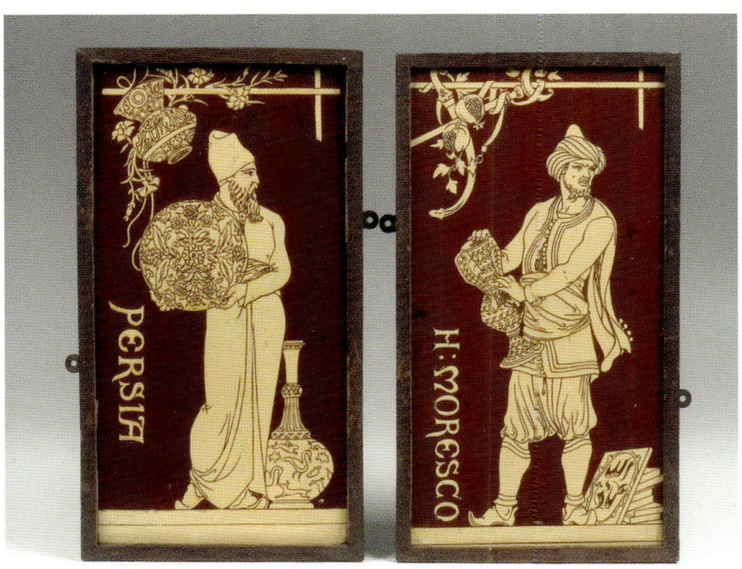

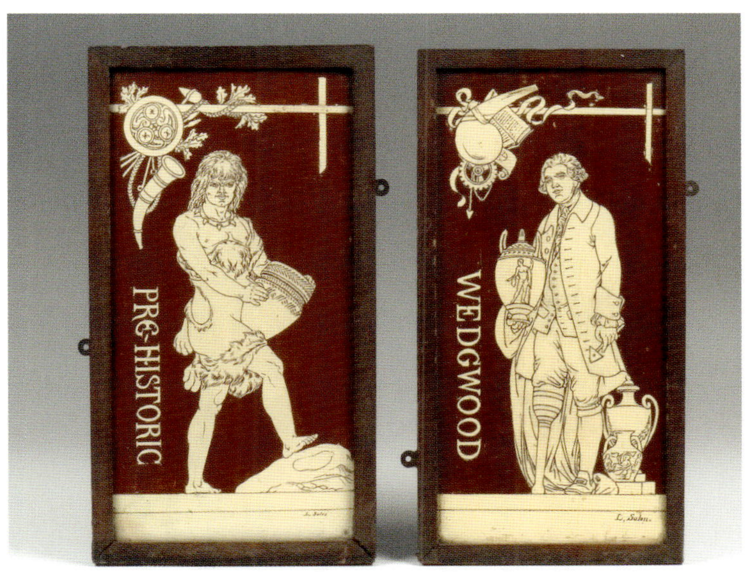

Tiles, c.1878, Staffordshire, Stoke-on-Trent, Mintons, **(683-691+693)** each height: 39.3cm, (15½in), **(692 + 694)** height: 42cm, (16½in), slip-decorated earthenware. Twelve tiles designed as a fireplace surround by Marc-Louis Solon, (1835-1913). They represent a global history of ceramic production from ancient China, Japan, and Persia, via Ancient Greece and Europe. Solon signed the first (**692**), (a cave-dweller) and the last, which depicts Josiah Wedgwood, with his wooden leg,[37] holding the famous 'First Day' vase and his copy of the Portland Vase at his feet (**694**). Solon showed the tiles at the Paris International Exhibition of 1878. In the Minton Archives is a document confirming that Henry Willett purchased the tiles of the caveman and Wedgwood for £20 in 1884.[38]

Clubs and Friendly Societies

The Beefsteak Club, also called the Sublime Society of Steaks, was founded around 1735 by Lord Peterborough and John Rich, manager of the Covent Garden theatre. This very exclusive dining club was limited to 24 members, many with literary and theatrical connections. Among the earliest were William Hogarth, David Garrick and John Wilkes. The Prince of Wales had to wait until 1785 for a vacancy. Members met at the theatre every Saturday from November to June, until it burned down in 1808. They wore uniform in Whig colours; blue coats and buff waistcoats, their buttons adorned with the gridiron symbol, and observed elaborate rituals. They saluted 'Beef and Liberty', and took turns to play officers with titles like 'Bishop', who dressed in full regalia, 'Recorder' and 'Boots', the newest member who had to wait upon the others.[40] The club was dissolved in 1867 but was relaunched and expanded from 1876.

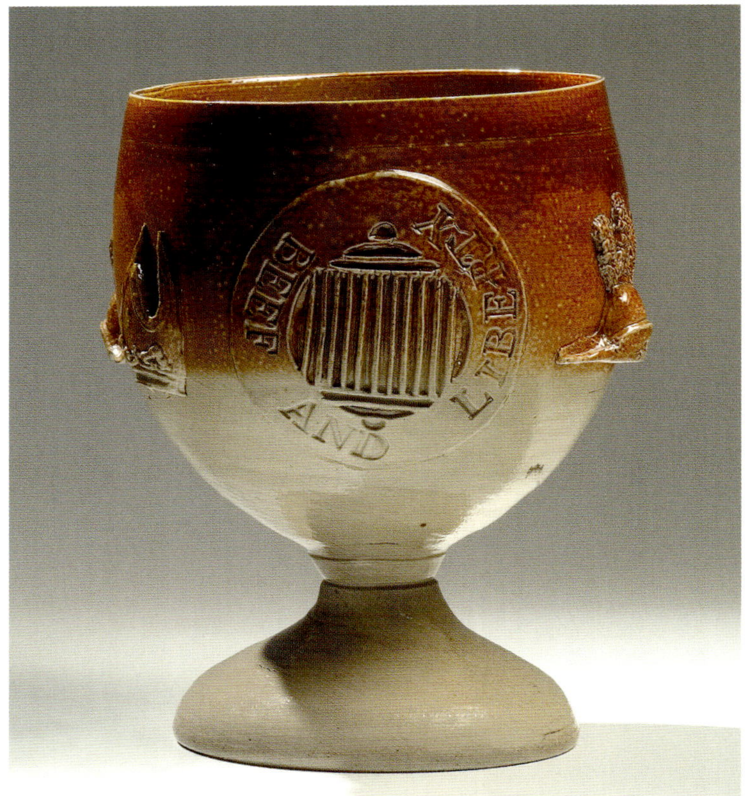

Goblet, (**575**), c.1810, London, Kishere's Mortlake Pottery, height: 17.8cm, (7in), saltglazed stoneware. Goblet embellished with medallion, impressed, 'BEEF AND LIBERTY', and a gridiron (symbolic of grilling). The sides applied with sprigged hats, including a bishop's mitre. Probably made as a special order for the Beefsteak Club.[41]

The Noble Order of Bucks

Another elite, convivial society was the Noble Order of Bucks. Founded in the 1730s, they traced their origins back to Nimrod, the Assyrian 'mighty hunter' of the Old Testament. By 1770 the best known of their 19 lodges, met at the Turk's Head tavern, Gerrard Street, Soho.[42] They aimed to promote, 'Fellowship, Freedom of Conversation, Innocent Mirth and every social Virtue' accompanied by prodigious consumption of wine! They had numerous badges, jewels and regalia and accessories designed incorporating their arms and symbols.

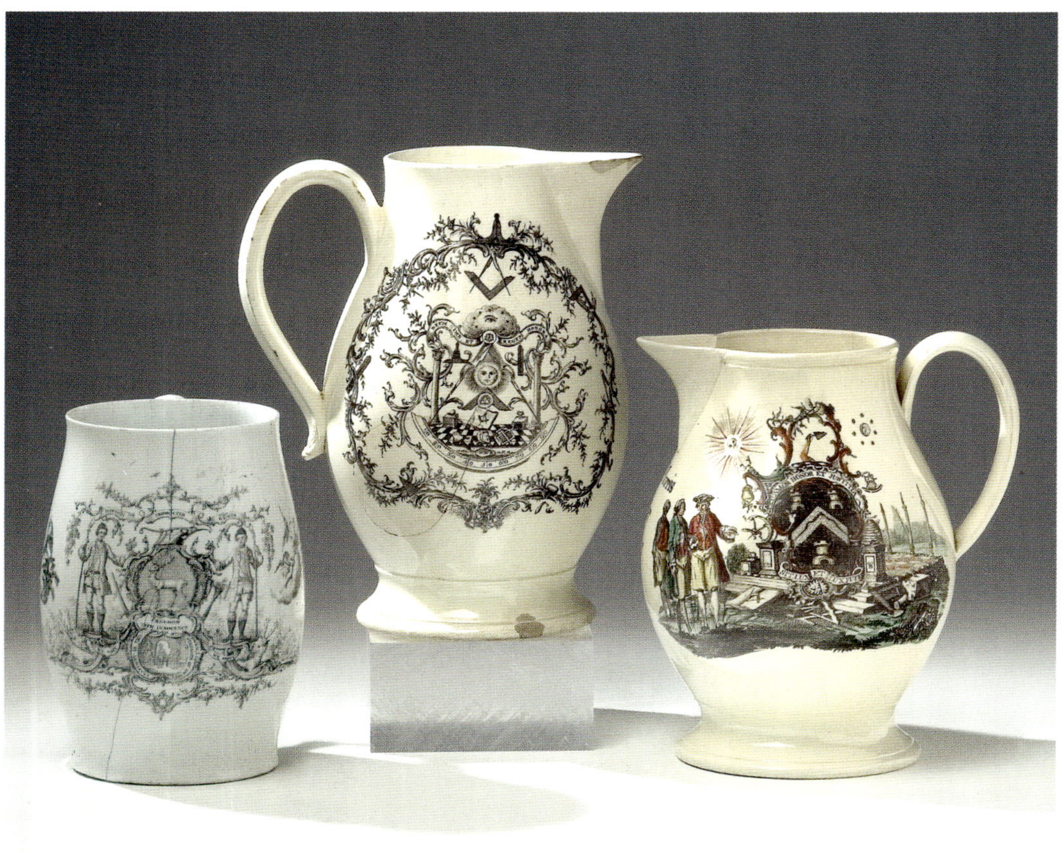

Mug, (**576**), c.1760, Staffordshire, Longton Hall, printed in Liverpool, height: 16.5cm, (6½in), printed, soft-paste porcelain. Printed with a complex coat of arms printed (and signed) by John Sadler. A shield, crested with a ploughshare and the motto, 'INDUSTRY PRODUCETH WEALTH', is emblazoned with the buck or stag above the tag, 'FREEDOM WITH INNOCENCE'. A tiny scene below shows figures enacting society rituals, inscribed, 'Unanimity is the / Strength of Society'. Two hunters or 'keepers' provide support.

Jug, (**578**), c.1790, Staffordshire, printed in Liverpool, height: 21.6cm, (8½in), printed creamware. Printed with many Masonic symbols, from tools and instruments directly related to building to the all-seeing eye of the Supreme Being.

Jug, (**579**), c.1796, Staffordshire, Wedgwood, height: 19.1cm, (7½in), creamware, printed and coloured. Masonic jug associated with East Sussex. Printed by William Greatbatch of Fenton, inscribed under the spout: 'To James Morris Master Builder, Lewes, Sussex'. Three men are shown in robes and aprons with symbols of Freemasonry. This print was designed by J. Ross, adapted around 1770 by Robert Hancock at Worcester and is often found on porcelain. In 1796, a James Morris leased a building in Lewes High Street so that the South Saxon Lodge could be installed at the Masonic Temple.

The Odd Fellows

The majority of the Friendly Societies were founded to be inclusive and supportive of large numbers of members. Unlike the Bucks, the Antigallicans, the Gregorians, and the Jerusalem Sols, (all now defunct), the Odd Fellows still flourishes as a benefit society today. Branches were set up in small towns where there were insufficient numbers of members of individual trade guilds to warrant separate associations. The earliest surviving lodge rules date from 1730 and refer to the Loyal Aristarcus Lodge in London. It met in the Oakley Arms in Southwark, the Globe Tavern in Hatton Garden or the Boar's Head in Smithfield.

The Freemasons

The best-known of the friendly societies, but the one with the most controversial reputation, largely for exclusivity and secrecy, is the Freemasons who derived from groups controlling the stonemasons' craft in the seventeenth century.[43] One of the first recorded Freemasons is Elias Ashmole, the antiquarian and herald, whose collections formed the basis of the Ashmolean Museum in Oxford. Organised Freemasonry was established in England on 24 June 1717 when four London lodges came together at the Goose & Gridiron Ale House, St Paul's Churchyard to formed a Grand Lodge. Initially the Grand Lodge was simply an annual feast for lodges in London but in 1721 John, Duke of Montagu, was elected Grand Master and thereafter the Grand Lodge met in 'quarterly communication'.

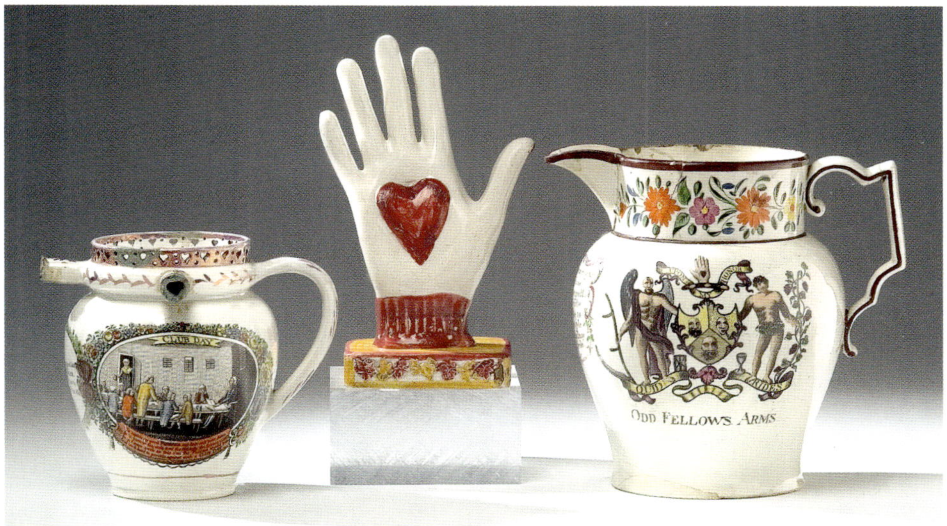

Puzzle jug, (**584**), c.1810, North East, height: 13.3cm, (5¼in), creamware, printed and coloured. Scenes inscribed, 'CLUB DAY', and 'FRIENDLY SOCIETY'S FEAST' with verses,

Come, come Brother Members both little and great,
Who in friendship partake of our annual treat
While happy and cheerful we sit here and sing
Each Tradesman and Labourer's blest as a King

Model, (**587**), c.1810, Staffordshire, height: 19.1cm, (7½in), enamelled pearlware. Model of the open hand with a red enamelled heart on the palm, denoting friendship and charity.

Jug, (**583**), c.1810, Staffordshire, height: 17.8cm, (7in), pearlware, printed and enamelled. Printed with the Odd Fellows' Arms. The shield is decorated with three masks, referring to those worn at initiation ceremonies, while Father Time and Bacchus act as supporters. The symbolic heart-in-hand is the crest ('What the hand gives, the heart proves') and beneath is the motto, 'QUID RIDES' (Why are you laughing?).

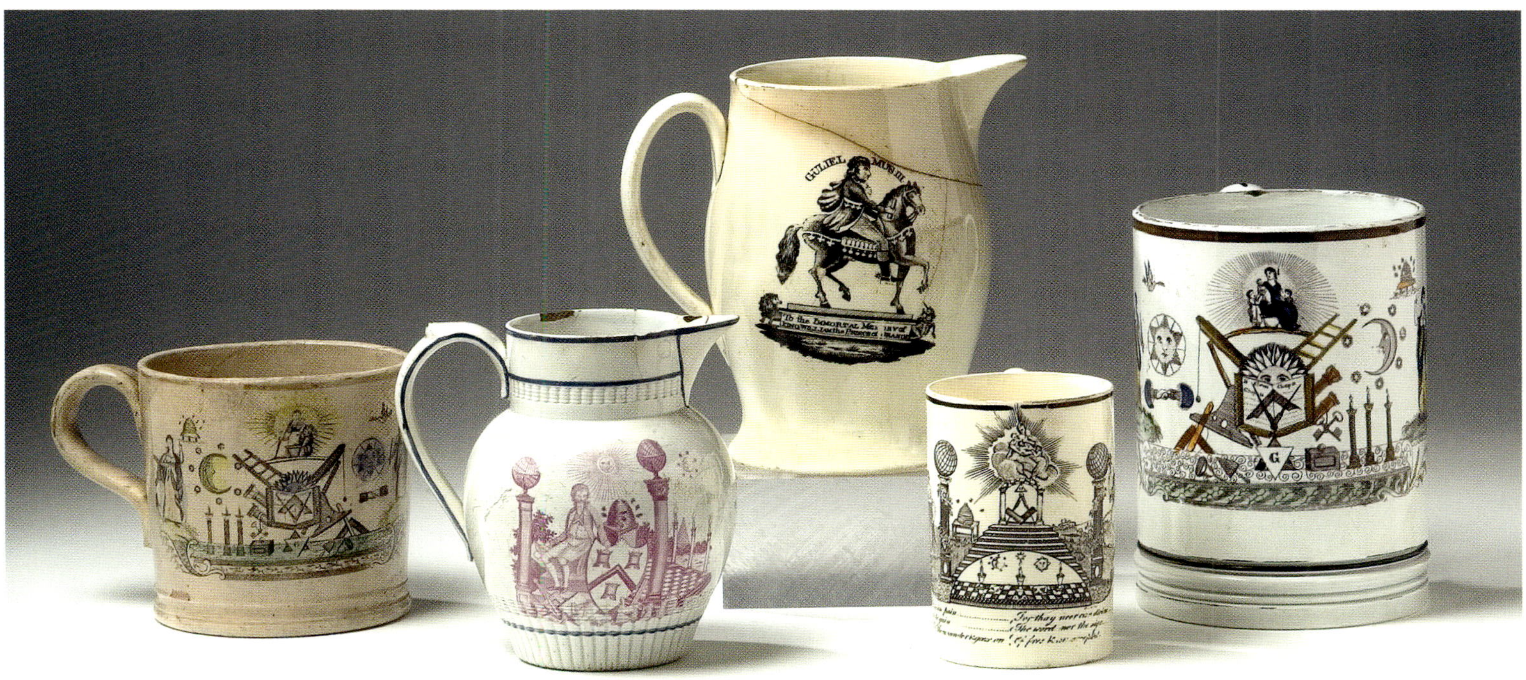

Mug, (**580**), c.1800, Staffordshire or North East, height: 15.3cm, (6in), drabware, printed and enamelled. Printed with Masonic symbols; tools and instruments directly related to building and stonemasonry, the sun and moon, the beehive of Industry, the all-seeing eye of the Supreme Being, the clasped hands of Friendship and a mother with children denoting Charity.

Jug, (**581**), c.1800, possibly Bristol, height: 12.7cm, (5in), puce-printed pearlware. Printed with Masonic symbols including a man wearing an apron, two large columns, the sun and moon and stonemasons' tools.

Jug, (**586**), c.1800, Staffordshire, height: 15.3cm, (6in), printed creamware. Printed with an equestrian monument inscribed, 'GUGLIEL/MUS III', William III. This was probably made for an Irish Orange Lodge.

Mug, (**582**), c.1800, Sunderland, Walter Cockburn,[44] height: 10.2cm, (4in), printed creamware. Printed with Masonic symbols; tools and instruments, two columns topped with globes, the beehive of Industry, the sun and moon and a mother with children denoting Charity.

Jug, (**R2454.18**), c.1800, North East, height: 9.7cm, (3¾in), creamware, printed and coloured. Printed with symbolic devices; tools and instruments, the sun and moon, the beehive of Industry and a mother with children denoting Charity.

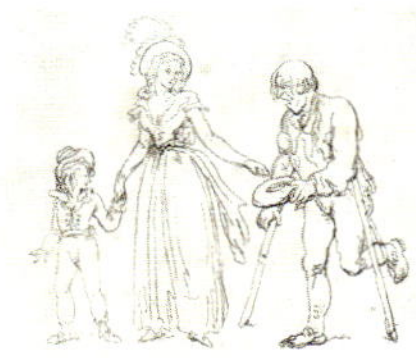

Chapter 9

PHILANTHROPY

The Campaign against Slavery

The notorious 'triangular trade' in human beings dominated the British economy during the eighteenth century and helped to build enormous private fortunes. From the ports of London, Bristol and Liverpool, arms, textiles and beads were exported to West Africa where they were exchanged for human cargo. Men, women and children were packed tightly into ships and despatched, in appalling conditions, to the West Indies. Around 20,000,000 Africans were transported in this way and up to 1,000,000 died in transit.

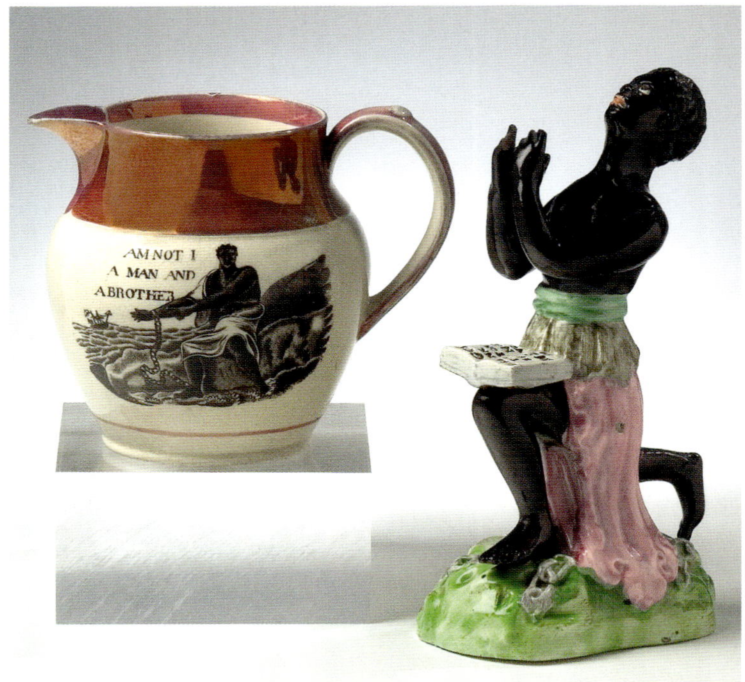

Jug, (**593**), c.1820, Staffordshire, height: 11.5cm, (4½in), pearlware, printed and lustred. Printed with a verse from *The Negro's Complaint* by William Cowper (published 1788) and an image of a slave, entitled, 'Am Not I a Man and a Brother' (misquoted from the motto of the Slave Emancipation Society), and The slave, sitting on a rock, was adapted from an illustration to the poem by Richard Westall, in an edition of 1817.[1] Abolitionists are known to have ordered copies printed, ' on the finest hot-pressed paper, and folded it up in a small, neat form, [and] gave it the title of 'A Subject for Conversation at the Tea-table'.[2]
Figure, (**589**), c.1835, Staffordshire, height 17.8cm, (7in), enamelled pearlware. Kneeling figure of a former slave, broken chains and manacles beside him. Open book on his raised knee impressed, 'BLESS GOD / THANK BRITTON [*sic*] / ME NO SLAVE'. Such figures were adapted from the famous jasperware relief medallion, designed by William Hackwood for Josiah Wedgwood, used by the Slave Emancipation Society from 1787.

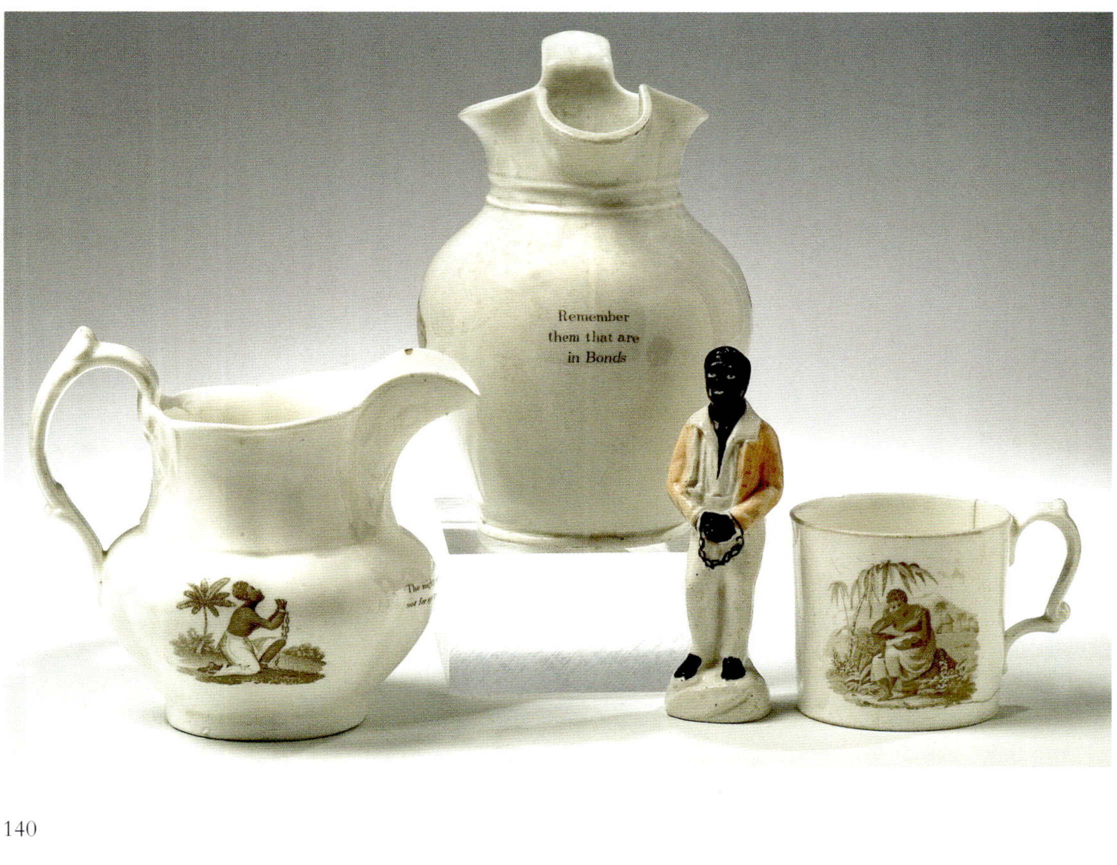

Clockwise:
Jug, (**594**), c.1830, Staffordshire, Stoke-on-Trent, Mintons, height: 17.8cm, (7in), sepia-printed bone china. Vignette of kneeling slave, inscribed 'This Book [the Bible] tell Man not to be cruel / Oh that Massa would read this Book'.
Jug, (**R2454.7**), c.1830, Staffordshire, height 14cm, (5½in), printed pearlware. Vignettes and, 'Remember / them that are / in Bonds'.
Figure, (**592**), c.1835, Staffordshire, Stoke-on-Trent, height 12.7cm, (5in), enamelled pearlware. Standing figure of a manacled slave, possibly made by the Dudson factory, (founded in 1830).[3] Probably intended to celebrate the abolition of slavery in the British islands of the Caribbean in 1833, although it was later called 'Uncle Tom in chains', in reference to *Uncle Tom's Cabin* (published in 1852).
Mug, (**595**), c.1820, Staffordshire, Stoke-on-Trent, Mintons, height 7.8cm, (3in), printed bone china. A black woman in distress, sits holding a sick or dead child.

Those who survived the notorious 'middle-passage' were sold as slaves and put to work on the plantations. Sugar products, spices, rum and tobacco were sent back to Europe to supply fashionable society with luxury goods, together with American cotton for clothing. It created great wealth for individual absentee plantation owners (such as William Beckford) and encouraged the expansion of trade and industry in the Midlands and north-west England, the heartlands of the Industrial Revolution.

Meanwhile the right to buy and sell human beings went largely unchallenged. The moral justification depended on a refusal to recognise black people (of African descent) as human beings. From about 1783 abolitionists investigated and began to publicise the inhumanity of slavery, using publications and mass-produced objects, such as printed pottery to advertise the cause. The campaign gathered momentum under the guidance of social reformers such as William Wilberforce. In addition public opinion was swayed by the shocking testimony of former slaves, such as Olaudah Equiano, who spoke in public of their ordeals. Slave memoirs were also published as books or tracts.

William Wilberforce (1759-1833)

Wilberforce founded the Church Missionary Society and in 1787 formed the Anti-Slavery Society. His influential campaign led eventually to the bill to abolish the slave trade in 1807. Despite his friendship with William Pitt, he remained politically independent. The slave trade was abolished in 1807 and, from 1834, slaves in British colonies were granted emancipation. Slavery continued in the United States for another 30 years.

Hannah More (1745-1833)

More was born in Bristol the fourth daughter of a schoolmaster. She was well educated at her older sister's school and taught there before moving to London in 1773, hoping to write for the theatre. She cultivated the patronage of intellectuals such as Dr Johnson, Horace Walpole and David Garrick, the great actor-manager, and his wife Eva. Garrick arranged to stage More's tragedy, *Percy,* at Covent Garden in 1777; after which he claimed there was, 'not a dry Eye in the House'. The staging of *The Fatal Falsehood* in 1779, however, was a failure and a rival playwright accused More of plagiarism.

She fled fashionable society for evangelical Christianity and campaigned against slavery alongside William Wilberforce. During the 1790s, she and her sister Martha invested in a network of Sunday schools in the Cheddar area. Between 1795 and 1798. More wrote fifty *Cheap Repository Tracts*, 'to promote good morals among the poor'. Published monthly they sold in millions. In addition, she wrote *Strictures on the Modern System of Female Education* (1799) and her only novel, *Coelebs in Search of a Wife* (1809) which sold particularly well in the United States. At her death Hannah More left £30,000, an unprecedented sum for a woman writer.

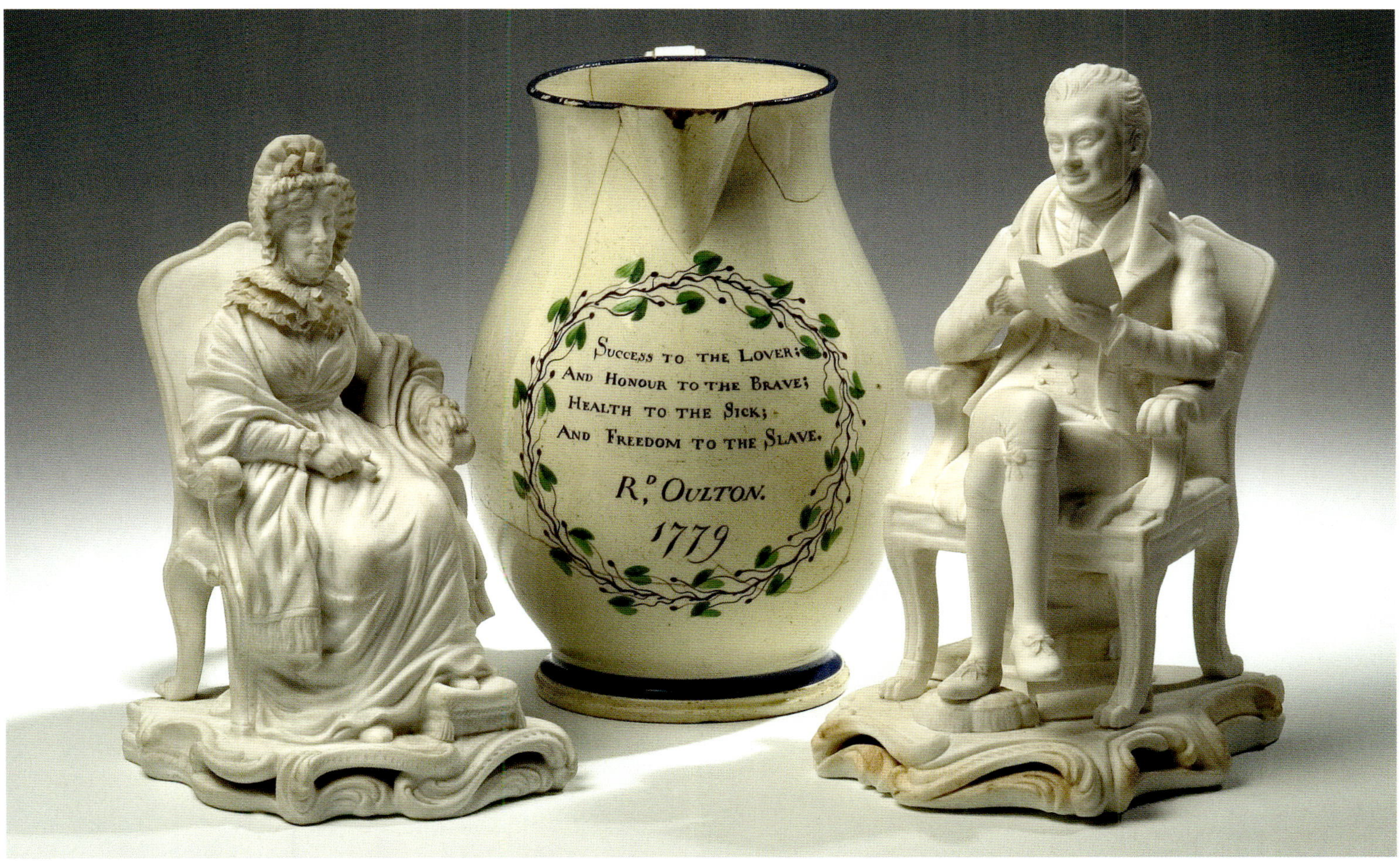

Figure, (**955**), c.1835, Staffordshire, Stoke-on-Trent, Mintons,[4] height 15.8cm, (6¼in), biscuit porcelain. Portrait of Hannah More, modelled soon after her death, by George Cocker. Based on a painted portrait of 1822 by H.W. Pickersgill.
Jug, (**588**), 1779, Staffordshire, height 16.5cm, (6½in), enamelled pearlware. Painted with a verse,

Success to the Lover; / And Honour to the Brave /
Health to the Sick; / And Freedom to the Slave.

and inscribed and dated for Richard Oulton, 1779. Despite the early date for such sentiments, during the American War of Independence in the late 1770s, the promise was made to slaves that if they defected to the British side they would be freed. Oulton remains unidentified but may be related to generations of brewers who became mayors of Chester in the seventeenth century or possibly to a Quaker family.
Figure, (**591**), c.1835, Staffordshire, Stoke-on-Trent, Mintons, height 19.7cm, (7¾in), biscuit porcelain. William Wilberforce, modelled in biscuit porcelain is based on a watercolour portrait of 1832-33, by George Richmond.[5]

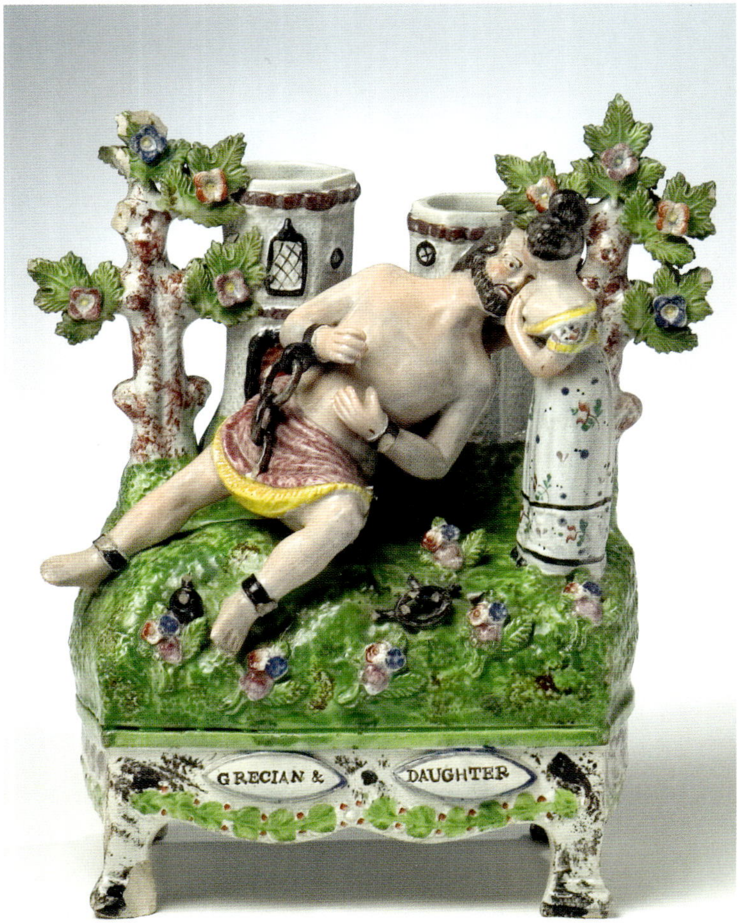

Figure Group, (**598**), c.1830, Staffordshire, height 25.4cm, (10in), enamelled pearlware. Table-based, spill vase depicts the large prone figure of a man, wearing a loincloth, manacles and leg irons, being breast fed by a small standing figure of a woman, fashionably dressed .The subject is inscribed on the base, 'GRECIAN & DAUGHTER', though it is better known as 'Roman Charity'. The original story concerned Cimon and his devoted daughter Pero, according to Valerius Maximus's *Memorable Acts and Sayings of the Ancient Romans.* A painting by Rubens, engraved by John Smith c.1700, may have been the inspiration for one of Mrs Salmon's famous waxworks. Her premises, established in Fleet Street in 1711, described 'Hermonia's father had offended the Emperor and was sentenced to be starved to death but was preserved by sucking his daughter's Breast.'

James Wood (1756-1836)

Jemmy Wood ran a family drapery business, (founded in 1716 by his grandfather) and the Gloucester Old Bank, one of the earliest private banks in England. He amassed great wealth, becoming one of the richest commoners in England but is chiefly remembered for his meanness. He served as Sheriff of Gloucester in 1811 and 1813 but never stood for mayor because of the expense involved. He dressed shabbily and was often mistaken for a vagrant. When he died his estate was valued at £900,000 and his will was disputed for five years – potential beneficiaries included Gloucester City Corporation.

Richard Reynolds (1735-1816)

Reynolds, a Quaker, married the daughter of ironmaster Abraham Darby and was a partner at his ironworks at Coalbrookdale. After Darby's death he pioneered new ways of producing the iron cylinders for the early Newcomen steam engines. Reynolds was involved with his friend Josiah Wedgwood on numerous public projects and donated annual sums of between £10,000 and £20,000 to charities. After Reynolds' death, James Montgomery wrote, 'Verses to the Memory of the late Richard Reynolds of Bristol' (published 1816).

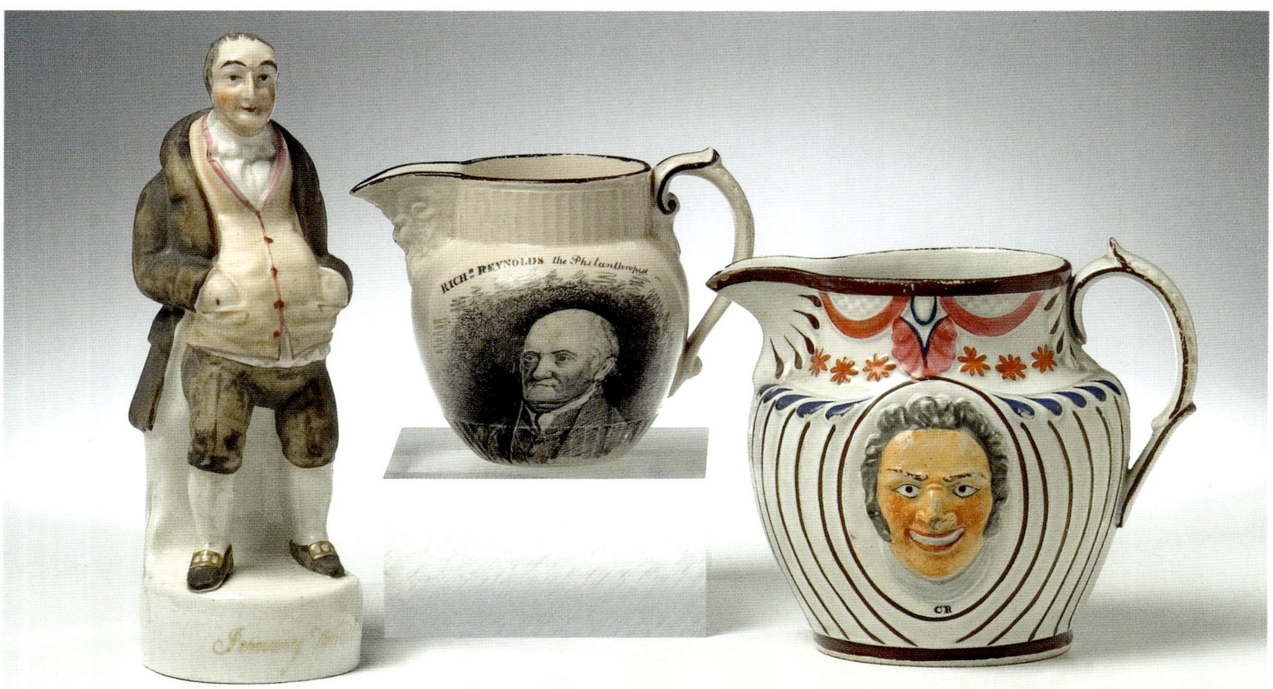

Figure, (**601**), c.1850, Staffordshire, height 20.3cm, (8in), enamelled earthenware. Humorous figure with large belly, inscribed 'Jemmy Wood'. 'Five years of wrangling over his will aroused national interest and inspired such figures to be made.
Jug, (**597**), c.1820, Staffordshire, height 12.1cm, (4¾in), printed creamware. Jug moulded with satyr-mask spout, portrays and commemorates the noted iron manufacturer and philanthropist, 'RICHD REYNOLDS the Philanthropist'. Portrait probably taken from engraving published 1817.[6] On the reverse are lines from Mongomery's eulogy, published 1816,
'widows' tears in sad bereavement, fall, / And foundling voices on their father call'
Jug, (**623**), c.1830, Staffordshire, height 14cm, (5½in), enamelled pearlware. Relief-moulded jug, contrasting the smiling face of a creditor, impressed 'CR', with the distress of the debtor, impressed 'DR'.

Jug, (**1559**), c.1800, Staffordshire, height: 11.5cm, (4½in), pearlware, red-printed and coloured. Inscription, 'May merit with / Regard be rais'd / Rewarded, honour'd / And be praised'.
Plate, (**1542**), c.1810, Staffordshire, diameter: 18.4cm, (7¼in), pearlware, printed and coloured. Alphabet plate inscribed, 'Those who dainties love shall beggers prove / Pride is as loud a begger as Want', shows a little girl giving alms to a woman and her child. Even young children were encouraged to give to the poor and needy.
Mug, (**599**), c.1800, North East, diameter: 5.7cm, (2¼in), earthenware, red-printed and yellow-glazed. A small girl makes a donation to an old man with a stick, begging alms.

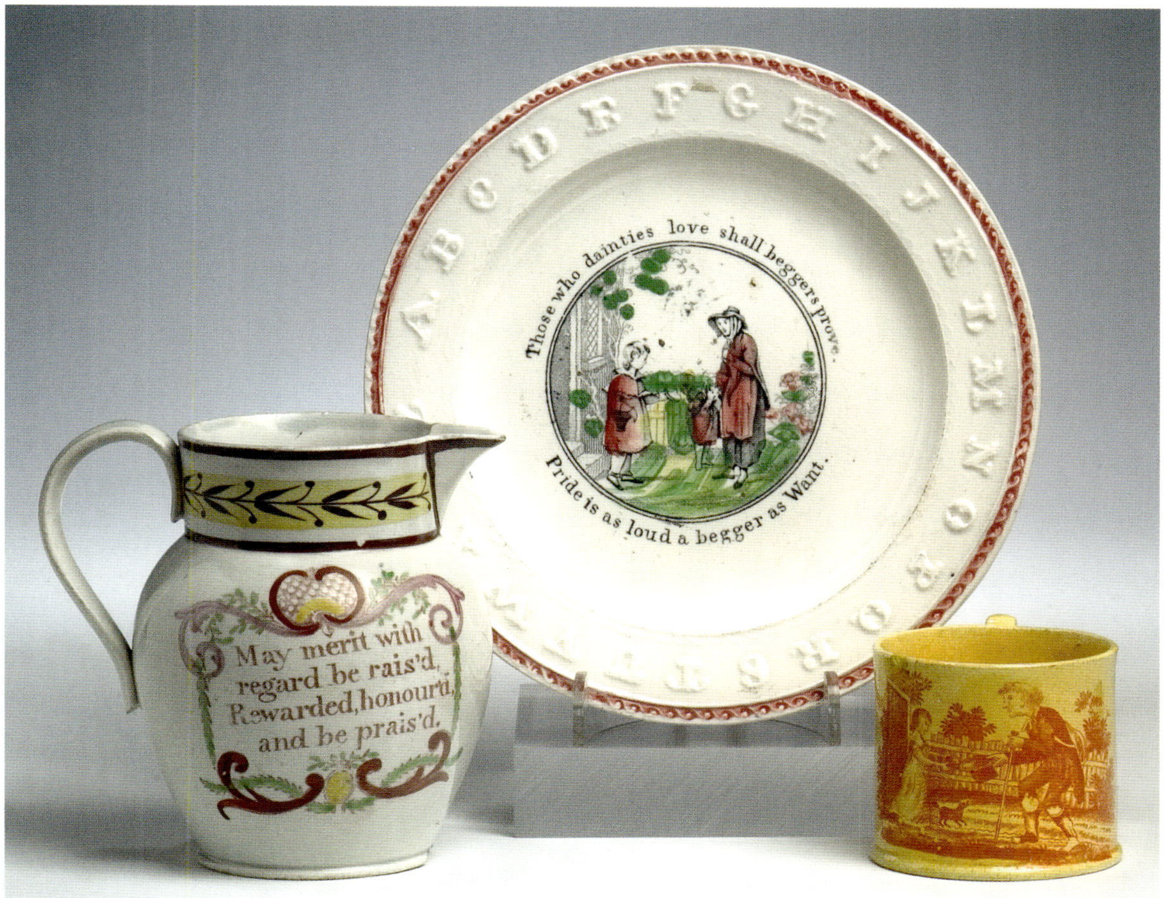

Pair of Figures, (**600 & A**), c.1870, Germany, height 17cm, (6¾in), height 20.3cm, (8in), coloured majolica. They represent a rich man in a fur-collared coat, searching his pocket for coins to give an emaciated pauper. Impressed on base: W&R, probably for Wittman & Roth, importers.
Figure Group, (**602**), c.1830, Staffordshire, height 25.4cm, (10in), enamelled pearlware. Group inscribed, 'Widow & Orphans' depicts a large female figure with two tiny children. Willett's group is missing one child (replaced by a mound of clay frit), who carries a bundle of twigs on his head as the homeless family is shown living rough.

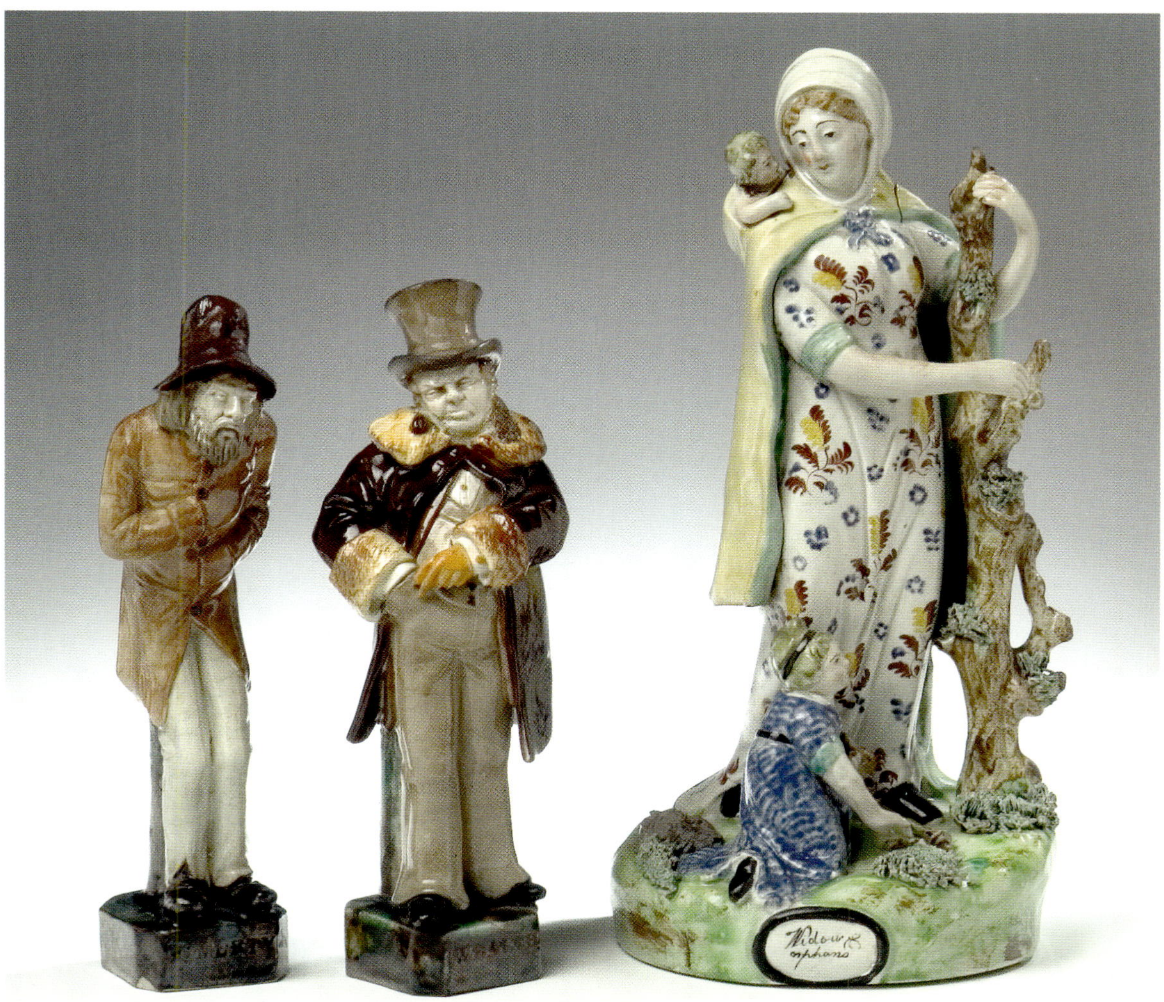

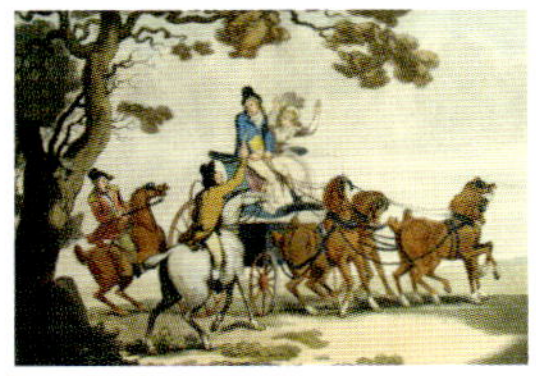

Chapter 10

CRIME

The public appetite in the eighteenth and nineteenth centuries for news of scandal, violent crime and scurrilous court cases was at least as great as it is today. Hundreds of anonymous printing presses produced cheap books, broadsheets and satirical images on topical issues. Libellous allegations, court reports and sensational stories were disseminated through such prints or 'penny dreadfuls' in the Victorian era.

A few of the most dramatic events were fictionalised and presented on stage. John Thurtell's story was dramatised as *The Gamblers* in 1824, even before his trial. The melodrama, *The Red Barn*, presented in 1830, re-enacted the murder of Maria Marten. Dick Turpin, the notorious horse thief, highwayman and murderer was hanged in 1739. *Rookwood*, the novel and stage play of 1834, a highly romanticised version of his life as a latter-day Robin Hood, relaunched his reputation as an anti-hero and revitalised his memory. Such propaganda led to a demand for souvenirs of the most lurid and controversial incidents, which the potteries were quick to supply.

Public interest in crime and criminal trials reached a peak during periods marked by a dearth of other newsworthy events such as patriotic wars or constitutional crises. The populace maintained a healthy streak of cynicism towards crime in public life and often supported the accused in their struggle against authority. An early case concerned the alleged abduction of the young housemaid Elizabeth Canning, by the gipsy woman, Mary Squires, and the brothel keeper, Susannah Wells. Controversy raged at all levels of society over the innocence or guilt of the parties involved, and, in addition to the pottery plaques made in Staffordshire, porcelain mugs with their likenesses were ordered from China.

The length of time involved in turning round an order to China indicates that interest in a particular case long outlived the actual event and was fuelled by wider issues, such as politics and religion. John Bellingham, who assassinated the Prime Minister, Spencer Perceval, in 1812 and was hanged within a week of the event, might not have excited much interest on his own account if he had not been a Catholic, a focus for discontent among the oppressed minority. Many more ceramic vessels were decorated with his portrait than that of the unfortunate Perceval. The latest of the cases represented in the group, the protracted Tichborne trials for fraud and impersonation, set the members of an ancient landed Catholic family against a working-class Anglican underdog and, once again, controversy raged.

The passion for souvenirs of hangings is a ghoulish subject. Officially, the removal of hanged corpses on behalf of surgeons was the only legal method of obtaining bodies for dissection. Supporters of Dick Turpin secretly disinterred his corpse at night to save it from this fate. John Thurtell was less fortunate; visitors queued for hours at St Bartholomew's Hospital in 1824 to see his body as it was 'anatomised'. Eventually his skull sat beside that of John Bellingham on a hospital shelf, after undergoing intensive phrenological observation.

Most gruesome of all was the fate of William Corder, who murdered Maria Marten. He was hanged at Bury St Edmunds in 1828 before a capacity crowd of 20,000. Published accounts of the trial sold out and during his execution, the hangman was besieged with offers of one guinea per inch of rope by souvenir hunters. The dissection was carried out at the Shirehall, while 5,000 waited to view the body. Messrs Miozz of Cambridge and Child of Bungay made casts of Corder's head and hands, now preserved at Moyse's Hall Museum in Bury, together with a unique account of the trial bound in his skin. His skeleton was still being used for instruction in anatomy at Bury Hospital in the 1940s.

The popular press thrived on producing souvenir editions of grisly crimes and executions. In 1849 James Catnach's London press sold over 2.5 million cheap broadside prints of the executions of the murderers James Rush in Norwich and George and Maria Manning in Southwark.[1] Throughout the Victorian period flat-back pottery figures of famous murderers proliferated. James Rush and his mistress, Emily Sandford, were commemorated in this way, together with Mr and Mrs O'Brian, Palmer the Poisoner and many others. Rush can be seen amongst a host of celebrated murderers at Madame Tussaud's display of waxworks in one of Dicky Doyle's illustrations for *Punch*.[2]

The Abduction of Elizabeth Canning

Canning, an eighteen-year-old London maidservant, claimed to have been abducted on New Year's Day, 1753 and forced into prostitution at the brothel run by 'Mother Wells' in Enfield. Canning alleged that Mary Squires, an elderly gipsy, had imprisoned her but that, after a month in captivity she had escaped and returned to her mother's house in the City. Her case was at first upheld by Henry Fielding, the Middlesex magistrate and novelist. Squires and Wells were tried at the Old Bailey and Squires was sentenced to death for stealing Canning's stays (corset). Squires was saved by the influential Sir Crisp Gascoyne, former Lord Mayor of London, who produced witnesses to confirm that Squires was in Abbotsbury, Dorset when the alleged abduction took place. She was granted a free pardon. The London mob, who regarded Canning as a plucky heroine for defending her honour, were incensed and there were violent clashes between the 'Canaanites' (for Canning) and the 'Egyptians' (who supported the gipsy Squires). Elizabeth Canning was tried in 1754, convicted of perjury and transported to America.

Numerous prints were issued in connection with this sensational story and several ceramic souvenirs were produced, including Chinese porcelain mugs and dishes bearing portraits of both women, some accompanied by the following couplet, confirming the case's popular appeal: 'One day for Liberty the Briton fires – the next he flames for Canning or for Squires'.[3] The image on the Willett plaque is taken from a print by Benjamin Cole, showing both women, published in the

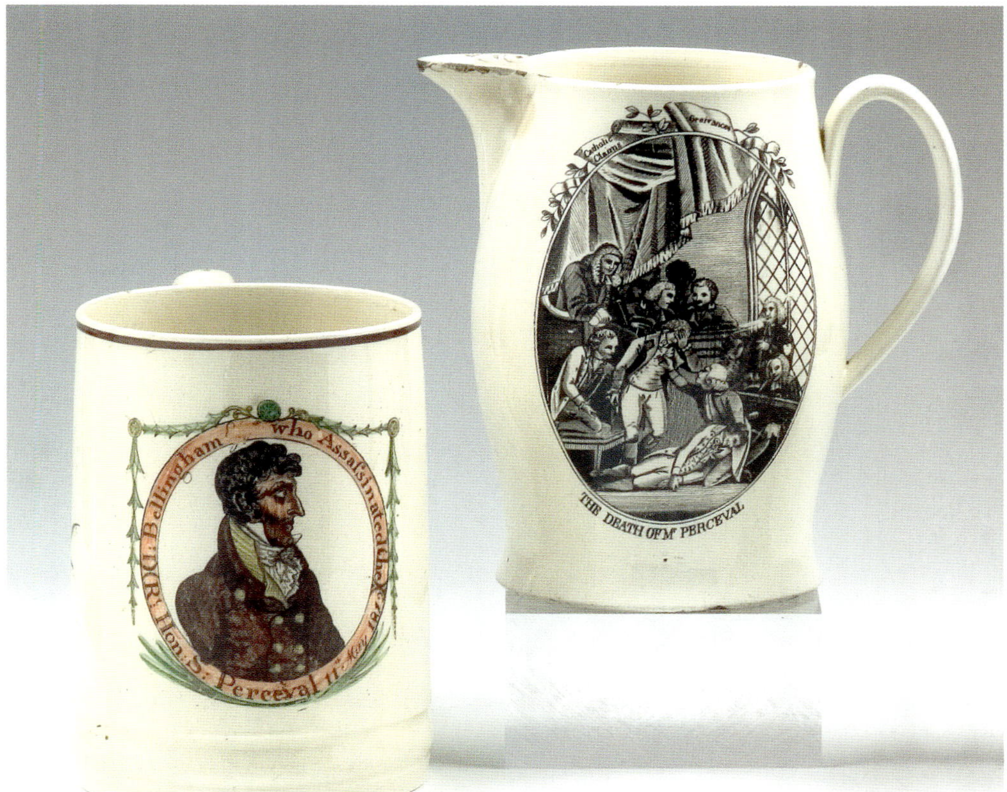

Mug, (**606**), 1812, Liverpool, height: 15.3cm, (6in), creamware, printed and coloured. Profile portrait inscribed 'I: Bellingham Esq. Who Assafsinated the / Rt Hon: S: Perceval 11th May 1812'. The portrait bears out the Rev. Croly's description of him. 'He was forty-two years of age, of a pale, intelligent countenance, and with the look of a gentleman … [He] died, frigid and fearless, a reasoning madman.'[4] The image is based on the portrait of Bellingham, etched by Denis Dighton at the Sessions House of the Old Bailey on 16 May. **Jug**, (**605**), 1812, Staffordshire, height: 17.2cm, (6¾in), printed creamware. 'The death of Mr Perceval', shows Perceval falling before his parliamentary colleagues in the House of Commons. Scrolls above inscribed; 'Catholic Claims' and 'Grievances', referring to the petitions for Catholic emancipation recently presented to the House. On the reverse of the jug is the 'Odd Fellows Arms'. The print sources are unknown.[5]

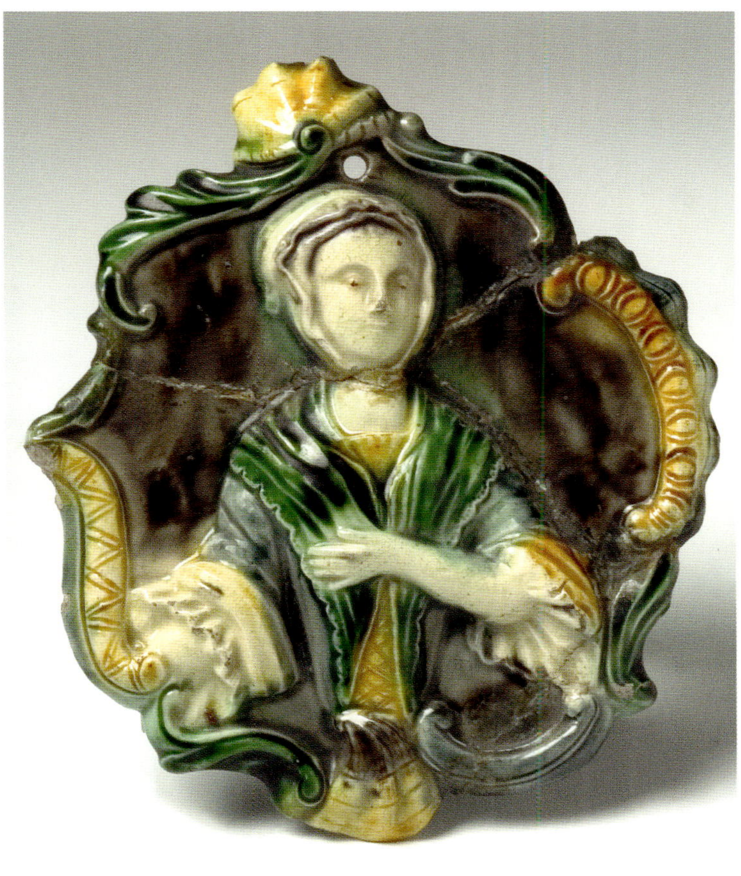

Plaque, (**603**), 1755-60, Staffordshire, height: 16.5cm, (6½in), earthenware, lead glazed and oxide-coloured. A half-length, female figure, moulded in low relief framed by asymmetrical scrolls. Willett thought the figure was Sarah Malcolm, a laundress executed in 1733 for the murder of three people in the Temple Chambers in London. The image was thought to be loosely based on an engraved portrait by William Hogarth.[9] In 1972 Bernard Watney correctly identified the likeness as that of Elizabeth Canning.

London Magazine of 1754. A companion plaque exists featuring a similar relief portrait of Mary Squires.[6] They were made either in Staffordshire or (given the possible link with its director, Nicholas Crisp) at the Indio Pottery at Bovey Tracey in Devon.

The Assassination of Spencer Perceval

The assassination of the Prime Minister, Spencer Perceval, caused shock countrywide. His assailant was John Bellingham, a Liverpool-born broker, who was imprisoned in northern Russia for five years for bankruptcy, after his business in Archangel had failed in 1804. He applied unsuccessfully to his insurers at Lloyds Coffee House in London and to the British Ambassador in St Petersburg, who was powerless to help. After his release, already deranged, he pursued the Ambassador, who was recalled to Britain, determined to shoot him. In London his letters to the Prince Regent and to the Prime Minister went unanswered so he decided to shoot the first minister he encountered.

On 25 April 1812 he had a tailor of Greys Inn Road sew a nine-inch breast pocket inside a dark overcoat, in which to conceal a pistol. On Monday 11 May he left his lodgings in King Street, St James's and made for the Palace of Westminster. There he waited for the Prime Minister, Spencer Perceval, who arrived at 5.15 p.m. to attend a committee. Bellingham shot him dead in the lobby of the House of Commons. Perceval 'uttered but the words "I'm murdered", tottered forwards a few steps and fell into the arms of some persons who had rushed to his assistance'.[7] Confident of vindication, Bellingham immediately gave himself up.

Only four days later, on 15 May, Bellingham was tried at the Old Bailey, and was condemned to death by Lord Mansfield, after a plea of insanity was quashed. The government was seriously shaken and wasted no time in having Bellingham hanged before a large crowd at Newgate Prison on 18 May.[8] After his execution, he became a focus for discontent among members of the oppressed Catholic minority.

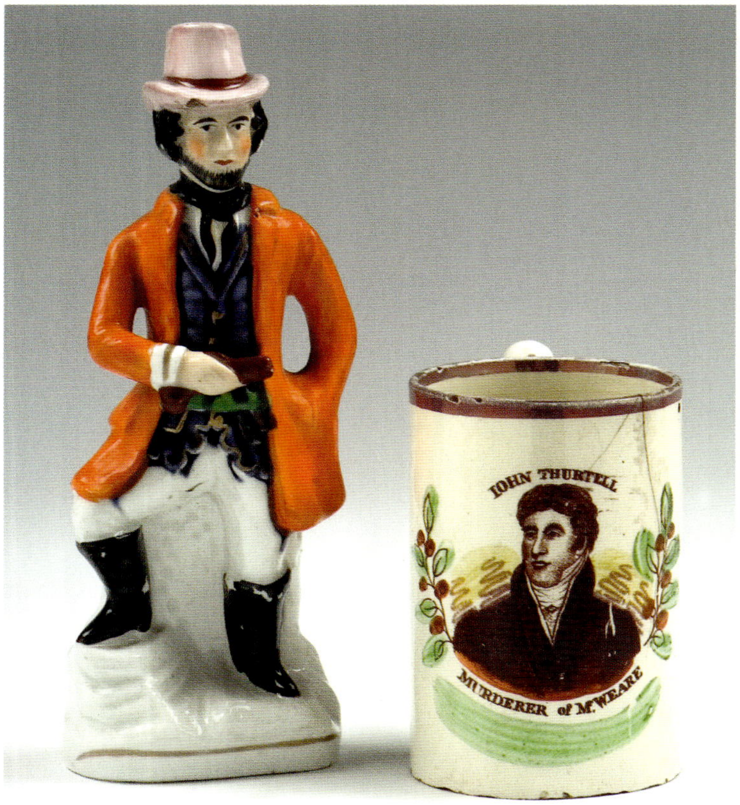

Figure, (**614**), c.1850, Staffordshire, height: 14cm, (5½in), enamelled earthenware. Figure of a highwayman, brandishing a pistol.
Mug, (**607**), c.1824, Staffordshire, height: 10.2cm, (4in), creamware, brown-printed and coloured. Portrait inscribed, 'John Thurtell murderer of Mr. Weare'. The print source is unknown.

John Thurtell, the 'Gigman'

Thurtell, from a respectable Norwich family, was a former lieutenant in the Royal Marines and a keen amateur boxer. He was also a bankrupt manufacturer of bombazine fabric and a failed publican. His financial situation worsened as he became addicted to gambling. Cheated of £300 by the former waiter and professional card sharp, William Weare, he planned his revenge. On 24 October 1823, on the pretext of a game-shooting expedition, he drove his victim in a gig to a country cottage owned by William Probert. Thurtell and an accomplice then murdered Weare at Gill's Hill, near Elstree.[10]

A melodrama, *The Gamblers*, was staged (until suppressed), before the trial took place in January 1824. It featured the very horse and gig used by Thurtell. Thurtell was dignified throughout his trial but was condemned to be hanged outside Hertford gaol the day after sentencing. The case had widespread press coverage and caught the public imagination. Thurtell was seen to have been ruined by evil acquaintance, pugilism and gambling. Following dissection before a large crowd at St Bartholomew's Hospital, a cast of his head was made for phrenological study while other parts of his corpse disappeared. Writing in 1836, Charles Dickens described him as, 'one of the murderers best remembered in England'.[11] The case inspired a popular rhyme,

They cut his throat from ear to ear, His head they battered in.
His name was Mr William Weare / Wot lived in Lyons Inn.

The Red Barn Murder

Maria Marten was murdered by her former lover, William Corder. Maria, the daughter of Thomas Marten, mole-catcher, from Polstead in Suffolk, was already a single mother when, in 1825, she became involved with William Corder. He was the younger son of a local farming family and a noted wastrel and womaniser. After Maria had borne his child, William suggested that she could be arrested for having illegitimate children, and she agreed to flee to Ipswich. They arranged to meet at the Red Barn on 13 May 1827 but Maria was never seen again. William went to London, married a respectable schoolmistress and began a new life.

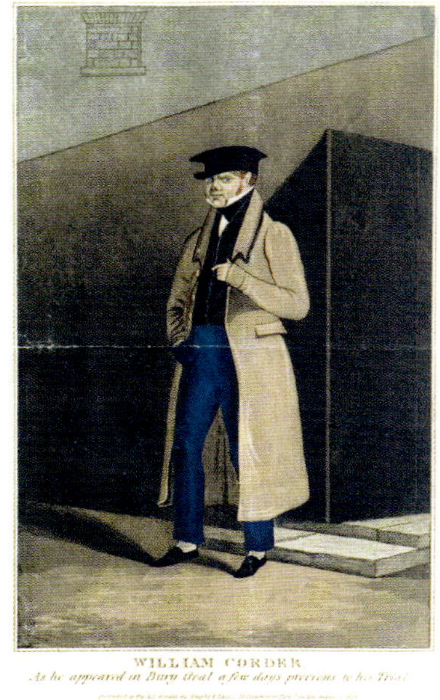

Print, (610), 1828, London, published 1 August 1828 by Knight & Lacey, hand-coloured aquatint, plate size: 21cm, (8¼in). Portrait of the murderer, inscribed; 'WILLIAM CORDER / As he appeared in Bury Gaol a few days previous to his trial'.

On 19 April 1828, prompted by a dream of his wife Anne, Thomas Marten dug up the floor of the Red Barn and discovered his daughter's body in a shallow grave. Corder was eventually tracked down to Brentford, arrested and held at Bury gaol. That summer up to 200,000 visitors tore the barn apart in a ghoulish quest for relics. The Rev. John Skinner noted that 'a dilapidation of the premises is still going on to such an extent that a person is paid to watch them.'[12] Corder was tried at Bury St Edmunds, found guilty and hanged outside Bury gaol on 11 August before a capacity crowd who clamoured for souvenirs. The Willett Collection includes a coloured print of Corder looking defiant, 'as he appeared in Bury Gaol a few days previous to his Trial'. The murder was presented in contemporary peepshow productions and published in broadsheets and 'penny dreadfuls'.[13] *The Red Farm, or The Well of St Mary*, (adapted from the French by W.T. Moncrieff) was presented at Sadlers Wells in 1842.[14] A film, *Maria Marten, or The Murder at the Red Barn* was made by MGM in 1935 and a melodrama by Brian J. Burton, *The Murder of Maria Marten, or, The Red Barn* published in 1964.[15]

William Corder's corpse was put on public display for a day before being removed for dissection. Most of his skin was sold in small sections as souvenirs to members of the public, except for his scalp, and a transcript of the trial was bound in his tanned hide, which remain at Moyse's Hall Museum, Bury St Edmunds. His skeleton continued to be used until the mid-twentieth century for anatomy lessons at the Royal College of Surgeons in London. In 2004 Corder's descendants arranged for some of these remains to be released for a private cremation and afterwards scattered his ashes at Polstead.[16]

The Rush Murders

James Rush, the illegitimate son of an affluent farmer, rented Stanfield Hall and mortgaged Potash Farm in Norfolk from the Jermy family. In 1842 he was widowed and hired Emily Sandford, who became his mistress, as governess to his nine children. By 1844 he was £5,000 in arrears on payments to the Jermys and in 1847 he was evicted from Stanfield Hall and the Jermys moved in. After supper on 28 November 1848 he left Potash Farm with his shotgun, ostensibly looking for poachers. He went straight to Stanfield Hall and shot dead Isaac Jermy and his son and wounded Mrs Jermy and their maid. Wooden models of the two buildings, now preserved at the Ancient House Museum in Thetford, were used in evidence during the trial in Norwich, which lasted six days. Rush was hanged from the bridge over the moat at Norwich Castle on 21 April 1849, before an enormous crowd.[17] Such was the celebrity of the case that a life-size figure was modelled of Rush and exhibited at Madame Tussaud's waxworks.[18]

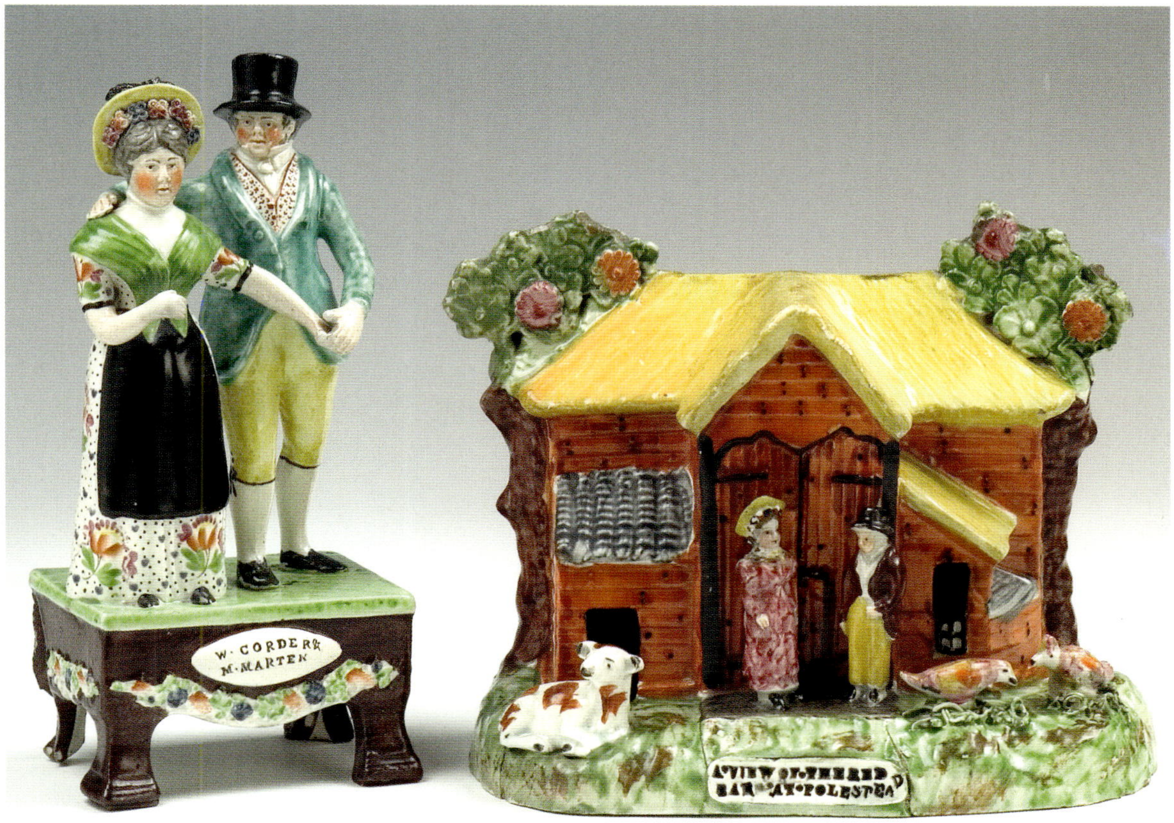

Figure Group, (**608**), c.1829, Staffordshire, height: 20.2cm, (8in), enamelled pearlware. The table base has an oval plaque inscribed, 'W. Corder & M. Marten'. Corder's right arm encircles Marten's shoulders while she holds his left hand in hers. The group is very rare.
Model of Red Barn, (**609**), c.1829, Staffordshire, height: 15.3cm, (6in), enamelled pearlware. Building with trees, farm animals and a pair of figures standing before the barn doors. Rectangular plaque inscribed, 'A.View.of.the.Red.Barn.at.Po lstead'. A print of the barn with its distinctive tall doors appears in James Curtis's, *An Authentic and Faithful History of the Mysterious Murder of Maria Marten,* (published 1828) a contemporary account of the incident which was probably the source image for the potters. Other examples are known with different details.[19]

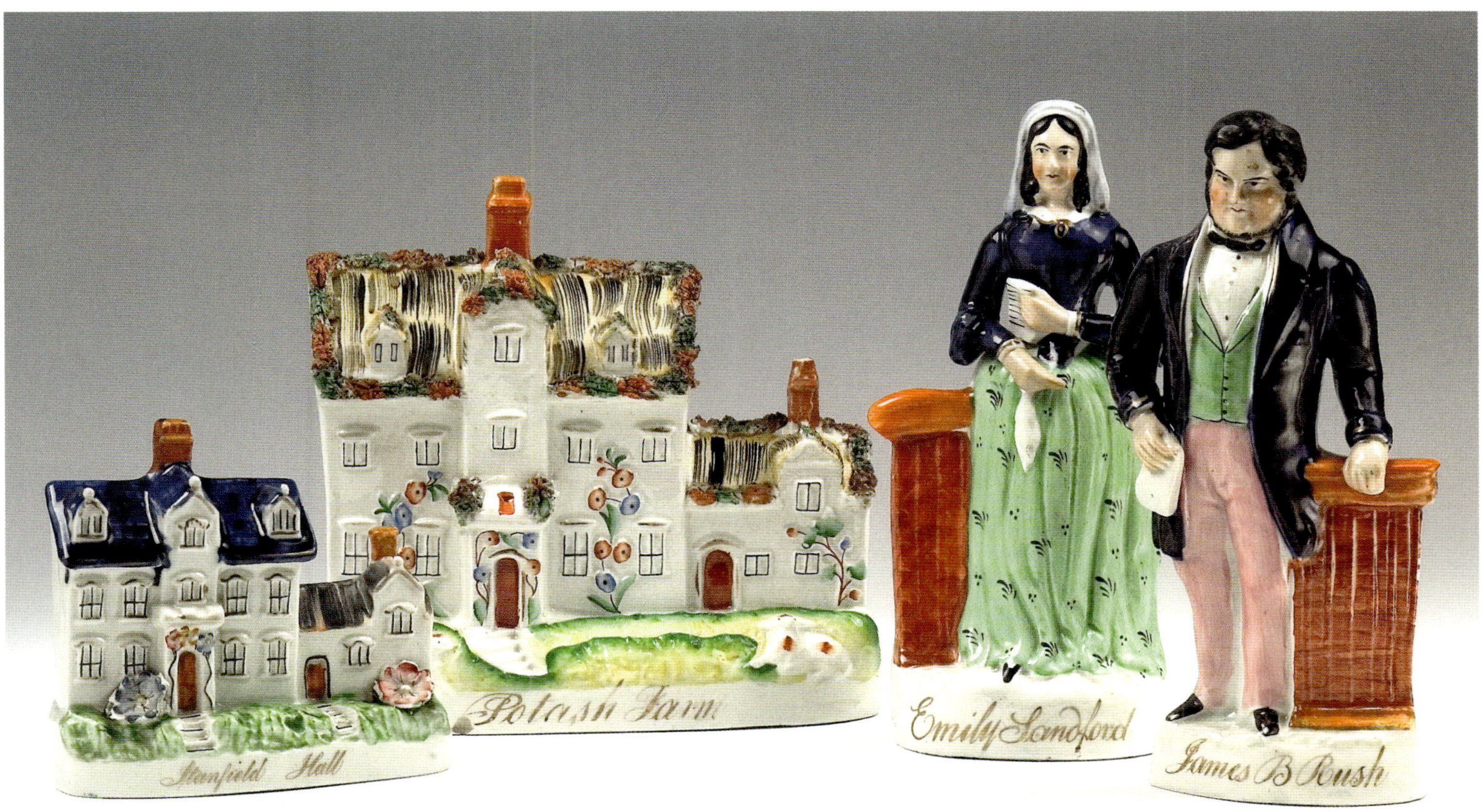

Model Building, (**613**), c.1850, Staffordshire, height: 14cm, (5½in), earthenware, enamelled and gilt.
Model Building, (**612**), c.1850, Staffordshire, height: 21.6cm, (8½in), earthenware, enamelled and gilt. The buildings, though inscribed 'Potash Farm' and 'Stanfield Hall' respectively, both derive from the same view of Potash Farm. The appearance of the buildings and the figures based on wood-block printed sketches of the trial by Earle, published in the 'Extraordinary' edition of the *Norfolk Chronicle and Norwich Gazette*, 4 April 1849 and in the *Illustrated London News*, 7 April 1849.[20] **Pair of Figures**, (**611 & A**) c.1850, Staffordshire, height: 26cm, (10¼in), height: 25cm, (9¾in), earthenware, enamelled and gilt. Slip-cast figures, each standing beside a witness box, inscribed: 'James B. Rush' and 'Emily Sandford'.

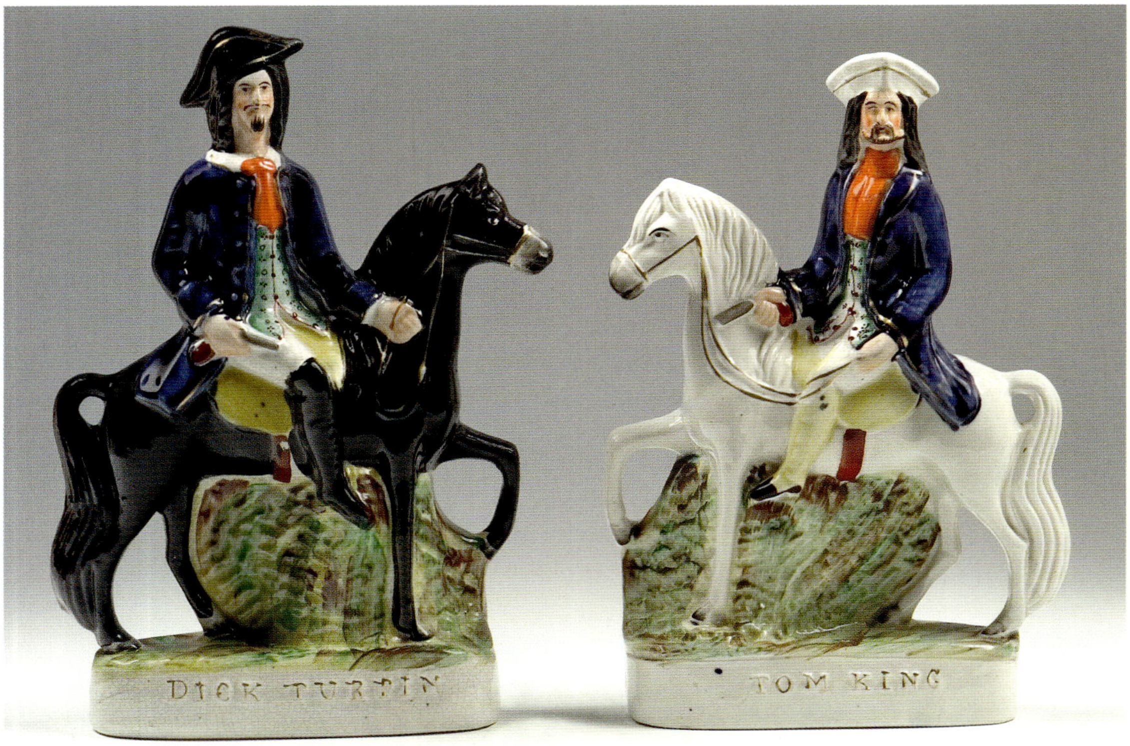

Pair of Figures, (**614* & A**), c.1850, Staffordshire, height: 30.5cm, (12in), height: 30.5cm, (12in), earthenware, enamelled and gilt.
Entitled 'Dick Turpin' and 'Tom King', the flat-back equestrian figures brandish their pistols. Turpin's horse (the famous Black Bess) is enamelled black while King's is white.

Dick Turpin, Highwayman

Richard Turpin was born in 1705 in Thaxted in Essex and trained as a butcher. His early crimes included cattle rustling and robbing smugglers before he became a member of the notorious Essex Gregory Gang. From 1735 he began a series of highway robberies, sometimes in the company of Matthew King (later known as Tom) whom he shot accidentally during a botched robbery. After that Turpin operated alone. Having murdered a keeper in Epping Forest, he hid in Holland for a while, before moving to Yorkshire. He managed to evade capture until 1738, when he was convicted at the York Assizes of horse stealing and hanged on 7 April 1739. [21]

Turpin's popularity underwent an astonishing revival in the 1830s following the success of W. Harrison Ainsworth's novel *Rookwood*, published in 1834, on a late wave of Romanticism. Three editions rapidly sold out and Ainsworth became the toast of literary London, entertaining writers such as Thackeray and Dickens, the illustrator George Cruikshank and the young Disraeli at Kensal Lodge on the Harrow Road. At a dinner given in his honour on 15 September 1881, the Mayor of Manchester announced that there were 250 volumes of his works at Manchester's free libraries which had been borrowed 7,660 times during the previous few months.[22] Turpin's cherished mare, Black Bess and episodes such as the famous ride to York were totally fictional.

George Barrington, (1755-1804)

George Barrington 'the gentleman pick-pocket', was born George Waldron in County Kildare, Ireland. He left home with a troupe of actors and infiltrated fashionable society in London in 1773, where he operated as confidence trickster. In 1777 the *London Chronicle* described him as the 'genteelest thief ever remembered at the Old Bailey' and in 1785 his portrait was painted by William Beechey.

Following his eighth conviction in 1790, (for stealing a gold watch from Henry Townsend at Enfield racecourse), he was transported to Australia, allegedly helping to quell a mutiny en route. His fame was such that London and provincial publishers used his name freely on a wide variety of publications relating to Australia. *Blackwood's Magazine* suggested in 1827 that 'ninety-nine out of one hundred English people' would associate New South Wales with 'ropes, gibbets, arson, burglary, kangaroos, George Barrington and Governor Macquarie'.[23] In the Antipodes Barrington became a pious Christian and a model citizen. In 1792 he won the first warrant of emancipation to be issued and was made chief constable of convicts at Parramatta, New South Wales. He may have written an early history of Australia and certainly penned the prologue to a play enacted by convicts in 1796, which included the lines:

> True patriots we, for be it understood, / We left our country for our country's good.

In 1800 he resigned his commission due to insanity, lived on a generous pension and died at Parramatta in 1804.[24]

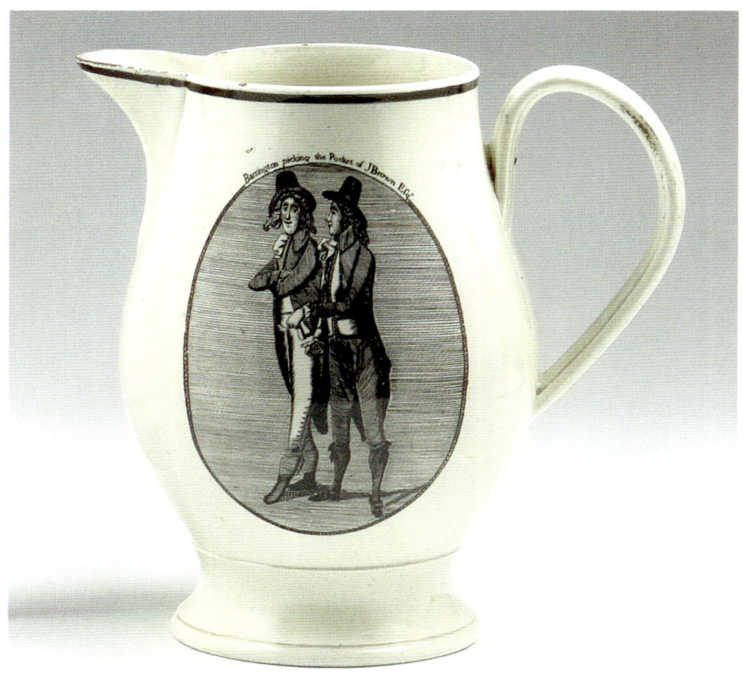

Jug, (**616**), c.1791, Staffordshire, height: 15.9cm, (6¾in), creamware, printed and enamelled. Scene entitled, 'Barrington picking the Pocket of J. Brown Esq.', shows, within an oval frame, one fashionably dressed man deftly stealing from another. A ship on the reverse.

The Tichborne Case

Roger Tichborne, the heir to the extensive Hampshire estates of the Catholic Tichborne family, was shipwrecked and disappeared while bound for South America in 1854.[25] In 1866 the Dowager Lady Tichborne received a reply to her long-running advertisement for news of him from Wagga Wagga in Australia, where one Thomas Castro, a butcher, claimed to be her son. Despite physical evidence to the contrary, Lady Tichborne accepted him as her son but after her death in 1868, he was repudiated by the rest of the family and a civil case was brought in 1871.

After losing the case in a trial that lasted 102 days, Castro was rearrested for perjury. The next, criminal trial for impersonation lasted 188 days in 1873 and 1874, making legal history both for its duration and cost, since official inquiries had to be conducted in Chile (where Sir Roger had disappeared) and in Wagga Wagga.[26] It excited controversy relating to class conflict and excited pro- and anti-Catholic feeling.[27] Castro and his blustering but inept counsel, Dr Edward Kenealy, lost the case for failing to prove that Castro, his client, was not Arthur Orton, a Wapping butcher. Castro/Orton eventually confessed his guilt and served ten years penal servitude. After his release in 1884, he retracted his confession and proceeded to tour, arguing his case in music halls and as a side show in travelling fairs.[28] A wide range of mass-produced souvenirs of the case was produced.

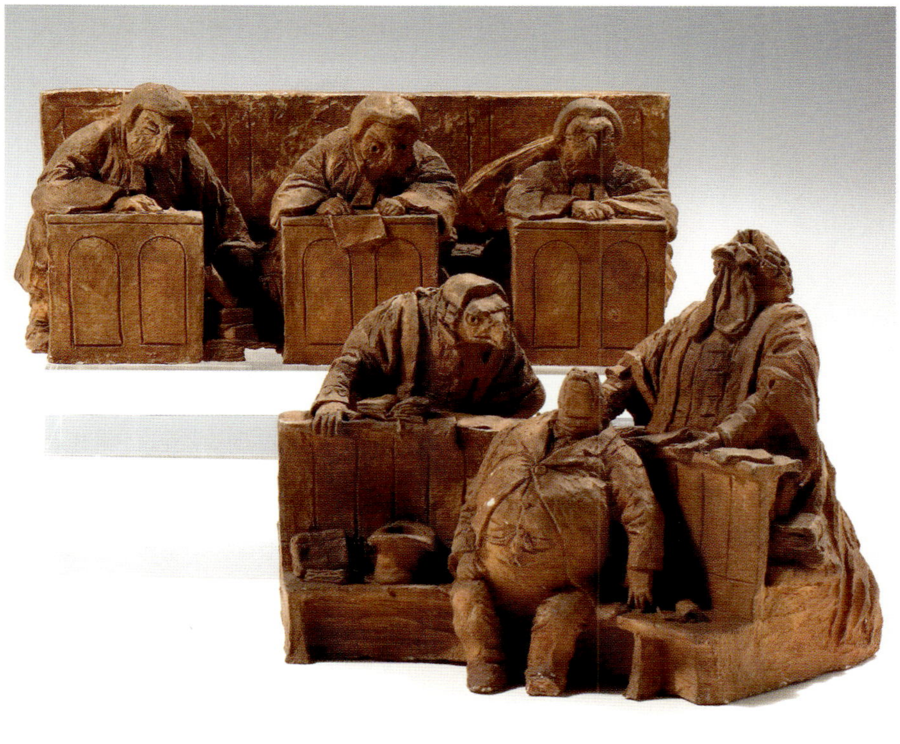

Pair of Figure Groups, (**618A & 618B**) c.1874, height: 17.2cm, (6¾in), judges height: 10.2cm, (4in), painted plaster. Two groups of plaster figures modelled by Randolph Caldecott, coloured to resemble terracotta, depicting participants at the second trial of the 'Tichborne Claimant', held in 1874. One group shows the prosecution and defence counsels as a hawk and a rooster respectively, standing behind the claimant, a seated tortoise. The other shows a bench of judges represented as owls. Caldecott, the celebrated illustrator of children's books, attended the trial as a 'special reporter' and made copious sketches of the main protagonists, caricatured as birds and animals.[29]

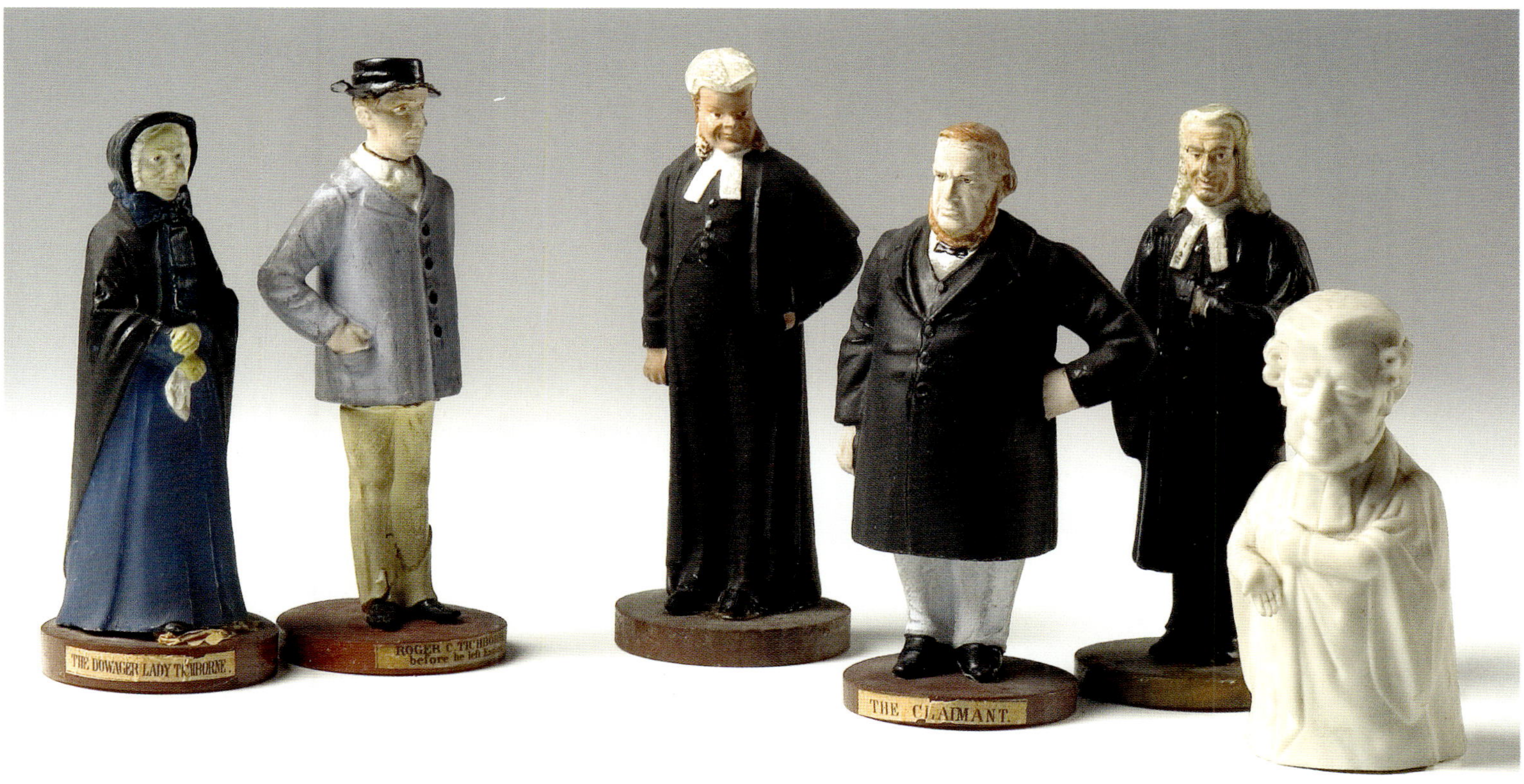

Five Figures, (**618***), c.1875, each height: 12.7cm, (5in), painted plaster. Figures represent participants (real and notional) in the Tichborne case. They include the judge, Lord Chief Justice Bovill, the claimant's lawyer Serjeant Ballantine and the Solicitor General (who has lost his spectacles).[30] Two further figures represent the young Sir Roger Tichborne, another, 'The Claimant', (Thomas Castro) together, with one of the late Lady Tichborne.[31]

Candle-snuffer, (**R2454.34**), c.1875, Royal Worcester, height: 9.5cm, (3¾in), biscuit porcelain. Modelled as the hollow figure of the prosecution counsel, Henry Hawkins, the piece is intended to 'snuff-out' a candle-shaped porcelain model of the claimant. (It was presented in 1923 by members of Willett's family.)

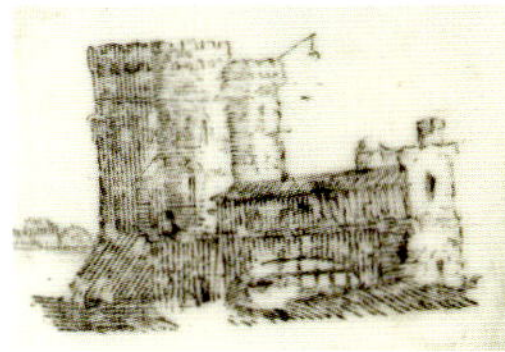

Chapter 11

ARCHITECTURE

Willett used the term 'architecture' fairly broadly. Some of the model buildings and images represented can be identified; several record major civic projects such as the 'Crow's Nest' on Newcastle's Guildhall, additions to the London Hospital and several cast-iron bridges. Others are rustic cottages, inspired by the taste for the 'Picturesque'. Pastille burners were often modelled as thatched or timber-framed *cottages ornés*, such as those built by John Nash, in 1811 at Blaise Hamlet, near Bristol.

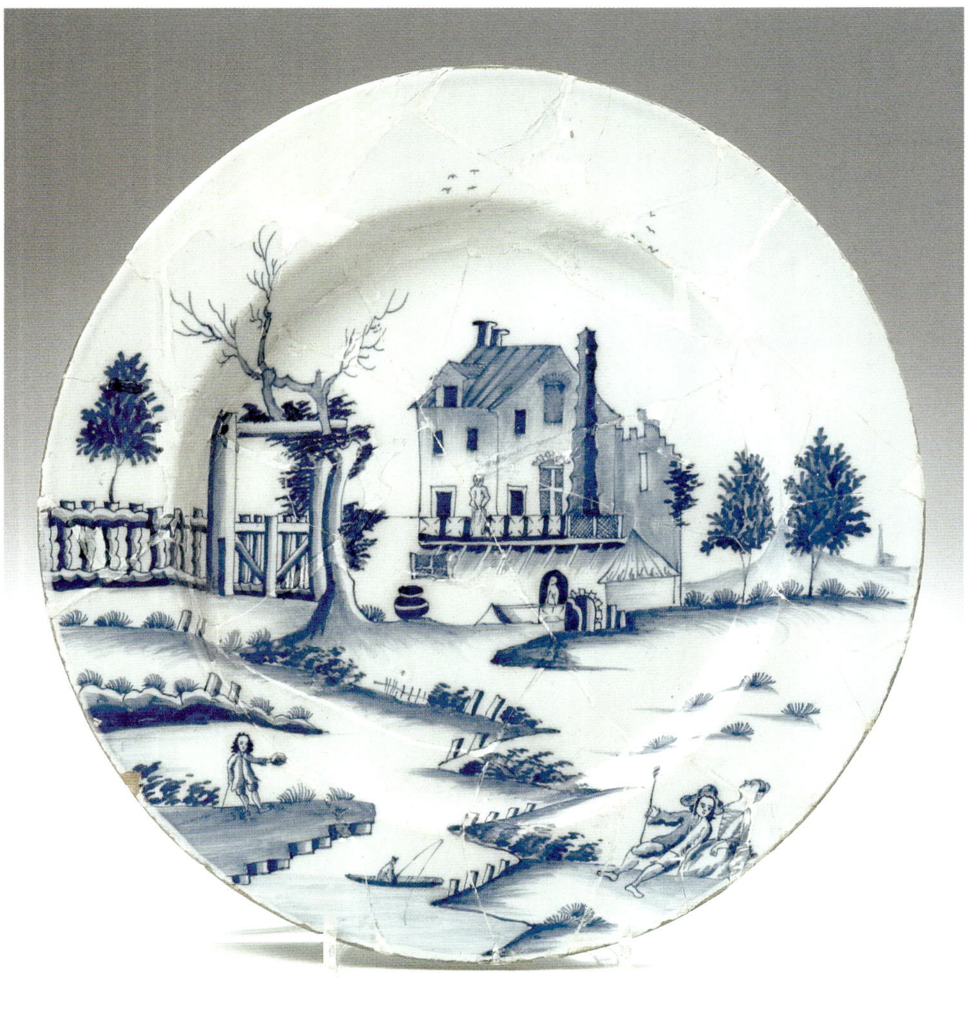

Dish, (698), c.1780, London?, diameter: 29.2cm, (11½in), tin-glazed earthenware. Dish, now badly damaged, decorated with a lively but confusing landscape scene featuring what appears to be a water mill.

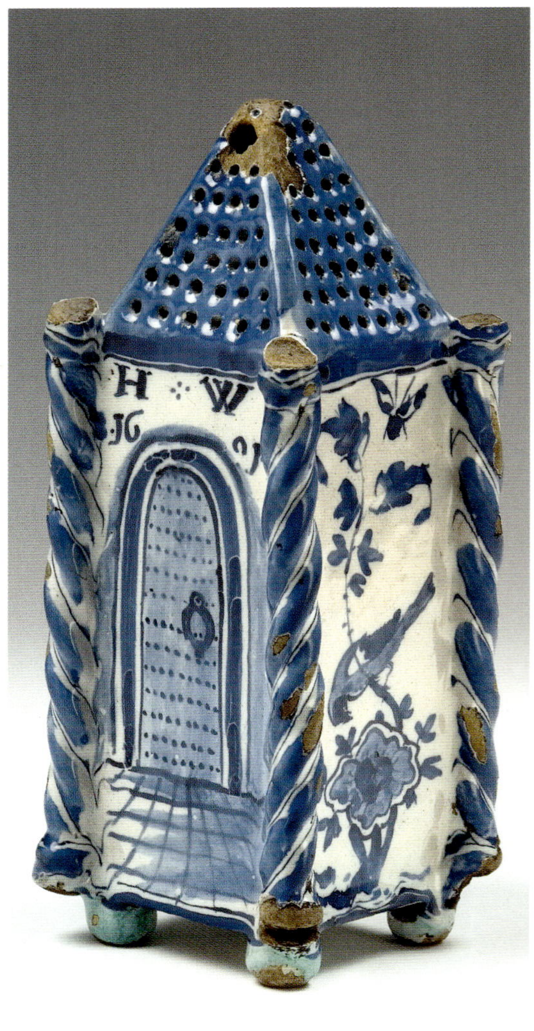

Pastille Burner, **(719)**, 1691, Holland, height: 21.6cm, (8½in), tin-glazed earthenware. Willett describes the burner, or sugar sifter, as a 'lock-up'. The four-sided tower, decorated with birds and foliage, has a pierced, pyramidal top and is inscribed HW, (which must have amused its owner) either side of a painted door.

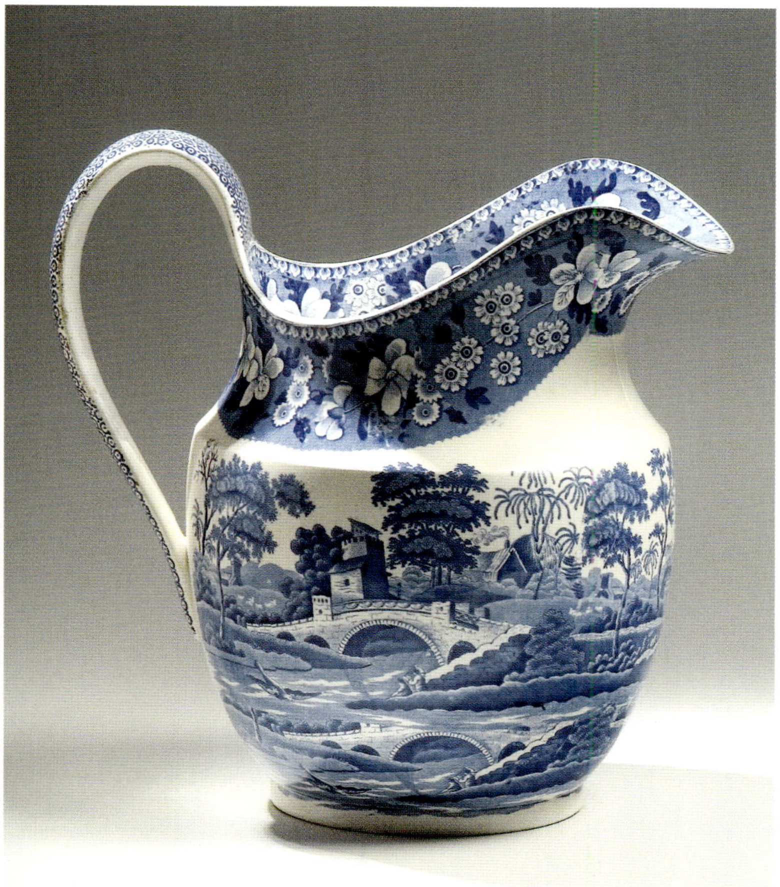

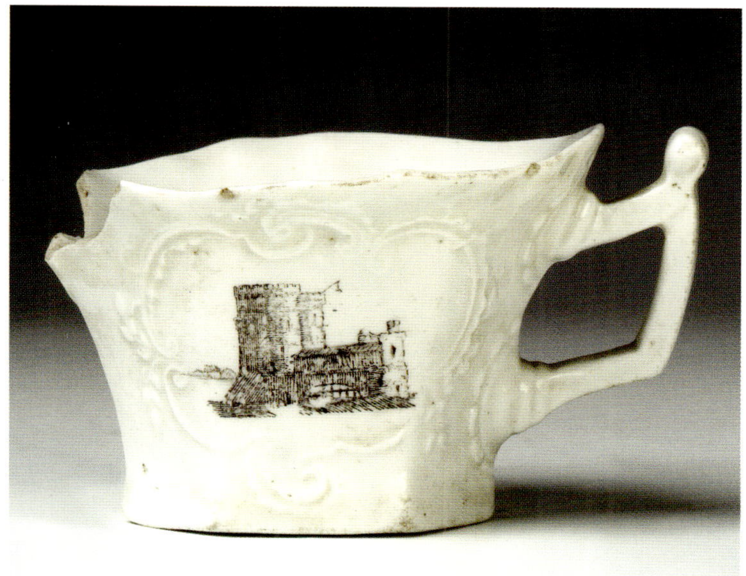

Cream Jug, (**715**), c.1755, Worcester, height: 5.1cm, (2in), printed,soft-paste porcelain. Tiny vignettes of a medieval castle keep and a villa are placed within moulded, rococo bordered reserves.

Ewer, (**732**), c.1825, Staffordshire, Stoke-on-Trent, Spode, height: 31.7cm, (12½in), blue-printed earthenware. Ewer, once part of a bedroom set with washbowl, printed with lush romantic landscapes, bridges and distant cottages.

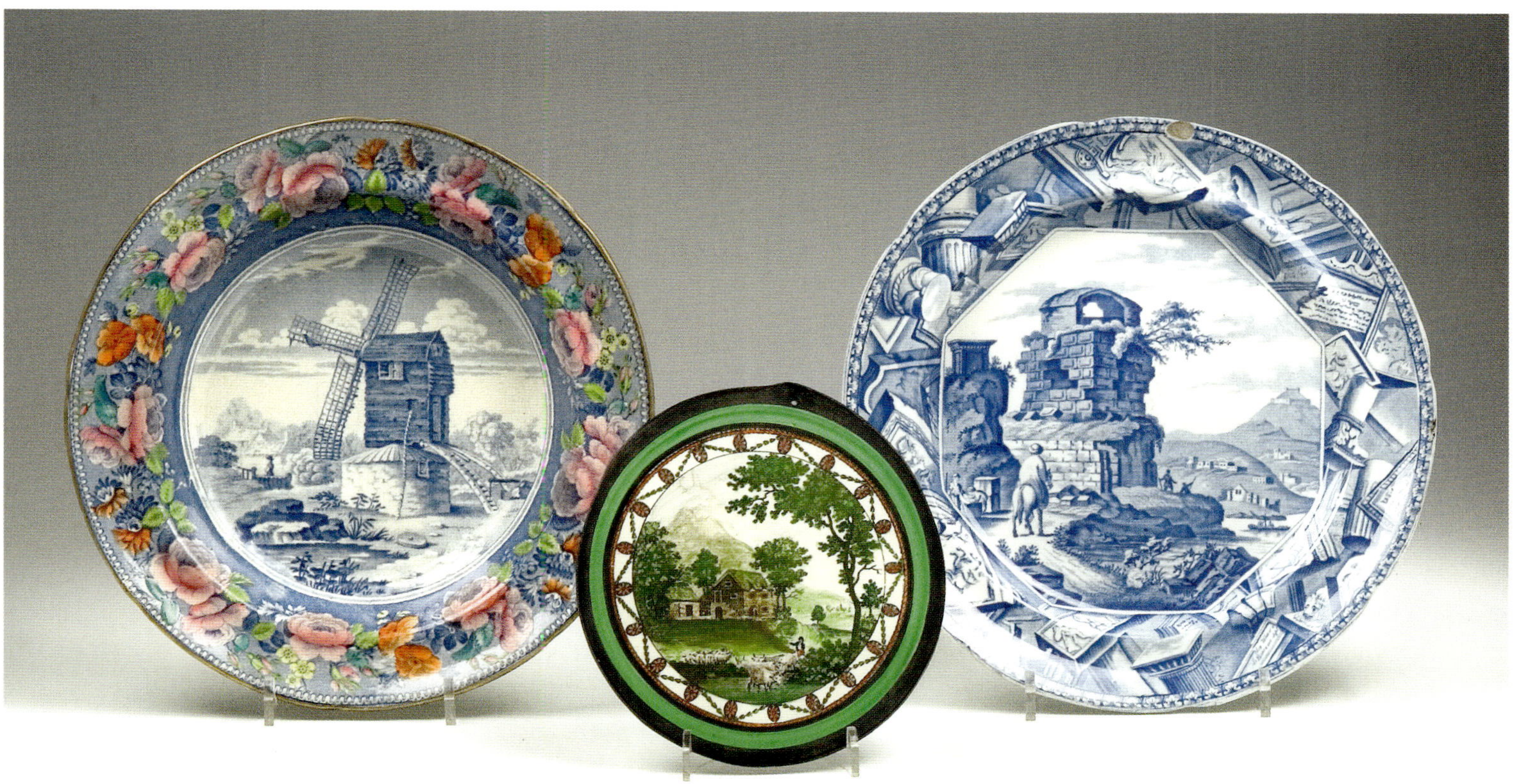

Soup Plate, (**696**), c.1820, Staffordshire, perhaps Lane Delph, height: 21.6cm, (8½in), blue-printed earthenware, coloured. Post mill, entitled on reverse, 'Powder Mill Hastings'. This mill ground the 'Black Powder' (gunpowder) for a factory on the Great Sanders Estate in Hastings . In the nineteenth century it was the scene of three explosions, in which several workers died, which led to its closure. An indistinct daisy mark on the reverse of the dish may be that of William Mason (fl.1812-16), of Lane Delph in Staffordshire.[1]

Teapot Stand, (**727**), c.1820, Staffordshire, height: 15.3cm, (6in), earthenware, printed and coloured. Stand or plaque (drilled for hanging) decorated with thatched farm buildings.

Plate, (**697**), c.1825, Staffordshire, diameter: 24.8cm, (9¾in), blue-printed earthenware. View of unspecific ruins in a hilly landscape, possibly within the Ottoman Empire.[2] Border of fragments of antique masonry and inscriptions. Marked 'Mason's Cambrian Argil', printed by Bentley, Wear and Bourne.[3]

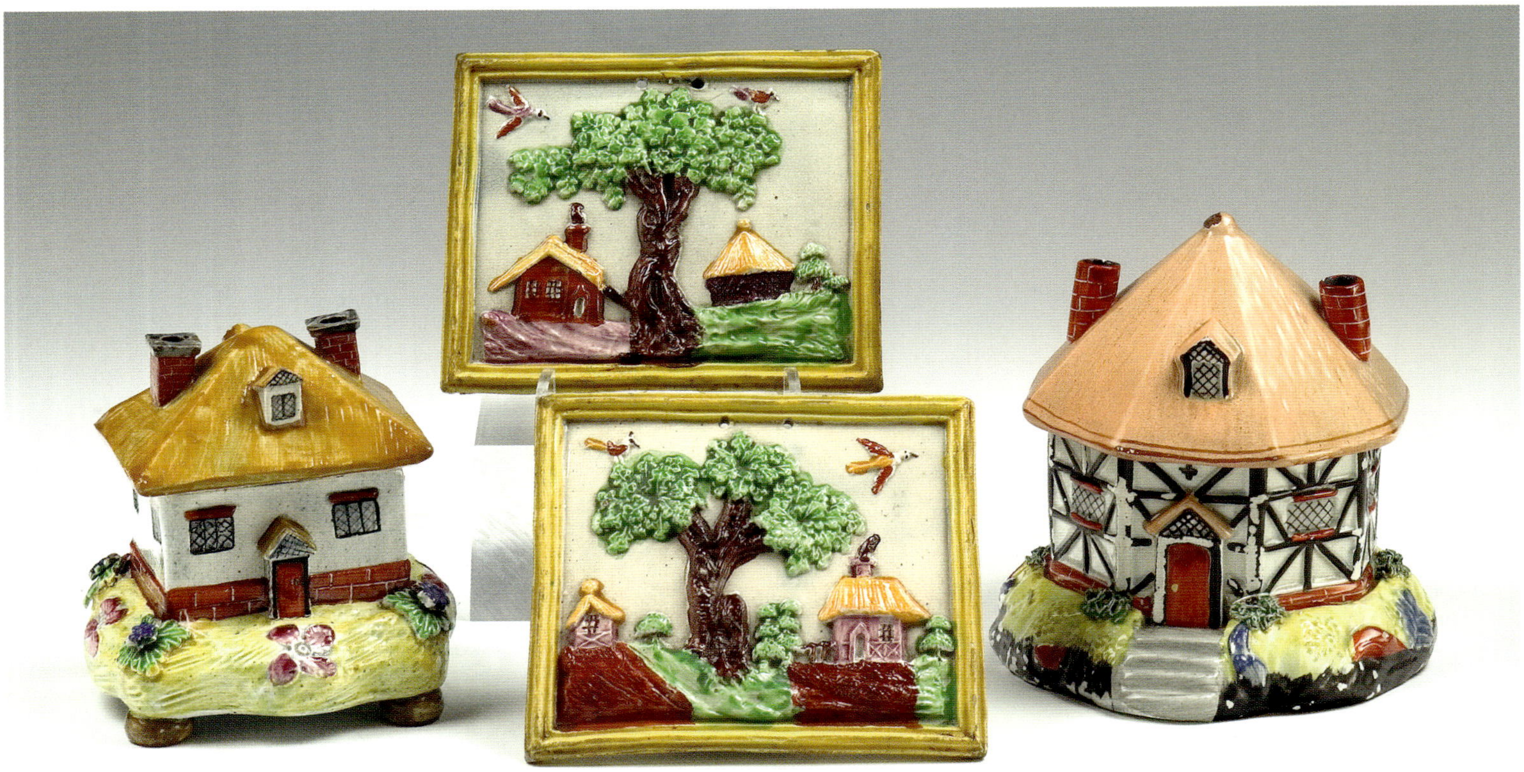

Pastille Burner, (**701**) c.1825, Staffordshire, height: 10.2cm, (4in), enamelled pearlware. Cottage on a grassy knoll with detachable thatched roof.
Pair of Plaques, (**724 + 725**), c.1810, Staffordshire, each height: 12.1cm, (4¾in), enamelled pearlware. Relief-moulded with thatched cottages separated by large trees.

Pastille Burner, (**702**), c.1825, Staffordshire, height: 13.3cm, (5¼in), enamelled pearlware. Octagonal, timber-framed cottage with detachable thatched roof.

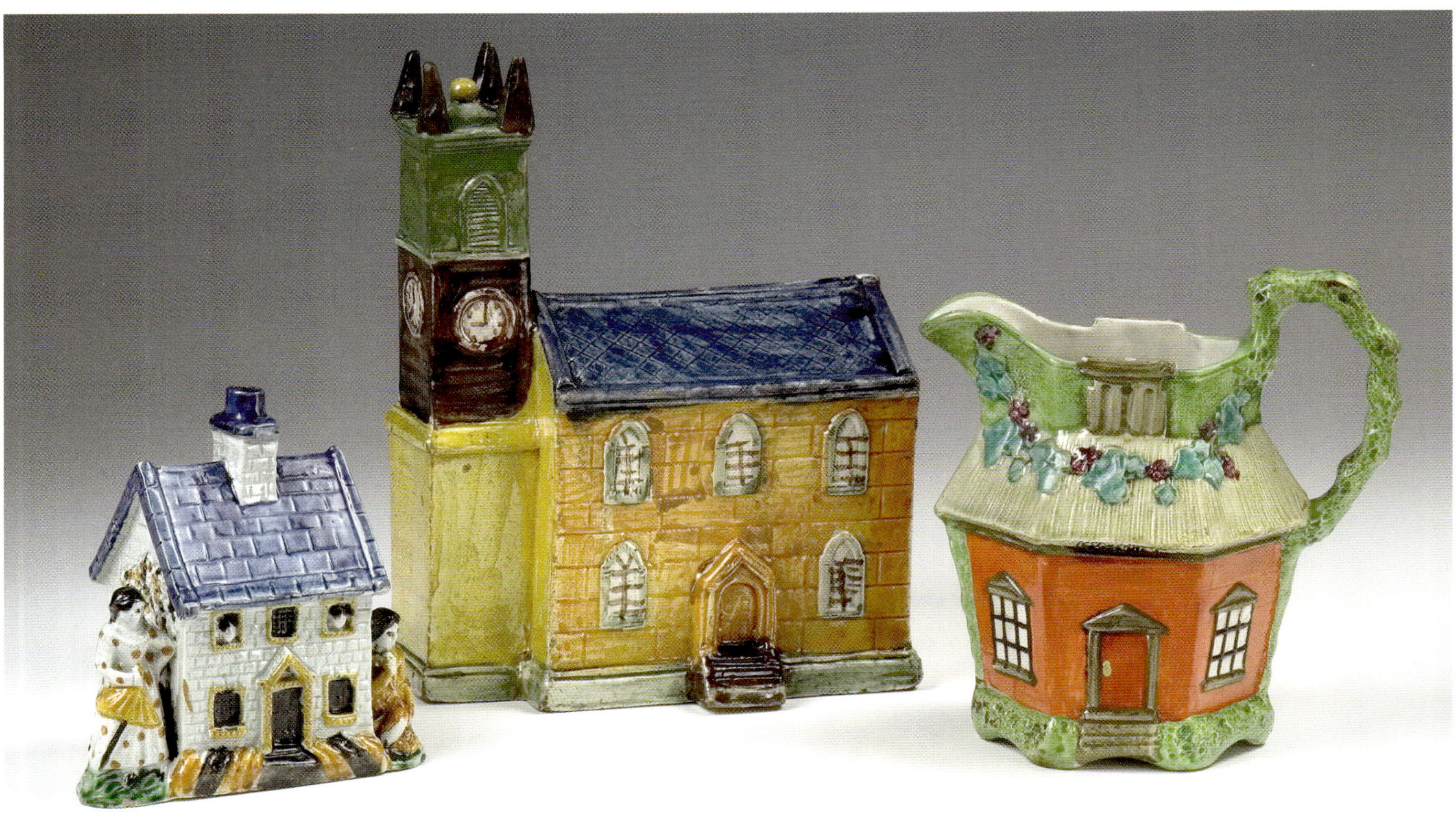

Money Box, (**703**), c.1820, possibly Scotland, height: 12.7cm, (5in), Pratt-coloured pearlware. Model house with slot in back of roof, flanked by large figures of children and faces at the first-floor windows.
Model Church, (**709**), c.1830, Staffordshire, height: 22.2cm, (8¾in), pearlware. Church, boldly decorated in Pratt colours, has no obvious function.
Jug, (**700**), c.1825, Staffordshire, height: 16.5cm, (6½in), enamelled pearlware. Relief-moulded as a hexagonal brick cottage, its thatched roof festooned with vines.

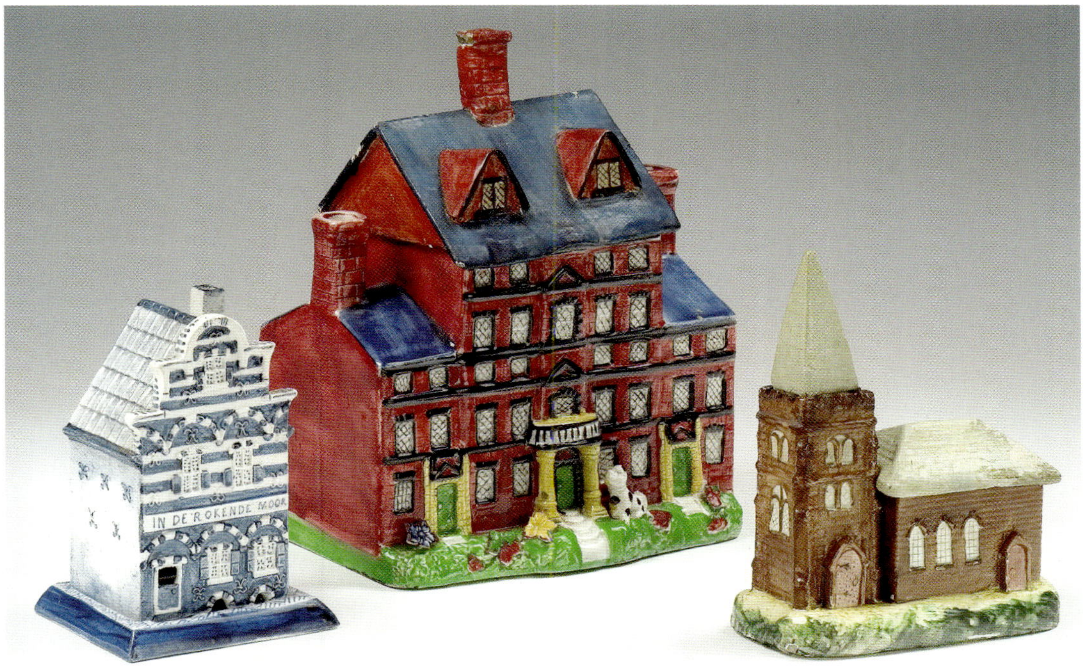

Pastille burner, (**717**), c.1870, Holland, Delft, height: 14cm, (5½in), blue-painted pearlware. Gabled house, inscribed, 'IN DE ROKENDE MOOR', detachable from its base. 'The Sign of the Smoking Moor' is a well-known building in Delft. Marked for De Porceleyne Fles (The Porcelain Bottle).
Model, (**733**), c.1830, North East?, height: 17.8cm, (7in), enamelled pearlware. Large building with a blue roof, described as a manor house but looks more like an institution or factory on six floors.
Model Church, (**734**), c.1830, Staffordshire, height: 14cm, (5½in), enamelled pearlware. Church has removable spire and nave roof tower and could be used as a pastille burner.

Model Church, (**706**), c.1850, Staffordshire?, height: 17.8cm, (7in), enamelled pearlware. Large but crude model of Westminster Abbey.

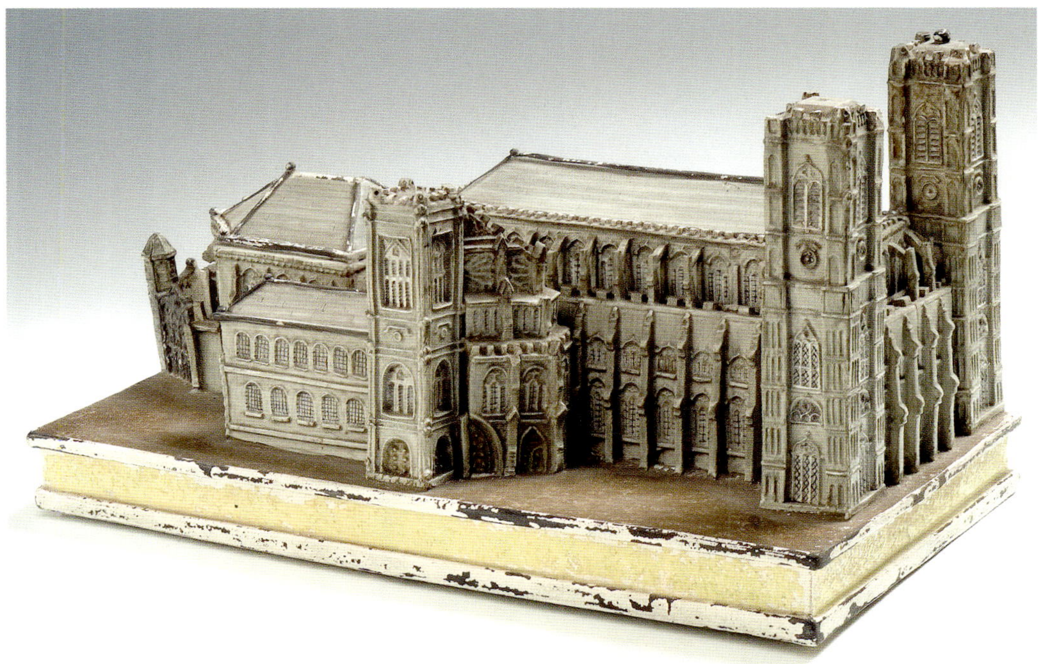

Model, (**728**), c.1840, Worcester, height: 18.4cm, (7¼in), soft-paste porcelain. Pastille burner or night light modelled as a two-storey house, detachable from its base. It has pierced dormer windows.
Model, (**729**), c.1840, Worcester, height: 10.2cm, (4in), soft-paste porcelain. Shallow roofed one-storey building, incised on the base; 'Chamberlains Royal Worcester Porcelain Manufactory … & 155 New Bond Street.'
Model, (**R.603/13**) c.1870, Germany?, height: 17.8cm, (7in), enamelled hard-paste porcelain. Pastille burner or night light from similar mould to (728).

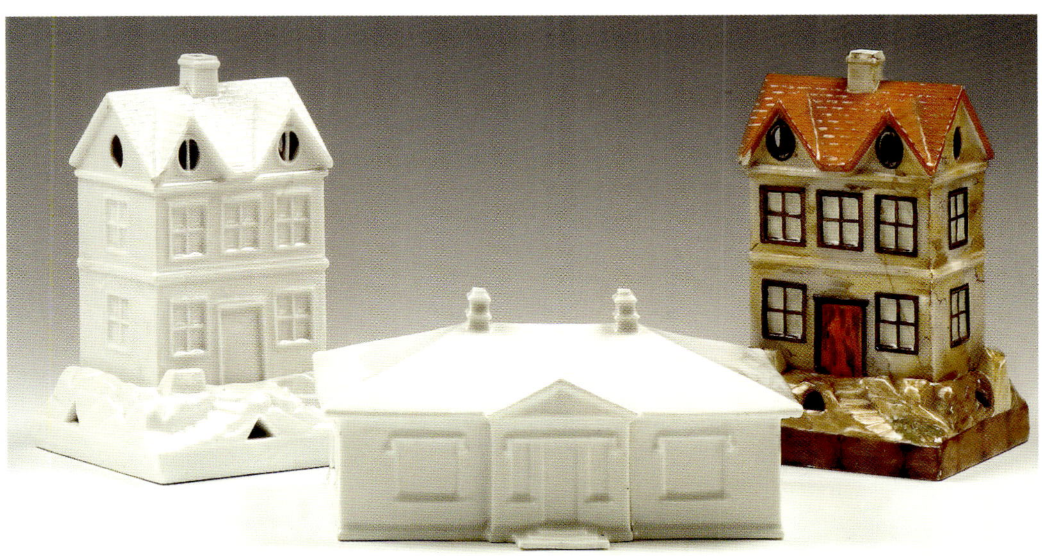

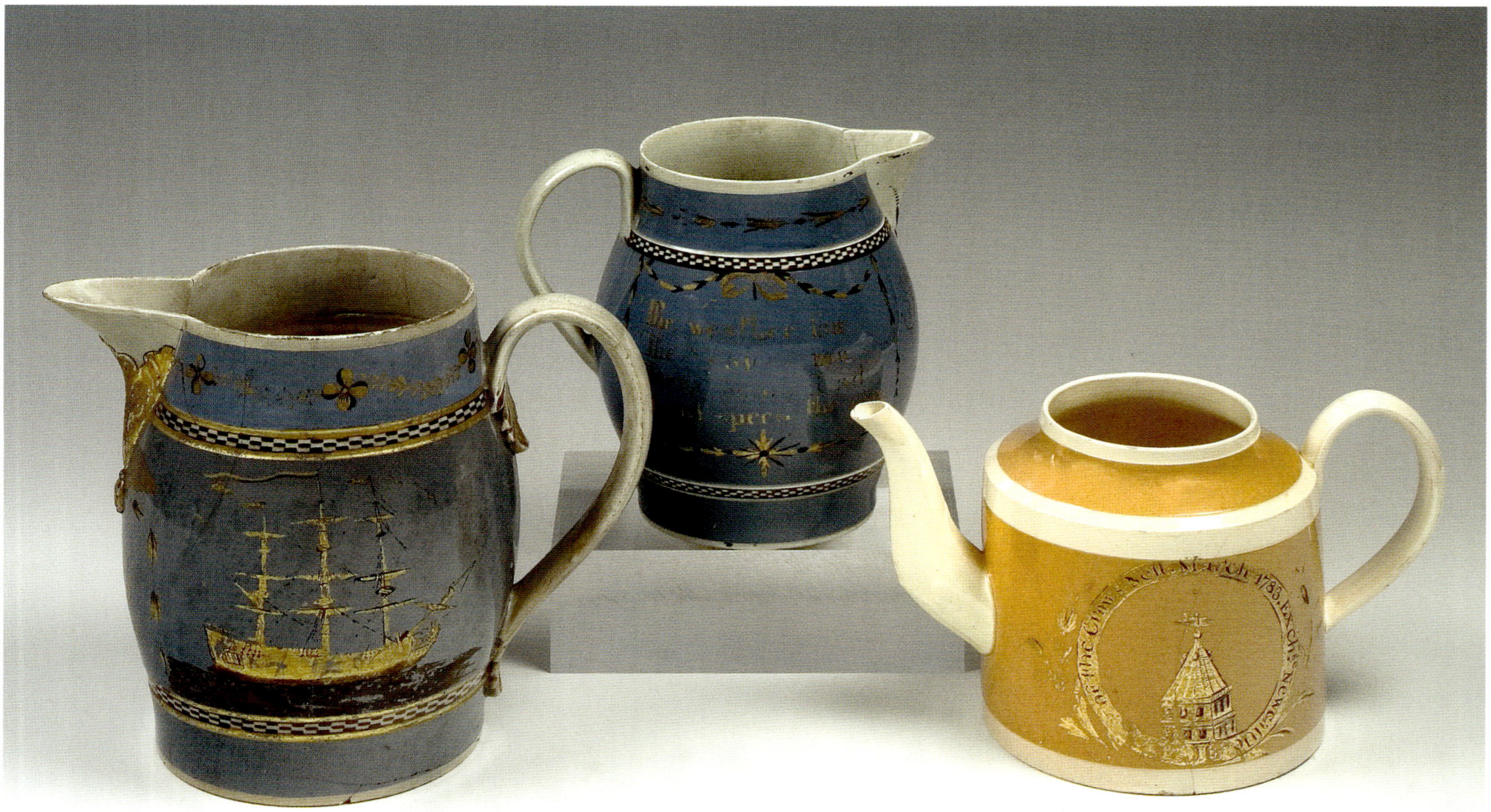

Jug, (**334**), 1788, possibly Liverpool, height: 18.4cm, (7¼in), pearlware, enamelled and gilt. Covered with blue slip but for narrow diaper bands around the neck and base. Gilt decoration of ship and on reverse (possibly) a coat of arms, very rubbed.

Jug, (**1248**), c.1790, possibly Liverpool, height: 15.3cm, (6in), pearlware, enamelled and gilt. Covered with blue slip but for narrow diaper bands around the neck and base. Decorated with verse, 'the weather's fine' now rather rubbed.[4]

Teapot, (**713**), probably North East, height: 13.3cm, (5¼in), creamware, painted and gilt. Broad bands of apricot slip on shoulder and sides. Painted with the apex of a tower inscribed, 'View of the Crows Nest. March 1783. Exch.ge. Newcastle'. The crow's nest was the lookout at the top of the tower of Newcastle upon Tyne's Guildhall, which was built at this date.[5]

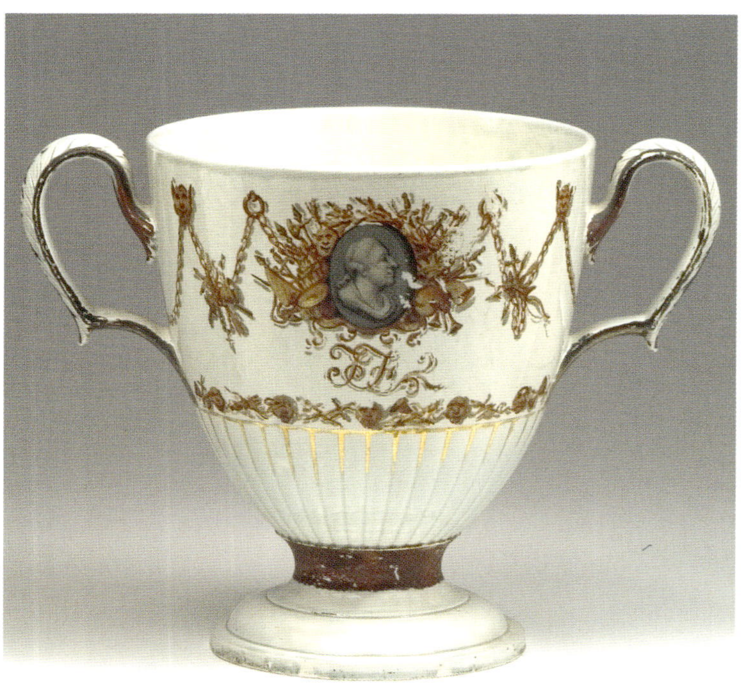

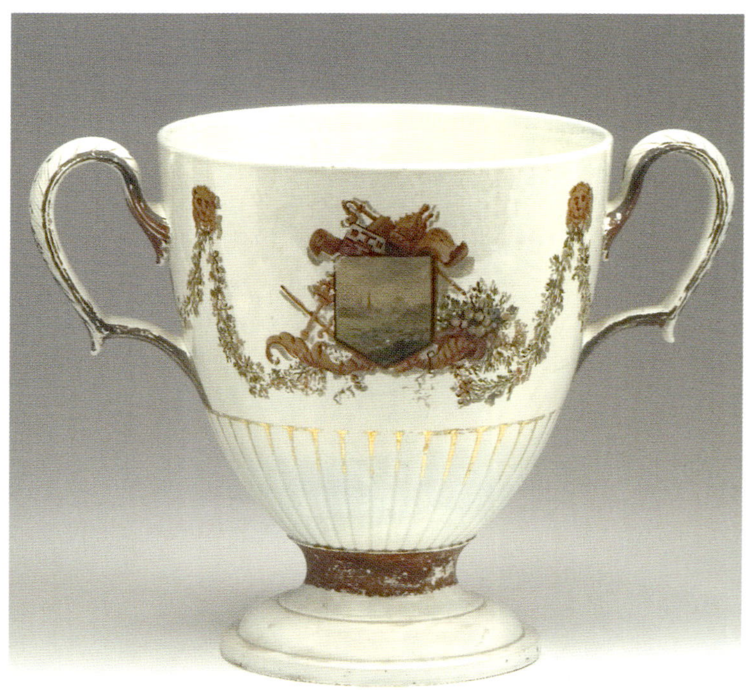

Loving Cup, (**723**), 1797, Staffordshire, height: 22.9cm, (9in), pearlware, enamelled and gilt. Decorated on one side, between looped chains and groups of arms, masks and musical instruments, an unidentified grisaille portrait plaque (and the monogram 'TF'). On the other, a shield with a tiny cityscape and distinctive church spires. At the base of each handle inscribed in gilt; 'HW' and '1797 Lichfield'.

Loving Cup, (730), c.1810, Staffordshire, height: 15.3cm, (6in), soft-paste porcelain, enamelled and gilt. A finely painted landscape and country mansion with a huge waterwheel and outbuildings, beside a waterway with a sailing boat and timber, awaiting shipment. On reverse, gilt monogram, 'IW'. Although unmarked it may be an early product (c.1810) of the Minton factory.

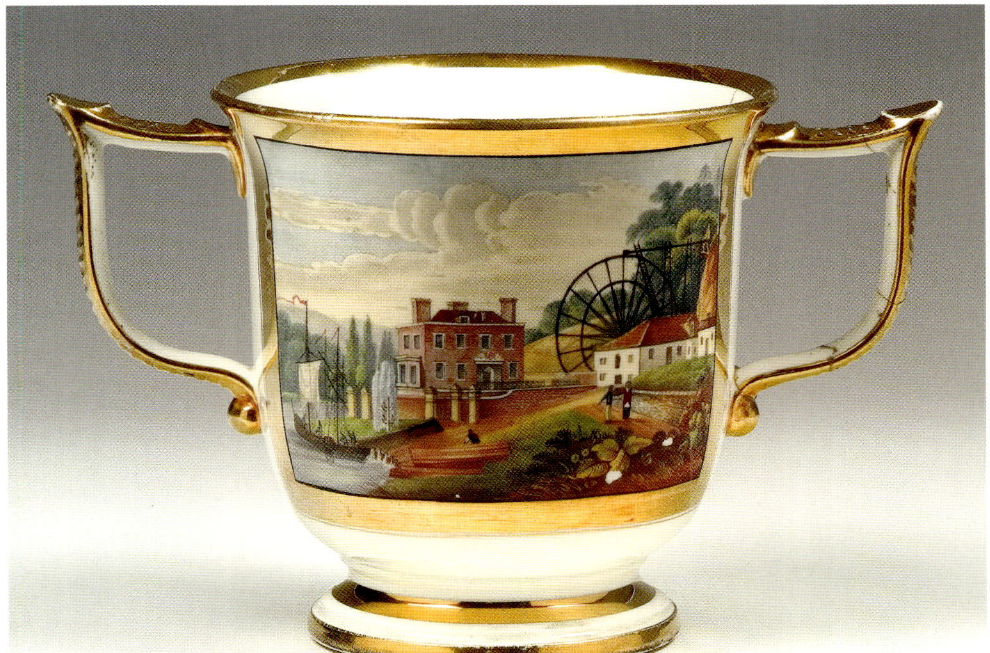

New London Bridge

Docks Acts of 1799 and 1800 authorised dock building at the Isle of Dogs and at Wapping, and involved replacing the medieval structure of London Bridge, as part of a scheme to modernise the Port of London. Thomas Telford proposed a single span bridge, allowing ships of 200 tons to pass beneath. The short listed designs were published in 1800 and included one for a 'proposed cast-iron bridge' by Thomas Wilson. He had designed the Wear Bridge in Sunderland, which opened in 1796. Pieces printed with iron bridges were something of a speciality for Sunderland potteries. All the submissions for iron bridges on the Thames, however, were rejected and eventually a stone bridge was erected in 1831.

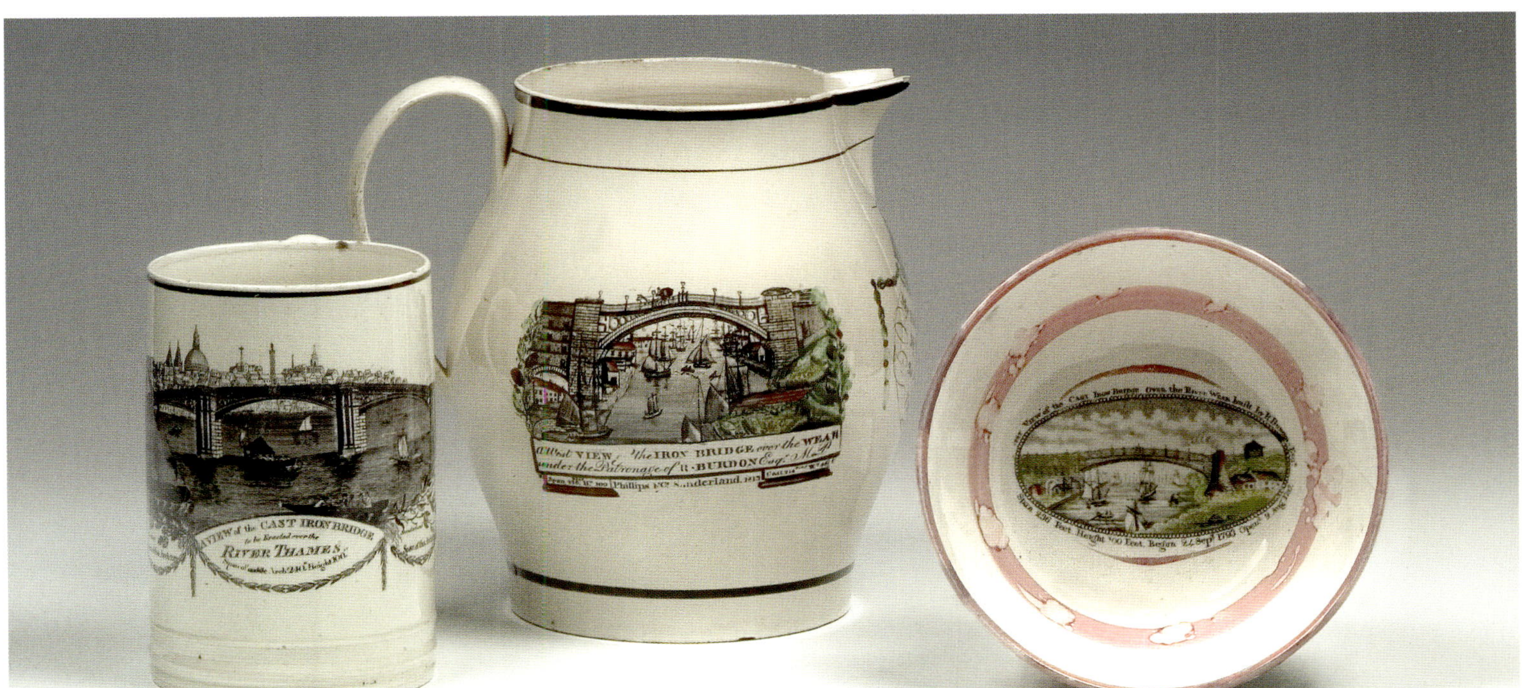

Mug, (714), c.1820, Sunderland, height: 15.3cm, (6in), printed creamware. View of a bridge over the Thames in London, inscribed 'A View of the Cast-Iron Bridge to be Erected over the River Thames, Span of middle Arch 240 ft' and other statistics relating to the bridge's dimensions. Signed by engraver Edward Barker, who worked either at Scott's Southwick Pottery or Dawson's at Low Ford.[6] This engraving actually shows John Rennie's iron bridge at Southwark, completed by Walkers of Rotherham in 1819. The London cityscape behind the bridge shows the dome of St Paul's and a couple of Wren churches (nowadays obscured by taller buildings).

Jug, (412), 1813, Sunderland, Phillips & Co.'s Garrison Pottery, height: 20.3cm, (8in), creamware, printed and enamelled. Printed with 'A West View of the Iron Bridge over the Wear' showing extensive river traffic and warehouses on both wharfs.

Bowl, (837), c.1850, Sunderland, diameter: 16.8cm, (6⅝in), earthenware, coloured and lustred. A popular print celebrating the bridge over the Wear, initiated by R. Burdon Esq. in 1793 and completed 1796. Smoking factory chimneys feature on the right bank.

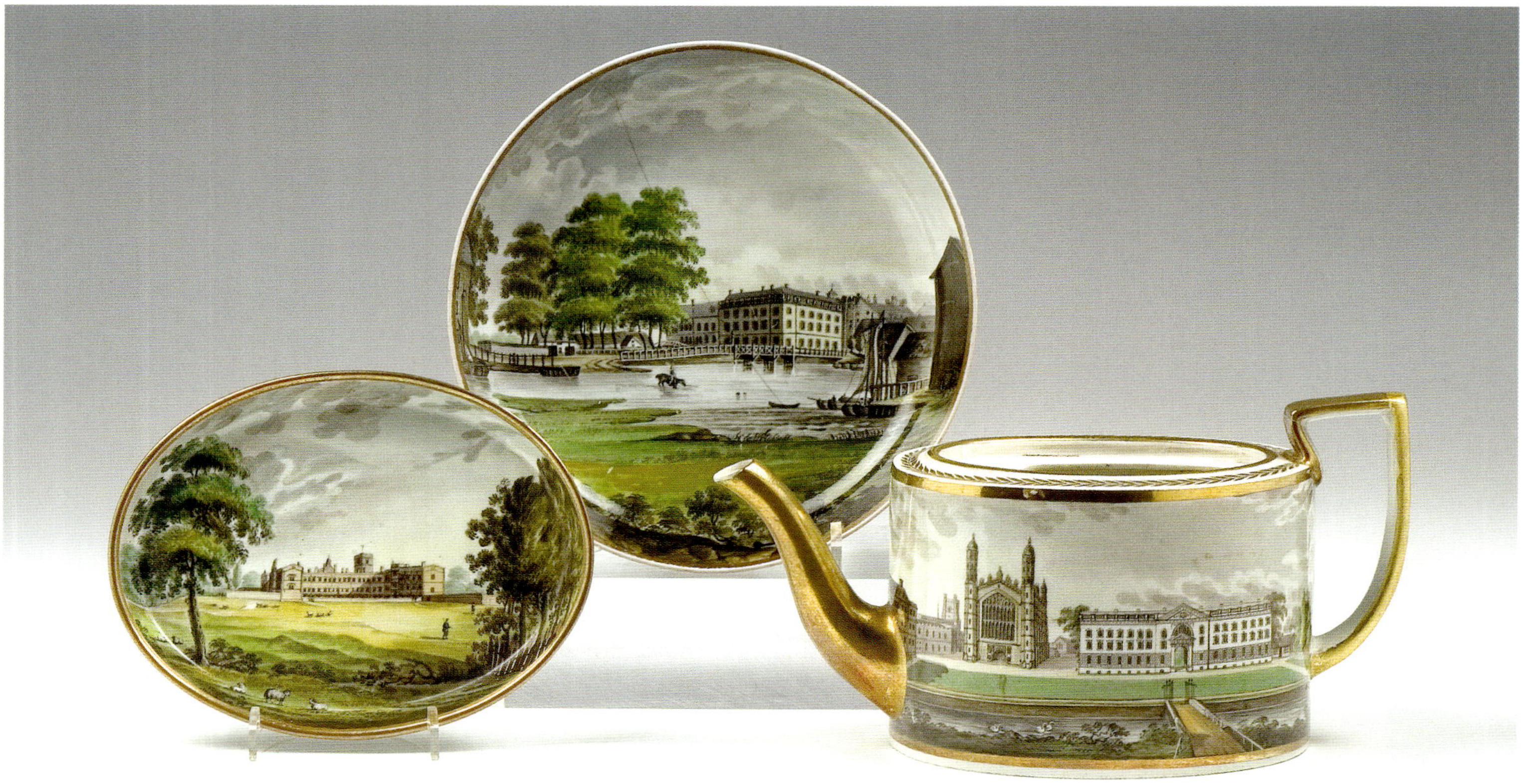

Tea Service, (**731**), c.1815, Stoke-on-Trent, Mintons, bone china, enamelled and gilt. Each piece painted with a Cambridge location, taken from etched views by Richard Harraden 1795-1810, published together as *Cantabrigia Depicta* in 1809.[7]
Teapot Stand, diameter: 14cm, (5½in). Painted with view entitled (beneath), 'Jesus College in the University of Cambridge', published 18 April 1798.[8]
Dish, diameter: 20.5cm, (8⅛in). Painted with view entitled (beneath), 'Queens College in the University of Cambridge', published 16 June 1798.[9]
Teapot, height: 11cm, (4⅜in). Painted with view entitled (beneath), 'King's College Chapel and Clare Hall in the University of Cambridge' published 12 October 1797.[10]

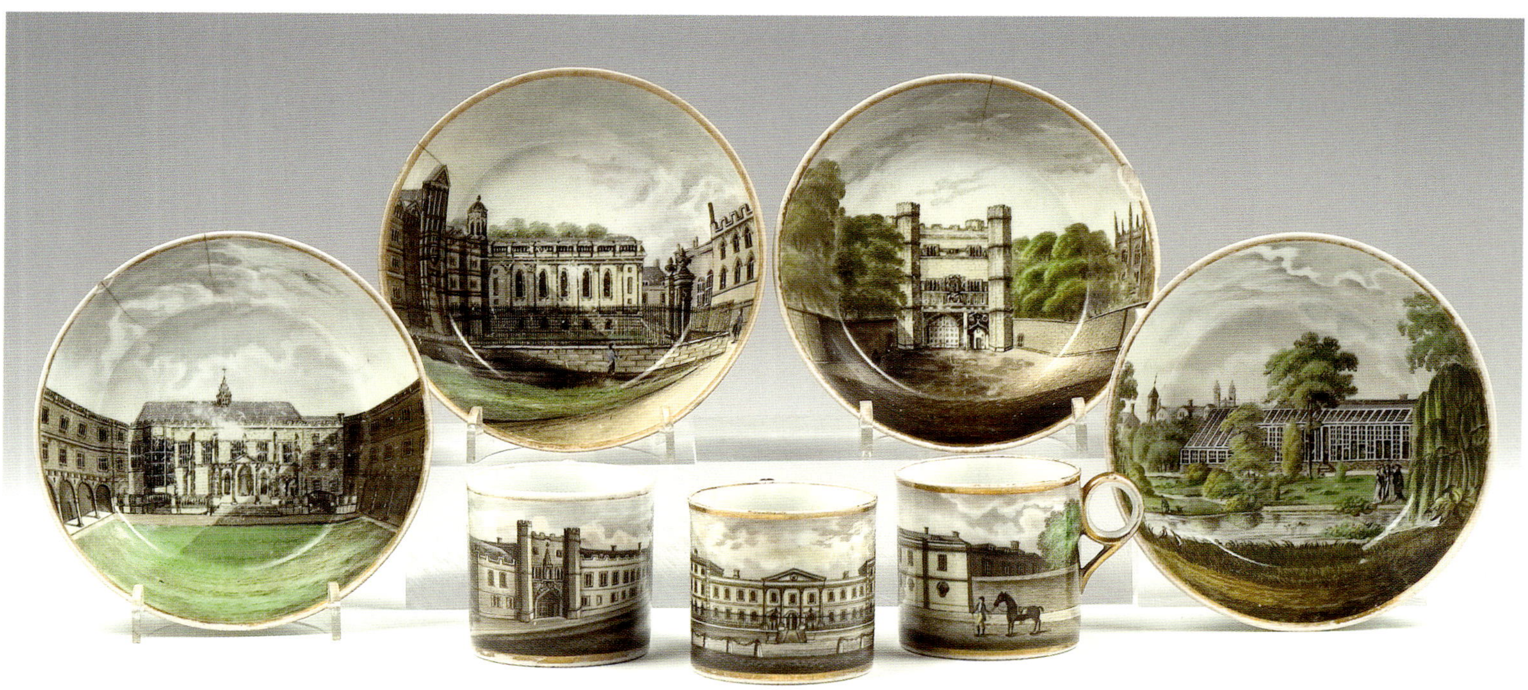

The views on the coffee cans and saucers all come from Harraden's smaller etchings of Cambridge, published in a bound volume in 1805.
Clockwise:
Saucer, diameter: 13.6cm, (5¼in), 'East-End of Nevill's Court', dated 5 November 1798.
Saucer, diameter: 13.6cm, (5¼in), 'Clare Hall & Chapel…', dated 1 February 1800.
Saucer, diameter: 13.6cm, (5¼in), 'The Gate of Trinity College', dated 5 November 1798.
Saucer, diameter: 13.6cm, (5¼in), 'The Green House and part of the Botanic Garden' dated 1800.
Coffee Can, height: 6cm, (2⅜in), 'Trinity Hall, Cambridge', dated May 1797.
Coffee Can, height: 6cm, (2⅜in), 'Emanuel College', dated 5 November 1798.
Coffee Can, height: 6cm, (2⅜in), 'Christ's College', dated 1800.

Printed Souvenir Wares

Teabowl and Saucer, (**720**), c.1800, Staffordshire, height: 5.1cm, (2in), diameter: 12.7cm, (5in), enamelled, soft-paste porcelain. Painted with romantic landscapes within oval reserves on a strong yellow enamel ground.
Slop Bowl, (**718**), c.1800, Staffordshire, diameter: 16cm, (6⅜in), printed, soft-paste porcelain. central vignette inscribed, 'Leasowes', a famous garden at Halesowen in Worcestershire, created in the 1740s by the poet William Shenstone. It was visited by Thomas Jefferson, Benjamin Franklin and John Wesley while Samuel Johnson described it as 'the envy of the great, and the admiration of the skilful'. The source may be a print of 1792 published by Harrison & Co after Samuel Evans.[11]
Teacup and Saucer, (**721**), c.1800, Staffordshire, New Hall, height: 6.4cm, (2½in), diameter: 14cm, (5½in), soft-paste porcelain, puce-printed and coloured. Unnamed country house on saucer and a romantic nymph and shepherd scene on the accompanying teacup.

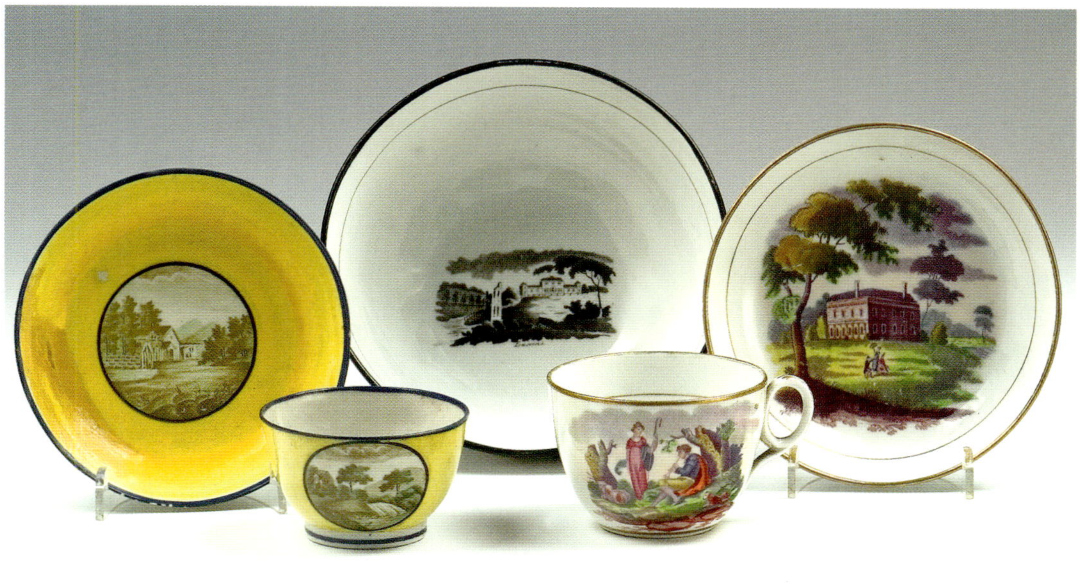

Mug, (**710**), c.1850, Staffordshire, height: 6.8cm, (2⅝in), printed earthenware. Entitled, 'CRANBROOK CHURCH', St Dunstan's, Cranbrook in Kent was sometimes known as 'the Cathedral of the Weald'.
Mug, (**722**), c.1880, Staffordshire, height: 8.9cm, (3½in), blue-printed earthenware. Entitled,'LONDON HOSPITAL, INCORPORATED MDCCLVIII' (1758) is marked beneath with a large blue '1'. In 1876 Queen Victoria opened a new wing at the London Hospital, (founded 1757), then the largest hospital in the country. The mug probably dates from this time.
Plate, (**699**), c.1845, Staffordshire, height: 17.2cm, (6¾in), printed bone china. Inscribed, 'St Alban's Abbey', the view may date from the 1840s, following an early restoration under the architect L.N. Cottingham, when the tower spike was removed.
Mug, (**711**), c.1860, Staffordshire, height: 8.3cm, (3¼in), printed earthenware. The view, entitled 'MARKET PLACE DEVIZES', shows the Gothic-style market cross, (1814), and to the right is the Corn Exchange, (1857) topped by an imposing statue of Ceres. (Stamped beneath with the name of Alfred Parsons, China Warehouse, Devizes).
Pair of Candlesticks, (**707 + 708**), c.1880, Germany, each height: 12cm,(4¾in), hard-paste porcelain, printed, enamelled and gilt. Inscribed, 'GUILDHALL PLYMOUTH' and 'THE ROYAL ALBERT BRIDGE SALTASH'. The bridge over the Tamar, designed by I.K. Brunel, was opened by the Prince Consort in 1859.

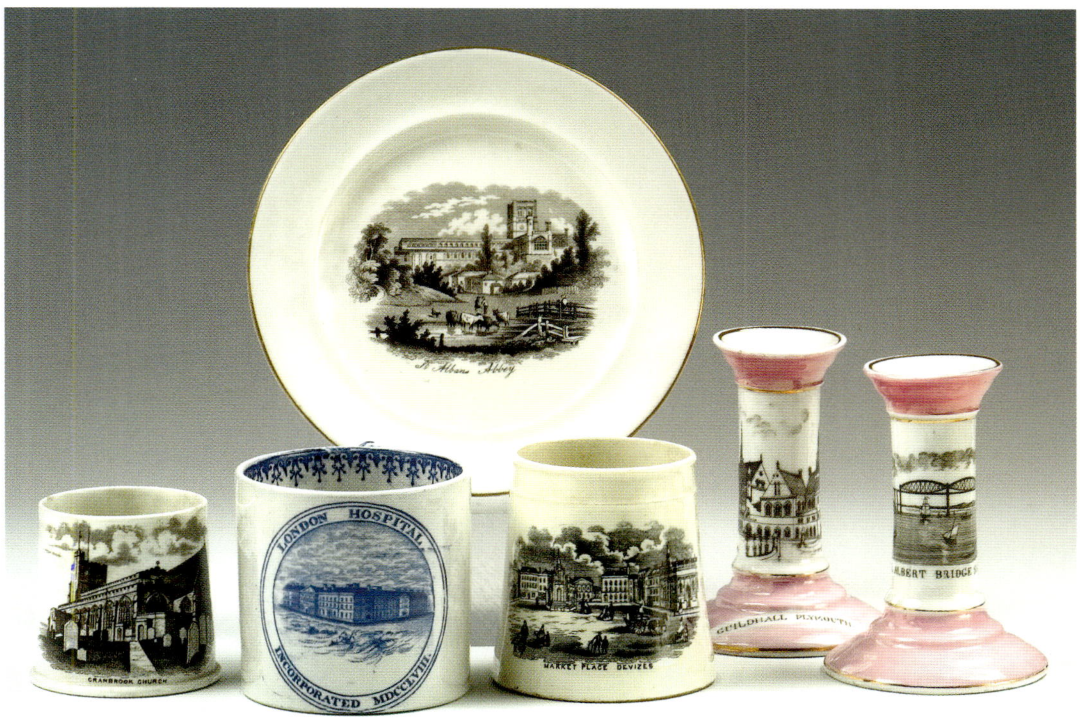

Pair of Bulb Pots, (**705 & A**), c.1810, each height: 19.1cm,(7½in), pearlware, enamelled and lustred. Modelled with bow fronts and four Corinthian capped pilasters, they are decorated with well-painted pink lustre landscapes and country cottages.

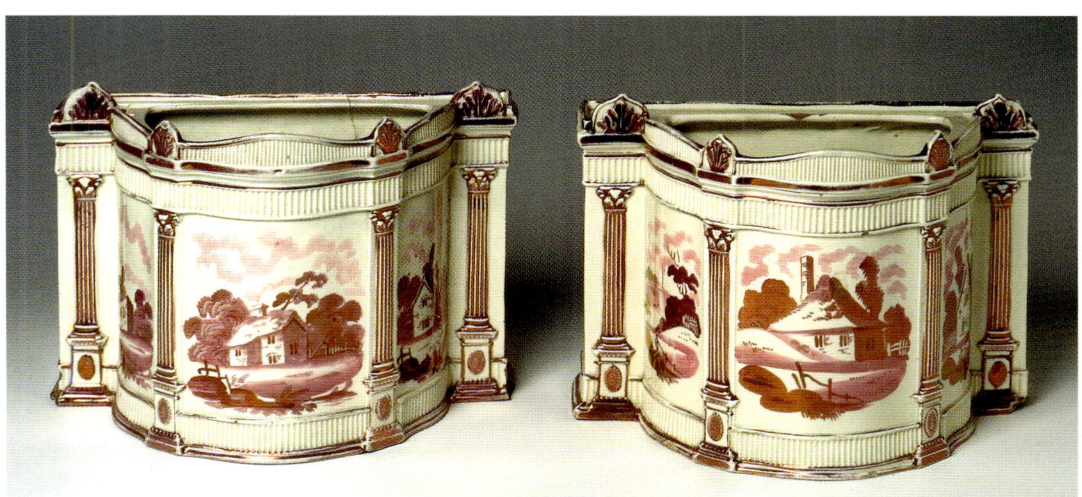

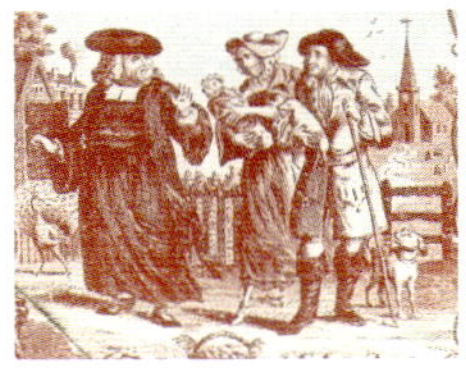

Chapter 12

SCRIPTURE HISTORY & RELIGION

Henry Willett separated his ceramic survey of religious practice in Britain into two parts. 'Scripture History' deals with the characters, events and parables of the Old and New Testaments, often interpreted in a very lively, contemporary way. Illustrations and three-dimensional realisations of these stories were important in the moral education of a visually sophisticated but partially illiterate society.

'Religion' comprises observations and caricatures of the established church and its employees from 1700 to 1900. The market for these pieces, which were produced in quite large editions and often savagely critical in tone, is less clearly defined but they reflect the anticlerical mood of the times. This section also includes representatives of the many groups who broke away from the established church during the period to set up and promote their own non conformist sects.

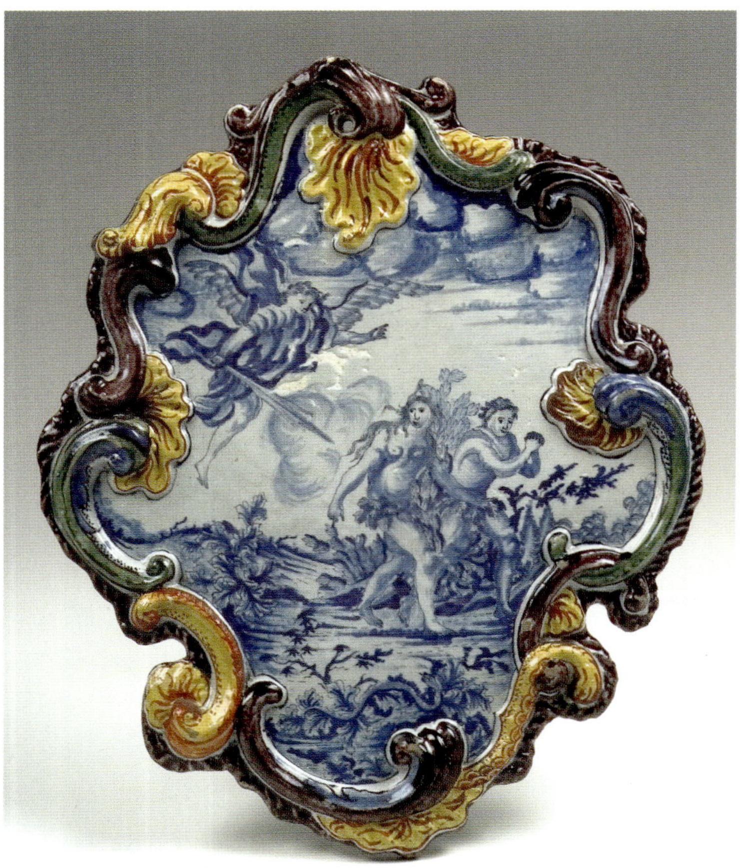

Plaque, (**735**), c.1760, Holland, height: 28.5cm, (11¼in), delftware. Within a scrolling frame, pierced for hanging, Adam and Eve are expelled from Eden. Wearing modest wreaths about their waists, they flee the Archangel Michael, who brandishes his sword.[1]

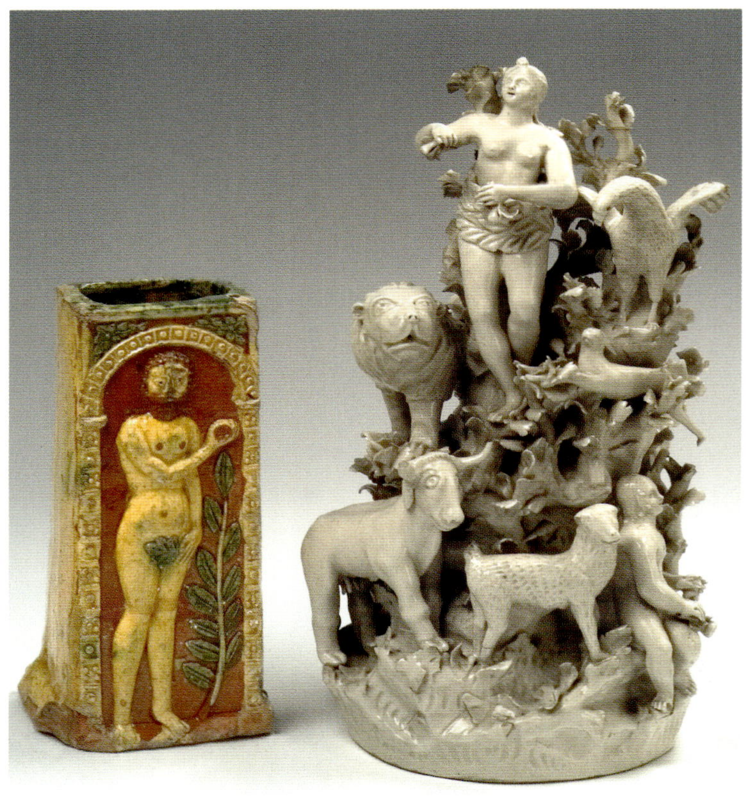

Candle-holder, (**737**), c.1700, Germany, height: 21.6cm, (8½in), earthenware, oxide-coloured. Heavily potted (with a lug for hanging), relief-moulded and slip decorated with the figure of Adam standing in a niche.
Figure Group, (**736**), c.1770, Italy, possibly Le Nove factory,[2] height: 31.8cm, (12½in), earthenware. Naively modelled figure of Eve (or an angel) hovering in a tree above the seated figure of Adam, together with an eagle, two lions, a goat, a pig, a cow and a hare.

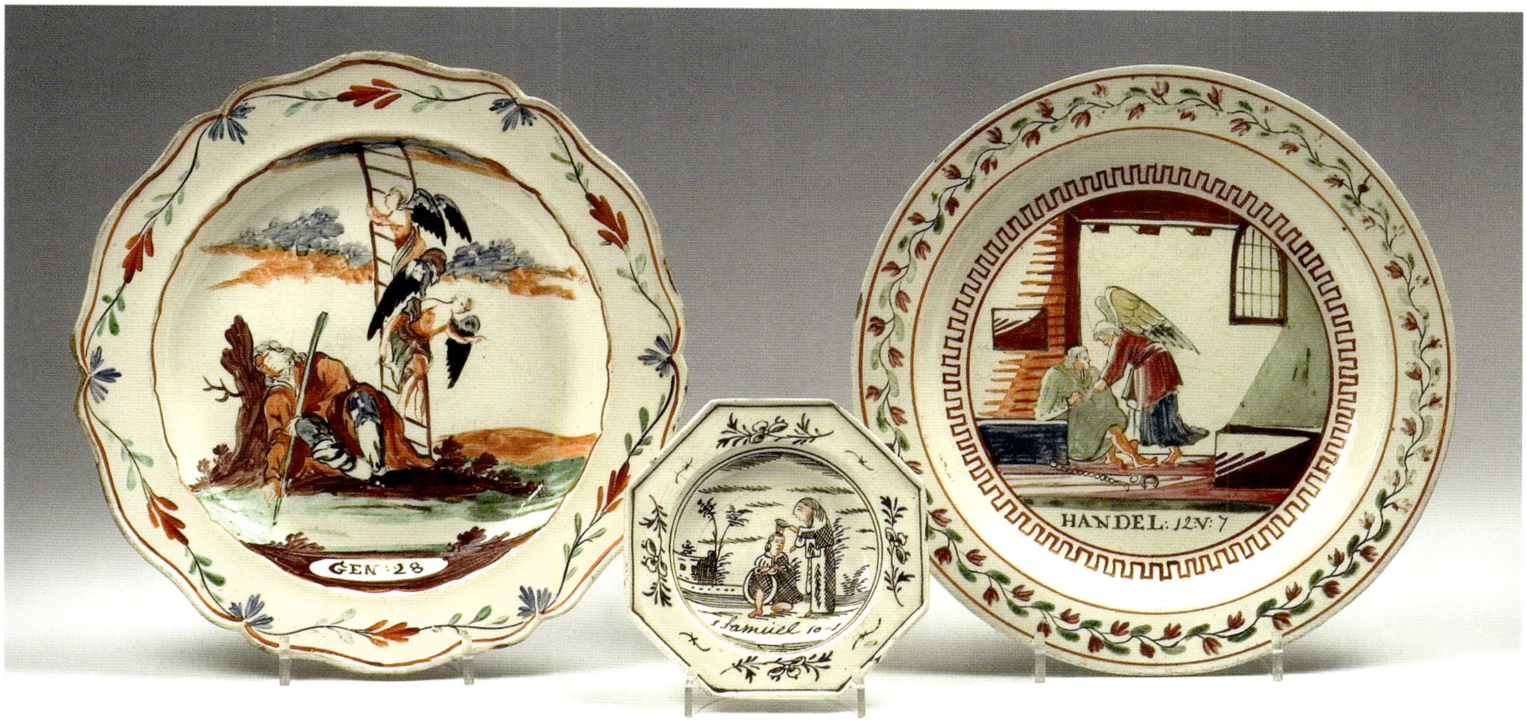

A number of pieces with religious subjects were made in Staffordshire or Yorkshire and exported for decoration in Holland.
Plate, (**747**), Staffordshire or Yorkshire, diameter: 25.4cm, (10in), enamelled creamware. Inscribed, 'Gen[esis] ch:28.', the sleeping Jacob dreams of angels climbing a ladder to and from Heaven. Possibly decorated in Holland.

Plate, (**742**), Staffordshire or Yorkshire, diameter: 12.7cm, (5in), enamelled creamware. Inscribed, '1 Samuel 10-1', Samuel anoints Saul, who kneels at his feet.
Plate, (**792**), Staffordshire or Yorkshire, diameter: 25.4cm, (10in), enamelled creamware. Inscribed, 'HANDEL: 12: v: 7' (Acts 12:7), an angel releases St Peter from prison. Decorated in Holland.

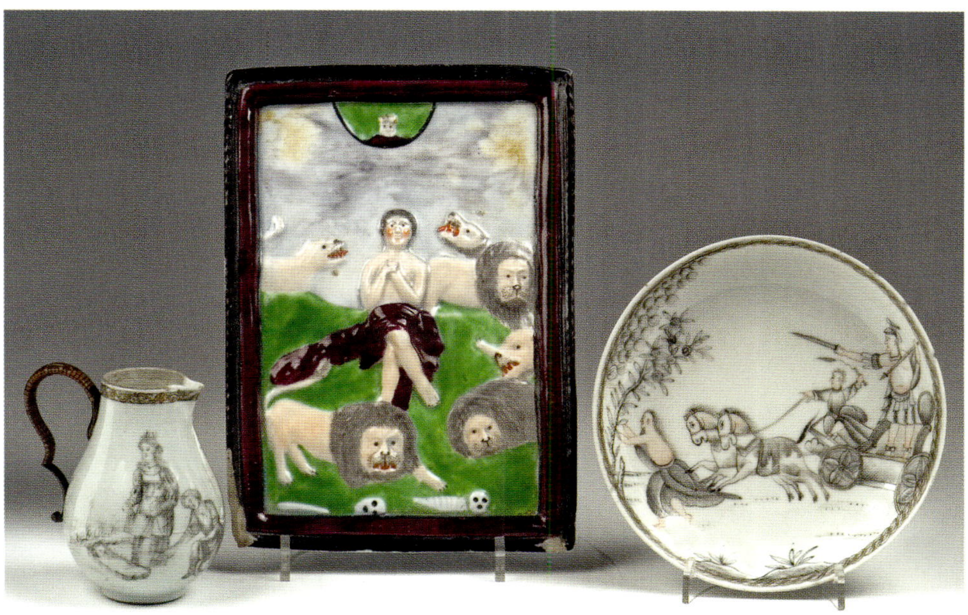

Cream Jug, (**741**), c.1760, China, height: 9.6cm, (3¾in), hard-paste porcelain. Painted with the story of the discovery of Moses in the bulrushes (Exodus 2: 1-10.) Replacement metal handle, delicately bound in woven cane.
Plaque, (**749**), c.1820, probably Staffordshire, height: 21.6cm, (8½in), enamelled, soft-paste porcelain. Relief-moulded with Daniel in the lions' den. Darius, King of Babylon, favoured Daniel but when the prophet prayed to the God of Israel, he was thrown to the lions. Daniel was found unharmed, since God's angel had 'shut the mouths of the lions'. (Daniel 6: 1-23). God looks down from the sky as Daniel sits, cross-legged, in the midst of a prowling pride. The bones of those less favoured by God lie in the foreground.
Saucer, (**748**), c.1770, China, diameter: 15.9cm, (6¼in), hard-paste porcelain. Ahab (seventh King of Israel) in his chariot, pursues the prophet Elijah, who had just denounced him as an idolater (who had allowed the worship of Baal) and a murderer. He has also told Ahab that none of his male heirs would survive (1 Kings 21: 17-24).

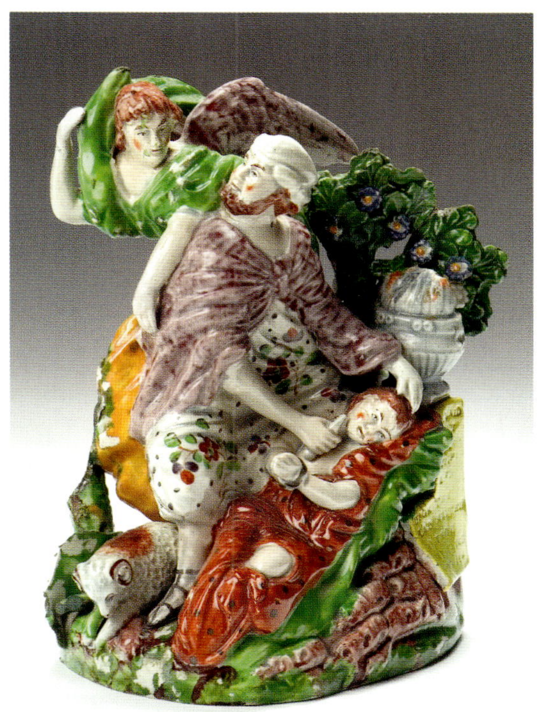

Figure Group, (**738**), c.1820, Staffordshire, height: 17.8cm, (7in), enamelled pearlware. An Angel touches Abraham as he prepares to cut the throat of his son, Isaac. 'God tested Abraham, and said to him, 'Abraham! Take your son, your only son Isaac, whom you love, and go to the land of Moriah, and offer him there as a burnt offering' (Genesis 22: 1-2). Impressed inscription has a touching note of informality, 'HE SAID LAY NOT THINE HAND UPON THE LAD NEITHER DO THOU ANY THING UNTO HIM'.

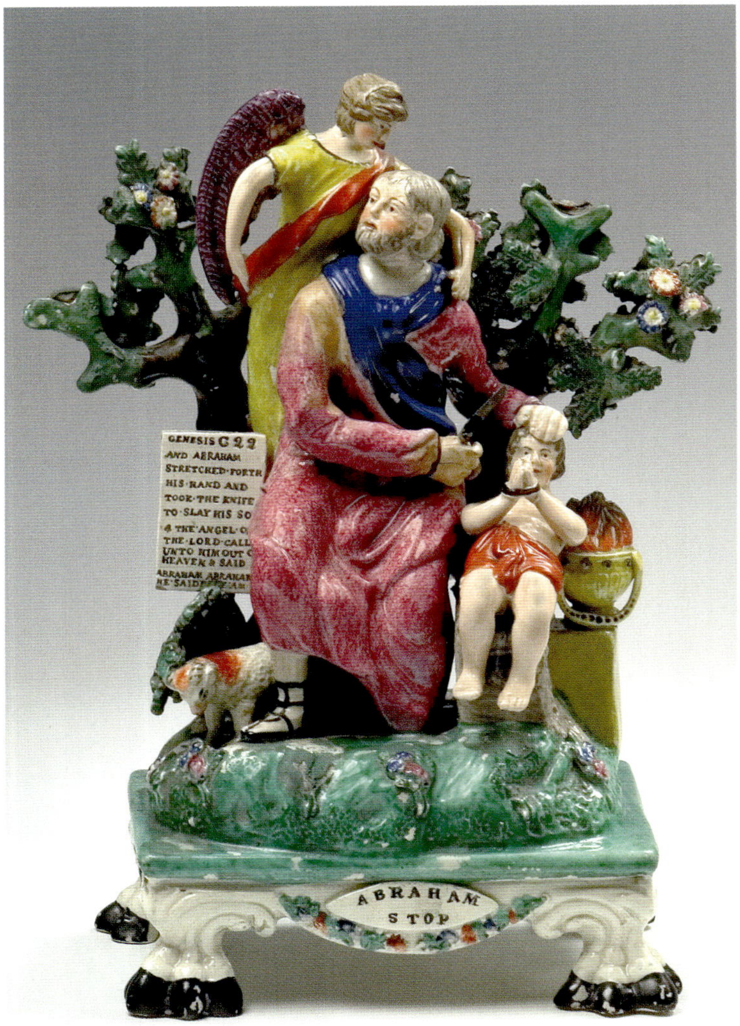

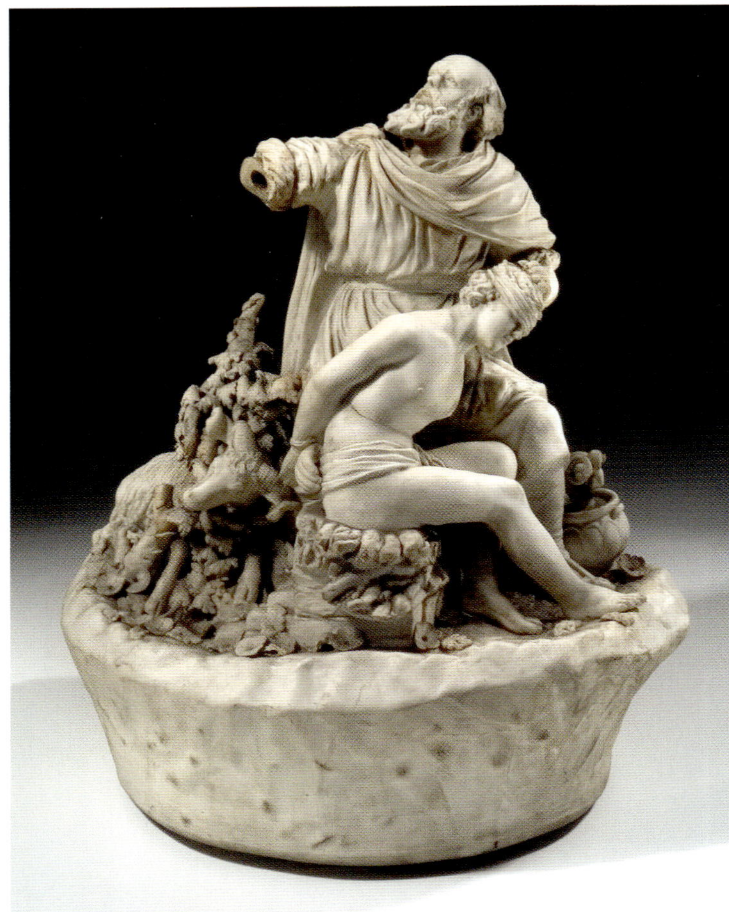

Figure Group, (**740**), c.1850, Staffordshire, height: 35.6cm, (14in), biscuit porcelain. Sculpted group, probably for installation in a church. Abraham gazes upwards as he raises his (missing) right arm to strike Isaac. The ram is caught in a thicket.

Figure Group, (**739**), c.1830, Staffordshire, height: 30.5cm, (12in), enamelled pearlware. Table-based group, impressed, 'ABRAHAM STOP'. The angel appears ready to enfold Abraham in his arms as he raises a (metal) knife to sacrifice the child. A tiny ram stands to the left. Above the ram a tablet reads, 'GENESIS C22 / AND ABRAHAM STRETCHED*FORTH HIS*HAND AND TOOK* THE KNIFE TO*SLAY HIS SON & THE*ANGEL*OF THE*LORD* CAME UNTO HIM' (Genesis 22:7).

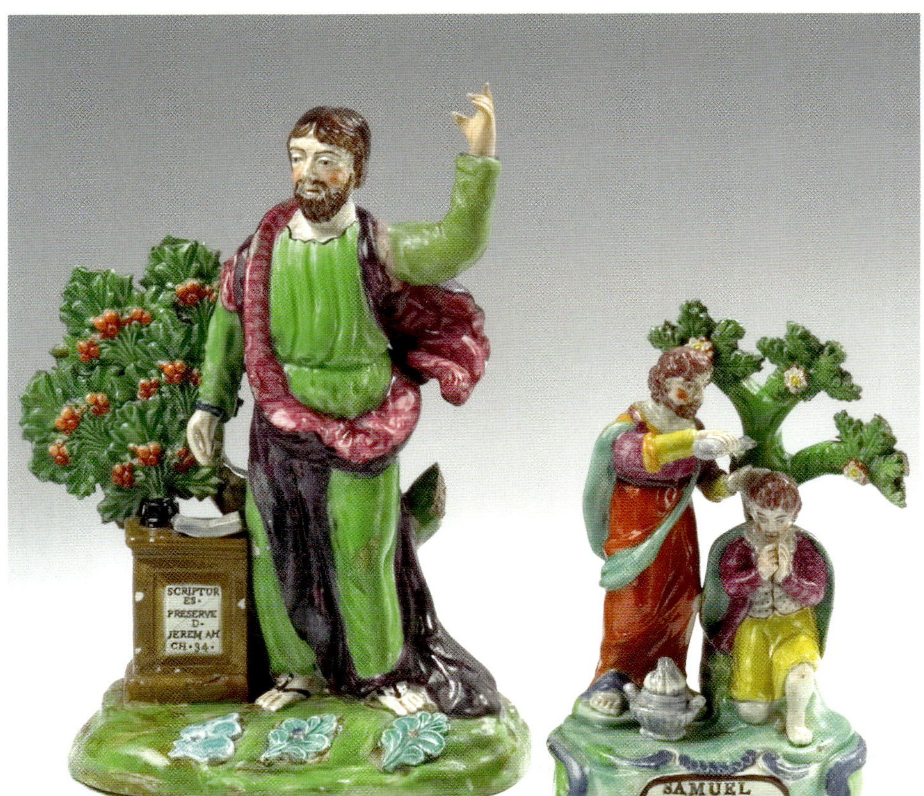

Figure Group, (**750**), c.1830, Staffordshire, height: 24.8cm, (9¾in), enamelled pearlware. The identity of a large Old Testament prophet is puzzling. Willett identified him as Hilkiah, High Priest in the time of King Josiah. But the inscription on the altar beside the declaiming figure reads, 'SCRIPTURES PRESERVED, JEREMIAH 34'. This chapter relates to God's command (through the prophet Jeremiah) to King Zedekiah of Judah to free all the Hebrew slaves in his kingdom.

Figure Group, (**743**), c.1830, Staffordshire, height: 18.4cm, (7¼in), enamelled pearlware. Entitled, 'SAMUEL ANOINTING DAVID', scene shows Samuel pouring oil onto the head of David, the youngest son of Jesse of Bethlehem, as king. (The story is told in 1 Samuel 16: 12-13).

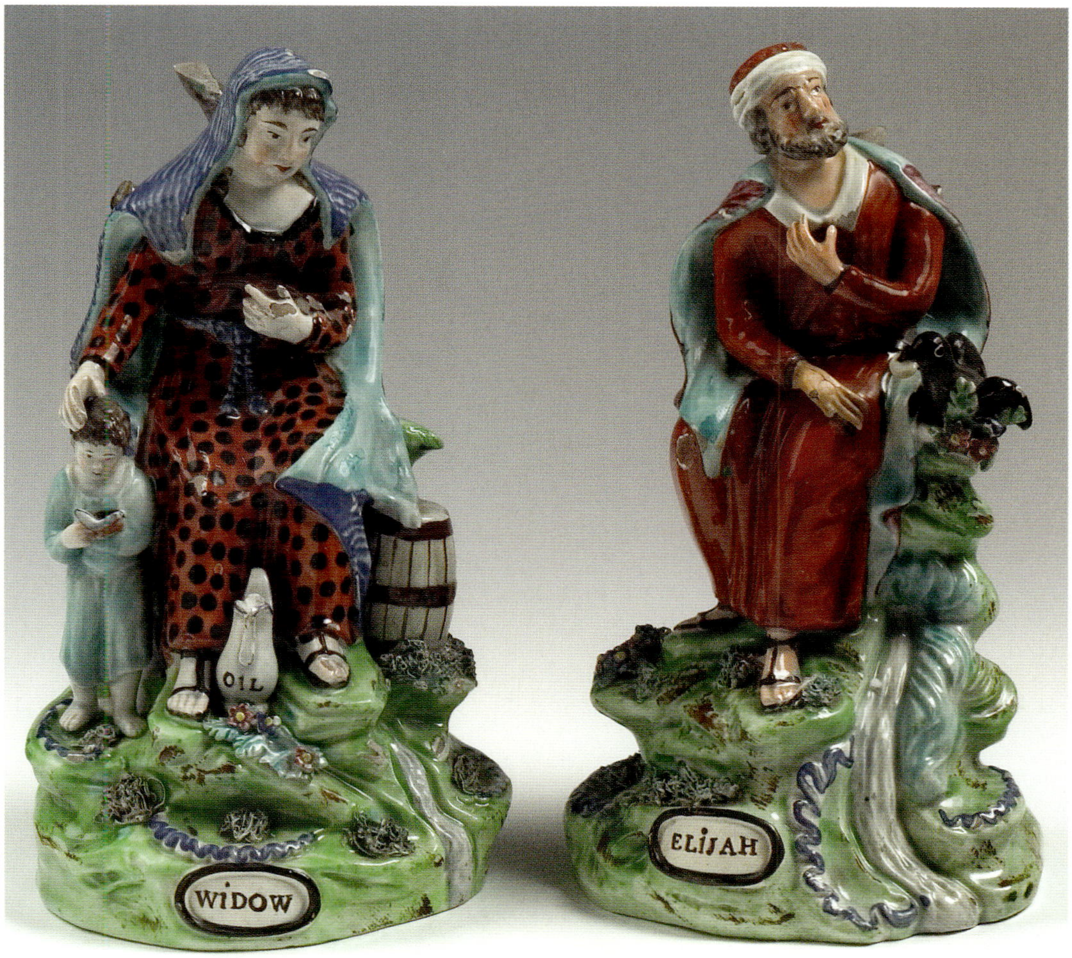

Pair of Figure Groups, (744 & A), c.1820, Staffordshire, John Walton, height: 25.4cm, (10in), height: 25.4cm, (10in), enamelled pearlware. Figures inscribed 'ELIJAH' and 'WIDOW', represent the story of the prophet Elijah and the Widow of Zarephath (I Kings 17: 7-24). A raven delivers bread from God to Elijah, in hiding from King Ahab. When the sustaining spring fails, God instructs Elijah to go and seek the Widow of Zarephath in Sidon. Elijah assures the widow, about to cook her last meal with a handful of flour and a few drops of oil, that if she shares it with him, 'The jar of flour will not be used up and the jug of oil will not run dry until the day the Lord gives rain on the land.' The widow stands beside a flowing stream, with a barrel of flour and a jug marked 'OIL'. She places a protective hand on the head of her son (whom Elijah would later raise from the dead).

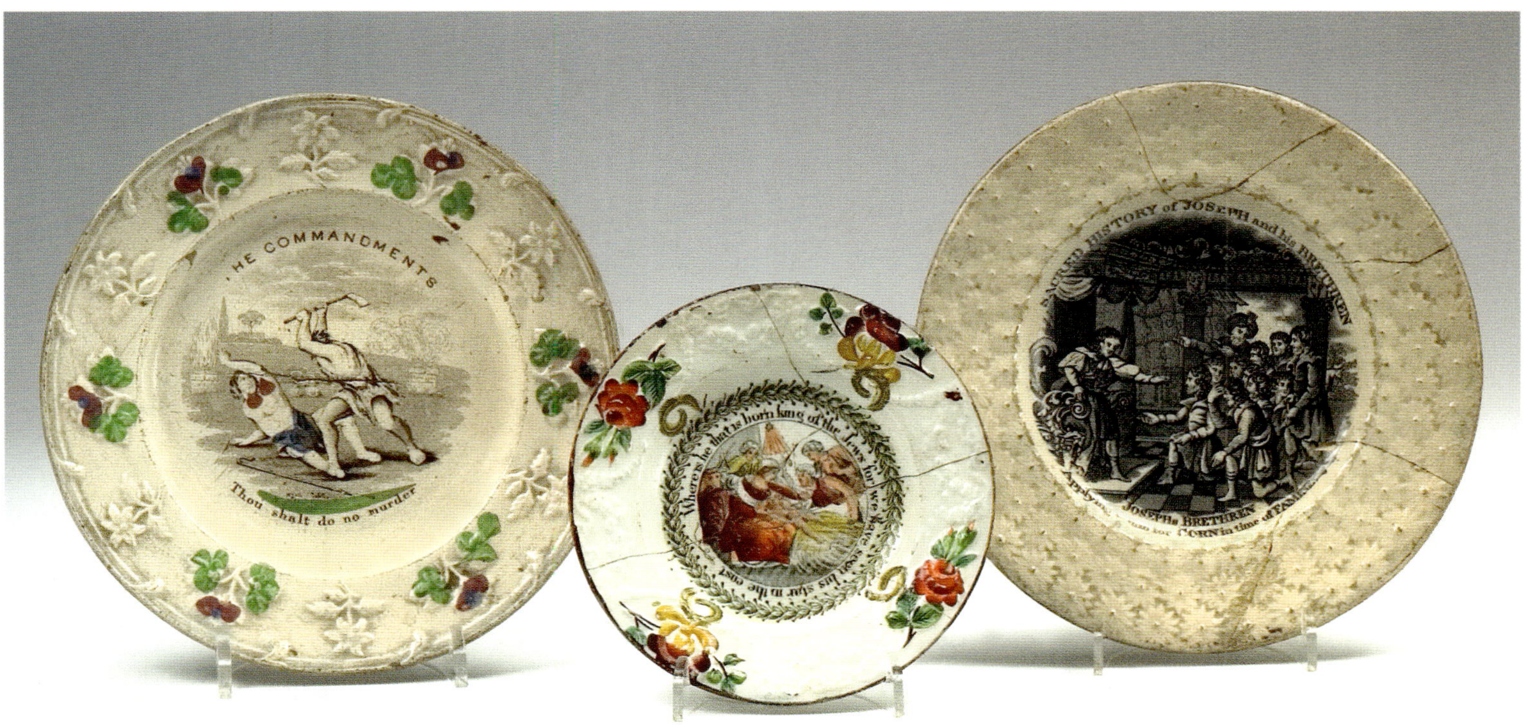

Nursery Plate, (745), c.1840, Staffordshire, diameter: 18.4cm, (7¼in), earthenware, printed and coloured. Entitled, 'THE COMMANDMENTS. Thou shalt do no murder,' shows Cain murdering his brother, Abel, with an axe.
Nursery Plate, (757), c.1830, Swansea, Glamorgan Factory, diameter: 14cm, (5½in), earthenware, printed and coloured. Inscribed,' Where is he that is born king of the Jews for we have seen his star in the east', it shows the arrival of the Magi at Christ's birthplace.
Nursery Plate, (746), c.1830, Staffordshire, diameter: 19.1cm, (7½in), printed earthenware. Inscribed, 'SACRED HISTORY OF JOSEPH AND HIS BRETHREN', illustrates the episode where Joseph's brothers petition him for corn, now that he is in a position of authority, during a period of a famine in Egypt.

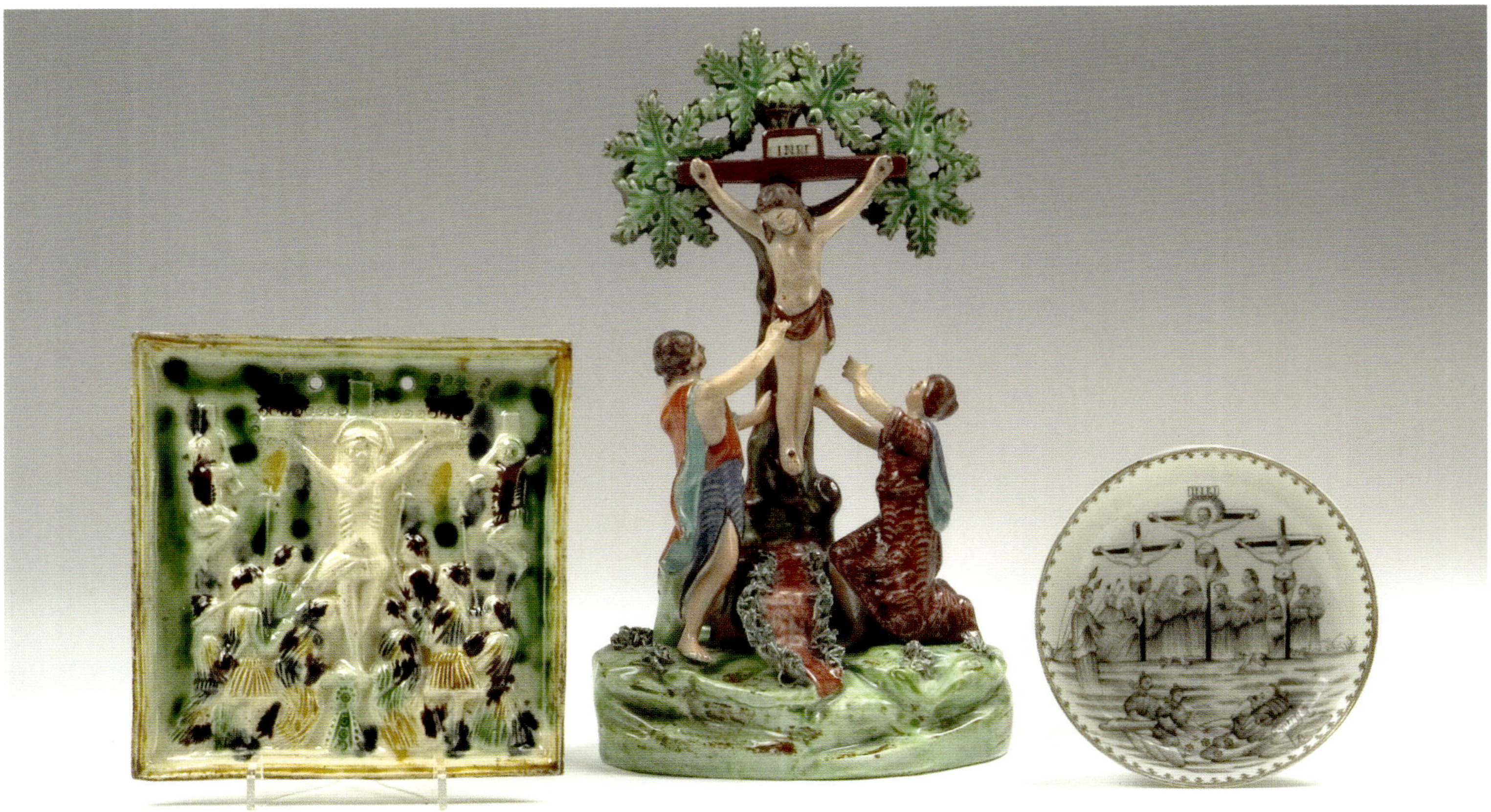

Plaque, (**772**), c.1770, Staffordshire, height: 31.8cm, (12½in), creamware, lead-glazed and oxide-coloured. Rare piece, relief-moulded with scene of Christ crucified between two robbers, surrounded by soldiers. Some of them throw dice for Christ's clothing.
Figure Group, (**771**), c.1820, Staffordshire, height: 26.7cm, (10½in), enamelled pearlware. Christ's Crucifixion; the agonised gestures of St John the Evangelist and Mary Magdalene, who kneels beside the Cross add to the drama.
Saucer, (**770**), c.1770, China, diameter: 12.7cm, (5in), hard-paste porcelain. Painted with Christ's Crucifixion, including the dice throwing.

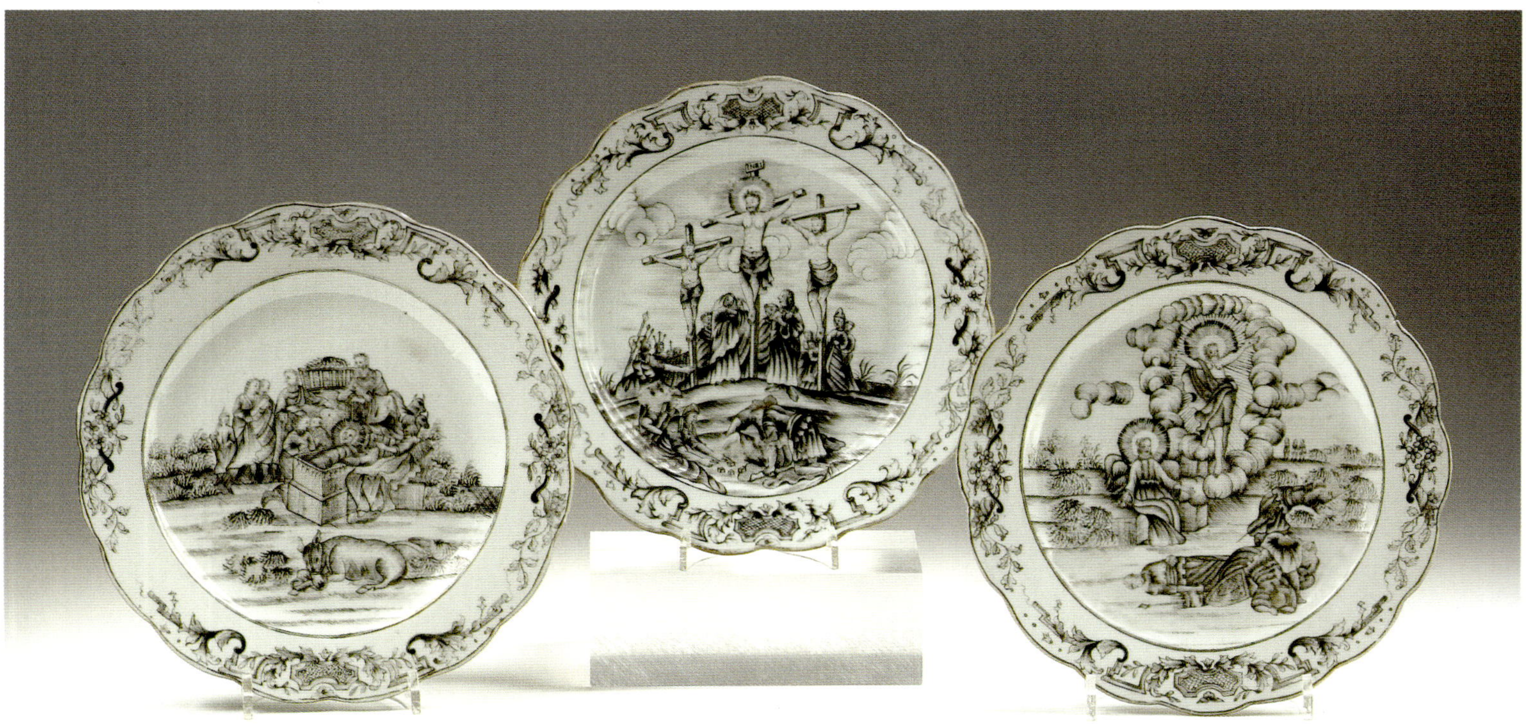

Plate, (**779**), c.1760, China, diameter: 22.9cm, (9in), hard-paste porcelain. Matching set of plates illustrating episodes in the Life of Christ. The Nativity depicted in a landscape.
Plate, (**780**), c.1760, China, diameter: 22.9cm, (9in), hard-paste porcelain. Christ's Crucifixion; the soldiers throw dice for his clothes.
Plate, (**781**), c.1760, China, diameter: 22.9cm, (9in), hard-paste porcelain. Christ's Resurrection; an angel attends as he rises from the tomb while the soldiers sleep.

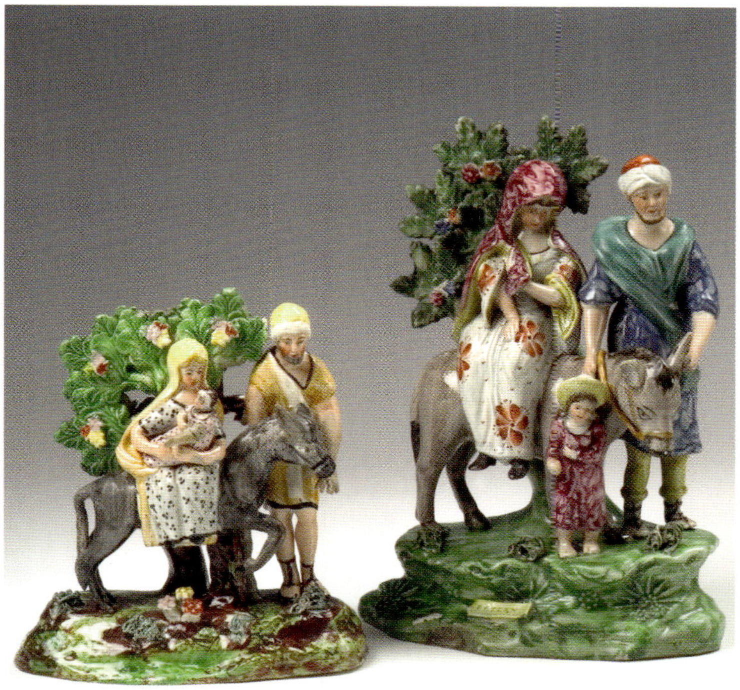

Figure Group, (**758**), c.1815, Staffordshire, height: 17.2cm, (6¾in), enamelled pearlware. Represents the flight of the Holy Family into Egypt. The bocage trees behind the donkey carrying Mary have distinctive curly leaves and its base is impressed 'S'.
Figure Group, (**759**), c.1820, Staffordshire, height: 24.2cm, (9½in), enamelled pearlware. Labelled, 'RETERN [*sic*]', the Holy Family are shown returning from Egypt to Israel. Jesus is shown as a little boy wearing a broad-brimmed straw hat or halo.

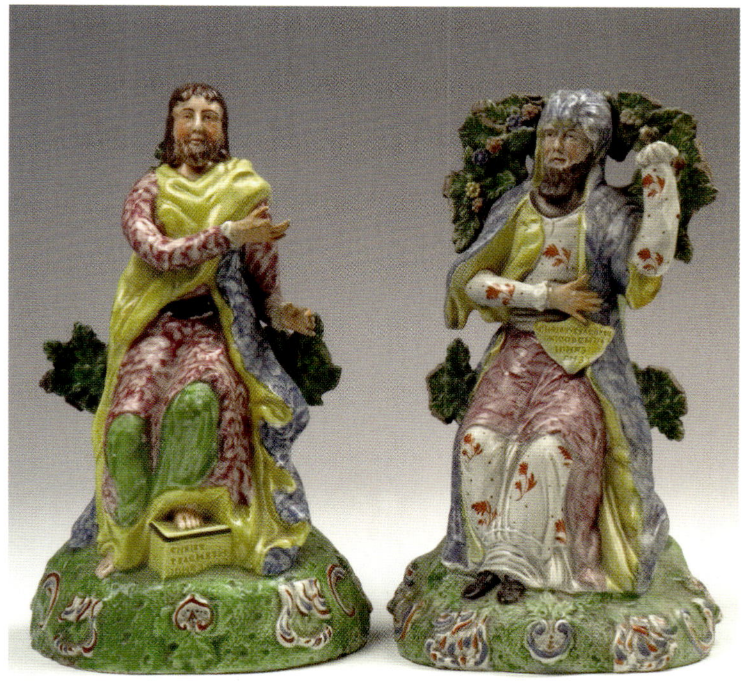

Pair of Figures, (**760 & 761**), c.1820, Staffordshire, height: 26.7cm, (10½in), height: 26.7cm, (10½in), enamelled pearlware. They represent Jesus, his foot on a plaque, impressed, 'CHRIST TEACHETH / JOHN 3' and Nicodemus, the Pharisee and member of the Sanhedrin, (the Jewish ruling council). The latter has a shield impressed, 'CHRIST TEACHETH / NICODEMUS / JOHN 3 / CH 3' and wears a 'tallit' or prayer shawl. Their discussion is recorded in John 3 1-21.

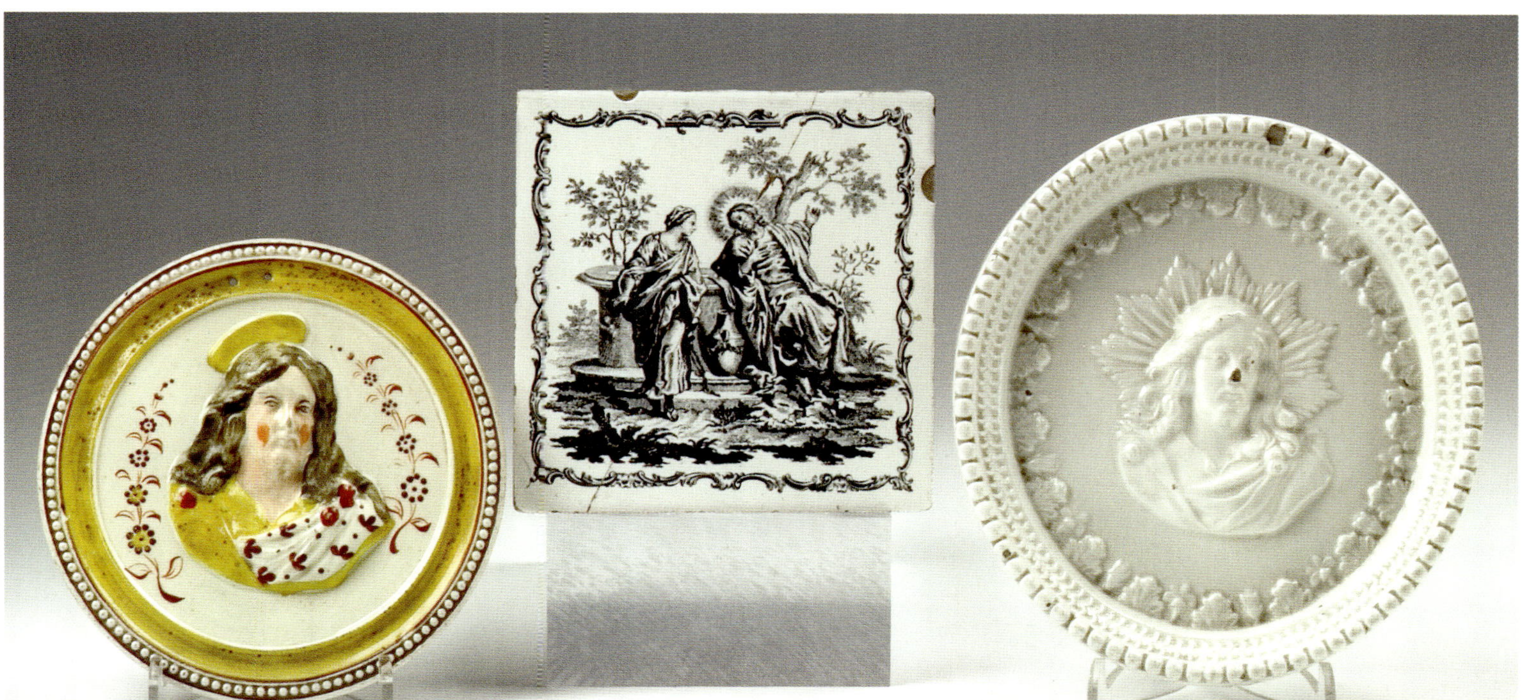

Plaque, (**769**), c.1800, Staffordshire, diameter: 13.6cm, (5⅜in), enamelled creamware.
Relief-moulded with a bust of Christ. Enamelled, giving Christ a floral-patterned robe and unusually pink cheeks.
Tile, (**762**), c.1770, Liverpool, height: 12.7cm, (5in), printed, tin-glazed earthenware. Christ sits at a well with a woman of Samaria. Relates to the incident when Jesus, asked a non-Jewish woman for water and convinced her that he was the Messiah (John 4: 4-29). The image derives from a print after Carlo Maratta.[3]
Plaque, (**768**), c.1810, Staffordshire, diameter: 16.5cm, (6½in), earthenware. Relief-moulded with distinctive oval frame, of a type found on other items in the Willett Collection (e.g. HW 050, 078).

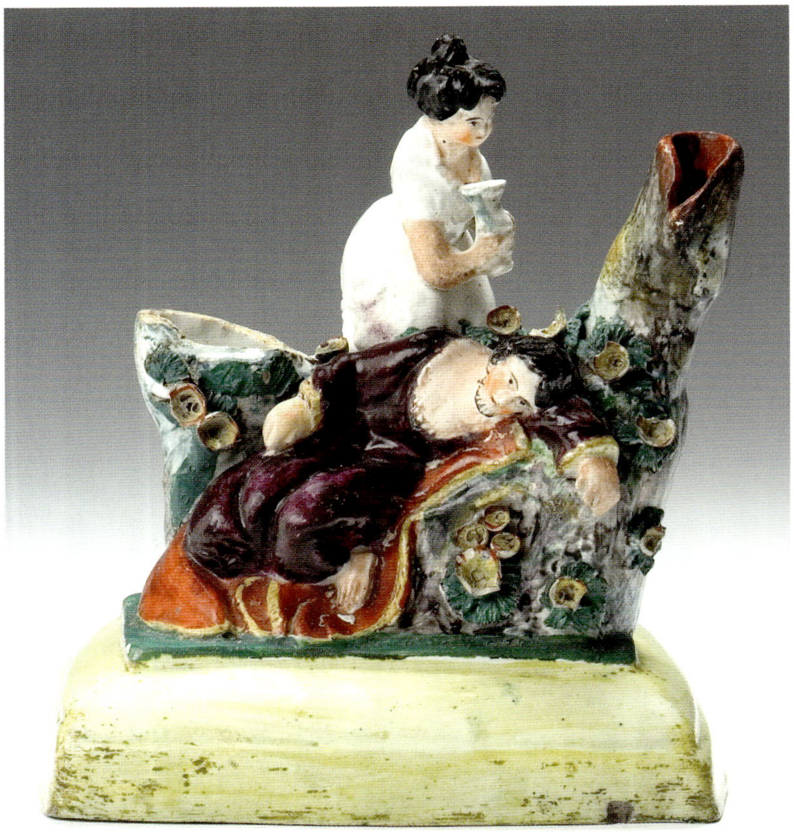

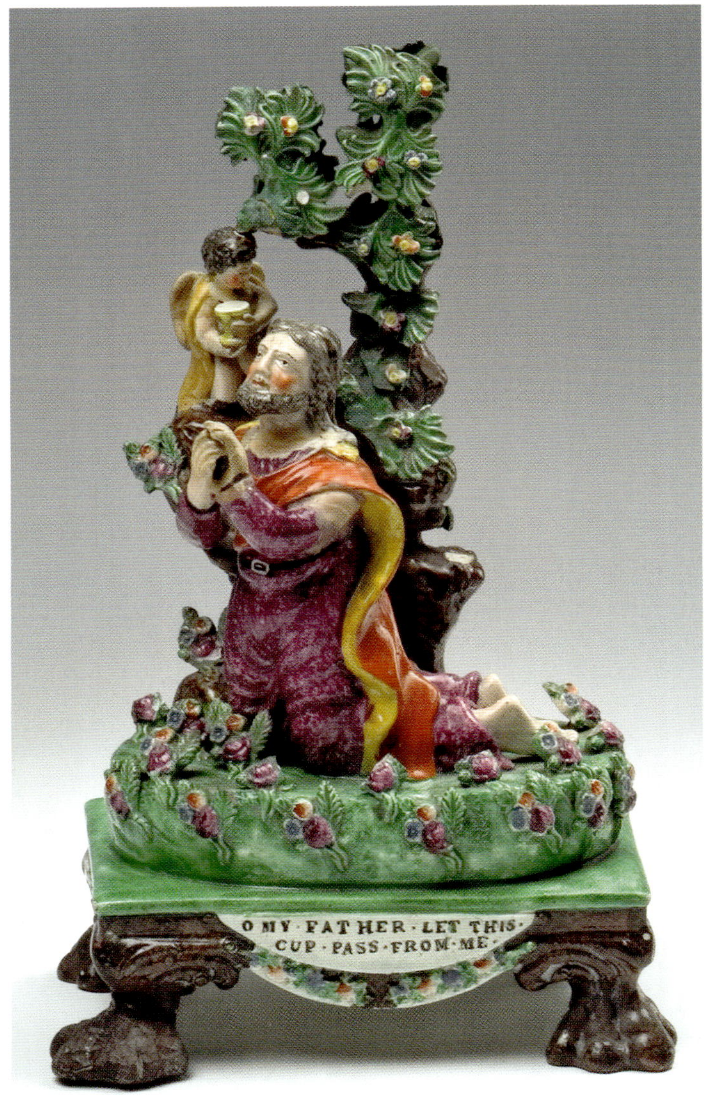

Figure Group, (**764**), c.1830, Staffordshire, height: 15.3cm, (6in), enamelled pearlware. Christ in the Garden of Gethsemane, on the Mount of Olives, before his Crucifixion. A small female figure (possibly intended to be an angel?) leans over his prostrate figure to offer a cup of water.

Figure Group, (**765**), c.1830, Staffordshire, height: 30.5cm cm, (12in), enamelled pearlware. Table-based group, shows Christ on his knees, praying in anguish as an angel offers him a cup. Plaque beneath impressed, 'O MY*FATHER*LET THIS*CUP*PASS* FROM*ME', (Matthew 26: 39 and Mark 14: 35).

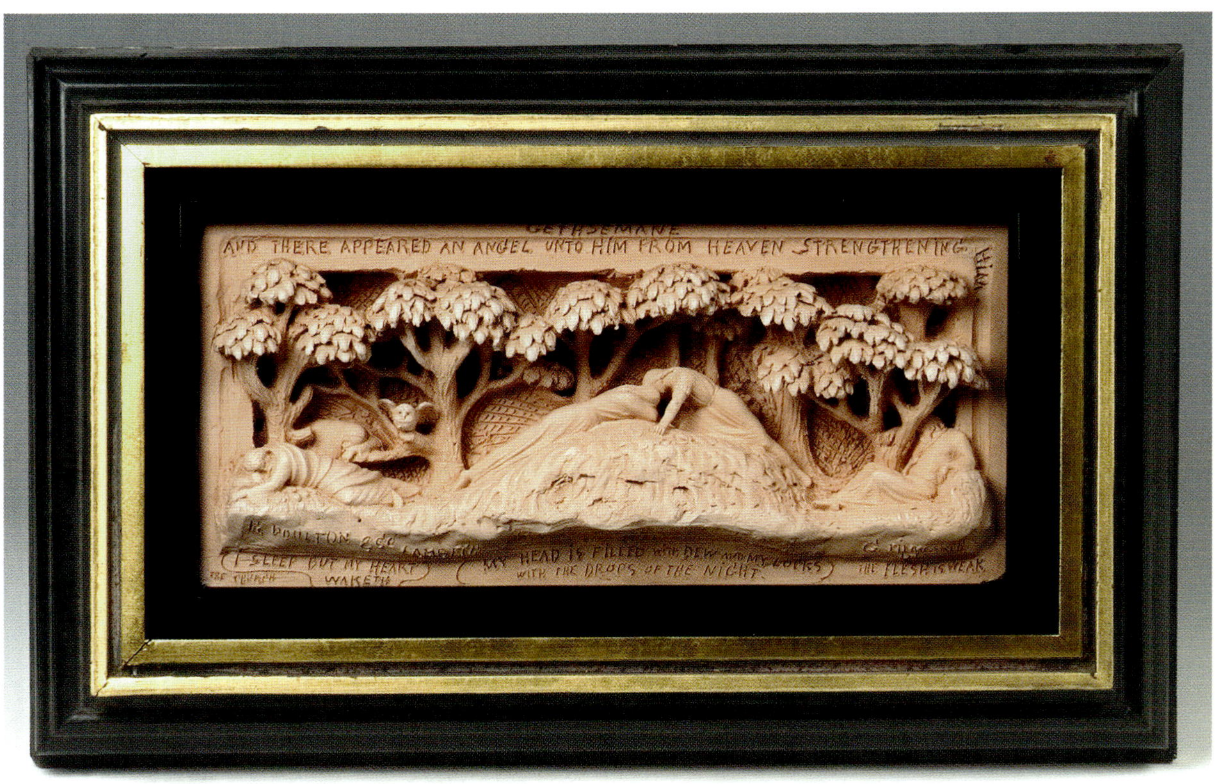

Sculpture, (**857**), c.1880, London, Doulton, height: 30.5cm, (12in), terracotta. Panel modelled by George Tinworth (1843-1913) showing Christ praying on the Mount of Olives among trees, as his disciples sleep. Tinworth included the title and a quotation from Luke 22:43 'GETHSEMANE / AND THERE APPEARED AN ANGEL UNTO HIM FROM HEAVEN, STRENGTHENING HIM'.

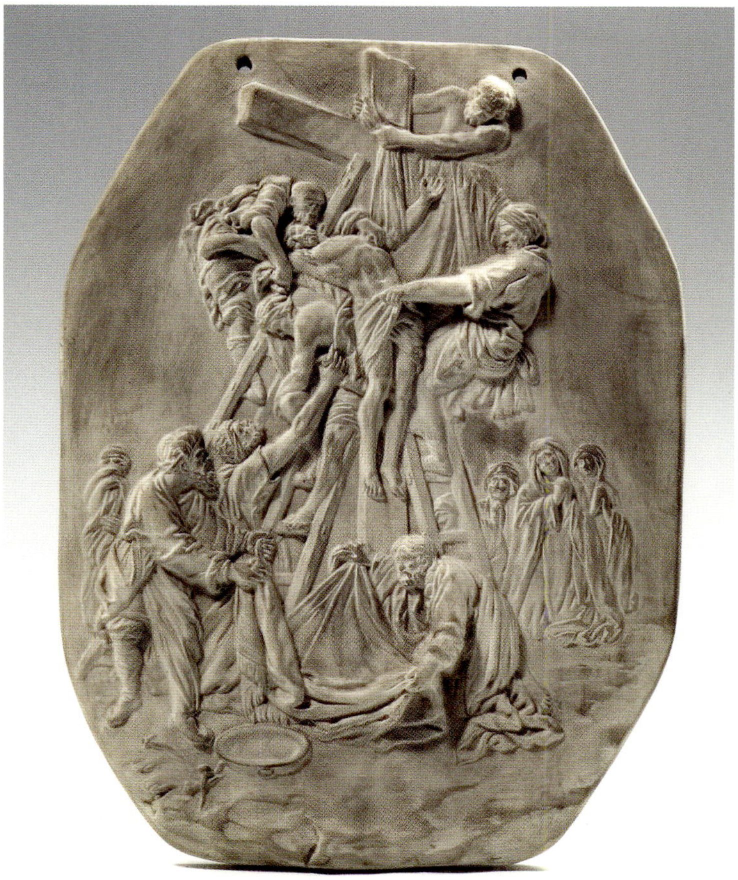

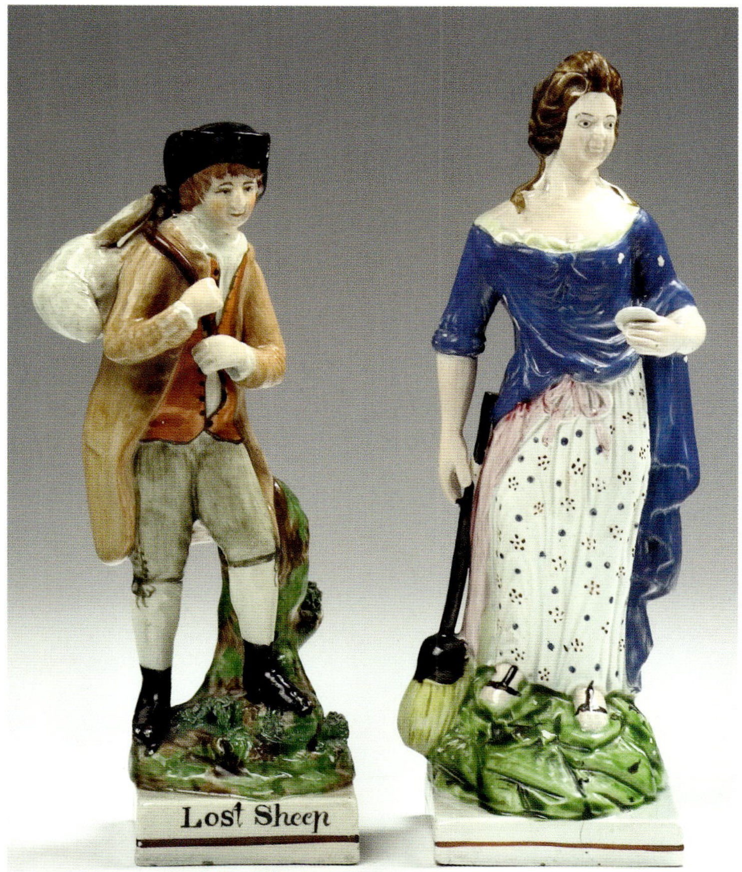

Plaque, (**773**), c.1800, height: 31.8cm, (12½in), plaster. Relief-moulded composition representing Christ's descent from the Cross. Crude cast taken from a well-known piece modelled by Enoch Wood in 1777, based on a work by Jean Jouvenet (1644-1717), rather than Rubens, to whom it is often acknowledged.[4]

Figure, (**777**), c.1820, Staffordshire, Wood factory?, height: 22.9cm, (9in), enamelled pearlware. Inscribed, 'Lost Sheep', a happy shepherd with a lamb slung across his shoulders illustrates God's joy at the redemption of a lost soul (Luke 15, 1-7).
Figure, (**778**), c.1820, Staffordshire, Wood factory?, height: 22.9cm, (9in), enamelled pearlware. A woman with a broom, her overskirt tucked up for housework, holds up the 'Lost Coin', another example of the redemption of a lost soul (Luke 15, 8-10).

Figure, (**775**), c.1800, Staffordshire, height: 24.2cm, (9½in), enamelled pearlware. Woman wearing classical robes, stands beside an altar (with a flame) holding a flagon.
Tile, (**776**), c.1800, London or Holland, height: 24.2cm, (9½in), tin-glazed earthenware. The story of the Wise and Foolish Virgins (Matthew 25: 1-13). Only the five wise virgins, who have remembered to bring oil for their lamps, are ready to escort the Bridegroom (or Christ) to his marriage. Christians should be ready for the arrival of Christ at any time.
Figure, (**774**), c.1800, Staffordshire, height: 20.3cm, (8in), enamelled pearlware. Woman wearing classical robes holds a flaming lamp in one hand and a jug in another. They are probably priestesses or Vestal Virgins, although Willett believed they were Wise and Foolish Virgins.

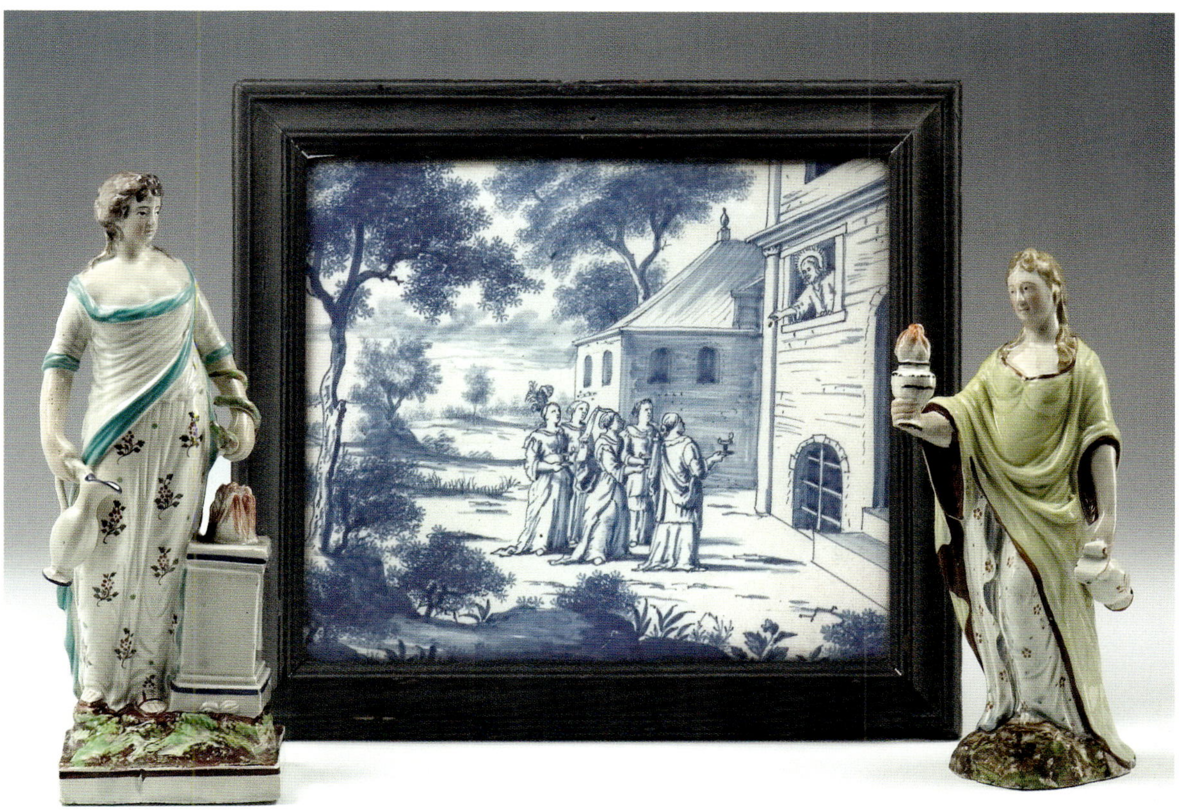

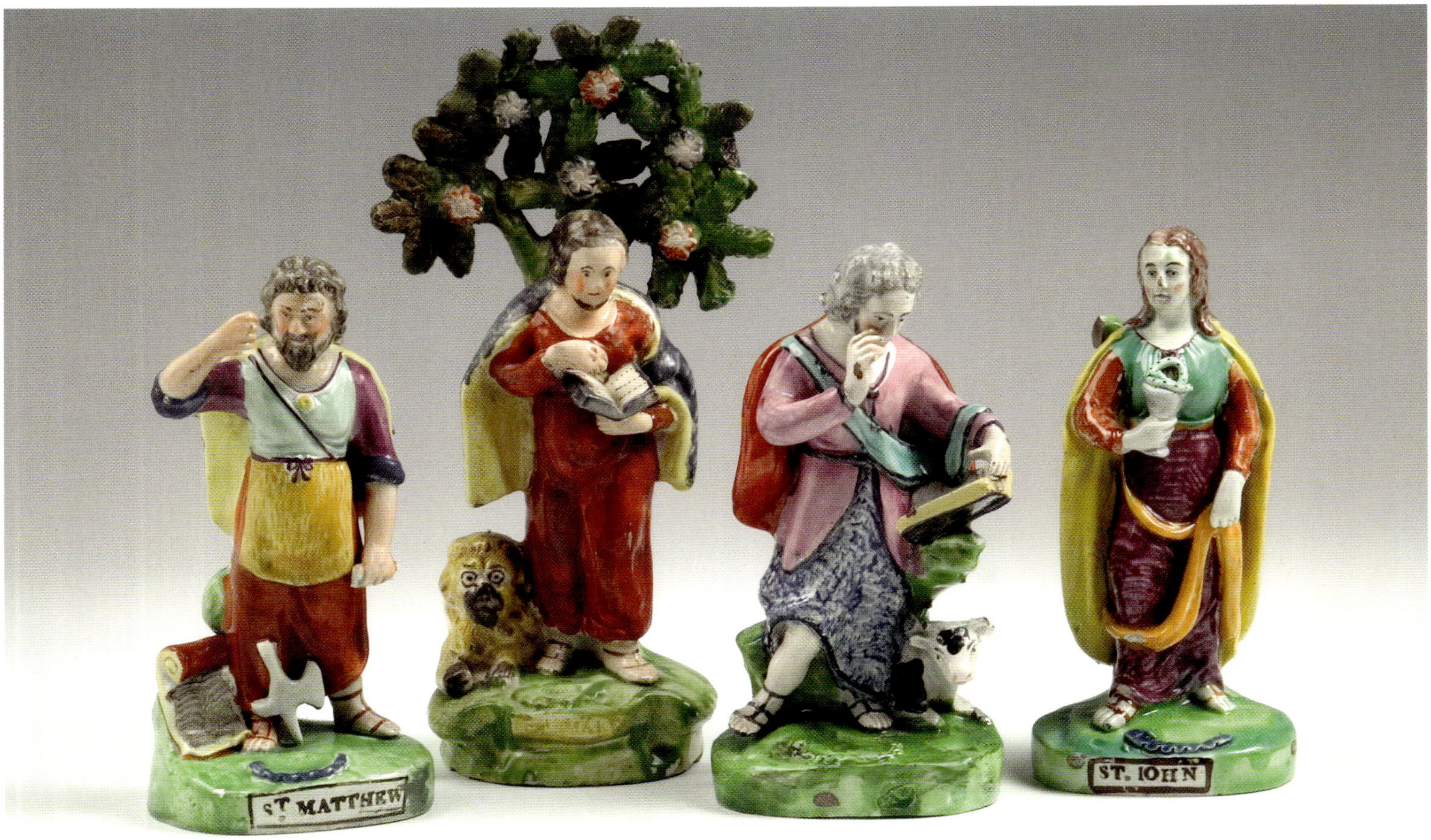

Figure, (**782**), c.1820, Staffordshire, height: 19.1cm, (7½in), enamelled pearlware. St Matthew is shown with a scroll and an axe head (the handle is missing), the instrument of his beheading.
Figure, (**783**), c.1820, Staffordshire, height: 25.4cm, (10in), enamelled pearlware. St Mark writes in a book with a lion at his feet, a bocage tree still intact.

Figure, (**784**), c.1820, Staffordshire, height: 19.1cm, (7½in), enamelled pearlware. St Luke also writes in a book, accompanied by a small ox.
Figure, (**785**), c.1820, Staffordshire, height: 19.1cm, (7½in), enamelled pearlware. St John the Evangelist holds a chalice from which a snake emerges, symbolising the legend of a poisoned cup from which he drank without harm.

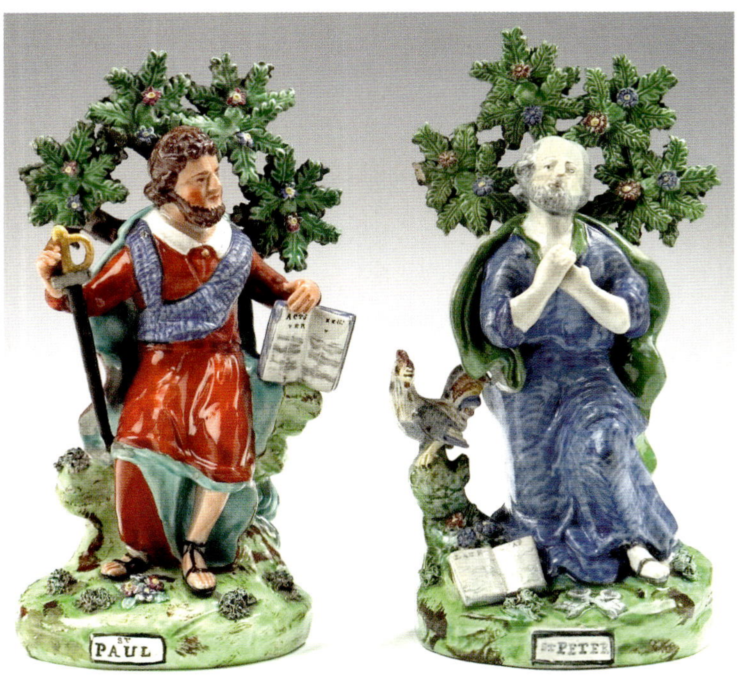

Figure, (**788**), c.1820, Staffordshire, height: 24.2cm, (9½in), enamelled pearlware. St Paul holds a sword, (a weapon with which he was entitled, as a Roman citizen, to be executed) and an open copy of the Acts of the Apostles marked 'Acts ch:xxiii v: v'. During Paul's interrogation by the Sanhedrin he declares, 'Thou shalt not speak evil of the ruler of thy people'.
Figure, (**789**), c.1820, Staffordshire, height: 25.4cm, (10in), enamelled pearlware. St Peter kneels in prayer, accompanied by the cockerel, which, as predicted, crowed after he had thrice denied knowing Christ.

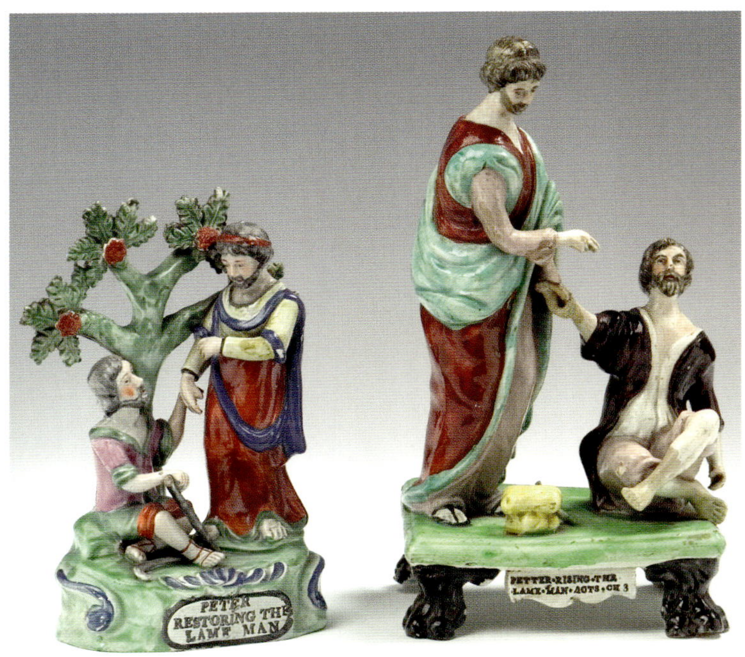

Figure Group, (**786**), c.1820, Staffordshire, height: 19.1cm, (7½in), enamelled pearlware. Impressed, 'PETER RESTORING THE LAME MAN', with a bocage tree.
Figure Group, (**787**), c.1820, Staffordshire, height: 26.7cm, (10½in), enamelled pearlware. Impressed, 'PETTER. [*sic*] RISING. THE. LAME. MAN. ACTS CH.3' enacted on a table-base with grotesque feet. Acts 3 1-10 relates to the miracle where St Peter cured a man who had been lame since birth.

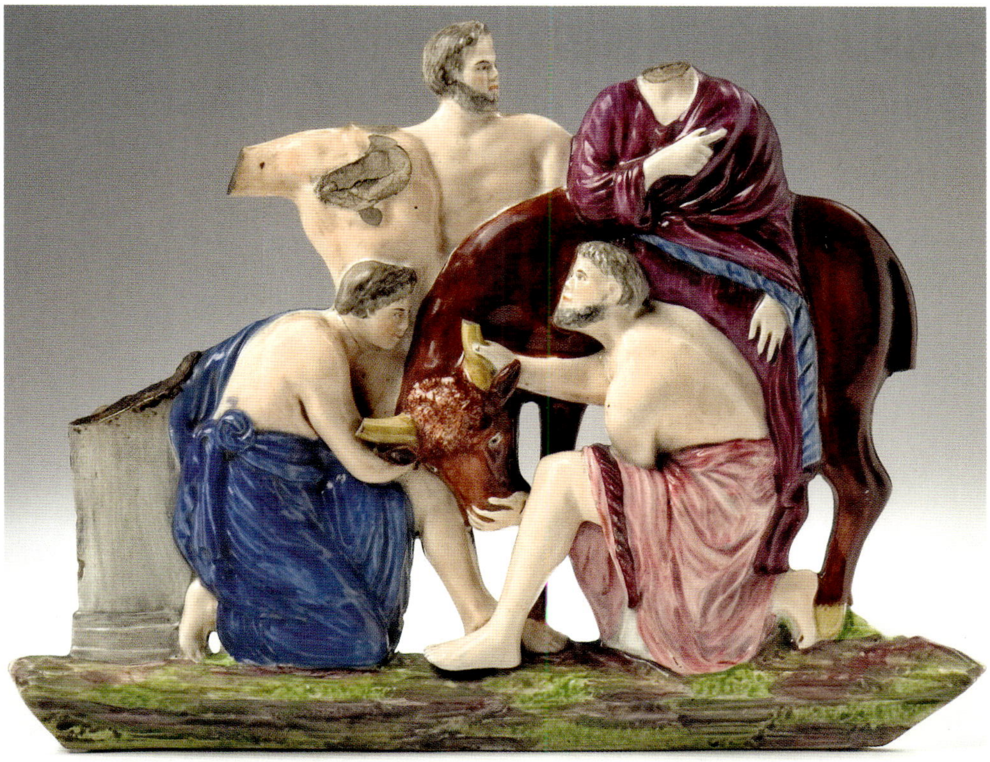

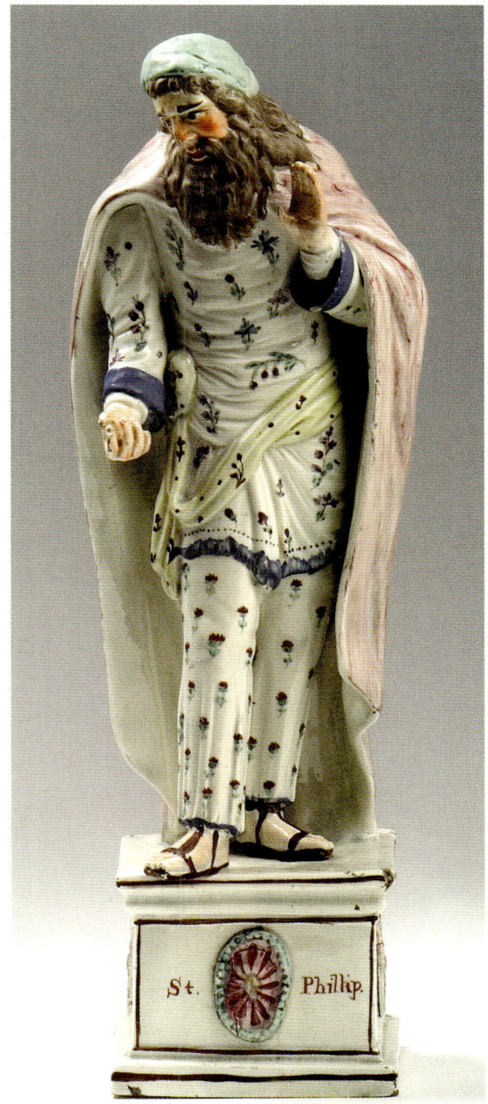

Figure Group, (**790**), c.1820, Staffordshire, height: 22.2cm, (8¾in), enamelled pearlware. Damaged relief-moulded plaque illustrating the 'Sacrifice at Lystra' (Acts 14: 8-15), where St Paul and St Barnabas were hailed as gods after healing a disabled man. They had to explain that they were mortal and dissuaded the Lystrans from sacrificing bulls in their honour. Image loosely based on a print after Raphael's cartoon (for tapestry) of the subject.[5]

Figure, (**791**), c.1790, Staffordshire, Wood factory, height: 36.2cm, (14¼in), enamelled pearlware. Entitled, 'St Phillip', the figure wears a slouch hat and loose clothing including trousers. Based on one modelled by Agostino Carlini for the Derby porcelain factory c.1760.[6] Stands on a neoclassical plinth similar to that supporting the figure of Benjamin Franklin (451).

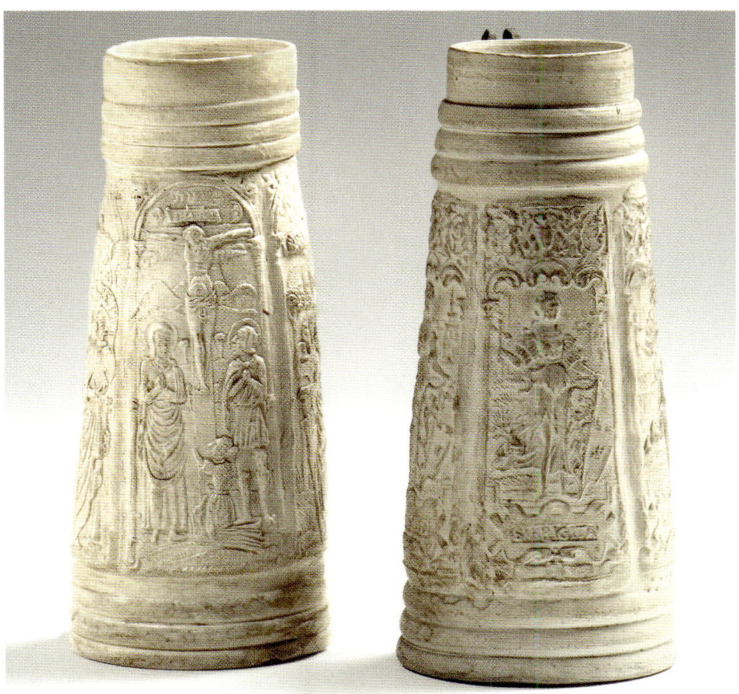

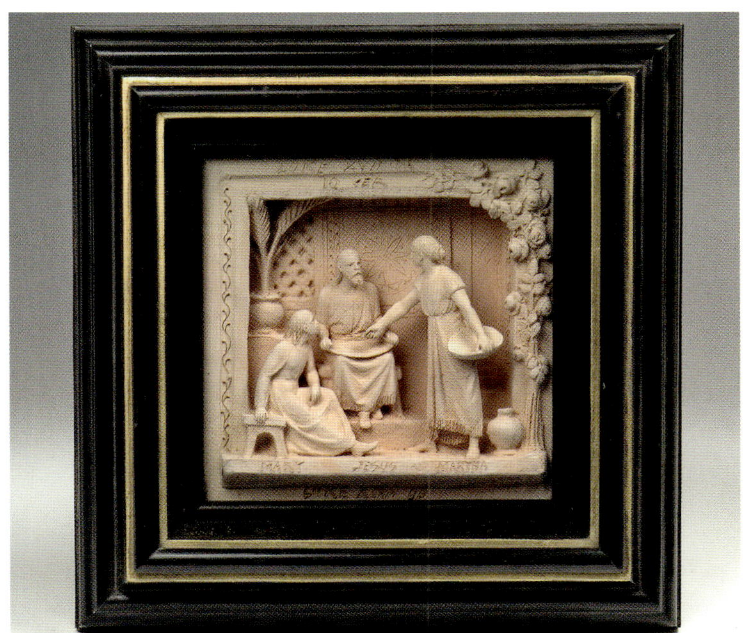

Tankard, (**766**), c.1590, Germany, Siegburg, height: 18.1cm, (7⅛in), stoneware. Tankard or or *Schnelle* , made in the Rhineland, relief-moulded with panels showing scenes of the Crucifixion, St Peter and St Paul.
Tankard, (**767**), c.1590, Germany, Siegburg, height: 18.1cm, (7⅛in), stoneware. Tankard or *Schnelle*, made in the Rhineland, relief-moulded with portraits of St Brigita, the fourteenth-century founder of the Order of Brigittines in Vadstena, Sweden.

Sculpture, (**858**), c.1880, London, Doulton, height: 17.8cm, (7in), terracotta. Panel modelled by George Tinworth (1843-1913) showing Christ in the house of Martha and Mary. Christ sits at the back of a room while Mary points an accusing finger at Martha who sits listening to Jesus. Participants' names incised on the frame with reference, 'LUKE XVII/ 10VER'. (The story is actually told in Luke 10 38-42.)

Virgin and Child

Despite the movement for plain worship, led by dissenters and non conformists and the strong current of anti-Catholic feeling through the eighteenth century, there are a surprising number of ceramic images of the Virgin and Child. Although some were exported to allies in Catholic Europe their proliferation suggests a continuing devotion to the Mother of God.

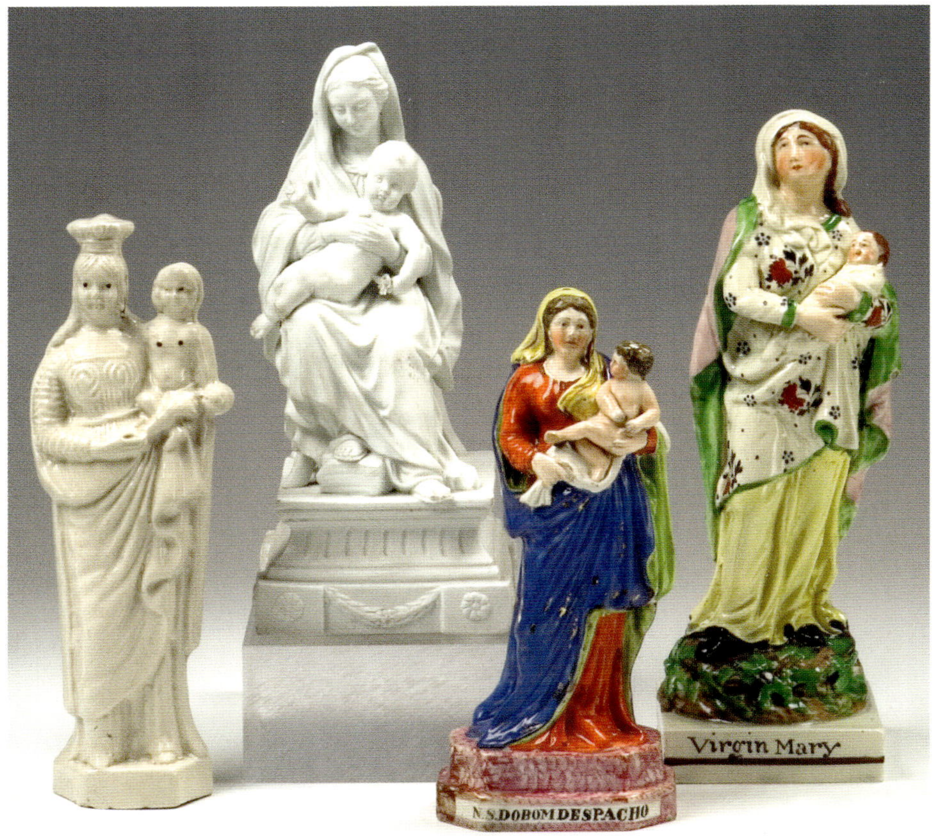

Figure Group, (**753**), c.1760, Staffordshire, height: 20.9cm, (8¼in), salt-glazed earthenware. Crowned Madonna and Child; spots of manganese oxide are applied to the eyes and the Christ Child's nipples.
Figure Group, (**756**), c.1810, Derby, height: 21.6cm, (8½in), biscuit porcelain. Seated Madonna and Child may be based on a print of a Madonna after Raphael.
Figure Group, (**752**), c.1800, Staffordshire, Burslem, height: 19.1cm, (7½in), enamelled pearlware. The inscription, 'N.S. DOBOM DESPACHO', indicates that this Madonna and Child was made for the Portuguese market. It is based on a print after Raphael's 'Sistine Madonna', from the Sistine Chapel in Rome. Similar shards excavated from beneath Burslem Town Hall confirm that it was made by Enoch Wood. [7]
Figure Group, (**751**), c.1820, Staffordshire, height: 24.8cm, (9¾in), enamelled pearlware. Madonna and Child inscribed, on the square base, 'Virgin Mary'.

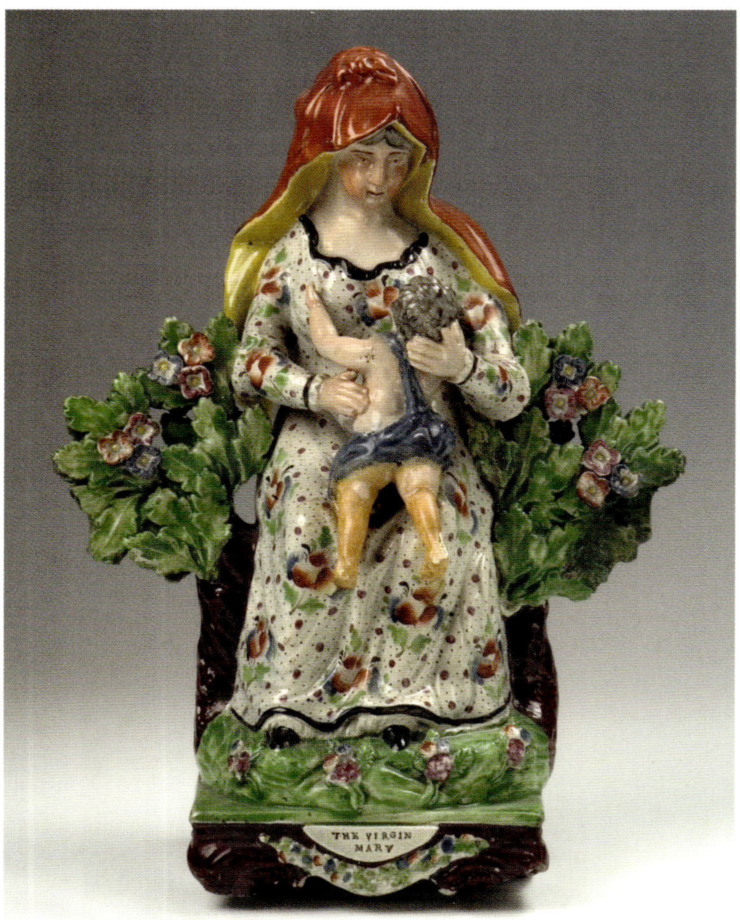

Figure Group, (**755**), c.1830, Staffordshire, height: 30.5cm, (12in), enamelled pearlware. Table-based group impressed, 'THE VIRGIN MARY'. The feet are missing from the base and Jesus' legs are badly damaged.

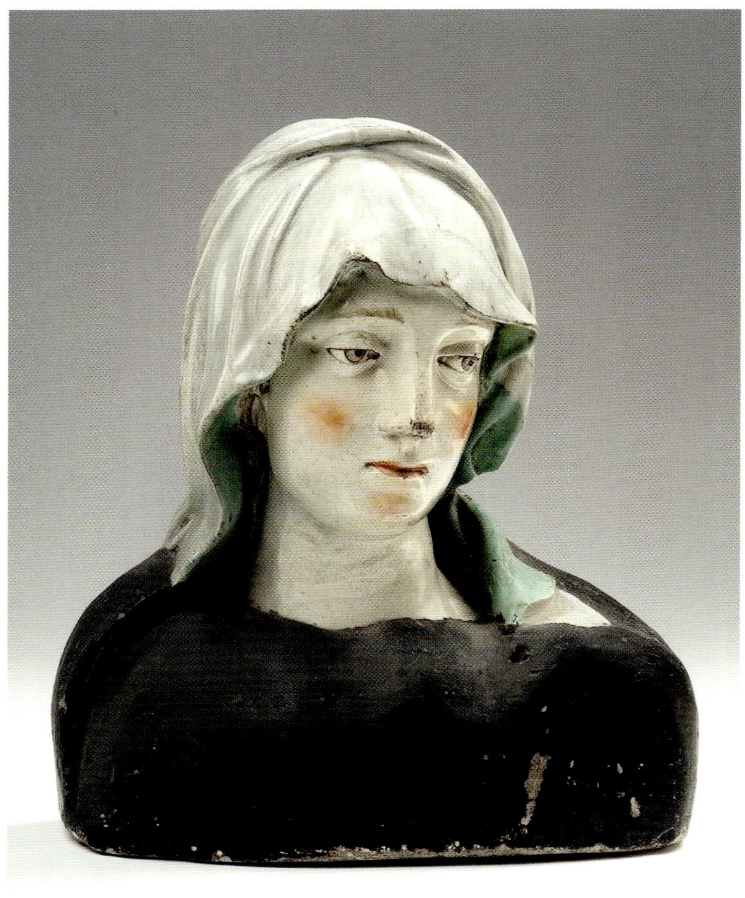

Bust, (**754**), c.1800, Staffordshire, Burslem? height: 28cm, (11in), enamelled porcelain. Finely modelled bust appears to represent the Virgin Mary but it may be related to a Wood factory piece entitled, 'Sadness', c.1790–c.97. The truncated head appears to have been set into a separate, matt-painted base.

The Prodigal Son

The parable of the Prodigal Son (Luke 14, 11-32) was very popular in the mid-eighteenth century and was applied to other media, such as embroidery. This story of riches to rags, repentance and redemption enjoyed lasting popularity as sequences of popular prints, which are mentioned by George Eliot as late as 1860.[8] The print series adapted by Greatbatch and others was based on French originals of the 1750s.[9]

The characters are dressed not in historical costume but in the height of contemporary fashion. The survival of so many of these teapots testifies to a marketing success story. It may owe something to the popularity of Hogarth's recent satires on modern morals and towards the end of the century became an oblique comment on the scandalous and extravagant behaviour of George, Prince of Wales.

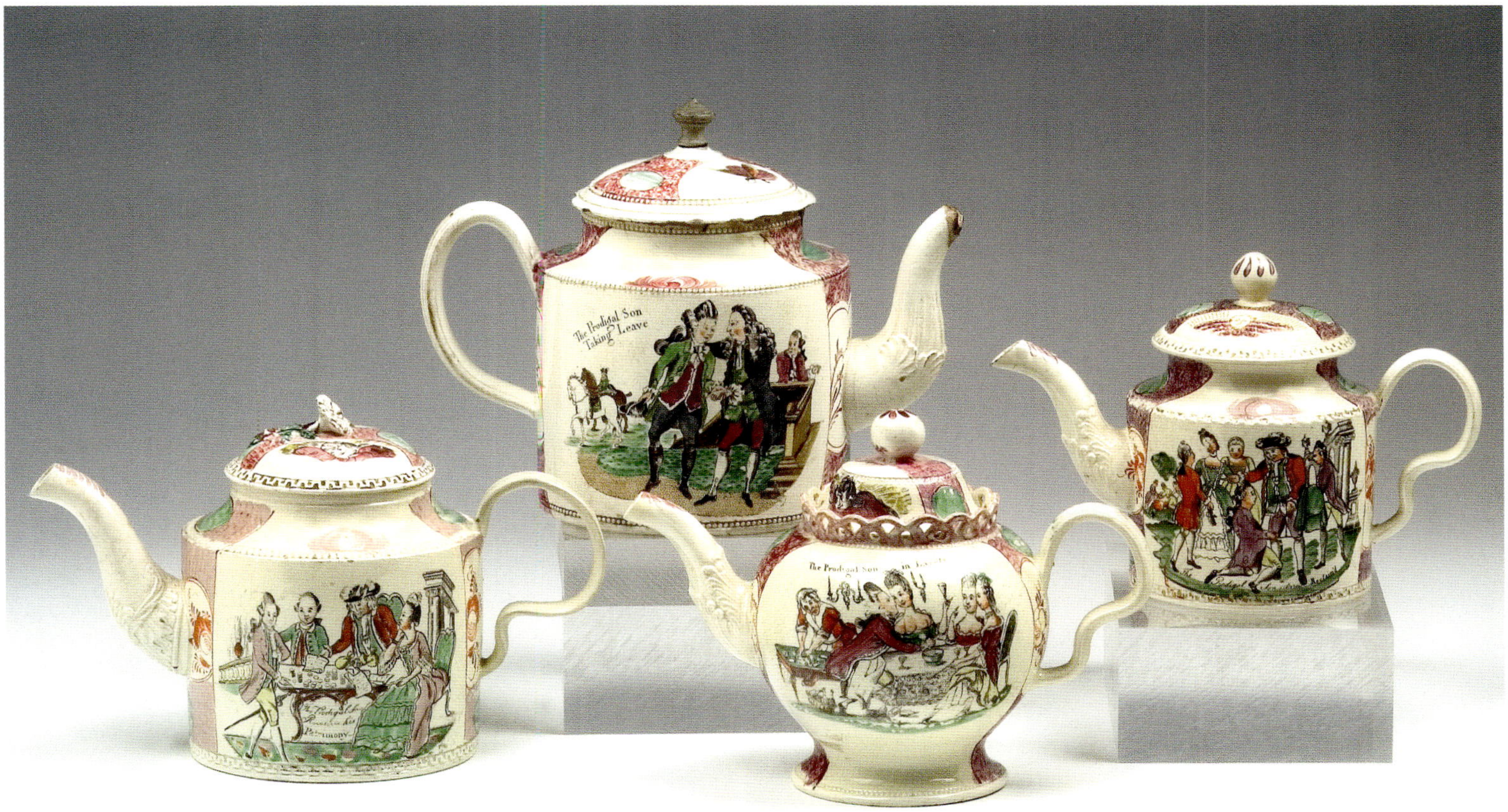

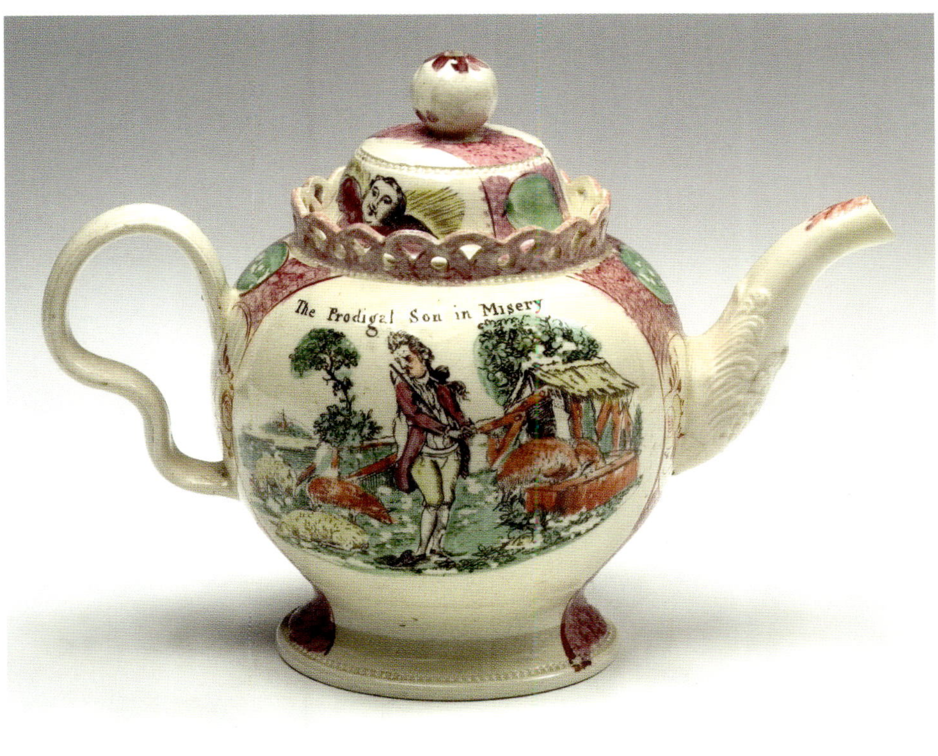

Teapot, (**793**), c.1780, Staffordshire, Fenton, height: 10.2cm, (4in), creamware, printed and enamelled. Printed by William Greatbatch with 'The Prodigal Son Receiving his Patrimony' (on reverse, 'The Prodigal Son Taking Leave').

Teapot, (**794**), c.1780, Staffordshire, height: 15.3cm, (6in), creamware, printed and enamelled. Printed with 'The Prodigal Son Taking Leave' (on reverse, 'The Prodigal Son Receiving his Patrimony'). The scenes feature characters even more fashionably dressed, macaroni-style, with huge wigs.[10]

Teapot, (**795**), c.1780, Staffordshire, Fenton, height: 14cm, (5½in), creamware, printed and enamelled. Printed by William Greatbatch with 'The Prodigal son in Excess',[11] where he squanders his inheritance.

Teapot, (**796**), c.1780, Staffordshire, Fenton, height: 12.7cm, (5in), creamware, printed and enamelled. Printed by William Greatbatch with 'The Prodigal Son Returns Reclaim'd'[12] (on reverse, 'the Prodigal Son Feasted on his Return').[13]

Teapot, (**795**), c.1780, Staffordshire, Fenton, height: 14cm, (5½in), creamware, printed and enamelled. Printed by William Greatbatch with 'The Prodigal Son in Misery', where he is reduced to living in poverty and squalor with pigs.[14]

Symbolic Virtues

Several pieces illustrate the essential Christian virtues, Faith, Hope and Charity. These were the names of a legendary family of female martyrs from the reign of Hadrian, now Catholic saints; the mother Sophia/Sapientia (Wisdom) and her three daughters, Pistis/Fides, Elpis/Spes, and Agape/Caritas (Faith, Hope and Charity). They took their names from St Paul's first Epistle to the Corinthians 13: 13, 'And now abideth Faith, Hope, Charity, these three; but the greatest of these is Charity'. 'Caritas' is generally identified with 'Love', of God and of humanity. From the sixteenth century onwards it found symbolic visual expression in art as maternal love for several infants.

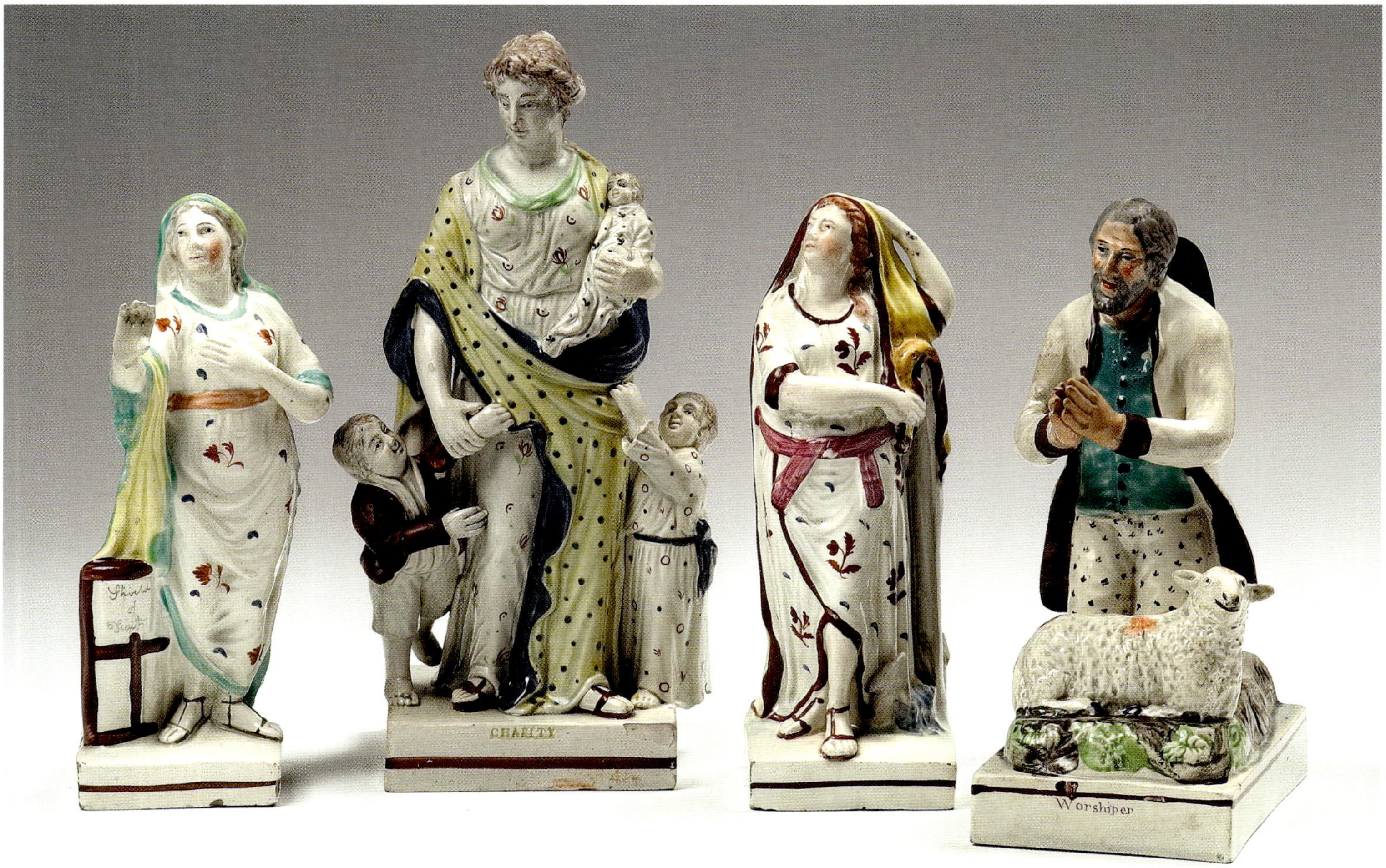

Figure, (**843A**), c.1800, Staffordshire, height: 17.8cm, (7in), enamelled pearlware. Figure in classical dress representing Faith with a shield inscribed, 'Shield of Faith'.
Figure Group, (**843**), c.1800, Staffordshire or Yorkshire, height: 22.2cm, (8¾in), enamelled pearlware. Base impressed, 'Charity' represents maternal love for children in a group marked by Ralph Wedgwood.

Figure, (**843B**), c.1800, Staffordshire, height: 17.8cm, (7in), enamelled pearlware. Figure in classical dress representing Hope with an anchor.
Figure, (**827**), c.1800, Staffordshire, Wood factory, height: 17.8cm, (7in), enamelled pearlware. Figure inscribed, 'Worshiper' [*sic*], a praying shepherd on his knees with a large sheep, inspired by figures of Spanish peasants.[15] Impressed beneath base, '70'.

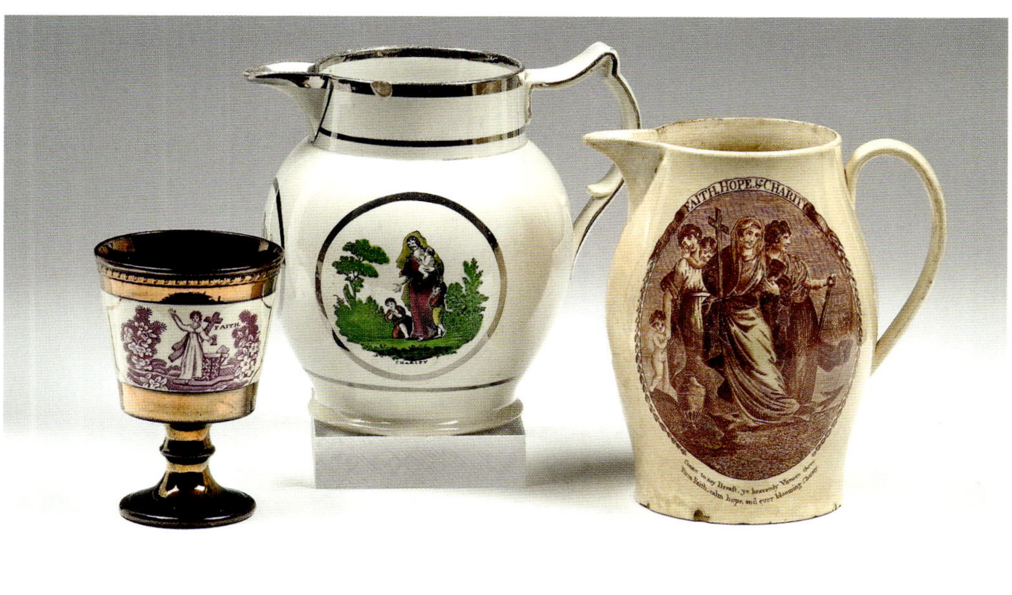

Goblet, (**836**), c.1820, Staffordshire, height: 12.7cm, (5in), earthenware, purple-printed and lustred. Printed with Faith with crucifix and communion cup before an altar.
Jug, (**844**), c.1810, Staffordshire, height: 17.8cm, (7in), earthenware, printed, coloured and lustred. Printed within a roundel, a mother with children, representing Charity.
Jug, (**842**), c.1810, Staffordshire, height: 17.1cm, (6¾in), red-brown printed drabwear. Symbolic figures of 'FAITH, HOPE & CHARITY', with the lines, 'Come to my Breast, ye heavenly Virtues three / Firm Faith, calm hope, and ever blooming Charity'. On reverse, Religion, with a chalice, stands before an altar.

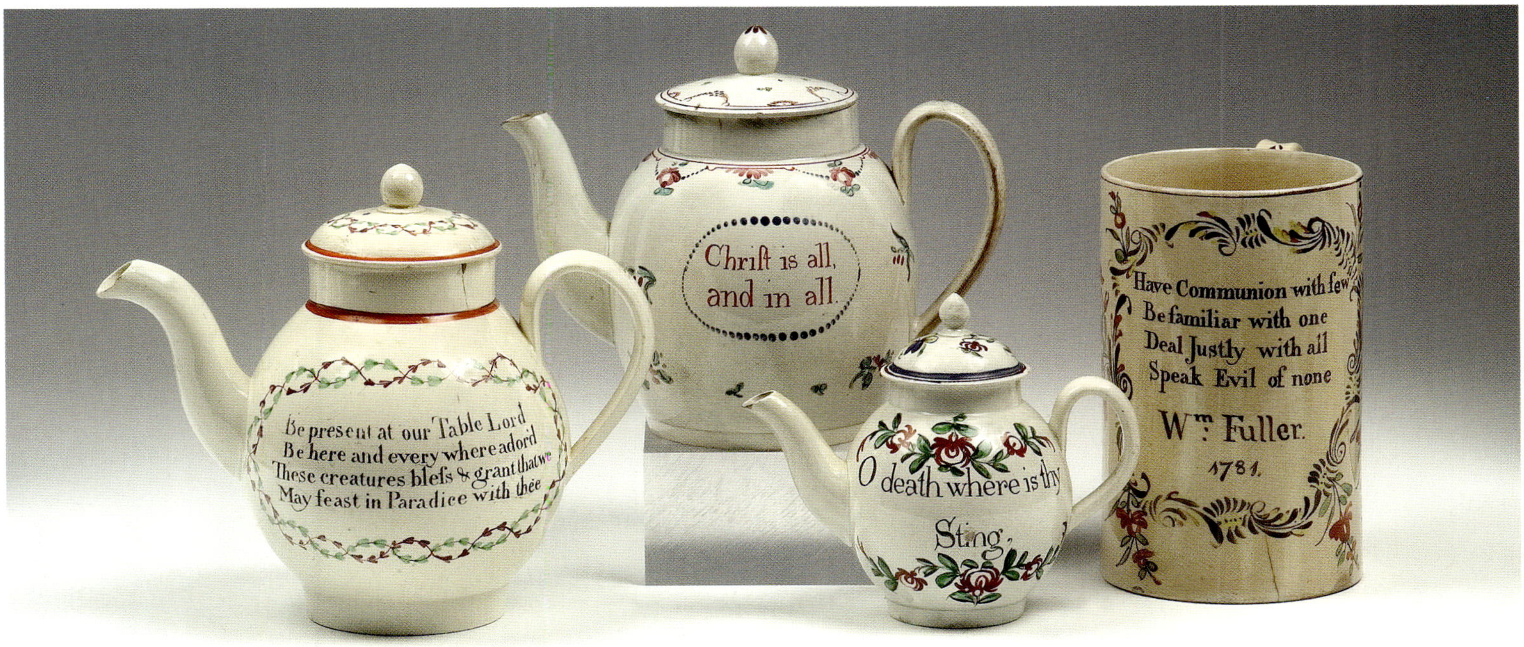

Teapot, (**R603.11**), c.1800, Staffordshire, height: 16.5cm, (6½in), creamware, printed and enamelled. Printed within foliate wreath, 'Be present at our table Lord', a typically pious sentiment applied to teaware.
Teapot, (**845**), 1802, Yorkshire, perhaps Leeds, height: 12.1cm, (4¾in), enamelled pearlware. Inscribed 'Christ is all and in all' (from Colossians 3:11), for 'Hannah Brecliff. Kirkstall 1802'. Kirkstall is a historic village, now a suburb of Leeds, where it may have been made.

Teapot, (**846**), 1802, Yorkshire, height: 12.1cm, (4¾in), enamelled pearlware. Inscribed, 'The Sting of Sin is Death' and 'O Death, where is thy sting.' (from Corinthians 15:55-56).
Mug, (**1420**), 1781, Yorkshire, height: 15.3cm, (6in), enamelled drabware. Inscribed, 'Have communion with few/ Be familiar with one / Deal Justly with all / Speak Evil of none / Wm. Fuller 1781'.[16]

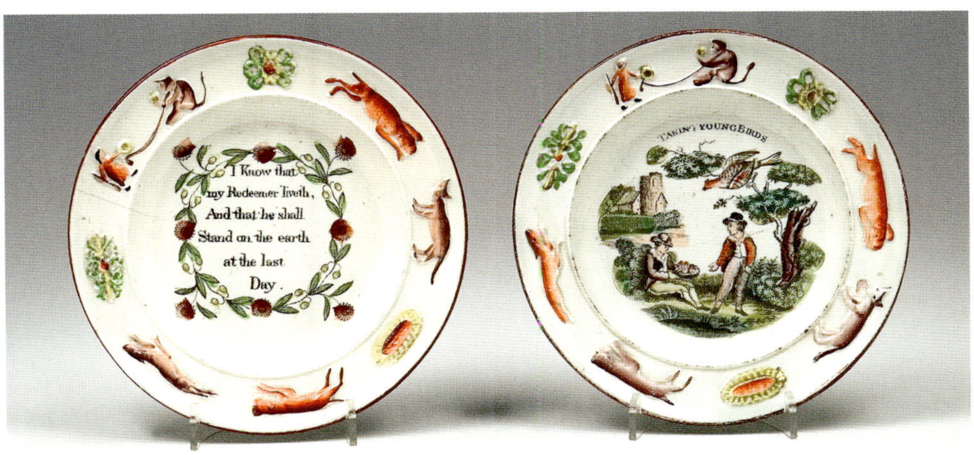

Plate, (**862**), c.1820, Swansea, Glamorgan Pottery, diameter: 17.8cm, (7in), pearlware, printed and enamelled. Inscribed 'I know that my Redeemer liveth, And that he shall Stand on the earth at the last Day' with the inspiring words from Job 19:25. Border relief-moulded with animal figures.
Plate, (**1607**), c.1820, Swansea, Glamorgan Pottery, diameter: 15.3cm, (6in), pearlware, printed and enamelled. Printed with, 'TAKING YOUNG BIRDS' showing two boys stealing a nest. Border relief-moulded with animal figures.

Nursery Plate, (**860**), Staffordshire, c.1850, diameter: 17.8cm, (7in), earthenware, printed and coloured. Inscribed within oval wreath, 'Since you are not certain OF AN HOUR throw not away A MINUTE', one of Benjamin Franklin's *Maxims*. Made for the American market.
Nursery Plate, (**861**), Staffordshire, c.1830, diameter: 17.8cm, (7in), pearlware, brown-printed and coloured. Printed with the Lord's Prayer within relief-moulded floral border. Another
Nursery Plate, (**859**), Staffordshire, c.1850, diameter: 17.8cm, (7in), earthenware, printed and coloured. Inscribed within oval wreath, 'Cherish your best hopes As a Faith, and abide by them In Action', a quotation from *Woman in the Nineteenth Century* (1845), the best-known work of Sarah Margaret Fuller (1810-1850). Fuller, a formidable intellectual studied languages at Harvard University Library and was close to fellow Transcendentalists such as Ralph Waldo Emerson, Thoreau and the Alcott family. Made for the American market.

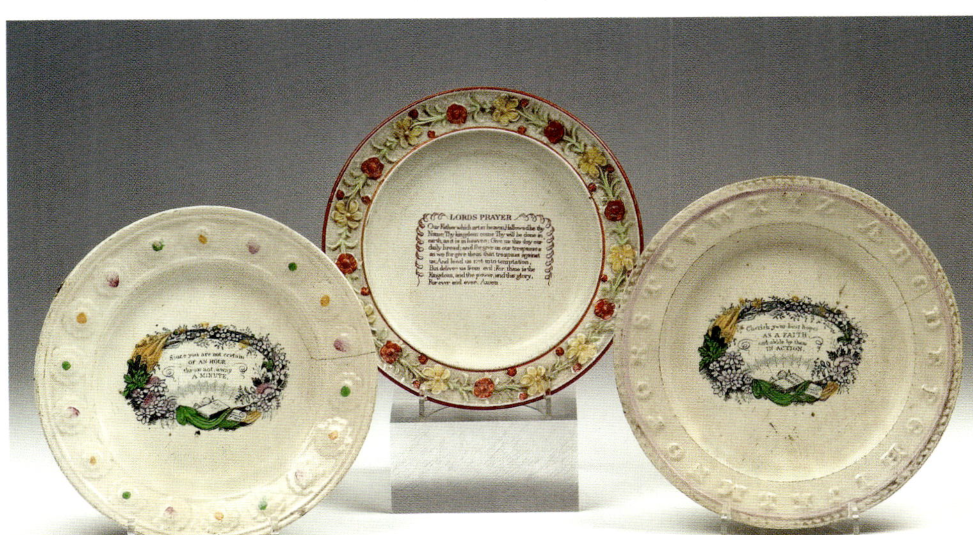

The Reformation

The sixteenth and seventeenth centuries were marked by unprecedented religious upheaval throughout Europe. During the Reformation, England, Scotland and parts of Germany and the Netherlands broke decisively from the Roman Catholic Church, leading to sporadic warfare throughout the period. The hurried departure of Catholic James II, and the arrival of Protestant William of Orange from the Netherlands in 1688, known as the Glorious Revolution, marked a watershed in the relationship between the state and religious orthodoxy in Britain. From this time associations between Protestantism and patriotism and Catholicism and treason were intensified. What was less clear-cut, however, was the official attitude towards nonconformity; the 'Toleration Act' of 1689 was an admission on the part of the Anglican establishment that it could not stamp out Puritanism and dissenters. Baptists and Quakers for example, flourished.[17]

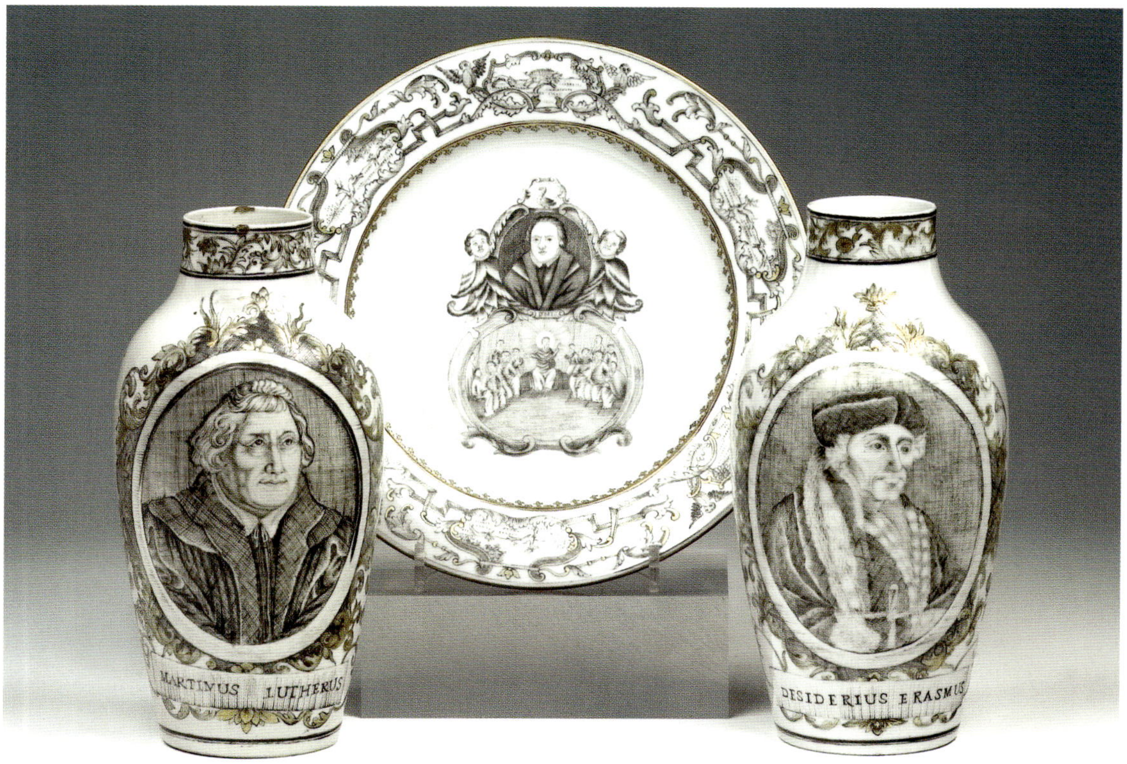

Vase, (**797**), c.1760, China, height: 22.2cm, (8¾in), hard-paste porcelain. Painted with portrait of Martin Luther (1483-1546), the German religious reformer.[18]
Plate, (**798**), c.1760, China, diameter: 22.9cm, (9in), hard-paste porcelain. Painted with small portrait of Martin Luther and scene of Christ appearing to the disciples at Pentecost.
Vase, (**797A**), c.1760, China, height: 22.2cm, (8¾in), hard-paste porcelain. Painted with portrait of Desiderius Erasmus, (1466-1536), the Dutch philosopher.[19] Both executed in careful hatching imitating source prints sent to China. As disagreement with the established Church increased during the eighteenth century, perhaps dissenters began to collect images of pioneer reformers?

The Plight of Catholics

Some of the anti-Catholic subjects represented are ambivalent in meaning. Catholicism was outlawed in Tudor England and a strong undercurrent of anti-Catholic feeling continued with periodic outbursts, such as the Gordon Riots of 1780. Catholics were actively discriminated against until the late eighteenth century, when the Catholic Relief Act of 1778 allowed them to join the armed forces without taking the oath of allegiance to the Church of England. The 1793 Relief Act allowed some Catholics to vote (for Anglican MPs) while finally, in 1829, Catholic emancipation granted equal rights to stand for political office.

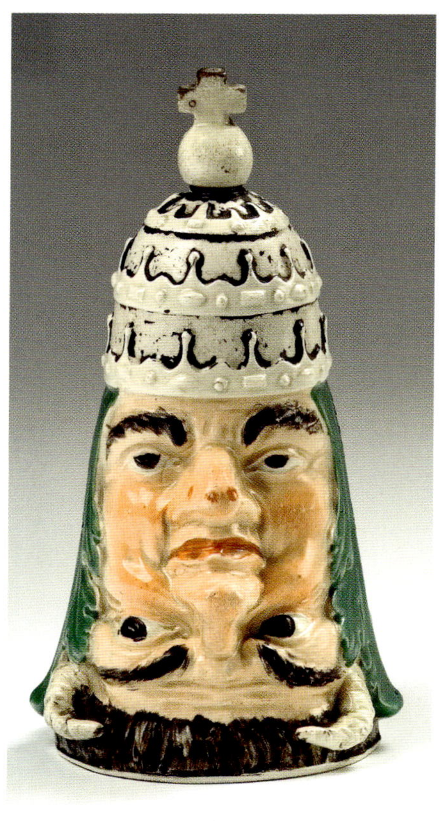

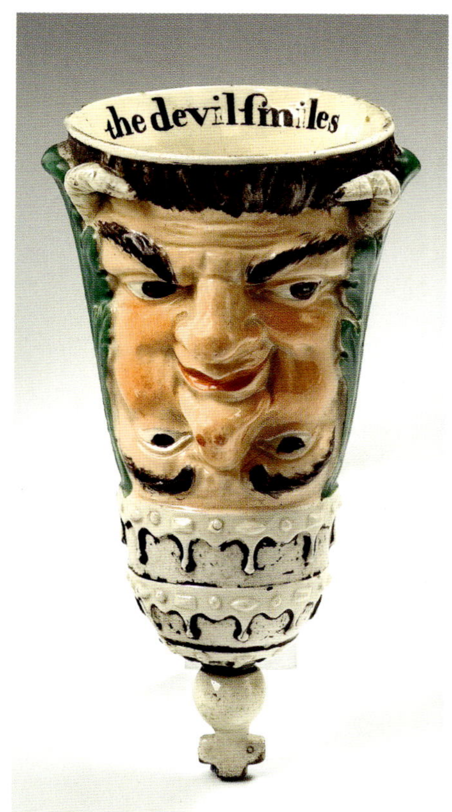

Stirrup Cup, (**823**), c.1790, Staffordshire, Burslem?, height: 14.5cm, (5¾in), enamelled pearlware. Cup relief-moulded as a reversible head; the Pope with his Triple Crown is interchangeable with the Devil grinning. The enamelled inscription within confirms these identities, 'While Pope absolves/ the devil smiles'.[20] The inverted image, a popular optical trick, is often found in children's puzzles and satirical cartoons.

Figure, (802), c.1850, Staffordshire, height: 22.9cm, (9in), earthenware, printed, enamelled and gilt. Young woman holding scroll printed with biblical quotations, e.g. 'Search the Scriptures. John 5.39', illustrates 'PROTESTANTISM'.
Figure Group, (**801**), c.1850, Staffordshire, height: 24.2cm, (9½in), enamelled earthenware. Modelled as Protestant Bishops, 'RIDLEY AND LATIMER / Be of good comfort, Master Ridley'. They were burned at the stake in 1555, during the reign of Mary I.
Figure, (**799**), c.1840, France, height: 13.4cm, (5¼in), enamelled earthenware. Modelled as a monk with a prayer book wearing a grey habit.
Figure, (**802A**), c.1850, Staffordshire, height: 21cm, (8¼in), earthenware, printed, enamelled and gilt. Black-frocked priest holding a scroll printed with incendiary remarks, such as 'The translators of the English Bible are to be abhorred to the depths of Hell'.[21] Plinth has been replaced; the original was inscribed 'POPERY'.

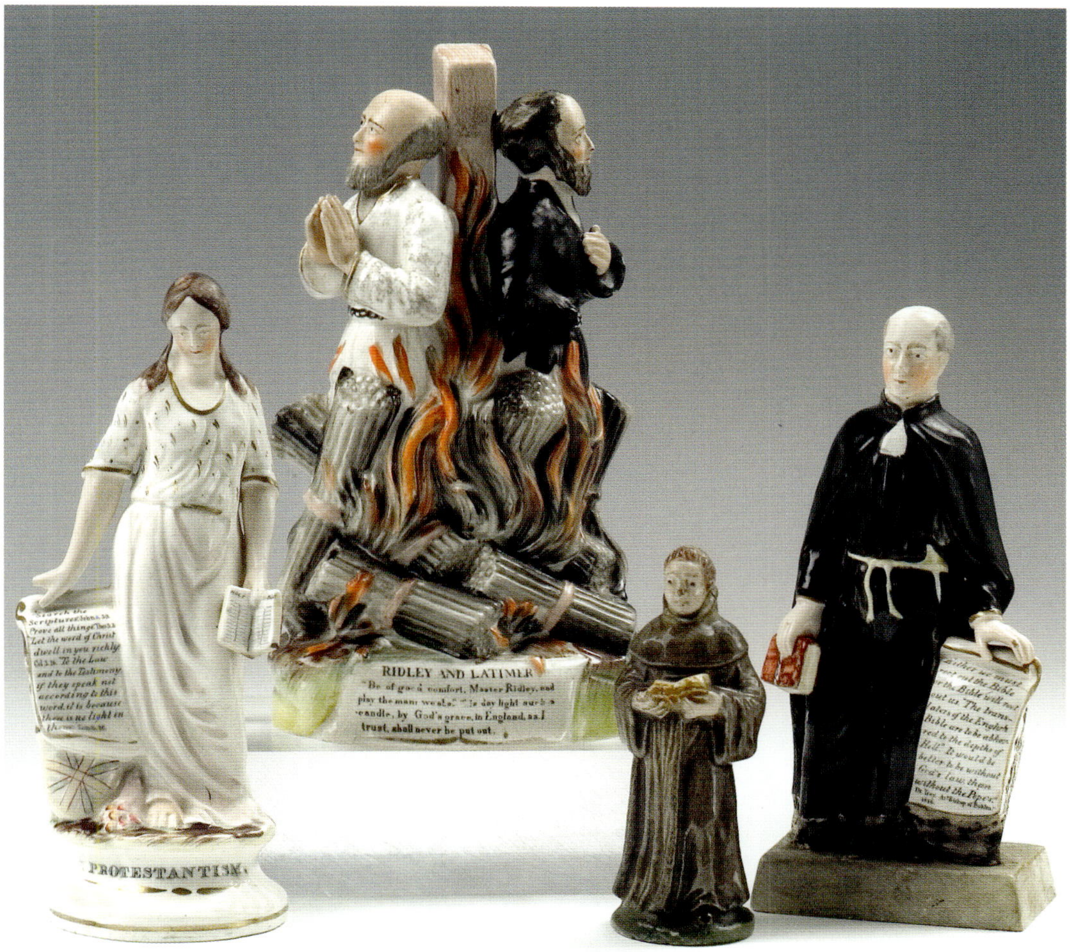

Anglican Church Abuses

The period following the Glorious Revolution and before the Test and Corporation Acts were repealed (in order to bring the power of the clergy under state control) could reasonably be called the 'Anglican Ascendancy'.[22]

The late eighteenth century saw members of the aristocracy snaffling lucrative bishoprics whenever they became vacant. In turn, bishops bestowed the choice appointments in their gift to members of their own families.[23] There was also a massive discrepancy between rich and poor prelates; in the mid-eighteenth century the see of Durham was worth £6,000 per year while Oxford was only worth £500. Further down the clerical food chain parsons and curates could be as poor as church mice.

Anti clericalism was rife. Pluralism was one of the most serious abuses, whereby priests accumulated parishes for their combined incomes. Many believed that clerics were slack in their work and failed to offer spiritual and practical support to their parishioners. Some spent too much time hunting or were notorious for over indulging in food and drink.

Dr Henry Sacheverell (1674-1724)

Sacheverell was chaplain of St Saviour's, Southwark, (later Southwark Cathedral) and a controversial churchman during the reign of Queen Anne. Already known as a charismatic orator, in 1709 he delivered an inflammatory sermon at Derby on 15 August and on 5 November at St Paul's Cathedral, warning of the threat to the Church from the Whig ministry's tolerance of dissenters. Printed version of the sermon sold 40,000 copies.[24] He was arrested, tried and convicted of seditious libel in 1710 and banned from preaching for three years. His huge popular following helped bring about the downfall of the Whigs.

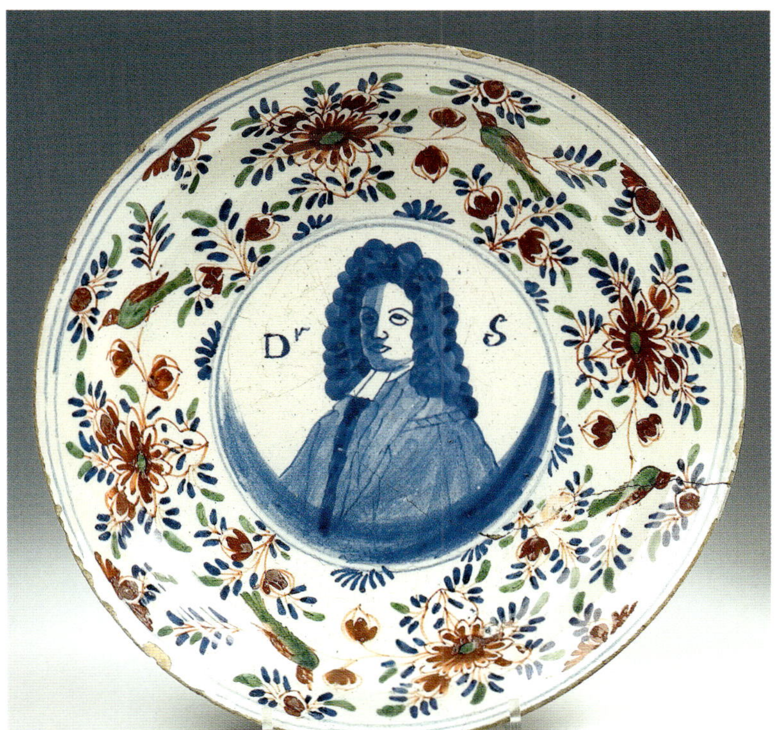

Charger, (**800**), c.1715, Liverpool or Belfast, diameter: 28cm, (11in), tin-glazed earthenware. Within broad floral border, a central portrait of a man wearing clerical dress and a full wig, inscribed, 'Dr S'.[25] The dish was probably made at the height of Sacheverell's celebrity, possibly in Belfast, where Sacheverell visited the delftware pottery in 1698.[26]

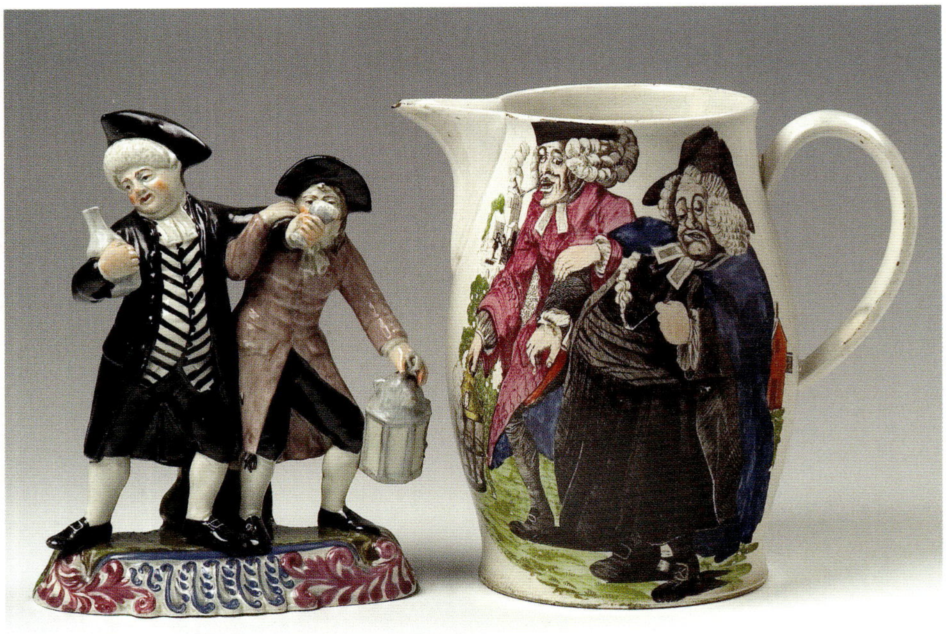

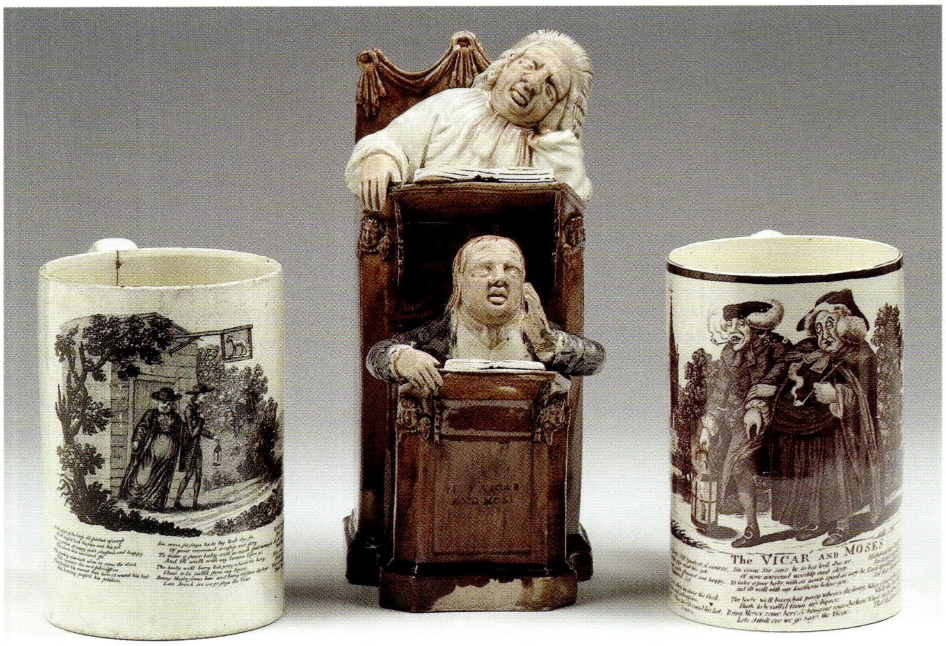

The Vicar and Moses

Perceived abuses within the church were frequently addressed in fictional writings. The poem, *The Vicar and Moses*, written around 1780 by George Alexander Stevens (1710-84), adapted from one of the Roxburghe Ballads, enjoyed enormous popularity over a long period and led to a number of ceramic representations. The story, told with coarse humour, concerns the attempts of the intoxicated parson and his clerk to attend the funeral of a dead baby.

Figure Group, (**807**), c.1790, Staffordshire, height: 24.2cm, (9½in), enamelled pearlware. Representing the staggering, drunken, clerics; the Vicar with a bottle and Moses, the clerk, with a lantern, on an ornate base.
Jug, (**803**), c.1790, Staffordshire, Lane End, height: 22.9cm, (9in), creamware, printed and enamelled. Printed with the entire poem, *The Vicar and Moses*, together with an oversized enamelled print, signed by John Aynsley. The lurching churchmen occupy the foreground while tiny figures of the distressed family gather beside the grave. The image derives from a painting by Robert Dighton (1752-1814).[27]

Mug, (**805**), Staffordshire, c.1800, printed in Liverpool?, height: 15.3cm, (6in), printed creamware. Two men are shown leaving a tavern, 'At the sign of the horse', above six of the sixteen verses of *The Vicar and Moses*, on what could be a Wedgwood mug.
Figure Group, (**809**), c.1790, Staffordshire, Wood factory, height: 26.7cm, (10½in), earthenware, lead-glazed, oxide-coloured. Impressed 'THE VICAR AND MOSES', a vicar sleeps at the top of a double-decker pulpit while his clerk, on the lower level, reads the lesson.[28] John Wood's factory ledger at Brownhills records the sale of five such pieces in 1786 while Ralph Wood at Burslem actually stamped or incised other known examples. In 1835, their descendant, Enoch Wood, sent a gift of 182 pieces of pottery to the King of Saxony in Dresden, including an early version of one of these pulpits.[29]
Mug, (**804**), Staffordshire, c.1800, printed in Liverpool?, height: 15.3cm, (6in), printed creamware. while the other is printed in dark brown, with a similar source print to that used for the large jug (803).

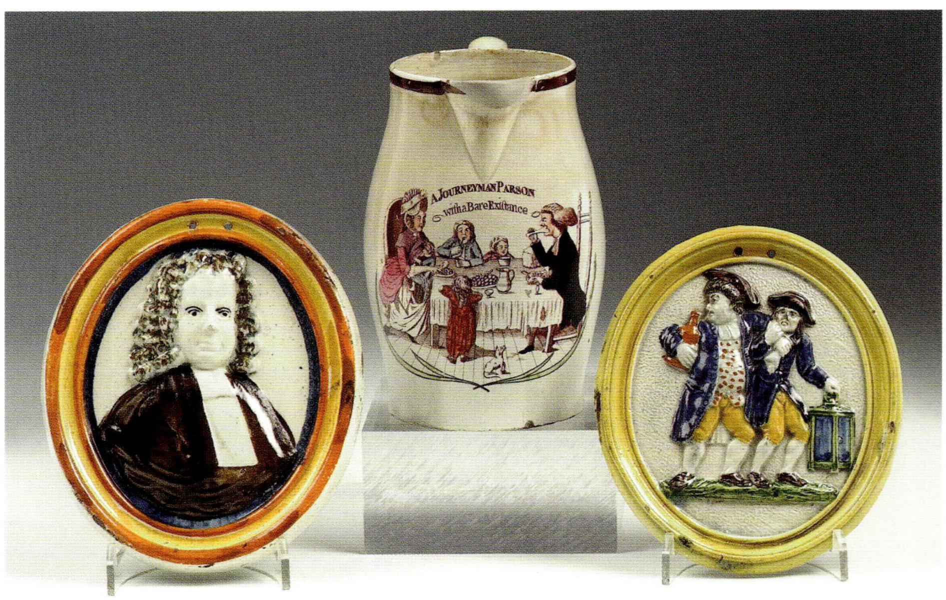

Plaque, (**850**), c.1790, Staffordshire, height: 14.6cm, (5¾in), pearlware, painted in high-temperature colours. Medallion, relief-moulded with the portrait of a cleric in a full-bottomed wig who could be Henry Sacheverell.[30]
Jug, (**815**), c.1790, Staffordshire, height: 14cm, (5½in), pearlware, brown-printed and coloured. Entitled, 'A JOURNEYMAN PARSON With a Bare Existance [*sic*]' shows the parson's family eating a frugal dinner. Taken from one of a pair of prints after Robert Dighton, which contrast the meagre meal at the poor Parson's house[31] with the lavish spread enjoyed by the Master Parson's family.
Plaque, (**808**), c.1790, Staffordshire, height: 14cm, (5½in), pearlware painted in high-temperature colours. Relief-moulded with a pair of staggering clerics, the vicar with a bottle, the clerk with a lantern.

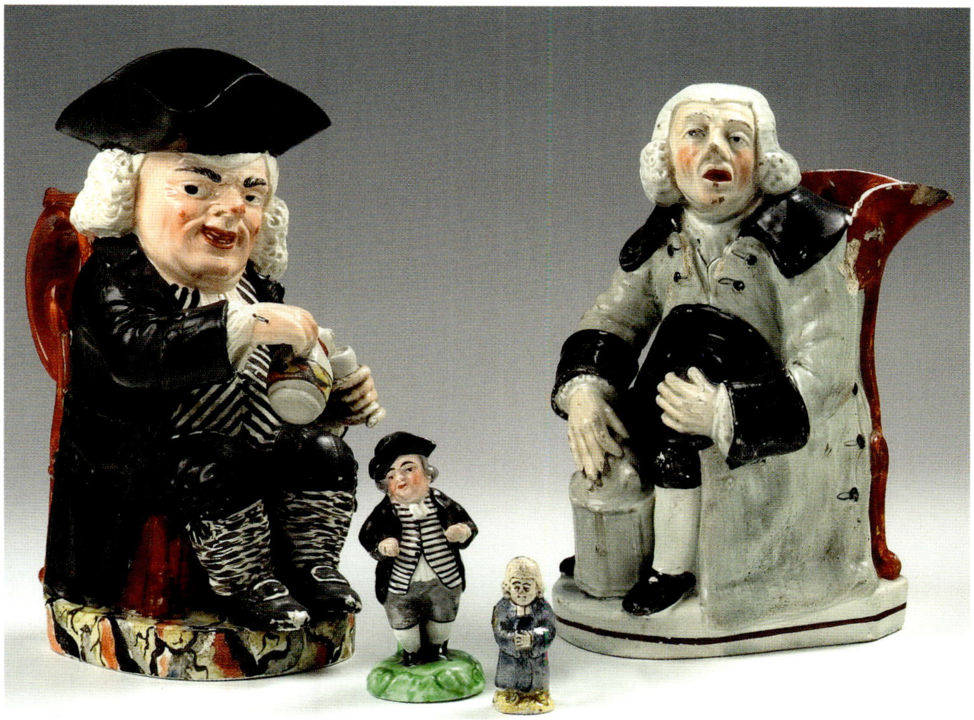

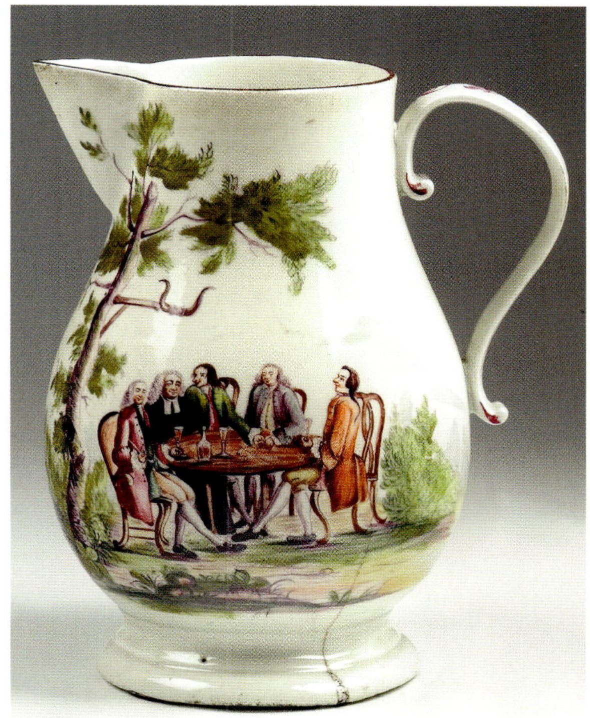

Toby Jug, (**810**), c.1800, Staffordshire, height: 25.4cm, (10in), enamelled pearlware. Modelled as a parson wearing Geneva bands over a diagonally striped black and white waistcoat. His cocked hat forms a pouring spout while his ruddy complexion and bulbous red nose indicate that he is a habitual drinker. The handle is attached to the back of the parson's chair.
Figure, (**812**), c.1800, Staffordshire, height: 11.5cm, (4½in), enamelled pearlware. Small figure of a priest in a striped waistcoat (similar to that worn by 810).[32]
Figure, (**813**), c.1800, Staffordshire, height: 6.4cm, (2½in), painted in high-temperature colours. Tiny figure, with a pierced head and lower opening forming a whistle, wears a cassock and falling neck bands.
Toby Jug, (**811**), c.1800, Staffordshire, height: 25.4cm, (10in), enamelled pearlware. Modelled as a fearful and querulous clerk (like 'Moses'), or night watchman, he holds a lantern and his broad-brimmed hat close to his chest. The chair back forms the pouring spout.

Jug, (**822**), c.1760, Derby, height: 20.3cm, (8in), enamelled soft-paste porcelain. Five gentlemen (including a cleric) meet out of doors to drink (they may be members of a drinking club), beneath the sign of a pair of ox horns, which are generally used to signify cuckoldry.[33]

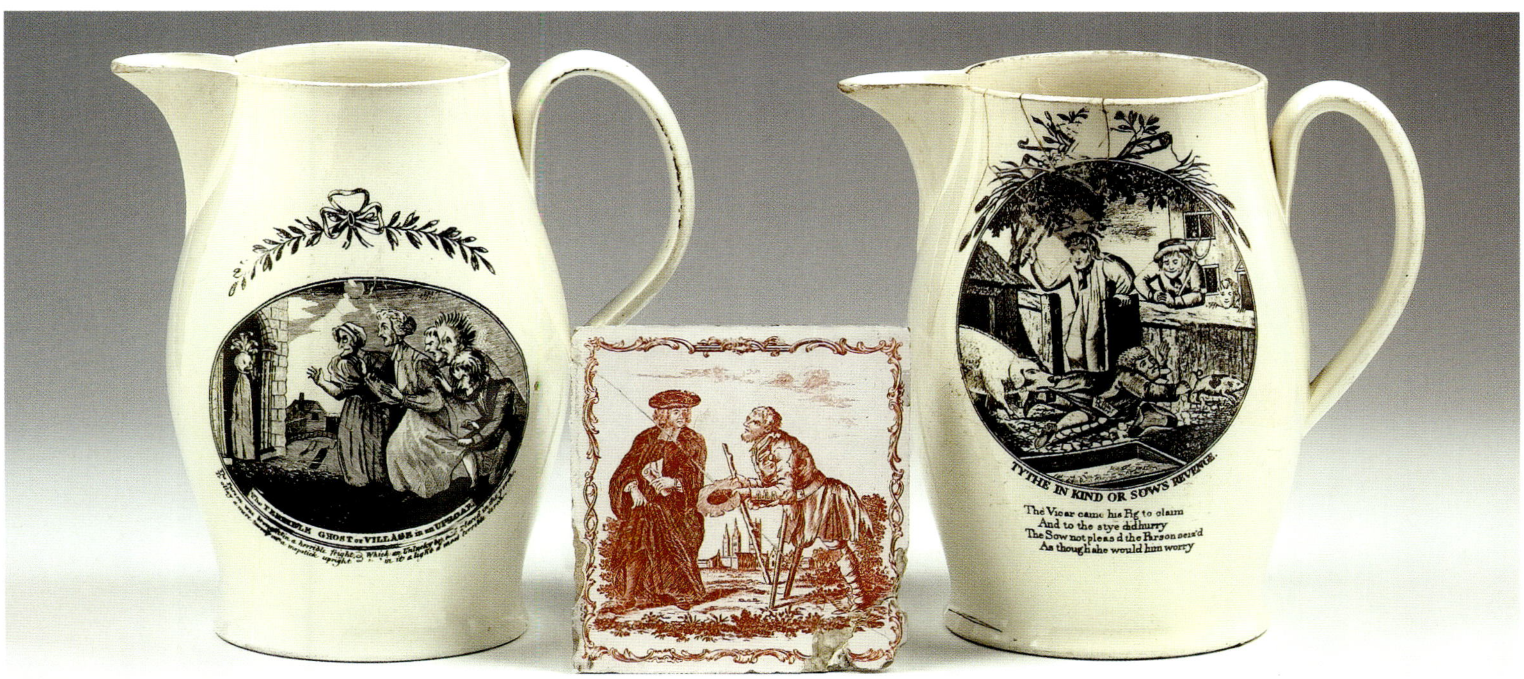

Jug, (**816**), c.1790, Staffordshire or Liverpool, height: 20.3cm, (8in), printed creamware. 'The TERRIBLE GHOST or VILLAGE in an UPROAR', illustrates a Hallowe'en caper with a turnip-headed mop causing the priest as much of a fright as the rest of the villagers .
Tile, (**814**), c.1775, Liverpool, height: 12.7cm, (5in), red-printed tin-glazed earthenware. A man with a wooden leg begs alms from an unwilling priest. It derives from a satirical print, entitled 'the Pluralist and the Old Soldier' drawn by 'Tim Bobbin' in 1770 and published in 1773.[34]
Jug, (**819**), c.1790, Staffordshire or Liverpool, height: 15.3cm, (6in), printed creamware. Entitled 'Tythe in Kind or the Sow's Revenge', the parson is being attacked by the sow as he attempts to claim his piglet. The farmer's family laugh at his humiliation. The subject, is based on a print by Collings, engraved by William Blake in Harrison & Co.'s *Wits Magazine,* of 1 March 1784.[35]

Tithes

Tithes, one-tenth parts of all agricultural produce, were levied as tax by the Anglican Church from the agricultural poor and were bitterly unpopular. They were authorised by the Bible, most explicitly in Leviticus 27: 30-32; 'And all the tithe of the land, whether of the seed of the land, or of the fruit of the tree, is the Lord's … of the herd or of the flock … the tenth shall be holy unto the Lord.' Tithes were made marginally more tolerable by satirical graphic treatment.

Legislation and Dissent: The New Marriage Act

Some figure groups comment on social issues or recent parliamentary legislation. Lord Hardwick's Marriage Act of 1754 made clandestine marriages illegal, and regulated weddings by instituting banns, issuing licenses, and recording details in parish registers. The New Marriage Act of 1823, which repealed it, was intended to reduce the abuses of the system, including a good many under age unions not approved by parents or guardians. This was the time when lovers ran away to marry in Gretna Green in Scotland, where the law was different. Under the 1823 Act, marriages performed without the benefit of banns or a licence could be valid but the officiating clergy would be guilty of a felony.

Figure Group, (**820**), c.1790, Staffordshire, height: 17.2cm, (6¾in), enamelled pearlware. Derby factory produced a porcelain group around 1765 and pearlware copies followed. The farmer, his wife (with a baby) and the parson stand in a regimented line with a heap of farm produce at their feet. Based on an original Derby porcelain group of c.1765.
Jug, (**818**), c.1780, Staffordshire or Liverpool, height: 19.1cm, (7½in), printed drabware. Verse begins, 'In country Village lives a Vicar / Fond – as all are – of Tythes and Liquor'. The parson turns from his parishioners in horror as the farmer's wife attempts to offer him her tenth child as well as the more usual 'tithe' piglet. The popularity of the subject lasted well into the 19th century; it is still found on a jug dated 1802.
Tile, (**821**), c.1765, Liverpool, height: 11.5cm, (4½in), red-printed tin-glazed earthenware. The print 'TYTHE PIG', drawn by Boitard first appeared on delftware tiles from 1758. It is also the source for jug (818). [36]

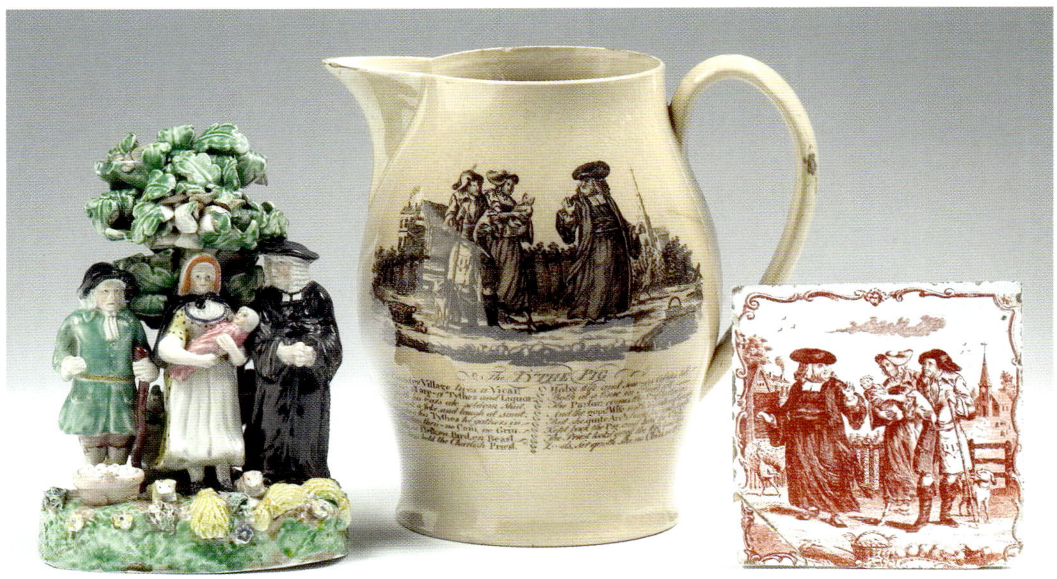

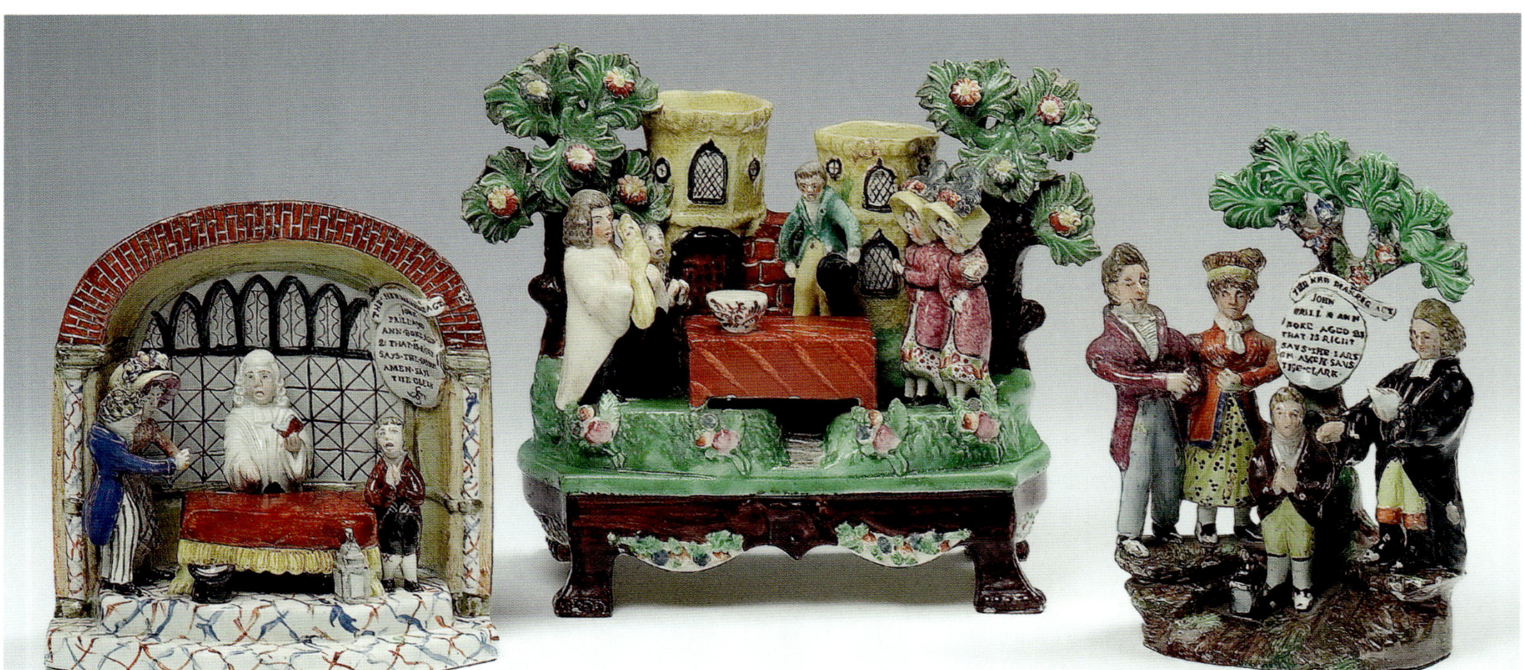

Figure Group, (**824**), c.1830, Staffordshire, height: 15.3cm, (6in), enamelled pearlware. Plaque inscribed, 'THE NEW MARRIAGE ACT'. The parson conducts a fashionable wedding ceremony within the apse of a church with the clerk as witness. Inscription continues; 'John Frill And Ann Boke. Aged 21. That Is Right. Says The Parson. Amen Says The Clerk'.
Figure Group, (**826**), c.1830, Staffordshire, height: 21cm, (8¼in), enamelled pearlware. Table-based spill vase tableau represents a christening scene with a punch-bowl as font.
Figure Group, (**825**), c.1830, Staffordshire, height: 17.8cm, (7in), enamelled pearlware. Marriage service enacted out of doors, beneath a tree. There is no altar; the clerk takes centre stage and an impressed plaque has exactly the same inscription as (824).

John Wesley (1703-1791)

A good proportion of the section on Religion concerns breakaway factions from the Established Church. Methodism was founded by John Wesley (1703-1791) in the mid-eighteenth century. There are said to be more pottery busts, figures and vessels commemorating Wesley than any other Briton except Queen Victoria. He was born in Epworth, in South Yorkshire, the eleventh of the nineteen children of the Rev. Samuel and Susanna Wesley. At the age of five, John was miraculously saved from a fire at the parsonage and from then on believed God had spared him for some special purpose.

After reading theology at Christ Church College, Oxford, Wesley was ordained, becoming a Fellow of Lincoln College and Moderator of Classics in 1726. He served as curate to his father at Epworth, before travelling to Georgia in the American colonies, hoping to convert indigenous Americans, but experienced doubts about his own faith. Back in England in 1738, he met Peter Bohler, a Christian from Moravia, who told him, 'to preach faith till you have it and then because you have it, you will preach faith.'

Wesley preached a doctrine of personal salvation through Christ alone, at open-air gatherings and became a celebrated charismatic orator. He travelled some 42,000 miles in his lifetime, mainly on horseback, helping to set up Methodist societies all over the country, although he never actually left the Church of England. Methodism became established in South Wales and the industrial Midlands where the manufacture of commemorative pottery reinforced Wesley's message. Together with printed tracts and pamphlets, it helped to spread the Word.[37]

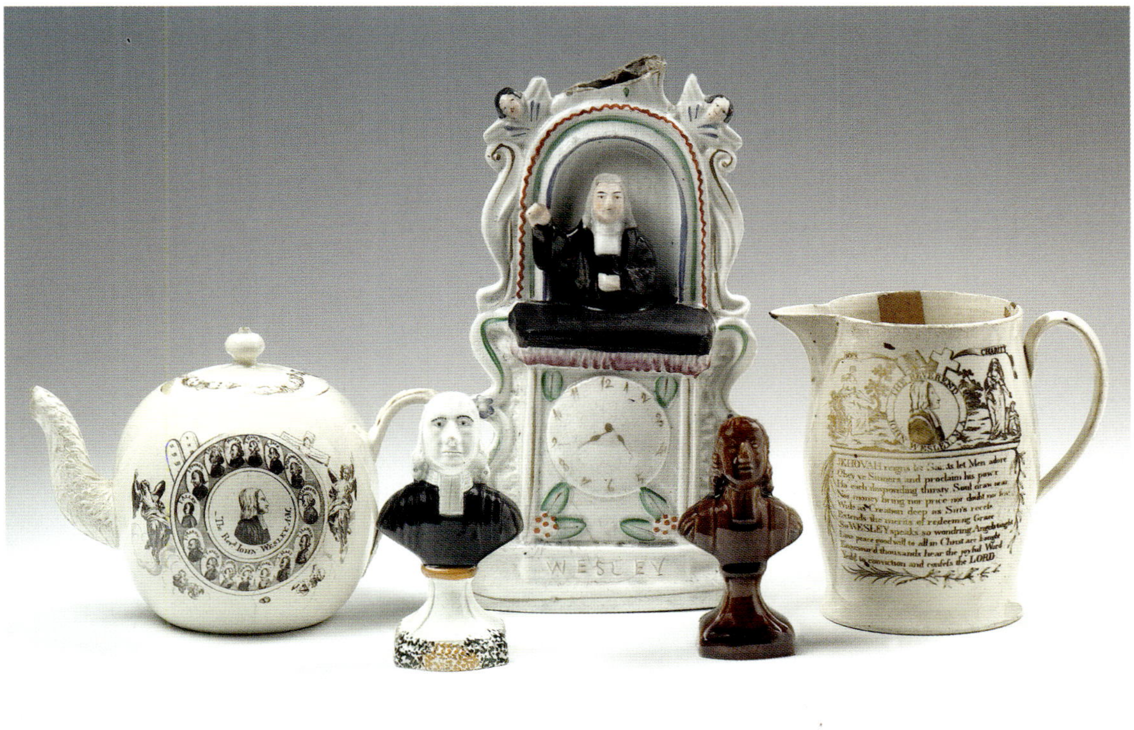

Teapot, (**841**), c.1790, Staffordshire, Etruria, height: 14cm, (5½in), printed creamware. Crudely printed with a portrait of John Wesley at the centre of a circle of 14 prominent Methodist preachers, such as I. Allen, T. Hanby and T. Taylor.
Bust, (**829**), c.1790, Yorkshire, height: 12.1cm, (4¾in), Prattware. Portrait bust of John Wesley.
Watch Stand, (**828**), c.1840, height: 25.4cm, (10in), enamelled earthenware. Damaged watch stand modelled as a pulpit where Wesley is shown preaching.
Bust, (**830**), c.1790, Yorkshire?, height: 11.5cm, (4½in), earthenware. Brown-glazed portrait bust of John Wesley, pierced as a pounce or pepper-pot.
Jug, (**839**), c.1790, Staffordshire, height: 14.6cm, (5¾in), printed creamware. Crudely printed and overfired with Wesley in profile (representing Faith) between Hope and Charity. Verses from Methodist hymns were probably written by his brother, Charles.

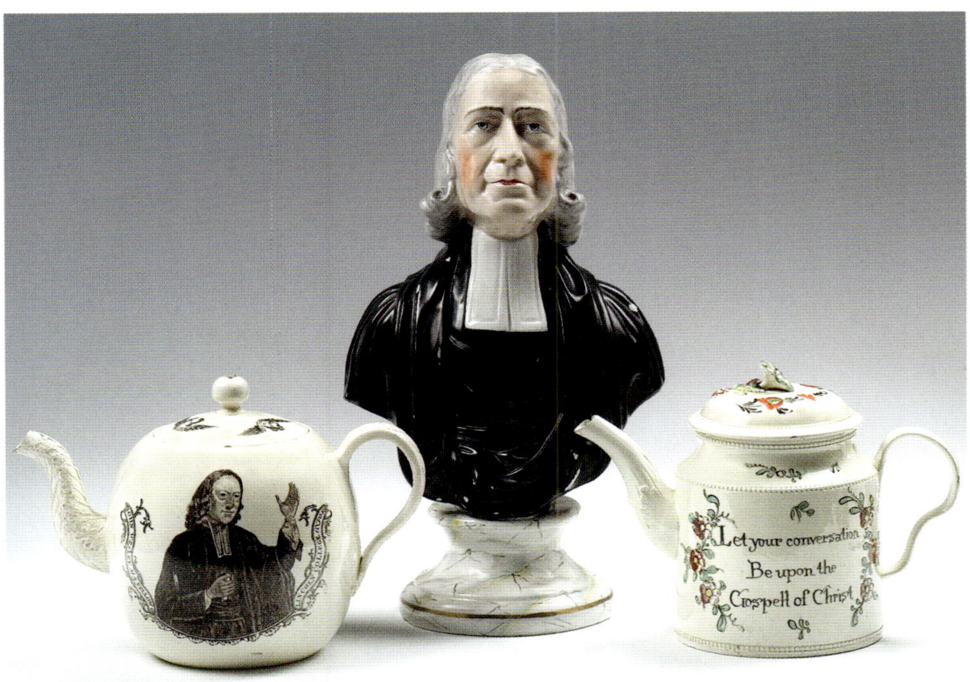

Teapot, (**840**), c.1780, Staffs, Etruria, height: 14cm, (5½in), printed creamware. Wedgwood teapot finely printed in Liverpool by Guy Green, with a portrait of John Wesley, his left hand raised in blessing. A banner identifies him as 'A Fellow of Lincoln College, Oxford'. Taken from a painting of 1765 by Nathaniel Hone.[38] Reverse inscribed; 'Let your conversation be on the Gospel of CHRIST' (from Philippians 1: 27) and a reference to 'Watts's Hymns'.
Bust, (**831**), c.1790, Staffordshire, Burslem, height: 29.2cm, (11½in), enamelled pearlware. Portrait bust of John Wesley issued by Enoch Wood, with an impressed plaque recording that Wesley had sat for the portrait in 1781. He wears his hair long and white and is smartly dressed in cassock and Geneva neckbands. Always concerned about his preachers' public appearance, he advised one, in a letter of 24 April 1769, 'Whatever clothes you have let them be whole; no rents, no tatters, no rags … let no-one ever see a ragged Methodist'.[39]
Teapot, (**847**), c.1780, Staffs, Greatbatch of Fenton, height: 14.7cm, (5¾in), enamelled creamware. Inscribed, 'Let your Conversation Be upon the Gospell [*sic*] of Christ'. Painted on reverse with a chinoiserie figure in a garden.

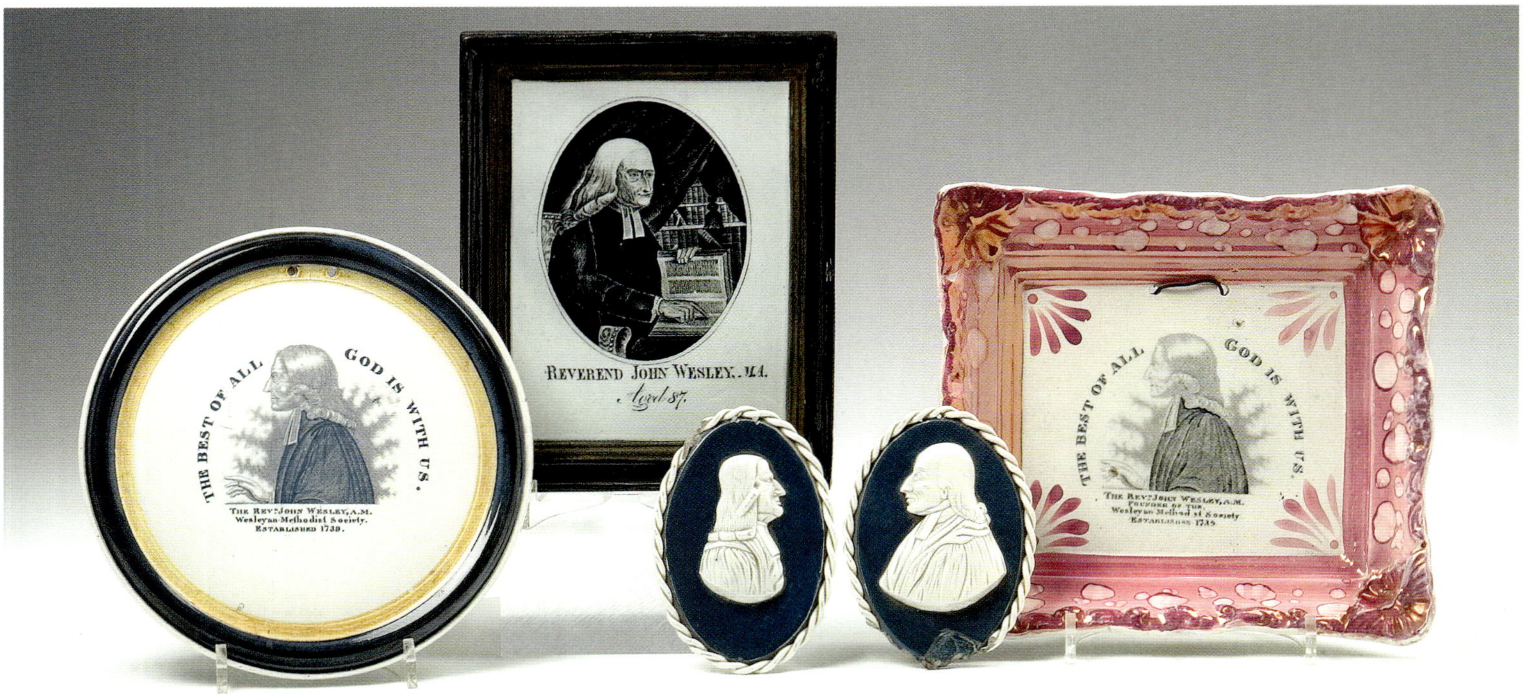

Plaque, (**DA322297**) c.1820, Sunderland, Dixon Austin & Co., diameter: 18.2cm, (7⅛in), pearlware, printed and enamelled. Inscribed, 'The best of all/ God is with us' beneath profile portrait of Wesley, probably based on a stipple engraving of 1792 by Ridley after Edridge.[40]
Plaque, (**833**), c.1800, North East, height: 19.1cm, (7½in), pearlware, printed and enamelled. Naive portrait of 'REVEREND JOHN WESLEY M.A. Aged 87' with integral moulded frame, based on an engraving by William Ridley after a miniature by R. Arnold.[41]
Pair of Plaques, (**834 + 835**), c.1800, Staffordshire?, each height: 10.8cm, (4¼in), pearlware. Crude relief-moulded portraits of John and Charles Wesley (1708-1788) inspired by Wedgwood jasperware medallions.
Card Tray, (**838**), c.1800, Sunderland, height: 20.3cm, (8in), earthenware, printed and lustred. Inscribed, 'The best of all / God is with us' beneath profile portrait of Wesley, probably based on 1792 print by Ridley after Edridge.

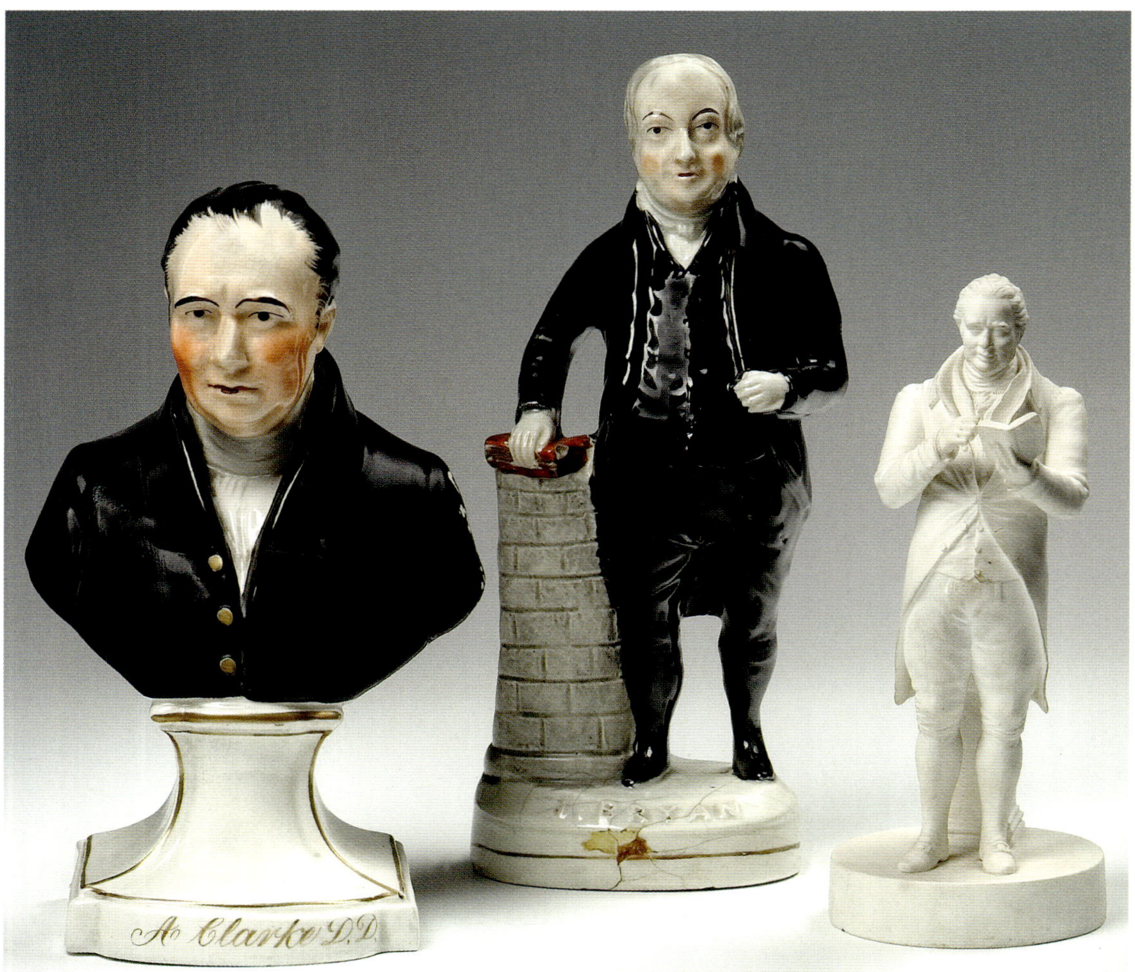

Bust, (**854**), c.1840, Staffordshire, height: 23.5cm, (9¼in), earthenware, enamelled and gilt. Entitled 'A. Clarke D.D.',[42] Adam Clarke (c.1760-c.1832), the most influential British Methodist in the generation after Wesley. Born in Northern Ireland, the son of a Church of Ireland minister, he converted to Methodism in 1778. Clarke, also an accomplished scientist and linguist, served an unprecedented three terms as President of the Wesleyan Conference.
Figure, (**855**), c.1850, Staffordshire, height: 26.7cm, (10½in), enamelled earthenware. The base for a caricature figure with short legs has moulded title, 'J. BRYAN', for the Rev. John Bryan, a Welsh Calvinist Methodist who subsequently became a grocer in Leeds and Caernarvon.[43]
Figure, (**853**), c.1835, Staffordshire, Stoke-on-Trent, height: 20.3cm, (8in), biscuit porcelain. Figure of Adam Clarke modelled by the Mintons Factory, No. 61 from the pattern book. It probably dates from the time of his death.

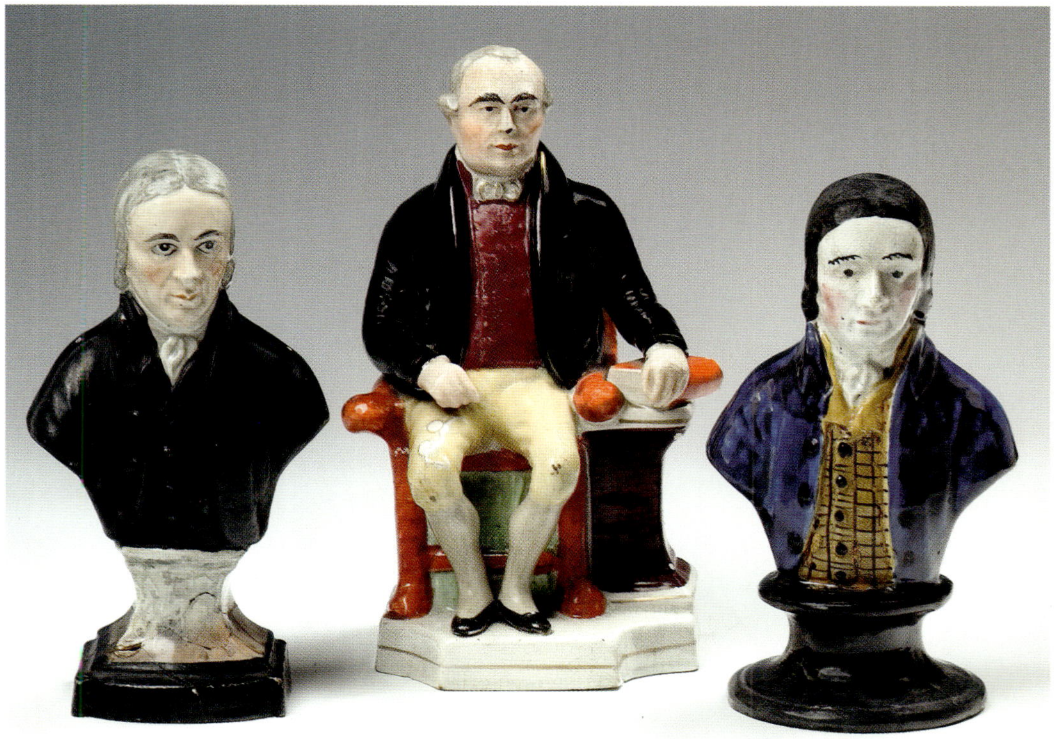

Bust, (**851**), 1826, Staffordshire, height: 19.1cm, (7½in), enamelled pearlware. Portrait bust, incised on the back, 'W. Thorn 1826', wears a clerical black coat.
Figure, (**848**), c.1840, Staffordshire, height: 21.6cm, (8½in), enamelled earthenware. Portrait figure said to represent the eccentric preacher, William Huntington (1745-1813). Born William Hunt, in Kent, he worked as an errand boy, coach driver and coal heaver before fleeing the district after the daughter of a Frittenden tailor became pregnant. He converted to Calvinism and added S.S. for 'Sinner Saved', to his new name. He was a prolific writer and died in Tunbridge Wells.
Bust, (**852**), c.1830, Staffordshire, height: 19.1cm, (7½in), Prattware. Portrait bust from similar mould to (851). The reference may be to James Thorne, (1795-1872) a follower of William O'Bryan, whom he succeeded as leader of the 'Bible Christian Connexion' in 1829. Thorn was their first itinerant preacher, known for his 'earnest eloquence and ready wit'.

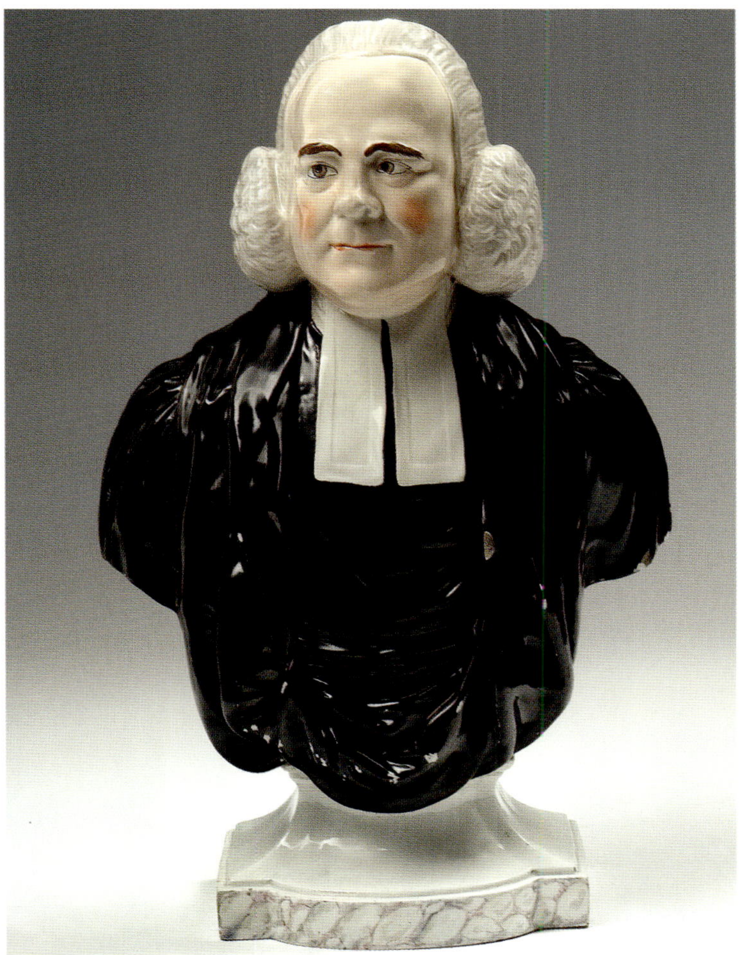

Bust, (**832**), c.1795, Staffordshire, Neale & Co. height: 27.9cm, (11in), enamelled pearlware. Portrait bust of the evangelical Calvinistic Methodist, Rev. George Whitefield (1714-70), one of Wesley's best known followers. Born in Gloucester he travelled widely in Britain and America and preached out of doors to crowds of thousands. He was acclaimed as a fiery orator who campaigned to save men from the fires of hell.[44] Bust modelled around 1791 and issued by Neale & Co. faithfully reproduces his full wig and the distinctive cast in one eye.

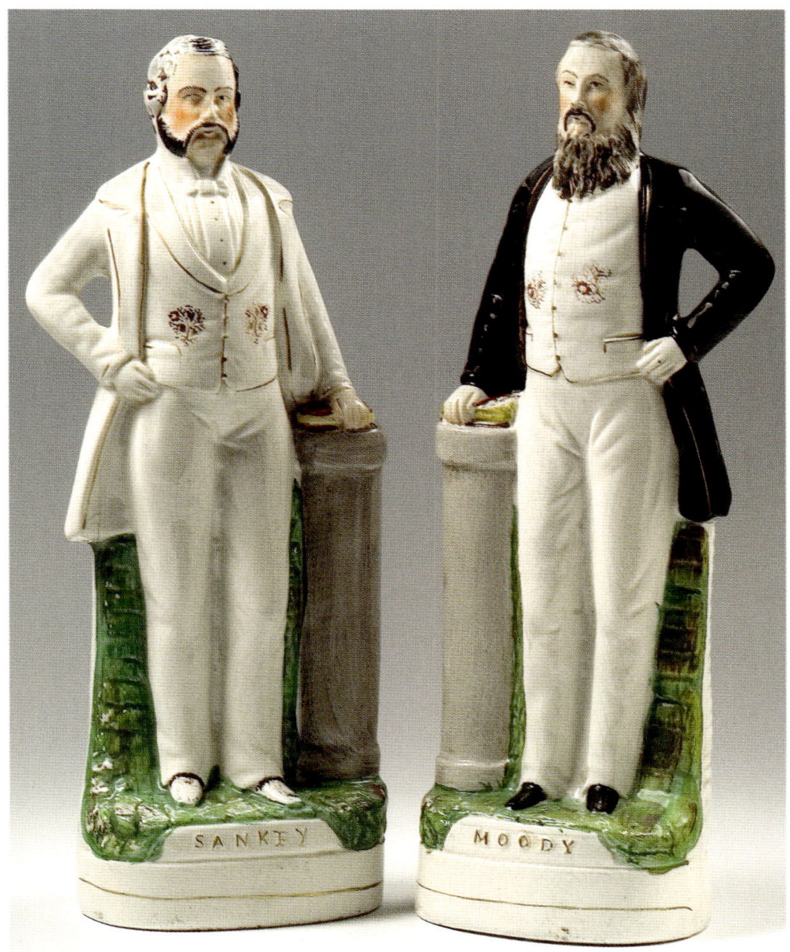

Pair of Figures, (**0863 & A**), c.1875, Staffordshire, each height: 43.5cm, (17in), earthenware, enamelled and gilt. Figures representing the American evangelists, Dwight Lyman Moody (1837-99) and Ira David Sankey (1840-1908). Moody, (right) a shoe salesman with an English wife, spent increasing amounts of time fund-raising for the YMCA. As a charismatic preacher, he embarked on a two-year tour of Britain with Sankey, (left), a gifted gospel singer, whose simple but soul-stirring hymns won them considerable celebrity.

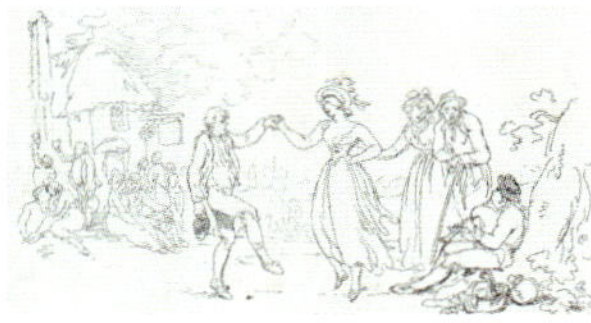

Chapter 13

MUSIC & DRAMA

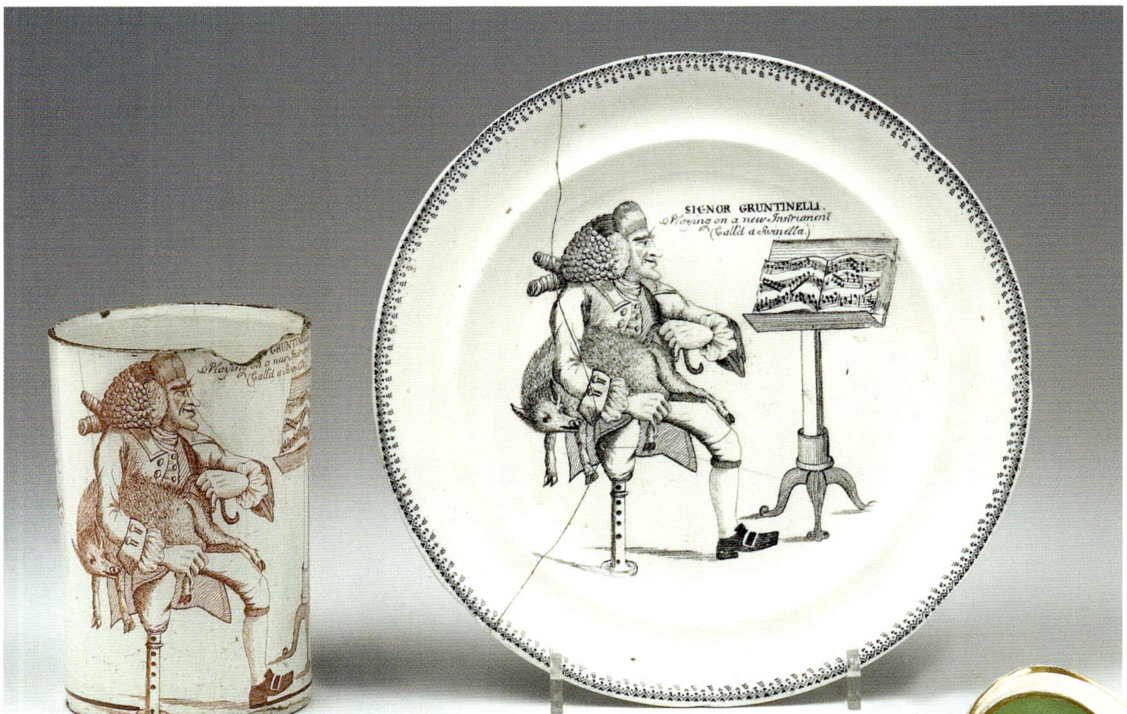

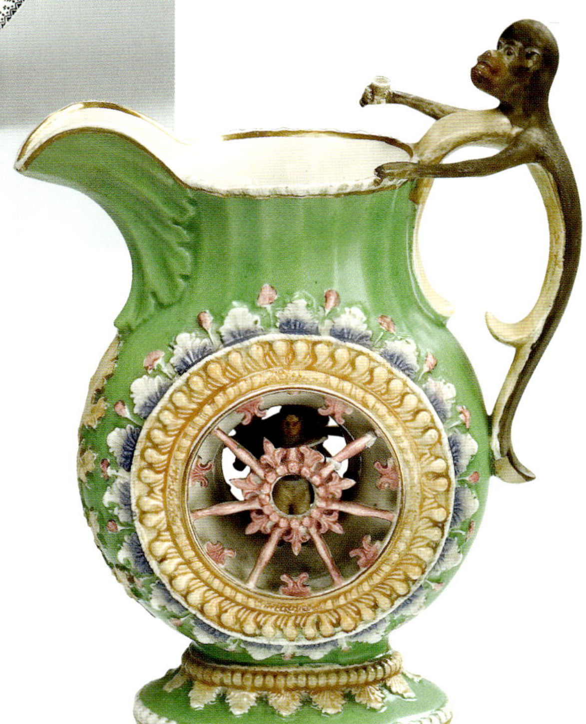

Mug, (**866**), c.1775, Staffordshire, height: 21.6cm, (8½in), red-printed creamware.
Plate, (**865**), c.1775, Staffordshire, diameter: 12.7cm, (5in), printed creamware.
Printed with, 'SIGNOR GRUNTINELLI Playing on a new Instrument (Call'd a Swinetta)'. An elderly man, balancing on a wooden leg formed of a pipe of his instrument, attempts to play a 'musette' or pastoral oboe, in the form of a wild boar that struggles as he pulls its tail. Source print published by Matthias Darly in 1774 and widely copied.[1] The identity of the musician being lampooned is unknown.

Jug, (**894**), c.1830, Staffordshire, diameter: 28cm, (11in), printed creamware.
Elaborately moulded novelty item, with monkey-headed handle, its central void containing tiny figures of musicians, partly obscured by a wheel-like tracery of spokes.

George Frideric Handel (1685-1759)

Handel was born in Saxony, but settled in London in 1712 and died a British hero. For nearly 50 years he produced prodigious quantities of operas, oratorios, concertos and chamber music. His *Messiah*, first performed in Dublin in 1742, became a national institution within his lifetime. In 1784 five days of commemoration concerts for Handel were held in Westminster Abbey with a choir and orchestra of over 500, unprecedented for England. These celebrations were so successful that they were repeated; the last in 1791 involved over 1000 performers.[2] His oratorios 'gave voice to the potent triad that supported English national identity: Protestantism, prosperity and power'.[3]

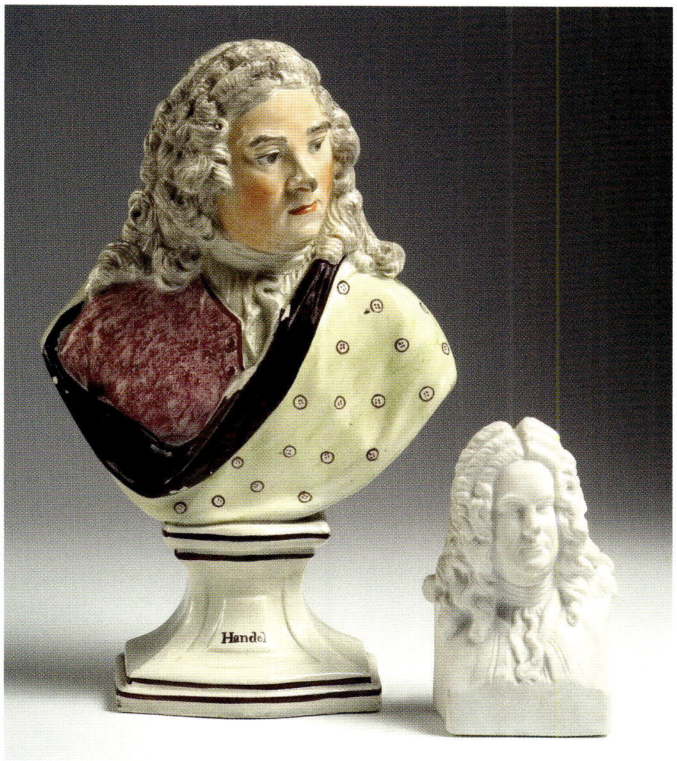

Bust, (**877**), c.1800, Staffordshire, Burslem, height: 20.3cm, (8in), enamelled pearlware. Portrait bust of Handel made by Ralph or Enoch Wood's factory (impressed: 80).
Bust, (**874**), c.1800, Germany, height: 10.5cm, (4⅛in), hard-paste porcelain. Portrait bust, impressed: Handel.

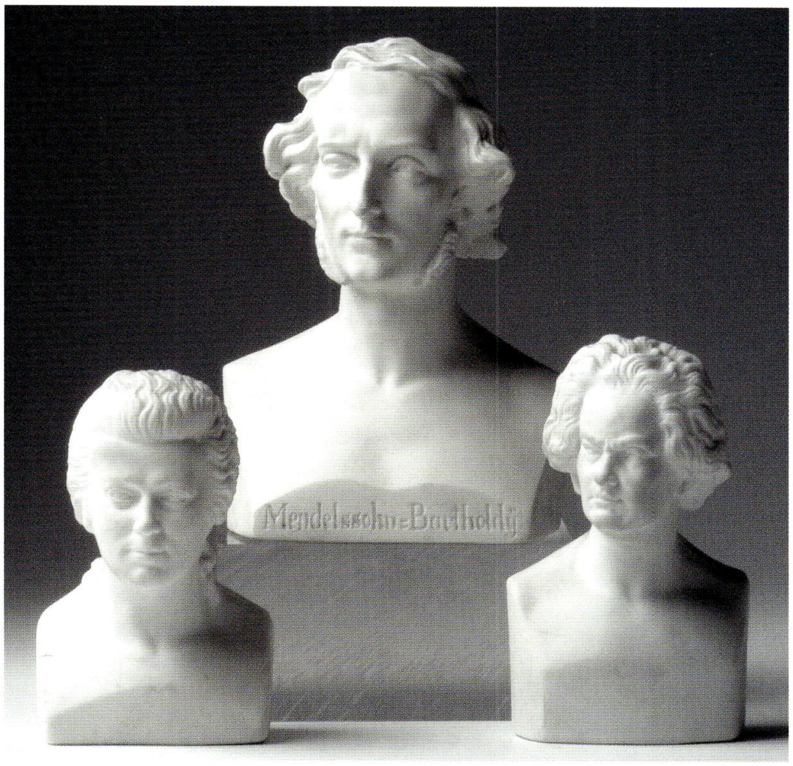

Bust, (**876**), c.1880, Germany, height: 8.9cm, (3½in), hard-paste porcelain. Portrait bust of Mozart (1756-91), named on back.
Bust, (**873**), c.1880, Germany, height: 14cm, (5½in), hard-paste porcelain. Portrait bust of Mendelssohn (1809-47), named on chest.
Bust, (**875**), c.1880, Germany, height: 11.5cm, (4½in), hard-paste porcelain. Portrait bust of Beethoven (1770-1827), named on back.

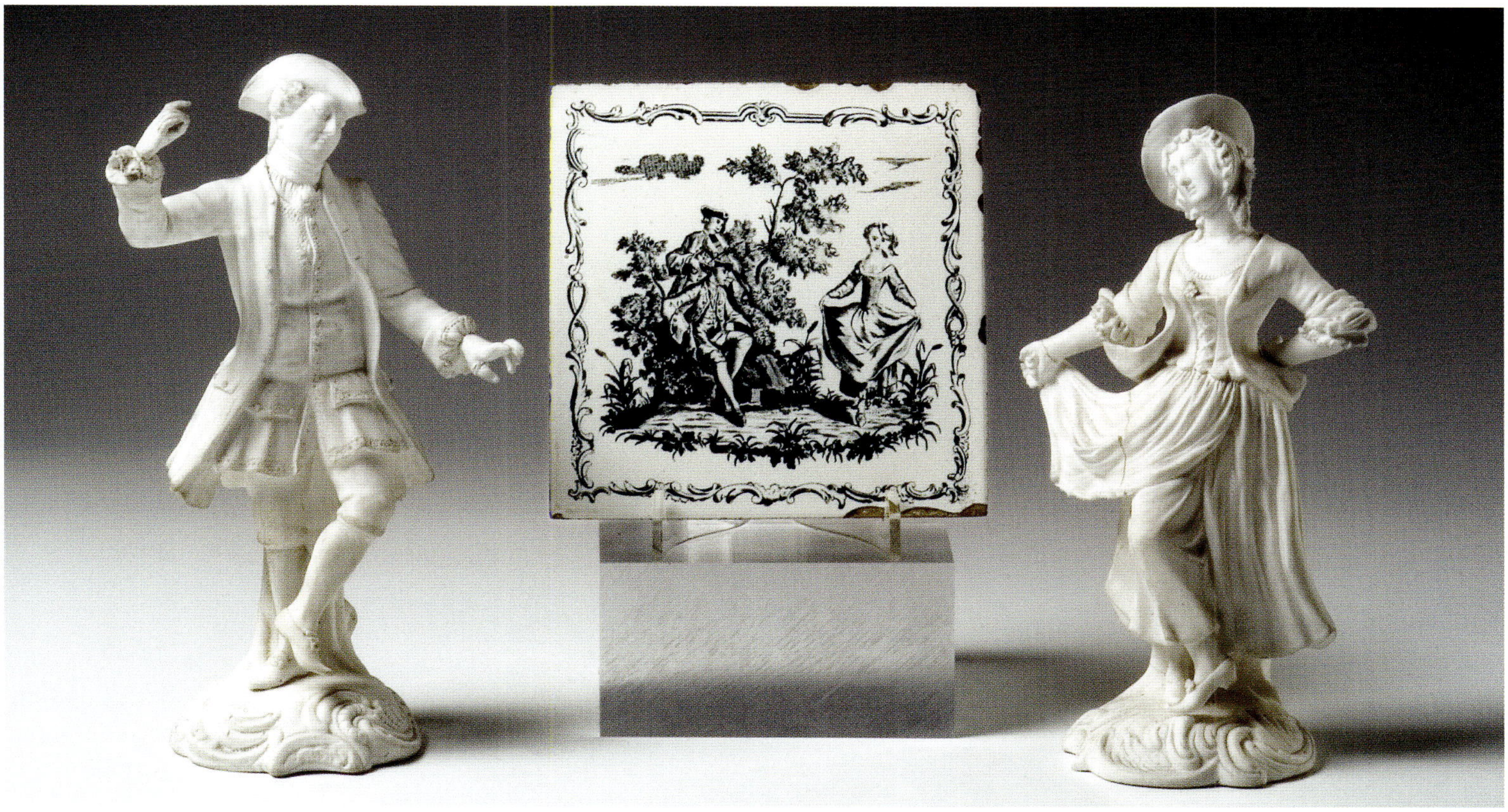

Pair of Figures, (**1195 & A**), c.1830, Staffordshire, Stoke-on-Trent, Mintons, height: 23.5cm, (9in), height 24.2cm, (9½in), biscuit porcelain. Pair of dancers (inscribed No. 108 and No. 109), wearing rococo fancy dress, recalling the nymphs and shepherds of Arcadia.
Tile, (**1196**), c.1770, Liverpool, height: 12.7cm, (5in), printed tin-glazed earthenware. Two gentlemen, (one of them playing a viol), watch a young woman dance. It is generally known as 'Nancy Dawson dancing a hornpipe', taken from *The Ladies Amusement*, plate 32.[4] Nancy Dawson (1728-1767), a dancer at Sadler's Wells Theatre (then at Covent Garden), was plucked from the chorus in 1759 to dance a hornpipe in *The Beggar's Opera,* to great acclaim. 'Miss Dawson's Hornpipe' composed by Thomas Arne became very popular.[5] She gave her name to a section of the Lancashire morris dance.

Emma Hamilton (1765-1815)

Emma, (née Hart), the wife of Sir William Hamilton, the British Envoy to Naples, enjoyed Europe-wide fame for her mimed 'Attitudes'. A pioneer performance artist, from 1786 she regularly entranced Grand Tourists and other distinguished visitors to Naples with movement and poses inspired by figures painted on the antique vases in her husband's collection. The German writer Goethe was deeply impressed and artists from Cosway and Romney to Mme Vigée le Brun sketched her dramatic improvisations. Her 'Attitudes' were recorded on a Berlin porcelain coffee service (c.1795), where each piece illustrated a different pose, based on Tommaso Piroli's portfolio of prints after original drawings by Friedrich Rehberg.[6]

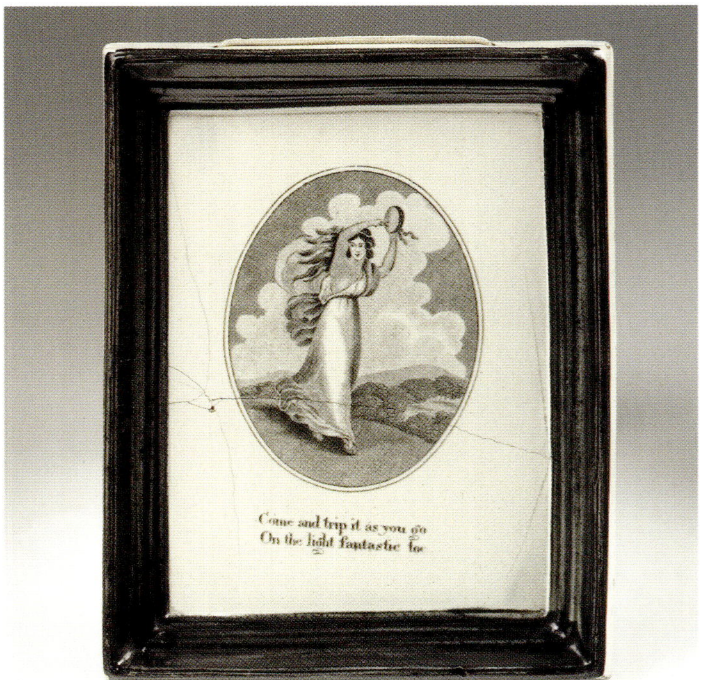

Plaque, (**1198**), c.1800, North East, height: 21.6cm, (8½in), earthenware, printed and enamelled. Printed with image of Emma performing with a tambourine, loosely based on Plate VIII of *Lady Hamilton's Attitudes*, engraved by Piroli. Inscribed 'Come and trip it as you go / On the light fantastic too', from Milton's poem, *L'Allegro*.

Black Performers

Billy Waters (c.1778-c.1823)

One of the best-known black, street musicians of the early nineteenth century was Billy Waters. After losing his leg on active service during the Napoleonic Wars, he was awarded a small naval pension but was later obliged to play his violin in London's Drury Lane to support his wife and two children.

Elected 'King of the Beggars', he featured in Pierce Egan's popular book, *Life in London* (1821) illustrated by George Cruikshank and was immortalised in a staged version of Egan's book. He died, destitute in St Giles's Workhouse in 1823, at the age of 45, 'having parted with his old friend the fiddle for a trifling sum at the pawnbrokers.'

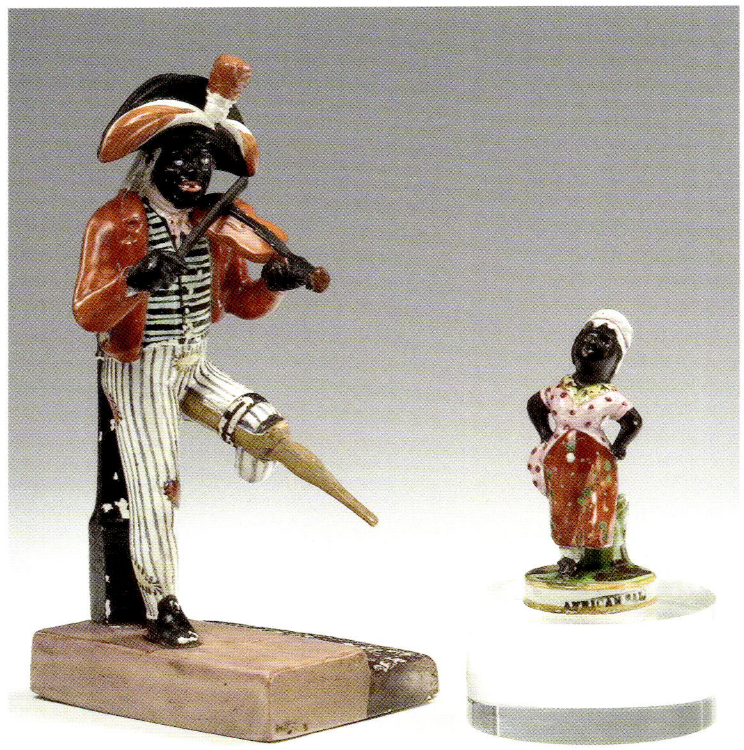

Figure, (**883**), c.1825, Staffordshire, Burslem, height: 21.6cm, (8½in), enamelled pearlware, marked 'H' on base. Portrait of Billy Waters, (after a Derby porcelain prototype), taken from images drawn by George Cruikshank for Pierce Egan's *Life in London*.
Figure, (**891**), c.1830, Staffordshire, Burslem, height: 9.6cm, (3¾in), enamelled pearlware. Portrait of 'African Sal', another character from *Life in London,* modelled on a Derby figure, (with a similar, coin-like base) and made by Enoch Wood. Sal, a single parent from 'foreign parts', was played on stage by a Mr Saunders. Cruikshank's illustration shows her dancing with 'Dusty Bob' at 'All Max', a drinking establishment where, 'Lascars, blacks, jack tars, coal heavers, dustmen, women of colour … were all Jigging together.'

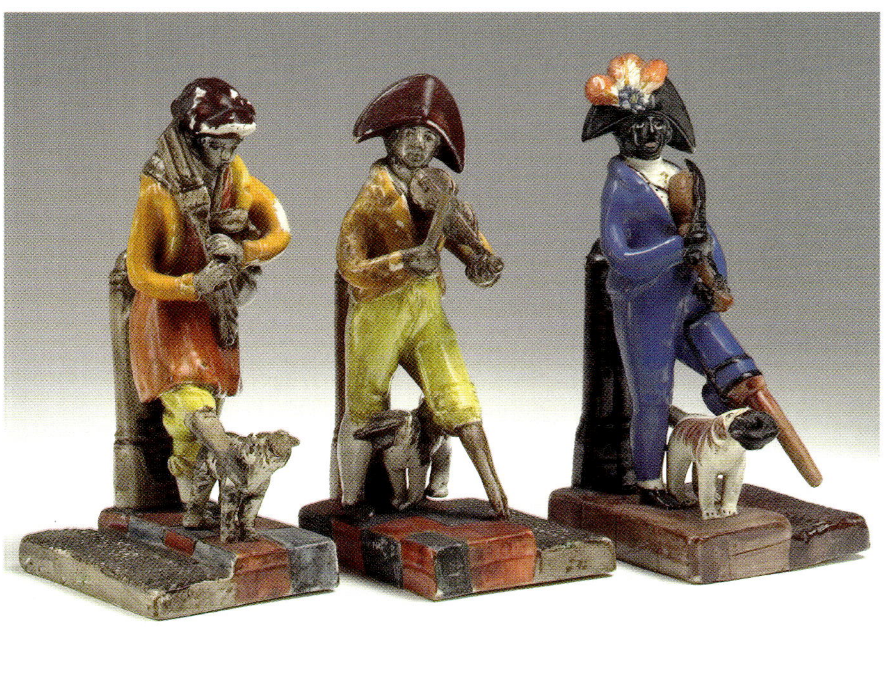

Figure, (**881**), c.1825, Staffordshire, height: 17cm, (6⅝in), enamelled pearlware.
Figure, (**882**), c.1825, Staffordshire, height: 17cm, (6⅝in), enamelled pearlware.
Figure, (**884**), c.1825, Staffordshire, height: 17cm, (6⅝in), enamelled pearlware. Three further figures (confirming Billy Waters's popularity) are based on Enoch Wood's portrait of Billy Waters, but are far more crudely executed.

Black Bandsmen

By the end of the eighteenth century several smart battalions had a corps of black musicians. Military bands often played for promenaders in London's fashionable Vauxhall Gardens, a favourite venue for masques and balls. In an illustration from *Life in London*, Cruikshank shows such a band entertaining the crowd and includes a black tambourine player and one playing the Chagana or 'jingling johnny'. Black musicians brought innovations of lasting importance to band music, from fancy footwork and the juggling of drumsticks to the complex rhythms they played.

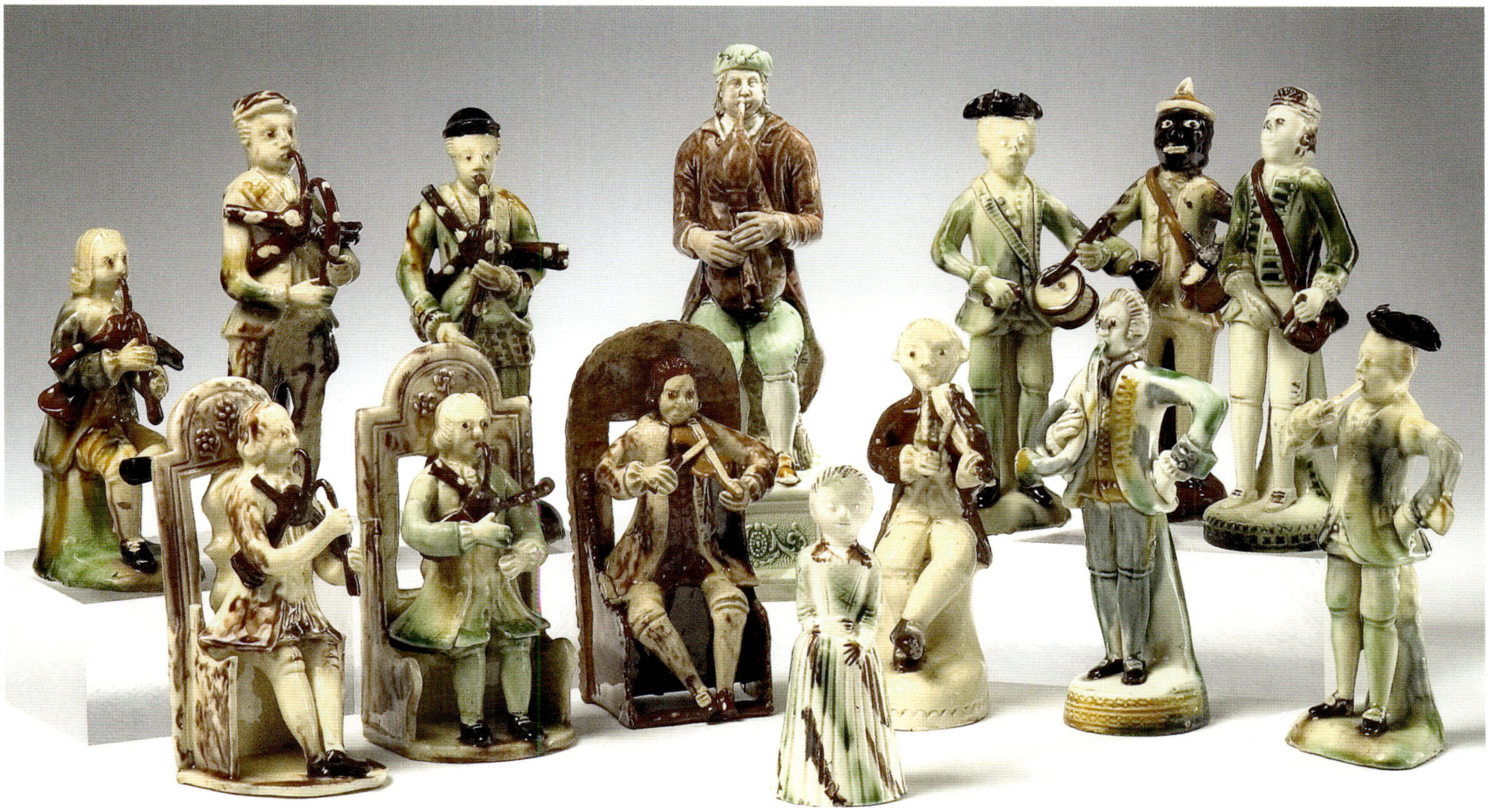

Thirteen Figures, (**888**), c.1760, Staffordshire, earthenware, lead-glazed and oxide-coloured. Museum visitors in the 1870s nicknamed this large, mixed group of early musicians, 'Nebuchadnezzar's Band'.[7] They comprise drummers, horn players, bagpipers, violinists and a small
Female Figure, height: 11.5cm, (4½in), cast as a singer![8]

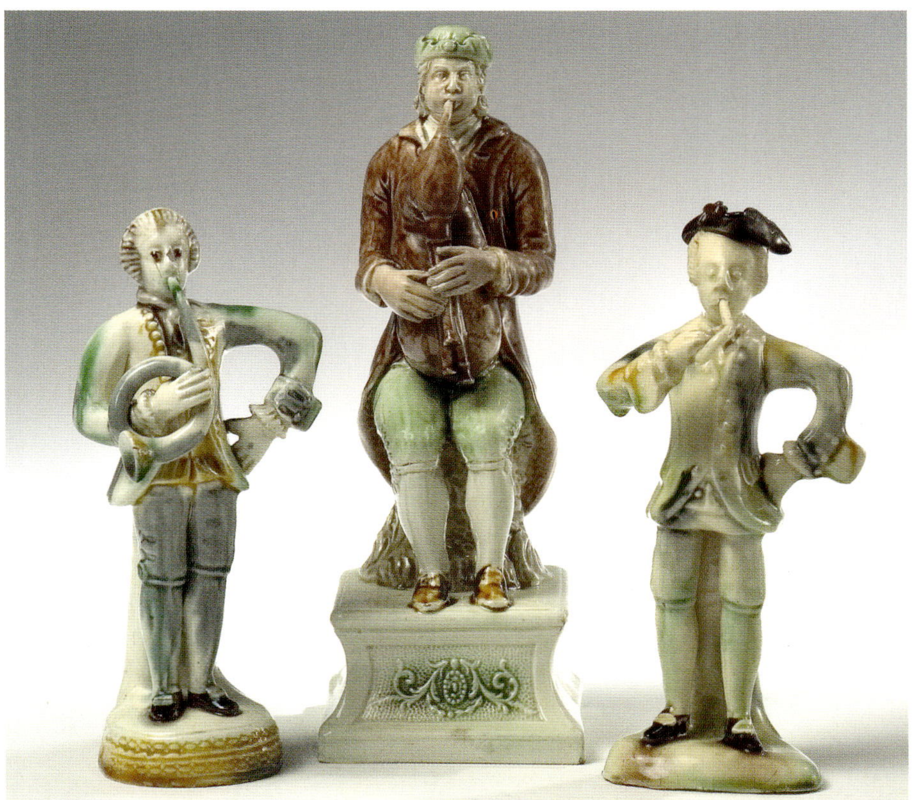

Horn-player, height: 15.5cm, (6⅛in),
Bagpiper, c.1780, probably Wood factory, height: 22cm, (8⅝in), Sitting, mounted on rectangular plinth.
Piper, height: 15.5cm, (6⅛in).

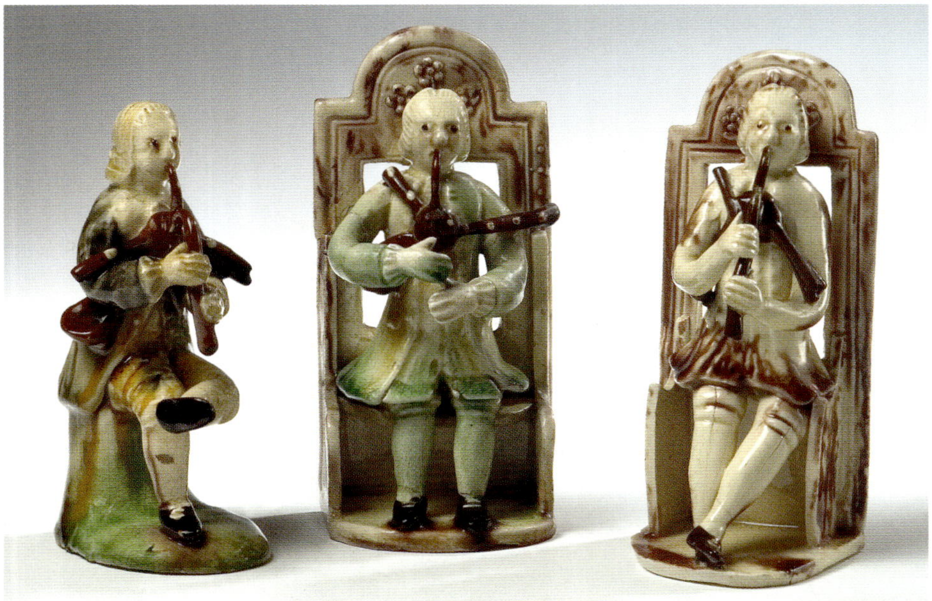

Bagpiper, height: 14cm, (5½in),
Two Bagpipers, each height: 15.3cm, (6in). They sit in high-backed chairs decorated with stamped floral designs.

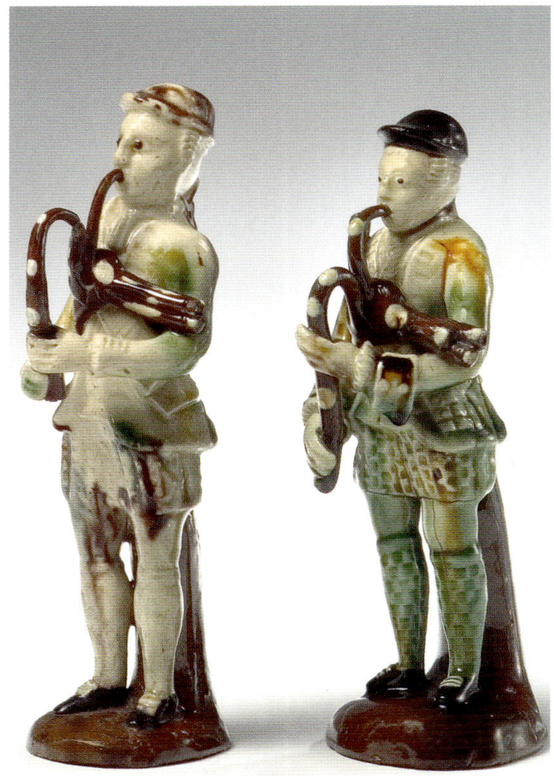

Scottish Bagpipers, height: 16.cm, (6½in), height: 15.7cm, (6¼in). They wear caps, plaid kilts and hose.

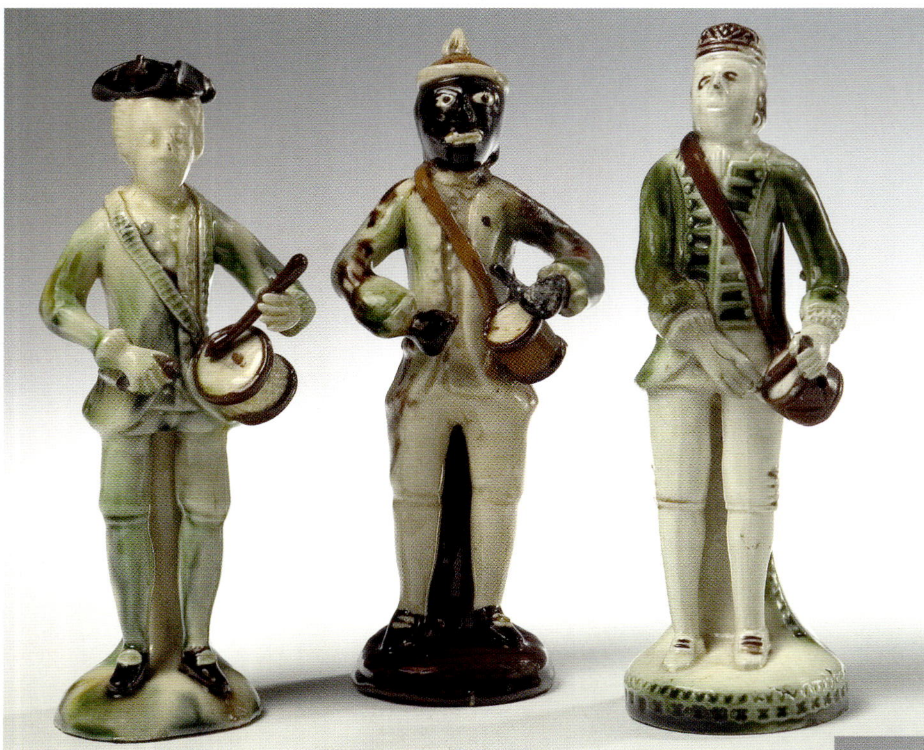

Drummer, height: 15.9cm, (6in),
Black Drummer, height: 15.9cm, (6in). The tradition of using black musicians in regimental bands began in the late 1600s when British regiments on duty in the West Indies 'acquired' black drummers.[9]
Drummer, height: 15.9cm, (6in).

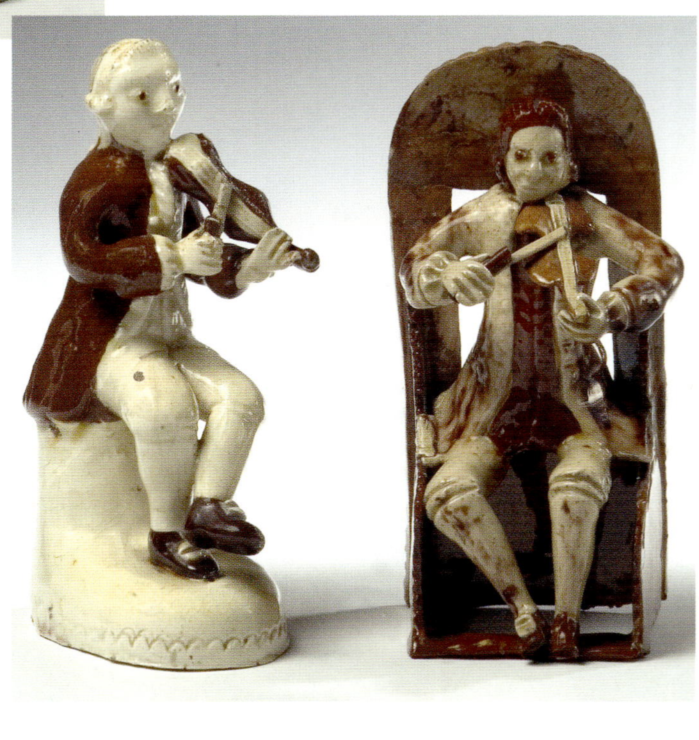

Violinist, height: 12.2cm, (4¾in).
Violinist, height: 15.5cm, (6⅛in). Sits on an armchair composed of marbled clays.

Jim Crow

The fictional American black character was invented by white actors. The Englishman, Charles Mathews, encountered the songs, movements and speech patterns of black Americans in New York in 1822. He was the first actor to 'black up' in order to imitate them in his London show, *A Trip to America*. The American, Thomas Dartmouth Rice, who performed in London in 1836, claimed to portray a real-life black singer, with a crooked right shoulder and left leg, who dressed in rags and sang,

> Weel about and turn about and do jus' so,
> Eb'ry time I weel about, I jump Jim Crow.[10]

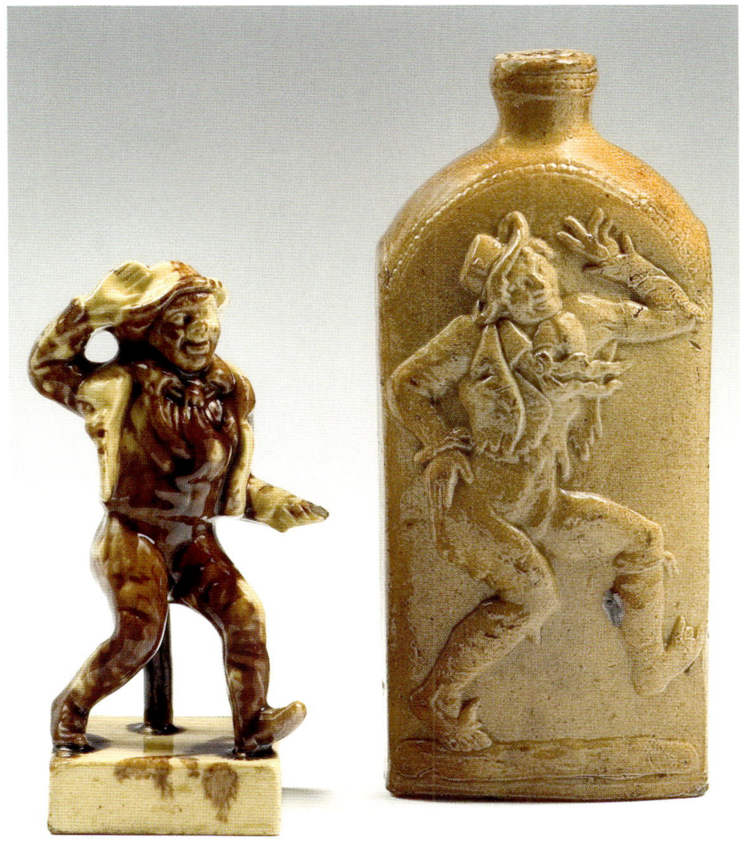

Figure, (**880**), c.1840, Staffordshire, height: 16.5cm, (6½in), treacle-glazed earthenware.
Flask, (**879**), c.1840, London, height: 22.3cm, (8¾in), stoneware. The dancing figure and the relief-moulded image of a dancing figure represent Jim Crow. Both are based on an engraving of Dartmouth Rice c.1832.[11]

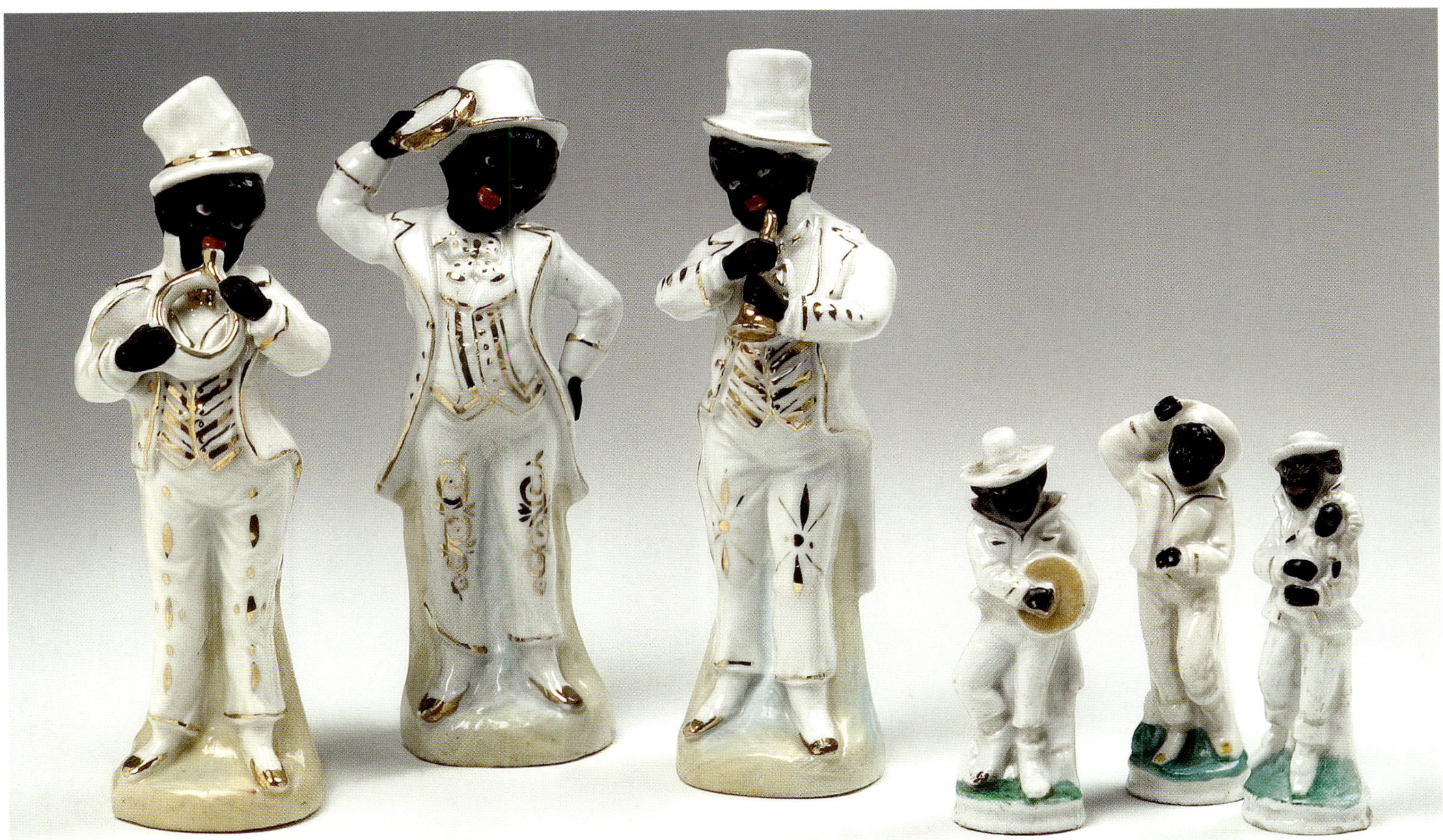

Three Figures, (**889**), c.1860, Germany, heights: 17.2cm/ 17.2cm /18cm, (6¾in/6¾in/7⅛in), hard-paste porcelain, enamelled and gilt. Of the group of larger figures, one dances while the others play trumpet and horn.
Three Figures, (**890**), c.1860, Germany, heights: 9.2cm / 9.9cm /9.5cm, (3⅝in/3⅞in/3¾in), enamelled, hard-paste porcelain. All figures dance, one with a tambourine, one with bells and one with a baby. Groups of black African musicians as well as white ones blacked-up, became something of a craze in the late 19th century. They were regular entertainers on street corners, in the music hall and on popular occasions like Derby Day.

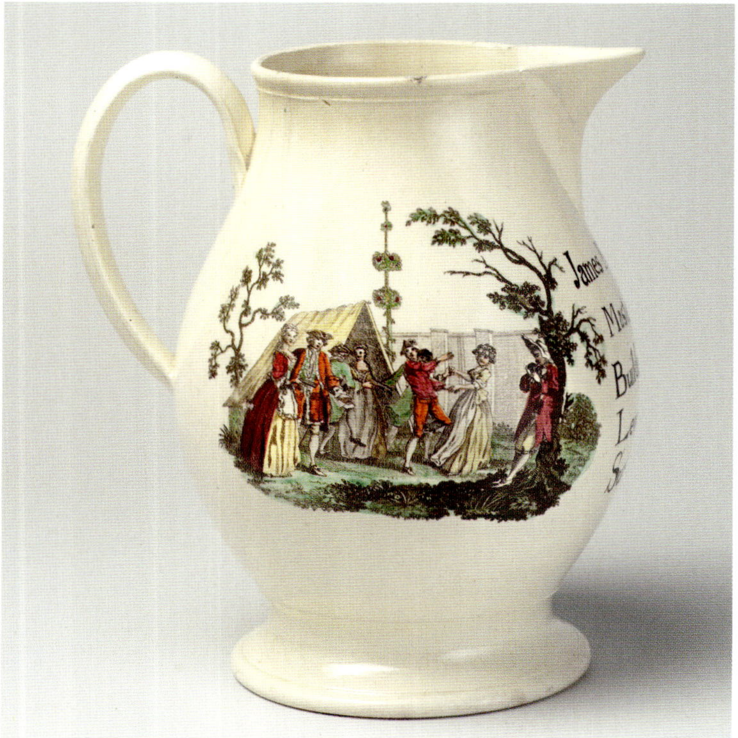

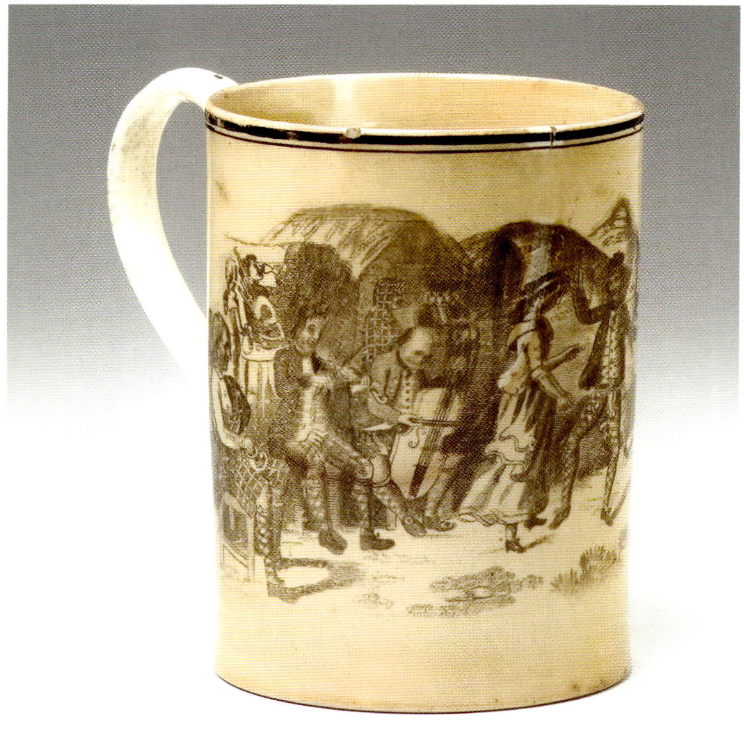

Amateur Music Making

Jug, (579), c.1796, Staffordshire, Wedgwood, height: 19.1cm, (7½in), creamware, printed and coloured. Jug decorated for a Freemason by William Greatbatch of Fenton, depicts May Day festivities. Well-dressed men and women are shown emerging from a tent to dance around a maypole – a famous folk symbol of fertility and marriage. Taken from a design by the French artist, Gravelot, engraved by George Bickham and first published in 1737.

Mug, (1197), c.1790, Staffordshire, height: 12.1cm, (4¾in), printed creamware. Lively scene of open air Scottish dancing on a wraparound print. Robert Burns praised its source, 'A Highland Wedding at Blair Atholl' painted in 1780 by David Allan, for its pastoral authenticity.[12] The participants include Neil Gow, the famous composer and fiddler, (retained by the Duke of Atholl for £5 a year) who wears tartan breeches.[13]

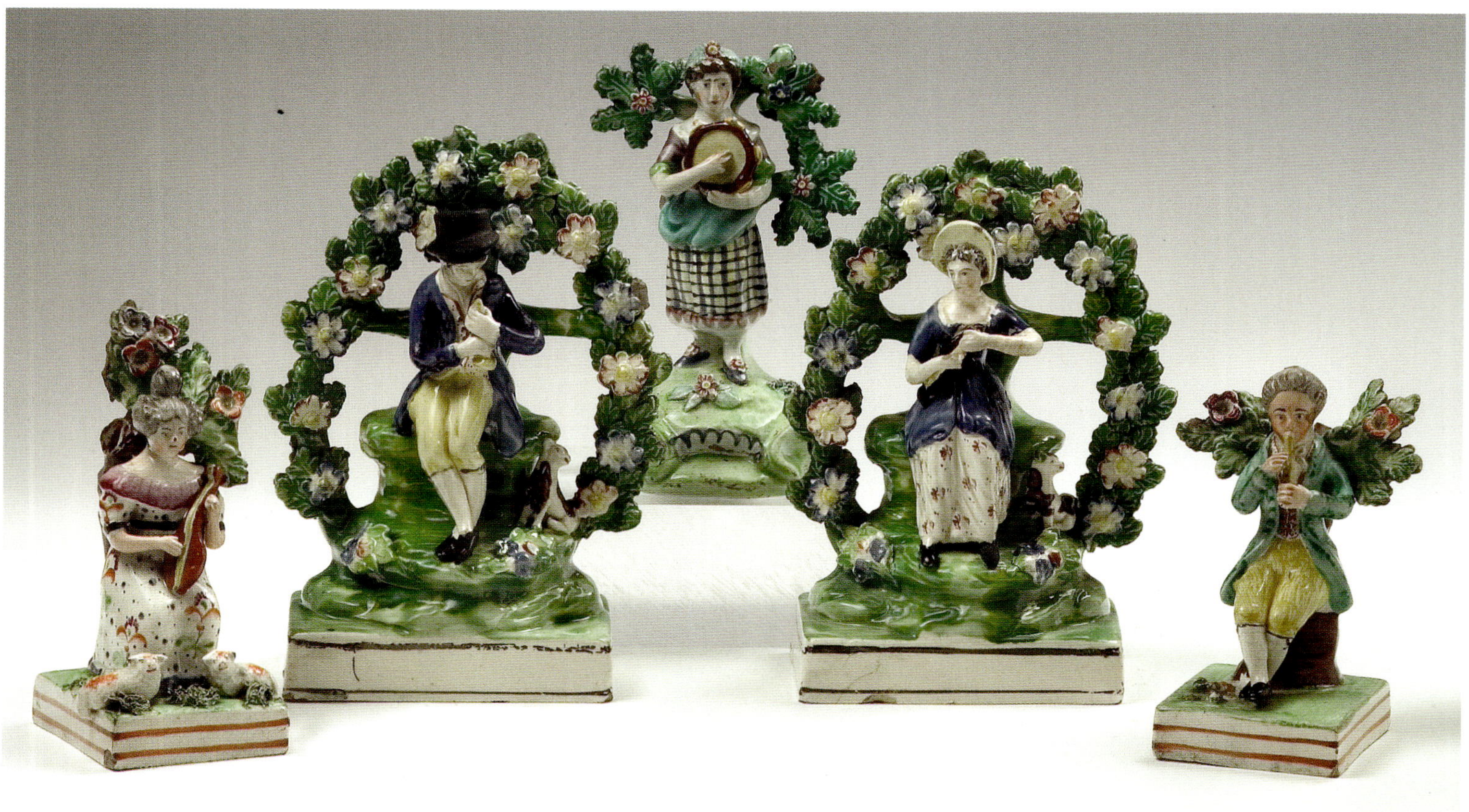

Figure, (868) pair to **(867)**, c.1830 Staffordshire, height: 14cm, (5½in), enamelled pearlware. A girl, in fashionable 1820s dress, plays the mandolin, accompanied by lambs.
Pair of Figures, (869 + 870), c.1830 Staffordshire, each height: 17.8cm, (7in), enamelled pearlware. A boy and girl play crudely modelled instruments each sitting within an arbour of flowers.
Figure, (885), c.1830, Staffordshire, height: 15.3cm, (6in), enamelled pearlware. A girl standing on a plinth, signed by Walton, plays a tambourine.
Figure, (867) pair to **(868)**, c.1830 Staffordshire, height: 11.5cm, (4½in), enamelled pearlware. A boy plays a recorder or penny whistle.

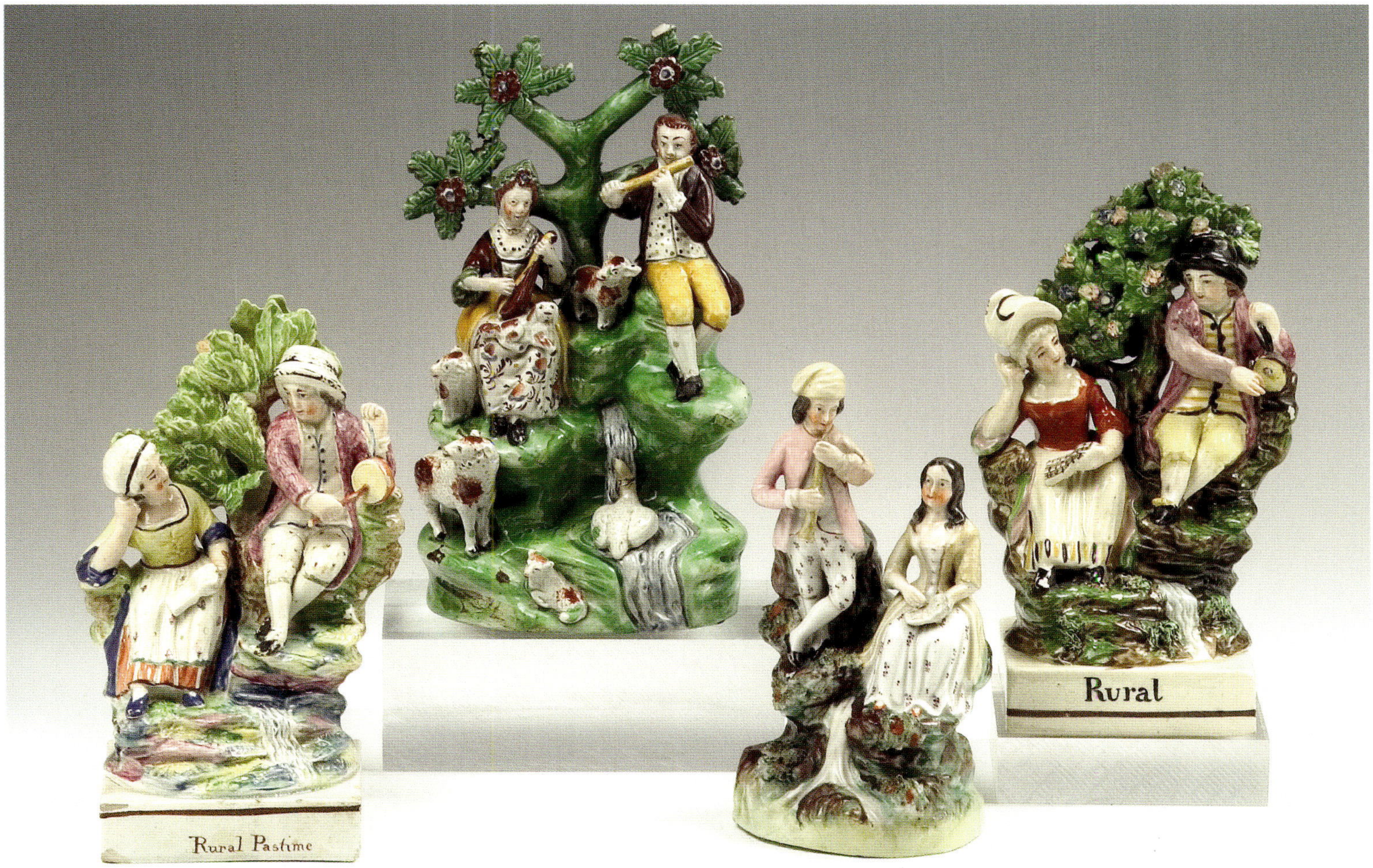

Figure group, (**871**), c.1830, Staffordshire, height: 17.8cm, (7in), enamelled pearlware. Couple sit beside a stream, she with a songbook and he with a small tambourine, inscribed, 'Rural Pastime'.
Figure group, (**887**), c.1830, Staffordshire, height: 22.9cm, (9in), enamelled pearlware. Complex bocage group; woman plays a mandolin, man plays a flute with four sheep, a lapdog and a swan.

Figure group, (**886**), c.1845, Staffordshire, height: 17.8cm, (7in), enamelled soft-paste porcelain. Couple sit beside a stream, he with a clarinet and she with a songbook.
Figure group, (**872**), c.1830, Staffordshire, height: 20.3cm, (8in), enamelled pearlware. Couple sit beside a stream, she with a songbook and he with a small tambourine, inscribed, 'Rural'.

Figure, (**901**), c.1790, France, Niderviller, height: 21cm, (8¼in), enamelled pearlware. A boy playing the cymbals (incised: 48) lacks a partner.
Pair of Figures, (**896 & A**), c.1800, Staffordshire or Scotland, height: each 21cm, (8¼in), pearlware decorated in Pratt colours. A woman dances while her companion plays a guitar or mandolin.
Figure, (**897**), c.1800, Staffordshire, height: 21cm, (8¼in), enamelled pearlware. A woman wearing a conical hat playing a friction drum, inscribed, 'Spanish Dancer'.

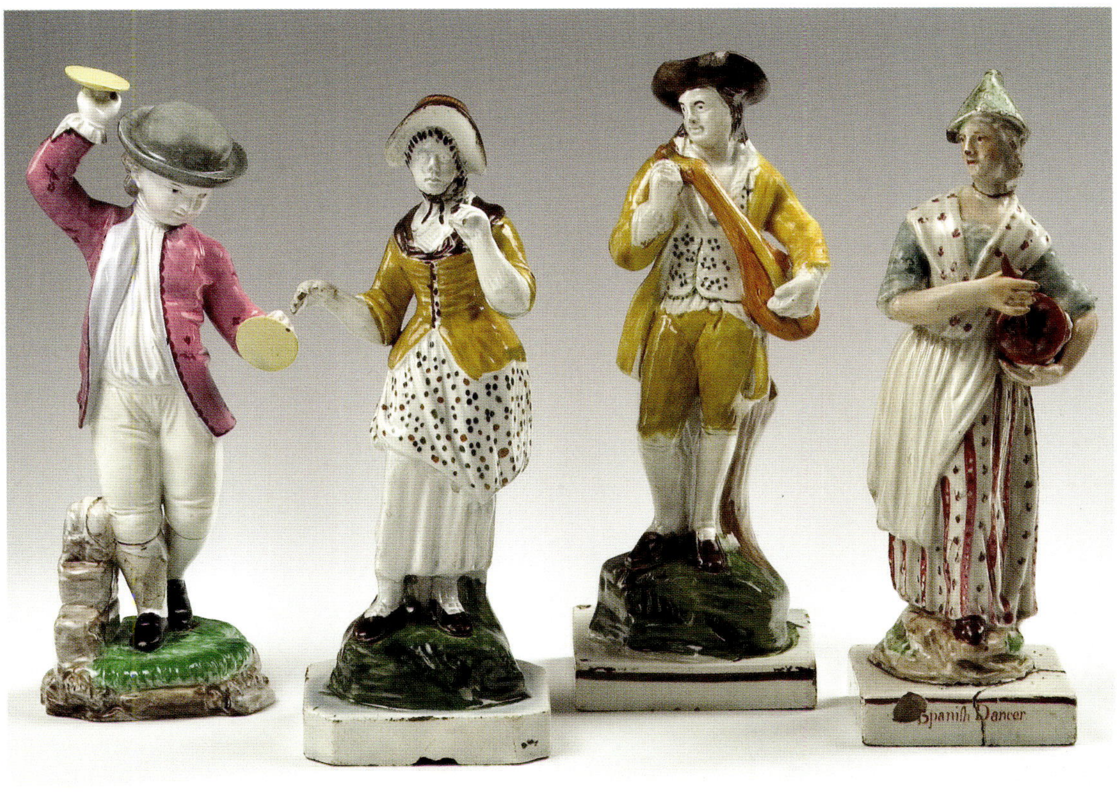

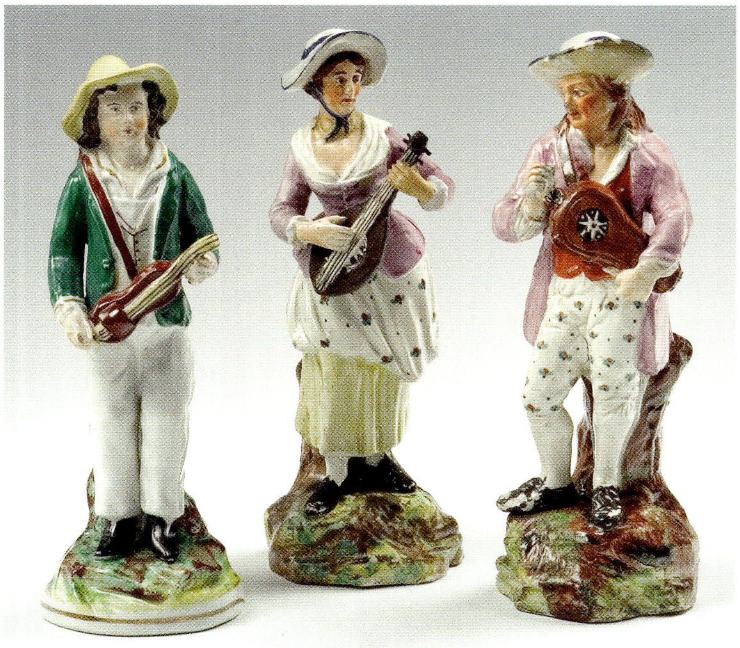

Figure, (**898**), c.1840, Staffordshire, height: 20.3cm, (8in), enamelled pearlware. Boy playing a ukulele.
Pair of Figures, (**899 & A**), c.1830, each height: 21cm, (8¼in), pearlware decorated in Pratt colours. Woman plays the guitar while man plays the hurdy-gurdy.

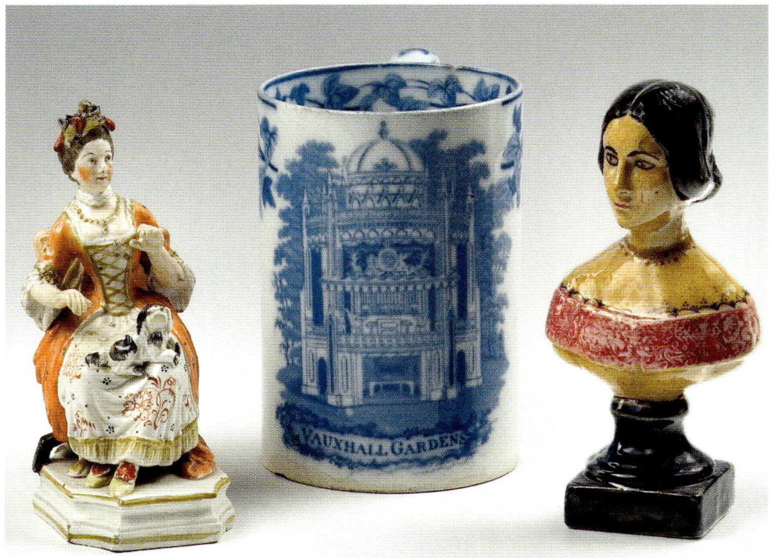

Figure, (**900**), c.1790, Staffordshire, height: 15.3cm, (6in), enamelled pearlware. A lady sits playing a guitar or mandolin, accompanied by a lapdog. She was one of a pair, (her male companion plays a flute), based on Derby porcelain models issued in the 1770s.[14]
Mug, (**1199**), c.1810, Staffordshire, height: 14.3cm, (5⅝in), blue-printed pearlware. Unattributed view of the central bandstand in Vauxhall Gardens, on whose balcony musicians performed.
Bust, (**878**), c.1850, Staffordshire, height: 16.5cm, (6½in), enamelled drab-ware. Woman with dark hair and an off-shoulder dress, said to represent Jenny Lind (1820-87), the celebrated soprano, known as the 'Swedish Nightingale'. It bears faint resemblance to a lithographic portrait of 1847 by Richard James Lane, after Conrad L'Allemand, which dates from her London debut.[15]

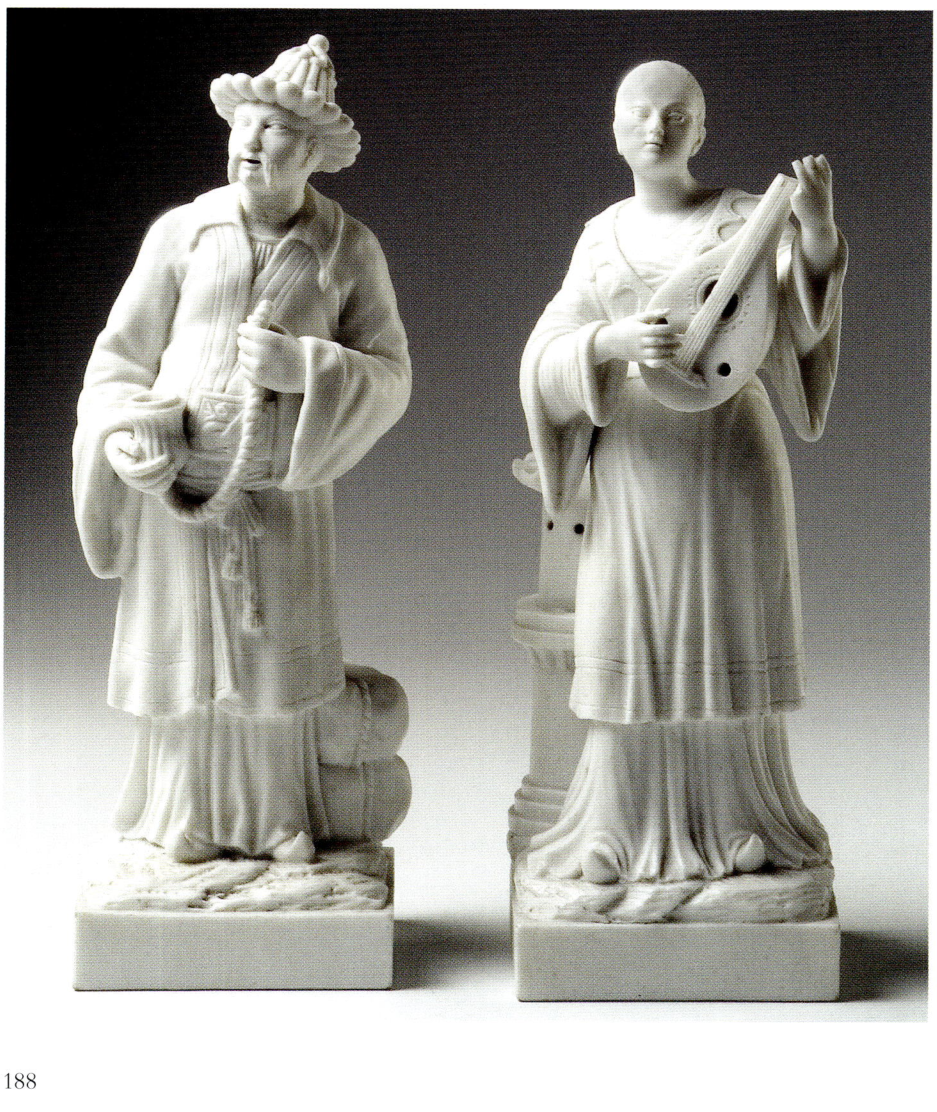

Pair of Figures, (**895 & A**), c.1800, height: 21.5cm, (8½in), height: 20.5cm, (8⅛in), hard-paste porcelain. Pair of oriental musicians modelled as pastille burners The woman plays a lute while her male companion carries a hookah or opium pipe. They may be related to so-called 'Malabar' figures, modelled in the mid-eighteenth century by J. J. Kaendler for Meissen.

Commedia dell'Arte and Pantomime

Commedia dell'Arte street theatre developed from the Italian carnival in the late Middle Ages and was soon absorbed into the popular cultures of most other European countries. The first troupe arrived in England from the French court in the 1670s. Harlequin (Arlecchino) originally wore a mock sword or cudgel and a black domino mask. His loose clothes became close fitting and the random patches evolved into a pattern of lozenges in symbolic colours; red for anger, blue for love, brown or mauve for constancy and yellow for jealousy. Harlequin was a clown, juggler and warm-up artist for other characters like Scaramouche, Pantaloon and Punch (Pulcinella) who was to become the most famous of them all. The harlequinade evolved into pantomime, which remains popular to this day.

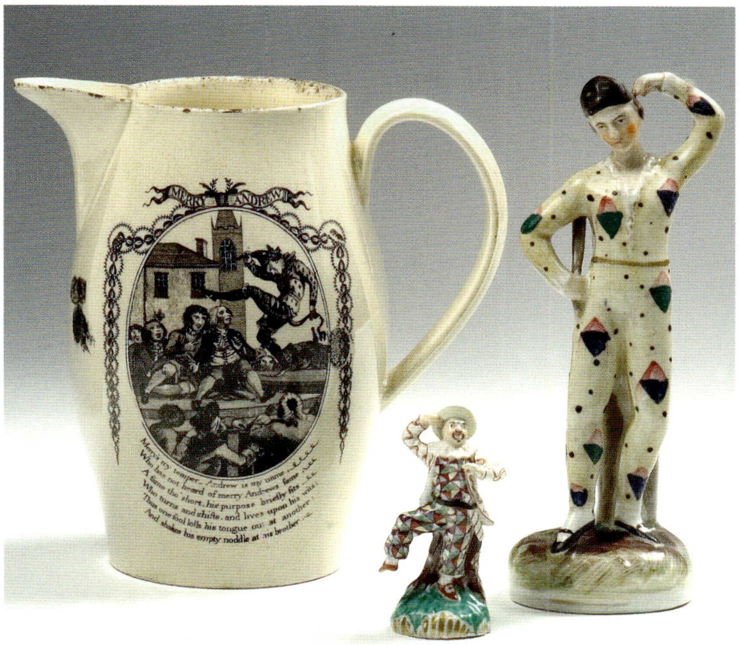

Jug, (1223), c.1780, Staffordshire, height: 17.8cm, (7in), printed creamware. Harlequin cavorts on a raised stage in the guise of 'MERRY ANDREW', a comic master of ceremonies; part Harlequin, part medieval jester. Verse includes, 'A fame tho' short, his purpose briefly fits / Who turns and shifts, and lives upon his wits'.
Figure, **(892)**, c.1780, European, height: 8.3cm, (3¼in), enamelled hard-paste porcelain. Some of the earliest porcelain figures produced by the Meissen factory in Dresden were *commedia dell'Arte* characters and may have provided a model for this tiny dancing Harlequin.
Figure, **(893)**, c.1845, Staffordshire, height: 19.1cm, (7½in), enamelled earthenware. This limp example of a Harlequin wears a black diabolo, a half-face mask, referring to Harlequin's satanic origins.

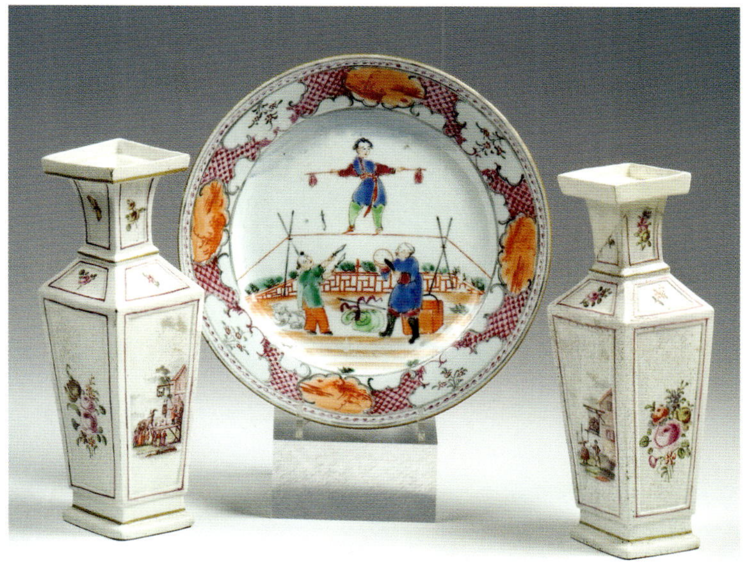

Pair of Vases, **(1233 & A)**, c.1760, Derby, each height: 22.9cm, (9in), enamelled soft-paste porcelain. Rare vases, with three of four sides painted with flower sprays.
Plate, **(1235)**, c.1780, China, diameter: 22.9cm, (9in), enamelled hard-paste porcelain. Painted with a tight rope walker performing above a crowd.

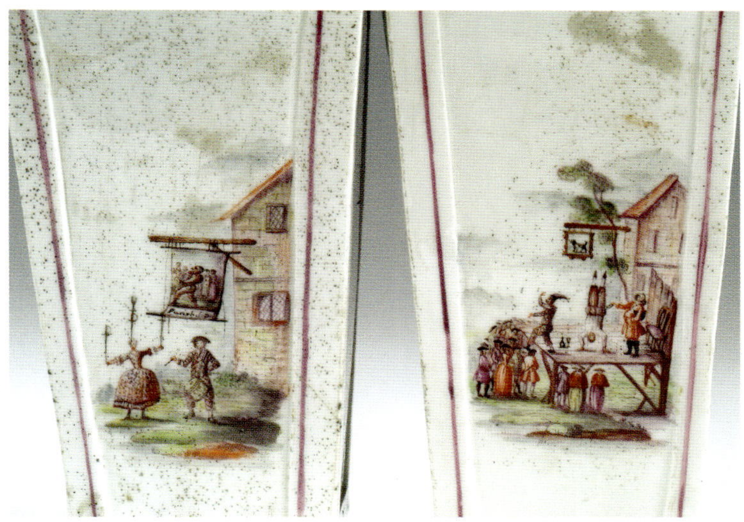

Pair of Vases, **(1233 & A - details)**, c.1760, Derby, each height: 22.9cm, (9in), enamelled soft-paste porcelain. Rare, four-sided vases, one side of each delicately painted with scenes at a country fair. One shows a pair of performers dressed as Harlequins, a woman sword-juggler and her male companion, playing drum rolls. They stand beneath an unusual inn sign featuring Mr Punch. The other shows 'Merry Andrew' bantering with the crowd while an acrobat tumbles on a stage.

Joseph Grimaldi (1778-1837)

Grimaldi was the most famous exponent of *Commedia*-derived pantomime in early nineteenth-century London and is regarded as the father of modern clowning.[16] Aged three he was already dancing at Sadlers' Wells. He was commended for his swordsmanship in *St George the Champion of England* in 1802 and in 1805 he was poached by the impresario Charles Dibdin for Covent Garden, where he first performed *Harlequin and Mother Goose*. He attained cult status and was described as 'the Michelangelo of buffoonery' and as 'the Garrick of Clowns'.

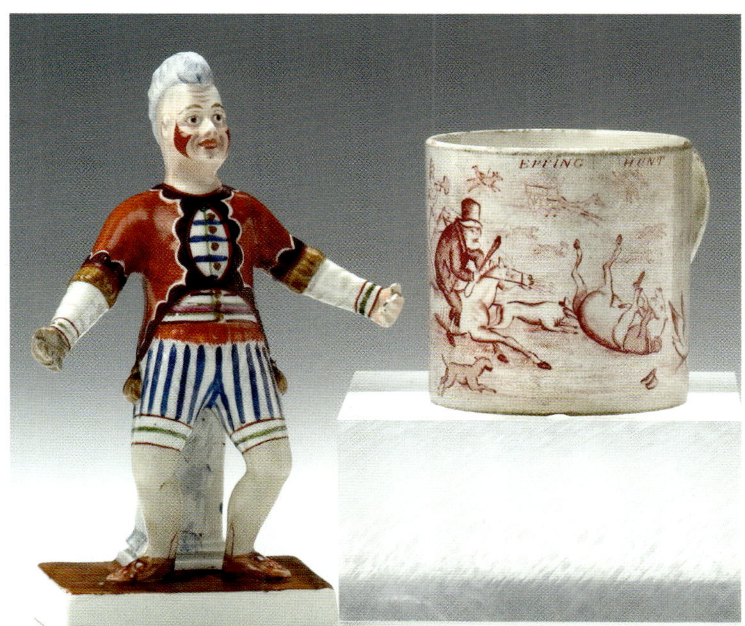

Figure, DA320000, (Hoare Collection), c.1828, Staffordshire, Burslem, height: 14cm, (5½in)**,** enamelled pearlware. Joseph Grimaldi playing Squire Bugle in *Harlequin and Mother Goose.* Made by Enoch Wood's factory around the time of his farewell benefit performances at Sadler's Wells and at Drury Lane. Numerous possible sources for his appearance in the role include Pierce Egan's *Life in London* (1821). His autobiography, *The Life and Adventures of Joseph Grimaldi* (1836) was edited by Charles Dickens.
Mug, **(1113)**, c.1830, Staffordshire, height: 6.7cm, (2⅝in), red-printed earthenware. Inscribed, 'Epping Hunt' printed with comic characters and lines of dialogue. Probably represents a scene called 'The Epping Hunt' in the popular stage pantomime, *The Red Dwarf*, which starred Grimaldi.

The London Stage

There are eleven tin-glazed tiles printed in Liverpool around 1780, with portraits of leading actors and actresses of the mid-eighteenth century, in some of their best-known roles. Most of the images come from Bell's *British Theatre* (1776-78) and Lowndes's *New English Theatre* (1777). For the first time many of them celebrate British actresses for whom the eighteenth century was a golden age.

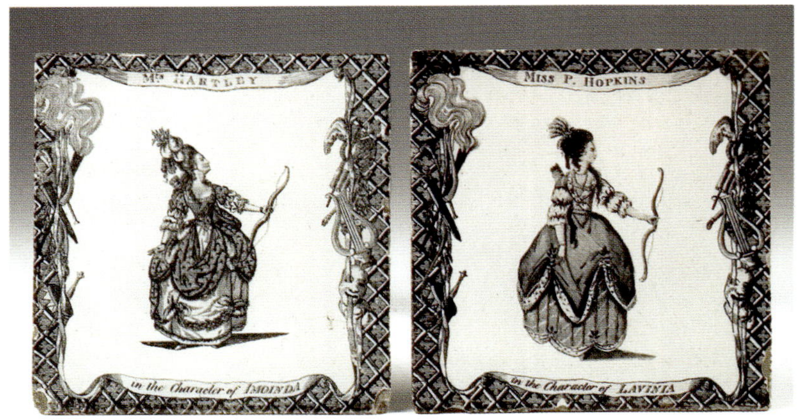

Each **Tile**, c.1780, Liverpool, height: 12.7cm, (5in), printed tin-glazed earthenware.
(**903**) Mrs Elizabeth Hartley (1751-1824) as the black princess, Imoinda, the heroine of Thomas Southerne's popular tragedy, *Oroonoko*, (based on Aphra Behn's novel of c.1670), first performed at Drury Lane Theatre in 1696.[17] Behn had spent her childhood in Surinam, South America, where she learned the history of the mythical African prince Oroonoko and his bride, Imoinda, described as the 'black Aphrodite'.
(**911**) Priscilla Hopkins (1756-1845), as Lavinia in Shakespeare's *Titus Andronicus*.[18] Daughter of David Garrick's prompter at Drury Lane, she attended the Bristol school run by Hannah More and her sisters before taking to the stage. She married the actors William Brereton and later, John Philip Kemble.

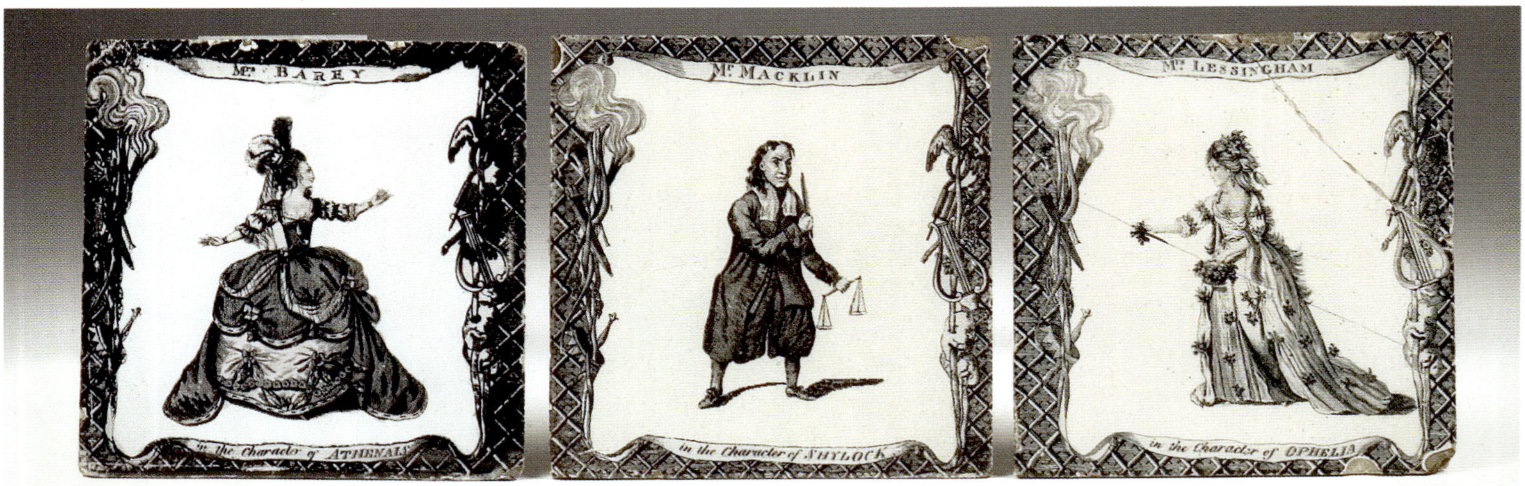

Each **Tile**, c.1780, Liverpool, height: 12.7cm, (5in), printed tin-glazed earthenware.
(**905**) Ann Spranger Barry (1734-1811) as Athenais in Nathaniel Lee's *Theodosius or the Force of Love* (1680).[19] Barry and her second husband, the Irish actor Spranger Barry, were part of Garrick's Drury Lane company.
(**904**) Charles Macklin (1699-1797) as Shylock in Shakespeare's *The Merchant of Venice*, his greatest role. The long-lived Irish actor (born McLaughlin), was an exuberant character who had a turbulent career. An early friend and ally of Garrick, he arrived in London in 1725 and was principal actor at Drury Lane Theatre until 1748. He had a violent temper and was constantly involved in law-suits over his contracts. In 1735 he was acquitted of killing a fellow actor in a greenroom brawl. His interpretation of Shylock brought unprecedented naturalism and sympathy to the role, of which Alexander Pope wrote, 'This is the Jew / That Shakepeare drew'.[20] However, during a performance at Covent Garden in 1772 the audience threatened to riot unless Macklin was removed from the stage.[21]
(**909**) Jane Lessingham (1739-83), as Ophelia in her madness from *Hamlet*.[22] In common with other actresses who had dubious personal reputations, Lessingham is mentioned in Harris's List of Covent Garden prostitutes.

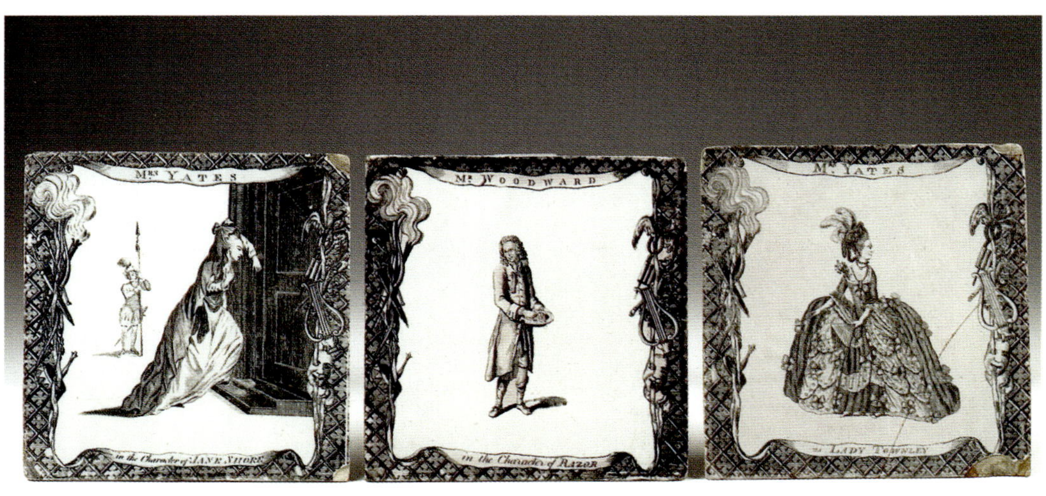

Each **Tile**, c.1780, Liverpool, height: 12.7cm, (5in), printed tin-glazed earthenware.
(**912**) Mary Anne Yates (1728-87) as the eponymous heroine in Nicholas Rowe's *Jane Shore* (first performed in 1714).[23] Yates (née Graham) a celebrated tragedienne, is shown leaning on a doorframe in the role of Shore, the beautiful mistress of Edward IV, who was forced to do public penance as a harlot and died in penury.
(**907**) Henry Woodward (1717-77) as Razor in Murphy's *The Upholsterer*. The image is taken from an anonymous print in *Dramatic Portraits of the English Stage in the Days of Garrick*, printed for Robert Sayer, 1769.[24]
(**906**) Yates also played Lady Townley in *The Provok'd Wife*, drafted by Sir John Vanburgh and completed by Colley Cibber in 1728. The print shows a reversed copy of an image by James Roberts.[25]

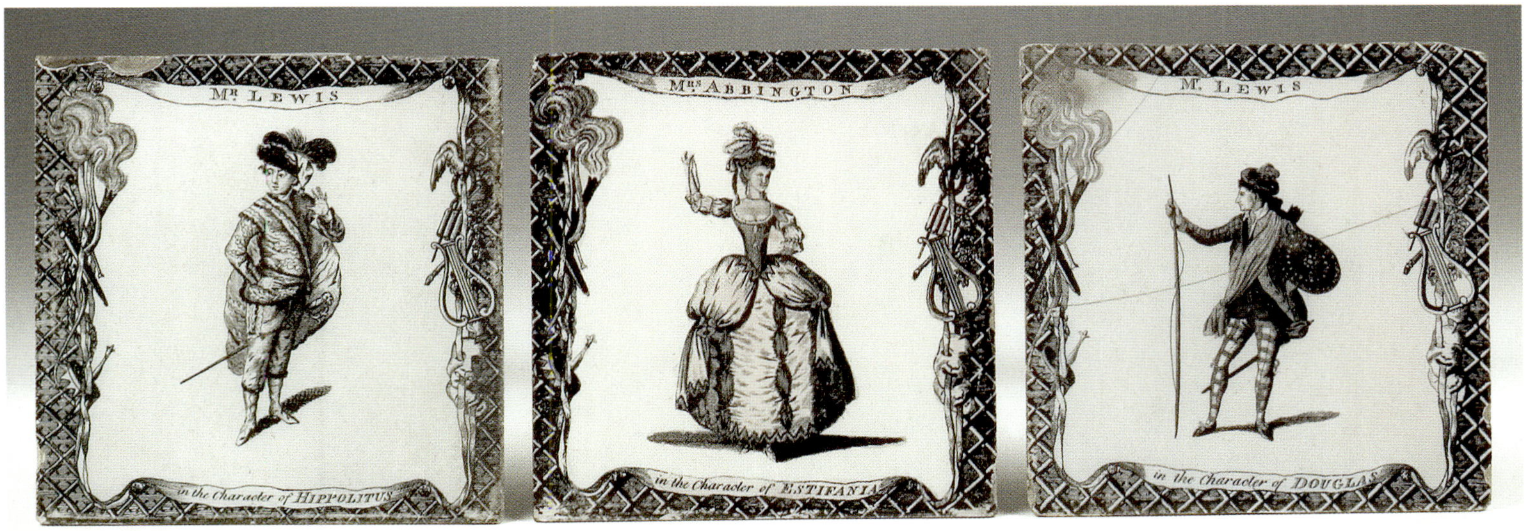

Each **Tile**, c.1780, Liverpool, height: 12.7cm, (5in), printed tin-glazed earthenware.
(**902**) William Thomas Lewis (1748-1811) as Hippolytus in *Phaedra and Hippolytus*.[26] Lewis was Deputy Manager of Covent Garden from 1782 to 1804 and lessee of Liverpool Theatre from 1803 to 1811. Based on the Greek tragedy by Euripides, the play was written by Edmund 'Rag' Smith, a friend of Addison, (founder of *The Spectator*) who defended it despite its disastrous reception when first performed in 1707.
(**910**) Frances Abington (1737-1815) as Estifania in *Rule a Wife and Have a Wife* by the Elizabethan team of Beaumont and Fletcher.[28] Abington was a flower girl, street singer and milliner's assistant before making her stage debut in 1755. Upstaged by Kitty Clive, she went to Ireland before being recalled by David Garrick. She created thirty important roles at Drury Lane Theatre. In 1775 Samuel Johnson explained to Boswell why, despite being unable to see or hear well, he had attended a benefit performance held for her. 'Because she is a favourite of the publick [*sic*]; and when the publick cares the thousandth part for you that it does for her, I will go to your benefit too'.[29]
(**908**) William Thomas Lewis playing the title role in John Home's *Douglas: A Tragedy*, wearing full Highland dress.[27] First performed at Canongate Theatre, Edinburgh, in December 1756, it 'had unbounded success for a great many nights in Edinburgh, and was attended by all the literati … the town in general was in an uproar of exultation that a Scotchman had written a tragedy of the first rate.' In 1757 it was produced at Covent Garden. Robert Burns said of the play in 1790, 'one Douglas lives in Home's immortal page'.

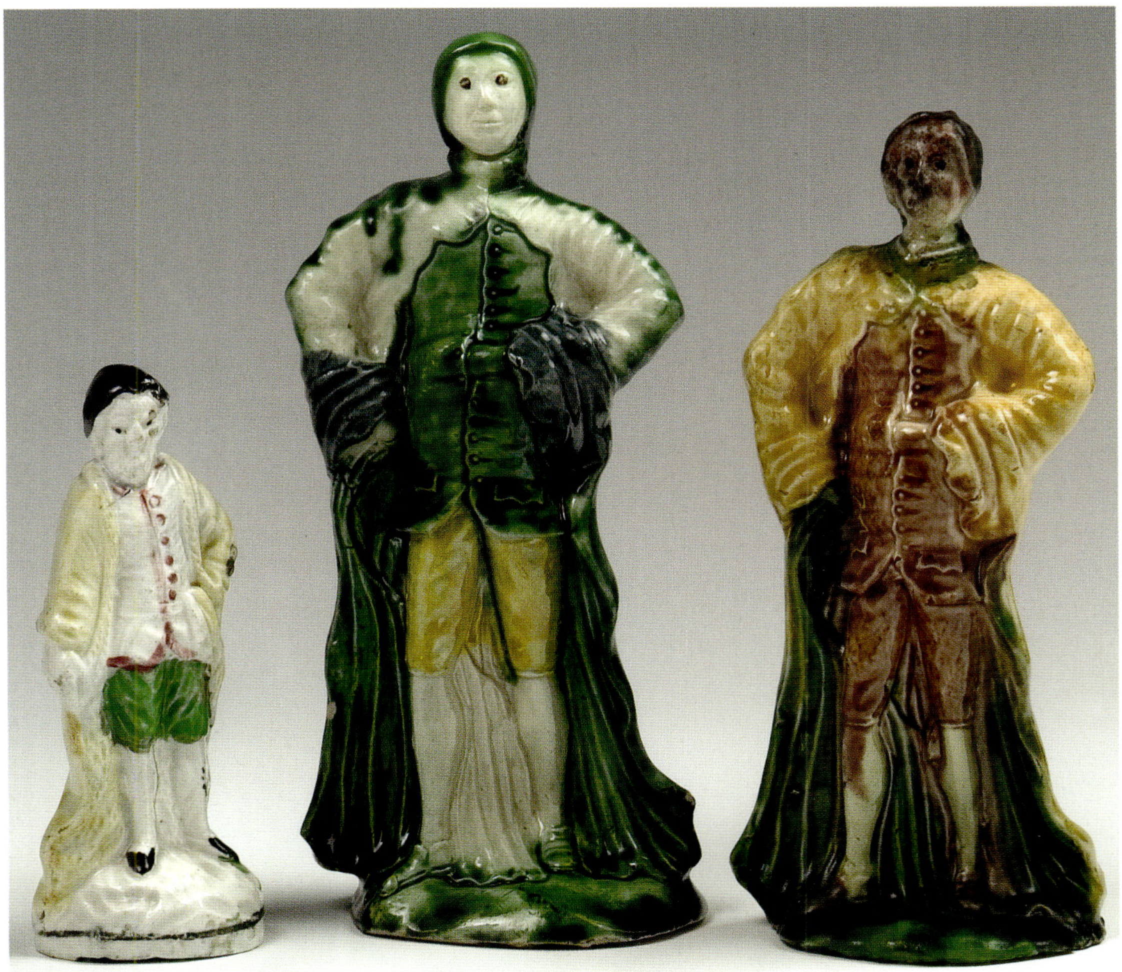

Figure, (**915**), c.1770, Staffordshire, height: 12.7cm, (5in), coloured earthenware. Old man with a mask-like face, thought to be be an actor.
Two Figures, (**913 + 914**), c.1770, Staffordshire, each height: 20.3 cm, (8in), lead-glazed earthenware. From similar moulds, they wear voluminous greatcoats and strike dramatic poses, but there is no proven link with the theatre.[30] They are traditionally linked with the first great actor-manager, Colley Cibber (1671-1757), who excelled in eccentric roles, was a shrewd administrator, and wrote some thirty plays but was a weak Poet Laureate. One figure has a restored head.

Henry Woodward (1717-1777) and **Kitty Clive** (1711-1785)

Woodward was considered one of the finest comedians of the eighteenth century, famed for his performances of Mercutio, Bobadil and Touchstone. A protégé of John Rich, he first appeared on stage at Covent Garden in 1730, while still a pupil at the Merchant Taylor's School. He went to Drury Lane in 1738 and became the regular stage partner of Kitty Clive; his Petruchio was said to have upstaged her Katherina in *The Taming of the Shrew*.

The Irish actress Kitty Clive was born Catherine Rafter in Kilkenny. Her marriage to the barrister, George Clive, was a failure and she made her name on the stage. In 1747 she was one of the founder-members of Garrick's company. She also sang, notably for Thomas Arne and in Handel oratorios. She joined the cast of *Lethe* as Mrs Riot, The Fine Lady, in 1749. She later chose to play Mrs Riot for her farewell performance in 1769. Mrs Clive retired to a cottage on the estate of Horace Walpole at Strawberry Hill in Middlesex, who described her as, 'Mrs Catherine Clive, the excellent commedian [*sic*].'.

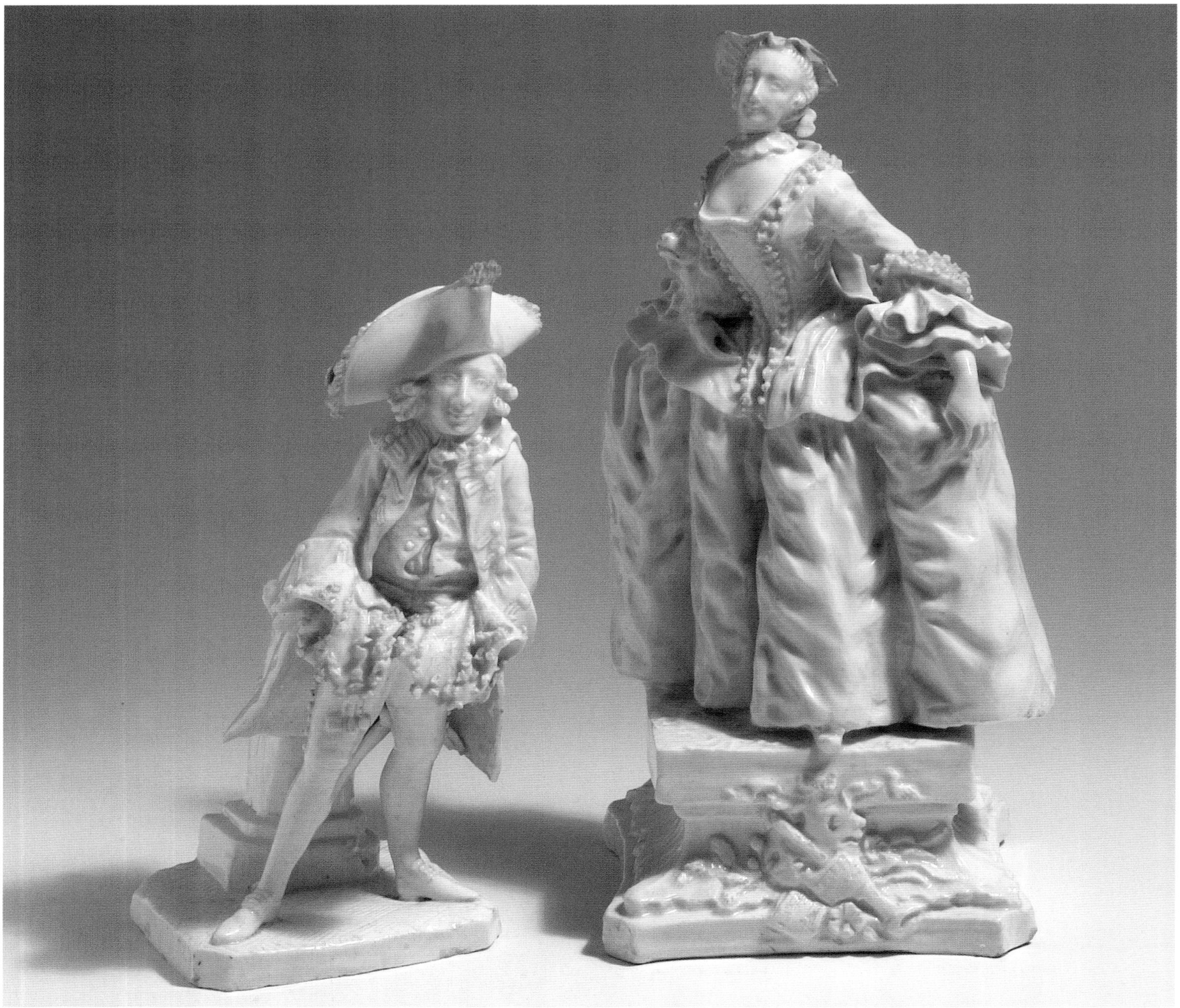

Figure, (**916**), c.1750, London, Bow, height: 25.4cm, (10in), soft-paste porcelain. Henry Woodward is modelled as a glazed porcelain figure from the Bow factory in the role of The Fine Gentleman in *Lethe, or Aesop in the Shade*, (1740), a mythological farce and David Garrick's first great play.[31] Garrick writes of the character, 'I dress, visit, study, taste, write sonnets; by birth, travel, education and natural abilities I am entitled to lead the fashion' The figure is taken from a drawing by Francis Hayman, c.1750.

Figure, (**917**), c.1750, London, Bow, height: 31.8cm, (12½in), soft-paste porcelain. Mrs Clive is shown very fashionably dressed in a sack-backed robe, her skirts supported on either side by huge panniers. She wears a frilled bonnet (damaged), a little ruff around her throat and carries a tiny lap dog under one arm. She stands on an elaborate plinth, moulded with musical trophies and theatrical masks. Garrick, who is known to have owned one of these figures, describes The Fine Lady: 'She lies abed all morning ... makes mischief, buys china, cheats at cards, (and) keeps a pug dog'. The popularity of the image is confirmed by the survival of tiny engraved copies on watchpapers.[32] Some of these popular figures were enamelled at William Duesbury's workshop; his London account book notes, 'for enamelling Mrs Clive three shillings'. This may be the first full-length portrait figure in English porcelain. The model is copied from an engraving of 1750, by Charles Mosley, either after a watercolour by Thomas Worlidge or after a painting by Pieter van Bleeck.

David Garrick (1717-1779)

David Garrick was the greatest actor-manager and playwright of the eighteenth century. The son of an army captain, Garrick was raised in Lichfield in Staffordshire. He briefly attended Dr Johnson's Academy in Edial before it was wound up and they both left for London in 1737. He registered as a law student at Lincoln's Inn and operated briefly as a wine merchant. *Lethe*, his first play, was staged in 1740 and, following his astonishing debut as *Richard III* in 1741, Alexander Pope said of him, 'that young man never had his equal an actor, and he will never have a rival.' In 1747 Garrick bought half the patent of Drury Lane Theatre, with which he was associated until his retirement, when he sold his share to Richard Brinsley Sheridan. He brought a new sense of realism to English stage productions.

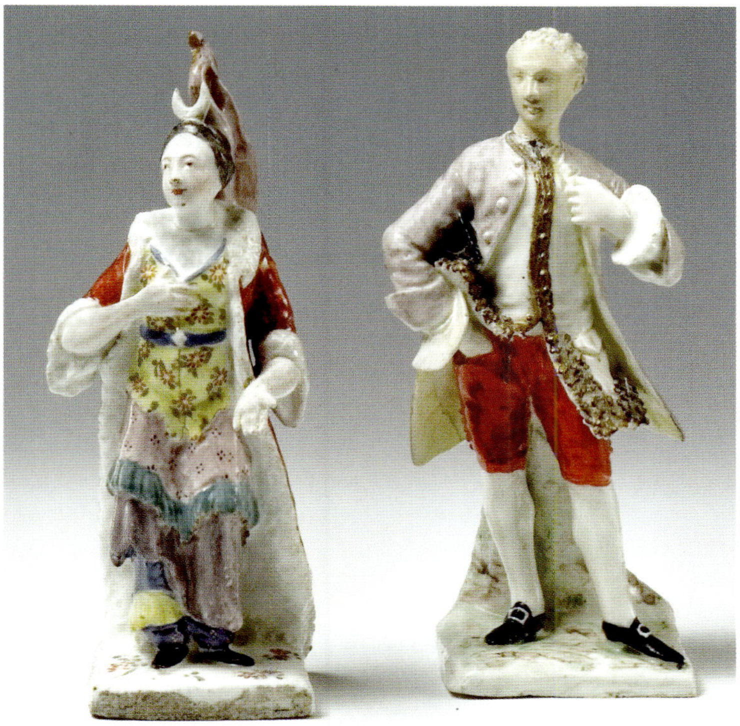

Figure, (**919**), c.1770, London, Bow, height: 22.3cm, (8¾in), soft-paste porcelain. Said to represent David Garrick. Female figure wears an exotic 'Turkish' costume and a conical headdress with a crescent moon.
Figure, (**920**), c.1770, London, Bow, height: 22.3cm, (8¾in), soft-paste porcelain. Said to represent David Garrick as Archer from George Farquhar's comic masterpiece *The Beaux Stratagem*.[33] Piece has a restored head.

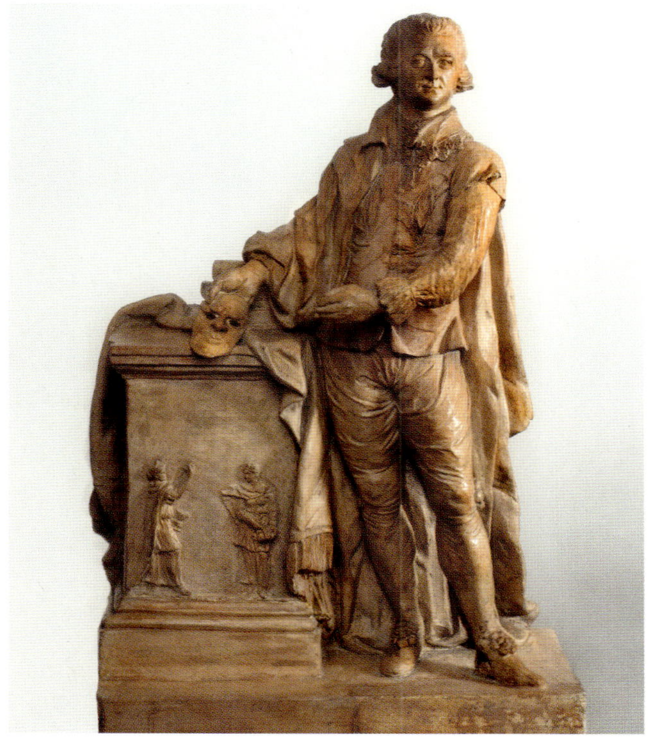

Sculpture, (**937**), c.1778, height: 38.1cm, (15in), terracotta. The final image of Garrick is unique. It is a terracotta maquette for a sculpture by John van Nost the Younger (based in Dublin). It represents Garrick as 'the English Roscius', an allusion to the famous actor of Ancient Rome, Roscius Gallus.[37] Garrick, holding a theatrical mask, stands beside an altar decorated with relief of classical figures.[38]

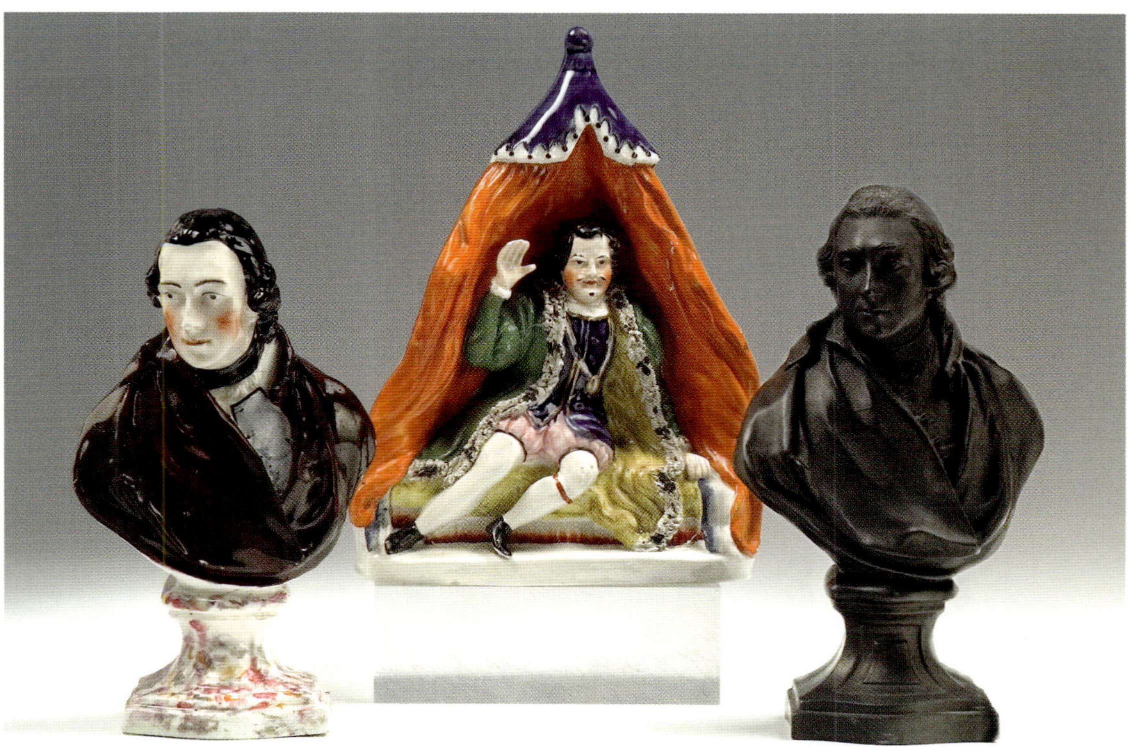

Bust, (**921**) c.1800, Staffordshire, height: 22.3cm, (8¾in), enamelled pearlware. Portrait bust impressed: Garrick.
Figure, (**927**), c.1855, Staffordshire, height: 24.2cm, (9½in), enamelled earthenware. Depicts Garrick as Richard III in his tent before the Battle of Bosworth, haunted by the ghosts of all those he had murdered. Based on prints after William Hogarth's famous painting of 1745.[34] It was engraved by Hogarth and Grignion, first published 20 June 1746, then again for Tallis's Shakespeare Gallery (1852-3).[35]
Bust, (**922**) c.1780, Staffordshire, height: 22.3cm, (8¾in), black basalt. Portrait bust incised: Garrick, (taken from the same source as 921) based on images of a sculpture by Roubiliac, 1757.[36]

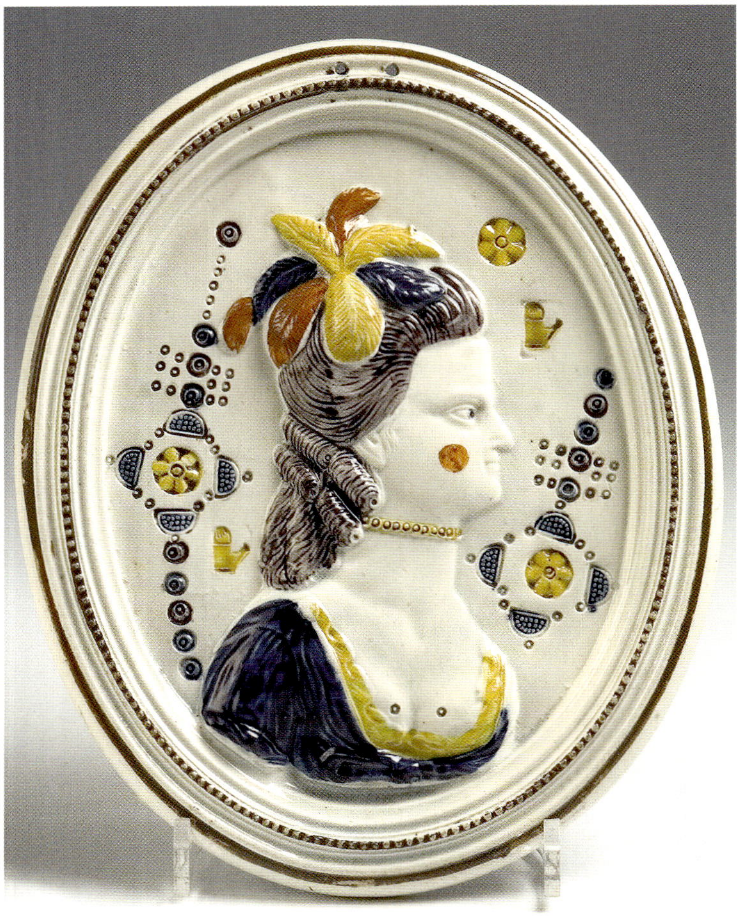

Plaque, (**368**), c.1800, Staffordshire, height: 22.3cm, (8¾in), Prattware. Relief-moulded with profile portrait of Sarah Siddons (1755-1831). Willett believed it portrayed Queen Marie Antoniette but it probably shows the esteemed Mrs Siddons as Euphrasia in Arthur Murphy's tragedy, *The Grecian Daughter*, first performed in 1772. It may be taken from an engraving of 1798 by J. Caldwell.[39] Part of the powerful Kemble dynasty of actors, she dominated the London stage from 1782 until her farewell in 1812. During this time she married the actor, Henry Siddons, and had seven children. The critic William Hazlitt proclaimed her 'tragedy personified'.

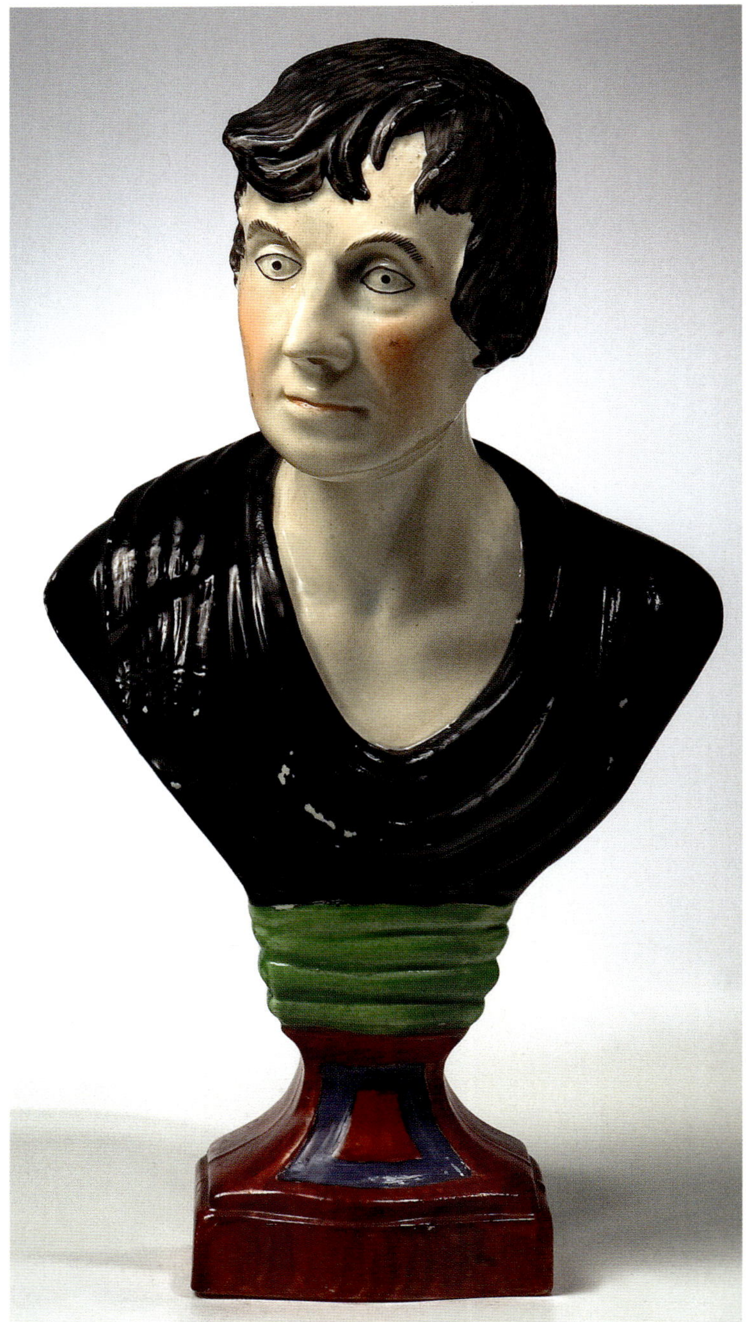

Bust, (**923**) c.1800-20, Staffordshire, height: 29.9cm, (11¾in), enamelled pearlware. Portrait of either John Philip Kemble (1757-1823) or Edmund Kean (as Willett believed) in the title role of Shakespeare's *Coriolanus*. Kemble's was the defining performance of the role in productions staged regularly from 1789 to 1817, an act Kean found hard to follow in 1820. The portrait of Kemble by Sir Thomas Lawrence (c.1798) shows him wrapped in his imposing black cloak.

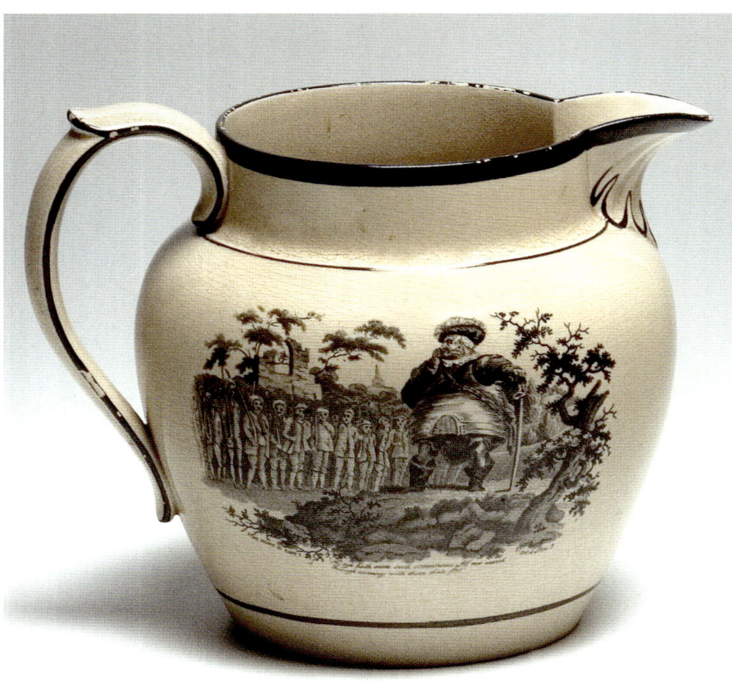

Jug, (**918**), c.1820, Staffordshire, Factory Z,[40] height: 15.9cm, (6¼in), printed drabware. Printed with scenes featuring Shakespeare's Sir John Falstaff. On one side he reviews his troops in *Henry IV part 2*, on the other he is shown in Windsor Forest in *The Merry Wives of Windsor*.

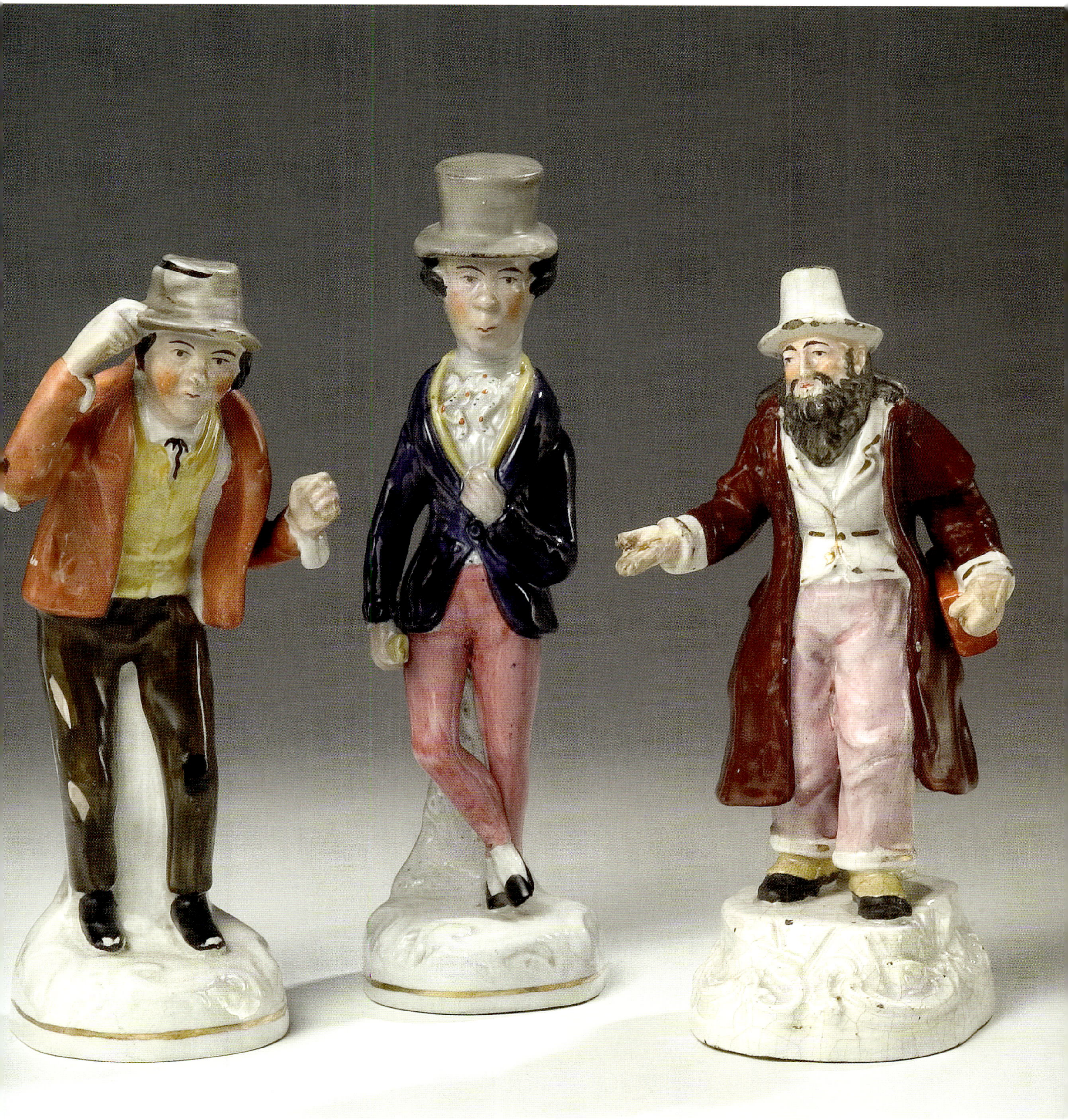

Figure, (**936**), c.1855, Staffordshire, height: 21.6cm, (8½in), soft-paste porcelain. Caricature figure touching his hat described as 'a ragged boy'. Perhaps the same actor as (934)?

Figure, (**934**), c.1855, Staffordshire, height: 22.9cm, (9in), soft-paste porcelain. Caricature figure standing with legs crossed, said to represent Dick Swiveller possibly from a dramatisation of Dickens's *The Old Curiosity Shop.*

Figure, (**935**), c.1840, Staffordshire, height: 20.3cm, (8in), soft-paste porcelain. Said to represent Robert William Elliston (1774-1831) as Shylock in Shakespeare's *The Merchant of Venice*. Elliston ran away from St Paul's School to join the theatre. He acted at Drury Lane from 1804 to 1809 and from 1819 was the lessee of the house until ill health and bankruptcy forced him to retire in 1826.

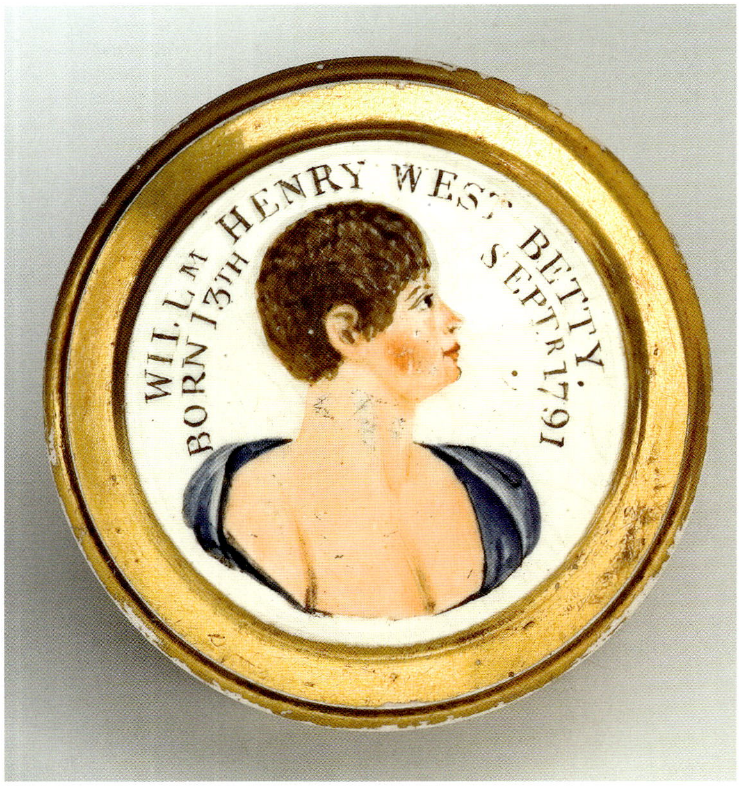

William Henry West Betty (1791-1874)

Henry West Betty was a child prodigy actor. From the age of eleven he trod the boards in Ireland and Scotland, playing tragic heroes such as Romeo, Hamlet and Richard III, before his London debut. He was a radiantly beautiful child but it is difficult to assess his real talent. His father and his theatrical mentor, William Hough, conducted a highly effective publicity campaign, heralding him as the 'Young Roscius', after the great Roman actor. Within 24 hours of arriving in London, Master Betty was mobbed by hysterical fans in the audience at Covent Garden.

He made his debut at Covent Garden on 1 December, 1804, as Achmet in the forgotten tragedy, *Barbarossa*, at 50 guineas a night (raised to 75). The army was needed to control the crowds outside the theatre. He was favoured by George III and the Prince of Wales while Prime Minister Pitt adjourned a parliamentary debate in order to see him perform. The child star provided a brief but welcome diversion from the threat from France; the *Morning Post* declared, 'the war and Buonaparte were for a time unheeded and forgotten'. Busts of Betty as Achmet, modelled by the sculptor Gahagan were issued and sold at three guineas each. He retired in 1824, aged 32, largely forgotten.

Patch Box, (**926**), c.1791, Derby?, diameter: 3.8cm, (1½in), soft-paste porcelain, enamelled and gilt. Tiny box for black face patches or for snuff, with a screw-thread lid modelled in low relief and painted with profile portrait, loosely draped about the shoulders. Encircled by inscription; 'William Henry West Betty / Born on the 13th September 1791'.

John Liston (1776-1846)

Originally a grammar school master, Liston's stage career began in serious drama opposite actresses such as Sarah Siddons. By 1808, however, he had found his true calling in comedy. His roles spanned Shakespeare's clowns to a wide range of modern roles. Liston's distinctive round, apple cheeks and retroussé nose are as recognisable in the many ceramic souvenirs of his famous roles as in their source prints.

Probably his most popular part was the title role in John Poole's comedy, *Paul Pry*, launched in 1825, with his famous catchphrase; 'I hope I don't intrude!' In his heyday he was paid up to £450 a week, a huge wage for the day. He played mainly at Covent Garden and the Haymarket Theatre until his retirement in 1837. He was a great favourite of George IV and the critics William Hazlitt and Charles Lamb. Many ceramic figures were produced to mark his best loved roles. They were made in porcelain by the Rockingham and Derby factories and by Charles Salt, [41] and in earthenware by John Walton and many anonymous Staffordshire potters.

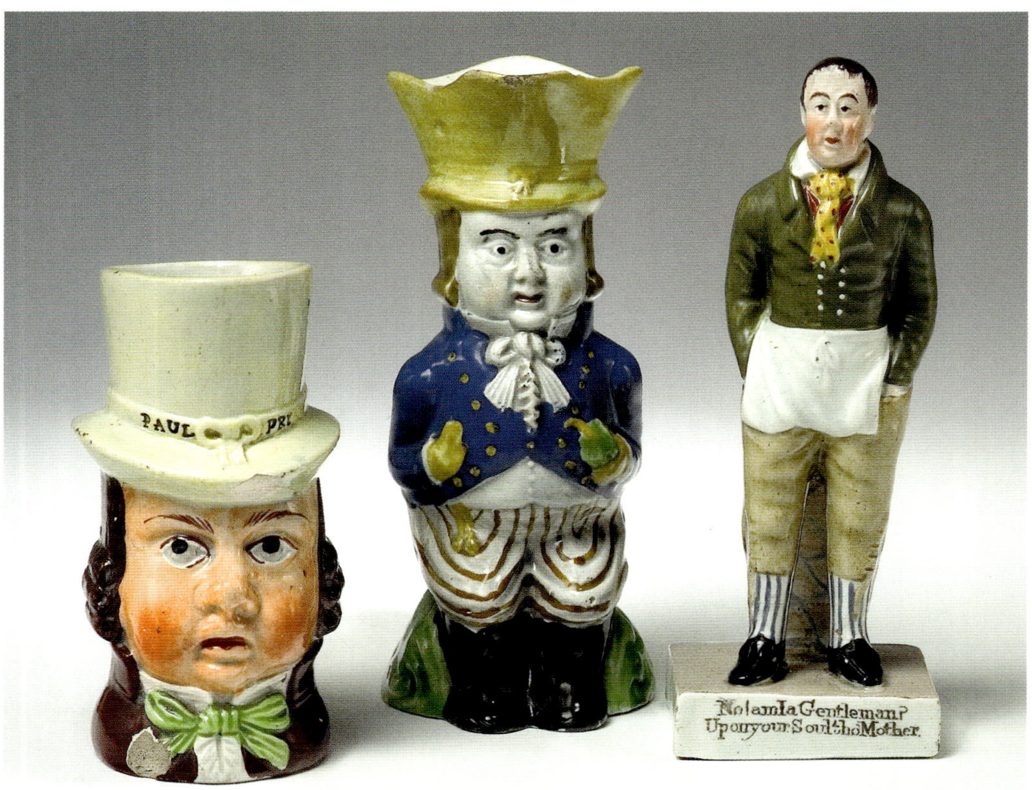

Jug, (**925**), c.1830, Staffordshire, height: 11.5cm, (4½in), enamelled pearlware. Portrait of John Liston in the title role of *Paul Pry*.

Toby Jug, (**924**), c.1830, Staffordshire, height: 15.3cm, (6in), enamelled pearlware. Portrait of John Liston in the title role of *Paul Pry*. Both pieces are based on prints after J.W. Gear of 1825 and are inscribed with his famous catchphrase, 'I hope I don't intrude?'[42]

Figure, (Hoare Collection), c.1830, Staffordshire, height: 16cm, (6¼in), enamelled pearlware. Portrait figure of John Liston as Sam Swipes in *Exchange no Robbery* by Theodore Hook. The plinth inscribed with Swipes's catchphrase, 'No! Am I a Gentleman? Upon your soul tho Mother'.[43]

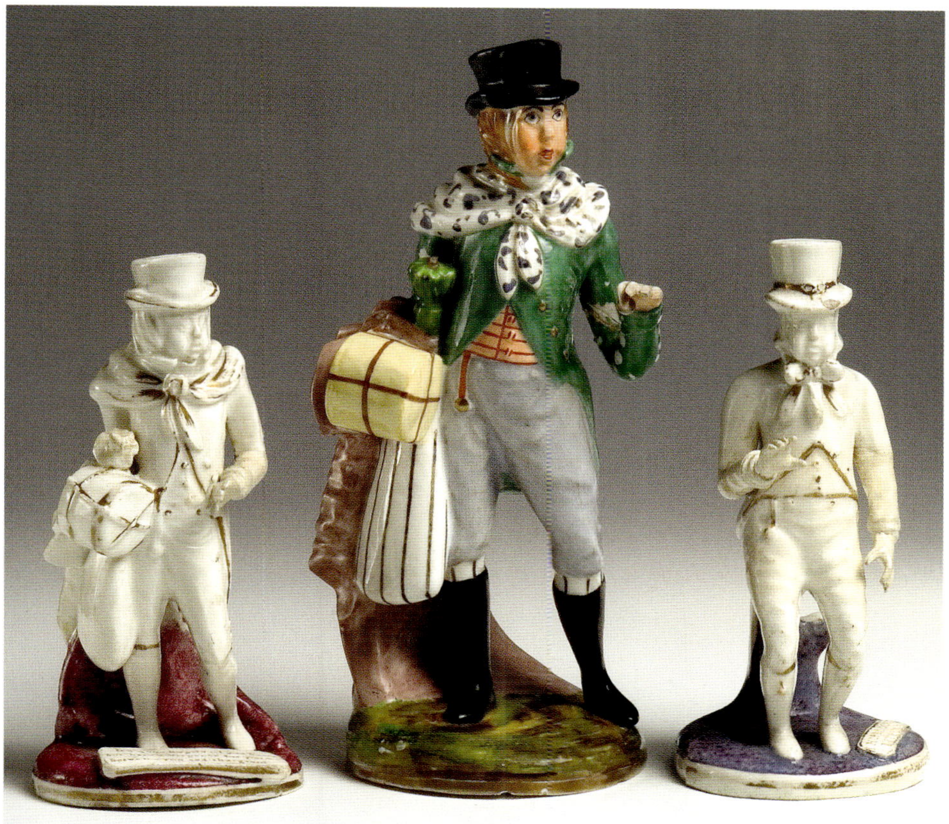

Two Figures, (**928 + 929**), c.1830, Staffordshire, each height: 15.9cm, (6¼in), enamelled pearlware. John Liston as Lubin Log from *Love, Law and Physic* by James Kenney (premiered in 1812) in two rare porcelain figures marked 'Salt'. Ralph Salt produced mainly earthenware.
Figure, (**930**), c.1830, Derby?, height: 21.6cm, (8½in), enamelled soft-paste porcelain. John Liston as Lubin Log from *Love, Law and Physic.*[46]

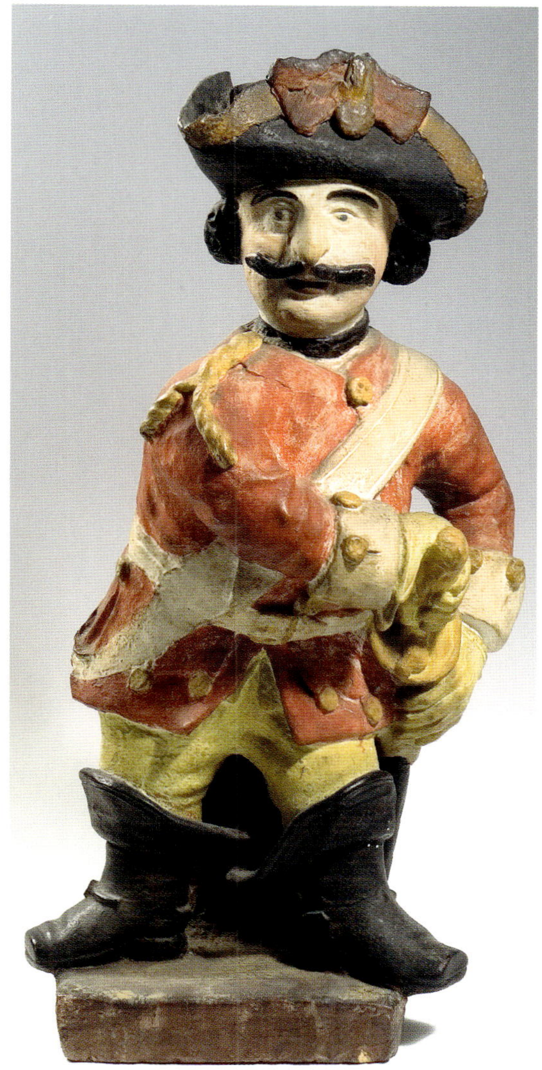

Figure, (**938**), c.1830, height: 53.3cm, (25in), painted plaster. Large caricature figure, said to represent the eponymous hero of *Bombastes Furioso.* This burlesque opera by William Barnes Jones parodied Ludovico Ariosto's Renaissance masterpiece *Orlando Furioso.* This piece may have been employed as an architectural detail.

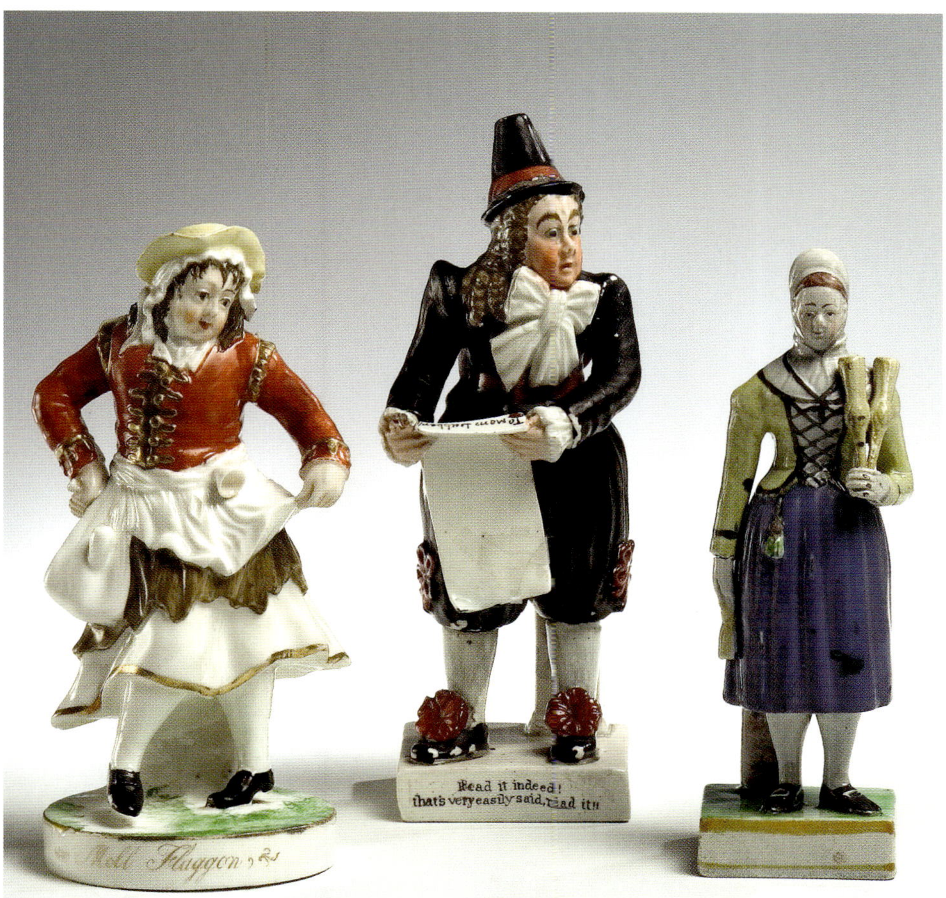

Figure, (**931**), c.1830, Yorkshire, height: 16.5cm, (6½in), enamelled soft-paste porcelain. Dancing woman (unmarked but probably Rockingham factory) is a portrait of John Liston. Liston here plays the female role of Moll Flaggon in Burgoyne's comic opera, *Lord of the Manor.*[44] Originally staged in 1780, Liston first performed in it in 1812. It was revived as a vehicle for him in 1823 and was so successful that it played on the London stage until 1826.
Figure, (**932**), c.1825, Staffordshire, height: 18.4cm, (7¼in), enamelled pearlware. John Liston as Van Dunder in *T'would Puzzle a Conjuror*, a successful comedy presented at the Haymarket Theatre in 1824.[45]
Figure, (**679**), c.1830, Staffordshire, height: 12.7cm, (6in), enamelled pearlware. Figure of a street vendor of besom brooms, possibly inspired by the popular stage duo of Madame Vestris and John Liston and their hit song of 1826, 'Buy a Broom'.

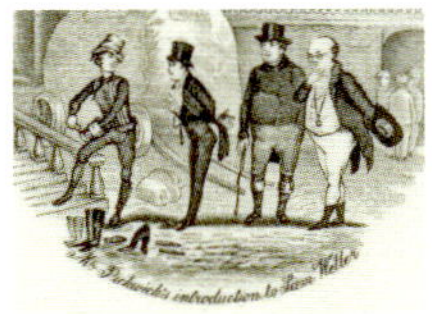

Chapter 14

POETRY, SCIENCE & LITERATURE

Reproduction of Celebrity Portraits

By the early eighteenth century a national pantheon of great men from British history and literature had been assembled, as well as an art establishment to record their likenesses. New technologies developed for copying and disseminating popular images of such figures.

The Engravers' Copyright Act of 1735, championed by William Hogarth, attested to the proliferation of popular print in London, in particular the sale of unauthorised copies (usually etched or engraved) of an artist's work. The ability to transfer printed images from the engraving plate to the surface of ceramics was developed independently in London and Liverpool in the 1750s. One of the pioneers of cheap reproductions of popular sculpture was John Cheere (1709-1787), younger brother of Henry Cheere, whose very successful sculpture workshop was based at Hyde Park Corner.

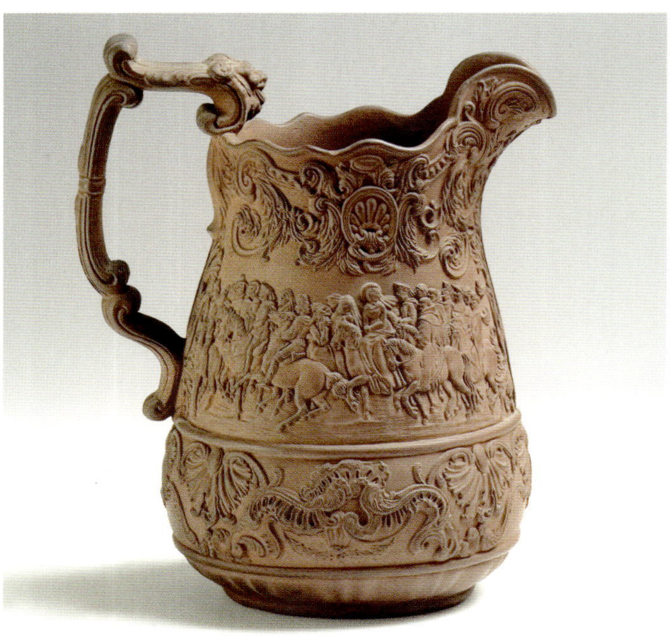

Jug, (**940**), c.1820, Germany? height: 23.5cm, (9¼in), red stoneware. Moulded with a central frieze of Canterbury pilgrims and applied with ornate scrolled decoration to rim, base and handle.

Figure, (**939**), c.1790, Staffordshire, Burslem, height: 30.5cm, (12in), enamelled pearlware. Figure of Chaucer modelled at Ralph Wood II's factory. He wears generalised seventeenth -century clothes and stands beside a marbled plinth on which rests a pile of his books.[1] In the absence of contemporary print sources the modeller may have copied Chaucer's loosely draped headdress from half-length portraits engraved by George Vertue.[2]

Poetry

Geoffrey Chaucer (c.1343-c.1400)

Regarded as the father of English literature, Chaucer wrote *The Canterbury Tales* in the 1380s, although it was not printed and published by William Caxton until 1475. Chaucer served the household of Prince Lionel, later Duke of Clarence as diplomat and spy, having to be ransomed after being captured in France in 1360. His official positions included comptroller of customs on furs, skins, and hides for the port of London (1374–86) and clerk of the king's works (1389–91). He was buried in Westminster Abbey.

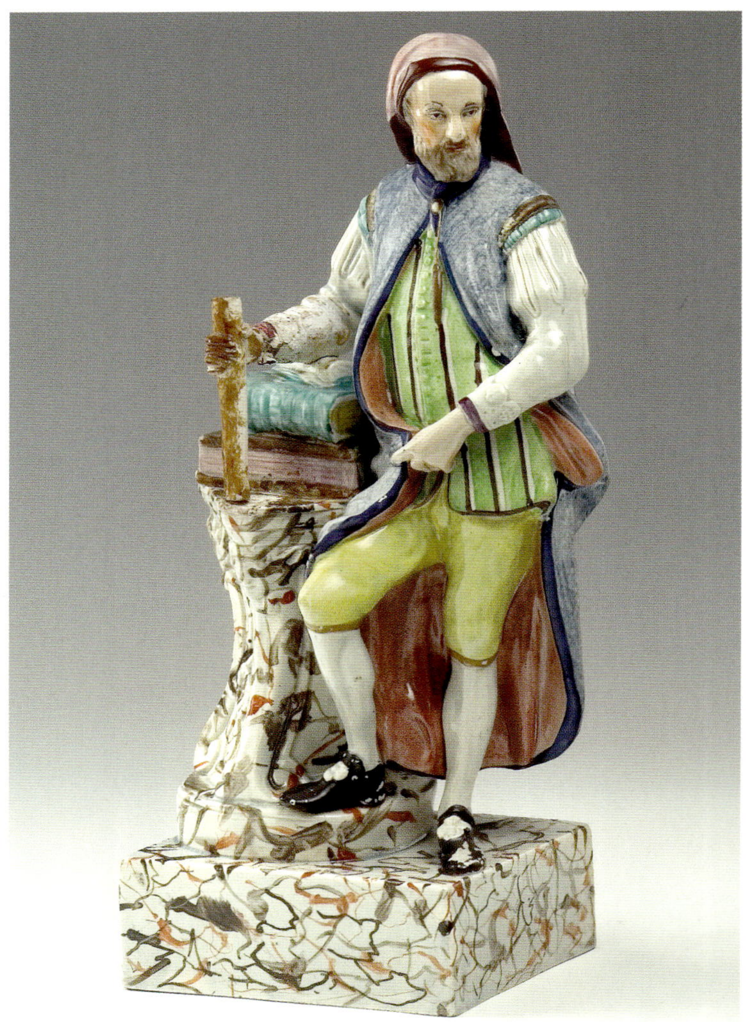

William Shakespeare (1564-1616)

Despite continuing disagreement about the details of his life and career, Shakespeare is widely regarded today as the greatest poet and dramatist of England's literary golden age. Unfortunately few of the ceramic souvenirs are of high quality. After a long period of neglect after his death, interest was rekindled in the 1760s. Oliver Goldsmith remarked in *The Vicar of Wakefield* (1766), 'Our taste has gone back a whole century, Fletcher, Ben Johnson [*sic*], and all the plays of Shakespeare, are the only things that go down'[3] In 1769 David Garrick held a Shakespeare Jubilee and in 1775 Georg Christoph Lichtenberg observed, during his visit to England: 'Shakespeare is not only famous but sacred; his moral maxims are heard everywhere'.[4]

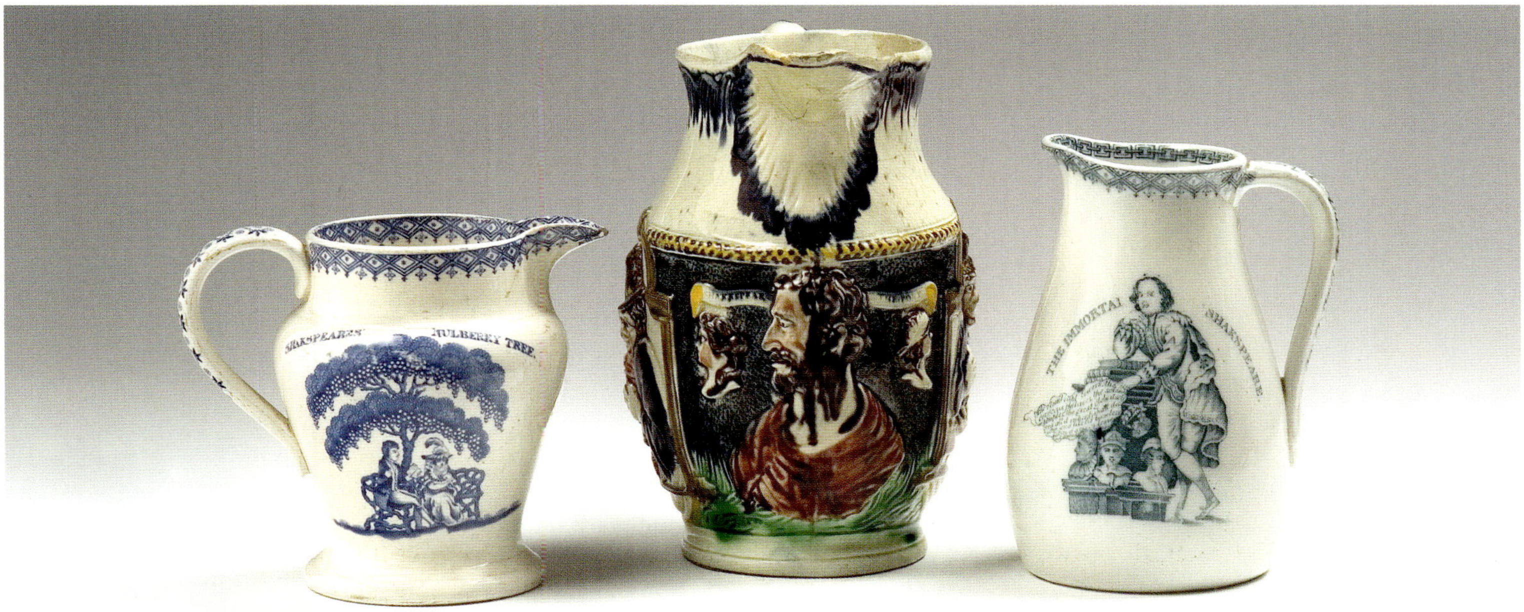

Jug, (**943**), c.1820, Staffordshire, height: 12.7cm, (5in), blue-printed earthenware. Printed with 'SHAKSPEARE'S MULBERRY TREE', with a fashionably dressed couple reading from the plays.[5]
Jug, (**941**), c.1790, Staffordshire, height: 19.1cm, (7½in), Prattware. Relief-moulded caricatures of 'the Miser', beneath the spout, 'The Spendthrift',[6] and a profile portrait of 'SHAKESPEAR / THE POET' all crudely coloured.
Jug, (**944**), c.1820, Staffordshire or Scotland, height: 15.3cm, (6in), blue-printed earthenware. Image adapted from the monument to Shakespeare by Peter Scheemakers after a design by William Kent, installed in Poets' Corner, Westminster Abbey, in 1740.[7] Shakespeare leans on books piled on a plinth carved with the heads of English monarchs, (including Queen Elizabeth I). He points to a cloud, inscribed with lines from act 4 of *The Tempest*, his last play. Despite the careful rendering of most of the sculptural details, Shakespeare's feet have suffered from a tuck in the transfer.[8]

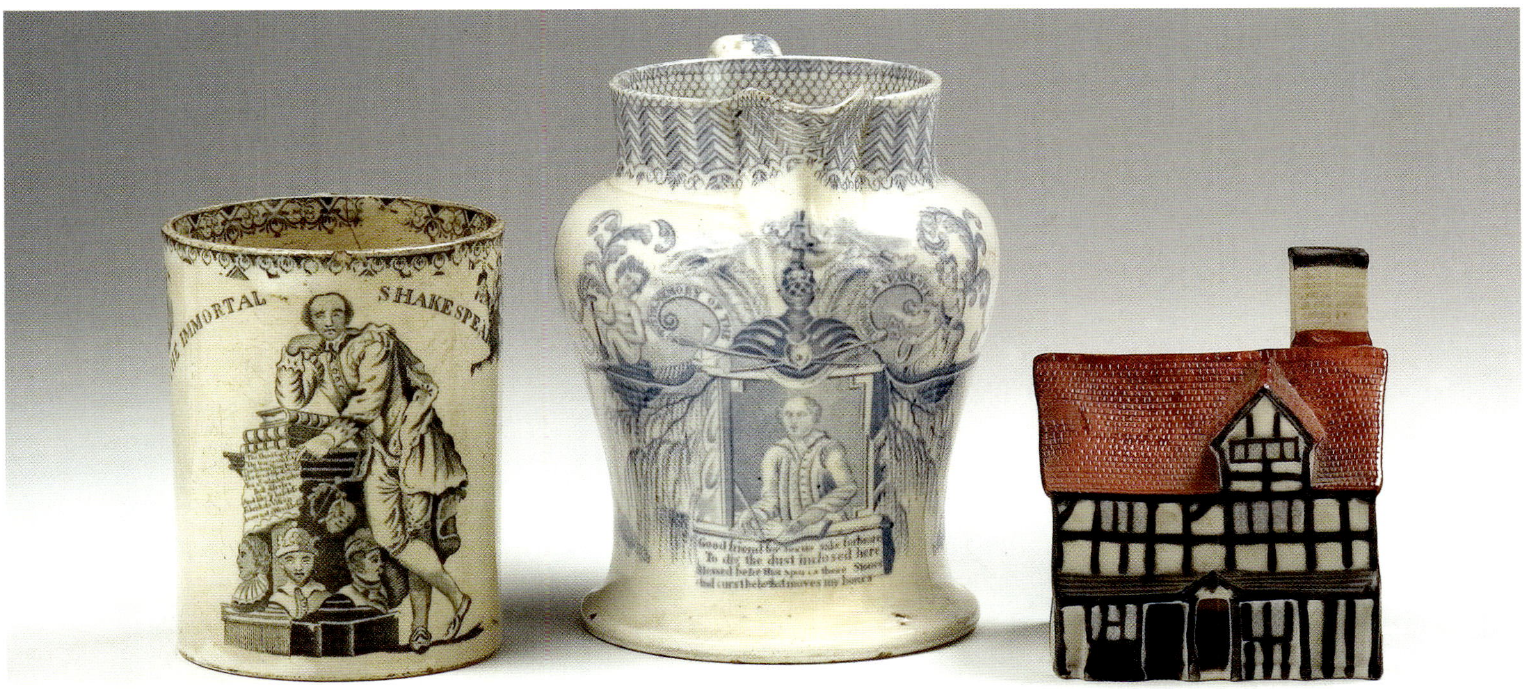

Mug, (**945**), c.1820, Staffordshire, height: 9.2cm, (3⅝in), sepia-printed earthenware. Entitled, 'THE IMMORTAL / SHAKESPEARE', image taken from the monument in Westminster Abbey (see 944), and small border scenes representing the Seven Ages of Man.[9]
Jug, (**942**), c.1820, Staffordshire, height: 12.1cm, (4¾in), blue-printed earthenware. Printed with figures and willows surrounding a framed portrait of Shakespeare, apparently based on his monument in Stratford-upon-Avon church.
Model, (**946**), c.1890, Staffordshire, height: 8.9cm, (3½in), enamelled biscuit porcelain. Souvenir model of Shakespeare's birthplace, the timber-framed house in Henley Street, Stratford, bought by John Shakepeare in 1552.

John Milton (1608-1674)

Milton, a composer's son, was born in Bread Street, London. He was a linguist, a devout Christian and an idealistic man of letters, the author of *Areopagitica* (1644), an impassioned defence of free speech. During the Commonwealth he served Cromwell as Latin Secretary and civil servant. After the Restoration of Charles II he was arrested, marginalised and impoverished in his later years. Now remembered as a great poet, he had to dictate the epic *Paradise Lost* (1664) to assistants, having lost his sight. His reputation dwindled after his death but his work was rediscovered and championed by Samuel Johnson, William Blake and Wordsworth. His biographer, William Hayley, regarded him (in 1796) as 'England's greatest author'.

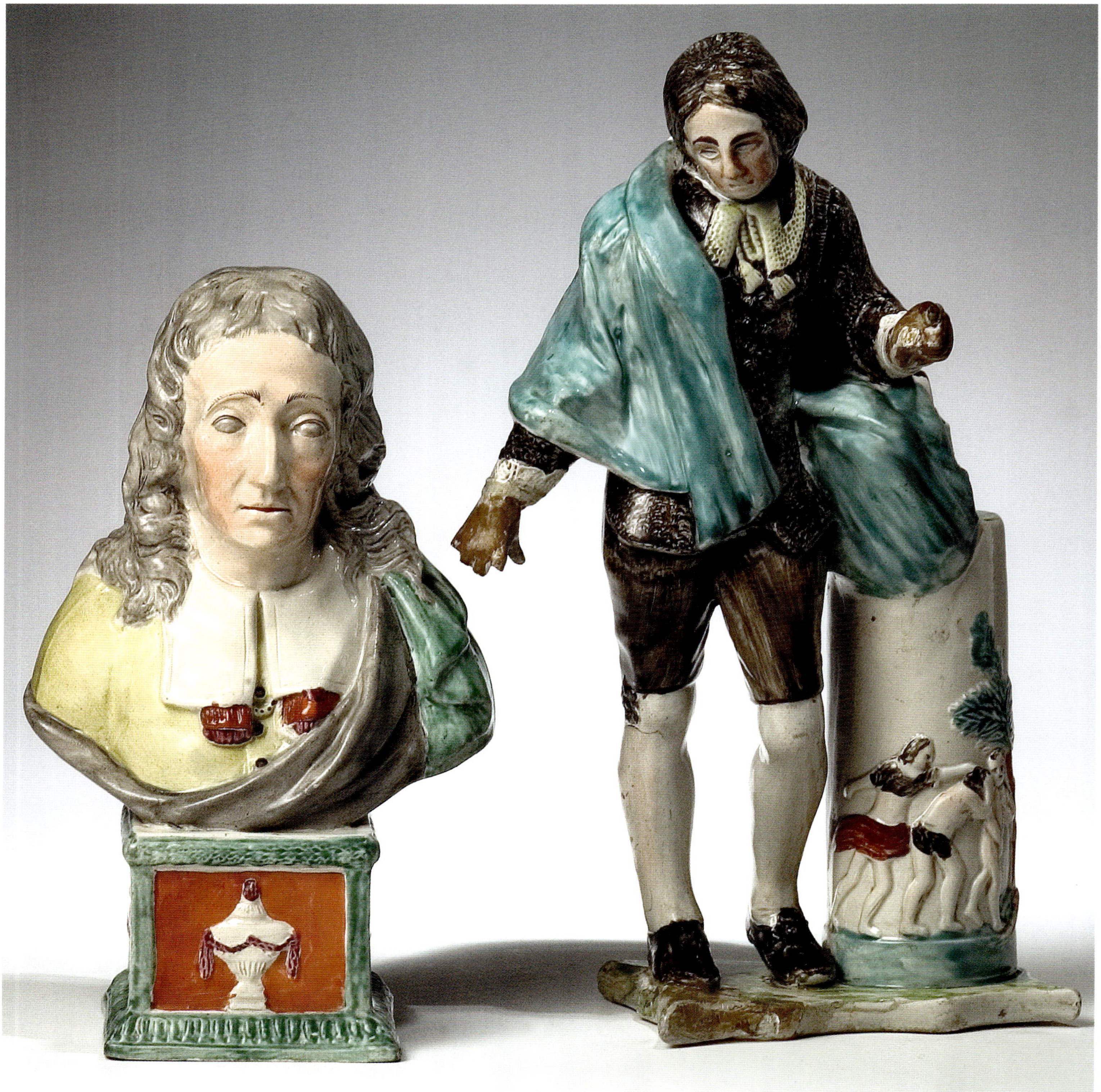

Bust, (948) c.1800, Staffordshire, height: 22.2cm, (8¾in), enamelled pearlware. Portrait bust, marked 'Milton' stands on plinth embellished with reliefs of classical urns. Related to a plaster bust, probably made by John Cheere,[10] it was copied from the portrait bust by John Michael Rysbrack (1694-1770) in Westminster Abbey (1737) and is very close to a marble example in the National Portrait Gallery.[11] They all emphasises his sightless eyes and include detail such as the tassels below his collar.

Figure, (949) c.1790, Staffordshire, height: 26.7cm, (10½in), enamelled pearlware. Milton stands beside a truncated column, relief-moulded with Adam and Eve being expelled from Eden, from *Paradise Lost*. Probably based on a sculpture of 1749 by John Cheere (itself perhaps inspired by a lost terracotta figure by Scheemakers) via a Chelsea-Derby porcelain figure of c.1775.[12]

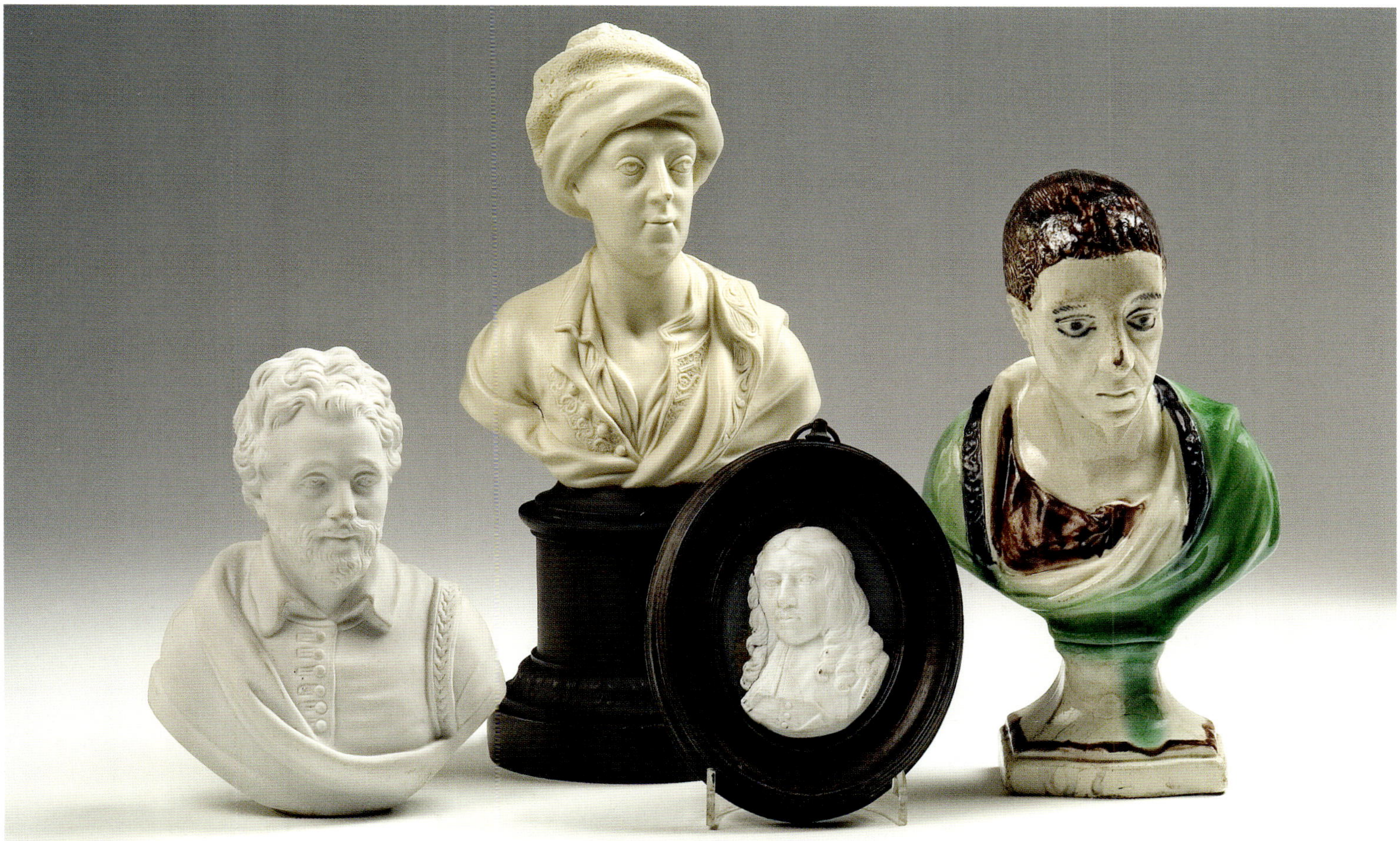

Bust, (947) c.1873, Staffordshire, height: 16.5cm, (6½in), biscuit porcelain. Portrait bust of Ben Jonson,(lacking a plinth), impressed on the back, J&BT / 817 (for James & Thomas Bevington). It may be based on an image such as that in John Simon's group portrait, 'Poets and Philosophers of England'.[13]
Bust, (951) c.1790, Staffordshire, height: 27.3cm, (10¾in), smear-glazed stoneware. Portrait of Matthew Prior, closely modelled on the bust sculpted by Antoine Coysevox (1640-1720) c.1700, for the monument in Westminster Abbey designed by James Gibbs and executed by John Michael Rysbrack in 1739.[14] It was carefully copied, first by John Cheere[15] and later by John Turner of Lane End. Prior is shown wearing an informal, open-necked shirt and an embroidered neglige cap or turban, worn at home in place of a wig.
Plaque, (950) c.1790, James Tassie, height: 14cm, (5½in), opaque glass paste. Finely-modelled relief portrait of Marvell, inscribed and signed by James Tassie.[16] The Glaswegian Tassie (1735-99) went to Dublin as a modeller and met Dr Henry Quin, with whom he developed his patent *pâte-de-verre*. He settled in London in 1767 and his portrait medallions and reproductions of antique gems were an immediate success. Many of the cameos and intaglios in Wedgwood's first catalogue of 1773 were cast from moulds supplied by Tassie, who published his own catalogue in 1775 listing over 3,000 items.[17]
Bust, (952) c.1790, Staffordshire, height: 21cm, (8¼in), Pratt coloured pearlware. Pope's portrait, despite its crude decoration, has the intense gaze and gaunt features of a man suffering ill health.[18] Almost certainly based on one of the celebrated marble portrait busts made from 1738 by the French-born sculptor, Louis François Roubiliac (1702-62) or an exact plaster replica by John Cheere.[19]

Ben Jonson (1572-1637)

The English poet and playwright was educated at Westminster School and Cambridge University. His first great success for the Admiral's Men at the Rose Theatre was *Every Man in his Humour* (1598). He is best known for his comedies *Volpone* (1607), *The Alchemist* (1610) and *Bartholomew Fair* (1614). Although esteemed in his day, his reputation suffered in comparison with Shakespeare and he was undervalued until the early twentieth century.

Andrew Marvell (1621-1778)

Marvell was a friend of Milton and assisted him as Latin Secretary during the Commonwealth. He is best known for poems such as *To his Coy Mistress* and *The Garden* and a Horatian *Ode on Cromwell's Return from Ireland*. After the Restoration, he turned to writing satires.

Matthew Prior (1664-1721)

The son of a nonconformist joiner from Dorset, Prior became a Fellow of St John's College Cambridge. As trade commissioner, his flair for French made him an able diplomat and ambassador to Paris, where he negotiated the Treaty of Utrecht in 1713. Impeached by the Whig Prime Minister, Robert Walpole, he was imprisoned from 1715 to 1717. Volumes of his poetry were published in 1709 and 1717. He originated the phrase 'The ends must justify the means.'[20] A monument to Prior by John Michael Rysbrack was installed in Poets' Corner, Westminster Abbey in 1723.

Alexander Pope (1688-1744)

Pope's father, a London linen merchant, was a Catholic convert, which caused difficulties for his family. Largely self-taught, Pope greatly admired Horace and Virgil, Roman poets of the Augustan age. Pope suffered serious illhealth, including asthma and tuberculosis of the spine that left him crippled and only 4'6" in height; his literary enemies called him the 'hunchbacked toad'. He is regarded as the greatest of the new 'Augustan' poets and the wittiest satirist of his time. His first great work, *An Essay on Criticism* (1711), contains the line, 'To err is human, to forgive divine' while his *Essay on Man* (1734) made him famous throughout Enlightenment Europe. He is best remembered for his translations of Homer's *Iliad* (1720) and *Odyssey* (1726), the satirical poem *The Rape of the Lock* (1714) and the savage burlesque, *The Dunciad* (1728).

William Cowper (1731-1800)

Cowper was born in Berkhamsted, Hertfordshire and qualified as a lawyer although severe depression prevented him from practising. On recovering he became an evangelical Christian and a supporter of William Wilberforce in the fight against slavery.[21] He is remembered for his translations of Homer, in which he hoped to improve on Pope's versions, the *Olney Hymns* and for the long poem, *The Task*, highly regarded by the Royal Family. His *Diverting History of John Gilpin*, an uncharacteristically light-hearted poem, was initially published anonymously in 1782, although Cowper later admitted authorship. It became enormously popular and was published in numerous illustrated editions.[22]

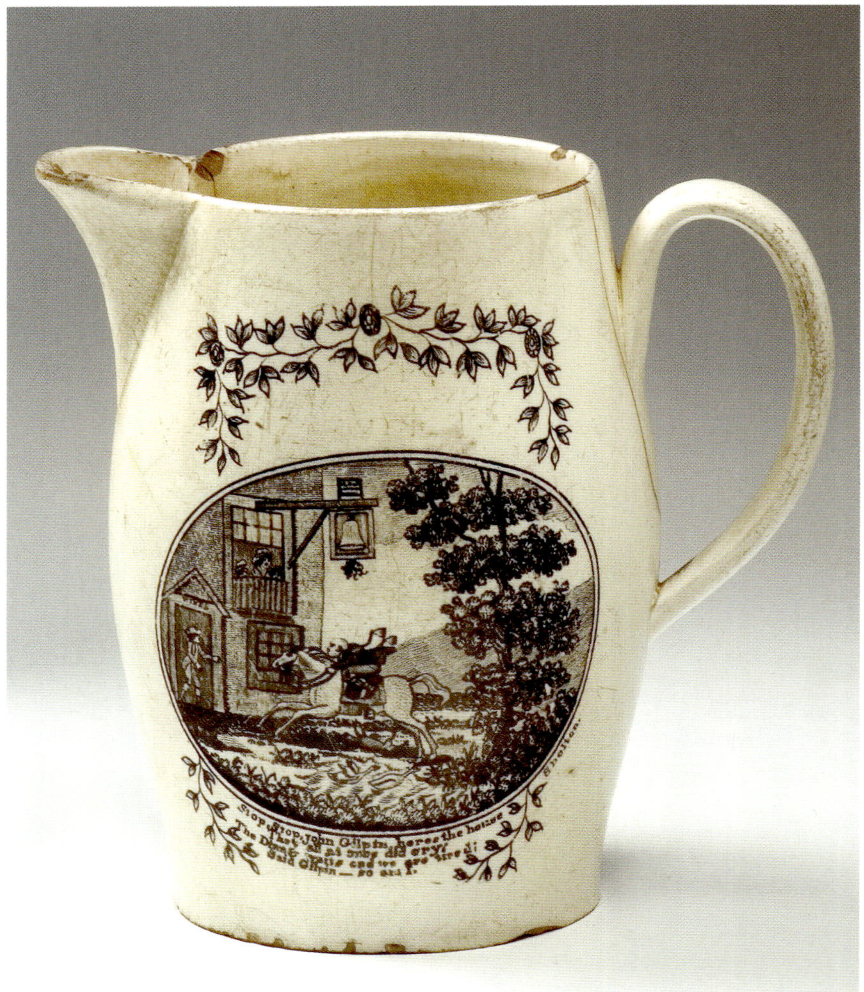

Jug, (954) c.1790, Staffordshire, Shelton, height: 14cm, (5½in), printed creamware. Printed by Thomas Fletcher with scene of John Gilpin on a runaway horse, flying past 'The Bell' at Edmonton, where he was to have enjoyed his wedding anniversary breakfast. Inscribed with verse 37: 'Stop, stop, John Gilpin!—here's the house!"/ They all at once did cry; "The dinner waits, and we are tired."/ Said Gilpin, "So am I!' On the reverse an unrelated scene of a man riding towards the visible spire of the church of Great St Mary.[23]

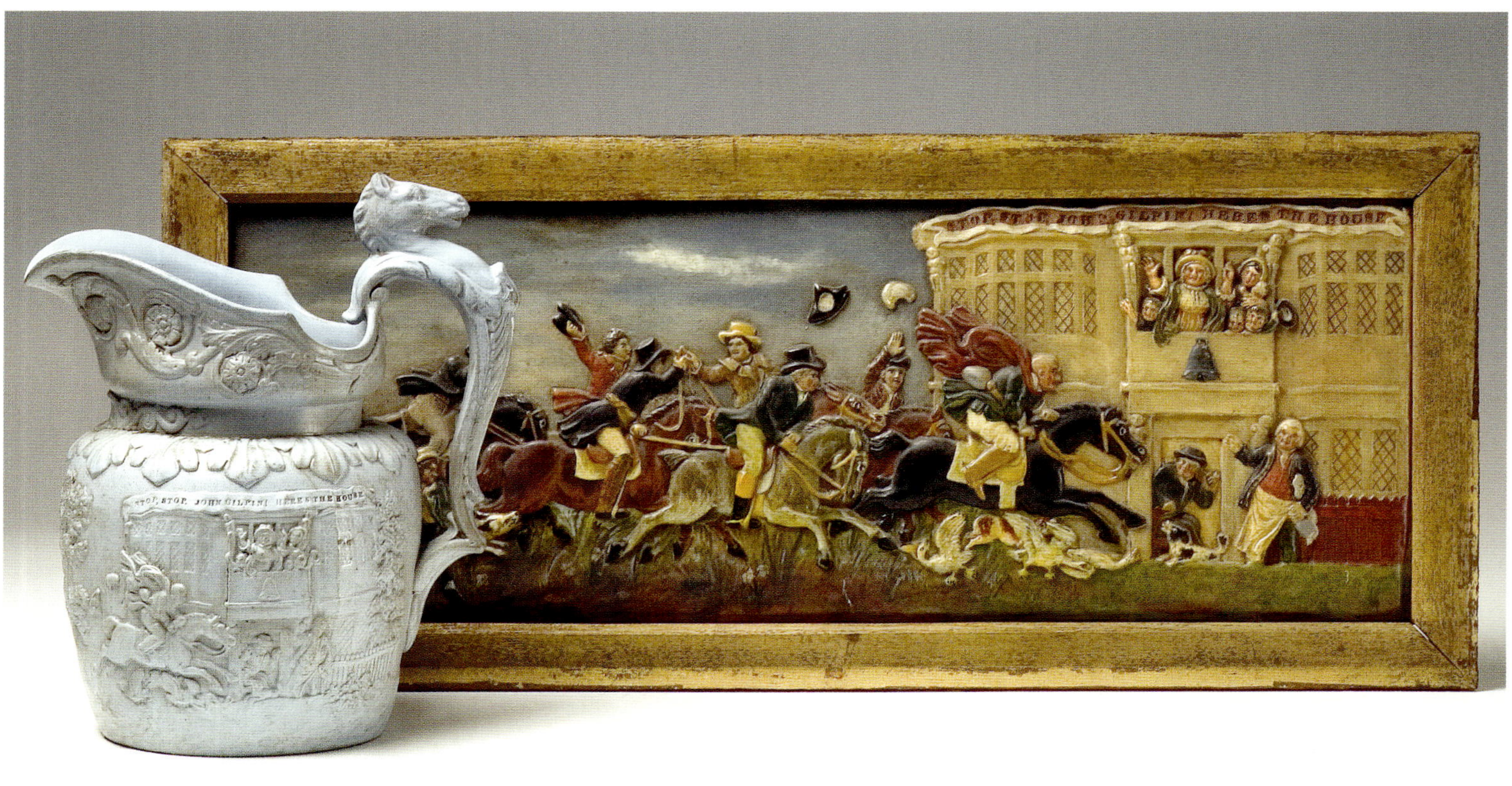

Jug, (**R.815**), c.1845, Staffordshire, height: 22.9cm, (9in), blue, smear-glazed stoneware. Relief-moulded with Gilpin's ride through Edmonton. **Plaque**, (**953**), c.1845, Staffordshire, height: 17.8cm, (7in), enamelled earthenware. Relief-moulded scene from *John Gilpin*, almost certainly based on 1844 illustration of 'Mr Wells, the popular equestrian', well known for his performance as Gilpin at Philip Astley's Circus.[24]

Robert Burns (1759-1796)

Scotland's most celebrated poet was born the son of a poor farmer in Alloway, South Ayrshire. After a succession of labouring jobs, including flax dressing, he began regularly writing poetry. The young Walter Scott met Burns in 1774 and described him as of, 'manners rustic, not clownish. ... [his] eye alone indicated the poetical character and temperament. It was large, and of a dark cast, and literally glowed when he spoke with feeling or interest'.[25] He visited Edinburgh in 1787 and was cultivated by influential members of society, such as Dugald Stewart, but refused to settle there or to move to London. Although he could write verse in standard English, he excelled in crafting poetry from everyday speech, songs and stories of his fellow Scots. This made him Scotland's favourite poet but antagonised the Scottish Establishment. In 1791 he took the post of Exciseman and later died of alcoholism.

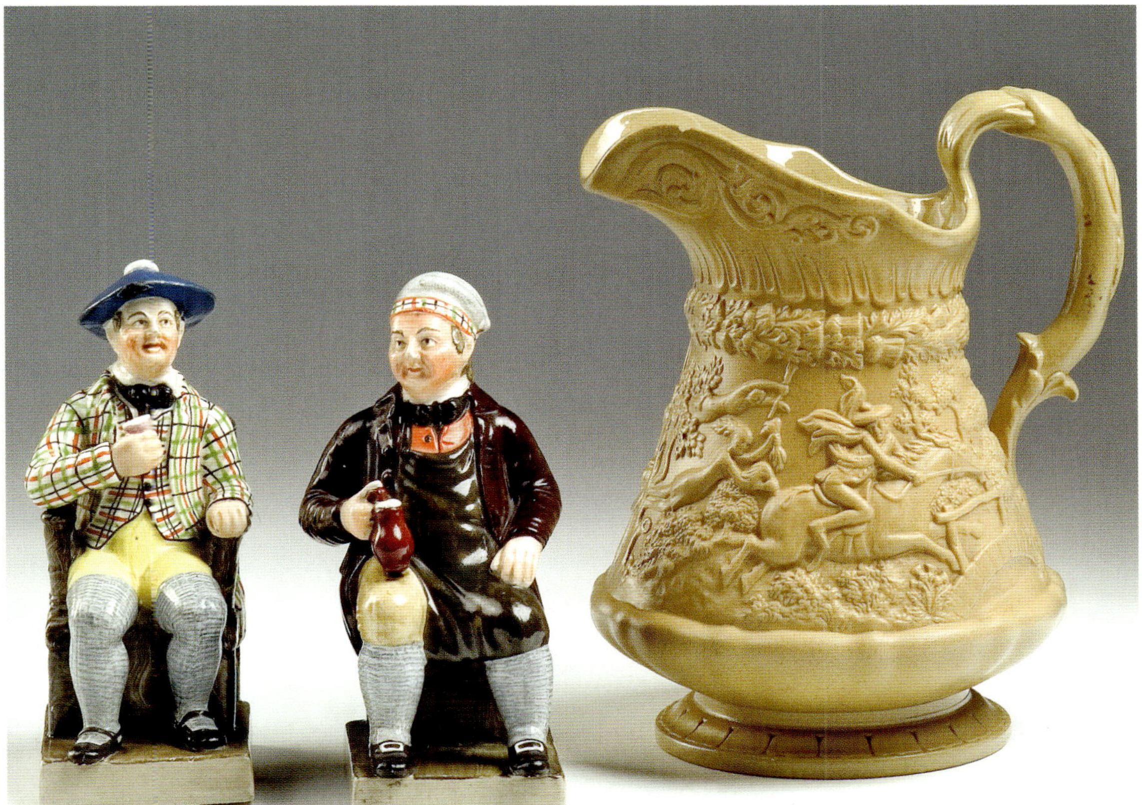

Pair of Figures, (958 + 959) c.1830, Staffordshire, height: 13.3cm, (5¼in), height: 13.3cm, (5¼in), enamelled pearlware. *Tam O'Shanter*, perhaps Burns's greatest narrative poem, was published in the *Edinburgh Herald* in 1791. It tells of the Ayrshire farmer, Tam, and his friend Souter Johnny, 'His ancient, trusty, drouthy crony,' enjoying a night of heavy drinking at their local alehouse. Then Tam must invent a story to explain to his wife why he has returned home so late. The figures are closely modelled on sculptures by James Thom that toured Scotland and were shown in London in 1829.[26] Engraved illustrations of them inspired the potters.[27]

Jug, (960), 1835, Staffordshire, Hanley, height: 17.8cm, (7in), buff stoneware. A dated jug made by William Ridgway & Co. of Hanley, relief-moulded with illustrations after Landseer. Tam O'Shanter has to ride home over the Brig O'Doon (the bridge over the River Doon) at Alloway. Stopping at the ruined kirk, Tam disturbs a witches' dance and is pursued across the bridge as the witches pull the tail of his grey mare, Meg.

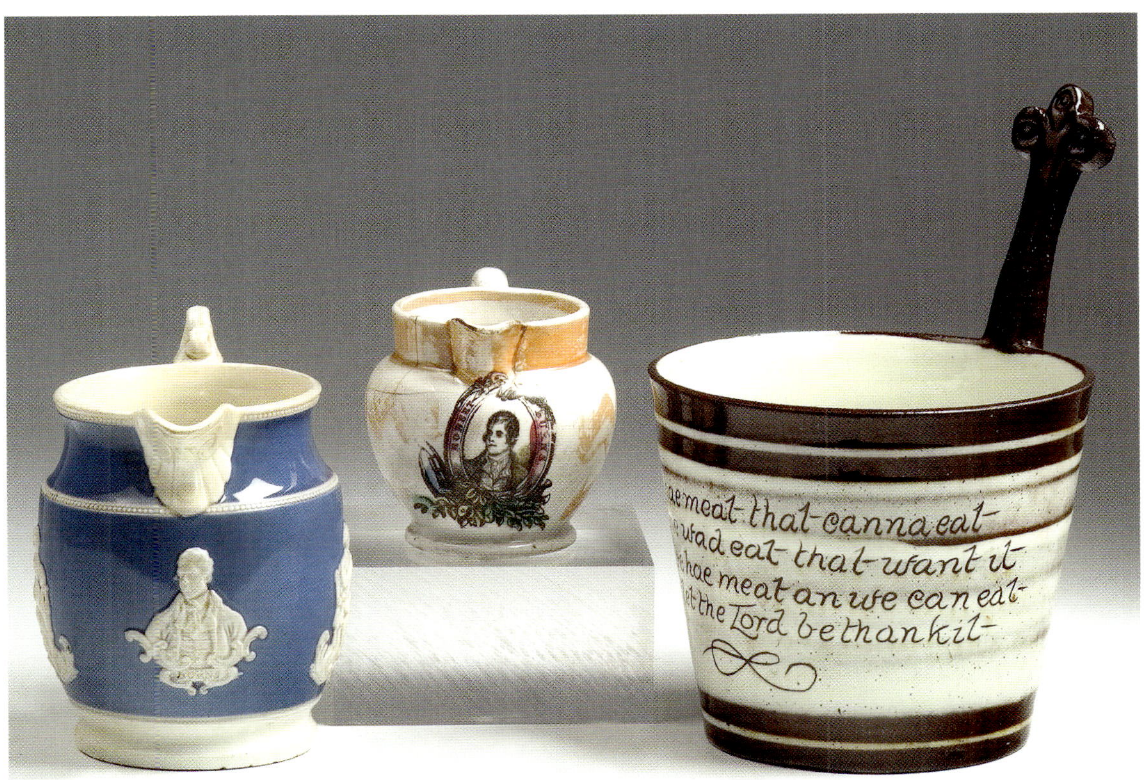

Jug, (956), c.1830, Staffordshire, height: 10.2cm, (4in), earthenware. Jug covered in blue slip with white relief sprig portrait of Burns under the spout. Sprigged portraits of Tam O'Shanter and Souter Johnny on each side.

Jug, (957), c.1860, Sunderland, height: 7.6cm, (3in), earthenware, printed and lustred. Jug with printed portrait of Burns[28] may be a centenary souvenir.

Luggie, **(961)**, c.1880, Ayrshire, Cumnock Pottery, height: 19.7cm, (7¾in), earthenware. Luggie, Scottish pail with a vertical handle, incised through cream slip with words from Burns's *Selkirk Grace*. Although this Grace is credited to Burns, there is a similar seventeenth-century version known as the Galloway or Covenanters' Grace, 'Some hae meat that canna eat / An some wad eat that want it / But we hae meat an we can eat / Sae let the Lord be thankit'.[29]

Sir Walter Scott (1771-1832)

Scott came from a Border family who had settled in Edinburgh. He studied law at Edinburgh University and in 1792, while waiting to enter the Bar, took a walking tour of the Borders. The next summer he explored Perthshire and the Eastern Highlands. The stories and ballads he collected were published in 1802 as *Minstrelsy of the Scottish Border.* They were followed in 1803 by *The Lay of the Last Minstrel*. The popularity of these works led to Scott being asked to organise George IV's memorable visit to Edinburgh in 1822.

Scott's publishing business, founded with James Ballantyne, went bankrupt in 1826. He spent the rest of his life paying off the debt by writing prodigiously. He had great success with romantic Scottish novels *Waverley* (1814), *Rob Roy* (1817) and *The Heart of Midlothian* (1818). The Medieval England evoked by such novels as *Ivanhoe (1819), Peveril of the Peak* (1824) and *The Talisman* (1825) boosted the popularity of the Gothic Revival in the mid-nineteenth century. *Ivanhoe* even inspired tournaments in southern England.

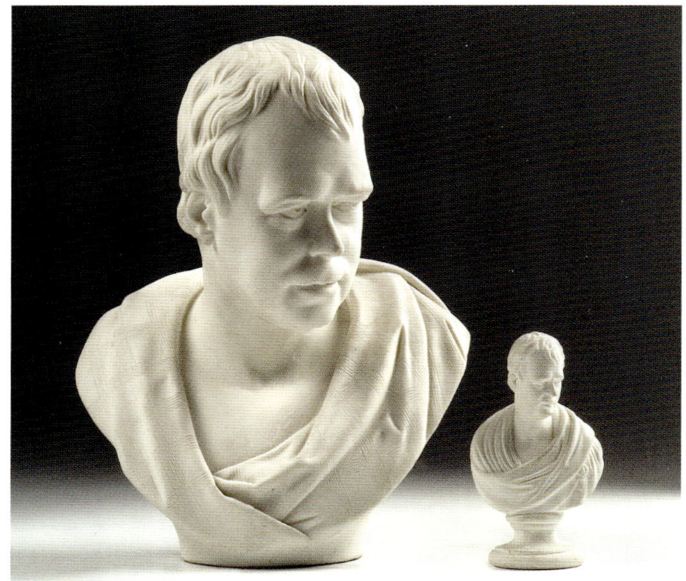

Bust, (962), c.1830, Staffordshire, Stoke-on-Trent, height: 25.4cm, (10in), biscuit porcelain. Portrait of Scott, probably made by Mintons. He is shown swathed in drapery, incised with a chequered design in imitation of tartan. **Bust, (963)**, c.1830, Staffordshire, height: 10.8cm, (4in), biscuit porcelain. The smaller version suggests the circular brooch attached to the plaid cloak. Both pieces based on a marble portrait of Scott by Sir Francis Chantrey, of 1820. The appearance of a plaster replica on the tray of 'images' to be sold by the sleeping *Italian Image Seller*, in the painting by Hugh Cameron, indicates the popularity of this view of Scott.[30]

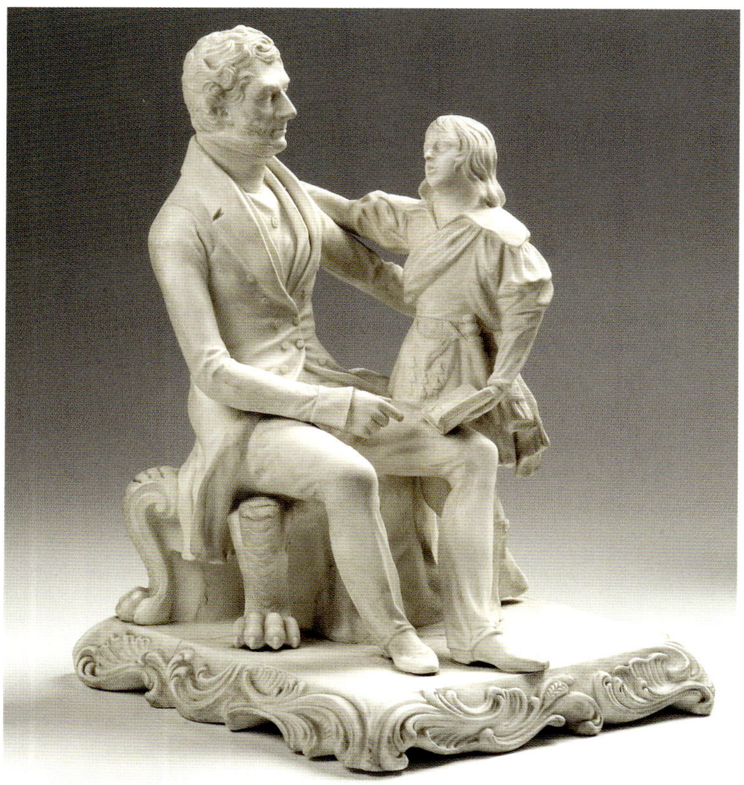

Figure Group, (964), c.1850, Derby, height: 31.8cm, (12½in), biscuit porcelain. Represents Scott's son-in-law, writer and critic, John Gibson Lockhart (1794-1854), who had married Scott's elder daughter Sophia, with his son, the delicate John Hugh ('Littlejohn'), who wears a plaid kilt. The family visited Brighton in 1826 for the therapeutic sea-bathing, and declared the air 'most healthful and the children are all day long on the beach'.[31] The boy, to whom Scott had dedicated *Tales of a Grandfather* (stories from Scottish history) in 1829, died tragically young in 1831.

Lord Byron (1788-1824)

George Gordon, 6th Baron Byron, was a Romantic poet famed for his scintillating satires and epic poems such as *Childe Harold, Don Juan* and *Manfred* and notorious for his charismatic, reckless personality. From 1816 he lived abroad in self-imposed exile, travelled extensively and became a legend throughout Europe. He died of fever at Missolonghi, supporting the Greeks in their fight for independence from Turkish rule. Owing to his scandalous private life it was only in 1969 that a memorial to him was finally placed on the floor of Westminster Abbey.

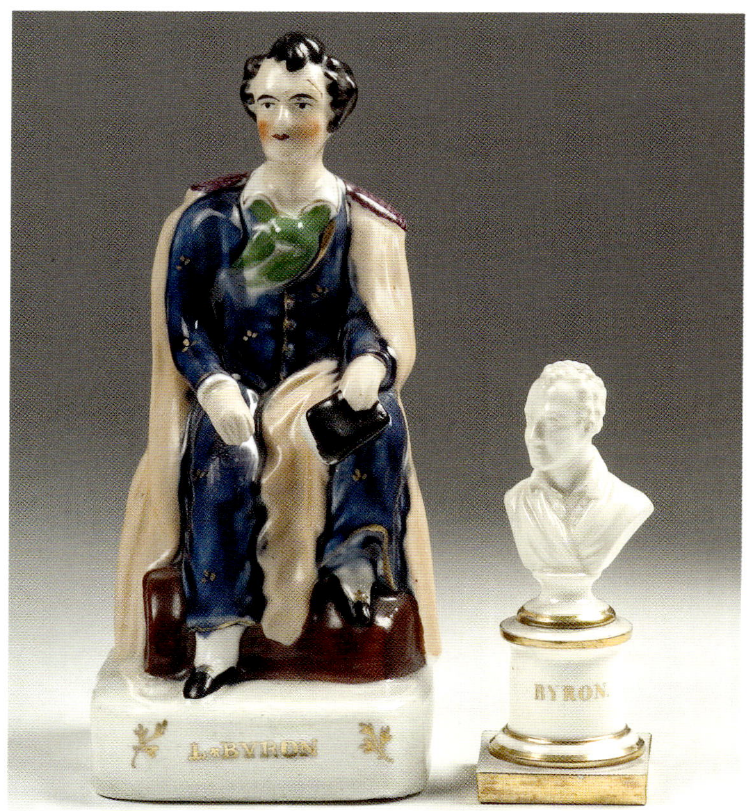

Figure, (965), c.1840, Staffordshire, height: 18.4cm, (7¼in), enamelled earthenware. Figure, entitled, 'L★BYRON', loosely based on the marble statue commissioned by the poet's admirers after his death, from the Danish sculptor, Bertel Thorvaldsen. Rejected by Westminster Abbey in 1829, it is now in the Wren Library at Byron's alma mater, Trinity College, Cambridge. **Bust, (966)**, c.1825, probably Derby, height: 10.8cm, (4in), soft-paste porcelain. Cylindrical plinth labelled in gilt, 'BYRON'.

Henry Wadsworth Longfellow (1807-1882)

Longfellow was the American poet best known to British readers. Born in Portland, Maine, the son of a lawyer and congressman, he travelled in Europe before settling at Harvard, where he taught from 1836. He is now best remembered for his narrative poems, *The Song of Hiawatha* and *Hyperion* but was celebrated in his lifetime for *The Hanging of the Crane*.

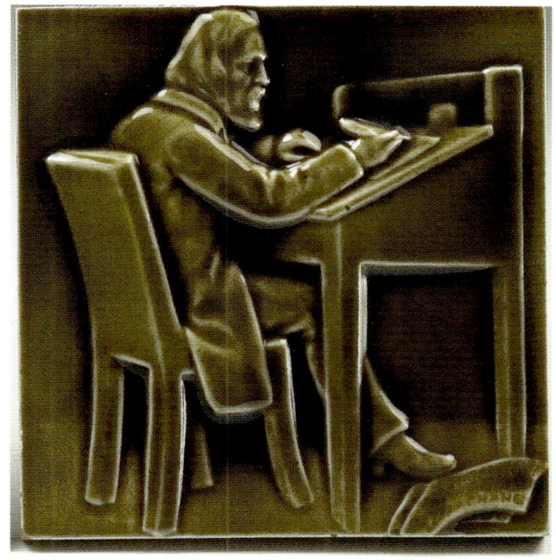

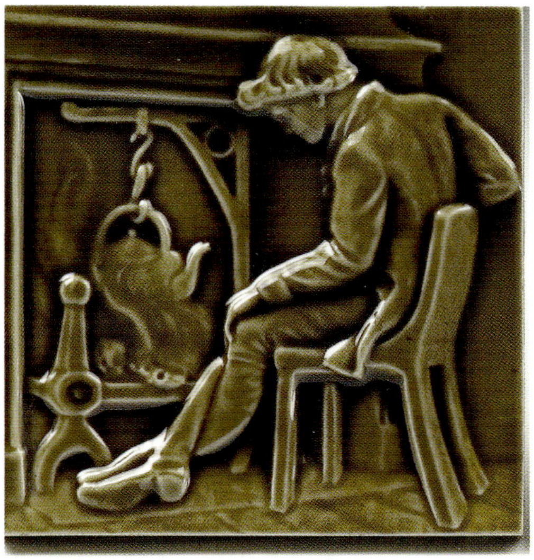

1

Tile, (**967**), c.1880, Shropshire, Broseley, height: 15.3cm, (6in), dust-pressed earthenware. Low-relief portrait of Longfellow writing at a desk. Discarded sheet of paper (lower right) inscribed: 'LONGFELLOW / THE HANGING / OF THE CRANE', linked to the series of scenes illustrating *The Hanging of the Crane*.[32]

Tiles, (1713a, b, c, d), c.1880, Shropshire, Broseley, each height: 15.3cm, (6in), dust-pressed earthenware. Tiles marked for Maw & Co. Benthall Works. The title relates to French expression, 'Pendre la Crèmaillière,' referring to the pot-hook hung above a stove, symbolizing a house-warming. Narrative scenes on each of the seven tiles match stanzas from the poem:

1713a 1. A young man watches a kettle on a hook over the stove, 2. A young couple take tea at a table.
1713b 3. A couple sit at a table with a child, 4. Two children eat from bowls at the table.
1713c 5. A man reads to the family gathered round a table.
1713d 6. Children present posies to their grandparents, 7. An older woman reads a letter and weeps.

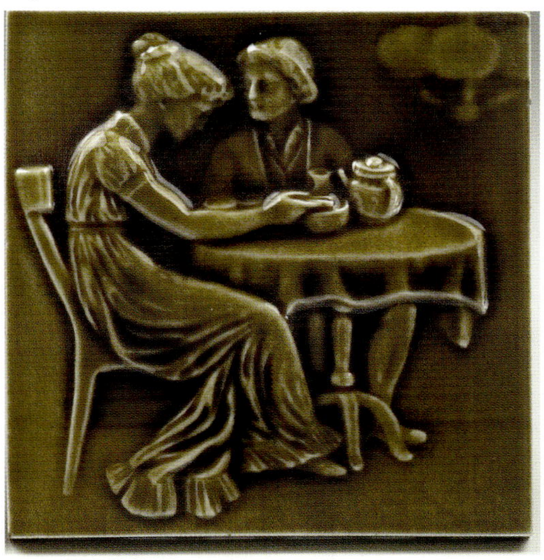

2

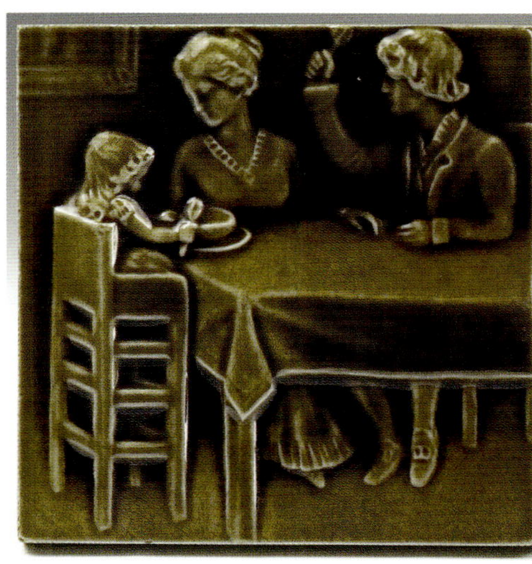

3

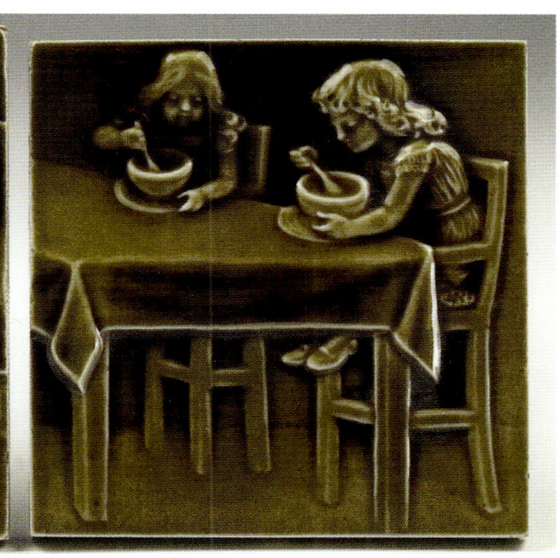

4

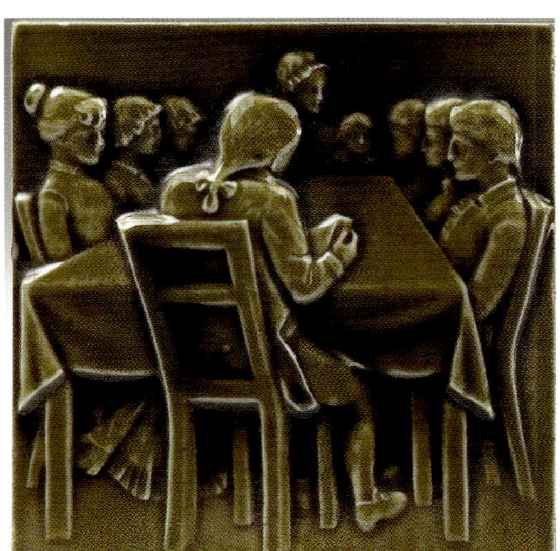

5

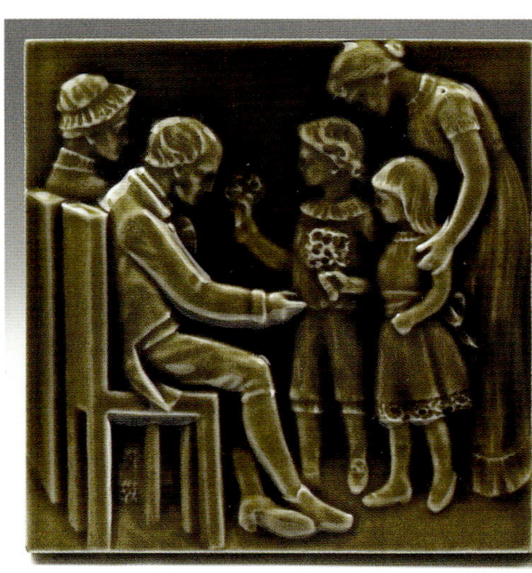

6

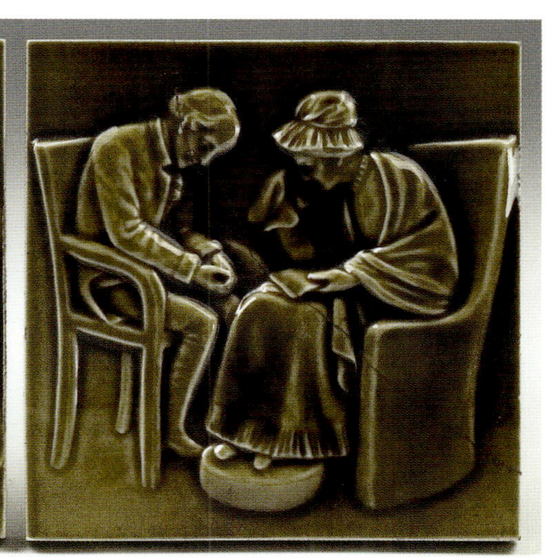

7

Science

Sir Isaac Newton (1642-1727)

Isaac Newton, the mathematician and astronomer attended Grantham Grammar School and Trinity College, Cambridge where he became a Fellow in 1667. In 1666, when driven from Cambridge by plague, Newton formulated a series of important theories concerning light, colour, calculus and the law of 'universal gravitation', His greatest works, *Philosphiae Naturalis Principia Mathematica,* was published in 1687, and *Optics* in 1704. He was knighted in 1705 and served as President of the Royal Society from 1703 until his death.

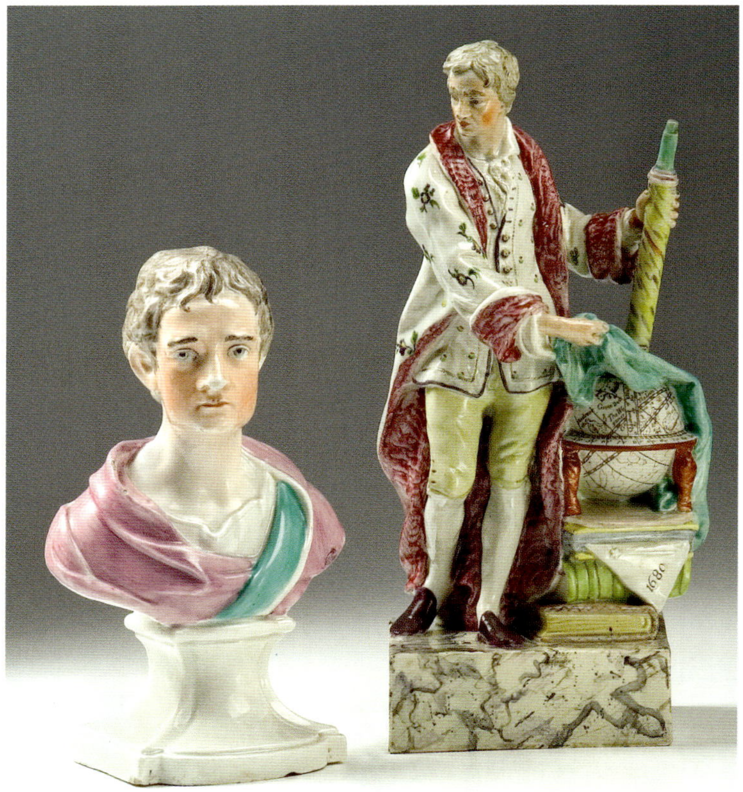

Bust, (969), c.1790, Staffordshire, Burslem, height: 22.9cm, (9in), enamelled pearlware. Portrait bust of Newton attributed to Enoch Wood, probably based on casts after a Roubiliac marble bust of 1751.[33]
Figure, (970), c.1790, Staffordshire, Burslem, height: 31.7cm, (12½in), enamelled pearlware. Figure, impressed 'Ra.Wood' and '137', probably modelled after one by John Smith. Newton, bare-headed, wears a long morning gown over his waistcoat and breeches. Such casual clothes, (charmingly decorated with floral sprigs), give him an air of informality and Romantic sensibility, at variance with the seventeenth century in which he lived. A piece of paper, decorated with a comet and the date, 1680, protrudes from beneath a celestial globe.

John Locke (1632-1704)

Locke was educated at Westminster and Christ Church College, Oxford, where he taught moral philosophy. A highly important Enlightenment thinker and 'Father of Classical Liberalism' his views influenced the American Declaration of Independence. He is best known for his *Two Treatises of Government* (1689), letter *Concerning Toleration* (1689) and *An Essay Concerning Human Understanding* (1690).

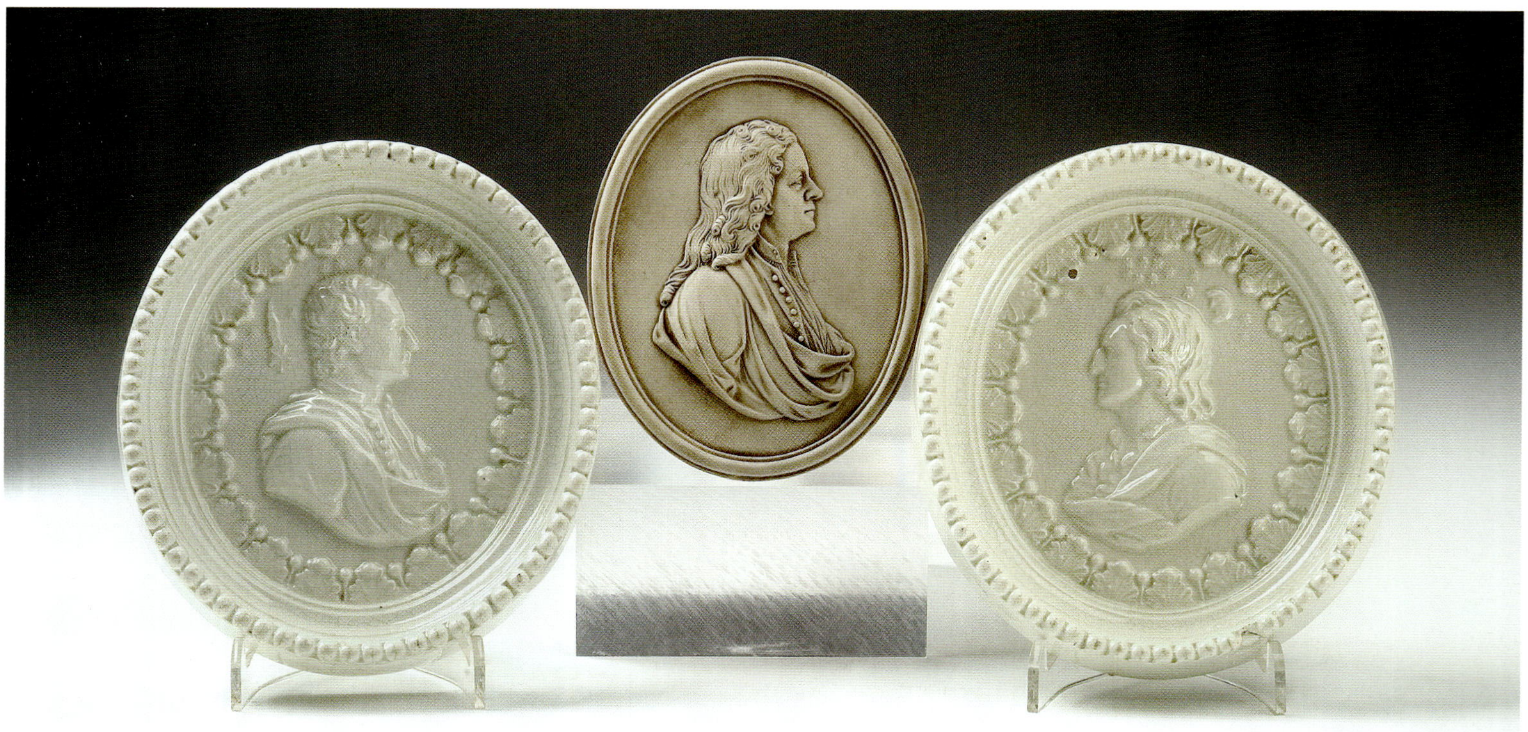

Plaque, (971), c.1815, possibly Glasgow, height: 15.3cm, (6in), pearlware. Relief-moulded portrait of Isaac Newton in deep, oval frame, possibly by Bagnal of Glasgow.[34] Newton faces right with a comet behind his head. He built the first reflecting telescope with a one-inch mirror in 1672, which enabled the Great Comet of 1680 to be observed.[35]
Plaque, (985), c.1800, Staffordshire, height: 12.1cm, (4¾in), white jasperware. A similar mould at the Wedgwood Museum is marked 'Newton'.[36]

Plaque, (968), c.1815, possibly Glasgow, height: 15.3cm, (6in), pearlware. Relief-moulded portrait of John Locke in deep, oval frame, (possibly by Bagnal of Glasgow). The left-facing profile features the moon and a specific constellation, (inappropriate for the philosopher). Both portraits however, are based on named Wedgwood jasperware medallions. The Newton design (971) is attributed to Hackwood, while that of Locke, produced in 1779, was probably modelled on a bust by Rysbrack.[37]

Joseph Priestley (1733-1804)

Priestley was a theologian, a chemist and a political radical. The son of a Leeds cloth-dresser, he studied history, science and philosophy at the new nonconformist Daventry Academy in Northamptonshire. He was made a Fellow of the Royal Society in 1766 and joined the Birmingham based group of intellectuals and innovators known as the Lunar Society, whose members included Erasmus Darwin and Josiah Wedgwood.[38] In 1774 he isolated oxygen and other gases including ammonia, sulphur dioxide and carbon dioxide (coincidentally inventing soda water in 1772).

In his writings he argued for extended civil liberties and in *A Political Dialogue on the General Principles of Government* (1791), he expressed radical political ideas similar to those of Tom Paine. After he publicly expressed support for the French Revolution in 1791, the Birmingham mob burned his house down. Among his losses, listed in a compensation claim from the Warwickshire Assizes, were modern luxury goods including 'colossal amounts' of new English ceramics.[39] His interest may have been kindled by his friendship with Josiah Wedgwood. He emigrated to America in 1794.

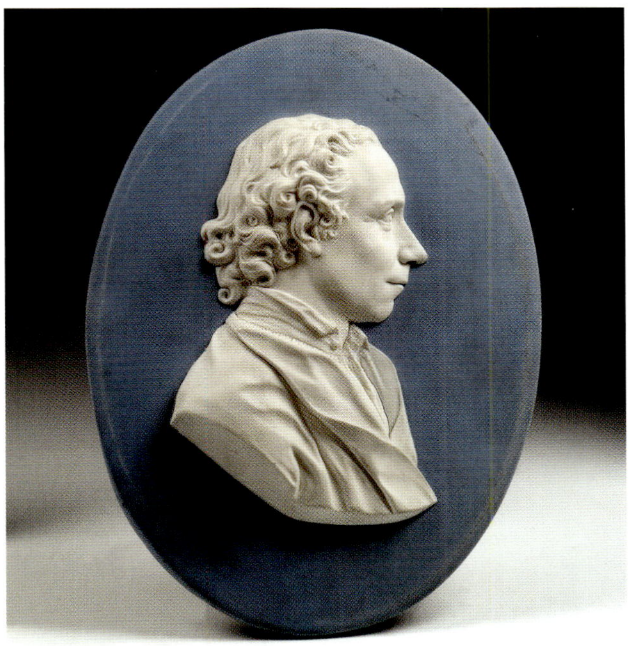

Literature

The rapid increase in literacy between the sixteenth and the eighteenth centuries was coincidental with rapid expansion in publishing. Book content gradually diversified from religious texts and instruction to philosophical and legal treatises, history, topical bulletins, practical advice and recreation. By 1700 fiction had emerged in the form of 'romances', full-length fantasies for which Cervantes' *Don Quixote* (1605-15), blazed a trail and 'nouvelles', short story collections, at which French aristocratic writers excelled. By the mid-eighteenth century, however, the English novel was dominant and the works of Daniel Defoe, Jonathan Swift, Samuel Richardson, Henry Fielding, Tobias Smollett and Laurence Sterne were read (in translation) throughout Europe. Women writers, such as Fanny Burney and Maria Edgeworth were almost equally successful although they often chose to publish under a male pseudonym.

Robinson Crusoe

Daniel Defoe's famous bestseller became one of the most popular books ever written. It was first published in 1719, six years after Alexander Selkirk's account of his five years as a castaway on an uninhabited island. Selkirk, a skilled navigator, was appalled by the behaviour of the tyrannical captain of his ship and demanded to be put ashore on the next island they came to, Juan Fernandez, 400 miles off the coast of Chile. (The ship later sank off the coast of Peru.)[40] Selkirk took ashore clothing, bedding, a musket and gunpowder, tools, a Bible and tobacco. He resigned himself to a long stay but was eventually rescued by a British privateer whose pilot, William Dampier, recognised the dishevelled Selkirk as a former shipmate. Selkirk returned to Scotland but, unable to adjust to life ashore he joined the Royal Navy in 1720 and died of fever off Africa shortly after.

Plaque, **(972)**, c.1780, Staffordshire, Wedgwood, height: 33cm, (13in), jasperware. Relief-moulded portrait impressed both 'Wedgwood' and 'Priestley'. Portrait based on one by Giuseppe Cerracchi. In 1779 Wedgwood wrote to Bentley, his then business partner, 'Dr Priestley arriv'd & we are with great reverence taking off his Presbyterian parson's wig & preparing a Sr I. Newton as a companion to him'.[41]

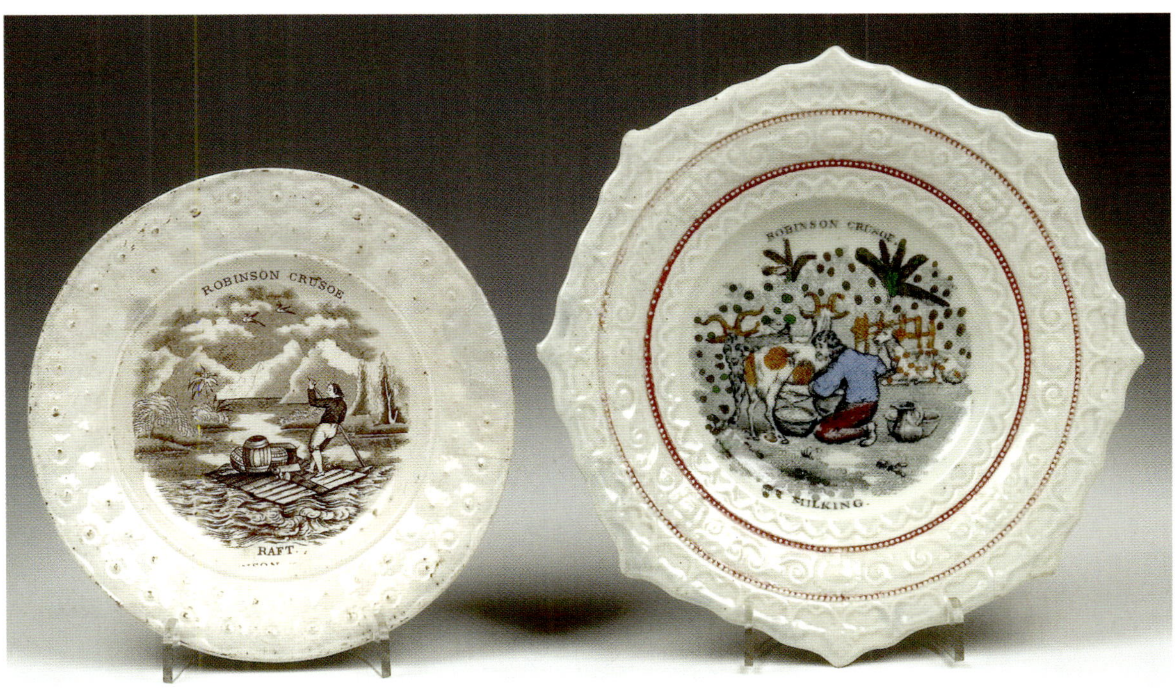

Nursery Plate, **(973)**, c.1855, possibly Middlesbrough, diameter: 15.3cm, (6in), brown-printed earthenware. Entitled, 'ROBINSON CRUSOE/ RAFT', Crusoe shown punting a laden raft to a palm-clad island.
Nursery Plate, **(974)**, c.1855, Staffordshire, diameter: 19.1cm, (7½in), earthenware, printed and enamelled. Octagonal plate (a design patented by the Staffordshire firm of Bailey & Ball in 1847) printed and sparsely coloured with Crusoe and goats, entitled, 'ROBINSON CRUSOE/ MILKING'.[42] Scenes on both plates based on J.J. Grandville's illustrations to a French edition of the story (1840), published by Routledge in England in 1853.[43]

Catherine Macaulay (1731-1791)

Catherine and John Sawbridge, her brother (later a radical politician), were largely self-taught. In 1760 she married a Scottish doctor who administered a London hospital. He died in 1776, leaving her a wealthy widow with a six-year-old daughter. In 1778, aged 47, she made a scandalous second marriage to James Graham, 26 years her junior.

Catherine Macaulay published her major work, *The History of England from the Accession of James I to that of the Brunswick Line*, in 8 volumes from 1763 to 1783. Unusually, for her time, she used primary source material but became notorious for her republican views. However, this made her a welcome guest of George Washington at Mount Vernon, during her 'triumphal tour' of the new United States in 1785. Macaulay was both revered (she was part of John Wilkes's circle) and reviled by her contemporaries (especially by Edmund Burke and David Hume). She was immortalised, however, together with the writer Hannah More, in Richard Samuel's painting of 1778, *The Nine Living Muses of Great Britain*. *Letters on Education*, her thoughts on the upbringing of girls was published in 1790 two years before Mary Wollstonecraft's *A Vindication of the Rights of Women*, which it profoundly influenced.

Dr Samuel Johnson (1709-1784)

Johnson has been described as 'arguably the most distinguished man of letters in English history.' The author of the ground-breaking *Dictionary of the English Language*, (first published in 1755) was born in Lichfield, Staffordshire and attended Oxford University until his funds ran out. After the failure of the Edial Hall School that he set up in 1735, he came to London and worked as a journalist. He was famously ugly, plagued by nervous tics and prey to depression but was surrounded by a devoted social circle. He produced a new edition of Shakespeare (1765), the travel memoir *A Journey to the Western Isles of Scotland* (1775), and *Lives of the Poets*, 1779-81 (some of which was written in Brighton at a house leased for the social season by his friend Mrs Hester Thrale). He was also the subject of a distinguished biography by James Boswell.

Edward Gibbon (1737-1794)

Gibbon was a historian, remembered for *The History of the Decline and Fall of the Roman Empire*, which was written mainly in London and published from 1776 to 1788. He was MP for Liskeard then for Lymington and Commissioner for Trade and Plantations, although he lived partly in Lausanne. He was elected Professor in Ancient History to the Royal Academy and belonged to 'the Club', the elite literary group which formed around Dr Johnson, and included Edmund Burke, David Garrick, Charles James Fox and Sir Joshua Reynolds. He was reviled by some for his condemnation of organised religion.

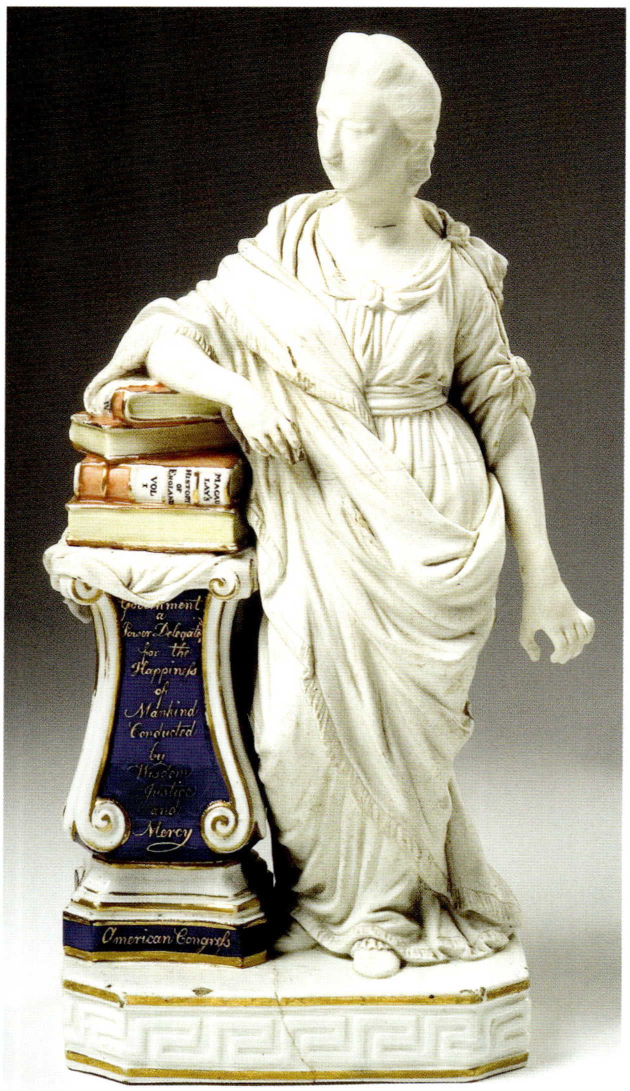

Figure, (976), c.1780, Derby, height: 31.7cm, (12½in), biscuit-porcelain, partly enamelled and gilt. The figure of Catherine Macaulay, incised No. 88, was adapted from a portrait of 1774 by Robert Edge Pine in which Macaulay wears Roman robes in the role of Clio, the Muse of History. She leans on a pile of her own publications holding a scroll copy of the radical 'Bill of Rights'. Such figures were expensive to produce; an example was sold in 1780 for 19/-.

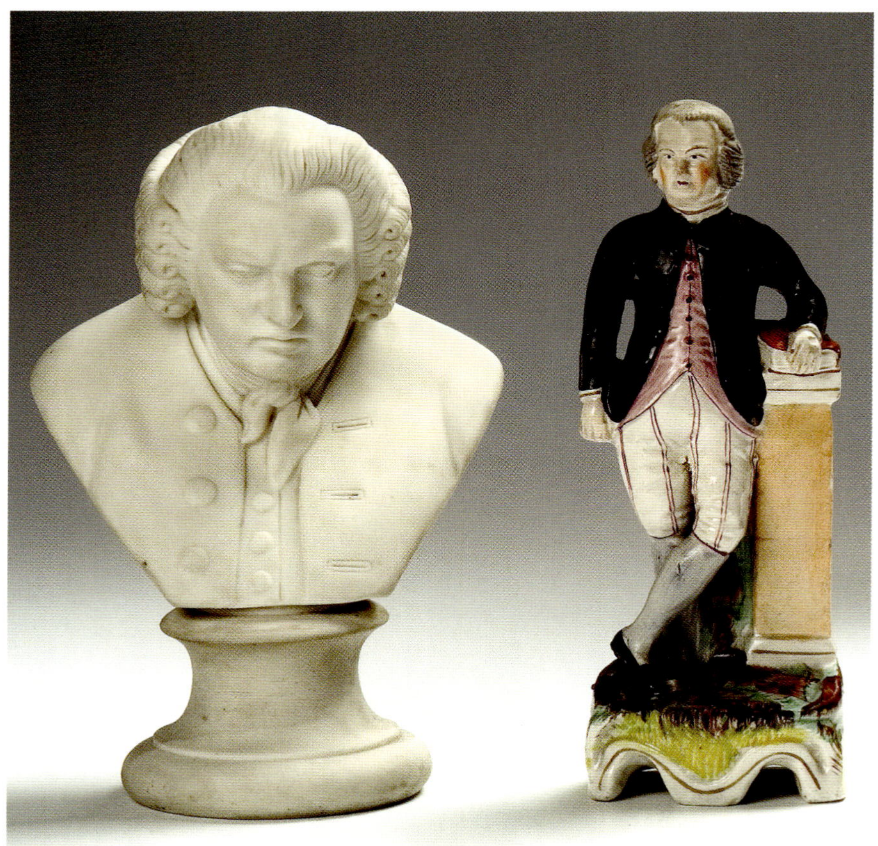

Bust, (975), c.1830, Staffs, height: 20.3cm, (8in), biscuit porcelain. Portrait bust of Dr Samuel Johnson. Most of the portraits produced during his lifetime reflect his ill-favoured looks. This later image, probably very loosely based on prints after paintings by his friend Joshua Reynolds, has softened his appearance.

Figure, (977), c.1830, Staffordshire, height: 20.3cm, (8in), enamelled pearlware. Said to represent Edward Gibbon. There is only passing resemblance to portraits of him with his chubby cheeks, double chin and short, tubby figure.

Thomas Carlyle (1795-1881)

Thomas Carlyle, the historian and political critic, was born at Ecclefechan in Dumfries and Galloway in 1795 and raised as a strict Calvinist. After graduating at eighteen from Edinburgh University he taught at several schools before becoming a full-time writer, specialising in the study of German literature. He and his wife, the writer Jane Welsh, moved to London in 1834 where his best-known works were published. These included *Sartor Resartus,* (1834), *The French Revolution* (1837), used by Charles Dickens as source material for *A Tale of Two Cities,* and *History of Friedrich II of Prussia* (1858). *On Heroes and Hero-Worship and the Heroic in History* (1841) must have been of great interest to Henry Willett, who entitled two of the commemorative sections of his early ceramic collection, 'Hero Worship'.[44]

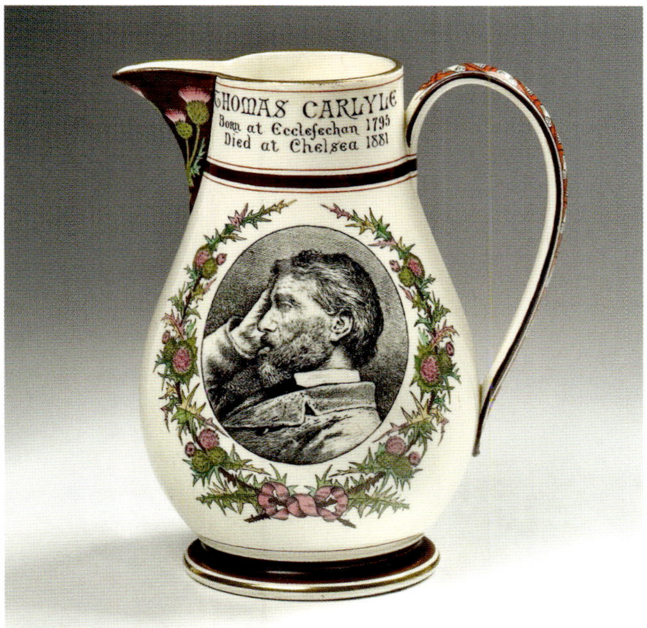

Jug, (**979**), 1881, Staffordshire, Wedgwood, height: 19.7cm, (7¾in), creamware, printed and enamelled. Portrait of Thomas Carlyle, based on a photograph of the writer, taken in the 1860s and produced as a cabinet card by Elliott & Fry.[45] The jug was produced to commemorate his life and work and has a backstamp for the retailer John Mortlock of Oxford Street. On the reverse, a quotation from *Past and Present* (1843) likening the idle man to a potter's botched vessel.[46]

Harriet Beecher Stowe (1811-1896)

The American author, Harriet Beecher was born into a religious family, passionately opposed to slavery. Inspired by the many slave narratives published in the early nineteenth century, *Uncle Tom's Cabin, or Life among the Lowly*, was published in instalments from 1851 to 1852. By 1853 it had sold an astonishing 300,000 copies in book form. On receiving Mrs Stowe at the White House in 1862, President Lincoln is said to have exclaimed (rather patronisingly), 'So this is the little lady who made this big war?' The book shocked Europe with its emotive story of the saintly Tom, a pious, loyal and honest slave and the horrors of slavery. Tom befriends the five-year-old white child, Evangeline, on a steamer travelling down river and, after saving her life, is bought for her. Eva later dies tragically and Tom is sold to a sadistic plantation owner called Legree, who beats Tom to death, convinced that he has helped two runaway slave women. Quantities of souvenirs attest to the popularity and influence of the novel.

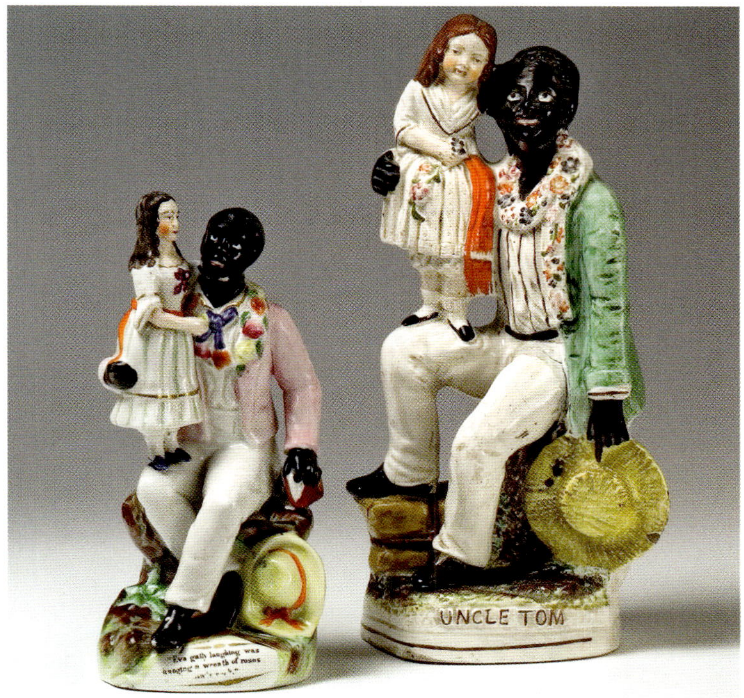

Figure Group, (**983**), c.1856, Staffordshire, height: 20.3cm, (8in), pearlware, enamelled and gilt.
Figure Group, (**984**), c.1856, Staffordshire, height: 25.4cm, (10in), enamelled pearlware. Two groups represent Uncle Tom, the eponymous black hero, with the plantation-owner's daughter, Evangeline, on his knee. The composition may be based on an illustration for the book by Adolph Jean-Baptiste Bayot.

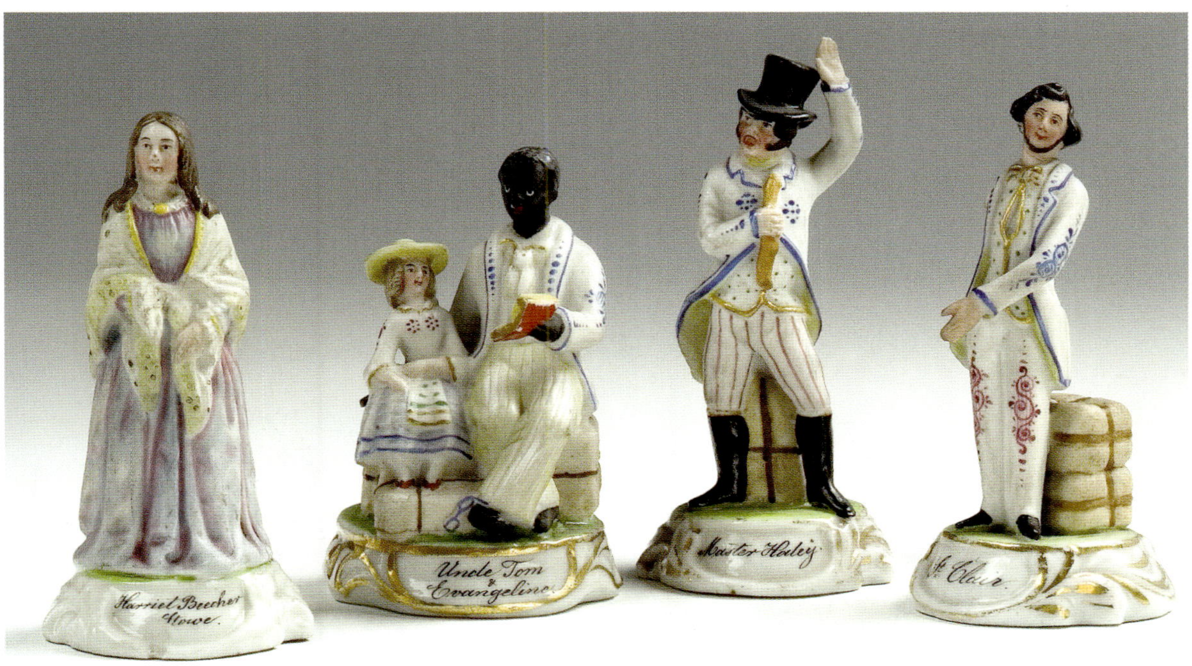

Figures, (**980 + 981 + 982 + 933**) c.1856, Germany, each height: 8.9cm, (3½in), hard-paste porcelain. Tiny figures in cheap porcelain are entitled, 'Harriet Beecher Stowe', 'Uncle Tom and Evangeline', 'St Clair' (Evangeline's father) and 'Master Haley' (**933**).

Charles Dickens (1812-1870)

In 1821, just as Dickens began school, his family, apart from Charles, were sent to London's Marshalsea prison, because his father was deeply in debt. For three years Charles endured appalling conditions in Warren's blacking factory coming near to despair. Although he returned to school, the experience became fictionalised in two of his best-known novels, *David Copperfield* (1849-50) in which his father was the model for Mr Micawber, and *Great Expectations* (1860-61). He began his literary career as a journalist, becoming parliamentary correspondent for the *Morning Chronicle* in 1833. In 1836 he published *The Pickwick Papers* which was hugely popular. Dickens himself spent time in Brighton and wrote *Dombey and Son* (1846-48) while staying at the Bedford Hotel. Phiz, (Hablot Knight Browne), his popular illustrator, who died in 1882, is buried in Brighton's Extra-Mural Cemetery.

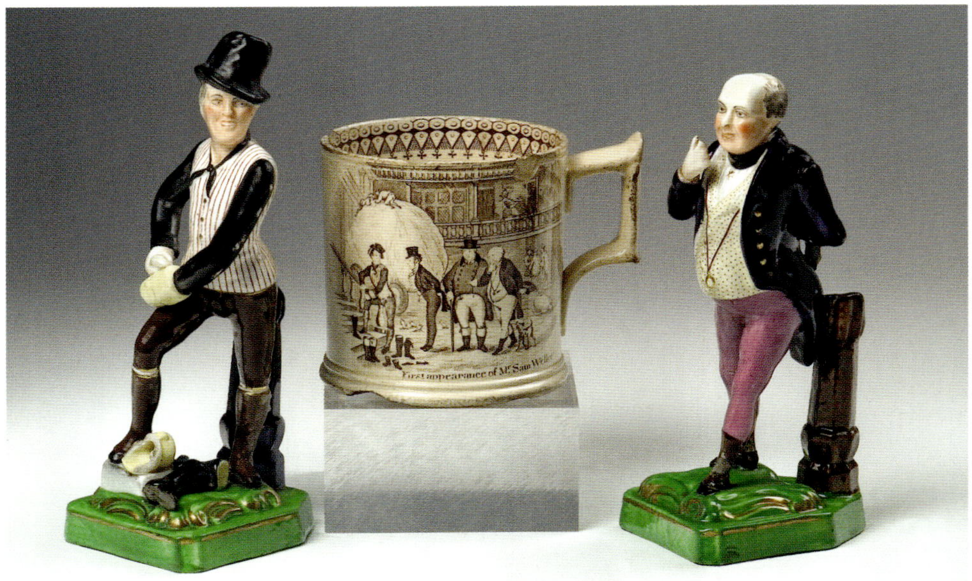

Pair of Figures, **(989 & A)**, c.1840, Staffordshire, height: 19.1cm, (7½in), height: 20.3cm, (8in), earthenware, enamelled and gilt. Individual figures of Sam Weller and Mr Pickwick echo the poses of the characters on the mug.
Mug, **(987)**, 1840, Staffordshire, Cobridge, height: 10.2cm, (4in), brown-printed earthenware. Mug, marked for John & Robert Godwin, printed with copies of Phiz illustrations for *The Pickwick Papers;* 'First appearance of Mr Sam Weller' and, on reverse, 'Mr Pickwick addresses the club'.

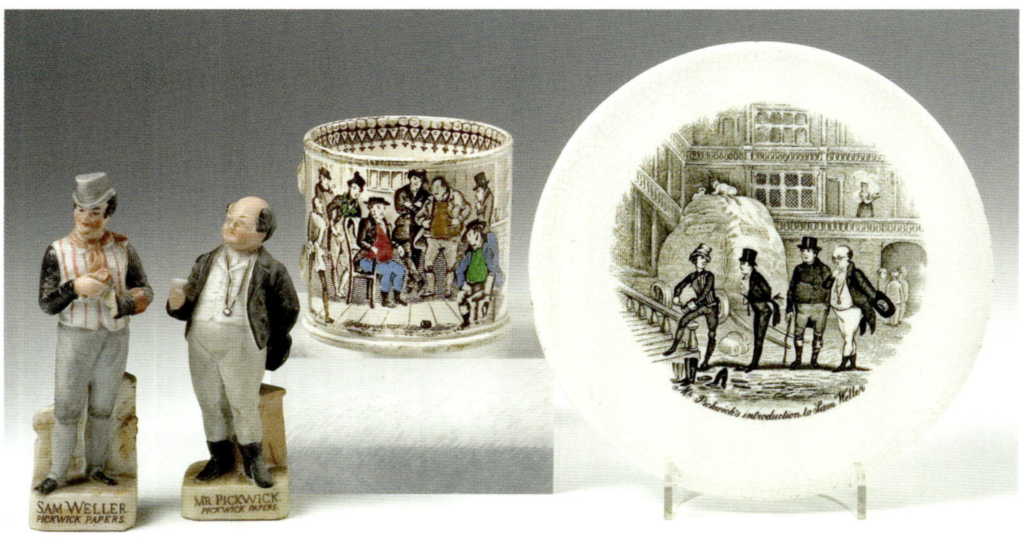

Pair of Figures, **(R2454.43 & 44)**,[47] c.1880, Germany, height: 11cm, (4⅜in), height: 12.7cm, (5in), hard-paste porcelain. Phiz's illustration inspired this pair of figures.
Mug, **(990)**, c.1840, Staffordshire, height: 7cm, (2¾in), brown-printed earthenware Scenes include, 'Mr Pickwick having his portrait taken in the Debtors' prison'.
Teapot Stand, **(988)**, c.1840, Staffordshire, diameter: 16.5cm, (6½in), brown-printed earthenware. Copy of Phiz illustration, 'Mr Pickwick's introduction to Sam Weller'.

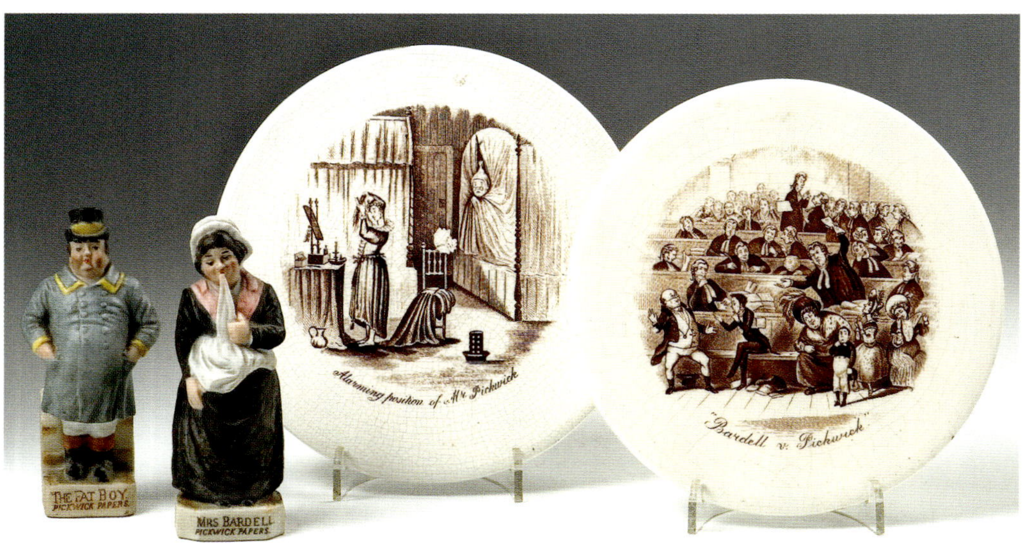

Pair of Figures, **(R2454.45 & 46)** c.1880, Germany, height: 11.5cm, (4½in), height: 12cm, (4¾in), hard-paste porcelain. Figures represent Mrs Bardell and The Fat Boy from *Pickwick Papers.*
Two Teapot Stands, **(992 + 993)**, c.1840, Staffordshire, each diameter: 16.5cm, (6½in), brown-printed earthenware. Printed with Phiz illustrations to *The Pickwick Papers.*

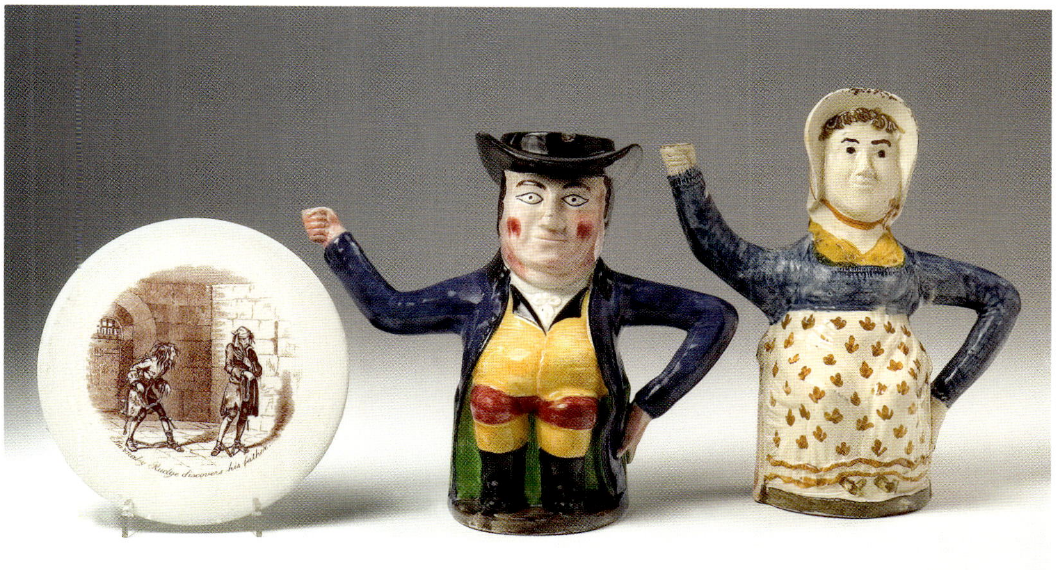

Teapot Stand, **(999)**, c.1845, Staffordshire, diameter: 16.5cm, (6½in), brown-printed earthenware. Printed with a scene from *Barnaby Rudge* (published 1841).
Two Teapots, **(994 & A)**, c.1840, Staffordshire, each height: 21.6cm, (8½in), enamelled earthenware and Prattware. Novelty teapots, modelled as a man and a woman, considered by Willett to represent 'Mr and Mrs Weller Snr.'

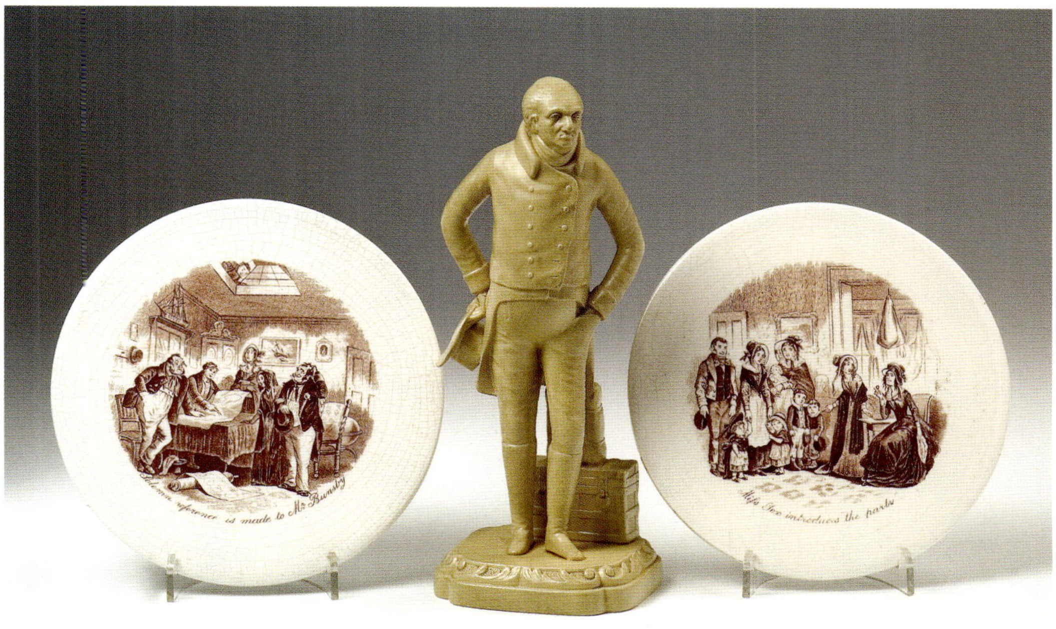

Two Teapot Stands, **(1000 + 1001)**, c.1850, Staffordshire, each diameter: 16.5cm, (6½in), brown-printed earthenware. Printed with scenes from *Dombey and Son* (1846-48).
Figure, **(995)**, 1840, Staffordshire, height: 22.9cm, (9in), smear-glazed stoneware. Figure of Ralph Nickleby, from *Nicholas Nickleby* (1838-39), impressed, 'Published by Ridgway, Son & Co. on 1 September 1840'.[48]

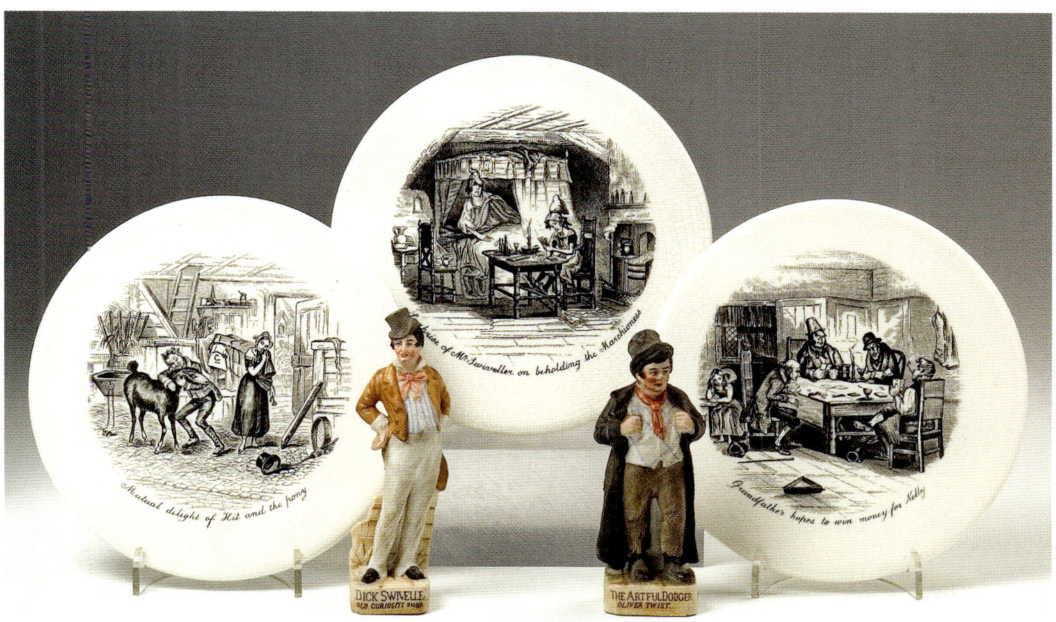

Three Teapot Stands **(996 + 997 + 998)** c.1850, Staffordshire, each diameter: 16.5cm, (6½in), printed earthenware. Printed with illustrations from *The Old Curiosity Shop* (1840).
Pair of Figures, **(R2454.47 & 48)**, c.1880, Germany, height: 12.3cm, (4⅞in), height: 11cm, (4⅜in), hard-paste porcelain. Two figures represent 'The Artful Dodger' from *Oliver Twist* (1837-39) and 'Dick Swiveller' from *The Old Curiosity Shop*.

Aesop's Fables

The first English translation of Aesop's Fables, *The Book of the Subtyle Historyes and Fables of Esope*, was published by William Caxton in 1484. The most popular edition and a publishing phenomenon, which remained in print for over 100 years, was *Fables of Aesop and Others*, published by Samuel Croxall in 1722, with engraved designs by Elisha Kirkall. They inspired the decoration of some of the earliest tiles produced in Liverpool using the new medium of transfer printing.[49]

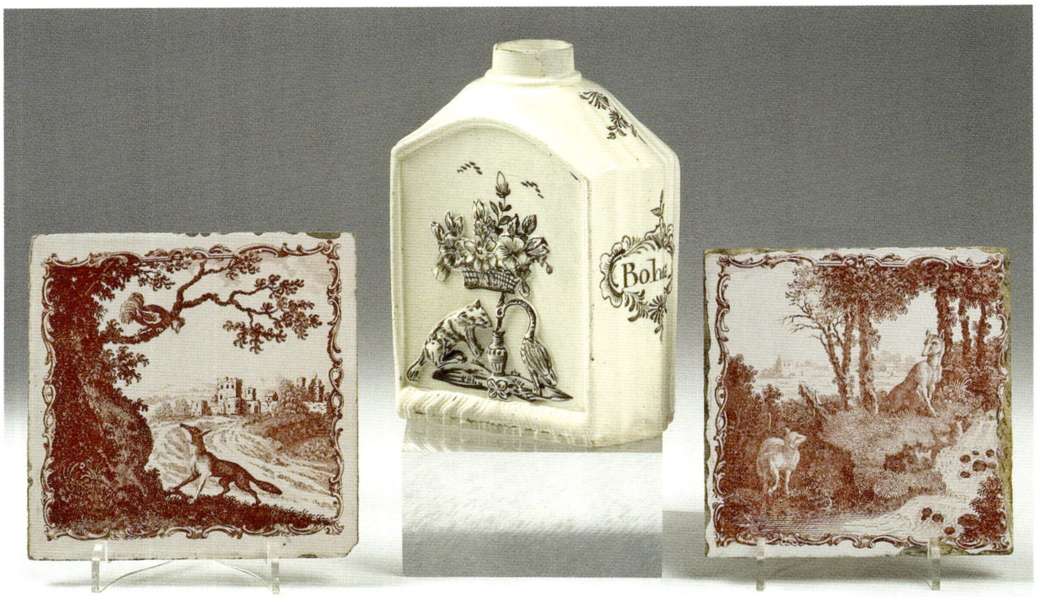

Tiles, (1003 + 1004) c.1765, Liverpool, each height: 12.7cm, (5in), printed, tin-glazed earthenware. John Sadler used Kirkall's illustrations for more than 40 transfer prints on tiles, including 'The Cock and the Fox', and 'The Wolf and the Lamb'.[50]

Tea Canister, (1002), c.1770, possibly Devon, height: 15.3cm, (6in), enamelled creamware. Relief-moulded with Elisha Kirkall's illustration to 'The Fox and the Stork'; the fox tries to drink from a bottle and the stork from a plate. Inscribed, 'Bohea', a type of black China tea.[51]

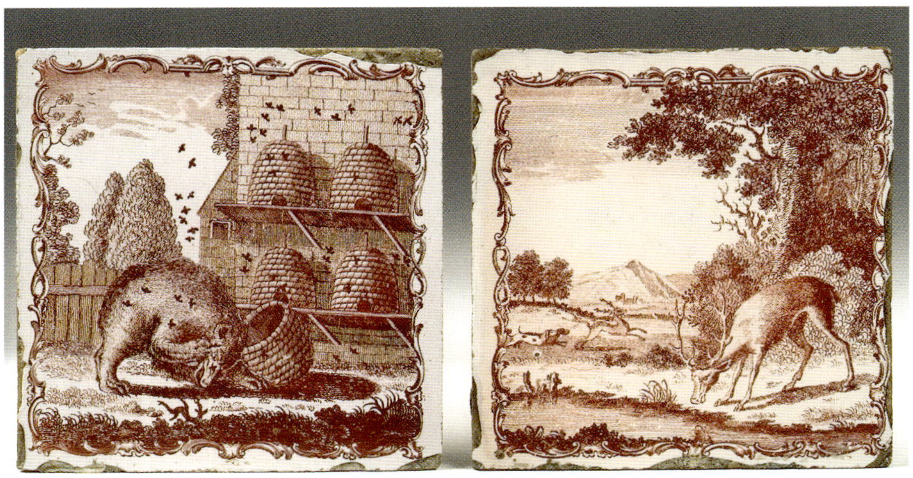

Tiles, (1005 + 1007) c.1765, Liverpool, each height: 12.7cm, (5in), printed, tin-glazed earthenware. John Sadler used Kirkall's illustrations for 'The Bear and the Beehives'[52] and 'The stag admiring his own reflection'.

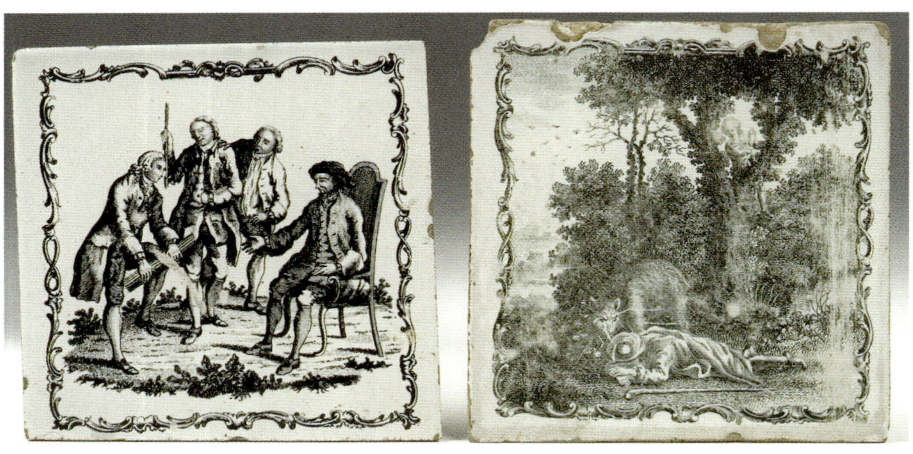

Tiles, (1008 + 1006) c.1765, Liverpool, each height: 12.7cm, (5in), printed, tin-glazed earthenware. 'The Man with the Bundle of Sticks' is not part of Sadler's main fable series and may be earlier.[53] Kirkall's image, 'The Bear and Two Travellers'[54] illustrated Aesop's Fables.

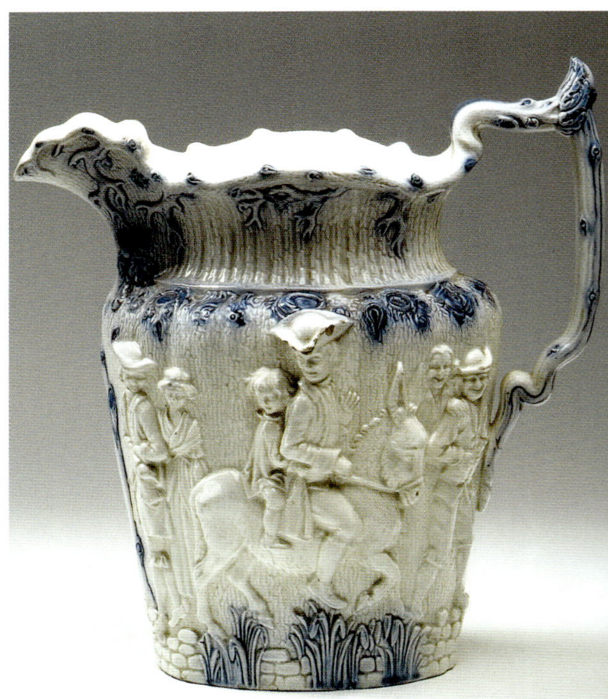

Jug, (1009), c.1850, Staffordshire, height: 25.4cm, (10in), earthenware, tinted underglaze. Relief-moulded with 'The Old Man and the Ass', after French fable-writer, La Fontaine. Jug marked for Mellon, Venables & Co. Royal Patent.

Dr Syntax

The fictional cleric and incurable Romantic was an immensely popular fictional character. Verses by William Combe (1742-1823), illustrated by Thomas Rowlandson (1756-1827), were first published in the *Poetical Magazine* from 1809 under the title *The Tour of Dr. Syntax in search of the Picturesque.* From 1812 they appeared as separate volumes, documenting the excursions of the comic curate and schoolmaster.

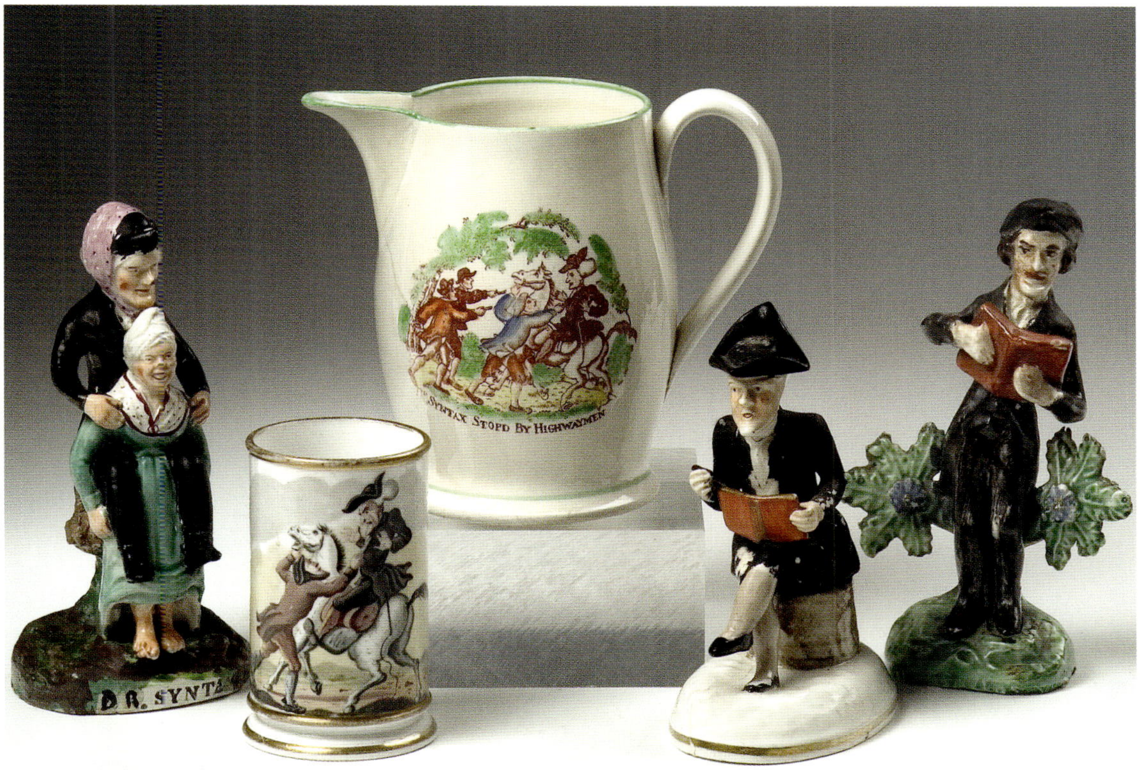

Figure Group, (1014), c.1820, Staffordshire, height: 15.3cm, (6in), enamelled pearlware. Dr Syntax being carried by an old woman, also called 'Debarquant à Calais'.[55]
Spill Vase, (**1013**), c.1810, Derby, height: 8.9cm, (3½in), enamelled, soft-paste porcelain.
Jug, (**1012**), c.1820, Staffordshire, height: 12.7cm, (5in), red-printed creamware, enamelled. Spill vase and jug both illustrate the dramatic incident, 'DR SYNTAX STOPD BY HIGHWAYMEN' while riding his trusty mare, Grizzle.
Figure, (1011), c.1830, Staffordshire, height: 13.3cm, (5¼in), earthenware, enamelled and gilt. Dr Syntax sits holding a pen and a sketchbook, 'Drawing after Nature' (published in *Ackermann's Repository* in 1813).
Figure, (1010), c.1820, Staffordshire, height: 14.6cm, (5¾in), enamelled pearlware. Dr Syntax stands reading a book.

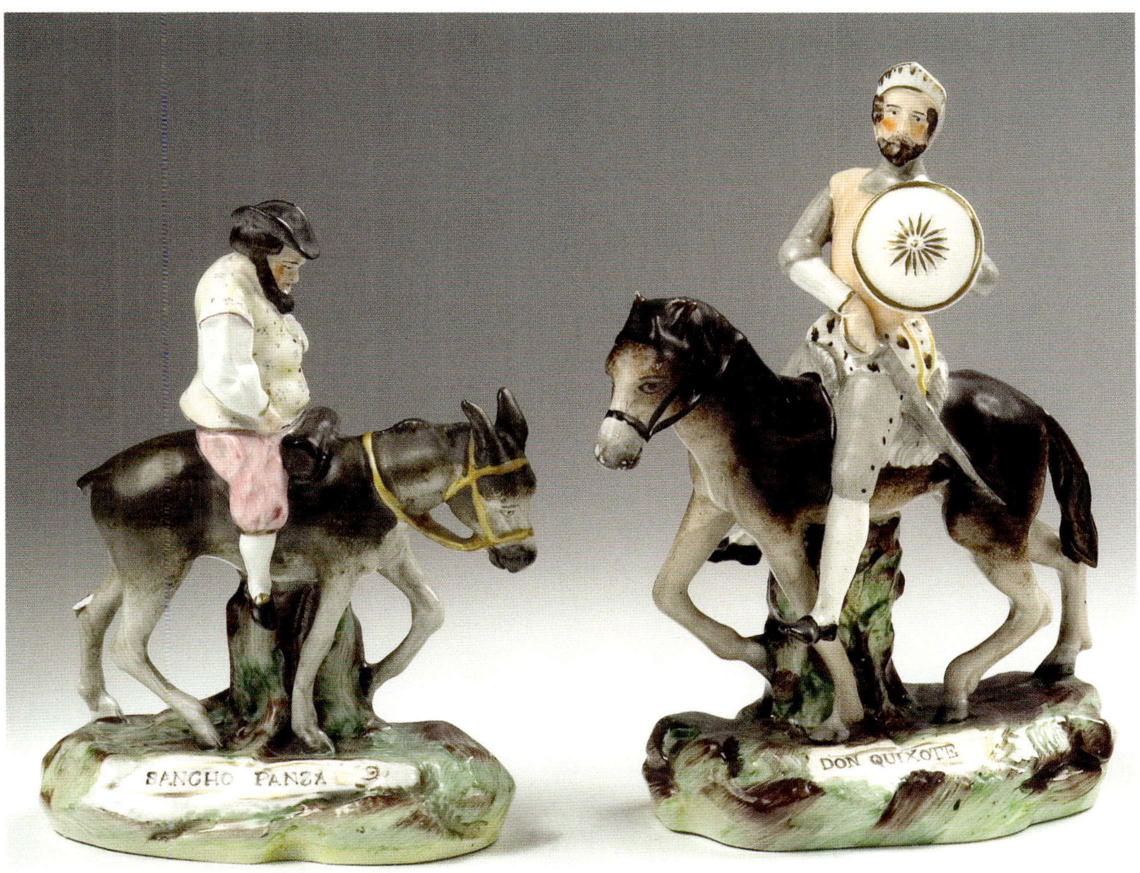

Figure, (**1016**), 1840, Staffordshire, height: 20.3cm, (8in), enamelled earthenware.
Figure, (**1015**), 1840, Staffordshire, height: 24.1cm, (9½in), enamelled earthenware. Pair of equestrian figures entitled, 'DON QUIXOTE' and 'SANCHO PANZA', the comic heroes created by Miguel Cervantes (1547-1616) in his masterpiece, *Don Quixote* (published in 1606) a classic of Spanish literature. The high-minded but eccentric cavalier, (in full armour) is mounted on his skinny horse Rosinante while his trusty squire, Sancho Panza rides his ass, Dapple.

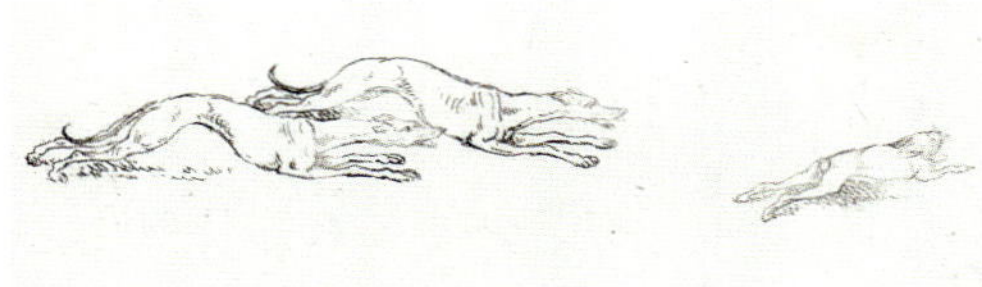

Chapter 15

COMBAT SPORTS & FIELD SPORTS

Animal Fights

Entertainments that exploited the natural aggression of animals were popular in England in the Middle Ages. The baiting of bears, bulls and badgers were highlights of the periodic 'wakes' or holidays, which punctuated the calendar of medieval village life, while cockfights were arranged throughout the year. Although these diversions were most popular with ordinary people, at first they were regularly attended by the nobility. Queen Elizabeth I was devoted to bear-baiting. In Shakespeare's day the Bear Gardens adjoined the Globe Theatre in Southwark. Animal baiting was temporarily banned by the Puritans during the Commonwealth but was revived after the Restoration of Charles II in 1660. Nearly a century later the London magistrate, Sir John Fielding, complained that diversions such as 'Bull-baitings, bear-baitings, cock-matches and such races as are contrary to the law ... are the thieves that rob the ... labourers of their precious time'.[1] Bear-baiting finally died out when bears became scarce.

Bears and bulls were baited by bulldogs. The original large mastiff was replaced around 1800 by the Staffordshire bull-terrier, a cross between the bulldog and the Old English terrier, attempting to combine the strength of the former with the agility of the latter. The hapless bull was tied to a stake in the market place, a publican's yard or a nearby field and was set upon by dogs, one by one. They went for the muzzle, the dewlap or the genitals, causing injury but not death. Butchers believed that beef-meat was tenderised by baiting before slaughter. The dogs, however, could be gored or have their backs broken when tossed on the bull's horns.

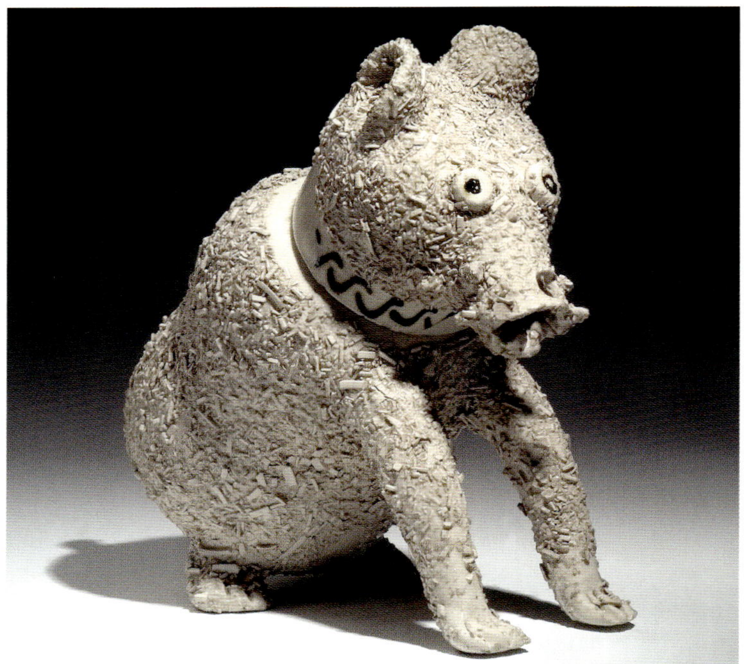

Bear Jug, (**1391**), c.1740, Staffordshire, height: 23.5cm, (9¼in), white salt-glazed stoneware. Bear's detachable head forms a cup. Head and body covered with shredded clay to indicate fur and its collar, decorated with manganese, forms the neck of the cup. Pierced snout once fitted with links of ceramic chain.

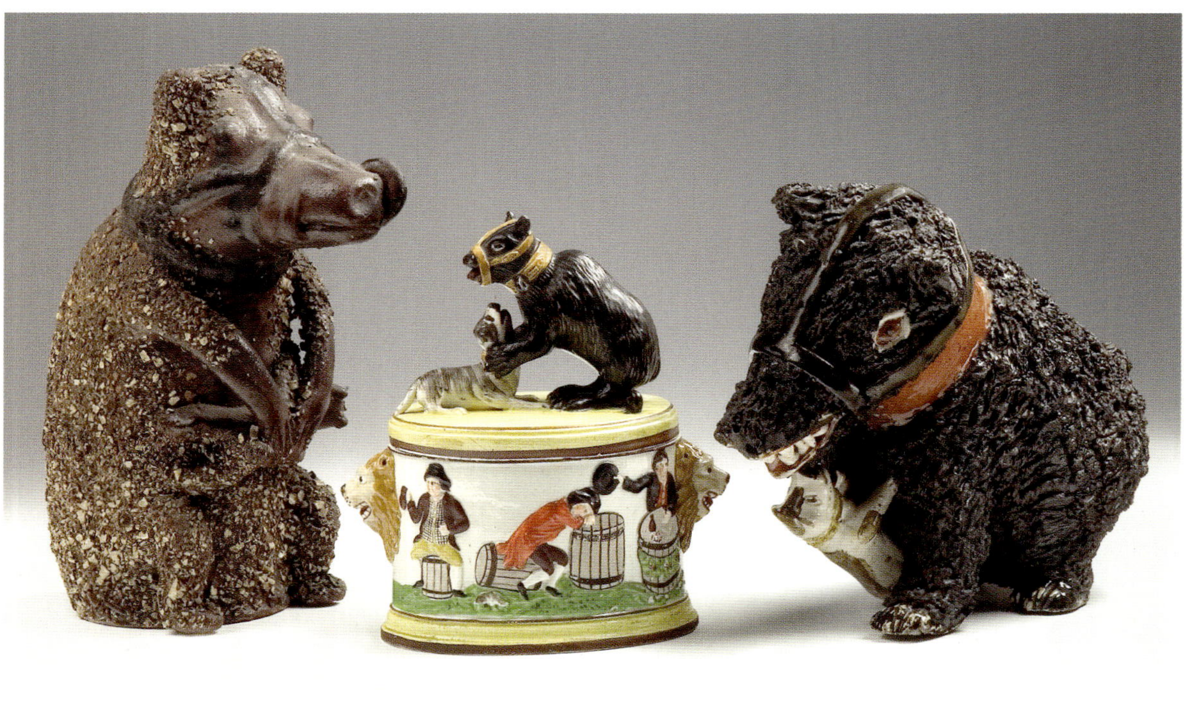

Figure, (**1027**), c.1780, Staffordshire, height: 25.4cm, (10in), earthenware. Bear with dark brown shredded clay for fur and a ring through its nose, as it overpowers a dog.
Tobacco Box, (**1024**), c.1820, Staffordshire, height: 19.1cm, (7½in), enamelled pearlware. Sides relief-moulded with scenes of men drinking and carousing, typical behaviour at a baiting contest. Figure of a bear, wearing harness and collar, pins down a bull terrier on flat lid. Side handles moulded as lion masks.[2]
Figure, (**1026**), c.1780, Staffordshire, height: 21.6cm, (8½in), earthenware. Bear with black, shredded clay as fur and a broad red collar. It fights a small black and white dog.

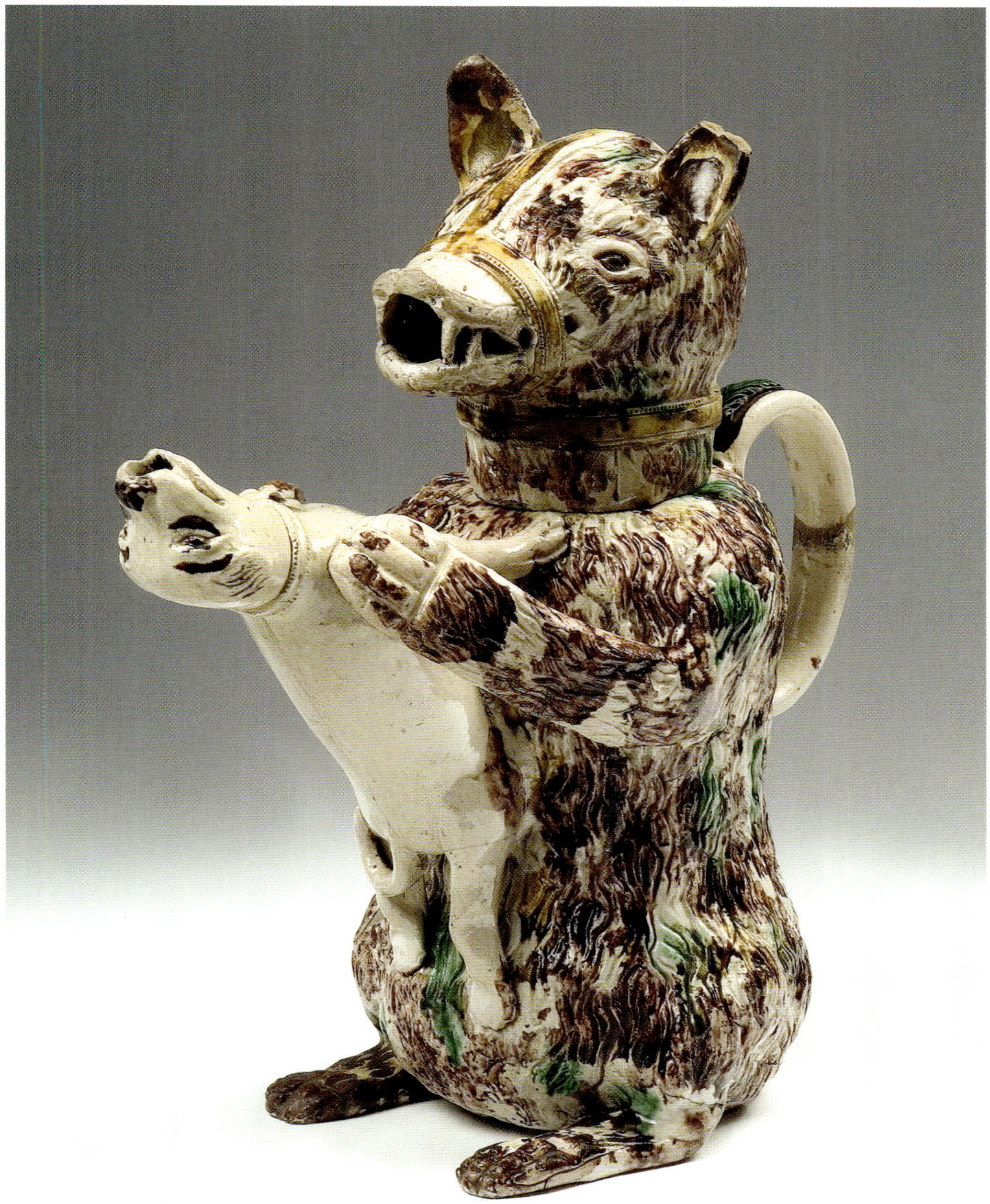

Bear Jug, (**1025**), c.1780, Staffordshire, height: 33cm, (13in), lead-glazed earthenware. Bear modelled grappling with a bull terrier, which forms the spout. The bear's muzzled head forms a cup.

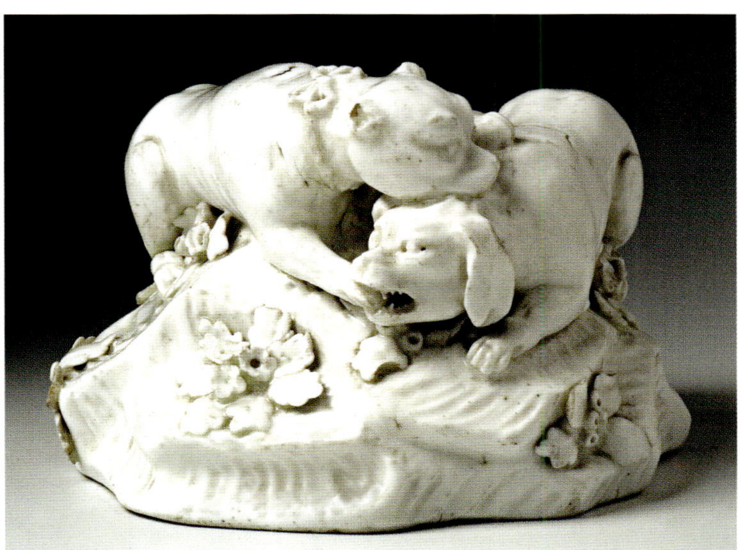

Inkwell, (**1028**), c.1760, London, Bow, height: 7.6cm, (3in), soft-paste porcelain. Group modelled as two dogs fighting on a rocky base around an inkwell. One muscular bulldog overpowers another dog, possibly a spaniel.

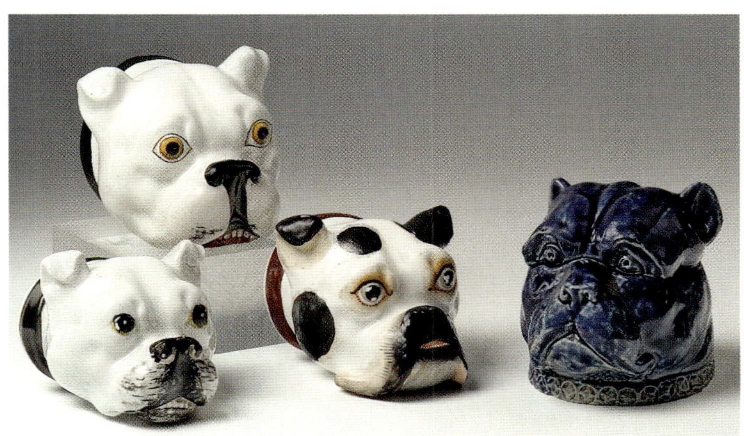

Three Stirrup Cups, (**1017 & A & B**), c.1810, Staffordshire, height: 10.2cm, (4in), enamelled pearlware. Modelled as the heads of bulldogs with collars and clipped ears; two are white while one has extensive black patches. Perhaps they were passed round at dogfights just as similar cups, modelled as foxes and hounds were at meets before the hunt set off?

Jar Lid, (**1018**), c.1800, Staffordshire, height: 9.5cm, (3¾in), earthenware. Crudely modelled head of a bulldog appears to be the lid of a tobacco jar.

Bull-baiting

By 1820 animal baiting was under threat but Staffordshire remained one of its last strongholds. In 1825 the *Pottery Mercury* remarked that the loss of bull-baiting 'would rejoice any person of humane feeling' and a truly horrific episode took place in 1833 at Rowley Regis Wake,

> a two-year old bull was worried in the most brutal manner. Either on Monday or Tuesday one of this bull's horns was broken off, and the following day the other shared the same fate and a portion of the tongue was also torn out of its mouth by one of the dogs. On the Thursday he was again dragged to the stake and worried for hours, the whole of his head and face being mangled and covered in blood, in a manner too shocking to describ. [3]

The disruptive behaviour of the spectators and the barbarity inherent in the spectacle of these activities became increasingly less tolerated. Tracts were circulated and sermons delivered condemning cruel sports. Eleven bills were presented to Parliament between 1800 and 1835 in an effort to suppress them. In 1824 the Society for the Prevention of Cruelty to Animals was founded. Even after the Cruelty to Animals Act was passed in 1835, there were numerous infringements of the law. Even today there are cases of illegal cockfights, dogfights and badger-baiting.

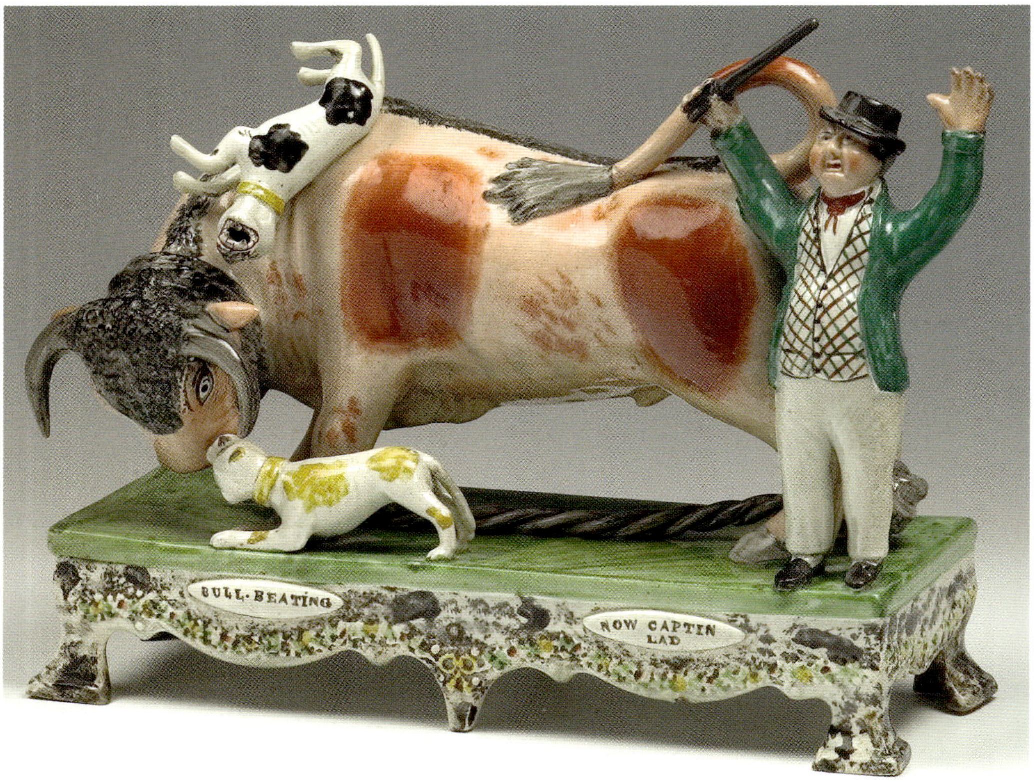

Figure Group, (**1019**), c.1825, Staffordshire, height: 29.2cm, (11½in), enamelled pearlware. Table-based plinth captioned, 'BULL.BEATING', and 'NOW CAPTIN LAD [*sic*]', shouted by a man, probably the owner of the dogs. Bull is tethered to a stake with a stout rope, while small bulldogs or bull terriers fearlessly attack it. The bull has tossed one of them over its shoulder.

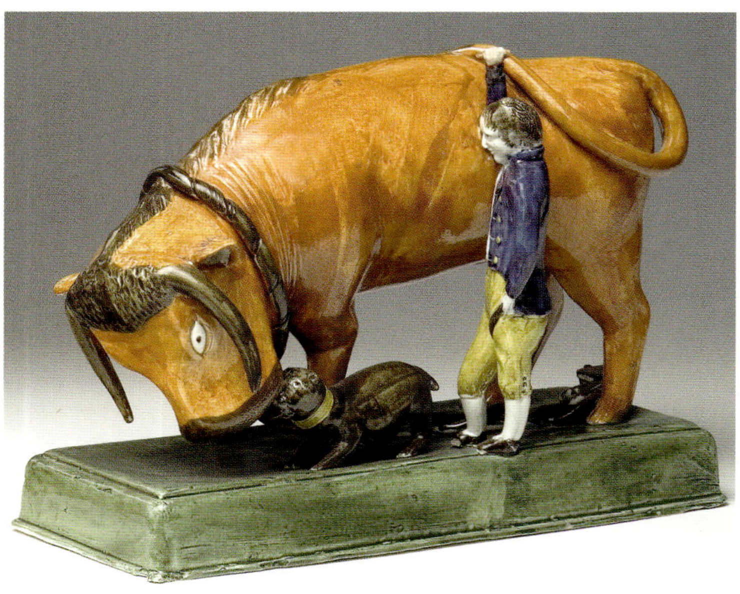

Figure Group, (**1020**), c.1825, possibly Yorkshire, height: 22.2cm, (8¾in), enamelled pearlware. Bull-baiting group; a small man and a single terrier stand beside a large, tethered bull.

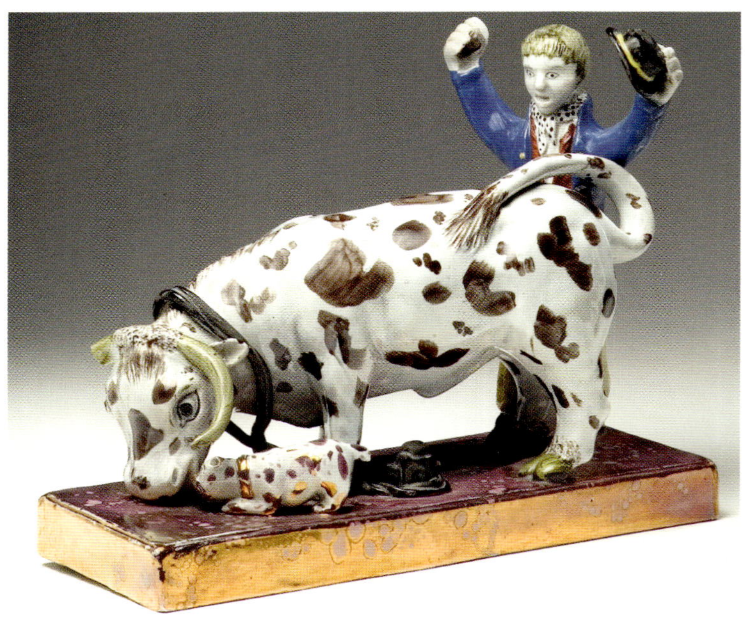

Figure Group, (**1021**), c.1825, Staffordshire, height: 21.6cm, (8½in), pearlware, enamelled and lustred. Bull-baiting group; large man waves his hat to encourage spotted terrier to attack a small, tethered bull.

Figure Group, (**1022**), c.1825, Staffordshire, height: 17.8cm, (7in), pearlware, enamelled and lustred. Bull-baiting group; a man waves his hat and gnarled cudgel to encourage two dogs to attack tethered bull.
Jug, (**1023**), c.1825, Staffordshire, height: 16.5cm, (6½in), pearlware, red-printed and enamelled. Naively decorated with scenes of bull-baiting and an interior with men at a table (probably betting). Scrolling monogram, 'JIR', beneath spout.

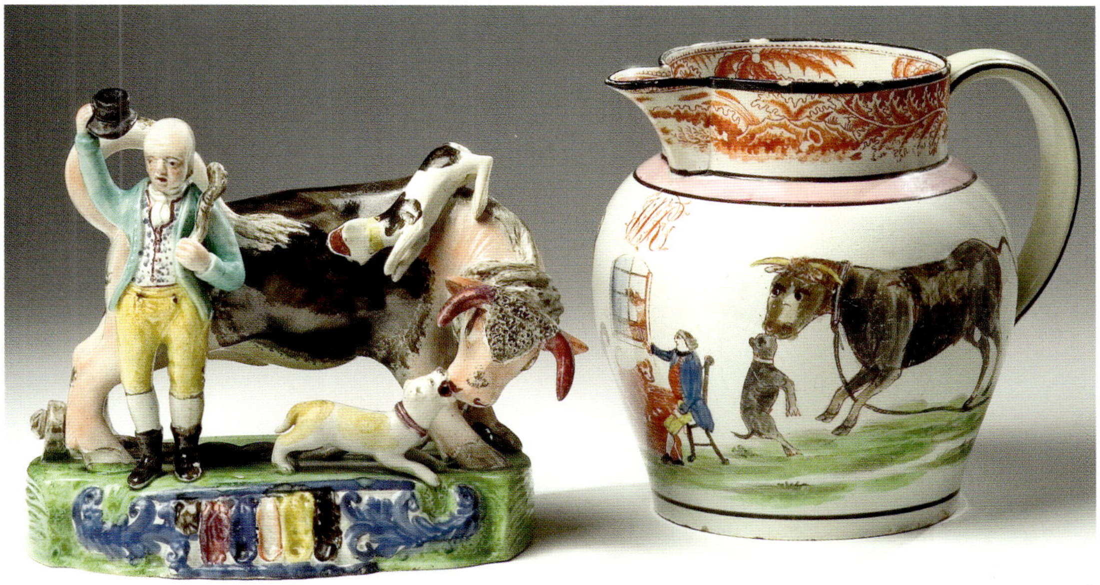

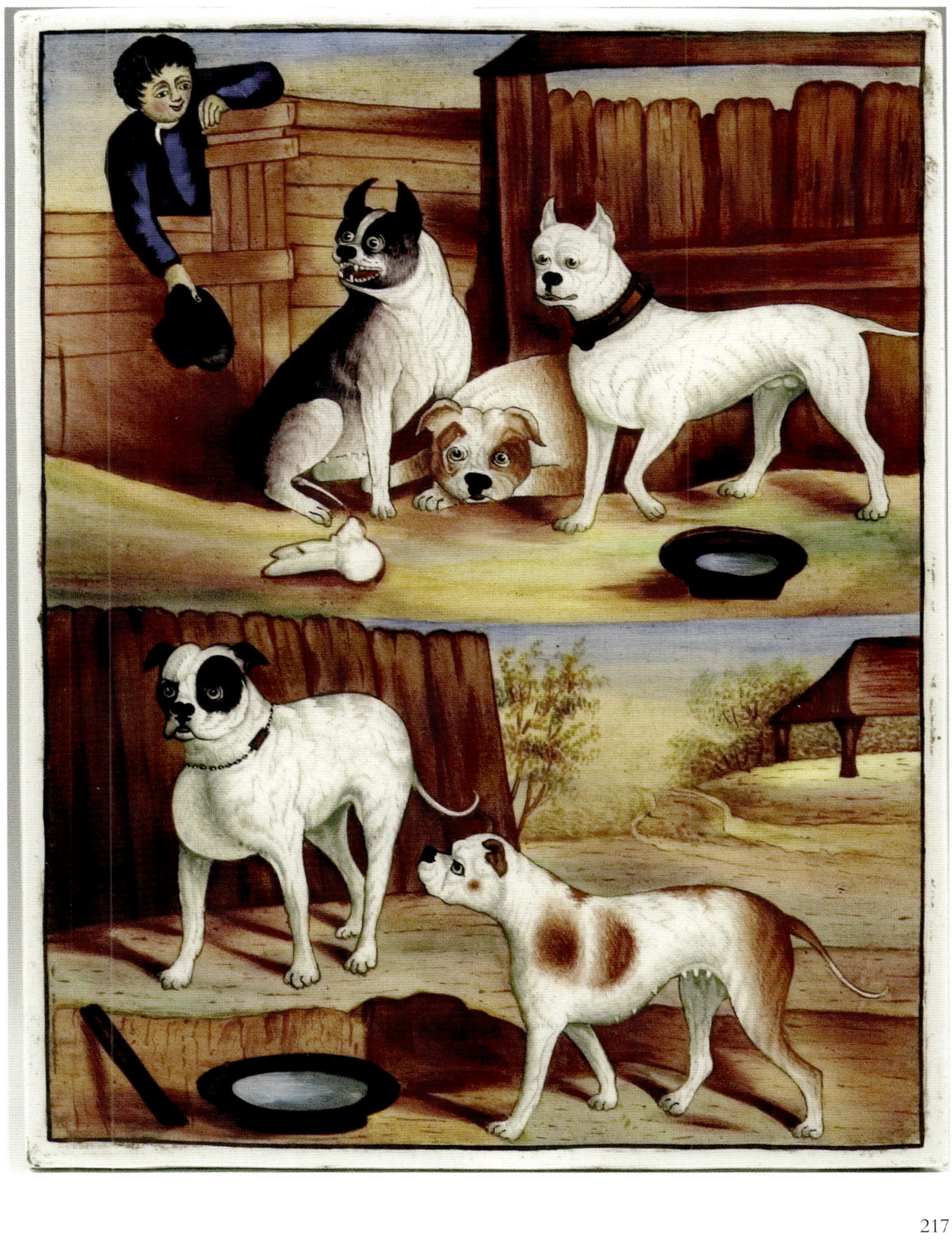

Plaque, (1204), c.1820, Staffordshire, height: 30.5cm, (12in), enamelled bone china. Painted with two group portraits of champion fighting dogs. Above: 'Wasp', 'Child' and 'Billy' (bred by the Duke of Hamilton), whose portraits were published in 1809.[4] 'Crib' and his mother 'Rosa', (owned by Harry Verelst Esq) were painted by Samuel Raven and published 1817.[5] According to the Kennel Club this print was the most popular early-nineteenth century image of dogs.

Cockfighting

The cruel but popular pastime of 'throwing at cocks', where a tethered cockerel was stoned (especially on Shrove Tuesday), died out in the early-eighteenth century but the popularity of cockfighting continued unabated well into the nineteenth century. Pairs of prize cocks, equipped with metal spurs, were set on each other and fought to the death in custom-built miniature amphitheatres. The cockpit was one of the few places where gentlemen and commoners mingled freely but it also became notorious for heavy drinking and furious betting. Cockfighting was made illegal in 1849, not only because of the cruelty involved but also because of the difficulty in controlling the gambling.

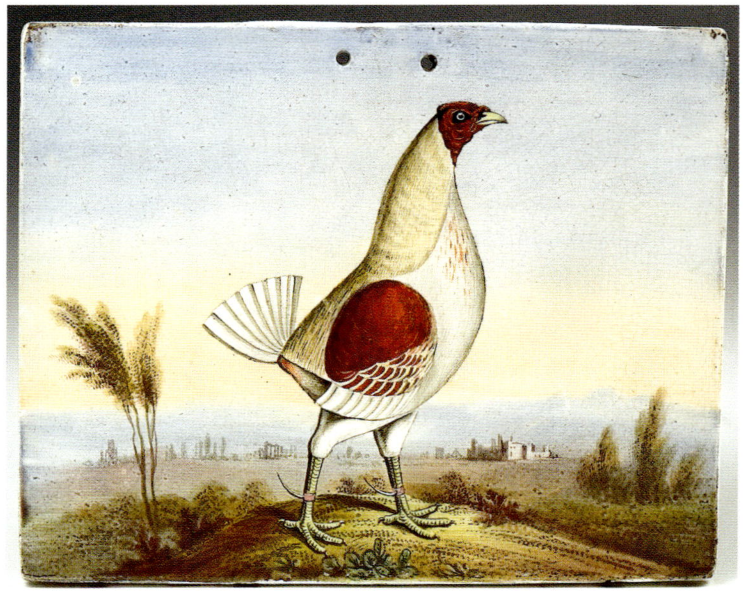

Plaque, (**1046**), c.1810, height: 21cm, (8¼in), enamelled, soft-paste porcelain. A beautifully painted portrait of a creamy white champion cockerel in fighting trim with red wings and spurs. The low viewpoint lets it dominate the distant landscape.

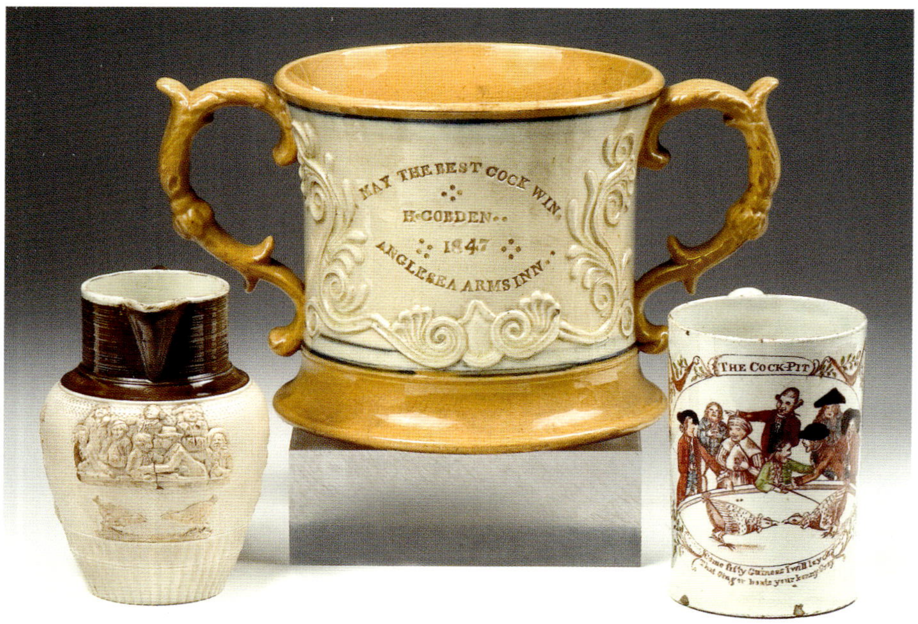

Jug, (1049), c.1790, Staffordshire, height: 13.4cm, (5¼in), part-glazed, cream stoneware. Applied with relief sprigs of Hogarth's cockpit scene, adapted by Sayer & Bennett whose print was published in 1776.[6] Possibly made by Turner of Lane End.
Two-handled Cup, (**1047**), 1847, Staffordshire, height: 15.3cm, (6in), slip-decorated earthenware. Relief-moulded and impressed, 'MAY THE BEST COCK WIN / H. COBDEN 1847 / ANGLESEA ARMS INN'. Cobden was the last trainer of fighting cocks for the Duke of Richmond. On retiring, he ran the Anglesea Arms, a tavern at Halnaker, near Goodwood, when this cup was presented to him by his admirers.[7]
Mug, (**1050**), c.1790, Staffordshire, Lane End, height: 12.1cm, (4¾in), pearlware, printed and enamelled. Print entitled 'THE COCK PIT,' adapted by John Aynsley from Sayer & Bennett's print of 1776. The cockfight takes place at the Royal Cockpit, Birdcage Walk, near St James's Park.[8] A man on the left gestures to the coins he has flung into the ring and probably speaks the lines inscribed beneath; 'Come fifty Guineas I will lay / That Ginger beats your bonny Grey'. This may refer to the famous Ginger Red, a celebrated cock that won against long odds at the Royal Cockpit and subsequently at Guildford.[9]

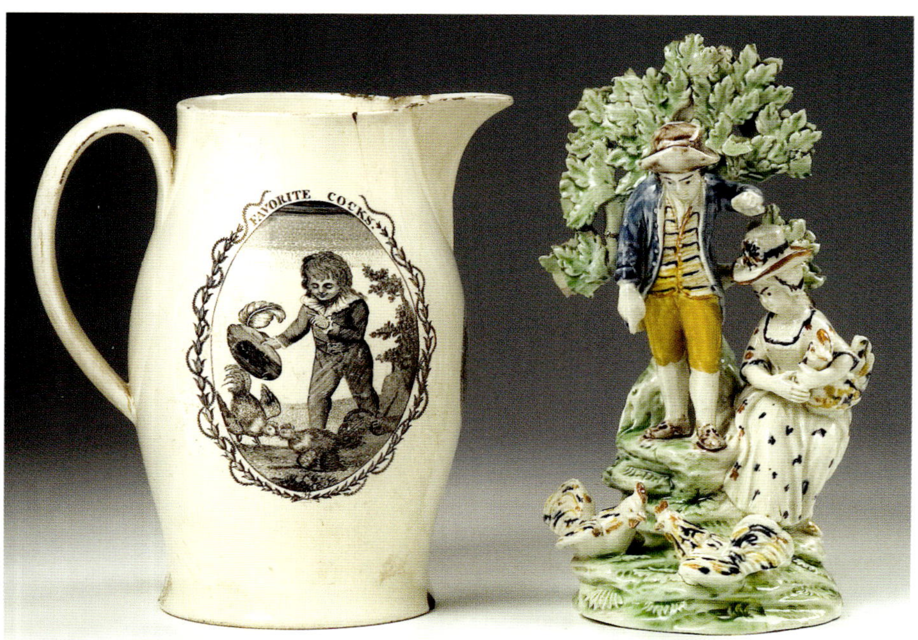

Jug, (1052), c.1796, Staffordshire, height: 21.6cm, (8in), printed creamware. Inscribed, 'FAVOURITE COCKS / (34)'[10] a well-dressed boy watches cocks fighting. The image is taken from an untitled print by Bartolozzi after William Hamilton, published in 1795.[11]
Figure Group, (1051), c.1800, Staffordshire, height: 23.5cm, (9¼in), Pratt coloured pearlware. Two cocks fighting, watched by a man and woman sitting on a rock. She has another cockerel under her arm.

Two-handled Cup, (1044), c.1850, Staffordshire, height: 13.4cm, (5¼in), earthenware, printed and enamelled. Printed with fighting cocks in different attitudes, inscribed, 'A Challenge / A Set To / Heeling / A Knock down blow / A Rally / the Death'.
Plate, (1043), c.1830, Staffordshire, diameter: 21.6cm, (8½in), soft-paste porcelain, red-printed, enamelled and gilt. Black fighting cock painted in the centre with motto: 'SEMPER PRONUS'. Printed border with vignettes of stags.
Jug, (1045), c.1850, Staffordshire, height: 20.3cm, (8in), earthenware, printed and enamelled. Printed with fighting cocks in different attitudes, (as 1044).

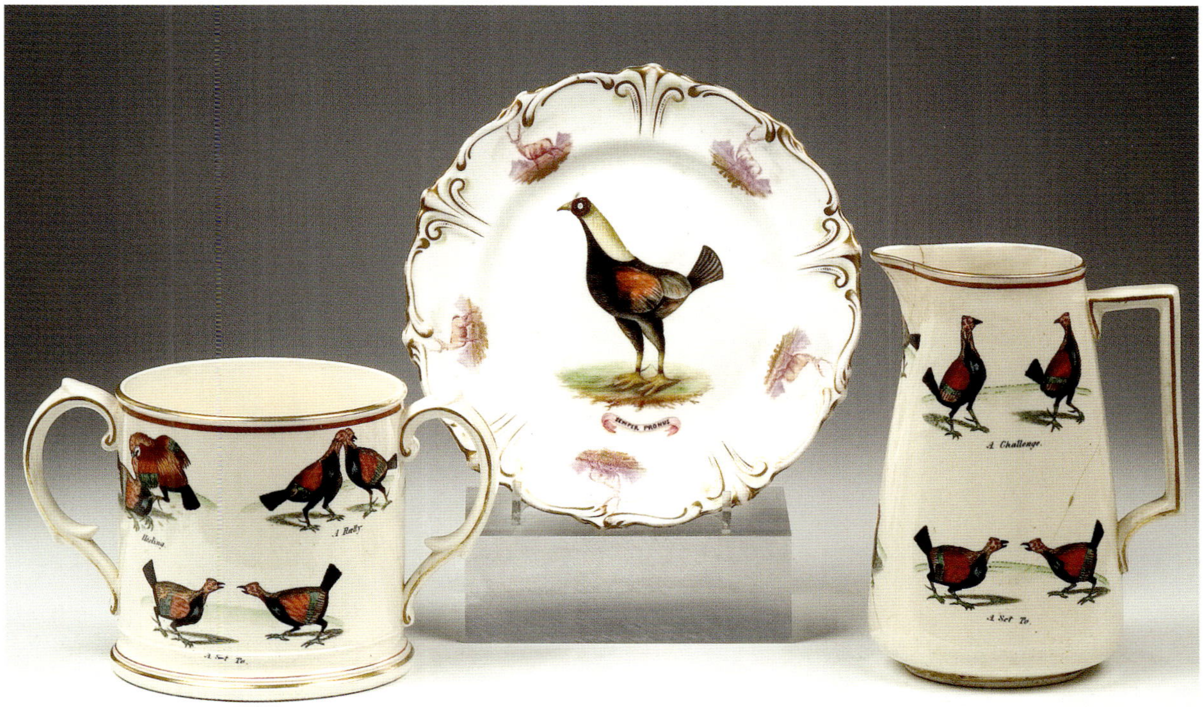

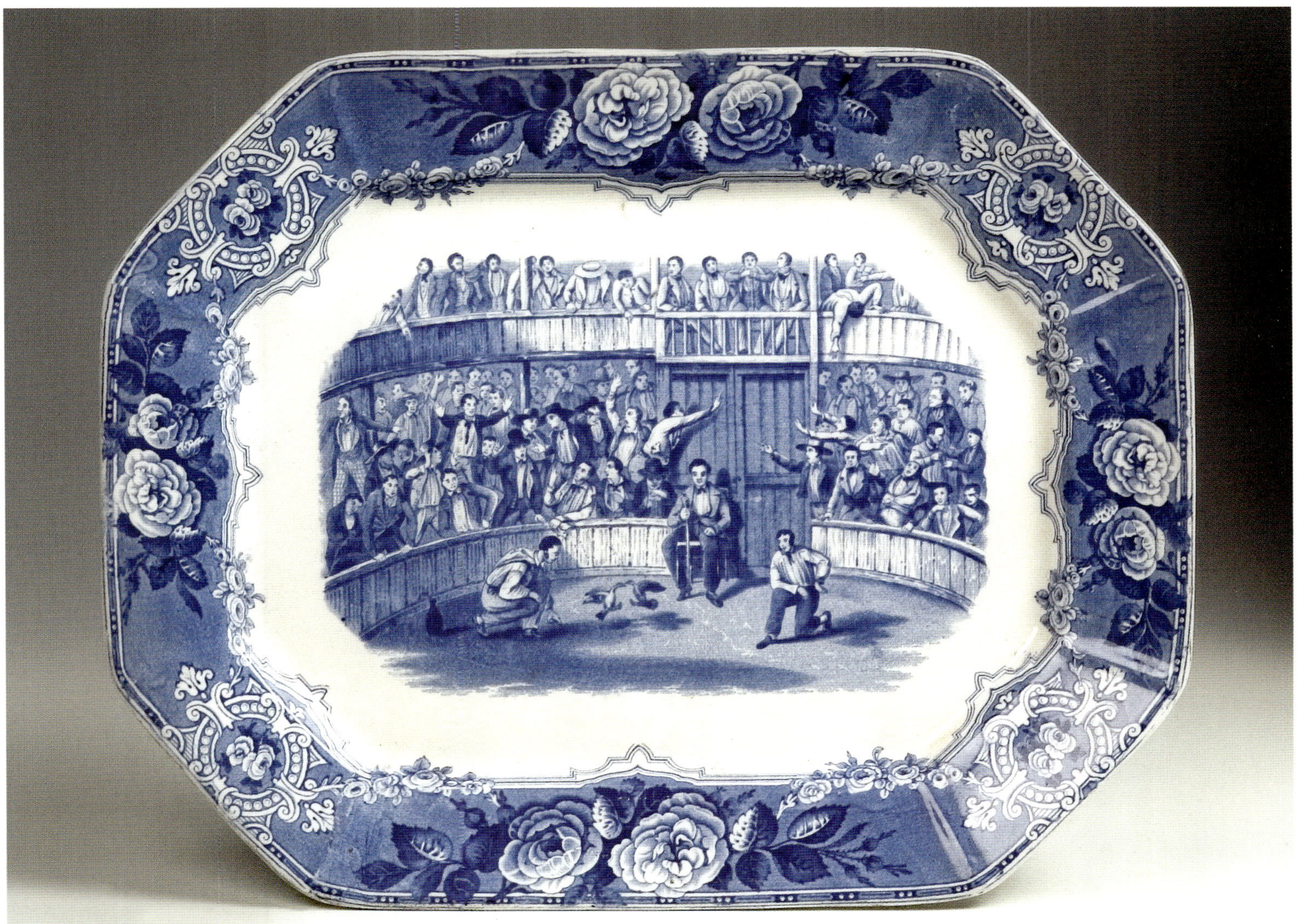

Serving Dish, **(1048)**, c.1890, Staffordshire, height: 34.3cm, (13½in), blue-printed, earthenware. Scene of cockfighting before a Spanish crowd, made by William Adams.

Prizefighting

'There are two things that an Englishman understands, hard words and hard blows', wrote William Hazlitt, in 1826. Pugilism (the forerunner of boxing), began at fairgrounds during village 'wakes' or holidays. James Figg, an itinerant showman, excelled at 'Cudgelling, single stick, back sword (fencing) and pugilism' in the early-eighteenth century. Jack Broughton, a pupil of Figg, drafted the first set of rules for the prize ring in 1743, after accidentally killing an opponent. This code proposed the appointment of seconds and umpires, set limits on hitting, allowed for time between rounds and falls and divided the prize money.

It was customary to fight within a 20-foot square or 'ring' (probably named after a popular sparring area in Hyde Park) bounded by eight posts and two rope rails, attended by seconds and bottle holders who dispensed water. Pugilists fought with bare fists which they 'pickled' in order to toughen the skin. The Championship of Tom Cribb from 1809-22 marked a golden age for prizefighting when the 'Fancy' or followers of the sport, included the Prince Regent, the Whig leader, Charles James Fox and many of the nobility. Strong links were established with the United States and the first of the great black boxers emerged, fighters like Bill Richmond and Tom Molineux. Other 'scientific' boxers included Daniel Mendoza and 'Gentleman' John Jackson, who numbered Lord Byron amongst the aristocratic pupils at his Bond Street Academy. Young hopefuls were often trained by successful champions; Mendoza was discovered by Humphries, Molineux was promoted by the more senior Bill Richmond and Tom Cribb nominated Tom Spring as his successor.

From the 1820s to the 1850s the game fell into disrepute at the hands of dishonest promoters and even the best contestants were open to bribes. Introduced in 1838, the New Rules of Prizefighting made the sport a little more humane but had little effect in moderating the depravity of the game at that time. Tom Sayers proved a worthy champion from 1857 and helped raise the status of the game. In 1864 the Marquess of Queensberry's Rules were drawn up to govern boxing contests with gloves although bare-knuckle fights were still held in secret and abroad.

Johnson and Perrins

Tom Johnson (1750-97), (born Tom Jackling in Derby), became Champion of England in 1783. After several successful title defences he met Isaac Perrins (1750-1800), the 'Birmingham Giant', on a turfed stage raised five feet from the ground at Banbury in Oxfordshire on 22 October 1789. They fought 62 rounds in 90 minutes before Johnson's experience and agility overpowered the larger man.[13]

Humphreys and Mendoza

Daniel Mendoza (1763-1836) was born to Jewish parents in Whitechapel, London and nicknamed 'the Star in the East'. He fought Richard Humphreys (or Humphries), 'the Gentleman Boxer', at Odiham, Hampshire in 1788 for a purse of 400 guineas. Mendoza was relatively inexperienced while Humphries had already performed before royalty. Mendoza was beaten in a bout lasting 29 minutes. 'It was acknowledged that there never was more skill and science displayed in any boxing match in the kingdom'.

When they met again, in 1789 and 1790, Mendoza's superior speed and skill triumphed and he became national champion from 1792 to 1795. He retired in 1820 and ran The Admiral Nelson pub, in Whitechapel, to

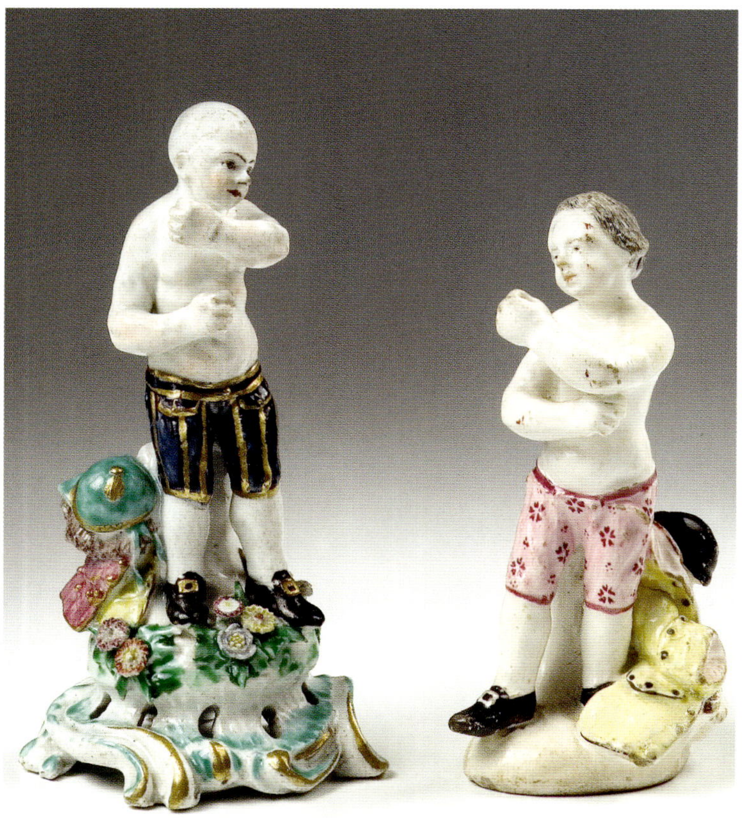

Two figures, (**1039 & A**), c.1755-c.1765, London, Bow, height: 14.5cm, (5¾in), height: 17.5cm, (6⅞in), enamelled, soft-paste porcelain. Unmatched pair of boys posed as pugilists. One is shaven-headed and stands on a scrolled rococo base. Both are stripped to their breeches, their discarded coats lying at their feet as they square up to fight.[12]

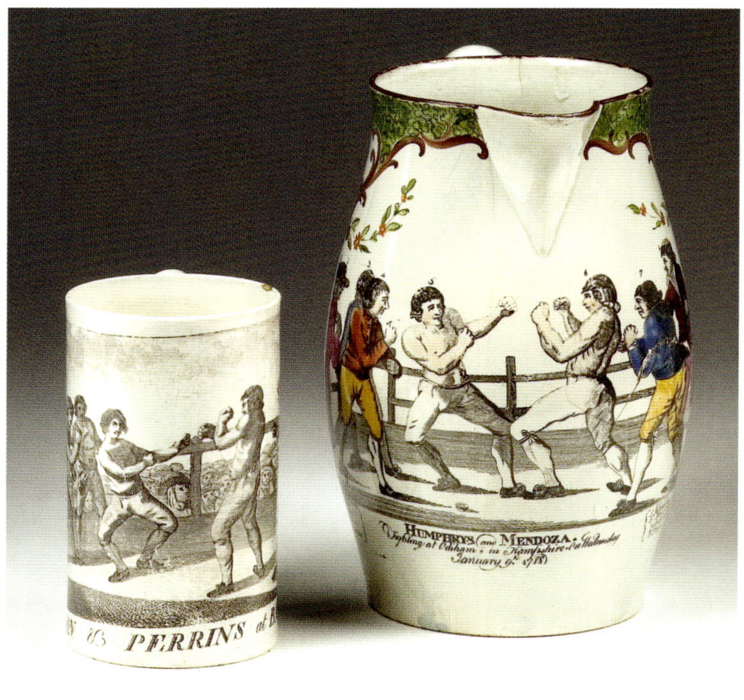

Mug, (**1033**), c.1790, Staffordshire, height: 12.7cm, (5in), printed pearlware. A wrap-around print entitled, 'JOHNSON & PERRINS at BANBURY',[14] shows the pugilists in the ring being urged on by seconds. Interestingly the print on the mug more closely resembles images of the match between Humphries and Mendoza than any of those produced for Johnson vs Perrins.
Jug, (**1035**), c.1788, Staffordshire, Lane End, height: 19.7cm, (7¾in), pearlware, printed and enamelled. The print, signed by John Aynsley of Lane End, is labelled: 'HUMPHRYS and MENDOZA, Fighting at Odiham in Hampshire on Wednesday January 9th 1788, 1.Umpire 2.Umpire 3.Isaac 4.Benjamin 5.Mendoza 6.Humphreys 7.Johnson 8.Tring'.[15] It shows the first of the three contests between Richard Humphreys and Daniel Mendoza.

support his wife and eleven children. He died in 1836 at the age of 73. Humphreys also lived to a good age, having retired early from the game to run a successful business as a coal merchant, probably from the 'Coal Hole', close to the Adelphi in the Strand. The match is the frontispiece to an early book on boxing, from which the print on the jug is loosely derived. On the title page is the following verse,

Black eyes, bloody nose / Cross buttocks, hard blows,
These Heroes sustain / Both for fame and for gain;
For pray who would fight / If they got nothing by't? [16]

Spring and Langan

Thomas Spring (1795-1851) was born Thomas Winter at Fownhope in Herefordshire and ruled as Champion of England from 1819 to 1824. The first contest between Spring and the Irish Champion, John Langan (b.1798) took place at Worcester on 7 January 1824 where Spring was declared the winner after 77 rounds, lasting 2 hours 29 minutes. When they met again at Chichester on 8 June 1824, Spring repeated his success in 'one of the fairest battles ever witnessed'.

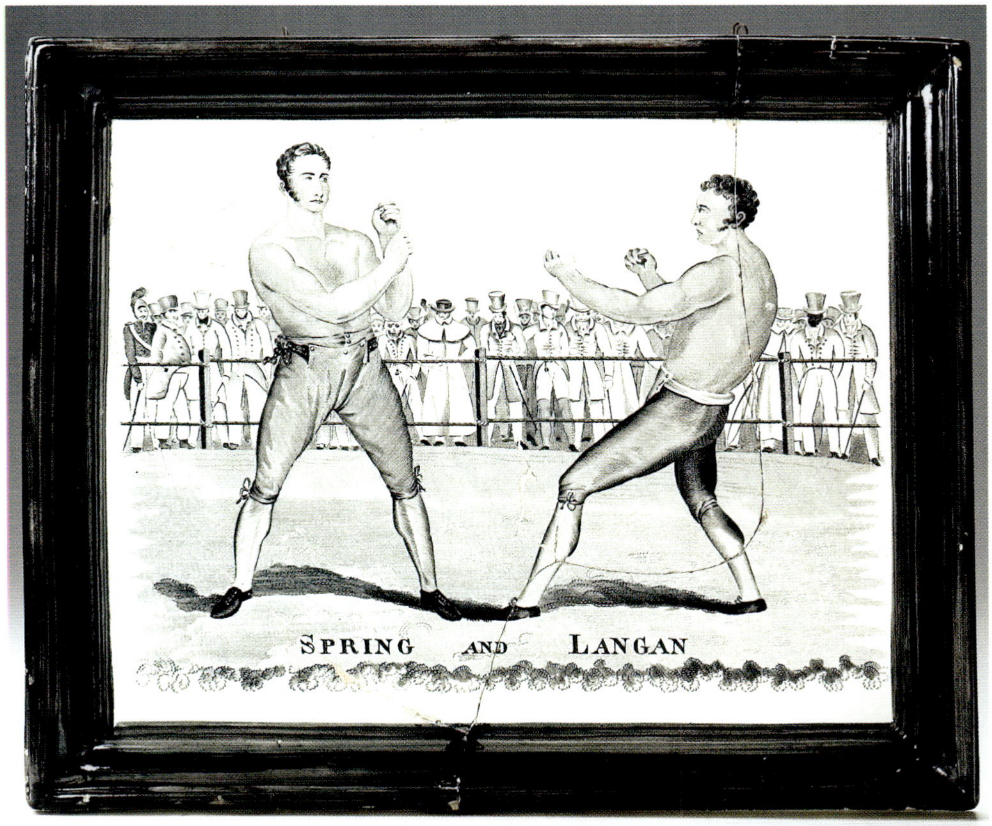

Plaque, (1029), c.1825, North East, height: 40.7cm, (16in), printed pearlware. Plaque with integral, black-glazed frame, printed with the contest between 'SPRING AND LANGAN'. The crowd of spectators includes a very well-dressed black man and a sinister character wearing dark glasses!

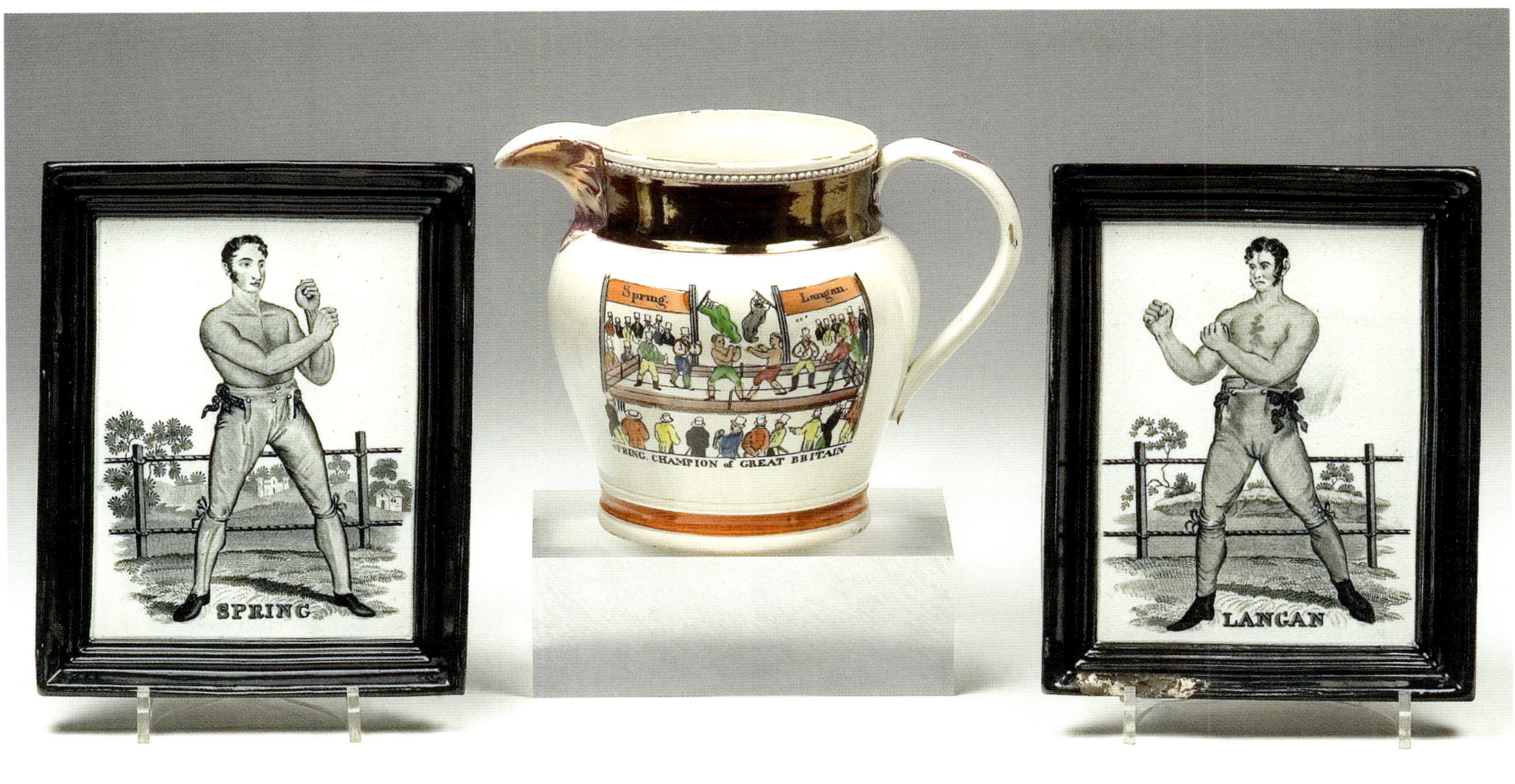

Pair of Plaques, (**1037 & A**), c.1825, North East, each height: 18.4cm, (7¼in), printed pearlware. Each plaque with integral, black-glazed frame, printed with individual portraits of 'SPRING' and 'LANGAN'.
Jug, (**1031**), c.1825, Staffordshire, height: 14cm, (5½in), pearlware, printed, enamelled and lustred. Jug, produced after the second contest, inscribed on each side, 'SPRING. CHAMPION of GREAT BRITAIN', and 'Drink to England's Champion. Gallant SPRING' and 'June 8 at Chichester in Sussex. 77 Rounds'.[17]

Cribb and Molineux

Gloucestershire-born, Thomas Cribb (1781-1867), Champion of England from 1805 to 1818, was challenged by Tom Molineux (1784-1818), a 26-year-old former slave from Virginia in the United States, nicknamed 'the Sable Gladiator'. They first met at Copthorne Common near East Grinstead on 18 December 1810 in a contest of 33 rounds lasting 55 minutes. Owing to the disputed outcome Molineux challenged a second time and they met again near Wymondham in Leicester on 18 September 1811. Cribb won the second match easily in eleven rounds lasting 19 minutes.

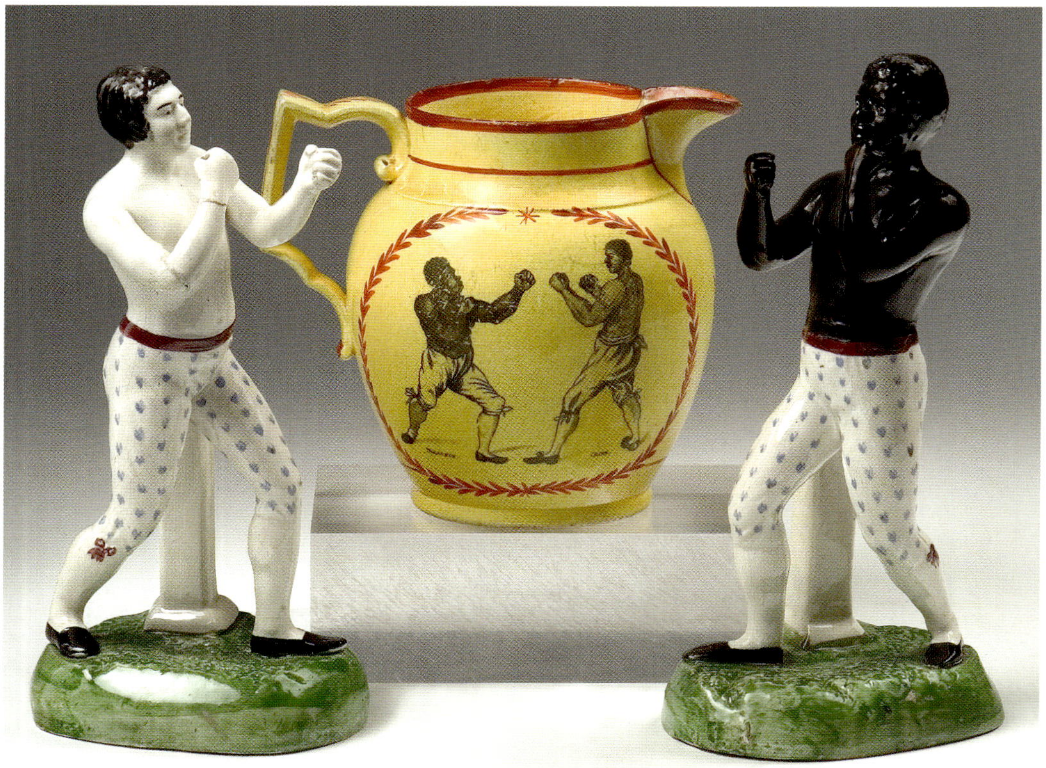

Pair of Figures, (**1034 & A**), c.1812, Staffordshire, height: 22.3cm, (8¾in), enamelled pearlware. The white and black pugilists each wear matching, spotted breeches. Figures probably modelled after a print of the second contest of 1811, published by George Smeeton on 17 December, 1812.[18]

Jug, (**1038**), c.1812, Staffordshire, height: 14cm, (5½in), yellow-glazed pearlware, printed and enamelled. Within enamelled wreath, print entitled, 'MOLINEUX' and 'CRIBB'. Image probably derives from a combination of the print published by Smeeton, 1812, and a print of Thomas Cribb after a painting by De Wild, 1811.[19]

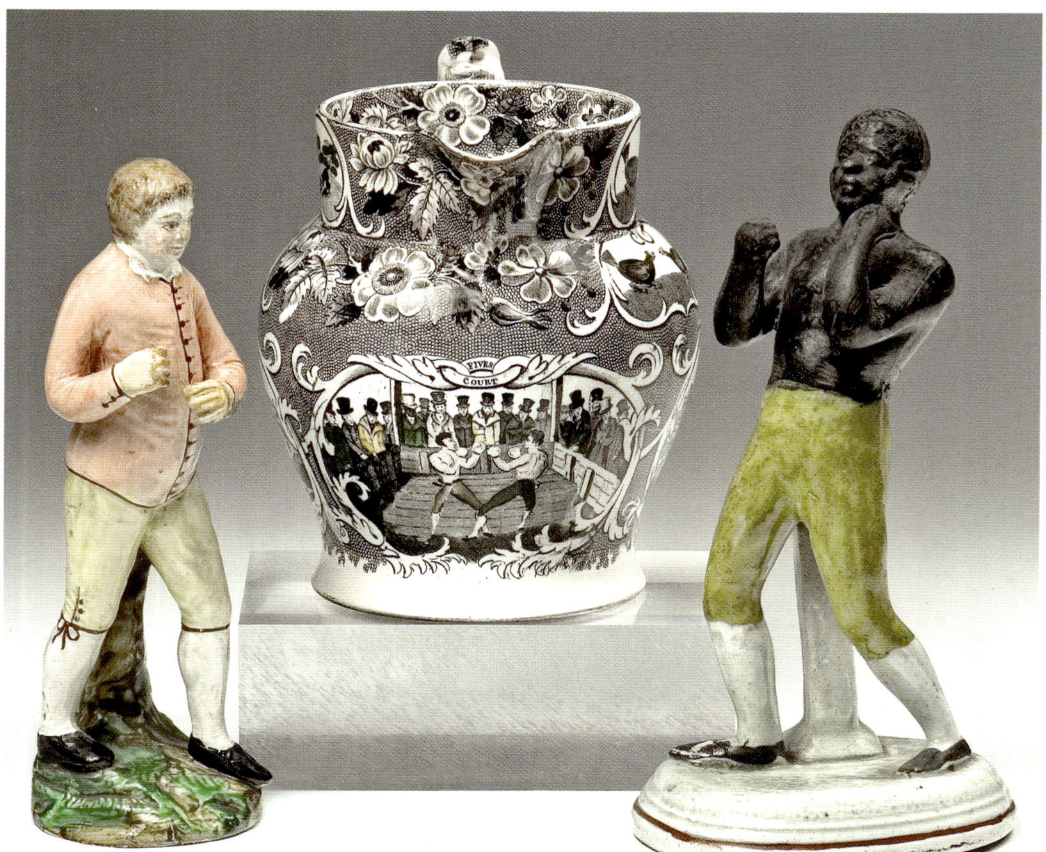

Figure, (**1040**), c.1790, Staffordshire, height: 21cm, (8¼in), enamelled pearlware. Figure, still wearing his pink jacket stands with raised fists.

Jug, (**1041**), c.1850, Staffordshire, height: 15.3cm, (6in), pearlware, printed and enamelled. Densely printed with sporting scenes including, 'FIVES COURT', (boxing), and vignettes of fighting cocks and tethered bulls around the neck.

Figure, (**1040A**), c.1812, Staffordshire, height: 21cm, (8¼in), enamelled pearlware. Figure of a black pugilist probably modelled on Molineux.

Benjamin Caunt (1815-1861)

Caunt was born in Hucknal Torkard, Nottinghamshire, where his parents were tenants of Lord Byron at Newstead Abbey. Caunt notably defeated the famous Bendigo, another Nottingham fighter in 1835 and 1838, before sailing for a tour of the United States in 1841. He returned in 1842 to win the Championship of England and, with his winnings, purchased the Coach and Horses public house in St Martin's Lane and retired from fighting. The chest infection he caught while tending his racing pigeons, 'coupled with late hours and the free living inseparable from his calling as a publican gave the powerful pugilist his final knockdown blow'.[20]

Tom Sayers (1828-1865)

Sayers reigned as Champion of England from 1846 to 1860, vanquishing opponents who were taller and heavier. In 1860 he was challenged by John Camel Heenan, the 'Benicia Boy' from the United States and a match lasting 37 rounds took place at Farnborough on 17 April. The outcome was disputed, so in the interest of international cordiality two identical silver belts were made by Hancock's of London and presented to the contestants in this first international championship match.[21]

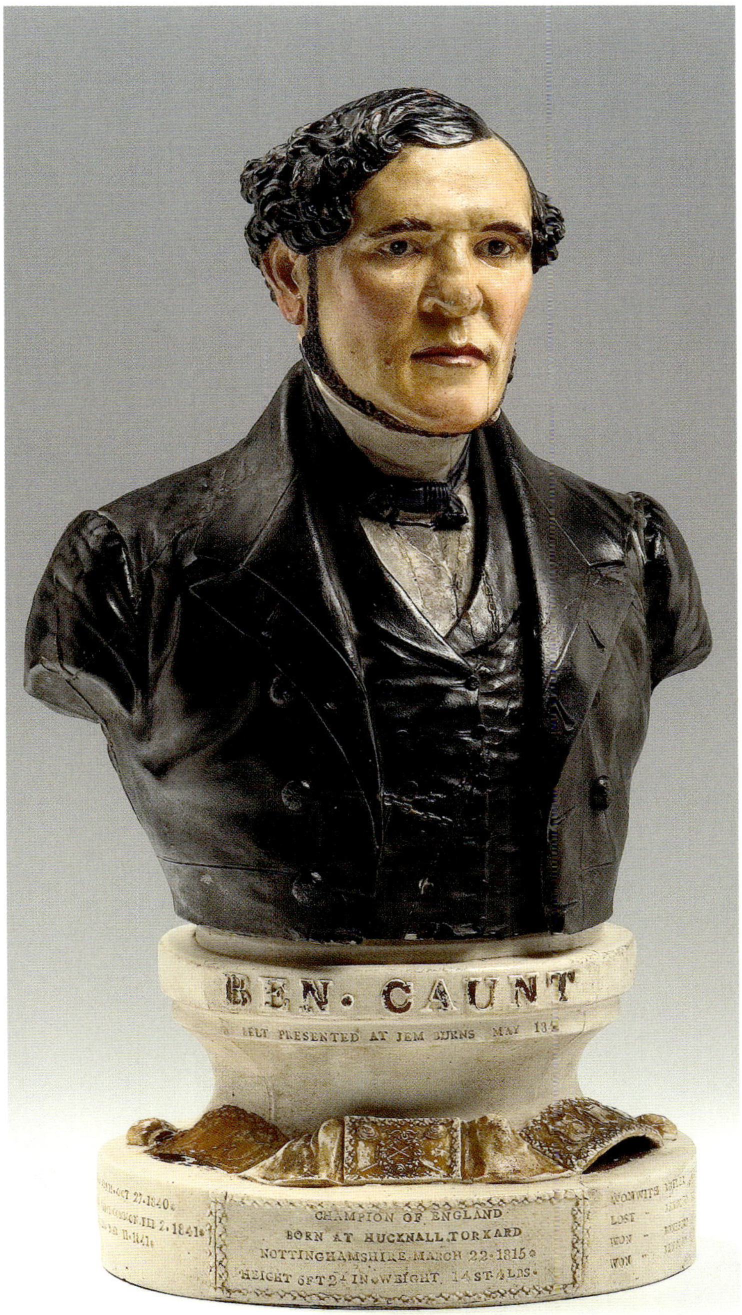

Bust, (**1030**), 1844, height: 39.4cm, (15½in), enamelled plaster. Portrait bust of Benjamin Caunt, signed by H. Bently, 1844. Circular plinth, moulded with impressed details of Caunt's life and a model of the championship belt. Another example in brown stoneware at the Castle Museum, Nottingham.

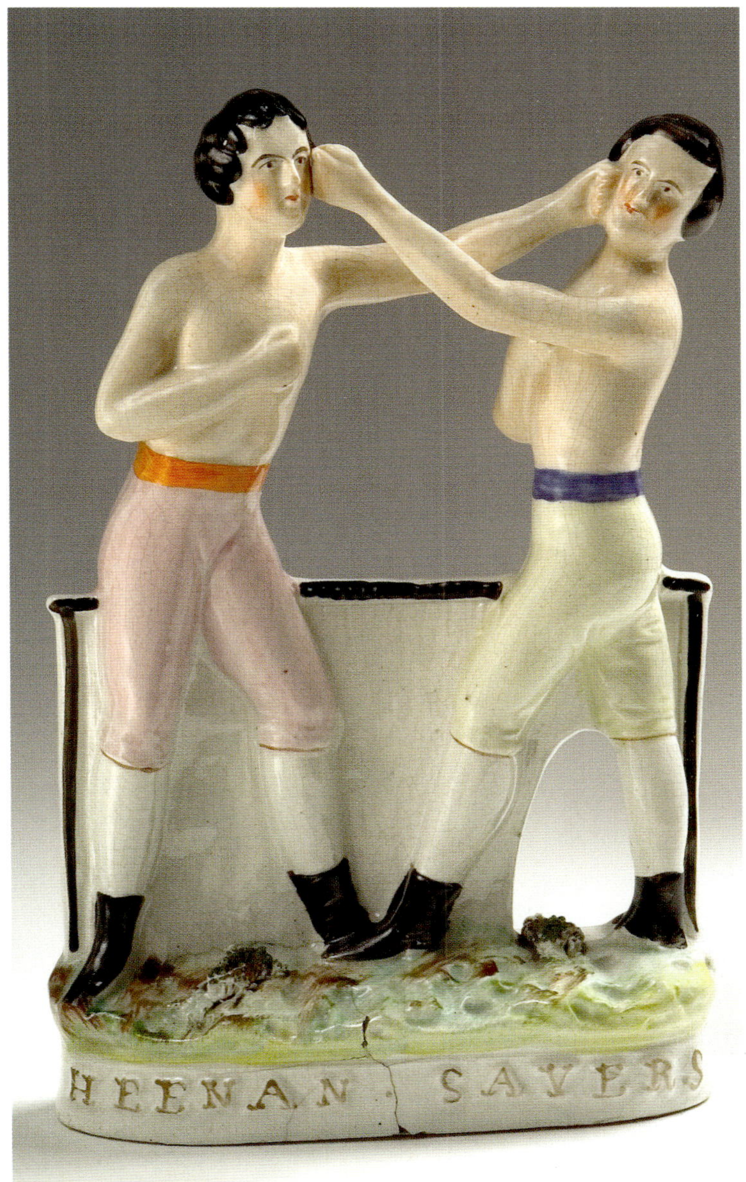

Figure Group, (**1032**), c.1860, Staffordshire, height: 24.2cm, (9½in), enamelled earthenware. Flat-backed group moulded with pugilists in close combat. Entitled 'HEENAN.SAYERS'. This group was widely forged during the twentieth century.

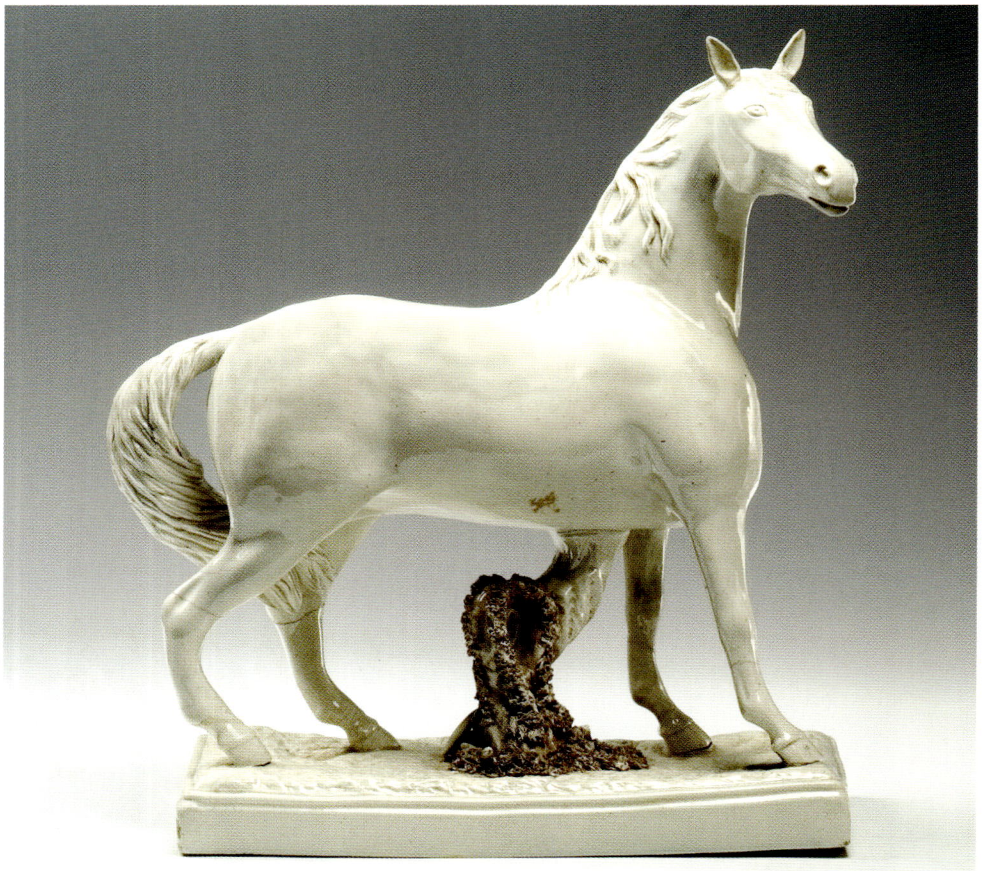

Figure, (**1054**), c.1790, Yorkshire, Leeds, height: 45.8cm, (18in), creamware. Figure of a stallion, popularly known as 'Eclipse', partly supported by a stump beneath the belly. While it is a virtuoso piece of potting there is no proof that this figure was intended as a portrait. Such figures may have been made for display in the windows of harness and tack makers, corn chandlers, horse doctors or veterinary suppliers.

Horse Racing; Eclipse

William, Duke of Cumberland, bred Eclipse at his Windsor Forest stud from Marske (a Jockey Club Plate winner) out of Spiletta (a descendant of the famous Godolphin Arabian). The chestnut foal was born during a solar eclipse on 1 April 1764. He had an Arab profile, a white blaze and a white stocking on one leg and was exceptionally powerfully built, standing over 15 hands. At the sale of Cumberland's stables, after his death in 1765, Eclipse was bought by William Wildman, a Smithfield meat dealer with a stud in Surrey.

Wildman recognised that the colt had great potential, despite his fiery temper and waited until May 1769 before racing him at Epsom. When challenged to place the front runners, Dennis O'Kelly, who bought the horse in 1770 for 1,750 gns, announced as he placed his bets: 'Eclipse first, the rest nowhere.' (At that time, a horse more than 240 yards behind the lead was said to be 'nowhere'). The stallion proved him right, beating the opposition by a huge distance. Eclipse was unbeaten in eighteen races and hardly ever ran at full stretch. He retired and went to stud at Clay Hill, near Epsom, in 1771, at a covering fee of 50 guineas, and sired the winners of 862 races. He died of colic in 1789. Most of today's British thoroughbred bloodstock can trace their line back to Eclipse.

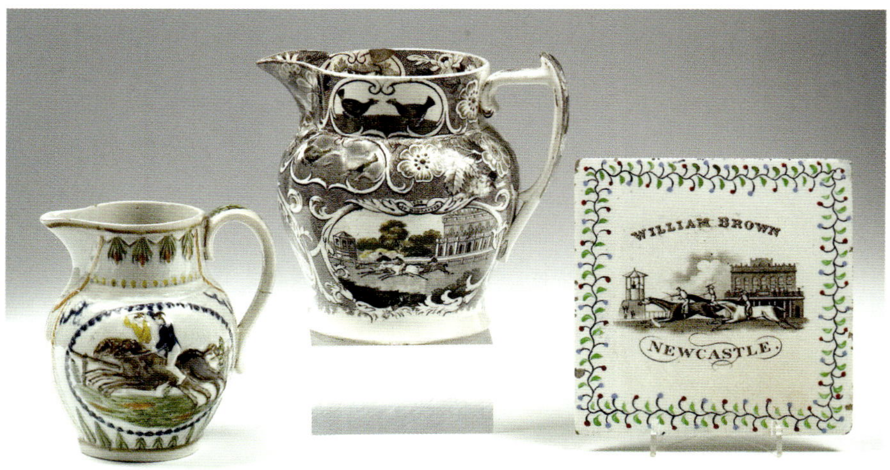

Jug, (**1059**), c.1800, Staffordshire, height: 12.7cm, (5in), Prattware. Has two relief-moulded scenes in reserves of jockeys mounting horses and galloping flat out in a race.
Jug, (**1041**), c.1850, Staffordshire, height: 15.3cm, (6in), pearlware, printed and enamelled. Densely printed with sporting scenes including, 'CUP AT DONCASTER', showing the finish of a horserace. The view is closely based on published views of Doncaster racecourse, notably a print of 1812 showing the famous St Leger Stakes.
Tile, (**1060**), c.1850, Staffordshire, height: 15.3cm, (6in), printed and enamelled earthenware. A horse-race takes place in front of a spectators' stand, inscribed 'WILLIAM BROWN' and 'NEWCASTLE'.

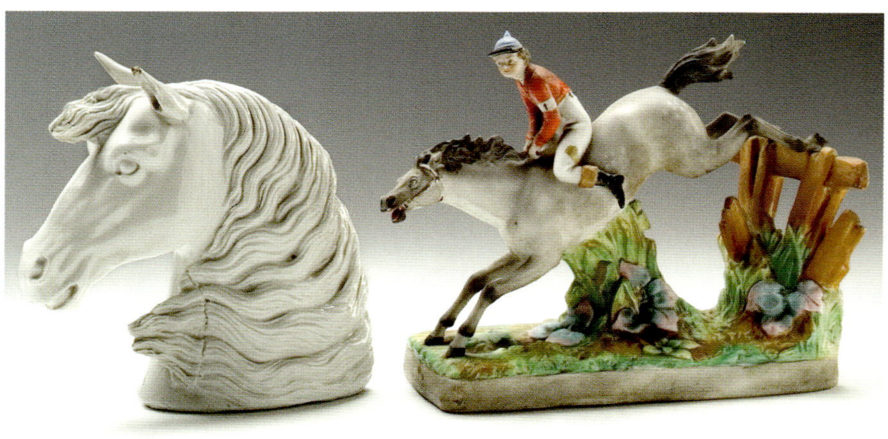

Horse Head, (**1053**), c.1790, Staffordshire, height: 15.3cm, (6in), soft-paste porcelain. Dramatically sculpted horse's head, probably based on a print after one of several paintings by George Stubbs, of a horse frightened by a lion.[22] The tension of the encounter created a 'sublime' subject for the Romantic Age. Stubbs himself adapted it in 1780 for jasperware reliefs by Wedgwood. Horace Walpole was inspired to write a poem, 'On seeing the celebrated Startled Horse, painted by the inimitable Mr. Stubbs'[23] which describes the horse, 'rooted' to the spot by 'apprehension, horror, hatred, fear', with 'ears shot forward' and 'stiff projected mane'.
Figure Group, (**1065**), c.1880, Germany, height: 16.5cm, (6½in), hard-paste porcelain. A horse and rider jumping a fence while steeple chasing.

Pair of Horses, (1055 & A), c.1800, Yorkshire, height: 16cm,(6¼in), height: 15.5cm,(6⅛in), Pratt-palette pearlware. Working horses with comic, startled eyes stand on thin, rectangular bases. Both have docked tails and saddle blankets secured with broad girth straps.
Figure group, (1058), c.1800, Staffordshire, height: 18.4cm,(7¼in), Prattware.
Horse and rider on grassy knoll with a tree; probably made by Charles Tittensor.[24]

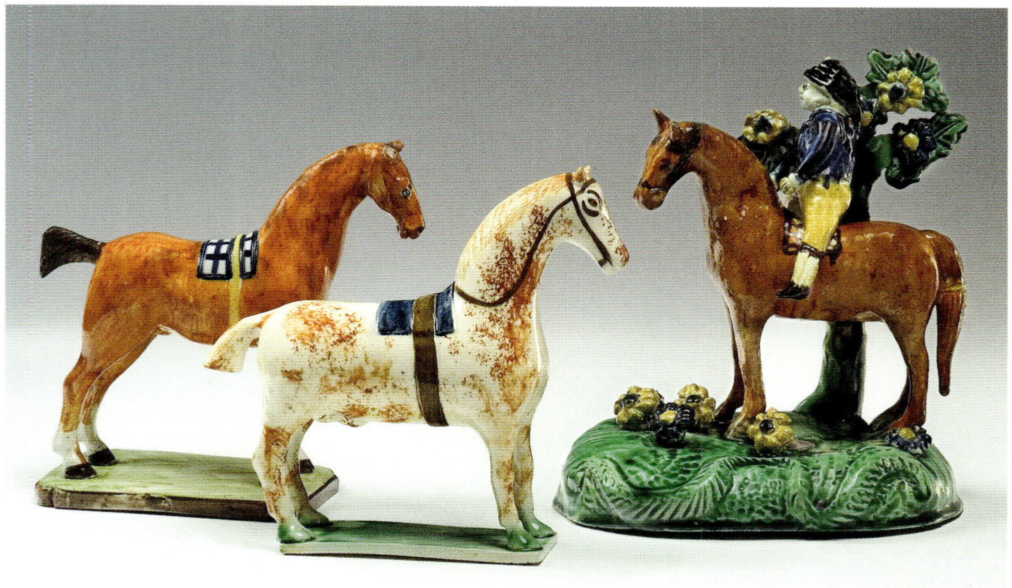

Mug, (1063), c.1850, Staffordshire, height: 10.5cm, (4⅛in), earthenware, brown-printed and coloured. Inscribed, 'STEEPLE CHASING', horses and jockeys gallop across ploughed fields. Steeple chasing; riding cross-country, jumping hedges and ditches, using a church steeple as a landmark, seems to have become popular in the 1820s.
Jug, (R2454.15), c.1840, Staffordshire, height: 14.5cm, (5¾in), blue-printed earthenware. Over fired print shows the culmination of a fox-hunt taking place in front of a country church.
Mug, (1064), c.1850, Staffordshire, height: 15.3cm, (6in), brown-printed earthenware, part-glazed. Print of steeple chasing through countryside, jumping laid hedges. Jockeys wear different coloured silks.

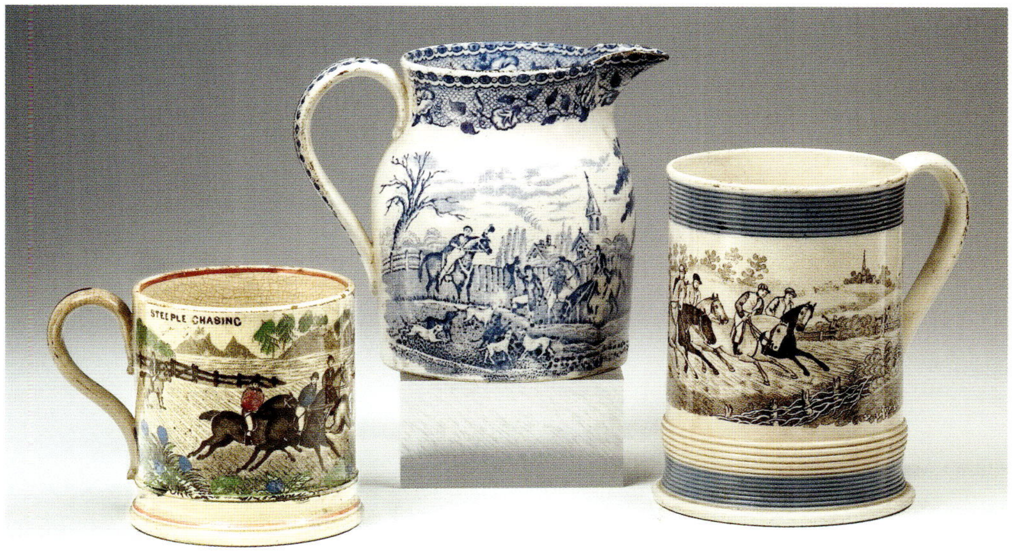

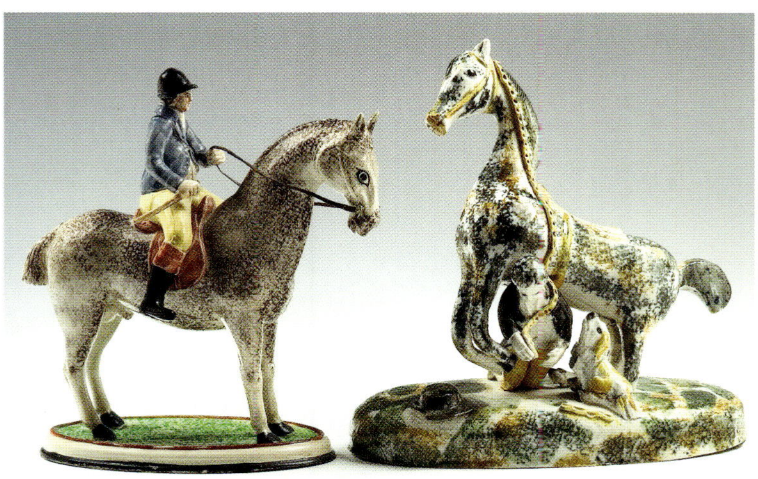

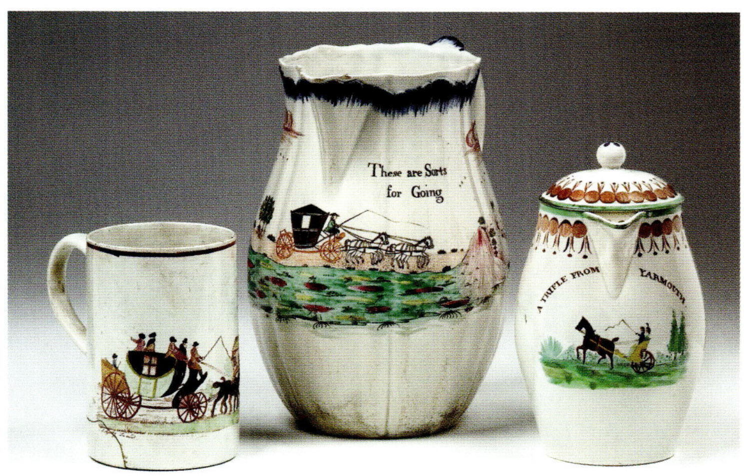

Figure group, (1056), c.1830, Yorkshire, height: 20.3cm, (8in), enamelled pearlware. Well-modelled horse with an enamelled rider who sits on a huntsman's saddle carrying a hunting horn, while dressed in the short jacket and hard cap of a jockey.
Figure group, (1057), c.1820, Staffordshire, height: 21.7cm, (8½in), Prattware. Represents a training session where the horse rears after throwing its rider. The rider picks himself up while still gripping the leading rein.

Mug, (1067), c.1805, Staffordshire, Lane End, height: 12.1cm,(4¾in), creamware, printed and coloured. A four-horse coach inscribed, 'Dover', marked for John Aynsley.
Jug, (1070), c.1805, Staffordshire, height: 21cm,(8¼in), enamelled pearlware. Jug perhaps made by Neale & Co. decorated with a four-horse coach in landscape inscribed, 'These are Sorts / for Going'.
Jug with lid, (1071), c.1800, Staffordshire, height: 17.2cm,(6¾in), enamelled pearlware. Decorated by William Absolon of Yarmouth with a couple in a one-horse gig, inscribed, 'A TRIFLE FROM YARMOUTH'.[25]

Field Sports

Stag-hunting

In Norman England, the hunting of deer and boar was reserved for royalty and courtiers. These quarry species were protected within Royal Forests and it was a serious offence to kill them there except as part of a Royal Hunt. Stag-hunting scenes appear as relief sprigs on salt-glazed stoneware vessels. Spotted hounds chase a stag amongst trees around the base of a large mug made at Vauxhall, dated 1721, dedicated to Queen Anne (018).[26] A jug, dated 1747, shows horsemen pursuing a stag with pairs of hounds and beaters on foot (113).[27] The privilege was extended to major landowners and senior churchmen but by the mid-eighteenth century stag-hunting (mainly fallow and roe deer) reverted to being a largely royal pastime once again.

The Duke of Rutland's Belvoir hunt was founded as late as 1730 expressly to hunt the stag and the Duke of Beaufort's pack at Badminton continued to concentrate on stags until the 1770s. However, agricultural and naval expansion had decimated forests that were the deer's main habitat and some hunts turned to fox-hunting. Farmers welcomed this development as a means of controlling the pests that preyed on their livestock. Stag-hunts, however, remained a popular subject for ceramic decoration until well into the nineteenth century.

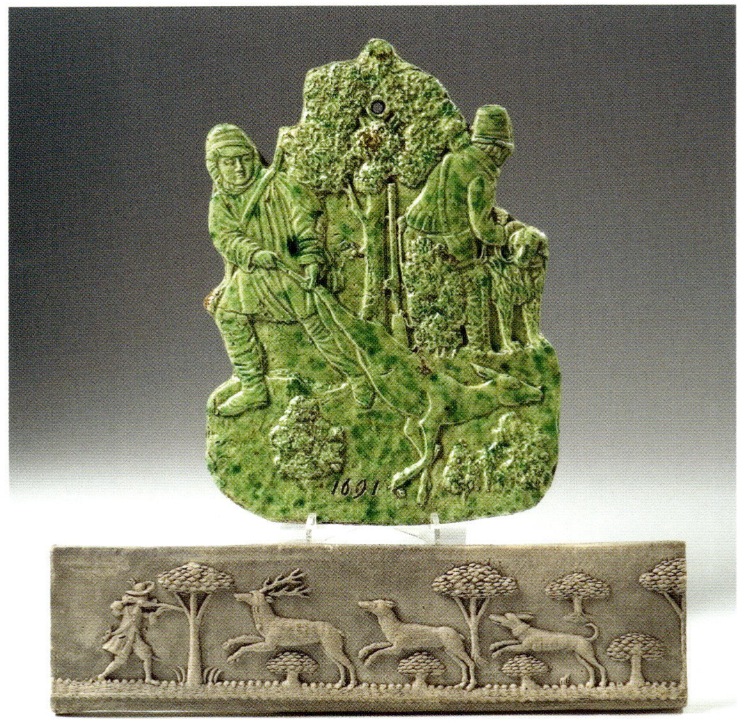

Tile, (**1112**), 1691 (date incised), Germany, height: 26cm, (10¼in), green-glazed earthenware. Tile pierced for hanging, relief-moulded with hunters dragging a young hind.
Plaque, (**1108**), c.1650, Germany, height: 8.3cm, (3¼in), biscuit terracotta. Relief-moulded with a frieze of a stag, pursued by hounds, being shot by a huntsman.

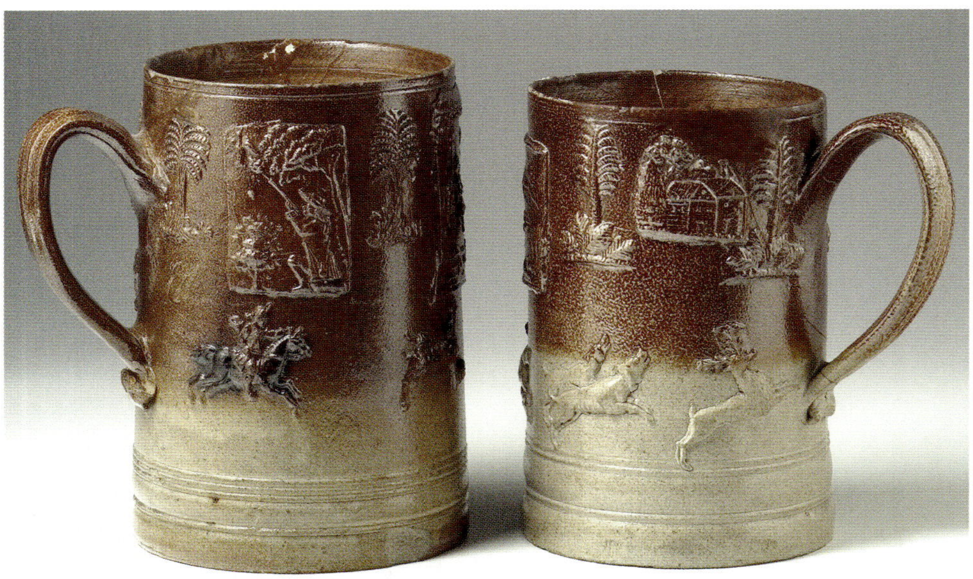

Mug, (**1132**), c.1740, London, height: 22.2cm, (8⅝in), salt-glazed stoneware. Relief-moulded sprigged plaque depicting pheasant shooting, while a stag-hunting party gallops round the circumference.[28]
Mug, (**1101**), c.1750, London, height: 20.8cm, (8⅛in), salt-glazed stoneware. Relief-moulded with figures taking part in stag-hunt.[29]

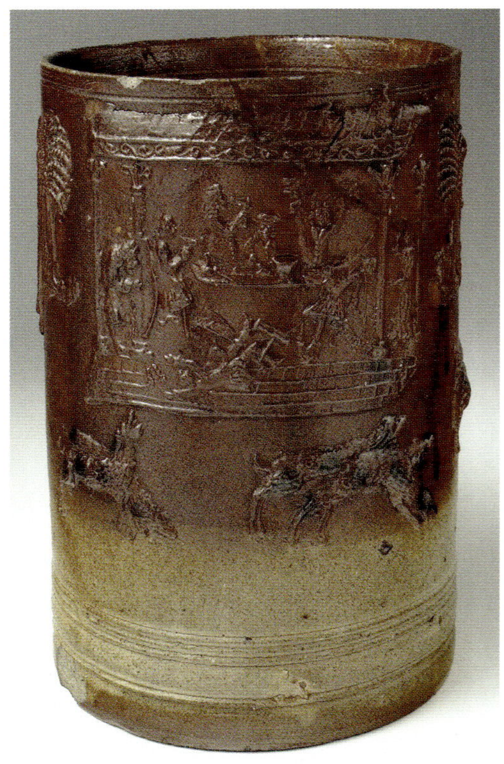

Mug, (**1132**), detail c.1740, London, height: 22.2cm, (8⅝in), salt-glazed stoneware. A relief moulded plaque of Hogarth's *A Midnight Modern Conversation*, framed by columns.

Jug, (**1102**), c.1780, London, Mortlake, height: 17.8cm, (7in), salt-glazed stoneware. The jug, with a metal rim, made at Joseph Kishere's Mortlake Pottery, relief-moulded with stag-hunting sprigs.
Figure, (**1109**), c.1820, Derby, height: 17.8cm, (7in), soft-paste porcelain. Figure of stag (with damaged antlers) lies beneath a blossom-covered tree.

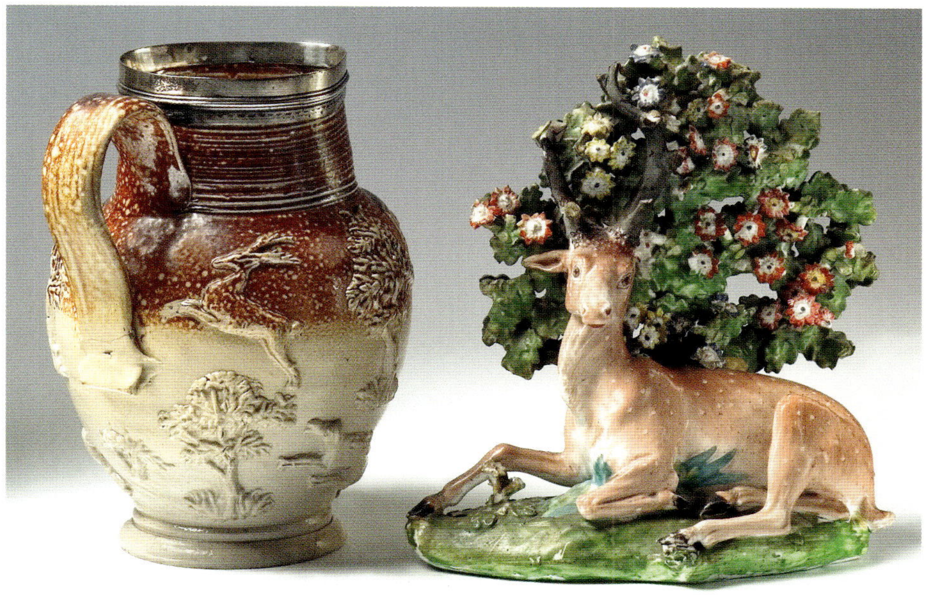

Jug, (**1104**), c.1810, Staffordshire, Hanley, height: 16.5cm, (6½in), enamelled pearlware. Jug, possibly by David Wilson & Sons, relief-moulded with a popular image of a rider dismounting at 'The Death of the Stag'.
Jug, (**1105**), c.1810, Swansea, probably Haynes, Dillwyn & Co., height: 18.4cm, (7¼in), earthenware, blue-printed, coloured and lustred. The same subject (as 1104) appears as an underglaze-blue print, on a silver lustre jug.

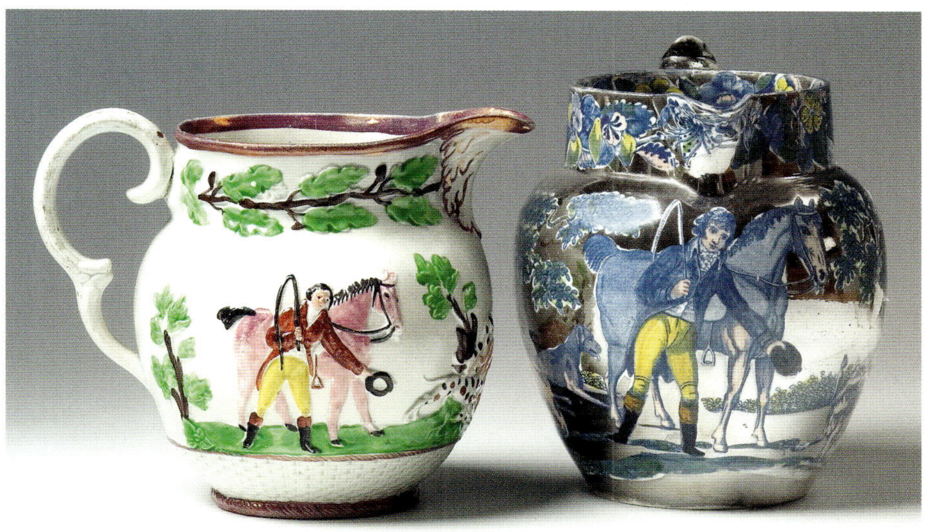

Jug, (**1104**), c.1810, Staffordshire, Hanley, height: 16.5cm, (6½in), enamelled pearlware. Jug, possibly by David Wilson & Sons, relief-moulded with hounds attacking a dying stag ('The Death of the Stag').
Ornament, (**1107**), c.1810, Staffordshire, height: 7cm, (2¾in), soft-paste porcelain. Relief-moulded and pierced with hounds attacking a dying stag.
Jug, (**1106**), c.1850, Staffordshire, Stoke-on-Trent, height: 13.3cm, (5¼in), white stoneware. Jug, probably by Copeland, applied with relief sprigs on a jasper slip ground.

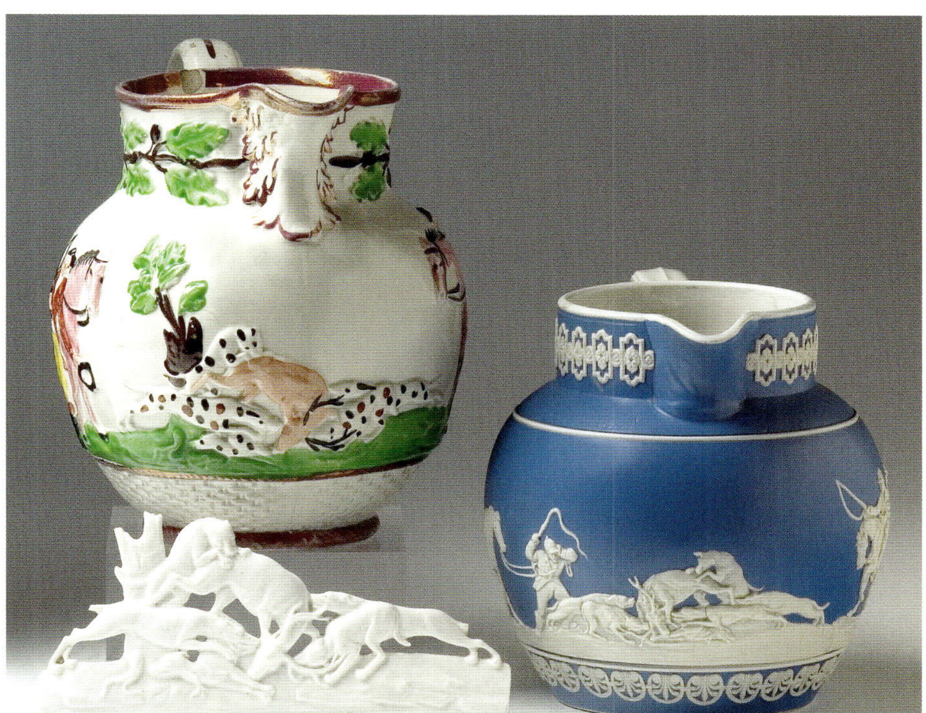

Jug, (**1152**), c.1795, Yorkshire, height: 17.2cm, (6¾in), creamware. Jug, possibly made at the Leeds Pottery, printed with 'PARTRIDGE SHOOTING', taken from an illustration by Samuel Howitt for the *Sporting Magazine*.[30]

Figure, (**1111**), c.1820, Staffordshire, height: 27.9cm, (11in), enamelled pearlware. A Scottish Highlander with a musket brandishes a small hunting horn, his jacket and kilt painted an inappropriate pink![31]

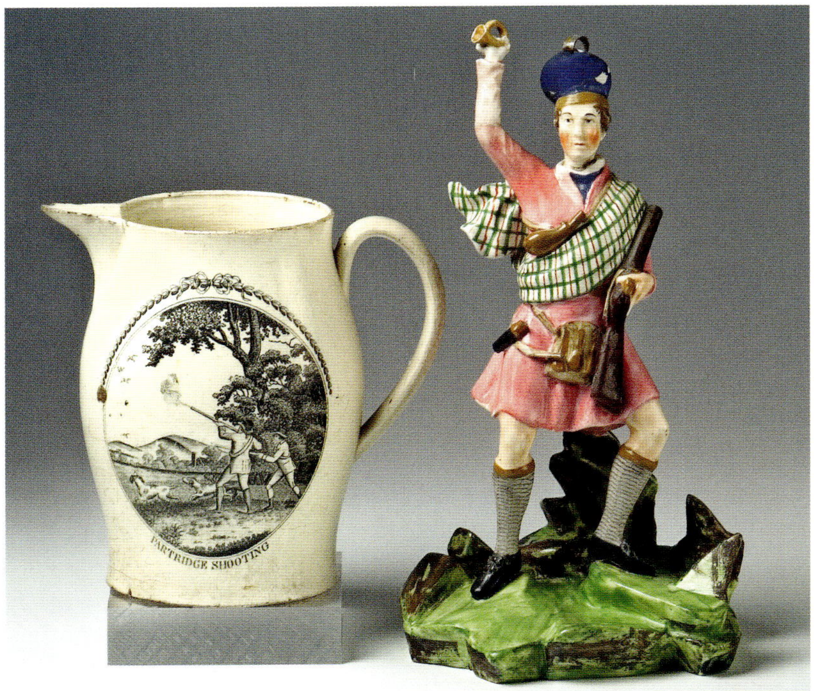

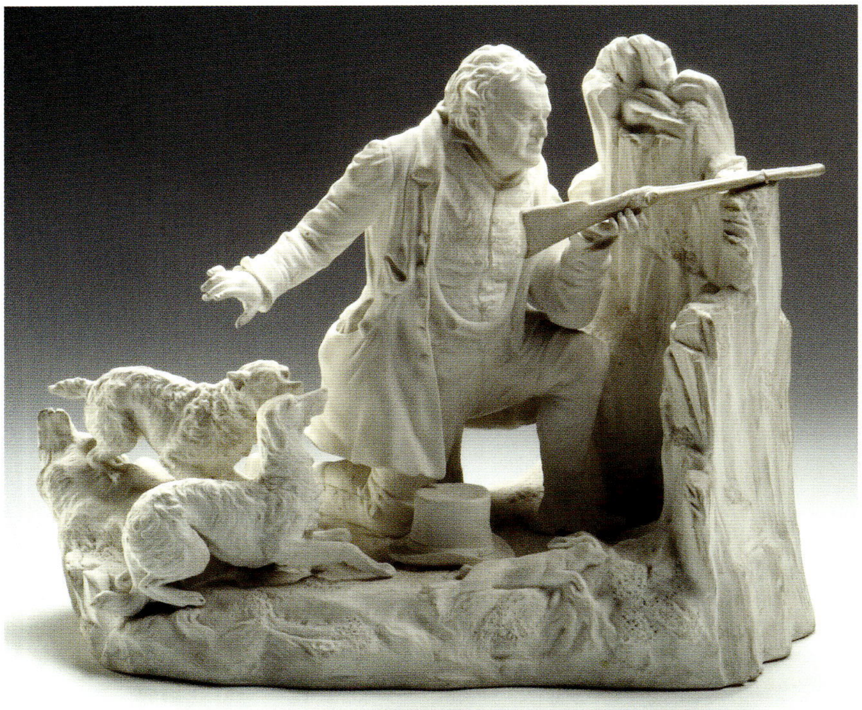

Figure, (**1110**), c.1830, Staffordshire, Stoke-on-Trent, height: 25.4cm, (10in), biscuit porcelain. A kneeling huntsman takes aim while quieting his dogs. 'The Gamekeeper', was made by Minton (model No. 112) who later issued it as their most expensive parian ware model at £3.6s.8d.

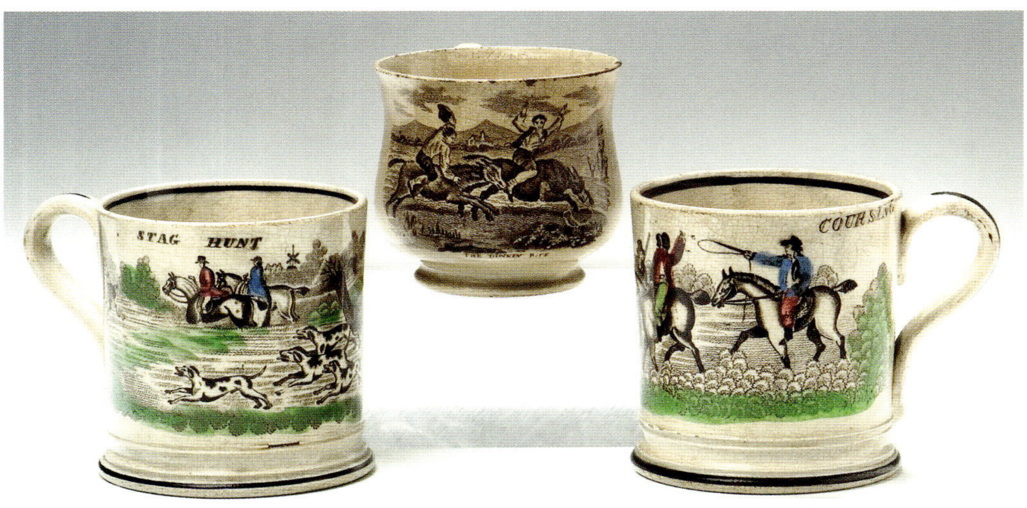

Mug, (**R.2454.21**), c.1850, Staffordshire, height: 9cm, (3½in), earthenware, brown-printed and coloured. Inscribed, 'STAG HUNT', with riders and dogs wading through a river.

Mug, (**1062**), c.1795, Staffordshire, height: 7.7cm, (3in), brown-printed earthenware. Inscribed, 'DONKEY RACE', two donkeys and riders gallop through a landscape.

Mug, (**R.2454.20**), c.1850, Staffordshire, height: 9.3cm, (3⅝in), earthenware, brown-printed and coloured. Inscribed, 'COURSING', with riders walking through landscape.

Fox-hunting

From the Middle Ages there were sharp distinctions between the quality of different types of quarry. The hart, the hind, the hare, the boar and the wolf were the superior 'beasts of venery', while the fox, the marten and the small roe deer were considered second-rate prey. Richard Blome states that 'the Quality' pursued deer in forests, chases and parks while men of lower rank diverted themselves with the hare.[32] Until the mid-eighteenth century the fox was dismissed as an inedible, verminous creature of low cunning, like the badger, worthy only to be 'stopped' or trapped in its earth by terriers. The nobility gradually took up fox-hunting, initially as gentle exercise. They met at dawn to take up a cold scent, pursue and kill the fox at a walking pace when it had a full stomach, and was therefore unable to run fast.

Leicestershire and its neighbouring counties, where woodlands had been cleared and arable fields transformed into grassland, became the best hunting country in England. Midland hunts, such as the Quorn, the Belvoir, the Cottesmore and the Pytchley were established. Hugo Meynell, a wealthy Leicestershire squire, was master of foxhounds with the Quorn Hunt from 1753 to 1800 and transformed the sport by breeding crack packs of foxhounds, renowned for speed, stamina and scenting powers. Faster hounds required faster horses and selective breeding was vigorously pursued. By 1800 English horses were the best in the world. The fox could be hunted through the day when it was fast, wily and hungry, by a pack of up to 100 pairs of hounds and horsemen.

The combination of the thoroughbred hunter and improved hounds (owned by subscription syndicates from the 1760s) made the sport swift and exciting. Peter Beckford wrote in his *Thoughts upon Hunting* (1781), 'Fox-hunting is now become the amusement of gentlemen nor need any gentleman be ashamed of it!' The hunt was widely celebrated in literary works such as William Somerville's lengthy poem, *The Chace* (1735) and in art. Painters John Wootton and James Seymour thrived on the demand for hunting scenes.

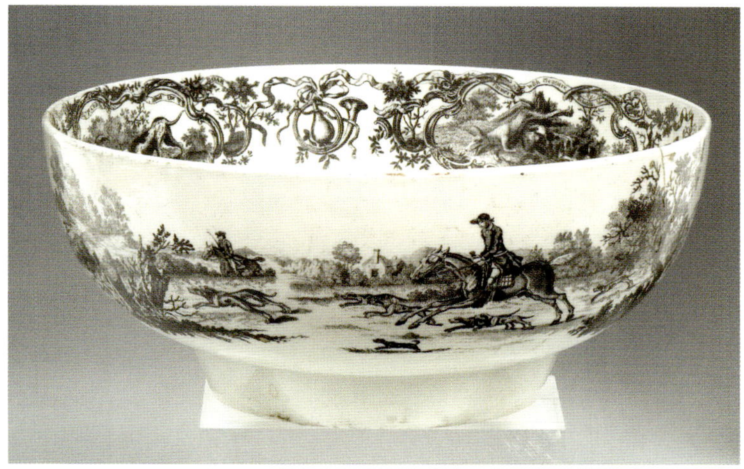

Punch Bowl, (1134), c.1770, Worcester, diameter: 27.9cm, (11in), printed, soft-paste porcelain. Wrap-around design of a fox hunt against a hilly landscape. Adapted by Robert Hancock from a print of 1757 by Thomas Burford after the painting, 'The Chace'[*sic*], by James Seymour.[33]

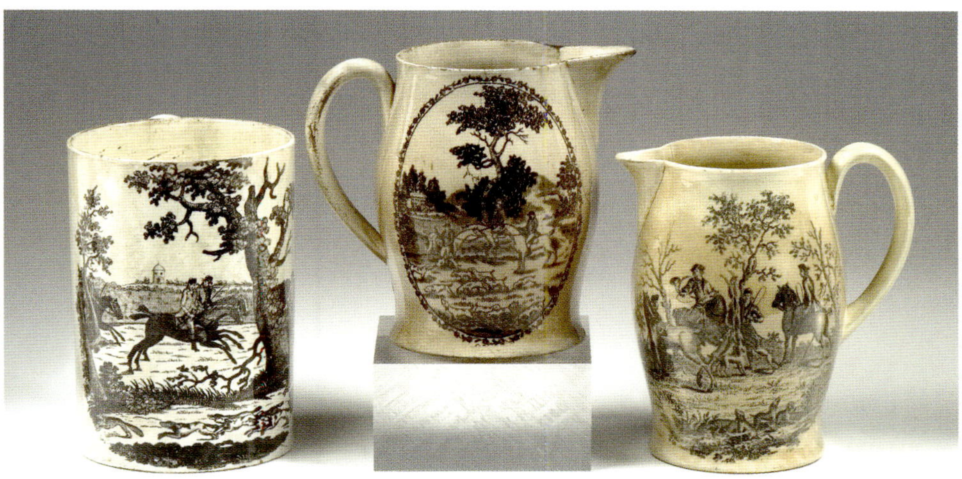

Mug, (1114), c.1800, Staffordshire, height: 15.3cm, (6in), printed creamware. The hunters gallop in one direction while the hounds go in another.
Jug, (1116), c.1800, Staffordshire, height: 14cm, (5½in), printed creamware. Within an oval frame, the death of the fox with a country house in the background.
Jug, (1115), c.1780, Staffordshire, Etruria, height: 14.7cm, (5¾in), printed creamware. Printed by Sadler & Green in Liverpool for Wedgwood. Delicately engraved scene of mounted huntsmen blowing horns in woodland and dogs scenting the air. One of a set of four 'Hare Hunt' prints engraved by Bernard Baron in 1727 after designs by John Wootton.[34] Although the Wootton / Baron originals are rare, they were readily available as pirated copies.[35]

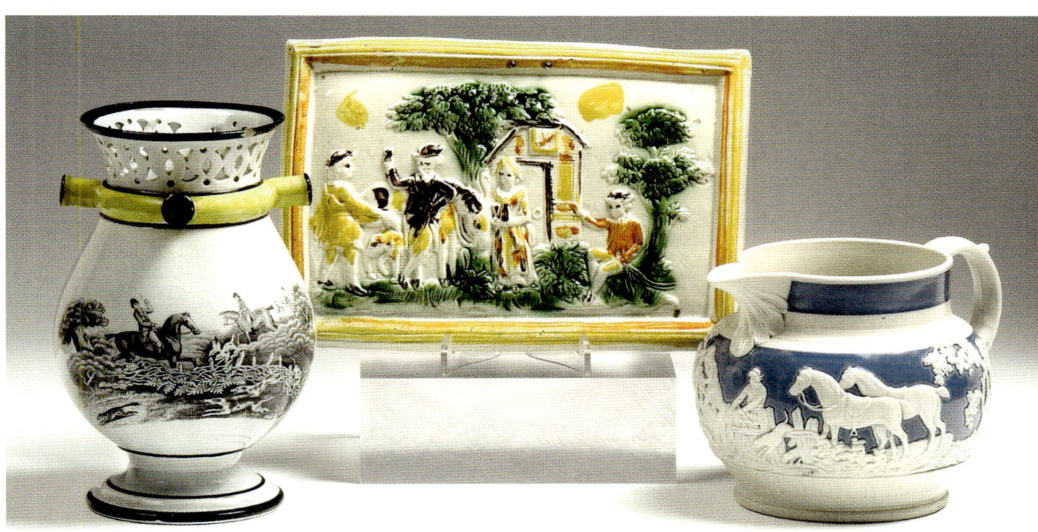

Puzzle Jug, (1117), c.1800, Staffordshire, height: 19.1cm, (7½in), pearlware, printed and enamelled. Print of riders and hounds chasing a fox over a laid hedge. Image closely based on a print of 1799 by Samuel Howitt.[36]
Plaque, (1133), c.1800, Staffordshire, height: 22.9cm, (9in), Prattware. Relief-moulded with huntsmen taking refreshment at an inn after the hunt is over.[37]
Jug, (1137), c.1840, Staffordshire, height: 11.4cm, (4½in), smear-glazed stoneware. Jug, probably made by Copeland, relief-moulded on a blue-glazed ground with dismounted huntsmen and hounds at the 'Death of the Fox'.

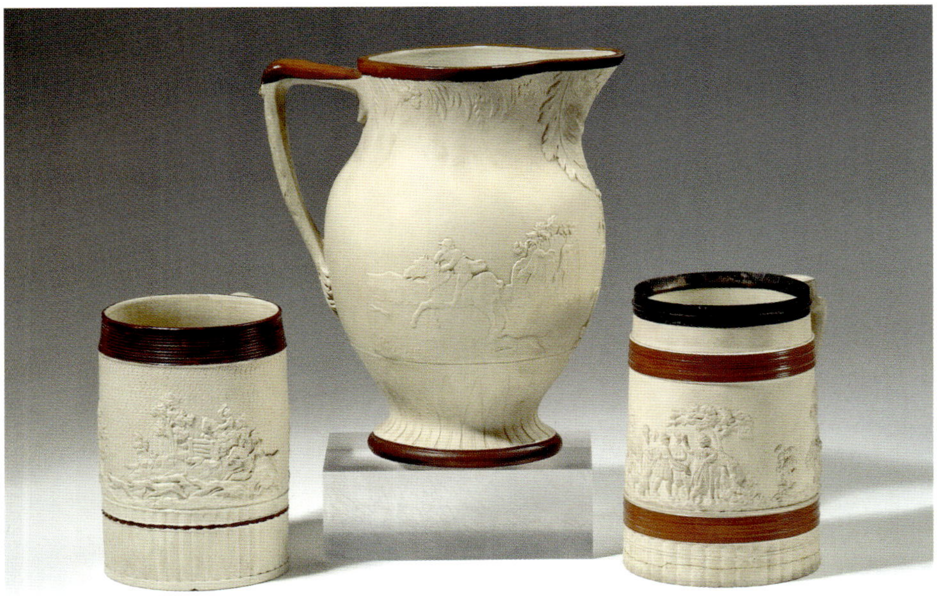

Mug, (**1126**), c.1795, Staffordshire, Burslem, height: 15.3cm, (6in), cream stoneware, enamelled. Mug, marked 'Wedgwood & Co.', for Ralph Wedgwood, sprig-moulded with a fox-hunting scene in a landscape on a textured ground.
Jug, (**1118**), c.1795, Staffordshire, Lane End, height: 24.1cm, (9½in), cream stoneware, enamelled. Jug made by John Turner, moulded in very low relief with galloping horses and hounds.
Mug, (**1127**), c.1795, Staffordshire, Lane End, height: 15.9cm, (6¼in), cream stoneware, enamelled. Tankard with metal rim, made by John Turner, sprig-moulded with huntsmen resting at an inn after the hunt is over.[38]

Figure, (**1138**), c.1800, Staffordshire, height: 7.6cm, (3in), Prattware. Small animal, assumed to be a fox but looks far more like a cat.
Figure, (**1135**), c.1790, Staffordshire, height: 10.2cm, (4in), enamelled pearlware. Figure of a seated fox, cast from a Derby porcelain original.
Stirrup cup, (**1129**), c.1790, Staffordshire, height: 12.7cm, (5in), enamelled pearlware. Head of a fox, crisply moulded and coloured.
Stirrup cup, (**1130**), c.1790, North East? height: 13.3cm, (5¼in), enamelled pearlware. Head of a fox, yellow-glazed with protruding tongue. Generally fox-mask cups were circulated among participants before the fox hunt. But 'forty-eight cream colour fox heads, twenty six brown fox heads' were part of a huge order supplied by Wedgwood for the open-air coming-of-age party of Sir Watkin Williams Wyn in 1770.[39]

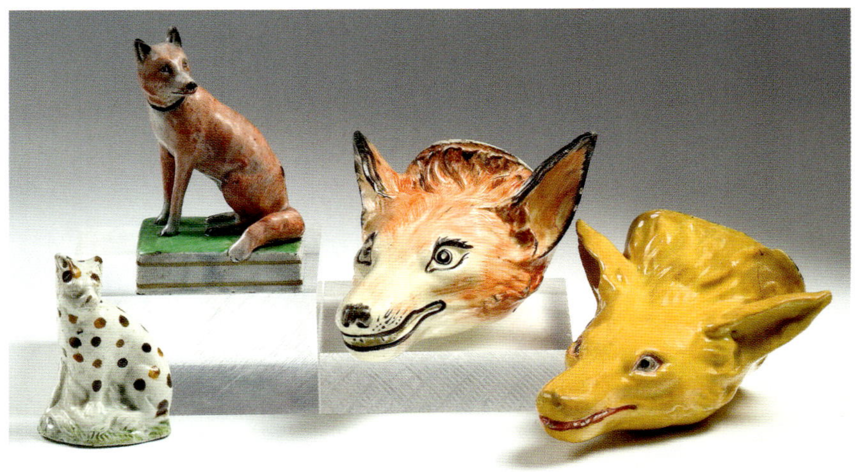

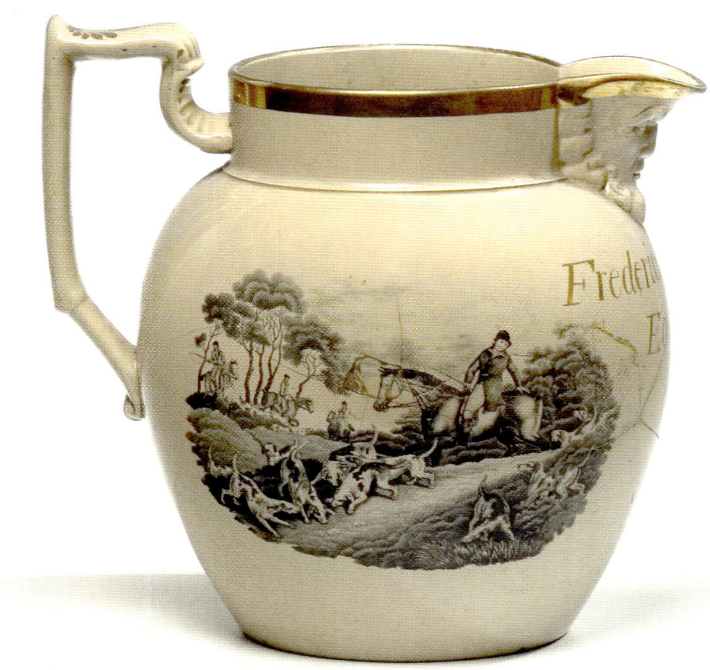

Jug, (**1136**), 1819, Staffordshire, height: 25.4cm, (10in), drab earthenware, printed and gilt. Jug, moulded with a mask spout, printed with fox-hunting scenes and inscribed, 'Frederick Augustus / Eaststaff / 1819'. One Frederick Eaststaff was born c.1781 in Middlesex and died in 1861.[40]

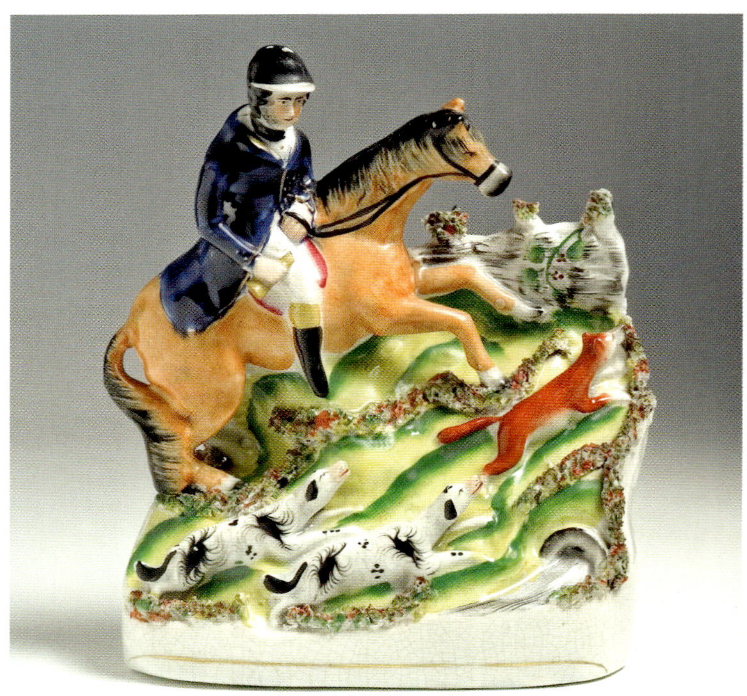

Figure Group, (**1131**), c.1850, Staffordshire, height: 25.4cm, (10in), enamelled earthenware. A huntsman and hounds in full cry as a little fox streaks ahead of them.

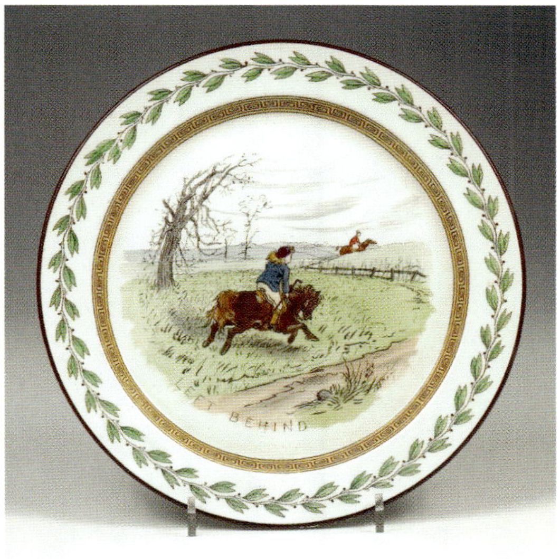

Plate, (1121), c.1875, Staffordshire, Stoke-on-Trent, diameter: 25.4cm, (10in), earthenware, printed and enamelled. One of a series of plates depicting comic hunting scenes, issued by Mintons. Inscribed, 'LEFT BEHIND', the efforts of the little pony, drawn by John Leech, prefigure the comic creations of twentieth-century cartoonist, Norman Thelwell. Leech (1817-64), who had a house at 16 Lansdowne Place in Hove was a regular contributor to *Punch*. His hunting scenes were used as lithographic illustrations to R.S. Surtees's books, *Mr Sponge's Sporting Tour* (1852) and *Handley Cross* (1853).[41]

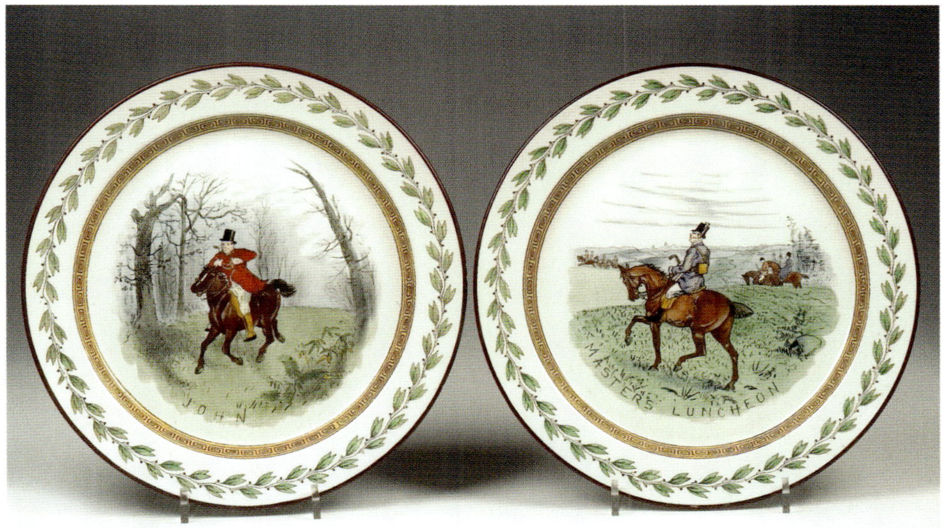

Plates, (1120 +1123), c.1875, Staffordshire, Stoke-on-Trent, each diameter: 25.4cm, (10in), earthenware, printed and enamelled. Humorous portraits of huntsmen, 'JOHN' and 'MASTER'S LUNCHEON'.

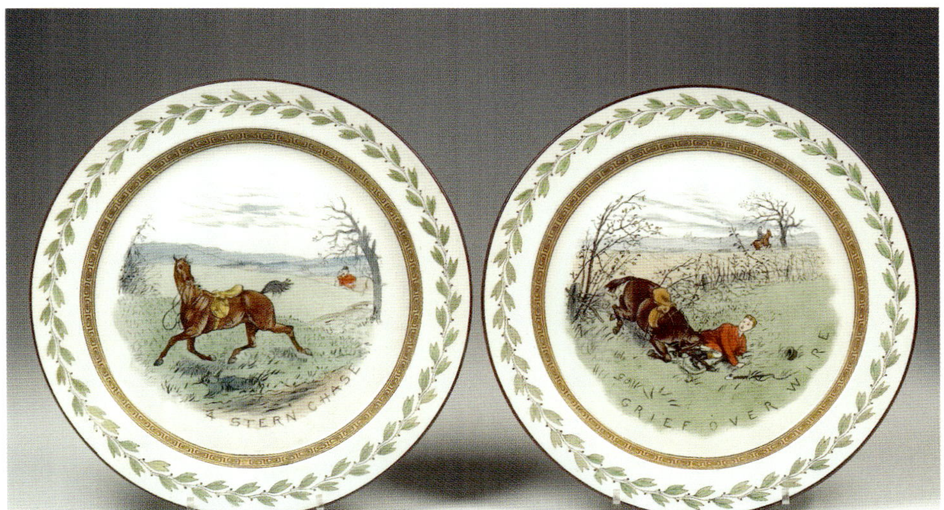

Plates, (1122 +1124), c.1875, Staffordshire, Stoke-on-Trent, each diameter: 25.4cm, (10in), earthenware, printed and enamelled. Humorous portraits of a runaway horse, 'A STERN CHASE' and 'GRIEF OVER WIRE', a fall at a fence.

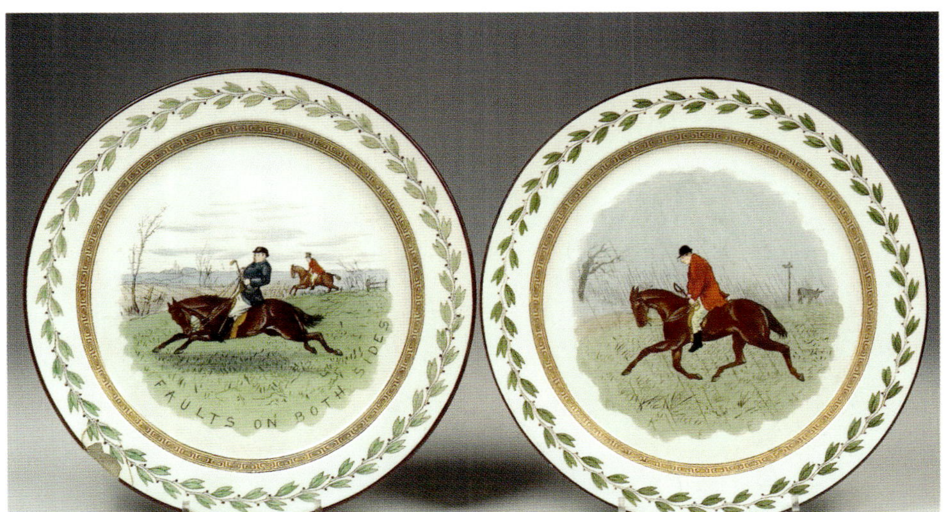

Plates, (1119 +1125), c.1875, Staffordshire, Stoke-on-Trent, each diameter: 25.4cm,(10in), earthenware, printed and enamelled. Humorous portraits of a runaway horse, inscribed 'FAULTS ON BOTH SIDES', and 'KEEN', depicting hunting in heavy rain.

Shooting

Even shooting game was originally restricted to the upper classes. The Game Act of 1671 restricted the shooting of pheasant, partridge and hare to freeholders with land worth £100 or more a year. The Act was followed by 24 further Game Laws, which created a legal thicket impossible to enforce and which was regularly broken, either by the silent assent of the landowner or, far more frequently, by the activities of poachers.

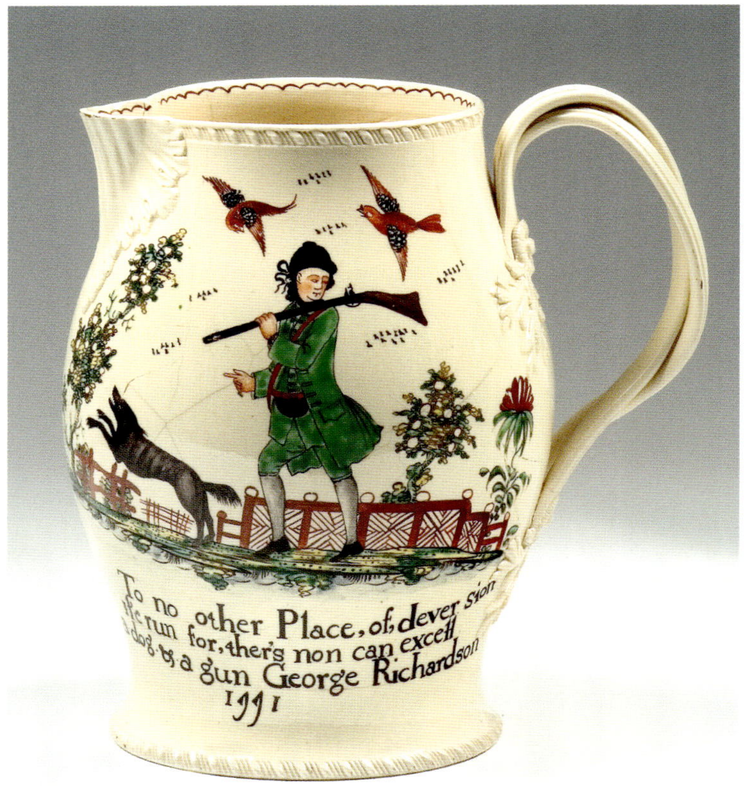

Jug, (1083), 1771, Yorkshire, Leeds, height: 19.1cm, (7½in), enamelled creamware. Rare creamware jug with moulded rim, its entwined handle has complex floral terminals. Inscribed for George Richardson, probably a Yorkshire landowner and keen sportsman, painted with a huntsman carrying a rifle, a powder flask hanging from his belt. His black dog leaps before him as they pass a chinoiserie fence and large chrysanthemum bushes while red birds fly overhead. The figure may be inspired by sporting subjects engraved after paintings by A.F. Desportes, from the early 1700s, also found as blue-printed decoration on Lowestoft porcelain of the period.[42]

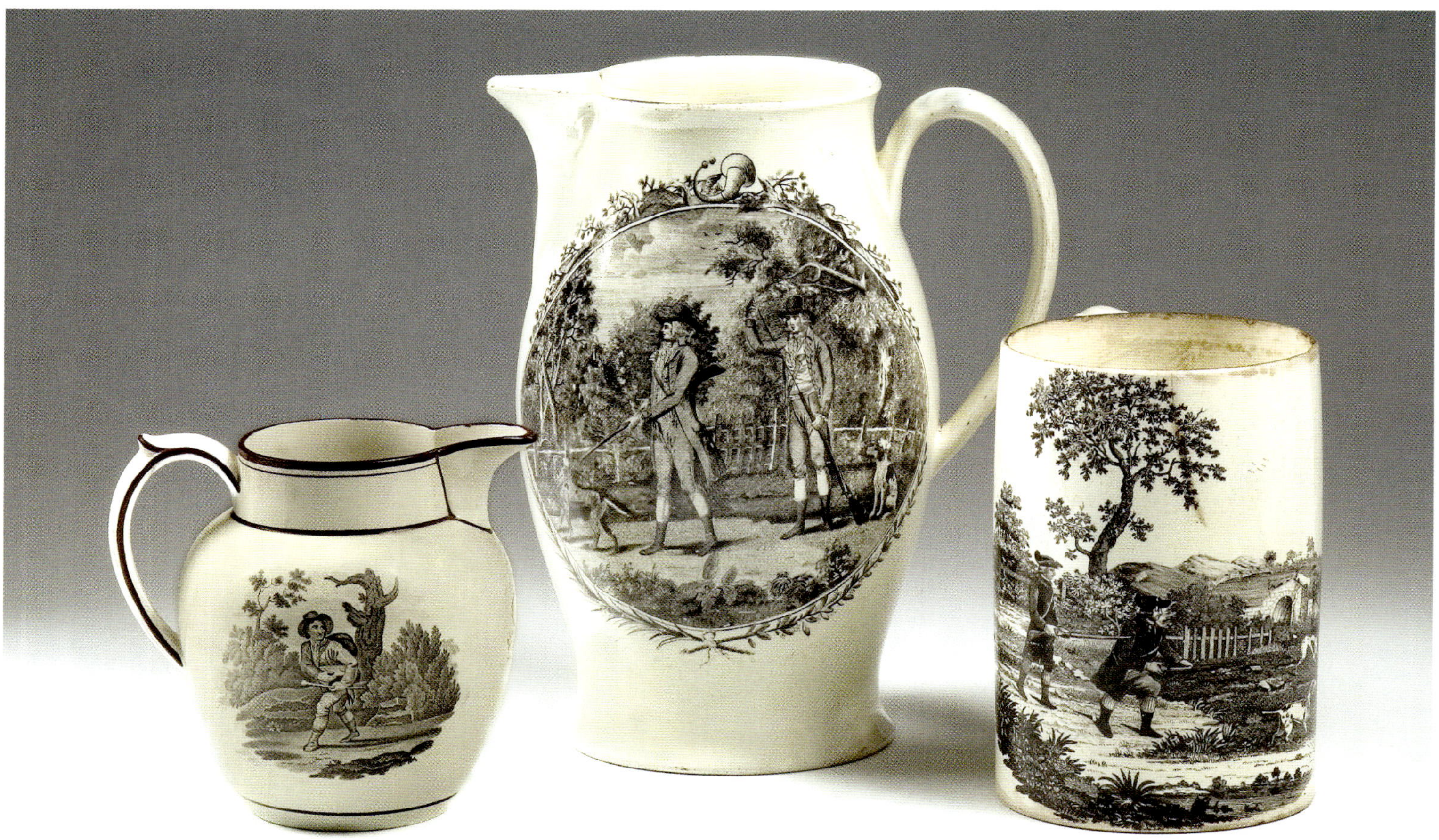

Jug, (270), c.1815, Staffordshire, Stoke-on-Trent, height: 13.3cm, (5¼in), printed bone china. Jug made by Spode, delicately printed with a poacher creeping cautiously through the landscape.
Jug, (1075), c.1790, Staffordshire or Liverpool, height: 24.2cm, (9½in), printed creamware. Oval reserve printed with two sportsmen with dogs, walking beside fenced woodland. One of the two tamps down the gunpowder in the barrel of his musket in anticipation of shooting game birds.[43]
Mug, (1076), c.1795, Staffordshire, Burslem, height: 16.5cm, (6½in), enamelled creamware. Mug, probably by Ralph Wedgwood, printed with a combination of figures and dogs from *Shooting II* and *Shooting III*, (from a quartet of paintings by George Stubbs), engraved by William Woollett in 1770.[44] The sportsmen are seen stalking and firing at game birds.

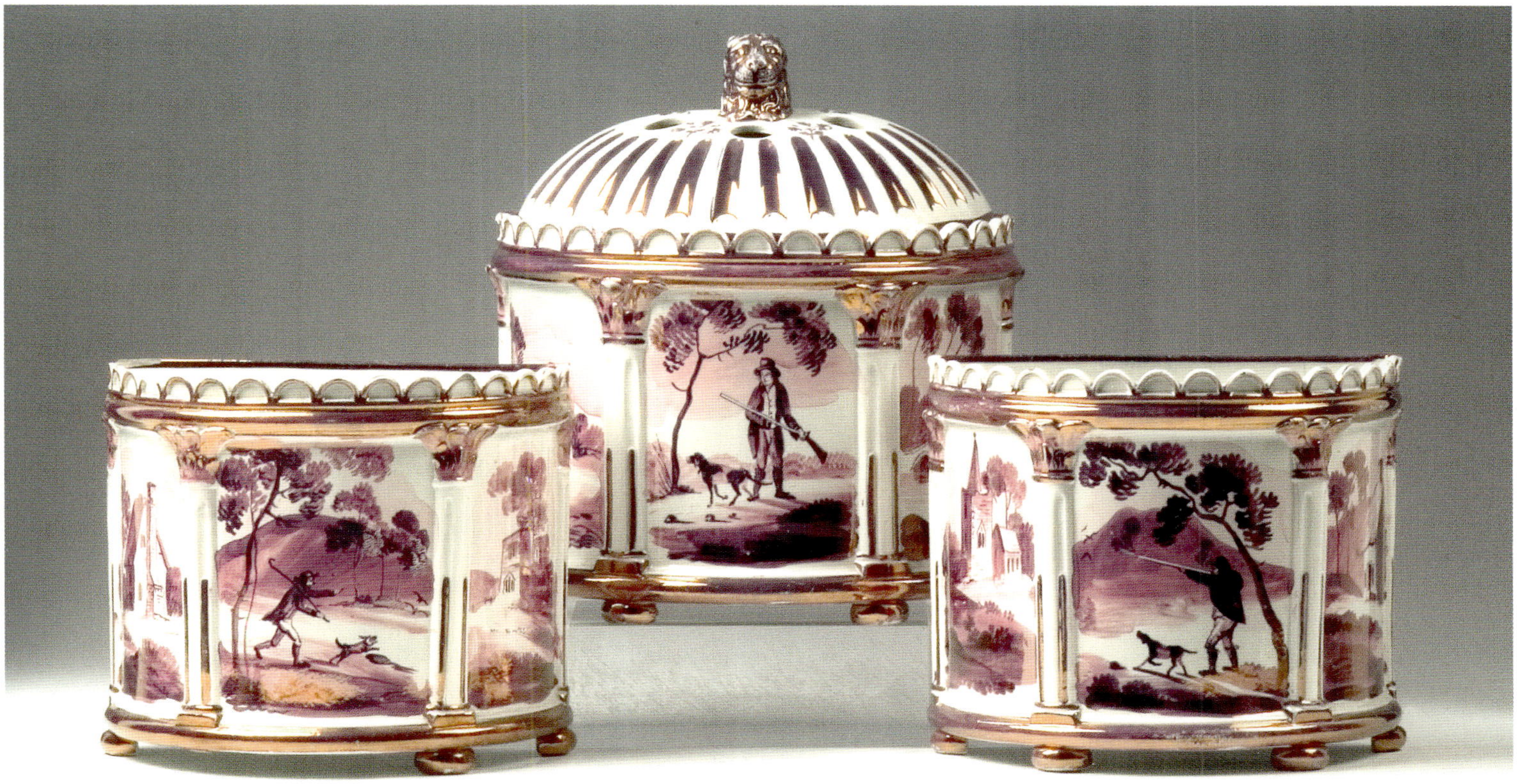

Three Bulbpots, (1077 & A & B), c.1800, Staffordshire, 2 x height: 16.8cm, (6⅝in), height: 25.4cm, (10in), lustred pearlware. D-shaped bulb pots, one with lid, painted with generalised scenes of sportsmen with guns and dogs.

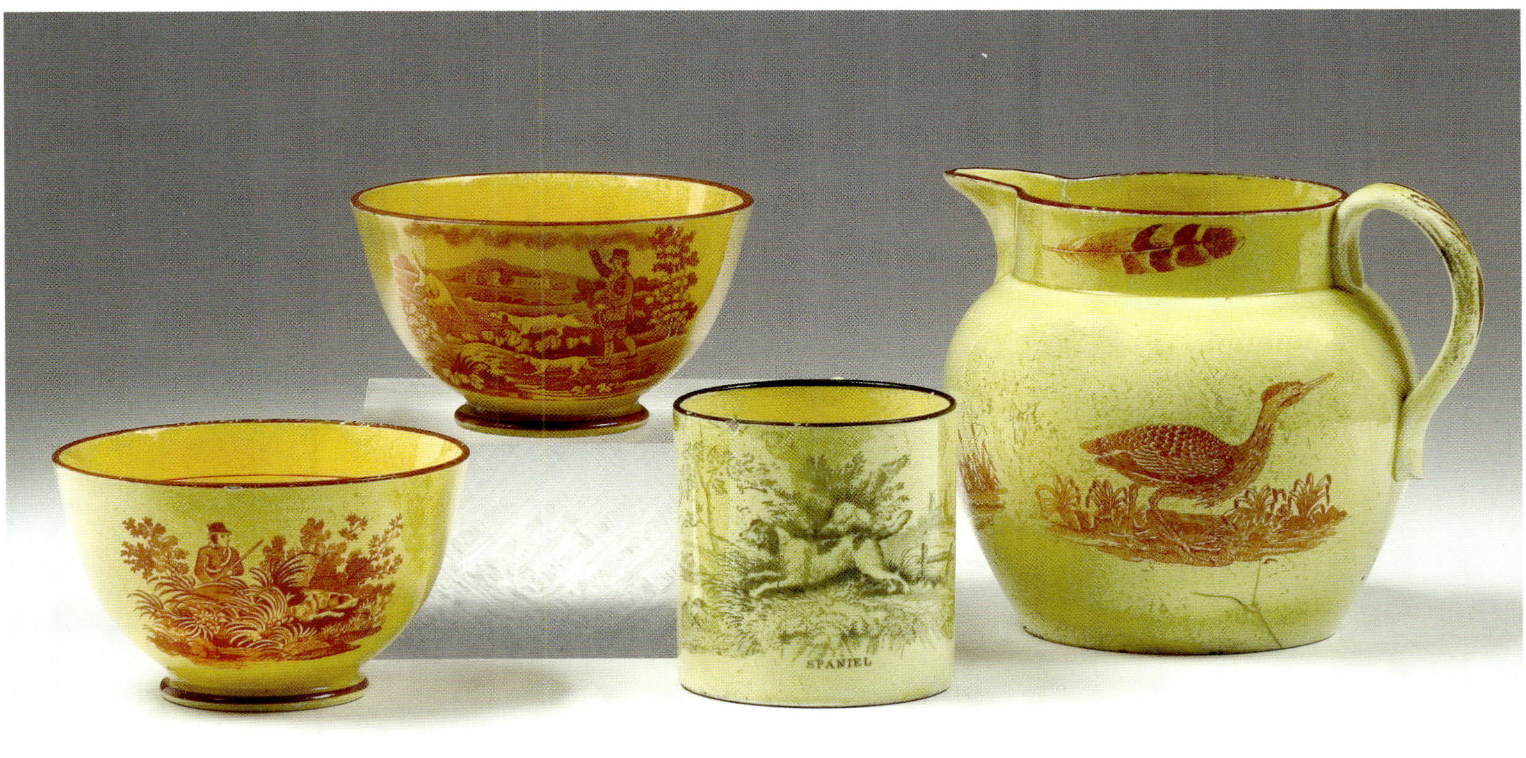

Two Teabowls, (**1078 & A**), c.1800, probably North East, each height: 5.7cm, (2¼in), red-printed, yellow-glazed earthenware. Each printed with vignettes, a huntsman and dog taking cover and another walking with dogs in a landscape.
Mug, (**1097**), c.1800, probably North East, each height: 6.4cm, (2½in), printed, yellow-glazed earthenware. Print entitled, 'SPANIEL', taken from image of the springer spaniel by Thomas Bewick (1753-1828).[45]
Jug, (**1094**), c.1815, Swansea, Cambrian Pottery, height: 10.8cm, (4¼in), red-printed, yellow-glazed earthenware. Printed with fine vignettes of a partridge, a woodcock and a snipe, and feathers around the rim. These images are clearly influenced by Bewick. Charlotte Bronte notes that Bewick's *History of British Birds* is one of Jane Eyre's favourite books at Lowood.[46]

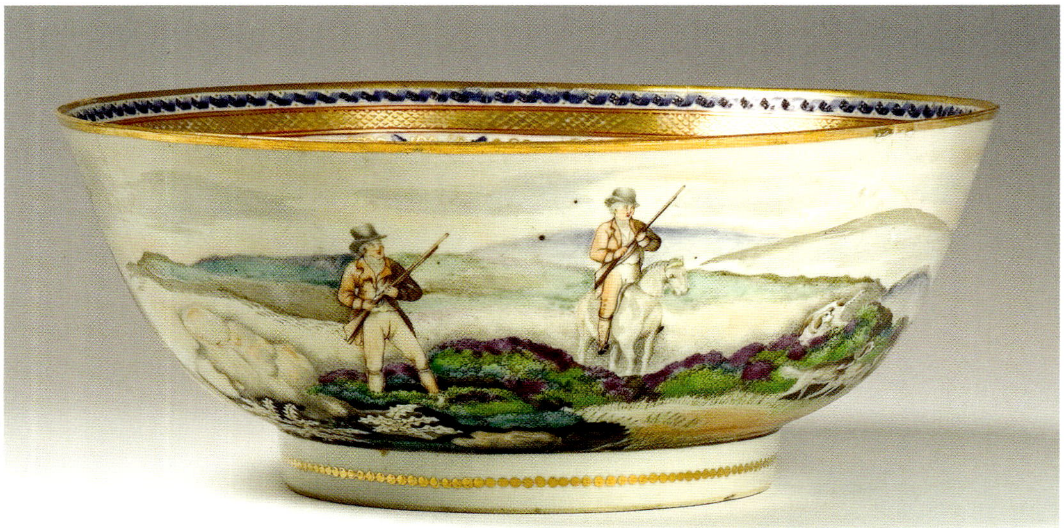

Punchbowl, (**1086**), c.1810, China, diameter: 30cm, (11¾in), hard-paste porcelain, enamelled and gilt. Delicately painted with hunting scenes, a horseman and dogs in the centre and on the exterior, sweeping open moorland and men with guns hiding among leafless trees. The image is taken from 'Grouse Shooting' by Samuel Howitt from Edward Orme's *British Field Sports*, published 1807.

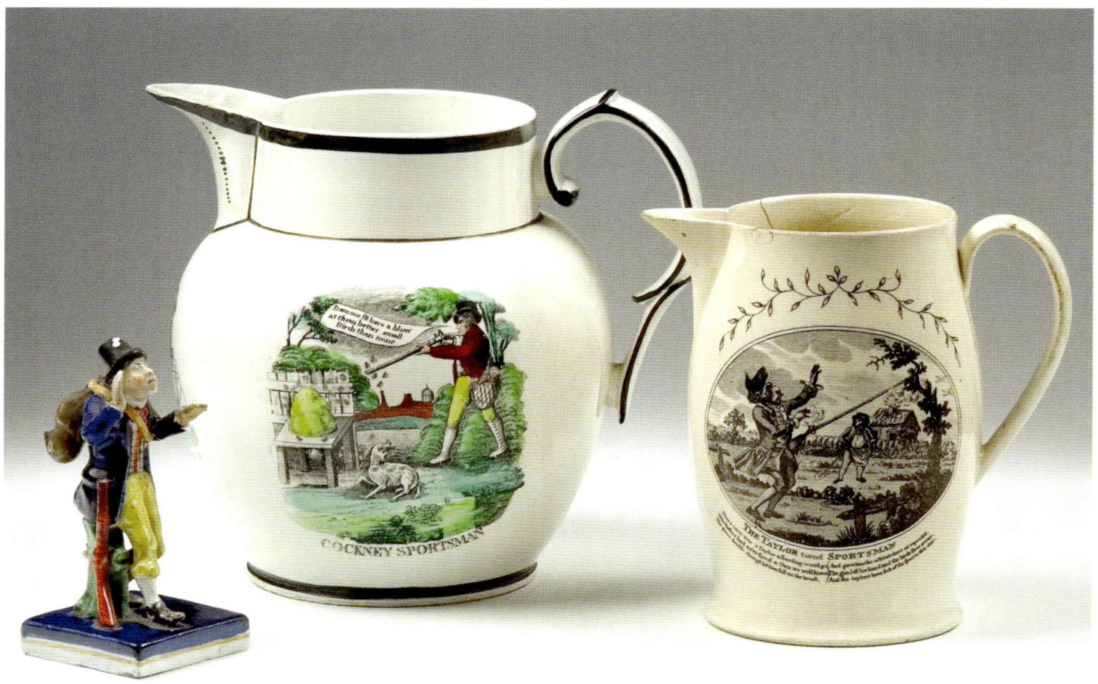

Figure, (**1098**), c.1810, Staffordshire, height: 14cm, (5½in), enamelled pearlware. Comic figure of a 'Cockney Sportsman' looking alarmed, with a large, dead owl hanging down his back. 'Cockney Sportsmen' was a series of caricatures of city dwellers making fools of themselves in the countryside. [47] It fed into the class snobbery around country sports.[48]
Jug, (**1099**), c.1800, Staffordshire, height: 14.6cm, (8½in), pearlware, printed and enamelled. Print entitled, 'COCKNEY SPORTSMAN',[49] shows a comic hunter shooting at a beehive exclaiming, 'better small birds than none.' It is taken, not from Gillray's famous series but from an earlier print published by Sayer, entitled 'The London Cockney's Attack on the Bee Hive', of 1791-2.[50]
Jug, (**1093**), c.1790, Staffordshire, height: 17.8cm, (7in), printed creamware. A comical scene inscribed, 'THE TAYLOR turn'd SPORTSMAN' after Robert Dighton and verses making fun of the tailor who has never before fired a gun and drops it.[51]

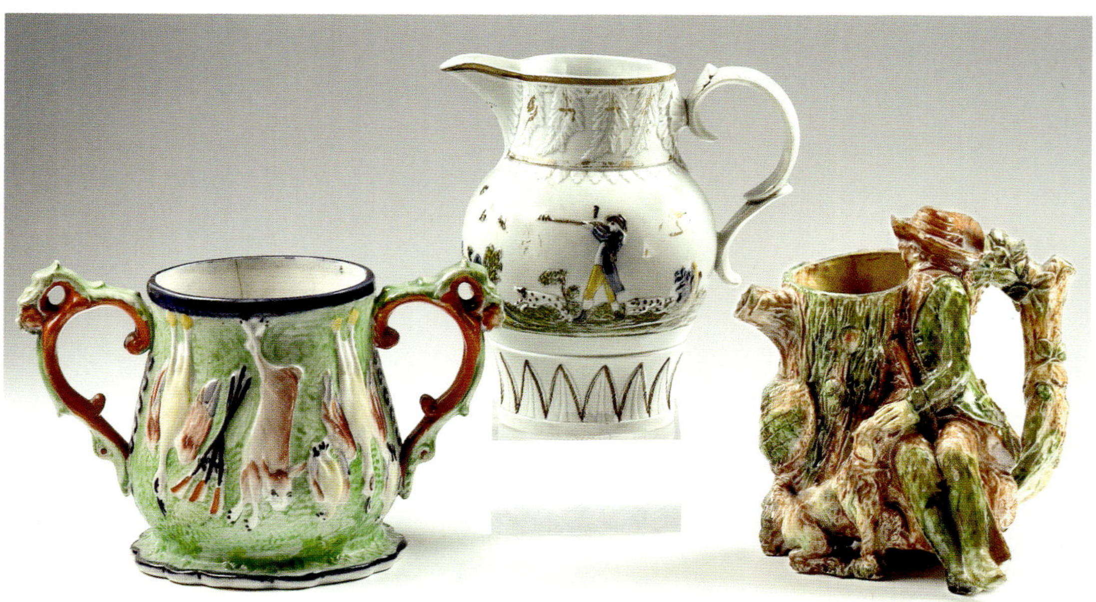

Two-handled Cup, (**1091**), c.1810, height: 15.9cm, (6¼in), enamelled pearlware. Relief-moulded with dead game (including a stag, a heron and a hare) and guns hanging from the rim.
Jug, (**1084**), c.1795, Staffordshire, height: 20.3cm, (8in), Prattware. Relief-moulded scenes of huntsmen with spotted dogs, shooting birds.
Teapot (lacking lid)**,** (**1072**), c.1790, Staffordshire, height: 12.7cm, (5in), lead-glazed and oxide-coloured. Moulded as a sportsman sitting at the base of a truncated tree trunk, his shotgun between his knees and his dog beside him. A pig peers from beneath the roots.

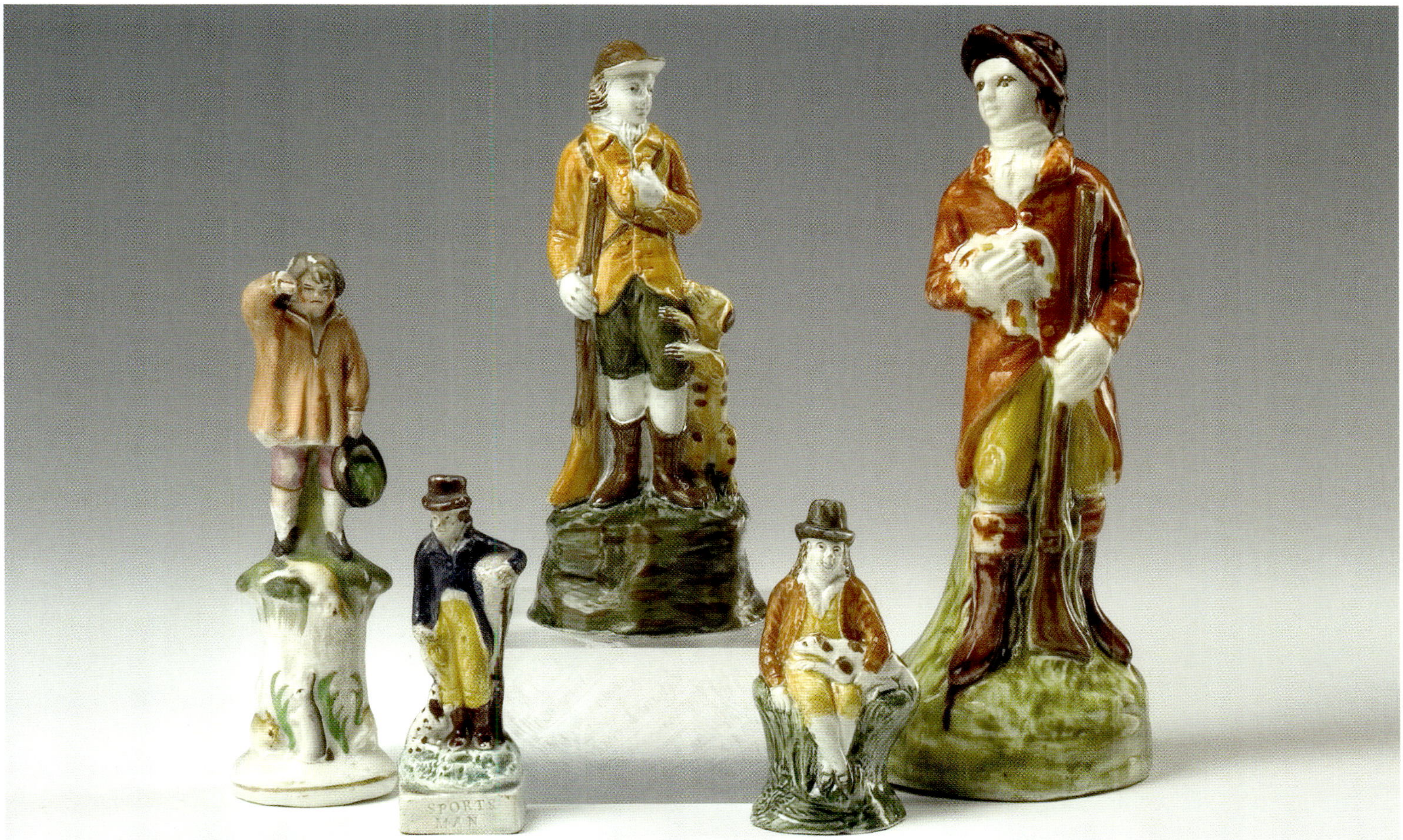

Figure, (1090), c.1810, Staffordshire, height: 17.8cm, (7in), enamelled soft-paste porcelain. A boy on a high pedestal moulded with a dead hare and other animals.
Figure, (1080), c.1810, Staffordshire, height: 10.8cm, (4¼in), Prattware. Figure with a gun and a dog standing on a base impressed: 'SPORTS / MAN'.
Figure, (1085), c.1810, Staffordshire, height: 17.7cm, (7in), Prattware. Hunt servant wearing peaked cap, with fawning spotted dog, carries gun.
Figure, (1079), c.1810, Yorkshire, Leeds? height: 10.2cm, (4in), Prattware. Figure sits on a tree stump with a dog on his lap. Similar figures were produced at the Leeds Pottery.
Figure, (1074), c.1810, Staffordshire, height: 24.2cm, (9½in), Prattware. Hunt servant wearing peaked cap, carries gun and holds dead bird.

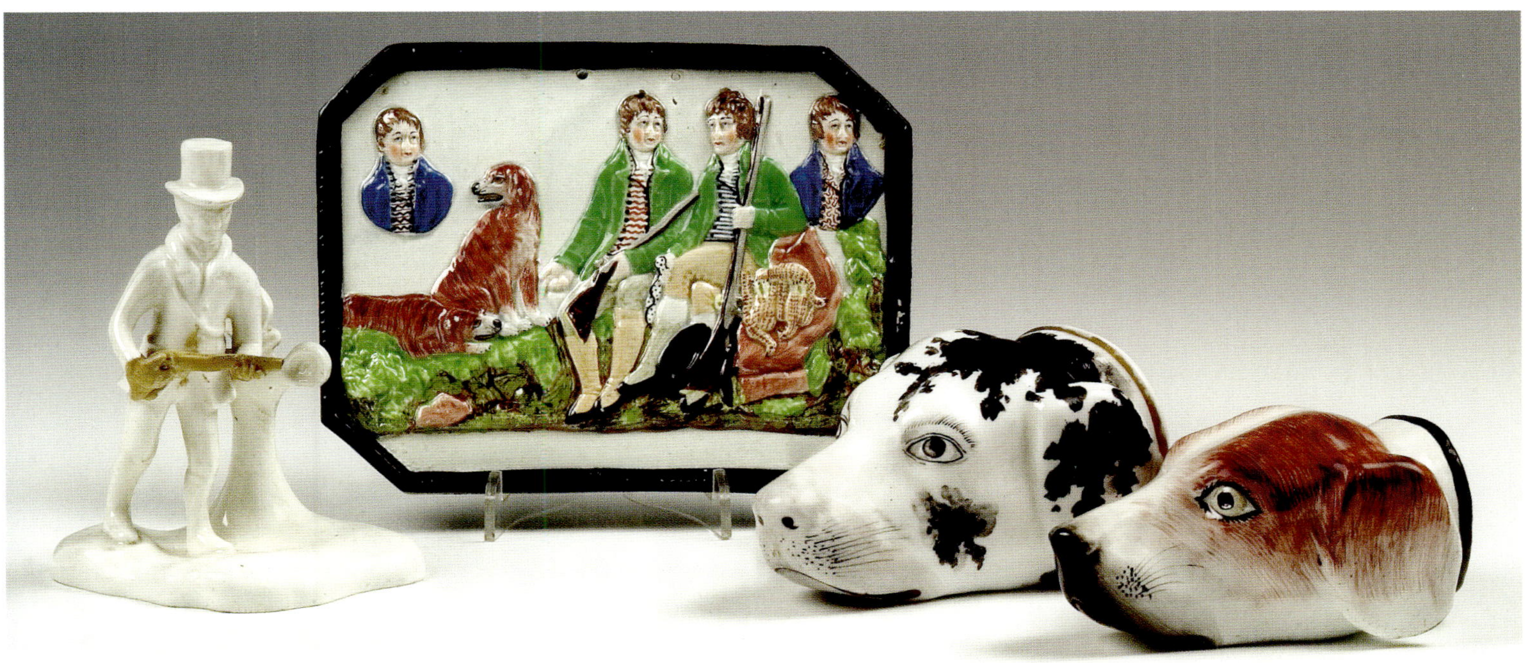

Figure, (1082), c.1840, Staffordshire, height: 21.6cm, (8½in), soft-paste porcelain. Crudely modelled figure of a man pointing an (overpainted) gun, possibly by Tittensor.
Plaque, (1089), c. 1810, Staffordshire, height: 17.1cm, (6¾in), enamelled pearlware. Relief-moulded with sportsmen, dogs, dead fowl and two disembodied busts. Subject taken from a popular mezzotint entitled 'Grouse Shooters in Bowland', by George Dawe published in 1804.[52]
Two Stirrup Cups, (1088 & A), c.1840, Staffordshire, each height: 12.1cm, (4¾in), soft-paste porcelain. Modelled as the heads of hounds, one with spotty black patches, the other with large brown patches over the eyes.

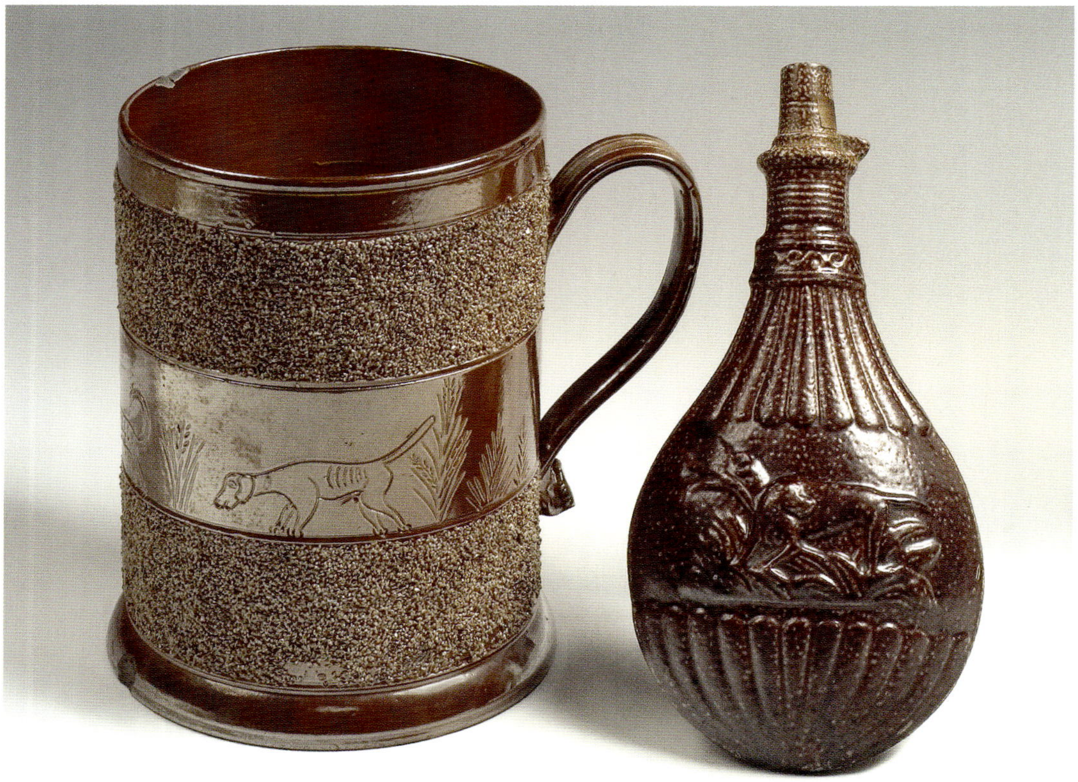

Mug, (**1103**), c.1800, Nottinghamshire, height: 21cm, (8¼in), salt-glazed stoneware. Smooth band around centre of mug with fritted surface, incised with outlines of fox hounds.
Spirit flask, (**1087**), c.1800, London, height: 24.8cm, (9¾in), salt-glazed stoneware. Flask, probably made at Lambeth, modelled as a powder flask, relief-moulded with a hound.

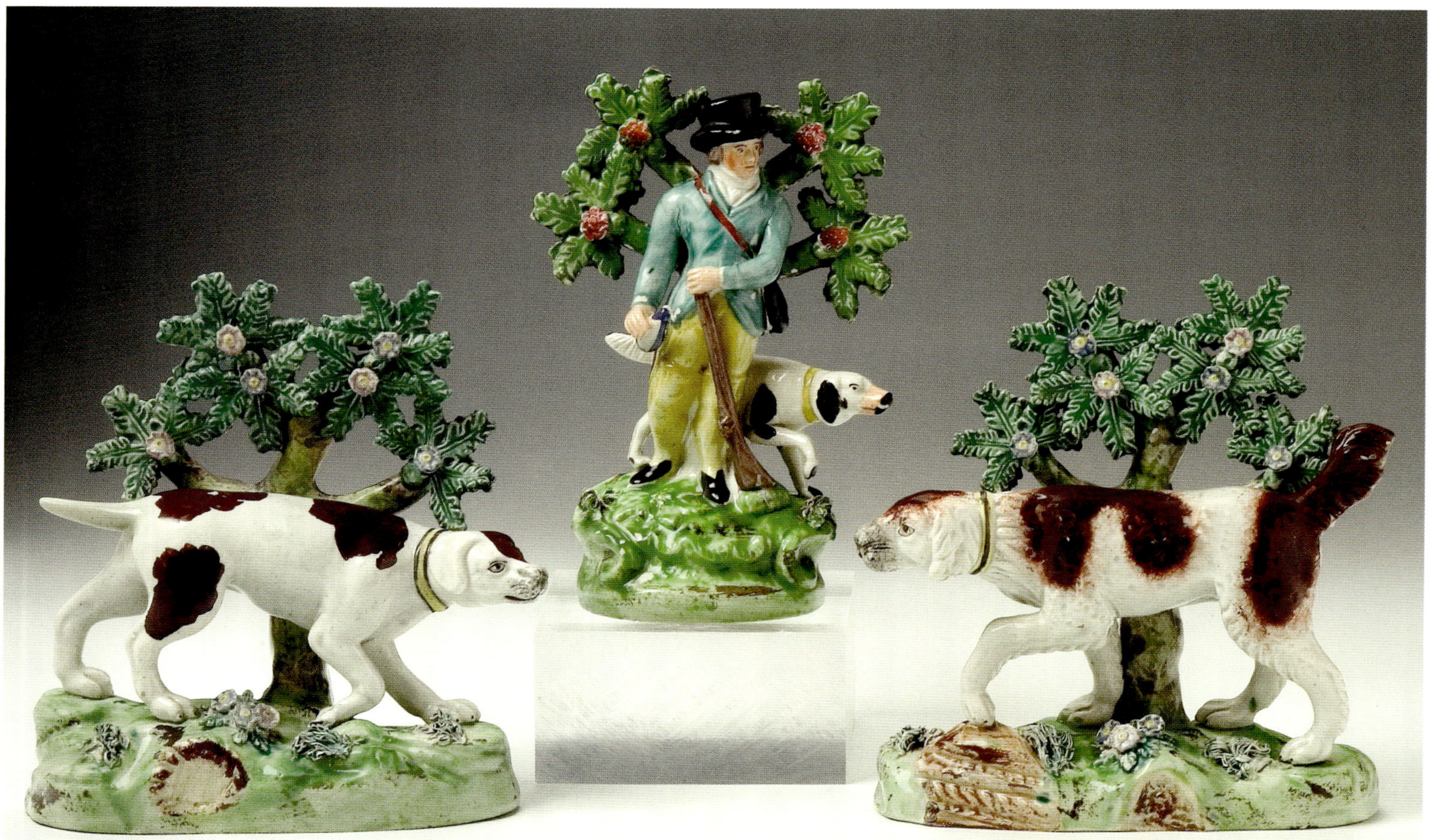

Figure, (**1081**), c.1820, Staffordshire, height: 13.3cm, (5¼in), enamelled pearlware. Figure of a pointer, with its characteristic hocked-paw gesture, adept at locating and retrieving pheasant and grouse on moorland.
Figure, (**1073**), c.1820, Staffordshire, height: 19.1cm, (7½in), enamelled pearlware. Between the two dogs is a small bocage group of a sportsman with his gun and powder bag and his pointer.

Figure, (**1081A**), c.1820, Staffordshire, height: 13.3cm, (5¼in), enamelled pearlware. Figure of a water spaniel (or otter hound), expert in finding waterfowl. They may owe something to Thomas Bewick's images of the pointer and large water spaniel.[53] *A Description of Three Animals*, (1744) states that, '[the water spaniel] is very excellent at hunting of Otters, Ducks, etc'.

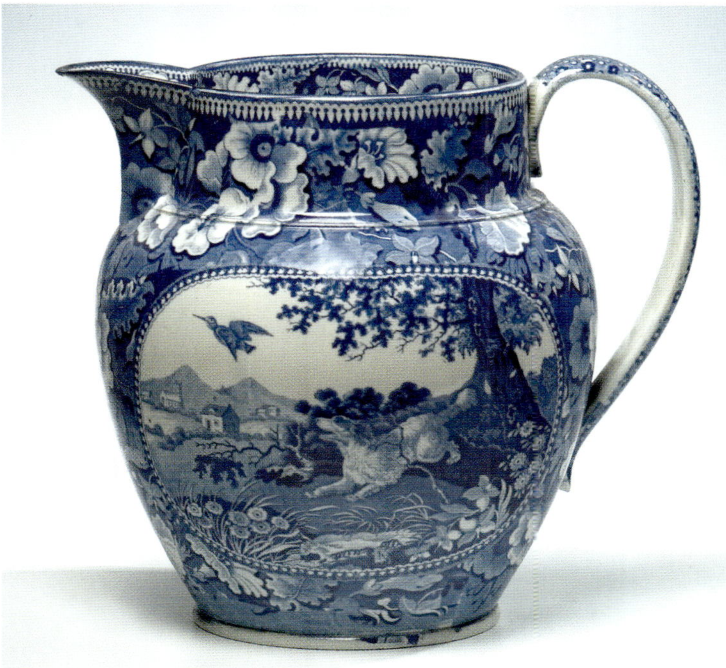

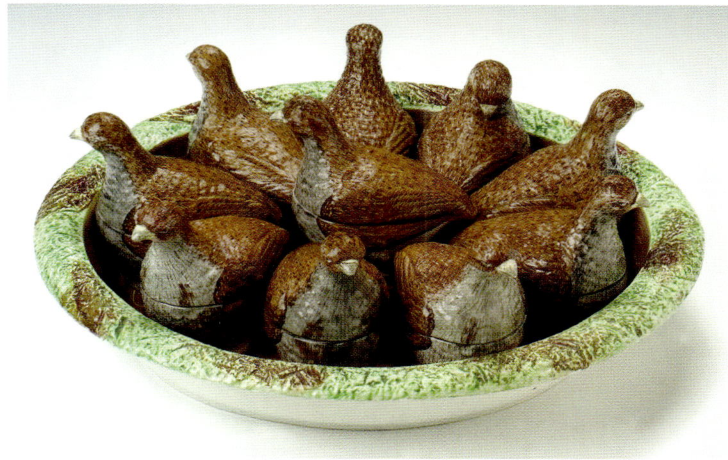

Jug, (**1100**), c.1810, Staffordshire, Burslem, height: 26.7cm, (10½in), blue-printed earthenware. Probably made by Ralph Stevenson. Image of springer spaniel flushing out a woodcock against floral background, taken from *The Sportsman's Cabinet,* 1803.[54]

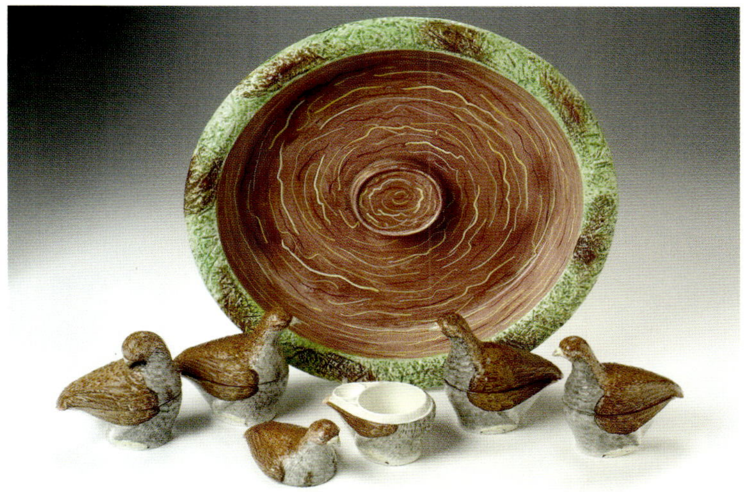

Dish, (**1095**), c.1815, Staffordshire, Longport, height: 34.3cm, (13½in), enamelled pearlware. An extraordinary dish, made by Davenport, modelled as a nest containing ten individual egg cups, each in the form of a quail with detachable lid. Each egg cup has a separate depression (at the tail end) for salt. Only one other example (smaller), has been noted.[55]

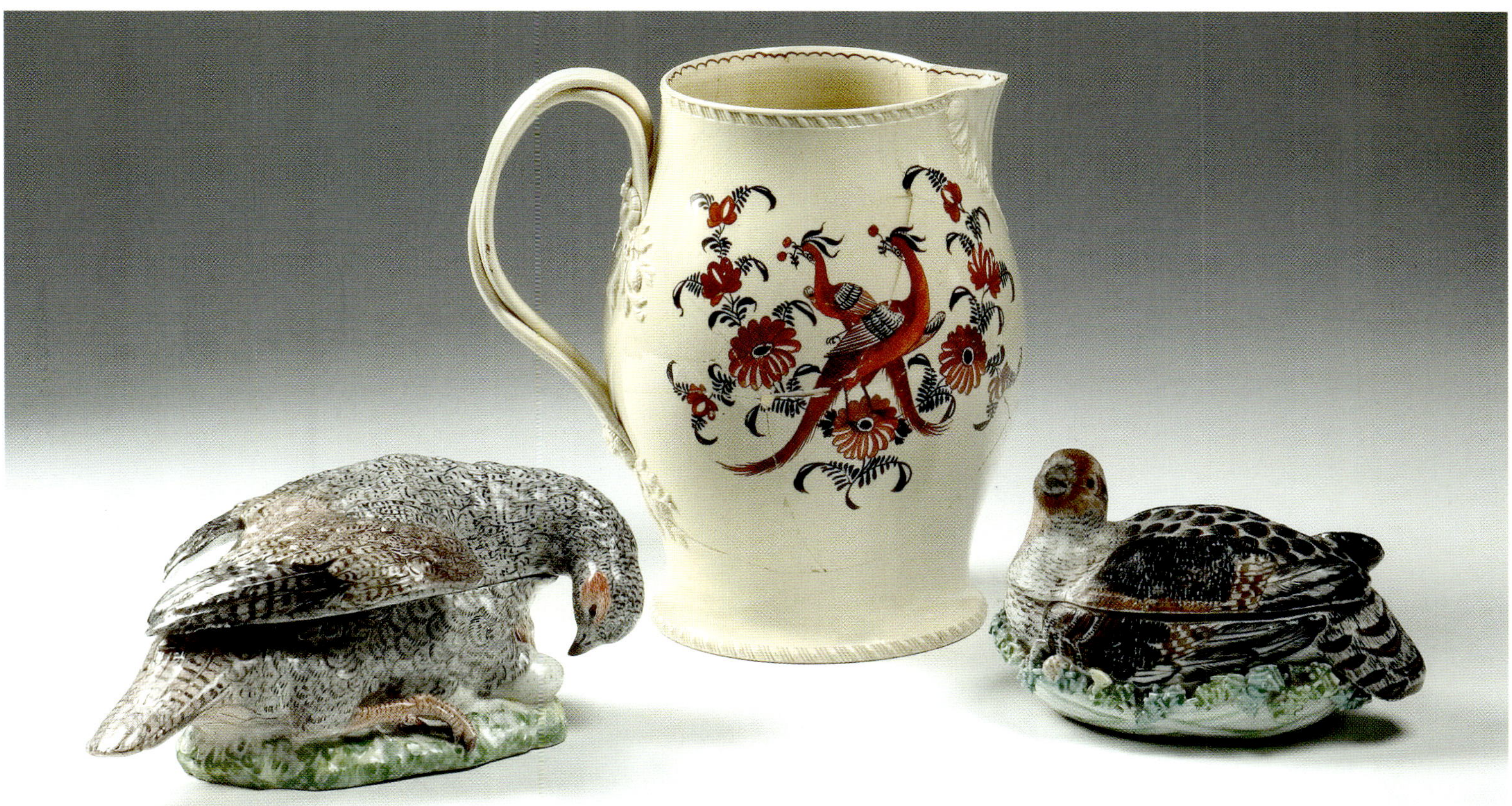

Box, (**1096**), c.1760, London, Bow, height: 8.4cm, (3⅜in), enamelled soft-paste porcelain. Modelled as brooding quail or partridge, the upper parts forming the lids. One tucks an egg beneath her breast with her beak. **Jug,** (**1083**), 1771, Yorkshire, Leeds, height: 19.1cm (7½in), enamelled creamware. Rare creamware jug with moulded rim, its entwined handle has complex floral terminals. Enamelled with exotic red pheasants and flowers. **Box,** (**1096A**), c.1760, Worcester, height: 9cm, (3½in), enamelled soft-paste porcelain. Modelled as brooding quail or partridge, looking up from her nest.[56]

Hare Coursing

By the late-seventeenth century, with the technical advances made in the accuracy and reliability of firearms, the hare was becoming increasingly rare. As the agricultural revolution progressed and wide-scale land clearance and drainage encroached upon the woodland habitat, modes of hunting changed accordingly. The hare, 'a subtle, clever beast with a sweet scent', had long been designated the quarry of the country squire and was hunted by pairs of matched greyhounds. Star greyhounds included Lord Orford's bitches, Czarina and Maria, who featured in the Rev. William Daniel's *Rural Sports* (1807). Coursing marked the origin of greyhound racing which has continued to be a popular sport until today.

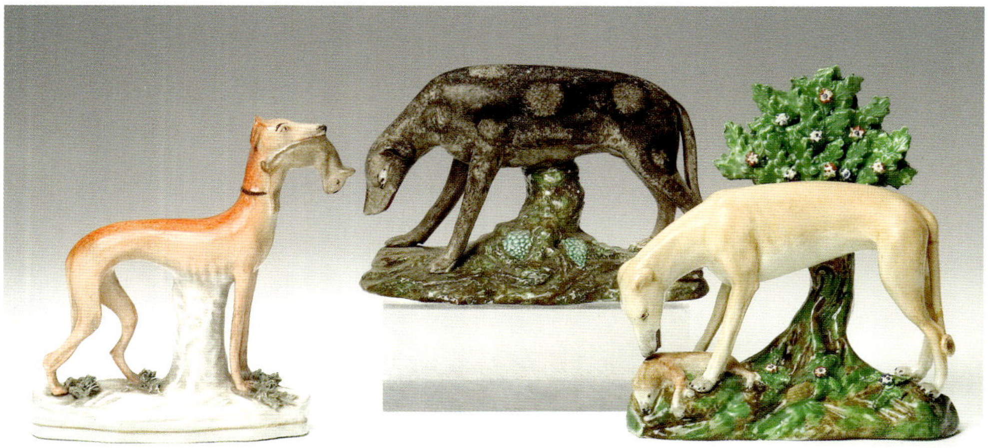

Figure, (**1150**), c.1840, Staffordshire, height: 17.8cm, (7in), enamelled bone china. Figure of a greyhound proudly holding its prey aloft.
Figure, (**1141**), c.1790, Staffordshire, height: 11.5cm, (4½in), enamelled pearlware. Crudely modelled figure of greyhound bending over a dead hare.
Figure, (**1149**), c.1820, Staffordshire, height: 15.3cm, (6in), enamelled pearlware. Greyhound, bending over a dead hare before an ornate bocage tree.

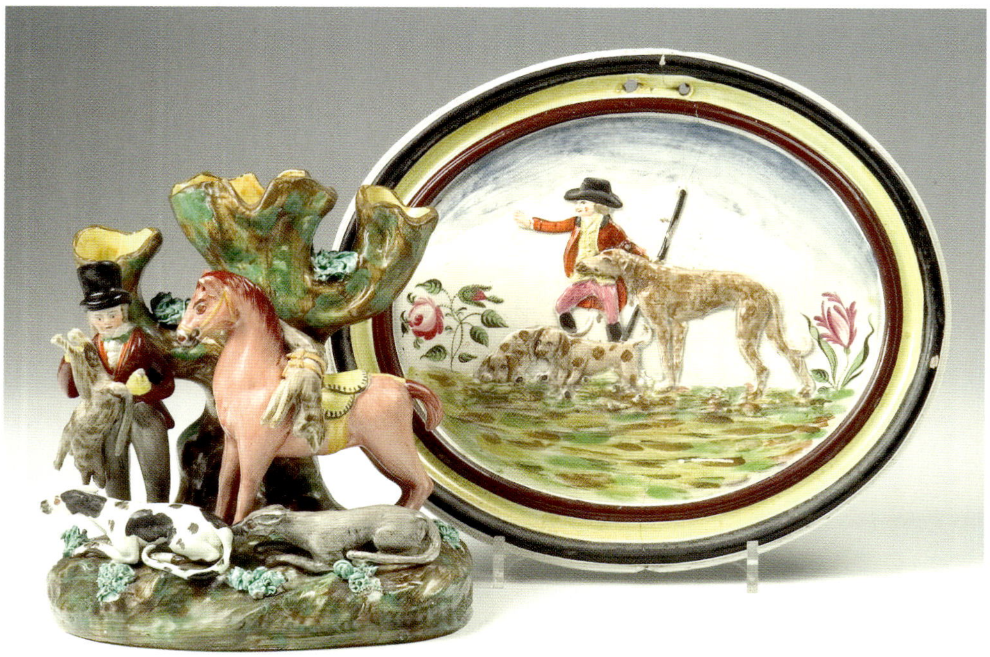

Flower-holder, (**1143**), c.1820, Staffordshire, height: 17.2cm, (6¾in), enamelled pearlware. Two greyhounds crouch on the ground as a huntsman holds up a dead hare; another is strapped to his horse's saddle. Gnarled, hollow tree behind contains three chambers for spills.
Plaque, (**1151**), c.1800, Staffordshire, height: 24.8cm, (9¾in), enamelled pearlware. Relief-moulded with a man holding a staff, a large greyhound and two beagles (not usually used for hare coursing).

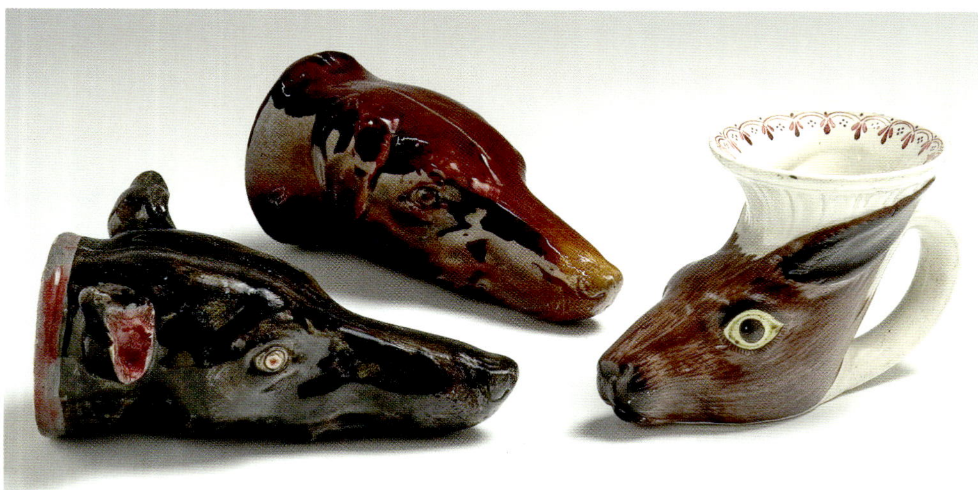

Stirrup Cup, (**1144**), c.1820, Staffordshire, height: 16.5cm, (6½in), enamelled pearlware. Head of a greyhound, enamelled with red inner ears and collar.
Stirrup Cup, (**1144A**), c.1840, Staffordshire, height: 16.5cm, (6½in), glazed earthenware. Head of a greyhound, treacle-glazed with flattened ears.
Stirrup Cup, (**1145**), c.1840, Staffordshire, height: 9.6cm, (3¾in), glazed earthenware. Head of a hare modelled as cup with a handle and upper rim, similar to a Greek rhyton.

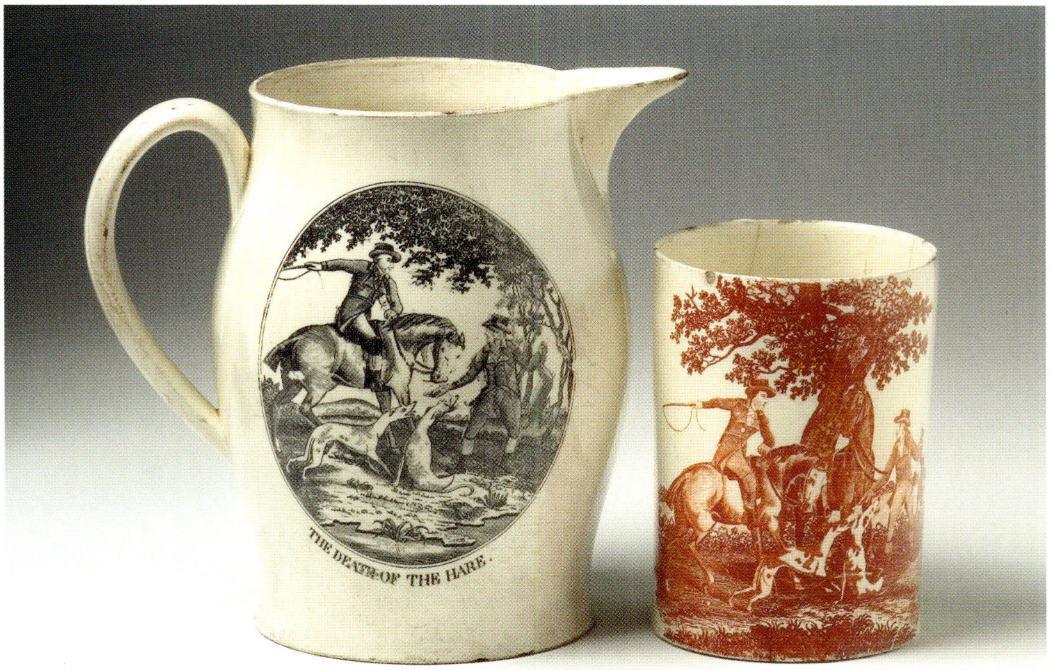

Jug, (**1152**), c.1795, Yorkshire?, height: 17.2cm, (6¾in), printed creamware.
Mug, (**1142**), c.1795, Staffordshire, height: 12.1cm, (4¾in), red-printed creamware. Both pieces decorated with same image, 'THE DEATH OF THE HARE', taken from the *Sporting Magazine,* engraved by Cook, probably after Samuel Howitt.[57] The jug may have been at the Leeds Pottery.

Plaque, (**1146**), c.1810, Staffordshire, height: 15.3cm, (6in), earthenware. Kidney-shaped plaque, (or male pitcher mould) moulded with sportsmen, and greyhounds at, 'The Death of the Hare'.
Plaque, (**1148**), c.1810, Staffordshire, height: 13.3cm, (5¼in), enamelled pearlware. Octagonal plaque relief-moulded with 'The Death of the Hare' (as 1146) and two disembodied busts.
Plaque, (**1092**), c.1810, Staffordshire, height: 15.3cm, (6in), earthenware. Kidney-shaped plaque, (or male pitcher mould) moulded with subject taken from a popular mezzotint, entitled 'Grouse Shooters in Bowland', by George Dawe published in 1804.[58]

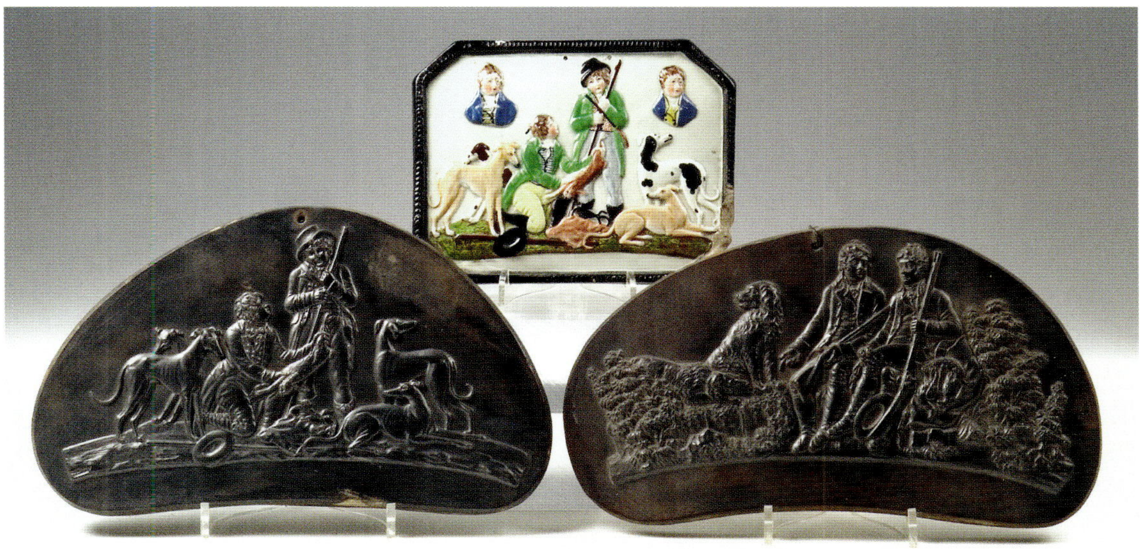

Jug, (**1139**), c.1810, Staffordshire, height: 14.6cm, (5¾in), Prattware. Relief-moulded with horsemen riding to hounds while the fox keeps just ahead.
Jug, (**1153**), c.1795, Staffordshire, height: 19.1cm, (7½in), Prattware. Relief-moulded with hare coursing through low thickets.
Jug, (**1140**), c.1810, Staffordshire, height: 14cm, (5½in), Prattware. Relief-moulded with horsemen riding to hounds while the fox keeps just ahead.

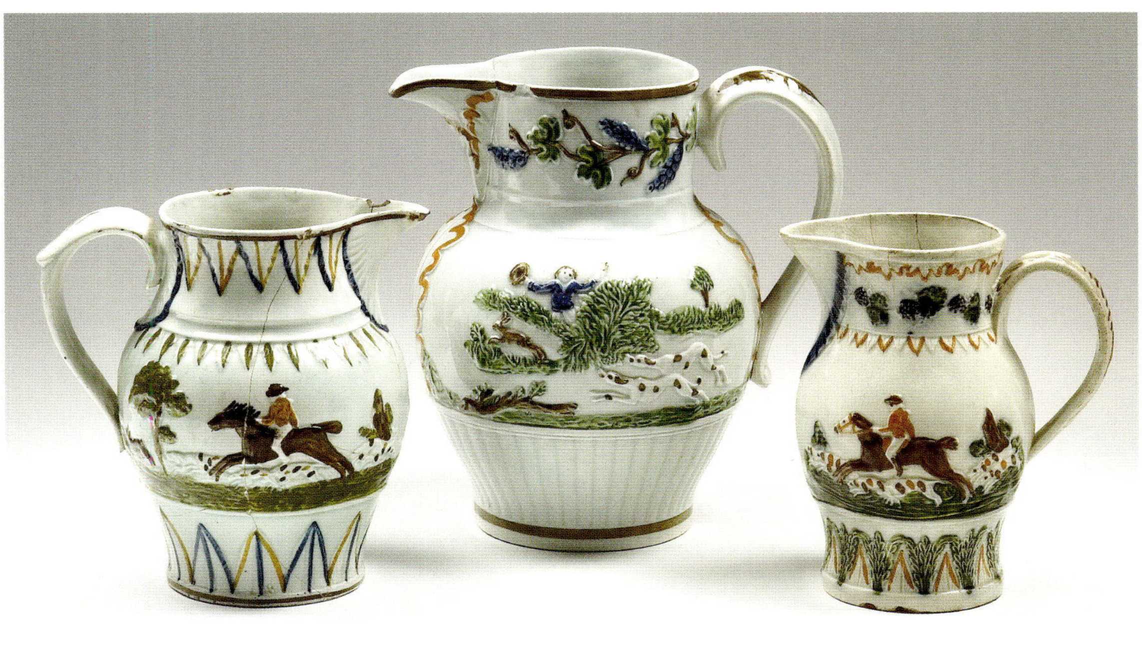

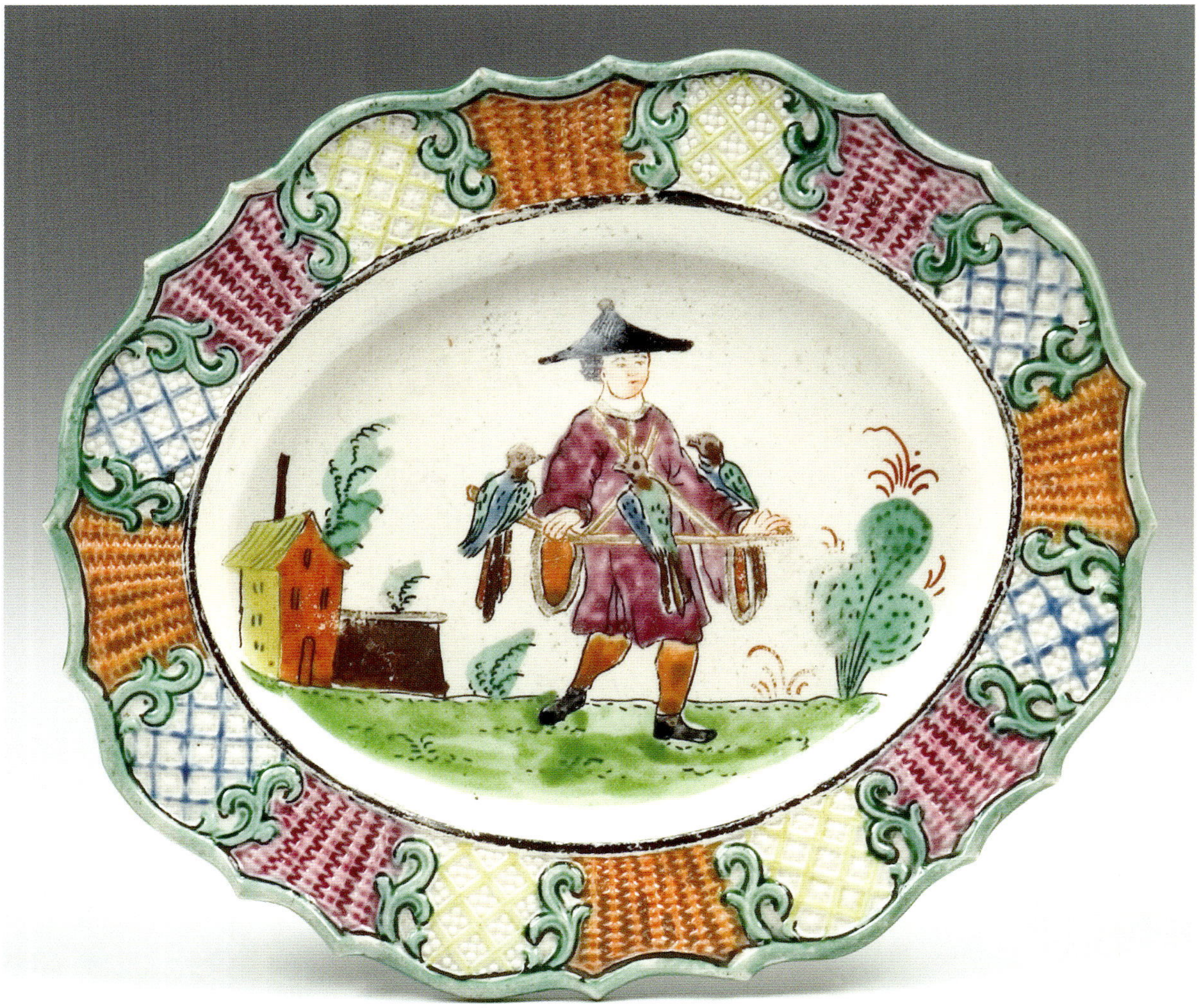

Stand, (**1156**), c.1760, Staffordshire, height: 15.3cm, (6in), enamelled, salt-glazed stoneware. Rare, basket-moulded stand for a butter tub, enamelled with a chinoiserie figure of a falconer holding a 'cadge' (a travelling frame of perches) on which the hooded birds sit.

Falconry

Hawking or falconry was also organised according to class distinctions. Medieval sumptuary laws allotted the gerfalcon to a king, the peregrine to an earl, the hobby to an esquire, the sparrow hawk to a priest, the goshawk to a yeoman and the kestrel to a servant. Although the sport declined sharply after the arrival of the musket, it never died out. In 1791 the Earl of Oxford revived the sport with some success in Yorkshire and Norfolk. The tiny merlin could kill quail and snipe. The peregrine was flown at hares, rabbits and most of the larger game birds and could even bring down a heron.

The falconer traditionally wears one buckskin gauntlet to which the hawk returns to be 'hoodwinked' or blinkered, with a close-fitting plumed hood, when not flying at game. The bird was tethered by 'jesses' or thongs attached to its legs, secured around the fingers of the glove. During the moulting season the birds were confined to mews; quiet, dark quarters in the owner's stables. The sport is only occasionally demonstrated at English fairs and practised on country estates but continues to be very popular in the Middle East and along the old Silk Road through central Asia.

Hunting in India

A deer-hunting expedition in India went badly wrong. On 22 December, 1792, Lieutenant or rather Mr Hugh Munro, (there is no record of him in the Army lists), the illegitimate, only child of General Sir Hector Munro, landed with friends on Saugor Island in the Sanderbanks, near Calcutta. It was rich in game but notorious for the game-hunting tigers that swam in the rivers. Munro and his companions lit a large fire (recommended to ward off predators) and were picnicking when they were surprised by a pair of ferocious tigers, which leapt from the undergrowth, seized Munro and killed him.

The incident was widely reported and published in the *Sporting Magazine* and in the *Gentleman's Magazine* in July 1793.

'I heard a roar, like thunder, and saw an immense royal tiger spring on the unfortunate Munro, ... In a moment his head was in the beast's mouth, and he rushed into the jungle with him, with as much ease as I could lift a kitten'.

> The friend shot the tiger, releasing Munro who staggered back, 'all over blood ... He lived 24 hours in the extreme of torture; his head and skull were torn, and broke in pieces, and he was wounded by the jaws all over his neck and shoulders; ... we have just read the funeral service over the body, and committed it to the deep'.[59]

There is a famous musical organ, known as Tipoo's Tiger, modelled as a tiger devouring a British soldier, now in the collections of the V&A. It was made around 1795 in Seringapatam in India for Tipu, Sultan of Mysore, the sworn enemy of the British in late-eighteenth-century India.[60] The organ was plundered by the British at the fall of Seringapatam in 1799 and displayed in London from 1808. The death of Munro may have inspired its construction or it may simply have reflected Tipu's obsession with tigers and his hatred of the European invaders. His father, Haidar Ali, had been defeated and humiliated by Sir Hector Munro at Porto Novo and he himself had been forced to hand over two of his sons as hostages to Lord Cornwallis in 1792.[61] The death of Sir Hector's son, mauled by Tipu's favourite beast, must have seemed just revenge.

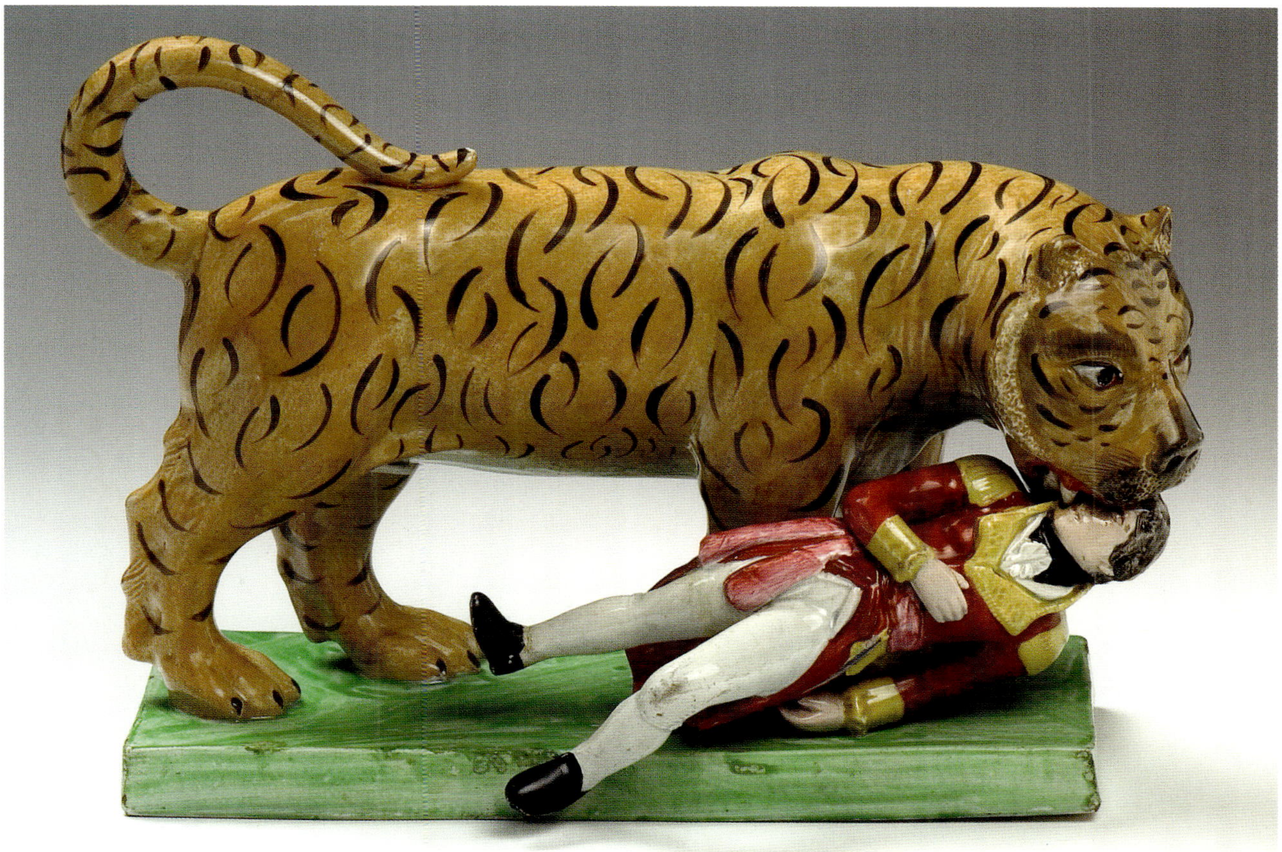

Figure Group, (**1155**), c.1825, Staffordshire height: 24.1cm, (9½in), enamelled pearlware. A tiger mauls a man wearing the uniform of a British soldier. Group inspired by the dramatic death of Munro in 1792 in Mysore, southern India. Such pieces, produced from the 1820s, were probably inspired by the wooden hand-organ known as 'Tipoo's Tiger'.

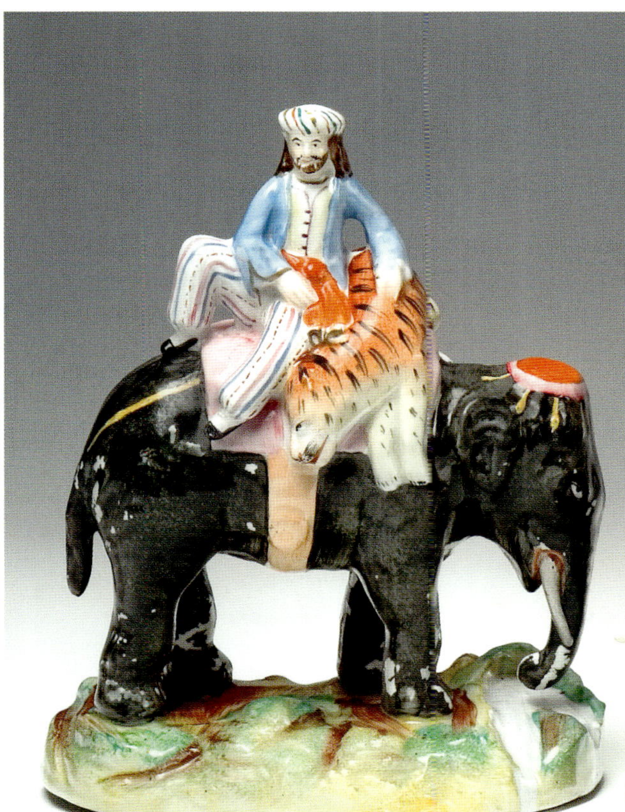

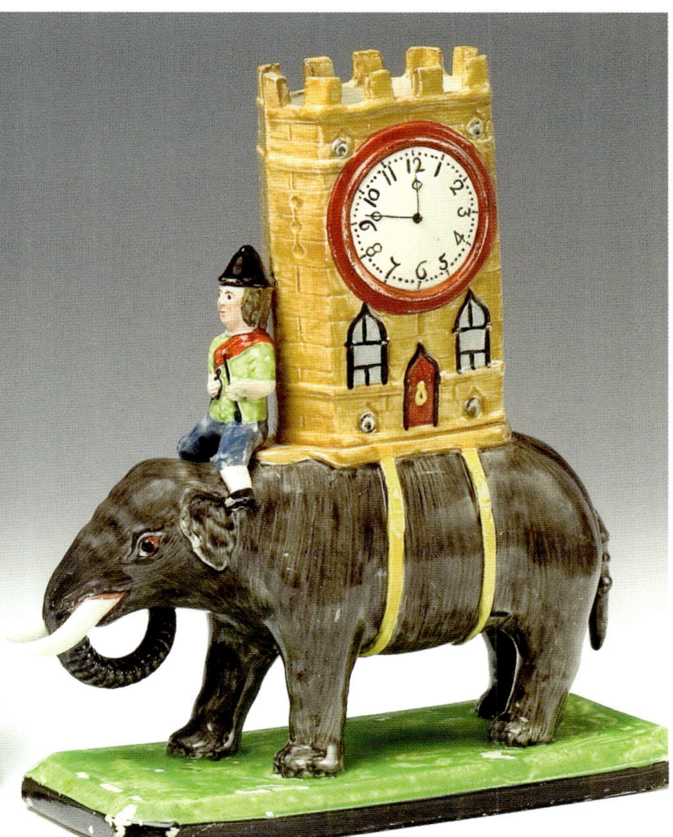

Figure Group, (**1154**), c.1840, Staffordshire, height: 22.2cm, (8¾in), enamelled pearlware. Man in exotic oriental costume sits on top of an elephant supporting a small dead tiger. Such pieces may be inspired by a stage production, such as *The Elephant of Siam*, staged at London's Adelphi Theatre on 3 December 1829.[62]

Flower-holder, (**1221**), c.1830, Staffordshire, height: 22.9cm, (9in), enamelled pearlware. Flower holder or spill vase in the form of an elephant with a howdah on its back, modelled as a clock tower.

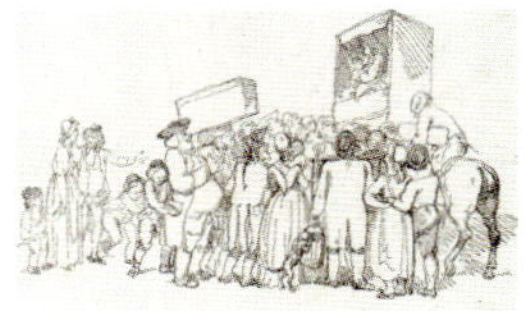

Chapter 16

PASTIMES & AMUSEMENTS

Archery

In the Middle Ages, archery practice with the longbow was obligatory rather than a pastime, so that men should be prepared for military combat. Idle pursuits, such as football, were accused of distracting men from archery. In 1545, Roger Ascham, tutor to the future Queen Elizabeth I, wrote the first treatise on the subject, *Toxophilus, the Schole of Shootinge*. King James I, author of *The Book of Sports* (pub. 1618), considered archery a very suitable pastime to follow Divine Service on the Sabbath. With the arrival of firearms, however, archery all but disappeared.

Interest revived in the late-eighteenth century when women were permitted to compete in contests on equal terms with men. In 1780 Sir Aston Lever and a Mr Waring founded the Toxophilites, a group who met regularly at Leicester House to shoot at butts. In October 1790 a Miss Littledale defeated her male opponents. Female participants adopted dress based on contemporary fashion with Tudor details, with a 'gay sash of toxophilite green'. Amelia, Lady Salisbury, hosted the first archery contest at Hatfield House in Hertfordshire on 6th July 1789 and the Union Society, which drew its members from Hertfordshire and Essex, was inaugurated in 1792. Its romantic motto was 'Archery, Freedom and Love'. Pierce Egan echoes these sentiments,

> the company of ladies must prove a great attraction to the admirers of archery ... but instead of hitting the target, their aim, I rather apprehend, is of a more tender nature – the hearts of the archers![1]

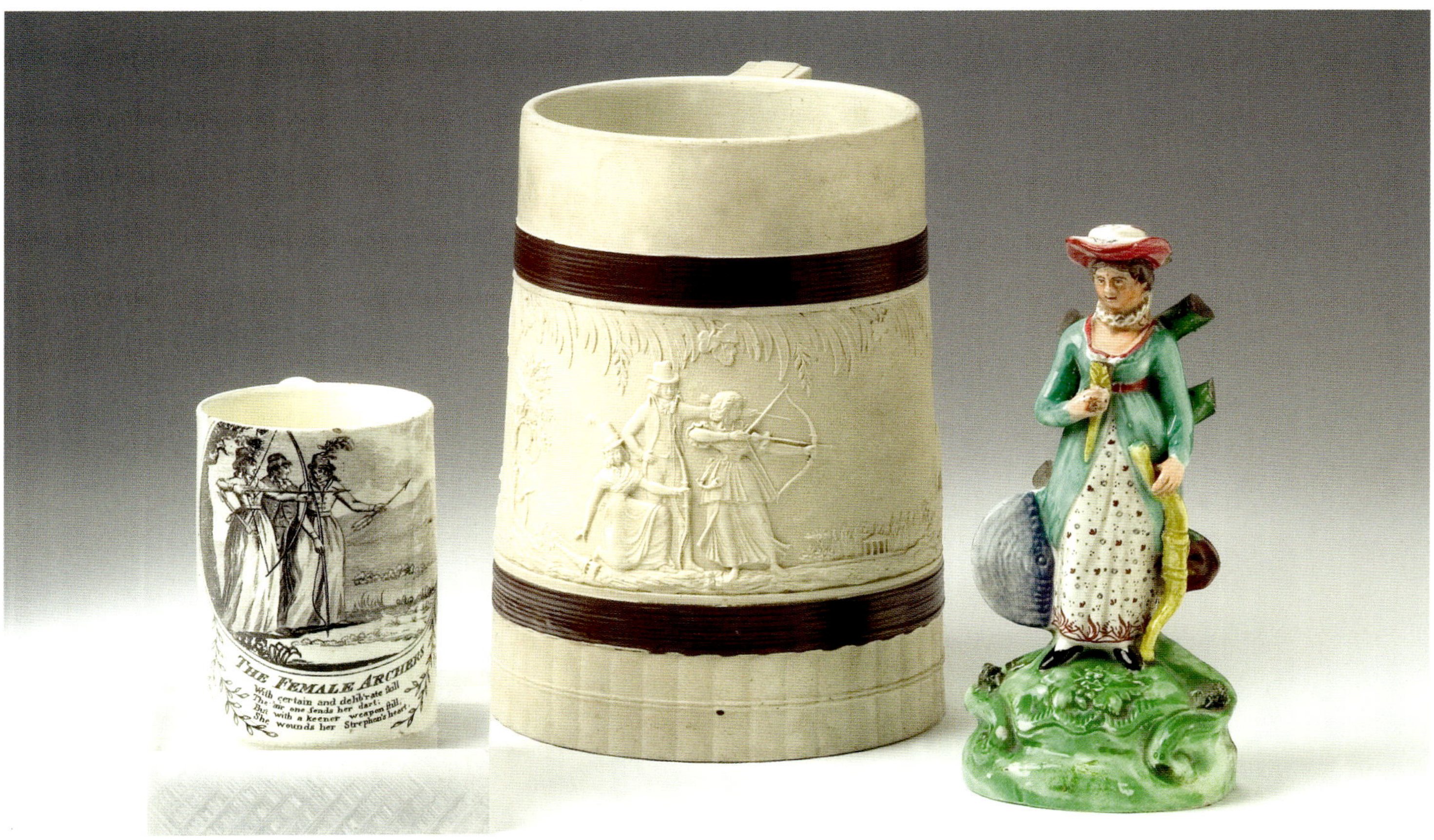

Mug, (1157), c.1795, Staffordshire, height: 12.7cm, (5in), printed creamware. Truncated print entitled, 'THE FEMALE ARCHERS', shows two women archers with a male companion and verse, 'With certain and delib'rate skill/ The fair one sends her dart / But with a keener weapon still / She wounds her Strephon's heart'[2] The scene is partly inspired by an illustration in the *Sporting Magazine*, 1792, showing 'Archery at Hatfield'. [3]

Mug, (1158), c.1795, Staffordshire, Lane End, height: 19.1cm, (7½in), cream stoneware. Mug made by John Turner, decorated with relief sprigs of female archers. The young woman aiming for a target on a butt is bare headed and dressed in fluttering, light weight clothes.

Figure, (1159), c.1825, Staffordshire, Lane End, height: 17.2cm, (6¾in), enamelled pearlware. Female archer, (title, 'ARCHAR', all but illegible), stands before a damaged bocage tree, a target beside her. Similar figures are marked for Ralph Salt.

Cricket

Cricket probably began as a diversion for shepherds. One shepherd used his crook to defend a wicket-gate in a paddock fence from being hit by stones thrown by another. One of the first references to a game of cricket is that held in 1300, between Prince Edward and his favourite, Piers Gaveston. The first recorded match was played at Coxheath in Kent in 1646 and the first county match on 29 June 1709, when Surrey played Kent at Dartford Brent. Shepherds' crooks and clubs were replaced by long, thin 'battes', resembling extended hockey sticks. By the eighteenth century, the batte had developed into a heavier, curved version of the one we know today, carved from a single piece of wood.

The first list of the laws of cricket (as revised by the MCC in 1788), was published on 1 July 1793. It included the following details;

> The Ball Must weigh not less than five ounces and a half, nor more than five ounces and three quarters.
> It cannot be changed during the game, but with the consent of both parties. / The Bat Must not exceed four inches and one quarter in the widest part. / The Stumps Must be twenty-two inches out of the ground, the bail six inches in length

Willett was a keen amateur cricketer and an active supporter of the Sussex County Cricket Club, formed in 1839, the oldest first-class county side in England. Hove has been at the centre of Sussex cricket since 1791 when George, Prince of Wales, granted local cricketers a parcel of land, used by the county team until 1847.[4]

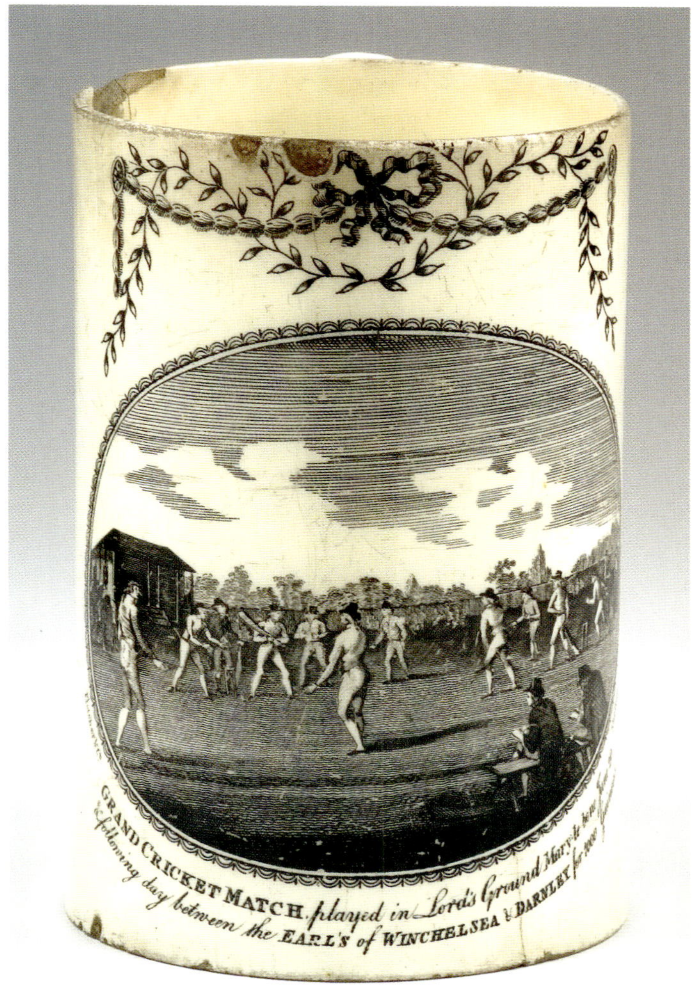

Mug, (1160), c.1795, Staffordshire, Thomas Fletcher, Shelton, height: 15.3cm, (6in), printed creamware. Print entitled, 'GRAND CRICKET MATCH played in Lord's Ground Mary le Bone June 20th & following day between the EARL'S of WINCHELSEA & DARNLEY for 1000 Guineas'. On 20 and 21 June 1793 the MCC under Winchelsea, with three powerful players from Hampshire, won by ten wickets. The image on the mug, taken from the *Sporting Magazine*, was published soon after.[5] The teams dressed in contemporary day clothes, while the brims of their top hats shaded their eyes from the sun. In 1786, a group of aristocrats had commissioned Thomas Lord, the son of a Yorkshire wine merchant and a useful under arm bowler, to provide new premises. Two decades later, Dorset Square was no longer secluded, so Lord developed new grounds in St John's Wood that opened in 1814, where the Marylebone Cricket Club has remained.

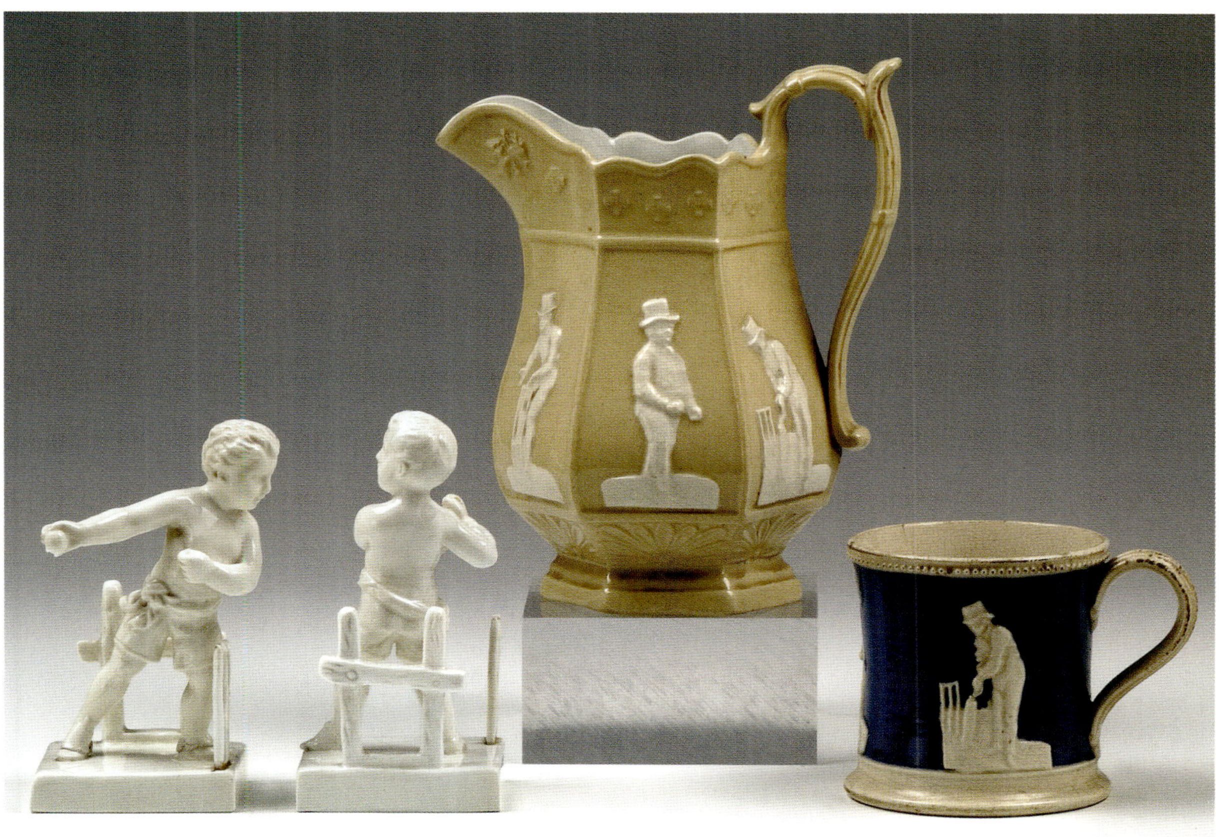

Pair of Figures, (1168 & A), c.1840, Staffordshire, each height: 12.7cm, (5in), soft-paste porcelain. The pair may have served as trophies or menu-holders; Minton made pairs of cupid cricketers for this purpose.
Jug, (1166), c.1850, Staffordshire, height: 18.4cm, (7¼in), slip-decorated earthenware. Jug applied with white relief sprigs of Tom Box (1808-1876), Sussex wicketkeeper for 24 years without missing a match, and F.W. Lillywhite (1792-1854), one of the first round-arm bowlers.[6]
Mug, (1167), c.1850, Staffordshire, height: 8.3cm, (3¼in), slip-decorated earthenware. Relief sprig of Fuller Pilch (1803-1870) the great Norfolk batsman.[7]

W.G.Grace (1848-1915)

Grace played cricket seriously from 1865, and began training as a doctor from 1868, taking ten years to qualify because of the pressure of his increasing cricket commitments. His burly 6'2 ½" frame and beard were instantly recognisable and for Victorians he personified cricket. He played for Gloucester County Cricket Club (which his family founded) and for England during his 43-year career. He broke all records, scoring 54,211 first class runs and 45,000 runs in club and minor fixtures. As a bowler he took 2,808 first class wickets and made more money as an amateur than many professionals. He toured America and Canada in 1872-73 and Australia in 1873-74, taking a great deal of time off from his medical work. He never really enjoyed medicine and was glad to resign from his Gloucester practice in 1899. His obituary in Wisden read: 'When he was in his prime, no sun was too hot and no day too long for him'.

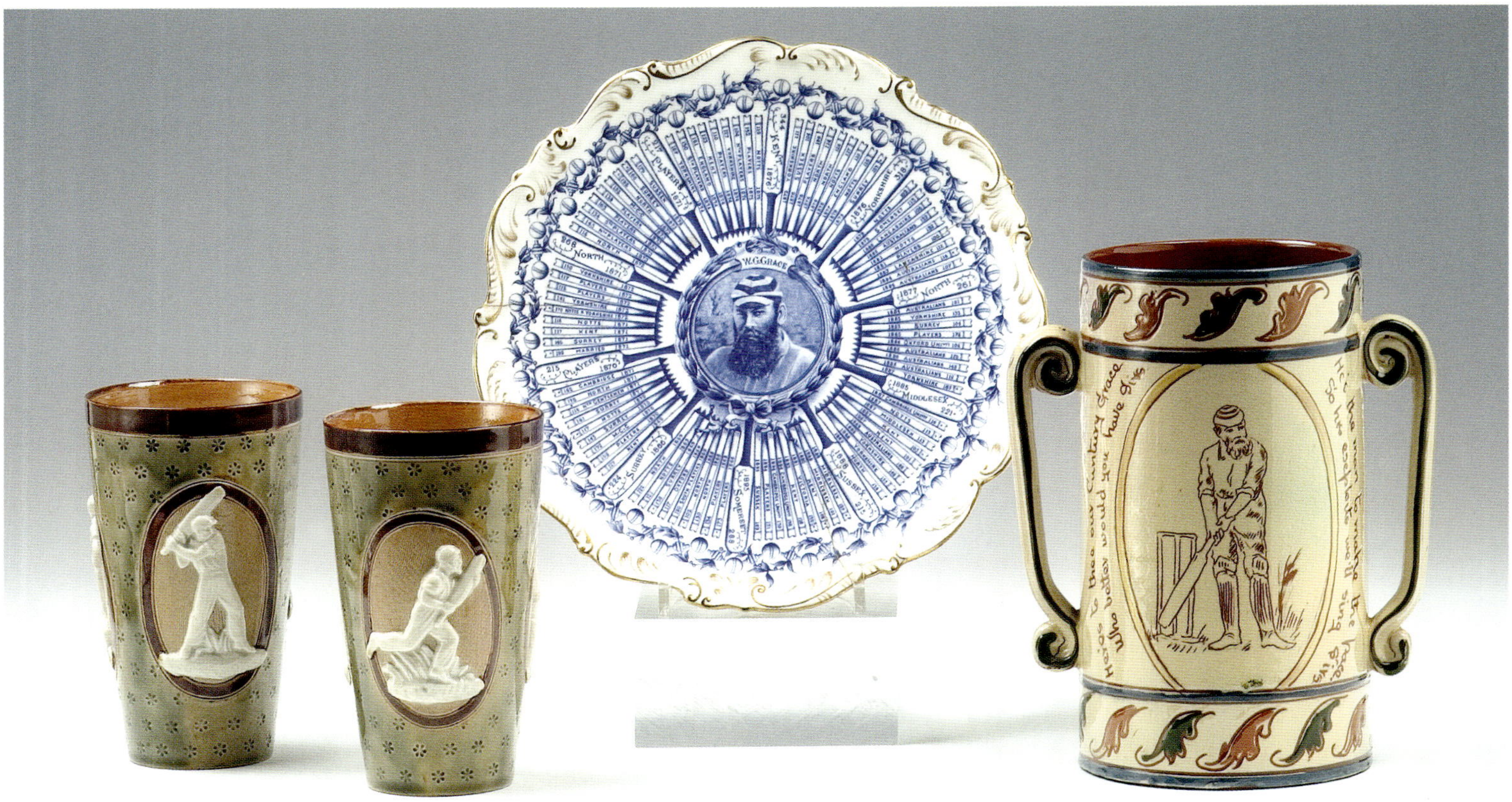

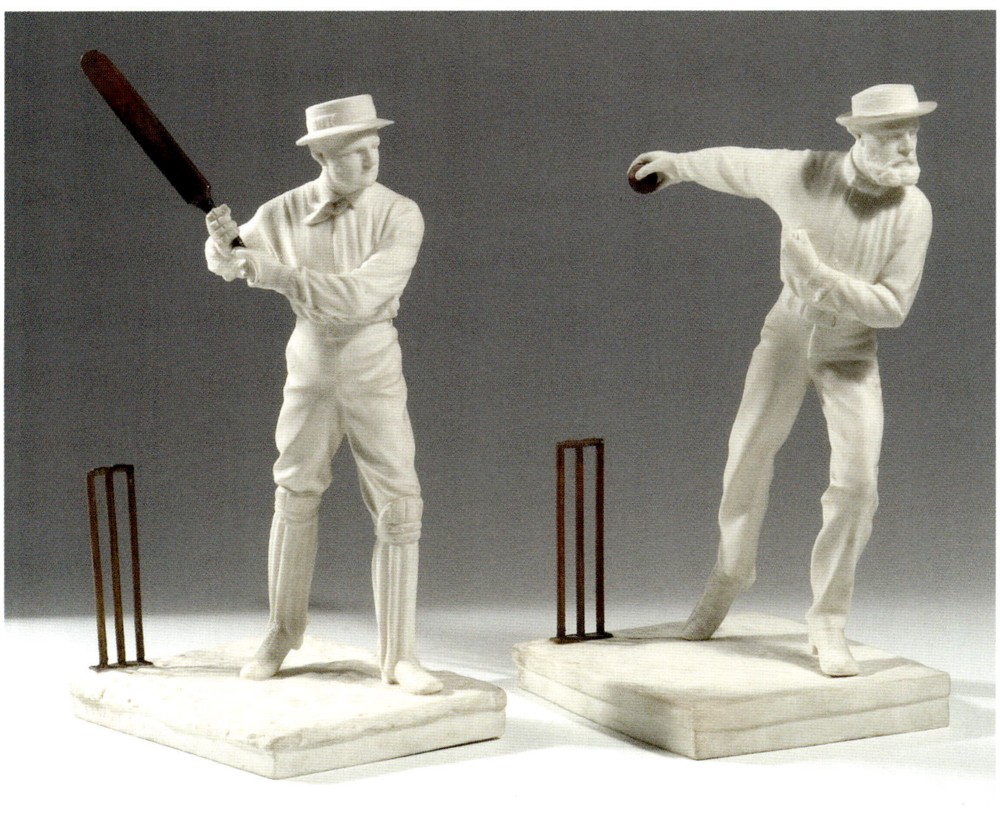

Pair of Beakers, (1169 & A), c.1895, London, each height: 14.6cm, (5¾in), stoneware. From a set of lemonade jug and beakers made by Doulton. Applied sprigs of batsmen, one standing at the crease and one taking a run.
Plate, (**1171**), 1895, Shropshire, diameter: 22.3cm, (8¾in), soft-paste porcelain, blue-printed and gilt. Issued by Coalport to commemorate W.G. Grace's 'Century of centuries', details of which surround his portrait. Design applied to standard, gilt-rimmed dessert plate.[8]
Two-handled Mug, (1170), c.1895, Devon, Aller Vale, height: 20.3cm, (8in), slip-decorated earthenware. Sgraffito decoration of W.G. Grace at the crease inscribed: 'Here's to thee our Century Grace / Who better would you have sirs / He's the man who makes the pace / So his exploits will sing sirs'. A pair of crossed cricket bats and sprays of leaves on the reverse.

Figure of Batsman, (**1172**), 1857, Staffordshire, Stoke-on-Trent, height: 28.3cm, (11⅛in), Parian porcelain.
Figure of Bowler, (**1172A**), 1857, Staffordshire, Stoke-on-Trent, height: 28.3cm, (11⅛in), Parian porcelain. Two large figures of cricketers, from Mintons' National Sports series. Each (unidentified) figure, modelled, signed and dated by Thomas Fowke, wears straw boater and stands before metal stumps.

Riding for Pleasure

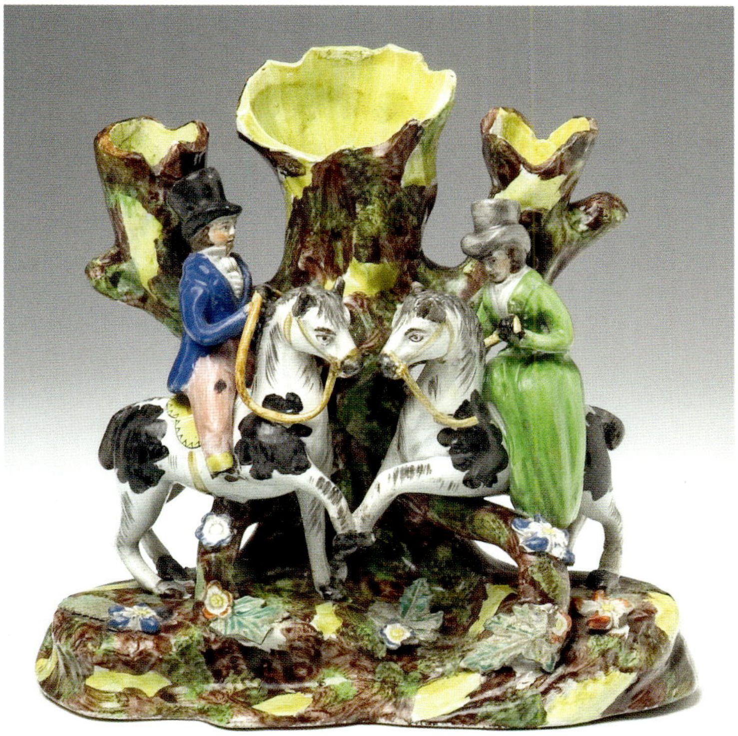

Flower-holder, (**1174**), c.1825, Staffordshire, height: 20.3cm, (8in), enamelled pearlware. Pair of equestrians perform dressage before a hollow tree. Both wear riding outfits; the woman, in tailored jacket and hat, rides side saddle.

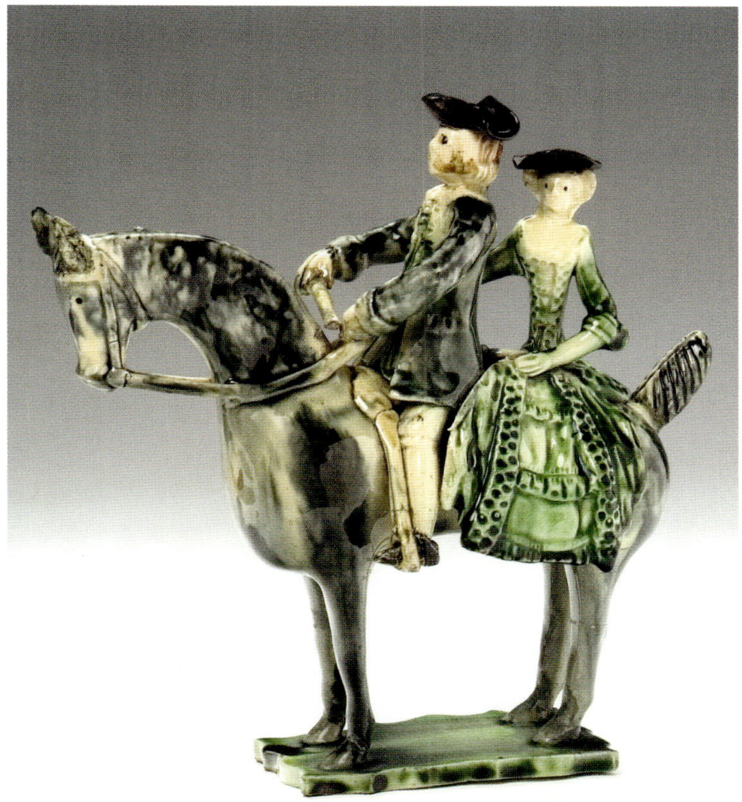

Figure Group, (**1173**), c.1750, Staffordshire, height: 20.9cm, (8¼in), earthenware, lead-glazed and oxide-coloured. Very rare, early equestrian group. The male rider sits astride the horse, his companion rides pillion, wearing wide, paniered skirts. Similar ladies were made sitting on chairs. The horse has a bulbous body, skinny legs, a long, neck and cropped tail, with a resemblance (entirely coincidental) to Chinese pottery horses of the Tang Dynasty.

Figure, (**1175**), c.1825, Staffordshire, height: 18.4cm, (7¼in), enamelled pearlware. Male rider before a bocage tree decorated with jam-tart flowers, prepares to jump.
Figure, (**1176**), c.1830, Staffordshire, height: 24.2cm, (9½in), enamelled pearlware. Equestrienne rides side saddle, apparently on a zebra. Although zebras were occasionally ridden in circus acts,[9] other examples of this model have a plain coloured horse; the stripes are assumed to be a decorator's caprice.

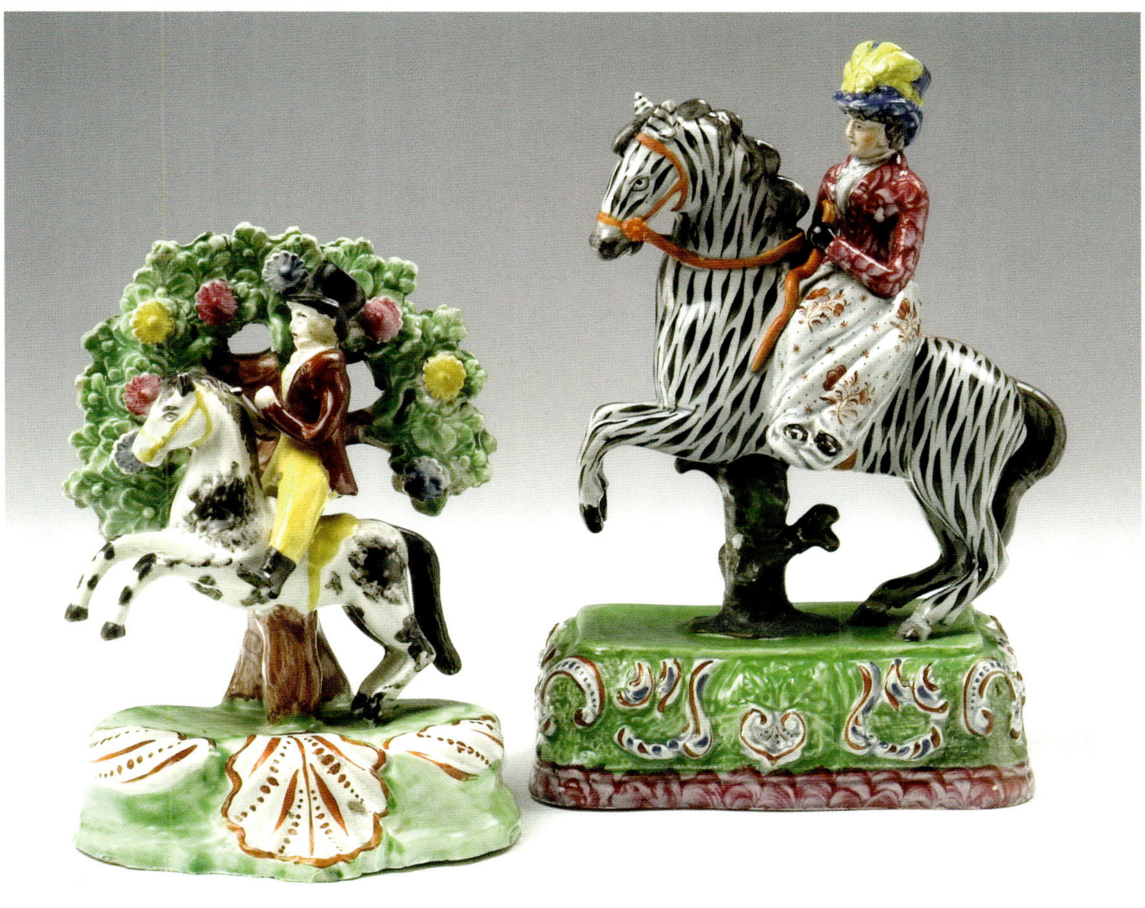

Cycling

A new method of riding for pleasure appeared in the early-nineteenth century. A machine, known as a velocipede, a 'hobby' or 'dandy'-horse was invented by the German Baron von Drais and patented in Britain in 1818 by Denis Johnson. The original velocipede lacked pedals so locomotion was very labour intensive; it involved pushing the ground on either side. Dandy-horses, named for their fashionable riders, could be hired for about £8 from Johnson's Repository in London's Long Acre. They weighed up to 50 lbs. and travelled at 8-10 miles per hour. The 50-mile journey from London to Brighton took around 9 hours.

Velocipedes proved so popular that, for a while, the Metropolitan Police considered them a threat to public safety and banned them. The following extract, taken from Fairburn's *Whimsical Description of the New Pedestrian Carriage or Dandy Horse* (1819), refers to velocipedes in Brighton:

> JOHNSON'S ROYAL HOBBY-HORSE CHARGERS.
> Four of them have been sent down to the Kremlin, at Brighton; when it was whispered they were on the go, numbers assembled to view this new addition to the royal stud, ... Sir Benjamin [Bloomfield], as Comptroller of the Stud-House, must rub down Johnson's Patent Charger to a brilliancy fit to dazzle royal eyes.

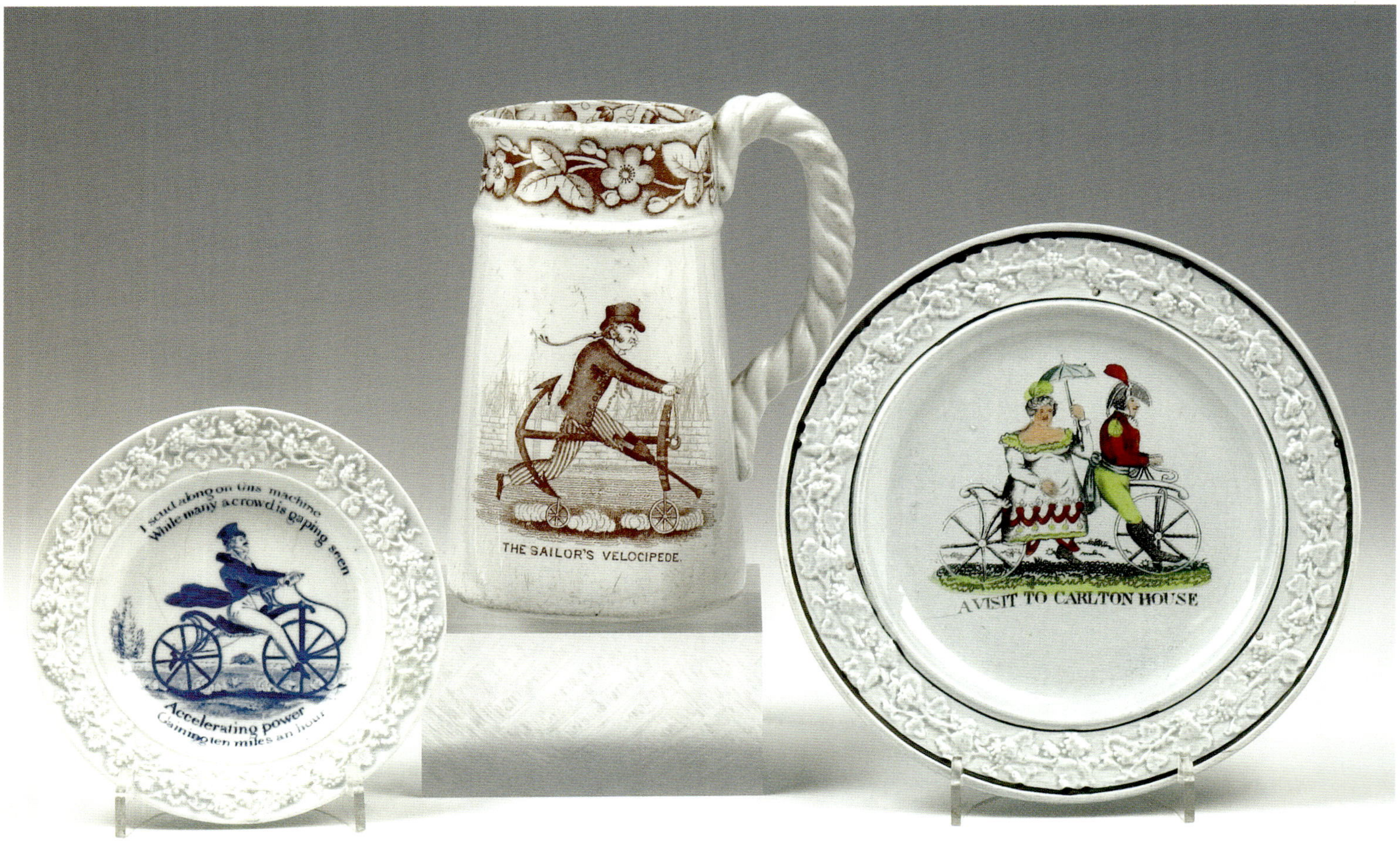

Nursery Plate, (**1179**), c.1825, Staffordshire, diameter: 12.1cm, (4¾in), blue-printed pearlware. A well-dressed young man speeds along a dusty road on an early bicycle inscribed, 'I scud along on this machine / While many a crowd is gaping seen Accelerating power / Gaining ten miles an hour'
Jug, (**1178**), c.1875, Staffordshire, diameter: 15.3cm, (6in), brown-printed pearlware. Printed with, 'THE SAILOR'S VELOCIPEDE' and 'THE WELSHMAN'S VELOCIPEDE'. This extensive series of comic vignettes where the vehicle is matched to its rider's occupation, first appeared on plates marked 'Brough' in the 1820s.
Plate, (**1177**), c.1820, Staffordshire, diameter: 17.1cm, (6¾in), blue-printed pearlware. Print entitled, 'A VISIT TO CARLTON HOUSE', shows a man in uniform (possibly a royal duke) and a plump, fashionably-dressed woman holding a parasol, perched on an elongated velocipede.[10]

Ballooning

An extraordinarily innovative form of transport took off in the 1780s. The Montgolfier brothers sent animals on their inaugural hot air balloon flight at Versailles in September 1783. The craze spread across the Channel and in August 1784, James Tytler made an ascent near Edinburgh. Subscribers who had enabled the construction of a balloon in London, for Vincenzo Lunardi (1759-1806), Secretary to the Neapolitan Ambassador, were entitled to see it suspended in the Lyceum dome. A bag made from 520 yards of red-and-white striped, oiled silk, 33 feet across with a gondola 11 feet long by 4 feet wide was admired by 20,000 people before the Lyceum's manager locked the door, demanding that Lunardi pay him a royalty on the subscriptions received. The police had to rescue the balloon so that the pioneer aeronaut, accompanied by a cat, could ascend on 15 September, from the Honourable Artillery Company's grounds at Moorfields in the City of London. This was witnessed by a crowd of 150,000 people and progressed to Ware, in Hertfordshire, where it landed.

The Frenchman, Jean-Pierre Blanchard, (1753-1809) undertook several balloon flights in Britain, the first at Lochée's Military Academy in Chelsea on 15 October 1784. Blanchard took a passenger named Sheldon, his dog and a basket of pigeons. He also carried oars and a rotating fan in the hope of influencing the balloon's course. Horace Walpole had a good view from Strawberry Hill,

'As I was writing this my servants called me away to see a balloon; I suppose Blanchard's … It appeared about a third of the size of the moon or less, when setting, something above the tops of the trees on the level horizon … I diverted myself with a sort of meditation on future airgonation, supposing that it will not only be perfected, but will depose navigation'.[11]

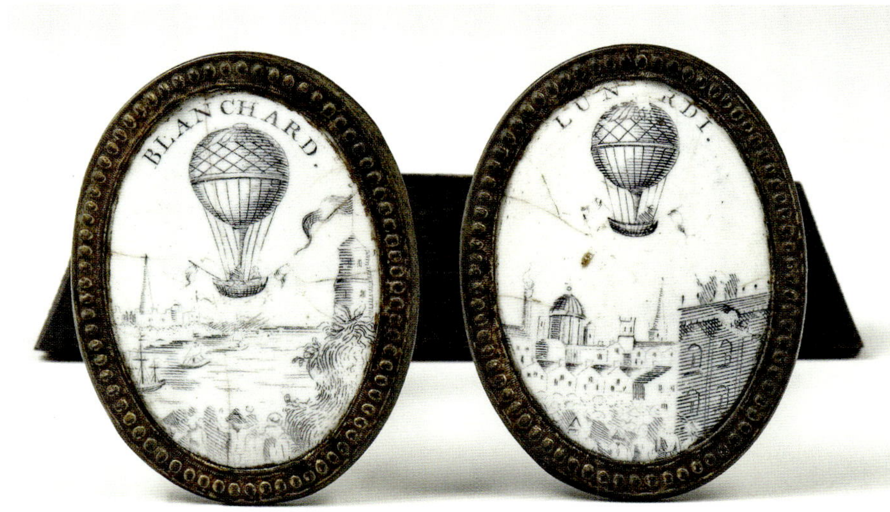

Door Handle, (**1181**), c.1785, height: 4.2cm, (1⅝in), copper, enamelled and printed. Print shows balloon entitled 'LUNARDI', hovering over Old London Bridge and St Paul's Cathedral. Engravings after the ascent and the balloon's exhibition in the Pantheon in Oxford Street show a cylindrical basket-cage, rather than a long gondola, as described. The following year Lunardi made further flights with a larger balloon, from St George's Fields, Southwark.
Door Handle, (**1182**), c.1785, height: 4.2cm, (1⅝in), copper, enamelled and printed. Print shows balloon entitled 'BLANCHARD' and more generalised scenery.

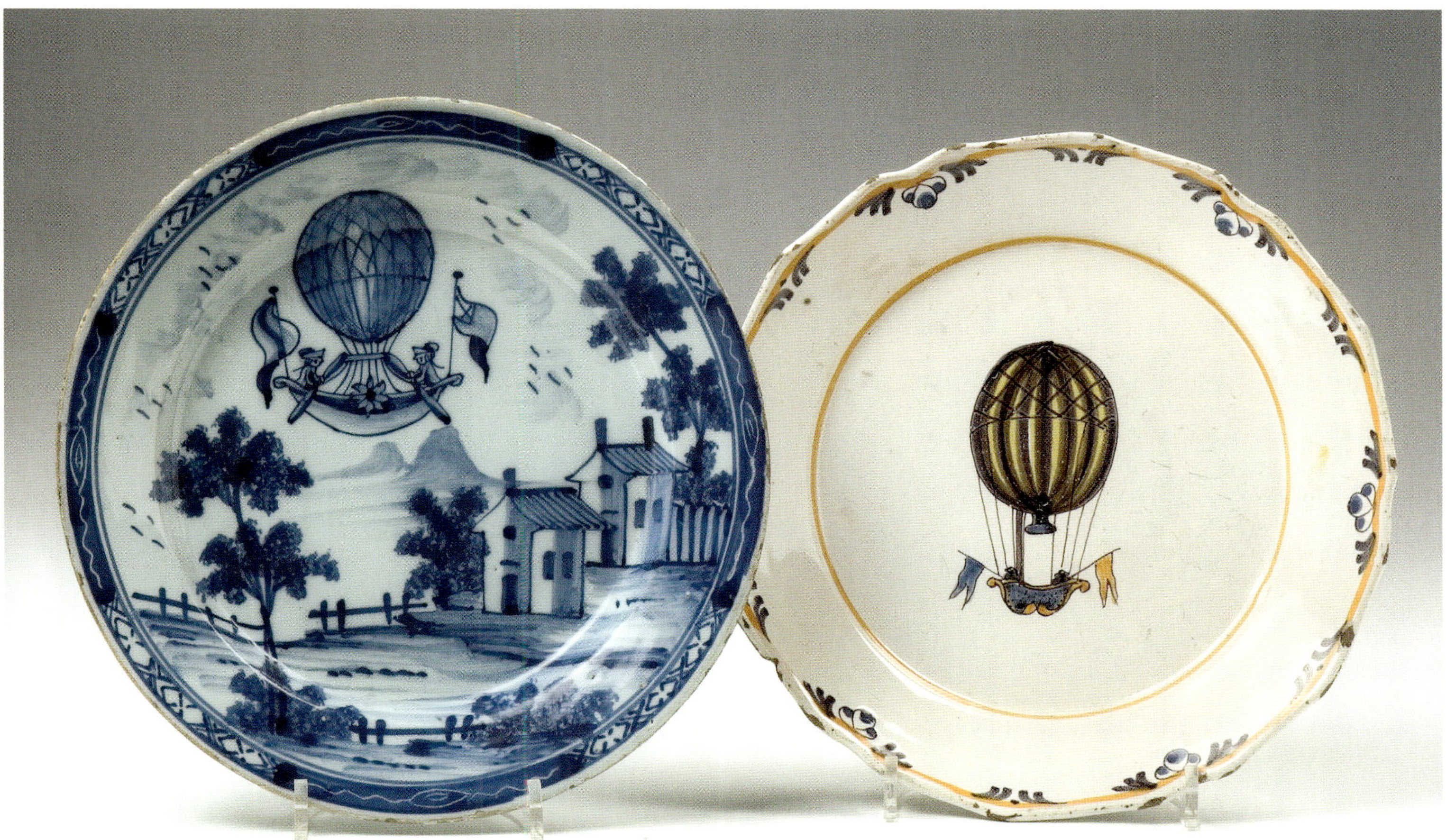

Plate, (**1180**), c.1785, Bristol or Liverpool, diameter: 23.5cm, (9¼in), tin-glazed earthenware. An unfeasibly small balloon floats over a landscape with buildings. Its basket contains two men, each carrying a national flag. This balloon, with its distinctive boat-shaped gondola and oars, closely resembles published images of Blanchard's machine. Some of his flights took place from the Stockwell Road where workers from the South Bank potteries, which produced much delftware, would have had a good view of the events.
Plate, (**1183**), c.1785, France, Nevers, diameter: 20.3cm, (8in), faience. A generalised decorative balloon with a boat-shaped gondola.

Fishing

The Compleat Angler The Contemplative Man's Recreation was published in 1653. Co-written by Izaak Walton (1593-1683) and Charles Cotton, it remains the classic work on fishing for pleasure. Sea-fishing was a major food-producing industry but angling in rivers and fishponds was a popular pursuit for gentry and commoners alike. Walton's protagonist, Piscator, debates the virtues of fishing with his friends Auceps, the falconer, and Venator, the huntsman, describing his pastime as 'honest, ingenuous, quiet and harmless', which explains why so little was published on the subject.

Colonel Venables, one of Walton's followers, sums up the delights of a sport that is cheap to pursue and involves little risk, in his book, *The Experience'd Angler: or Angling Improv'd* (1683),

> The Angler when he hath the worst success, loseth but a Hook or a Line or perhaps a Fish, and suppose he take nothing, yet he enjoyeth a delightfull walk by pleasant Rivers in Sweet Pastures, among odiferous Flowers.

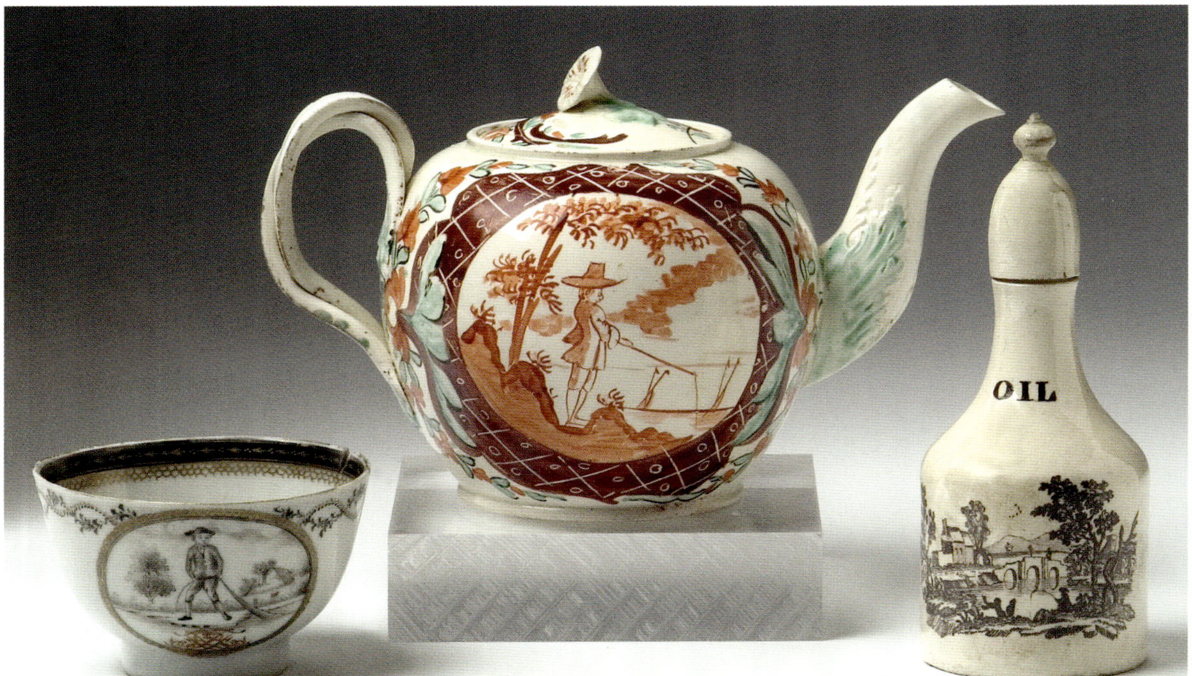

Teabowl, (**1188**), c.1770, China, height: 5.1cm, (2in), enamelled hard-paste porcelain. Painted with a fisherman pulling a drag-net onto a riverbank.
Teapot, (**1186**), c.1770, Leeds, height: 10.2cm, (4in), enamelled creamware. Painted on both sides with a fisherman on a riverbank.
Oil Bottle, (**1193**), c.1780, Leeds, height: 12.7cm, (5in), creamware, printed and enamelled. A seated fishermen on a riverbank, a three-arch bridge behind.

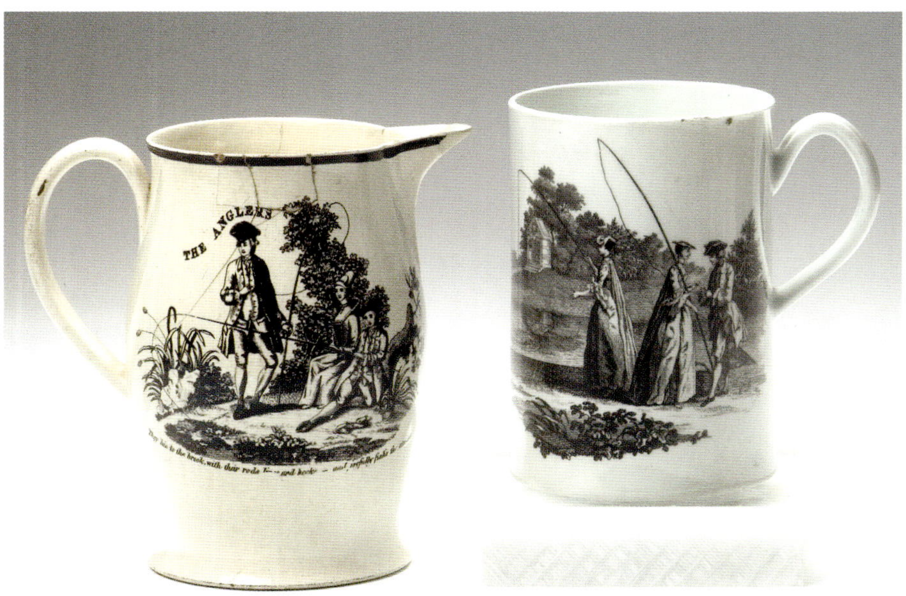

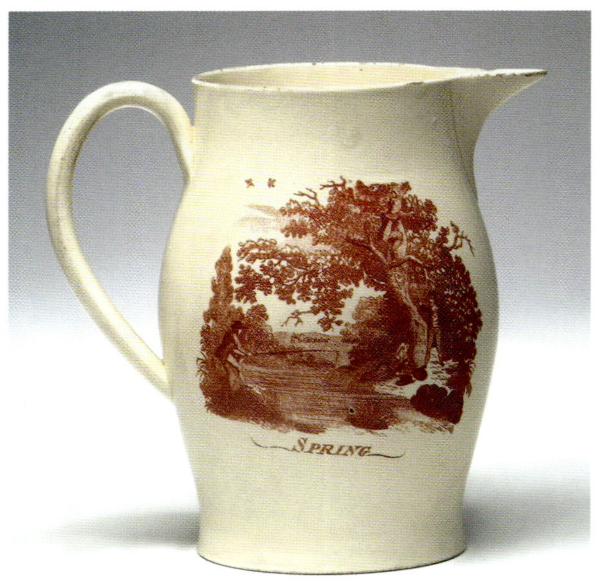

Jug, (**1190**), c.1780, Staffordshire, height: 14cm, (5½in), creamware, printed and enamelled. Print entitled, 'THE ANGLERS' shows two men and a woman, inscribed, 'They hie to the brook with their rods, lines and hooks – and joyfully fish the stream'. The design comes from *The Ladies Amusement*, 1762, pl.32.[12]
Mug, (**1187**), c.1760, Worcester, height: 12.1cm, (4¾in), printed soft-paste porcelain. Printed with 'The Whitton Anglers', engraved by Robert Hancock, taken from one drawn and engraved in 1757 by William Woollett, 'A View of the Canal and of the Gothic Tower in the Garden of His Grace the Duke of Argyle at Whitton in Middlesex'.[13] Two elegantly dressed women in sack-backed dresses stand at the water's edge holding rods while their male companion ties a fly.
Jug, (**1673**), c.1790 Staffordshire or Liverpool, height: 17.8cm, (7in), red-printed creamware. River landscape, inscribed 'SPRING'; a man fishes from the left bank while three youths climb or sit beneath a tree.

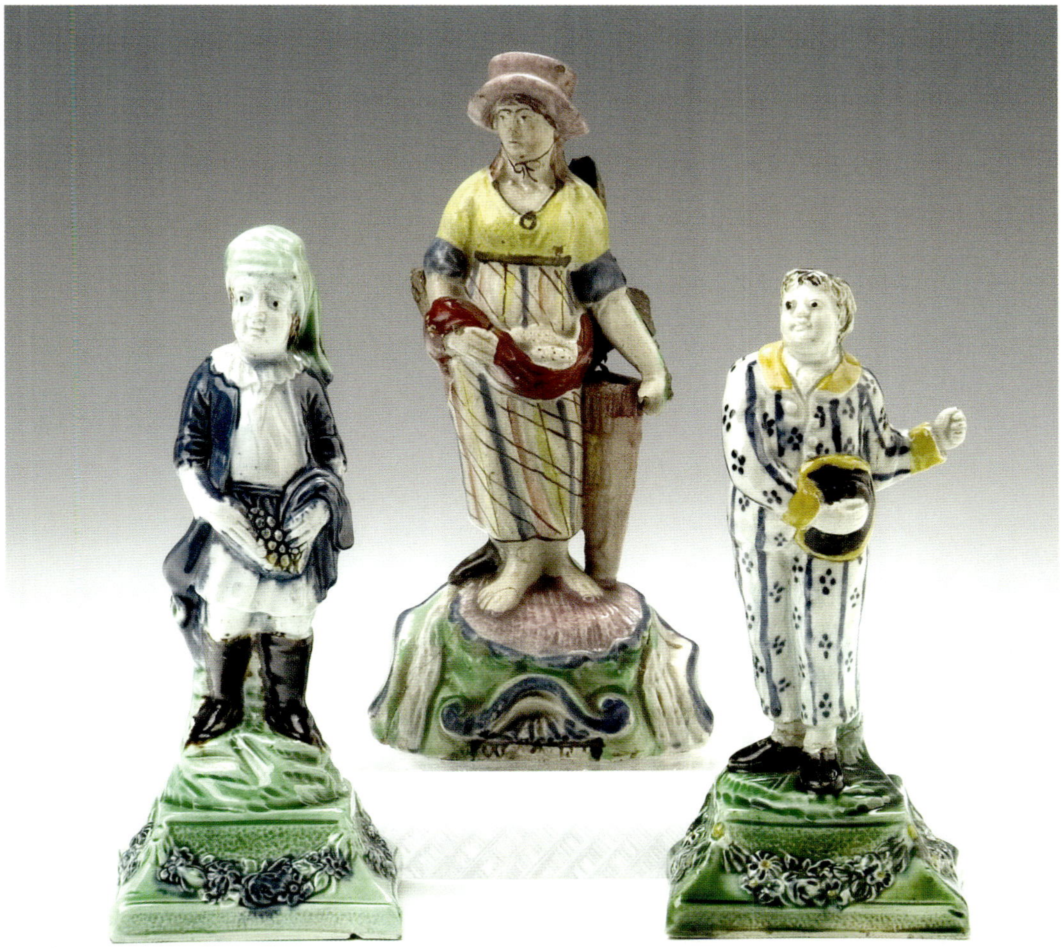

Two Figures, (**1194 & A**), c.1800, Staffordshire, height: 16cm, (6¼in), height: 15.3cm, (6in), Prattware. One wears long, black boots and has an apron full of shellfish. The other, dressed in a blue striped suit is more likely to be a sailor.
Figure, (**1191**), c.1820, Staffordshire, height: 16.5cm, (6½in), enamelled pearlware. Young woman with an apron full of fish must be involved with the fishing industry.

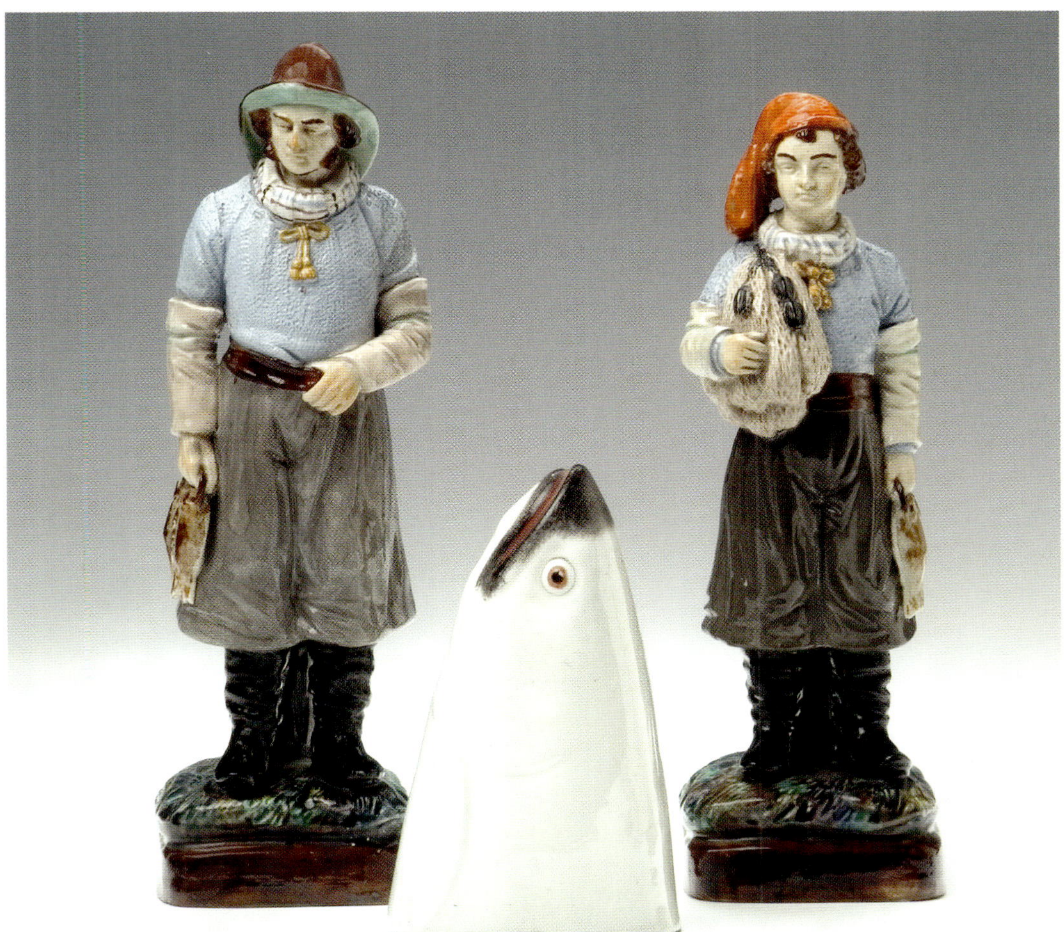

Figure, (**1185**), 1880, France, height: 24.2cm, (9½in), enamelled earthenware. Fisherman wears a knitted, woollen hat and carries nets over his shoulder and fish in his hand. Impressed import marks for Wittman & Roth of London.
Stirrup Cup, (**1192**), c.1790, Derby, height: 12.7cm, (5in), enamelled soft-paste porcelain. Modelled as the head of a trout and made by Duesbury & Keen.
Figure, (**1184**), 1880, France, height: 22.2cm, (8¾in), enamelled earthenware. Fisherman wears long boots, wide, waterproof trousers waterproof sleeves and a sou'wester hat. Impressed import marks for Wittman & Roth of London.

The Lottery

The national lottery was as popular in the late-eighteenth century as it is today.[14] Once purchased, tickets were negotiable, as good as bank notes. After the first draw the value of the remaining tickets was enhanced. Many prizes were paid against annuities, thus allowing the government to borrow without paying interest. Lottery offices were open to fraud and often sold fractions of lottery tickets and insured numbers against proving blanks.

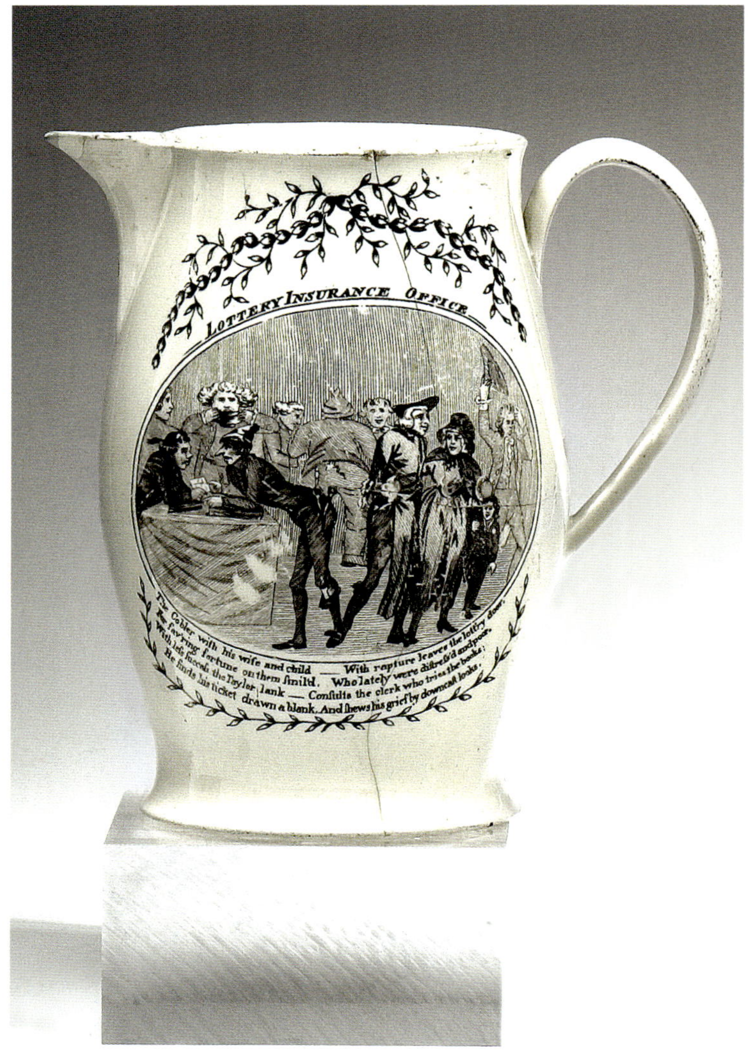

Jug, (**1242**), c.1792, Staffordshire, height: 17.8cm, (7in), printed creamware. 'THE LOTTERY INSURANCE OFFICE', illustrates a financial settlement. On the right a tailor, '.. finds his ticket drawn a blank, / And shows his grief by downcast looks' rushes away to the right. A gleeful cobbler and his family leave with a purse of money, 'For fav'ring fortune on them smil'd / who lately were distressed and poor'. The next contender leans eagerly towards the clerk at the desk. The original print was published by Bentley & Co. in 1790, based on a drawing by Collings.[15]

Menageries

King Henry I kept a collection of exotic animals, including lions, leopards, lynxes and camels at Woodstock in Oxfordshire. In 1252 Henry III transferred the animals, which included a polar bear, to the Tower of London and made the City Sheriffs responsible for them. The collection was augmented in 1254 by an elephant, a gift from the king of France. By the eighteenth century members of the public could visit for a fee of 1½d or the donation of a dog or cat to be fed to the lions! In 1835 the Tower menagerie was combined with the Duke of Cumberland's in Windsor Great Park to form London Zoo in Regent's Park.

Apart from Royal menageries, other animal collections toured provincial towns and villages and were very popular attractions at 'wakes' week or holiday fairs. A permanent display of rare species was situated at the 'Exeter Change' (Exchange) on London's Strand in 1800. It owed its celebrity to the energetic marketing campaign of its proprietor Gilbert Pidcock, self-styled the 'Modern Noah', 'Here the Majestic African Lion roars in concert with the dread Bengal Tyger' The display was noisy and frequently noisome, according to contemporary reports. The *European Magazine* remarked in 1826 it was; 'a great annoyance at all times and a perfect nuisance in warm weather'.

Pidcock, who died in 1810, was succeeded by Stefani Polito, a veteran Italian menagerist, who toured the country during the summer and showed the animals at the Exeter Change during the winter. The animals were confined in cramped cages, little better than their travelling trucks. They were not taught tricks and the high point was feeding time. Poets Lord Byron and Wordsworth, and artists such as Landseer, and the Frenchman, Agasse, haunted the menagerie. Around 1817 Polito sold the menagerie to Edward Cross who hung a huge banner across the entrance to the Exeter Change, illustrating the animals within. The door man who stood beneath a brilliantly coloured macaw, was dressed as a Yeoman of the Guard, recalling the Tower menagerie. Thomas Frost recorded that, in 1825, the entrance to Atkins's Menagerie had show-cloths 40 feet long and a 'brass band of eight performers wearing scarlet tunics and leopard-skin caps, played on the outside',[16] a scene evoked by the earthenware menageries.

George Wombwell, best known of the showmen, quit cobbling in London's Commercial Road in 1804 in order to import and exhibit animals. His 40 caravans of animals cost over £100 a day to feed, but during Bartholomew Fair, held at Smithfield in 1828, he made £1,700. By 1825 he had four lions and lionesses, two leopardesses with cubs, a hyena, a wolf and cubs, a polar bear and a pair of zebras. Wombwell continued touring until his death in 1850, when his remains were returned from Northallerton in Yorkshire and were buried in some style at Highgate Cemetery in London. John Ruskin recalled, in *Flors Clavigera*, that the nearest he came to disobeying his parents as a child was, 'in passionate effort to get to play with the lion's cubs in Wombwell's menagerie'.

Many of the animals had limited life expectancy. One elephant at the Exchange, called Chunee, turned rogue and had to be shot, while another, from Wombwell's, died on the road from Newcastle to London. Its carcase was exhibited to great acclaim at Smithfield Market as 'the only dead Elephant at the Fair'!

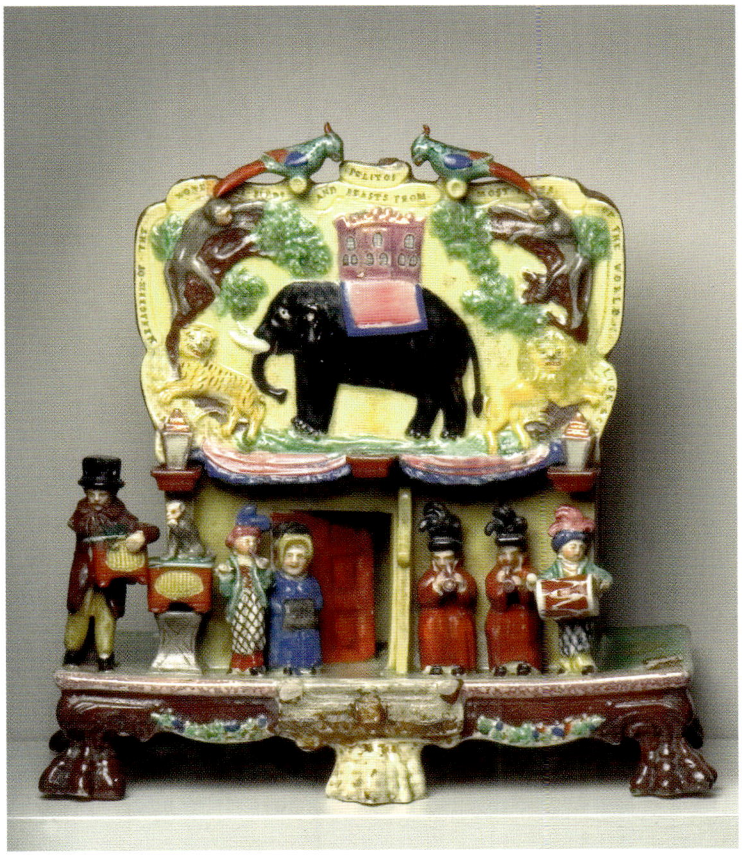

Figure Group, (**1220**), c.1830, Staffordshire, height: 31.2cm, (12¼in), enamelled pearlware. Table-based menagerie group inspired by prints of Exeter Change and the temporary booths at Bartholomew and Southwark Fairs. Base stands on six grotesque crocodile feet. Banners decorated with portraits of the animals inside. The entrance crowded with barkers and musicians with instruments, drumming up interest. The doorway was left slightly ajar to lure the paying public inside.

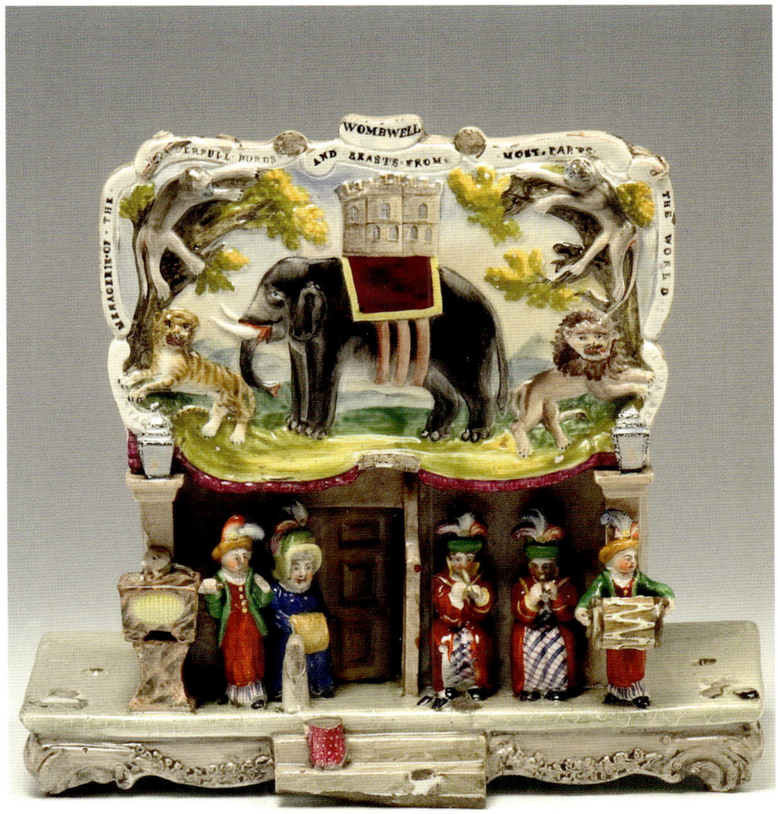

Figure Group, (**1219**), c.1830, Staffordshire, height: 29.2cm, (11½in), enamelled pearlware. Table-based menagerie group very similar to Polito's, substituting the name of Wombwell. Like the Polito's example the show-cloth impressed around the edge: MENAGERIE.OF.THE.WONDERFULL. BURDS.AND.BEASTS.FROM. MOST. PARTS.OF.THE.WORLD'. Sadly, the green macaws from the top of the cloth, several of the musicians and all the paw feet beneath the base are missing.

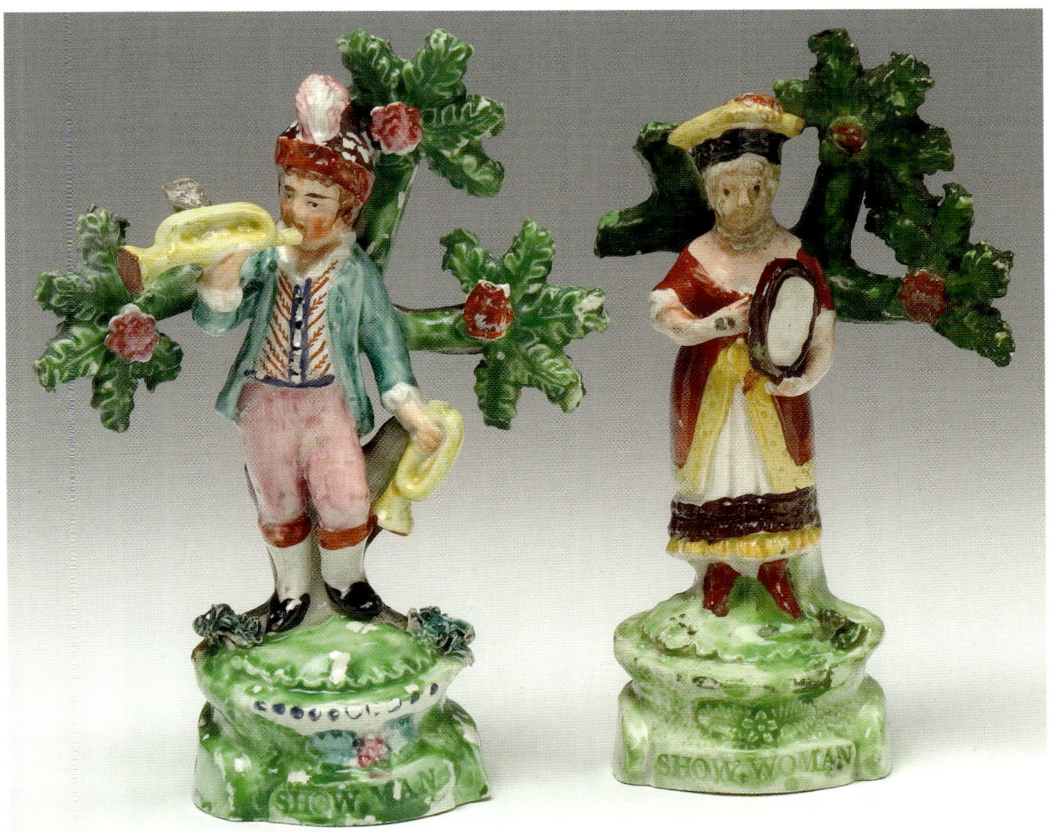

Figure, (**1229**), c.1820, Staffordshire, height: 16.6cm, (6½in), enamelled pearlware. Possibly by Ralph Salt, c.1820, depict a 'SHOW.MAN', blowing a bugle.
Figure, (**1230**), c.1830, Staffordshire, height: 15.3 cm, (6⅛in), enamelled pearlware. Figure impressed, 'SHOW.WOMAN' bangs a tambourine. Their role at fairs was to attract the paying public into the tents that contained the travelling menageries.

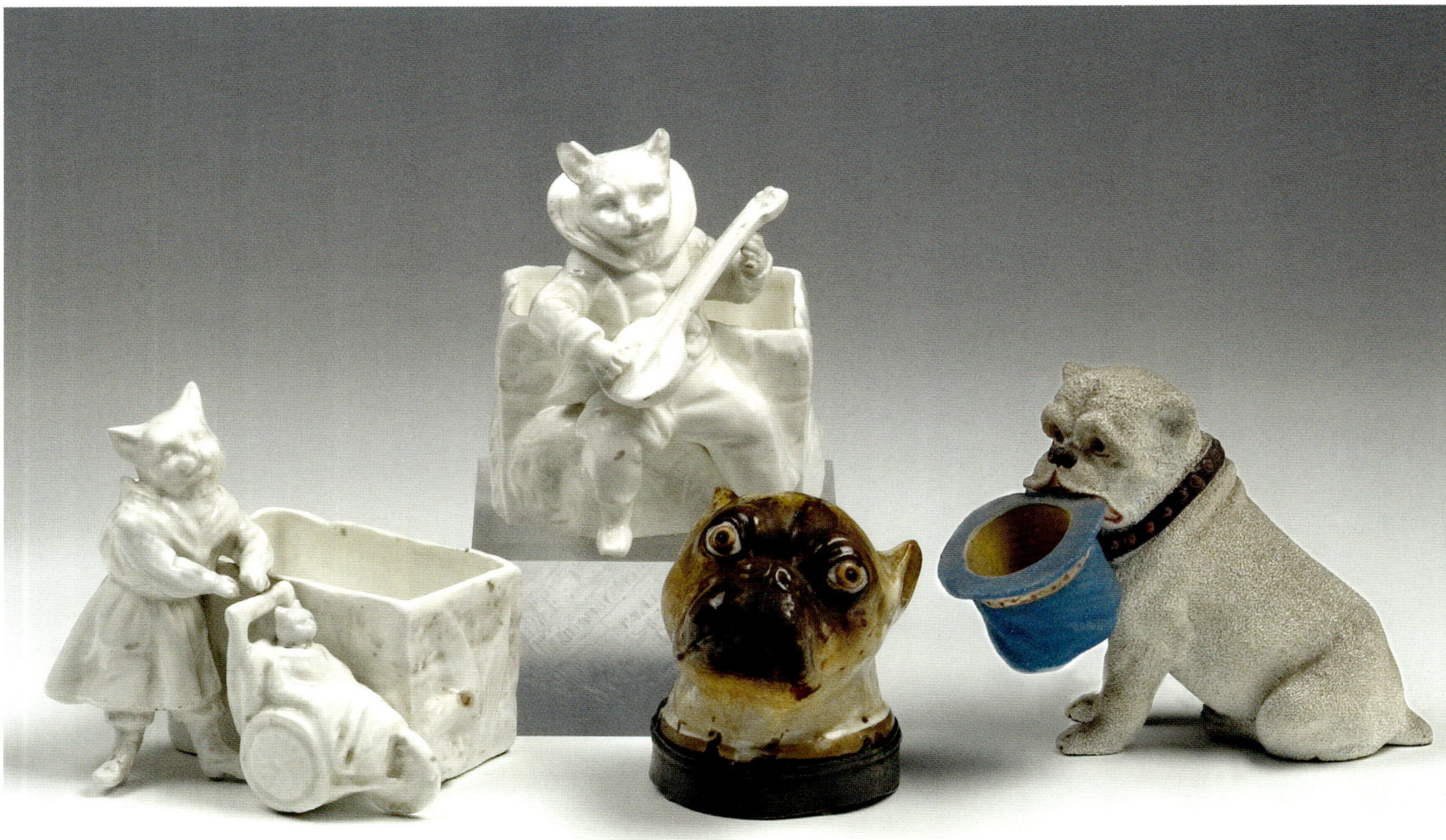

Two Flower-boxes, (**1209 & A**), c.1880, Staffordshire, height: 10.5cm, (4⅛in), height: 11.5cm, (4½in), bone china. Modelled as cats in fancy dress, female wheels a kitten in a baby carriage and the tom plays a mandolin. According to a handbill of 1832, Signor Cappelli's 'Learned cats' that performed regularly at Bartholomew Fair, could 'beat a drum, turn a spit, grind knives, play music … roast coffee … and grind rice in the Italian manner.'[17] Cats are very difficult to train.

Tobacco Box, (**1206**), c.1880, Staffordshire, height: 8.9cm, (3½in), bone china. Box with a metal lid, modelled as the head of a pug.
Figure, (**1202**), c.1880, Germany?, height: 10.2cm, (4in), hard-paste porcelain. Model of a bulldog holding brim of a top hat, to solicit donations for a street performance or circus act.

Nursery Plate, (**1208**), c.1850, Staffordshire, height: 16.5cm, (6½in), printed earthenware. A cat and a dog appear to smoke churchwarden pipes.
Figure, (**1203**), c.1850, Staffordshire, height: 21.6cm, (8½in), enamelled earthenware. Figure of a muscular dog, possibly a boxer or bulldog, sitting to attention.
Plaque, (**1236**), c.1850, Staffordshire, diameter: 17.2cm, (6¾in), enamelled pearlware. Relief-moulded with monkey wearing a feathered cap, smoking a pipe. A late nod to the eighteenth-century taste for *singeries.*

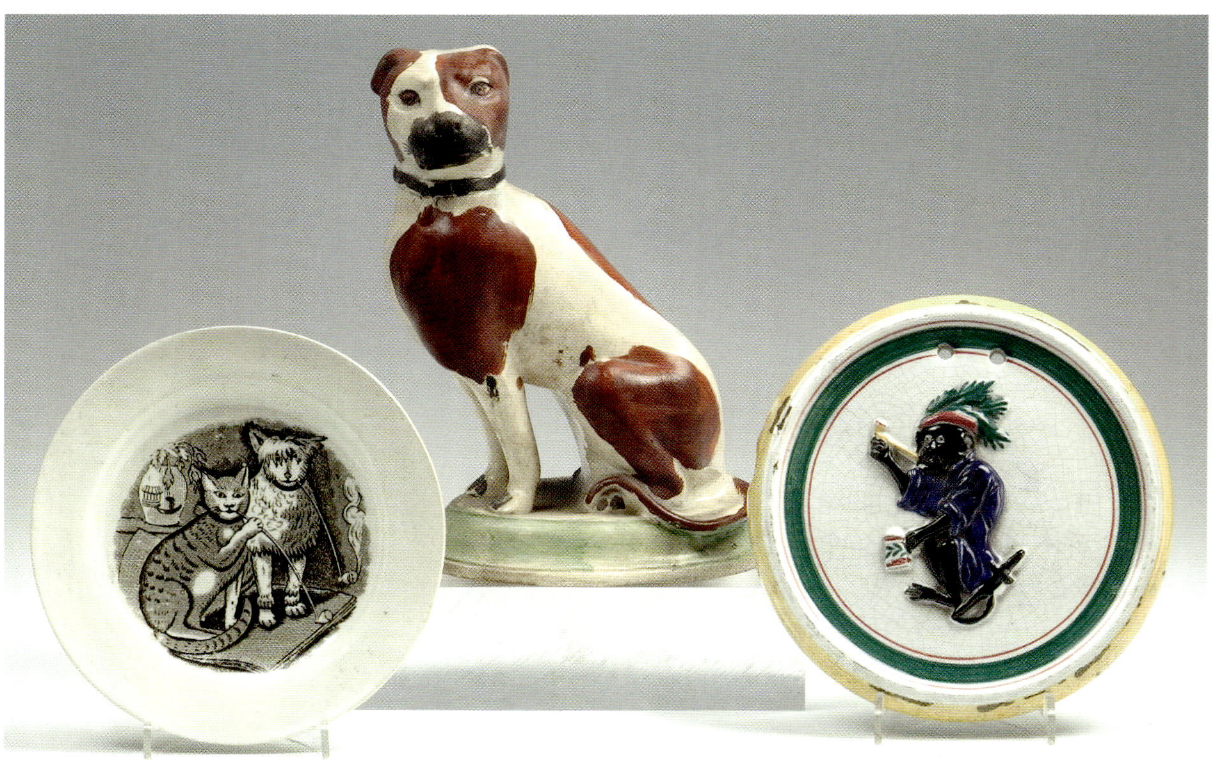

Dancing dogs

Dogs are easily taught tricks and dog acts were very popular. They performed regularly at fairs and in city streets and from 1784 to 1785 there were competing troupes of dancing dogs performing at the Sadlers' Wells Theatre.[18] They continued to give street performances well into the nineteenth century. The anonymous author of *The Menageries* (1829) mourned their gradual disappearance, although 'in some obscure street of London, boys gather around for wonder at the sight of dogs turning a spinning-wheel and dancing a cotillion'. Dancing dogs were frequently portrayed by artists from Hogarth (in *Southwark Fair*, 1733) to Rowlandson (a detail on a sheet of etchings published by Fores in 1790) and by George Cruikshank.[19]

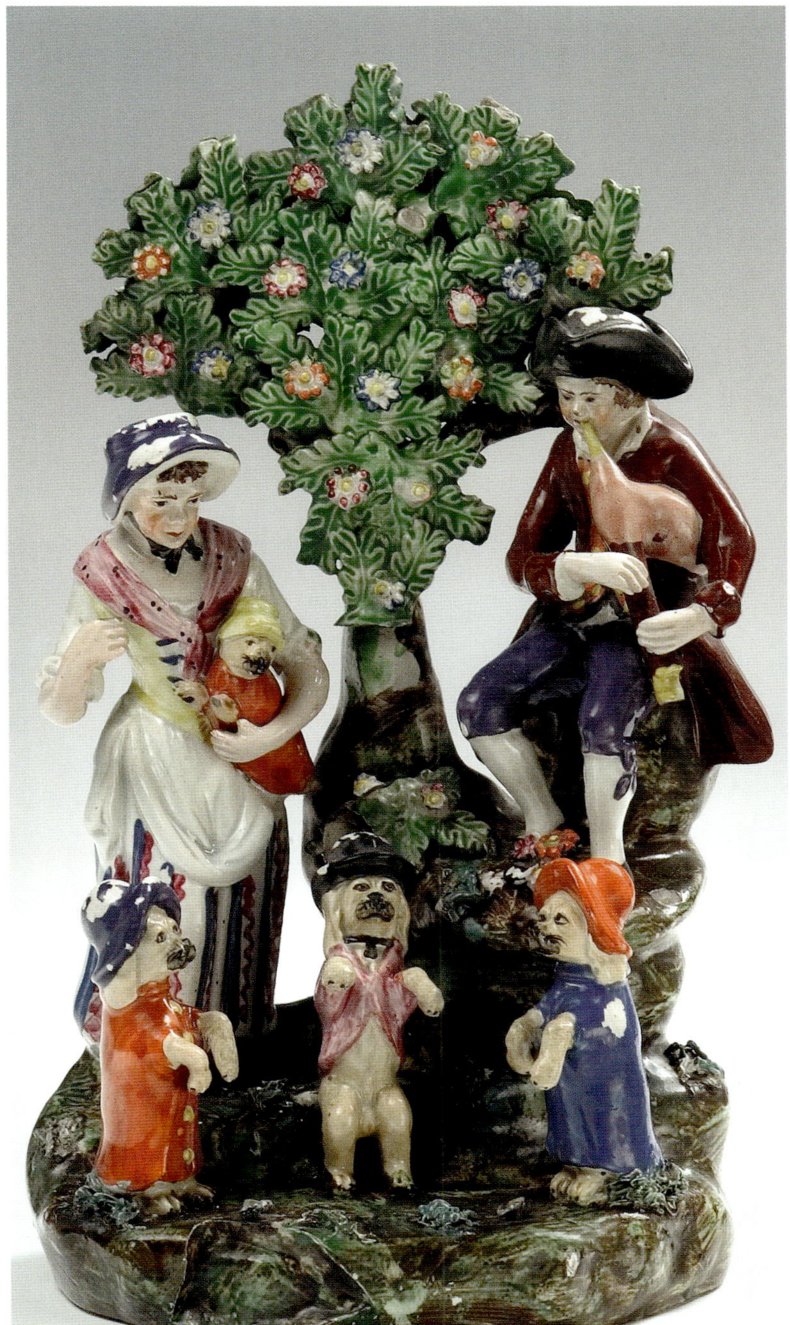

Figure Group, (**1207**), c.1820, Staffordshire, height: 24.2cm, (9½in), enamelled pearlware. A man stands on a rock playing the bagpipes while a woman beats time for her canine protégés. The dogs dressed in coats and hats, hop about on their back legs.

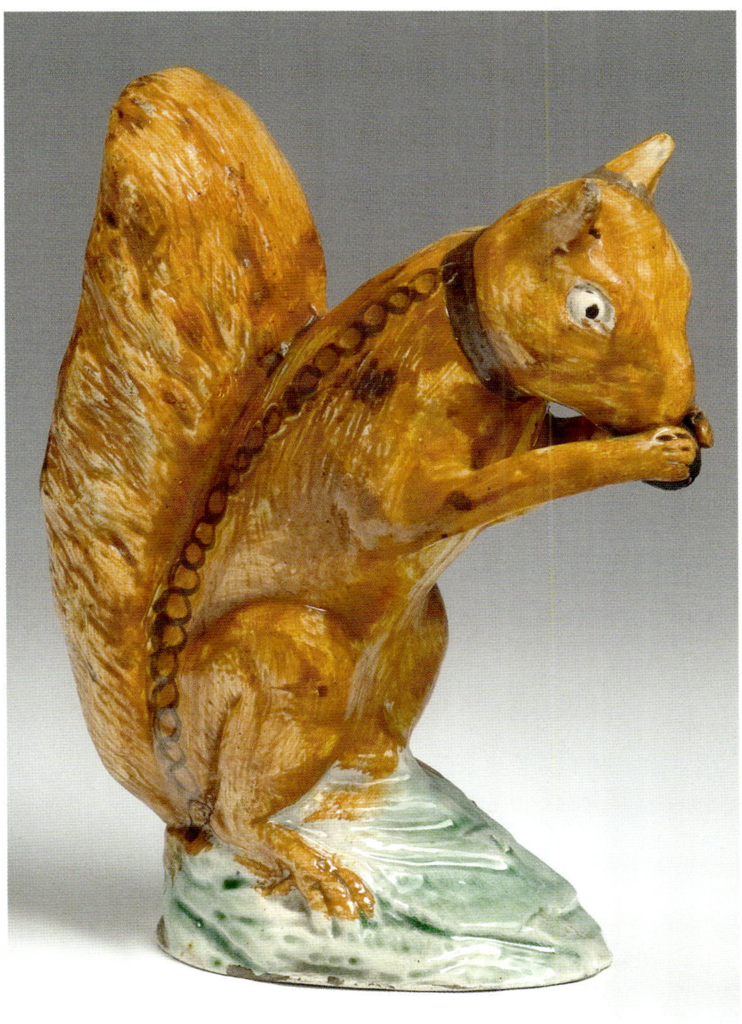

Figure, (**1210**), c.1790, Staffordshire, height: 20.3cm, (8in), Pratt-coloured pearlware. Model of a red squirrel wearing a collar and chain, reminds us that squirrels were surprisingly popular domestic pets.[20] Squirrel-shaped teapots were an early novelty form in white salt-glazed stoneware. Lead-glazed earthenware squirrel figures survive, initiated by the Wood family.

Isaac Van Amburgh (1811-1865)

Given the passive nature of visits to the menageries, wild beast shows and circuses provided more obvious excitement. Van Amburgh and his arch-rival, Manchester Jack, the 'Lion King' of Wombwell's Menagerie, were the best-known celebrity trainers of wild animals. Van Amburgh was a lion tamer from Kentucky who toured Britain in 1838 and 1842 to great acclaim.

On his second visit he was painted by Landseer and presented to Queen Victoria, who went to view his show five times. She noted that '[the animals] all seem actuated by the most awful fear of him ... he takes them by their paws, throws them down, makes them roar and lies upon them after enraging them'.[21]

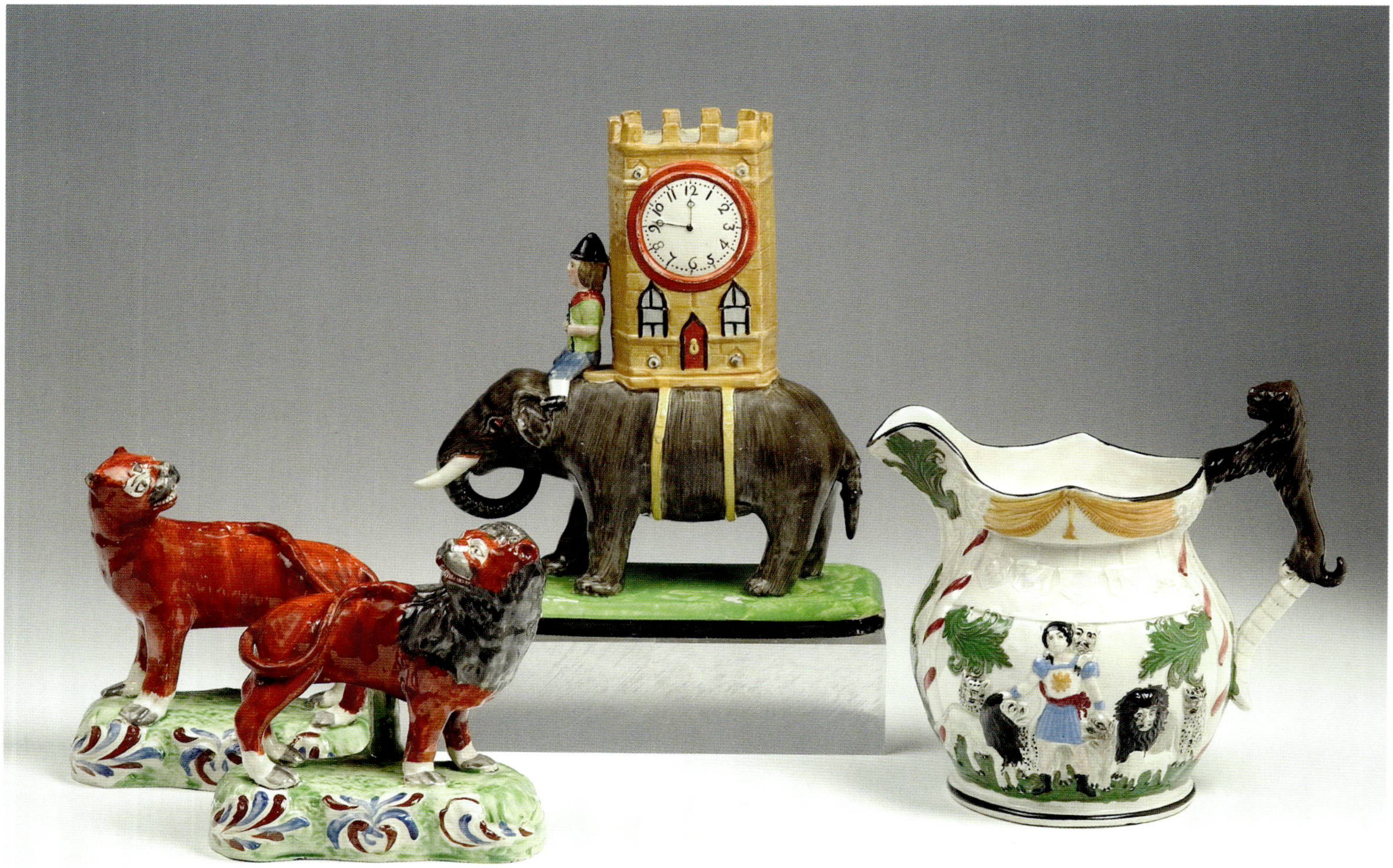

Pair of Figures, (1222 & A), c.1830, Staffordshire, height: 14cm, (5½in), height: 14.6cm, (5¾in), enamelled pearlware. Models of a red-painted lion and lioness on colourful bases.
Flower-holder, (1221), c.1830, Staffordshire, height: 22.9cm, (9in), enamelled pearlware. Flower holder or spill vase in the form of an elephant with a howdah on its back, modelled as a clock tower.

Jug, (1234), c.1845, Staffordshire, height: 16.5cm, (6½in), enamelled pearlware. Relief-moulded with Isaac van Amburgh in Roman gladiator costume, surrounded by lions, leopards and a sheep! Image probably taken from a poster or flier for his show. Draped curtain, stage scenery and brightly striped poles frame the group.

Travelling performers

William Wordsworth, in *The Prelude* (1805), recalls witnessing street performances in London, 'A raree-show is here, / With children gathered round; another street Presents a company of dancing dogs, / Or dromedary, with an antic pair/ Of monkeys on his back; a minstrel band / Of Savoyards; or, single and alone, An English ballad-singer'.[22]

Many travelling entertainers were Savoyards from Northern Italy, nomadic Roma, or Turks from the Ottoman Empire, which covered a vast area of Eastern Europe and the Middle East at this time. Although bear-baiting had largely disappeared, bears were still wild in Europe and were caught or captive bred for street performance. Bern in Switzerland is named after bears and still has a public bear pit and there are still performing bears in Eastern Europe.

Thomas Bewick (1753-1828), in tiny wood engravings in the 1790s, depicted troupes of travelling entertainers doing the rounds of fairs and animal shows.[23] Methods used to train bears to dance were often barbaric. Bewick records, 'Some of them are taught to perform by setting their feet on hot iron plates, and then playing to them whilst in this uneasy situation'. They soon learned to hop from foot to foot. He condemns, 'The excessive cruelties practised upon this poor animal ... its eyes are put out, and an iron ring being put through the cartilage of the nose to lead it by, it is kept from food and beaten, till it yield obedience'.[24]

Figure, (1214), c.1790, Staffordshire, height: 8.3cm, (3¼in), lead-glazed earthenware. Tiny figure of a muzzled bear.
Inkwell, (1218), c.1790, Staffordshire, height: 15.3cm, (6in), earthenware. Novelty inkwell crudely modelled as a bear holding a hat-shaped container for sand, its fur suggested by shredded clay.
Two Stirrup Cups, (1216 + 1217), c.1820, Staffordshire, each height: 8.9cm, (3½in), enamelled pearlware. Cups or box lids modelled as the muzzled heads of bears.

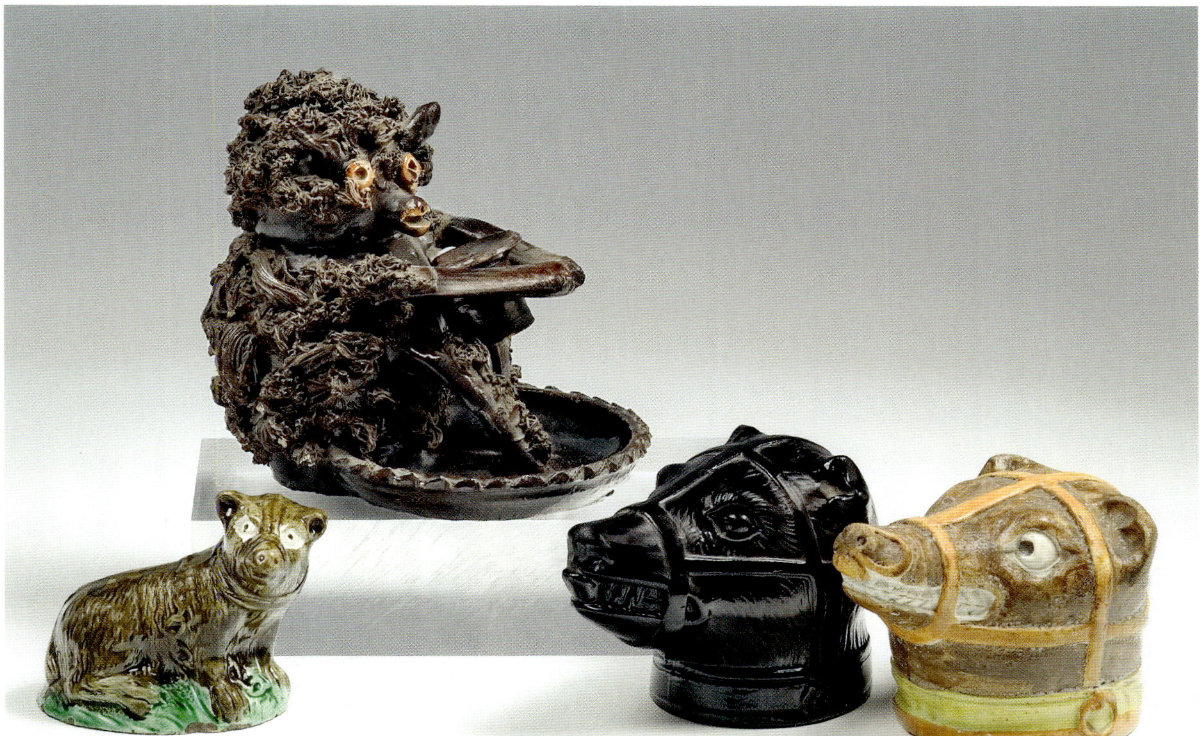

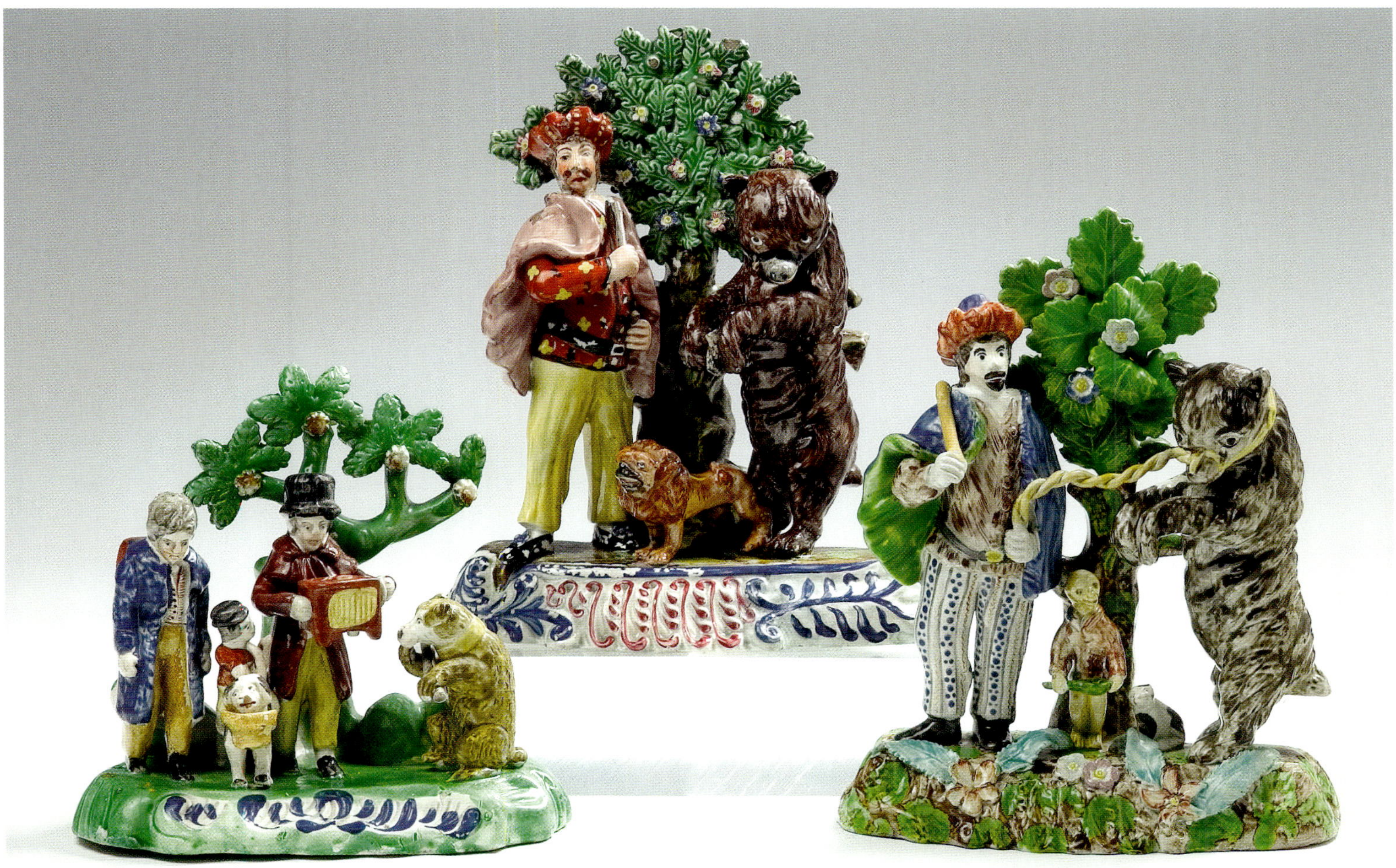

Figure Group, (**1213**), c.1830, Staffordshire, height: 14.7cm, (5¾in), enamelled pearlware. Two men (one with hand organ), a dog carrying a hat in its mouth and a clothed monkey on its back, and a small bear.
Figure Group, (**1211**), c.1830, Staffordshire, height: 21.6cm, (8½in), enamelled pearlware. Man in oriental costume with a stick, a tethered bear standing on its hind paws and a dog-sized lion.

Figure Group, (**1212**), c.1830, Staffordshire, height: 20.3cm, (8in), enamelled pearlware. Man in oriental costume with a stick, a tethered bear on its hind legs, a dog and a monkey wearing clothes, trained to collect money from spectators. The varying size of the figures, particularly the small lion suggests that these pieces were compiled from an ad hoc assemblage of components in the potters' workshops, rather than to a planned design.

Punch and Judy

Punch evolved from Pulchinella, one of the stock *commedia dell'arte* characters and became one of the most popular sideshows at country fairs. By 1800 Punch together with his battered wife Judy and their much-abused baby, were part of an established puppet show. There was a new surge of interest in Mr Punch after the launch, in 1841, of *Punch or the London Charivari*, the humorous magazine.

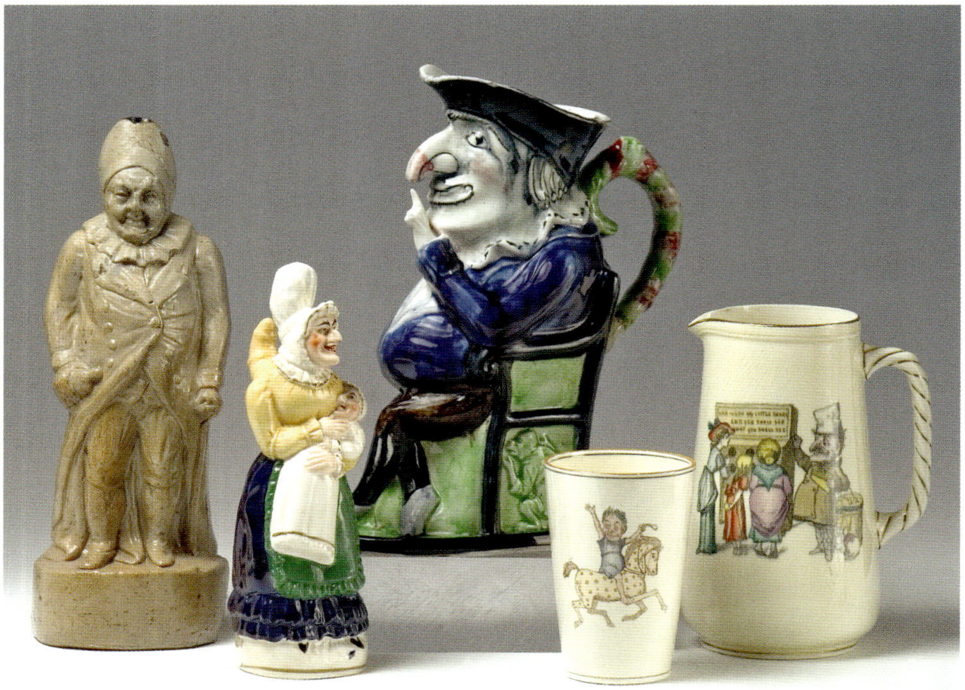

Spirit Flask, (1224), c.1850, London?, height: 28cm, (11in), salt-glazed stoneware. Modelled as Mr Punch.
Figure, **(1225)**, c.1850, Staffordshire, height: 21.7cm, (8½in), enamelled earthenware. Modelled as Mr Punch's wife Judy carrying her baby, a pronounced hump on her back.
Toby Jug, **(1226)**, c.1820, Staffordshire, height: 30.5cm, (12in), enamelled pearlware. Jug modelled as figure of Punch with hook nose and a finger to his lips, sitting on a chair, the sides of which are relief-moulded with monkeys wearing plumed hats, a relic of the fashion for *singeries*.
Beaker and Jug, **(1226 + 1227)**, c.1878, Staffordshire, Wedgwood, height: 12.7cm, (5in), height: 30.5cm, (12in), earthenware, printed and coloured. Beer or lemonade jug and beaker by Wedgwood, (design registered 1878) based on a cover design for *Punch* magazine of 1864.[25]

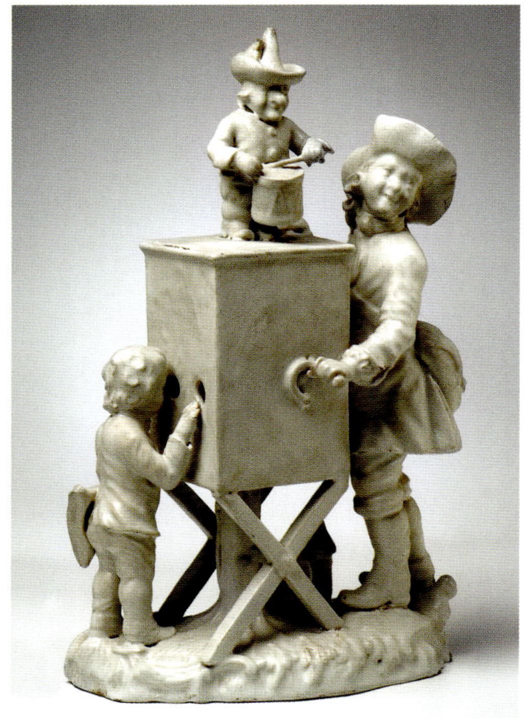

Figure Group, **(1232)**, c.1780, France, height: 30.5cm, (12in), matt-glazed earthenware. Model of a peep show, very popular at country fairs. A little boy looks through the peep-hole while the showman operates the handle and a dwarf with a Punch-like nose plays the drum.

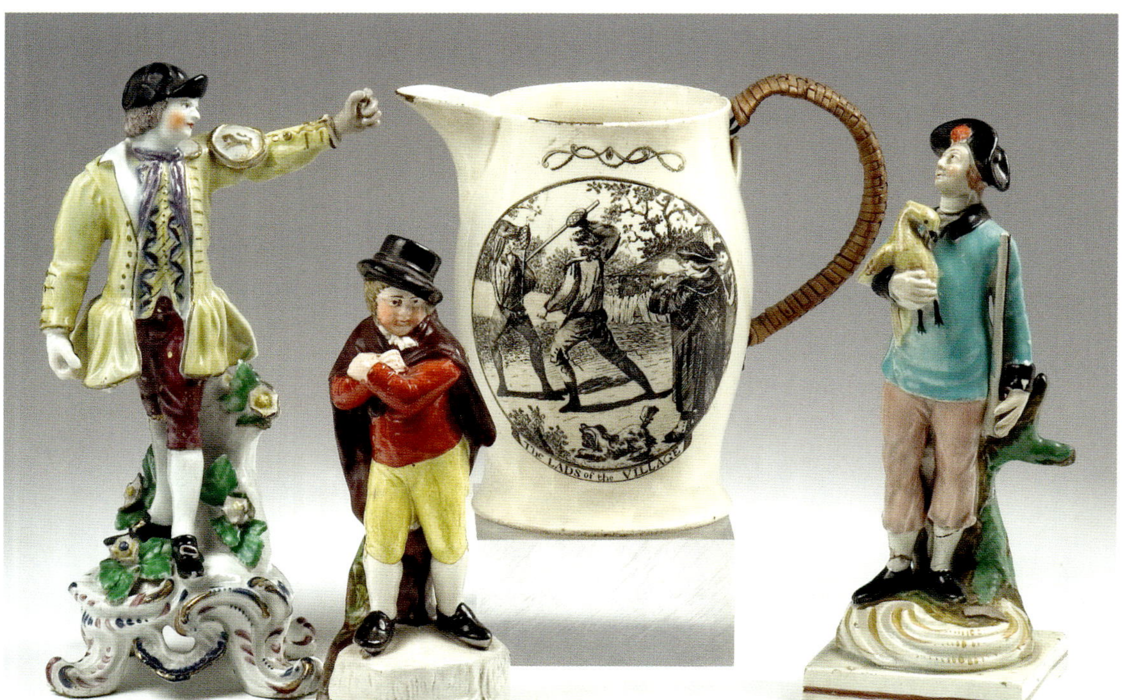

Figure, (1237), c.1760, London, Bow, height: 24.2cm, (9½in), enamelled, soft-paste porcelain. Figure of Thames waterman wearing Doggett's Coat and Badge. From 1696 Thames watermen were regulated and their boats licensed to ply their trade from an approved place; printed tables of fares soon appeared. In 1715, Thomas Doggett set the famous rowing race, (still run today) for young watermen who had completed their seven-year apprenticeships. The prize was a special coat and large circular medallion, embellished with a galloping Hanoverian horse.[26]
Figure, (1241), c.1800, Staffordshire, height: 19.1cm, (7½in), enamelled pearlware. Figure, wearing warm clothes and ice skates for skating on a frozen waterway.
Jug, **(1240)**, c.1800, Staffordshire, height: 17.2cm, (6¾in), printed creamware. 'The LADS of the VILLAGE', taken from a print by Robert Dighton,[27] illustrates the combat sport of 'single sticks', a forerunner of fencing, where participants bound their sword hands. Jug has replacement handle.
Figure, **(1239)**, c.1790, Staffordshire, height: 22.9cm, (9in), enamelled pearlware. An informal man holds a stick (or musket) in one hand and dead duck in the other.[28]

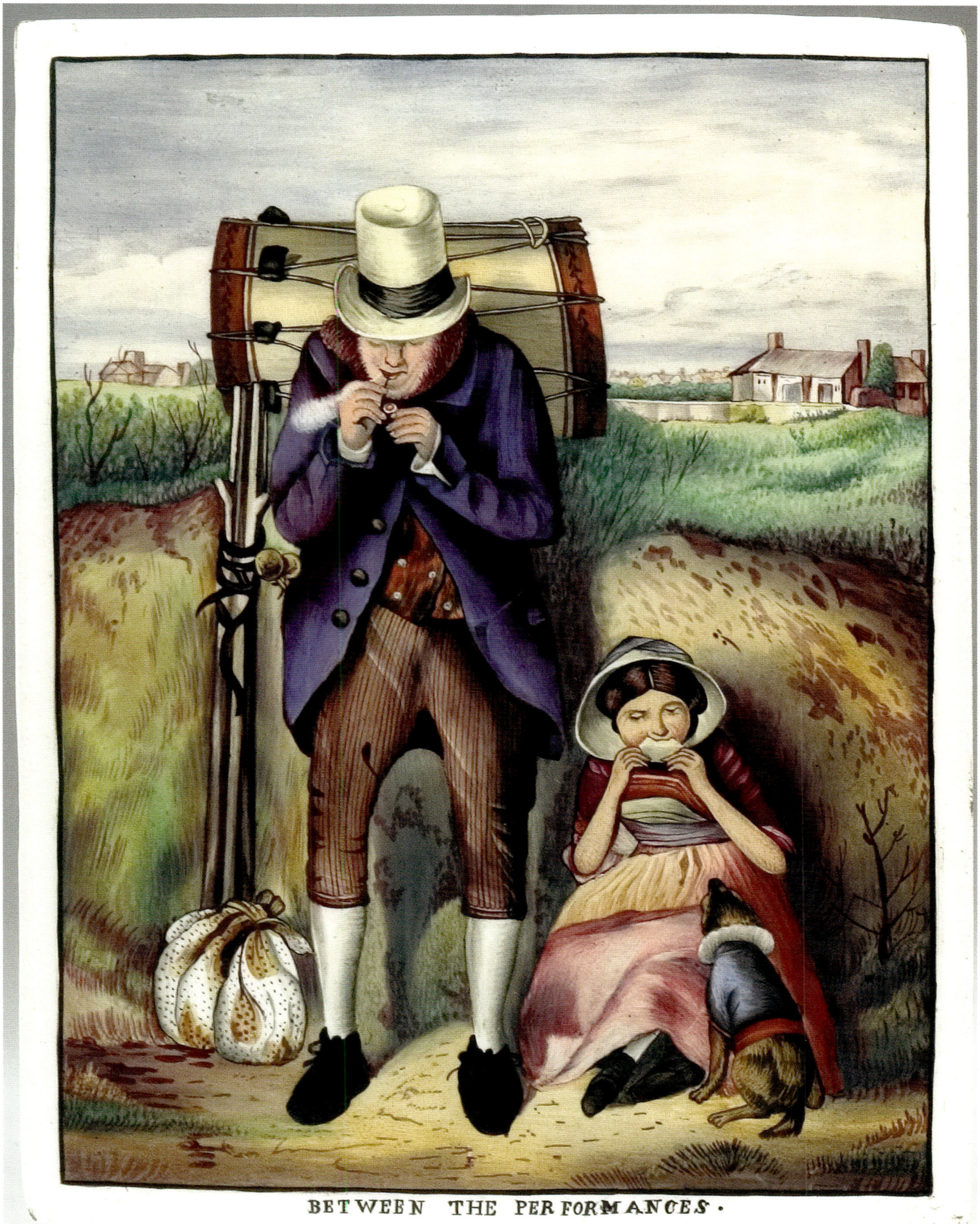

Plaque, (**1231**), c.1850, Staffordshire, height: 30.5cm, (12in), enamelled bone china.
Entitled, 'BETWEEN THE PERFORMANCES', a group of travelling entertainers, (probably a father and daughter), pause for a roadside picnic while their performing dog looks hopefully at their food. Street performers and itinerant showmen were becoming rare by the mid-Victorian period since most animal acts had been absorbed into circuses.

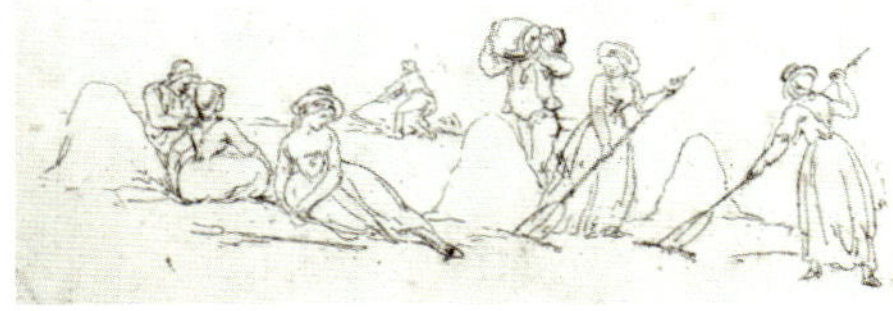

Chapter 17

AGRICULTURE

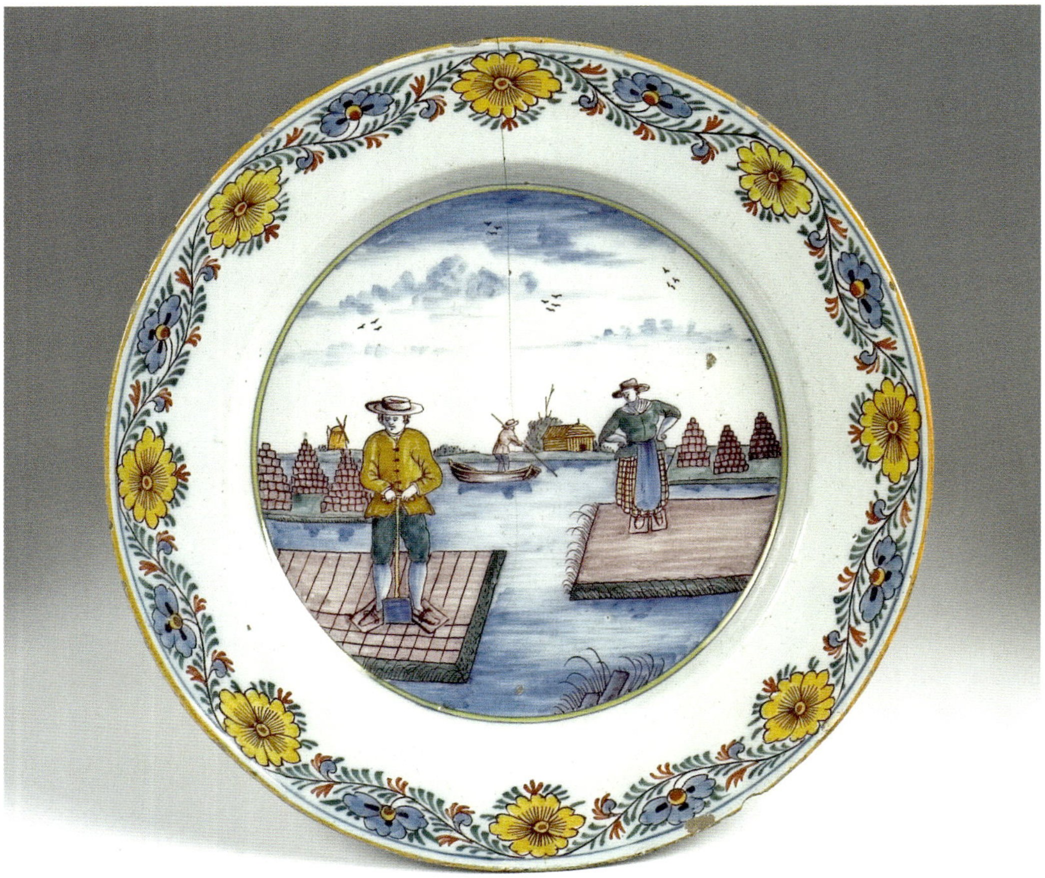

Dish, (**1279**), c.1730, Holland, height: 34.9cm, (13¾in), tin-glazed earthenware. Dish, marked K:V:B, shows labourers wearing large overshoes for walking on boggy land. They are in the polders, cutting peat for fuel. Before reclaimed land could be worked, it had to be deforested, drained or cleared of stones.

Agricultural Revolution

'Nothing separates the modern world more from the old regime than the relative importance of agriculture and the countryside'.[1] Of the 80 per cent of the population who lived in the countryside in 1700, 66 per cent worked directly on the land (compared to 2 per cent in 2000). The importance of agriculture to the eighteenth century state cannot be overestimated. Frederick the Great of Prussia made the point that, 'agriculture comes first among human activities, and without it there would be no merchants, no courtiers, no kings, no poets, no philosophers'.[2] Monarchs, from Empress Maria Teresa of Austria to 'Farmer' George III, made well publicised expressions of enthusiasm for agriculture.

Major changes in land management during the late-eighteenth century amounted to an agricultural revolution. Open pastures were enclosed into rectangular fields bordered by hedges and crops were rotated annually using new scientific principles. This created the now familiar chequer board pattern, still a hallmark of the British landscape. Premier landowners took pride in trying out new technologies. Men like Charles 'Turnip' Townshend, a retired statesman in George II's reign, alternated turnips with crops instead of leaving land fallow, in order to provide animal fodder. Thomas Coke of Norfolk introduced new crops and techniques, propelling his backward county to the forefront of English farming.

Arable Farming and Harvesting

The age of enclosure brought new methods of drilling and sowing seed, draining, fertilising and nourishing the land. This improved its quality so that sufficient barley and wheat could be produced to feed a rapidly growing population. Wheat could now be grown in areas where only oats, rye and spelt would grow before, creating a nationwide demand for refined wheat bread. William Cobbett wrote enthusiastically about his wheat field, 'the handsomest piece of wheat I ever saw … it has white straw, white ear and small brown grain. It is the very sort of wheat that is grown in Virginia, and that makes the finest flour'.[3]

It was no wonder that agricultural abundance was celebrated on pottery, reflecting farmers' achievements and increasing the prosperity of the landowners.

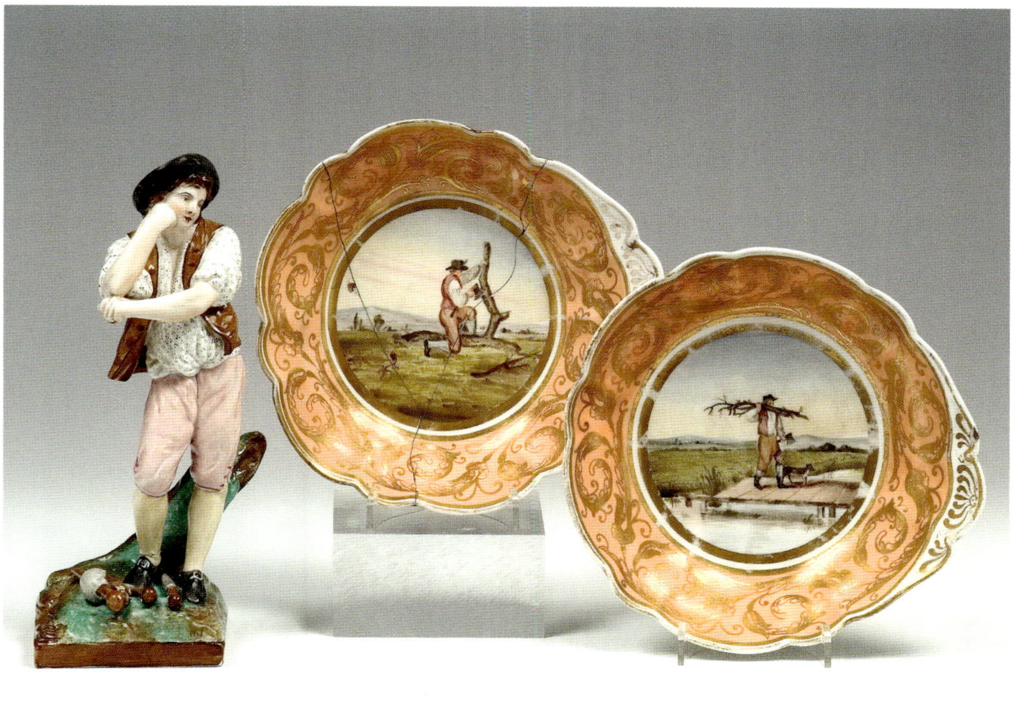

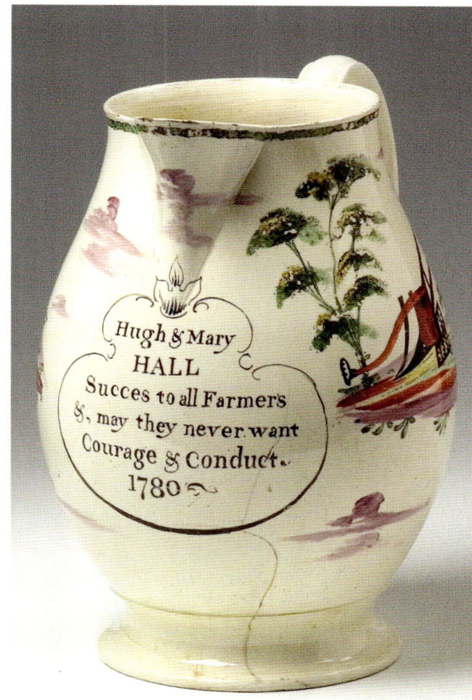

Figure, (**1267**), c.1790, French?, height: 24.2cm, (9½in), enamelled pearlware. A young man (modelled after P.L. Cyfflé) rests on his missing spade, his drainage tools at his feet.
Pair of Dessert Dishes, (**1269 & A**), c.1830, Worcester, each diameter: 19.7cm, (7¾in), enamelled soft-paste porcelain. Dishes with gilt scrolls on salmon borders, marked for Flight, Barr & Barr. Each painted with woodcutters; one man chops logs, the other carries a bundle of branches.

Jug, (**1249**), 1780, Yorkshire, height: 25.4cm, (10in), enamelled creamware. Jug finely painted with a ploughshare on one side and a wheatsheaf on the other. Inscribed for 'John & Mary HALL Succes [*sic*] to all Farmers &, may they never want Courage & Conduct 1780'.

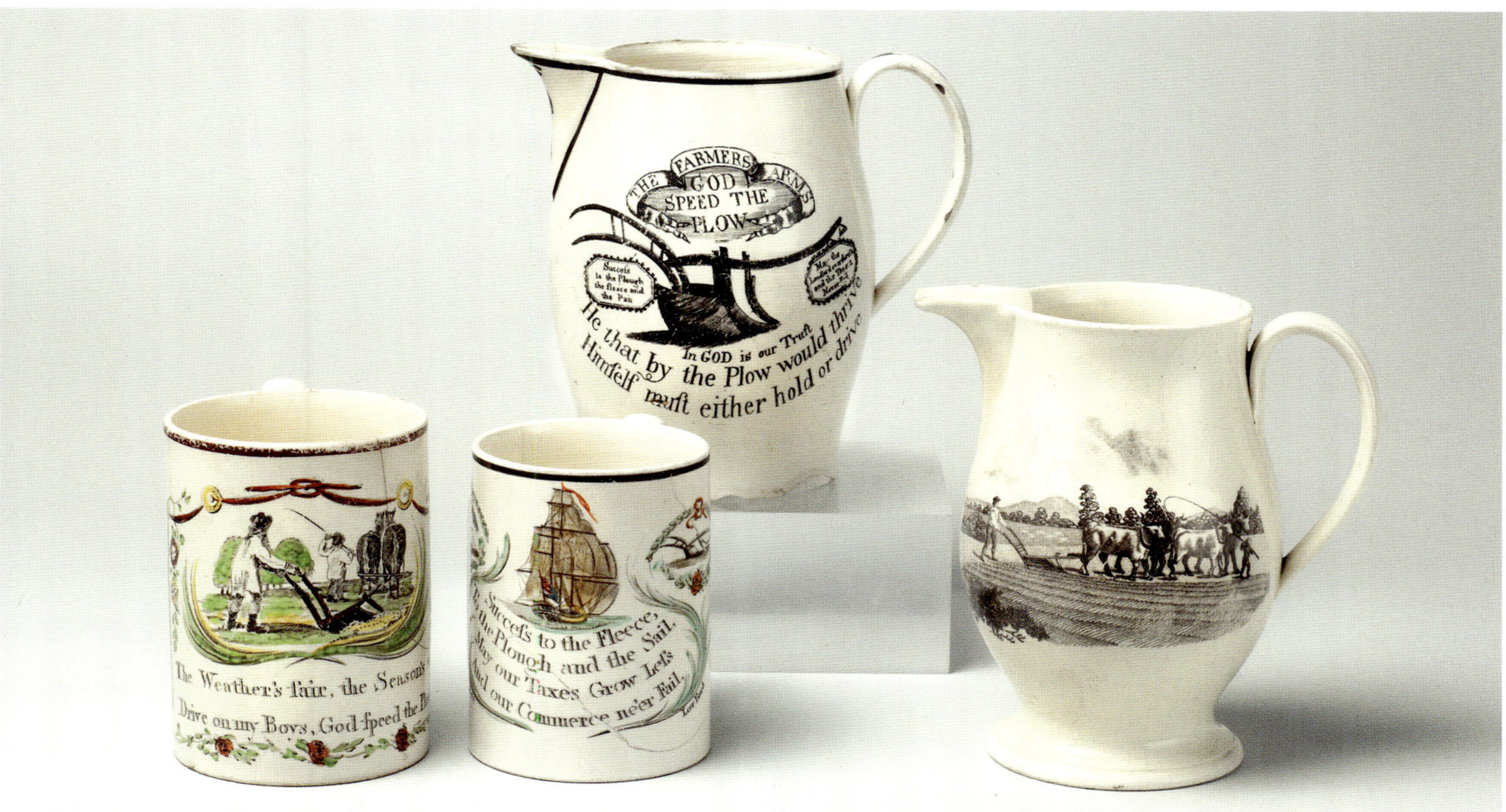

Mug, (**1266**), c.1810, Sunderland, height: 10.2cm, (4in), creamware, printed and enamelled. Mug made at Dawson's Low Ford Pottery. The ploughman guides a two-horse plough, inscribed, 'The Weather's fair, the Season's now, Drive on my Boys, God speed the Plough'.
Mug, (**1268**), c.1810, Sunderland, height: 11.5cm, (4½in), creamware, printed and enamelled. Mug made at Dawson's Low Ford Pottery, features a sailing ship and verses, and a sheep on the reverse.

Jug, (**1265**), c.1810, Staffordshire, height: 13.3cm, (5¼in), printed creamware. Printed with large ploughshare and inscribed, 'He that by the plough would thrive, Himself must either hold or drive'.
Jug, (**1263**), c.1810, Staffordshire, height: 13.3cm, (5¼in), printed creamware. Finely printed with ploughshare pulled by four oxen in an open field. William Cobbett was 'decidedly for the using of oxen'. They were stronger, hardier and ate less than horses and did not require the services of a blacksmith.[4]

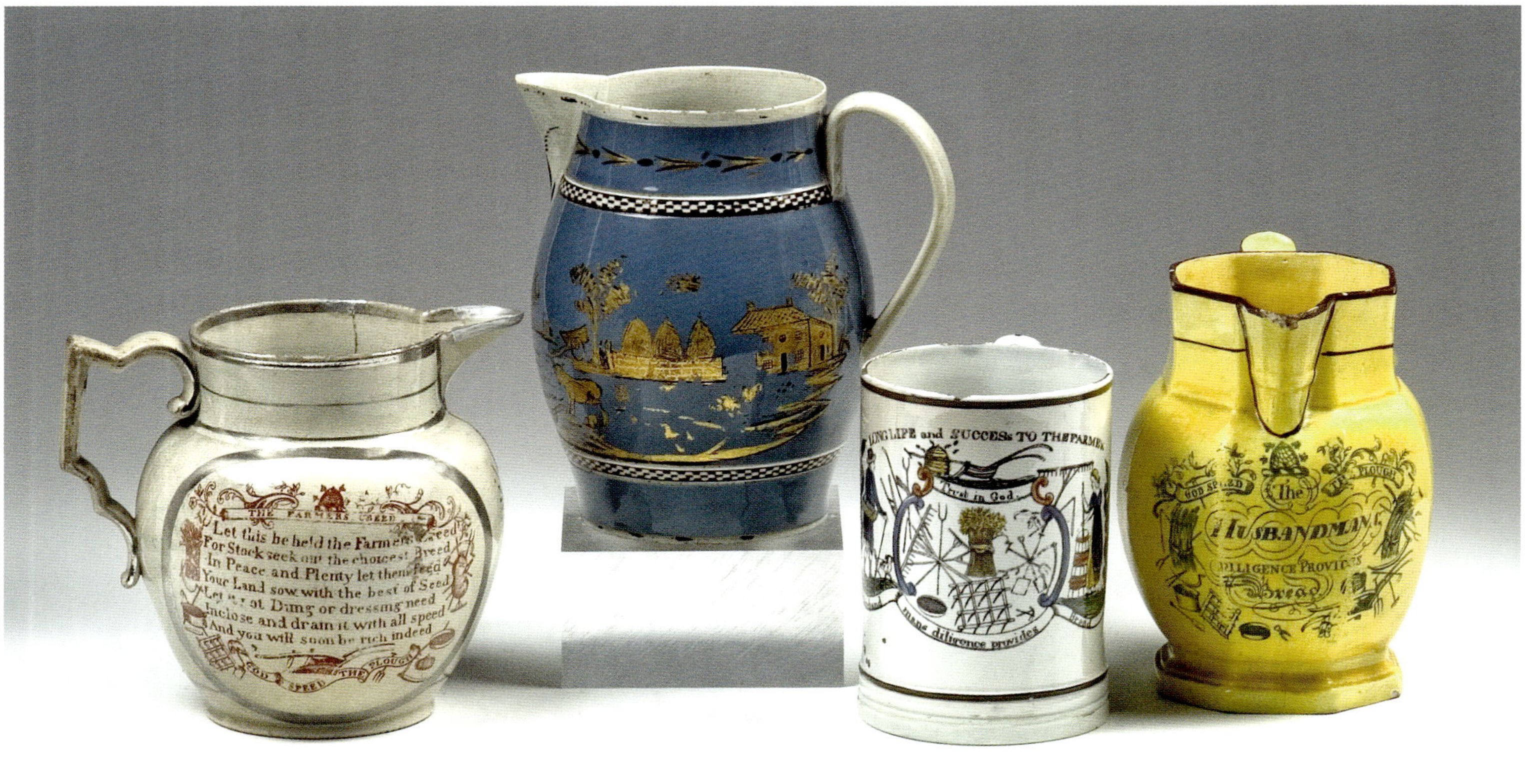

Jug, (**1243**), c.1810, Staffordshire, height: 14cm, (5½in), pearlware, brown-printed and lustred. Jug printed with 'THE FARMER'S CREED', 'GOD SPEED THE PLOUGH' and agricultural implements.

Jug, (**1248**), c.1790, probably Liverpool?, height: 15.3cm, (6in), lustred pearlware. Covered with blue slip but for narrow diaper bands around the neck and base. Embellished in black and gilt with a farmyard, animals and hayricks. Reverse inscribed, 'The Weather's fair, the Season's now'.

Mug, (**1246**), c.1800, North East, height: 12.7cm, (5in), pearlware, printed and Pratt-coloured. Printed with farm workers, utensils and, 'LONG LIFE and SUCCESS TO THE FARMER'.

Jug, (**1245**), c.1800, Staffordshire, height: 15.3cm, (6in), earthenware, yellow-glazed and printed. Faceted body printed, 'The HUSBANDMAN'S DILIGENCE PROVIDES Bread'.

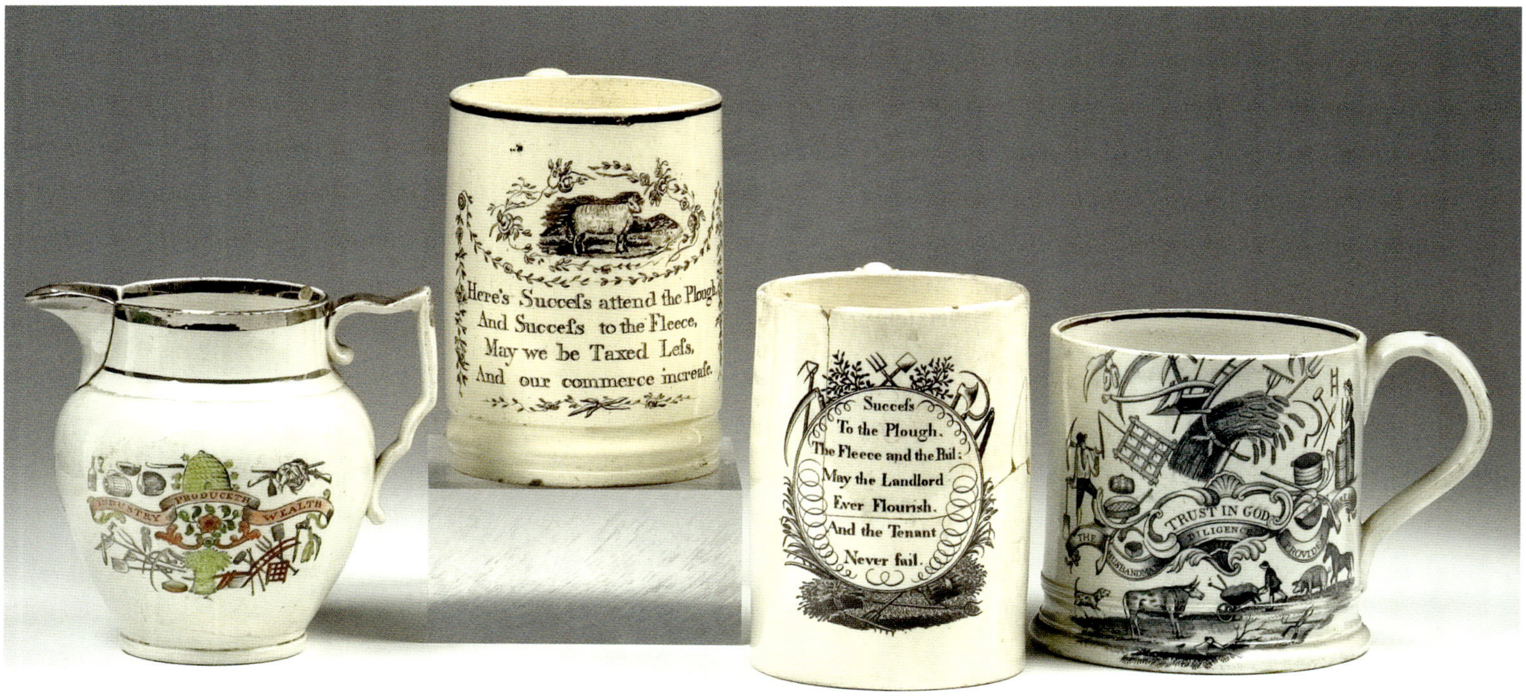

Jug, (**1254**), c.1800, Staffordshire, height: 11.5cm, (4½in), pearlware, printed coloured and lustred. Printed with farm tools united by a banner inscribed, 'INDUSTRY PRODUCETH WEALTH'.

Mug, (**1253**), c.1800, Sunderland, Low Ford, height: 12.7cm, (5in), printed creamware. Made by Dawson & Co., printed with vignette of a sheep and the plea, 'Success to the Fleece / May we be Taxed Less, / And our Commerce increase'.

Mug, (**1251**), c.1800, Staffordshire, height: 12.1cm, (4¾in), printed creamware. Within a circular frame, flanked by tools; 'Success to the Plough, the Fleece and the Pail,[5] May the Landlord Ever Flourish And the Tenant Never Fail'.

Mug, (**1250**), c.1820, North East, height: 10.2cm, (4in), printed earthenware. Numerous farming tools and symbols, 'TRUST IN GOD' and, 'Let the wealthy and great / Roll in splendour and state / I envy them not I declare it / I eat my own lamb / My own chickens and ham / I shear my own fleece and I wear it'.

Mug, (1264), c.1830, North East, height: 6.4cm, (2½in), earthenware, printed and coloured. Ploughing with oxen and sowing seed inscribed 'SPRING'.
Mug, (R2454.35), c.1830, North East, height: 7.2cm, (2⅞in), brown-printed earthenware. Depicts haymaking carts and tools in summer.
Plate, (1258), c.1820, North East, diameter: 20.3cm, (8in), printed earthenware. Plate with rose relief border printed, 'IN GOD IS ALL OUR TRUST. Let the wealthy and great / Roll in splendour and state / I envy them not I declare it'.
Jug, (1281), c.1800, Staffordshire, Lane End, height: 14cm, (5½in), pearlware, printed and enamelled. Print signed by John Aynsley, shows produce transported to market in a covered wagon, marked 'Cotton', drawn by eight horses.[6] In the background a tiny but chilling vignette; to the left of windmill hangs a figure on the gallows circled by crows.

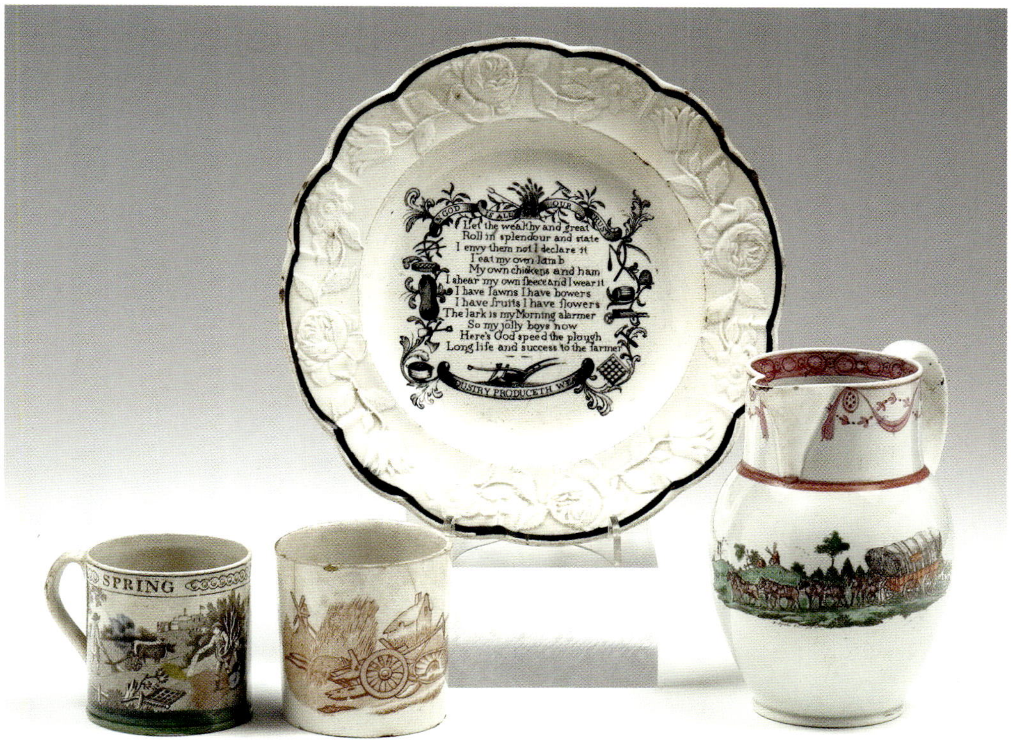

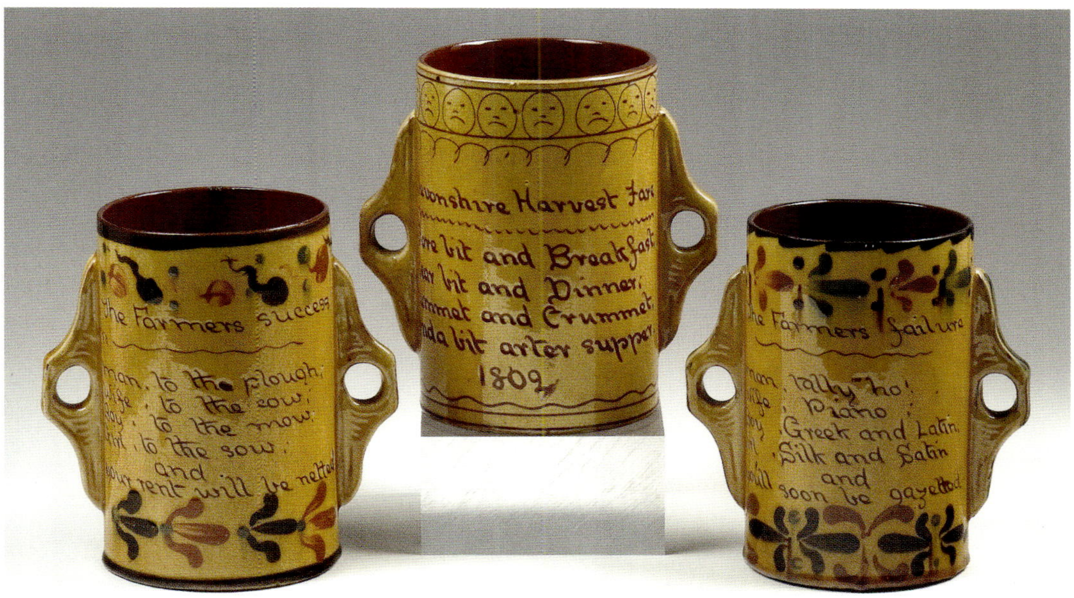

Pair of Cups, (1247 & A), c.1890, Devon, each height: 15.3cm, (6in), coloured slipware. Two cylindrical cups with side handles, made at the Aller Vale, inscribed in sgraffito with shrewd observations, contrasting 'The Farmer's Success: Man to the plough, Wife to the cow, Boy to the mow, Girl to the sow, and your rent will be netted'; with, 'The Farmer's Failure: Man, tally ho! Woman, piano, Boy, Greek and Latin, Girl, Silk and Satin, and will soon be gazetted'.[7] These epigrams were published by Nathaniel Hone in his *Table Book*, 1828, where they contrasted farming mores of 1722 with those of 1822.
Cup, (1361), c.1890, Devon, height: 15.3cm, (6in), coloured slipware. Cup with side handles, made at Aller Vale, inscribed in sgraffito with border of sad faces, 'Devonshire Harvest Fare … And a bit arter supper/ 1802'.

Beaker, (1369) c.1790, Staffs, Etruria, height: 8.9cm, (3½in), printed creamware. Probably made by Wedgwood.
Plate, (1363) c.1790, Staffordshire, height: 22.3cm, (8¾in), printed creamware. Marked 'Drab Porcelain',[8] printed with a pair of haymakers. Both pieces printed with versions of a very popular print. Man with rake and woman with wheat-sheaf amble past farm buildings and hayricks. Subject first appeared as a vignette header to a song in *Clio and Euterpe or British Harmony* first published in 1758.
Mug, (1358) c.1760, Worcester, height: 12.7cm, (5in), enamelled soft-paste porcelain. Very rare mug painted with sinuous figures of man with a rake over his shoulder and a woman carrying wheat sheaf, farm buildings and hayricks behind them.[9]

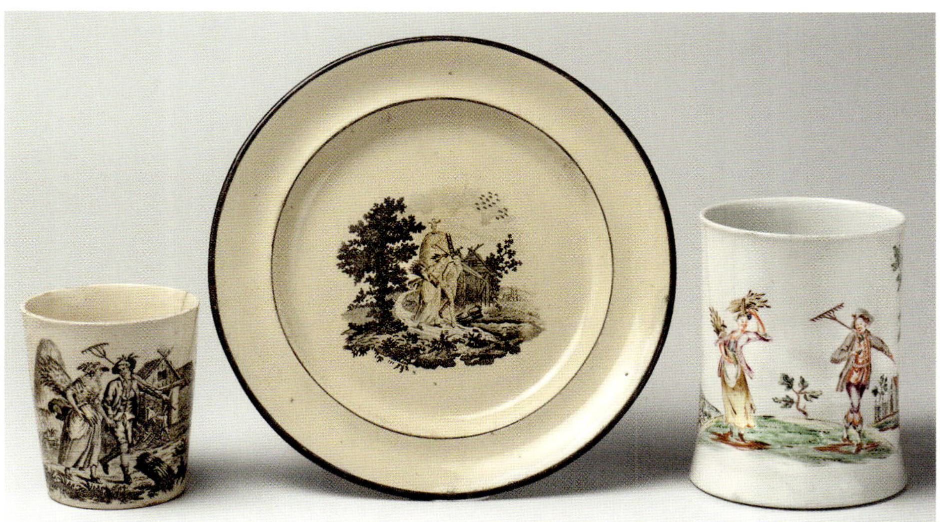

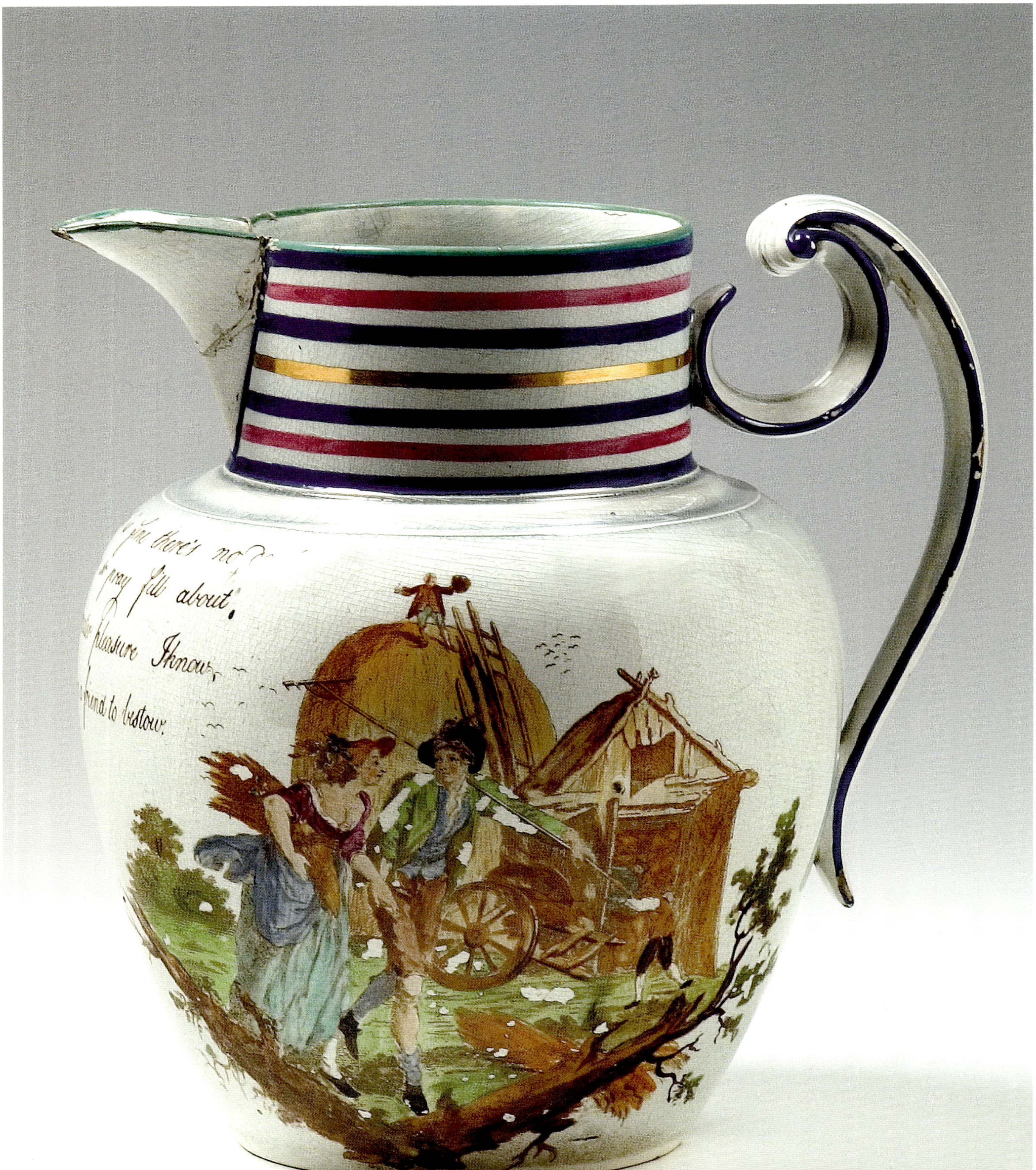

Jug, (**1365**) c.1800, Staffordshire, height: 20.3cm, (8in), pearlware, printed and enamelled. Jug printed and coloured with 'Harvest Home'. A young man carrying a rake and a young woman with a wheat sheaf walk in front of a huge hayrick, a barn and a farm cart. Design derives from the header to 'My Grandmother's Cat' from *Clio and Euterpe or British Harmony* (volume II), first published in 1758,[10] and a 1763 printed song sheet, entitled 'Harvest Home', signed by Grimm and published by Robert Sayer of Fleet Street.[11] Design also used by Hancock on Worcester porcelain, by Thomas Rothwell on creamware in Hanley[12] and by John Sadler on delftware tiles in Liverpool, all in the 1760s.[13]

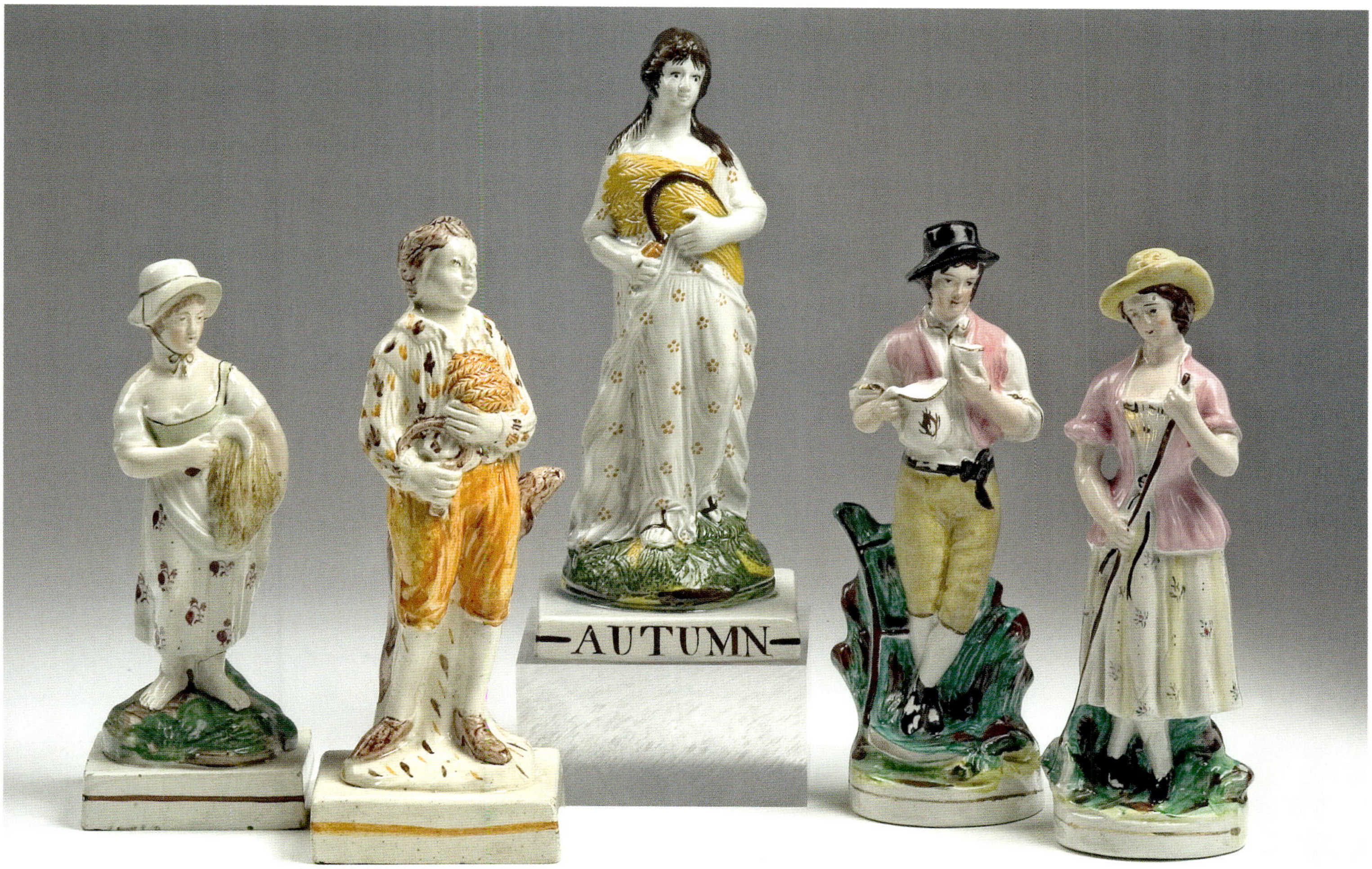

Figure, (1367), c.1800, Staffordshire, height: 19.1cm, (7½in), enamelled pearlware. Figure of girl in bonnet holds sickle and wheat-sheaf. She may symbolise summer in a set of seasons.[14]

Figure, (1368), c.1800, North East, height: 22.3cm, (8¾in), Pratt-coloured pearlware. Figure of boy holds sickle and wheat-sheaf.

Figure, (1366), c.1800, Sunderland, height: 21.7cm, (8½in), Pratt-coloured pearlware. Symbolic figure of 'AUTUMN', made by Dixon, Austin & Co. also carries sickle and wheat sheaf.

Pair of Figures, (1360 & A), c.1840, Staffordshire, height: 20.5cm, (8⅛in), height: 19.5cm, (7⅝in), enamelled earthenware. Pair of farm workers making hay, a high summer activity. Woman leans on her pitchfork while her male companion pauses from scything for liquid refreshment.

Figure Group, (1354), c.1820, Staffordshire, height: 19.1cm, (7½in), enamelled pearlware. A gardener and his wife stand either side of a stream. He leans on a spade, she holds a watering can.

Figure Group, (1359), c.1820, Staffordshire, height: 25.4cm, (10in), enamelled pearlware. A couple sits on rocks, taking a picnic break; he holds a bag of food and there is a small cask at their feet.

Figure, (1350), c.1800, North East or Scotland, height: 20.3cm, (8in), pearlware, lead-glazed and sponged. A boy holds a cup of grapes.

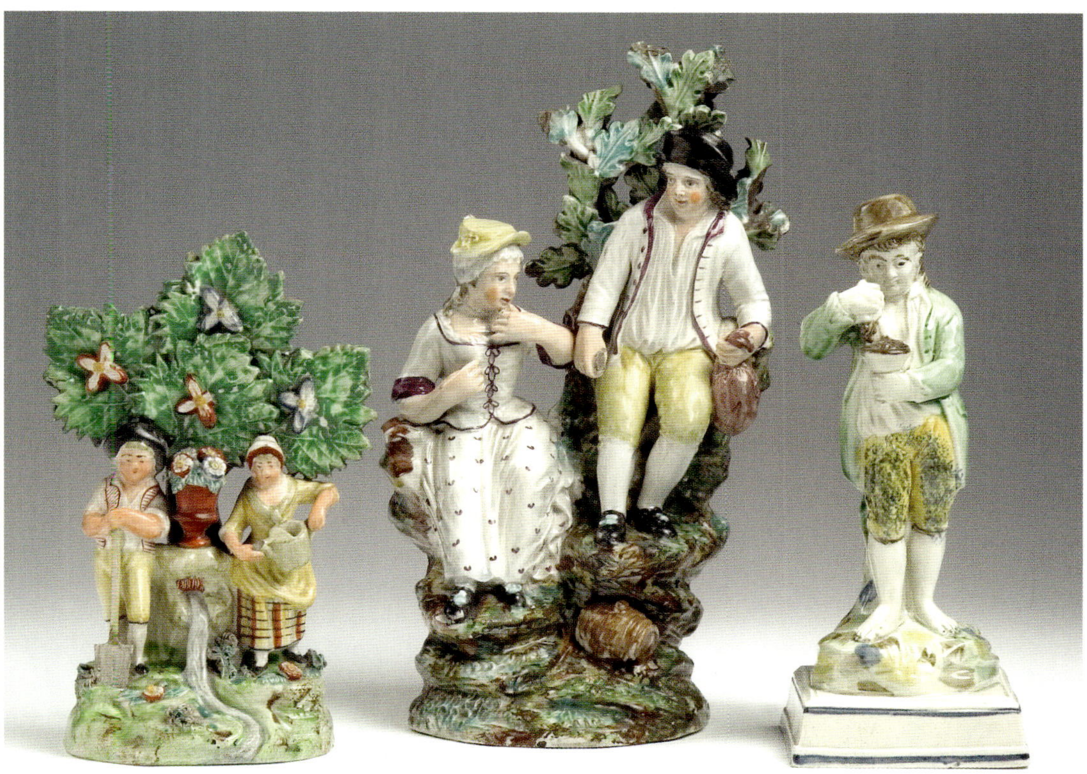

Animal Husbandry

Livestock were subject to intensive breeding programmes during the eighteenth century. Robert Bakewell of Dishley Grange, Leicestershire, worked with Longhorn cattle and Leicester sheep, Robert and Charles Collings developed Shorthorn cattle and John Ellman of Glynde in Sussex greatly improved Southdown sheep, a breed native to Suffolk. Thomas Coke's 'sheep shearings' on his Holkham estate in Norfolk, to which he succeeded in 1776, attracted experts from all over Europe, eager to learn his innovatory methods. Arthur Young, Secretary to the Board of Agriculture actively promoted Southdowns and they rapidly became the premier English downland sheep. At Lewes Fair in the main market, 30,000 sheep were sold in 1793.

As winter crops for animal fodder were developed, farmers could cease the wholesale slaughter of livestock at the end of autumn. In addition, animal size and meat quality improved dramatically. The average weight of cattle and sheep sold at Smithfield Market in London doubled between 1710 and 1795. Successful breeders, with justifiable pride, had themselves painted with their prize specimens. William Cobbett, who recommended cottagers to keep a pig rather than any other farm animal, declared his intention to, 'send a fat hog to the *cattle* show at Smithfield on Monday next. She has by no means finished her fatting; but … when she is fat I will bet a hundred pounds she will weigh … five hundred pounds, a weight much about equal to that of a fat Scotch ox.'[15]

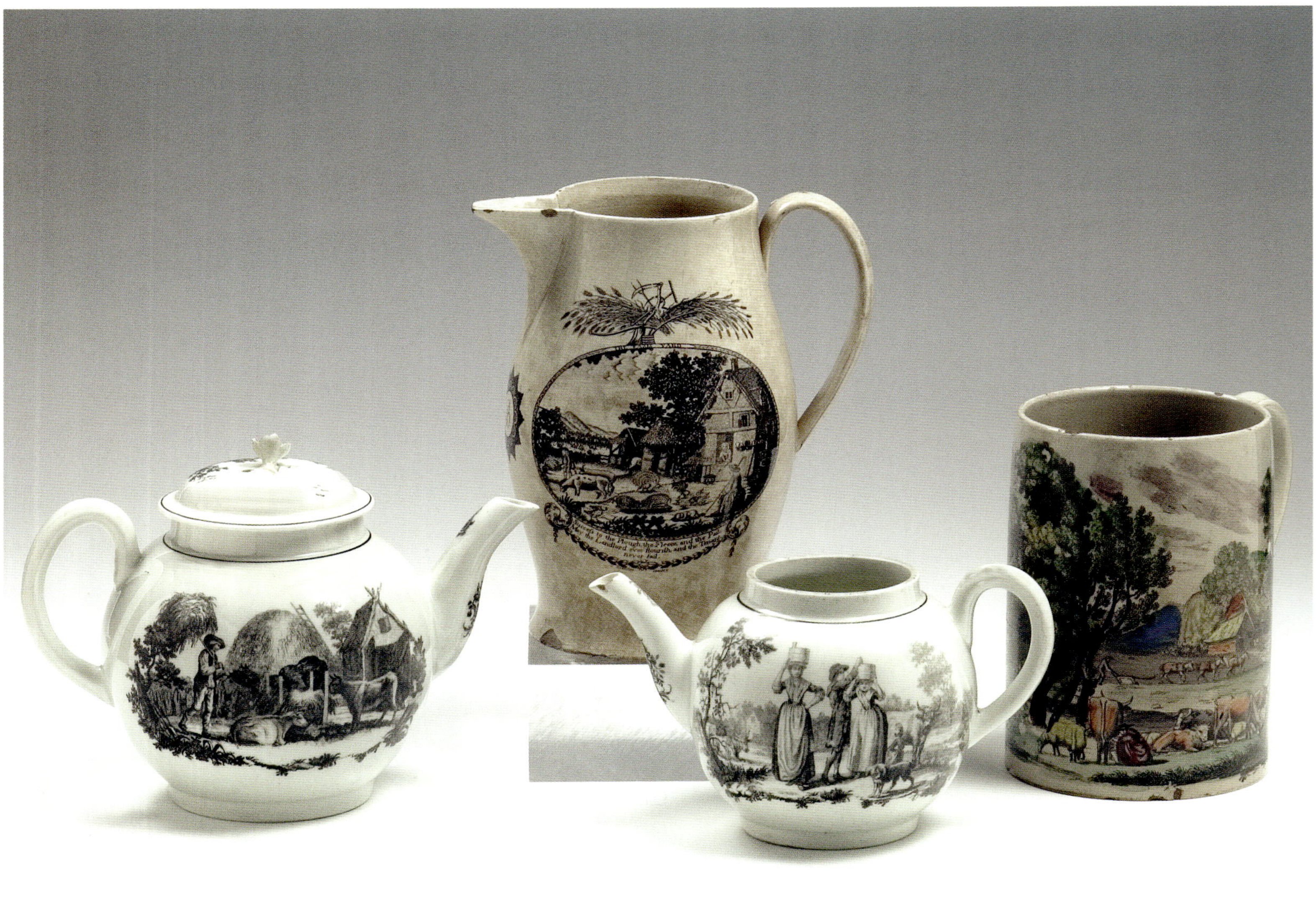

Teapot, (**1338**), c.1770, Worcester, height: 15.3cm, (6in), printed soft-paste porcelain. A cowherd brings hay on a pitchfork to his cattle before hayrick and barn.
Jug, (**1244**), c.1770, Staffordshire, Hanley, height: 19.1cm, (7½in), printed creamware. Oval print entitled, 'THE FARMYARD' with pigs, chickens, cattle and a turkey, signed by Thomas Baddeley.
Teapot, (**1257**), c.1770, Worcester, height: 11.5cm, (4½in), printed soft-paste porcelain. Two dairymaids have pails of milk placed on their heads while a third continues to milk a cow. Based on a print published by Robert Sayer in 1766.[16]
Mug, (**1255**), c.1800, Staffordshire, height: 15.3cm, (6in), creamware, printed and coloured. Panoramic wrap-around print of a farm, from a flock of sheep led home by horsemen, to cattle grazing and being milked while the farmer ploughs a distant field.

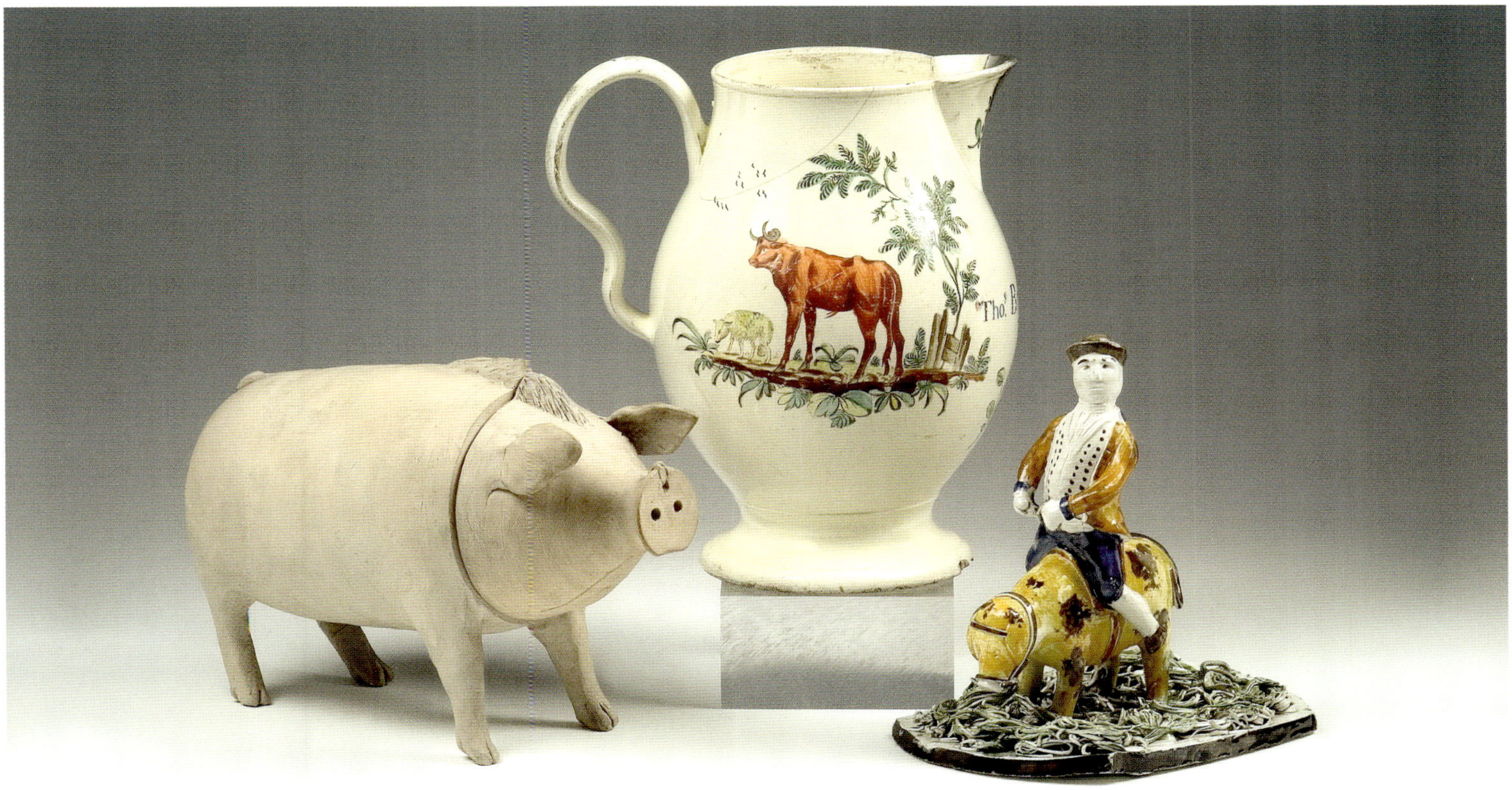

Flask and Cup, (**1261**), c.1850, Sussex, height: 17.2cm, (6¾in), biscuit clay. Modelled as a pig from an unusual mix of pale Dorset and Sussex clays, giving the vessel a naturalistic pale pink appearance. Made as a souvenir of the Sussex pig breed, its head detaches to form a drinking cup. It is doubtful whether it was used to hold liquid since it is unglazed and porous. It may be a late nod to the old hogs head of ale; a barrel holding 54 gallons!

Jug, (**1252**), c.1780, possibly Yorkshire, height: 22.3cm, (8¾in), enamelled creamware. Inscribed for 'Thomas Bryon' with a prize ox and a horse painted on each side.

Figure Group, (**1261**), c.1800, Staffordshire or North East, height: 17.2cm, (6¾in), Pratt-coloured pearlware. Very unusual group, described as 'An Irishman riding a pig'; the pig wears a harness.[17]

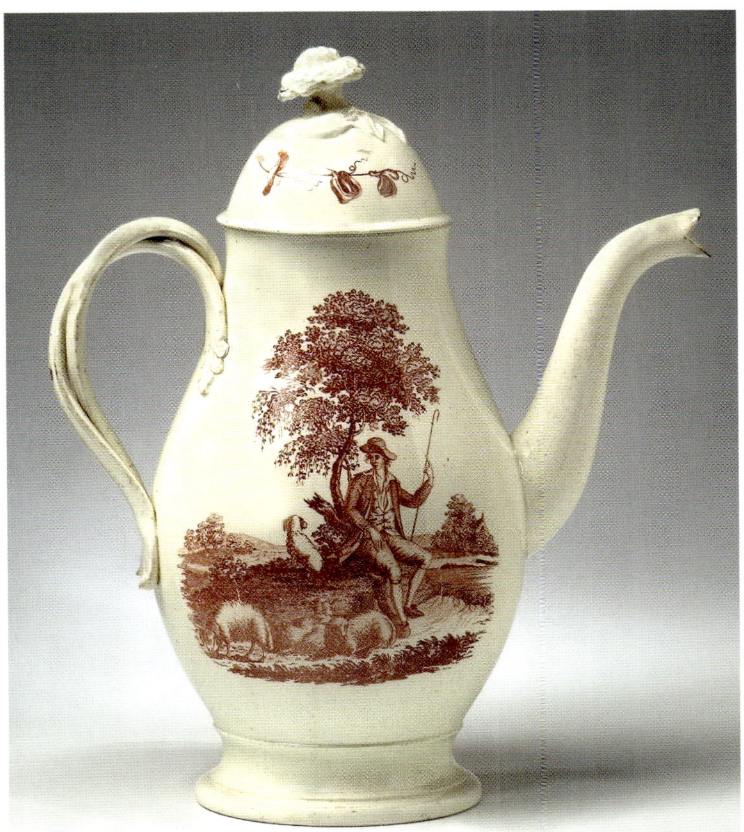

Coffee Pot, (**1690**), c.1780, Wedgwood and Liverpool, height: 28cm, (11in), red-printed creamware. Printed by Sadler and Green with a shepherd minding his flock. Sweet peas adorn the lid.

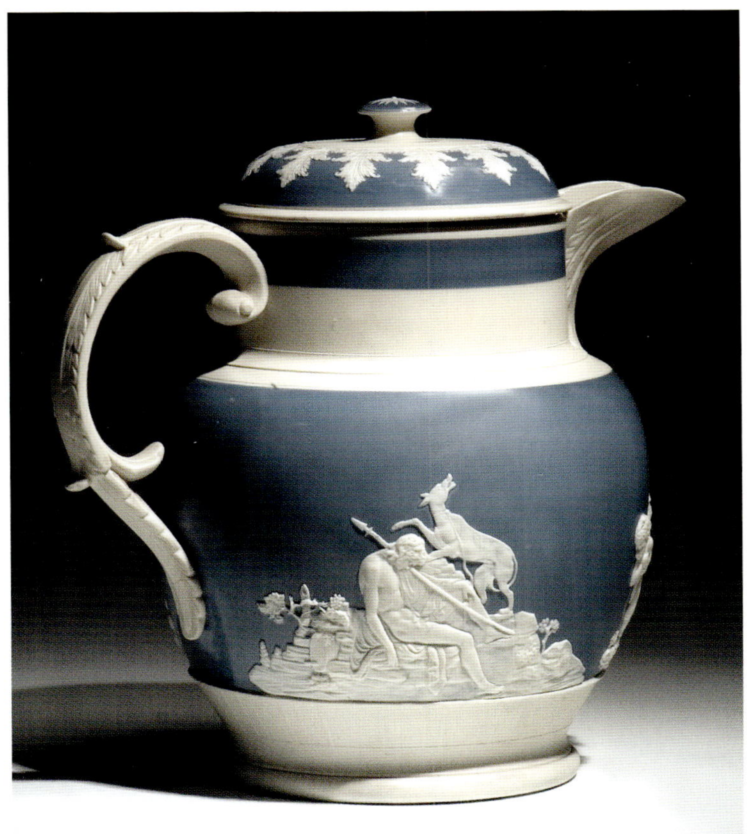

Jug, (**1462**), c.1810, Staffordshire, height: 29.2cm, (11½in), smear-glazed stoneware. White relief sprig on blue slip of Endymion, the beautiful shepherd of Greek mythology, loved by Selene, goddess of the moon.

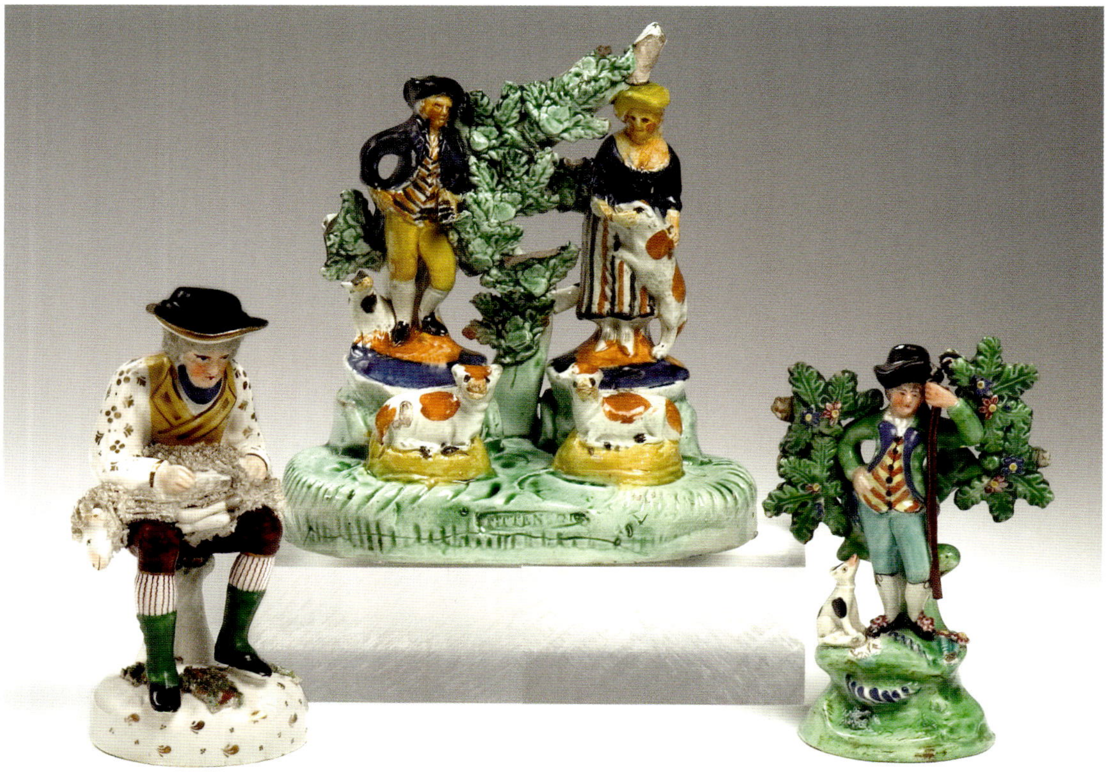

Figure, (**1318**), c.1840, Staffordshire, height: 15.9cm, (6¼in), enamelled soft-paste porcelain. Seated man balances a sheep on his knees as he shears its fleece.
Figure Group, (**1321**), c.1800, Staffordshire, height: 17.8cm, (7in), Pratt-coloured pearlware. Crudely modelled group, comprising shepherd, shepherdess and several sheep, stamped several times, back and front, 'TITTENSOR'. This may indicate that the component parts were also sold separately.
Figure, (**1317**), c.1820, Staffordshire, height: 14.7cm, (5¾in), Pratt-coloured pearlware. Figure of shepherd, with his dog, leaning on his crook.

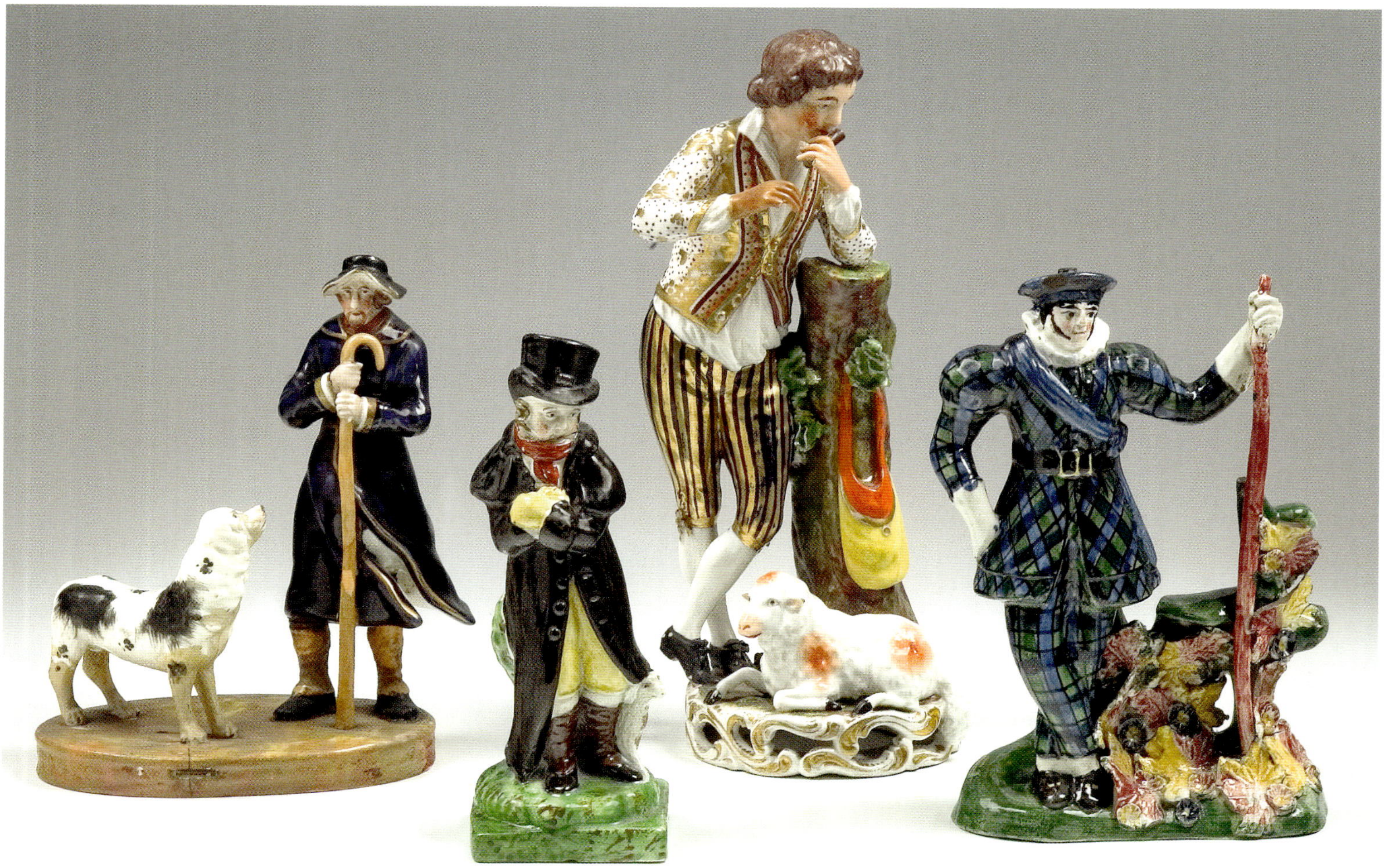

Figure Group, (**1316**), c.1830, Staffordshire, height: 17.8cm, (7in), enamelled soft-paste porcelain. Wind swept shepherd and his dog, said to be inspired by a painting (as yet unidentified) by Thomas Barker of Bath, who specialised in wild elemental scenes.
Figure, (**1327**), c.1820, Staffordshire, height: 17.8cm, (7in), enamelled pearlware. Male youth wears a greatcoat, scarf and top hat to withstand heavy weather. He has a dog but no further evidence to suggest he is a shepherd.
Figure, (**1320**), c.1830, Derby, height: 25.4cm, (10in), soft-paste porcelain, enamelled and gilt. Figure of a romanticised shepherd, wearing elaborately decorated clothing, plays the flute to his sheep.
Figure, (**1327**), c.1800, Scotland, height: 17.8cm, (7in), Pratt-coloured pearlware. Highland shepherd, c.1800, wears an elaborate tartan outfit.

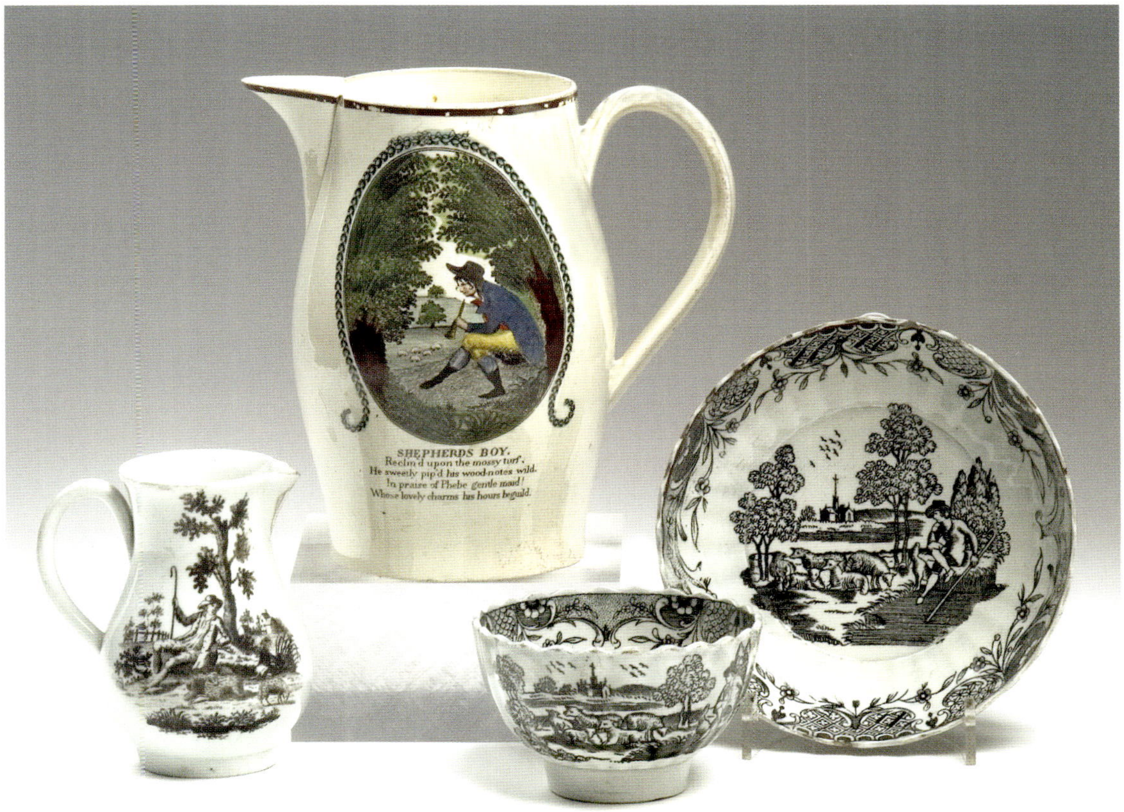

Jug, (**1328**), c.1800, Staffordshire, height: 15.3cm, (6in), creamware, printed and enamelled. Printed, 'SHEPHERDS BOY', in a framed Arcadian setting, 'sweetly pip'd his wood-notes wild / In praise of Phebe gentle maid!'[18]

Jug, (**1323**), c.1770, Worcester, height: 8.9cm, (3½in), printed soft-paste porcelain. A shepherd reclines beside diminutive sheep.

Cup and Saucer, (**1324 & A**), c.1820, Staffordshire, height: 3¼cm, (8.3in), diameter: 12.7cm, (5in), printed pearlware. A shepherd sits meditating beside his flock in a landscape.

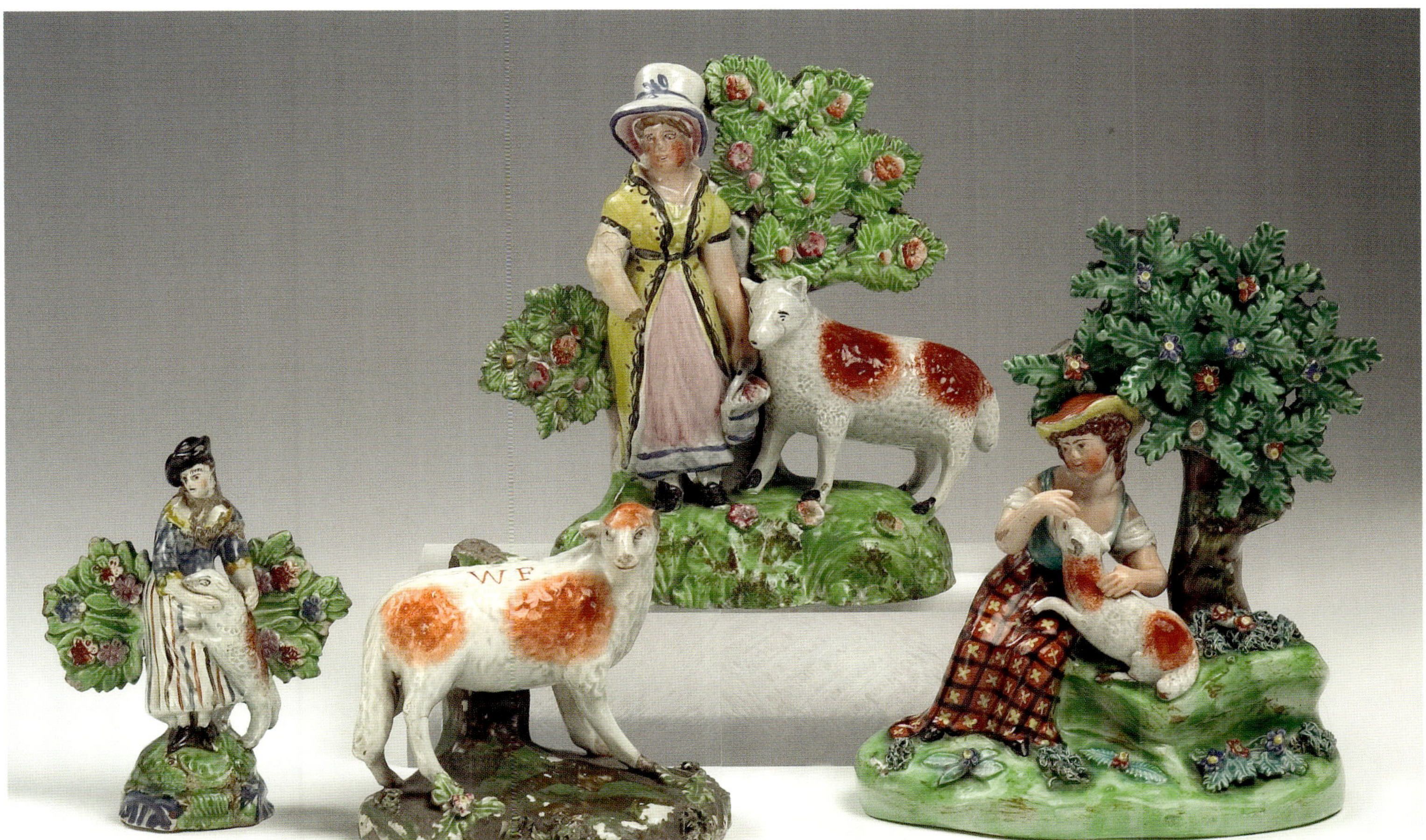

Figure, (**1614**), c.1800, Staffordshire, height: 12.1cm, (4¾in), enamelled pearlware. The female figure with a sheep climbing up her skirt, derives from a Derby prototype of c.1780.[19]

Figure, (**1313**), c.1820, Staffordshire, height: 14cm, (5½in), enamelled pearlware. Sheep with russet patches has been branded 'WF' for its owner.

Figure Group, (**1312**), c.1820, Staffordshire, height: 17.2cm, (6¾in), Pratt-coloured pearlware. A fashionably dressed shepherdess with a sheep.

Figure Group, (**1612**), c.1800, Staffordshire, height: 19.1cm, (7½in), enamelled pearlware. Made in the style of John Walton, a girl sits beneath a tree, petting a lamb.

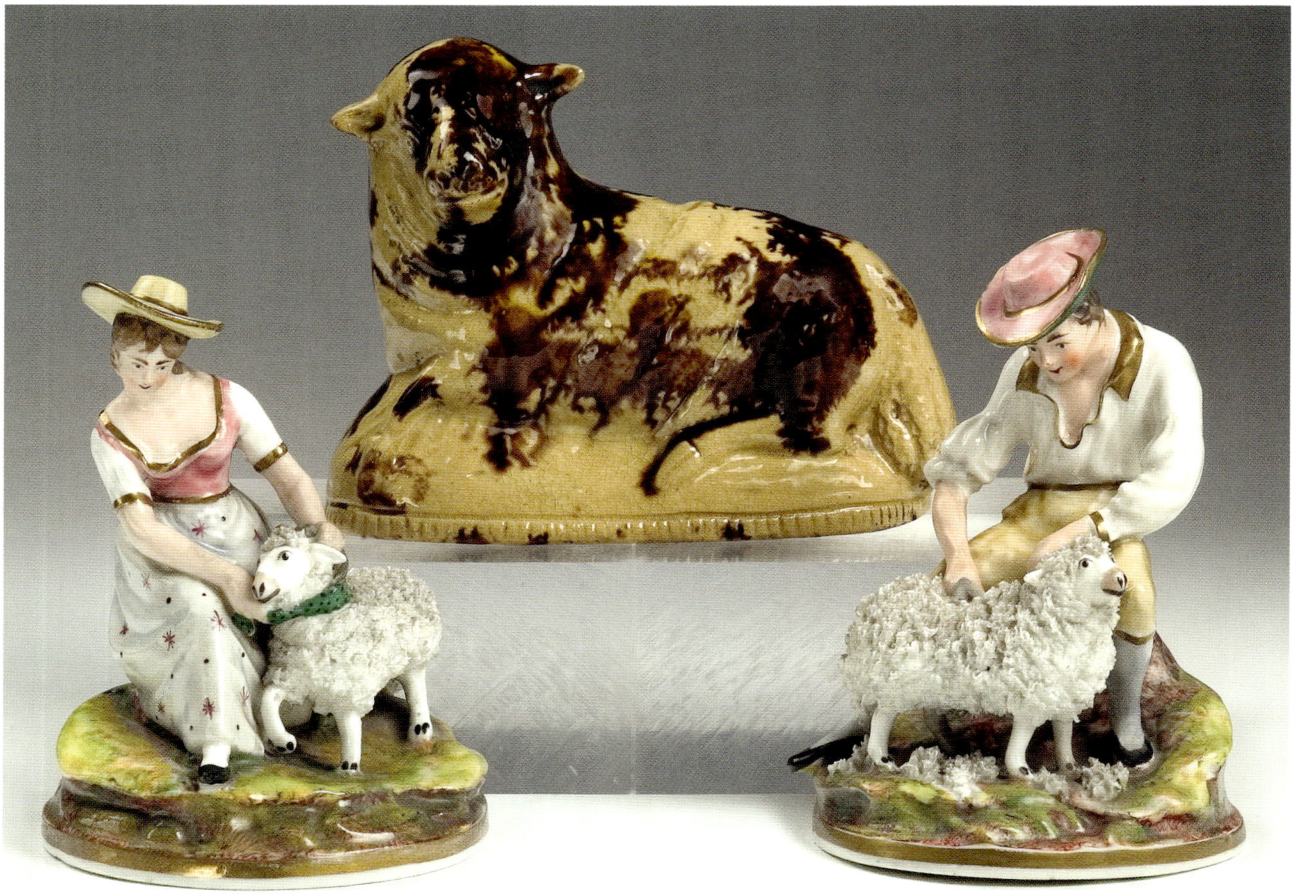

Pair of Figure Groups, (**1319&A**), c.1835, Staffordshire, height: 12.2cm, (4¾in), height: 11.6cm, (4⅝in), soft-paste porcelain, enamelled and gilt. A woman wraps a garland around the neck of a sheep while the man clips a docile sheep, using shredded clay to suggest the fleece.
Figure, (**1314**), c.1840, Staffordshire, height: 11.5cm, (4½in), sponged earthenware. Slip-cast figure of a recumbent sheep.

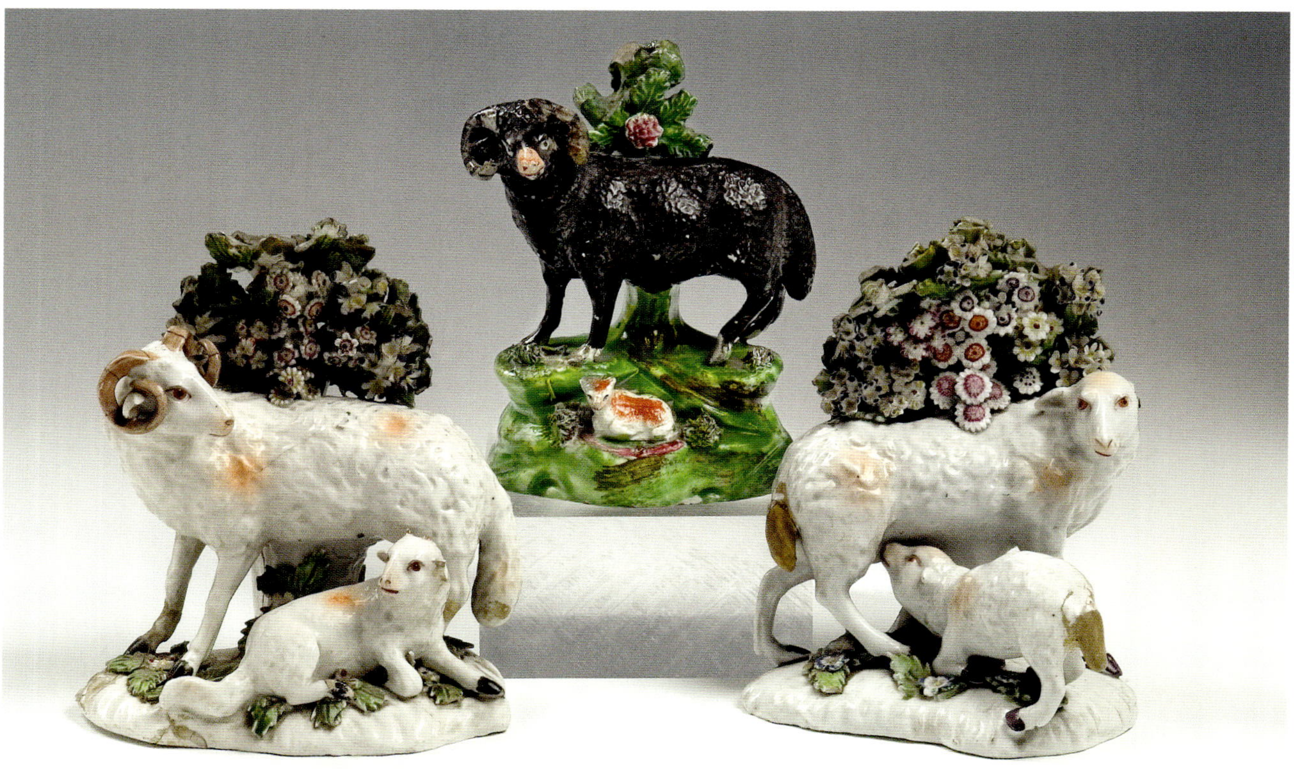

Pair of Figure Groups, (**1322 & A**), c.1775, Derby, each height: 14cm, (5½in), soft-paste porcelain. Sheep and ram, each with a lamb, their fleece lightly touched with blush-coloured patches; densely flowering trees behind them.
Figure Group, (**1315**), c.1825, Staffordshire, height: 14cm, (5½in), enamelled pearlware. Imposing figure of black ram and tiny lamb, marked for Ralph Salt.

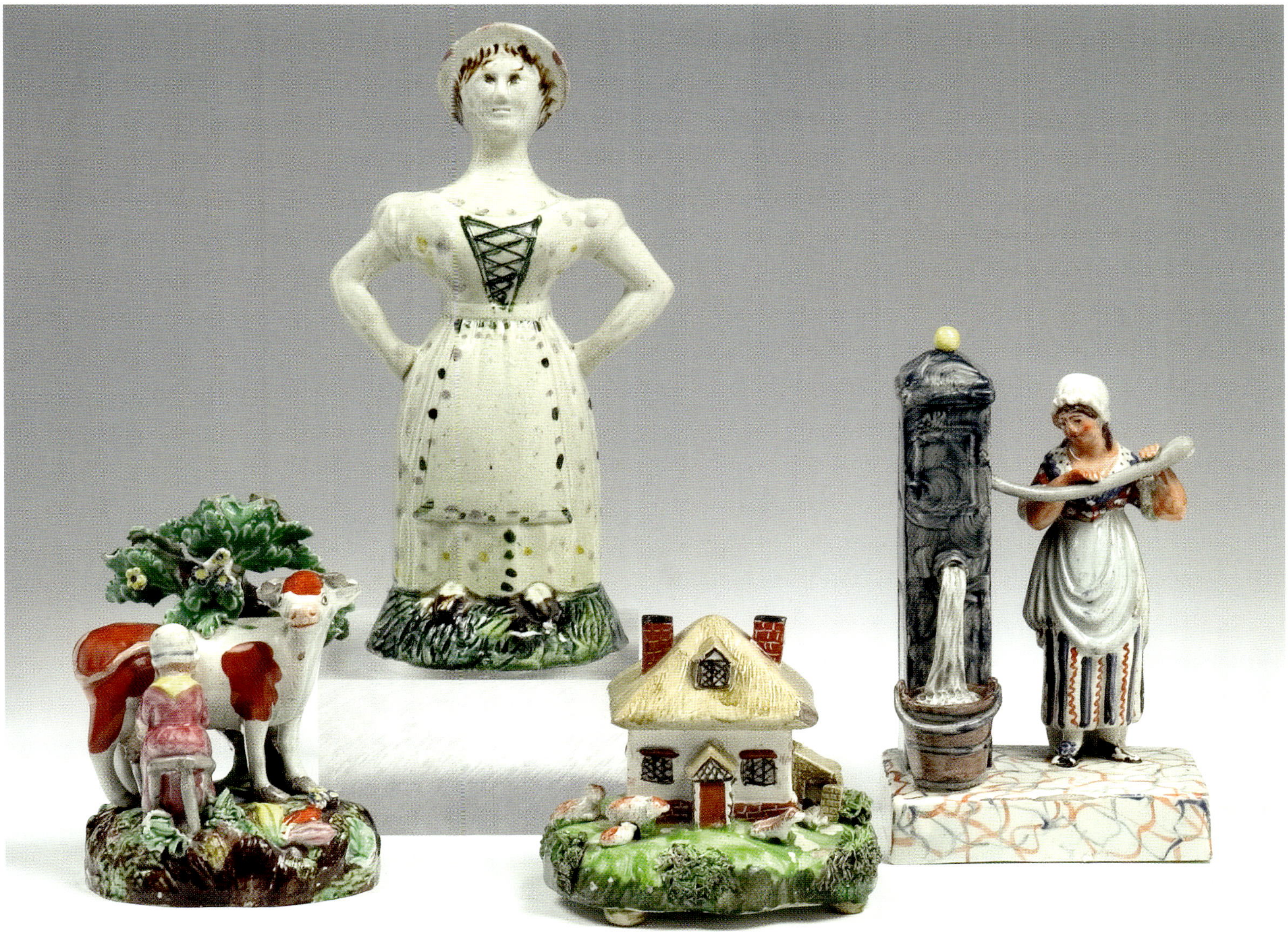

Figure Group, (**1341**), c.1820, Staffordshire, height: 12.1cm, (4¾in), enamelled pearlware. A dairymaid sits on a three-legged stool milking a happy cow.
Figure, (**1347**), c.1800, Staffordshire, height: 20.3cm, (8in), Pratt-coloured pearlware. Naively modelled dairymaid stands with arms akimbo.
Pastille Burner, (**1270**), c.1820, Staffordshire, height: 14cm, (5½in), enamelled pearlware. The grassy knoll outside this thatched cottage is occupied by several sheep and a sheepdog.
Figure Group, (**1346**), c.1820, Staffordshire, height: 16.5cm, (6½in), enamelled pearlware. Young woman pumps water into pail from 'the cow with the iron tail'.[20]

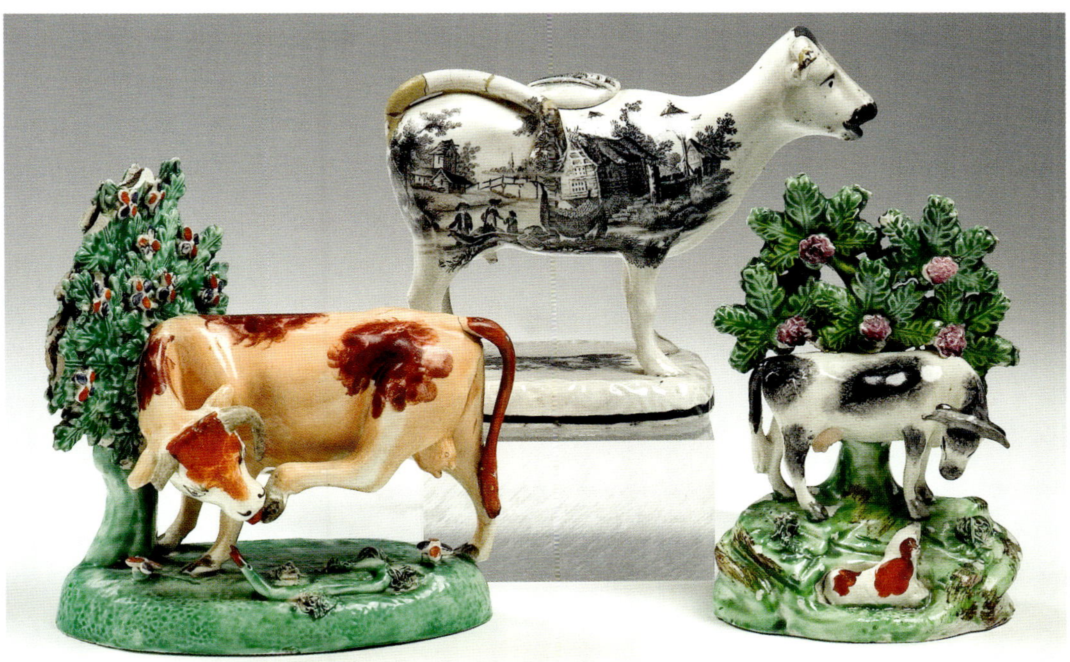

Figure Group, (**1343**), c.1820, Staffordshire, height: 16.5cm, (6½in), enamelled pearlware. A cow has been bitten by a viper, perhaps alluding to a mythological tale.[21]
Cream Jug, (**1342**), c.1830, Swansea, height: 14cm, (5½in), printed earthenware. Novelty cream jug modelled as a cow, made by Baker, Bevans & Irwin, Glamorgan Pottery, printed with river scenes.[22]
Figure Group, (**1345**), c.1820, Staffordshire, height: 15.3cm, (6in), enamelled pearlware. A cow and calf beneath a tree.

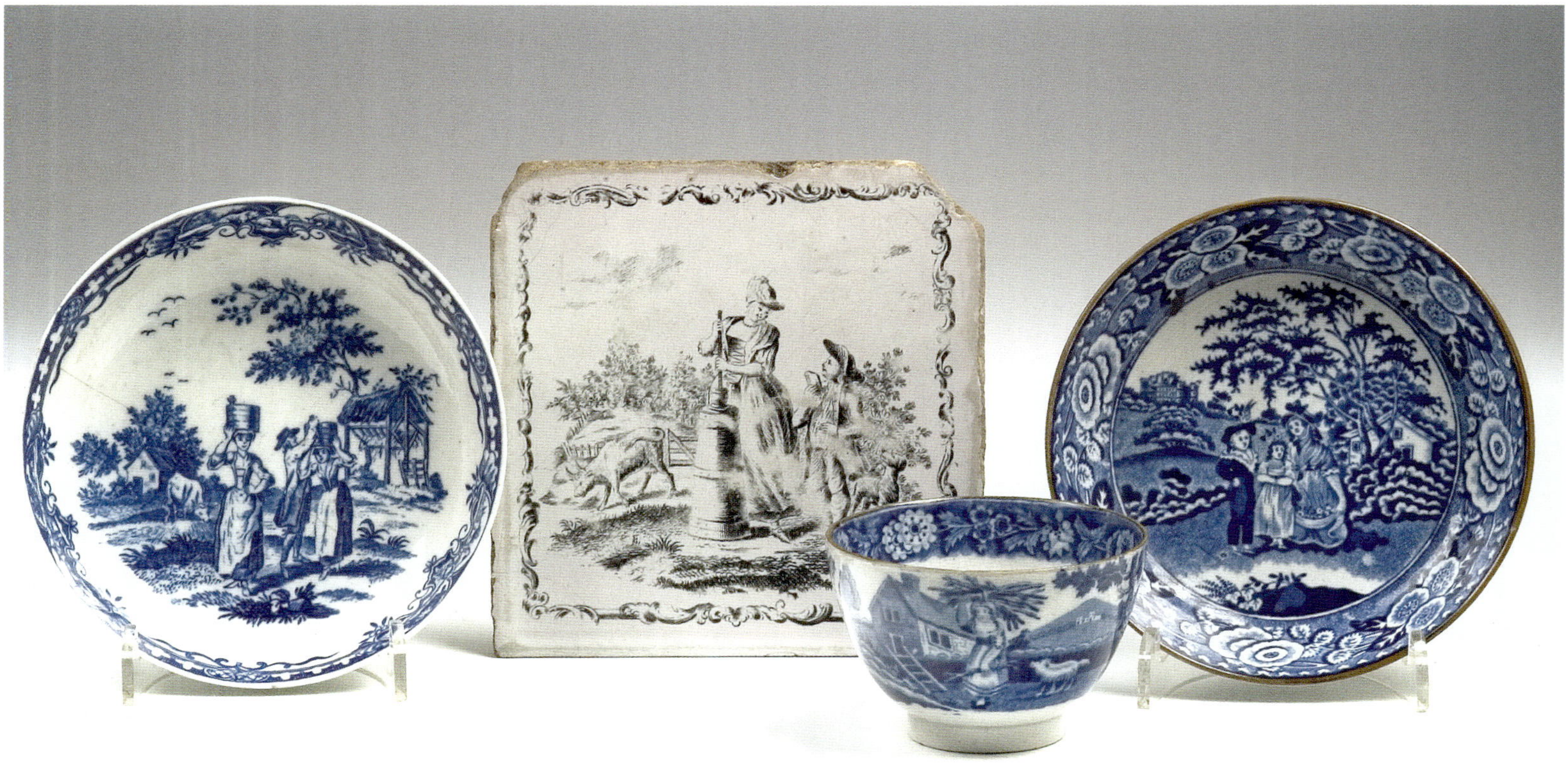

Saucer, (**1344**), c.1780, Worcester, height: 12.1cm, (4¾in), blue-printed soft-paste porcelain. Dairymaids with pails placed on their heads.
Tile, (**1340**), c.1760, Liverpool, height: 12.7cm, (5in), printed tin-glazed earthenware. A dairymaid churns butter, print by Sadler, taken from a drawing book published by John Bowles.[23]

Cup and Saucer, (**1356 & A**), c.1820, Yorkshire, height: 5.1cm, (2in), diameter: 12.7cm, (5in), blue-printed pearlware. Cup shows small girl carrying a bundle of firewood while (unmatched) saucer shows three children gathering flowers. Possibly made at the Don Pottery.[24]

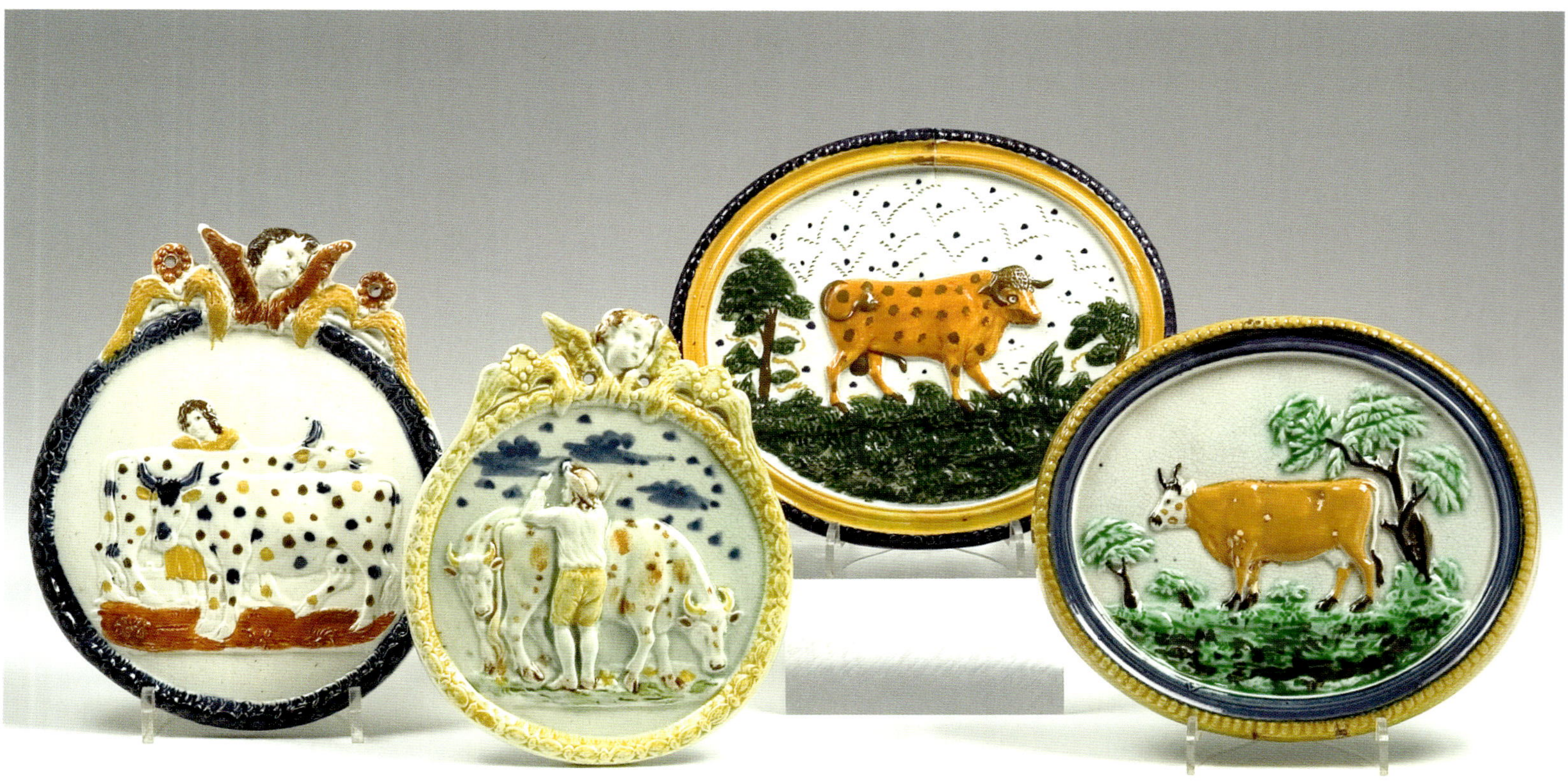

Two Plaques, (**1336 + 1337**), c.1800, Staffordshire, height: 17.7cm, (7in), height: 15.3cm, (6in), Pratt-coloured pearlware. Relief-moulded circular medallions with cherub heads, one with milkmaid and cows, one with a herdsman.

Pair of Plaques, (**1339 & A**), c.1800, Staffordshire, each height: 15.9cm, (6¼in), Pratt-coloured pearlware. Relief-moulded oval plaques, one with a bull, one with a cow and trees.

The Durham Ox

A very large meat dish features the Durham Ox, one of the most famous examples of intensive cattle breeding. A Shorthorn bull, bred from Dutch stock in Teeswater, by Charles and Robert Colling, it was sired by the famous bull, Favourite, in 1796. At the age of five, weighing 1456 kg, the Durham Ox was sold for £140 to Mr Bulmer, who toured it in an open cart for five weeks. He then sold it for £250 to Mr John Day who continued to exhibit it for six years, refusing offers of up to £2000. In 1807 it fell, broke a hip and had to be destroyed. George Garrard, the animal sculptor, claimed that it was 'no less distinguished for its uncommon beauty than for its weight, being an example of perfection in every way.'

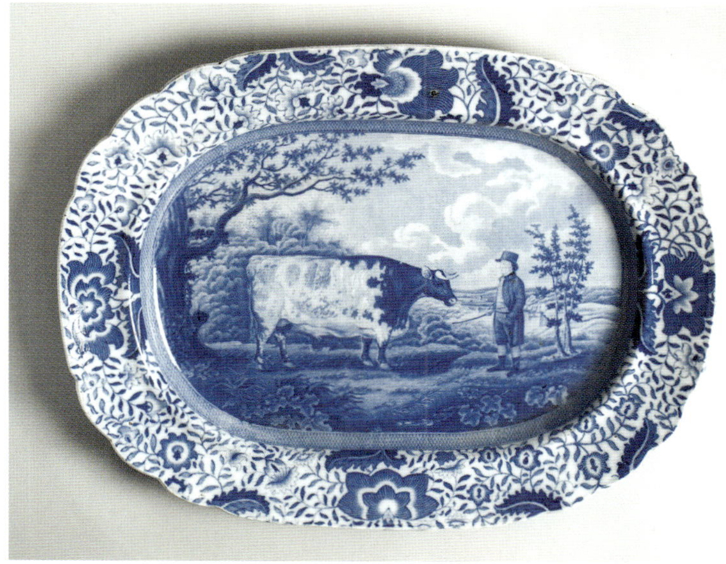

Meat Dish, (**R.2454/2**), c.1810, Staffordshire, height: 15.9cm, (6¼in), blue-printed earthenware. Portrait of the Durham Ox in its prime, with a man, probably John Day, its then owner. Day also published the popular print by J. Whessel after Boultbee's portrait of the Durham Ox, painted in 1802.

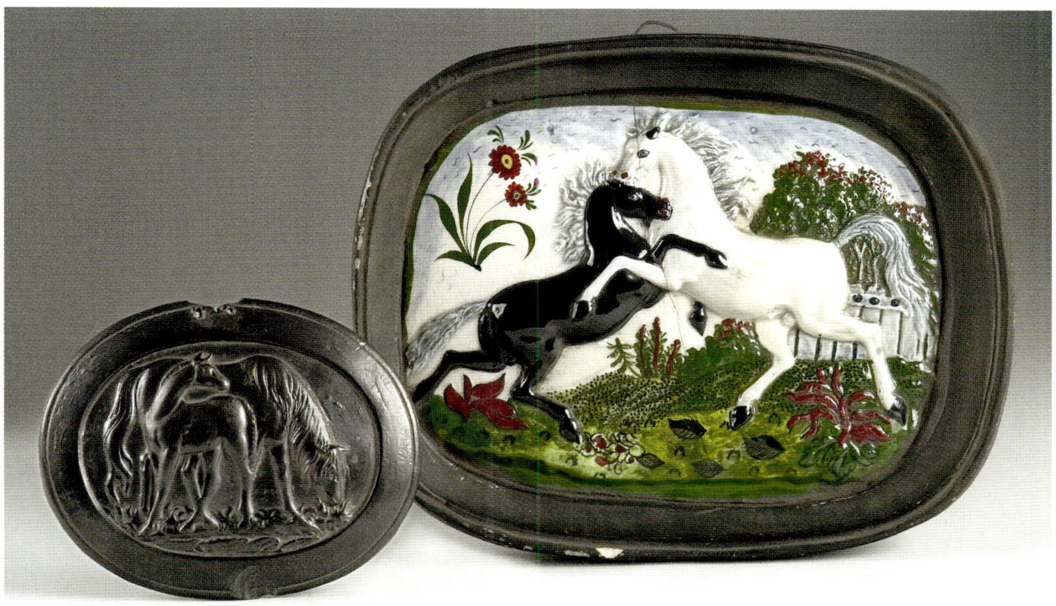

Plaque, (**1272**), c.1800, Staffordshire, height: 12.7cm, (5in), enamelled earthenware. Oval plaque relief-moulded with a mare and foal.
Plaque, (**1273**), c.1790, Staffordshire, height: 24.1cm, (9½in), Pratt-coloured earthenware. Relief-moulded design of a fight between white and black stallions, based on a print after a painting by George Stubbs, engraved in 1788.[25]

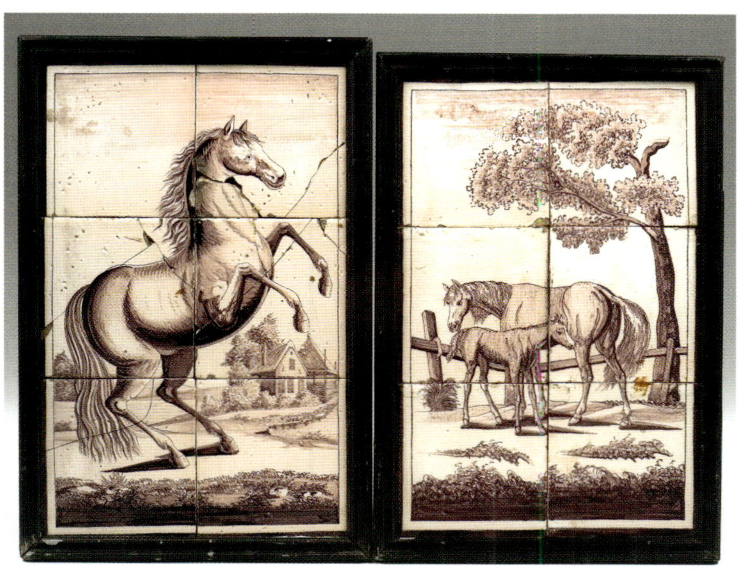

Six-Tile Panel, (**1277**), c.1850, Holland, Rotterdam, height: 34.3cm, (13½in), manganese painted delftware. A rearing stallion and houses.
Six-Tile Panel, (**1274**), c.1850, Holland, Rotterdam, height: 34.3cm, (13½in), manganese painted delftware. A mare and foal in a paddock.

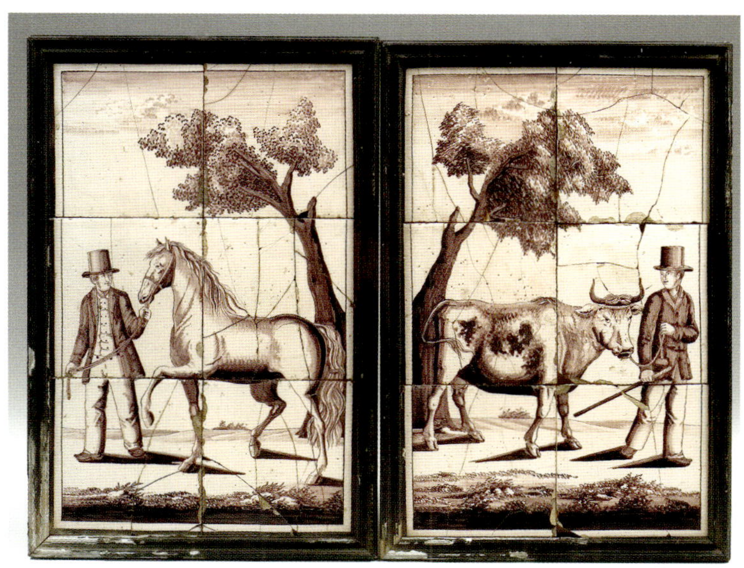

Six-Tile Panel, (**1275**), c.1850, Holland, Rotterdam, height: 34.3cm, (13½in), manganese painted delftware. A man in a top hat leading a horse to the left.
Six-Tile Panel, (**1276**), c.1850, Holland, Rotterdam, height: 34.3cm, (13½in), manganese painted delftware. A farmer leads a cow or bull to the right.

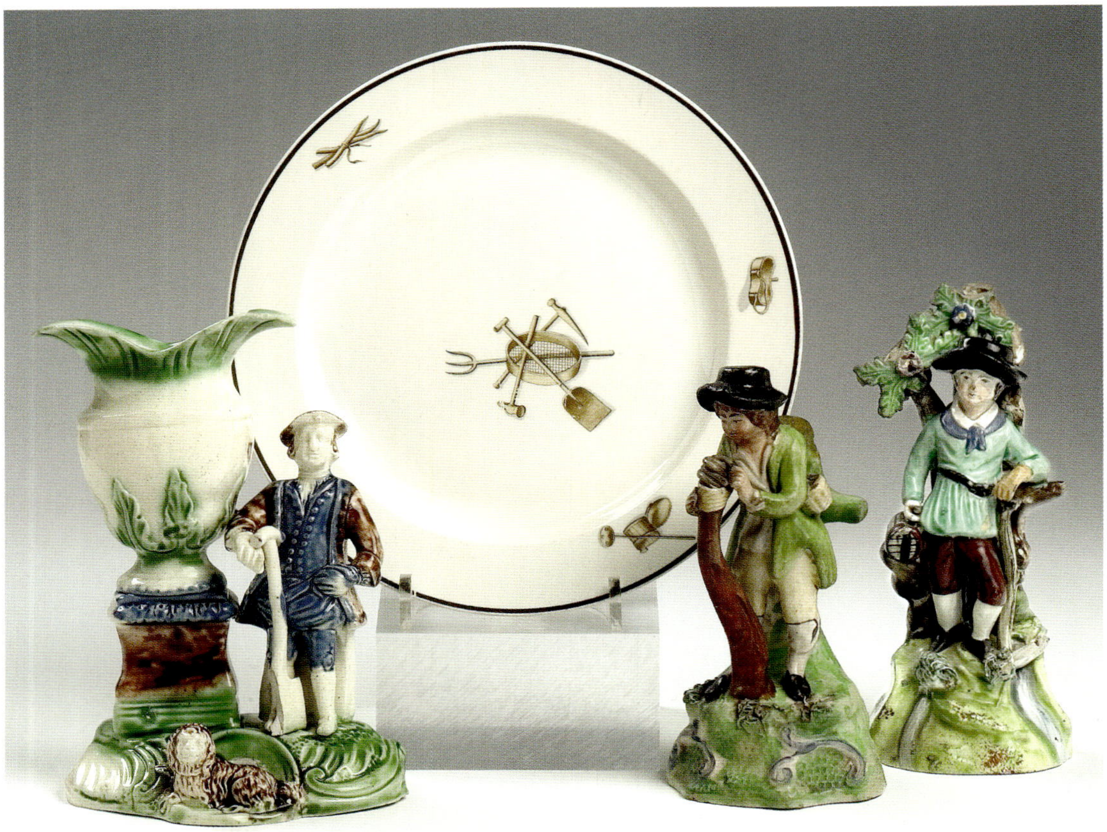

Figure Group, (**1353**), c.1800, Staffordshire, height: 16.5cm, (6½in), lead-glazed earthenware. A gardener, who appears to be working on a grand estate, stands beside a large urn on a plinth with his spade and his dog.
Plate, (**1256**), c.1805, Staffordshire, Wedgwood, diameter: 21cm, (8¼in), creamware, printed and enamelled. A plate delicately printed with a selection of farming and gardening tools including a pickaxe, a mallet, a spade, a pitchfork and a sieve.[26]
Figure, (**1355**), c.1820, Staffordshire, height: 15.3cm, (6in), enamelled pearlware. A man prepares the stump of a fruit tree for grafting.
Figure, (**1361★**), c.1820, Staffordshire, height: 17.2cm, (6¾in), enamelled pearlware. A man pauses for rest beside a gushing stream, a gnarled-handled scythe in one hand and a cask in the other.

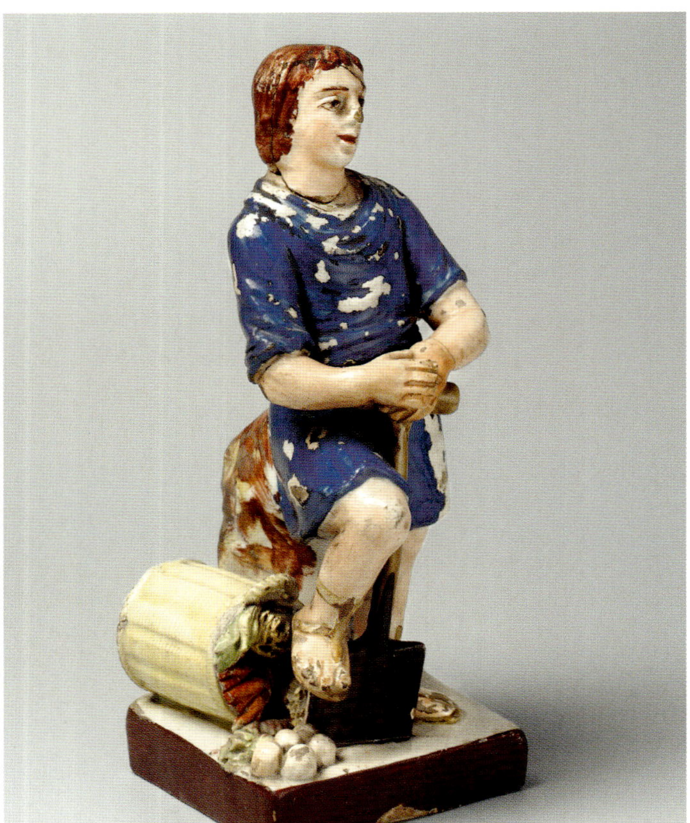

Figure, (**1357**), c.1820, Staffordshire, height: 21cm, (8¼in), enamelled porcelain. Man with a spade is digging vegetables, the fruits of his labours.

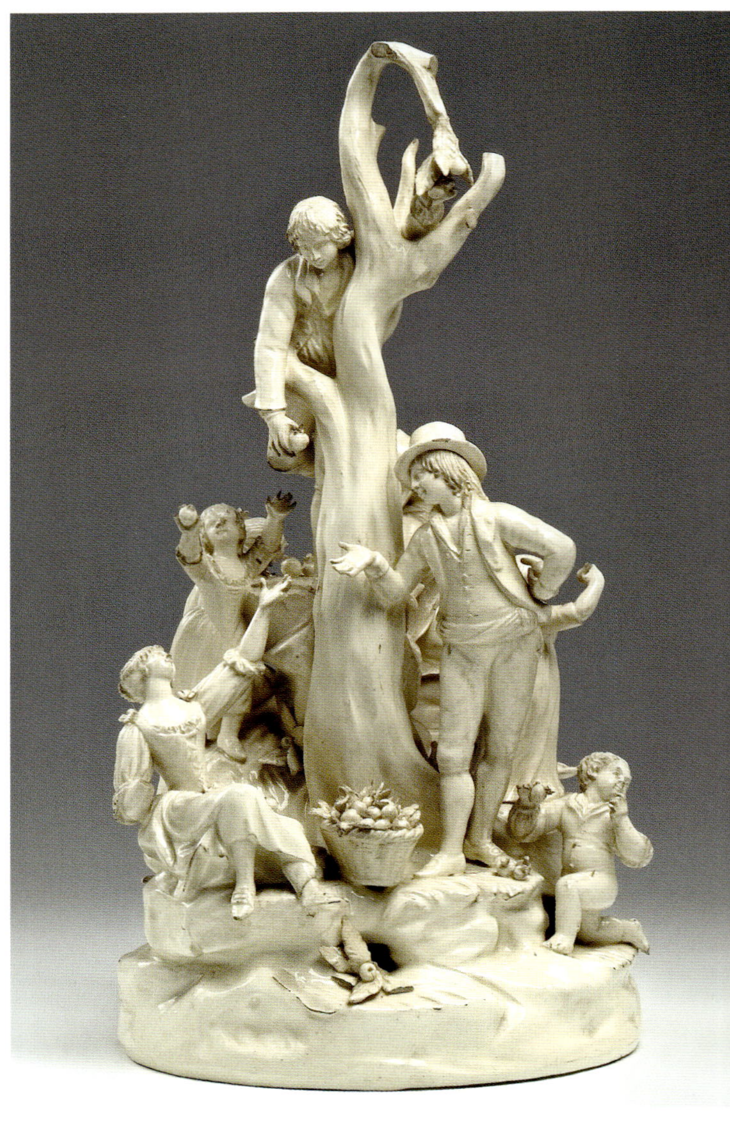

Figure Group, (**1351**), c.1770, Italy, possibly Le Nove factory,[27] height: 35.5cm, (14in), earthenware. Adults and children seem to perform a stately dance as they pick apples from a pollarded tree.

Pair of Figures Groups, (**1348 & A**), c.1800, Staffordshire, each height: 19.7cm, (7¾in), underglaze painted pearlware. Male and female gardeners each support a mantelpiece vase, from which fountains flow. He holds a spade, she has an apron of flowers.
Stirrup Cup, (**1352**), c.1800, Staffordshire, height: 8.9cm, (3½in), salt-glazed stoneware. Cup modelled as half a potato. As well as maize (or Indian corn), potatoes were the most important new crop to arrive from the Americas. The tuber did not become established in northern Europe until the mid-eighteenth century. Adam Smith, writing in *The Wealth of Nations* (1776), noted its high yield and calorific value; 'The food produced by a field of potatoes is not inferior to … a field of rice and far superior to that produced by a field of wheat.'[28]
Figure, (**1349**), c.1820, Staffordshire, height: 15.3cm, (6in), enamelled pearlware. A young man, delicately modelled, labelled 'Gardener', leans on his spade.

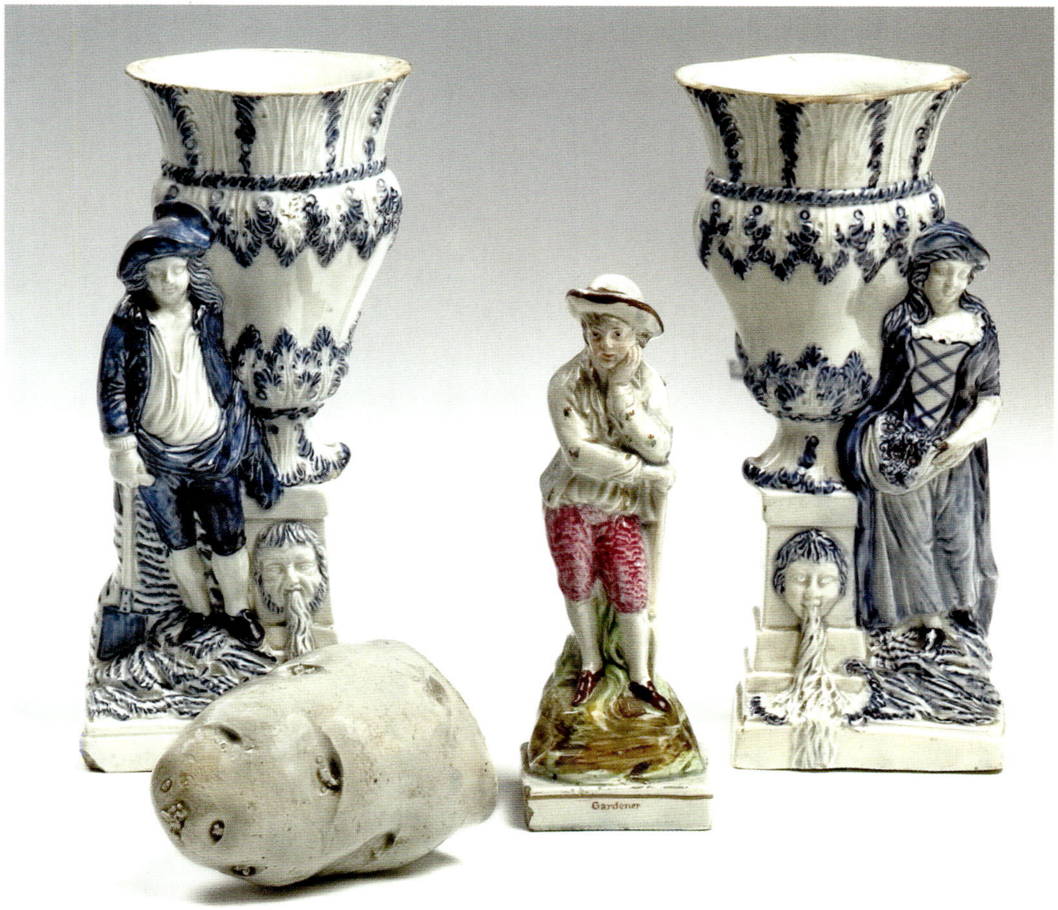

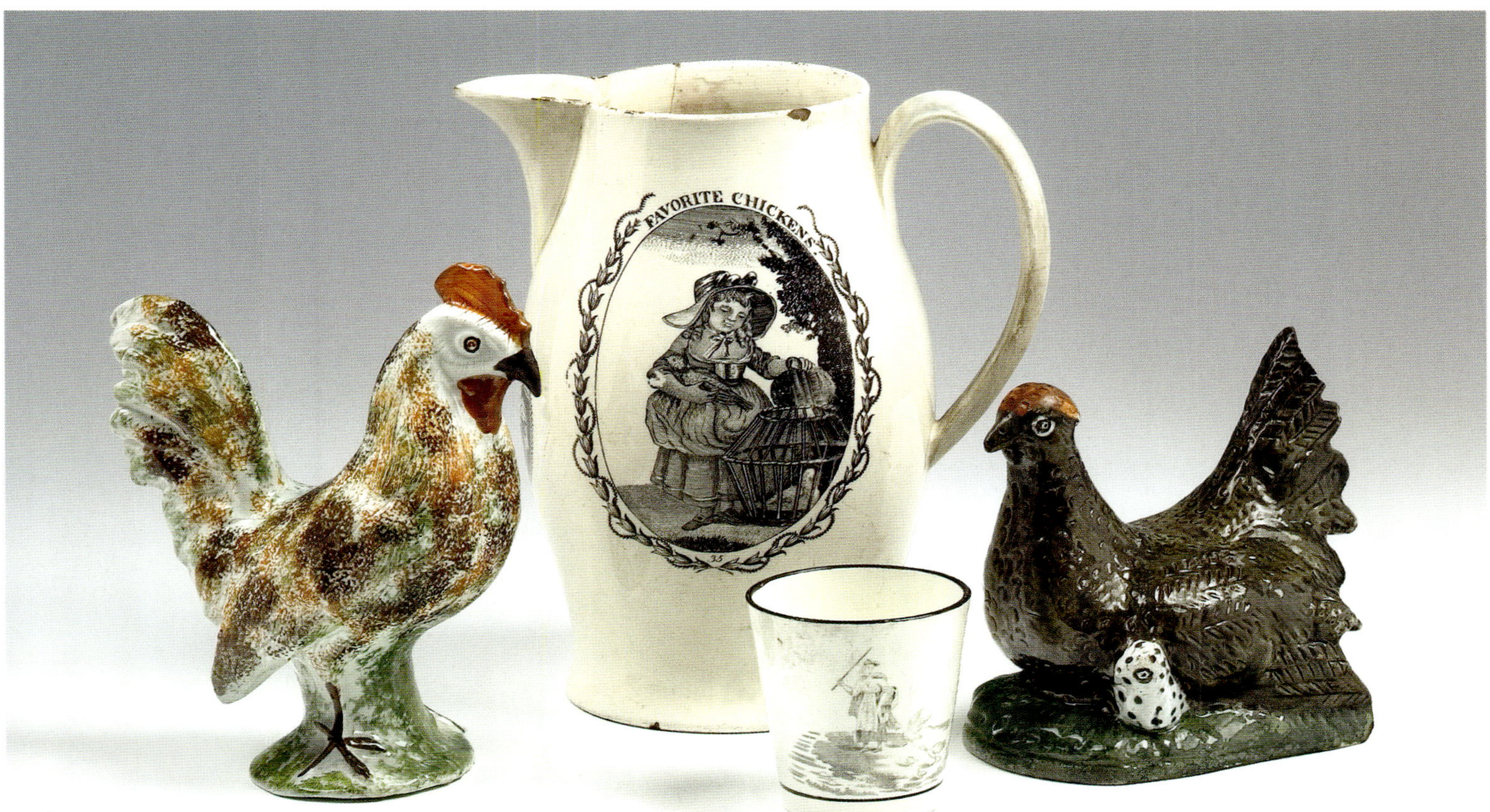

Two Figures, (**1280 & A**), c.1800, Staffordshire or Scotland, height: 12.7cm, (5in), height: 16.5cm, (6½in), Prattware. Two (unrelated) models of chickens; the plumage of the brood hen with spotted chicks incised and punched to indicate feathers.
Jug, (**1052**), c.1795, Staffordshire, height: 20.3cm, (8in), printed creamware. Oval print entitled 'Favourite Chickens', shows a girl taking hens from a coop. It may be related to detail in a print with the same title by Brydon after William Bigg, 1793.[29]
Beaker, (**1259**), c.1780, Staffordshire, Wedgwood, height: 7cm, (2¾in), printed creamware. Tiny beaker faintly printed with a woman feeding geese.

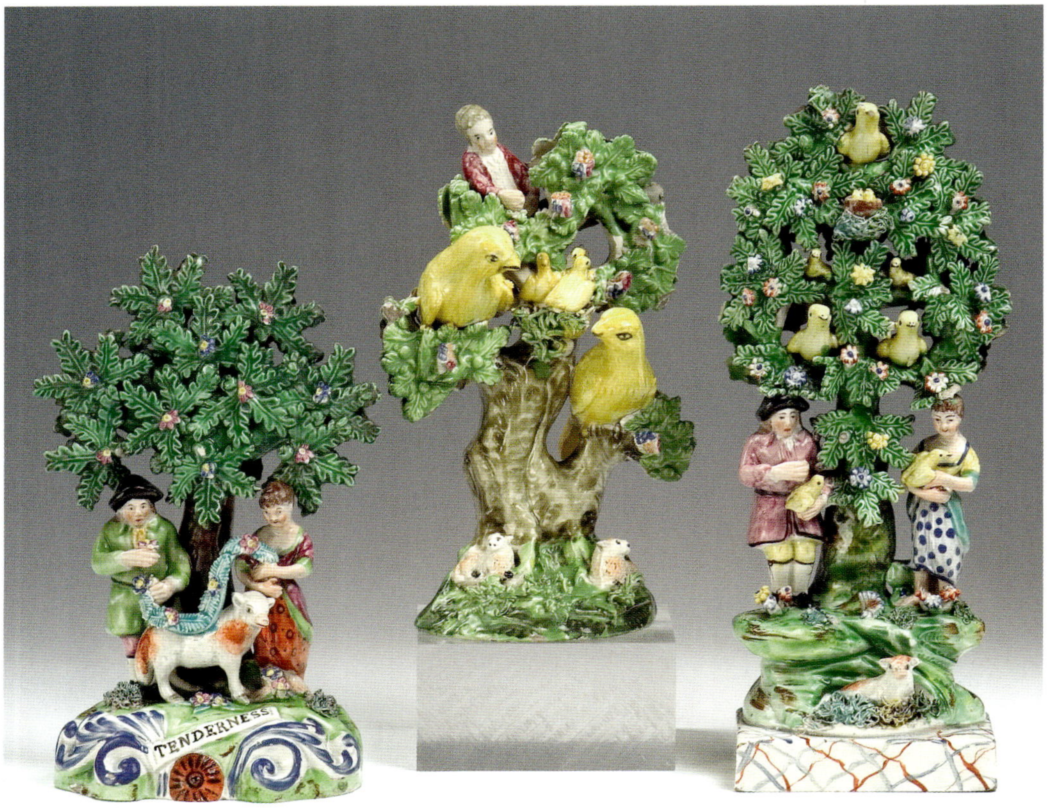

Figure Group, (**1617**), c.1820, Staffordshire, Burslem, height: 21cm, (8¼in), enamelled pearlware. Group inscribed, 'TENDERNESS' and marked 'Walton'. A boy and girl wind a garland around a lamb's neck.[30]
Figure Group, (**1609**), c.1820, Staffordshire, height: 21cm, (8¼in), enamelled pearlware. A diminutive boy at the top of a tree about to rob the nest of a pair of giant canaries!
Figure Group, (**1326**), c.1820, Staffordshire, height: 26.7cm, (10½in), enamelled pearlware. A man and woman hold yellow birds at the base of a large, ornate tree in which larger canaries roost.

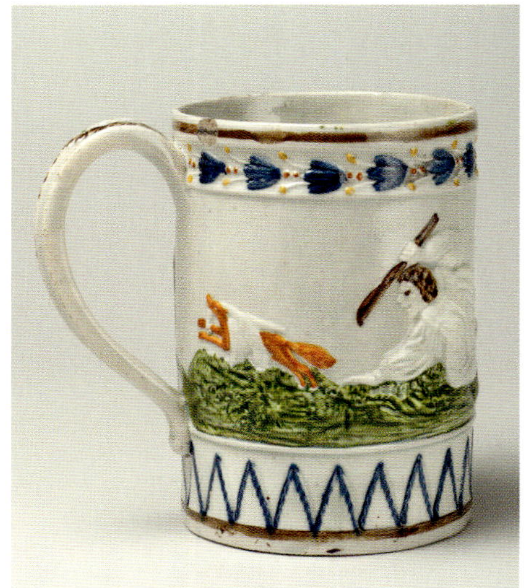

Mug, (**1331**), c.1800, Staffordshire, height: 11.5cm, (4½in), Prattware. Relief-moulded with figures illustrating nursery rhyme of the Grey Goose. The farmer pursues a fox as it carries off a goose while the farmer's wife, Old Mother Slipper Slopper, releases her dog. A large brown frog inside.

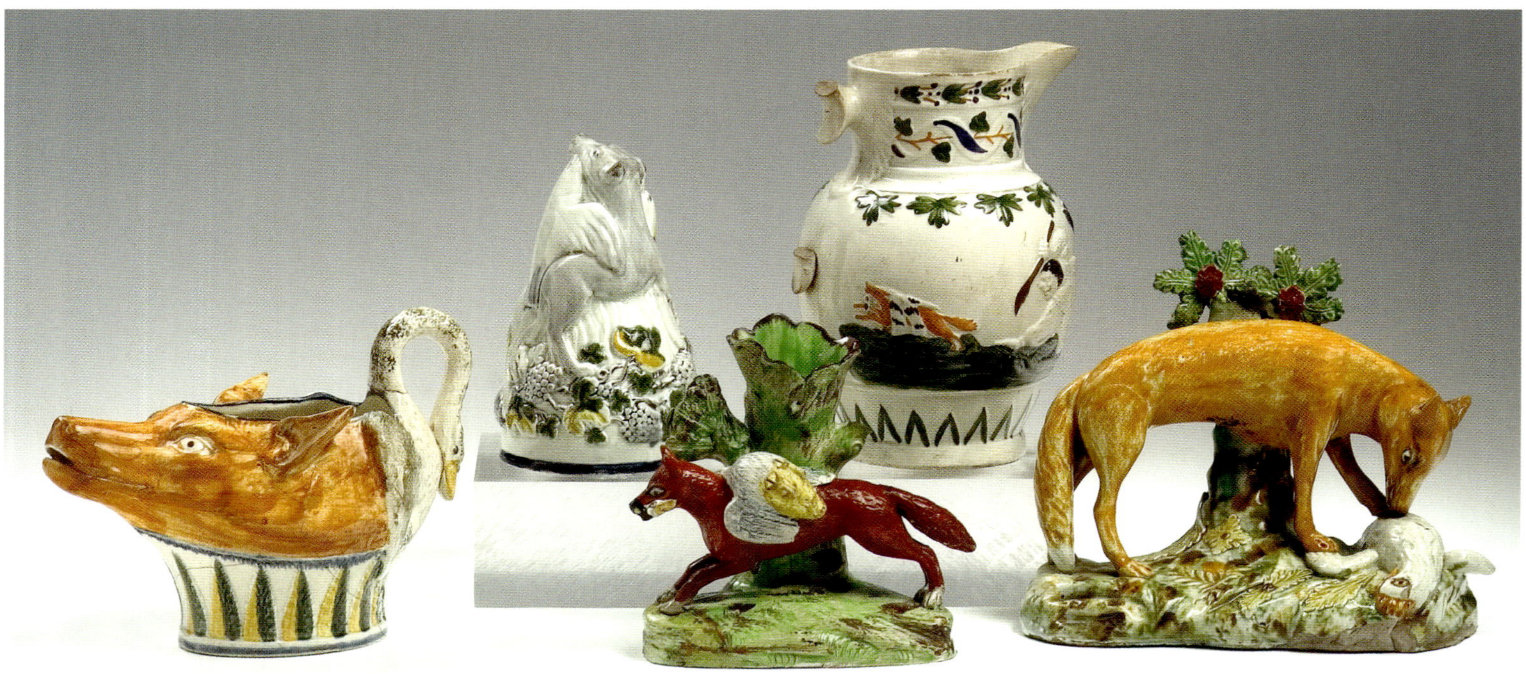

Sauce Boat, (**1335**), c.1800, Staffordshire, height: 12.7cm, (5in), Prattware. Novelty sauce boat uses the goose's neck as a handle and the fox's mouth as the spout.
Jug, (**1332**), c.1795, Staffordshire, height: 13.3cm, (5¼in), enamelled pearlware. Stirrup cup moulded with a dog catching a fox, still with a goose in its mouth.
Jug, (**1330**), c.1800, Staffordshire, height: 15.3cm, (6in), Prattware. Relief-moulded with figures illustrating nursery rhyme of the Grey Goose. The farmer pursues a fox as it carries off a goose while the farmer's wife, Old Mother Slipper Slopper, releases her dog.
Spill Vase, (**1333**), c.1810, Staffordshire, height: 12.7cm, (5in), enamelled pearlware. Fox on the run, with spill vase behind.
Figure Group, (**1334**), c.1810, Staffordshire, height: 15.3cm, (6in), enamelled pearlware. Fox prepares to devour a chicken.

Selling Garden Produce

Bee-keeping was an important cottage industry. In the late eighteenth century sugar was still an expensive commodity and honey remained the main sweetener of food. Bees and beehives have always symbolised hard work. They appear elsewhere on mugs intended as rewards for children and as Masonic symbols of productivity.

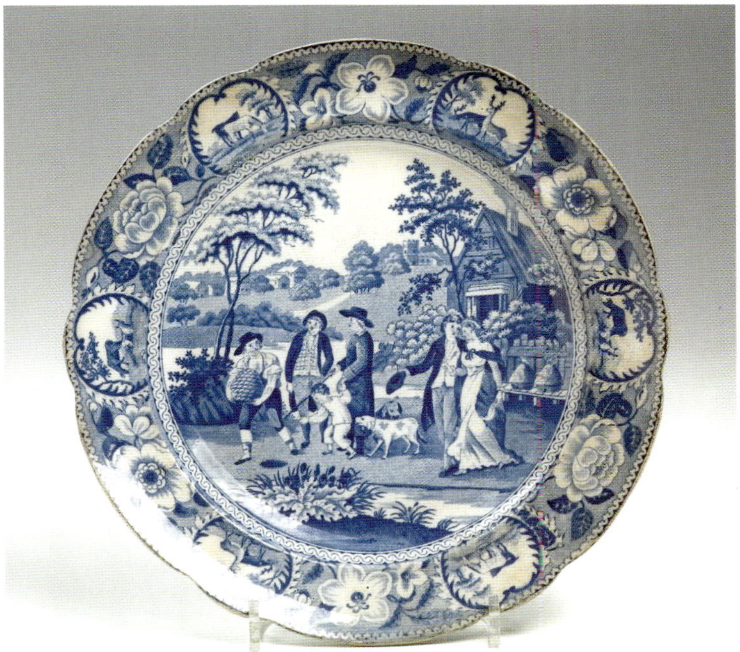

Plate, (**1278**), c.1820, Staffordshire, diameter: 24.8cm, (9¾in), blue-printed pearlware. Printed design known as 'The Beemaster', taken from a watercolour painting *Swarm of Bees, Autumn*, by George Robertson, now in the Cecil Higgins Museum.[31] The piece has been attributed to William Adams. A group of figures in front of a farmhouse, with a row of beehives or skeps before it. They accompany a labourer with a large bee skep, which must contain or be intended to capture a swarm of bees.

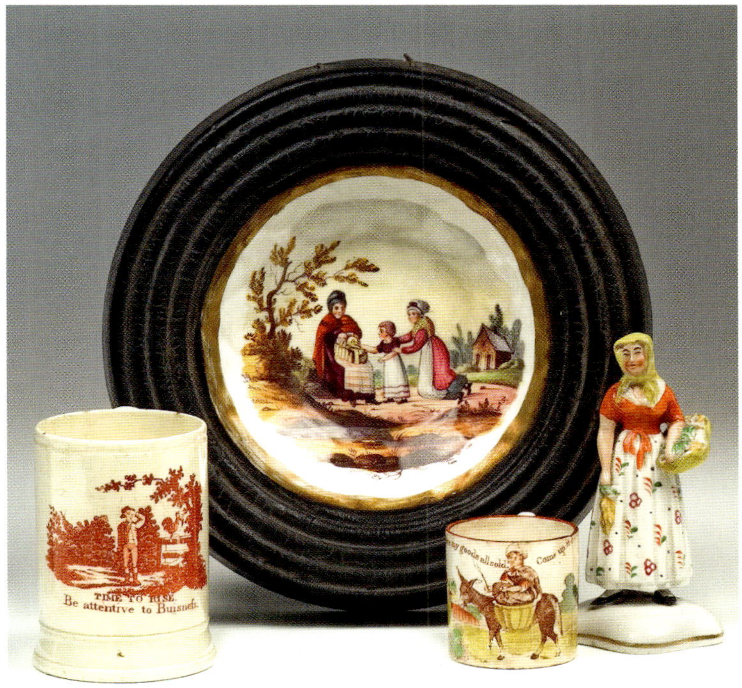

Mug, (**1297**), c.1820, Staffordshire, height: 8.9cm, (3½in), red-printed creamware. A boy rubs his eyes beside a stile where a cockerel crows. Beneath is another of Franklin's 'Poor Richard' sayings, 'TIME TO RISE Be attentive to Buisnefs [*sic*]'.
Saucer, (**1290**), c.1800, Staffordshire, height: 14cm, (5½in), enamelled bone china. A framed bone-china saucer shows an old pedlar woman sitting by the roadside selling knick-knacks from a basket.
Mug, (**1298**), c.1820, Staffordshire, height: 5.1cm, (2in), bone china, brown-printed and coloured. Printed with a young woman riding a donkey, her feet resting in the empty side pannier, 'Market's done my goods all sold', adding rather suggestively, 'Come up here for I am cold'.
Figure, (**1295**), c.1840, Staffordshire, height: 11.5cm, (4½in), enamelled earthenware. A woman wearing a headscarf selling vegetables including carrots and brassicas from a basket.

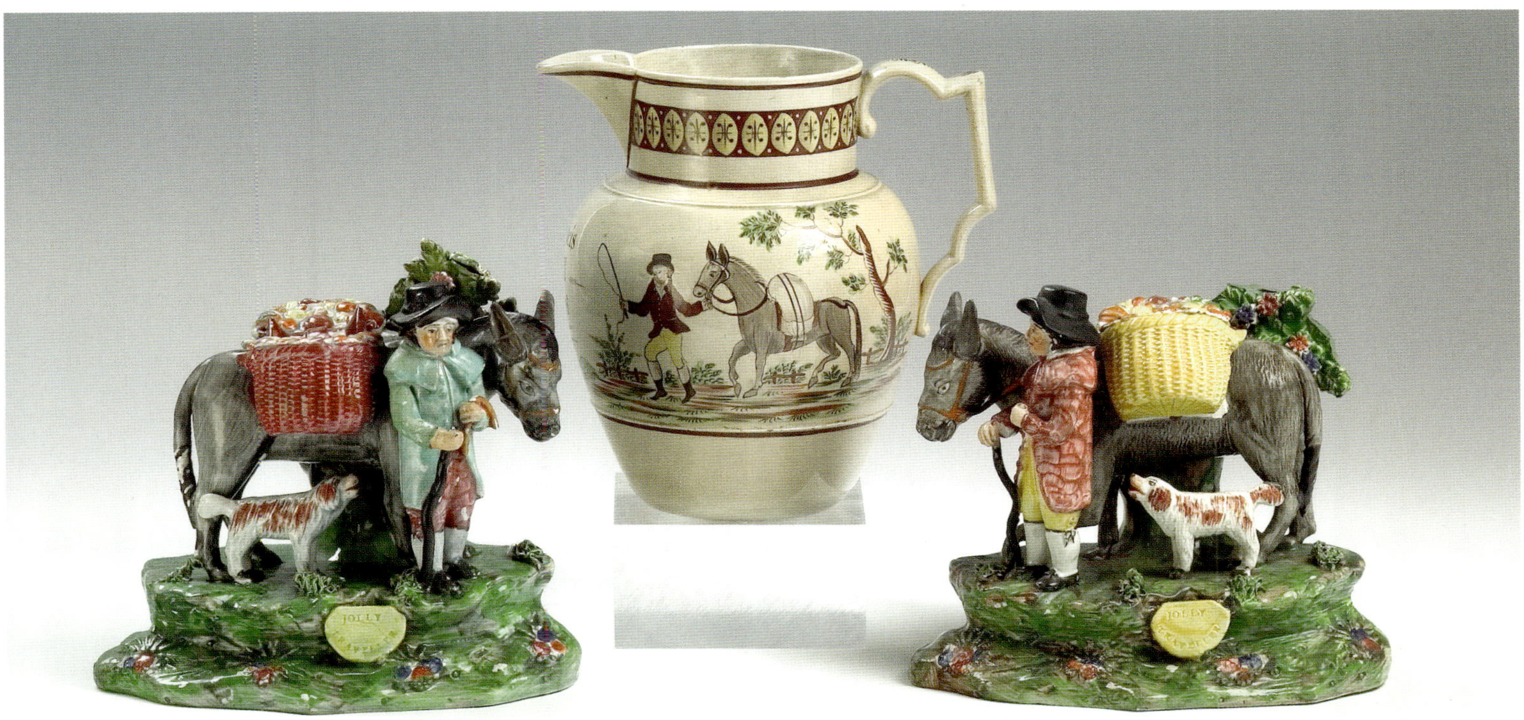

Pair of Figure Groups, (1306 & A), c.1820, Staffordshire, height: 15.3cm, (6in), height: 17.2cm, (6¾in), enamelled pearlware. Two groups of farmer with pack horse and dog inscribed 'JOLLY TRAVELLER'. Each horse or mule carries side panniers full of produce.
Jug, (**1282**), 1806, Staffordshire, height: 17.8cm, (7in), enamelled drabware. Jug inscribed, 'Francis Hall 1806', shows farmer leading his pack mule to market.

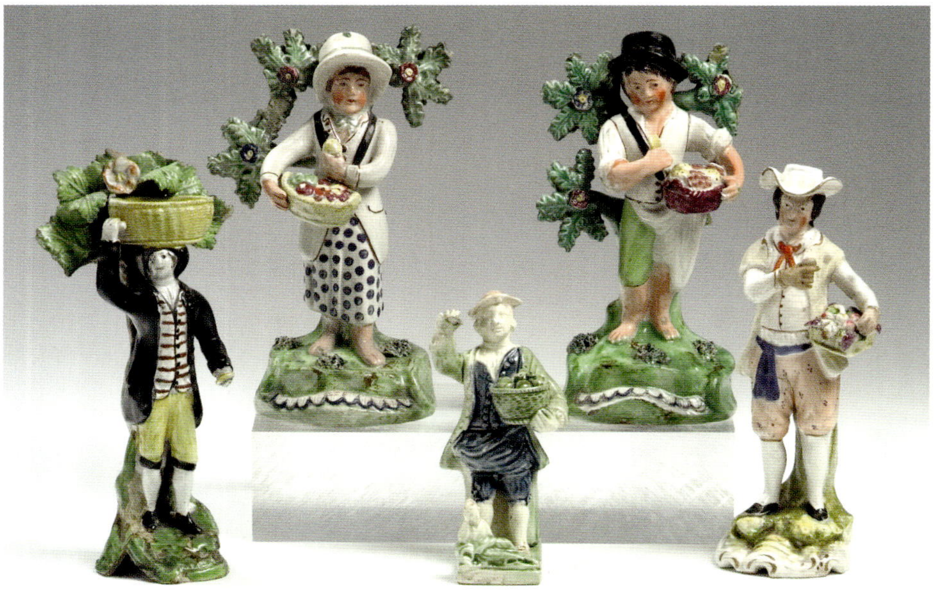

Clockwise:
Figure, (**1292**), c.1820, Staffordshire, height: 17.8cm, (7in), enamelled pearlware. A young man (marked for Tittensor) carries large basket of fruit on his head.
Pair of Figures, (**1286 & A**), c.1820, Staffordshire, Burslem, each height: 17.8cm, (7in), enamelled pearlware. Girl and boy with baskets slung from straps over their shoulders, selling their wares (she has fruit, he has cakes and buns). Each marked on reverse for John Walton.
Figure, (**1307**), c.1840, Staffordshire, height: 17.8cm, (7in), enamelled earthenware. Male figure wearing a white Stetson holds a basket of fruit.
Figure, (**1302**), c.1790, Staffordshire, height: 11.5cm, (4½in), lead-glazed earthenware. Small man offers fruit from finely woven basket while a tiny water nymph reclines at his feet.[32]

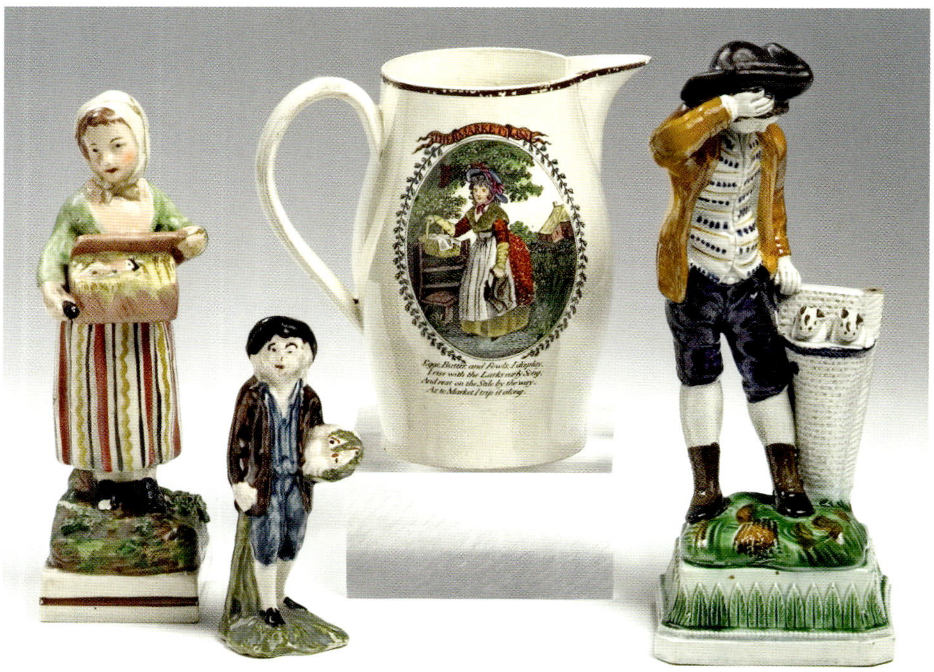

Figure, (**1294**), c.1810, Staffordshire, height: 19.7cm, (7¾in), enamelled pearlware. A girl opens the lid of a hay-filled hamper where a piglet nestles.[33]
Figure, (**1303**), c.1800, Staffordshire, height: 12.1cm, (4¾in), Prattware. Tiny boy holds a basket of fish.
Jug, (**1328**), c.1800, Staffordshire, height: 15.3cm, (6in), creamware, printed and coloured. 'THE MARKET LASS', stands beside a stile, a covered basket in one hand and a brace of game birds in the other, and verse, 'Eggs Butter, and Fowls, I display / I rise with the Larks early Song / And rest on the Stile by the way / As to Market I trip it along'. It appears loosely related to a print with the same title, issued by Laurie & Whittle in 1794.[34]
Figure, (**1288**), c.1790, Staffordshire, height: 22.3cm, (8¾in), Prattware. Boy stands beside a finely modelled, woven backpack from which rabbits peep.

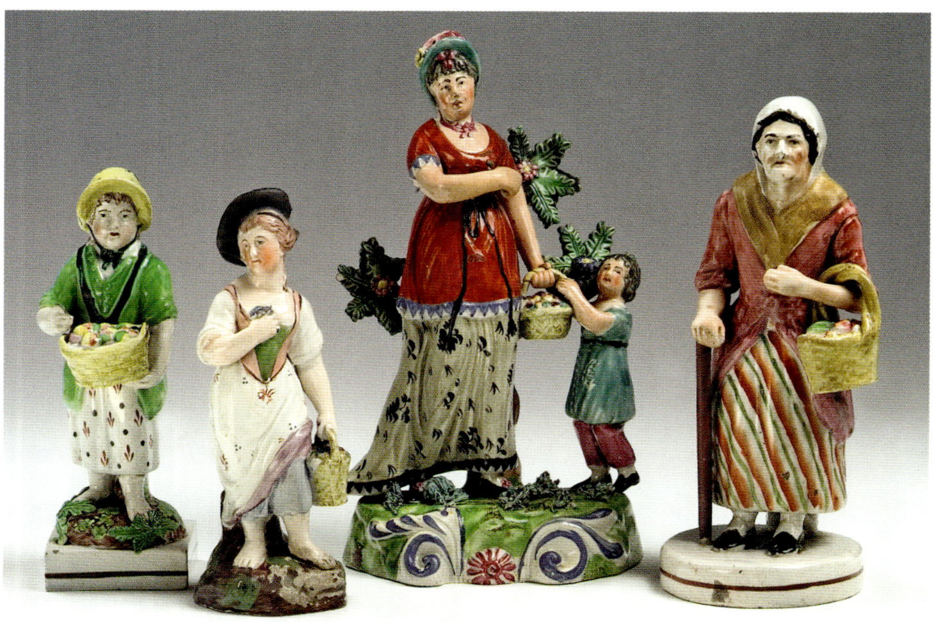

Figure, (**1308**), c.1810, Staffordshire, height: 17.8cm, (7in), enamelled pearlware. A small girl sells fruit from a basket slung from straps over her shoulders.
Figure, (**1291**), c.1800, Staffordshire, height: 17.8cm, (7in), enamelled pearlware. A girl in a black hat carries a basket of flowers.
Figure Group, (**1305**), c.1820, Staffordshire, height: 22.9cm, (9in), enamelled pearlware. Group marked by John Walton; fashionably dressed woman with a child, she carries a small basket and may be shopping rather than selling.
Figure, (**1301**), c.1840, Staffordshire, height: 21cm, (8¼in), enamelled earthenware. An old woman staggers to or from market, leaning on a stick with a basket over her arm.

Figure, (**1283**), c.1810, Staffordshire, height: 16.5cm, (6½in), enamelled pearlware. Girl with basket of flowers.
Figure, (**1284**), c.1830, Staffordshire, height: 14cm, (5½in), enamelled pearlware. Girl with basket of flowers.
Figure Group, (**1287**), c.1830, Staffordshire, height: 20.3cm, (8in), enamelled pearlware. Shepherdess with basket of flowers and a sheep.
Figure, (**1289**), c.1820, Staffordshire, height: 13.3cm, (5¼in), enamelled pearlware. Old woman with a stick and basket on her arm.
Figure, (**1296**), c.1820, Staffordshire, height: 15.3cm, (6in), enamelled pearlware. Girl holding a plant in an urn.

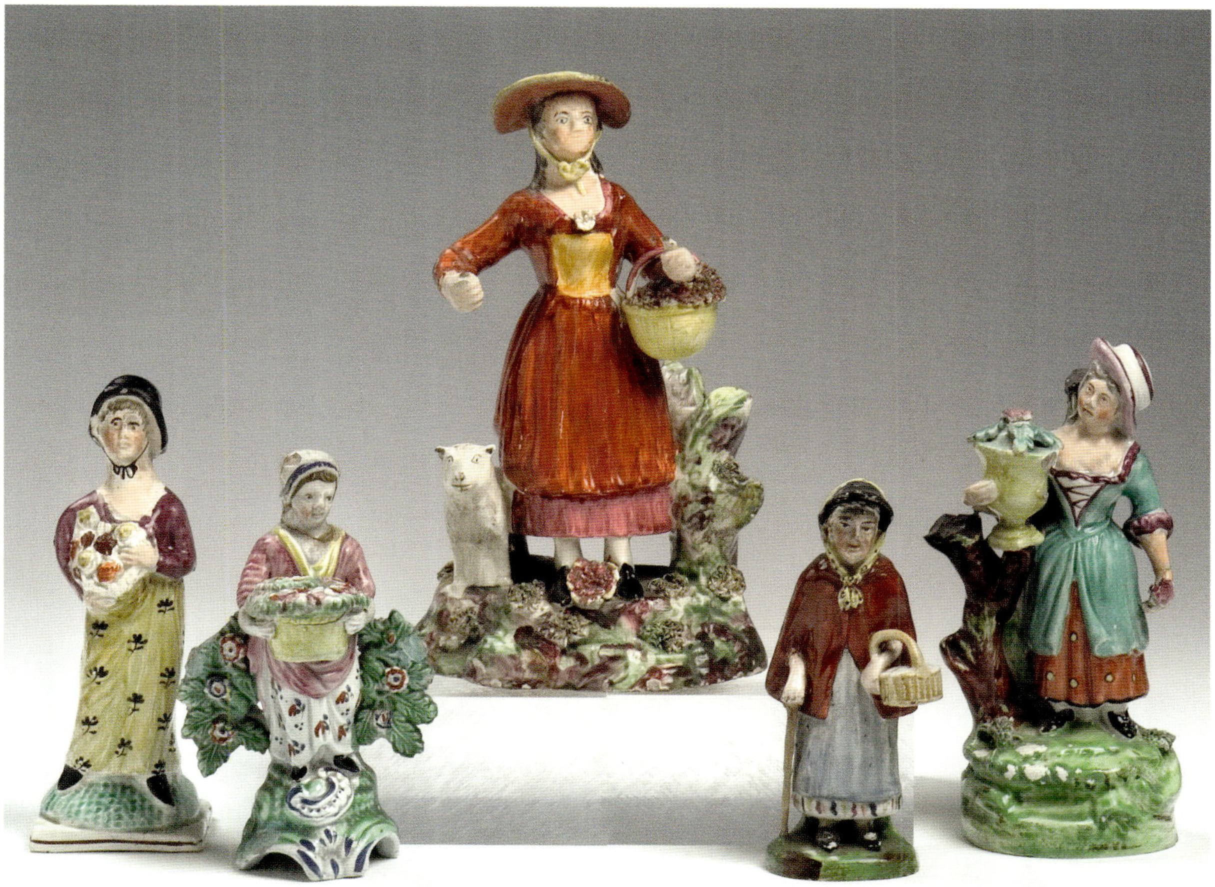

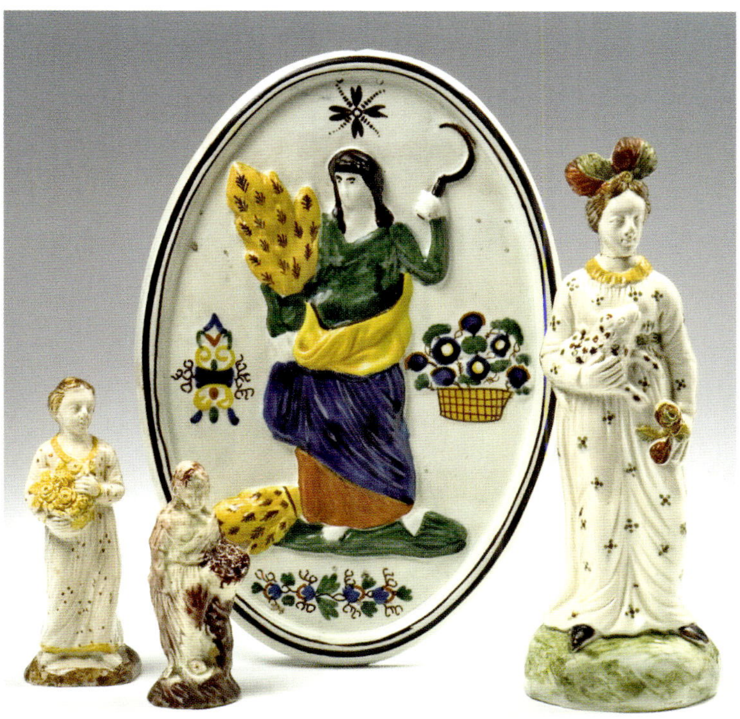

Figure, (**1300**), c.1800, Staffordshire, height: 14.6cm, (5¾in), Pratt-coloured creamware.
Figure, (**1293**), c.1800, Staffordshire, height: 11.5cm, (4½in), lead-glazed earthenware. Tiny figures in classical robes carrying bouquets; nymph or representations of the goddess Flora.
Plaque, (**1364**), c.1800, North East, height: 30.5cm, (12in), Prattware. Relief-moulded with Autumn or Ceres, goddess of harvest with scythe and wheat-sheaves.
Figure, (**1325**), c.1820, Staffordshire, height: 27.3cm, (10¾in), Pratt-coloured creamware. Woman with plumes in her hair carries a rose and a spotted sheep.

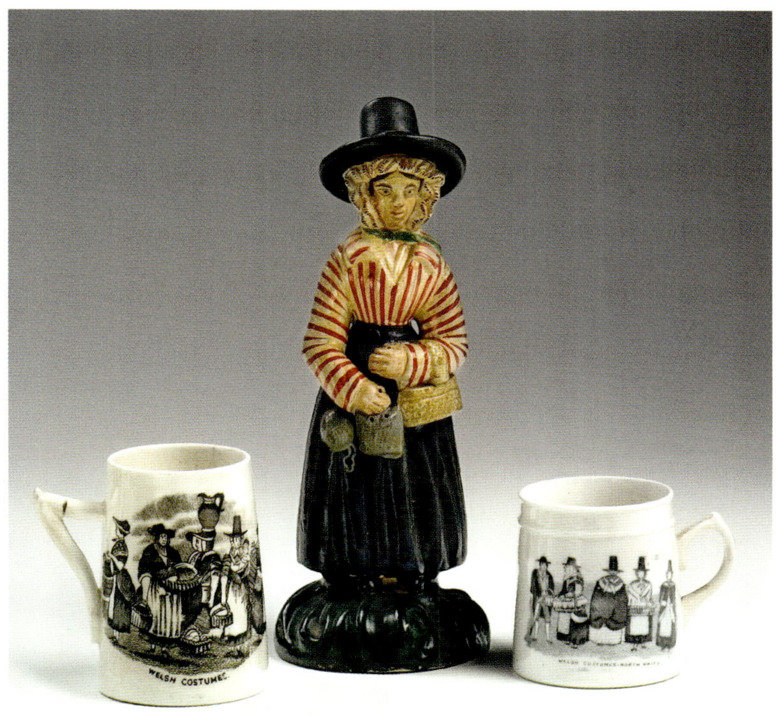

Mug, (**1310**), c.1870, Staffordshire, height: 8.9cm, (3½in), printed earthenware. Printed with 'WELSH COSTUMES' taken from Welsh Costumes No. 2, published by Newman & Co. c.1869.[35]
Figure, (**1309**), c.1850, Staffordshire, height: 22.9cm, (9in), enamelled earthenware. Woman in tall, black hat carries a basket, ball of wool and knitting (metal needles missing?).
Mug, (**1311**), c.1880, Staffordshire, height: 7cm, (2¾in), printed earthenware. Printed with 'WELSH COSTUMES' taken from Welsh Costumes No. 6, published by Newman & Co. c.1869.[36]

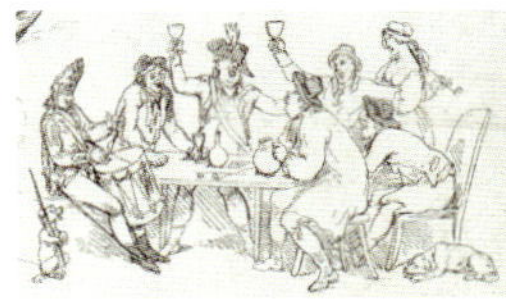

Chapter 18

CONVIVIALITY & TEETOTALISM

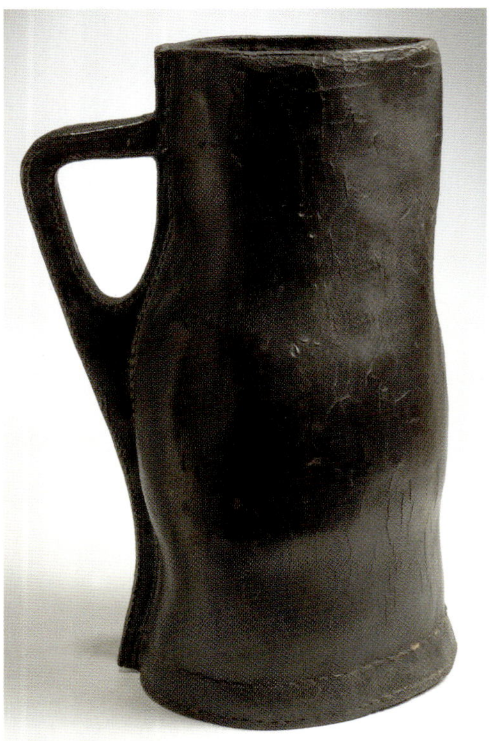

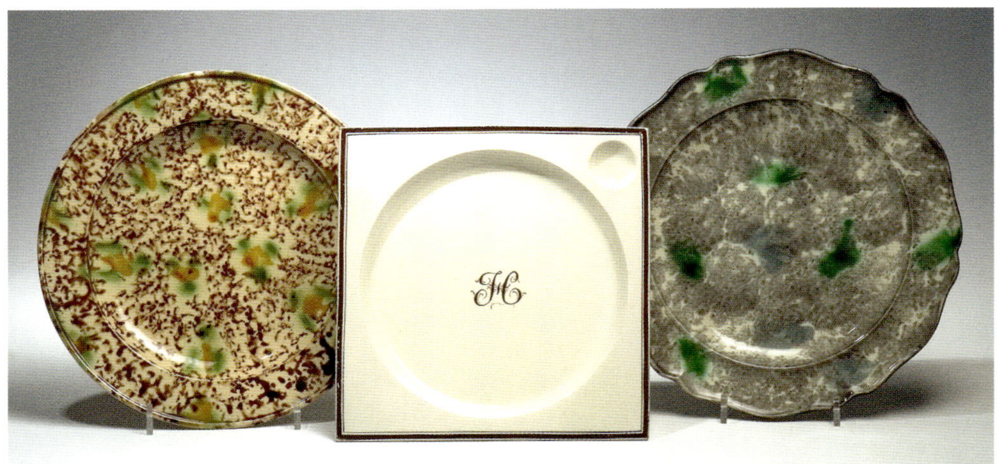

Plate, (1471), c.1780, Staffordshire, diameter: 24.2cm, (9½in), creamware, oxide-coloured.
Plate, (1468), c.1780, Staffordshire, height: 21cm, (8¼in), enamelled creamware. Square with painted border and central initial 'H'. Many medieval plates were rectangular wooden platters. Note small corner depression for salt.
Plate, (1472), c.1780, Staffordshire, diameter: 24.2cm, (9½in), creamware, oxide-coloured. Gently scrolling, incised profile recalls contemporary metalwork; at this time most plates were made of pewter.

Jug, (**1465**), c.1700, height: 51cm, (20¼in), leather. Large leather jugs, known as 'Black Jacks' were in general use from c.1350-1750. Made like shoes, they were doubled and stitched through the welts, the overlap cut to form a handle. Their dark colour is due to age and the pitch used for waterproofing. This one is alleged to have come from Kensington Palace.[1]

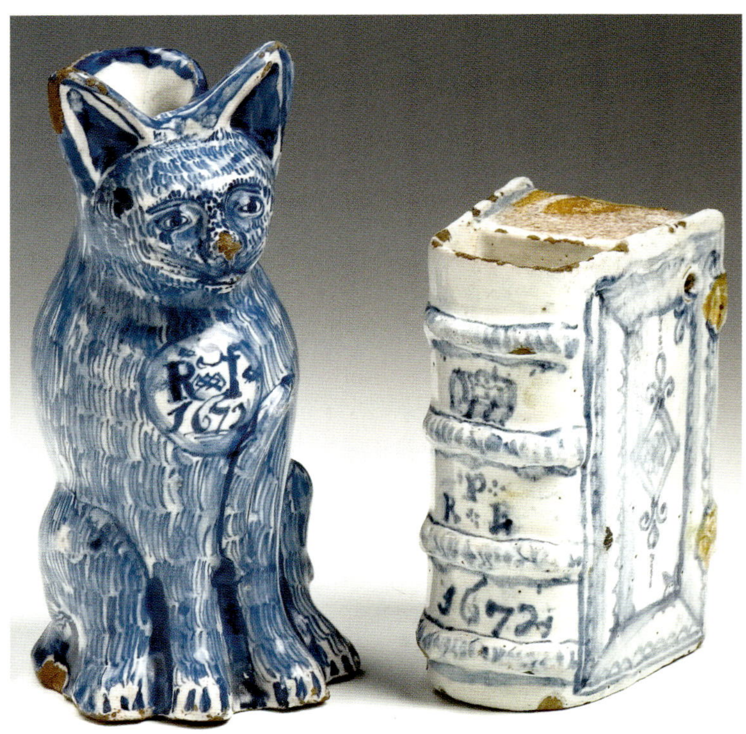

Jug, (**1370**), 1672, London, height: 17.8cm, (7in), tin-glazed earthenware. Jug modelled as a cat, (without handle), probably made in London. Inscribed, within a medallion, 'SRI 1672'. The dozen or so dated cat jugs that survive (1657-1677) are inscribed with three initials in triangular format. They are believed to be sentimental gift items, probably to commemorate a marriage. (The letter at the apex is the groom's surname with the initials of the groom and bride below, viz. R. and I. S.). In 1884, Lady Charlotte Schreiber purchased a similar cat jug, dated 1676, which she presented to the Victoria & Albert Museum, 'My cat belonged, as I suspected, to Mr Willett – I can only suppose he parts with it because he has two older and better specimens – viz.1672 and 1674'.[2] Shortly after this date, Henry Willett sold the later of his two specimens to the British Museum.[3]
Flask, (**1374**), 1672, height: 12.1cm, (4¾in), tin-glazed earthenware. Flask or handwarmer, modelled as a prayer book with a hollow spine, inscribed, 'PRE 1672'. Probably a marriage gift, recording when E. married P.R. There is a small bung hole on the 'front cover' and a drain hole at the base of the hollow chamber in the spine.

Posset, Punch and Drinks for Special Occasions

Caudle and posset were hot alcoholic beverages drunk on celebratory occasions or at a club or society meeting. Recipes vary though caudle was usually made from oatmeal or crushed biscuits beaten with egg yolks, mixed with wine or ale, sweetened, spiced and boiled – a sort of alcoholic porridge. It was considered particularly suitable for strengthening the sick.

Alcoholic (milk-based) posset could be made by heating a quart of cream, seasoned with cinnamon, nutmeg and sugar, adding six egg yolks and pouring the mixture into the heated sack (sherry). Posset pots were designed so that the base of the spout was located below the scummy head of the beverage. Posset seems to have died out around 1850. Hot wine punch, which gradually replaced caudle in popularity, was unsuitable for tin-glazed earthenware, which reacted with the acid in the wine.

By the early-eighteenth century punch (from an Indian word for five - the typical number of ingredients, usually including wine, brandy, fruits and spices) succeeded posset and caudle as the alcoholic mixture of choice. Clubs and societies consolidated their unity by drinking toasts. The punch bowl was an important adjunct to official functions in local government and judicial matters. At a dinner held in 1740 by James Brockman Esq of Beachborough in Kent, following a court hearing, the bill of expenses included; '29 Pound of Beef at 3d. per pound - 7/3 / For One Bowl of Punch for the Jury - 5/- / For Beer and Tobacco - 3/9'.

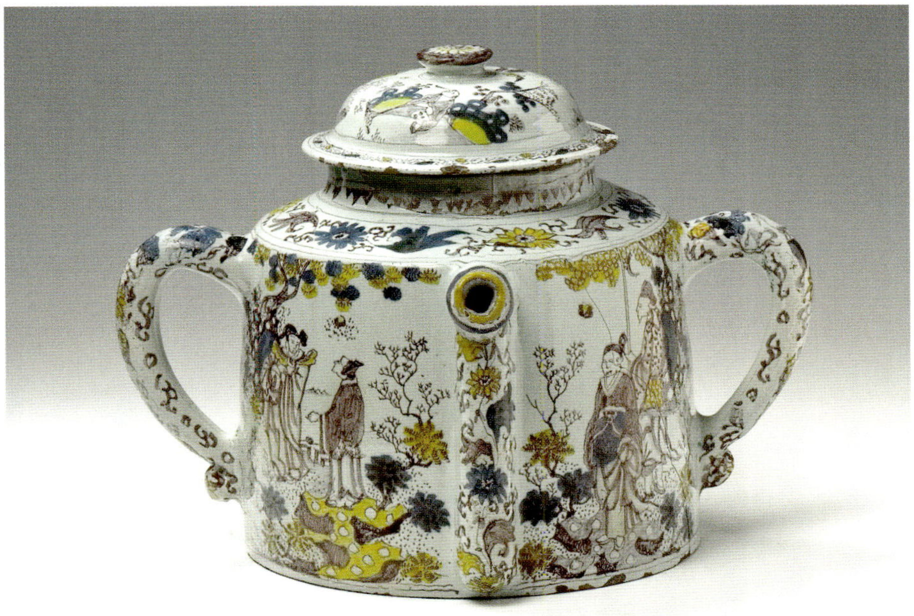

Caudle or Posset Pot, (1686), c.1680, Bristol, Liverpool or Holland, height: 24.2cm, (9½in), tin-glazed earthenware. Lidded pot for caudle or posset with small spout and side handles. This shape was made extensively in silver and pewter before 1700 when ceramic vessels became more readily available. Finely painted with pairs of Chinese worthies in gardens; on reverse a group of warriors in a landscape of volcanic rocks, banana palms and abundant flora.

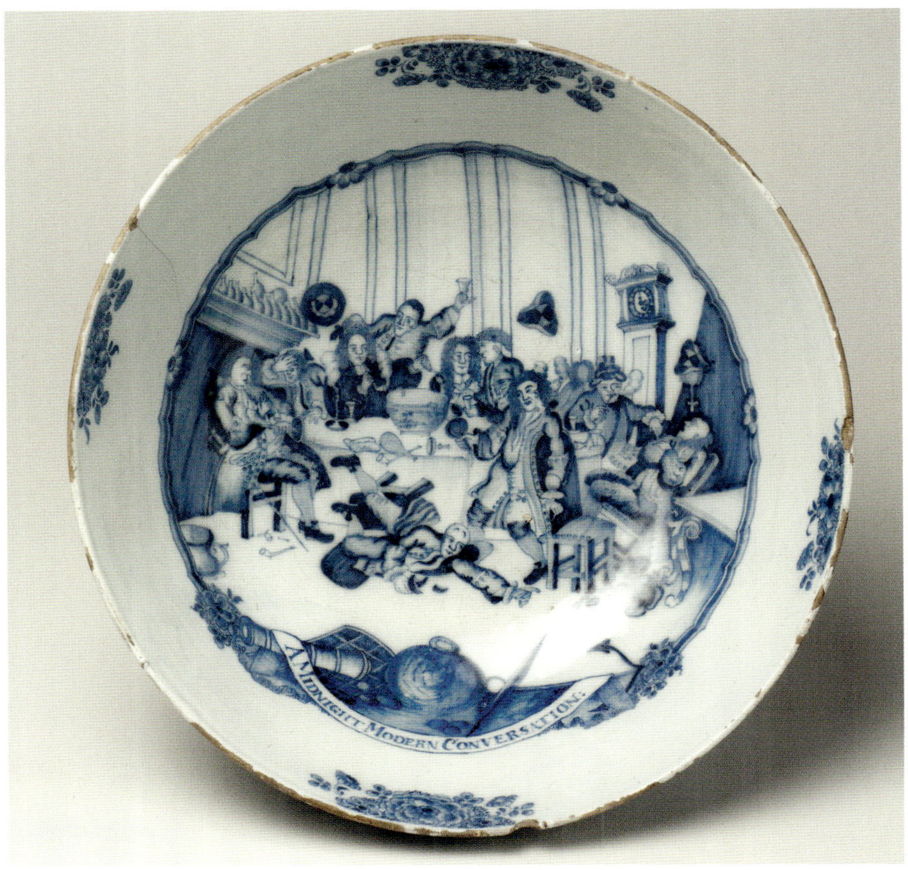

Punch Bowl, (1384), c.1750, Liverpool, diameter: 25.4cm, (10in), tin-glazed earthenware. Interior of bowl painted with a careful copy of *A Midnight Modern Conversation,* one of William Hogarth's most famous prints.[4] It shows a group of men proposing toasts while already very drunk. Hogarth probably painted the subject in response to the announcement of the impending Excise Bill, taxing wine and tobacco. The scene is probably set at St John's Coffee House, Temple Bar, at a meeting of a gentlemen's drinking club. Many of the figures may be portraits, the best-known being James Figg, the prize fighter, who has fallen from his chair and lost his wig. At the centre of the composition is the oversized punch bowl decorated with a fashionable chinoiserie design. The floor is littered with lemon peel and empty wine bottles.

Hogarth's print was published in March 1733 and sold by advance subscription of 5/- and was available after publication, for 'three half-crowns'. More pirate copies were made of this print than any other of his designs so the subject quickly became familiar to the public. Within a month of publication, makers of relief-moulded stoneware had adapted the design. Later it became a favourite subject for the inside and outside of punch bowls. Hogarth's international popularity was such that the design is also found on punch bowls of Dutch delftware, Meissen porcelain and Chinese export porcelain.[5]

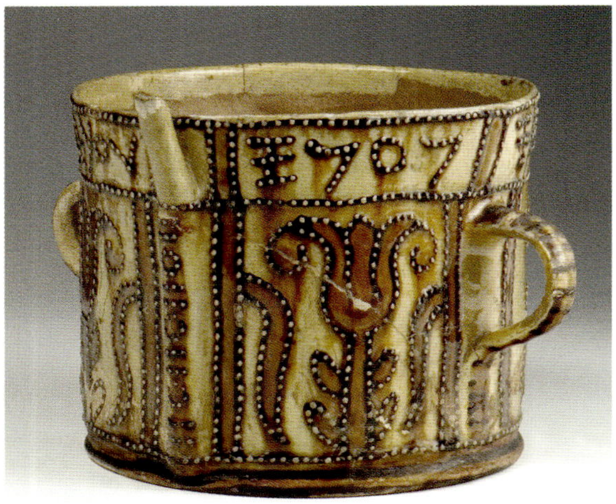

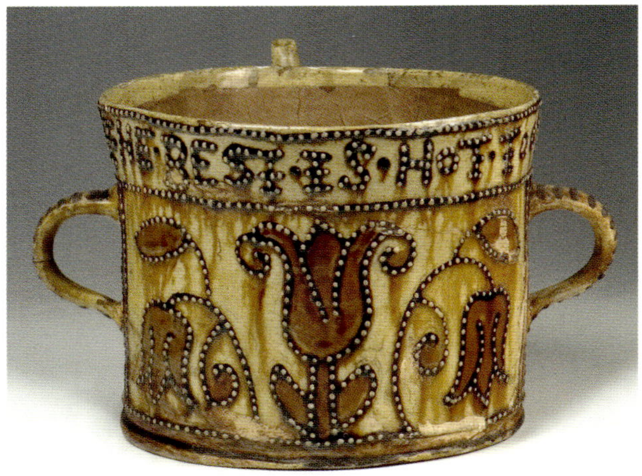

Caudle or Posset Pot, (**1689**), 1707, Staffordshire, height: 20.3cm, (8in), slipware. The squat, drum-shaped pot slip-decorated with large tulips and inscribed 'THE.BEST.IS.NOT TOO.GOOD.FOR.YOU.', a very popular motto, since a large number survive.[6] This form was well suited to serving bragget, a late-seventeenth century concoction of ale and honey fermented with spices, drunk on Bragget Sunday, which fell in the middle of Lent.

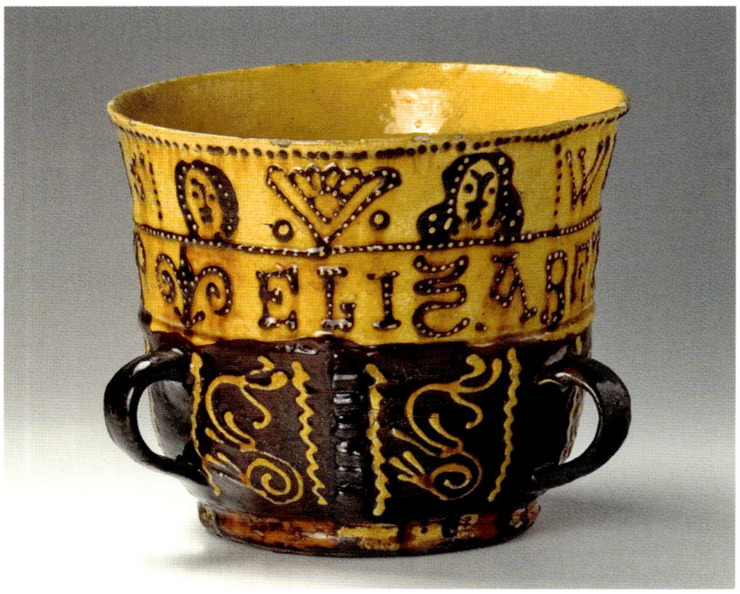

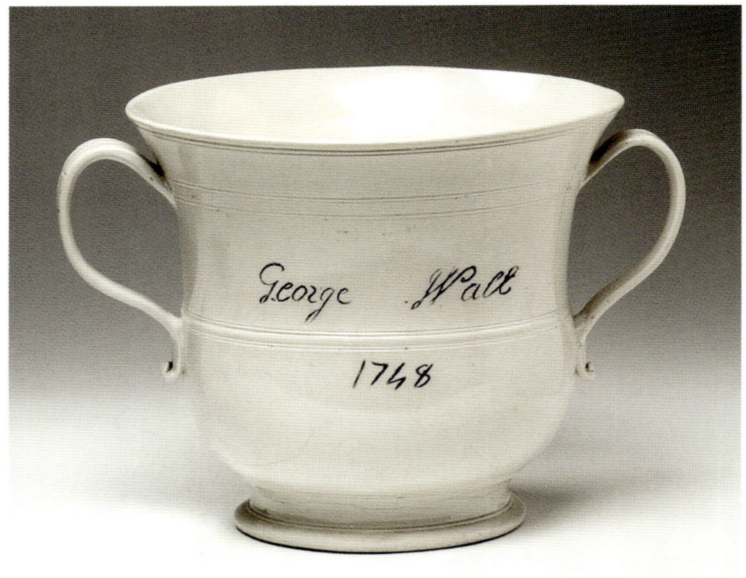

Loving Cup, (**1397**), 1715, Staffordshire, height: 20.3cm, (8in), slipware. Cup applied with four small C-shaped handles around the base decorated bands of small faces and grotesques, inscribed, 'WILLIAM LEY 1715 / ELIZABETH LEY HER CUP'. It is similar to another loving cup, dedicated to Ann Draper in 1707, sold by Willett to the British Museum in 1887.

Loving Cup, (**1433**), 1748, Staffordshire, height: 19.7cm, (7¾in), salt-glazed stoneware. Two-handled loving cup incised in scratch blue, 'George Wall 1748 / Elizabeth Wall 1748'. It was probably created for a wedding feast although such vessels were also passed round for guests to take a ritual sip on other special occasions such as Christmas and anniversaries.

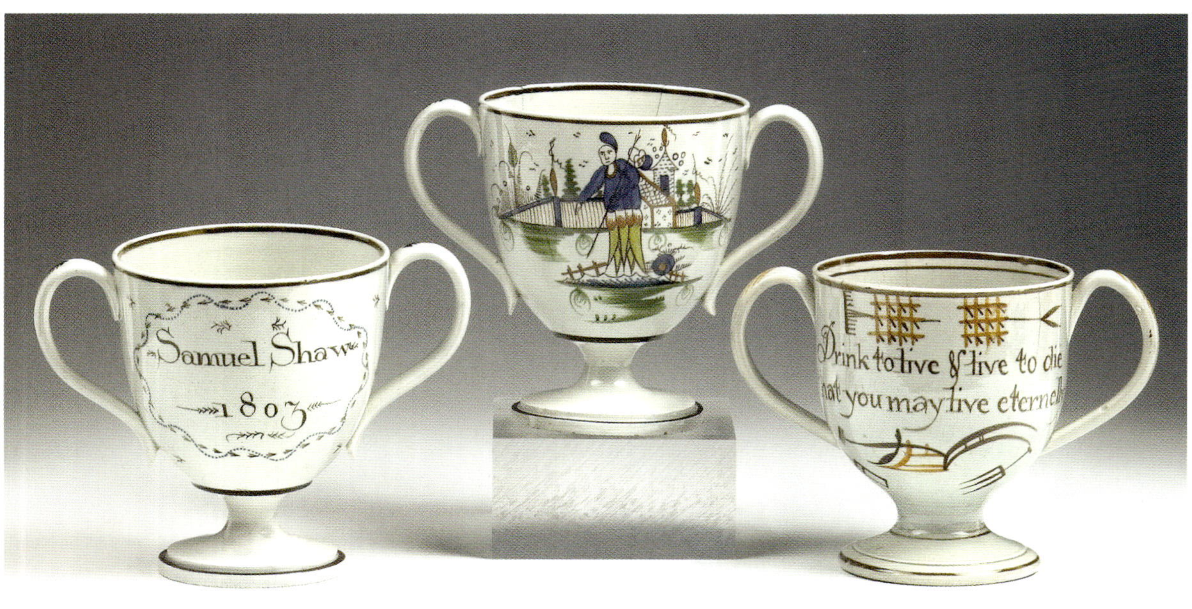

Pair of Cups, (**1429 & A**), 1803, Yorkshire, each height: 13.3cm, (5¼in), Pratt-coloured pearlware. Small two-handled cups inscribed 'Samuel Shaw 1803' (chinoiserie buildings on reverse) and 'Mary Shaw 1803', decorated with a Chinese figure in a garden. Probably made for the Shaws' marriage or anniversary.
Cup, (**1428**), c.1805, Yorkshire, height: 12.7cm, (5in), Pratt-coloured pearlware. Similar cup decorated with a plough and farm tools and inscribed, 'Drink to live and live to die / That you may live eternally.'

Wine Bottles

A large number of tin-glazed earthenware wine bottles survive, labelled with their contents. Their globular shape derives from imported German stoneware bottles from Siegburg or Cologne in the Rhineland. Their modest size, given the drinking capacities of the day suggests that they were probably intended as Christmas or New Year gifts. Samuel Pepys frequently mentions sack (sherry) in his diary.

By Pepys's time most wine was decanted from casks into glass bottles. On 23 October, 1663 Pepys inspected his 'new bottles ... with my crest upon them'.[7] From around 1650 many bottles had seals applied to the body of the bottle stamped with names, dates, crests or symbols denoting the names of inns. This safeguarded tavern property or provided a prestigious form of identification for the contents of a gentleman's wine cellar.

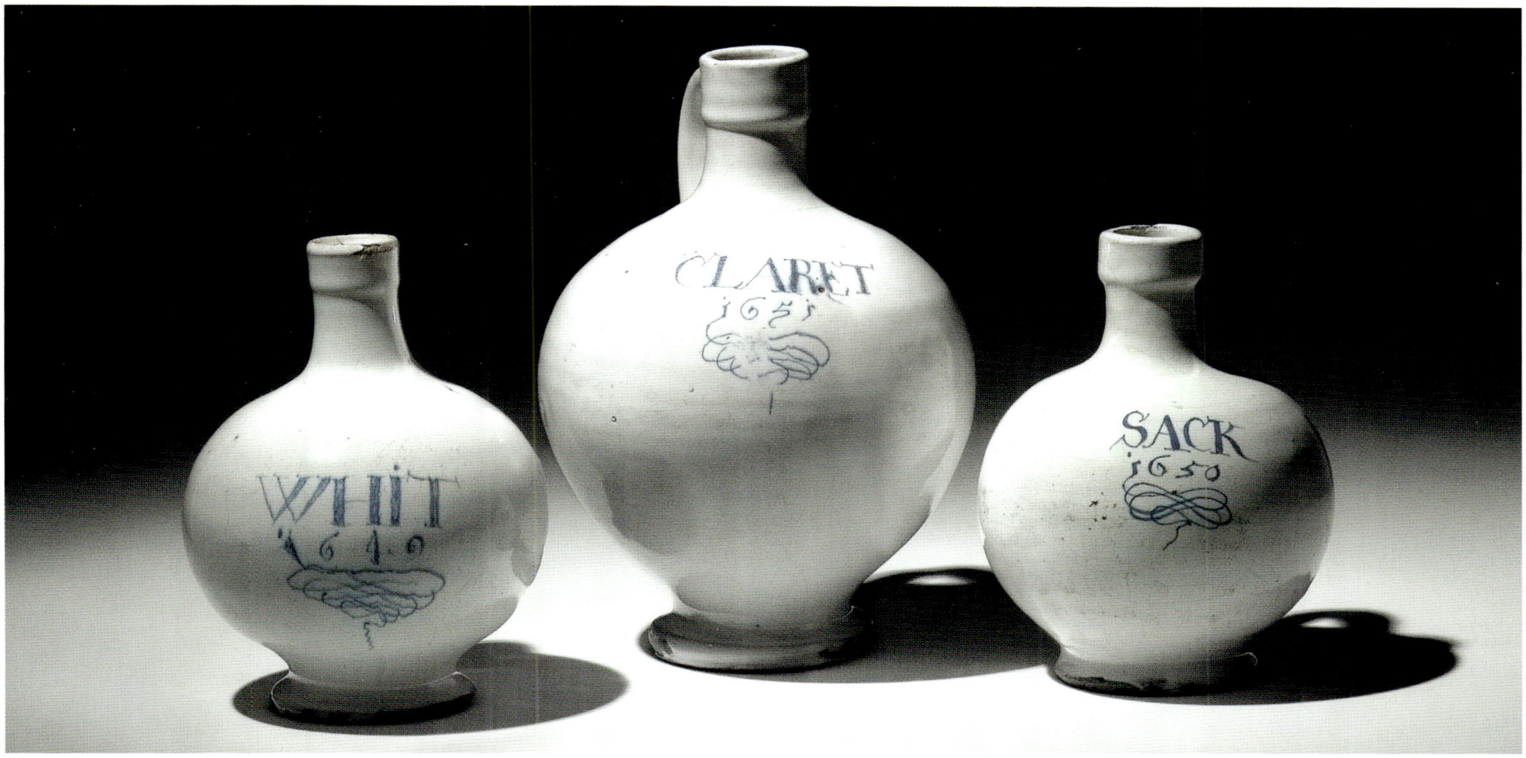

Wine Bottle, (**1371**), 1642, London?, height: 15.6cm, (6⅛in), tin-glazed earthenware. Inscribed underglaze, 'WHIT 1642', for white wine, usually from Germany.
Wine Bottle, (**1371A**), 1651, London?, height: 20.5cm, (8⅛in), tin-glazed earthenware. Inscribed underglaze, 'CLARET 1651', for clarified red wine, mainly from Bordeaux.[8]

Wine Bottle, (**1371B**), 1650, London?, height: 15.3cm, (6in), tin-glazed earthenware. Inscribed underglaze, 'SACK 1650'. 'Sack', (*secco* – dry) covered sherry-sack (from Jerez) Canary-sack (from the Canary Islands), Madeira-sack etc., fortified wines imported from southern Europe.

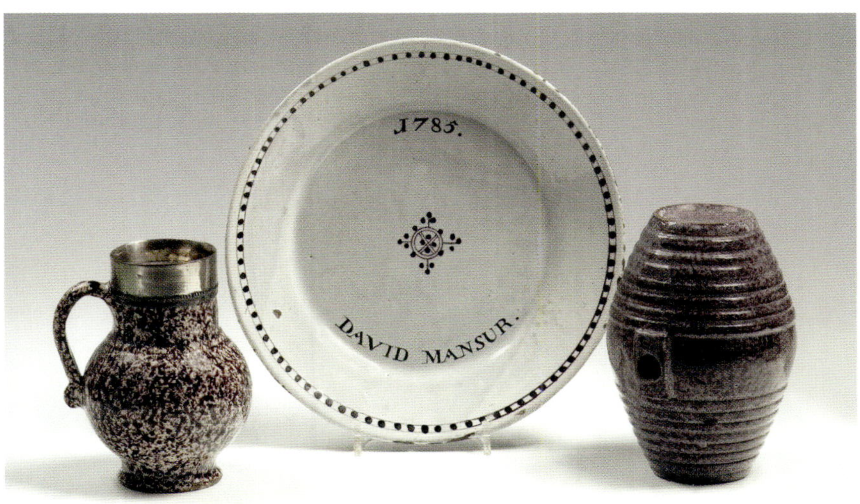

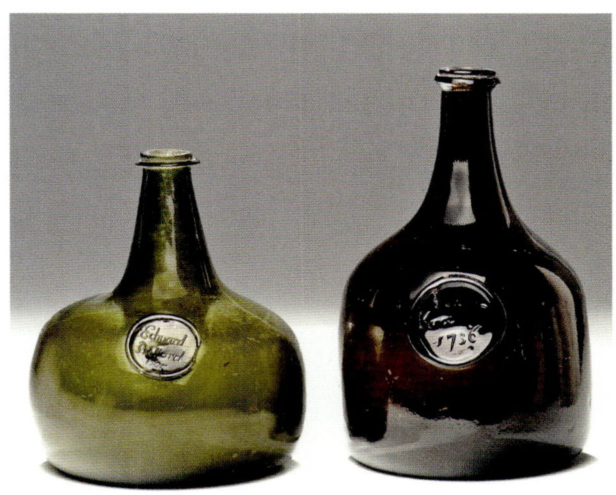

Drinking Jug or Mug, (**1373**), c.1630, London, height: 13.3cm, (5¼in), tin-glazed earthenware. Mug, sponged underglaze with manganese oxide and fitted with a silver-coloured metal collar.[9]
Plate, (**1469**), 1785, London, diameter: 23.5cm, (9¼in), tin-glazed earthenware. Commemorative plate is inscribed in manganese, 'David Mansur' and dated 1785.
Bottle, (**1372**), c.1750, London or Bristol, height: 15.3cm, (6in), tin-glazed earthenware. Bottle modelled as a wine cask, sponged underglaze with manganese oxide. incised with concentric rings, has a central bung hole.[10]

Wine Bottle, (**1380**), 1705, London?, height: 17.8cm, (7in), green glass. Onion-shaped bottle with a seal impressed, 'Edward Ballard / 1705'.
Wine Bottle, (**1381**), 1736, London?, height: 18.3cm, (8½in), brown glass. Cylindrical bottle with a seal impressed, 'John Knoteford / 1736' Such bottles would be filled by the vintner and returned to their owners or used by the owner to decant his own wine from the cask.

Mineral Water

Until the advent of technology that allowed access to clean drinking water, it was usually safer (even for small children) to drink beer. Bonwick, the landlord of a Surrey ale house, sank a well on his land, adjacent to an old pear tree, intending to make beer. The resulting brew was distasteful so Bonwick sold the untreated water as a medicinal cure for gout. Two- and three-gallon bottles were advertised in the *General Evening Post* in 1752. They could be sent to London, charged at 2/- per gallon for the contents and 2/- deposit on the bottle.[11] The water is mentioned by Horace Walpole to Sir Horace Mann in 1753, 'You might have doctors for every one of them [nervous complaints] from Dr. Meade to Dr. Thomson & from Bath to *the iron pear tree*'.[12]

Tavern Culture

There are numerous proverbs and rhymes associated with inns and alehouses in the eighteenth and nineteenth century and numerous exhortations to take a drink inscribed on ceramics.

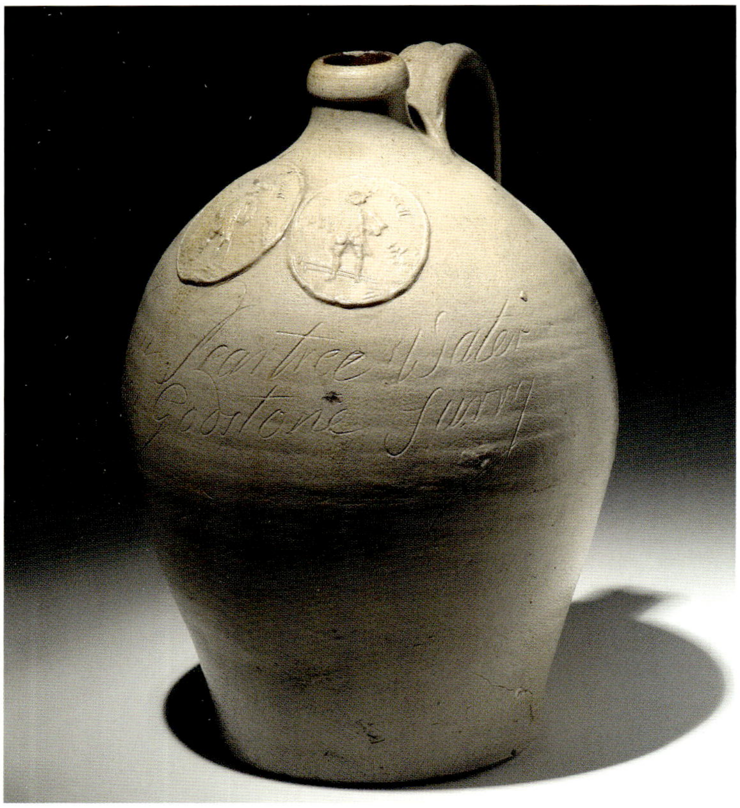

Bottle, (1393), c.1752, London, height: 34.3cm, (13½in), salt-glazed stoneware. A two-gallon bottle inscribed, 'Iron peartree Water / near Godstone Surry [*sic*]'. Relief-moulded medallions on the shoulder show two figures. One holds crutches and moans, 'Oh! The Gout' while the other has discarded the crutches and holds a tankard, proclaiming, 'Drink and be well'. Since at least a dozen of these bottles survive in public and private collections sales were obviously brisk but it is not known for how long.

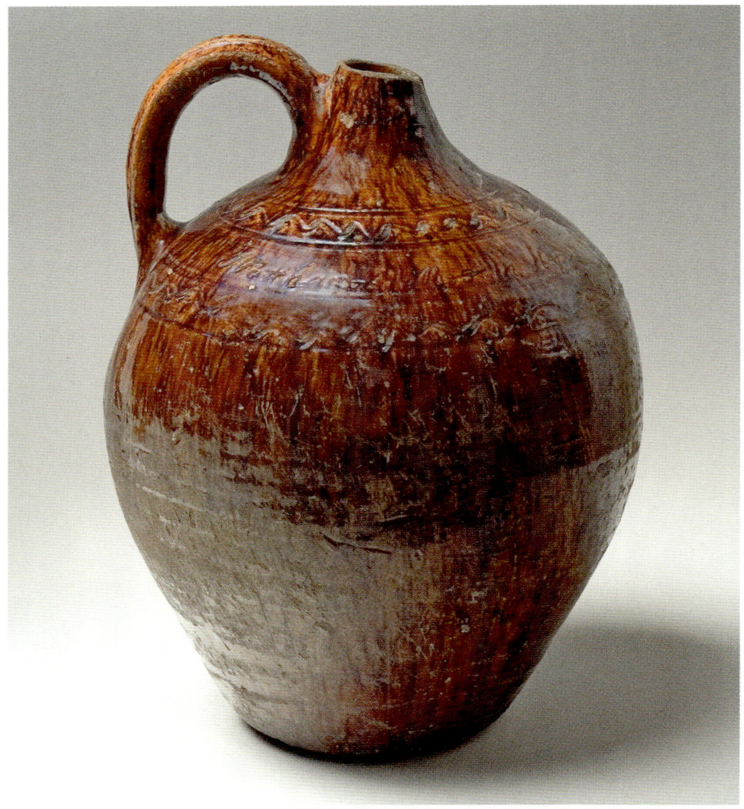

Bottle, (1394), c.1734, Suffolk, height: 35.6cm, (14in), red earthenware. A two-gallon bottle with incised geometric decoration, inscribed, 'Nathaniel Mos in Hepworth October 2nd 1734'. Described as 'Wattisfield' ware, after a Suffolk village near Hepworth, ten miles north-east of Bury St Edmunds. A Roman pottery site at Wattisfield was leased by John Death from John Cogisdale in 1734 and he and his descendants worked the pottery until it was taken over by Thomas Watson in 1808.

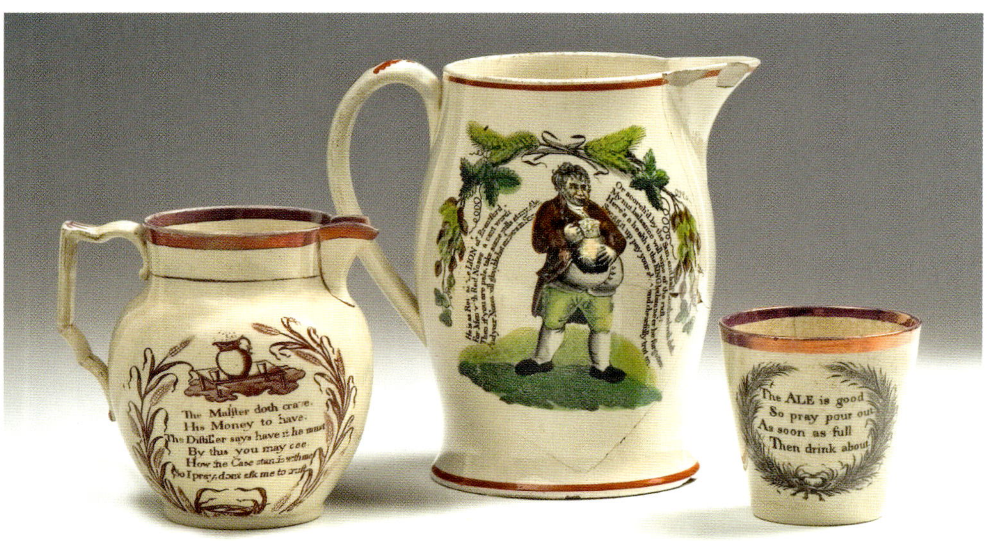

Jug, (1399), c.1810, Staffordshire, height: 10.8cm, (4¼in), creamware, brown-printed and lustred. Jug printed with verse, 'The Maltster doth crave / His money to have/ The distiller says have it he must / By this you may see / How the case stands with me / So I pray don't ask me to trust'.
Jug, (1432), c.1800, Staffordshire, height: 15.3cm, (6in), creamware, printed and coloured. Jug printed with drinker holding jug of ale beneath a festoon of hops and verse, 'He is as red as the LION of Brentford'. The old Red Lion tavern at 318 Brentford High Street opened before 1670.
Beaker, (1398), c.1800, Staffordshire, height: 7cm, (2¾in), creamware, printed and lustred. Beaker printed, 'The ALE is good / So pray pour out; / As soon as full / Then drink about'. On reverse the infant Bacchus, astride a barrel.

Mug, (**1414**), c.1800, Staffordshire, height: 9.6cm, (3¾in), pearlware, printed and coloured. Printed with toast, 'Money to him / who has spirit to ufe it / And courage to him / Who has courage to lofe it'.
Mug, (**1418**), c.1800, Staffordshire, height: 12.7cm, (5in), pearlware, printed and coloured. Printed, 'A friend that is Social / And makes not too free / to a pot of my liquor / Right welcome shall be'.
Mug, (**1419**), c.1800, Staffordshire, height: 10.2cm, (4in), pearlware, printed and coloured. Printed, 'To my best my friends are free / Free with that and free with me'.

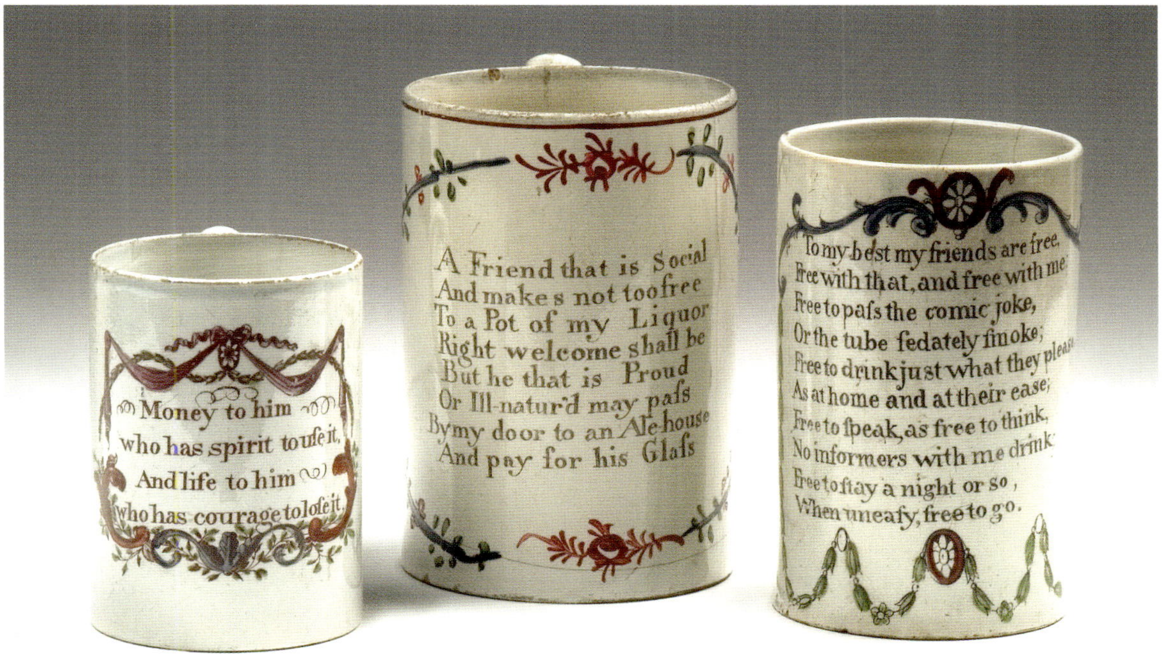

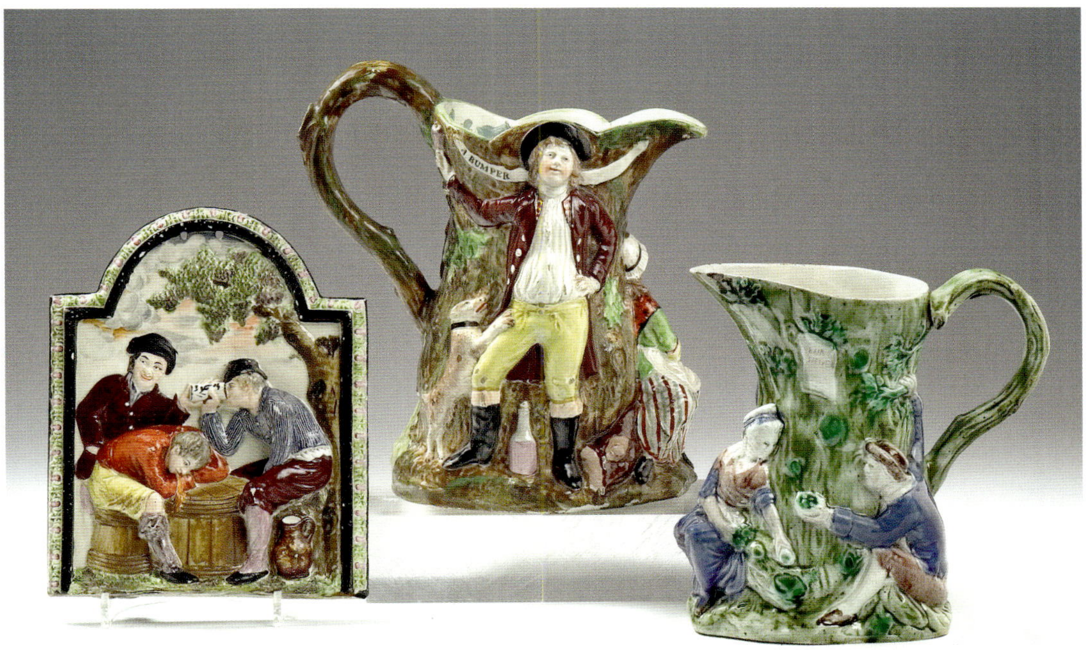

Plaque, (**1494**), c.1790, Staffordshire, height: 22.3cm, (8¾in), enamelled pearlware. Probably made by the Wood family. Relief-moulded with drinking scene. One man vomits colourfully over the half barrel they use as a table. The subject taken from paintings by the seventeenth-century Dutch artist, Adriaen Brouwer.[13]
Jug, (**1464**), c.1800, Staffordshire, height: 25.4cm, (10in), enamelled pearlware. Jug, relief-moulded as a tree trunk, designed in 1788 by Jean Voyez (1735-1800), who worked as modeller and translator for Wedgwood. A man stands holding up a glass, beneath a ribbon impressed, 'A BUMPER', his dog and a bottle at his feet. On reverse, a woman and man with bird's nest beneath a notice impressed, 'Fair Hebe' (which gives the jug its nickname).
Jug, (**1463**), c.1790, Staffordshire, height: 22.3cm, (8¾in), pearlware, oxide-coloured. A woman with fruit and flowers and man with bird's nest beneath a notice impressed, 'Fair Hebe'.

Jug, (**1697**), c.1800, Staffordshire, height: 17.2cm, (6¾in), pearlware, printed, yellow-glazed and coloured. Printed with verse, 'How happy is he / Who contented can be … In a prudent & fenfible Wife.'
Figure Group, (**1674**), c.1830, Staffordshire, height: 15.3cm, (6in), enamelled pearlware. Group comprises a small man and a large woman and dogs in front of quasi-heraldic lion and unicorn, flanking a tree full of red squirrels. Willett said it represented 'love at first sight'.
Jug, (**1664**), c.1790, Staffordshire, height: 17.7cm, (7in), enamelled pearlware. Small jug with a woman with fruit and flowers and man with bird's-nest beneath a notice impressed, 'Fair Hebe'.[14]

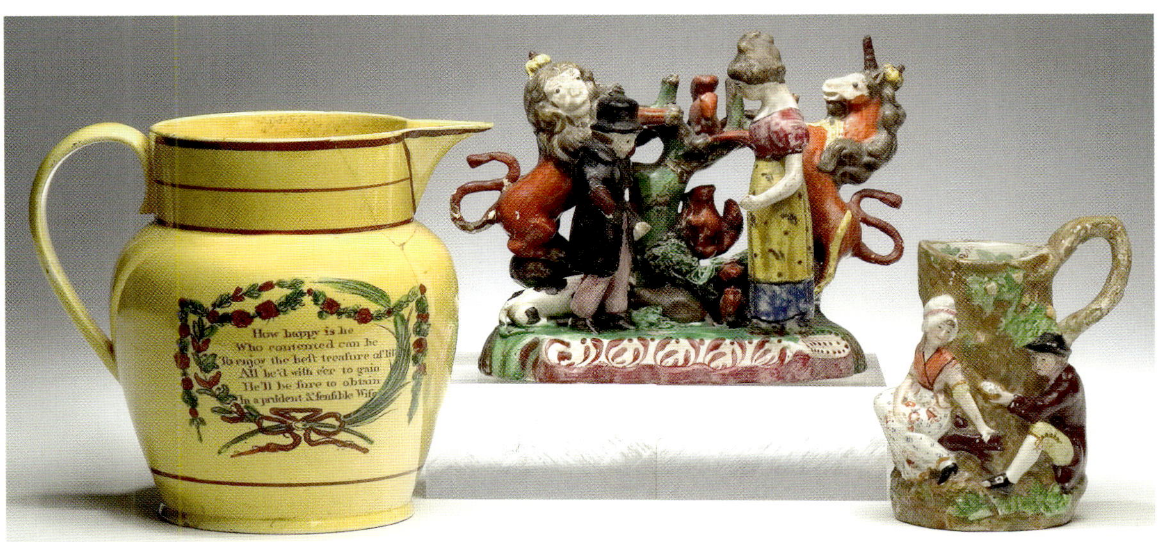

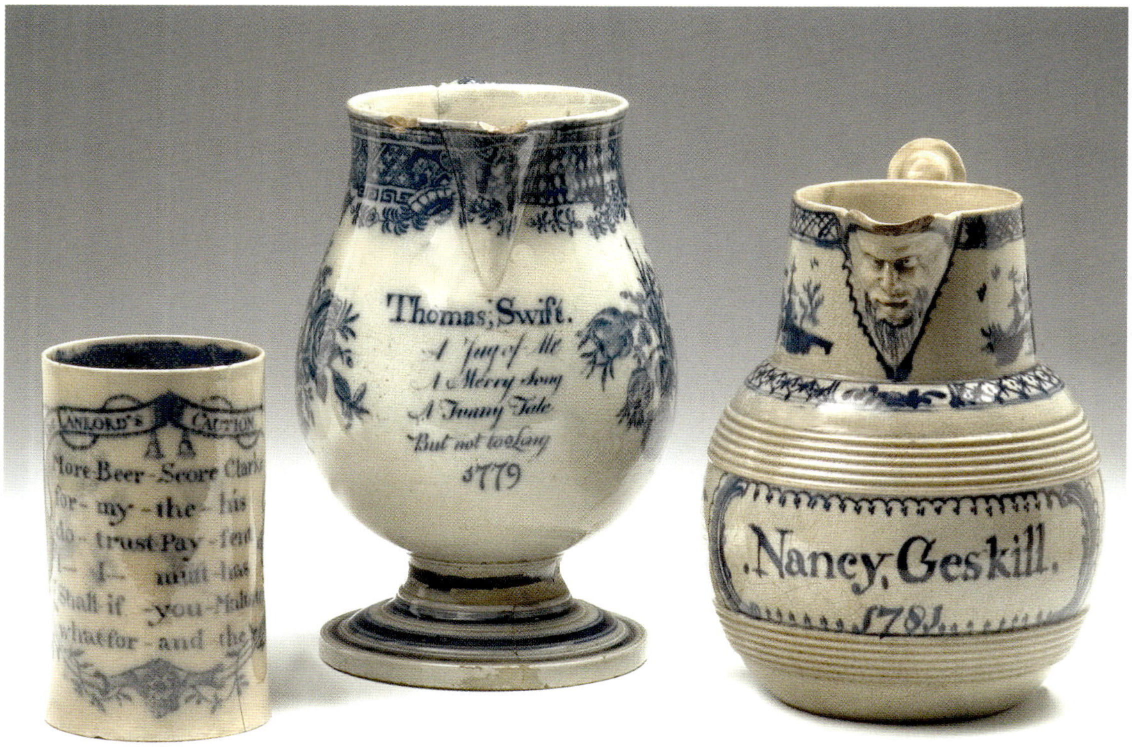

Mug, (**1413**), c.1790, Staffordshire, height: 12.7cm, (5in), blue-printed drabware. Mug, printed underglaze riddle (words in reverse order), 'The Maltster has sent his Clark / And you must Pay the Score / For if I trust my Beer / What shall I do for More' (as 1439).
Jug, (**1425**), 1779, Staffordshire, height: 20.3cm, (8in), blue-printed pearlware. Jug on waisted foot, dedicated to 'Thomas Swift 1779' and inscribed; 'A Jug of Ale/ A Merry Song/ a Funny Tale/ But not too Long'.[15]
Jug, (**1426**), 1781, Staffordshire, height: 17.7cm, (7in), blue-printed drabware. Jug with a mask spout and handle moulded with the figure of a sailor, is painted, 'Nancy Geskill' and dated 1781.

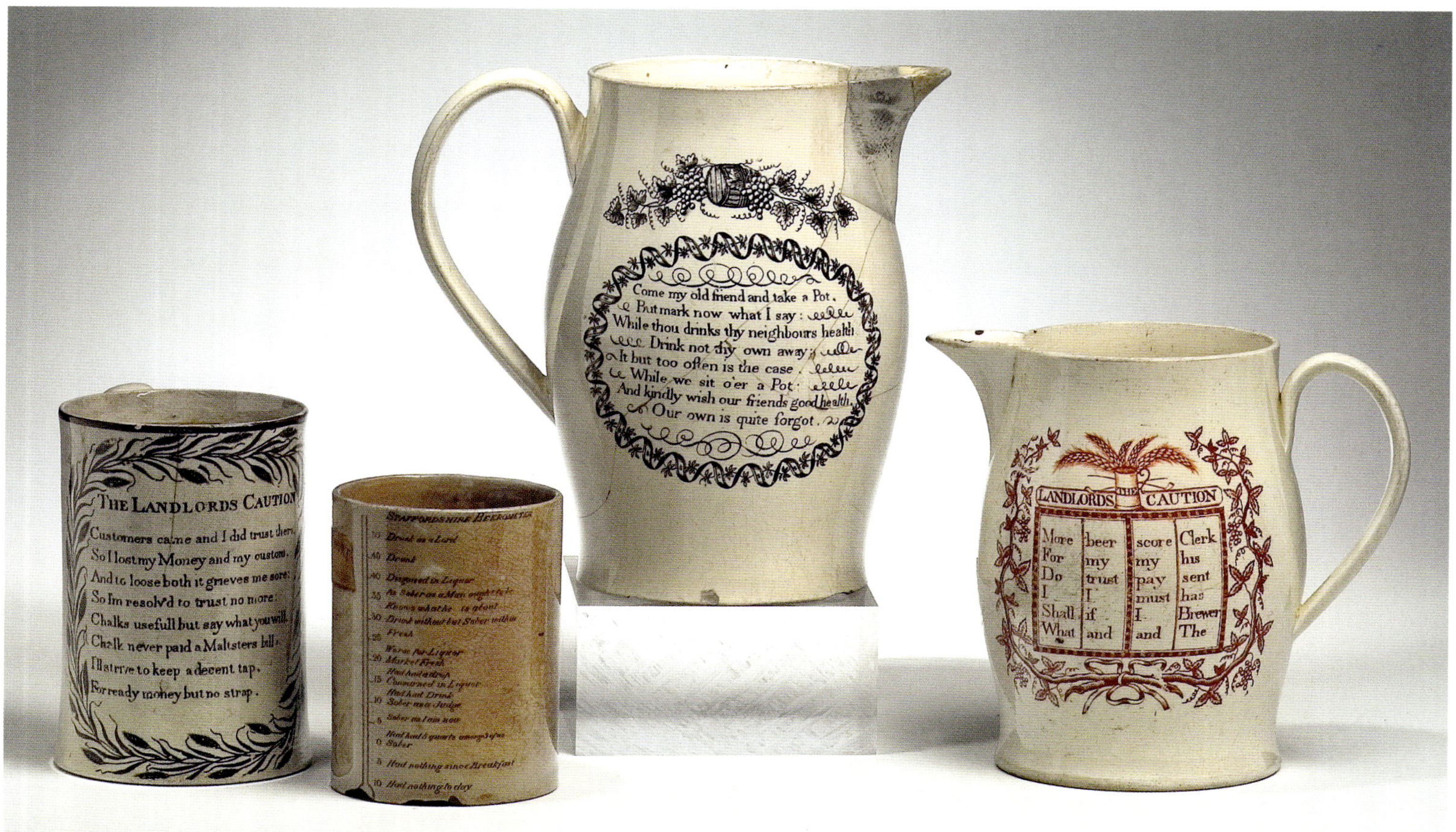

Mug, (**1416**), c.1800, Staffordshire, height: 12.1cm, (4¾in), printed drabware. Mug printed with 'THE LANDLORDS CAUTION / Customers came and I did trust them / So I lost my Money and my custom … Chalks usefull but say what you will / Chalk never paid a Maltsters bill'.
Mug, (**1439**), c.1820, Staffordshire, Longport, height: 10.2cm, (4in), red-printed drabware. Mug made by Davenport printed, 'STAFFORDSHIRE BEEROMETER'. The vertical scale, imitating a thermometer, ranges from '– 10 – Had nothing all day', to '0 – Sober' to '50 – Drunk as a Lord'.

Jug, (**1427**), c.1800, Staffordshire, Longport, height: 17.8cm, (7in), printed creamware. Printed with a health warning, 'Come my Old Friend /… While that thou drinkst thy / neighbours health / Drink not thine own away'.
Jug, (**1439**), c.1820, Staffordshire, Longport, height: 10.2cm, (4in), red-printed creamware. Jug printed with riddle (words in reverse order), 'The Maltster has sent his Clark / And you must Pay the Score / For if I trust my Beer / What shall I do for More' (as 1413).

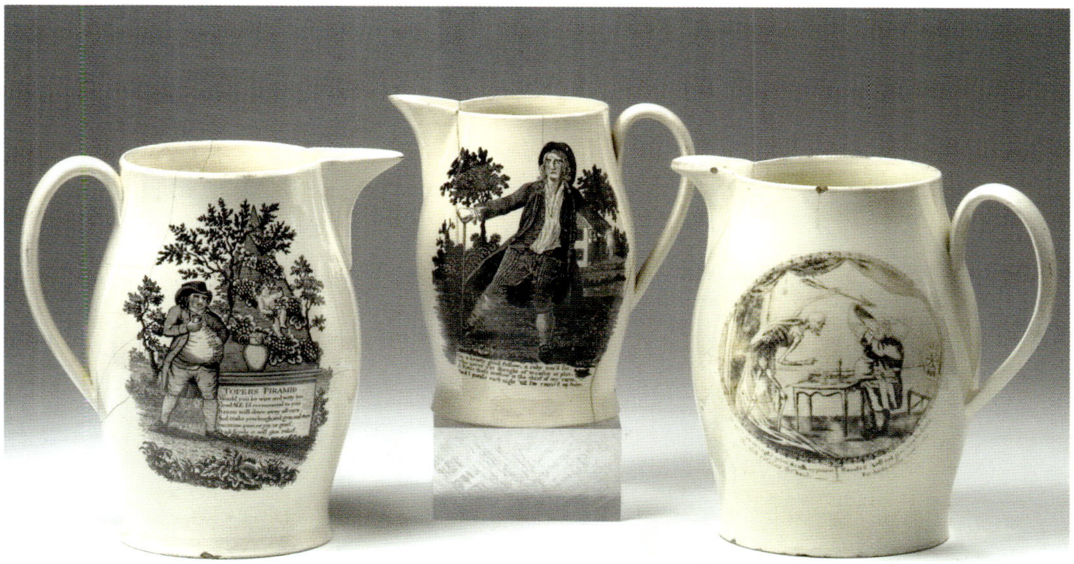

Jug, (**1435**), c.1800, Staffordshire, height: 20.3cm, (8in), printed creamware. Rotund drinker stands beside the, 'TOPERS PIRAMID' extolling the beneficial effects of ale. 'It soon will drive away all care / And make you laugh and grin and stare'.
Jug, (**1430**), c.1790, Staffordshire, height: 17.2cm, (6¾in), printed creamware. Large figure lurching home from the inn, proclaiming, 'I'm a hearty good fellow, a ruby-nos'd sot'. The lines come from a popular drinking song.[16] On the reverse a 'Caution', 'sit and spend as you desire/ But do not stand before the fire'
Jug, (**1436**), c.1780, Staffordshire, probably Shelton, height: 20.3cm, (8in), printed creamware. Death points an arrow at a heavy drinker who drains a large punchbowl inscribed, 'To speed his draught grim death appears'. The image is probably by Thomas Fletcher and entitled elsewhere, 'The Last Drop'.[17]

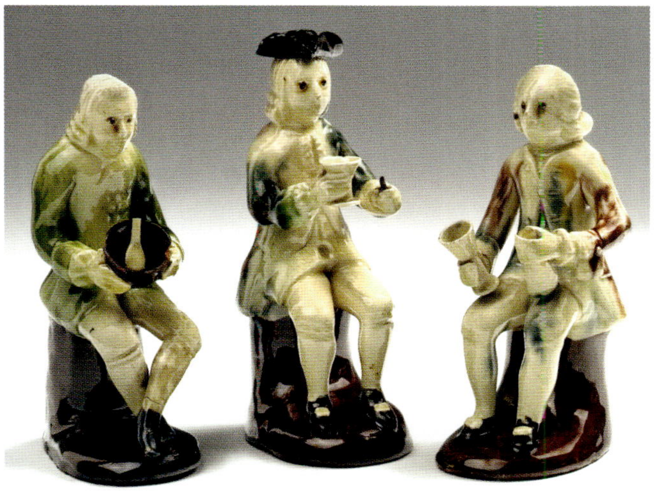

Three Figures, (**1485**), c.1760, Staffordshire, height: 2 x 12.2cm, (4¾in), height: 13.2cm, (5¼in), lead-glazed and oxide-coloured. Three companionable drinkers sit on brown glazed stumps, one with a bowl and spoon, one (wearing a hat) with a goblet and broken pipe stem, the third with a goblet and bottle.

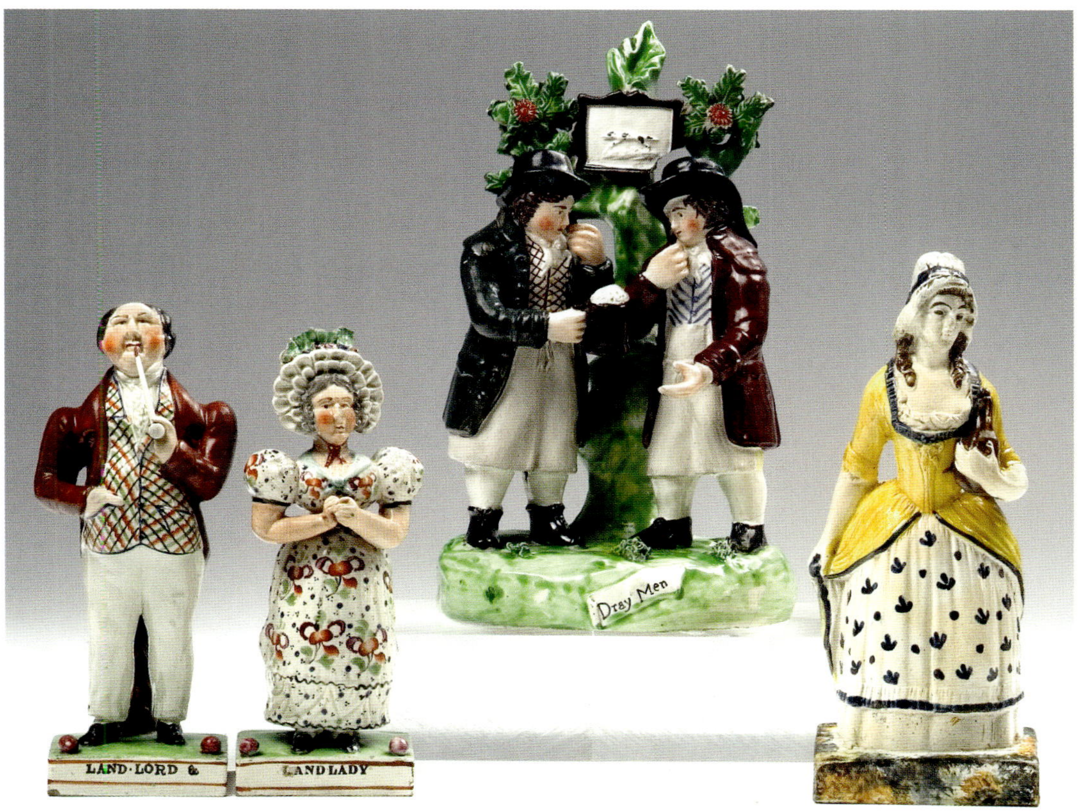

Pair of Figures, (**1473 & A**), c.1830, Staffordshire, height: 18.4cm, (7¼in), height: 17.6cm, (6⅞in), enamelled pearlware. Humorous figures, entitled, 'LANDLORD &' 'LANDLADY'. The landlord closely related to the farmer from table-based, bull-baiting groups (see 1019).
Figure Group, (**1478**), c.1820, Staffordshire, height: 23.5cm, (9¼in), enamelled pearlware. Two draymen (who delivered beer from the breweries), drinking beneath an inn sign depicting a dog.
Figure, (**1474**), c.1790, Staffordshire, height: 21.6cm, (8½in), Pratt-coloured pearlware. A winsome barmaid holds a bottle beneath her arm.

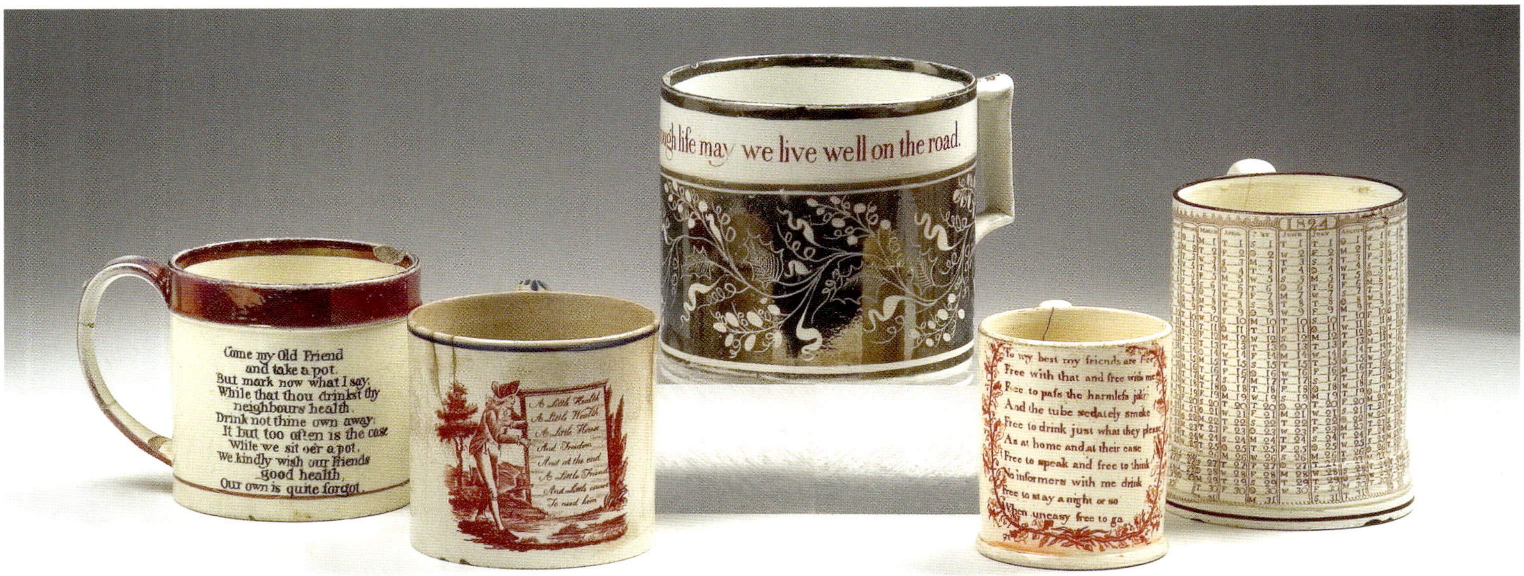

Mug, (**1417**), c.1800, Staffordshire, height: 11.8cm, (4⅝in), creamware, printed and lustred. Printed, 'Come my Old Friend / And take a pot / But mark now what I say / While that thou drinkst thy/ neighbours health / Drink not thine own away', see (also HW 1427).
Mug, (**1437**), c.1800, Staffordshire, height: 8.2cm, (3¼in), red-printed creamware. Man supports billboard printed, 'A little Health / A little Wealth / A little House and Freedom'.

Mug, (**1415**), c.1800, Staffordshire, height: 11.5cm, (4½in), pearlware, red-printed and lustred. Inscribed on a large mug, decorated with sgraffito holly sprigs, 'On our journey through life may we live well on the road'.
Mug, (**R2454.17**), c.1800, Staffordshire, height: 8.8cm, (3½in), red-printed creamware. Printed 'To my best my friends are free'.[18]
Mug, (**1408**), c.1823, Staffordshire, height: 12.1cm, (4¾in), brown-printed creamware. Printed with a complete calendar for 1824.

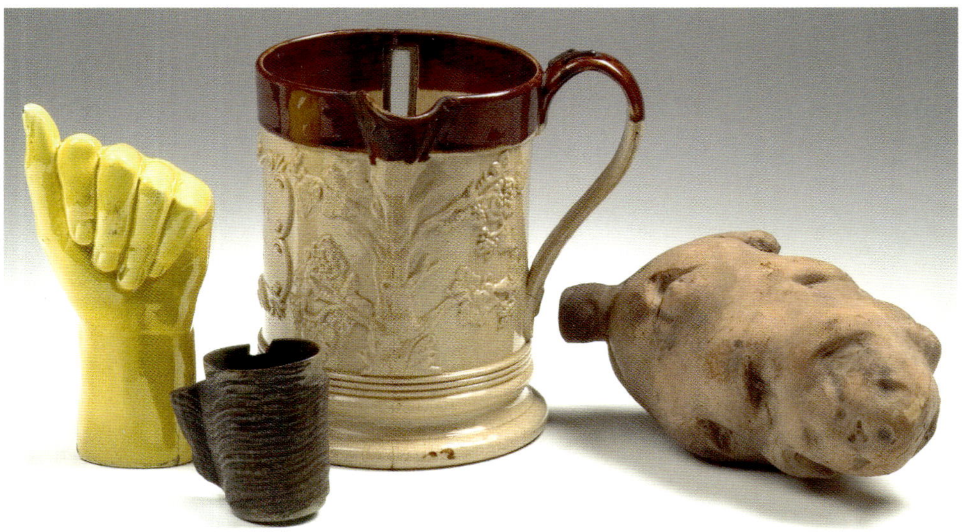

Cup, (**1401**), c.1800, North East, height: 16.5cm, (6½in), brown-printed creamware. Cup moulded as a human hand, clenched in a soft fist. Probably used as a stirrup cup or at club ceremonies.
Beaker, (**1389**), height: 7cm, (2¾in), ram horn. Found object with inserted base. Circular surface grooves formed by yearly growth.
Jug, (**1403**), c.1860, Bristol, height: 17.2cm, (6¾in), brown-dipped earthenware. Jug with side handle, relief-moulded with fanned vines. A small glass window with engraved horizontal line inserted near the top, opposite the spout. Made by J. & J. White's Baptist Mills Pottery in Bristol. 'Sidney's Patent Imperial Quart',[19] was an important technical innovation for the accurate measurement of capacity to satisfy new weights and measures legislation.
Bottle, (**1390**), c.1790, Staffordshire, height: 21cm, (8¼in), terracotta. Bottle or spirit flask (glazed within), realistically modelled as a whole potato or yam.[20] Such flasks may have been intended to hold potcheen (high-quality ethyl alcohol that can be distilled from potatoes), banned in Ireland since 1661.

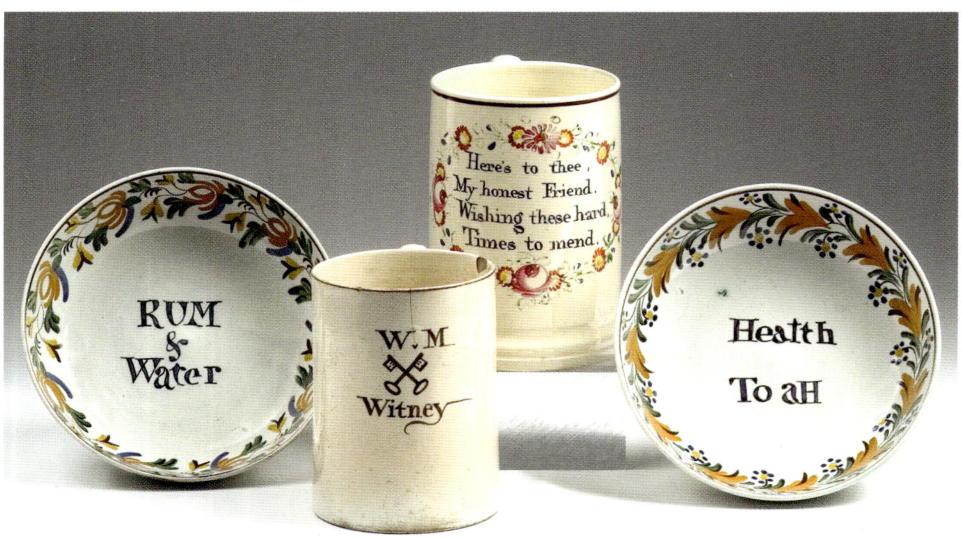

Two Bowls, (**1421 & A**), c.1790, Sunderland?, each diameter: 16.5cm, (16½in), Pratt-coloured pearlware. Bowls, possibly made by the Garrison Pottery, decorated with bands of flowers and inscribed with drink-related phrases, 'Rum & Water' and 'Health To aH [*sic*]'.
Mug, (**1407**), c.1790, Staffordshire, height: 12.1cm, (4¾in), enamelled creamware. Mug is enamelled, 'W.M. / Witney' with a pictogram of crossed keys. Probably made for the Crossed Keys public house in Witney in Oxfordshire.
Mug, (**1411**), c.1790, North East, height: 14cm, (5½in), enamelled creamware. Mug painted with floral garland and inscribed, 'Here's to thee, / My honest Friend. / Wishing these hard, /Times to mend.' The drinker, however, will be shocked by the glazed ceramic frog within.

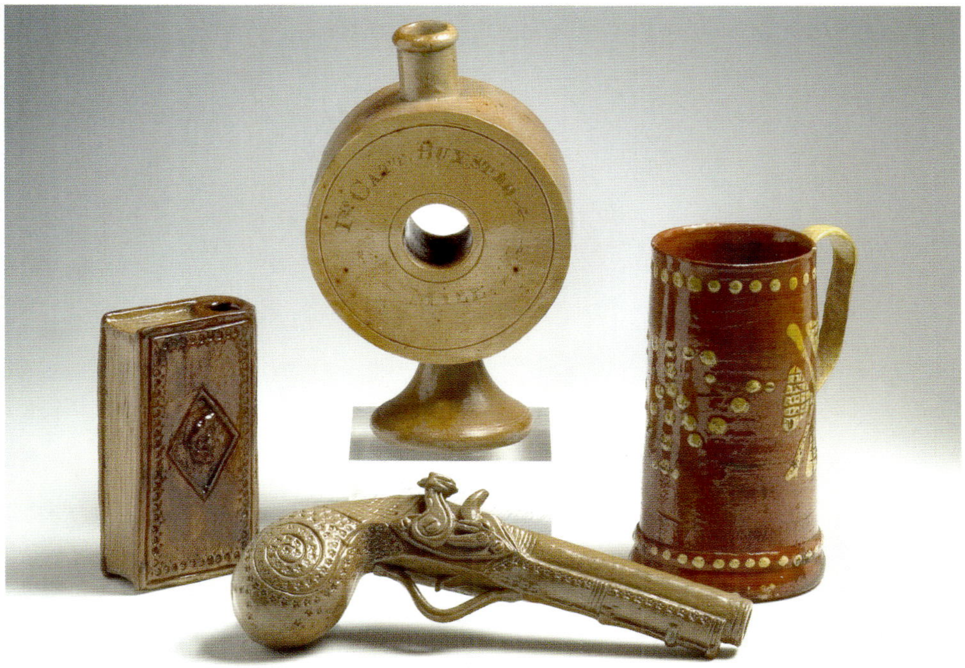

Flask, (1388), c.1820, Scotland?, height: 7.7cm, (3in), salt-glazed stoneware. Flask or hand-warmer modelled as a leather-bound book. Impressed tooling includes a thistle motif, suggesting a Scottish connection.
Flask, (1383), c.1840, London, Lambeth, height: 24.2cm, (9½in), salt-glazed stoneware. Flask marked for Stephen Green, modelled as a pistol with incised and stamped decoration.
Bottle, (1395), c.1790, Staffordshire, height: 21.6cm, (8½in), salt-glazed stoneware. Bottle with mill-wheel shaped body inscribed, 'INO. CATT. BUXSTED MILL'. This watermill beside the River Uck, was first mentioned in 1655. Later owners included John Catt of Robertsbridge, from a well-known milling family. John Catt married Elizabeth Willett of Buxted in 1770 and William, (Henry Willett's father) was their fourth child, born in 1776.
Mug, (1378), c.1840, Sussex, height: 17.2cm, (6¾in), red earthenware. Tall mug, crudely potted and decorated in cream slip with patterns and a monogram, 'WT'.

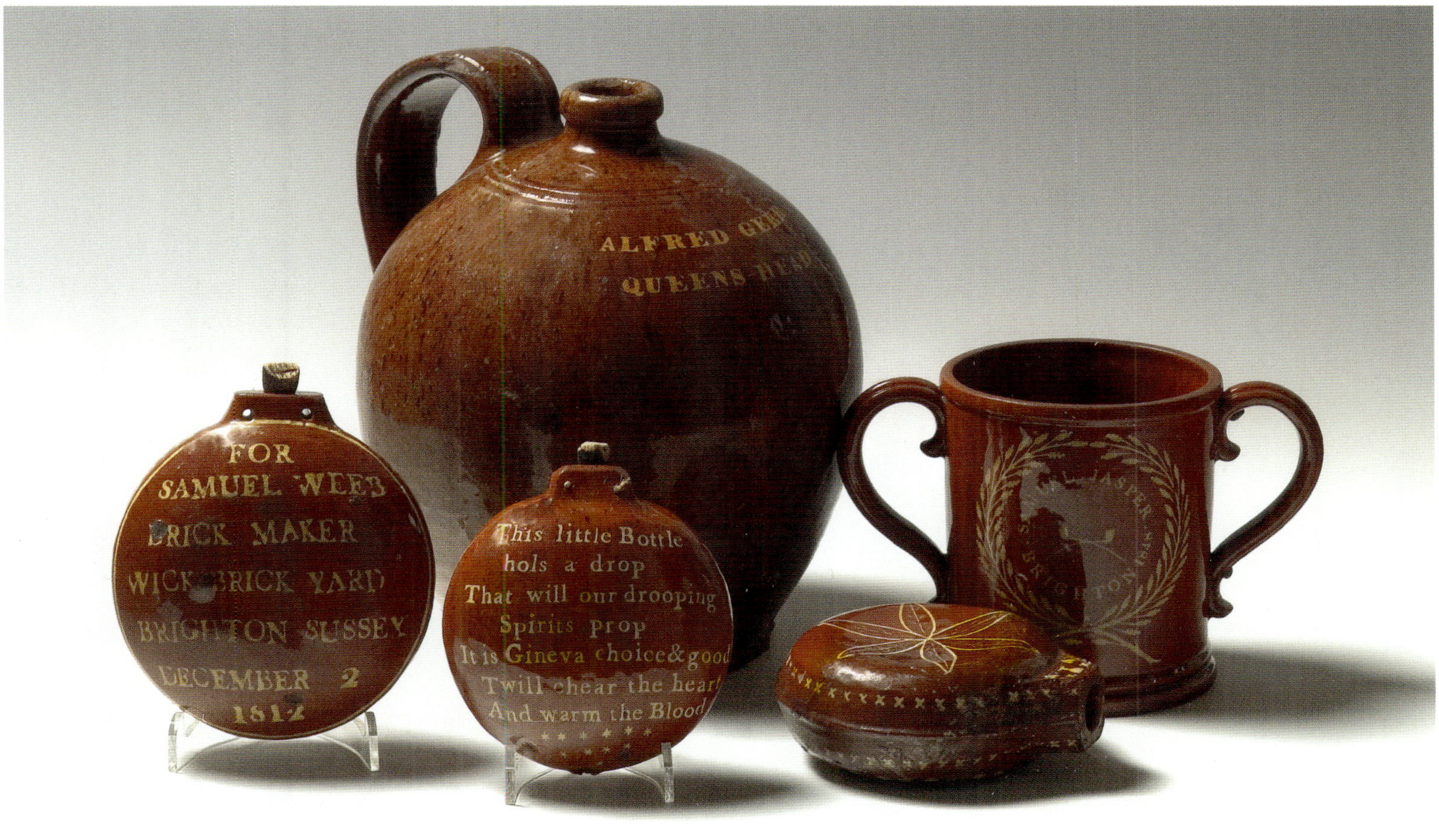

Flask, (1385), 1812, Sussex, height: 11.5cm, (4½in), red earthenware. Pill-shaped flask, inscribed in cream slip, 'FOR / SAMUEL WEEB/ BRICKMAKER / WICK BRICKYARD / BRIGHTON SUSSEX / DECEMBER 2 / 1812, backed by the popular ditty, 'A LITTLE HEALTH / A LITTLE WEALTH / A LITTLE HOUSE TO /LIVE IN'.
Flask, (1386), 1800, Sussex, height: 10.2cm, (4in), red earthenware. Pill-shaped flask inscribed in cream slip, 'This little Bottle / hols [*sic*] a drop / That will our drooping / Spirits prop / It is Gineva [gin] choice and good / T'will cheer the heart / And warm the blood'. Its owner was, 'Fanny Foster / Her Bottle/ Ditchling / 1800'.[21] Probably made at the Chailey, a few miles from Ditchling. Neck pierced like (1385) either to suspend the flask around the neck or to secure the bung.
Bottle, (1379), c.1875, Sussex, height: 21.6cm, (8½in), red earthenware. Balloon-shaped bottle holding up to a gallon, made for tavern keeper, 'ALFRED GEER / QUEENS HEAD'. Geer is a fairly common name in Sussex. An Alfred Charles Geer married at St Peter's Church in Brighton on 10 June 1875, about the right date for this piece.
Flask, (1387), c.1830, Sussex, height: 10.2cm, (4in), red earthenware. Pill-shaped flask decorated in cream slip with a six-petal flower and tiny wine glasses, hearts, diamonds and crosses. Inscribed round the circumference, 'MADE BY JOHN SIGGERY POTTER WISTON SUSSEX'. Wiston is a parish west of Steyning. Apart from Brickfields, this is the only evidence of potting in the area. By the 1830s Siggery had moved to Hurstmonceux.
Two-handled Cup, (1496), 1848, Sussex, height: 15.3cm, (6in), red earthenware. Slip decorated with a wreath of wheat and inscribed, around crossed churchwarden pipes, 'SAMUEL JASPER / BRIGHTON 1848'. On the other side is, 'Success to the Fleece / The Plough and the Flail'.

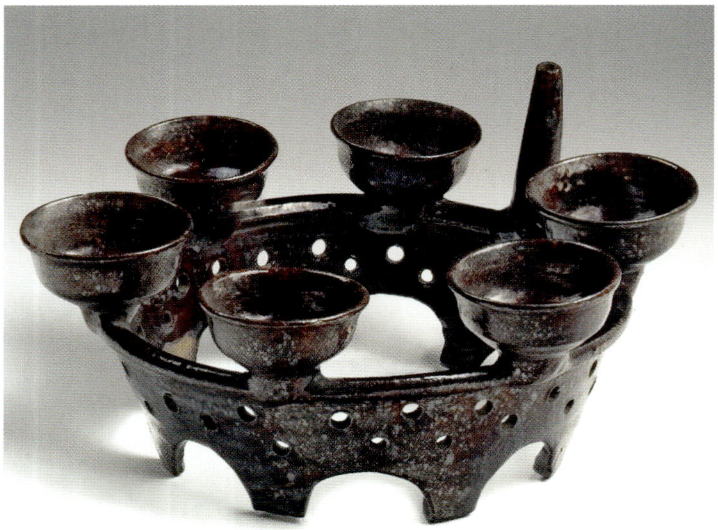

Puzzle or Fuddling Cup, (**1392**), c.1750, height: 14.6cm, (5¾in), earthenware. A rare piece comprising six shallow cups, the size of tea-bowls, pierced through each base and interconnected via a hollow ring and a spout. Fuddling cups are usually formed of three vessels (occasionally more), closely entwined and can be drained simultaneously. The term 'fuddling' suggests rapid inebriation. Michael Archer says, whereas with 'fuddling cups the whole contents were unexpectedly available, puzzle jugs were intended to frustrate the drinker'[22]. He suggests that they were probably made for taverns since very few have dates or initials.

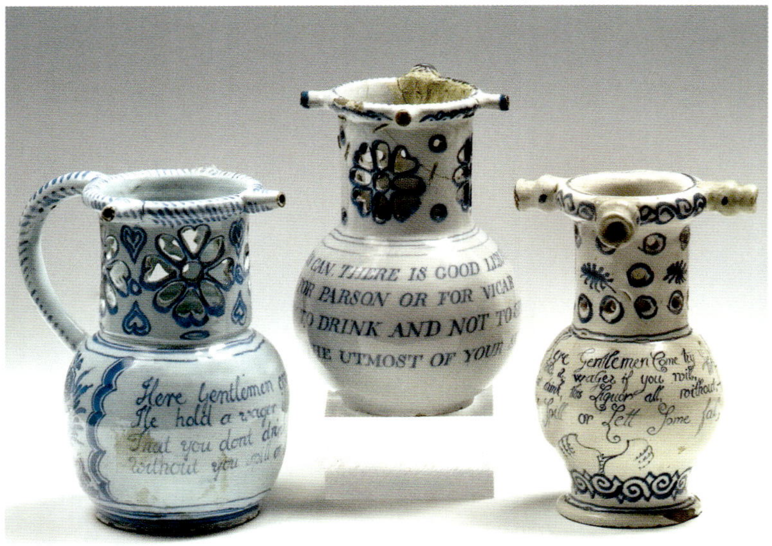

Puzzle Jug, (**1377**), c.1765, Liverpool, height: 20.3cm, (8in), tin-glazed earthenware. Neck pierced with petal-shaped holes and body inscribed, 'Here Gentlemen come try your skill / Ile hold a wager if you will / That you don't drink this Liquor all / Without you Spill or Lett some fall'.
Puzzle Jug, (**1376**), c.1765, Liverpool,height: 19.7cm, (7¾in), tin-glazed earthenware. Neck pierced with with petal-shaped holes and body inscribed, 'IN THIS CAN THERE IS GOOD LIQUOR / FIT FOR PARSON OR FOR VICAR / BUT HOW TO DRINK BUT NOT TO SPILL / WILL TRY THE UTMOST OF YOUR SKILL'.
Puzzle Jug, (**1375**), c.1765, Liverpool,height: 19.7cm, (7¾in), tin-glazed earthenware. Neck pierced with crude holes and decorated with cursive willow trees is inscribed in untidy script, 'Here Gentlemen come try your skill' Though produced in different workshops, the jugs have similar circulatory systems through a hollow handle, partly hollow neck and three nozzles around the rim.

Frog Mugs

Another very popular type of tavern joke was the 'surprise' frog mug. The origins of this bizarre form are obscure but since they are also called 'ague' mugs, it may have been believed that amphibians had medicinal properties. On 16 September 1666, Samuel Pepys recorded a trick played on a drinking companion, 'Pinchbacke did begin a frolick to drink out of a glass with a toad in it ... he did it without harm'.[23] There are examples of frog mugs in other sections of the Willett collection[24] but here they are linked to drinking slogans.

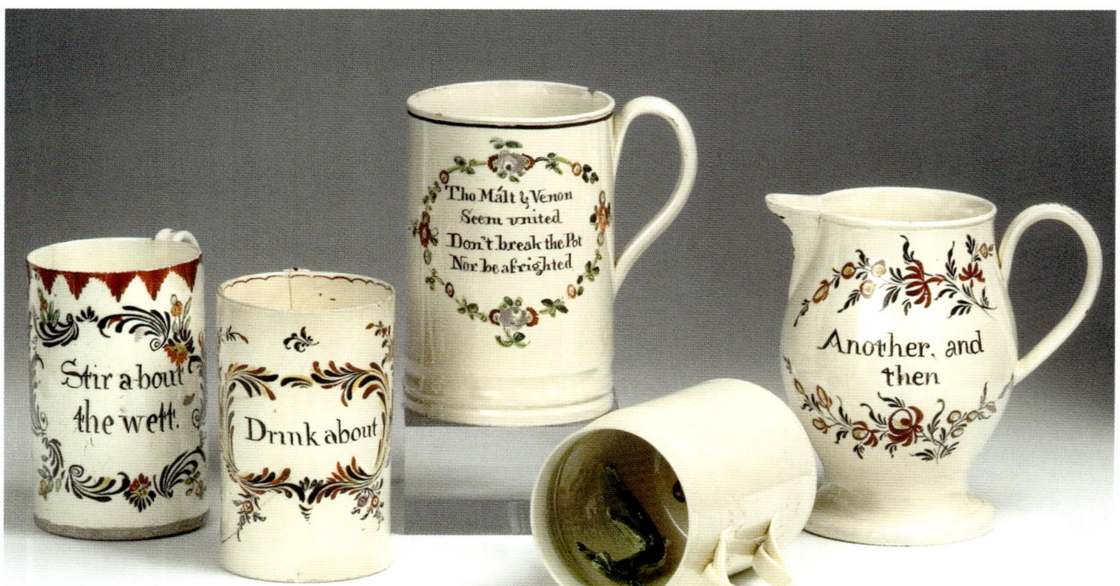

Two Mugs, (**1402&A**), c.1800, Yorkshire, each height: 12.7cm, (5in), enamelled creamware. Painted with bold foliate flourishes and inscribed with brief toasts: 'Stir a-bout / the wett' and 'Drink about'.
Mug, (**1405**), c.1780, Yorkshire or North East, height: 14.6cm, (5¾in), creamware, enamelled and printed. Inscribed within a flower garland, 'Tho Malt & Venon [*sic*] / Seem united / Don't break the Pot / Nor be afrighted'. A large brown-glazed toad inside.
Mug, (**1409**), c.1780, Yorkshire, Leeds, height: 12.1cm, (4¾in), enamelled creamware. Mug has elegant entwined handle with floral terminals. It contains not only a mottled frog but also a green glazed lizard or newt, crawling up the side.
Jug, (**1406**), c.1780, Yorkshire, height: 15.3cm, (6in), enamelled creamware. Inscribed within boldly painted flower sprays, 'Another / and then'.

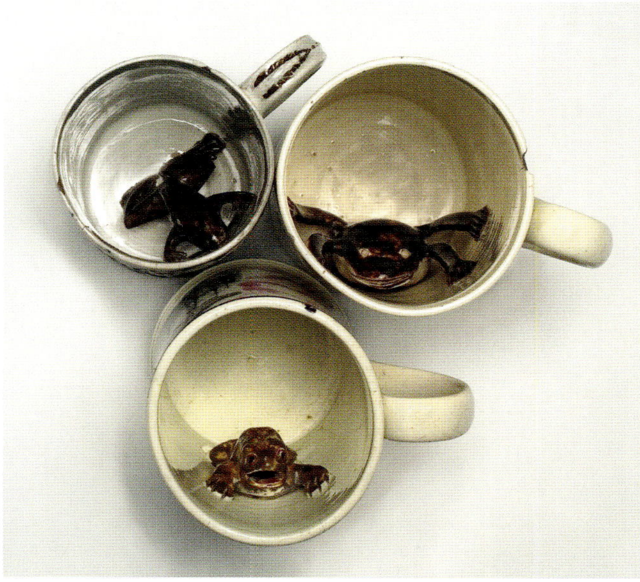

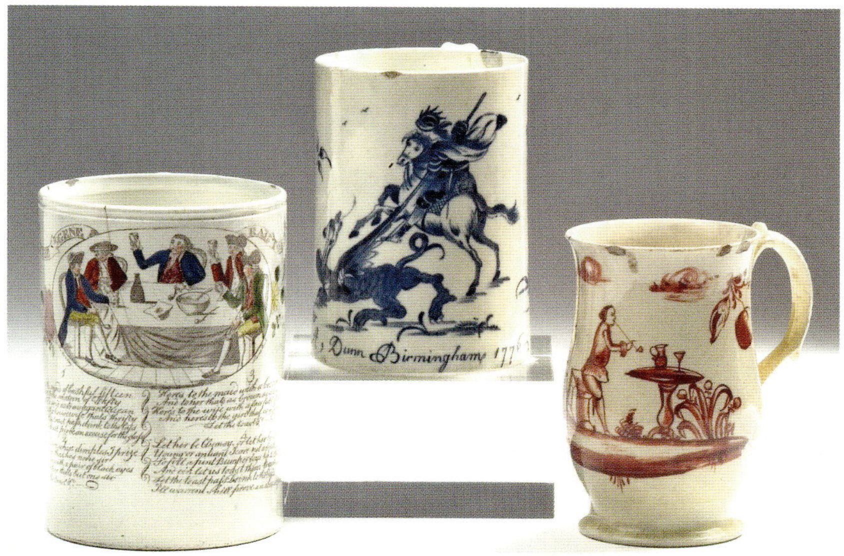

Clockwise from top left:
Mug, (**1331**), c.1800, Staffordshire, height: 11.5cm, (4½in), Prattware. Grey goose mug with large brown frog inside.
Mug, (**1405**), c.1780, Yorkshire, Leeds, height: 14.7cm, (5¾in), creamware, printed and enamelled. Crudely modelled, large brown-glazed toad inside.
Mug, (**394**), c.1805, Newcastle upon Tyne, height: 12.7cm, (5in), pearlware, printed, coloured and lustred. Napoleon mug with small tan-coloured frog inside.

Mug, (**1440**), c.1780, Staffs, Lane End, height: 12.7cm, (5in), pearlware, printed and coloured. Printed with a drinking party, entitled 'THE GENERAL TOAST', signed by John Aynsley. Verses begin, 'Here's to the maid of bashful fifteen / Likewise to the matron of Fifty'.
Mug, (**1404**), 1776, Worcester, height: 11.5cm, (4½in), soft-paste porcelain, painted underglaze. Inscribed, 'A Dunn, Birmingham, 1776', and painted with St George on horseback, killing the dragon.[25] Five mugs and a bowl are recorded with the same decoration, perhaps intended as a punch set. At this time William (publican) and Sarah (inn keeper) Dunn lived at the George Inn, 141-2, Digbeth, with their daughter Ann.[26]
Mug, (**1410**), c.1780, Derbyshire, Cockpit Hill, height: 11.5cm, (4½in), enamelled creamware. Painted with a solitary drinker and pipe-smoker accompanied by a large cherry, suggesting the piece was decorated at Cockpit Hill in Derbyshire.

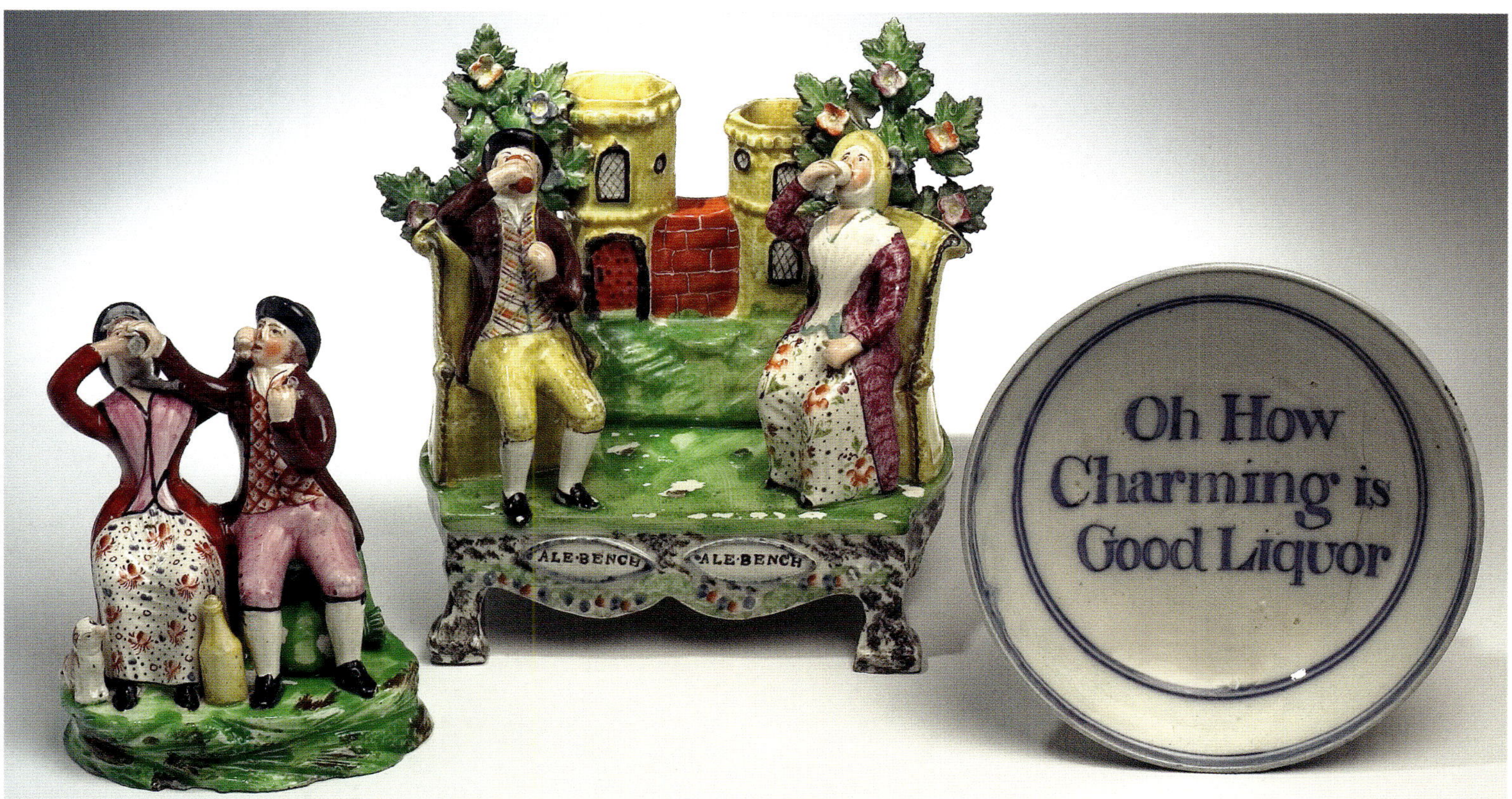

Figure Group, (**1479**), c.1825, Staffordshire, height: 14cm, (5½in), enamelled pearlware. A couple tussle over drink. A woman drains her beaker while a man holds a stick to her throat. A small dog and a bottle are at their feet.
Figure Group, (**1476**), c.1825, Staffordshire, height: 20.3cm, (8in), enamelled pearlware. Table-based spill holder twice titled, 'ALE.BENCH'. A couple (missing their table) draining their glasses.
Bowl, (**1422**), c.1825, Staffordshire, height: 11.5cm, (6½in), pearlware, painted underglaze. Bowl decorated with concentric bands and inscribed, 'Oh How / Charming is / Good Liquor'. Such bowls, often used instead of glasses, can be seen in use at the King of Prussia ale house on a Liverpool delftware tile (299).

Toby Fillpot

The origins of the legend of Toby Fillpot are uncertain and may go back beyond Sir Toby Belch from Shakespeare's *Twelfth Night*. The chubby, good-humoured ale drinker of Francis Fawkes's poem, which begins,

Dear Tom, this brown jug that now foams with mild ale, …
Was once Toby Fillpot, a thirsty old soul,
As e'er drank a bottle or fathom'd a bowl'.[27]

Fawkes was probably inspired both by Uncle Toby in Laurence Sterne's great comic novel, *Tristram Shandy*, (published between 1759 and 1767) and perhaps the Yorkshireman Henry Elwes, who died in 1761, having drunk an estimated 2,000 gallons of beer from such a brown jug. The poem inspired a print issued by Carington Bowles, listed in his catalogue of 1786.[31] The character is a worthy peacetime counterpart of the stalwart patriot John Bull.

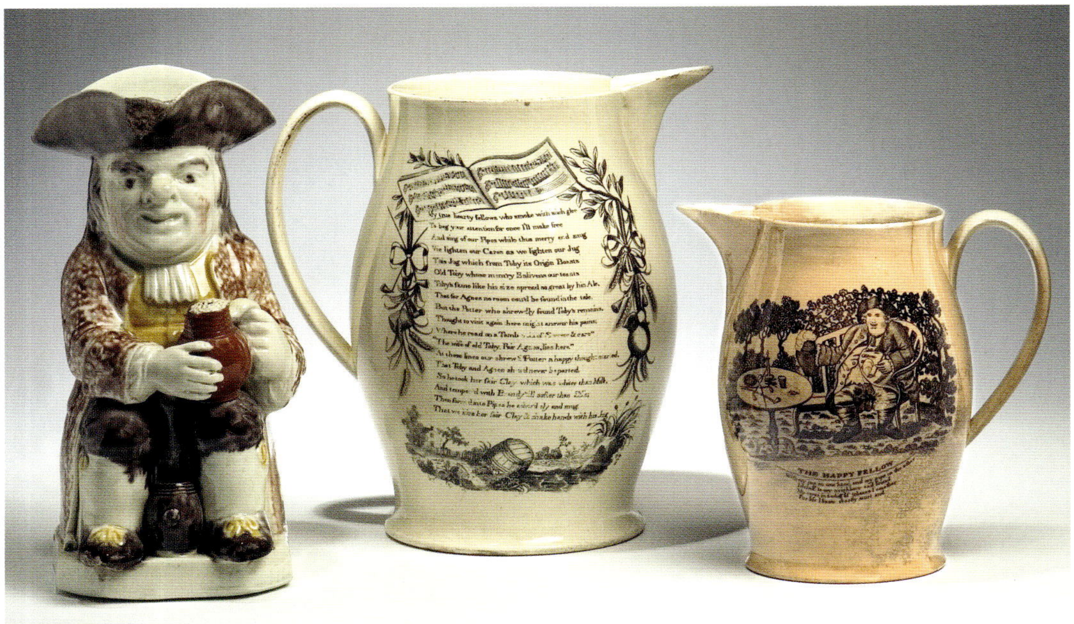

Toby Jug, (**1446**), c.1825, Staffordshire, height: 25.4cm, (10in), lead-glazed earthenware. Toby jug (known as a 'Ralph Wood' type), sponged in metal-oxide colours, holds a brown jug, a cask at his feet.
Jug, (**1438**), c.1790, Staffordshire or Liverpool, height: 24.2cm, (9½in), printed creamware. Jug printed with a music score, garlands and verses about Toby Fillpot, whose remains became clay to make future pottery, 'This jug which from Toby its origin Boasts'.
Jug, (**1434**), c.1790, Staffordshire, height: 17.8cm, (7in), printed creamware. Image of Toby Fillpot, sitting at a table, foaming beer mug in hand, based on Carington Bowles's print of 1786. Inscribed, 'THE HAPPY FELLOW / With my jug in one hand and my pipe in the other / I drink to my neighbour and friend…To my best my friends are free / Free with that and free with me'.

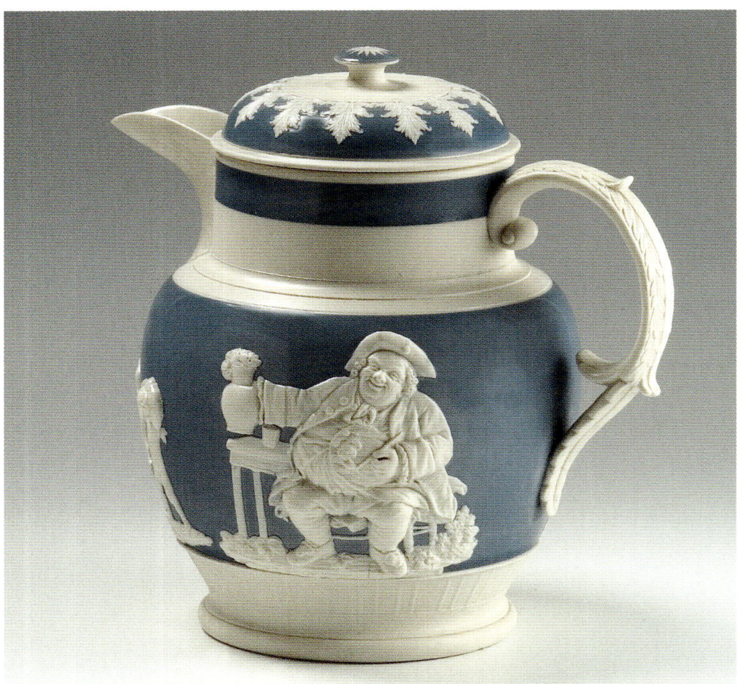

Jug, (**1462**), c.1810, Staffordshire, height: 29.2cm, (11½in), smear-glazed stoneware. Oversized jug, covered in blue slip, applied with three white sprigged vignettes. Relief sprig of Toby Fillpot raising his foaming tankard, based on Carington Bowles's print of 1786. Additional sprigs comprise four Bacchanalian boys with a goat and the sleeping shepherd Endymion and his dog.[28] The sprig moulds probably originated with the Turner family but the subjects are also found on pieces by Ridgway, on a very similar jug marked 'Mist' and by Chetham & Woolley.[29] There is a tantalising reference in the 1899 catalogue to the jug having been owned by George Osborne the 6th Duke of Leeds, who, from 1775 to 1838 was Master of the Horse to George IV.[30]

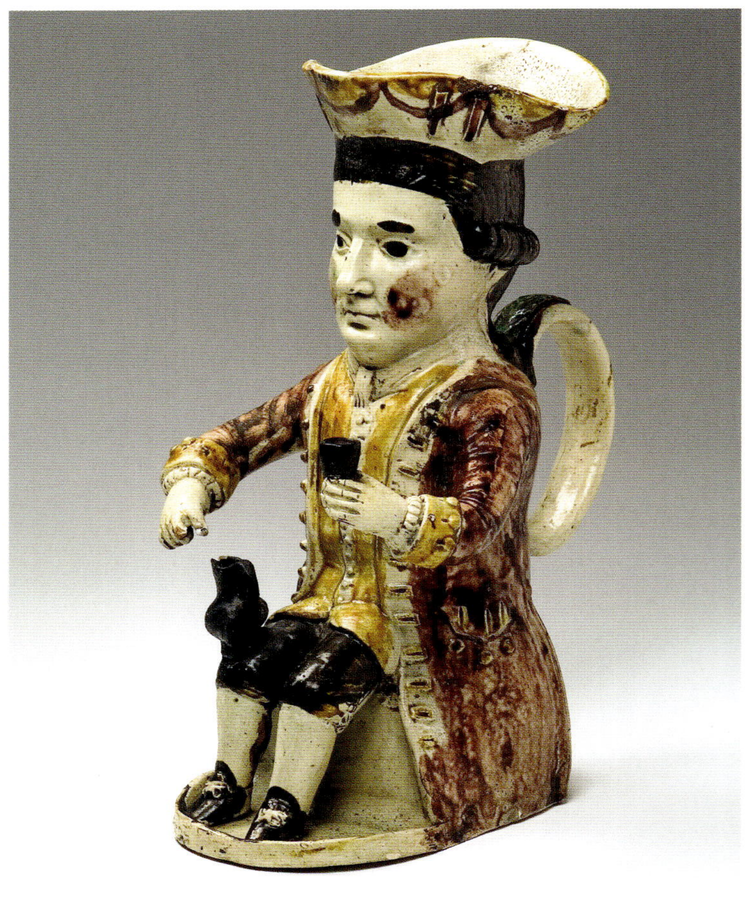

Toby Jug, (**1444**), c.1780, Staffordshire, height: 29.2cm, (11½in), Pratt-coloured pearlware. Thin, seated figure (sometimes known as the 'Thin Man'), amongst the earliest type of toby jug. He holds a glass in one hand and a jug on his knee.

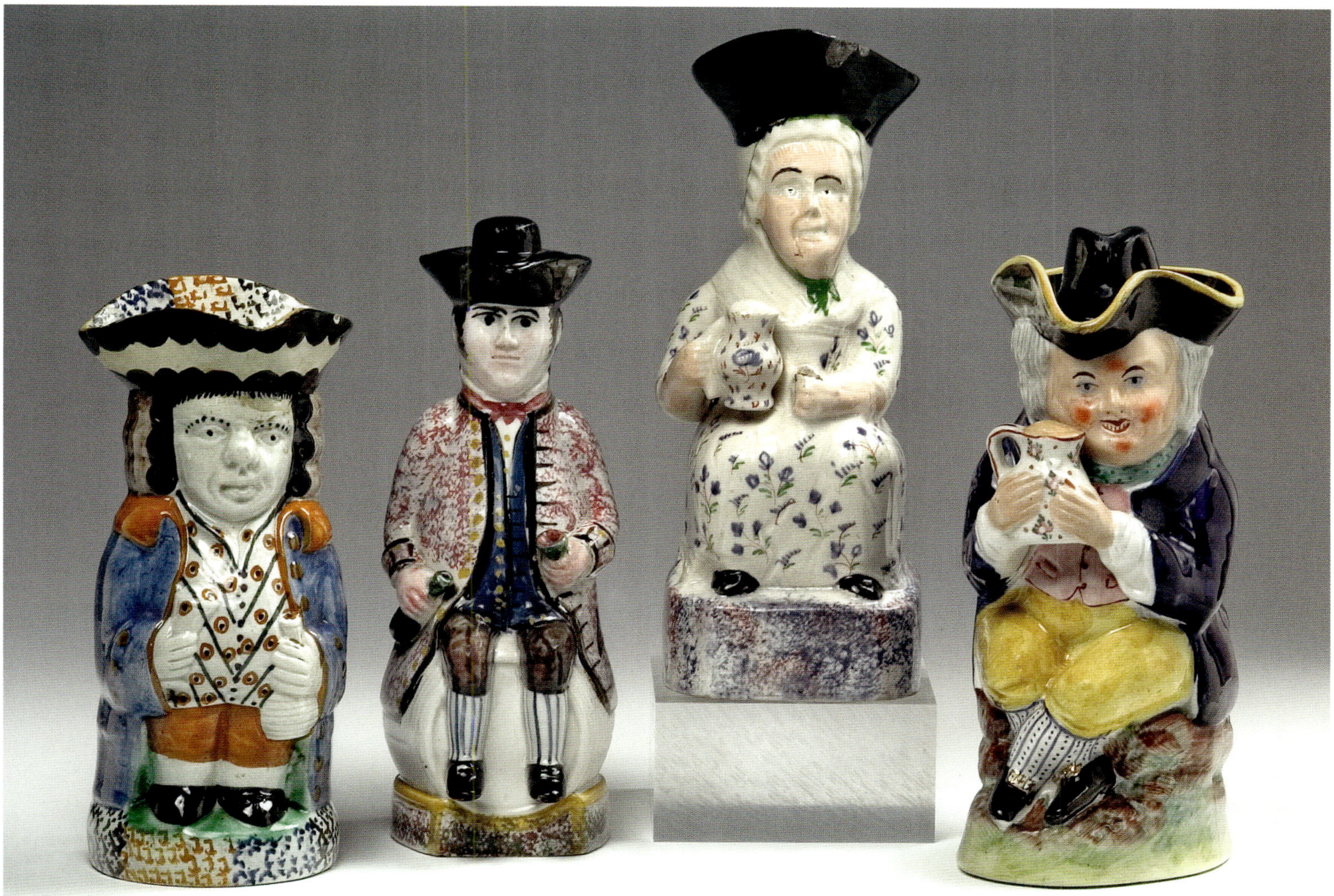

Toby Jug, (**1448**), c.1780, Yorkshire or Scotland, height: 20.3cm, (8in), Pratt-coloured pearlware. Figure, perhaps made at Swillington Bridge, Yorkshire, holds relief-moulded bottle and glass (camouflaged by painted waistcoat).[32]
Toby Jug, (**1453**), c.1780, Yorkshire?, height: 22.9cm, (9in), enamelled pearlware. Figure wears tricorne hat with crown (lid), and long topcoat sponged pink. He sits on an undecorated barrel.

Toby Jug, (**1457**), c.1780, Staffordshire, height: 24.2cm, (9½in), enamelled pearlware. Female Toby (traditionally known as 'Martha Gunn' after the Brighton bathing woman), is marked T. Burnell.
Toby Jug, (**1452**), c.1840, Staffordshire, height: 22.9cm, (9in), enamelled pearlware. Figure wears tricorne hat with crown (lid), and holds patterned jug.

Toby Jug, (**1449**), c.1800, Staffordshire, height: 24.2cm, (9½in), enamelled pearlware. Figure twists on his barrel seat, one foot on his dog, known as 'Admiral Lord Howe' type of Toby.
Toby Jug, (**1445**), c.1780, Staffordshire, height: 24.8cm, (9¾in), earthenware, lead-glazed and oxide-coloured. Skinny figure smoking a pipe sometimes known as the 'Thin Man'.
Toby Jug, (**1447**), c.1820, Staffordshire, height: 27.3cm, (10¾in), enamelled pearlware. Standing figure, holding a mug and a pipe, known as 'the Hearty Good Fellow', from one of several poems associated with Toby Fillpot.

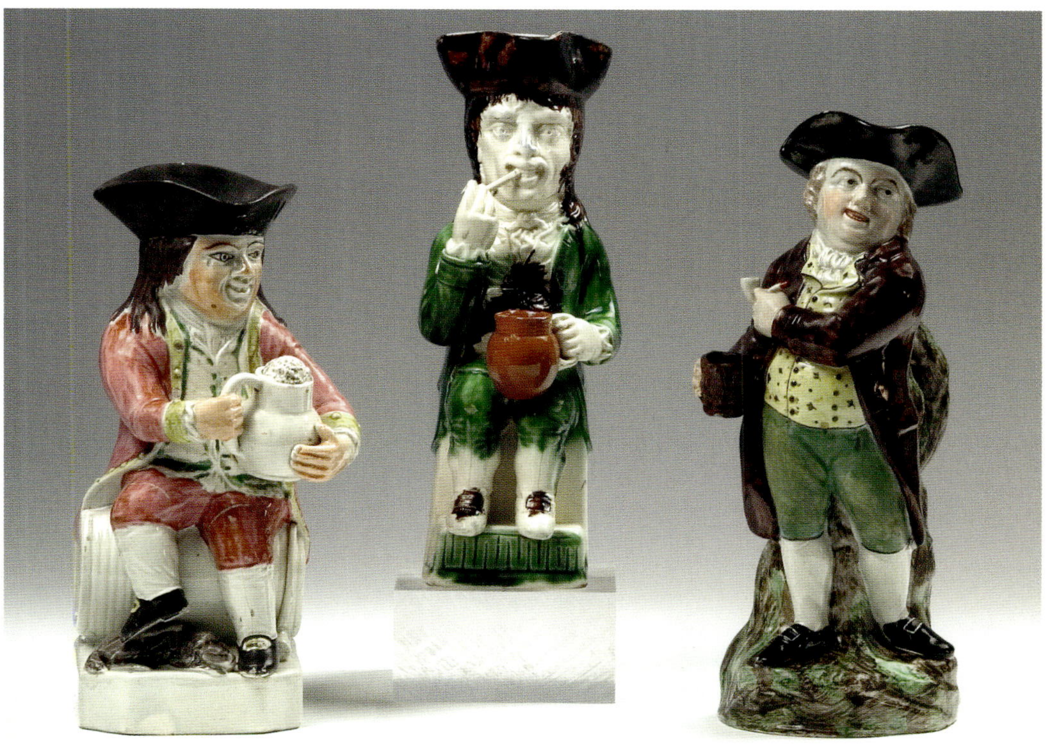

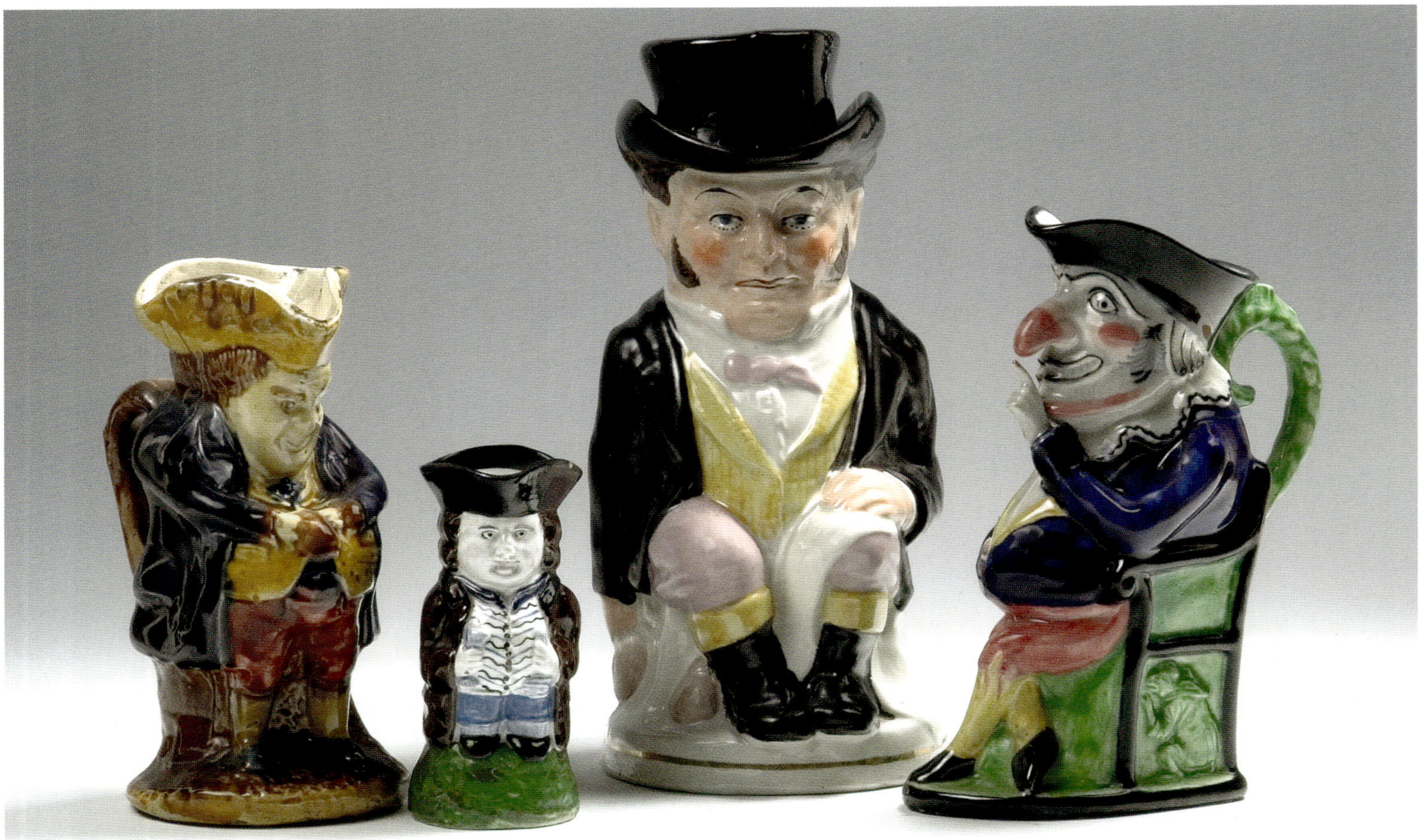

Toby Jug, (**1458**), c.1800, Staffordshire, height: 19.1cm, (7½in), enamelled pearlware. Figure crudely modelled as a standing figure with a hunched back.
Toby Jug, (**1450**), c.1820, Staffordshire, height: 12.7cm, (5in), Pratt-coloured pearlware. Small simplified form of Toby.

Toby Jug, (**1451**), c.1880, Staffordshire, height: 27.3cm, (10¾in), enamelled earthenware. Figure, described as 'John Bull', wears top hat.
Toby Jug, (**1454**), c.1820, Staffordshire, height: 20.3cm, (8in), enamelled pearlware. Jug modelled as figure of Punch sitting on a chair (see 1226).

Smoking

Despite James I's *Counterblaste against Tobacco*, published in 1604, smoking tobacco has been endemic in western society until the present. A group of novelty pipes modelled as sailors has already been discussed.[33] These and other pipes from this section of Willett's collection were illustrated in *The Connoisseur* in 1906.[34] Many of the images of smokers demonstrate that smoking tobacco was inseparable from drinking alcohol. Smoking could be an excitably social occupation or a solitary one. Tables are littered with long-stemmed churchwarden pipes, together with bottles, jugs, glasses and mugs.

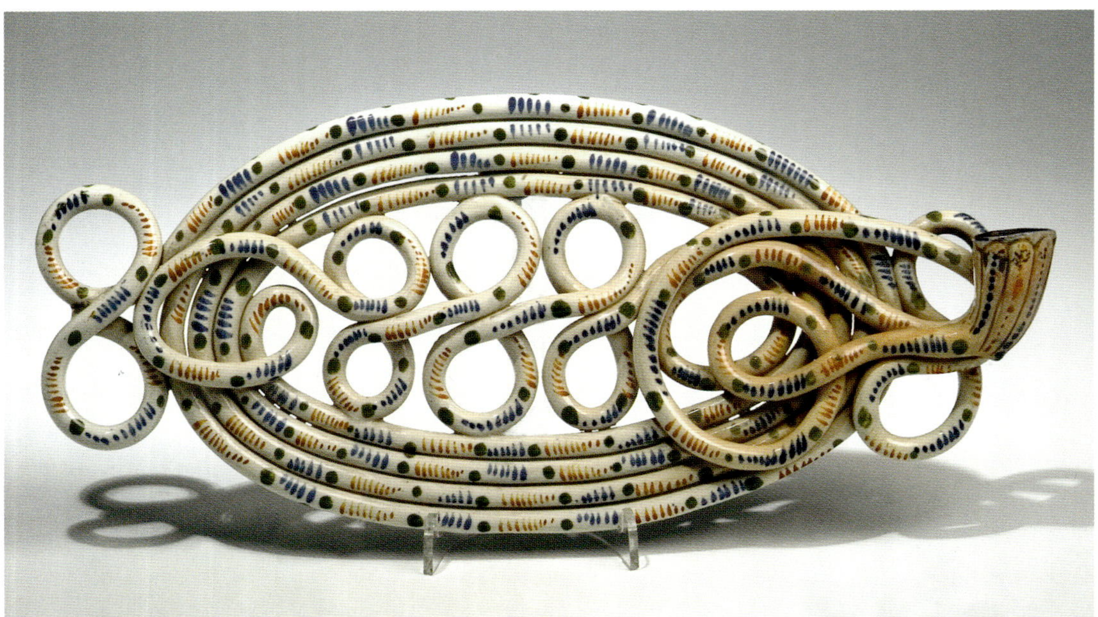

Pipe, (1500), Devon, length: 34.3cm, (13½in), Pratt-coloured pearlware. A novelty pipe, composed of metres of clay tubing, 'curiously twisted' (a little like that of a stopped brass instrument). Such pieces long thought to be Welsh but excavations on Indeo Pottery site, near Bovey Tracey, have revealed similar shards.[35]

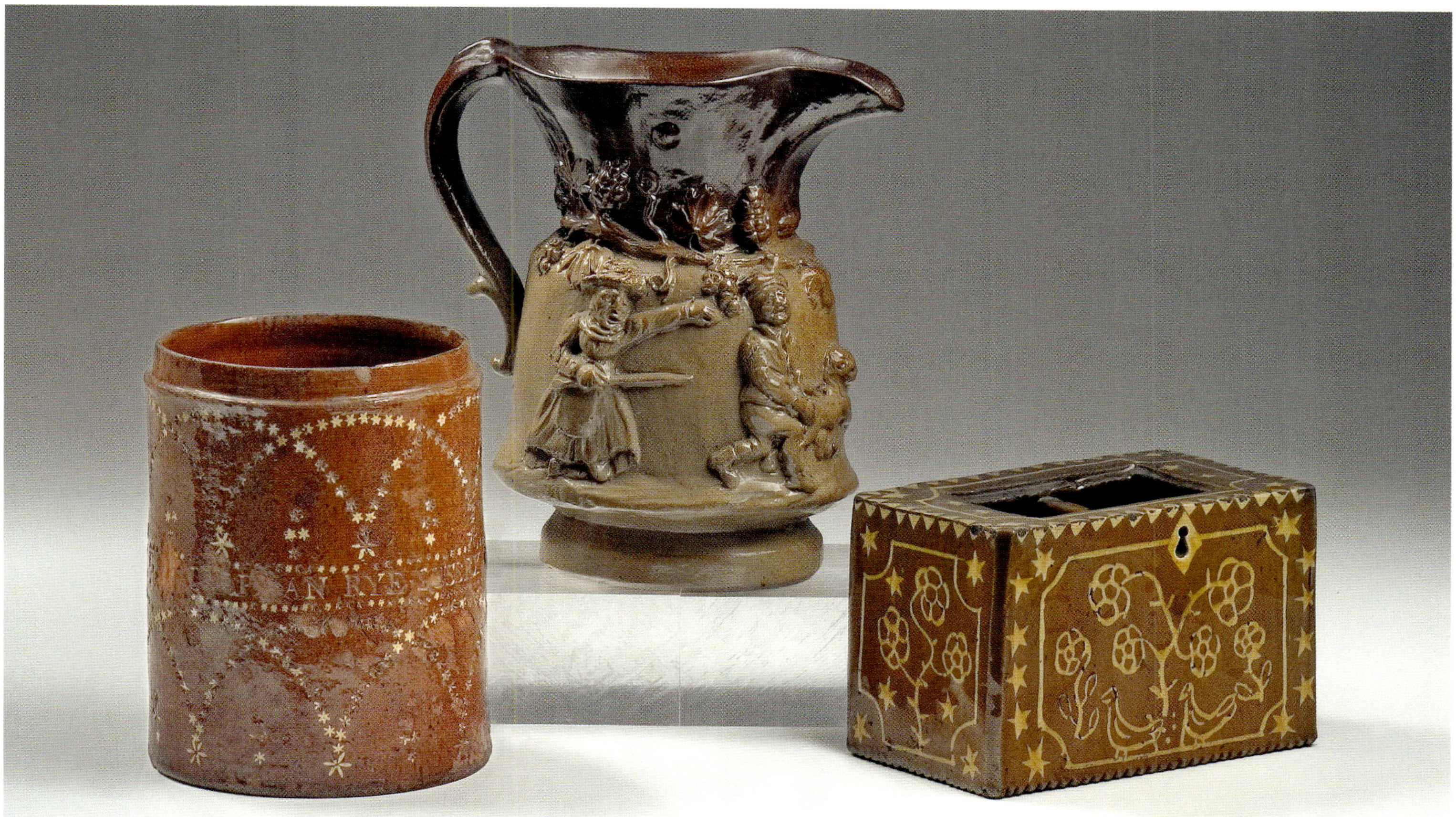

Tobacco Jar, (**1495**), 1808, Sussex, height: 15.9cm, (6¼in), red earthenware. Inlaid in cream slip with arcs of stars and barely legible inscription, 'G & E CHAPMAN RYE SUSSEX, APRIL 22 1808'. It was probably made for a tavern by Meeds Pottery, Burgess Hill.
Jug, (**1459**), c.1850, London?, height: 20.3cm, (8in), salt-glazed stoneware. Heavy, stoneware jug moulded with vines and comic characters; a woman with a pointed weapon or umbrella chases a man with a dog.
Tea Canister, (**1506**), c.1830, Sussex, height: 10.2cm, (4in), red earthenware. Brick-shaped canister (now lacks a lid) with two compartments, inlaid with flowers and birds in cream slip.

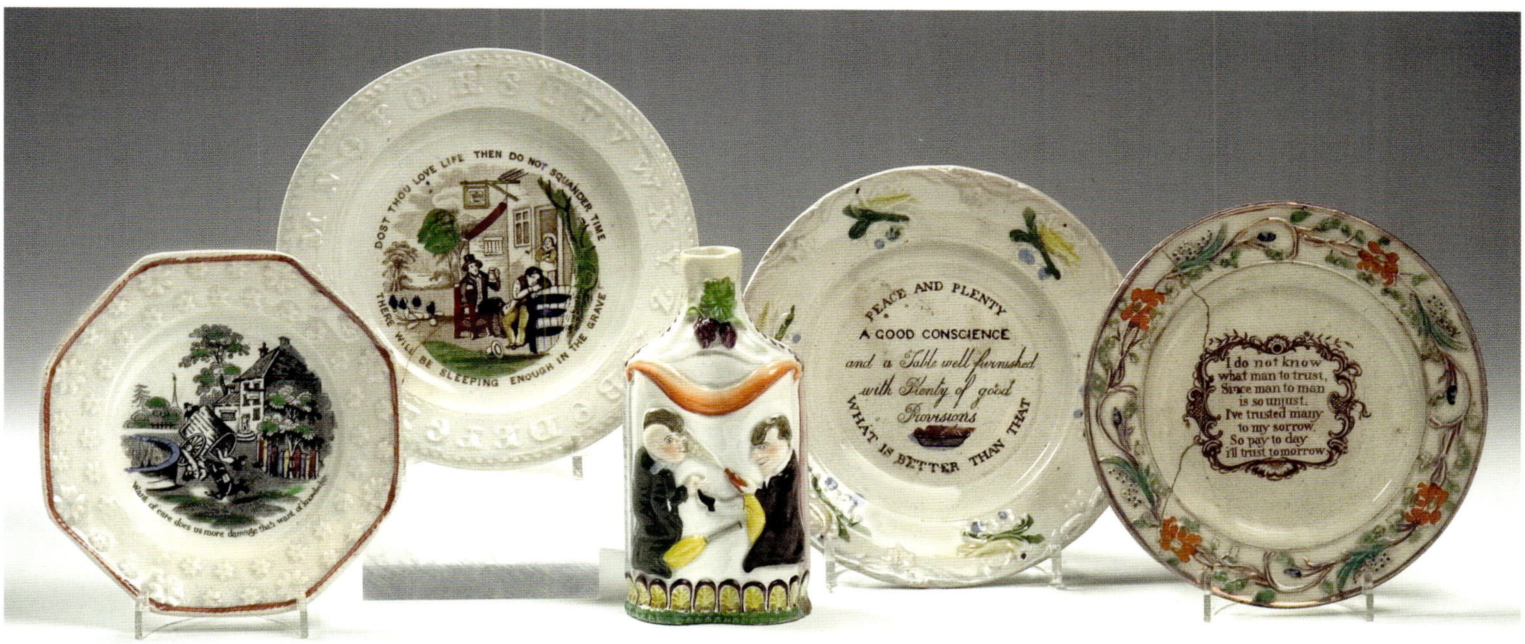

Nursery Plate, (**1509**), c.1850, Staffordshire, diameter: 18.4cm, (7¼in), earthenware, printed and coloured. Printed with illustration of a wagon overturning and one of, 'Poor Richard's Sayings', inscribed, 'Want of care does us more damage than want of knowledge'
Nursery Plate, (**1508**), c.1850, Staffordshire, diameter: 15.3cm, (6in), earthenware, printed and coloured. Printed with illustration to one of, 'Poor Richard's Sayings', exhorting a sleeping youth not to, 'squander time / There will be sleeping enough in the grave'.
Bottle, (**1441**), c.1800, Staffordshire, height: 15.3cm, (6in), enamelled pearlware. Relief-moulded with grotesque figure kicking another with his wooden leg while his opponent aims an opened bottle of fizzy liquid into his face. Adapted from tooth-drawing scene by Tim Bobbin, 'the Lancashire Hogarth'.[36]
Plate, (**1466**), c.1840, Staffordshire, diamter: 18.4cm, (7¼in), earthenware, printed and coloured. Printed with homily, 'Peace and Plenty / A good Conscience / What is better than that'.
Plate, (**1467**), c.1840, Staffordshire, diameter: 17.2cm, (6¾in), earthenware, printed, coloured and lustred. Printed with variant on the Landlord's Caution.

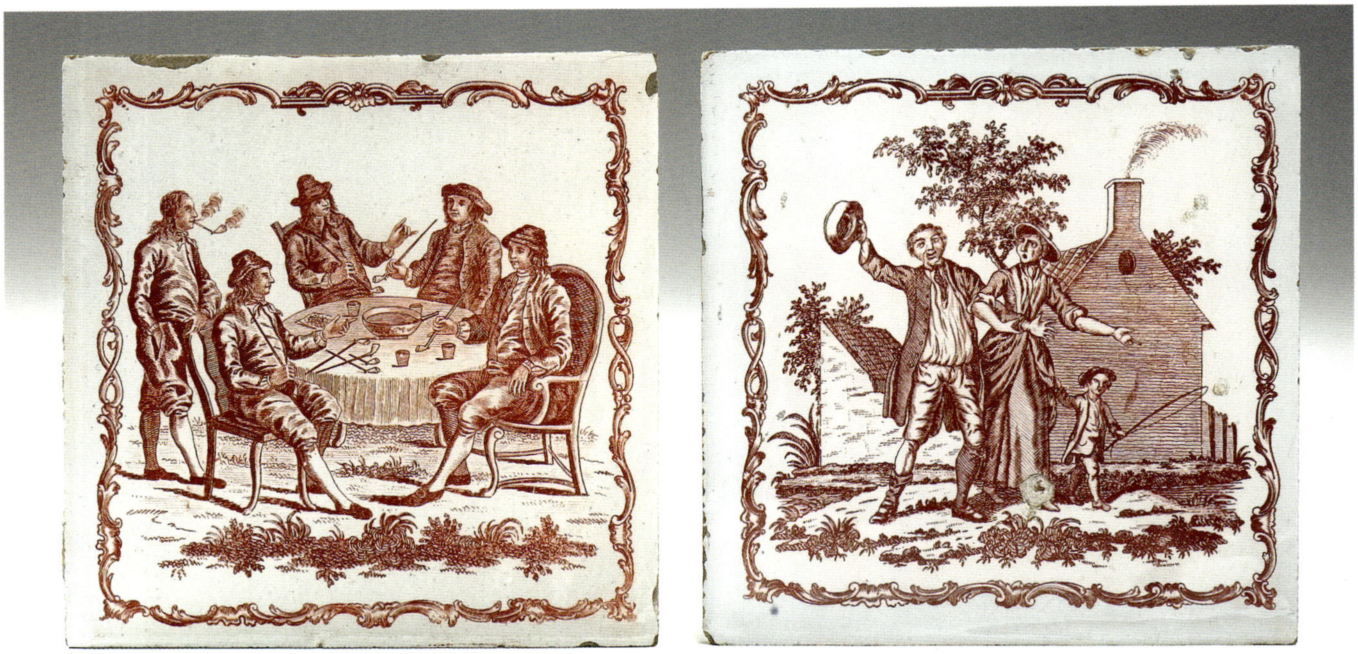

Tile, (**1492**), c.1770, Liverpool, height: 12.7cm, (5in), red-brown printed, tin-glazed earthenware. Printed by Sadler and Green, with a pipe and punch party.
Tile, (**1491**), c.1780, Liverpool, height: 12.7cm, (5in), red-brown printed, tin-glazed earthenware. Printed by Sadler and Green with drunk and disorderly man, being led home from the inn by his angry wife.

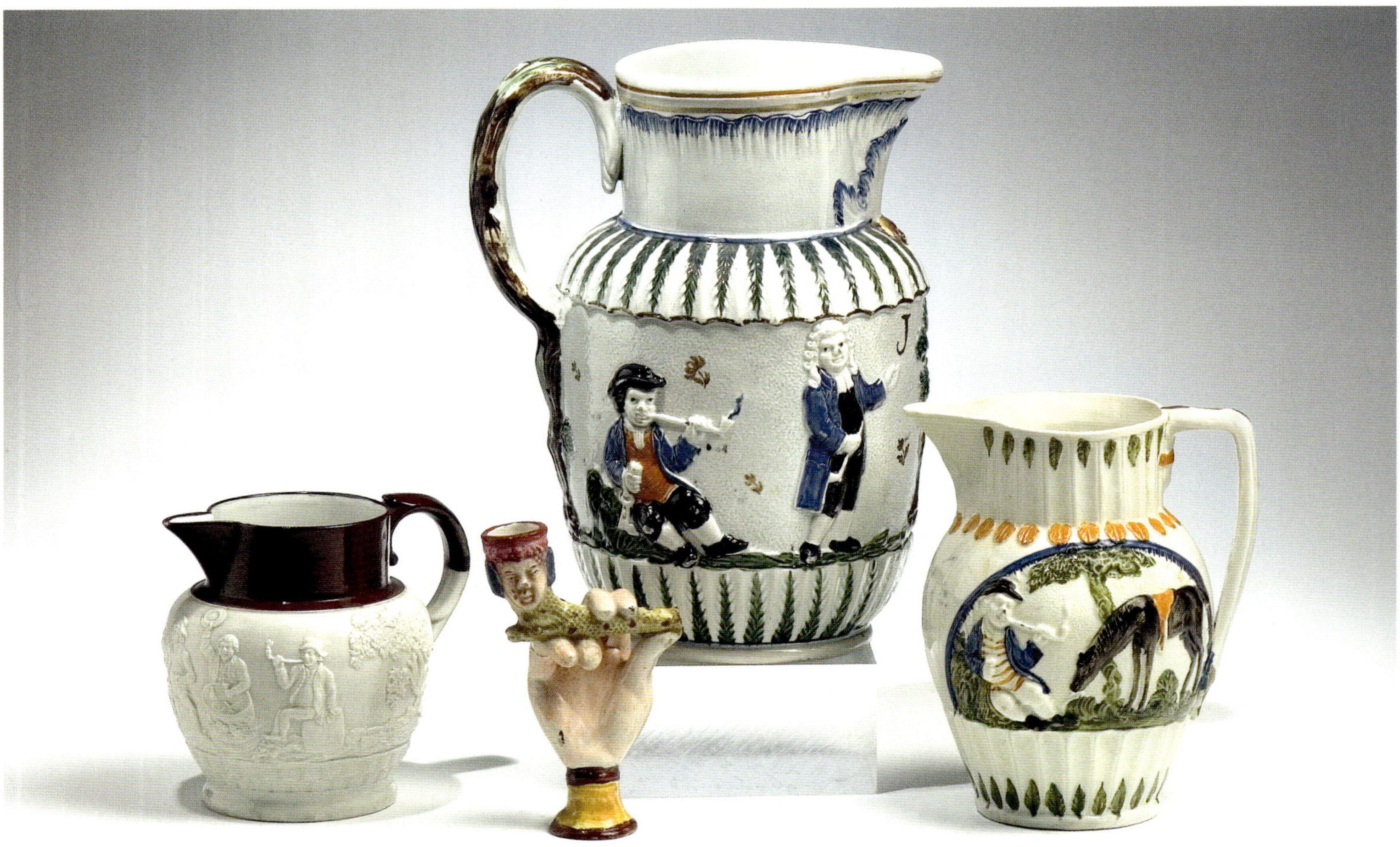

Jug, (**1461**), c.1800, Staffordshire, Longport, height: 11.5cm, (4½in), smear-glazed and enamelled stoneware. Relief-moulded jug made by Davenport, with figures drinking and smoking pipes.
Pipe, (**1498**), c.1850, Staffordshire, height: 5.1cm, (2in), enamelled pearlware. Novelty pipe, bowl modelled as a human head, supported by a larger hand.

Jug, (**806**), c.1790, Scotland, height: 22.9cm, (9in), Prattware. Relief-moulded with pipe-smoking clergymen and initials, 'JE'. Probably made c.1790 in Glasgow, where very similar shards have been found.
Jug, (**1460**), c.1830, Staffordshire, height: 15.3cm, (6in), Prattware. Relief-moulded with resting smoker and his horse.

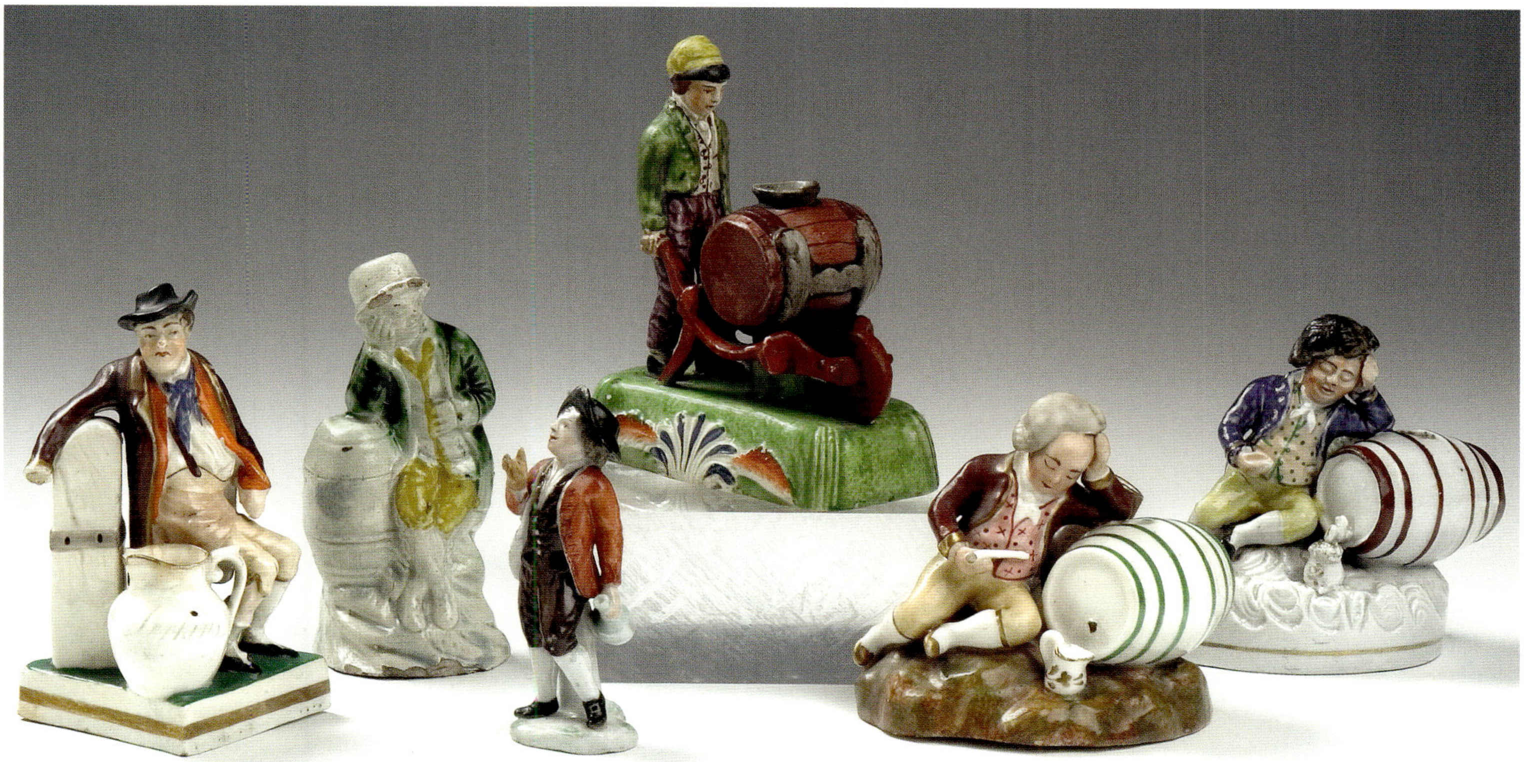

Figure, (1488), c.1810, Staffordshire, height: 12.7cm, (5in), enamelled soft-paste porcelain. Dishevelled man sits leaning on an upright post a large jug inscribed 'Perkins & Co.' beside him.
Figure, (1487), c.1800, Staffordshire, height: 12.7cm, (5in), coloured pearlware. Figure stands resting his elbow on an upright barrel.
Figure, (1484), c.1800, Staffordshire, height: 10.2cm, (4in), enamelled soft-paste porcelain. Boy in a red coat carries a large wine bottle.
Figure, (1362), c.1830, Staffordshire, height: 12.7cm, (5in), enamelled pearlware. Boy pushes a barrel on a wheelbarrow.
Two Inkstands, (1489 + 1490), c.1840, Staffordshire, each height: 10.8cm, (4¼in), enamelled earthenware. Two humorous, sleepy figures, their wigs askew, leaning on the barrels from which they have been drinking.[37]

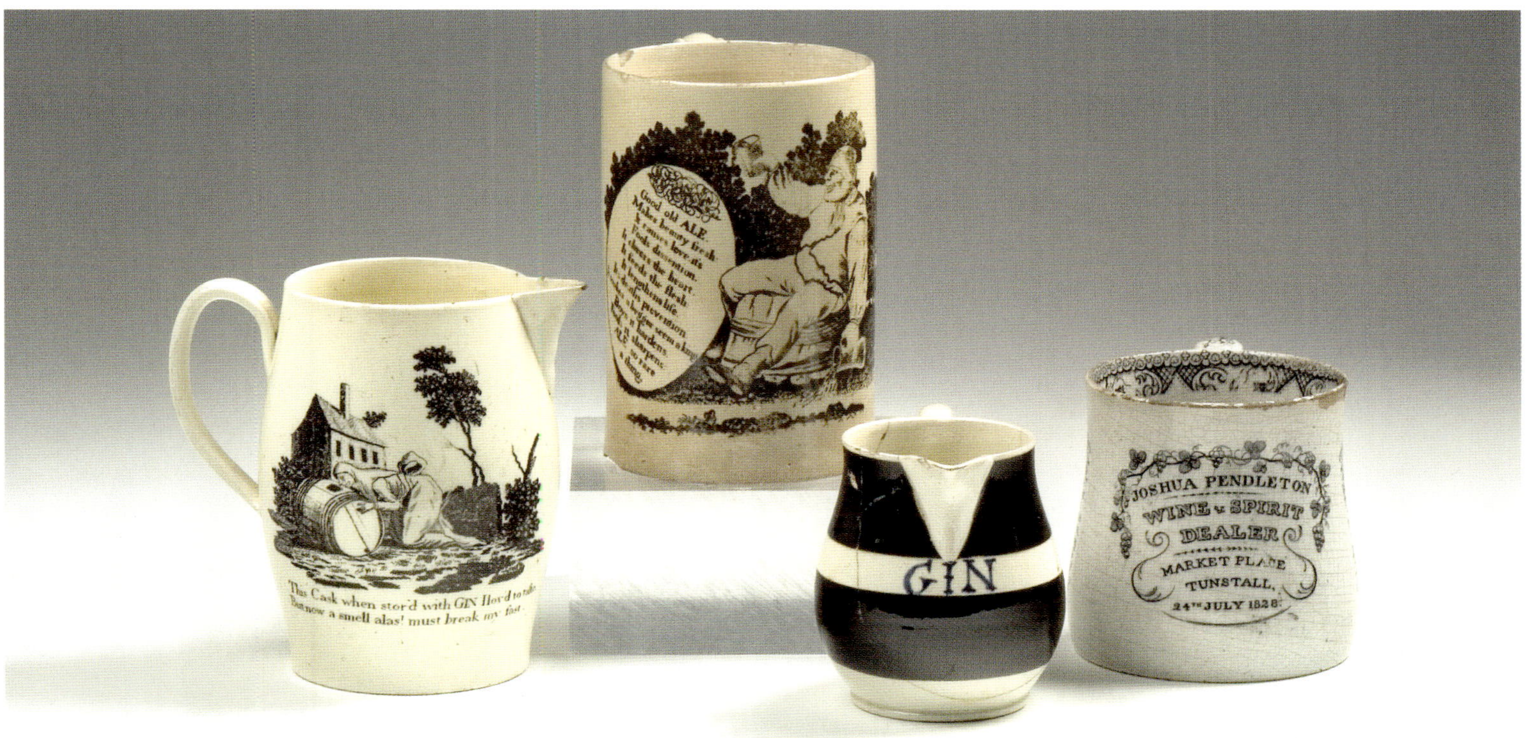

Jug, (1424), c.1790, Staffordshire, height: 11.5cm, (4½in), printed creamware. Printed with kneeling, hooded figure sniffing the bung hole of an empty barrel, 'This cask when stor'd with GIN I lov'd to taste / but now a smell, alas! must break my fast'. Reverse inscribed, 'Good liquor I can hold / Will make a coward bold' .
Mug, (1442), c.1790, Staffordshire, height: 12.7cm, (5in), printed creamware. A drinker spills both a glass and tankard, saluting, 'Good old ALE … It cheers the heart. / It feeds the flesh: / It lengthens life / It's death's prevention'.
Jug, (1400), c.1800, Staffordshire, height: 8.3cm, (3¼in), enamelled creamware. Brown-striped jug inscribed in blue 'GIN'.
Mug, (1412), c.1830, Staffordshire, height: 8.3cm, (3¼in), printed earthenware. Squat mug printed with doggerel verses for 'JOSHUA PENDLETON / WINE & SPIRIT DEALER' of Market Place, Tunstall, 24 July, 1828. Pendleton does not appear in Pigot's Directory of businesses in the Potteries for 1828-29; perhaps he had just arrived.

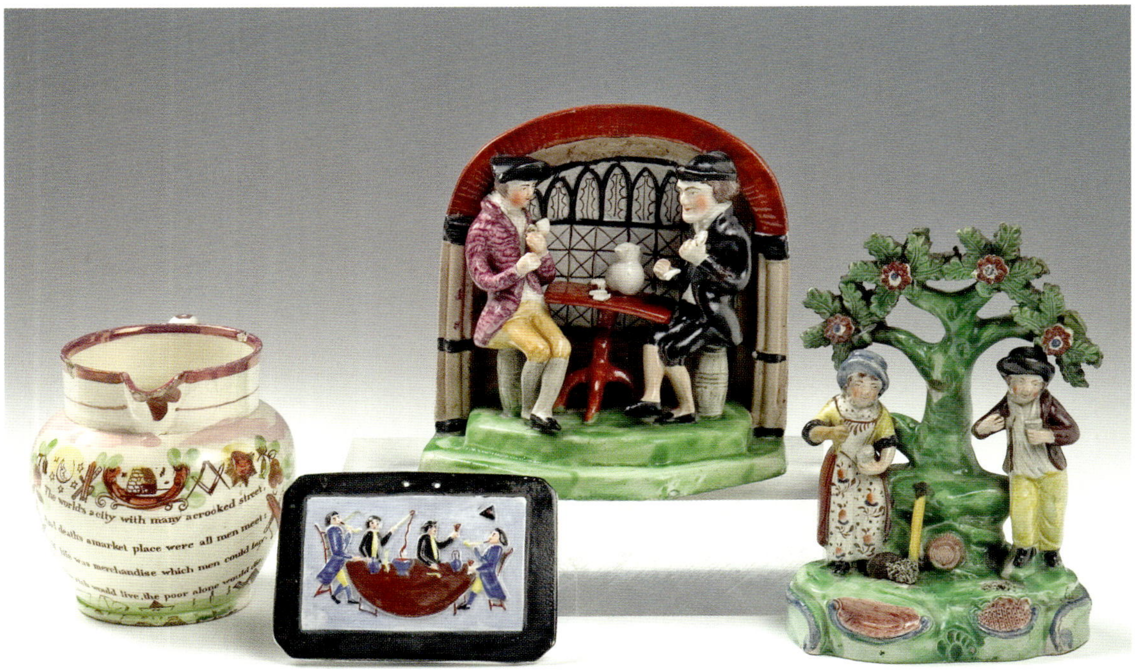

Jug, (**1443**), c.1820, Sunderland, height: 11.5cm, (4½in), pearlware, printed, coloured and lustred. Made at Lowlights Pottery, inscribed, among Masonic symbols, 'The world's a city with many crooked streets / And death's a market place where all men meet / If life were merchandise which men could buy / The rich would live, the poor alone would die'.
Plaque, (**1493**), c.1820, Staffordshire, height: 8.9cm, (3½in), enamelled pearlware. Relief-moulded with drinking party based on Hogarth's *A Midnight Modern Conversation*.
Figure Group, (**1475**), c.1820, Staffordshire, height: 15.3cm, (6in), enamelled pearlware. Dish-backed group features Dr Syntax playing cards with a friend in the tavern 'snug'.[38]
Figure Group, (**1486**), c.1820, Staffordshire, height: 17.8cm, (7in), enamelled pearlware. A man and woman hold beakers, a cask at their feet, as they pause from their work in the countryside.

The Campaign against Alcohol

'Teetotal' was the term adopted in the 1830s by those who limited themselves to drinking tea and water rather than beer, wine and spirits. Tea was an expensive novelty in the seventeenth and early eighteenth centuries when its consumption was limited to the affluent classes, who were often painted taking tea. By 1820 tea was widely available and cheap enough to be drunk by everyone. Tea houses and tea shops were set up by anti-alcohol campaigners, as alternatives to the pub. In addition technical advances enabled the provision of clean water supplies and public drinking fountains were built throughout the country.

Father Theobald Mathew (1790-1856)

In 1838 Father Mathew, an Irish Capuchin friar, agreed to lead the Teetotal Society of Cork. Cork was a centre for brewing and distilling, where many of the social problems of the poor could be linked to excessive drinking. Having travelled a good deal in Ireland administering the Pledge to abstain from alcohol, Mathew made successful visits to Scotland in 1842 and England in 1843. His controversial visit to the United States in 1849 was very taxing and he stopped travelling. W.M. Thackeray, who met him in 1842, described him as 'a stout, handsome, honest-looking man'.[39]

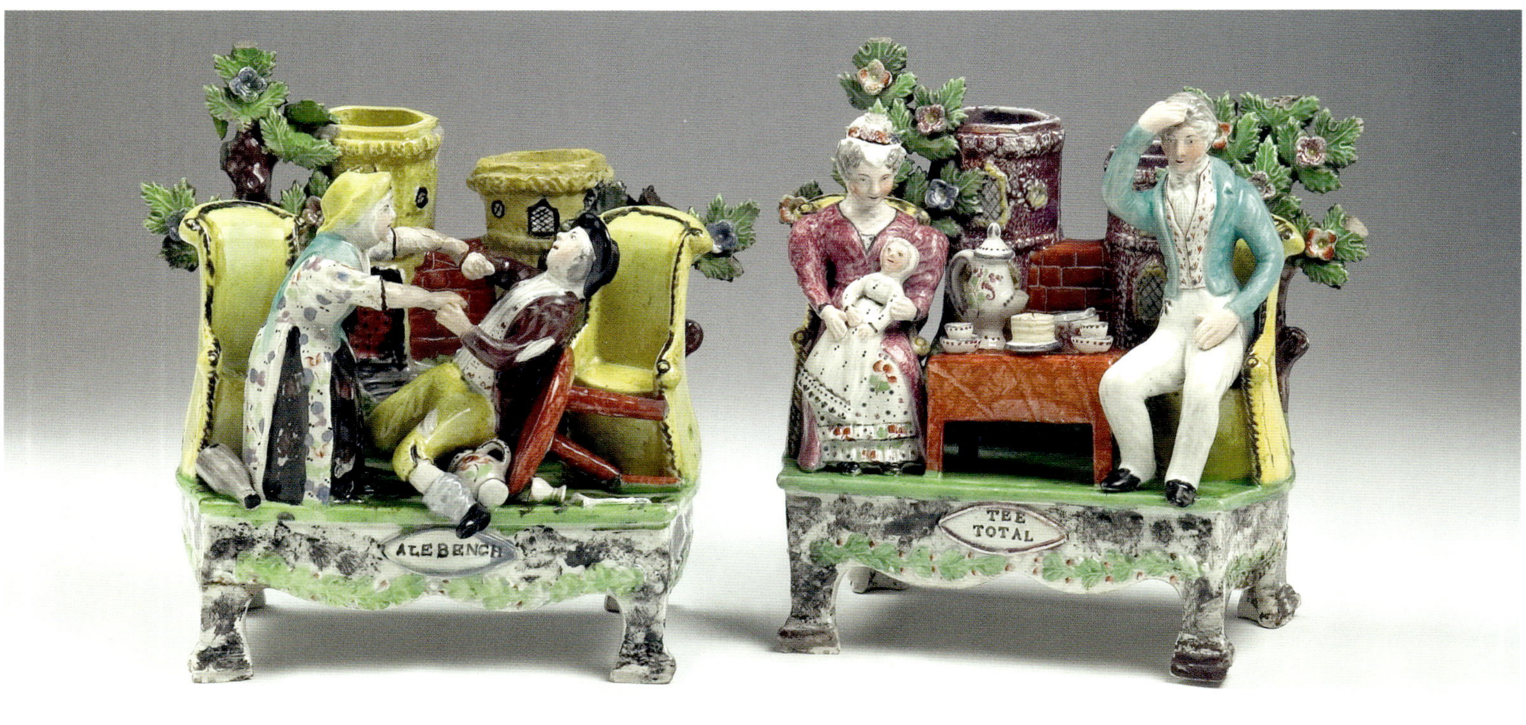

Two Figure Groups, (**1477 + 1521**), c.1830, Staffordshire, each height: 20.3cm, (8in), enamelled pearlware. Two table-based spill-holder groups contrast a destructive life of inebriation with the prosperity of those who have taken the pledge to abstain from alcohol. 'ALEBENCH' shows a drunken couple fighting, breaking the furniture and crockery. The affluent 'TEE.TOTAL' family is well dressed and calmly consumes tea and cake.

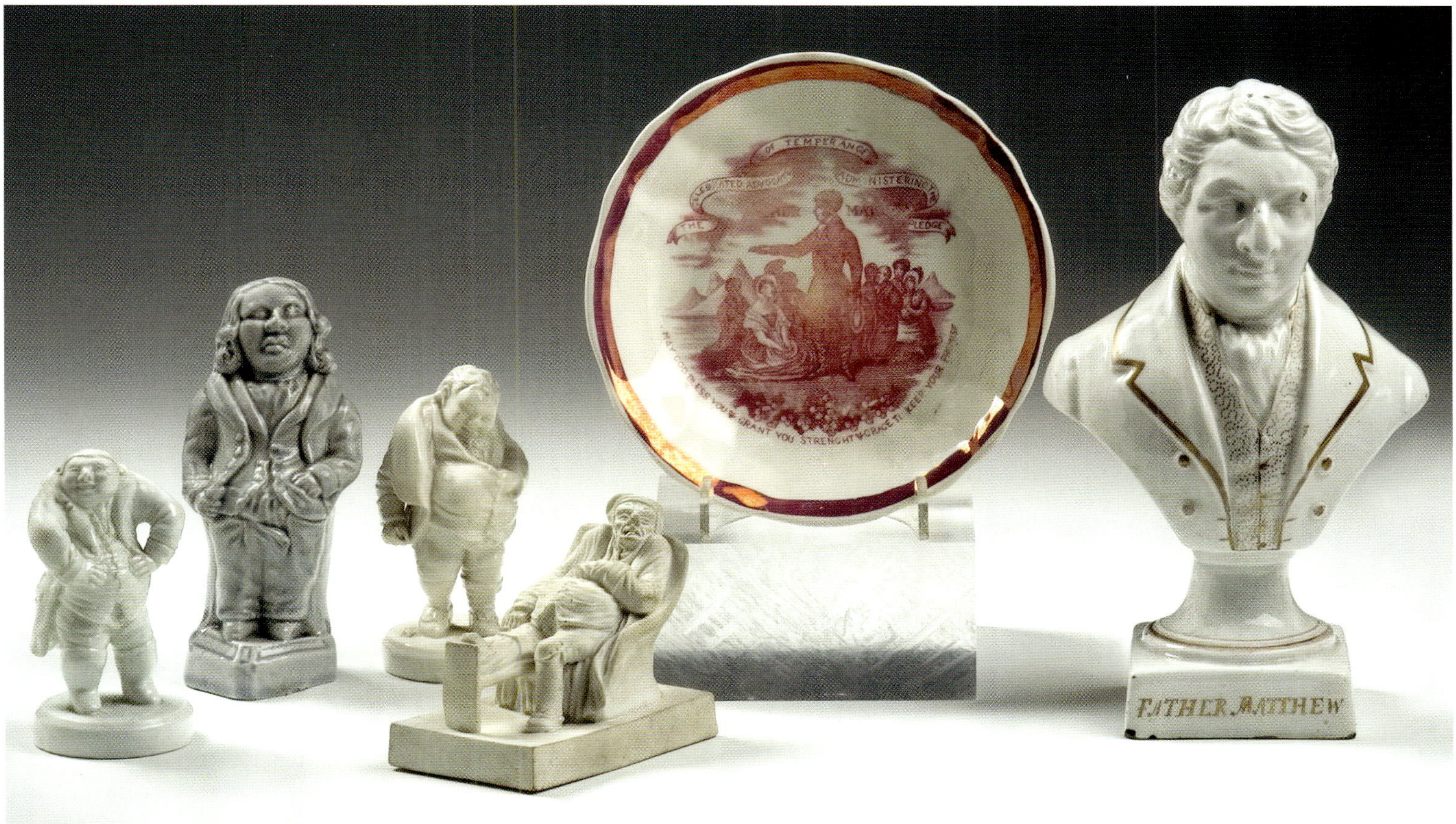

Three Figures, (**1502 & A & B**), c.1820, Derby, height: 9.3cm, (3⅝in), height: 7.7cm, (3in), height: 7.5cm, (2⅞in), biscuit porcelain (one glazed). Figures modelled by George Cocker, apparently commissioned by one Douglas Fox, 'a popular surgeon' to demonstrate the three stages of alcoholism.[40] The first looks stupidly cheerful, the second, with distended abdomen appears to be in pain. The third (inscribed 'Cocker/ Derby') inscribed 'The Dying Drunkard'.
Figure, (**1483**), c.1820, Staffordshire, height:13.3 cm, (5¼in), pearlware. Caricatured man perhaps inspired by Cocker's figures.
Saucer, (**1504**), c.1842, Staffordshire, diameter: 14.6cm, (5¾in), pearlware, red-printed and lustred. Printed with Father Mathew preaching, inscribed, 'FATHER MATTHEW / THE CELEBRATED ADVOCATE OF TEMPERANCE ADMINISTERING THE PLEDGE'.
Bust, (**1503**), c.1842, Staffordshire, height: 20.3cm, (8in), gilded soft-paste porcelain. Portrait bust, inscribed on base, 'FATHER MATTHEW [*sic*]'.

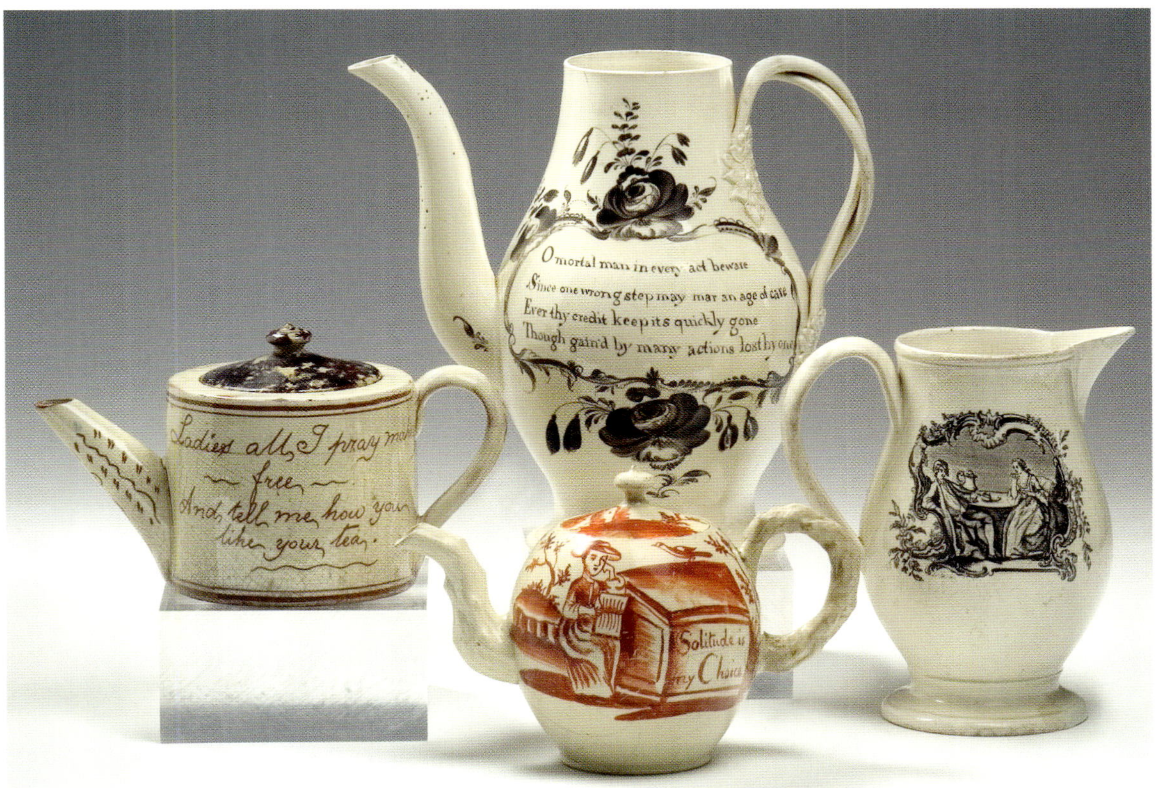

Clockwise:
Teapot, (**1507**), c.1880, Staffordshire, height: 10.8cm, (4¼in), red earthenware. Inscribed through cream slip, 'Ladies all I pray make / free / And tell me how you/ like your tea'.
Coffeepot, (**1501**), c.1780, probably made in Leeds, height: 19.1cm, (7½in), enamelled creamware. Coffee pot with entwined handle and elaborate terminals. Inscription warns against carelessly losing one's fortune or good name.
Cream Jug, (**R2454.12**), c.1780, Staffordshire, height: 14.7cm, (5⅜in), printed creamware. Finely printed with an informal scene of smoking and coffee drinking. Image signed TRS (for Thomas Rothwell sculpsit), copied from a design by Johann Esaias Nilson of Augsburg.[41]
Teapot, (**1704**), c.1770, Yorkshire, height: 11.5cm, (4½in), enamelled creamware. Painted with a seated woman reading beside a tomb inscribed, 'Solitude is my Choice'.

John Bartholomew Gough (1817-1886)

J.B. Gough was a celebrated temperance preacher. Born in Sandgate, Kent, to an impoverished soldier's family, aged twelve he emigrated with another family to the United States. He became an alcoholic and lived recklessly for many years until the temperance promoter, Joel Stratton, persuaded him to take the Pledge. He became a temperance lecturer, touring England from 1853 to 1855 and from 1857 to 1860. A handsome man and a charismatic orator, he enjoyed great success and revived the fortunes of the National Temperance League.

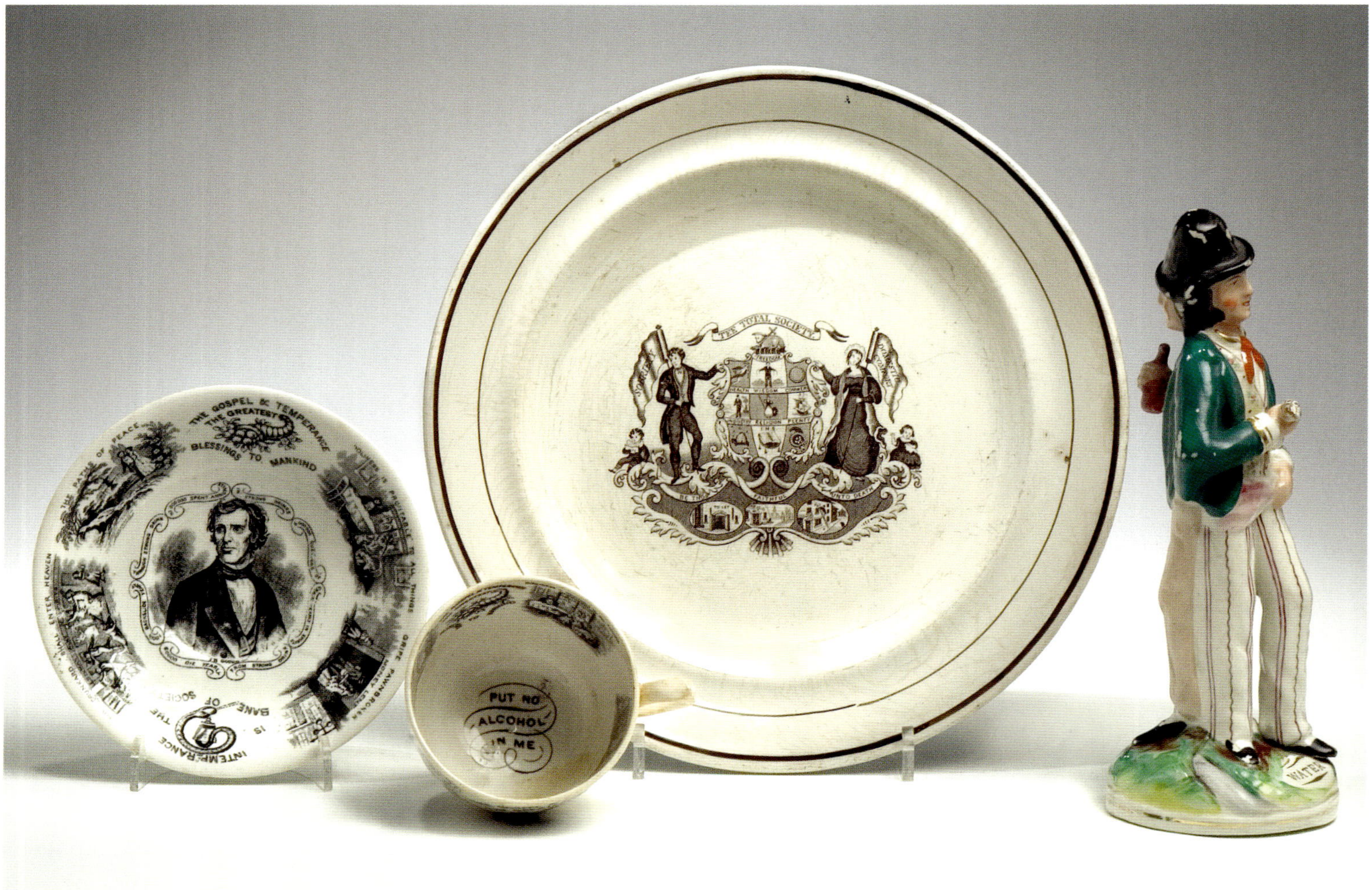

Teacup and Saucer, (**1510 & A**), c1860, Staffordshire, height: 8.3cm, (3¼in), diameter: 14cm, (5½in), printed earthenware. Printed with little scenes and mottoes. Base of the cup inscribed, 'PUT NO ALCOHOL IN ME'. Saucer, with a central portrait of J.B.Gough is printed, 'THE GOSPEL & TEMPERANCE / THE GREATEST / BLESSINGS TO MANKIND'
Plate, (**1511**), c.1840, , Staffordshire, diameter: 26cm, (10¼in), printed earthenware. Printed with arms of the 'TEE TOTAL SOCIETY', supported by a man with a banner marked, 'SOBRIETY' and a woman holding, 'DOMESTIC COMFORT'.
Figure, (**1505**), c.1850, Staffordshire, height: 22.3cm, (8¾in), earthenware, enamelled and gilt. A double-sided figure, inscribed, 'GIN' on one side and 'WATER' on the other, where the figure is much better dressed.

George Cruikshank (1792-1878)

Cruikshank was one of the best known and most prolific of nineteenth-century illustrators. His long career began with political satire during the Napoleonic Wars but he later turned to book illustration, the production of the famous *Comic Almanack* and a creative collaboration with Charles Dickens until they quarrelled.

A hard drinker in his youth George targeted the evils of alcohol, particularly gin, long before he decided to renounce it. Acknowledging it as a pernicious influence on health and public order, in 1847 he was commissioned to produce a series of prints demonstrating the ruin of a family through alcohol. This series of eight prints became *The Bottle,* which caused a marketing sensation, selling 100,000 copies in just a few weeks. Shortly after publication, when challenged by William Cash, Chairman of the National Temperance Society, Cruikshank himself took the Pledge. Cruikshank then allowed the prints to be applied to ceramics and sold in aid of Temperance charities. Henry Mayhew, author of *London Labour and the London Poor,* reported that '*The Bottle* was much admired among the poor', and cheap editions sold well. The popularity of the series led Cruikshank to produce a sequel, chronicling the fate of *The Drunkard's Children.*

Eight Plates, c.1850, Yorkshire, Middlesbrough Pottery, each diameter: 20.3cm, (8in), earthenware, brown-printed and coloured.
Two Plates, Plate I, '**THE BOTTLE** / PLATE I – THE BOTTLE IS BROUGHT OUT FOR THE FIRST TIME / THE HUSBAND INDUCES HIS WIFE JUST TO TAKE A DROP'. Plate II, the husband is sacked for drunkenness. The family pawn their clothes 'TO SUPPLY THE BOTTLE'.
Three Plates, Plate III, the family lose their furniture to the bailiffs. Plate IV, unemployed, they are forced to beg on the streets. Plate V, their youngest child dies.
Three Plates, Plate VI, quarrels and violence within the family. Plate VII, in a drunken fury the husband kills his wife with a bottle. Plate VIII, 'THE BOTTLE HAS DONE ITS WORK' The son and daughter take to 'vice' while the father is confined in a lunatic asylum.

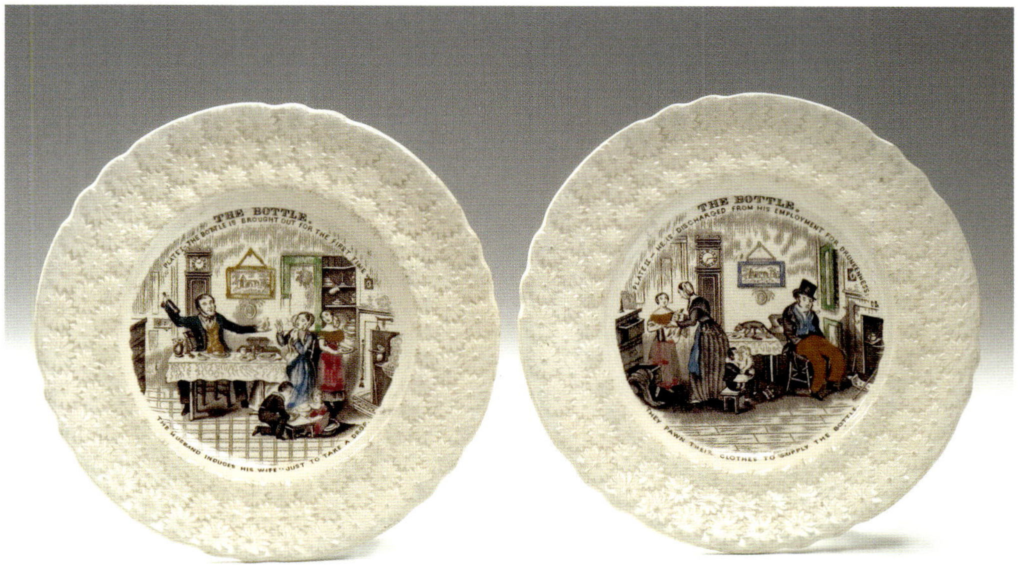

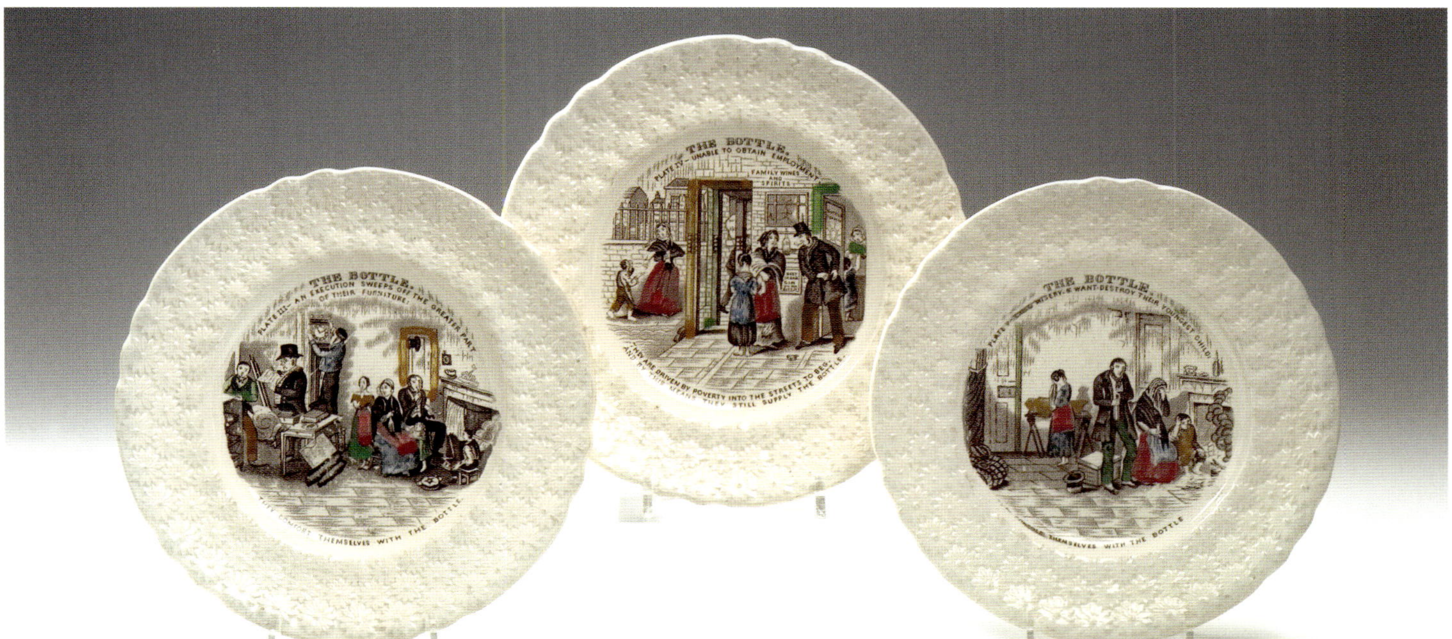

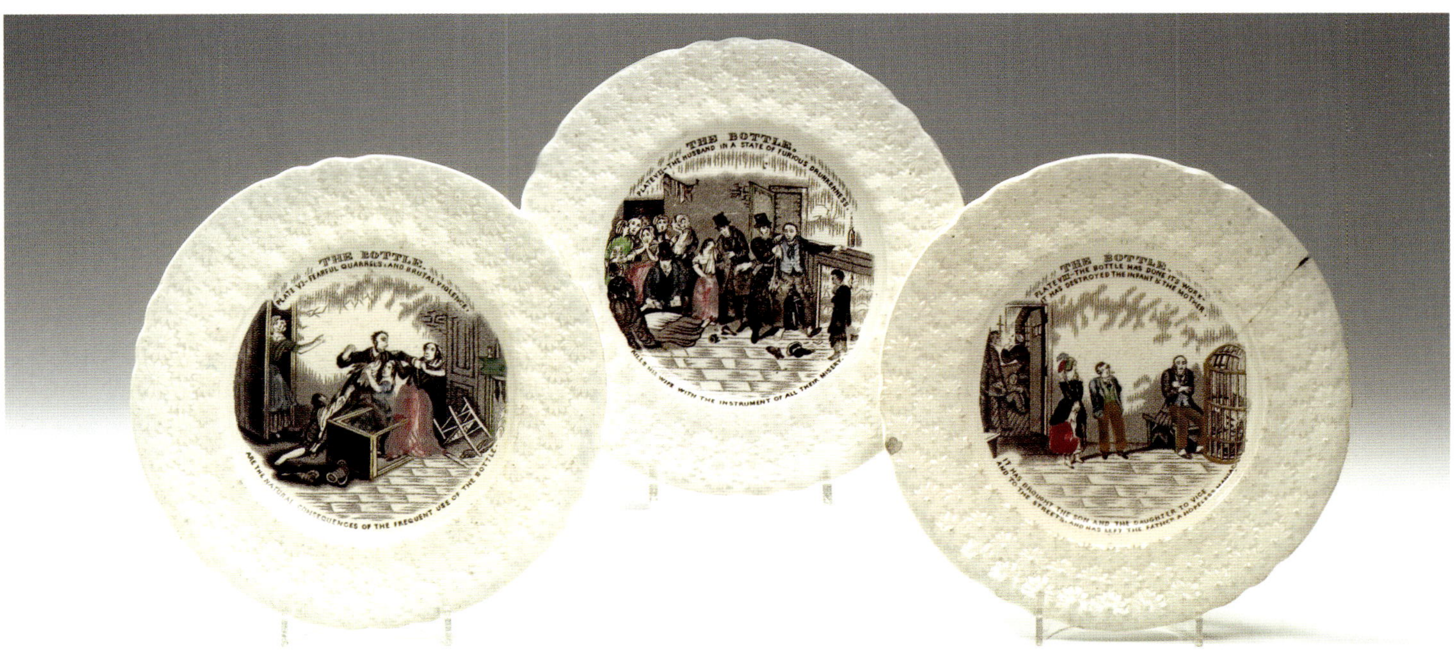

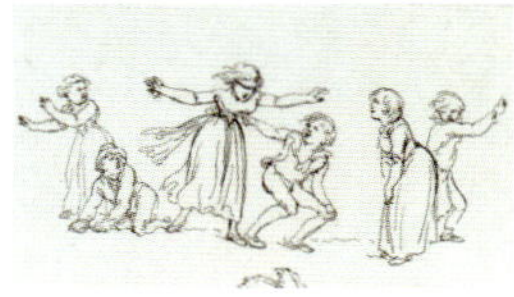

Chapter 19

DOMESTIC INCIDENTS

Infancy and Childhood

'As soon as the child is born it must be swathed; lay it to sleep in its cradle and you must have a nurse to rock it to sleep'. (Walter de Bibblesworth, late 1200s)[1]. By the late eighteenth century, influenced by ideas published in *Emile* (1762), by Jean-Jacques Rousseau, childcare guru of the Enlightenment, newborn babies ceased to be trussed in swaddling bands and 'rocker' nurses fell out of fashion. Wicker or basket-work cradles were popular from the middle ages, being light weight, well ventilated and cheap to produce. Catherine Naish supplied several for the children of George III.[2]

Models of hooded cradles, dating from around 1800 are all moulded with shallow rockers beneath. None is marked and they were probably made in different parts of the country. Replica pottery cradles modelled with babies were probably given as gifts to newly married couples. Some empty cradles may have contained token amounts of coal and slat, to ensure fertility and that the family would never lack for food or a warm fire. They may also have been given to parents filled with gifts for a new baby. The absence of porcelain examples suggests the market was the middle classes and working people.

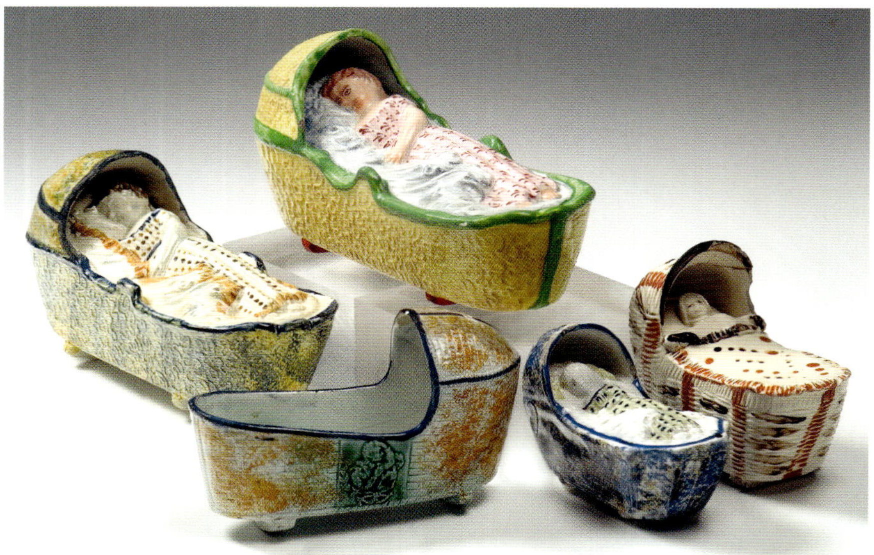

Clockwise:
Two Cradles, (1523 & A), c.1810, Staffordshire, height: 10.2cm, (4in), height: 9.2cm, (3⅝in), enamelled pearlware. Moulded with vermiculated surfaces; sleeping children half covered by wave-like blankets.
Cradle, (**1525**), c.1810, Staffordshire, height: 12.7cm, (5in), Pratt-coloured creamware. Moulded as basketwork; thick blanket folded back to reveal a baby wearing a bonnet.
Cradle, (**1524**), c.1810, Staffordshire, height: 11.5cm, (4½in), Pratt-coloured pearlware. Moulded as rug weave; baby half covered by wave-like blanket.
Cradle, (1526), c.1810, Staffordshire, height: 14cm, (5½in), enamelled pearlware. Empty cradle moulded as brickwork. Each side applied with relief profiles of a man and a woman expressing distress. Such a piece may have marked a stillbirth or an infant death, which occurred all too frequently.

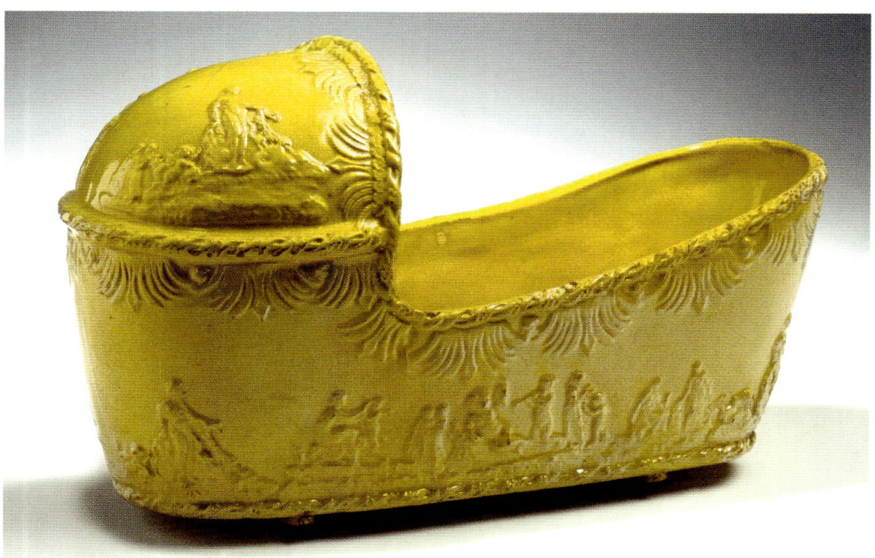

Cradle, (**1522**), c.1810, North East, height: 17.2cm, (6¾in), yellow-glazed earthenware. Large, empty cradle moulded with foliate frieze and sprigged motifs of classical figures.

Figure Group, (**1564**), c.1820, Staffordshire, height: 19.1cm, (7½in), enamelled pearlware. A lucky child is supervised by nurse or mother while riding on a large dog.
Figure Group, (**1684**), c.1825, Staffordshire, height: 19.1cm, (7½in), enamelled pearlware. A couple with a new baby sit on a garden bench flanked by their dog and cat.
Figure Group, (**1527**), c.1755, London, Bow, height: 15.3cm, (6in), soft-paste porcelain. A girl carries a baby in a cradle, (detached from its rocker), on a strap around her neck.

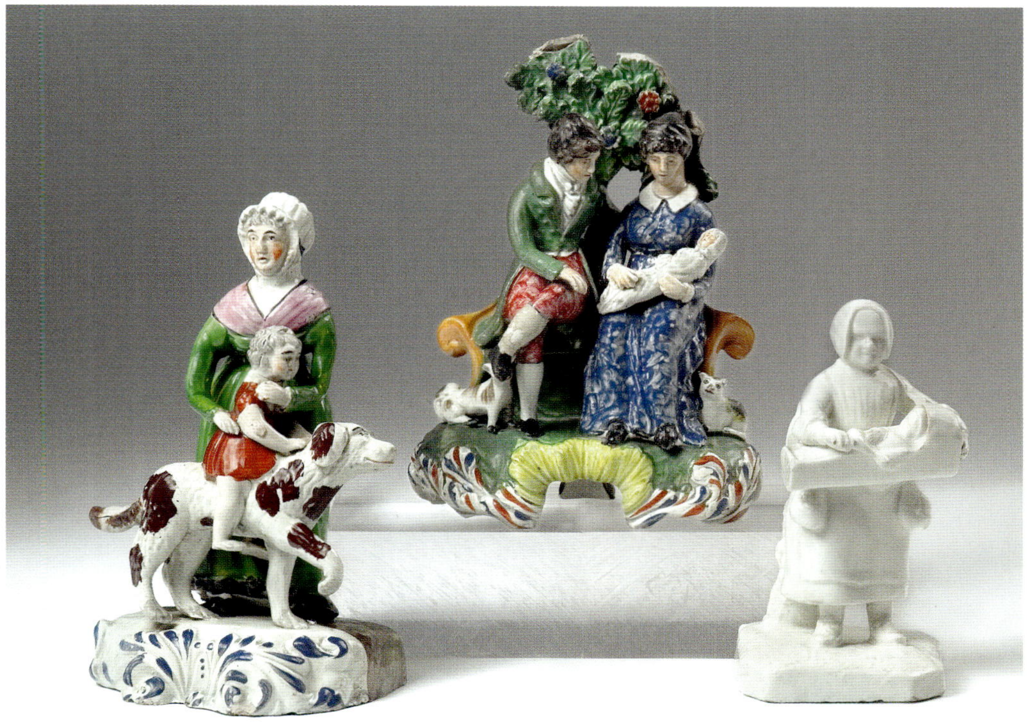

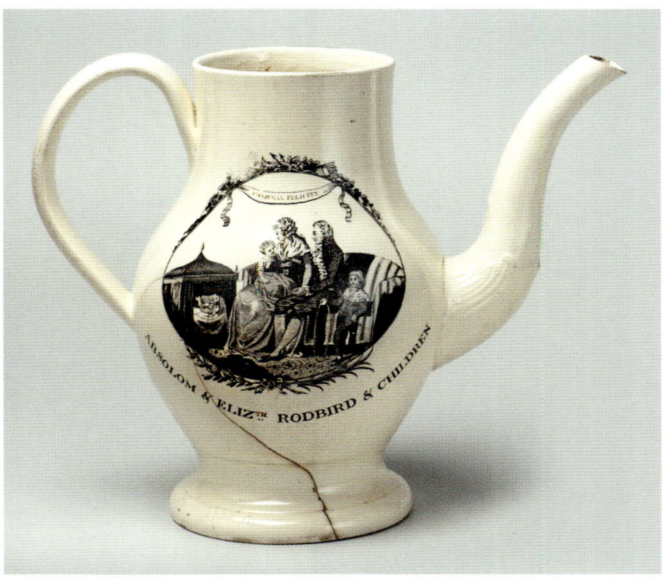

Coffee Pot, (**452**), c.1797-1803, Staffordshire, height: 21.6cm, (8½in), creamware, printed and enamelled. Printed with interior inscribed, above, 'CONJUGAL FELICITY', an intimate family group of parents and three children. It reflects William Ramsden's fond description of his family life at Charterhouse School in 1773, 'On my left sits Madam darning of stockings, on my right is our heir apparent reading the news; Betsy is making a cap for her doll, Tom and Dick are playing at Marbles on the carpet'.[3] Inscribed beneath, 'ABSOLOM & ELIZth. RODBIRD & CHILDREN', the scene either celebrates this happy family, c.1797 or commemorates them at a later date when the wife and two of the children had died.[4]

Mug, (**1691**), c.1805, Liverpool, probably Herculaneum Pottery, height: 12.7cm, (5in), brown-printed creamware. Young woman wearing classical dress sits with her children in a garden. Scene inscribed, 'The MOTHER_From Rofcoes Nurfe'. William Roscoe (1753-1831) was a prominent Liverpool historian, philanthropist, poet and a pioneer champion of Italian culture. In 1798 he translated Luigi Tansillo's poem, *The Nurse*, written to encourage women to breast-feed their own babies, at a time when those who could afford to hired wet-nurses. Roscoe considered that the subject, 'is treated in a manner peculiarly pointed and direct, yet without violating that decorum which is due to the public at large, and in particular to the sex to whom it is addressed.'
Plaque, (**1688**), c.1805, Sussex, Heathfield, height: 15.9cm, (6¼in), earthenware. Relief-moulded with a woman, probably a widow, and three young children sitting beside a tomb, with a weeping willow behind. Made by Jonathan Harmer (1762-1849) of Heathfield. Harmer, a stonemason, also made ornamental terracotta relief panels for insertion into tombstones. After his death, Harmer's moulds were used by other potters.

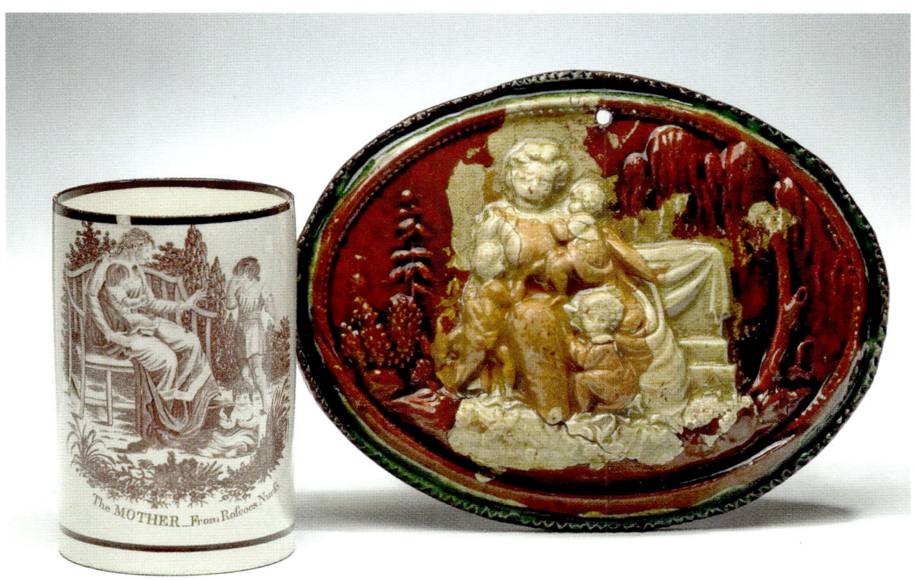

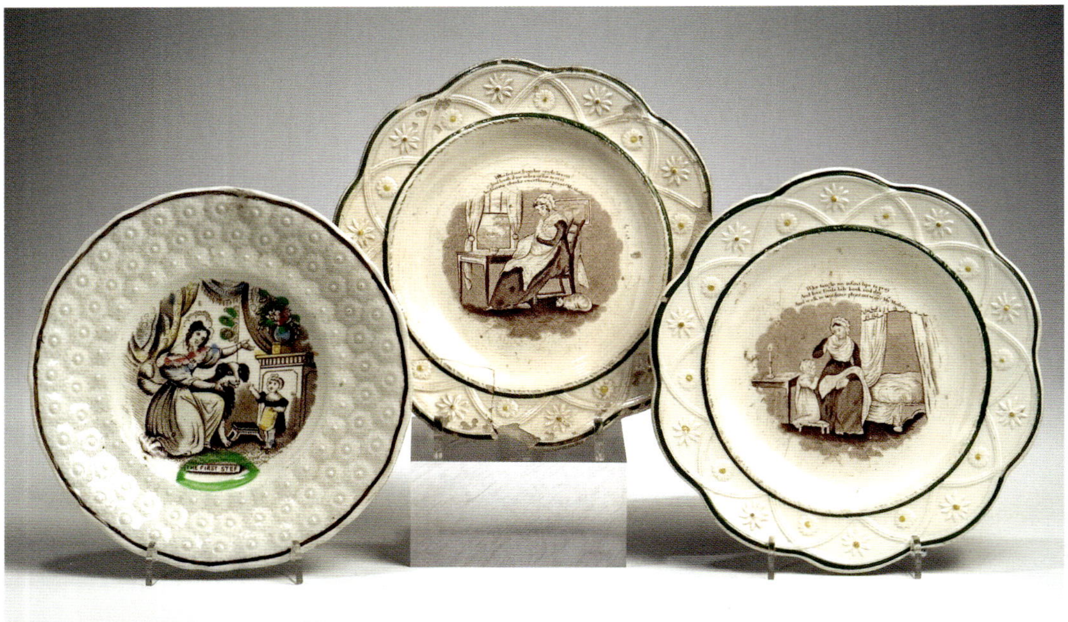

Plate, (**1528**), c.1840, Yorkshire, Middlesbrough Pottery, diameter: 17.8cm, (7in), earthenware, brown-printed and coloured. A mother restrains a dog as she encourages a toddler to take, 'THE FIRST STEP'.[5]

Two Plates, (**1540 &A**), c.1815, Staffordshire, each diameter: 18.4cm, (7¼in), earthenware, brown-printed and coloured. Within crisply moulded lobed border, scenes of mother and child inscribed, 'Who fed me from her gentle breast'. And 'Who taught my infant lips to pray'[6], verses from the poem, 'My Mother', by Ann Taylor (1782-1866), published as a picture sheet by William Darton Jnr February, 1812.[7]

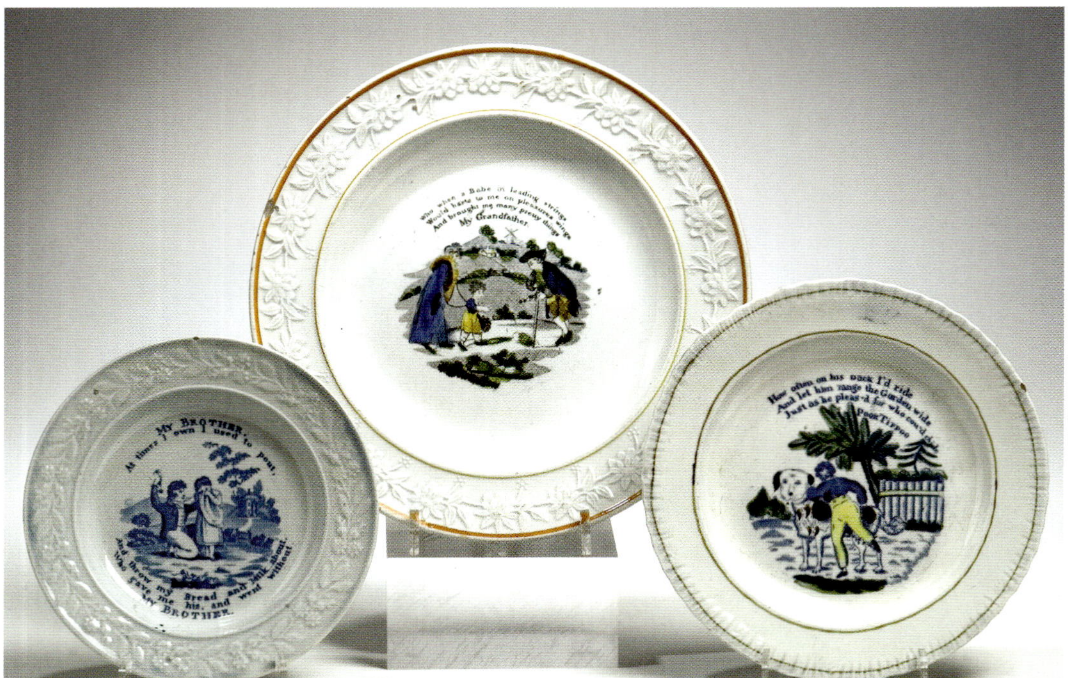

Plate, (**1541**), c.1812, Staffordshire, diameter: 15.3cm, (6in), blue-printed pearlware. A little girl is comforted by her brother, inscribed, 'At times I own I used to pout / And throw my bread and milk about, / Who gave me his and went without / MY BROTHER'. Verse written by Mary Belson Elliott and published by William Darton, Jnr in July 1811.

Plate, (**1572**), c.1815, Staffordshire, Cobridge, diameter: 22.3cm, (8¾in), pearlware, printed and coloured. Plate made by Andrew Stevenson of Cobridge. An old couple with a child in a walking harness, inscribed, 'Who when a babe in leading strings / Would hast to me on pleasure's wings… My Grandfather', from an illustrated poem by William Upton, published c.1813.[8]

Plate, (**1578**), c.1820, Staffordshire, diameter: 17.8cm, (7in), pearlware, blue-printed and coloured. A boy with a large dog inscribed, 'How often on his back I'd ride … Poor Tippoo', presumably named after the infamous Sultan of Mysore.

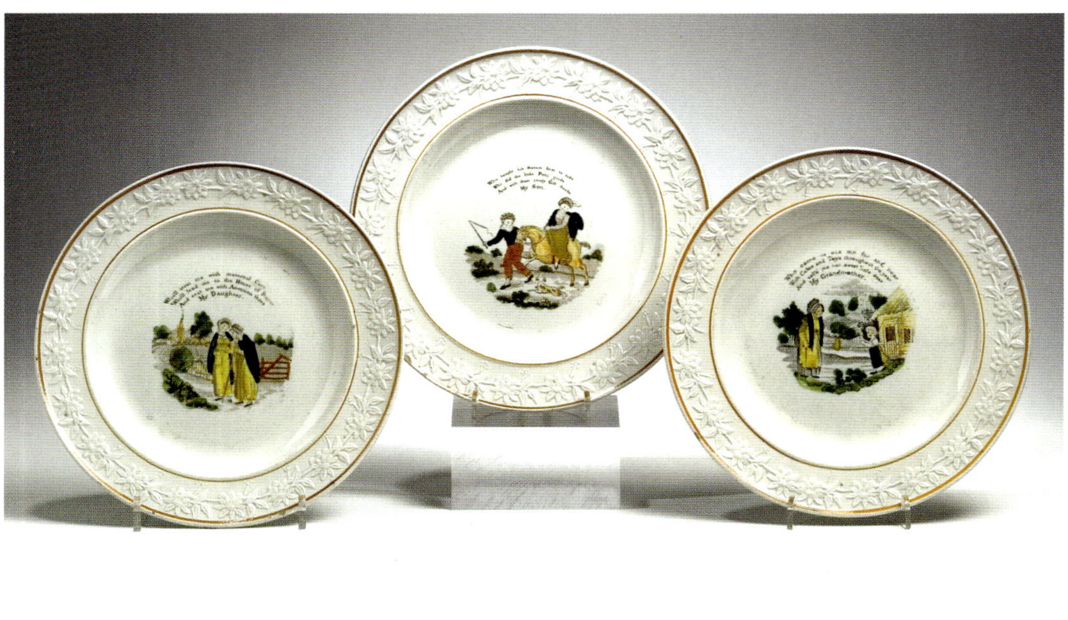

Three Plates, (**1569 + 1570 + 1571**), c.1815, Staffordshire, Cobridge, each diameter: 22.3cm, (8¾in), pearlware, printed and coloured. Plates made by Andrew Stevenson of Cobridge. Within crisply moulded borders, printed with family scenes; a young woman supports an older one, 'Who'll treat me with maternal care … My Daughter' (**1570**), (poem by Richard Gregory)[9], children and a pony, 'Who taught his sisters first to ride … My Son' (**1569**) (poem by Richard Gregory)[10] and an old woman giving presents to a child, 'Who came to see me near and far … My Grandmother' (**1571**) (poem by William Upton).[11]

Figure, (**1534**), c.1830, Staffordshire, height: 15.2cm, (6in), enamelled pearlware. Boy sitting on anvil-shaped seat, reading tiny book.
Figure Group, (**1529**), c.1770, Derby, height: 21.6cm, (8½in), biscuit porcelain. Group known as, 'The Prudent Mother', shows seated woman teaching a child to read.
Figure, (**1533**), c.1830, Staffordshire, height: 17.8cm, (7in), enamelled pearlware. Boy sitting on anvil-shaped seat, reading large book; entitled 'Cottage Boy'.

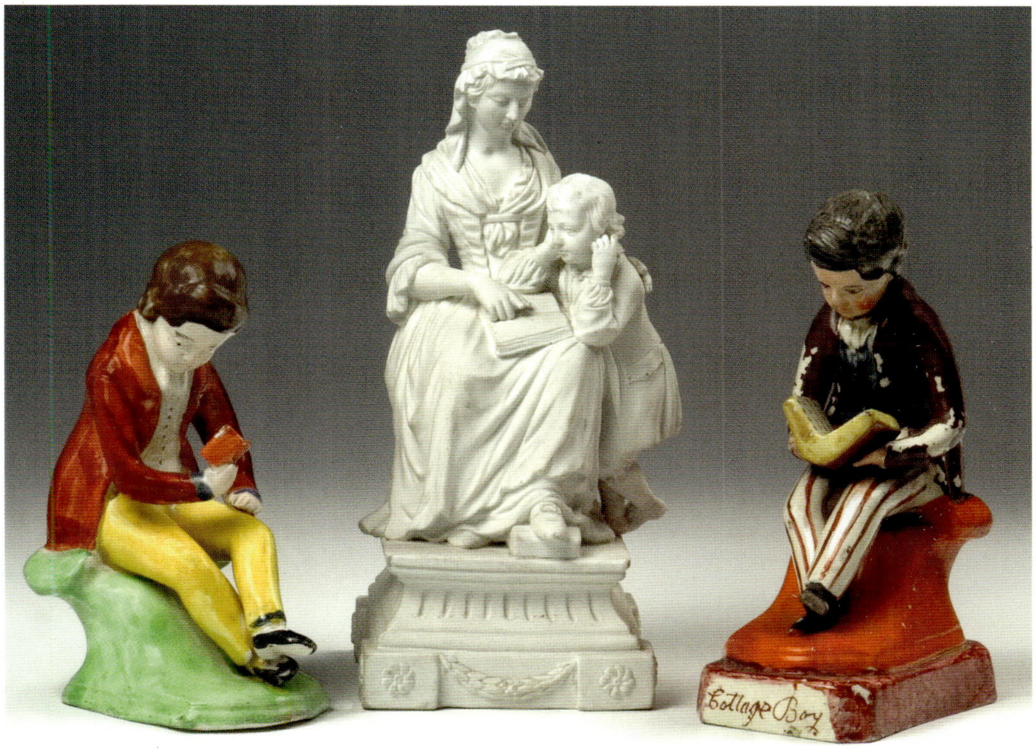

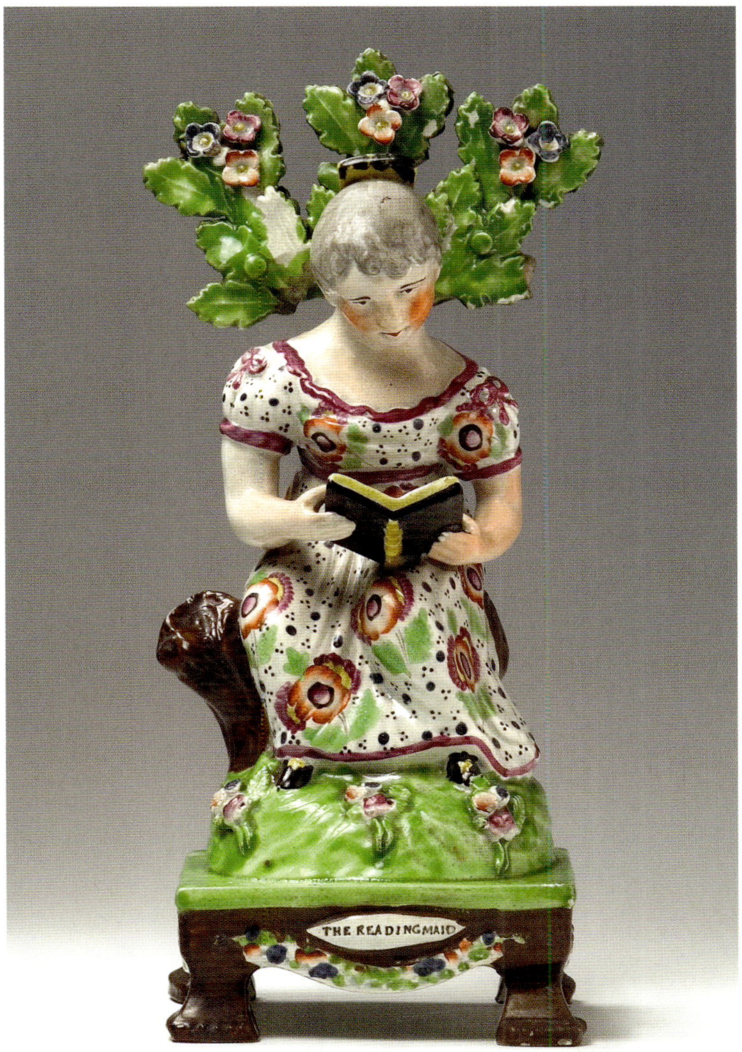

Figure, (**1532**), c.1825, Staffordshire, height: 30.5cm, (12in), enamelled pearlware. Large table-based figure of girl reading under a tree, entitled, 'THE READING MAID'.

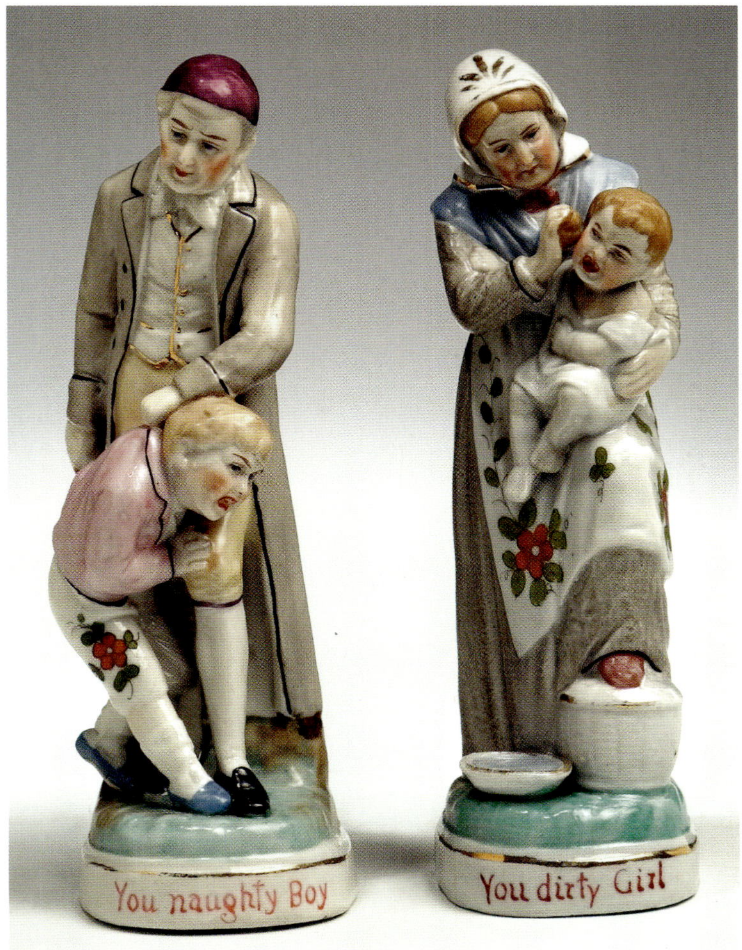

Pair of Figure Groups, (**1538 & A**), c.1880, Germany, each height: 16.5cm, (6½in), enamelled, hard-paste porcelain. Figures made by Springer and Oppenheimer of Elbogen. A grandfather wields the cane to punish, 'You naughty Boy' and the grandmother soaps the ears of 'You Dirty Girl'. They may be loosely linked to a well-known terracotta group, 'You Dirty Boy!', modelled by Giovanni Focardi, 1878, and made by the Watcombe Pottery in Devon as an advertisement for Pears Soap.[12]

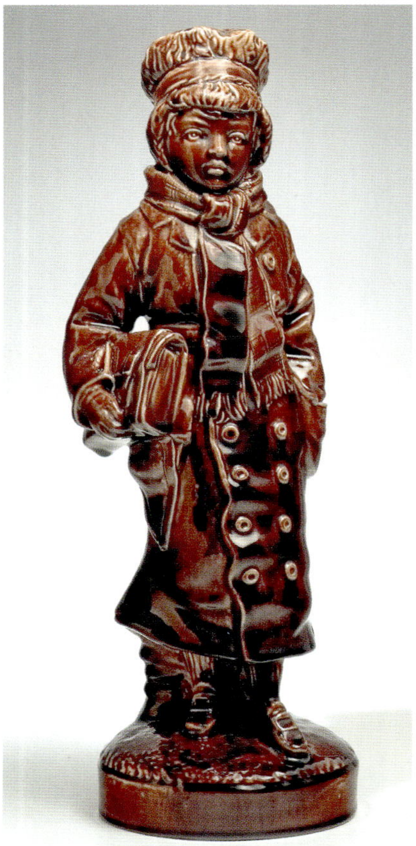

Figure, (1536), c.1850, Staffordshire, height: 38.1cm, (15in), treacle-glazed earthenware. Figure of a boy dressed for cold weather and carrying a satchel under his arm.

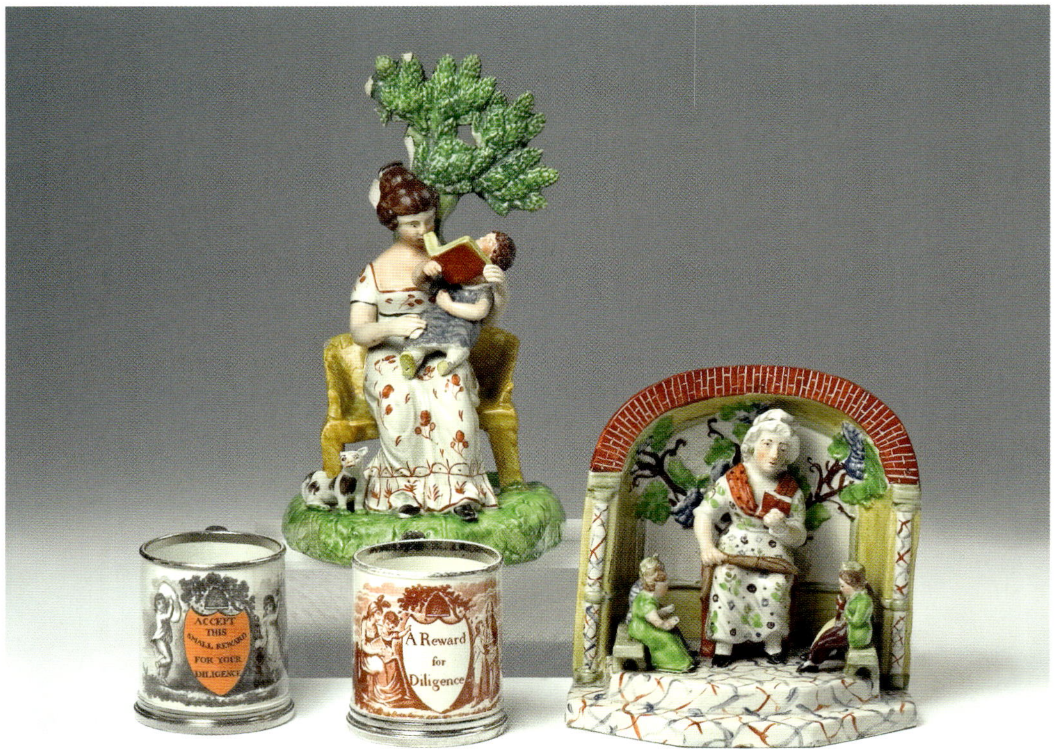

Two Mugs, (**1554 + 1555**), c.1830, Staffordshire, Burslem, each height: 7.6cm, (3in), pearlware, printed, enamelled and lustred. Each of two mugs made by Enoch Wood bears a shield inscribed, 'ACCEPT THIS SMALL REWARD FOR YOUR DILIGENCE' (the shield painted orange) (**1554**), and 'A Reward for Diligence' (printed in red) (**1555**). Design also includes a beehive, traditional symbol of industry and hard work.
Figure Group, (**1531**), c.1820, Staffordshire, height: 22.9cm, (9in), enamelled pearlware. A mother, sitting on a garden bench, reads a book to a very young child.
Figure Group, (**1530**), c.1830, Staffordshire, height: 16.5cm, (6½in), enamelled pearlware. Dish-backed tableau shows giant teacher with a switch on her knee, invigilating tiny children who are learning to read.

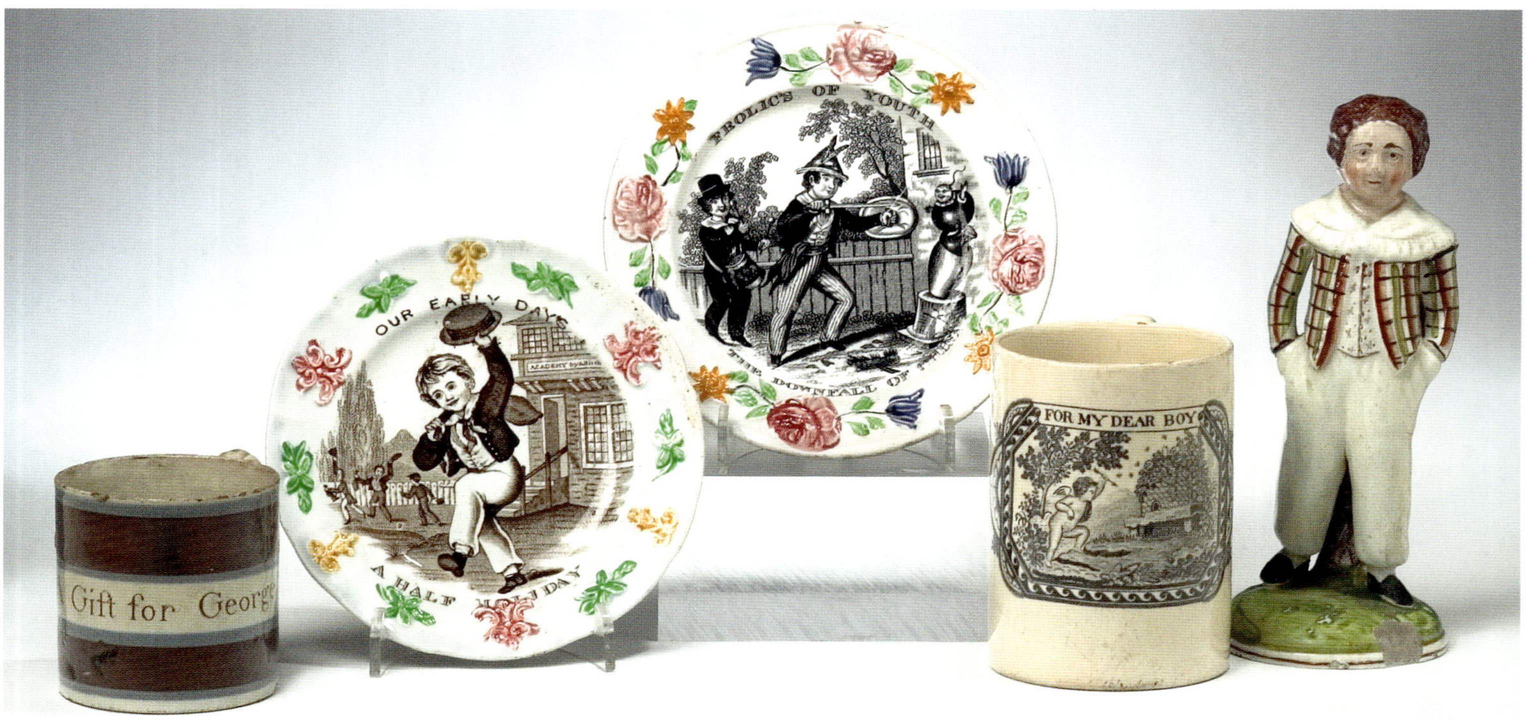

Mug, (**1547**), c.1810, Staffordshire, height: 6.4cm, (2½in), enamelled earthenware. Inscribed between broad enamelled bands, 'A Gift for George'.
Nursery Plate, (**1585**), c.1840, Staffordshire, diameter: 13.3cm, (5¼in), earthenware, printed and coloured. A boy skips out of school waving his hat, entitled 'OUR EARLY DAYS / A HALF HOLIDAY'. No. 6 from 'Our Early Days', an extensive series printed by Clerk and published by Orlando Hodgson (n.d.).[13]
Nursery Plate, (**1582**), c.1845, Staffordshire, Longport, diameter: 14cm, (5½in), earthenware, printed and coloured. Made by Davenport, inscribed, 'FROLICS OF YOUTH / THE DOWNFALL OF CHINA, in punning reference to the Opium Wars of 1839-42.
Mug, (**1543**), c.1810, Staffordshire, height: 10.2cm, (4in), printed creamware. Printed , 'FOR MY DEAR BOY' and image of Cupid attacking a beehive.
Figure, (**1535**), c.1840, Staffordshire, height: 16.5cm, (6½in), enamelled earthenware. Figure of schoolboy with his hands in his pockets.

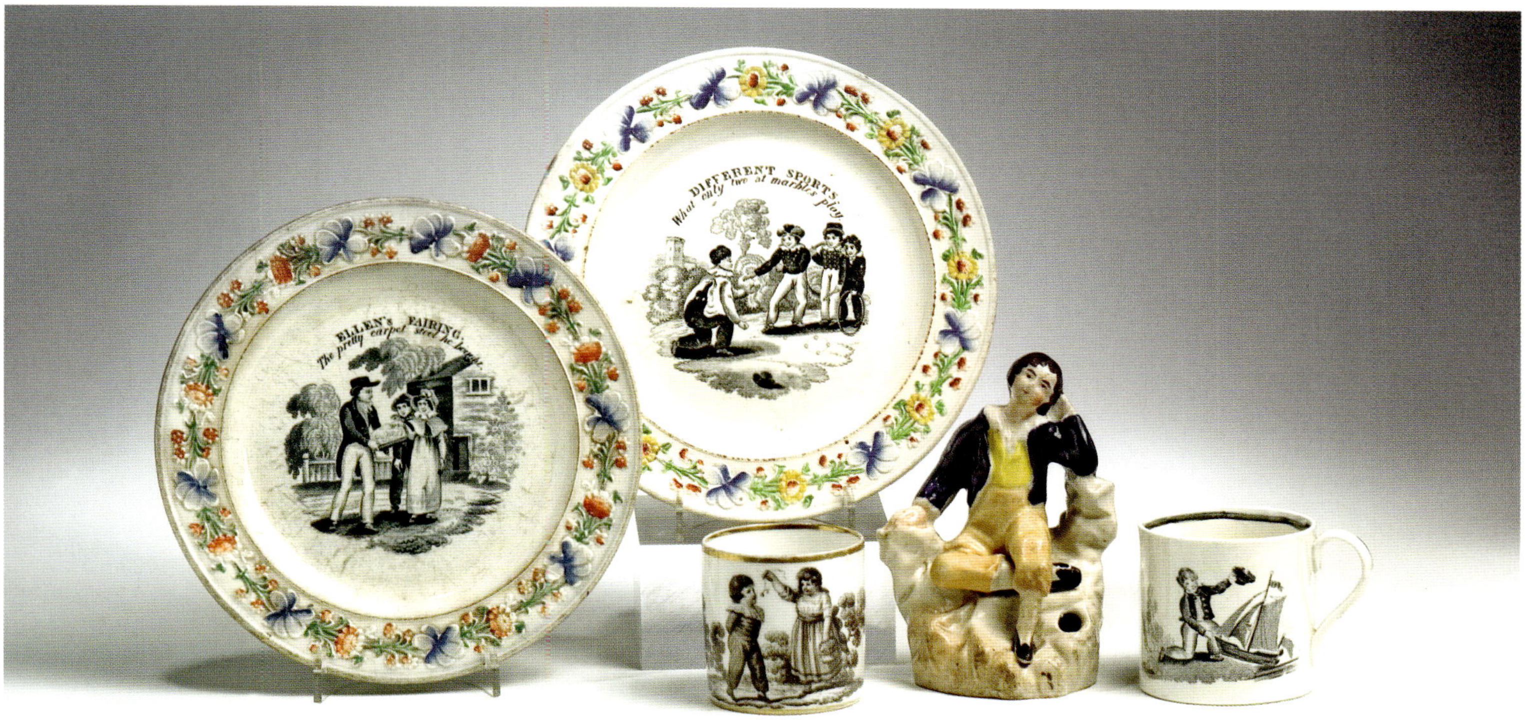

Nursery Plate, (**1672**), c.1840, Staffordshire, diameter: 19.1cm, (7½in), earthenware, printed and coloured. Distinctive relief-moulded floral border, possibly made by James Clews of Cobridge. Printed with scene entitled, 'ELLEN'S FAIRING / the pretty carpet stool [s]he bought'. Taken from a didactic poem in the collection, *The Rose*, by Mary Belson Elliott (c.1790–c.1860) first published in 1813.[14] Ellen (not her admirer) bought the carpet stool so her father could rest his gouty foot upon it.
Nursery Plate, (**1586**), c.1840, Staffordshire, diameter: 19.1cm, (7½in), earthenware, printed and coloured. Distinctive relief-moulded floral border, possibly made by James Clews of Cobridge. Children playing, entitled, 'DIFFERENT SPORTS / What only two at marbles play', taken from another of Elliott's poems in *The Rose*.[15]
Mug, (**1581**), c.1800, France, height: 6.4cm, (2½in), enamelled hard-paste porcelain. Painted in black with a boy and girl playing 'bob-cherry'.
Figure, (**1537**), Staffordshire, c.1840, Staffordshire, diameter: 12.7cm, (5in), enamelled earthenware. Small boy with crossed legs sits dreaming, taken from the pose of 'Master Lambton', c.1825, painted by Sir Thomas Lawrence.
Mug, (**1574**), c.1815, Staffordshire, height: 6.4cm, (2½in), printed earthenware. A boy launching a model boat inscribed, 'No shipbuilder famed for his skill / Can feel more delight than Will'.

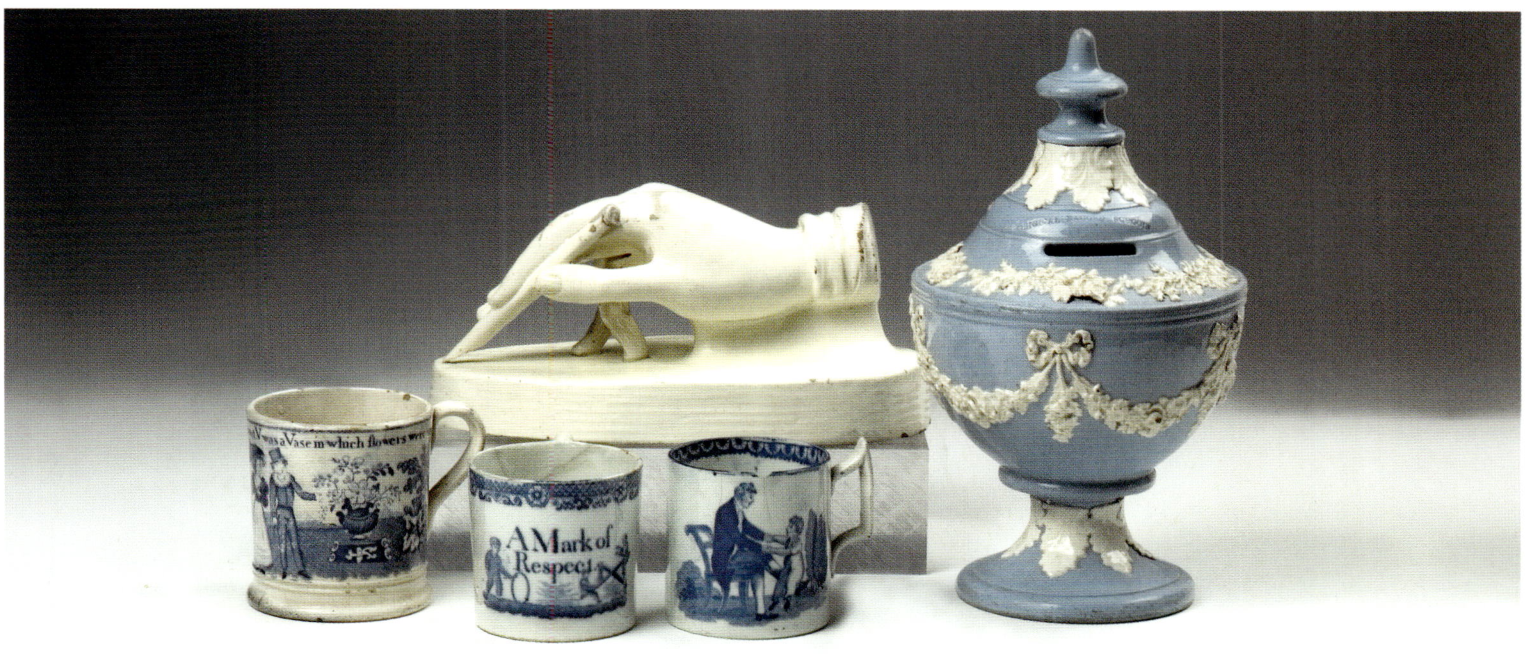

Mug, (**1546**), c.1830, Staffordshire, height: 7.7cm, (3in), blue-printed earthenware. Inscribed, 'U was an Umbrella saved Betsy from wet, V was a Vase'.
Mug, (**1592**), c.1815, Staffordshire, height: 6.4cm, (2½in), printed earthenware. Inscribed, 'A Mark of Respect', (probably a reward or prize) showing boys playing with a hoop and on the see-saw.
Mug, (**1544**), c.1815, Staffordshire, height: 6.4cm, (2½in), printed earthenware. Inscribed, 'Who placed me on his foot, to ride … My Father',[16] showing father and son playing together.
Model, (**1539**), 1812, Liverpool, Herculaneum, height: 20.3cm, (8in), creamware. Model of a hand holding a pen, may have been commissioned as a prize for handwriting. Incised on base, 'Designed for Circus Street School, Frd. LEGE Sculpt. Liverpool 1812'. Modelled by Frederick Lege, a freelance artist working for the Herculaneum factory. Four examples are known.
Money Box, (**R2454/5**), c.1850, Staffordshire, height: 22.2cm, (8¾in), slip-decorated earthenware. Urn-shaped money box applied with white-sprigged garlands to resemble Wedgwood jasperware. Stamped above slot, 'ORIGINAL RAGGED SCHOOLS'. These were founded in 1844 to deliver basic education to destitute children in inner cities.

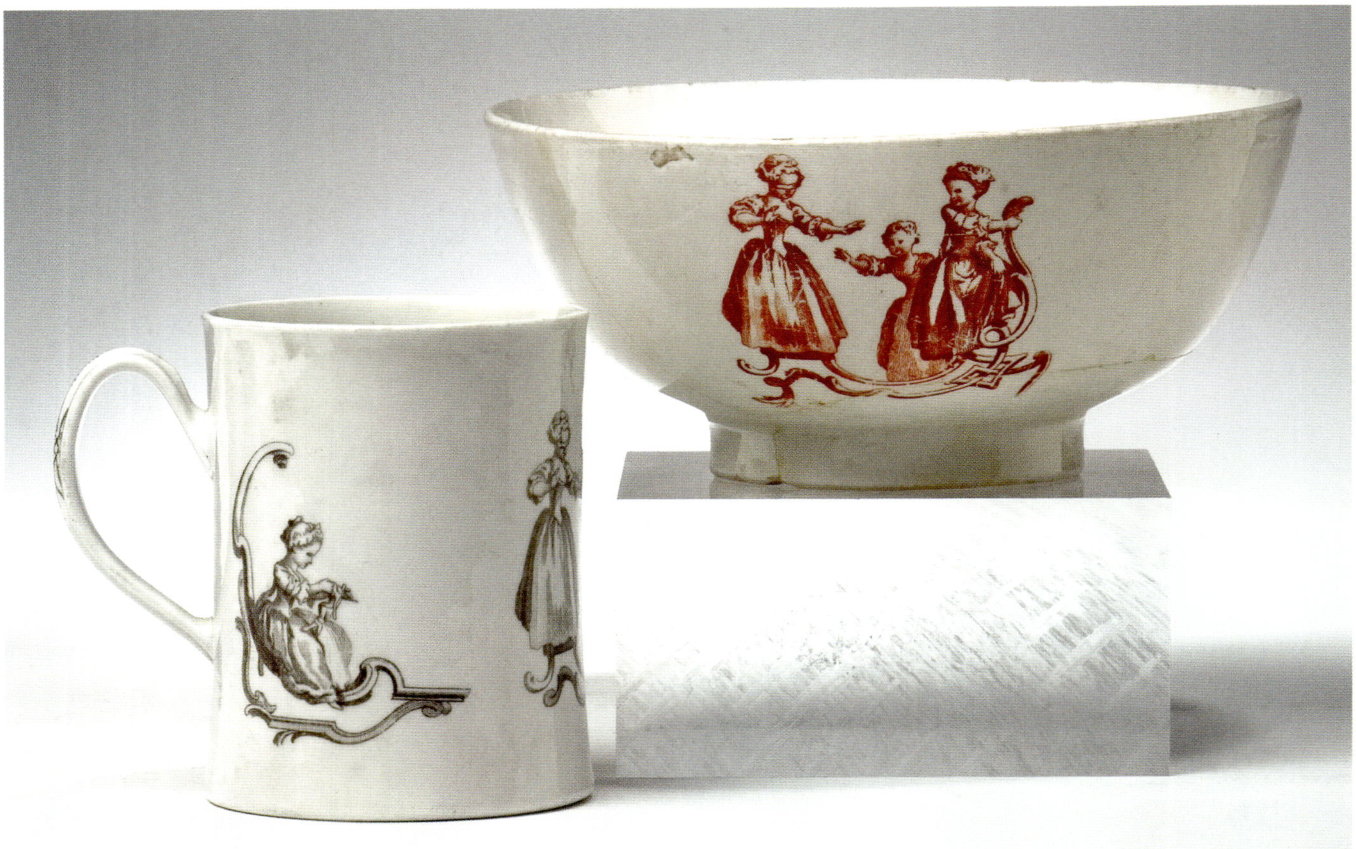

Mug, (1573), c.1760, Worcester, height: 8.9cm, (3½in), printed, soft-paste porcelain. Delicate vignettes of a girl playing with a doll and a boy blowing bubbles, adapted by Robert Hancock from designs by Hubert-François Gravelot (1699-1773), a French engraver working in London during the 1740s.[17]

Slop Bowl, (1575A), c.1755, London, Bow, diameter: 15.3cm, (6in), red-printed, soft-paste porcelain. Rare bowl printed with design after Gravelot including a game of 'Blind Man's Buff' (*Le Colin Maillard*), which also appears on the mug. Other vignettes comprise 'The Tea Party' and 'The Wheeling Chair'.

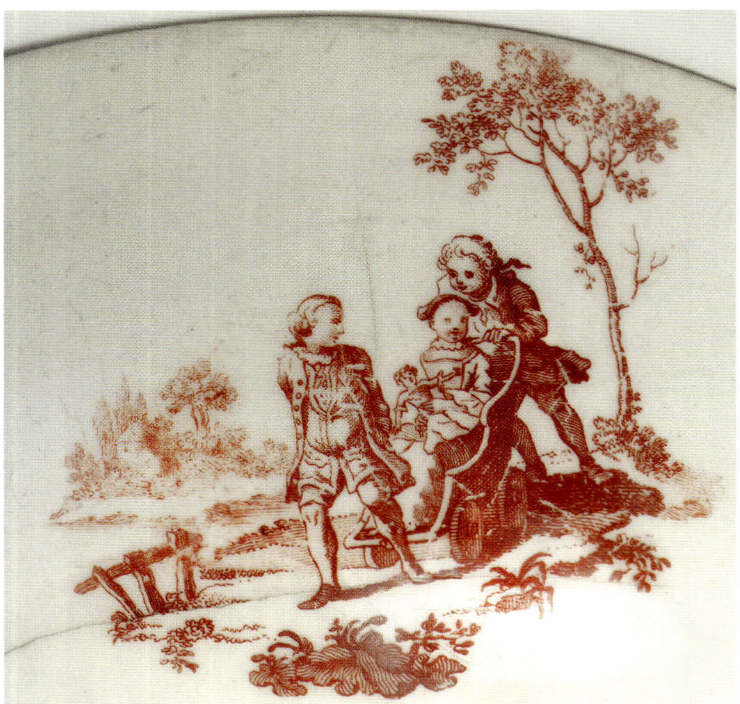

Slop Bowl (detail), (1575), c.1755, London, Bow, diameter: 15.3cm, (6in), red-printed, soft-paste porcelain. Vignette called 'The Wheeling Chair', shows little girl and her doll in a pushchair with sides, pushed by two boys. Design by Robert Hancock used at Bow and Worcester, on creamwares from Cockpit Hill in Derbyshire and on Battersea enamels.[18]

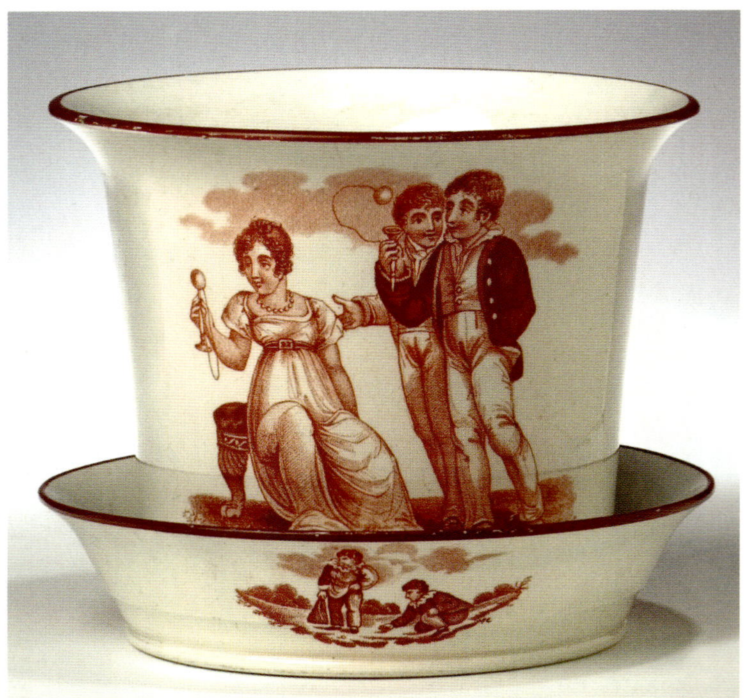

Flower Pot and Saucer, (1588), c.1810, Staffordshire, height: 9.9cm, (3⅞in), diameter: 12.9cm, (5⅛in), red-printed, pearlware. Made by Shorthose & Co. showing children at play. Three girls dress dolls and a girl and two boys play cup-and-ball.[19]

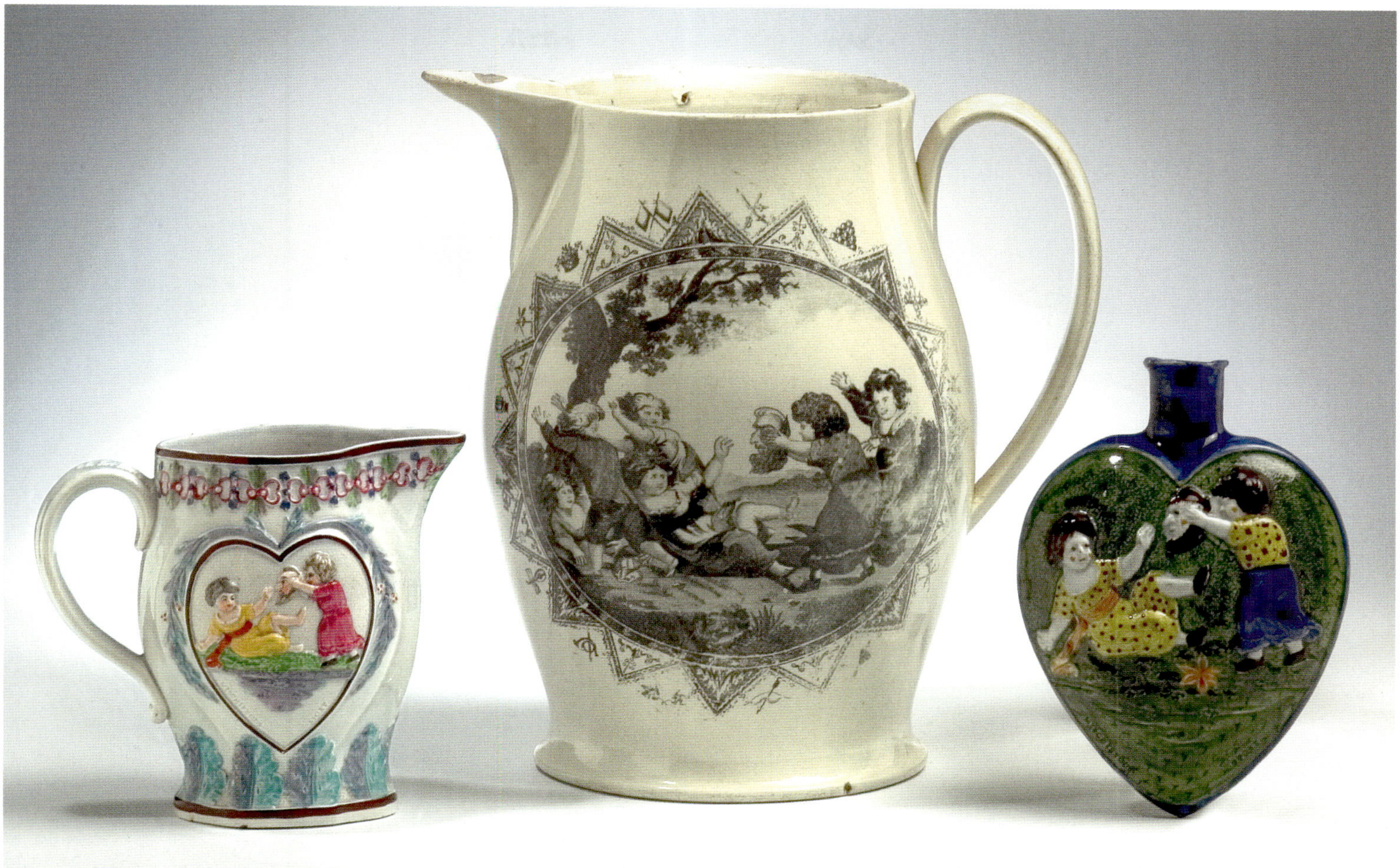

Cream Jug, (**1566**), c.1810, Staffordshire, height: 12.7cm, (5in), enamelled pearlware. Relief-moulded, within heart-shaped reserve, a child frightens another with a theatrical mask, impressed, 'MISCHIEVOUS SPORT'. [20]
Jug, (**1438**), c.1800, Staffordshire, height: 24.2cm, (9½in), printed creamware.

A more detailed depiction of 'Mischievous Sport' with several children in a landscape.
Flask, (**1567**), c.1810, Staffordshire, height: 15.3cm, (6in), Prattware. Heart-shaped flask relief-moulded, with a depiction of 'Mischievous Sport'.

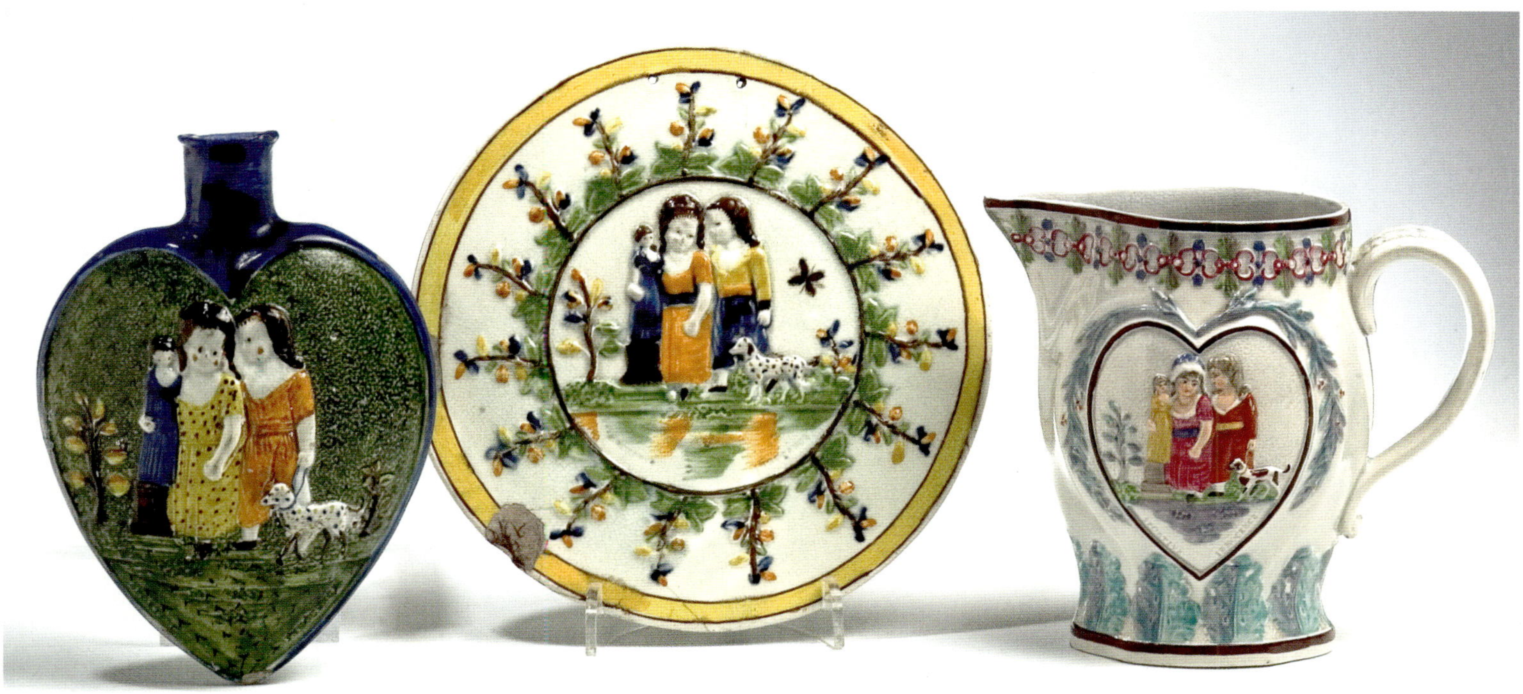

Flask, (**1567**), c.1810, Staffordshire, height: 15.3cm, (6in), Prattware. Relief-moulded with two children, a doll and a dog, impressed, 'SPORTIVE INNOCENCE', taken from Bartolozzi's print after a painting by William Hamilton.[21]

Plaque, (**1568**), c.1810, Staffordshire, diameter: 16.5cm, (6½in), Prattware. Relief-moulded with 'Sportive Innocence'.
Cream Jug, (**1566**), c.1810, Staffordshire, height: 12.7cm, (5in), enamelled pearl-ware. Relief-moulded, within heart-shaped reserve, with 'Sportive Innocence'.

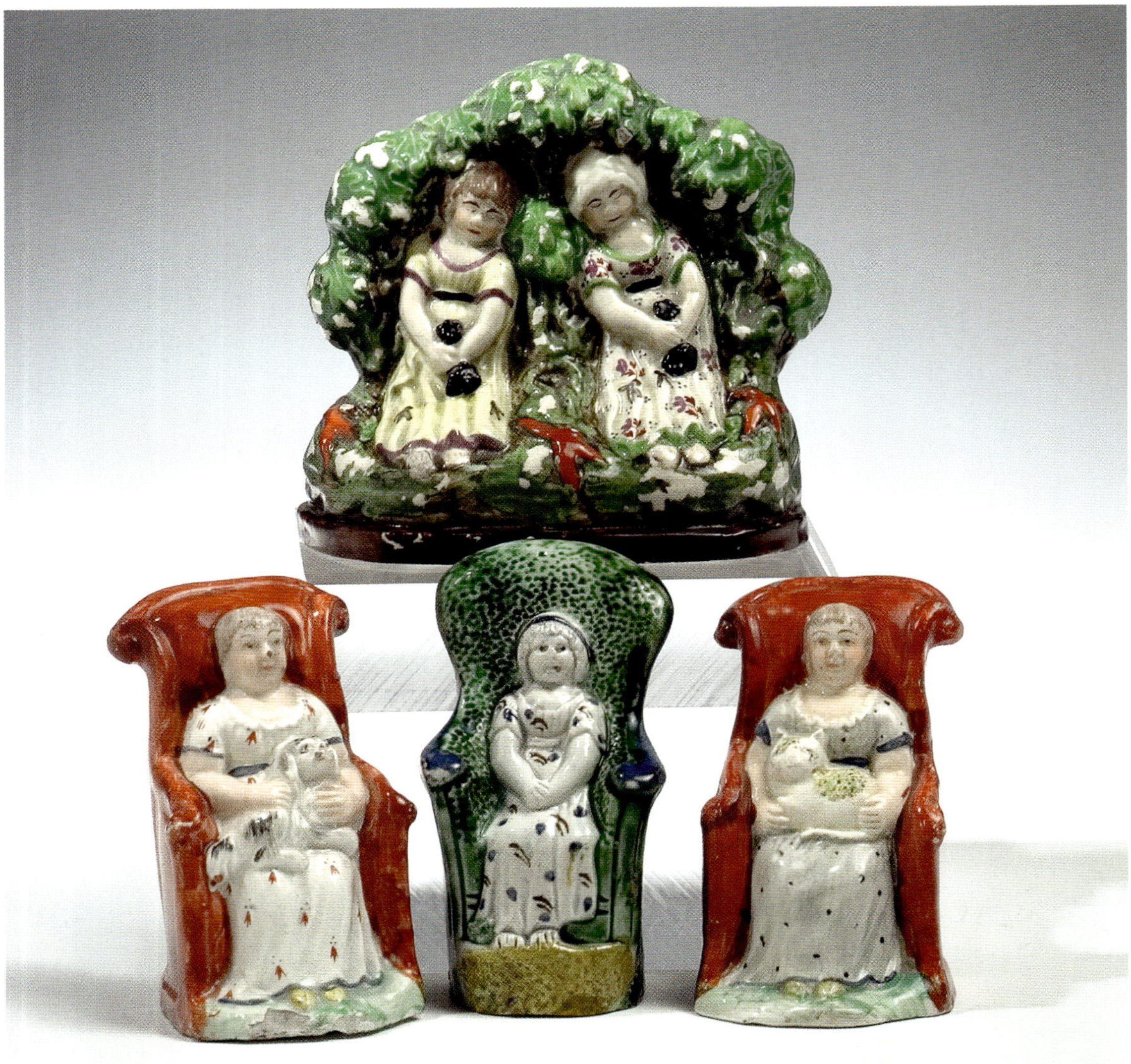

Three Figures, (**1618 & A & B**), c.1820, Staffordshire, height x 2: 7.6cm, (3in), height: 8.5cm, (3⅜in), Prattware and enamelled pearlware. Three little girls sit in armchairs; one holds a dog, one a cat.

Figure Group, (**1560**), c.1820, Staffordshire, height: 9.5cm, (3¾in), enamelled pearlware. Appears to illustrate the 'Babes in the Wood'; two sleeping children nestled in a bush.

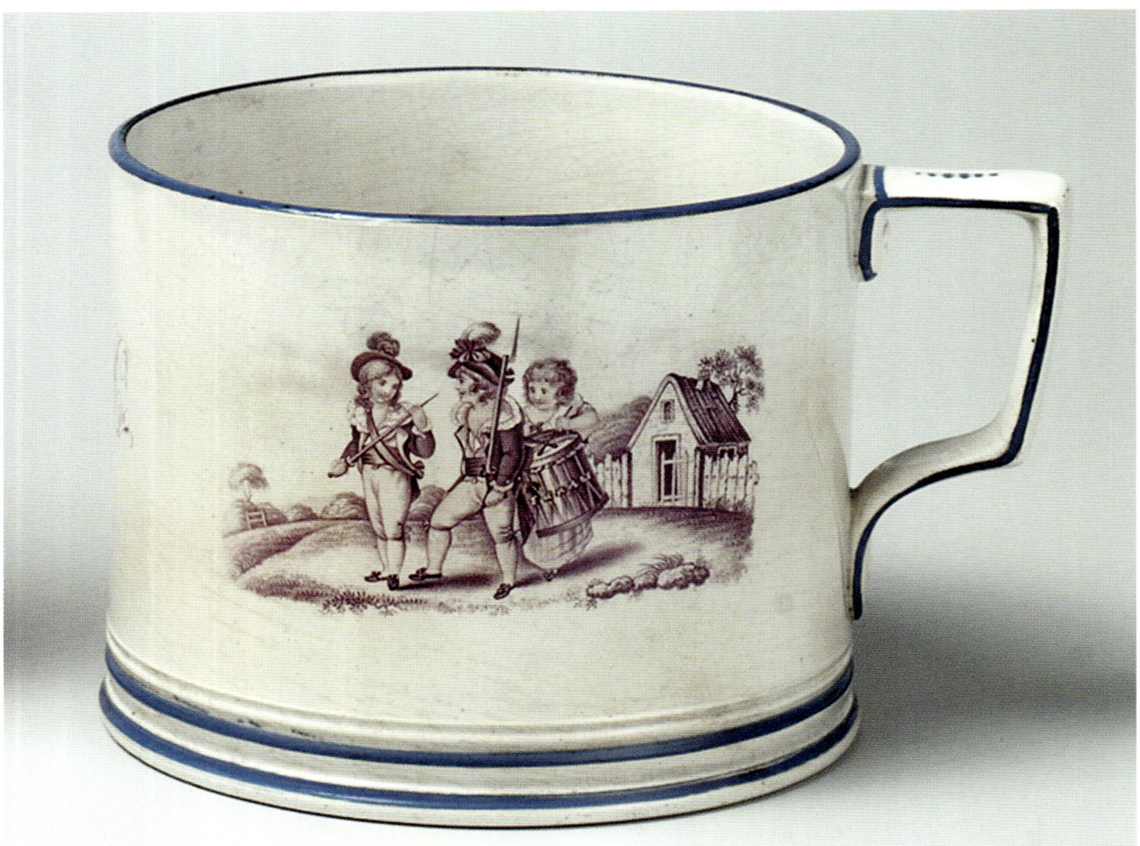

Large Mug, (327), c.1790, Liverpool, Herculaneum, height: 11.4cm, (4½in), pearlware. Printed in puce. On one side, three children dressed as soldiers practise army drill (image taken from the print, 'Children at Play', published in 1782); on the other, a seascape with warships.

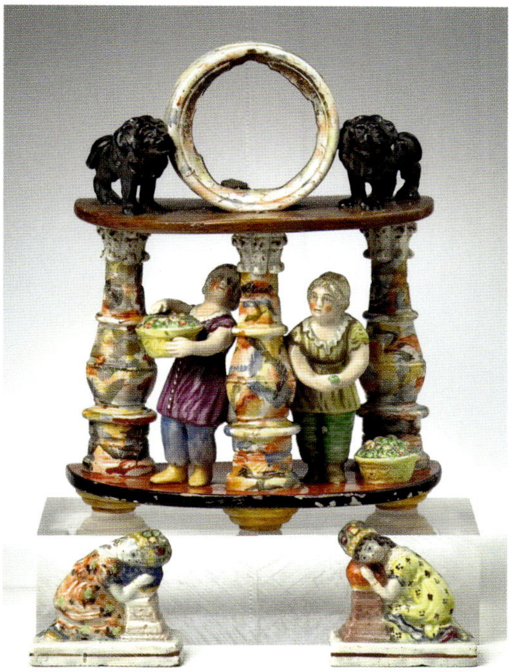

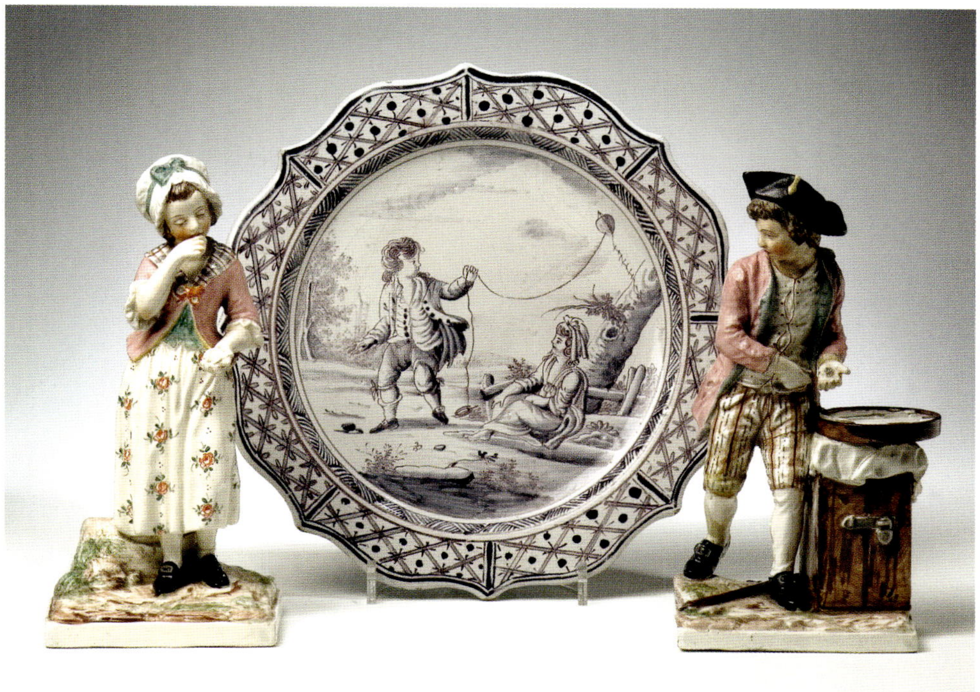

Two figures, (**1576 & A**), c.1810, Staffordshire, each height: 6cm, (2⅜in), enamelled pearlware. Tiny girls wearing floral wreaths, rest their heads on cushioned plinths. Such figures sometimes used as knops for box lids.
Watchstand, (**1577**), c.1820, Staffordshire, height: 22.3cm, (8¾in), enamelled pearlware. Watch-holder flanked by small black lions. Two children with baskets of fruit beneath.

Pair of Figures, (**1593 & A**), c.1850, France, height: 21cm, (8¼in), height: 22cm, (8⅝in), enamelled earthenware. A girl tastes a delicacy and a boy stands beside a roulette clock-faced games board, holding money. Copied from late-eighteenth century models by Pierre Stephan at St Clément or Niderviller.[22]
Plate, (**1583**), c.1780, France, diameter: 24.8cm, (9¾in), tin-glazed earthenware, painted in manganese oxide. A girl watches a boy in rumpled clothing fly his kite.

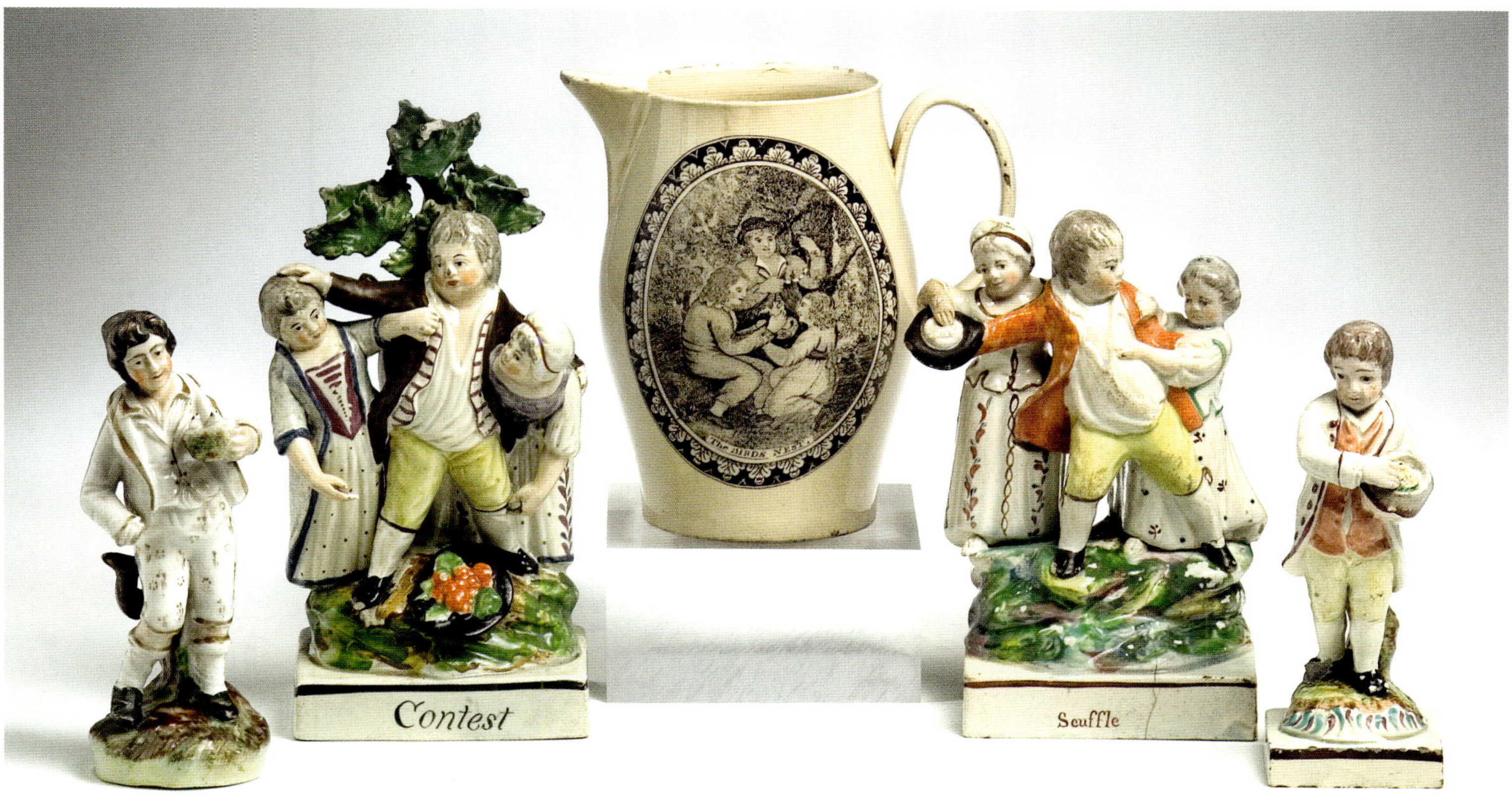

Figure, (**1605**), c.1840, Staffordshire, height: 15.3cm, (6in), bone china, enamelled and gilt. A boy holds a nest containing two white fledglings.
Figure Group, (**1591**), c.1820, Staffordshire, height: 20.3cm, (8in), enamelled pearlware. Entitled 'Contest', three children fight over a hatful of fruit.
Jug, (**1598**), c.1800, Staffordshire, height: 15.3cm, (6in), printed creamware. 'The BIRDS NEST', shows three children handling nestlings.

Figure Group, (**1602**),[23] c.1820, Staffordshire, height: 16.5cm, (6½in), enamelled pearlware. Entitled 'Scuffle', three children fight over a hatful of bird's eggs.
Figure, (**1599**), c.1820, Staffordshire, height: 14cm, (5½in), enamelled pearlware. A boy guards a nest of eggs or newly hatched chicks inside his hat. Children regularly stole songbirds' eggs (for eating or collecting) and fledglings to sell as caged pets.

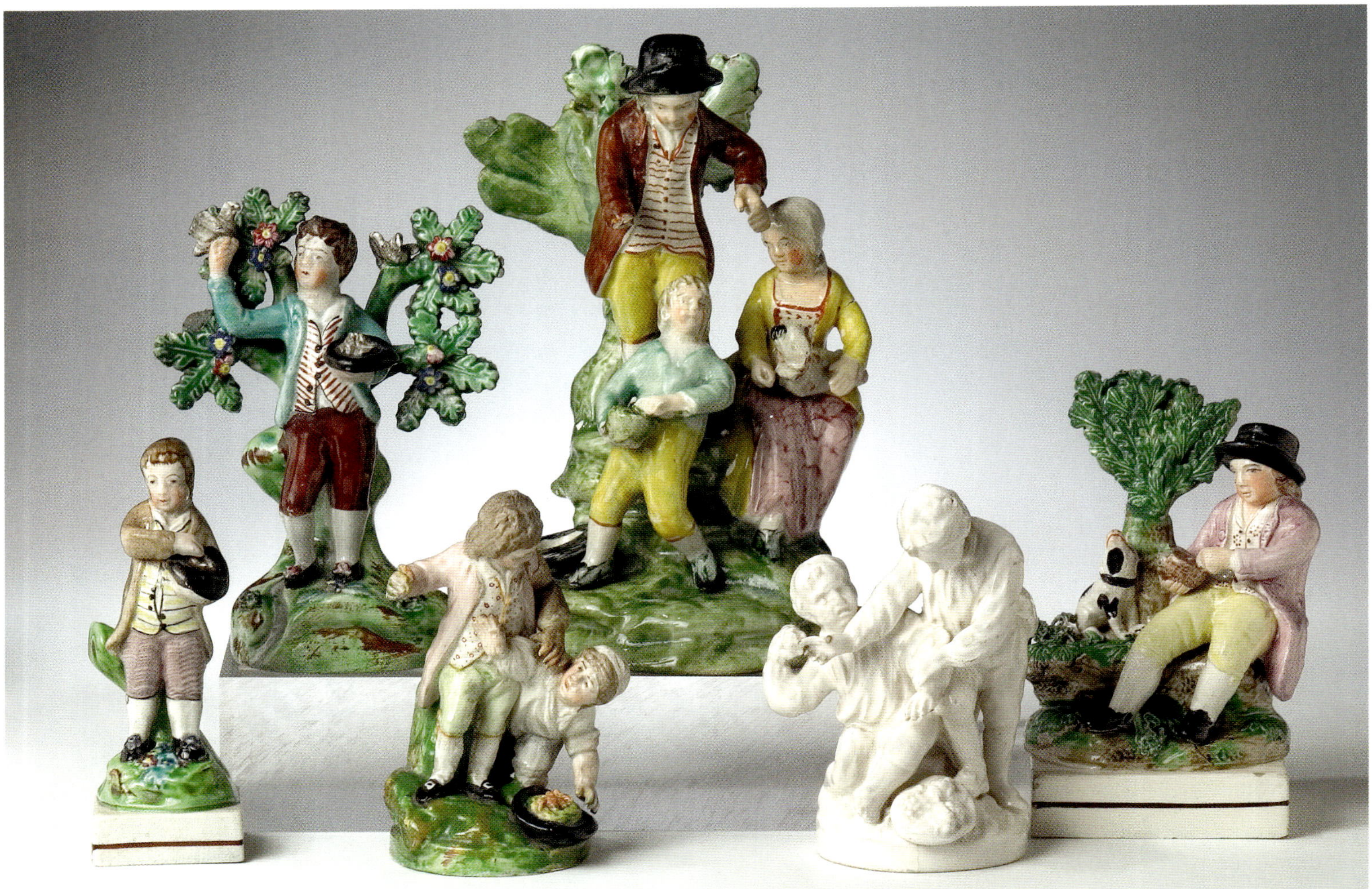

Figure, (**1600**), c.1820, Staffordshire, height: 14.6cm, (5¾in), enamelled pearlware. A boy guards a nest of eggs or newly hatched chicks inside his black hat.
Figure, (**1601**), c.1820, Staffordshire, height: 14cm, (5½in), enamelled pearlware. A boy stands before a tree, fighting off a mother bird whose fledglings he has stolen.
Figure Group, (**1604**), c.1820, Staffordshire, height: 12.7cm, (5in), enamelled pearlware. Two boys tussle over a bird's nest.
Figure Group, (**1608**), c.1820, Staffordshire, height: 20.3cm, (8in), enamelled pearlware. Two adults with a dog observe a boy holding a green nest.
Figure Group, (**1590**), c.1820, Staffordshire, height: 12.7cm, (5in), soft-paste porcelain. Two boys fight over a hat full of grapes.
Figure Group, (**1606**), c.1820, Staffordshire, height: 14cm, (5½in), enamelled pearlware. A boy holding a nest, and his dog sit beneath a tree.

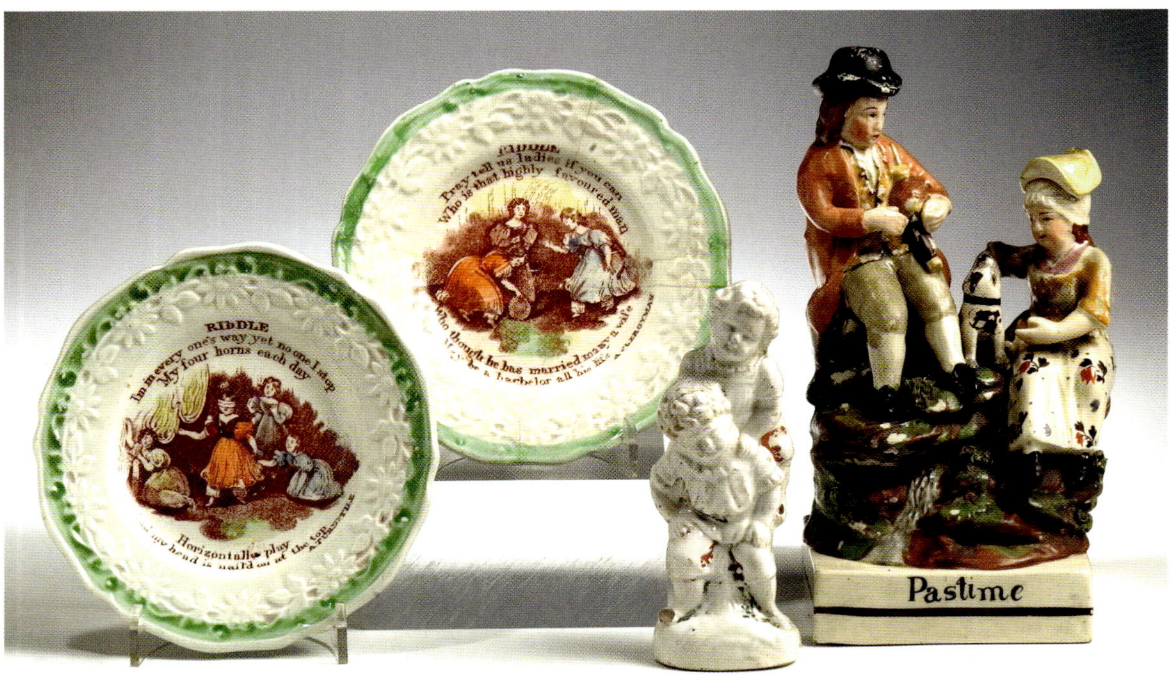

Pair of Nursery Plates, (**1587 & A**), c.1840, Staffordshire, each diameter: 13.4cm, (5¼in), pearlware, red-printed and coloured. Each is inscribed with a riddle and illustrates a game; 'blind man's buff' and 'spinning the trencher'.
Figure Group, (**1589**), c.1840, Staffordshire, height: 12.7cm, (5in), bone china. Two boys play piggy back.
Figure Group, (**1629**), c.1820, Staffordshire, height: 19.1cm, (7in), enamelled pearlware. Entitled 'Pastime', a boy and girl teach their dog to perform tricks.

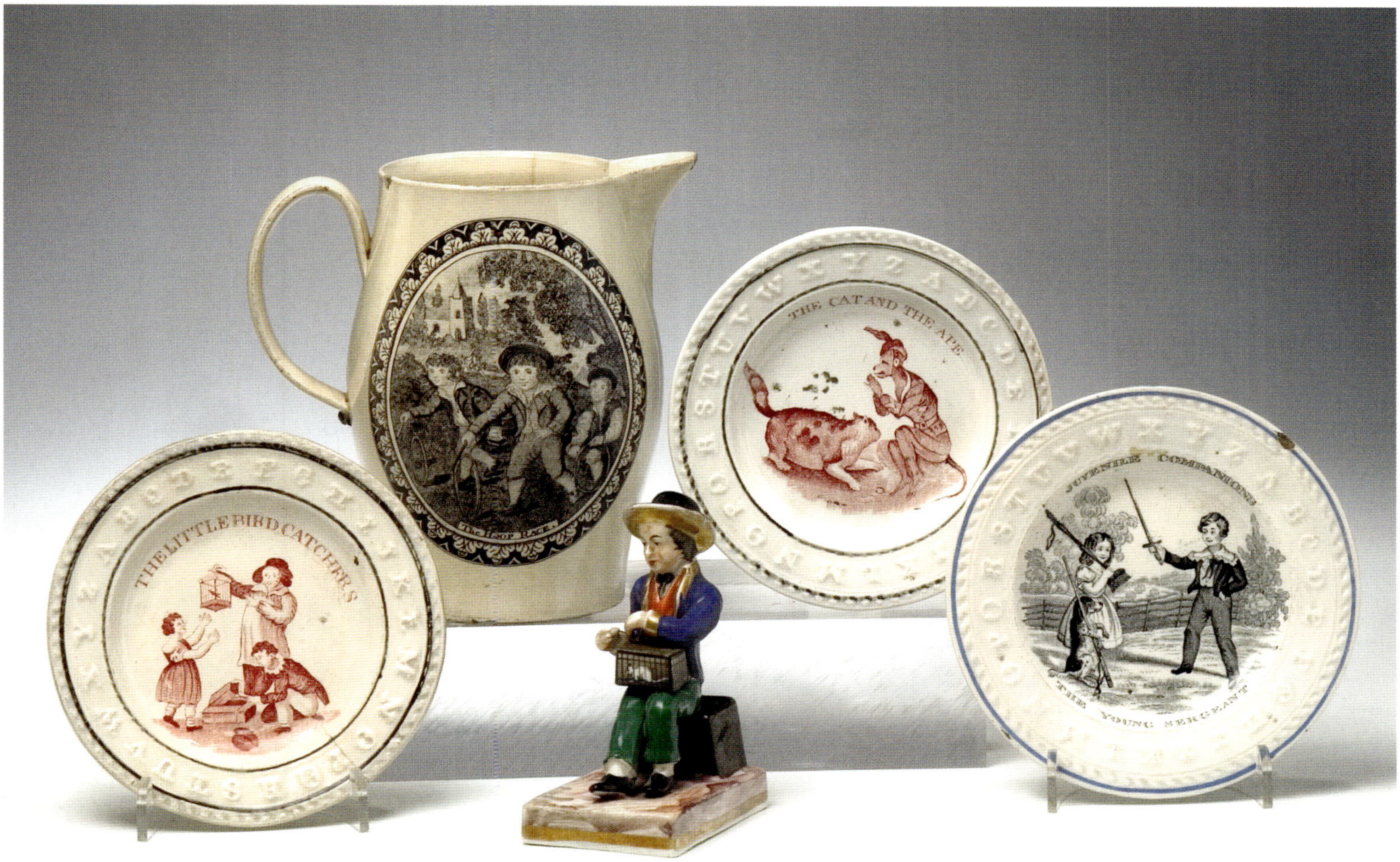

Nursery Plate, (**1610**), c.1830, Staffordshire, diameter: 12.7cm, (5in), red-printed earthenware. 'LITTLE BIRD CATCHERS', shows children transferring a bird from a trap to a cage.
Jug, (**1598**), c.1800, Staffordshire, height: 15.3cm, (6in), printed creamware. 'THE HOOP RACE', is based on a print published 26 August 1795 by John Fairburn.
Figure, (**1620**), c.1830, Italian?, height: 10.2cm, (4in), porcelain, enamelled and gilt. A boy holds a cage containing a white, pet rat.
Nursery Plate, (**1579**), c.1830, Staffordshire, diameter: 12.7cm, (5in), red-printed earthenware. 'THE CAT AND THE APE' shows the ape dressed in clothes.
Nursery Plate, (**1584**), c.1860, Staffordshire, Tunstall, diameter: 13.3cm, (5¼in), red-printed earthenware. Inscribed, 'JUVENILE COMPANIONS / THE YOUNG SERGEANT' shows a boy a girl and their dog playing soldiers. Probably by Elsmore & Forster of Tunstall.[24]

Plate, (862), c.1820, Swansea, Glamorgan Pottery, diameter: 17.8cm (7in), pearlware, printed and enamelled. Inscribed 'I know that my Redeemer liveth, And that he shall Stand on the earth at the last Day' with the inspiring words from Job ch:19 v:25. Border relief-moulded with animal figures.
Nursery Plate, (**1607**), c.1830, Glamorgan Pottery, diameter: 15.3cm, (6in), pearlware, printed and enamelled. Border relief-moulded with animals. Shows two boys 'TAKING YOUNG BIRDS' while the mother bird gazes down in distress.

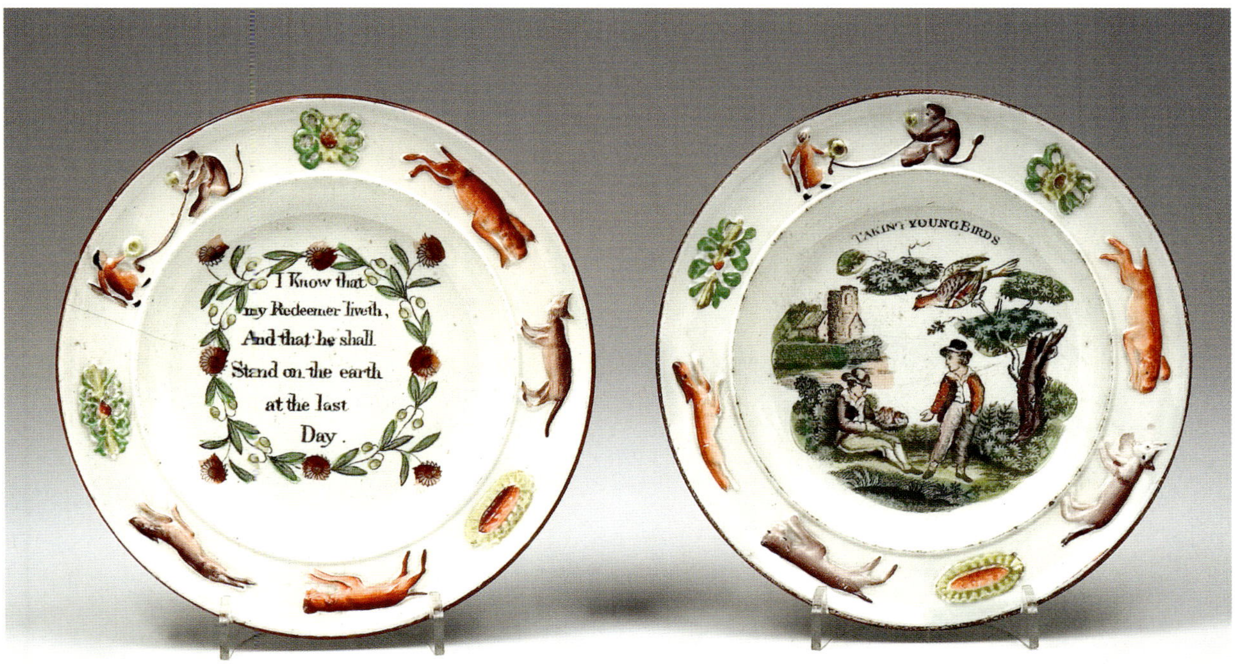

Animal Companions

Models of canine and feline companions were made in Ptolemaic Egypt and are found among Chinese grave goods of the Tang dynasty. Lap dogs, especially pugs, were great favourites in the eighteenth century and are represented as essential accessories in portraits of society women and actresses. Samuel Johnson was devoted to his cat Hodge, and Hogarth's trusty pug, Trump, was not only drawn by the artist but modelled at the Chelsea porcelain factory, based on a terracotta portrait by the sculptor Louis-François Roubiliac.

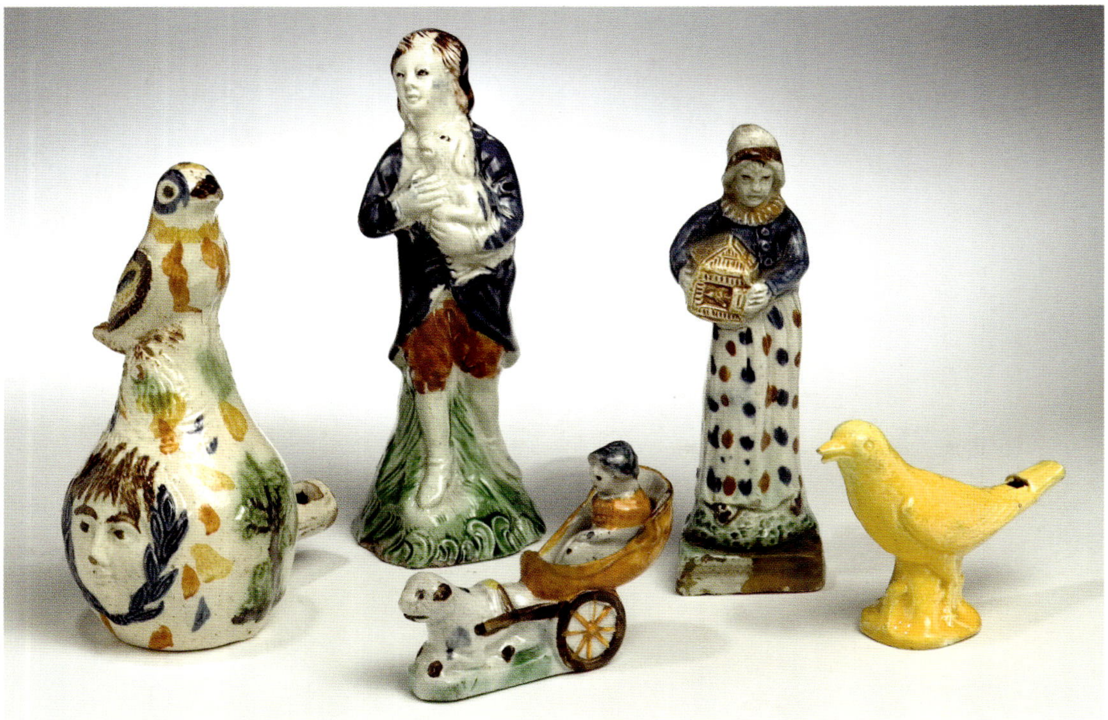

Whistle, (**1580**), c.1810, Staffordshire, height: 14cm, (5½in), Prattware. 'Fountain' whistle with a bird perched on top. Air is blown through a chamber full of water.
Figure, (**1628**), c.1800, Staffordshire, height: 15.7cm, (6¼in), Prattware. A boy hugs a puppy.
Figure Group, (**1563**), c.1800, Staffordshire, height: 8.9cm, (3½in), Prattware. Child in a small cart being pulled by a dog or goat.
Figure, (**1621**), c.1800, Staffordshire, height: 14cm, (5½in), Prattware. A girl holds a birdcage.
Whistle, (**1597**), c.1810, Staffordshire, height: 7.7cm, (3in), yellow-glazed earthenware. Model of a canary.

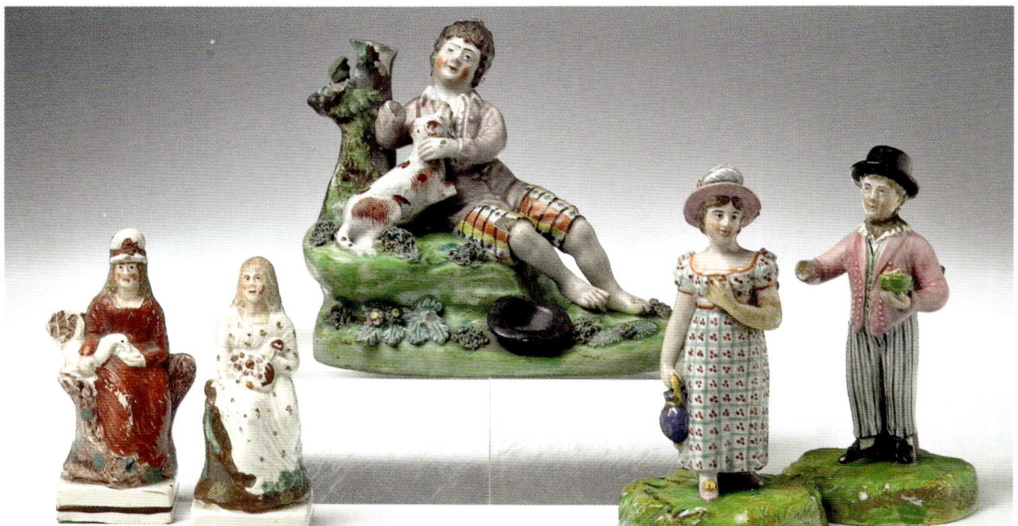

Two Figures, (**1627 & A**), c.1800, Staffordshire, each height: 10.8cm, (4¼in), enamelled pearlware. The girl in red feeds a chicken; the other holds a basket of flowers.
Figure Group, (**1634**), c.1820, Staffordshire, height: 13.3cm, (5¼in), enamelled pearlware. A youth with a dog lies beside a tree stump.
Pair of Figures, (**1603 & A**), c.1820, Staffordshire, height: 14cm, (5½in), height: 14.5cm, (5¾in), enamelled pearlware. An adolescent boy (missing a hand) tries to impress a girl with a bird's nest.

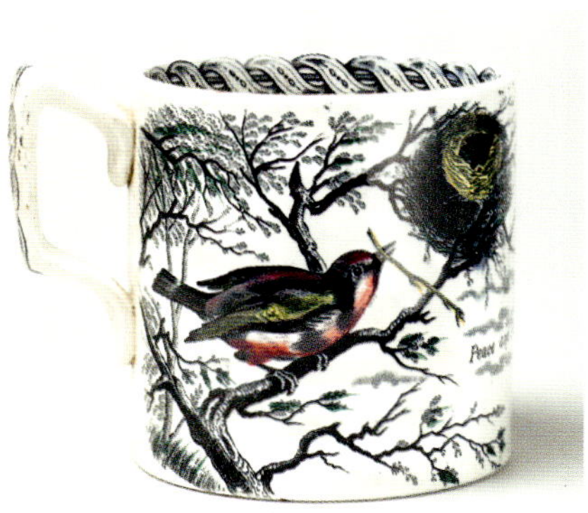

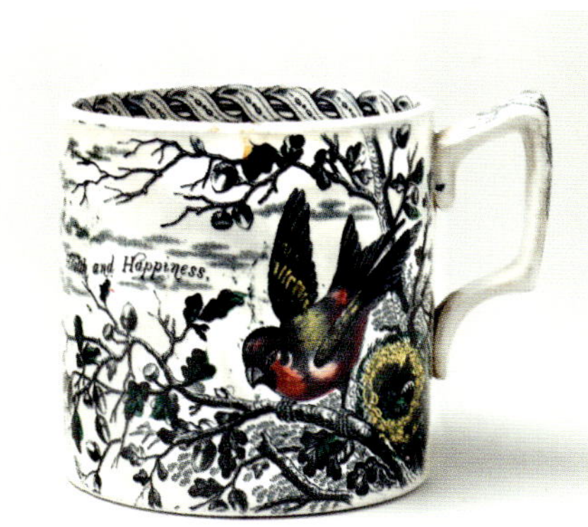

Mug, (**1611**), c.1880, Staffordshire, height: 10.2cm, (4in), printed earthenware. Designs of a bullfinch and another bird with their nests, representing, 'Peace and Plenty / Health and Happiness'.

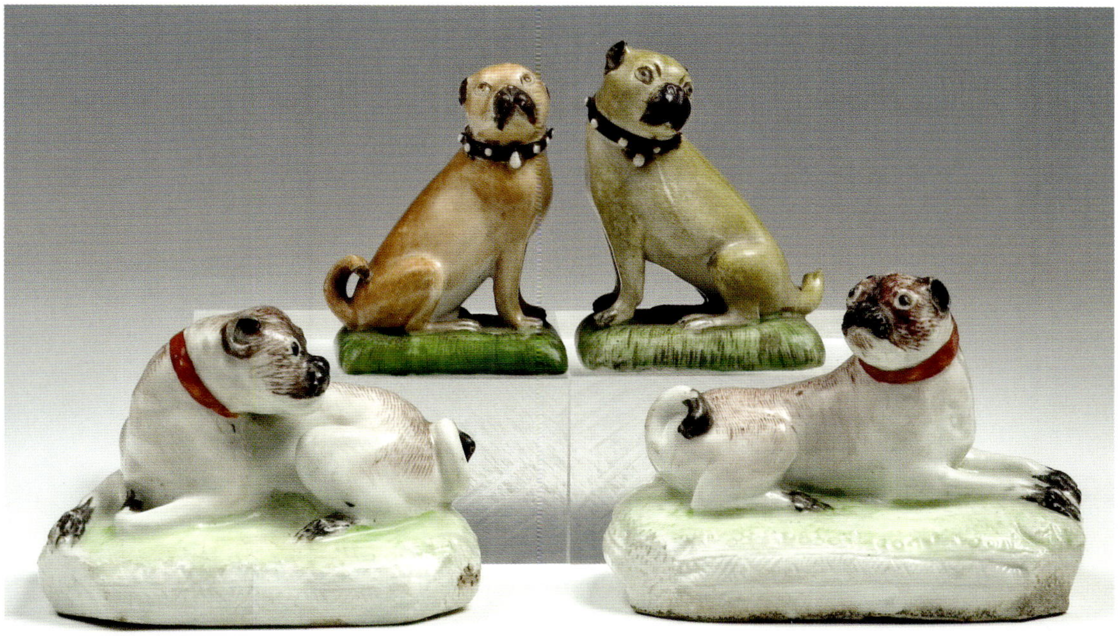

Pair of Dogs, (**1201 & A**), c.1755, London, Bow, each height: 8.2cm, (3¼in), enamelled soft-paste porcelain. Pair of pugs with red collars, lying on cushions incised with chevron patterns.
Pair of Dogs, (**1200 & A**), c.1800, Derby, each height: 8.2cm, (3¼in), enamelled soft-paste porcelain. The dogs, wearing studded collars, sit upright on grassy knolls.

Pair of Dogs, (**1619 & A**), c.1840, Staffordshire, each height: 11.5cm, (4½in), soft-paste porcelain, enamelled and gilt. Children clamber on each of two spaniels.
Pair of Inkwells, (**1205 & A**), c.1840, Staffordshire, each height: 7.7cm, (3in), soft-paste porcelain, enamelled and gilt. Modelled with spaniels lying on footstools suckling puppies.

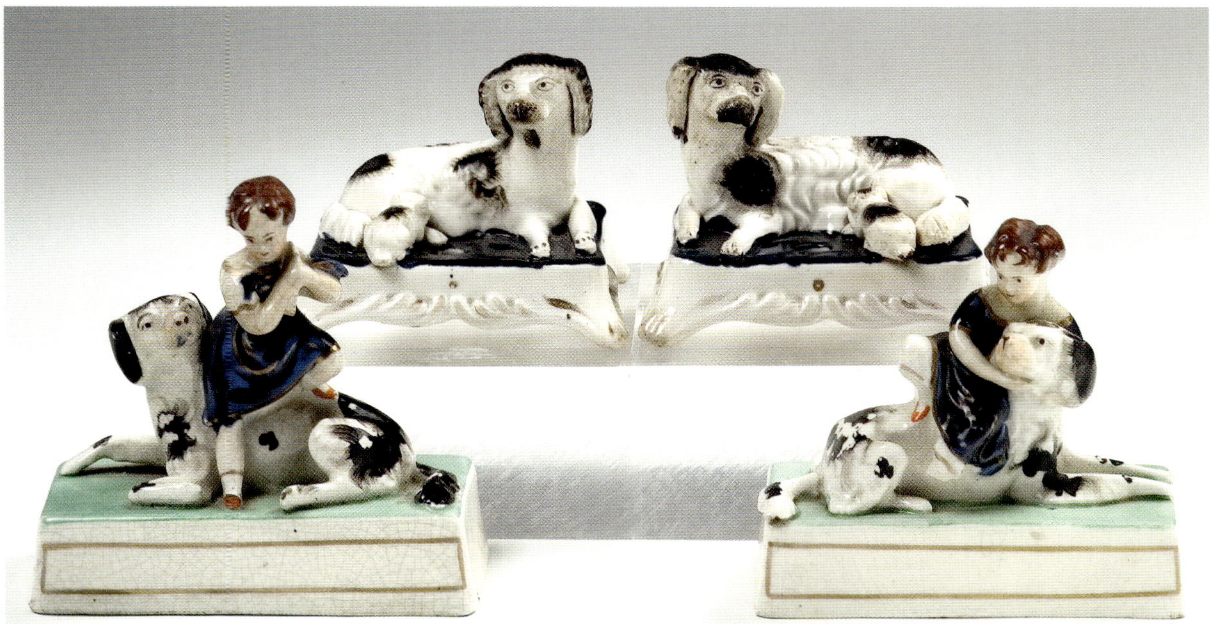

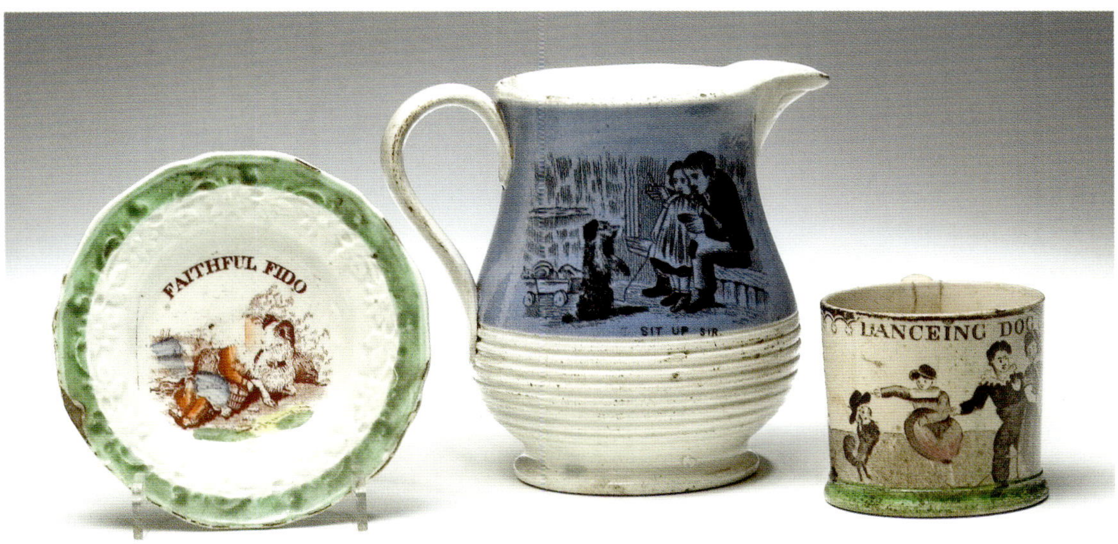

Nursery Plate, (**1624**), c.1840, Staffordshire, diameter: 11.5cm, (4½in), pearlware, red-printed and coloured. 'FAITHFUL FIDO'; shows a girl nuzzling into a dog's back.
Jug, (**1630**), c.1830, Staffordshire, height: 12.7cm, (5in), printed and slip-decorated pearlware. A man and a small child train a dog; 'SIT UP SIR'.
Mug, (**1626**), c.1830, Staffordshire, height: 6.4cm, (2½in), brown-printed earthenware. Crude print entitled, 'DANCEING DOGS [*sic*]'.

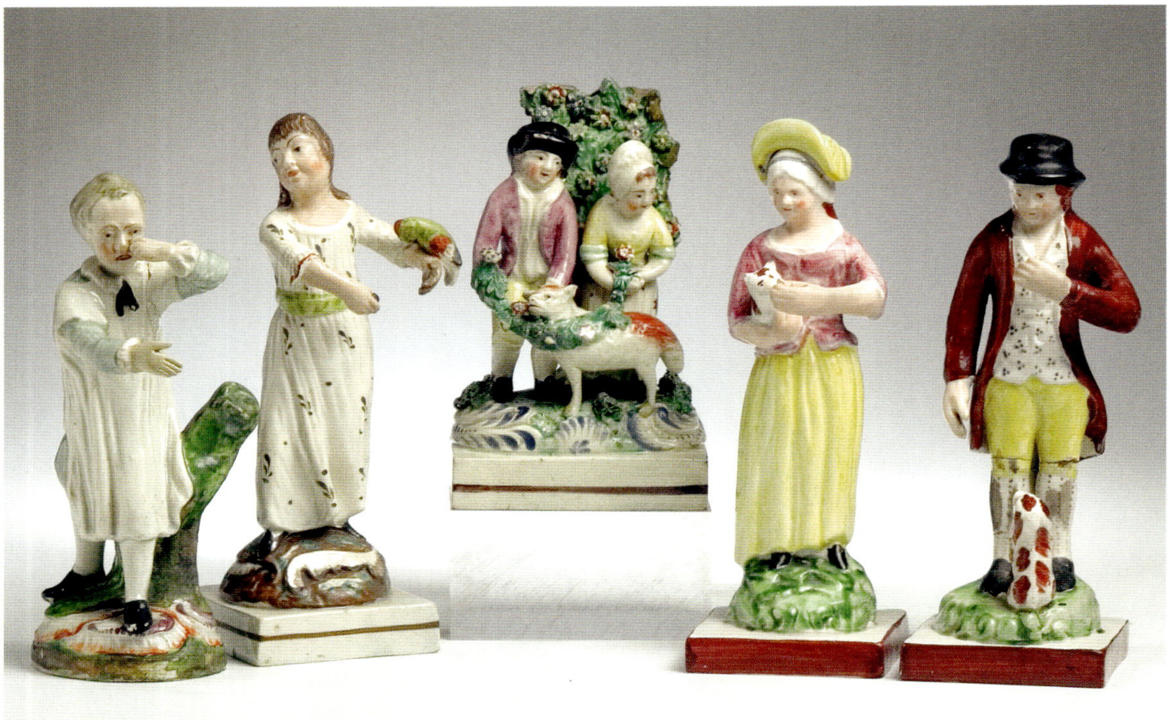

Figure, (**1595**), c.1810, Staffordshire, height: 19.1cm, (7½in), enamelled pearlware. A boy cries over a broken jug (having spilt milk).
Figure, (**1631**), c.1810, Staffordshire, height: 20.3cm, (8in), enamelled pearlware. A laughing girl with a parrot on her arm. Both inspired by pair of Derby porcelain figures where the girl steals her brother's ball, making him cry.[25]
Figure Group, (**1615**), c.1810, Staffordshire, height: 16.5cm, (6½in), enamelled pearlware. A boy and girl twining a garland round a lamb's neck; there were always orphaned lambs to care for.
Pair of Figures, (**1633 & 1632**), c.1820, Staffordshire, height: 16.5cm, (6½in), height: 20.3cm, (8in), enamelled pearlware. A young woman feeds a cat and a young man teaches a dog to beg.

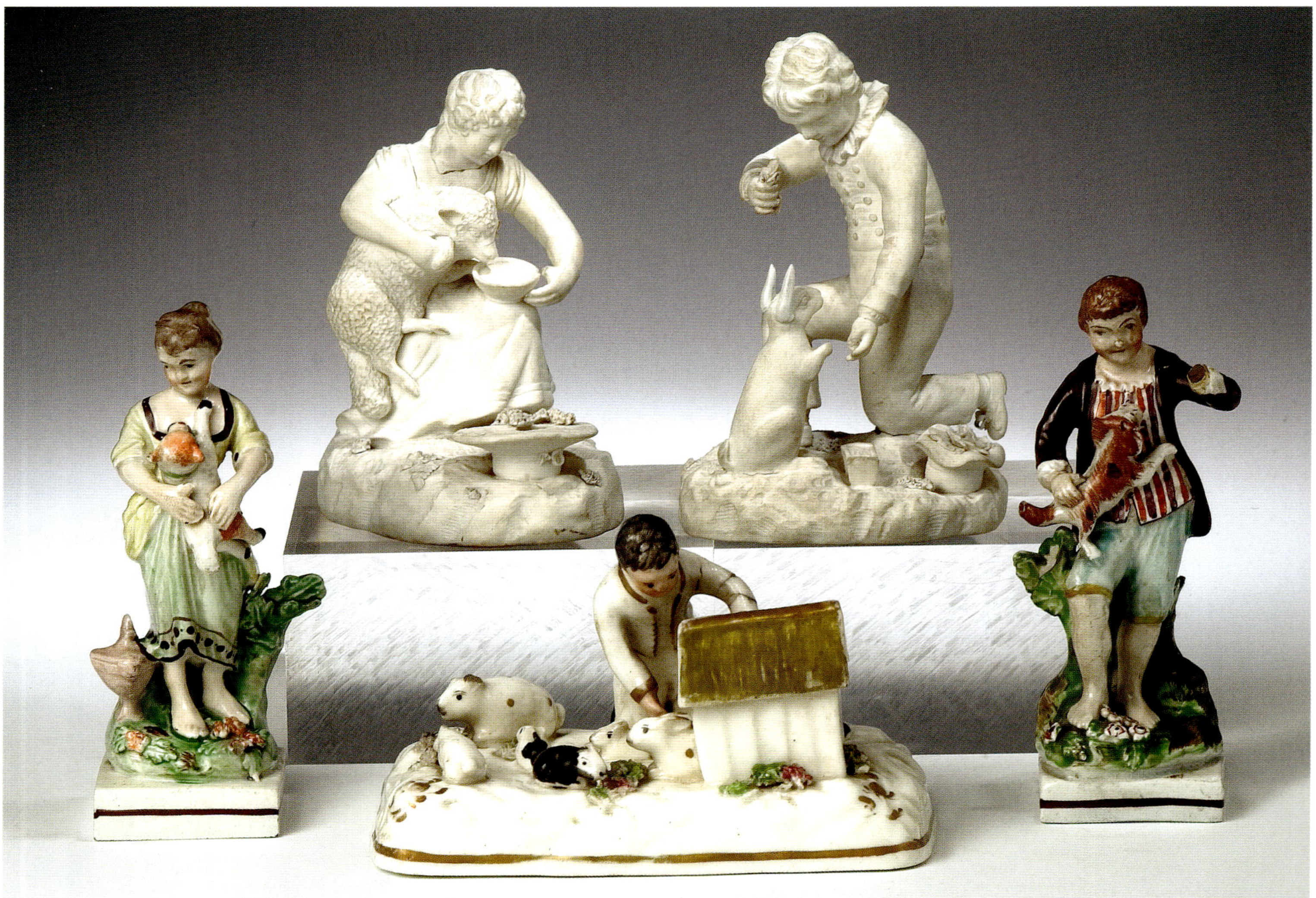

Clockwise:
Pair of Figures, (**1625 & A**), c.1810, Staffordshire, each height: 12cm, (4¾in), enamelled pearlware. A girl holds a lamb and (on far right) a boy plays with a dog.
Pair of Figures, (**1623 & 1622**), c.1830, Yorkshire, Rockingham, height: 10.2cm, (4in), height: 12.1cm, (4¾in), biscuit porcelain. A girl sits to feed a lamb and a boy kneels to feed a rabbit.
Figure Group, (**1616**), c.1840, Staffordshire, height: 12.7cm, (5in), enamelled soft-paste porcelain. A boy tends a hutch full of rabbits, which were kept as pets as well as for meat and fur.

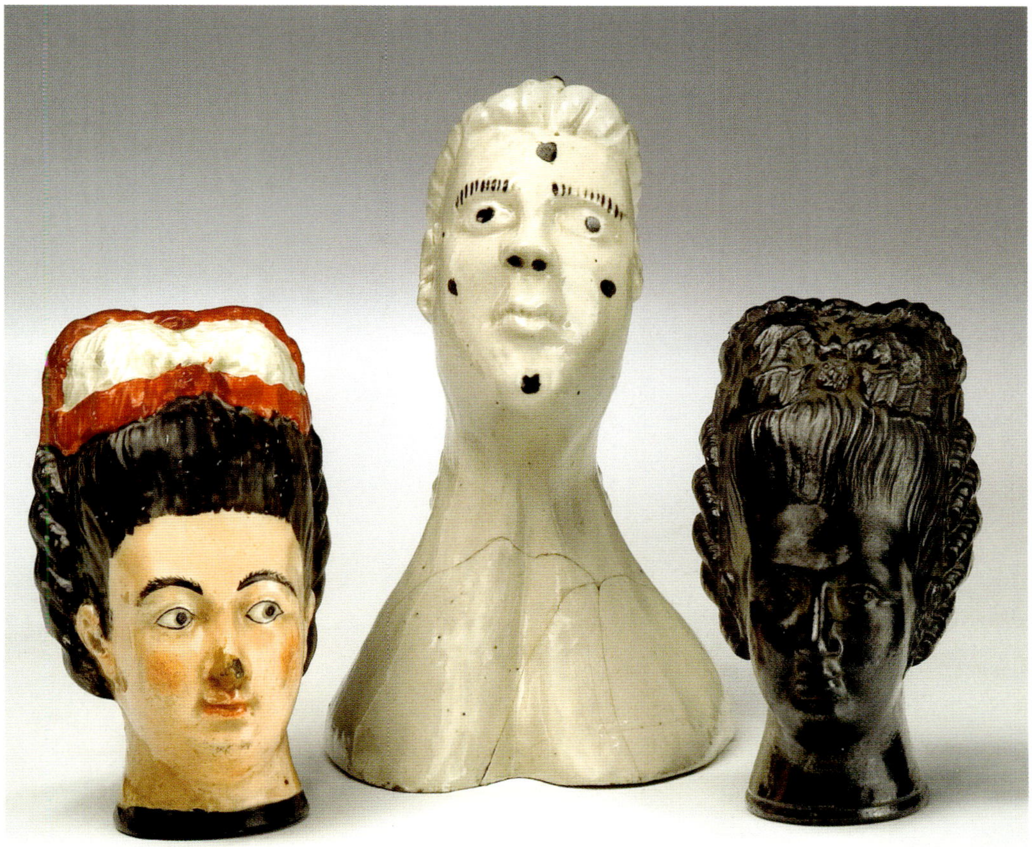

Two Patch-boxes, (**1682 & A**), Staffordshire, each height: 8.2cm, (3¼in), enamelled earthenware. Snuff boxes, or patch boxes, modelled as the heads of court ladies with their exaggerated hair styles, would have had screw-threaded ceramic lids.
Bust, (**1637**), c.1760, Staffordshire, height: 12.1cm, (4¾in), salt-glazed stoneware. A woman, painted with fashionable face patches, worn as 'beauty spots' or to cover scars.

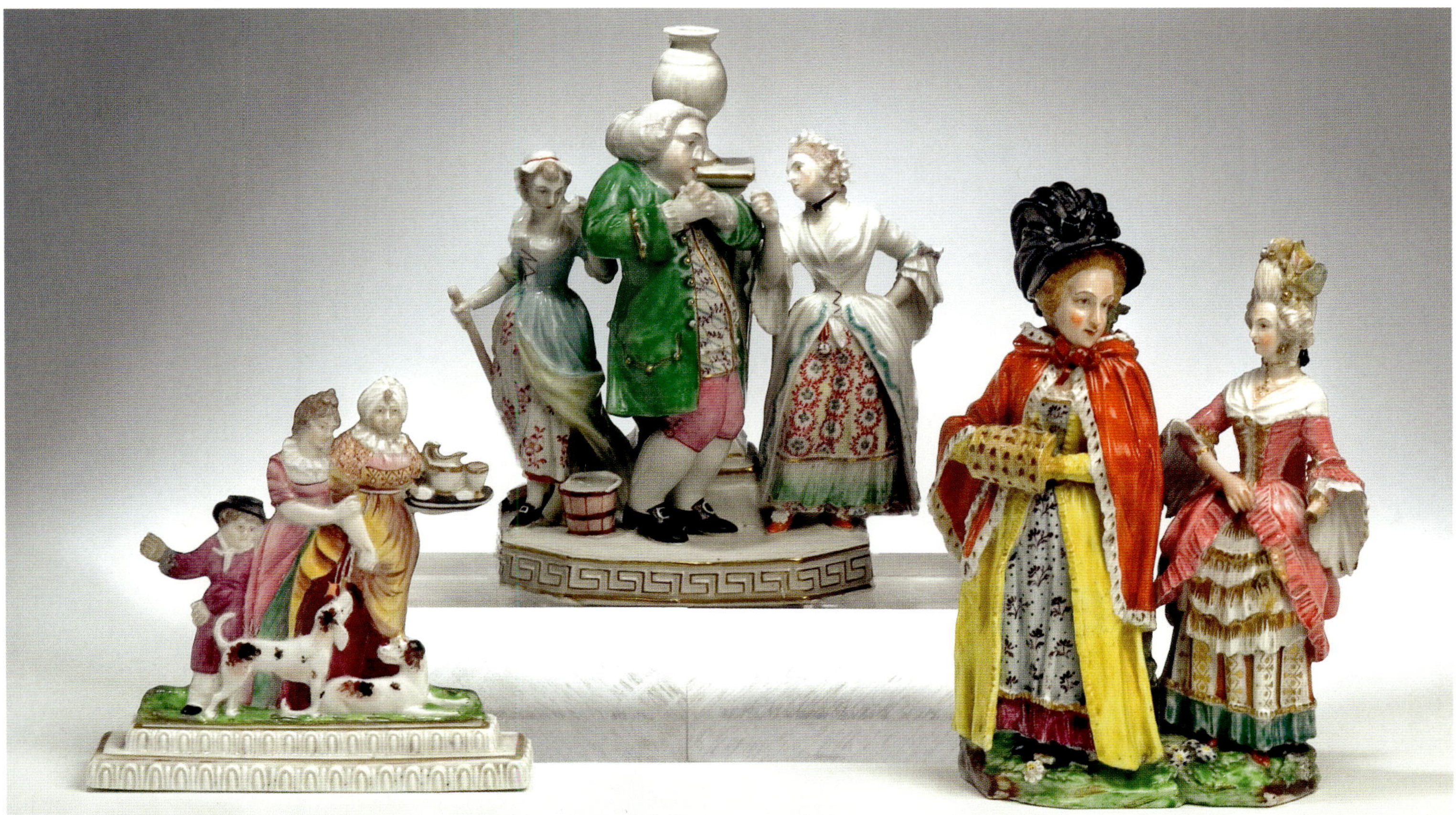

Chimney Ornament, (**1683**), c.1820, Staffordshire, height: 12.7cm, (5in), enamelled, soft-paste porcelain. Ornament on a narrow, stepped base (very similar to the figure of Queen Caroline (058), depicts a boy, two dogs and two women, one wearing a turban and carrying a tea tray.
Figure Group, (**1695**), c.1780, Derby, height: 18.3cm, (7¼in), enamelled, soft-paste porcelain. Known as 'The Unfaithful Husband', the group, (incised beneath No. 89) shows a dramatic confrontation between an enraged wife and her corpulent husband; sobbing maid cowers in the background. It may be based on a play.
Figure Group, (**1638***), c.1780, Chelsea-Derby, height: 19.7cm, (7¾in), enamelled, soft-paste porcelain. Two fashionable women are known in the Derby pattern book as 'The female Macaronis', or 'town and country beauties'. Modelled out of scale with one another, they appear to wear fashions of different decades.[26]

Fortune-Telling

Several items treat the absorbing topic of fortune-telling, with particular regard to finding husbands for young women. Publications such as '*Every Lady her own Fortune-teller; or An infallible Guide to the hidden Decrees of Fate* … price 1 shilling' were best-sellers.[27]

Tile, (**1637**), c.1760, Liverpool, height: 12.7cm, (5in), red-printed, tin-glazed earthenware. An astrologer prepares a chart for a young woman while a young man hides beneath the surprised astrologer's chair.
Tile, (**1705**), c.1760, Liverpool, height: 12.7cm, (5in), red-printed, tin-glazed earthenware. An astrologer predicts, 'A Brisk Husband soon', for one young woman while the other leaves in distress since she is, 'Never to be Married'.

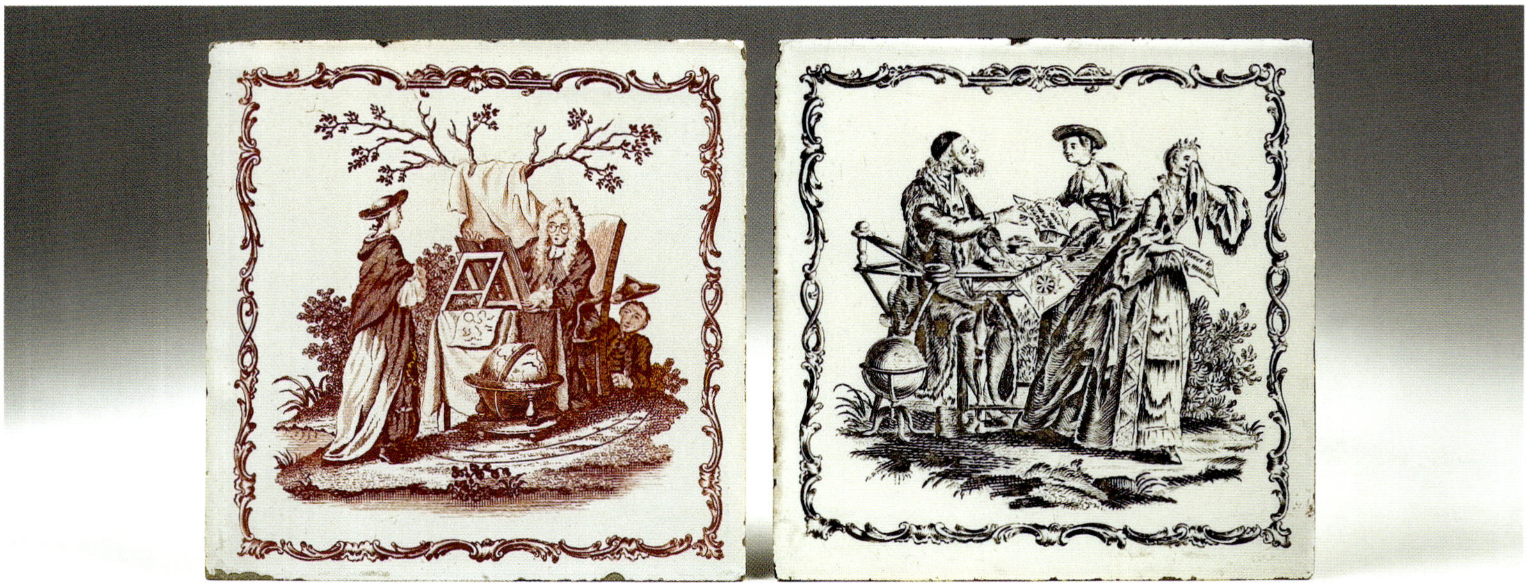

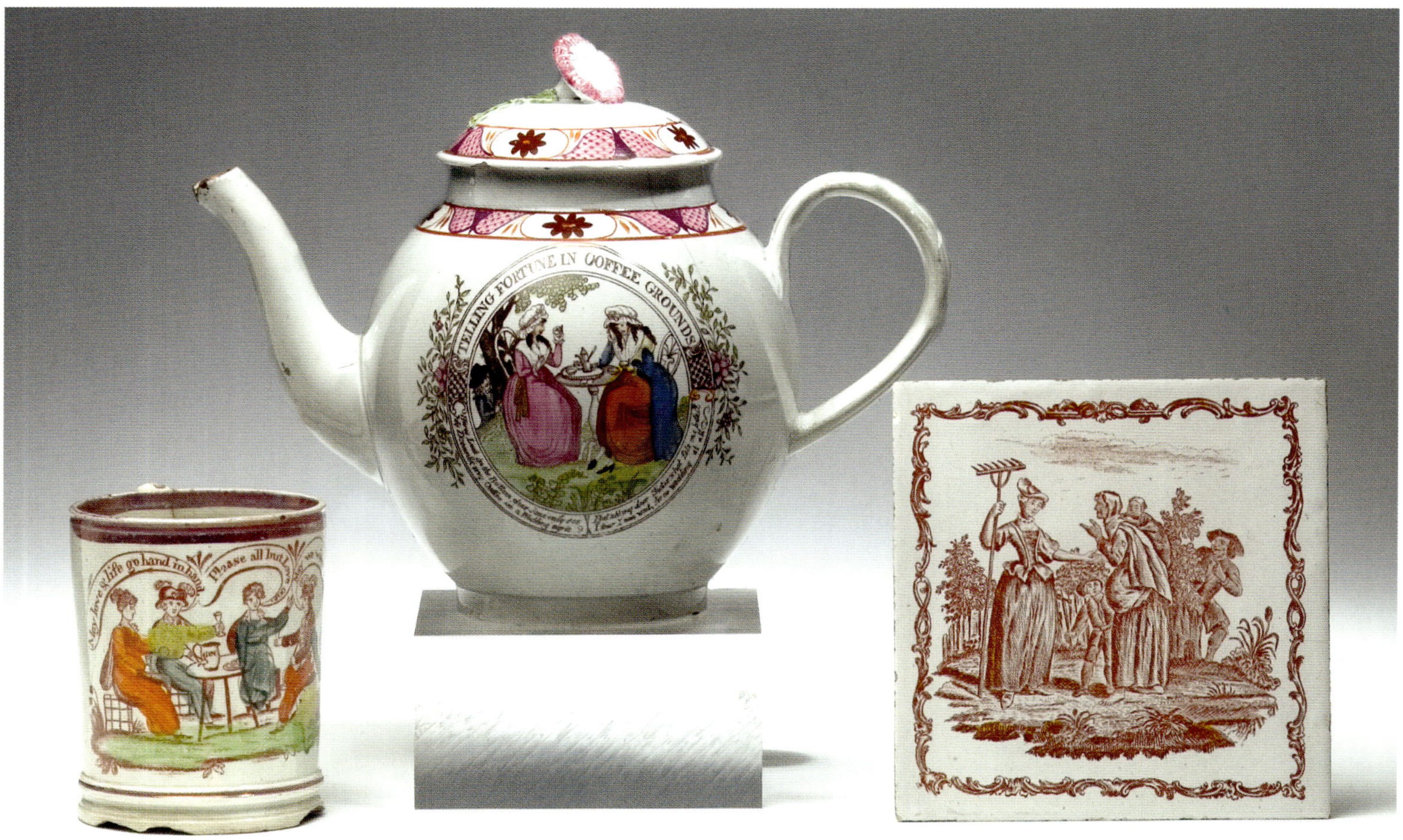

Mug, (**1660**), c.1810, Staffordshire, height: 8.9cm, (3½in), earthenware, printed, coloured and lustred. Four people drinking gin propose toast, 'May Love & Life go hand in hand…'
Teapot, (**1638**), c.1790, Staffordshire, Lane End, height: 17.8cm, (7in), pearlware, printed and enamelled. 'TELLING FORTUNE IN COFFEE GROUNDS' shows two young women gazing into coffee cups. Print signed by John Aynsley, based on one published by Robert Sayer.[28]
Tile, (**1636**), c.1770, Liverpool, height: 12.7cm, (5in), red-printed, tin-glazed earthenware. An old woman reads the palm of a haymaking girl.[29]

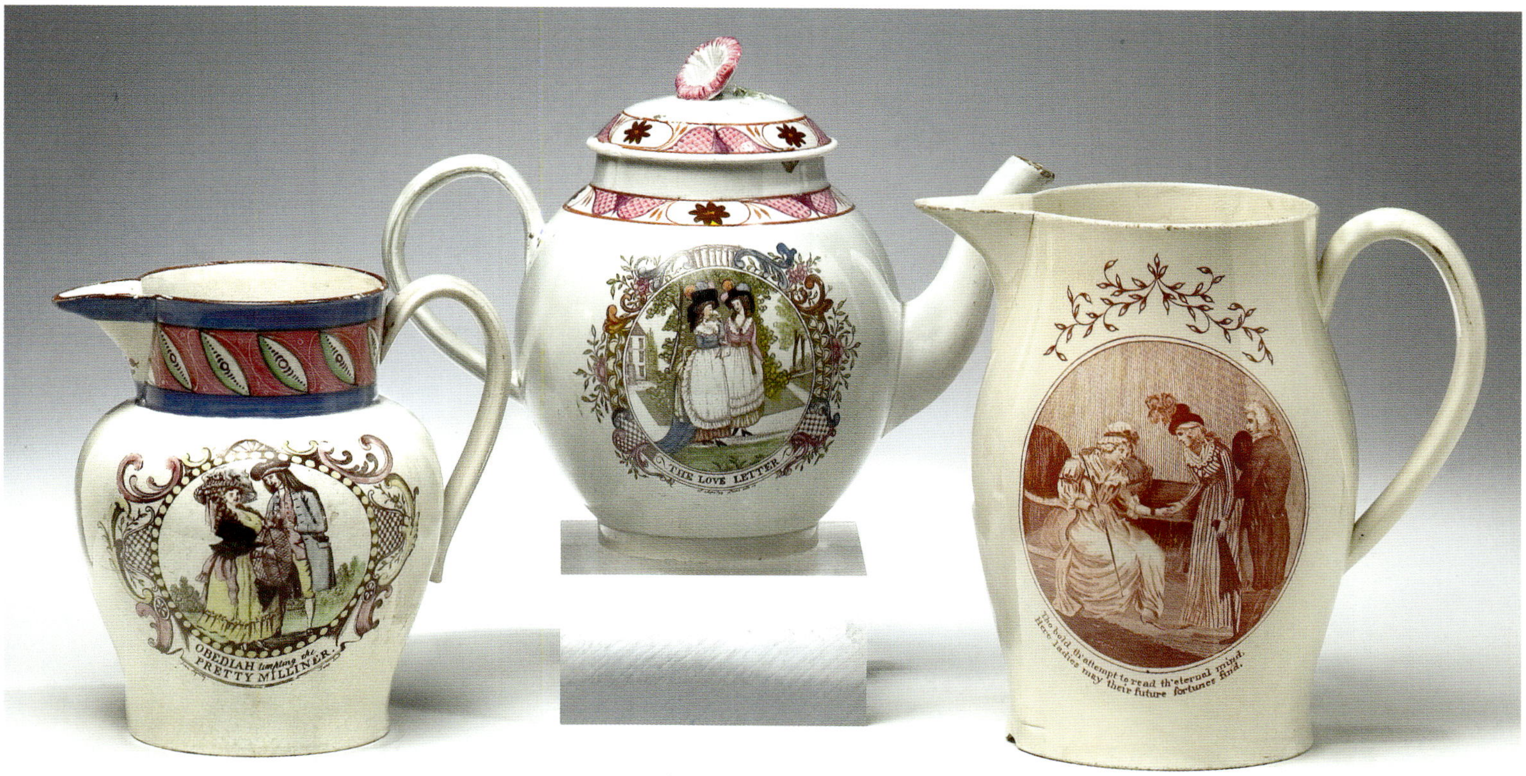

Jug, (**1667**), c.1790, Staffordshire, Lane End, height: 17.8cm, (7in), pearlware, printed and enamelled. 'OBEDIAH tempting the PRETTY MILLINER',[30] signed by John Aynsley, is taken from a mezzotint published by Robert Sayer in 1788.
Teapot, (**1638**), c.1790, Staffordshire, Lane End, height: 17.8cm, (7in), pearlware, printed and enamelled. 'THE LOVE LETTER', signed by John Aynsley, is based on a mezzotint of 1787 by Robert Sayer.[31]
Jug, (**1673**), c.1790, Staffordshire or Liverpool, height: 17.8cm, (7in), red-printed creamware. Inscribed, 'Tho bold th'attempt to read th'eternal mind. / Here ladies may their future fortunes find'. Shows a fashionable woman having her palm read.

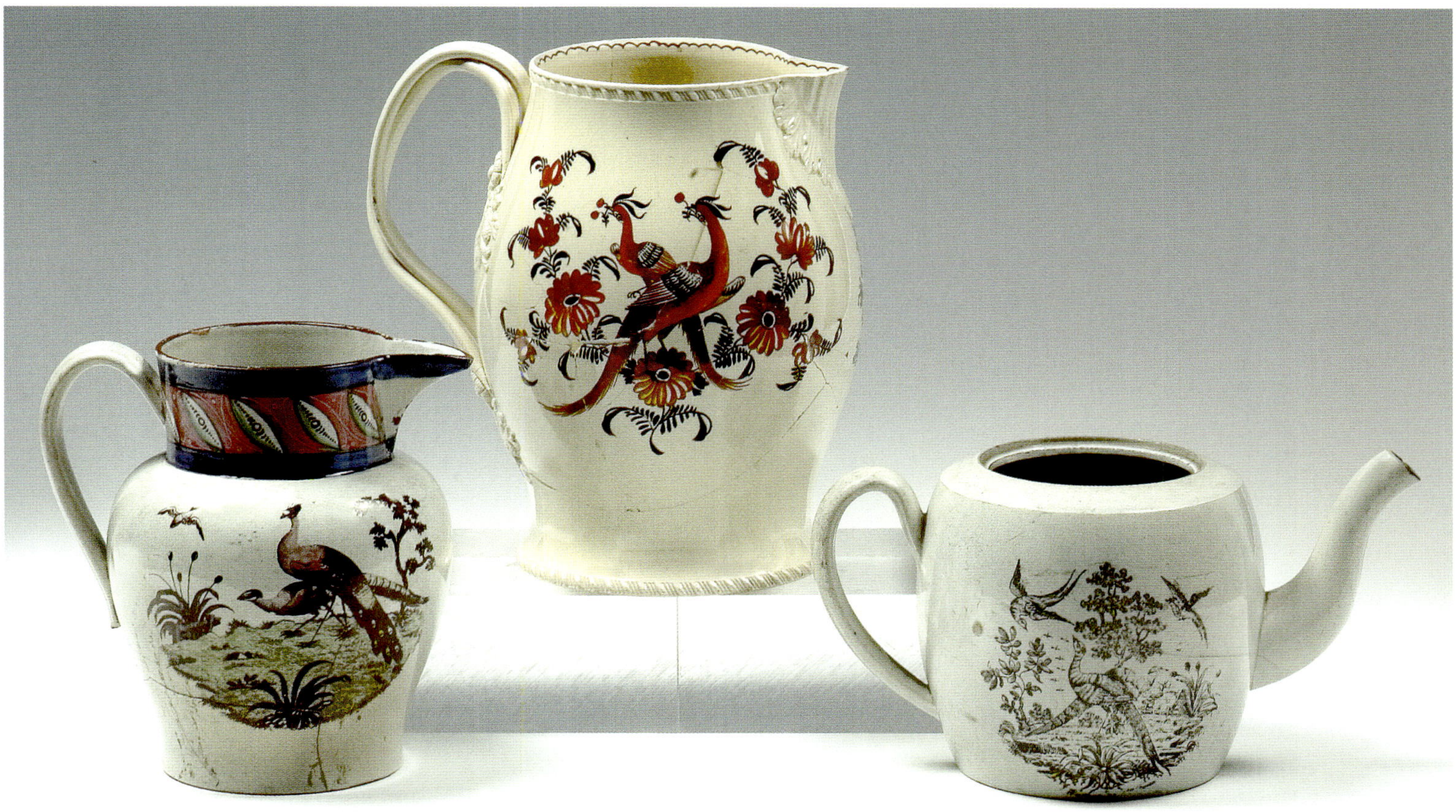

Jug, (**1667**), c.1790, Staffordshire, John Aynsley, Lane End, height: 14.6cm, (5¾in), pearlware, printed and enamelled. Printed with a pair of peafowl in landscape.
Jug, (1083), 1771, Yorkshire, Leeds, height: 19.1cm, (7½in), enamelled creamware. Boldly painted pair of red pheasants.

Teapot, (**1669**), c.1790, Newcastle upon Tyne, height: 10.8cm, (4¼in), printed pearlware. Pheasants in landscape, on teapot marked, 'J. Warburton, N.C. Tyne', (for engraver James Warburton). Based on a Liverpool print for Wedgwood they may, like doves, be linked to love.

Courtship, Opposition and Elopement

Courtship was closely monitored among the middling sort and gentry, where property and social standing were at stake. Thwarted by family opposition, some desperate couples ran away to be married, famously to Gretna Green, the Scottish town closest to the border with England. In 1753 the Hardwicke Marriage Act had been passed 'for the better preventing of Clandestine Marriages' such as the notorious Fleet weddings.[32] The New Marriage Act of 1823 closed further loopholes but until the law was changed in 1856, in Scotland anyone over sixteen could plight their troth without parental consent before a witness such as the blacksmith.

Two Fragments, (1670), c.1760, Worcester, each height: 15.3cm, (6in), printed soft-paste porcelain. Two sides of a coffee pot printed with designs after Watteau; one of a couple standing beside a fountain[33] the other with a man playing the lute to a shepherdess with sheep.

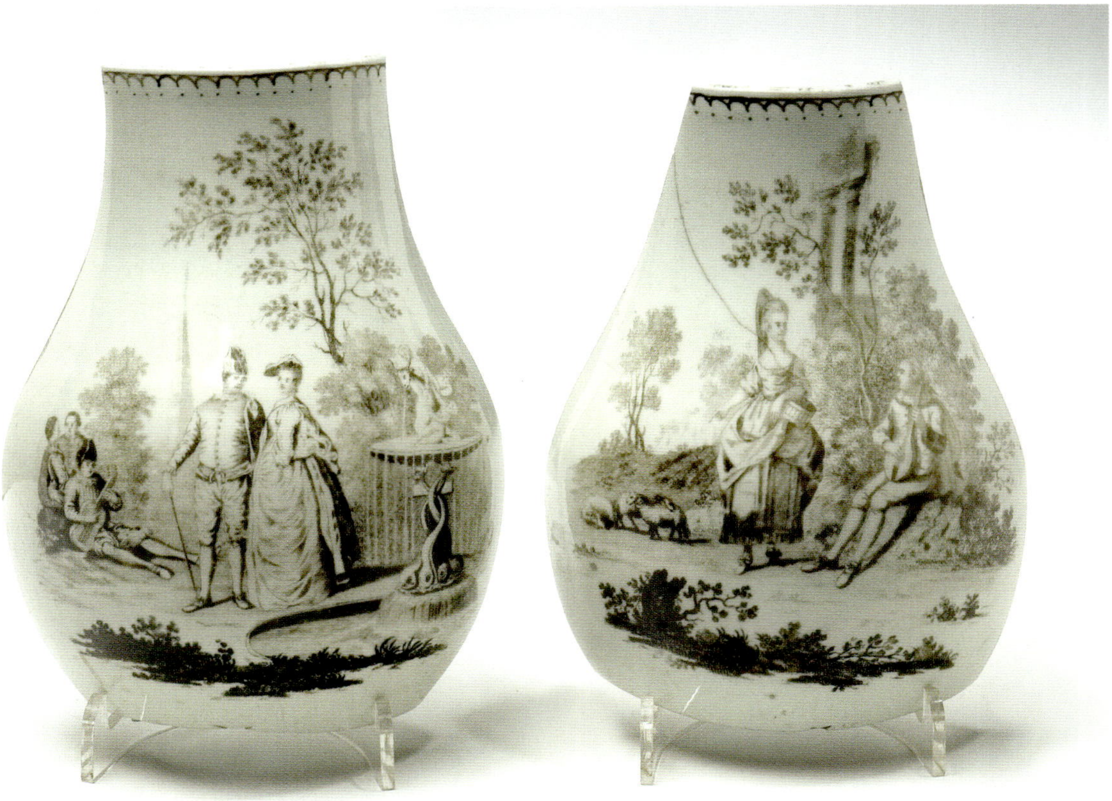

Two Plates, (1681 + 1712), c.1840, Swansea, Baker, Bevans & Irwin, each diameter: 17.8cm, (7in), earthenware, printed and coloured. Within relief-moulded floral borders, one inscribed, 'Jump Man / Follow woman. A marriage', the ancient ritual of jumping over a broomstick to propose marriage. The second printed with a grieving woman at a tomb, holding a crucifix, inscribed, 'There is Rest in Heaven'.

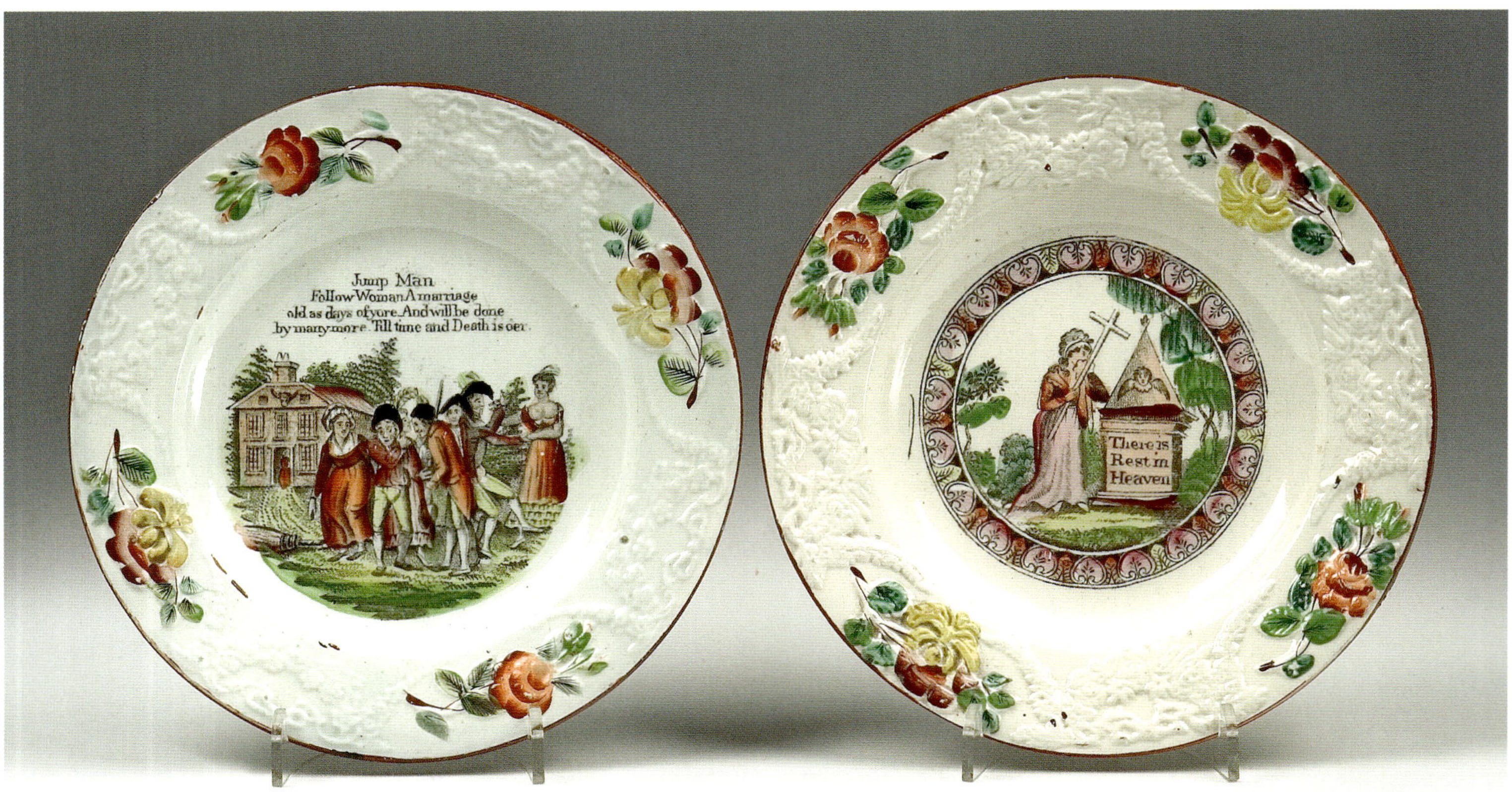

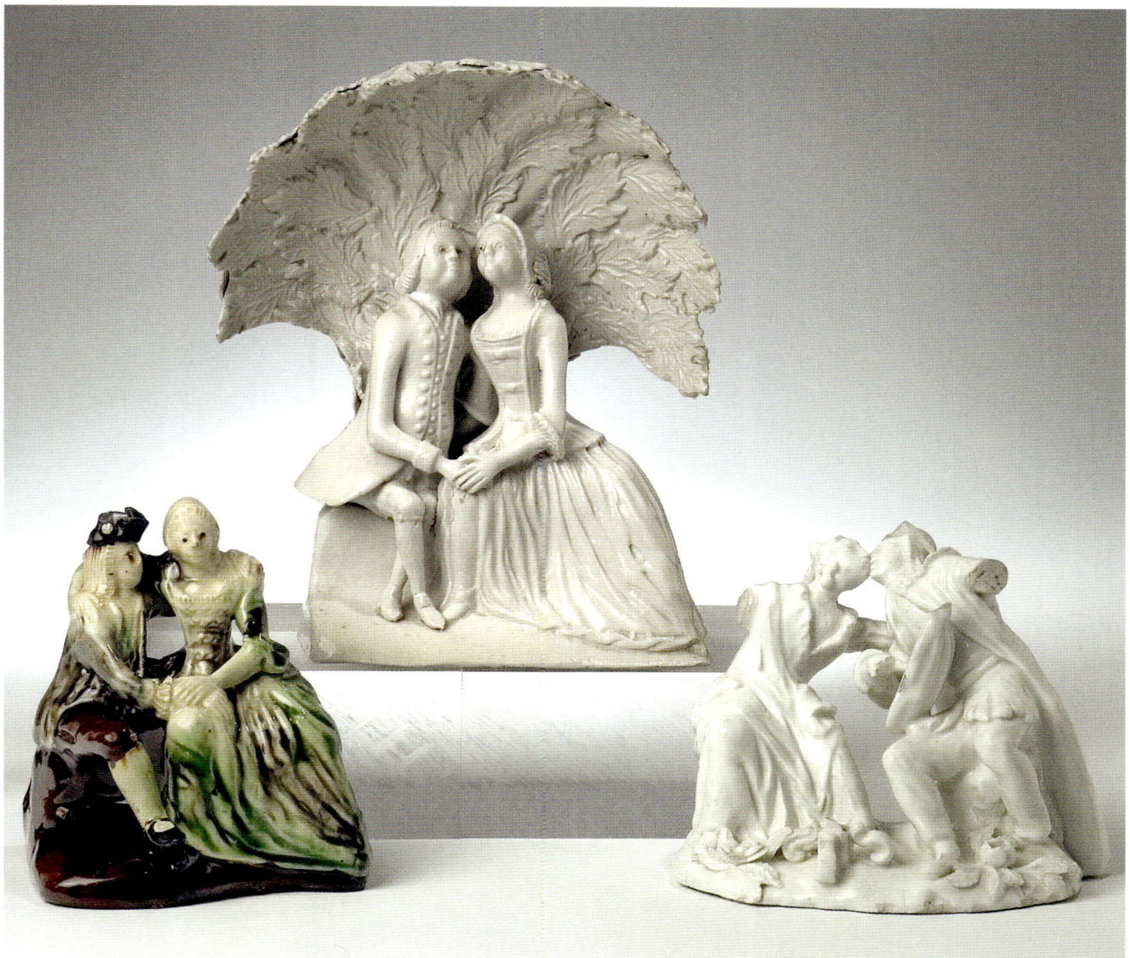

Figure Group, (**1639**), c.1760, Staffordshire, height: 11.5cm, (4½in), earthenware, lead-glazed and oxide-coloured. Pair of lovers embracing; her leg is slung over his knee.
Figure Group, (**1640**), c.1760, Staffordshire, height: 17.8cm, (7in), white salt-glazed stoneware. A couple sit beneath a tree, whose branches have been assembled in a curved mould.[34]
Figure Group, (**1641**), c.1752, London, Bow,[35] height: 10.2cm, (4in), soft-paste porcelain. A pair of lovers (badly damaged), lean in to kiss as he plays a lute.

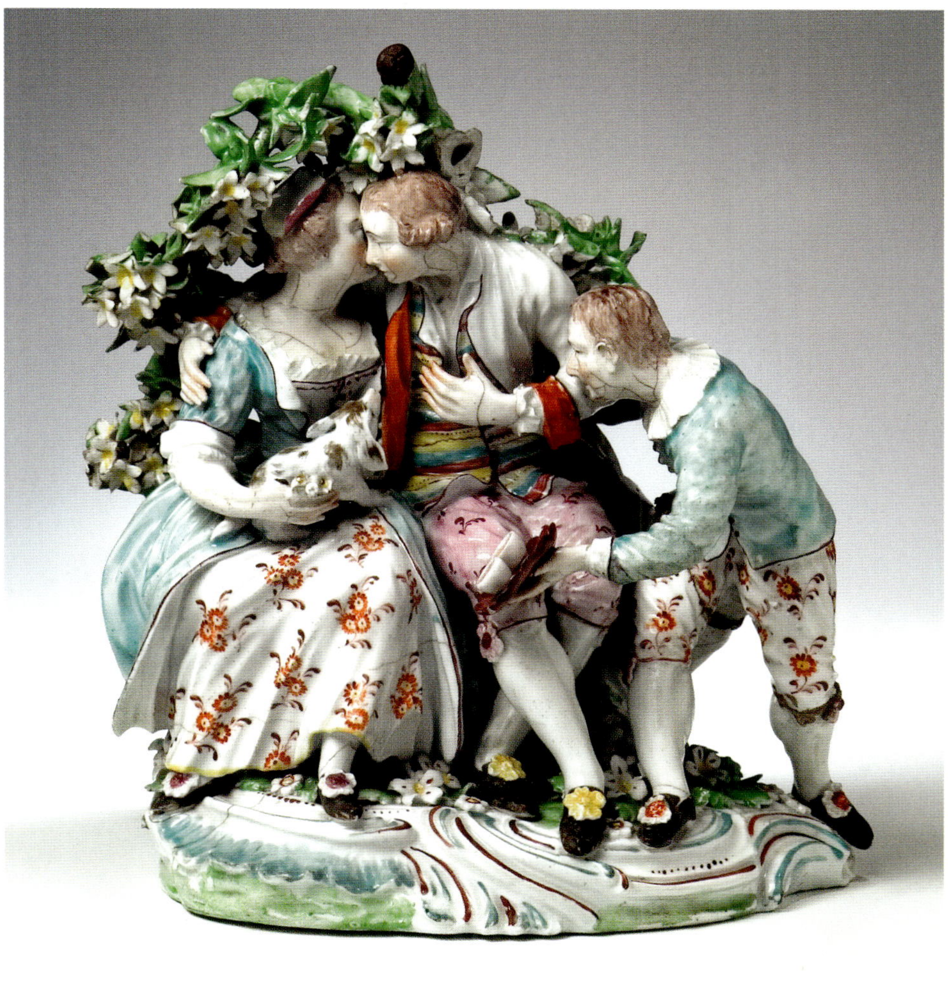

Figure Group, (**1652**), c.1765, Derby, height: 25.4cm, (10in), enamelled, soft-paste porcelain. Known as 'Isabella, Gallant and Jester', a couple are surprised in their flowery bower by a servant, who tips cups of tea over them. Derby modellers made a careful copy from an original by J.J. Kaendler for the Meissen factory at Dresden. The subject derives from the knockabout performances of *commedia dell'arte* troupes.

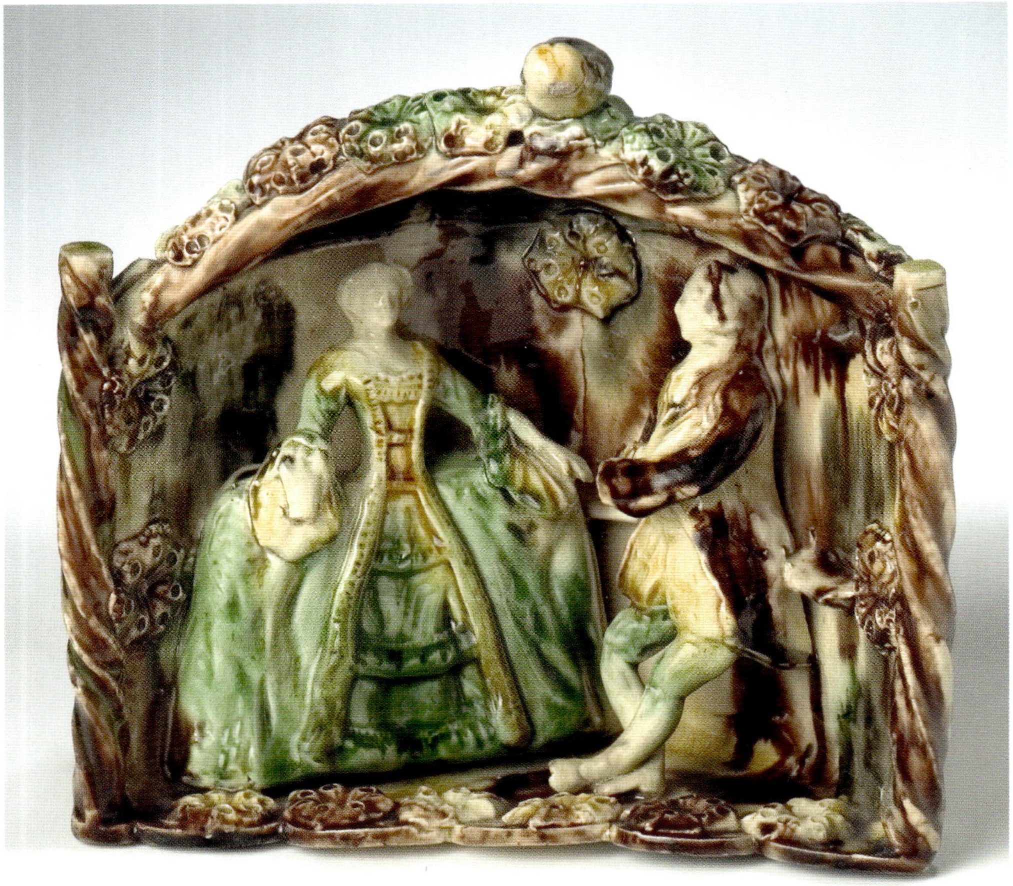

Figure Group, (**1654**), c.1760, Staffordshire, height: 17.7cm, (7in), earthenware, lead-glazed and oxide-coloured. A fashionable couple meet privately in a dish-shaped arbour whose back and roof are stamped with geometric patterns and applied flowers.

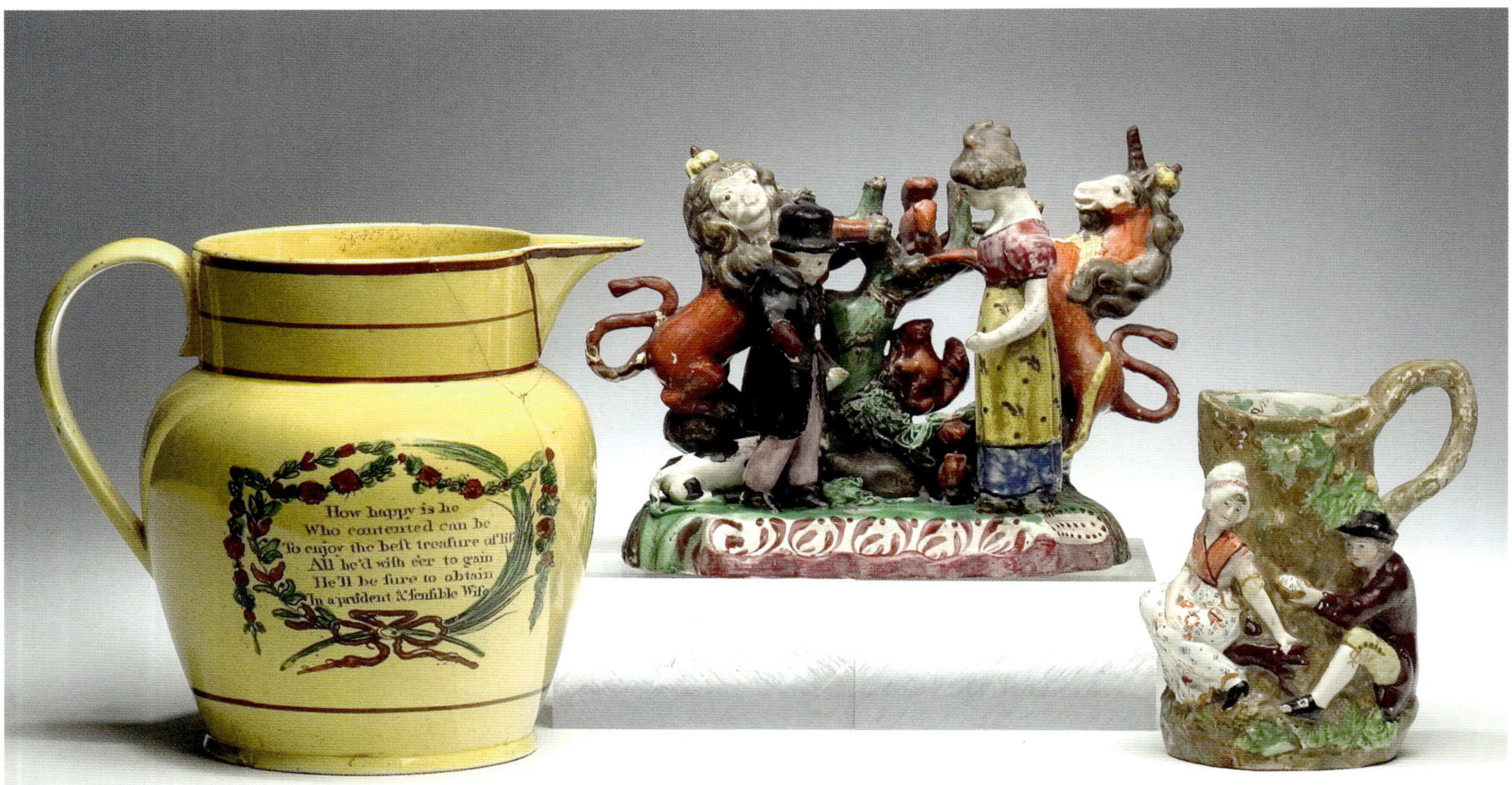

Jug, (**1697**), c.1810, Sunderland, height: 17.2cm, (6¾in), yellow-glazed earthenware, printed and coloured. Verse reads, 'From Rocks and Sands / And barren lands / Kind Fortune keep me free' and 'How happy is he / Who contented can be'.
Figure Group, (**1674**), c.1820, Staffordshire, height: 15.3cm, (6in), enamelled pearlware. A couple stand before a heraldic lion and unicorn that flank a tree, with a pair of greyhounds and several red squirrels. According to the 1899 catalogue it represents 'love at first sight' and may also symbolise fertility.
Jug, (**1664**), c.1800, Staffordshire, height: 17.8cm, (7in), enamelled pearlware. Relief-moulded with a man offering a nest to a young woman. Related to jugs designed by John Voyez (see 1463 +1464).

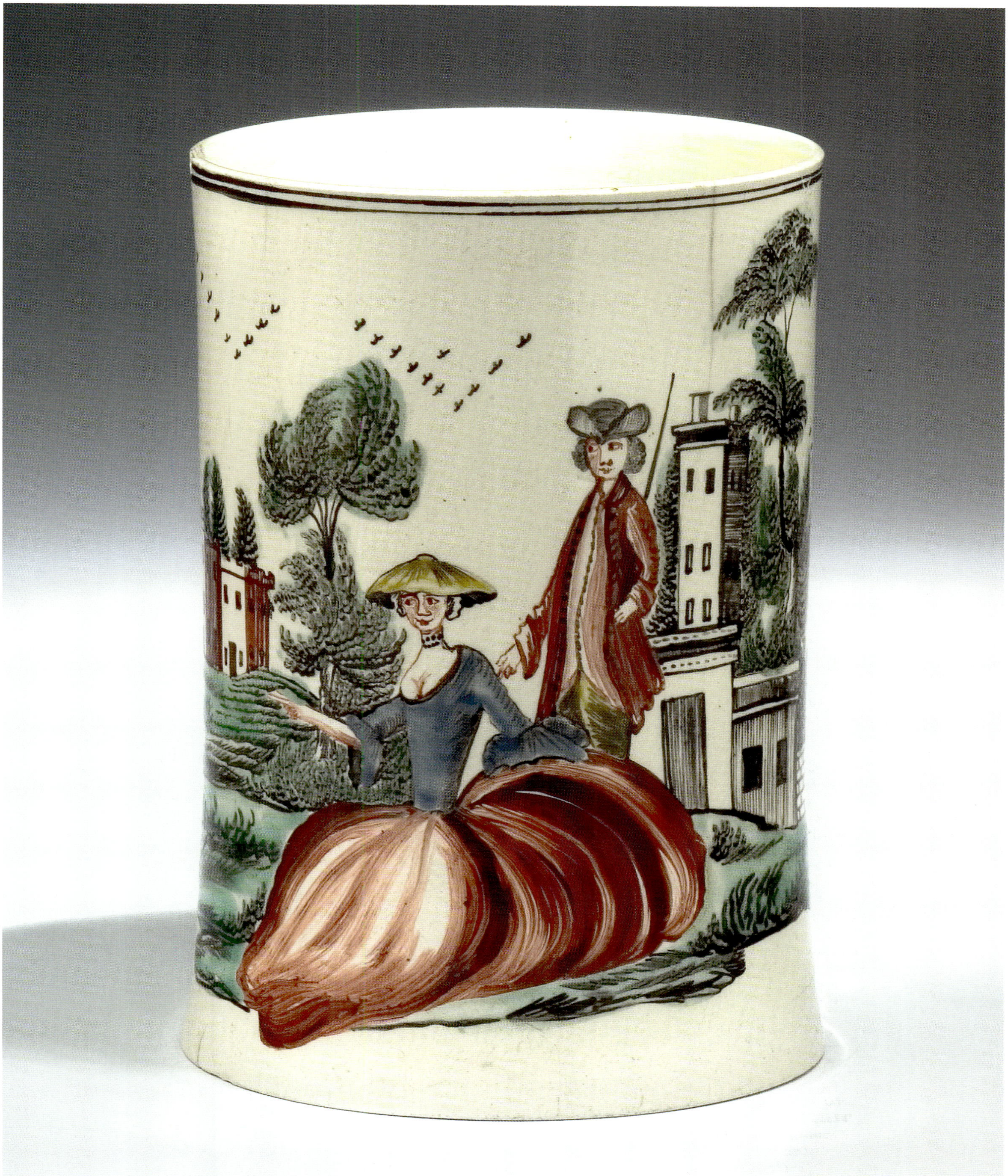

Mug, (**1662**), c.1770, North-East?, height: 14cm, (5½in), enamelled creamware. Painted with wrap-around image, whose distinctive style suggests James Robinson's workshop. A gentleman stands beside a seated woman who indicates the buildings and landscape behind her. The buildings bear a marked resemblance to Hylton Castle, near Sunderland.[36] The composition, which reinforces notions of visible wealth and social status, may be influenced by the type of society portrait popularised by Gainsborough in the early eighteenth century. The woman's mushroom-like straw hat was worn by gentlewomen to preserve a pale complexion.

Dandy Figures

A number of groups and pairs of figures promenade in the exaggerated dandy styles of 1810 to 1820, inspired by the caricatures of Robert Cruikshank. Women wear high-waisted gowns, puff-sleeved jackets and huge, coal-scuttle bonnets. Men in top hats wear cut away tailcoats with high, nipped-in waists, wide, striped trousers and high-collared, frilled shirts. Men and women carry interchangeable accessories, umbrellas and handbags!

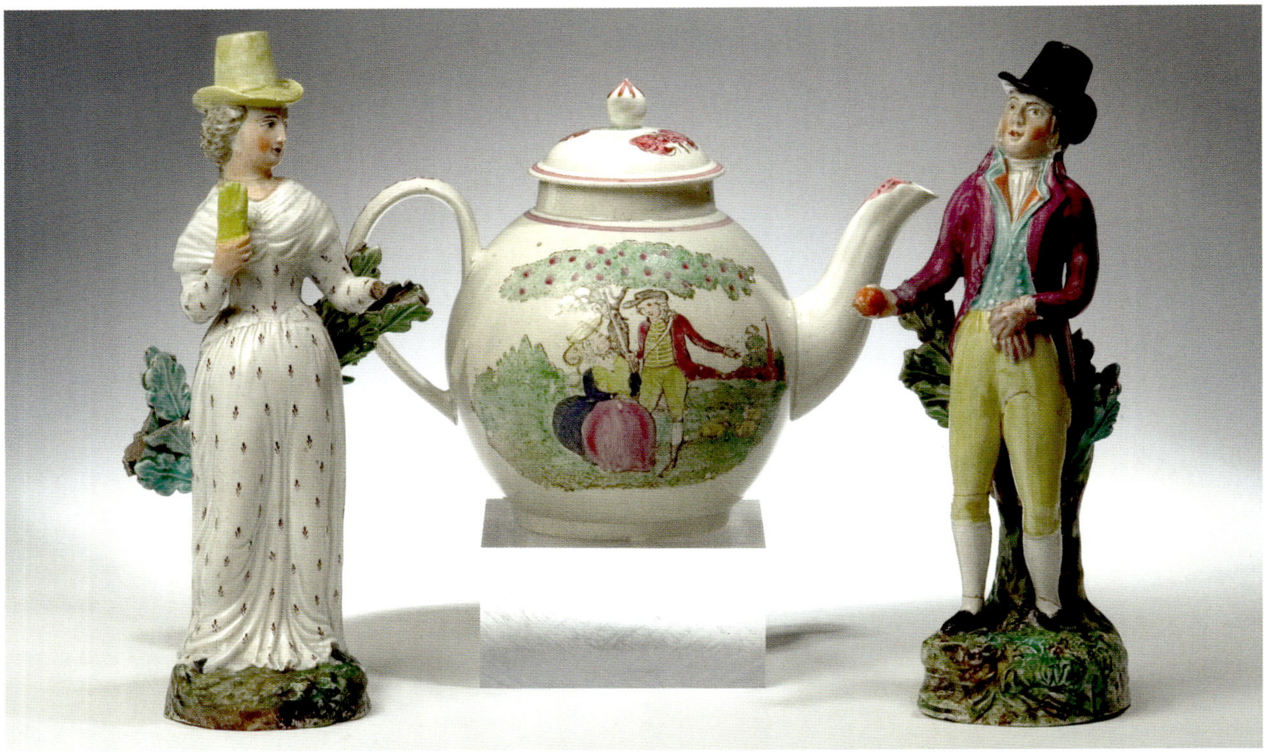

Pair of Figures, (**1656 & A**), c.1790, Staffordshire, each height: 24cm, (9½in), enamelled pearlware. A fashionably dressed woman, with curled and powdered hair, holds gloves while her long-haired beau, wearing knee breeches, holds an apple.
Teapot, (**Hove 62.35**), c.1790, Staffordshire, height: 16cm, (6¼in), pearlware, printed and enamelled. A fashionable couple with a shepherdess's crook meet beneath an apple tree.

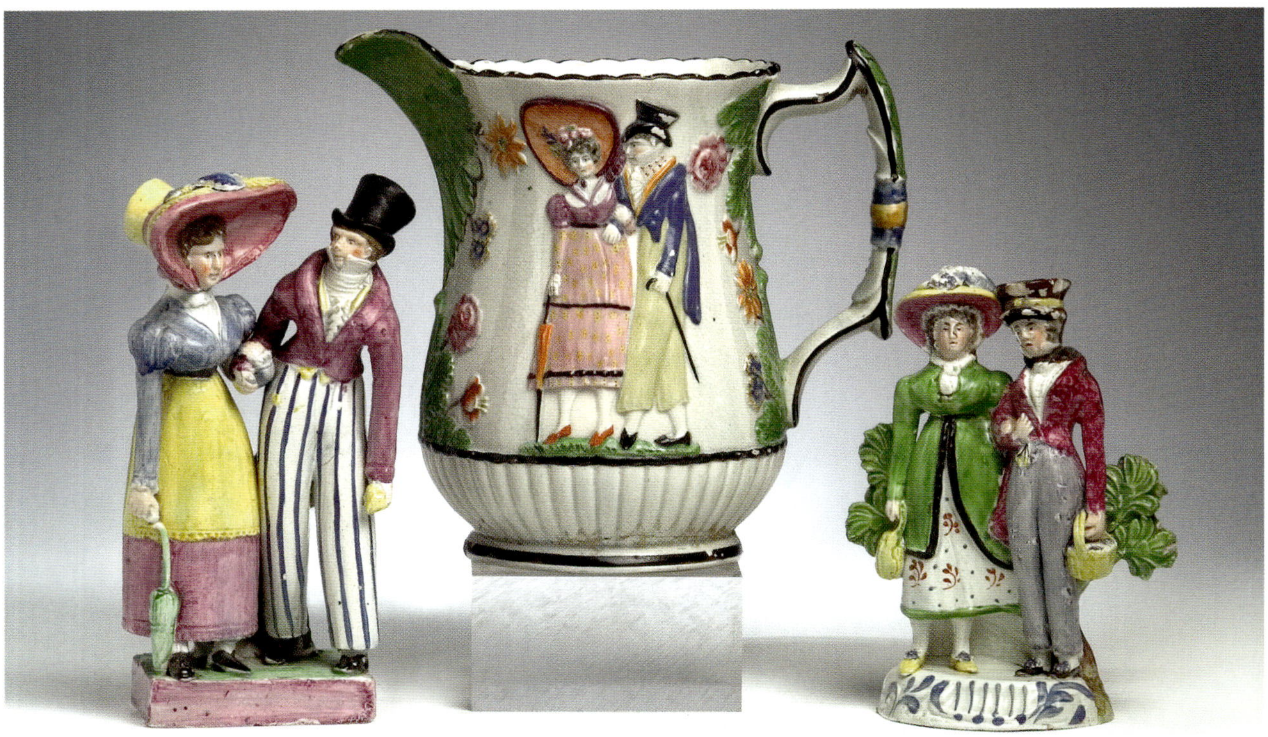

Figure Group, (**1647**), c.1825, Staffordshire, height: 16.5cm, (6½in), enamelled pearlware. Dandy couple wear fashionable clothes of exaggerated proportions and unusual colours.
Jug, (**1655**), c.1825, Staffordshire, height: 20.3cm, (8in), enamelled pearlware. Relief-moulded with a similar dandy couple flanked by foliage.
Figure Group, (**1648**), c.1825, Staffordshire, height: 20.3cm, (8in), enamelled pearlware. A couple walk arm in arm, both carry hand bags!

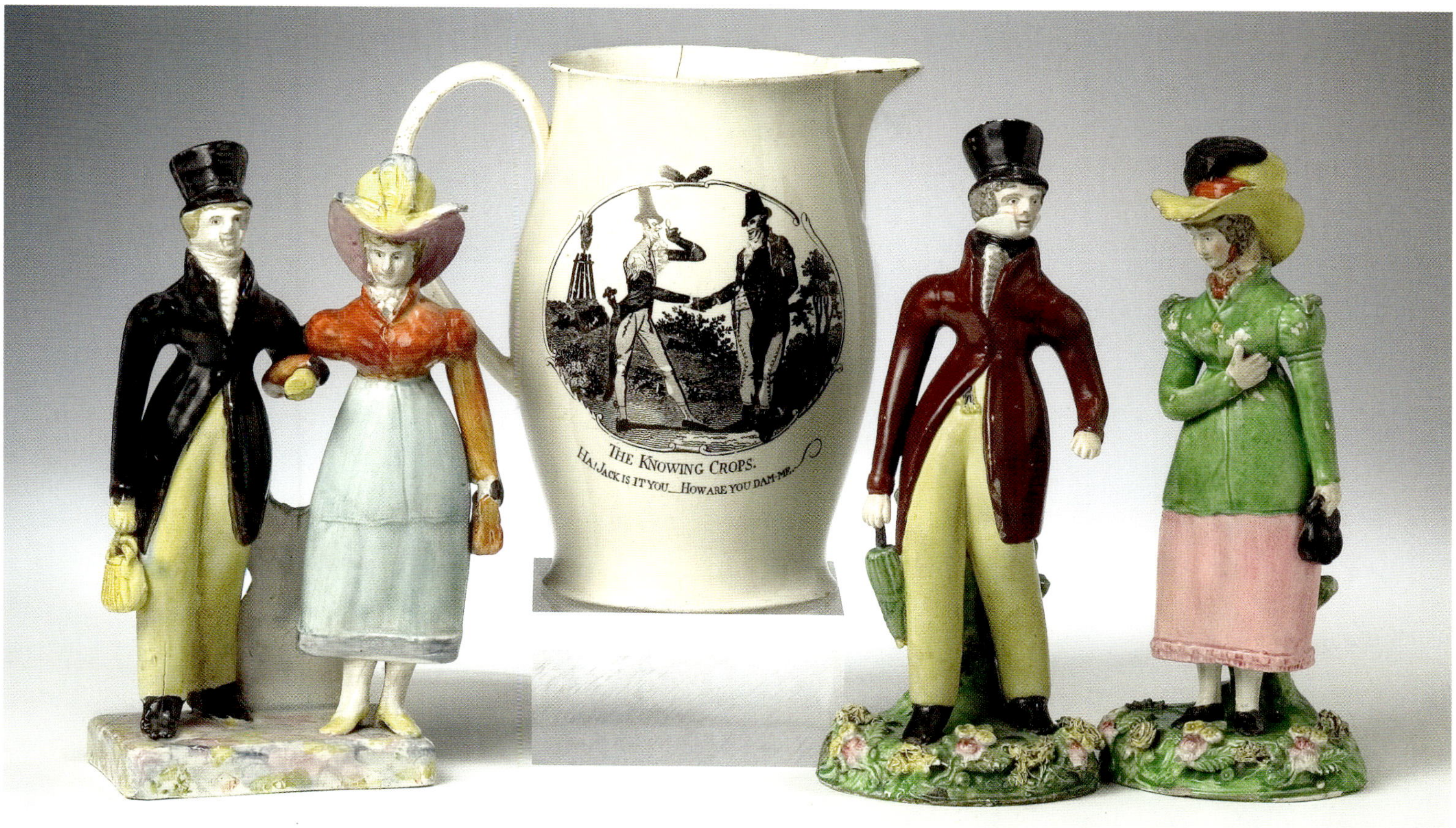

Figure Group, (**1649**), c.1825, Staffordshire, height: 17.8cm (7in), enamelled pearlware. Dandy couple promenades with linked arms, both carrying handbags. **Jug**, (**1242**), c.1792, Staffordshire, height: 17.8cm, (7in), printed creamware. Two fashionable fops greet one another, 'THE KNOWING CROPS / Ha! Jack is it you? How are you dam me', based on prints of 1791.[37] The new fashion for short hair was inspired by the French revolutionaries' nod to the republicans of Ancient Rome. A writer in the first edition of the *Observer,* 4 December 1791, deplores the style; 'In one thing, it is clear, the CROPS have been mistaken – they fancied they had left their enemies *nothing to lay hold on!!!*' .[38] **Pair of Figures**, (**1657 & A**), c.1825, Staffordshire, height: 23.5cm, (9¼in), enamelled pearlware. A couple acknowledge one another from individual bases applied with flowers.

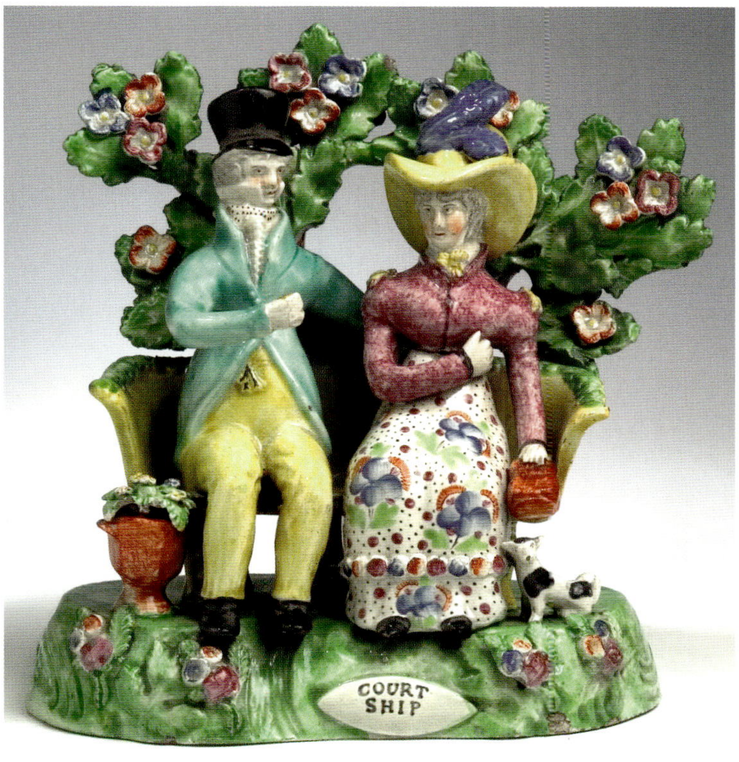

Figure Group, (**1650**), c.1820, Staffordshire, height: 19.7cm, (7¾in), enamelled pearlware. 'COURTSHIP', shows a fashionably dressed couple, sitting on a bench beneath a flowering arbour, a flowerpot on his side and a lapdog on hers.

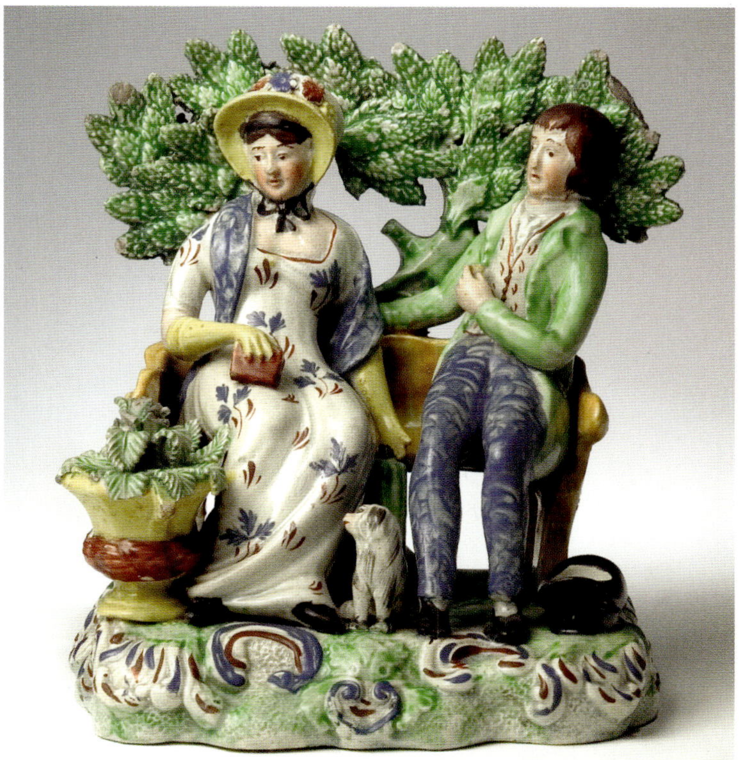

Figure Group, (**1651**), c.1820, Staffordshire, height: 20.3cm, (8in), enamelled pearlware. A group known as 'Perswaition [*sic*]', shows a naturalistic pair of lovers. The woman, sitting on a bench averts her eyes demurely as her lover offers a ring. Although unmarked, it was probably made by John Walton's workshop.

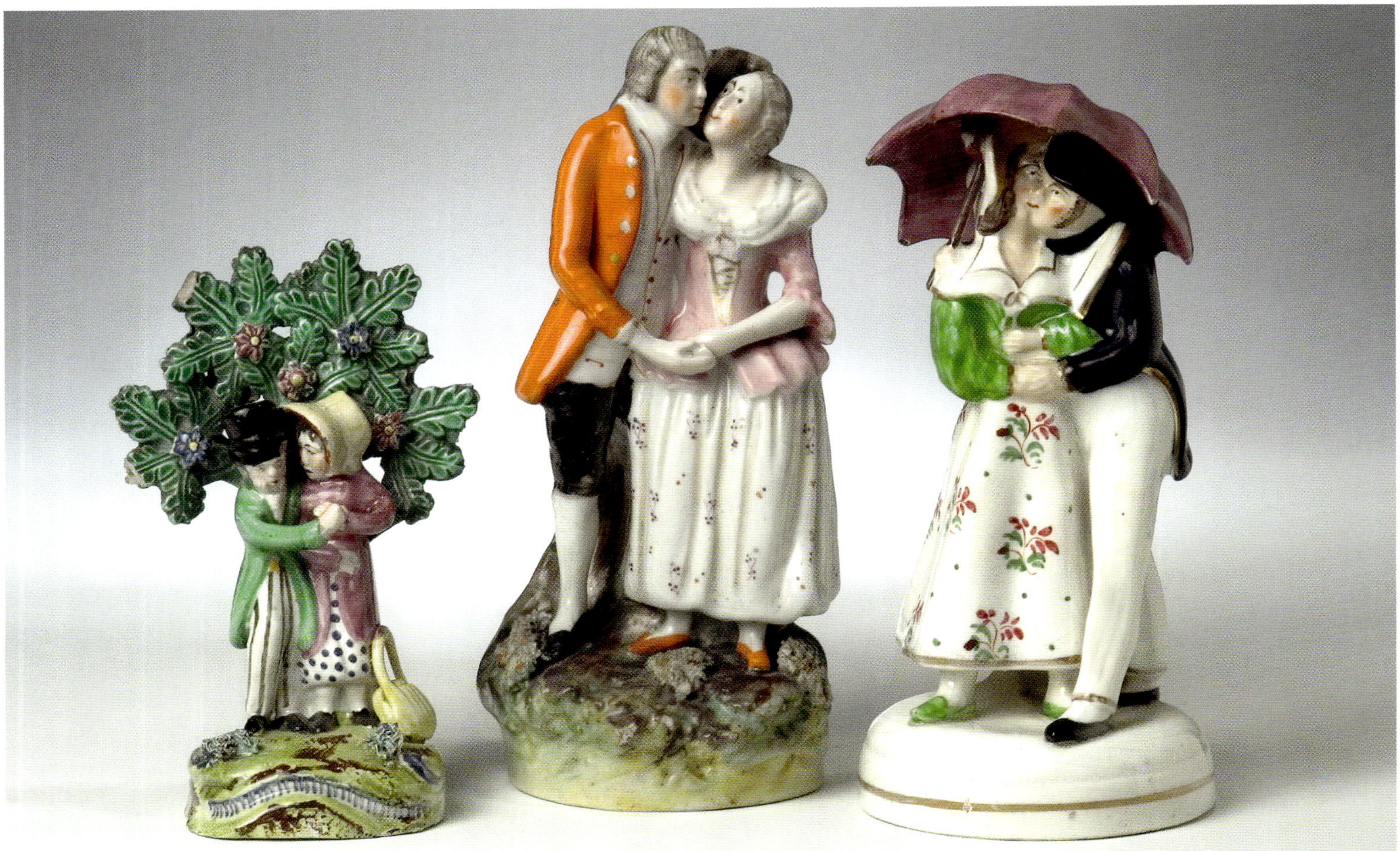

Figure Group, (**1646**), c.1820, Staffordshire, height: 12.7cm, (5in), enamelled pearlware. A small-scale pair embrace beneath a tree; she has sensibly placed her handbag on the ground.
Figure Group, (**1675**), c.1840, Staffordshire, height: 17.8cm, (7in), soft-paste porcelain, enamelled and gilt. A courting couple wear eighteenth-century dress.
Figure Group, (**1643**), c.1850, Staffordshire, height: 17.1cm, (6¾in), enamelled bone china. Lovers kiss under an umbrella, known as 'Umbrella Courtship'.

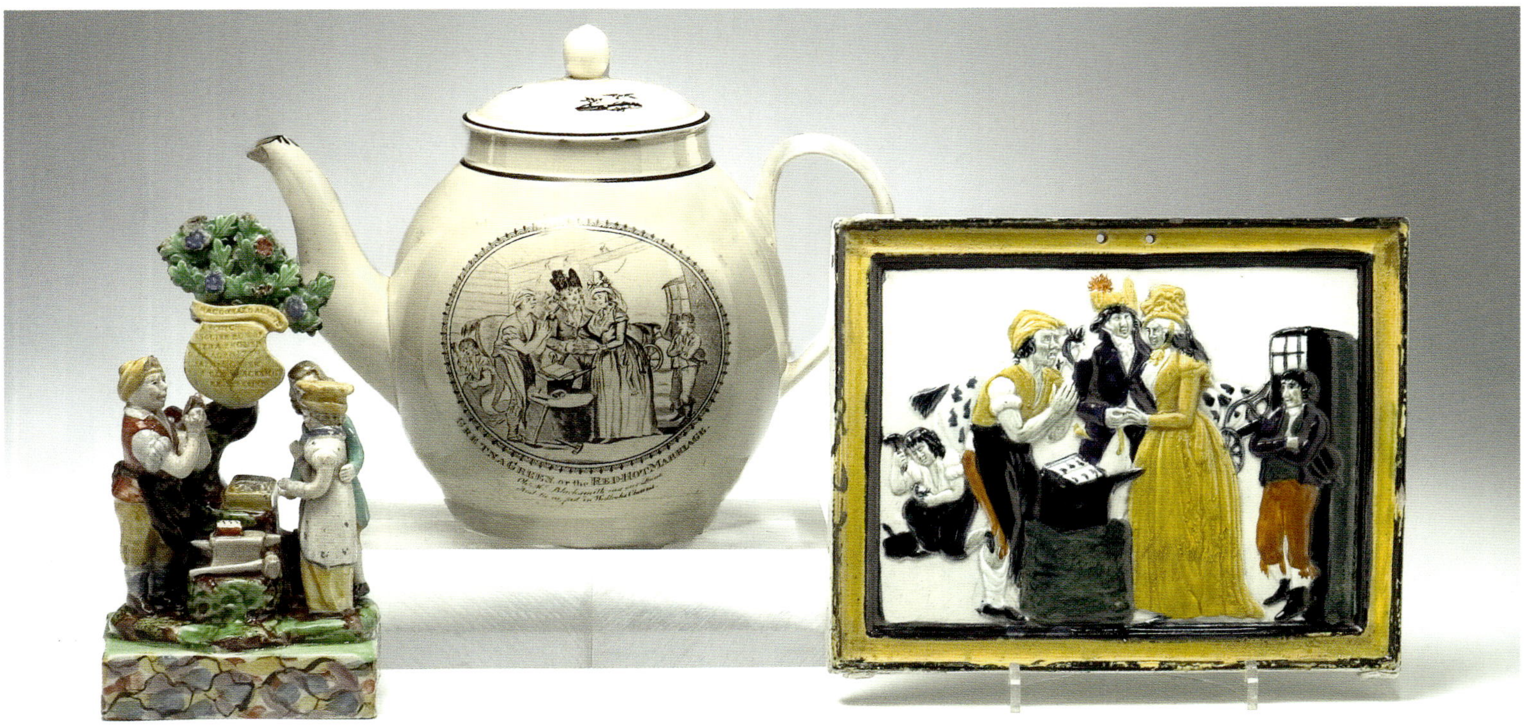

Figure Group, (**1679**), c.1820, Staffordshire, height: 19.1cm, (7½in), enamelled pearlware. A marriage takes place at the Gretna Green blacksmith's, inscribed, 'JOHN MACDONALD AGED 79 A SCOTCH ESQUIRE RAN OFF WITH AN ENGLISH GIRL AGED 17 TO GRETNA'.
Teapot, (**1680**), c.1795, Staffordshire, height: 28cm, (11in), printed creamware. Wedding scene at the blacksmith's, entitled, 'GRETNA GREEN or the RED-HOT MARRIAGE'. Based on print issued by Robert Sayers on 27 March 1793.
Plaque, (**1678**), c.1800, Staffordshire or Scotland, height: 18.4cm, (7¼in), Prattware. Plaque, drilled for hanging, relief-moulded based on the same print.

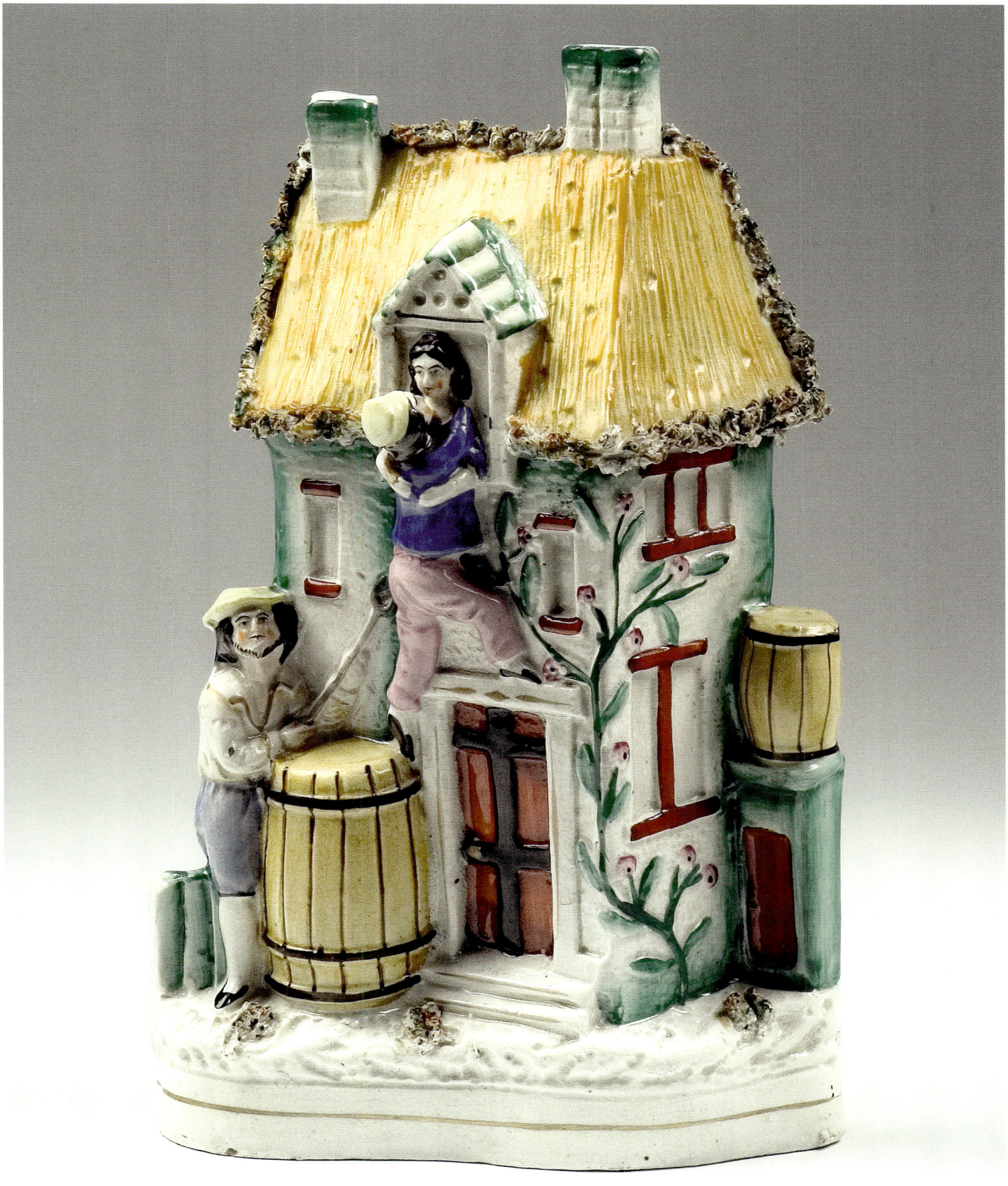

Figure Group, (**1658**), c.1840, Staffordshire, height: 30.5cm, (12in), enamelled earthenware. A lover, wearing a military cap, clambers up the front of a timber-framed house for a tryst with a young woman at an open window. Her father waits below with a pitchfork. The piece, known as, 'Courting under Difficulties' may derive from an anonymous print of 1835, entitled 'MILITARY INCIDENTS – The Preventive Check'; the couple are about to elope when her father appears in his nightshirt with a pistol.

Mug, (**1659**), c.1810, Staffordshire, height: 12.7cm, (5in), creamware, printed and coloured. 'VILLAGE MAID / Here I sit and sing and sigh / Here I muse and think on love', indulges in the exquisite melancholy of unrequited love.
Jug, (**1661**), c.1795, Staffordshire, Tunstall, height: 15.3cm, (6in), printed creamware. Jug signed by Thomas Baddeley. A distressed woman repulses Cupid, 'LOVE REJECTED / Deceitfull [*sic*] Boy with Flattery away'. Based on print by Bartolozzi, published in 1783, after a painting by Cipriani.[39]
Spill Vase, (**1663**), c.1790, Staffordshire, height: 19.1cm, (7½in), enamelled pearlware. A distressed young woman sits beside a hollow tree trunk (a spill vase) with her dog. She wears a loose robe and is usually identified with 'Poor Maria', a character mentioned by Laurence Sterne in his extraordinary novel, *Tristram Shandy* and his best-selling memoir, *A Sentimental Journey through France and Italy*, published in February 1768, weeks before his death. Figure based on prints after Angelica Kauffmann's painting of 'Poor Maria'.[40]

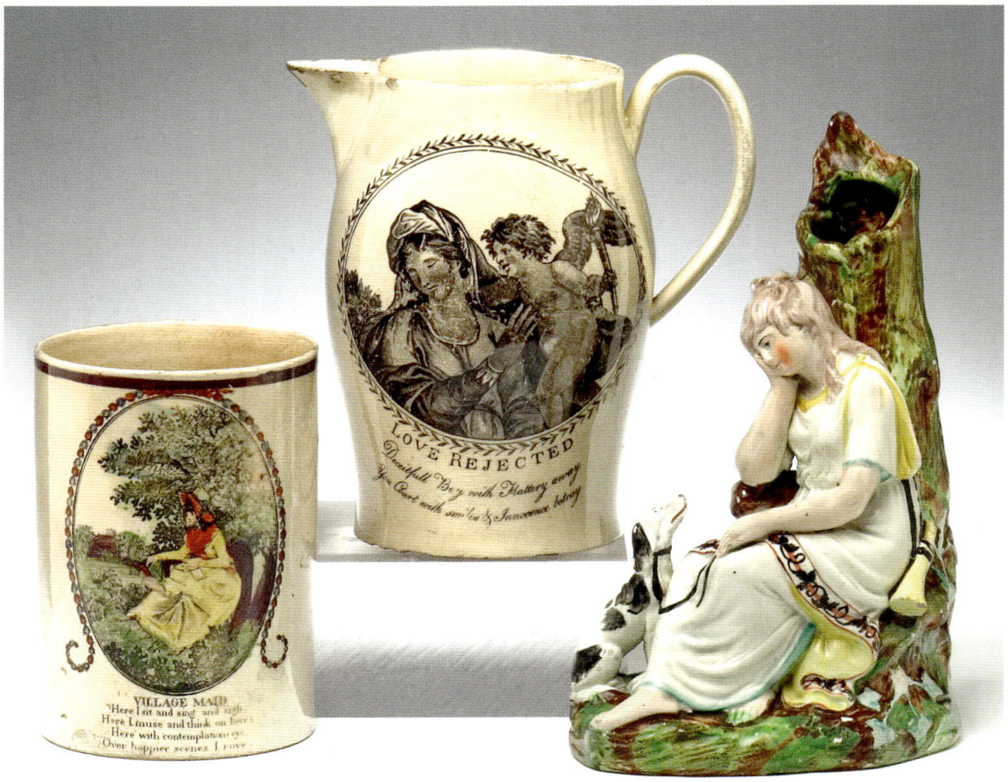

Marriage

A number of cynical comments on behavioural changes observed during courtship and after marriage appear on ceramics. The battle for power in the domestic sphere is not a recent phenomenon and has featured in literature since ancient times. The tussle had been symbolised by a tug of war over the wearing of the breeches since at least the late sixteenth century. When a woman leapt to her husband's defence in a conflict of 1594, his opponent taunted him, 'lett thy wife weare thye breeches, for she is worthie of them, she is the better man.'[41]

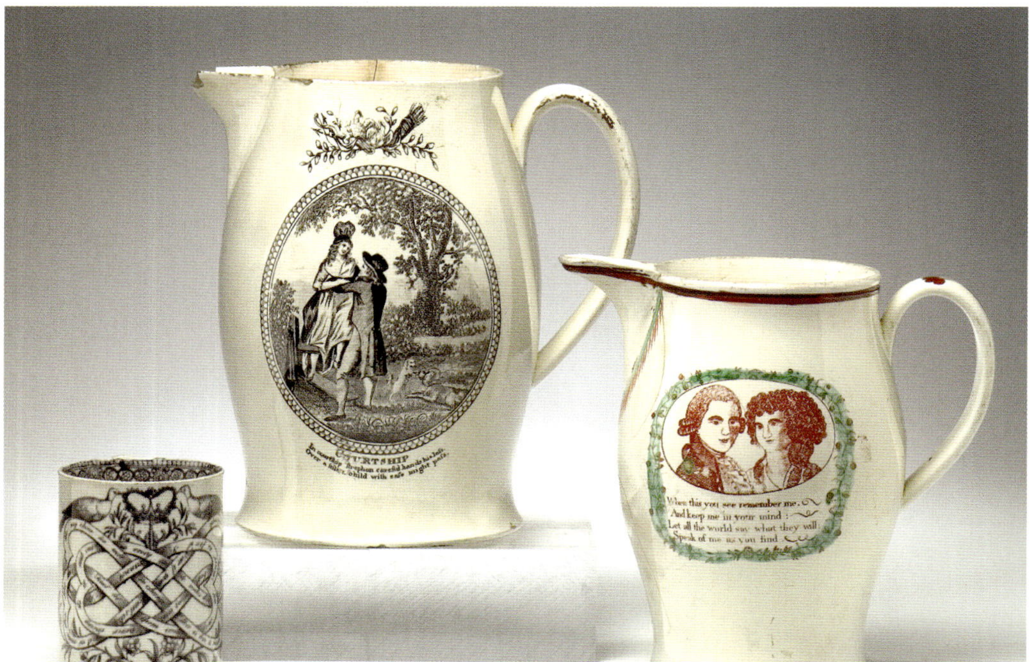

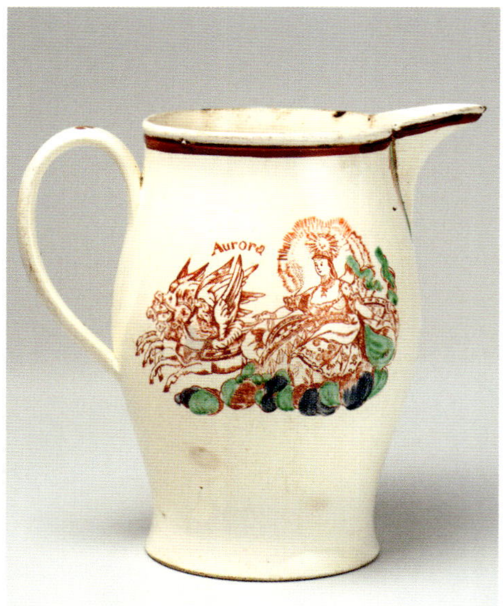

Mug, (**1653**), c.1850, Staffordshire, height: 9.6cm, (3¾in), purple-printed earthenware. Printed with symbols of courtship, including two doves perched on a woven lovers' knot inscribed with sentimental sayings, 'I like my choice too well to change'.
Jug, (**1676**), c.1790, Staffordshire, height: 20.3cm, (8in), printed creamware. Printed with contrasting scenes, 'COURTSHIP'. A young man helps his fiancée over a low stile, while their dogs frisk with one another. ('Matrimony' illustrated on reverse.)
Jug, (**1671**), c.1790, Staffordshire, height: 18.4cm, (7¼in), creamware, red-printed and coloured. The heads of a man and woman inscribed, 'When this you see remember me / And keep me in your mind' On the reverse 'Aurora', goddess of the dawn, in a winged chariot.

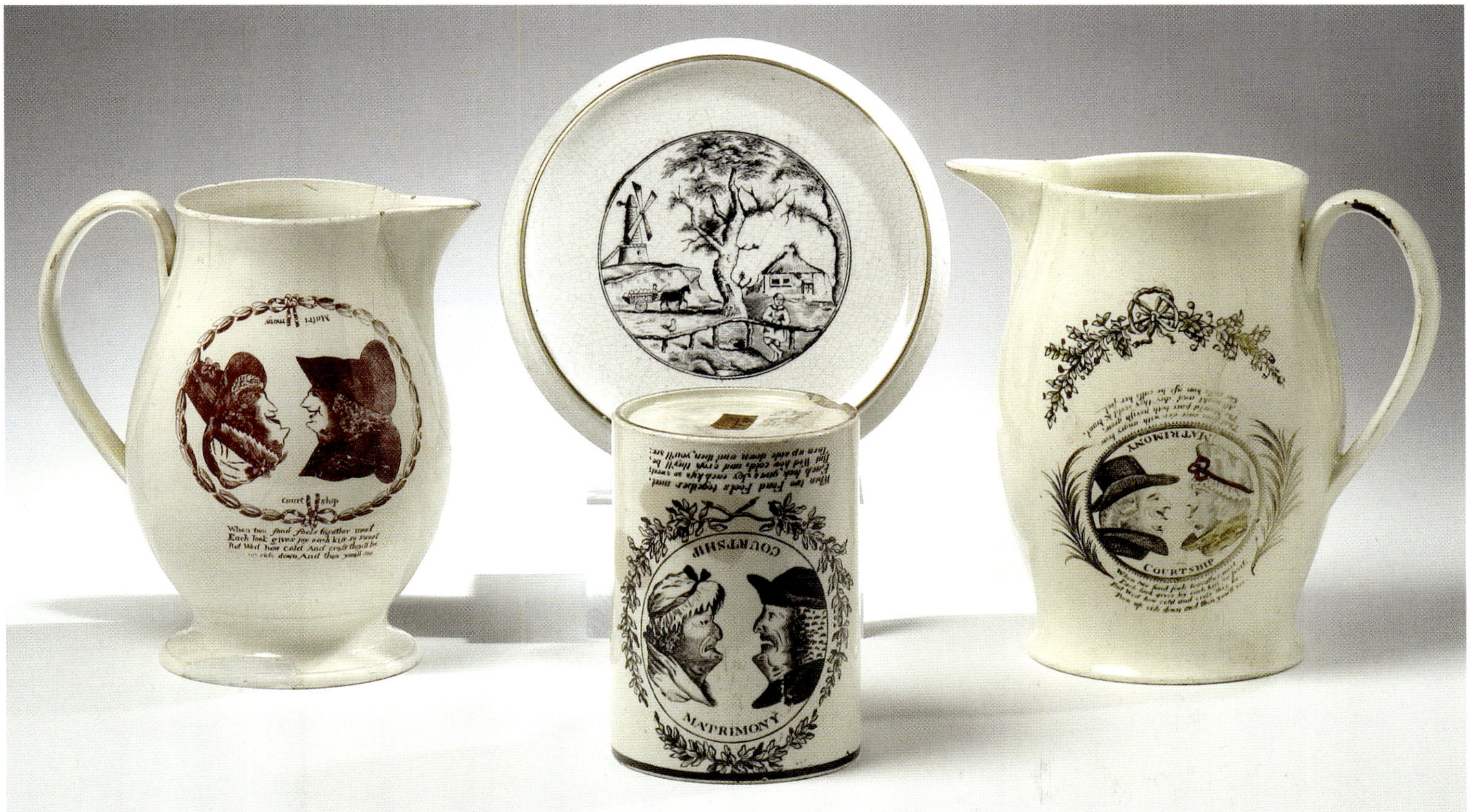

Clockwise:
Jug, (**519**), c.1800, Staffordshire, height: 17.1cm, (6¾in), brown-printed creamware. Printed with reversible portraits illustrating the change between, 'COURTSHIP / MATRIMONY / When two Fond Fools together meet / Each look gives Joy each kiss so sweet / But wed how cold and crofs they'll be? Turn upside down and then you'll see'.
Teapot Stand, (**667**), c.1820, Staffordshire, height: 17.2cm, (6¾in), earthenware, printed and gilt. Printed with a teasing optical riddle, 'THE MILL. THE HOUSE. THE MILLER. BUT WHERE IS HIS DONKEY'. The donkey's profile is hidden between the outline of the central tree and the miller's house.[42]
Jug, (**335**), c.1795, Staffordshire, height: 17.8cm, (7in), creamware, printed and coloured. 'COURTSHIP / MATRIMONY / When two Fond Fools' with additional verse.
Mug, (**1677**), c.1800, Staffordshire, height: 12.1cm, (4¾in), printed creamware. This crudely drawn image of 'COURTSHIP / MATRIMONY' (inverted) is closely based on a print published by J. Wallis in 1789.[43]

Spill-holder, (**1696**), c.1820, Staffordshire, height: 19.1cm, (7½in), enamelled pearlware. A couple have a domestic tug of war over a pair of breeches; their baby and dog lie between them. Above the fireplace a clock and two plaques proclaim, 'Conquer or Die' and 'Who shall Wear the trousers'.
Jug, (**1676**), c.1790, Staffordshire, height: 20.3cm, (8in), printed creamware. 'MATRIMONY' illustrates that familiarity breeds contempt, 'But wedded Strephon now neglects his dame'.[44] The husband now ignores his wife as she struggles to scale a gate while their dogs mate roughly.[45] ('Courtship' illustrated on reverse).
Mug, (**1036**), c.1790, Staffordshire, height: 12.1cm, (4¾in), pearlware, printed and coloured. Decorated in the manner of John Aynsley, with a domestic fist fight entitled, 'Peggy PLUMPER proving / her MAN before MARRIAGE OR / WHO WEARS ye BREECHES' it is accompanied by verses, 'Peggy Plumper, a lass, well made tall & pretty / Was courted by sweet Sammy Spar of ye City / They jog'd on in courtship, Sam would have gone faster / But Peg wo'd not Wed, till she knew who was master'.[46] Intriguingly there were famous women boxers. On June 22, 1768, 'two women fought for a new chemise valued at half a guinea, in the Spa fields, near Islington. The battle was won by a woman called 'Bruising Peg', who beat her antagonist in a terrible manner.'[47]

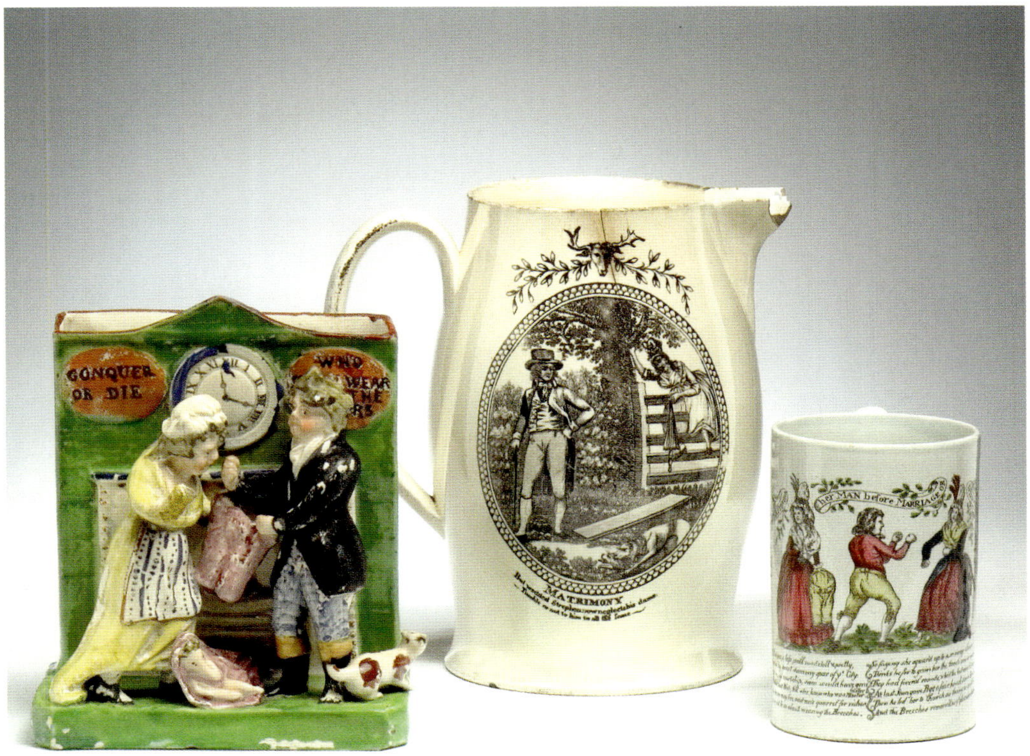

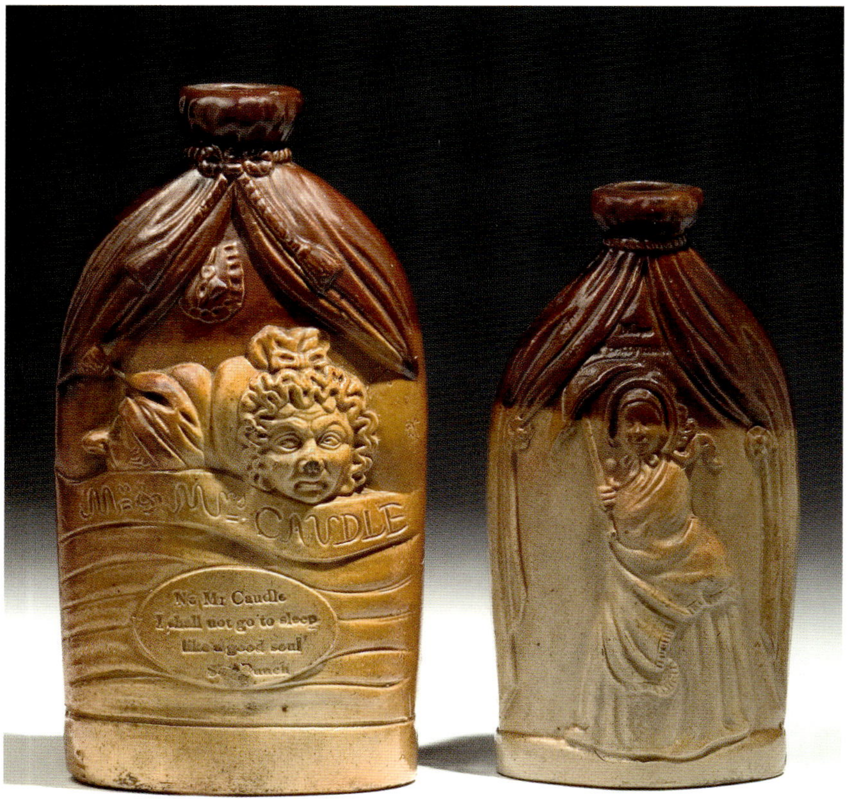

Flask, (**1702**), c.1850, London, height: 21.7cm, (8½in), salt-glazed stoneware. Relief-moulded with the faces of 'Mr & Mrs CAUDLE' in bed, inscribed, 'No Mr Caudle / I shall not sleep / Like a good soul'. The 'Mrs Caudle's Curtain Lectures', were immensely popular contributions to *Punch* Magazine by Douglas Jerrold (1803-57) in 1845. She was a domestic bully of whom Thackeray wrote, 'Almost all the events and perplexities of Cockney domestic economy pass before her'.[48]

Flask, (**1703**), c.1850, London, height: 17.8cm, (7in), salt-glazed stoneware. Similar flask relief-moulded (on reverse) with a woman with an umbrella inscribed, 'Miss Prettyman', (the daughter of Mr Caudle's friend).

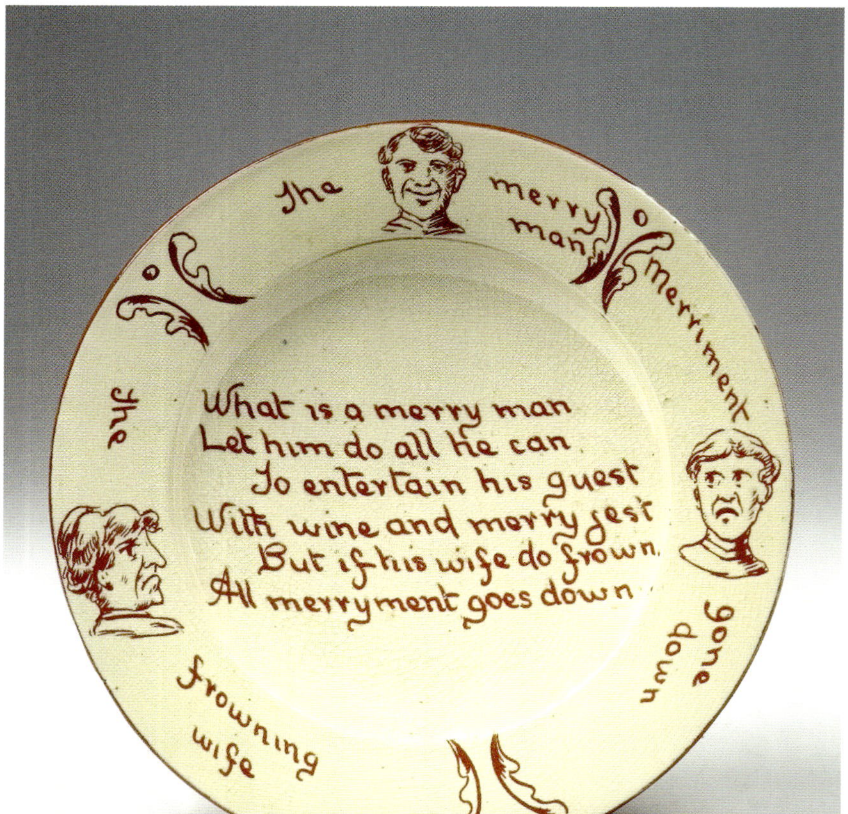

Dish, (**1698**), c.1880, Devon, Aller Vale, diameter: 24.8cm, (9¾in), slip-decorated earthenware. Dish is sgraffito-decorated with cartoon heads and verse, referring to a kill-joy wife, 'What is a merry man / Let him do all he can / To entertain his guest / With wine and merry jest / but if his wife do frown / all merriment goes down'.

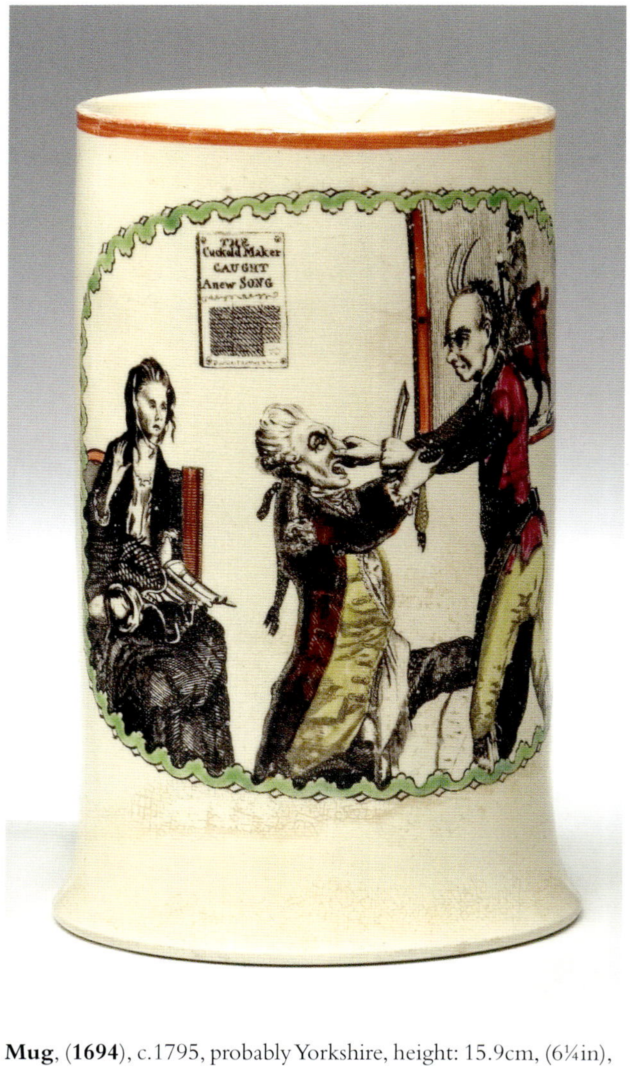

Mug, (**1694**), c.1795, probably Yorkshire, height: 15.9cm, (6¼in), creamware, printed and enamelled. An adulterous couple (the guilty woman has removed her stays) has been caught by the woman's husband, branded a cuckold by the horns of the Welsh tailor's goat, in the picture on the wall. The adjacent song-sheet entitled, 'THE / Cuckold Maker / CAUGHT / A New SONG' Scene based on a rare print published by Laurie & Whittle in October 1795. Ornate floral terminals for the missing handle suggest it was made in Leeds.

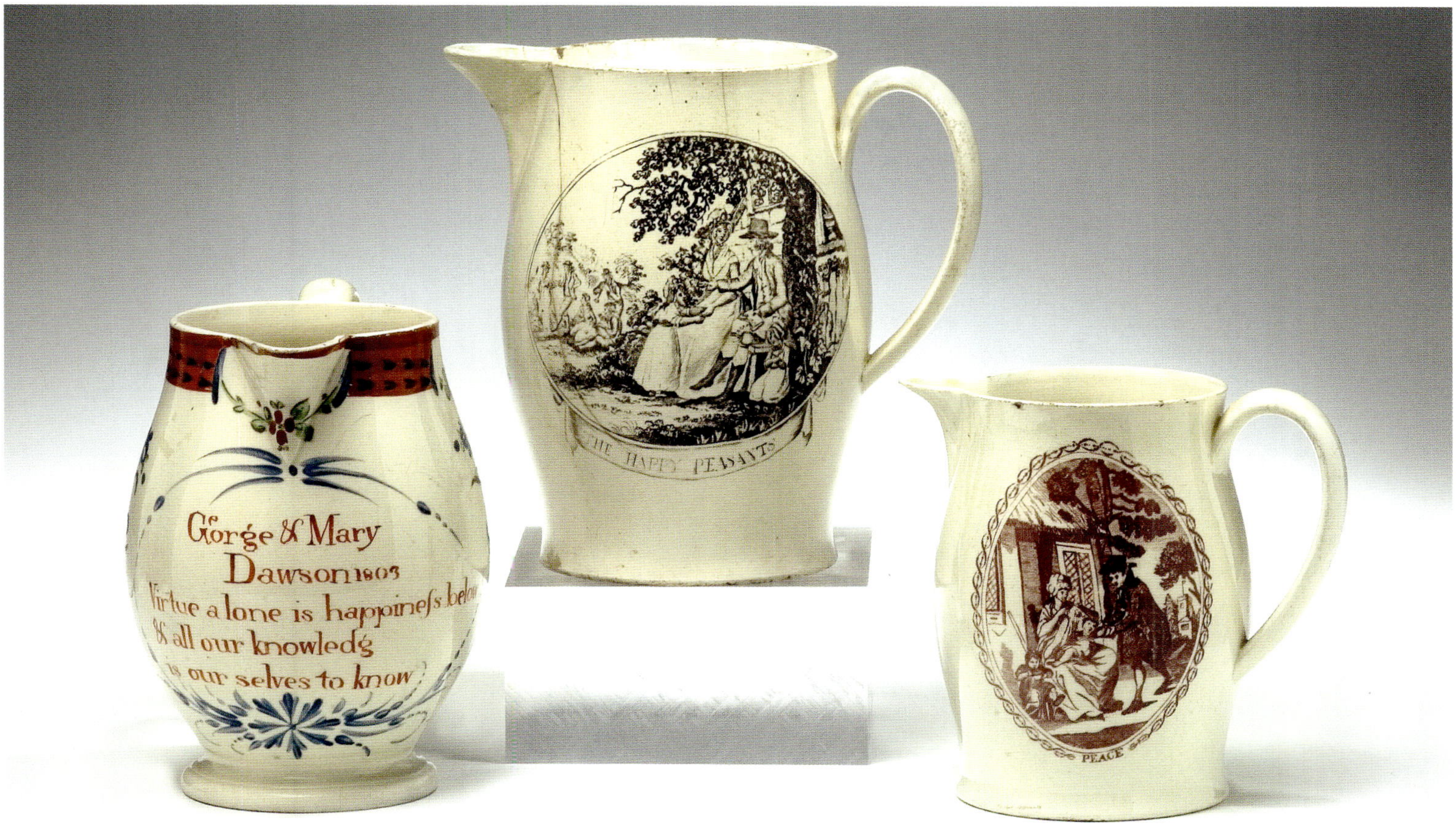

Jug, (**1693**), 1803, Leeds, height: 12.7cm, (5in), enamelled creamware. Enamelled with floral sprays and inscribed: 'George & Mary Dawson 1803 / Virtue alone is happinefs below / & all our knowledge / is ourselves to know'.[49]

Jug, (**1692**), c.1800, Staffordshire, height: 14.6cm, (5¾in), printed creamware. Printed with a family gathered at a cottage door with dancing in the background, inscribed, 'THE HAPPY PEASANTS'. Such images are loosely based on prints after George Morland or William Hamilton.[50]

Jug, (**1685**), c.1800, Staffordshire, height: 11.5cm, (4½in), brown-printed creamware. Printed with a family sitting at the door of their thatched cottage inscribed, 'PEACE'. On the reverse is, 'When this you see / Remember me'. Reassuring images of flourishing families were popular in the 1790s, a time of political uncertainty over war with France and George III's failing health.

Three Cups, (**1700, 1699, 1700A**), c.1890, Devon, Aller Vale, height x 2: 15.3cm, (6in), height: 20.3cm, (8in), earthenware, slip-decorated and coloured. Three-handled cups sgraffito-decorated with homespun mottoes, such as, 'They can Who think they can / If you can't be aisy Be aisy as you can', 'Stout heart Strong bow And steady eye / A Penny saved is a penny gained' 'Wast [*sic*] not want not' etc.

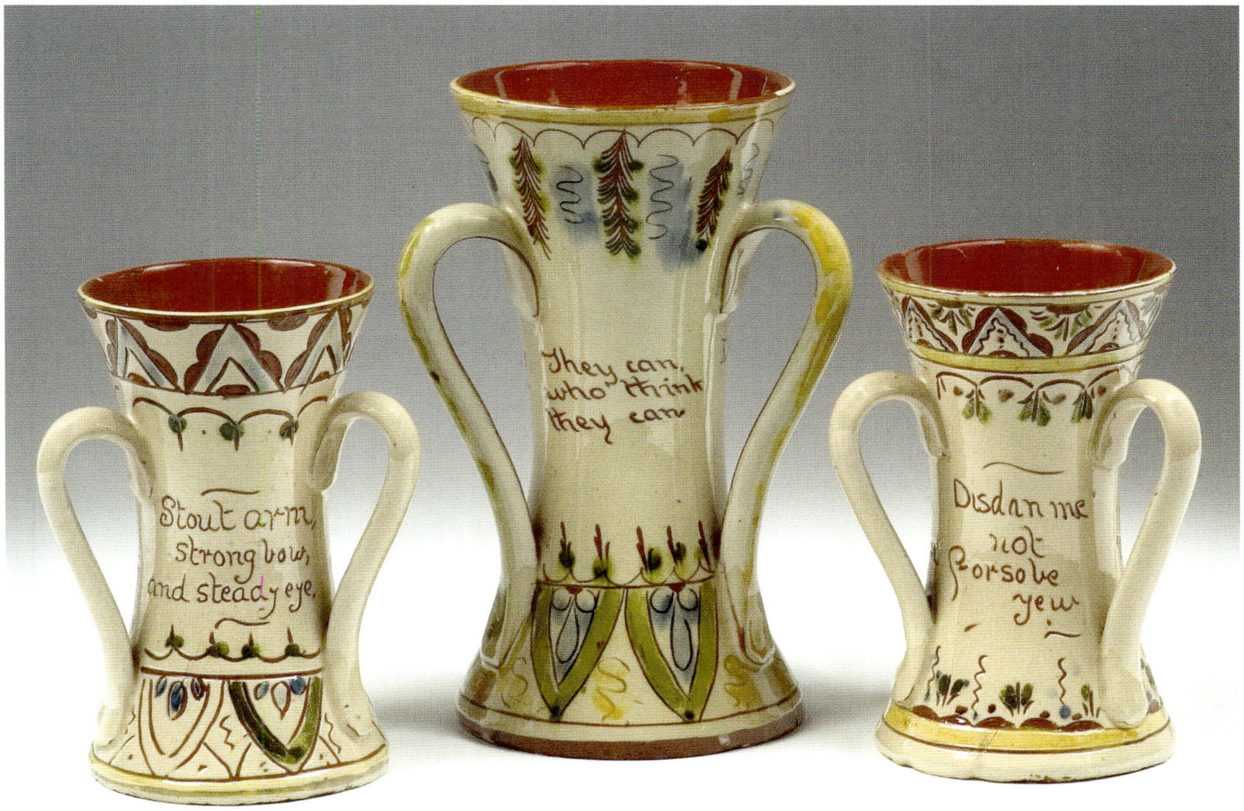

'Keep Within Compass'

The desirable outcome of marriage was, of course, mutual respect and a harmonious family life. A pair of prints, generally referred to as 'Keep within Compass' are used to outline the moral framework for a successful union.[51] The phrase and image were used on the title page of a book published in 1619.[52] The Birmingham painter, Samuel Lines (1778-1863) attests to their enduring popularity, recalling that the subject was 'frequently to be seen on the walls of farmhouses and cottages'.[53]

The design emphasises the importance of integrity as the moral heart of the family and women were considered key to upholding standards. Among the best known of the many conduct books available in the mid-eighteenth century was James Fordyce's *Sermons to Young Women* (1765) in which the author asserts optimistically that 'A roomful of riotous men could be "checked all at once into decency" by an accidental entrance of a virtuous woman'.[54]

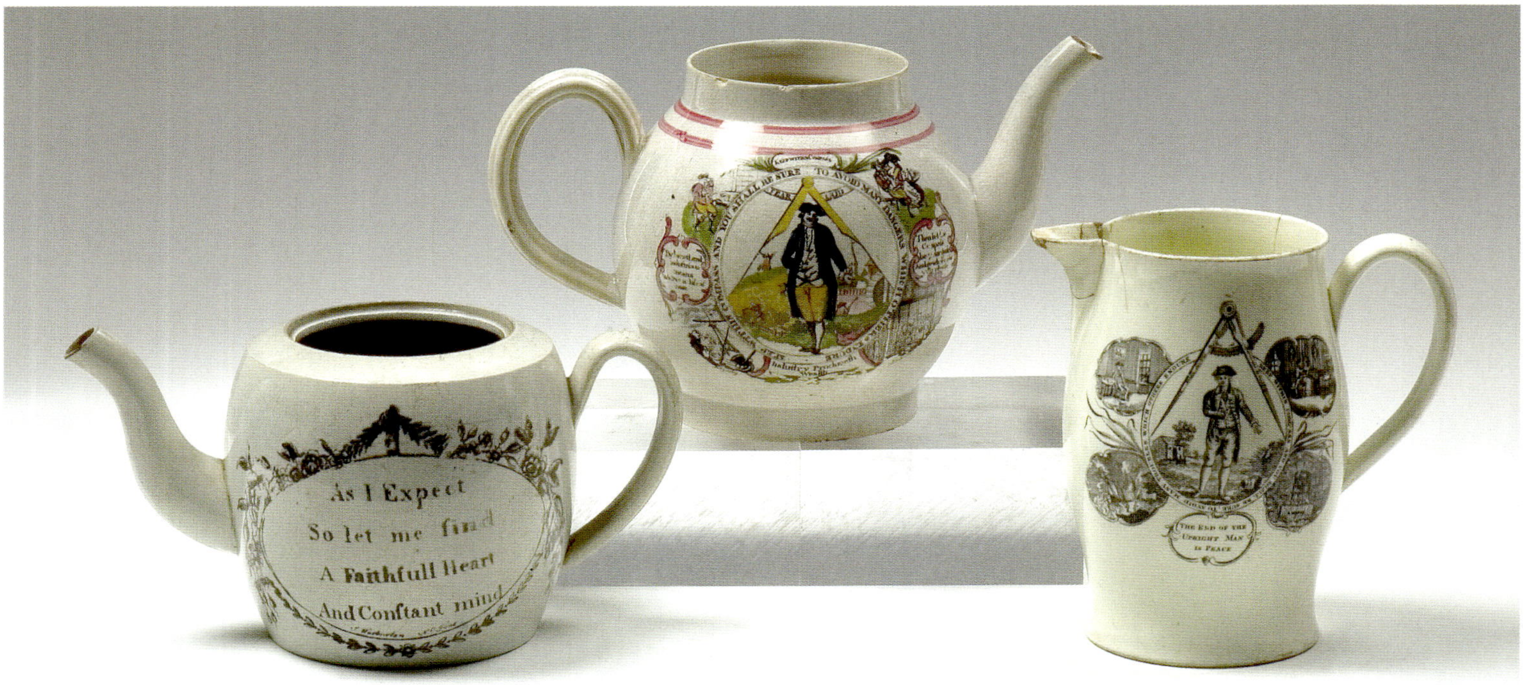

Teapot, (**1669**), c.1790, Newcastle upon Tyne, height: 10.8cm, (4¼in), printed pearlware. One side of teapot, marked, 'J. Warburton, N.C. Tyne', (for engraver James Warburton), a verse, 'As I Expect / So let me find / A Faithfull Heart / And Confant mind'.
Teapot, (**1558**), c.1790, Staffordshire, Lane End, height: 12.7cm, (5in), pearlware, printed and enamelled. Teapot made by John Aynsley, printed with a man standing within the angle of a pair of compasses, ringed by inscription, 'KEEP WITHIN COMPASS AND YOU SHALL BE SURE TO AVOID MANY TROUBLES WHICH OTHERS ENDURE'.

Jug, (**1556**), c.1790, Staffordshire and Liverpool, height: 14cm, (5½in), printed creamware. Crisply printed, probably by Guy Green, for Wedgwood, with a man and compasses, surrounded by tiny vignettes of proper and improper behaviour and their consequences.[55] It is inscribed, 'THE END OF THE UPRIGHT MAN IS PEACE' and 'KEEP WITHIN COMPASS AND YOU SHALL BE SURE'. Versions of the source prints were published by Bowles and Carver and by Carington Bowles in 1785 after a design by Robert Dighton. The text is from Psalm 37: 37, 'Mark the perfect man and behold the upright for the end of that man is peace'.[56]

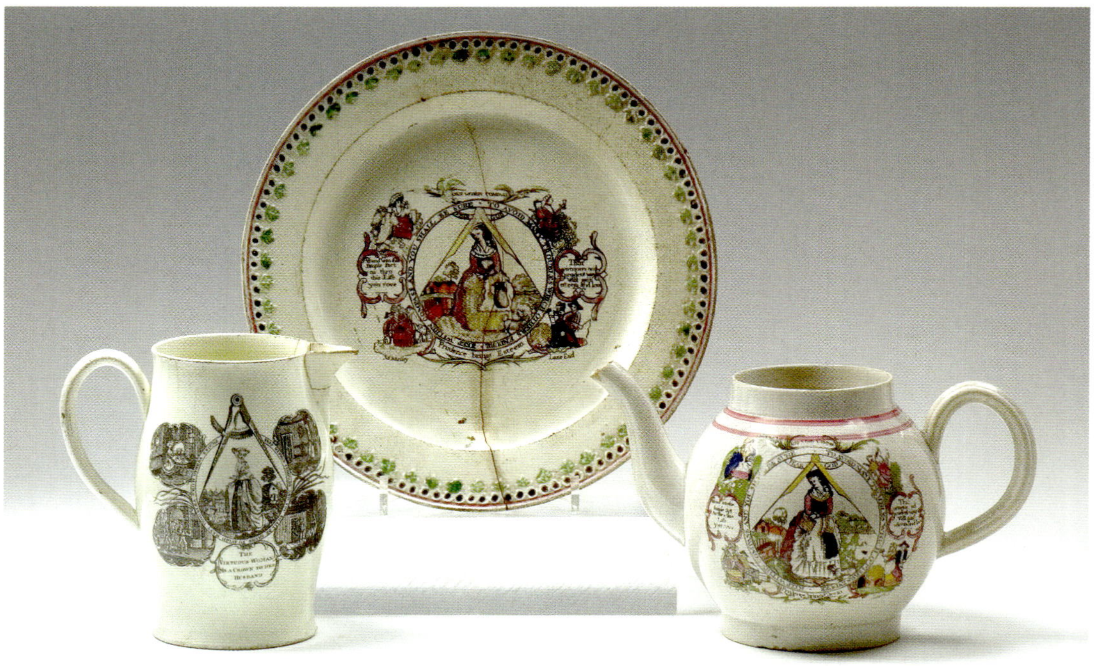

Jug, (**1556**), c.1790, Staffordshire and Liverpool, height: height: 14cm, (5½in), printed creamware. Crisply printed, probably by Guy Green for Wedgwood, with a woman standing within compasses, flanked by small scenes,[57] inscribed, 'THE VIRTUOUS WOMAN IS A CROWN TO HER HUSBAND' and 'KEEP WITHIN COMPASS'.
Plate, (**1557**), c.1785, Staffordshire, Lane End, diameter: 24.2cm, (9½in), pearl-ware, printed and enamelled. Plate signed M.[Michael] Shelley, Lane End, and printed with a similar scene of the woman and compasses.[58] Its inscriptions include, 'KEEP WITHIN COMPASS' and 'Prudence brings esteem'.
Teapot, (**1558**), c.1790, Staffordshire, Lane End, height: 12.7cm, (5in), pearlware, printed and enamelled. Teapot made by John Aynsley, printed with woman and compasses.

Hot Beverages and Old Age

Coffee was established as a social drink from the late seventeenth century but, like tea, it was expensive; only the affluent could afford to drink it. Coffee cups, known as coffee cans, are distinctively cylindrical with handles whereas early tea cups, (like their Chinese prototypes), lacked handles and are known as tea bowls. Frequently tea was so hot that, given the lack of a handle, it was poured into a saucer in order to cool it. It may have been drunk straight from the saucer, which nowadays would be considered ill-mannered.

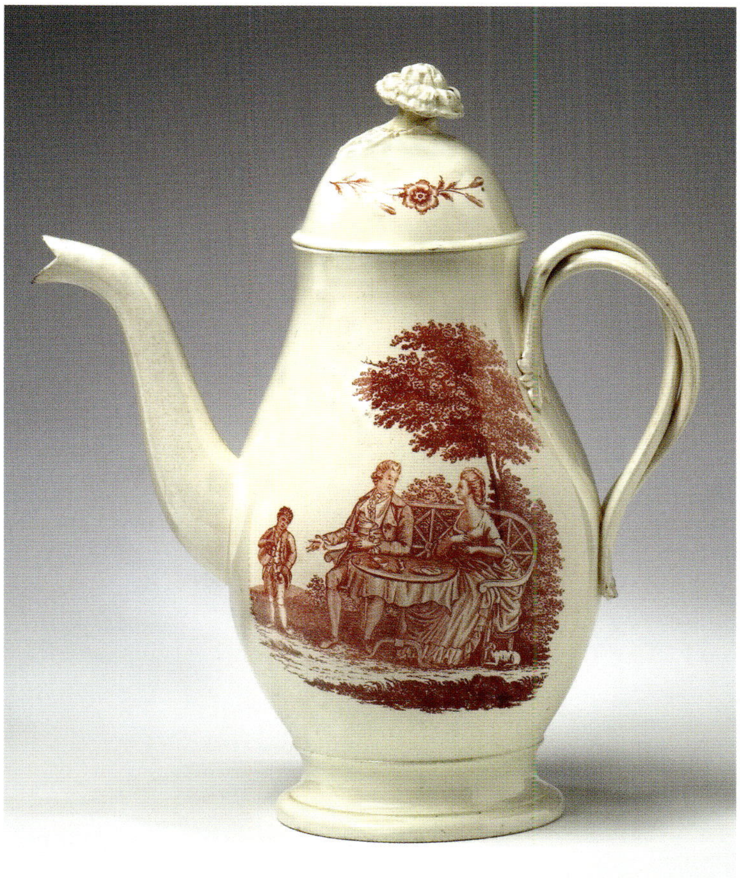

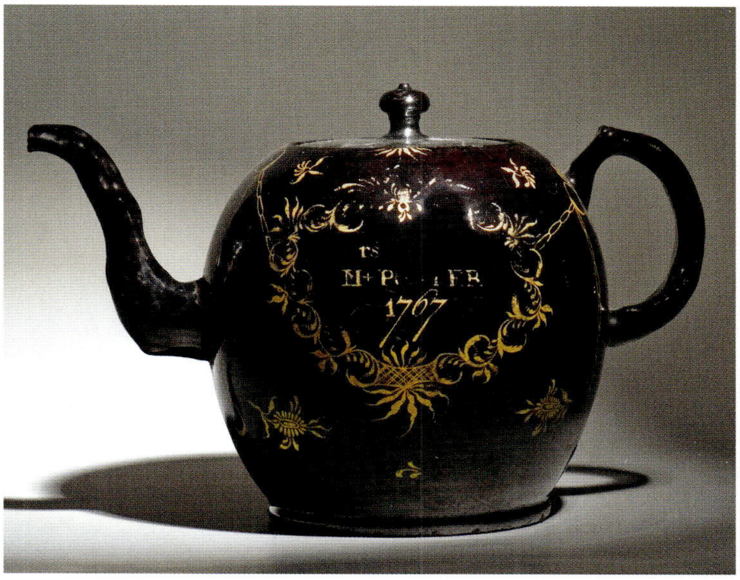

Teapot, (**1701**), 1767, Staffordshire, height: 20.3cm, (8in), earthenware, black glazed and gilt. Teapot gilt with swags and inscribed on both sides, 'Mrs M Porter 1767'.

Coffee Pot, (**1690**), c.1780, Wedgwood and Liverpool, height: 28cm, (11in), red-printed creamware. Printed by Sadler and Green with one of many versions of *The Tea Party*. An affluent couple take tea in their garden, served by a little black page who pours hot water from a kettle into the teapot.

Clockwise: **Figure**, (**1635**), c.1882, Germany, height: 17.8cm, (7in), coloured, hard-paste porcelain. A young woman offers a brown teapot, based on a greetings card designed by Albert Ludovici Jnr in 1881, intending gentle mockery towards the Aesthetic Movement. The original card was captioned, 'May you have a quite too happy time'.
Figure, (**1561**), c.1850, height: 12.1cm, (4¾in), painted plaster. Figure representing 'Red Riding Hood', one of many tales gathered and popularised as 'Little red-cap', by the Brothers Grimm in the early 1800s.
Figure, (**1565**), c.1870, Germany, height: 10.2cm, (4in), coloured, hard-paste porcelain. Sentimental model of a toddler hugging a terrier.
Nursery Teacup, (**849**), c.1810, Staffordshire, height: 3.8cm, (1½in), blue-printed pearlware. Printed with verse, 'RIGHTEOUS ART THOU O LORD / AND JUST ARE THY JUDGEMENTS', conflating verses from Revelations 16:5-7.

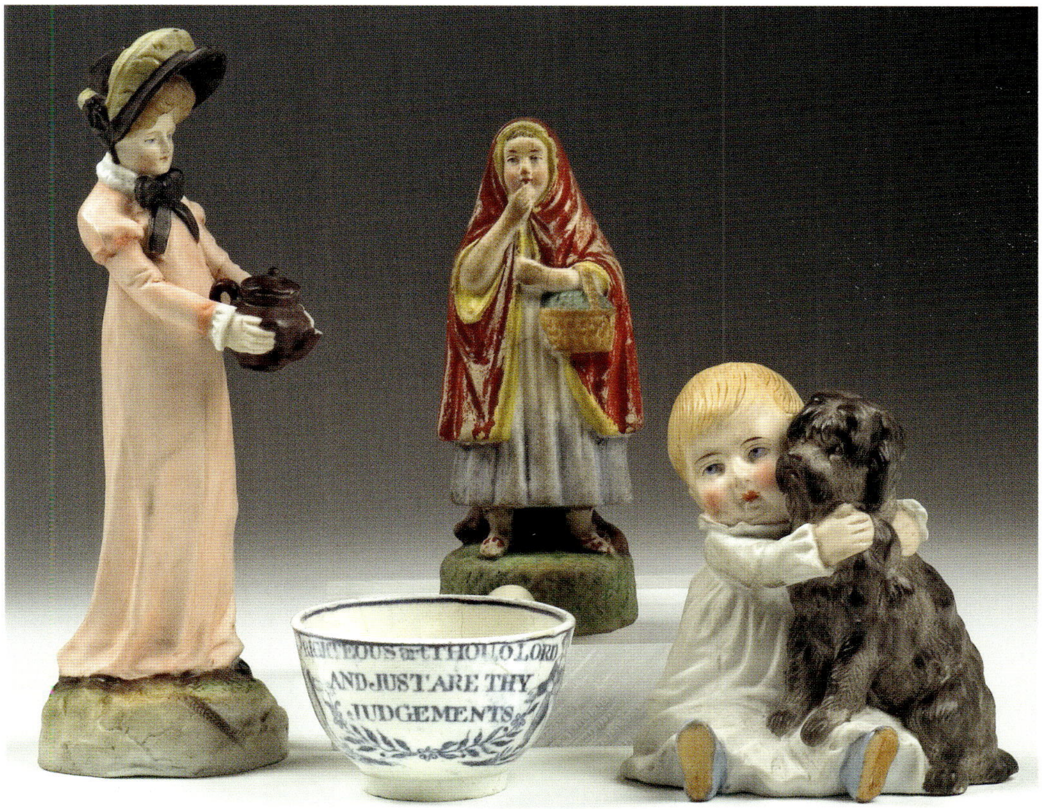

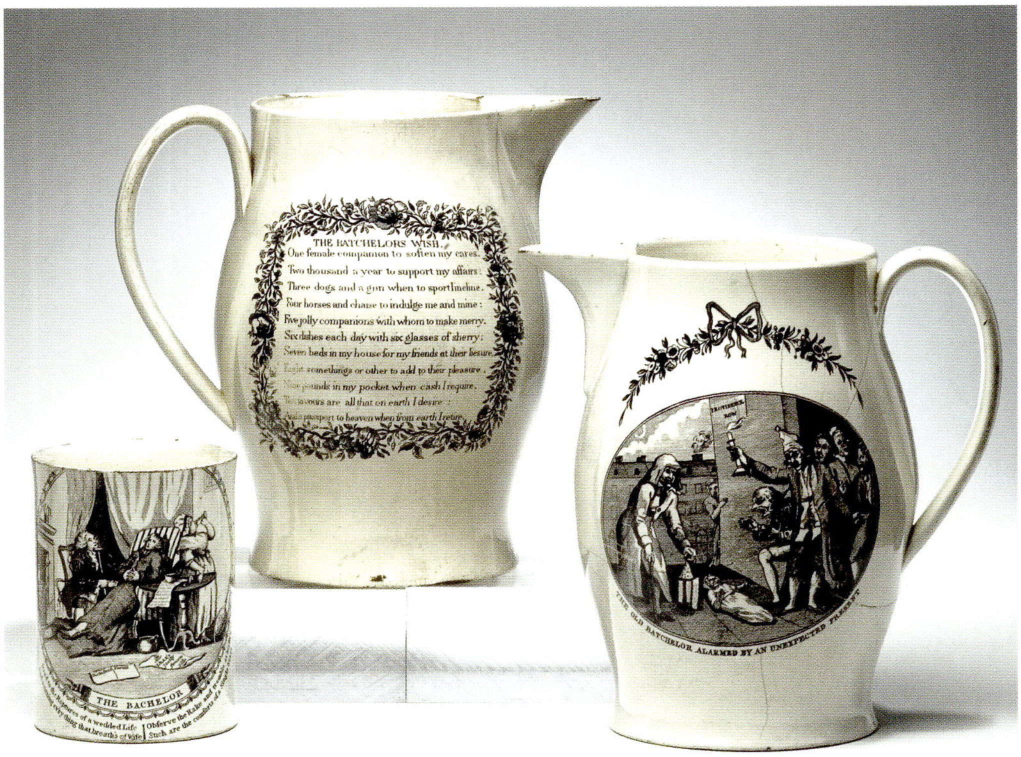

Mug, (**1706**), c.1780, Staffordshire, height: 11.5cm, (4½in), printed creamware. 'THE BACHELOR … Dead to the Raptures of a wedded Life…', appears to be in extremis. He lies ill, fleeced by his doctor, who sells him quack remedies, while a nurse drinks his liquor. The Earl of Rochester's pornographic poems lie on the floor.
Jug, (**1707**), c.1780, Staffordshire, height: 20.7cm, (8⅛in), printed creamware. 'THE BATCHELORS [*sic*] WISH', a cheerful, optimistic poem begins, 'One female companion to soften my cares, / Two thousands a year, to support my affairs / Three dogs and a gun when to sport I'm inclin'd …Ten favours are all that on earth I desire / And a passport to heaven, when from earth I retire'.
Jug, (**1435**), c.1780, Staffordshire, height: 20.3cm, (8in), printed creamware. 'THE OLD BACHELOR ALARMED BY AN UNEXPECTED PRESENT', shows an old man, (with a party of friends and a night watchman) horrified to find a newborn baby on his doorstep. J. Beresford's lists this enduring worry as a 'misery of human life', '4.(S.) On returning to your house very late at night, … discovering that, in the act of rapping at the door, you are rocking the cradle of a natural child, very unnaturally suspended at your knocker'.[59]

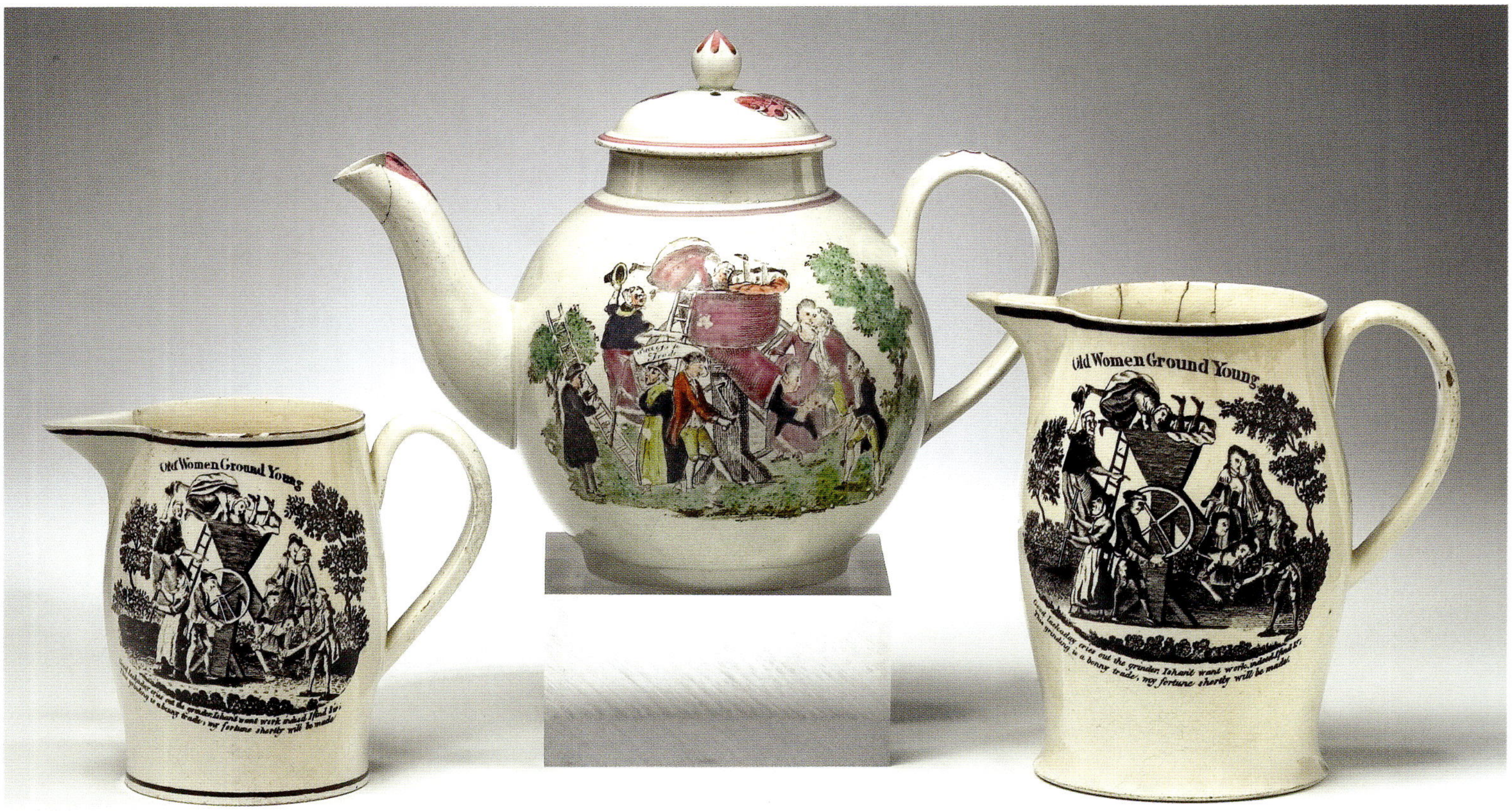

Cream Jug, (**1714**), c.1780, Staffordshire, height: 10.8cm, (4¼in), printed creamware. The satirical print entitled, 'Old Women Ground Young' was a hugely popular visual satire of the late eighteenth century. Old women are forced to climb a ladder and jump into a hopper at the top of an agricultural machine from which they emerge young and amorous! The grinder declares, '...This grinding is a bonny trade, my fortune shortly will be made'.
Teapot, (**Hove 62.35**), c.1790, Staffordshire, Lane End, height: 16cm, (6¼in), pearlware, printed and enamelled. Untitled print of 'Old Women Ground Young'. The grinder wishes 'Success to Trade'.

Cream Jug, (**1190**), c.1780, Staffordshire, height: 14cm, (5½in), printed creamware. Print very similar to that on (1714), entitled, 'Old Women Ground Young'. The earliest version of the subject, called 'The Miller's Maid', shows old men being ground young.[60] Old women first appear in Sayers & Bennett's 1775 catalogue, where 'Old Women and Old Men Ground Young' is listed with 'moral and instructive Emblems for the entertainment of Children'.[61] The idea probably originates in the medieval legend of 'The Fountain of Youth' that rejuvenates the old and disabled.

Cream Jug, (**1714**), c.1790, Staffordshire, height: 10.8cm, (4¼in), printed creamware. Inscribed, 'INKLE and YARICO', the scene shows a woman who has rescued a man from drowning, a ship in the background. The legend of Inkle and Yarico was first published in the *Spectator* in 1711 and was featured in poems, essays and plays. George Colman's comic opera *Inkle and Yarico*, presented at Covent Garden in 1787, enjoyed enormous popularity.[62] The story concerns the English trader, Inkle, who was shipwrecked in North America. He falls in love with a Native American (or black) woman who saves their lives.
Jug, (**1682**), c.1794, Staffordshire or Liverpool, height: 8.3cm, (3¼in), printed creamware. Inscribed under spout, 'W.Lancaster/ Wateryet Blawith- / July 8th 1794'; Water Yeat is at the southern end of Coniston Water, on the road to Ulverston. A gentleman plays the flute to a woman sitting in a garden, inscribed, 'The softest tones his flute can give – he chuses for her voice / Resolved in concert still to live with her he's made his choice.'
Jug, (**1423**), c.1790, Staffordshire, height: 14.7cm, (5¾in), printed creamware. The verse on (1682) is inscribed on this jug, and an image of lovers, named 'Edwin & Julia'. This refers either to the hero of James Beattie's celebrated poem *'The Minstrel'*, (1771-74) or to the protagonists of *The interesting story of Edwin and Julia; being a rational and philosophical enquiry into the nature of things. In a series of letters.* Written by 'a doctor of physic, M.A. &c' it was published by J. Wilkey in 1774.

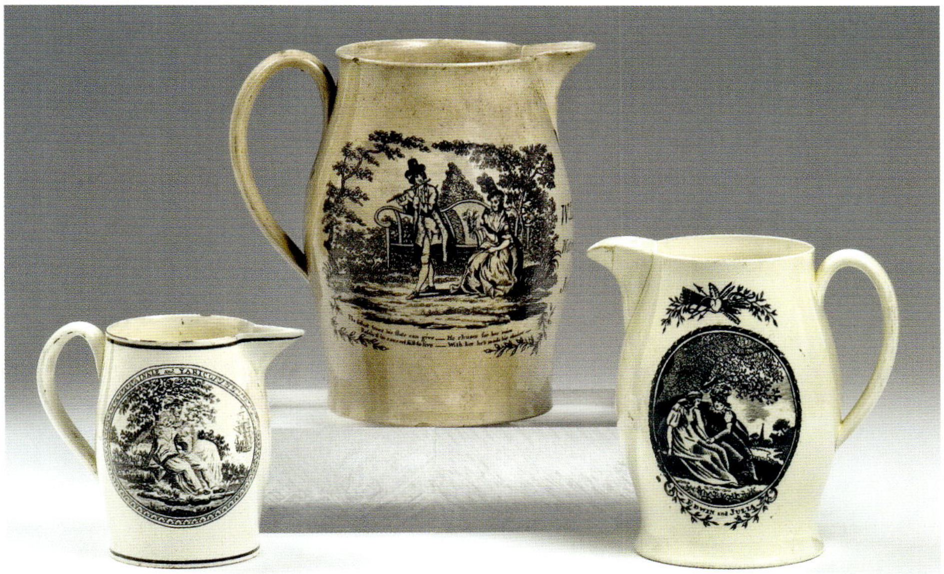

Figure, (**1715**), c.1760, Staffordshire, height: 15.3cm, (5in), soft-paste porcelain. Figure of an old man, symbolising Winter, sits on a log, warming his hands over a brazier (now missing). Made at Longton Hall. His grizzled face can still be seen beneath his hood.
Two Money Boxes, (**1708 & A**), c.1840, Staffordshire, each height: 5.1cm, (2in), enamelled, soft-paste porcelain. Modelled as the caricature heads of old women.

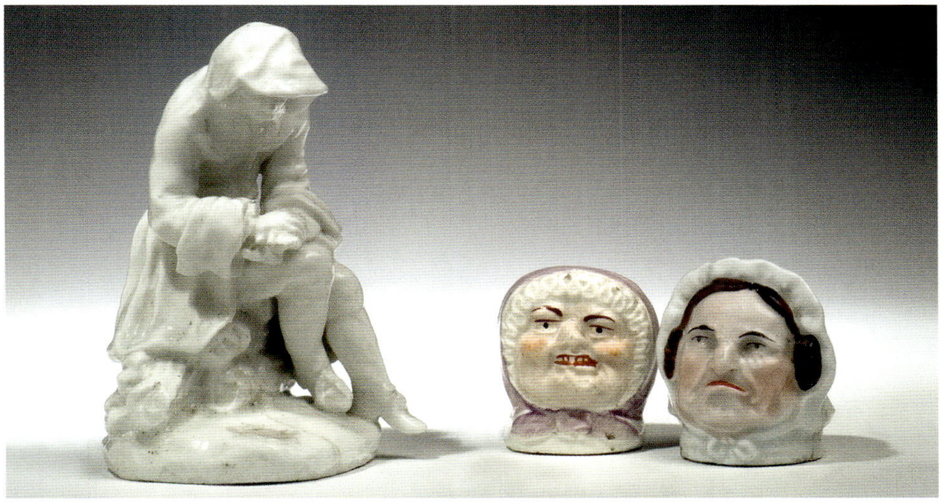

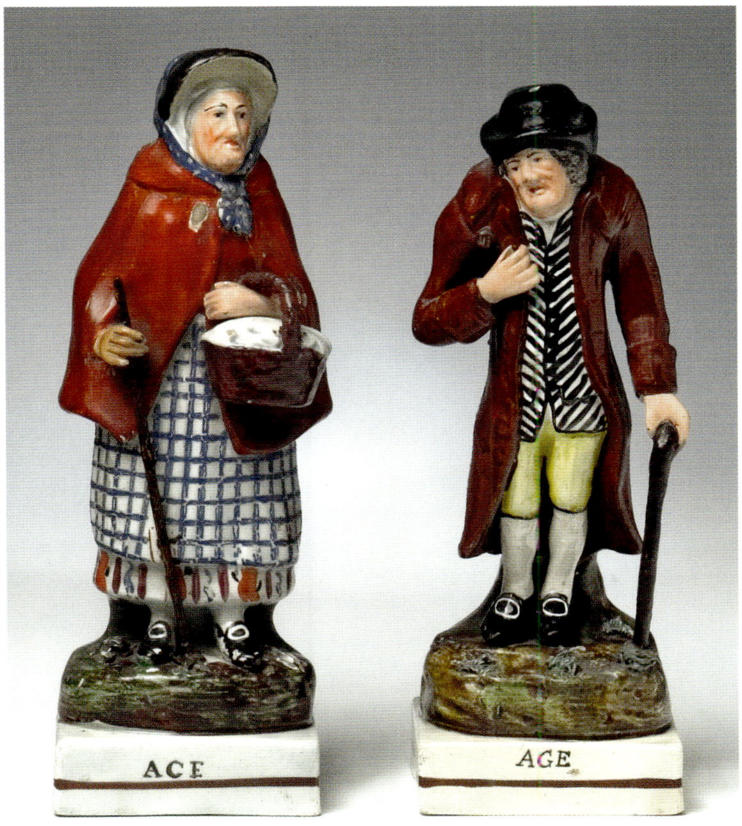

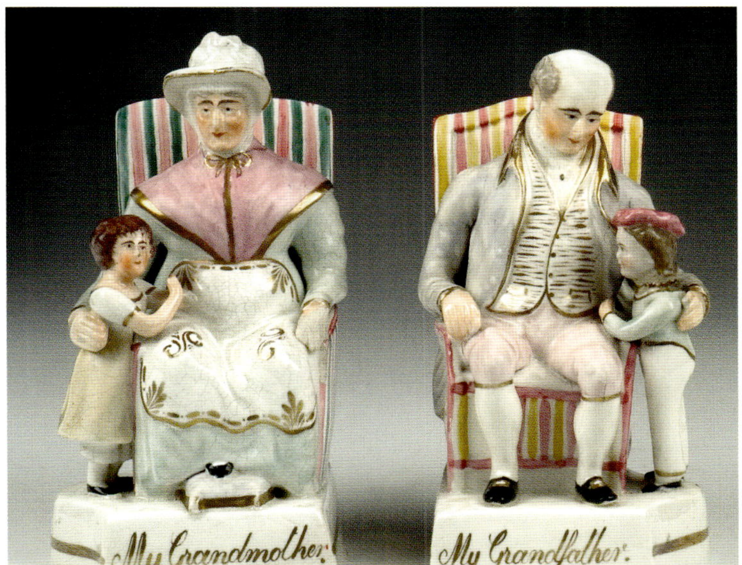

Pair of Bookends, (**1710 & A**), c.1860, Staffordshire, height: 16.9cm, (6⅝in), height: 16.3cm, (6⅜in), soft bone china, enamelled and gilt. Modelled as an old couple sitting in armchairs, each with a small child; inscribed, 'My Grandfather' and 'My Grandmother'.

Two Figures, (**1711 & A**), c.1820, Staffordshire, height: 19.1cm, (7in), height: 20cm, (7⅞in), enamelled pearlware. Old woman with stick and basket and old man with two sticks, both inscribed, 'AGE'.

GLOSSARY

Agateware
Pottery of marbled appearance, resembling the semi-precious stone; achieved by combining coloured clays in the body, or by blending coloured slips on the surface.

Applied sprigs
Relief decoration, moulded or stamped separately and attached to the surface of an object or vessel with liquid slip.

Basalt(es)
Black stoneware imitating the hard black stone used in Ancient Egypt; developed and named by Josiah Wedgwood c.1768.

Bat printing
See Printing

Body
The composite clay material from which earthenware, stoneware and porcelain are made.

Biscuit
Porcelain or earthenware fired without glaze.

Bone china
See Soft paste porcelain

Casting
The batch-production of ceramics by pouring liquid slip into a dry plaster mould that absorbs the water and deposits the clay.

Creamware
Cream-coloured earthenware, made with light-coloured Devon clay combined with calcined flint. A transparent lead glaze was developed, 1730–40.

Delftware
Earthenware, covered in opaque white tin glaze. First developed in Italy (maiolica), it was also made in France (faience) and in Holland. The English version is named after the Dutch town of Delft.

Drabware
A non-porous stoneware or stained earthenware.

Earthenware
A porous clay body fired at temperatures between 500° and 1150°C, requiring glaze to make it waterproof.

Enamel colours
Powdered, glassy pigments coloured with metal oxides, applied over the glaze. They are fired in a muffle kiln at between 700° and 900°C.

Faience
See Delftware

Frog mug
Drinking vessel, usually from Staffordshire or the North East, containing a three-dimensional model of a frog, toad or newt; also called a 'surprise' mug.

Glaze
Powdered glass dusted over or painted in suspension onto the ceramic surface and fired in a glost kiln, giving a glossy, waterproof finish.

High temperature colours
Certain colours (blue, green, yellow, brown) may be applied to the clay under the glaze, before firing at around 1100 to 1450°C in a high-temperature kiln. *See also* Prattware.

Impressed
Inscription or decoration applied to soft clay with a stamp.

Incised
Inscription or decoration applied to soft clay with a sharp instrument.

Jackfield ware
A type of pottery made at Jackfield in Shropshire around 1750. The red clay body was black-glazed and oil-gilt.

Jasperware
A dense, white stoneware that can be stained in a range of colours (blue is best known), developed by Josiah Wedgwood in the 1770s.

Lead glaze
A transparent, honey-coloured glaze containing lead oxide, used especially on creamware, fired to around 1050°C.

Loving cup
A large ornamental drinking vessel with two or more handles, to be passed around a table at weddings and banquets.

Lustre
A thin metallic film on a glazed surface giving off multi coloured reflections. This is achieved by depositing a metal oxide or sulphide to a pre-glazed surface and firing in a reduction kiln at around 600°C. Gold oxide produces pink lustre, platinum - silver lustre, and copper - red brown lustre but the result also depends on the underlying colour of the clay.

Maiolica
See Delftware

Moulding
The batch-production of ceramics by pressing soft clay into Plaster of Paris or fired clay moulds.

Oxide colours
Metal compounds were used for glazes, e.g. lead oxide (transparent) or tin oxide (opaque white). Also used as pigments for decorating ceramics either over or under the glaze: chrome (yellow), cobalt (blue), copper (green), manganese (purple-brown).

Parian porcelain
A creamy white unglazed body, resembling marble, pioneered by Copeland & Garrett in the 1840s. Composed of china clay and feldspar, it is named after the marble quarried on the Greek island of Paros.

Pearlware
Pearl-glazed earthenware, developed after creamware, covered in a lead glaze, tinted blue with cobalt oxide.

Pitcher mould
A mould of lightly fired clay used for making sprigged relief decoration to be applied to vessels.

Polychrome
Decoration using two or more colours.

Porcelain: True/Hard paste
A hard, translucent, non-porous body made from a mixture of china clay (kaolin) and china stone (petunse – feldspathic rock), fired at a high temperature, around 1450°C. It was pioneered in China and much imitated in Europe.

Porcelain: Soft paste
A ceramic body approximating to true porcelain but using substitute materials, e.g. powdered glass, soap rock and, in England, bone ash (for bone china). Fired to a temperature around 1300°C.

Posset pot
A multi-handled vessel with a cover, used for making and drinking posset or caudle (hot milk curled with wine, ale and spices).

Prattware
Generic term for figures and relief-moulded vessels in pearlware, decorated underglaze with high-temperature colours. Named after William Pratt of Lane Delph.

Pratt colours
Metal oxide pigments: brown, yellow, green and blue applied under the glaze and fired at high temperatures.

Printing
Mass-production method of decorating ceramics. A copper plate, engraved with the design, is inked and transferred to thin paper, which is applied to the surface of a vessel. A flexible glue bat, directly impressed by the copper plate and inked, may also be used for complex curved surfaces.

Puzzle jug
A novelty vessel with pierced openwork and multiple spouts, which makes pouring or drinking all but impossible.

Queen's ware
Creamware named in honour of Queen Charlotte by Josiah Wedgwood, from 1765.

Relief-moulding
Moulded decoration that stands proud of the object's surface.

Salt-glaze
A colourless glaze formed by throwing common salt into the kiln at 1000°C during firing. It forms a characteristic, pitted, 'orange peel' effect.

Slip
Clay mixed with water to a creamy, liquid state. Used for casting, to attach parts and (coloured) for decoration.

Sgraffito
Decoration made by scratching the design through slip before glazing, so as to reveal the body beneath.

Socle
A low block used to attach a bust to its plinth or base.

Smear-glazed
A very thin glaze, or faint gloss, applied to porcelain or stoneware.

Stirrup cup
An English drinking vessel lacking a handle or foot, usually moulded as an animal head. It was traditionally used by a mounted rider or huntsman about to depart.

Stoneware
A ceramic body midway between earthenware and porcelain, made from clay and a fusible stone, fired to around 1300°C to form a non-porous, waterproof material. Varieties include white salt-glaze, brown stoneware, jasperware, etc.

Stone China
A fine, white porcellanous stoneware, hard and compact. First developed by John Turner around 1800, extensively produced by Spode.

Terracotta
Earthenware body made of reddish clay, usually unglazed.

Transfer printing
See printing

Tin-glaze
See Delftware

Underglaze
See High-temperature colours

ENDNOTES

Introduction

[1] I am very grateful to Douglas Catt for access to his unpublished and regularly updated Catt family history document, *Descendants & Connections of Thomas Catt of Buxted from 1596.*

[2] See M.A. Lower, 'Mr William Catt', *The Worthies of Sussex*, 1865, pp. 217-19, also mentioned by Willett in a letter to Ruskin, published by Ruskin in *Fors Clavigera*,Vol. 28, p. 293.

[3] Colin Brent, *Georgian Lewes, 1714-1830*, Colin Brent Books, Lewes,1993, p. 28.

[4] See David Lyndhurst, *Bishopstone and the Lost Village of Tide Mills*, S.B. Publications, Seaford, 2001, p.24.

[5] Lower, op.cit., 1865, p.219.

[6] See the front page of the *London Gazette*, 28 August 1863.

[7] See *The Times*, 28 April 1864, p.12, the *Daily Telegraph*, 28 April 1864, p. 6. Charles Catt later married Mary Anne Mew from the Isle of Wight, causing a good deal of amusement in Brighton.

[8] Charles, an asthmatic, could not participate in farming and milling.

[9] Ruskin mentions him frequently, publishing several of his letters in *Fors Clavigera* (1871 onwards) and expresses his gratitude to Willett in prefaces to the reissue of *The Ethics of Dust* (1877) and *The Two Paths* (1878). Willett also contributed material and opinions to *Deucalion*, a series of geological essays, published in 1879. My thanks to Stephen Wildman of the Ruskin Library, Lancaster University, for references and copies of letters.

[10] See 'Obituary: Henry Willett', the *Oxford Magazine*, 1 March 1905.

[11] See J.G. Bishop, 'The Late Mr. Henry Willett', the *Brighton Herald*, 4 March 1905.

[12] J.G.Bishop, *Brighton Pavilion and its Royal and Municipal Associations 1783-1903*, 1903, pp.189-196.

[13] Kingsley, possibly fearing damage to sales, actually took out an injunction to stop the readings.

[14] Dickens himself had read aloud from *David Copperfield* at the Brighton Town Hall in 1861 (see Harrison, op.cit., 1906, p.68).

[15] 'The Late Mr. H. Willett', *Sussex Daily News*, 1 March 1905, p. 5.

[16] *Catalogue of the Cretaceous Fossils in the Brighton Museum, presented by Henry Willett*, 1871, Brighton, p. iv.

[17] Willett's frequent reports and appeals for funding are noted in *Nature,* until 1875, when funds were exhausted. By this date the first of two borings had reached 1500 ft. See *Nature,* 8 July, 1875, p. 194.

[18] The colours used to decorate the piece include Reckitt's Washing Blue.

[19] See J. Rutherford, 1982, op.cit. pp.176-81.

[20] The first two busts named were included in the subsequent ceramic collection but the bust of Dickens was lost.

[21] *The Graphic*, 24 August, 1872. See S. Beddoe, 'The British Association at Brighton: A page from the Graphic' in *The Royal Pavilion & Museums Review*, 1995, no.1, pp. 4-5.

[22] *The Brighton Herald*, 20 September 1873.

[23] *Catalogue of a Collection of Pottery and Porcelain illustrating Popular British History…*, 1899, London, HMSO.

[24] A.H. Church, *op.cit.*,, 1884, (a South Kensington Museum Art Handbook).

[25] *Introductory catalogue of the Collection of Pottery & Porcelain in the Brighton Museum Lent by Henry Willett,* 1879, Brighton.

[26] L. Jewitt, op.cit.,1883, p.210, Church, op.cit., 1884, p.69 and Solon, op.cit., 1885 all mention it.

[27] See R.H. Soden-Smith, 'Notes on Remarkable kinds of English Pottery, Salt-glazed white ware', *The Magazine of Art*, 1878, pp.107-10, examples from Willett's collection illustrated fig. 2, p. 108.

[28] Many of the illustrations feature early pieces from Willett's collection subsequently sold to the British Museum. See also Rogers, op.cit., 1970, p.11.

[29] See *Catalogue of English Pottery and Porcelain exhibited on loan at the Alexandra Palace*, ed. R.H. Soden-Smith,1873. A delftware plate showing figures in a landscape (signed by Bowen and dated 1761) is among those of Willett's pieces known to have been burned; see Lipski, op.cit.,1984, item 616, pp. 138-39.

[30] It is likely that Sir Augustus Franks played an active role in helping Willett to shape his innovative collecting policy. See D. Wilson, *The Forgotten Collector: Augustus Wollaston Franks of the British Museum*, Walter Neurath Memorial Lecture, London, 1984.

[31] Letter from Henry Willett, read to meeting 11 May 1874, Proceedings of the Pavilion Committee, vol. 8, pp.51-52.

[32] *Willett,* op.cit., 1879.

[33] See *Notes and Queries*, 6 March, 1880, p.189.

[34] Published in the *Brighton Herald*, 8 July 1899 and later issued as an offprint.

[35] Introduction to *Willett,* op. cit., 1879, reprinted in Introduction to *Willett,* op. cit.,1899.

[36] M.L. Solon, *Ceramic Literature: an Analytical Index* London, 1910, p. 217.

[37] See A. Lee, *Portraits in Pottery: with some account of the pleasant occasions…incident to their quest,* Boston, Mass., 1931, p. 108.

[38] Ibid. p.120.

[39] *Brighton Standard and Fashionable Visitors' List,* 11 November, 1902, p.10.

Chapter 1

[1] Its previous owner, Dr Hugh Diamond, believed it had been made in Isleworth for Hampton Court Palace.

[2] B. Rackham in *Trans ECC* vol. 2, No 6, 1938, pp. 20-21. Only one other candle sconce produced from the same mould is known; Brit. Museum [B.278]. There are stove tiles with similar decoration at the British Museum, Truro Museum (1925.193), The Greg Collection, Manchester etc.

[3] D. Askey, *Stoneware Bottles*, Brighton, 1981.

[4] A similar example, dated 1653, showing Charles I with his children, was sold by Chequers to the Victoria & Albert Museum for £155,000. See National Art Collections Fund *Review*, 1998, p.147.

[5] See G. Davidson in *Trans ECC*, vol.7, pt.1, 1968, pl. 82d., p. 76.

[6] By John Hall and William Woollett, (published1781).

[7] G.K. Whitehead, *Hunting and Stalking Deer in Britain through the Ages*, 1980, pp. 22-3.

[8] Title bestowed for the longest unbroken service to Parliament.

[9] The symbolic 'pelican in her piety' pecks her breast in order to nourish her young with her blood.

[10] She actually died in 1737 (Gregorian calendar).

[11] See Cook, op.cit. 1948, Item 52.

[12] See Aubrey Toppin in the *Trans ECC*, vol.1, Part 3, 1935, pp.12-13, Plate IV. A similar mug in the Greg Collection (no.1923-485) is discussed in *The Incomparable Art*, op.cit., 1969, pp. 54-5.

[13] The piece was discussed in *Fire and Form*, 2013, notably by John Mallett, pp.139-44 and by Anton Gabszewicz, pp.222-23. For a detailed discussion of the possibilities and a persuasive argument that the Willett example is an early waster from Bow, produced in 1745 in response to the king's personal victory at Dettingen, with an edition issued after Culloden, see Pat Daniels, op. cit. 2013, especially pp. 32-39.

[14] Royal Collection, RCIN 31614.

[15] See A. N. Newman, ed., 'Leicester House politics, 1750–60, from the papers of John, second earl of Egmont', *Camden miscellany, XXIII*, 1969, pp. 85–228.

[16] See Chapter IV, 'The Grand National Jubilee of King George III, 1809', *Jubilee Royal*, Commemorative Collectors Society, 1977, unpaged.

[17] See S. Benjamin, *English Enamel Boxes from the Eighteenth to the Twentieth Centuries*, London, 1978, p. 63.

[18] One was sold by Sotheby's from the Radford Collection in 1943 and is now at Wimpole Hall in Cambridgeshire. The other is at Colonial Williamsburg, Virginia, USA.

[19] The design source is a painting of 1792, *L'Urne Mystérieuse*, where the monarchs' profiles are hidden in the silhouette of a garden urn.

[20] Diana Edwards, op.cit., 1987, pp.100-105, lists portrait basalt plaques by Neale but does not mention George III or William Pitt the Younger (489). See Chapter 4, Statesmen.

[21] See May, op.cit., 1972, pp.33-35. The quotation was displayed around the walls of the Borough Road School in Southwark.

[22] This makes an ironic riposte to the design on a small cream jug, c.1780, (436) where a pug dog, symbolising France, pees on the sleeping British lion). See Chapter 6, England and America.

[23] The figure is based on a bronze, issued by L. Gahagan in 1811.

[24] The design is based on an illustration in Thomas Green, *Memoirs of her late Royal Highness Charlotte Augusta of Wales and Saxe-Coburg*, 1818, p. 320.

[25] Housman describes it as a Twelfth Cake ornament, to decorate a traditional confection made for the Twelfth Night after Christmas. Housman, op.cit., 1893, p.8.

[26] Atterbury & Batkin, op.cit., 1990, p.57.

[27] For further information see Binns, op.cit., 1877, pp.159-61, Prentice, op.cit., 1994, p.105 and for illustrations of a range of pieces see Sandon, op.cit., 1973, p. 25.

[28] See Godden, op.cit., 1968, p. 90.

[29] See Bromley after Hayter, NPG D33567.

[30] A.R. Freebairn after H. Weigall, NPG D33610.

[31] See engraving of 1834 by Bromley after Hayter, NPG D33567.

[32] Recorded in J.G. Bishop's *A Peep Into the Past: Brighton in the Olden Time, with Glances at the Present,* 1892. Archive.org/details/apeepintopastbr00bishgoog. Saunders was still recorded as landlord in Leppard & Co., *Brighton Directory*, 1845.

[33] Engraved by Wm Skelton, NPG D19586.

[34] Loosely based on a print after a portrait by Fanny Corbaux (pub. 1831. NPG D16074).

[35] See NPG D21979. Tony Lonton, 'George Potts Cocker's and Douglas Potts Cocker's Chenies Street Biscuit Porcelain Manufactory, London c.1840-45', *NCS Journal* Vol. 23, 2006-07, pp111.

[36] See Atterbury and Batkin, 1990, p. 284-5.

[37] F.C. Lewis after J.D. Francis, 1838, NPG D35045.

[38] See NPG D21979. It is likely that HW88, 89 and possibly 91 are all designs c.1840-c.1846 by Douglas Potts Cocker, who marked very few pieces. See Tony Lonton, 'George Potts Cocker's and Douglas Potts Cocker's Chenies Street Biscuit Porcelain Manufactory, London c1840-45', *NCS Journal* Vol 23, 2006-07, pp. lll.

[39] Lloyd Thomas *Old Torquay Potteries*, 1977, fig. 46, p. 269.

Chapter 2

[1] Published in the *Flying-Post* on 2 November 1714, see Black, 2005, p. 9.

[2] NPG D31532.

[3] H. Walpole, (Ed. D. Jarrett) *Memoirs of the Reign of George III*, Yale, 2000, Year 1765 pp.180-81.

[4] Errol Manners suggested (2005) in the absence of other painted examples, the bright enamelling may date from the 19th century.

[5] He is recorded as a successful bidder at the regular sales of Chelsea and Derby porcelain, had 'bespoke a set [of Chelsea china] for his own table' and owned a Chelsea chandelier said to be worth £500; see Young, op.cit., 1999, p.192 and note 88, p.196.

[6] The availability of copies in cheaper materials confirms Cumberland's general popularity. See V&A A.12-1947.

[7] At least one other design, featuring Charles Edward Stuart, was produced in China for the Scottish market. See Godden, op.cit., 1979, p.231.

[8] Engraved by John Faber and Thomas Hudson, NPG D32910. See *London 1753*, op.cit., 2003, item. 411, p.191.

[9] See D. Edwards, 'English White Salt-glazed stoneware for the American Market', *Trans ECC*, Vol.18, pt. 2, 2003, p.320, who notes advertisements for commemorative wares in the *Boston Gazette* and broken plates excavated at Williamsburg.

[10] Quoted in A. Vickery, *The Gentleman's Daughter*, London, 1998, p.123.

[11] Quoted in Hobson, op.cit., 1903, p.188, no. G112.

[12] Now in the Gemäldegalerie, Berlin.
[13] In fact Frederick, Duke of York died in January 1827. The plaque is in an earlier style.
[14] G.E. Hart, *Fall of New France: 1755-1760* Montreal, 1888, p.487.
[15] Schama, op.cit., 2001, Ch. 6 'The Wrong Empire', p.431.
[16] Hart, op.cit, 1888, p.487.
[17] See also 235, 236, 263.
[18] Reproduced as needlework panels and on cheap trays made of tole (painted and lacquered tin), its enduring popularity was such that Charlotte Brontë notes in *Jane Eyre,* that a copy of the image hangs alongside a portrait of George III at the George Inn at Millcote. (*Jane Eyre*, 1847, Chapter XI).
[19] The National Army Museum purchased, in 2008, a version of Schaak's painting. NAM 2008-05-25.
[20] NPG D8784.
[21] Two versions are at The Ashmolean Museum, Oxford and the National Army Museum, London.
[22] For discussion of images of Granby, see David H. Solkin, Ch. 5 'Exhibitions of Sympathy' in *Painting for Money, The Visual Arts and the Public Sphere in Eighteenth-Century England*, Yale, 1992, pp. 199-207.
[23] See E. Manners, 'A Documentary 'Girl in the swing' Seal', *Trans ECC*, vol.18, pt. 3, 2004, pp. 403-7. Half-length portrait engraved by Richard Purcell: NPG D39974.
[24] See Chapter 7, Politics; Revolt & Reform.
[25] See Rogers, op.cit., 1970, p.13.
[26] In enamelled versions, this is decorated with his family crest.
[27] Uglow, 2014, op.cit. pp. 43-44.
[28] Identified and illustrated by Lewis, op.cit., 1984, p.168.
[29] Illustrated in *The French Revolution*, op.cit. 1990, p.192, Cat. No. 146; Drakard, op.cit., 1992, p.172, fig. 466.
[30] *Letters of Charles Lamb*, Vol I p. 397 (28 March 1809) quoted in Gattrell, 2006, p. 496.
[31] See L.A. Compton, 'A Newcastle Mug', NCS *Newsletter*, No.76, December 1989, pp.46-8.
[32] Published by Thomas Tegg on 2[illegible] April. A copy in the British Museum: BM 1868,0808.7809.
[33] Home's painting is at the National Army Museum, Brown's is at the Bowes Museum, Barnard Castle.
[34] The figure's identity is doubtful. Two similar figures supporting a cruet in the Earle Collection, are identified as Napoleon. op.cit., 1915, (pp.182-3, figs.576 and 578). Haggar, op.cit., 1955, illustrates a slight variant as Nelson (pl.39) while a similar figure in the Willett Collection (184) is described as Lord Howe.
[35] V&A 90-1874.
[36] A large painting of *The Death of General Abercromby* (in Alexandria) was cut into six portrait fragments in the 1930s. The portrait of Moore is in the National Galleries of Scotland.
[37] Possibly inspired by clothes worn by Sicilian marionettes (*I Pupi*) which had become popular around 1800.
[38] NPG 4835.

Chapter 3

[1] In the 18th century, 'naval officer' referred to the civilian officials of the Naval Board. For more on the Naval career structure see Rodger, op.cit. 2004 pp. 380-81.
[2] Janice Wallace alerted me to T. Freeman, 'Dramatic Representations of British Soldiers and Sailors on the London Stage, 1660-1800', *Studies in British History*, vol.36, p. 122-24. 1995, New York.
[3] Quoted by Amanda Vickery, *The Gentleman's Daughter*, 1998, p. 203.
[4] From Horace Walpole, *Memoirs of George II*, ed. John Brooke, Yale, 1985, pp. 68-9, note 6.
[5] Ibid. pl.15B.
[6] Published by Amhurst and Rayner: BM 1854,0614.268.
[7] BM 1934,0201.6.
[8] Master mould for (165), found concealed in Enoch Wood's house on demolition, illustrated by Miranda Goodby, 'Moulds and Modellers in the early18th-century Staffordshire Potteries', *Trans ECC*, vol.17 pt.2, 2000, p.217. (166).
[9] Adams and Redstone, op.cit., 198[illegible], pp. 46, 101, illustrated p. 47, fig.7.
[10] Walpole, op.cit., 1985, book 1, p.128.
[11] NPG D760.
[12] NPG D1081.
[13] John Sykes, *Historical Register of Remarkable Events*, 1833, pp. 314-15.
[14] Probably engraved by Thomas Cook, published by Fielding & Walker. Collection of NMM PAD2942.
[15] See Freeman, 1995, op.cit., 'Dramatic Representations' p. 124.
[16] Identified by Lewis, op.cit., 1984, p. 164. NPG D16900.
[17] The print, engraved by Corbutt after R. Purcell was published by John Morris, 10 November 1777, (BM 1902,1011.7217). It was reissued by Laurie & Whittle, 1794.
[18] NPG D36353.
[19] See Chapter 6: England and America, p. 97.
[20] Uglow, 2014, op.cit. p. 65.
[21] See *Glorious Victory, Admiral Duncan and the Battle of Camperdown*, the exhibition organised by Dundee City Council in 1997.
[22] See example in the collection of the NMM AAA5954.
[23] See John Bentley, 'Three Aynsley black prints' in *NCS Newsletter,* no.77, March 1990, pp. 59-60.
[24] BM 1902,1011.7155.
[25] NMM PAD5622.
[26] It was part of a large dinner service. Similar items from a service made for Nelson in Paris porcelain are at the National Maritime Museum, Greenwich. See Prentice, op.cit., 1994, p. 101 and Col. Pl.155.
[27] Image actually shows HMS *Buckingham* in a sea battle of 3 November 1758 (published by Robert Sayer). The print was re-used to depict not only the Battle of the Nile but also the Battle of Trafalgar. See Prentice, op.cit., 1994, p. 30.
[28] *Nelson & Napoleon*, op.cit., 2005, p. 194.
[29] Lockett, T., & Godden, G. A., op.cit., 1989, p.106.
[30] The Abbott portrait is NPG 394.
[31] Prentice, op.cit., 1994, p.30, notes that these moulded jugs were reused after Trafalgar and 'Collingwood' was painted over the moulded name of Captain Berry.
[32] Mentioned, with 215 and 216 as examples of North Eastern pottery by Rev. E.A. Downman, *English Pottery & Porcelain*, 1910, pp.114-15. The profile portrait of Nelson is taken from one by Simon de Koster and the whole image was originally published by Laurie & Whittle, 12 December 1805.
[33] Now in the Walker Art Gallery, Liverpool WAG_3132.
[34] See *London World City 1800-1840,* op.cit., 1992, p. 237, cat.17.
[35] See for instance, 'Voyage in Search of Sir John Franklin', in *Harpers New Monthly Magazine*, Vol II, 1850-51, pp.588-97.
[36] The figure of Lady Franklin was damaged in the 1970s and her head was lost.
[37] See the *Illustrated London News*, 13 September, 1851.

Chapter 4

[1] 'The cap is superficially similar to that adopted by the Light Dragoons but the clothing details are purely decorative… [They] may have been devised from illustrations of foreign troops.' letter from National Museum quoted by Halfpenny, op.cit., 1991, p.38.
[2] Donald Towner attributed two similar creamware groups, at the V&A and at Colonial Williamsburg, Virginia, to the Leeds pottery, because of the addition of characteristic floral knobs. He suggested the Brighton salt-glaze group predates them. Towner, op.cit., 1978, p.146.
[3] See Colley, op.cit., 1992, ch.7 'Manpower', pp. 302-26.
[4] Pieter van der Merwe in *Nelson & Napoleon,* 2005, op.cit., p.164, cat. 181.
[5] See Chapter 5: England & France (399), p.59.
[6] See Harrison, op.cit., 1906, p. 69.
[7] See Lewis, op.cit., 1984, p. 169.
[8] Gaye Blake Roberts (Wedgwood Museum) to L.A. Compton, 26 January 1998: 'The mounted officer, listed in our Crest Book Index as Colonel Leigh [sic].' See portrait at Lyme Park, Cheshire, of Col. Thomas Peter Legh (1753-97) of Lyme Park, painted by Cranke, 1795. (NT Inventory Number 500011).
[9] Previously attributed to Liverpool, Newcastle, Staffordshire, Yorkshire or Portobello, Scotland.
[10] Harold Blakey alerted me to J.A. Fleming's *Scottish Pottery*, 1923, pl.XXX1 (opp. p. 150) where a similar figure is confidently identified.
[11] Illustrated versions of the ballad were published by Robert Sayer in the 1780s with Jemmy dressed as a sailor, rather than a Scotsman.
[12] Published by Fores, 22 September 1803. BM 1935,0522.12.20.
[13] Cameronian Regiment was raised in South Lanarkshire in 1689 and took the name of Richard Cameron, a Covenanter, whose efforts to protect the Presbyterian faith led to his death. The Regiment took part in worldwide campaigns before being disbanded owing to defence cuts in 1968.
[14] H. Sandon, op.cit., 1973, pl. 94 &95.
[15] See Rodger, op.cit., 2004, pp. 314-17.
[16] Print engraved by T. Booth after the French artist, L.P. Boitard. Published 18 December, 1744. 'Sailor's Return': BM 1871, 1209.2744.
[17] Drawn by Collings, etched by Barlow and published by Bentley. NMM_ PAD4732.
[18] BM 1861,0518.943.
[19] Blanning, 2007, Ch.3 p.107.
[20] My thanks to David Atherton for summarising documents at the National Archive.
[21] Jonathan Horne, *Collecting Early English Pottery*, pt. XV, 1995, fig. 441.
[22] 'Children at Play', engraved and published by C.W. White, 21 February 1782. It is also inscribed 'Man above others is the Animal of Imitation'.
[23] The sailor's clothes are very similar to those worn by a group of sailors in, 'Saturday Night', a print by T. Jones, published by Novello for their pocket edition of *Dibdin's Songs* (c.1840).
[24] Prints of the mariners' compass demonstrate very clearly any distortions of the glue bat employed to apply the print to the curved surface of the vessel.
[25] Each individual's flag had its own position on a specified flagpole and was raised when one of the owner's ships was identified. By 1825 there were fifty flagpoles.
[26] See NCS *Newsletter* No.86, June 1992, p.38.
[27] A coffee can with similar decoration was attributed to Pennington's Liverpool factory. Sotheby's, London, 14 April 1992, Lot 328.
[28] Tantalizingly a brown stoneware mug, c.1820 in the Fitzwilliam Museum, Cambridge (Glaisher Collection, C.1212-1928) is impressed, 'Simon Heaselwood/ Ship/ Woolpitt' where a Simon Hazelwood was christened in 1786.
[29] Charles Brannam's factory specialised in producing idiosyncratic art pottery. A similar beaker is illustrated in Liberty's *Yule-Tide Gifts* catalogue for 1904-5, p.76, no.2, where beakers are priced at 1/9d each and sold in pairs with a jug (with a novelty fish spout and handle) as a 'water set'.
[30] I am very grateful to David Atherton for scouring the records at Lloyds Register of Shipping for information about named ships represented in the collection.
[31] Nick Dolan, 'Sunderland Pottery', in NCS *Journal*, vol. 9, 1992, pp. 58-60.
[32] A very similar plate was sold at Jacksons Auction Rooms, Cedar Falls, Iowa, (no date) lot 218.
[33] Mankowitz, op.cit., 1953, fig.42, publishes a similar jug where the *Lucy* is shown with sails unfurled.
[34] Lionel Burman mentions that by 1790 it was widely available as a Bowles & Carver 'Catchpenny Print' (no.134). See also 659, which bears a similar design.
[35] An orange lustred jug with both prints was sold from Sotheby's, London, 9 July 2009, lot 135.
[36] Quoted in Rodger, op.cit., 2004, p. 504.
[37] Ibid., p. 504.
[38] See Beddoe, 'Life on the Ocean Wave', in Dunsmore, ed., 2011 pp. 108-112.
[39] *Bagnio,* from the Italian for bath-house, was synonymous with brothel.
[40] An example of the print on a creamware plate is known, dated 1769. See Prentice, op.cit., 1994, p. 61, fig,100.
[41] See Chapter 2 Military Heroes Nos. 116-122.
[42] Print published by Robert Sayer, April 1791. BM 2010,7081.1068. See also Beddoe, 'Life on the Ocean Wave', in Dunsmore, ed., 2011 pp.108-112. The third instance of 'THE FLOWING CAN' is on jug (1682).
[43] BM1935,0522.1.68. It features in a print shop window display in a print after Dighton.
[44] Also known as 'Jack Oakham throwing out a Signal for an Engagement', the print was first published by Sayer & Bennett in 1780. BM 2010,7081.1178.
[45] Ibid.
[46] Jane Austen, *Pride and Prejudice*, Chapter VII, (1813).
[47] The British Museum holds Bunbury's original drawing (BM 1900,0717.64) and a print by Knight, pub. 1786 (BM 1917,0208.2957).

[48] See also (277), for further information about 'Poor Jack'.
[49] Emmerson, op.cit., 1992, shows a teapot with a similar print marked for Ralph Wedgwood, p. 103, fig.113.
[50] The print inscribed, 'Tis Comical' was engraved after Robert Dighton, published by Bowles & Carver, 12 August, 1800. BM 2010,7081.2156.
[51] A similar jug in the Glaisher Collection, Fitzwilliam Museum, Cambridge: C.1096-1928.
[52] The poignant lines are taken from the poem, 'The Negro Boy's Tale', by Mrs Amelia Opie, first published in *The New Annual Register or General Repository*, 1803, pp. 226-230.
[53] Engraved by Charles Knight. A copy in the Yale Center for British Art, B1977.14.12020.
[54] A very similar image was taken from an engraving by Thomas Stothard, illustrating a poem about the Press Gang. See Williams Wood, op.cit., 1981, pp. 228-9, figs.153 &154.
[55] Source print published by Robert Sayer, December 1790. BM 1877,0113.162. Drakard, 1992, pp. 95-6, illus. fig. 243.
[56] The source print was published by Robert Sayer on 2 October 1791. The revellers are discreetly captioned 'Folly' while the destitute sailor is labelled 'Merit'. BM 2010,7081.3047.
[57] Source print published by Laurie & Whittle 12 May 1794: BM 2010,7081.3131.
[58] Identified by Nick Dolan, of Tyneside Museum Service, c.1990. The image was used subsequently on lustred jugs of the 1840s. The first lifeboat in the UK was launched from South Shields in 1789, and was painted several times by Luke Clennell.
[59] See M. Gibson, 'Black-Ey'd Susan', NCS *Newsletter*, No. 86, June 1992.
[60] The source print was published (with ten verses) by Robert Sayers, 2 October 1792, BM 2010,7081.3047.
[61] Janice Wallace alerted me to T. Freeman, 'Dramatic Representations of British Soldiers and Sailors on the London Stage, 1660-1800', *Studies in British History*, vol.36, pp.122-24. New York, 1995.
[62] Identified by Godden as by Mintons, See Godden, op.cit., 1968, fig. 136.
[63] Atterbury & Batkin, op.cit., 1990, p. 120.
[64] See Freeman, op.cit., 1995, 'Dramatic Representations' p.240.

Chapter 5

[1] Blanning, 2008, pp. 337-8.
[2] For the most comprehensive and readable account of the Revolution see Simon Schama, *Citizens, a Chronicle of the French Revolution,* 1989, especially ch. 10, 'Bastille, July 1789', p. 369 onwards.
[3] Hogarth includes one in his portrait of the radical politician, John Wilkes; see the teapot made at Cockpit Hill, which features a portrait of Wilkes (496). It was used extensively in the imagery of the American Revolution, see (440).
[4] Many similar French plates are described and illustrated in *Rue de la Revolution: Images Populaires de la Revolution Francaise Vol 2: Faiences patriotiques*, Nevers, 1989.
[5] The plate was included in the exhibition *Shadow of the Guillotine*, op.cit., 1989, cat. 31, p. 5.
[6] Example of the print: BM 1851,0901.630. Similar jugs sold at Christies, South Kensington, 6/12/1990, (243) and at Phillips, 8/4/1998, (384).
[7] See William Hague, *William Pitt the Younger*, 2004, pp. 329 onwards.
[8] Pieces concerning Paine are discussed in Chapter 7 Statesmen.
[9] A very similar pair, in white, salt-glazed stoneware, is in the Schreiber Collection at the Victoria & Albert Museum. Sotheby's sold a similar bust of Francis I on 16/2/1982 lot 6 and a similar bust of Maria Theresa on 6/3/1990 lot 238 and on 19/2/1991 lot 161.
[10] The sharp blade, weighing 40 kilos, fell at 7m. per second, from a height of 2.3m., achieving decapitation in less than half a second.
[11] Parson James Woodforde of Weston Longeville, Norfolk, recorded in his diary on 26 January 1793, 'The King of France Louis 16 inhumanly and unjustly beheaded by his cruel, blood-thirsty Subjects The poor King of France bore his horrid fate with manly fortitude'.
[12] See Rodger, op.cit., 2004, p.501.
[13] See Uglow, op.cit., 2014, p.159.
[14] See also Chapter 1: Royalty and Loyalty. Other examples illus. by Nance, op.cit., 1942, Pl. IX and by Grant Davidson, 'Early Swansea' in *Trans ECC*, vol 7, pt. 1,1968, p.68, pl. 77.
[15] The print is illustrated, together with a Chinese-export porcelain teabowl and saucer bearing the same design in *A Tale of Three Cities*, op.cit., 1997, exh.cat. 57, p.60.
[16] Published by Fores after Isaac Cruikshank, 12 Feb 1793. BM 1871,0812.2930.
[17] See Harrison, op.cit., 1906, p. 6.
[18] The jug featured at the British Museum, op.cit.,1989, cat.110, p. 36, illus. pl. 37.
[19] See Semmel, op.cit., 2004, p. 27.
[20] From *The Journals and Letters of Fanny Burney*, vol. 5 p. 313, quoted by Claire Harman in *Fanny Burney, A Biography*, 2000, p. 297.
[21] BM 1873,0208.147. An engraving of the image was used as the frontispiece of Hewetson's *The Life of Napoleon Bonaparte*, published 1815.
[22] There is a jug with a similar print in the collections of the New York Historical Society: 1951.136.
[23] Many examples from the Willett Collection are discussed extensively and illustrated by David Drakard, firstly in *Trans ECC*, vol. 13, 1, 1987, pp. 40-59 and later in Drakard, op.cit., 1992, ch.11: '1802-1804 Napoleon and the Great Invasion Scare', pp. 184-206.
[24] Presented by Arthur du Cane in 1942 (322140).
[25] Published by Fores after Charles Williams,16 April 1803: BM 1868,0808.7101.
[26] It is one of the earliest references to the nickname for the naval port of Portsmouth.
[27] A print, published by McCleary, Dublin, 1801-02, in John Johnson Coll. Bodleian Library, Oxford.
[28] Another example was published and illustrated by Jonathan Horne, *Catalogue*, 2002, p. 32. Perhaps the ingenious potters were finding new uses for stockpiles of the outmoded heroic portrait?
[29] 'The Governor of Europe' print illus. by Robert H. McCauley, *Liverpool Transfer Designs on Anglo-American Pottery*, Portland, Maine, 1942, pl.VI.
[30] Published by William Holland 16 August, 1803. BM 1868,0808.7175. Illus. by Robert H. McCauley,1942, op.cit., pl. VI.
[31] Published by Piercy Roberts, 1803. BM 1868,0808.7230.
[32] The image of the beast derives from an engraving by G. Sauley after Rowlandson, (published by Ackermann's on 22 July, 1808) who may have been inspired by the Hydra illustrated in Edward Topsell's *History of Four-footed Beasts,* 1607, p. 736, pl.157, one of the most popular books of the 17th century.
[33] See Semmel, op.cit., 2004, p. 72, 83 and notes. A number of caricatures, printed broadsides and polemics of the time echo this link between Napoleon and the Beast of the Apocalypse. A chaotic pamphlet entitled, *The Book of Remembrance* (1814), written by Ralph Wedgwood (no known relation), included complex mathematical tables for calculating the 'number of the Beast'.
[34] A similar print with explanation was published by Orme after Voltz in 1814. BM 1917,1208.4116.
[35] See Nick Dolan, 'Sunderland Pottery; some new views', *NCS Journal*, Vol 9, 1992 pp. 58-65 and *NCS Newsletter*, No. 92, Dec 1993, p. 47.
[36] Drawn and published by Piercy Roberts, May 1803. BM 1868,0808.7124.
[37] Published by Ackermann after Woodward (engraved by Isaac Cruikshank) July 1803. BM 1865,1111.2042.
[38] Published by Ackermann after Woodward (engraved by Isaac Cruikshank) 7 August 1803. BM 1868,0808.7167. A Spode jug with this print is illustrated in Henrywood, op.cit., 1998, p. 58 pl.151.
[39] BM 1851,0901.1148. It was still sufficiently popular to be included in her window display that forms the backdrop to Gillray's print, 'Very Slippy Weather', published in 1808.
[40] Although unmarked, the designs on four printed vessels were identified as Spode products by David Drakard, from surviving original engraved copperplates. They are: 393/396/398/401.
[41] Published by Thomas Tegg after Piercy Roberts, c.1805. BM 1948,0214.683.
[42] Published by Fores after Charles Williams, 14 June 1803: BM 1868,0808.7138.
[43] Published by Fores 22 October 1803: BM 1868,0808.7207.
[44] Published by William Holland, 3 May 1803. BM 1985,0119.381.
[45] A similar jug was sold from the Lewinson Collection, Bonhams, 8/4/98 (lot. 382).
[46] Published by Fores after Charles Williams, 1 November 1804: BM 1868,0808.7295.
[47] See Drakard, op. cit., 1992, ch. 13, '1812 Russia, a steppe too far', pp. 226-240.
[48] Similar examples were sold at Christies, 13/2/1989 lot 30 and 1/6/1995.
[49] Examples of both prints: BM–1868,0808.12693 and BM 1868,0808.12692. Several similar jugs were sold at Phillips, 8/4/1998, (lots 395, 397, 403, 406).
[50] Print made by Elmes published by Thomas Tegg, 1813. BM 1935,0522.12.48.
[51] Jug illus. Drakard, 1992, op.cit., Col.Pl.VIIIa.
[52] Published by Thomas Tegg after William Elmes, in December 1812. BM 1868,0808.8033.
[53] An example from the Williams-Wood collection was sold at Phillips, 8/4/1998 lot 408.
[54] Published by Knight & Walker after George Cruikshank, January 1813: BM J,4.203.
[55] Published by Knight & Walker after George Cruikshank. BM 1991,0720.47.
[56] 'The Ascent of the Aerial Balloon', discussed in Chapter 17, Pastimes & Amusements.
[57] There is a jug with a similar print in the Fitzwilliam Museum, Cambridge: C.736-1928.
[58] Examples were published by E.M.Nance, op.cit., 1942, pl. LII and another jug is illustrated by Henrywood, 1997 op.cit. p. 59, pl. 156. Further examples, inscribed with the date, 1 April 1814 were sold at Sotheby's, 14-16/5/1992 (925/927) and at Phillips, 8/4/1998 lots 399/400.
[59] A similar figure illus. in Pugh, 1970, op.cit., pl.40, fig.99.
[60] The figure is illustrated by Lewis, op.cit., 1969, p. 176, fig. 329. It was identified by Anthony Oliver, op.cit.,1971, p. 91 pls. 137/38, as based on an engraved portrait of the Empress in *Cassell's Illustrated Family Paper*, 26/07/1856.
[61] See Harrison, op.cit., 1906, p.7.

Chapter 6

[1] More than 100 people founded Jamestown, Virginia, in 1607, the first permanent English settlement. By 1624, 1200 inhabitants were thriving on the proceeds of the tobacco trade.
[2] The print was widely copied by Chinese glass painters and as decoration for ceramics. See Grossman, *Decorative Arts of the China Trade*, 1991, p. 213, pl. 116.
[3] A reversed image published April 1790.
[4] BM 1868,0808.10082.
[5] See also a similar bust of Napoleon (403) discussed in Chapter 5: England & France.
[6] Image published on 4 September 1798 by John Fairburn: BM 2010,7081.599.
[7] In the Museum of Fine Arts, Boston. Left unfinished, it was the model for all subsequent portraits of Washington by Stuart and his daughters. Engraved image published by William Nutter, 1798.
[8] Numerous versions, (Wedgwood also issued it in jasperware) based on the original plaster modelled by Houdon in 1786, now in the Smithsonian NPG.
[9] Quoted by Young, op.cit.,1999, p. 192.
[10] Probably derived from Joseph Wright's drypoint (see 441).
[11] Published in London by R. Wilkinson on 15 May 1783.
[12] Print after Cochin, published by Humphrey, c.1780: BM 2010,7081.1545.
[13] See *Success to America*, op.cit., 2010, item 20, pp. 102-3.
[14] Nini had a pottery in the stable block of the Chateau de Chaumont on the Loire near Blois. Nini's portrait was later used as the model for Wedgwood's portrait plaque in jasperware.
[15] There is some similarity to anonymous French maquettes for portrait sculptures of Franklin, c.1790, in the Walters Art Museum, Baltimore.
[16] Many of these were published around 1793, as a large sheet of oval prints with inscribed borders, under the heading, *Bowles's Moral Pictures or Poor Richard Illustrated*, crediting Franklin.
[17] For further examples see Riley, op.cit., 1991, pp. 270-83.
[18] The bald eagle was adopted as a symbol of the United States in June 1782; from 1800 it was spread eagled.
[19] 'Tennassee'[*sic*] which joined the Union in 1796, shares a ring with Kentucky (joined 1791).

[20] The source is a printed portrait of 1801 by Desnoyers after Bouch: BM 1867,0309.1167. The same image was used for James Madison when he succeeded Jefferson in 1809, illus. by McCauley, op.cit., 1942, pl. XX, fig. 38.
[21] See *Success to America*,op.cit., 2010, item 13. p. 86.
[22] A similar jug, signed by Thomas Radford, (who worked at Cockpit Hill, Derbyshire, until its closure in 1779) describes Washington as 'His Excellency, General Washington ... President of the Congress'.
[23] Similar jugs with both prints are known where the eagle print is dated 1802 or 1804. Both sides illus. by McCauley,1942, op.cit., pl.VII, figs. 178,192.
[24] Many of these portraits first appeared in *The Analectic Magazine* or *The Portfolio*, both published in Philadelphia.
[25] The portrait is based on one from the *Analectic Magazine*, (March 1813) by David Edwin after Gilbert Stuart. A copy in the Smithsonian, IAP 9E980001.
[26] It is taken from an illustration by Cornè, engraved by Hoogland, (dated 25 November, 1815), to *The Naval Monument*, published by Abel Bowen of Boston in 1816.
[27] Copy in Library of Congress.
[28] Illustration to *The Naval Monument*, (pub. 1816, as above). A copy of the print at the Library of Congress, Washington DC LOT 4413-A.
[29] The *Constitution's* indomitable record during the War of 1812 earned her the nickname, 'Old Ironsides'.
[30] Based on engraving by G. Delleker in the Smithsonian NPG.79.13.
[31] Printed portrait of Pike, c1813 at the Smithsonian_NPG.2002.
[32] There is a printed portrait (after Stuart) of Decatur at the Smithsonian _NPG.79.5.
[33] The image was drawn and engraved by Samuel Maverick.
[34] See http://patrioticamerica.citrusstaging.com/pottery/printed-designs/patterns/places.
[35] See Robert Hughes, *American Visions, The Epic History of Art in America*, 1997, pp. 120-23.
[36] The portrait is similar to that on one of 1851 by C.C.Wright, (a copy in the Smithsonian: NPG.77). I am grateful to Ted Gallagher for information on Henry Clay commemoratives including a reference to a plate in Dr E.A. Barber, *Anglo-American Pottery: Old English China with American Views*, 1901. Such pieces are very rare.

Chapter 7

[1] Simon Schama, *A History of Britain, The British Wars, 1603-1776*, 2001, p. 432.
[2] Quoted in William Hague, *William Pitt the Younger*, 2004, Prologue, p. xxii.
[3] Mezzotint by Richard Houston after Hoare, pub. Ryall & Withy BM 1902,1011.2687.
[4] See Cook, op.cit., 1948, items 32, 67, 84.
[5] Ibid. item 33.
[6] In the V&A Collections are a preparatory drawing, by J.F. Moore, c.1767 (V&A_4910_12) and a maquette by Nathaniel Smith (V&A_A.48-1928). Falkner. 1912, illustrates a similar figure, which leans to the right!
[7] Thanks to Perry Gauci of Lincoln College, Oxford for alerting me to a 1767 engraving of the figure.
[8] William Hague, op.cit., 2004, p. 589.
[9] In the collection of the Palace of Westminster. Portrait engraved by Cardon after Edridge, 1801. NPG 14503.
[10] From the collection of the late Tony Banks MP. Portrait engraved by S.W. Reynolds after Smith, 1806. NPG D18432.
[11] John Kenworthy-Browne, 'The Temple of Liberty at Woburn Abbey', *Apollo*, July 1989, pp. 27-32.
[12] Sold at Sotheby's, New York, 20/10/93, lot 55.
[13] This mistake was repeated by the Macmillan government in the case of Anthony Wedgwood Benn MP in 1961. See Anthony Howard, reviewing Peter D.G.Thomas, *Wilkes: A Friend to Liberty*, in the *Sunday Times*, 31 March 1996, section 7, p. 3.
[14] Published by Carington Bowles after J.S. Miller. NPG D37521.
[15] See Towner, *Creamware*, 1978, p. 94 where he mistakenly states that the reverse of the teapot is printed No. 45.
[16] 'English Liberty established or a Mirrour for Posterity' published by J.Lee, sold by J.Williams. NPG D21661.
[17] A very similar portrait and framing devices are relief-moulded on the lid of a creamware tobacco box, 1765-70, BM 2013,8007.1.
[18] See Harrison, op.cit., 1906, p. 10.
[19] George Croly, *The Personal History of his late Majesty George IV*, vol, 1841, p. 200-204.
[20] Image engraved by Sharp, published by Hullmandel c.1832: NPG D7802.
[21] John Priestley, 'British Election Ceramics', *Antiques*, June 1987, pp. 1300-1311.
[22] Willett himself owned two of these mugs and gave the other to the British Museum in 1874.
[23] Six other dated examples are discussed by Lipski & Archer, op.cit.,1984, pp130-131, no 579 See also Archer, 1997, pp. 150-51.
[24] Hugh Owen, 1873, *Two Centuries of Ceramic Art in Bristol*, London.
[25] There is another example inscribed identically but on a white ground at Clive House Museum, Shrewsbury, Messenger, op.cit.,1988 pp.195-197.
[26] Messenger, op.cit.,1988, pp. 60, 62.
[27] H.T.Weyman, *Shrewsbury Members of Parliament*, 1896.
[28] Described thus by James Mackintosh author of *Vindiciae Gallicae*, part of an ensuing pamphlet war.
[29] This image has also been noted on a large cotton kerchief.
[30] 'To Lady Ossory, 27 June 1792', from *Selected Letters of Horace Walpole*, 1973, p. 295.
[31] Revd. Heber of Shropshire, writing 27 January 1793, quoted by Uglow, op.cit., 2014, p. 28.
[32] Quoted in Claire Harman, op.cit., 2001, p.186.
[33] Lewis, op.cit. 1984, pl.41.
[34] *The Recollections of Mrs Mary Anne Clarke*, unpub. typescript, (Brighton) pp. 54-56. See also Chapter 2 Military Commanders, (133).
[35] Illustrated in Lewis, op.cit., 1984, p.142.
[36] Engraved by William Sharp after Northcote, published 1811. BM 1841,0313.112.
[37] Interestingly, Henry Willett presented two watercolour portraits of Hunt, by Adam Buck, to the National Portrait Gallery. One, dated c.1810, is catalogued as NPG 956.
[38] Engraved after Jarvis after Gilbert Stuart, published 1817-20, Smithsonian_NPG.79.1.
[39] *A Slap at Slop*, published by William Hone, 1821. BM 1870,1008.1321.3.
[40] A 'pocket borough' was in the gift of the local landowner or patron. A 'rotten borough' was similar but had usually dwindled in size and had very few voters.
[41] Details found on handkerchief from Lennox Boyd Coll. Christie's sale no. 5437,2008.
[42] Detail from print published by Catnach in 1832. BM 1868,0808.1298.
[43] A late addition to the collection from Willett's descendants in 1923. Print published by E.King in 1831: BM 1868,0808.9457.
[44] Geoffrey Godden believes it was made locally at the Whitehaven Pottery in Cumbria. Florence Sibson illustrates a blue-printed jug and beaker with similar wording. See F. Sibson, *West Cumberland Potteries*, Albert Chan, 1991, p. 39.
[45] Illustrated in Godden, op.cit., 1980, p. 16, pl. 29.
[46] Stella Tillyard, *Aristocrats*, 1994, pp. 369-373.
[47] Simon Schama, *A History of Britain*, Vol III, 2002, p. 96.
[48] The windswept portrait of Hely-Hutchinson is taken from one published by P. Dillon c.1810.
[49] The revised identification was published on G.K. Chesterton's 'Notebook' page in the *Illustrated London News*, 29 November, 1909, p. 710. I am grateful to Deborah Hedgcock for alerting me to it.
[50] Cobden was a close friend of Henry Willett. They both came from very large families and combined great flair for business with radical political views.
[51] NPG 134612.
[52] Newtown, once a prosperous market town, by 1832 had only fourteen cottages.
[53] NPG 3953.
[54] Like Peel he also attended Christchurch College, Oxford, and also achieved a double first in classics and mathematics.
[55] From a small group of pieces presented by Willett in 1904.

Chapter 8

[1] Quoted by Charles Gross in *The Gild Merchant*, 1890.
[2] Blanning, op.cit., 2007, p.109.
[3] Boyd Hilton, *A Mad, Bad and Dangerous People?: England 1783-1846*, 2006, p.13.
[4] The dish is discussed by Lionel Burman, 'Motifs and Motivations: The Decoration of some 17th century Delftwares' *Trans ECC*, vol 15: 1, pp. 103-04.
[5] Willett mistook it for the Fishmongers' Company. Exh. BFAC, op.cit., 1913, (case E.81).
[6] Nick Dolan suggests this may be printed by Edward Barker.
[7] See Dr Minnie Holdaway, 'Early Swansea Printed Earthenwares', in J. Gray, op.cit., 2003, pp. 66-67.
[8] The mug is discussed in detail by Howarth and Hildyard, op.cit. 2004, p. 46, illus. p. 36 (pl. 19 & 20).
[9] The Butchers' Arms are also found on another jug, together with a humorous print entitled, 'The Terrible Ghost'. See Chapter 12 Scripture History & Religion, p. 175.
[10] See Donald, 2002, op.cit., e.g. 'Pantheon Macaroni' of 1773, cat. 24, p. 35.
[11] Illustrated by Schkolne, op.cit., 2006, p. 306. I am indebted to Ruth Ure for the social history of wig-making and for sharing some satirical images of wig makers and their London clients from as early as 1680.
[12] Such bowls were made between 1680 and 1750.
[13] The British Museum has a copy: BM 1878,0511.1381.
[14] A copy in the British Museum BM 1935,0522.2.136.b.
[15] Published by Tabart & Co., 1804-5.
[16] The popular proverbs were originally penned by Benjamin Franklin. See Chapter 6 England & America (e.g. 455-56).
[17] Illustrated in Halfpenny, op.cit., 1991, p.213 and by Schkolne, op.cit., 2006, p. 306.
[18] The Society for the Superseding of the Necessity for Climbing Boys campaigned for the abolition of their use, gaining partial success in 1842. Disraeli's Climbing Boys Act of 1875 achieved a total ban.
[19] Lewis Walpole Lib: lwlpr07733 published 27 January 1793 (Call No. 793.01.27.01).
[20] Published by Laurie & Whittle, 12 May 1794. It also appears on a creamware jug: HW 1707. 'Mittimus' is a pun on a legal writ.
[21] Source print published by Bowles & Carver after John Collet. BM 1877,0210.44. Illustrated by Schkolne, op.cit., 2006, p. 306.
[22] BM 1877,0210.44.
[23] Source published by Bernard Watney, 'Some Liverpool Printed Tiles', in *The Burlington Magazine*, May 1987, p. 316.
[24] BM 1958,1006.2558. The scene, one of the, 'Human Passions of Laughter and Experiment'. It was originally published with a poem attached. Verse 8 describes the scene on the plate, 'Now string's put fast on tooth that aches,/ Which round his hand he wraps,/ A glowing coal o'th tongs he takes,/ And to his nose he claps. The sight and smell of fire drove back/ the patient's head in fright/ Who drew his own tooth in a crack/ And proved the Doctor right.' I am very grateful to Lionel Burman for information on John Collier.
[25] Print illus. by McCauley,1942, op.cit pl.XIV fig.193.
[26] See Simon Cottle, 'The Creamware of North East England', NCS *Newsletter*, No. 61,1986, pp. 31-44.
[27] See Tim Blanning, op.cit., 2007, p. 35.
[28] Harold Blakey discovered that the Lancaster Directory for 1825 lists Peter Bretherton, coach proprietor, at 35 Redman Street, Liverpool while D. &T. Bretherton, coach builders, were at 61 Shaws Brow. T. Williams & Co. were carriers at Kings' Dock. An earthenware jug, printed with a similar mail coach, marked for F. Bretherton, was sold at Christie's, 15/2/88, Lot No. 89.
[29] Rosemary Shields from the Bretherton family kindly supplied the identities of the original four brothers, Francis, Peter, Bartholomew and Joseph. She has a jug printed with the name of P. Bretherton (for Peter, 1771-1844). A branch of the family still manufactures luxury horseboxes in Leyland, Lancashire.
[30] It is also suggested that it may have been made by Thomas Pardoe after he moved to Bristol in 1809.
[31] The Fort was a well-known visitor attraction at Yarmouth in Norfolk. (see 1071).
[32] The aqueduct ran over the Irwell, not the Mersey.
[33] It is based on a print of 1843 by T.H. Ellis. Museum of London has a copy.
[34] He spent £220,000 on constructing canals which earned him only £80,000 per year.
[35] Sources identified and further examples illustrated in Noel Riley, op.cit., 1991, pp.178-79.

[36] Purchased by the V&A Museum from Sir William Hamilton's collection in 1864. See Bilby & Trusted, op.cit., 2002, cat. 102, pp. 76-77.
[37] The smallpox Wedgwood had suffered as a boy left him with an infection in his right knee known as 'Brodie's abscess'. He had his right leg amputated, without anaesthetic, on 28 May 1768 but made a speedy recovery. He had a wooden leg made by Mr Addison of Long Acre, who made 'lay figures for artists'.
[38] See also L. & J. Rakow, 'Wedgwood's Peg-leg Portraits', *Ars Ceramica*, No. 1, 1984, pp.10-13.
[39] R.W. Binns op. cit., 1877, opp. p.185.
[40] See Ben Rogers, *Beef and Liberty*, 2003, pp. 80-86.
[41] See Blacker, op.cit., 1922, p.108, and Howarth and Hildyard, op.cit., 2004, pp. 42-3, illus. p. 33 (pl.16).
[42] Their history and relics are well documented by Colin Wyman, *Trans ECC*, vol. 10 pt. 4&5, 1980 pp. 293-304 and William Reid, *Trans ECC*, vol 15 pt 2, 1994, pp. 209-221.
[43] For a full discussion of constructions and iconography see James Stevens Curl, *The Art and Architecture of Freemasonry*, London, 1991.
[44] Identified by Nick Dolan.

Chapter 9

[1] Westall's image engraved by John Romney. Identified by L.A. Compton, NCS *Newsletter* No. 72, p. 12.
[2] Quoted in Gretchen Gerzina, *Black England, Life before Emancipation*, 1995, pp. 186-87.
[3] The late Audrey Dudson showed me a shard (now lost) from excavations on the site, which closely resembles the figure.
[4] Mentioned by Church, op.cit., 1884, p. 117.
[5] Willett believed that all such biscuit porcelain figures were made at the Derby factory.
[6] The portrait, engraved by Sharp after William Hobday: BM 1841,0313.183. Reynolds was sufficiently well known that Samuel Percy modelled a wax portrait of him in 1817: NPG 4674.

Chapter 10

[1] See O'Connell, 1999, op.cit., pp. 97-98.
[2] *Punch*, 15 September 1849. The accompanying text includes mention of commemoratives, 'There was likewise a Model of Stanfield Hall, and Rush his Farm, as though the Place were as famous as Waterloo'.
[3] See Patrick Conner, ed., 'The Decorative Arts', *The China Trade 1600-1800*, exh. cat., Brighton Museum, 1986, pp. 98-99.
[4] Croly, op.cit., p. 128.
[5] Rodney Hampson has noted that Hamilton, a Staffordshire potter, was in the process of giving evidence to the House at the time of the murder and may have been responsible for the design or production of the jug.
[6] There are two similar plaques of Canning and one of Squires in the Weldon Collection. See Grigsby, op.cit., 1990, no.143, p. 255.
[7] Rev. George Croly, *The Personal History of George IV*, Vol II, 1841, pp. 126-129. An anonymous watercolour records the moment: BM 1872,1012.5158 and George Cruikshank etched a dramatized version of events: BM 1871,0429.727, published 1812.
[8] Walbrook, H. M., *Murder and Murder Trials 1812-1912*, London, 1932, Gillen, *Assassination: the Shocking Death of Spencer Perceval*, London, 1972.
[9] A similar plaque in the Glaisher Collection in Cambridge was similarly identified. *Glaisher Collection*, op.cit.,1935 [1987], No. 697, p. 97.
[10] Walbrook, op.cit., 1932. Borowitz, Albert, *The Thurtell-Hunt Murder Case*, London, 1988. Mug illustrated in *Art & Antiques Weekly*, 23-29 January 1981, p. 28.
[11] See Mary Cowling, *Victorian Figurative Painting*, 2000, pp. 123-25.
[12] Skinner's *Journal of a Somerset Rector 1772-1839* (1930) quoted by Scholkne, op.cit., 2006, p. 47.
[13] James Catnach, publisher of cheap prints, who had already produced a best-selling broadside on Thurtell's murder of William Weare, is said to have sold over 1,000,000 copies of his *Confession and Execution of William Corder* 1828.
[14] D. Gibbs, & H. Maltby, *The True Story of Maria Marten*, London, 1949, illus. fig. 20, opp. p. 129. Haining, Peter, *Buried Passions: Maria Marten and the Red Barn Murder*, London, 1980.
[15] See entry for William Corder by Alsager Vian (revised by J. Gilliland) in Oxford *DNB*, op.cit., 2004-6.
[16] See *Arts Industry*, 27 August, 2004, p. 6.
[17] T. Shore, *The Trial of J. Blomfield Rush*, London, 1928.
[18] See 'Madame Tussaud Her Wax Werkes. Ye Chamber of Horrors!!', illustration by Richard Doyle published in *Punch*, 15 September 1849.
[19] There are similar pieces at Moyse's Hall Museum, Bury St Edmunds, at the Saffron Walden Museum and another in the *Glaisher Collection*, op.cit., (no.962).
[20] There is a pair of figures at the Castle Museum, Norwich and examples of the model buildings in the Glaisher Collection (Nos. 1015, 1015A).
[21] D. Barlow, *Dick Turpin and the Gregory Gang*, London, 1973, Hilary and Mary Evans, *Hero on a Stolen Horse*, pp. 79-85, London, 1977.
[22] For highwaymen in their social context see J. Sharpe, *Dick Turpin, The Myth of the English Highwayman*, 2004.
[23] See S. Rickard's entry on George Barrington in the Oxford *DNB*, 2004-05.
[24] Drakard, op.cit.. 1992, pp. 92-3.
[25] D. Woodruff, *The Tichborne Claimant*, London, 1957. See also R. McWilliam's entry in the Oxford *DNB*, 2004-06.
[26] The length of the two cases was only surpassed by that of the McDonald's libel trial, held in London in 1996.
[27] A cartoon, entitled 'The Beggar's Petition', from *Judy, or the London Serio-Comic Journal* of 24 April 1872 shows the Claimant begging on the street, a souvenir model of Tichborne Hall beside him.
[28] His visit to the Brighton Dome on 21 January 1873, is recorded by J.G.Bishop, in his 'Chronological Table of Events associated with the Brighton Pavilion', *Brighton Pavilion (1783-1903)*, sandwiched between the opening of the Brighton Picture Gallery and Willett's presentation of Cobden's papers to the Victoria Reference Library. Kenealy died in 1880 and is buried at St Helen's churchyard, Hangleton where Willett himself is interred. They may have been acquainted.
[29] Illustrated in B. Hillier, *Pottery and Porcelain 1700-1914*, London, 1968, pls.207-8, NCS *Newsletter*, No.74, June 1989, p.17. The groups were included in the small exhibition of "terracottas" held by Caldecott (1846-86), at the Arts Club, Hanover Square, London, in 1875. The pieces were purchased by a Mr Stanley Baldwin of Manchester before they were acquired by Henry Willett.
[30] Thanks to Neil Hyman, of Hampshire Museum Service for identifying the unnamed figures.
[31] There are similar groups of figures in a private collection in Rotherfield, E. Sussex and at Wagga Wagga City Council, New South Wales, Australia.

Chapter 11

[1] Information kindly supplied by David Gawthorpe via J.A. Knowles.
[2] Suggested by the loose robe and turban worn by the rider in the foreground.
[3] For a similar plate and mark, see Godden, op.cit., 1970, pl.32, p. 46.
[4] Similar ware has been excavated at Hunslet, Leeds. This jug appears to come from the same pottery as 344, which is dated 1788.
[5] See Simon Cottle, 'Creamware of North East England', *NCS Newsletter*, No. 61, pp. 31-44 cites other examples.
[6] Identified by Nick Dolan, *NCS Journal*, Vol. 9, 1992, pp. 66-68.
[7] I am indebted to Duncan Langford and Peter Stovin for their research and identification of Richard Harraden's views of Cambridge.
[8] BM 1917,1208.3146.
[9] BM 1917,1208.3143.
[10] BM 1917,1208.3144.
[11] BM 1862,0712.903.

Chapter 12

[1] A similarly moulded plaque, with floral decoration was sold at Christies, 9/7/01, lot 134.
[2] Thanks to Aileen Dawson, for alerting me to an Italian porcelain group with animals similarly modelled, representing Africa at the British Museum, BM 1935,0416.2.CR.
[3] See *Trans ECC* vol. 9 Pt.1, 1973, p.58, illus. Pl.D 1-4.
[4] A documentary example, inscribed by Enoch Wood's youngest son Thomas, was published by Jonathan Horne, c.1990.
[5] The famous series of tapestries was acquired by Charles I in 1623 and was accessible to visitors when displayed at Hampton Court 1699-1763. Since 1865 they have been on loan to the Victoria & Albert Museum.
[6] See example at V&A_C.299-1940.
[7] See Halfpenny, 1991, op.cit., p. 200.
[8] In *The Mill on the Floss* when Maggie Tulliver observes a group on the wall of Luke Moggs's cottage.
[9] The prints were engraved by Richard Purcell after French originals of the 1750s by Sebastien Leclerc II. They were published by Robert Sayer in the 1760s and still available in Sayer's & Bennett's catalogue of 1775.
[10] Based on an engraving after Sebastien Leclerc II; BM 2010,7081.617.
[11] Based on an engraving after Sebastien Leclerc II; BM 2010,7081.619.
[12] Loosely based on an engraving after Sebastien Leclerc II; BM 2010,7081.621.
[13] Based on an engraving after Sebastien Leclerc II; BM 2010,7081.622.
[14] Loosely based on an engraving after Sebastien Leclerc II; BM 2010,7081.620.
[15] See Grigsby, op.cit., 1990, p. 460, item 294.
[16] Mentioned by Church, op.cit., 1884, p. 117.
[17] Blanning, 2008, pp. 262-3.
[18] The source is one of many engraved portraits of Luther, such as that on Jakob Winter's woodcut leaflet of 1615: BM Bb,13.318.
[19] The portrait of Erasmus is probably based on a later print after Hans Holbein, such as that by Faber of 1714 BM 1879,0510.407. There is a reference to another pair of vases (Luther and Calvin), formerly in the Ionides Collection. See Jourdain & Jenyns, *Chinese Export Art in the Eighteenth Century*, 1967, pl. 82 p. 115.
[20] A similar item, decorated in high-temperature colours at the British Museum: 1981,0101.453.
[21] Remark made by Dr Troy, Archbishop of Dublin in 1816.
[22] Blanning, 2008, p. 373.
[23] Ibid. p.374. Blanning cites Bishop Willes of Bath and Wells who, between 1749 and 1764, appointed only his sons and sons-in-law as Archdeacons and Chancellors.
[24] See Black, 2005, p.6.
[25] Illustrated in Rackham & Read, op.cit., 1924, pl. LIX, Tharp, op.cit., 1997, p. 43, fig. 27.
[26] Suggested by Dr Peter Francis. The source may be printed portraits such as one engraved by Gucht after Gibson in 1710: BM 1881,0611.261.
[27] The print was published in 1785 by Bowles & Carver after Dighton: BM 1935,0522.1.174.
[28] It may be inspired by a celebrated Hogarth cartoon, *The Sleeping Congregation*, 1736, which also features a double pulpit.
[29] See Taggart, op.cit., 1967, p. 133-4.
[30] See HW 800.
[31] The print was published in 1782 by Carington Bowles after Robert Dighton: BM 2010,7081.189422.1.49.
[32] On 2 April 1790, Parson Woodforde, (who was in the habit of handing down his clothes), 'Gave to my clerk, Js Smith, a good black striped Coat and Waistcoat'; there is little other evidence for this jazzy garment. It may have been invented by the decorators at the potteries.
[33] Another Derby jug, similarly decorated is illustrated by Simon Spero, *ECC Trans*. vol. 19, pt.2, 2006, p. 317.
[34] Print after Tim Bobbin (John Collier), 1770 – in the Wellcome Collection. Identified by Bernard Watney, *Burlington Magazine*, December 1972, figs. 11-12.
[35] BM 1872,1109.323.
[36] The source is a print of 1751 by Muller after Boitard: BM 1948,0214.500.
[37] For a full discussion of ceramic souvenirs of Wesley and other dissenters see Stephen Duckworth, 'Preacher Ceramics – Figures and Plaques' in *ECC Trans*, vol 24, 2013, pp. 63-87.
[38] Engraved by Greenwood and published by Robert Sayer in 1770: BM 1856,0712.250.
[39] From J. Downey, *The Eighteenth Century Pulpit*, 1969, quoted in Janet Mayo, *A History of Ecclesiastical Dress*, 1984, p.79.
[40] See NPG D2979.
[41] See Duckworth, op.cit., p. 84.

[42] An honorary Doctorate in Divinity.
[43] See Duckworth, op.cit. pp. 74-75.
[44] A mezzotint of 1742, by John Faber after J. Wollaston, shows him in action before a rapt congregation. See *London 1753*, op.cit., 2003, item. 3.29, p. 151.

Chapter 13

[1] V&A_S.1220-2009.
[2] Black, 2005, p. 222.
[3] Tim Blanning, ch.10, 'The Culture of Feeling…', *The Pursuit of Glory, Europe 1648-1815*, 2008, p. 527.
[4] See Anthony Ray, *Trans ECC.*, vol 9, pt.1, 1973, p. 42, pl.B4-3.
[5] It was used for Carey & Bickerstaffe's *Love in a Village* (1762) and was mentioned by Oliver Goldsmith in his epilogue to *She Stoops to Conquer*.
[6] Horace Walpole pointed out that Emma's fame enabled Sir William to marry his 'Gallery of Statues' (Walpole Correspondence, vol. XI, p. 349) See Christies, London, 9/7/2001, pp. 180-81, Lot no. 267.
[7] Their presence in the collection at this early date has been important for the authentification of other examples of these rare figures, which were widely forged in the early 20th century.
[8] They are discussed at length by Ross E. Taggart, 'John Astbury – 1730 or 1930?' in *The Art Quarterly*, Vol. XXX No.1, 1967 pp. 3-18.
[9] This type of figure was also used for slaves or servants in very rare early tavern pew groups (there is an example at Colonial Williamsburg, Virginia, USA) and tea-party scenes (one was sold at Sotheby's, New York, 20/10/1993, lot 102).
[10] See Honour, op.cit., 1989, pp. 61-4.
[11] 'Mr T. Rice as Jim Crow', published by Fairburn, London.
[12] The painting is on long loan to the National Galleries of Scotland, Acc. No. NGL001.81.
[13] The wearing of plaid was illegal at this time, since the 1745 proscription of wearing Highland dress was not lifted until 1782.
[14] See Bradshaw, op.cit., 1990, p. 176, No.11.
[15] National Portrait Gallery, NPG D22246.
[16] See *Circus & Sport*, op.cit., 1990, no.15, p. 24.
[17] Print engraved by Thornthwaite after Roberts for Bell's. V&A_S.28-2013.
[18] Print after Roberts for Bell's V&A_S.1090-2013.
[19] Print engraved by Thornthwaite after Roberts for Bell's. V&A_S.51-2013.
[20] See *The Georgian Playhouse*, op.cit., 1975, (unpag.) item no.31. NPG D5177.
[21] Black, 2005, p. 102.
[22] Print engraved by C.Grignion after Roberts for Bell's. V&A_S.1978-2013.
[23] J.Collyer after D.Dodd for Lowndes's, 1776. NPG D8915.
[24] An engraving of 1771 at University of Illinois. W911h-24.
[25] NPG D8932.
[26] Print engraved by Grignion after Dodd for Lowndes's. University of Illinois. L673w-13.
[27] Print engraved by Dodd after Goldar for Lowndes's, 1777. University of Illinois. L673w-11.
[28] Print engraved after Roberts for Bell's, 1776. BM Ee,5.23.
[29] Quoted by Martin Postle in *Joshua Reynolds, the Creation of Celebrity*, Tate, 2005, p. 190, cat. 54.
[30] Several surviving examples including BM 1887,0307,I.6. See Grigsby, op.cit., 1990, item no. 251, p. 409.
[31] Several surviving examples including BM 1887,0307,I.7. Engraved by James Macardell after Hayman. BM Ee,5.91.
[32] Circles of paper or fabric were inserted into watch cases to protect against dust. See London 1753, op.cit., 2003, p. 138, item. 3.10.
[33] A print of 1771, published by Robert Sayer and John Smith, shows Thomas Weston and Garrick as Scrub and Archer.
[34] Now in the Walker Art Gallery, Liverpool.
[35] See Pugh, op.cit., 1970, p. 66.
[36] National Portrait Gallery has a plaster cast of the sculpture, NPG 707a. The Garrick Club has a painting by Andrea Soldi, 1757, of Roubiliac sculpting the bust.
[37] Discussed by Homan Potterton, 'Garrick as Roscius?', *Country Life*, 7 February, 1974, p. 260.
[38] Lent to *The Georgian Playhouse*, op.cit., 1975, no. 63 and *David Garrick in Portrait and in Performance*, Buxton Museum and Art Gallery, 1981, no. 19.
[39] Identified by Lewis, op.cit., 1984, p. 138. A similar plaque was sold at Sotheby's on 14/11/1995 lot 199. See also *A Passion for Performance, Sarah Siddons and her Portraits*, Exhibition catalogue, J.Paul Getty Museum, Los Angeles, 1999.
[40] See Trevor Markin, 'More Factory Z Earthenware Jugs', in *NCS Newsletter* no. 96, Dec. 1994, p. 37-8.
[41] See Godden, op.cit., 1988, p. 681.
[42] V&A S.669-1997.
[43] Print engraved by J.W. Gear, published by Madeley, 182: BM 1868,0808.1757.
[44] Print published by Madeley, c.1830: BM 1868,0808.1759.
[45] Print published by Madeley, c.1826: BM 1868,0808.1754.
[46] Print published by Maclean, 1819, after Robert Dighton: NPG D34474.

Chapter 14

[1] Unmarked but would be impressed: Ra.Woodm/ Burslem no 155. He should be holding another book in his right hand rather than a scroll, part of a mistaken restoration.
[2] There are a number of early 18th century engravings by Vertue e.g. NPG D32930, NPG D24073.
[3] Black, 2005, p. 22.
[4] Blanning, 2008, p. 305.
[5] Today the gardens at New Place, Stratford, still boast a tree grafted from the famous white mulberry tree planted by Shakespeare himself in 1602. Many were planted at this time as part of James I's initiative to encourage the silk industry. In 1758 the famous mulberry tree was cut down by the Rev. Francis Gastrell, which provoked an angry crowd to smash his window panes.
[6] Possibly after prints by 17th-century Dutch artists, David Teniers or Adriaen Brouwer.
[7] Engraving of 1741 by Andrew Miller after Scheemakers: NPG D27949.
[8] Nick Dolan believes they may be made by J.P. Bell & Co. of Glasgow.
[9] From a speech of Jacques in *As You Like It*, Act 2.
[10] A similar bust first appeared in the Wren Library, Cambridge, in 1750.
[11] NPG no 3781, by an anonymous sculptor, probably late 17th - 18th century.
[12] See *Trans ECC* vol.7 Pt.2, 1969, pl.126b) and *The Man at Hyde Park Corner*, 1974, item 54.
[13] Mid-18th-century mezzotint: NPG D41665.
[14] Illustrated in Whinney, op.cit., 1964, pl. 56.
[15] See *The Man at Hyde Park Corner*, 1974, item 57.
[16] Possibly modelled on a print such as Basire's etching of 1776: NPG D20190.
[17] See E.M.Elville, 'Portraits in Powdered Glass', *Country Life*, 8 June, 1961, pp. 1351-52.
[18] Illustrated in Lewis, op.cit., 1984, p. 140.
[19] From the poem, 'Hans Carvel', 1701.
[20] See also *The Man at Hyde Park Corner*, 1974, item 64.
[21] He was the author of *The Negro's Complaint*, applied to a jug (593), see Chapter 9 'Philanthropy'.
[22] Sothebys, London sold a collection of over 300 early editions, prints, translations, musical settings and related games and ephemera, including fifteen ceramic items, on 3/12/87 (lot120).
[23] Whether this is the famous Cambridge University Church (which lacks a spire) or that at Sawbridgeworth in Yorkshire (with a fine spire) is unclear.
[24] *Illustrated London News*, 28 December 1844, illustrated in Oliver, op.cit., 1971, p. 82.
[25] Quoted by Lockhart in his *Life of Burns,* 1828.
[26] Schkolne, op.cit., 2006, devotes a chapter (pp. 42-45) to figures inspired by the poem, which was disseminated through Francis Grose's *Antiquities of Scotland,* vol.2, 1791.
[27] Illustrated in Halfpenny, op.cit., 1991, p. 204.
[28] Based on prints after Alexander Nasmyth's 1798 portrait of Burns, such as NPG D32441.
[29] An English version reads: Some have meat and cannot eat, / Some would eat that have no meat; / But we have meat and we can eat, / So let the Lord be thanked.
[30] Shown at the Fine Art Society in 1992 and illustrated in *Country Life*, 6 February, 1992, p. 99.
[31] See Harrison, op.cit., 1906, p. 33.
[32] Willett included the portrait of the poet in 'Literature' while placing the family scenes from the poem in 'Domestic Incidents'.
[33] Roubiliac bust at the Wren Library, Cambridge. See Milo Keynes, *The Iconography of Sir Isaac Newton to 1800*, Cambridge, 2005, p. 108, cat E.12.
[34] The group includes portraits of Princess Charlotte (050) and probably Prince Leopold (078), Empress Maria Theresa (370) and Christ (768). See J.A. Fleming, *Scottish Pottery*, 1923, pl. XXII facing p. 124.
[35] Discovered by Gottfried Kirch it is also known as Newton's Comet.
[36] See Keynes, op.cit., p. 104 cat E.2.
[37] An example in the collection of Birmingham City Art Gallery: 1885M2709. See Reilly and Savage, op.cit., 1973, p. 258 and pp. 217-8.
[38] See Jenny Uglow, *The Lunar Men*, London, 2002.
[39] See Berg, 2005, op.cit., Introduction, pp. 1-4. The ceramics included valuable china ornaments, a service of 108 pieces of Nankeen (Chinese export) porcelain, three sets of Wedgwood (with blue edges, green edges and yellow), three dozen plates and twelve dishes in Queensware in the kitchen and several sets of tea china.
[40] Chile has recently changed the name of Juan Fernandez to Robinson Crusoe Island in order to realise its tourist potential!
[41] Reilly and Savage, op.cit., 1973, p. 284.
[42] See Godden, op.cit., 1974, p. 247, figs. 327-8.
[43] See Riley, op.cit., 1991, pp. 88-91, figs. 322, 337.
[44] See Housman, 1879, op.cit. pp. 9-11,12-16.
[45] A copy of the sepia albumen cabinet card is in the National Portrait Gallery, NPG x5659.
[46] *Past and Present* (1843), book III, chapter XI.
[47] Presented by Willett's family in 1923.
[48] The edition included two companion figures, Smike and Nicholas Nickleby (two were sold at Christie's, 21/5/1990, lot 285).
[49] Kirkall's designs were based on Francis Barlow's illustrations for an edition of 1666.
[50] See Bernard Watney, 'Origins of Designs for English Ceramics of the Eighteenth Century', *Burlington Magazine*, December 1972, pp. 818-826, figs 7-8. An example of Kirkall's illustration: BM 2011,7084.47.13.
[51] See Leslie Grigsby, 'Aesop's Fables on English Ceramics', *The Magazine Antiques*, June 1994, pp. 871-5.
[52] An example of Kirkall's illustration: BM 2011,7084.47.8.
[53] See Anthony Ray, 'English Delftware Tiles', *Trans ECC.*, vol.9, Pt.1, 1973, pl. 46.
[54] An example of Kirkall's illustration: BM 2011,7084.47.22.
[55] Disembarking boat passengers were often rowed ashore where there was no pier, or in this case, given a lift to keep their feet dry.

Chapter 15

[1] Sir John Fielding, *An Account of the Origins and Effects of a Police*, 1758, quoted in Gattrell, 2006, p. 195.
[2] See *Circus & Sport*, op.cit., 1990, p. 54, no. 45 and illustrated by Lars Tharp, 'Potted History', *Antique Collecting*, October 1993, p. 19.
[3] *Staffordshire Advertiser*, 23 November 1833, quoted in Haggar, op.cit., 1955, p. 91.
[4] Engraved by W.Ward, *New Sporting Magazine,* 1809.
[5] Engraved by John Scott, 1817.
[6] Sayer & Bennett, British Museum: J,7.41.
[7] *Pottery Gazette*, 1 February, 1893. There is still an Anglesey Arms at Halnaker.
[8] See E.N. Stretton, 'The Turners of Lane End 1762-1803', *Apollo*, October 1958, p. 108.
[9] A portrait of Ginger Red by Cook was illustrated in the *Sporting Magazine,* vol I, 1792/3, opp. p. 118.
[10] The number probably refers to the pagination of the book of prints they came from.
[11] British Museum: 1868,0808.2871.
[12] Similar figures are illustrated by Gabszewicz, op.cit.,1982, p. 133, fig. 214. and p.142, fig. 235.
[13] Miles, H.D., *Pugilistica. The History of British Boxing*, vol.II, Edinburgh, 1906, pp. 60-3.
[14] A mug with a similar print was sold at Sotheby's, Belgravia, 6/12/1979, lot 160.
[15] See BM 1896,1118.109.
[16] See *Athletic Exercise: On the Science of Boxing displayed*, London, 1788, pp.31-2. Miles, H.D., op.cit, vol.I, pp. 86-7.

[17] Miles, op.cit., 1906, pp.1-52.
[18] For a portrait of Molineux see Pierce Egan, *Boxiana, Sketches of Ancient and Modern Pugilism*, London, 1813, p. 480. See also Miles, op.cit., vol.I, 1906, pp. 242-278. portrait of Tom Cribb after a painting by De Wild, 1811, faces p. 242.
[19] Published in Miles, op.cit, 1906, vol.I, ill. facing p.242.
[20] Miles, op.cit., 1906, vol.I, pp.48, 78-9.
[21] See Miles, op.cit., 1906, vol.III, pp. 359-433.
[22] See example at Tate, 1763 (T06869), adapted as an engraving by Stubbs in 1777.
[23] Published in *The Public Advertiser*, 1763.
[24] Suggested by Halfpenny, op.cit., 1991, p. 111.
[25] A mug with the same image, dated 1796, was included in *Shipwrecks and Marriages*, 2009 (item C29).
[26] See Chapter 1, Royalty & Loyalty, p.16.
[27] See Chapter 2, Military Heroes, p.33. The mug features the Duke of Cumberland, the victor of Culloden.
[28] See W.W. Hamilton Foyn, 'Dated London Brown Saltglazed Hunting Mugs 1713-75', *Trans ECC*. vol. 17, Part II, 2000, p. 254.
[29] Similar sprigs suggest that it may come from London Factory B, see Oswald, Hildyard & Hughes, op.cit., 1982, p. 47, fig. 16.
[30] 'Partridge Shooting', engraved by Cook was published in *The Sporting Magazine*, vol II, 1793, opp. p. 299.
[31] The decorator has omitted to apply tartan designs to his pink skirt!
[32] In *The Gentleman's Recreation* (1686).
[33] See Cook, op.cit., 1948, Item 42.
[34] Identified by G & S Guy-Jones, 'The Hare Chase' in *Trans ECC*, vol 15, part 3, 1995, pp. 346-48. Further information published by Helen Wyld, 'Bradshaw and Stranover's Hare Hunt Tapestries' in *National Trust Historic Houses and Collections Annual* 2014, pp. 4-9.
[35] Baron later gave evidence to the House of Commons in support of Hogarth's petition for artist's copyright. He stated that soon after he had engraved the copper plates for Wootton, they 'were copied by another Person; and that the copies were sold at a very Low Rate'.
[36] Howitt's series: 'Fox-Hunting' Pl. 2. British Museum: 1850,1014.678.
[37] See also HW 1127.
[38] See also HW 1133.
[39] Quoted by O. Fairclough, 'Buying Ceramics and Glass in the 1770's', *Trans ECC.*, vol.19, pt.1 2005, p. 54.
[40] Ancestry.com.
[41] See Harrison, op.cit., 1906, p. 69.
[42] See Smith, op.cit., 1975, p.152, pl. 239.
[43] Another example of this unusual print is dated 1792. See Henrywood, op.cit., 1997, p. 47 pl.118.
[44] See BM 1840,0808.182 and BM 1852,0705.208.
[45] Thomas Bewick *A General History of Quadrupeds*, 1790, p. 363.
[46] Bronte, *Jane Eyre*, 1847, Chapter I.
[47] By James Gillray after Isaac Cruikshank, published 1800.
[48] See Deuchar, op.cit., 1988.
[49] On the reverse is a humorous scene of two figures on a bicycle inscribed, 'A VISIT TO CARLTON HOUSE' (see also 1177).
[50] BM 935,0522.2.137.b.
[51] Published by Robert Sayer, 1782: BM 1861,0518.957.
[52] After the painting by James Northcote, of William Assheton of Downham Hall, Lancs. and the Rev. Dixon Hoste with their dogs and dead grouse.
[53] Bewick, op.cit.,1790, pointer p.355, large water spaniel. p. 361.
[54] Identified in Coysh and Henrywood, op.cit., 1981.
[55] A seven-quail dish sold at Christies, 2010, sale 7880, lot 62.
[56] These bird boxes probably derive from Meissen forms; a pair of Meissen quail tureens (c.1745) was sold at Sothebys, 16/10/1989, lot 319.
[57] *The Sporting Magazine*, vol IV, 1794, opp. p. 272.
[58] After the painting by James Northcote. See HW 1089.
[59] Quoted in *The Gentleman's Magazine*, July 1793, from 'a Letter from a Gentleman to his friend at Calcutta… 23 December 1792'. 'The Death of Mr Munro' was also the leading article in *The Sporting Magazine*, July 1793, pp. 199-201.
[60] See M. Archer, *Tippoo's Tiger*, 1959, V&A, London, who mentions the Brighton group, p.14.
[61] See Chapter 2, Military Heroes (132).
[62] See Pugh, op.cit., 1971, p. 407, pl.78A.

Chapter 16

[1] *The Finish to the Adventures of Tom and Jerry*, 1828, quoted in Halfpenny and Beddoe, op.cit., 1990, p. 62.
[2] Strephon, taken from Sir Philip Sidney's *Arcadia*, was a standard name for a rustic lover.
[3] Published 1 December, 1792, p. 55, drawn by Corbould, engraved by Cook, pub. J. Wheble.
[4] Croly, op.cit., 1841, p.172, records in 1787 that 'the prince was fond of manly sports; and cricket was often played in the lawn before the Pavilion'. John Wisden, Sussex and England cricketer and the originator of the *Almanach*, was born in Brighton in 1826.
[5] Published 1 July, 1793, p.135, engraved by Cook, pub. J. Wheble.
[6] In 1862 one of his sons founded Lillywhites sportswear and sporting goods store in Regent Street in London.
[7] Taken from engraved portraits in *The Illustrated London News*, Box and Pilch on 15 July, 1843, and Lillywhite on 22 July, 1843.
[8] See Messenger, op.cit., 1988, p. 340 pl. 291.
[9] Zebras can only be trained when raised as foals together with horses.
[10] The same group also appears on the pearlware jug (1099) - See chapter 16.
[11] Letter to the Hon. Henry Seymour Conway, 15 October 1784, from *Selected Letters of Horace Walpole*, 1973.
[12] Reverses design on a delftware tile printed by Sadler & Green. See Anthony Ray, 'Liverpool Delftware Tiles', *Trans ECC*, vol.9, pt.1, 1973, pl.38 B4-7.
[13] See Cook, op.cit., 1948, item 118. An example of the print at the British Museum: BM 1849,0328.31.
[14] Also on the reverse of HW 1680. Harold Blakey has found reference to the 'Lottery Insurance Office' in the *Sunday Observer* for 4 December 1791. An advertisement for Phillips' Royal Lottery Bank at 83 St Martin's Lane recommends buying lottery tickets by instalment well in advance of the draw.
[15] British Library no. 7750.
[16] Frost, *The Old Showmen and the Old London Fairs*, 1874, quoted by Schkolne, op.cit., 2006, p.111, who devotes a chapter to the menageries (pp.100-15).
[17] See Altick, *The Shows of London*, 1978, p. 307, fig.103.
[18] Black, 2005, p. 24.
[19] Illustration to the 'Dog Days' of July, published in his *Comic Almanach* for 1836.
[20] For example Holbein's portrait, c.1530, of the *Lady with a Squirrel and Starling* (National Gallery, London) Joseph Highmore's *Sir Eldred Lancelot Lee and family*, 1736, (Wolverhampton Art Gallery).
[21] Quoted in G. Speaight, *A History of the Circus*, 1980, p. 81.
[22] *The Prelude*, Book 7, lines 174-78.
[23] See Bewick, *A General History of Quadrupeds*, 1790, p. 292, footer to 'The Brown Bear'.
[24] Ibid. p. 290.
[25] See David Atherton, 'Mr Punch', *NCS Newsletter* no.145, March 2007, pp. 42-44.
[26] See Rogers, op.cit., 1970, p.14.
[27] *Twelve Elegant and Humorous Prints of RURAL SCENES adorned with COMIC FIGURES* by Robert Dighton, No.1, 'The LADS of the VILLAGE', c.1800, pub. Bowles & Carver.
[28] The 1899 catalogue links the figure with the custom of 'Throwing at Cocks' on Shrove Tuesday.

Chapter 17

[1] Blanning, 2007, ch.4, p.142.
[2] Ibid. p. 187.
[3] From ed. Richard Ingrams, *Cobbett's Country Book*, 1975, p.123 (entry for 18 December 1830).
[4] Ibid. pp.134-35.
[5] 'Pail' is also interchangeable with 'sail' and 'flail'.
[6] William Cotton was listed as a corn factor and hop merchant in High Street, Longton around 1800. See Norman Stretton, 'William Cotton', in *NCS Newsletter*, no. 74, p. 26.
[7] To be published in the *London Gazette* as a bankrupt.
[8] Identified by Harold Blakey as made by Thomas Lakin, see NCS *Newsletter*, no. 30, p. 20.
[9] One other is known painted with the same subject, sold from the Zorensky Collection at Bonhams, 22/2/06, lot 24.
[10] The song was 'My Grandmother's Cat', by Thomas Arne, which appears on p.176. The 1762 edition of *Clio and Euterpe* Vol II has been digitised by the National Library of Scotland. https://archive.org/details/clioeuterpeorbri1762ingl See also Cook, op.cit., 1948, Item 51.
[11] See Drakard, op.cit., 1992, p.101, who attributed the design to S.H. Grimm. The problem is that the topographical artist Grimm did not arrive in England from Switzerland until 1768.
[12] Williams Wood, op.cit., 1979, pl. 94, p. 169.
[13] Anthony Ray, 'Liverpool Delftware Tiles' *ECC Trans*, vol 9, pt.1, 1973, pl.44, C3-5.
[14] A similar figure in the Stoke collections is stamped P&F Warburton. See Halfpenny, 1991, op. cit., p. 53.
[15] Ingrams, op.cit., p. 133-34.
[16] This is a rare variant according to Cook, op.cit., 1948, item 73.
[17] Maev Kennedy suggests the phrase refers to a state of euphoria, resulting from a stroke of good luck. There is a mechanical toy in the V&A Museum of Childhood, MISC.28-1967, where a rider tries to stay on a bucking pig's back.
[18] Phoebe, in Greek mythology, was one of the early Titans, associated with the moon and the grandmother of Apollo and Artemis.
[19] The figure can also be found in a compilation group of shepherds, marked Tittensor (1321).
[20] Illustrated by Schkolne, op.cit., 2006, p. 174, who cites a print of a girl at a water pump by W.H. Pyne from his *Microcosm* (1803-06), as a possible source for the figure.
[21] Illustrated by Halfpenny, op.cit., 1992, p. 259.
[22] Illustrated in Godden, op.cit., 1980, p.16, fig. 29. A similar cow creamer is illustrated in Gray, op.cit., 2003, p.112, fig. 6.30.
[23] See Anthony Ray, 1973, op.cit., p. 40.
[24] See *NCS Newsletter*, no. 83, September 1991, p. 20.
[25] An example at the Mellon Center: Acc. no. 85.1437.2.
[26] A page of intricate design sketches for such tools shown at *This Land is Our Land*, at the Mall Galleries in 1989, (cat. no. 411). The central motif on this plate is numbered 39.
[27] Thanks to Aileen Dawson, for alerting me to the Italian Le Nove factory.
[28] Quoted in Blanning, 2007, p. 154.
[29] See example: BM 1917,1208.2936.
[30] Illustrated in Halfpenny, op.cit., 1991, p. 232.
[31] It must have been engraved, since it was used many times. See Coysh & Henrywood, op.cit., vol.1,1982, p. 38.
[32] He is from the same mould as the gardener attending an urn of flowers (1348).
[33] Willett thought it was a guinea pig but the animal is indistinct.
[34] Example at BM 2010,7081.1287.
[35] Website of Carmarthen Archive Service.
[36] Ibid.

Chapter 18

[1] Willett, op.cit., 1899, p. 105.
[2] V&A_ 414:821-1885. Church, op.cit., 1884, p. 40 mentions both cats to which Lady Charlotte refers. See Archer, op.cit., 1997, p. 255, for full discussion of the function and symbolism of cat jugs.
[3] BM 1887,0210.127.
[4] Mentioned by J. Mallett, *Trans ECC*, vol. 6. Pt. 2, 1966, p. 130.
[5] The image is also found in relief decoration on large brown stoneware mugs, for example HW 1102 and HW 1132.
[6] There are examples, bearing initials at Stoke-on-Trent, in the Greg Collection, Manchester; the Glaisher Collection, Cambridge; Temple Newsam House, Leeds; the Burnap Collection, Kansas; Colonial Williamsburg, Virginia, USA etc.
[7] See M. Slocombe, 'Message on a Bottle', *Country Life*, 17 April, 2003, p. 86.
[8] Listed with other known examples in Church, op.cit., 1884, p. 37.
[9] Church, op.cit., 1884, p. 40.
[10] For other examples see Britton, op.cit., 1982, p. 253 and Lipski & Archer, op.cit., 1984, p. 278.
[11] See Jonathan Horne, *A Catalogue of English Brown Stoneware*, 1985, Nos. 36 and 37, pp. 18-19.
[12] Quoted in Hobson, op.cit., 1903, in the entry to the example in the British Museum collections, given by Henry Willett in 1887, f. 8, p. 167.
[13] See Lewis, op.cit., 1984, p. 196.
[14] See Godden, op.cit., 1980, pp. 10, 163, who mentions Richard Meir Astbury and possibly Robert Gardner as makers.
[15] Church, op.cit., 1884, p. 117.

[16] As sung at Sadler's Wells by Mr Prentice in 1764, published in *The New Vocal Enchantress*, 1788.
[17] An example of 'The Last Drop', published by Robert Sayer, 1773: BM 1861,0518.496.
[18] See also HW 1418/1419/1434.
[19] Granted in August 1853 (no.1537).
[20] The NMM has a potato flask with a silver collar inscribed, 'Admiral Boyd's favourite yam,1783'. Brighton's generous holdings of such flasks are discussed by Salaman, op.cit., 1949, p. 598.
[21] In 2005 Gary Atkins had a similar flask inscribed for another member of the Foster family of Ditchling.
[22] See Taggart, op.cit., 1967, pp. 132-3, where a similar piece, described as a 'Drinking Vessel for the purpose of exhibiting Tricks in Legerdemain', formed part of the 1835 gift from Enoch Wood to the King of Saxony in Dresden. See also Archer, op.cit., 1997, p. 258.
[23] See D. Skinner, 'Hops and Venom, or Looking into Frog Mugs', exhibition leaflet for the Marjorie N. Davies Collection of 300 frog mugs, Stoke-on-Trent City Museum, 1985.
[24] For example, 266, 394, 548, 714, 1331, all from the North East.
[25] Mentioned in Branyan, et. al, op. cit., 1981, I.A.34, p. 89.
[26] See Dr N.T. Cooke, 'Dated 18th Century Worcester Porcelain – An Update', NCS *Newsletter*, 112, Dec. 1998, pp. 25-6. Another mug, inscribed, 'Ann Dunn. Birmingham, 1776' was included in *Shipwrecks and Marriages*, 2009 (item P7).
[27] The Rev Francis Fawkes, *Original Poems and Translations*, 1761.
[28] Example at the British Museum: BM 2010,7081.1369.
[29] Discussed in Chapter 18, Agriculture.
[30] Such pieces researched and discussed by A.Thomas, 'A Few Thoughts on Mist', NCS *Newsletter*, September 1982, pp. 21-23, H.Blakey, NCS *Newsletter*, No.85, March 1992, p.31, J.Bentley, NCS *Newsletter*, December 1992, No.88, p.13 and Rodney Hampson. See also P. Halfpenny, 'Smearglazed stonewares' in *Stonewares and Stone Chinas of Northern England*, NCS, 1982, pp.109-10. The case for Chetham and Woolley's extensive output of dry-bodied stonewares and MIST-type wares is persuasively argued by C.Wyman, 'The Stoneware of Chetham & Woolley: c.1795 - c.1820', *Trans ECC*. vol. 18, pt. 2, 2003, pp. 208-47.
[31] Willett, op.cit., 1899, p. 105.
[32] Similar examples illustrated in Lewis, op.cit., 1984, pl.18, p. 85.
[33] See Chapter 4 (items 273, 274, 294).
[34] See M.H.H. Macartney, 'Old English Pipes', *The Connoisseur*, Sept. 1906, pp. 12-16.
[35] B.Adams & A.Thomas, *A Potwork in Devon*, 1996, Sayce Publishing, Devon, p. 59.
[36] A digitised example, from *Human Passions Delineated*, 1773 is in the Wellcome Collection.
[37] A similar figure of a sleeping toper losing his wig, made at the short-lived French factory of Crépy-en-Valois was sold at Sotheby's, London, 17/02/1991, lot. 40.
[38] For further discussion of Dr Syntax see Chapter 14, p. 213.
[39] W.M.Thackeray, *The Irish Sketchbook*, 1843, p.113.
[40] Willett, op.cit., 1899, p.108. See also Tony Lonton, 'George Potts Cocker's and Douglas Potts Cocker's Chenies Street Biscuit Porcelain Manufactory, London c1840-45', *Northern Ceramic Society Journal* vol 23, 2006-07, pp. 113-14.
[41] Nilson's designs were popular on English enamels and creamware. See teapot in Fitwilliam Collection, C.9 & A-1963 and Bevis Hillier, John de Lanauze and others associated with the 'Bow factory', *ECC Trans*, vol 24 2013, pp. 157-8.

Chapter 19

[1] Kevill-Davies, op.cit., 1991, p. 106.
[2] Kevill-Davies, op.cit., 1991, p. 112.
[3] Quoted by A.Vickery, op.cit. 1998, p. 121.
[4] Records of gravestones removed long ago from the graveyard of Manchester Cathedral include the following : 'Here resteth the body of Betty wife of Absolom Rodbird who departed this life Jan 22 1798 aged 4 also Absolom their son who departed this life April 27 1800 aged 6yrs and 9mos also Jane their daughter who departed this life April 12 1802 aged 13yrs'. http://www.mlfhs.org.uk/member area/member docs finder.php?doc id=cathedral mis owens.pdf .
[5] See Riley, op.cit., 1991, p. 50. It is taken from a print in a scrapbook, bearing the same title, c.1830.
[6] Ibid. Illustrated pl.52(A), p. 69.
[7] Ibid., items 64-66, p. 30.
[8] Ibid., p. 38. From an illustrated poem by William Upton, published as a picture sheet by William Darton Jnr. c.1815. Illustrated in Kevill-Davies, op.cit., 1991, p. 155.
[9] Riley, op.cit., 1991, p. 32.
[10] Ibid., p. 34. Published by William Darton Jnr, 1812.
[11] Ibid., p. 36. Published by William Darton Jnr, 1813.
[12] See Lloyd Thomas, *Old Torquay Potteries*, 1977, fig. 16, p. 255.
[13] An example at the British Museum: BM 19152,0517.50.
[14] Mary Belson Elliott, *The Rose, containing Original Poems for Young People*, 1813, pp. 53-54.
[15] See Riley, op.cit., 1991, item 233, p. 68 Taken from 'Different Sports', in Mary Elliott, *The Rose*, op.cit. pp. 37-38.
[16] By Mary Belson Elliott, published by William Darton, c.1812.
[17] Illustrated in Cook, op.cit., 1948, items 14, 17, 28. also in *Trans ECC*, vol 3 pt.1, 1952, pl. 21-22.
[18] Cook, op.cit., 1948, item. 116.
[19] Illustrated in T. Markin, Anthony Keeling & co. Part II', the *NCS Journal*, no.19, 2002, p. 115.
[20] The subject may be loosely linked to a detail from the celebrated group portrait of 'The Marlborough Family' by Sir Joshua Reynolds (1723-92), exhibited at the Royal Academy in 1778. The young Lady Charlotte Churchill deliberately frightens her younger brother, still in a dress, with the Greek mask of Comedy. This detail was separately engraved by L. Schiavonetti, (1807) and the print freely adapted by other engravers and the potters. (An example in Brighton & Hove Museums Print Collection.)
[21] Pair of prints, 'Sportive Innocence' and 'Mischievous Sport', by Francesco Bartolozzi after William Hamilton sold at Moore Allen & Innocent, Cirencester, 10 May 2013, lot 410.
[22] I am indebted to Howard Coutts of the Bowes Museum for this information.
[23] Such groups may be inspired by prints such as 'The Quarrelsome Boys Tricked out of the Birds Nest', published by Robert Sayer, 1790, BM 2010,7081.3158.
[24] This is based on no.11 of the Juvenile Companions series, published by Hodgson after C.Wilson. BM 1952,0517. See Riley, op.cit., 1991, item 174, p. 56.
[25] See Bradshaw, op.cit., 1990, item.260, pls. 272-73, p. 330.
[26] See Bradshaw, op.cit., 1990, item 91, pp. 243-44.
[27] *The Observer*, 4 December 1791. This was the first edition to be published.
[28] Lewis Walpole Library_790.04.10.01.
[29] The design comes from the John Bowles Drawing Book, see Anthony Ray, op.cit., 1973, pl. 31d.
[30] BM 2010,7081.3071.
[31] There is a copy in the Lewis Walpole Library, Yale University: lwlpr06162.
[32] Unsuitable marriages, often with prostitutes, were conducted in the Fleet Street area, east of central London, see *London 1753*, items 1.69-70, pp. 87-89.
[33] A reversed version of 'La Cascade', (Wallace Collection, London) taken from an engraving by Scotin after Watteau.
[34] See Rogers, op.cit., 1970, p.12. The piece is mentioned in Charleston & Towner, *English Ceramics* 1580-1830.
[35] Opinion of Errol Manners and Anton Gabszewicz, 2005.
[36] Thanks to the late Tom Walford for this suggestion. A sketch of Hylton Castle appears in the *Illustrated Travel Diaries of R.R.*
[37] One published by Sayer in November 1791, copied and elaborated from the original by Isaac Cruikshank, 'A Crop of 1791', published by Fores in September 1791; British Museum: BM 1948,0214.494.
[38] Harold Blakey alerted me to the reference in the *Observer*, the first newspaper to be published on Sundays.
[39] Copy of source print in the British Museum: BM 1868,0808.2763.
[40] Kauffmann's painting of *Poor Maria* was wildly popular, and 'was transferred to an incalculable variety of articles of all sorts and sizes from a watch-case to a tea-waiter' – note to J.Moser 'Memoirs of the Late Angelica Kauffmann', *European Magazine*, April 1809.
[41] Alexandra Shepard, *Meanings of Manhood in Early Modern England* (Oxford University Press, 2003), p. 127.
[42] Similar visual puzzles, issued as games or published in books for children, are illustrated in Mrs Neville Jackson, *Toys of Other Days*, 1908, p. 307.
[43] BM J,11.116.
[44] The name Strephon probably comes from the mysogynistic poem, 'The Lady's Dressing Room', by Jonathan Swift, published in *The Daily Post*, 16 June 1732.
[45] These images are loosely based on a pair of watercolours with similar titles by Thomas Rowlandson, c.1785, which were copied by other artists and disseminated as prints from 1787. See J. Hayes, Rowlandson, *Watercolours and Drawings*, 1972, illustrated pp. 94-95.
[46] Quoted in full by Schkolne, op.cit., 2006, p. 92.
[47] Quoted in the *Daily Advertiser* and in *The Journal of Margaret Molloy (1768-69)* actually written by P. Creswick (pub.1898). *Angerstein 1753-55*, published by the Science Museum, 2001.
[48] W. M. Thackeray, *Contributions to the 'Morning Chronicle'*, ed. G.N. Ray, p. 94.
[49] Several similarly decorated pieces (several dated 1802) illustrated in Griffin, op.cit., 2005, p. 188. Shown in *Pots About People*, 1990, no 102.
[50] See Hamilton's 'Happy Cottagers' in *The Shadow of the Guillotine*, op.cit., 1989, fig. 208 p. 64.
[51] The earliest use of the theme can be found on slipware dishes by Samuel Malkin of Burslem. One, dated 1726, shows a man standing between compasses with medallions impressed with the main inscription, 'Keep with:in Cumpas'. Sold at Christies, London, 16 November 1992, lot 1.
[52] John Trundle, *Keepe within Compasse: or, the Worthy Legacy of a Wise Father*...See O'Connell, 1999, p. 80.
[53] S. Lines, *A Few Incidents in the life of Samuel Lines*, 1862, p.10, quoted in O'Connell, op.cit, p. 77 note 26.
[54] Quoted in Claire Harman, *Fanny Burney*, 2000, ch. 2 'A Romantick Girl', p. 41.
[55] Scenes of dissipation and fornication will lead to (moral) shipwreck and prison.
[56] See *Creamware and Pearlware*, op.cit., 1986, item 107, p. 85.
[57] Scenes of extravagance and vanity will lead to arrest and hard labour. See Emmerson, op.cit., 1992, item 112, p. 102.
[58] Shelley is discussed by R. Hampson, 'Michael Shelley of Lane End', NCS *Newsletter*, no. 74, p. 31.
[59] J. Beresford, *Miseries of Human Life*, 1825, p. 132. See also print, published by Sayer after Boitard, c.1765, 'The ENRAG'D BATCHELOR, or the PLAGUE of a SINGLE STATE', BM 1948,0214.508.
[60] See Emmerson, op.cit., 1992, item 57, p. 75.
[61] Anonymous version c.1775, is inscribed 'The Miller Grinding of Old Women Young'. BM 1999,0926.4. Even the young George Cruikshank produced a version of 'The Wonderful Mill' c.1805.
[62] The essayists William Hazlitt, Charles Lamb and the poet Robert Burns were moved by performances and Charles James Fox, the great Whig leader, wrote a version of his own.

Key

Collections

BM – British Museum
NMM – National Maritime Museum
NPG – National Portrait Gallery
NT – National Trust
V&A – Victoria & Albert Museum

Publications

DNB – Oxford dictionary of National Biography
NCS – Northern Ceramic Society
Trans ECC – Transactions of the English Ceramic Circle

SELECT BIBLIOGRAPHY

Adams, E., & Redstone, D., 1981, *Bow Porcelain*, London.

Archer, M., 1997, *Delftware, the tin-glazed earthenware of the British Isles*, (collection of the Victoria & Albert Museum) HMSO, London.

Atterbury, P. and Batkin, M., 1982, *Wedgwood Ceramics 1846-1959,* Richard Dennis.

Atterbury, P. and Batkin, M., 1990, *The Dictionary of Minton,* Woodbridge.

Baker, J., 1984, (revised by) *Sunderland Pottery*, Tyne and Wear.

Barker, D., 1991, *William Greatbatch a Staffordshire Potter*, London.

Berg, M., 2005, *Luxury and Pleasure in Eighteenth Century England*, Oxford.

Berkowitz, M. & Ungar, R., 2007, *Fighting Back? Jewish and Black Boxers in Britain*, University College, London and the Jewish Museum, London.

Bethnal Green, 1899, *Catalogue of a Collection of Pottery and Porcelain Illustrating Popular British History, lent by Henry Willett*, HMSO, London.

BFAC, 1913, *Catalogue of the Collection of Early English Earthenware*, Burlington Fine Arts Club, London.

Bilbey, D., & Trusted, M., 2002, *British Sculpture 1470-2000,* Victoria & Albert Museum, London.

Bills, M., 2006, *The Art of Satire, London in Caricature,* Museum of London.

Binns, R. W., 1877, *Worcester Pottery and Porcelain, 1751-1851*, London.

Black, J., 2005, *Culture in Eighteenth-century England, a Subject for Taste*, London.

Blacker, J. F., 1922, *The ABC of English Salt-Glaze Stoneware from Dwight to Doulton*, London.

Blanning, Tim, 2007, *The Pursuit of Glory, Europe 1648-1815*, London.

Bradshaw, P., 1981, *Eighteenth Century English Porcelain Figures 1745-95*, London.

Bradshaw, P., 1990, *Derby Porcelain Figures*, London.

Bradshaw, P., 1992, *Bow Porcelain Figures 1748-1774*, London.

Branyan, L., French, N. & Sandon, J., *Worcester Blue and White Porcelain, 1751-1790: an Illustrated Encyclopaedia of the Patterns.* London, 1981.

Britton, F., 1982, *English Delftware in the Bristol Collection*, London.

Britton, F., 1987, *London Delftware,* London.

Browne Muggs, 1985, *English Brown Stoneware,* ed. R. Hildyard, (exhibition catalogue), Victoria & Albert Museum, London.

Charleston, R. J. (ed.), 1965, *English Porcelain 1745-1850*, London.

Church, A. H., 1884, *English Earthenware*, London.

Church, A. H., 1911, *English Porcelain*, London.

Circus & Sport, English Earthenware Figures 1780-1840, 1990, exhibition catalogue, P. Halfpenny and S. Beddoe, J.B.Speed Museum, Louisville, Kentucky.

Colley, L., 1992, *Britons, Forging the Nation 1707-1837*, London.

Cook, C., 1948, *The Life and Work of Robert Hancock*, London.

Cowling, M., 2000, *Victorian Figurative Painting, Domestic Life and the Contemporary Social Scene*, London.

Coysh, A.W. and Henrywood, R.K., *The Dictionary of Blue and White Printed Pottery, 1780-1880.* vols 1 & 2. Woodbridge [Suffolk], UK: Antique Collectors' Club, 1981-1989.

Creamware & Pearlware, 1986, NCS Exhibition, Stoke-on-Trent City Museum & Art Gallery.

Croly, Rev. G., 1841, *The Personal History of His Late Majesty George IV.*

Chinese Whispers, 2008, exhibition catalogue, ed. D. Beevers, Brighton Museum & Art Gallery.

Daniels, P., Ramsay R. & G., 2013, *The George II Busts and Historic Wall Brackets,* Oxfordshire.

Deuchar, S., 1988, *Sporting Art in Eighteenth Century England*, Yale.

Dolan, B., 2004, *Josiah Wedgwood: Entrepreneur to the Enlightenment*, London.

Donald, D,. 1996, *The Art of Caricature, Satirical Prints in the Reign of George III,* Yale.

Donald, D., 2002, *Followers of Fashion, Graphic Satires from the Georgian Period*, National Touring Exhibitions, London.

Drakard, D. & Holdway, P. 1983, *Spode Printed Wares.*

Drakard, D. 1990, 'Sailors Afloat and Ashore', *Transactions of the English Ceramic Circle,* vol. 14 pt. 1, pp. 62-82.

Drakard, D. 1992, *Printed English Pottery, History and Humour in the Reign of George III.*

Dunsmore, A. (ed.), 2011, *This Blessed Plot, this Earth, English pottery studies in honour of Jonathan Horne,* Yale.

Earle Collection, 1915, Of early Staffordshire Pottery by Major Cyril Earle, London.

Edwards, D., 1987, *Neale Pottery and Porcelain,* London.

Emmerson, R., 1992, *British Teapots and Tea Drinking*, HMSO, London.

Falkner, F. 1912 (1972), *The Wood Family of Burslem*, London.

Freeth, F., 1905, 'The Willett Collection at the Brighton Museum', *The Connoisseur*, June 1905, pp.69-73.

Gabszewicz, A., 1982, *Bow Porcelain, the Collection formed by Geoffrey Freeman*, London.

Gatrell, V., 2006, *City of Laughter: Sex and Satire in Eighteenth-Century London*, Atlantic Books.

George, M. D., (& F. D. Stephens) 1870-1954, *Catalogue of Political and Personal Satires*, Vols. I-XI, British Museum, London.

The Georgian Playhouse, Actors, Artists, Audiences and Architecture 1975, Hayward Gallery, London.

Glaisher Collection, 1935, *Catalogue of the Glaisher Collection of Pottery and Porcelain in the Fitzwilliam Museum, Cambridge.* vols I & II by B. Rackham. Cambridge. (Reprinted Woodbridge, 1987).

Godden, G., 1966, *Encyclopaedia of British Pottery and Porcelain Marks*, (reprinted 1980) London.

Godden, G., 1968, *Minton Pottery and Porcelain of the First Period 1793-1850*, London.

Godden, G., 1970, *Coalport and Coalbrookdale Porcelains*, London.

Godden, G., 1979, *Oriental Market Export Porcelain*, London.

Godden, G., 1980, *Illustrated Encyclopaedia of British Pottery and Porcelain,* London.

Godden, G., 1988, *Encyclopaedia of British Porcelain Manufacturers,* London.

Godden, G. & Gibson, M., 1993, *Collecting Lustreware*, London.

Gray, J., 2003, *Welsh Ceramics in Context, Part 1*, Royal Institution of South Wales.

Gray, J., 2006, *Welsh Ceramics in Context, Part II*, Royal Institution of South Wales.

Greg Collection, 1923, *The Thomas Tylston Greg Collection of English Pottery,* by E. J. Sidebotham, Manchester.

Griffin, E., 2007, *Blood sport, Hunting in Britain since 1066,* New Haven & London.

Griffin, J.D., 2005, *The Leeds Pottery, 1770-1881*, Leeds.

Grigsby, L., 1990, *English Pottery 1650-1800, the Henry H. Weldon Collection*, London.

Haggar, R., 1955, *Staffordshire Chimney Ornaments*, London.

Halfpenny, P. et al., 2010, *Success to America, Creamware for the American Market*, Woodbridge.

Halfpenny, P., 1991, *English Earthenware Figures 1740-1840*, Woodbridge.

Halfpenny, P., and Beddoe, S., 1990, *Circus and Sport, English Earthenware Figures 1780-1840*, Louisville, Kentucky.

Harrison, F., 1906, *Historical & Literary Associations of Brighton & Hove,* Hove.

Henrywood, H.K., 1984, *Relief Moulded Jugs*, Woodbridge.

Henrywood, H.K., 1997, *An Illustrated Guide to British Jugs from Medieval Times to the Twentieth Century,* Woodbridge.

Hobson, R. L., 1903, *Catalogue of the Collection of English Pottery in the Department of British and Medieval Antiquities and Ethnography of the British Museum,* London.

Hodgkin, J.E. & E., 1891, *Examples of Early English Pottery, Named, Dated and Inscribed*, London. (Reprinted Wakefield, 1973).

Honour, H., 1989, *The Image of the Black in Western Art*, vol IV.

Hops & Venom, 1988, The Marjorie Davies Collection of Frog Mugs, Stoke-on-Trent.

Housman, H., 1893, *Notes on The Willett Collection of Pottery in the Brighton Museum*, Brighton.

Howarth, J. & Hildyard, R., 2004, *Joseph Kishere and the Mortlake Potteries*, Woodbridge.

Hume, I. N., 1975, 'Stoneware gin flasks: Legacy of the damned', *Antiques*, vol. CVII, February 1975, pp.304-313.

Hurlbutt, F., 1926, *Bow Porcelain*, London.

Jewitt, L., 1883, *The Ceramic Art of Great Britain*, London.

Jones Collection, 1991, *The Tristan Jones Collection of Commemorative Ceramics*, Phillips sale, 26 January, 1991, London.

Kensington Palace, 1987, *Anniversary of Accession and Jubilee of Queen Victoria* (no catalogue), Kensington Palace, London.

Kevill-Davies, S., 1991, *Yesterday's Children, The Antiques of Childcare*, Woodbridge.

Keynes, M., 2005, *The Iconography of Isaac Newton*, Boydell Press, Cambridge.

Lee, A., 1931, *Portraits in Pottery: With some account of the pleasant occasions incident to their quest,* Boston, Mass.
Lee, A., 1931, 'Possibilities in Ceramic Portraiture', November 1931, pp.159-60.
Lewis, G., 1956, *A Picture History of English Pottery*, London.
Lewis, G., 1969, *A Collector's History of English Pottery*, London.
Lewis, J. & G., 1984, *Pratt Ware 1780-1840*, Woodbridge.
Lipski, L. & Archer, M., 1984 (ed. M. Archer), *Dated English Delftware 1600-1800*, London.
Lockett, T., & Godden, G. A., 1989, *Davenport, China, Earthenware and Glass 1794-1887*, London.
London World City 1800-1840, 1992, (ed. Celina Fox), Yale and Museum of London.
Made in Liverpool, 1993, Liverpool Pottery and Porcelain 1700-1850, NCS Exhibition, Walker Art Gallery, Liverpool.
Mankowitz, W., 1953, *Wedgwood*, London.
Marno, F. and Massey, R., 2013, *Fire and Form, The Baroque and its Influence on English Ceramics c1660-c1760,* papers given at a Symposium organized by the English Ceramics Circle.
May, J. & J., 1972, *Commemorative Pottery 1780-1900*, London.
May, J., 1975, 'The Famous on the Bottle', *Art & Antiques*, 15 November, 1975, pp. 22-28.
McWilliam, R., 2007, *The Tichborne Claimant*, London.
Messenger, M., 1988, *Coalport 1795-1926*, Woodbridge.
Miller, J. J. II, 1979, *English Yellow-glazed Earthenware*, Smithsonian Institution.
Mountford, A. 1971, *The Illustrated Guide to Staffordshire Saltglazed Stoneware*, London.
Nance, E. M., 1942, *The Pottery and Porcelain of Swansea and Nantgarw,* London.
Nelson & Napoleon, 2005, (exhibition catalogue, ed. M. Lincoln, National Maritime Museum, Greenwich).
NCS Newsletter, 1975 onwards, *Newsletter of the Northern Ceramic Society*.
O'Connell, S., 1999, *The Popular Print in England*, exh. cat. British Museum Press, London.
The Proceedings of the Old Bailey, 1674-1913, at www.oldbaileyonline.org.
Oliver, A., 1971, *The Victorian Staffordshire Figure*, London.
Oliver, A., 1981, *Staffordshire Pottery The Tribal Art of England*, London.
Oswald, Hildyard & Hughes, 1982, *English Brown Stoneware 1670-1900*, London.
Oxford Dictionary of National Biography, 2004, Oxford DNB and www.oxforddnb.com/index.jsp.
Pots about People, Named and Dated Creamware and Pearlware 1760-1820, 1990, exhibition and leaflet, S. Bidgood and P. Walton eds. Bar Convent Museum, York.
Prentice, R., 1994, *A Celebration of the Sea*, (National Maritime Museum) HMSO, London.
Price, R. K., 1922, *Astbury Whieldon & Ralph Wood Figures and Toby Jugs*, London.
Pugh, P. D. & M., 1971. *Naval Ceramics*, Bath.
Pugh, P. D. Gordon, 1970, *Staffordshire Portrait Figures*, New York.
Rackham, B. & Read, H., 1924, *English Pottery*, London. (Reprinted Wakefield, 1972.)
Reilly, R., and Savage, G., 1973, *Wedgwood, The Portrait Medallions*, London.
Reilly, R., 1995, *The New Illustrated Dictionary of Wedgwood*, London.
Richards, S., 1999, *Eighteenth-century Ceramics, Products for a Civilised Society*, Manchester.
Riley, N., 1991, *Gifts for Good Children*, Richard Dennis, London.
Rococo, 1984, *Rococo, Art and Design in Hogarth's England* (exhibition catalogue, ed. M. Snodin), Victoria & Albert Museum, London.
Rodger, N.A.M., 2004, *The Command of the Ocean, A Naval History of Britain 1649-1815*, London.
Rodgers, D., 1975, *Coronation Souvenirs,* Wolverhampton.
Rogers, D., 1970, 'Mr Henry Willett and his English pottery', *The Connoisseur*, Jan. 1970, pp.10-16.
Rous Lench, 1986, *The Rous Lench Collections, Volume One English Pottery and Porcelain*, Sotheby sale 1 July, 1986, London.
Rous Lench, 1990, *Ceramics from the Rous Lench Collection*, Christie's sale, 19 May, 1990, London.
Rutherford, J., 1982, 'Henry Willett as a Collector', *Apollo*, March 1982, pp.176-81.
Salaman, R., 1949, *The History and Social Influence of the Potato*, Cambridge.
Sandon, H., 1969, *Worcester Porcelain 1751-1793,* London.
Sandon, H., 1973, *Royal Worcester Porcelain: From 1862 to the Present Day,* London.
Schama, S., 2001, *A History of Britain: Vol. 2: The British Wars 1603-1776*, BBC, London.
Schama, S., 2003, *A History of Britain: Vol. 3: The Fate of Empire 1776-2000*, BBC, London.
Schkolne, M., 2006, *People, Passions, Pastimes and Pleasures,* Winston Salem, N. Carolina.
Schreiber Collection, 1928/30, *Catalogue of English Porcelain, Earthenware, Enamels and Glass Collected by Charles Schreiber, Esq, MP, and the Lady Charlotte Schreiber,* vols I & II by B. Rackham. Victoria and Albert Museum, London.
Semmel, S., 2004, *Napoleon and the British*, Yale.
Sharpe, J., 2004, *Dick Turpin, the Myth of the English Highwayman,* London.
Shipwrecks and Marriages, Dated and Documentary ceramics, 2009, (ECC Exhibition, Massey, R. & Marno, F., (eds) Brian Haughton Gallery, London.
Smith, A., 1970, *The Illustrated Guide to Liverpool Herculaneum Pottery,* London.
Smith, S., *Lowestoft Porcelain in Norwich Castle Museum*, vol.1, 1975, vol.2, 1985.
Solkin, D.H. 1992, *Painting for Money, The Visual Arts and the Public Sphere in Eighteenth Century England*, Yale.
Solon, L. M., 1883/5, *The Art of the Old English Potter.*
Stoneware & Stone Chinas, 1982, NCS Exhibition, Stoke-on-Trent City Museum & Art Gallery.
Success To America, Creamware for the American Market, 2010, Teitelman, Halfpenny, Fuchs et al., Woodbridge.
Sunderland Pottery, 1984, (catalogue revised by J. Baker), Tyne & Wear.
Taggart, R., 1967, *The Burnap Collection, The Frank P. and Harriet C. Burnap Collections of English Pottery in the William Rockhill Nelson Gallery, Nelson Atkins Museum,* Kansas City.
A Tale of Three Cities, 1997, ed. D. S. Howard, Exhibition Catalogue, Sotheby's, London.
Tharp, Lars, 1997, *Hogarth's China, Hogarth's Paintings and Eighteenth-Century Ceramics,* London.
The French Revolution (version anglaise), 1990, (exhibition catalogue) Musée de la Revlolution Française, Château de Vizille, France.
The Incomparable Art, 1969, The Greg Collection, Manchester City Art Gallery.
The Man at Hyde Park Corner, Sculpture by John Cheere, 1709-87, 1974, (exhibition catalogue) Temple Newsam House, Leeds and Marble Hill House, Twickenham.
The Shadow of the Guillotine, 1989, ed., D. Bindman, (exhibition catalogue), British Museum, London.
Trans ECC, *English Ceramic Circle, Transactions*, 1933 onwards, London.
Transfer-Printed Worcester Porcelain at Manchester City Art Gallery, 1976 (catalogue by E. Leary and P. Walton), Manchester.
Uglow, J., 1997, *Hogarth, a Life and a World,* London.
Uglow, J., 2002, *The Lunar Men, The Friends who made the Future 1730-1810,* London.
Uglow, J., 2014, *In These Times, Living in Britain through Napoleon's Wars, 1793-1815,* London.
Vickery, A. 1998, *The Gentleman's Daughter, Women's Lives in Georgian Britain,* New Haven.
Vickery, A, 2009, *Behind Closed Doors, At Home in Georgian England*, New Haven.
Walford, T. & Massey, R., 2007, *Creamware and Pearlware Re-Examined*, English Ceramic Circle.
Walpole, H., 1973, *Selected Letters of Horace W.*
Walpole, H., 1985, *Memoirs of George II,* ed. John Broke, Yale.
Walpole, H., 2000, *Memoirs of George III,* ed. D. Jarrett, Yale.
Walton, P., 1976, *Creamware and Other English Pottery at Temple Newsam House, Leeds.* Leeds.
Watney, B., 1963, *English Blue and White Porcelain of the Eighteenth Century*, London (re-printed 1978/1979).
Watney, B., 1997, *Liverpool Porcelain*, Richard Dennis, London.
Weinreb, B. & Hibbert C., 1983 (reprinted 1992), *The London Encyclopaedia,* London.
Whinney, M., 1964, *Sculpture in Britain, 1530-1830*, London.
Willett, 1879, *Introductory Catalogue of the Collection of Pottery and Porcelain in the Brighton Museum, Lent by Henry Willett*, Brighton.
Willett, 1899, *Catalogue of a Collection of Pottery and Porcelain illustrating Popular British History,* HMSO, Bethnal Green Museum.
Willett, H., 1899, 'Museums and their Uses', address to the Congress of Curators held at Brighton, reprinted from the *Brighton Herald*, 8 July.
Williams-Wood, C., 1981, *English Transfer-Printed Pottery and Porcelain*, London.
Yarborough, R., 1996, *Bow Porcelain and the London Theatre*, Hancock, Michigan.
Young, H. 1999, *English Porcelain, 1745-95, Its Makers, Design, Marketing and Consumption,* V&A Museum Studies, London.

INDEX OF NAMES

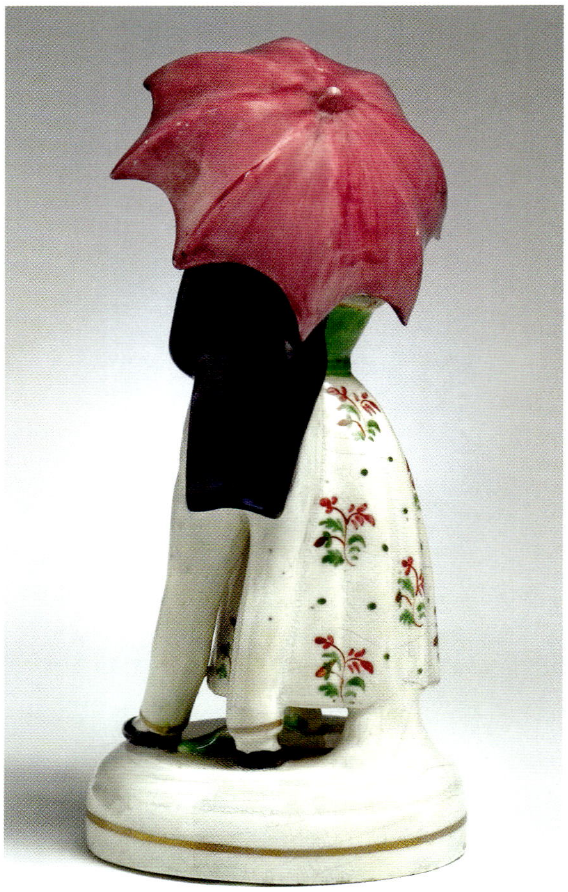

Figure Group, (**1643**), c.1850, Staffordshire, height: 17.1cm, (6¾in), enamelled bone china. Lovers kiss under an umbrella, known as 'Umbrella Courtship'.

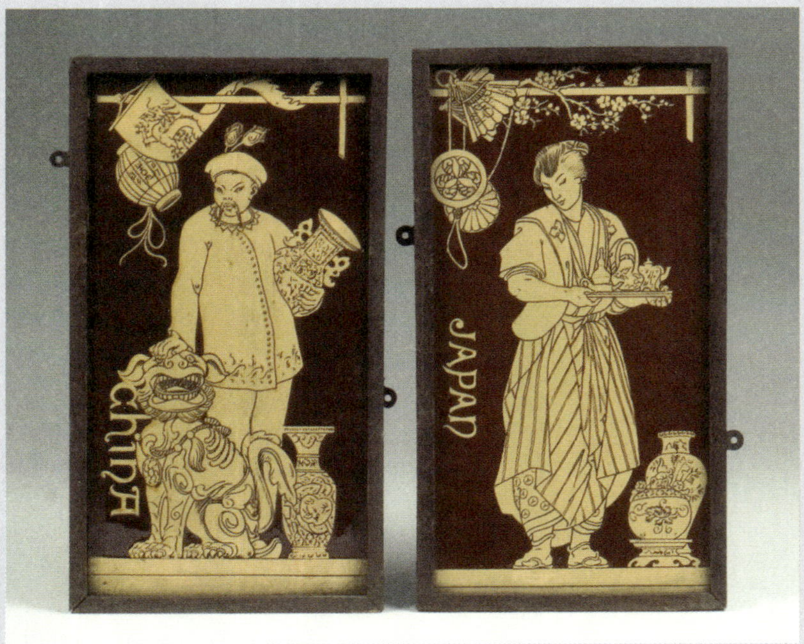
CHINA
JAPAN

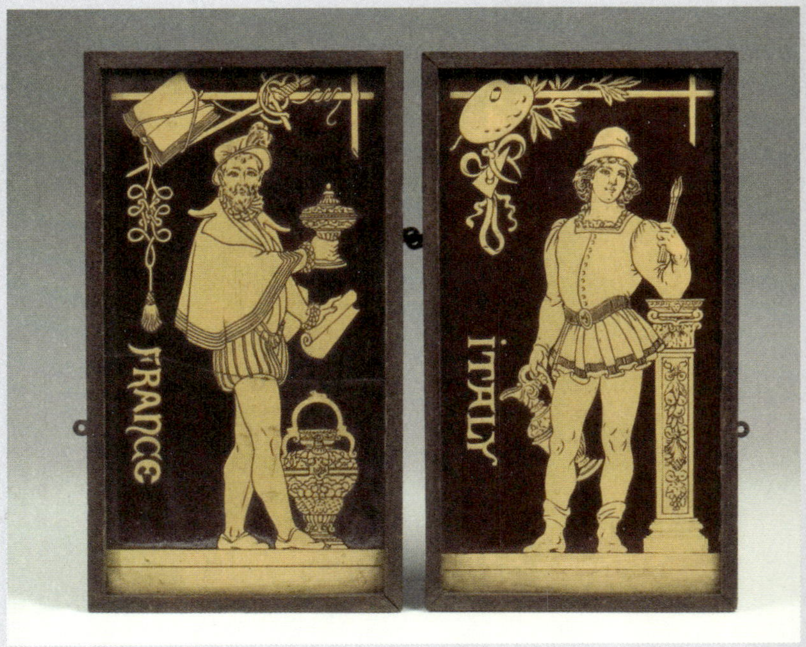
FRANCE
ITALY

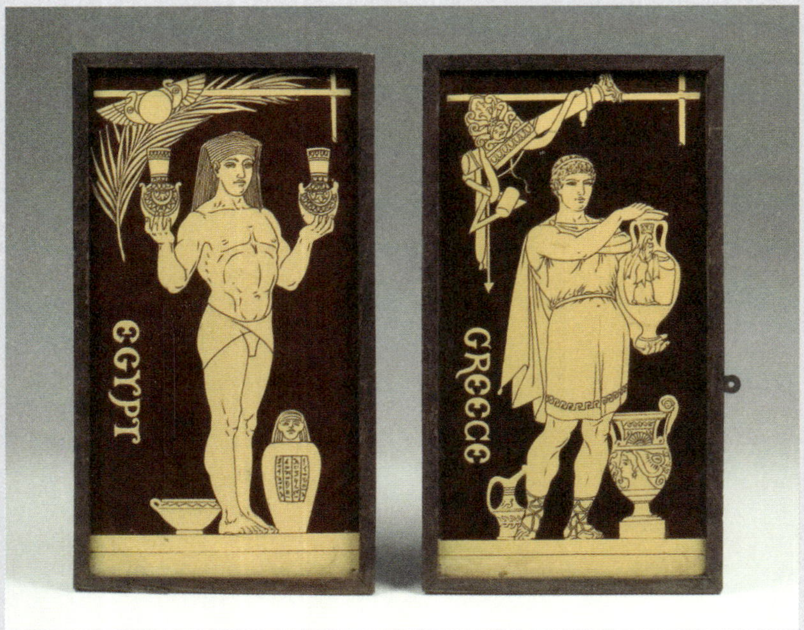
EGYPT
GREECE

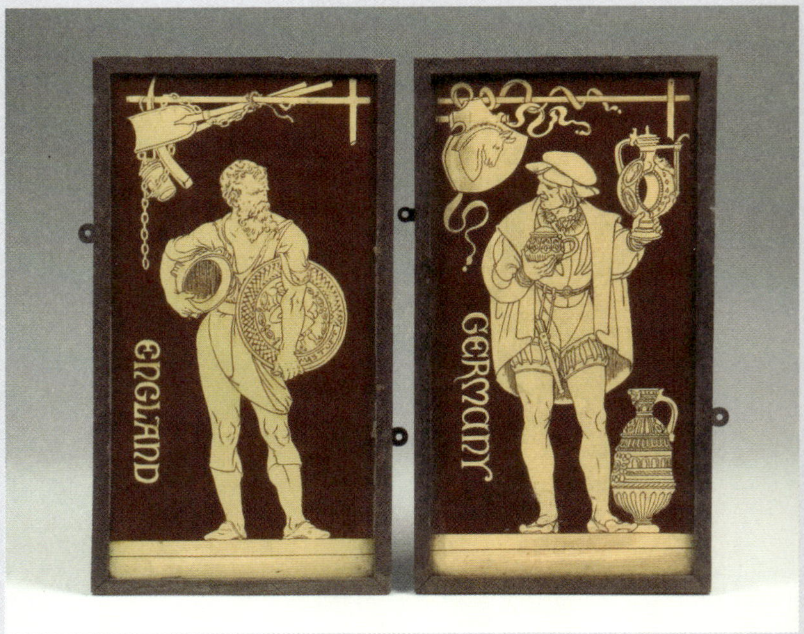
ENGLAND
GERMANY

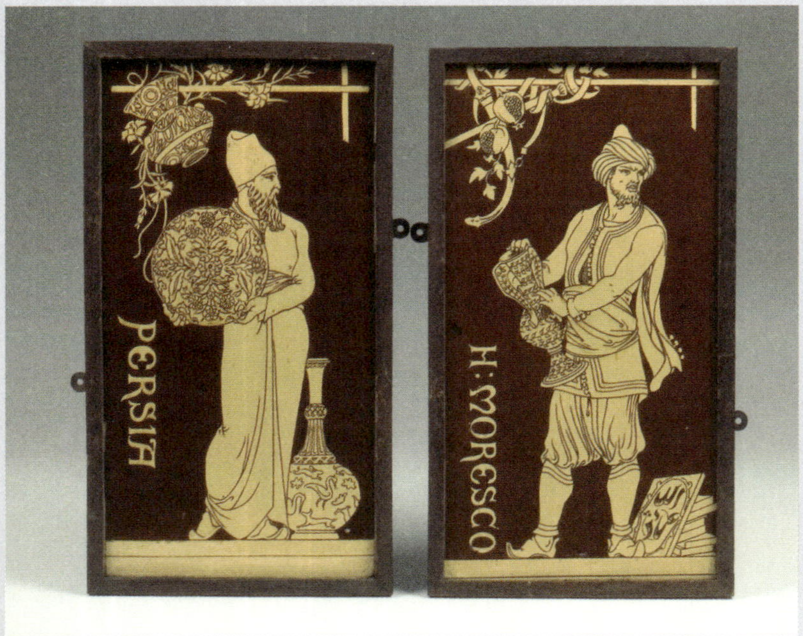
PERSIA
H:MORESCO

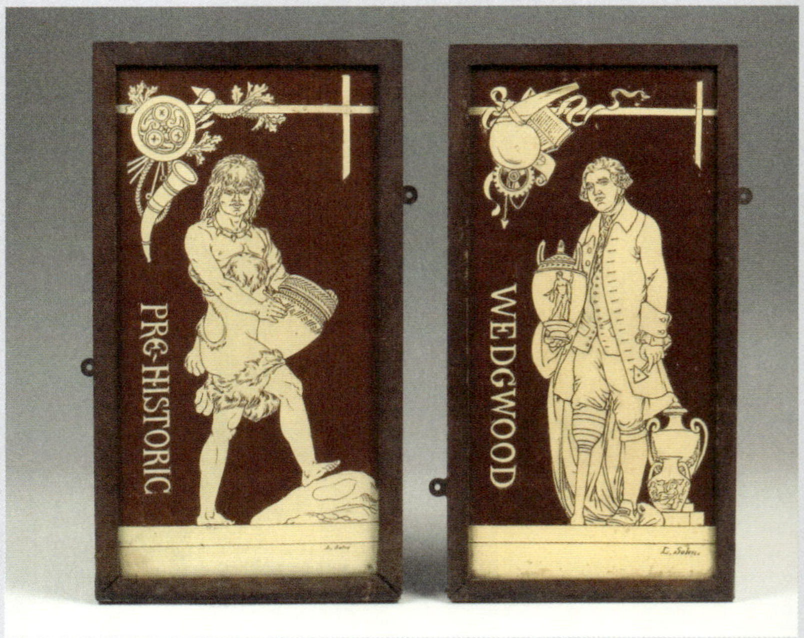
PRE-HISTORIC
WEDGWOOD